## Chapter 11    Multiple Regression and Correlation

Multiple regression model $E(y) = \alpha + \beta_1 x_1 + \beta_2 x_2 + \cdots + \beta_k x_k$

Global test $H_0 : \beta_1 = \cdots = \beta_k = 0$

$$\text{Test statistic } F = \frac{\text{Model mean square}}{\text{Error mean square}} = \frac{R^2/k}{(1 - R^2)/[n - (k + 1)]}$$

$$df_1 = k, df_2 = n - (k + 1)$$

Partial test $H_0 : \beta_i = 0$,   test statistic $t = \dfrac{b_i}{se}$,   $df = n - (k + 1)$

## Chapter 12    Comparing Groups: Analysis of Variance Methods

$H_0 : \mu_1 = \cdots = \mu_g$,  One-way ANOVA test statistic

$$F = \frac{\text{Between-groups sum of squares}/(g - 1)}{\text{Within-groups sum of squares}/(N - g)}, \, df_1 = g - 1, df_2 = N - g$$

## Chapter 13    Combining Regression and ANOVA: Analysis of Covariance

$E(y) = \alpha + \beta x + \beta_1 z_1 + \cdots + \beta_{g-1} z_{g-1}$,  $z_i = 1$ or $0$ is dummy variable for group $i$

## Chapter 14    Model Building with Multiple Regression

Quadratic regression $E(y) = \alpha + \beta_1 x + \beta_2 x^2$

Exponential regression $E(y) = \alpha \beta^x$  (log of mean is linear in $x$)

## Chapter 15    Logistic Regression: Modeling Categorical Responses

Logistic regression $\text{logit} = \log(\text{odds}) = \log\left(\dfrac{P(y=1)}{1-P(y=1)}\right) = \alpha + \beta x$

$P(y = 1) = \dfrac{e^{\alpha+\beta x}}{1+e^{\alpha+\beta x}} = \dfrac{\text{odds}}{1+\text{odds}}$

# Key Formulas for Statistical Methods

**Chapter 3   Descriptive Statistics**

Mean $\bar{y} = \dfrac{\Sigma y_i}{n}$ 　　　　 Standard deviation $s = \sqrt{\dfrac{\Sigma(y_i - \bar{y})^2}{n - 1}}$

**Chapter 4   Probability Distributions**

$z$-score $z = \dfrac{y - \mu}{\sigma}$ 　　　　 Standard error $\sigma_{\bar{y}} = \dfrac{\sigma}{\sqrt{n}}$

**Chapter 5   Statistical Inference: Estimation**

Confidence interval for mean $\bar{y} \pm z(se)$ with $se = \dfrac{s}{\sqrt{n}}$

Confidence interval for proportion $\hat{\pi} \pm z(se)$ with $se = \sqrt{\dfrac{\hat{\pi}(1-\hat{\pi})}{n}}$

**Chapter 6   Statistical Inference: Significance Tests**

$H_0 : \mu = \mu_0$ test statistic $t = \dfrac{\bar{y} - \mu_0}{se}$ with $se = \dfrac{s}{\sqrt{n}}, df = n - 1$

$H_0 : \pi = \pi_0$ test statistic $z = \dfrac{\hat{\pi} - \pi_0}{se_0}$ with $se_0 = \sqrt{\dfrac{\pi_0(1 - \pi_0)}{n}}$

**Chapter 7   Comparison of Two Groups**

Compare means: $(\bar{y}_2 - \bar{y}_1) \pm t(se)$ with $se = \sqrt{\dfrac{s_1^2}{n_1} + \dfrac{s_2^2}{n_2}}$

Test $H_0 : \mu_1 = \mu_2$ using $t = \dfrac{\bar{y}_2 - \bar{y}_1}{se}$

Compare proportions: $(\hat{\pi}_2 - \hat{\pi}_1) \pm z(se)$ with $se = \sqrt{\dfrac{\hat{\pi}_1(1-\hat{\pi}_1)}{n_1} + \dfrac{\hat{\pi}_2(1-\hat{\pi}_2)}{n_2}}$

**Chapter 8   Analyzing Association Between Categorical Variables**

Chi-squared test of $H_0$: Independence, $\chi^2 = \sum \dfrac{(f_0 - f_e)^2}{f_e}, \quad df = (r - 1)(c - 1)$

Ordinal measure $\hat{\gamma} = \dfrac{C - D}{C + D}, -1 \le \hat{\gamma} \le 1, z = \dfrac{\hat{\gamma}}{\hat{\sigma}_{\hat{\gamma}}}, \hat{\gamma} \pm z\hat{\sigma}_{\hat{\gamma}}$

**Chapter 9   Linear Regression and Correlation**

Linear regression model $E(y) = \alpha + \beta x$, prediction equation $\hat{y} = a + bx$

Pearson correlation $r = \left(\dfrac{s_x}{s_y}\right)b, -1 \le r \le 1$

$r^2 = \dfrac{\text{TSS} - \text{SSE}}{\text{TSS}}, \text{TSS} = \sum(y - \bar{y})^2, \text{SSE} = \sum(y - \hat{y})^2, 0 \le r^2 \le 1$

Test of independence $H_0 : \beta = 0, \quad t = \dfrac{b}{se}, \quad df = n - 2$

# STATISTICAL METHODS FOR THE SOCIAL SCIENCES

Fourth Edition

**Alan Agresti**
*University of Florida*

**Barbara Finlay**
*Texas A & M University*

PEARSON

Prentice
Hall

*PEARSON EDUCATION INTERNATIONAL*

Editor-in-Chief: *Deirdre Lynch*
Vice President and Editorial Director, Mathematics: *Christine Hoag*
Sponsoring Editor: *Dawn Murrin*
Editorial Assistant/Print Supplements Editor: *Joanne Wendelken*
Senior Managing Editor: *Linda Behrens*
Associate Managing Editor: *Bayani Mendoza de Leon*
Project Manager, Production: *Traci Douglas*
Senior Operations Supervisor: *Diane Peirano*
Executive Marketing Manager: *Kate Valentine*
Marketing Manager: *Wayne Parkins*
Assistant Manager, Marketing Support: *Diana Penha*
Marketing Assistant: *Kathleen DeChavez*
Art Director: *Jayne Conte*
Cover Designer: *Kiwi Design*
Cover Painting: *"Harvest" by Albina Felski*
Composition/Art Studio: *Laserwords*

© 2009, 1997 by Prentice Hall, Inc.
Pearson Prentice Hall
Pearson Education, Inc.
Upper Saddle River, New Jersey 07458

Previous edition copyright © 1986 and 1979 by Dellen Publishing Company, a division of Macmillan, Inc.

Printed in the United States of America

10 9 8 7

1006481646

ISBN-13: 978-0-13-713150-1
ISBN-10:    0-13-713150-X

Pearson Education Ltd., *London*
Pearson Education Australia Pty. Ltd., *Sydney*
Pearson Education Singapore, Pte. Ltd.
Pearson Education North Asia Ltd., *Hong Kong*
Pearson Education Canada, Inc., *Toronto*
Pearson Educación de Mexico, S.A. de C.V.
Pearson Education—Japan, *Tokyo*
Pearson Education Malaysia, Pte. Ltd.
Pearson Education, *Upper Saddle River, New Jersey*

To my parents

*Louis J. Agresti and Marjorie H. Agresti*

# Contents

*Sections or subsections marked with an asterisk have less importance for a first introduction to statistics and are optional.

# Preface

When I undertook the first edition of this book nearly three decades ago, my goal was to introduce statistical methods in a style that emphasized their concepts and their application to the social sciences rather than the mathematics and computational details behind them. I did this by focusing on how the methods are used and interpreted rather than their theoretical derivations.

This fourth edition of the book has an even stronger emphasis on concepts and applications, with greater attention to "real data" both in the examples and exercises. I continue to downplay mathematics, in particular probability, which is all too often a stumbling block for students. On the other hand, the text is not a cookbook. Reliance on an overly simplistic recipe-based approach to statistics is not the route to good statistical practice.

### Changes in the Fourth Edition

Since the first edition, the increase in computer power coupled with the continued improvement and accessibility of statistical software has had a major impact on the way social scientists analyze data. Because of this, this book does not cover the traditional shortcut hand-computational formulas and approximations. The presentation of computationally complex methods, such as regression, emphasizes interpretation of software output rather than the formulas for performing the analysis. The text contains numerous sample printouts, mainly in the style of SPSS and occasionally SAS, both in chapter text and homework problems. This edition also has an appendix explaining how to apply SPSS and SAS to conduct the methods of each chapter and a Web site giving links to information about other software.

Exposure to realistic but simple examples and to numerous homework exercises is vital to student learning. This edition has added many new exercises and updated old ones, with major emphasis on real data. Each chapter's homework set is divided into two parts, straightforward exercises on the text material in *Practicing the Basics*, and exercises dealing with open-ended data analyses, understanding of concepts, and advanced material in *Concepts and Applications*. The large data sets in the examples and exercises, including a data set introduced in Exercise 1.11 that appears again in exercises at the end of each chapter, are available at

http://www.stat.ufl.edu/~aa/social/data.html

This edition contains several changes and additions in content, directed toward a more modern approach. The main changes are as follows:

- There is stronger focus on *real examples* and on the integration of *statistical software*. This includes some new exercises that ask students to use applets at the Prentice Hall Web site to help learn the fundamental concepts of sampling distributions, confidence intervals, and significance tests.
- The book has a somewhat *lower technical level* in the first nine chapters, to make the book more easily accessible to undergraduate students. To help with this, some notation has been simplified or eliminated.
- Chapter 3, on descriptive statistics, has a separate section for measures of position, such as percentiles and related topics such as the box plot and outliers. It also has a short section on bivariate descriptive methods. This gives students

an early exposure to contingency tables and to regression and the point that, in practice, there's almost always more than one variable of interest. This section also introduces them to the concepts of association, and response and explanatory variables.

- Chapter 4 has a new section that introduces the relative frequency concept and briefly summarizes three basic probability rules that are occasionally applied in the text.
- The inference material on means in Chapters 5–7 has been changed to rely completely on the $t$ distribution, rather than using the $z$ for large samples and $t$ for small samples. This makes results consistent with software output. I continue to emphasize that the normality assumption for the $t$ distribution is mainly needed for small samples with one-sided inference.
- Partly because of the change in using the $t$ distribution always for inference about the mean, Chapter 5, on confidence intervals, now presents methods for the proportion (which relies only on the normal distribution) before the mean. This way, the students can learn the basic concept of a confidence interval using the information they've just learned at the end of Chapter 4 about the normal distribution as a sampling distribution (i.e., for a proportion, the margin of error multiplies the standard error by a $z$-score rather than a $t$-score). This delays introduction of the $t$ distribution by a section, so students are not confronted with too many new topics all at once.
- Chapter 7, on comparing two groups, has a new section introducing ideas of bivariate analysis, reminding students of the distinction between response and explanatory variables, defining independent and dependent samples, discussing how to compare two groups with a difference or a ratio of two parameters, and showing the general formula for finding a standard error of a difference between two independent estimates. Section 7.3 introduces the concept of a model.
- Chapter 12, on analysis of variance (ANOVA), explains the ideas behind the $F$ test and gives an example before presenting the sums of squares formulas.
- Chapter 15 provides a less technical explanation of logistic regression and introduces its extensions for nominal and ordinal response variables.
- Chapter 16 includes new sections on *longitudinal data analysis* and *multilevel (hierarchical) models*.

### Use of Text in Introductory Statistics Courses

Like the first three editions, this edition is appropriate for introductory statistics courses at either the undergraduate or beginning graduate level, and for either a single-term or a two-term sequence. Chapters 1–9 are the basis for a single-term course. If the instructor wishes to go further than Chapter 9 or wishes to cover some material in greater depth, sections that can easily be omitted without disturbing continuity include 2.4, 5.5, 6.6–6.7, 7.5–7.7, and 8.5–8.6. Also, Chapters 7–9 and Sections 12.1–12.2 are self-contained, and the instructor could move directly into any of these after covering the fundamentals in Chapters 1–6. Four possible paths for a one-term course are as follows:

- Chapters 1–9 (possibly omitting sections noted above): Standard cross-section of methods, including basic descriptive and inferential statistics, two-sample procedures, contingency tables, and linear regression
- Chapters 1–7, 9, 11: Emphasis on regression

- Chapters 1–7, 9, 12.1–12.2: After two-group comparisons, introduction to regression and analysis of variance
- Chapters 1–8, 10: Emphasis on categorical data, basic issues of multivariate relationships

Regardless of the type of data, my belief is that a modeling paradigm emphasizing parameter estimation is more useful than the artificial hypothesis-testing approach of many statistics texts. Thus, the basic inference chapters (5–8) explain the advantages confidence intervals have over significance testing, and the second half of this text (starting in Chapter 9) is primarily concerned with model building. The concept of a model is introduced in Section 7.5 in describing the two methods for comparing means. The modeling material forms the basis of a second course.

Some material appears in sections, subsections, or exercises marked by asterisks. This material is optional, having lesser importance for introductory courses. The text does not attempt to present every available method, since it is meant to be a teaching tool, not an encyclopedic cookbook. It does cover the most important methods for social science research, however, and it includes topics not usually discussed in introductory statistics texts, such as

- Methods for contingency tables that are more informative than chi-squared, such as cell residuals and analyses that utilize category orderings
- Controlling for variables, and issues dealing with causation
- The generalized linear modeling approach, encompassing ordinary regression, analysis of variance and covariance, gamma regression for nonnegative responses with standard deviation proportional to the mean, logistic regression for categorical responses, and loglinear association models for contingency tables

I believe that the student who works through this book successfully will acquire a solid foundation in applied statistical methodology.

# Acknowledgments

I am grateful to Barbara Finlay for her contributions to the first two editions of this text. I hope that the combination of our respective fields of expertise provides a book that is statistically sound as well as relevant to the social sciences.

I thank those who invested a considerable amount of time in helping this book to reach fruition. Thanks to Sarah Streett for updating data in many of the examples and exercises, to Jackie Miller for her excellent job on accuracy checking, and to Traci Douglas for serving as Production Editor. Thanks to Arne Bathke, David Most, Youqin Huang, and Michael Lacy for providing comments for this edition. Other individuals who provided advice or data sets include Roslynn Brain, Beth Chance, Brent Coull, Alfred DeMaris, Mary Gray, Brian Gridley, Ralitza Gueorguieva, John Henretta, Ira Horowitz, Harry Khamis, Bernhard Klingenberg, Jacalyn Levine, Michael Radelet, Paula Rausch, Euijung Ryu, Paul Smith, Robert Wilson, and Zoe Ziliak. Thanks also to the many people whose comments helped in the preparation of the first three editions, especially Burke Grandjean, Susan Reiland, Maureen Hallinan, Shirley Scritchfield, Sonja Wright, Douglas Zahn, Jeff Witmer, E. Jacquelin Dietz, Dorothy K. Davidson, and Mary Sue Younger. My editors for this and the previous edition, Petra Recter and Ann Heath at Prentice Hall, provided outstanding support and encouragement.

Finally, extra special thanks to my wife, Jacki Levine, for assistance with editing and style in the third edition and with overall encouragement during the preparation of the fourth edition.

*Alan Agresti*
Gainesville, Florida

CHAPTER 1

# Introduction

1.1   INTRODUCTION TO STATISTICAL METHODOLOGY
1.2   DESCRIPTIVE STATISTICS AND INFERENTIAL STATISTICS
1.3   THE ROLE OF COMPUTERS IN STATISTICS
1.4   CHAPTER SUMMARY

## 1.1   INTRODUCTION TO STATISTICAL METHODOLOGY

The past quarter-century has seen a dramatic increase in the use of statistical methods in the social sciences. There are many reasons for this. More research in the social sciences has taken on a quantitative orientation. Like research in other sciences, research in the social sciences often studies questions of interest by analyzing evidence provided by empirical data. The growth of the Internet has resulted in an increase in the amount of readily available quantitative information. Finally, with the evolution of evermore powerful computers, software, and statistical methodology, new methods are available that can more realistically address the questions that arise in social science research.

### Why Study Statistics?

The increased use of statistics is evident in the changes in the content of articles published in social science research journals and reports prepared in government and private industry. A quick glance through recent issues of journals such as *American Political Science Review* and *American Sociological Review* reveals the fundamental role of statistics in research. For example, to learn about which factors have the greatest impact on student performance in school or to investigate which factors affect people's political beliefs or the quality of their health care or their decision about when to retire, researchers collect information and process it using statistical analyses. Because of the role of statistics in many research studies, more and more academic departments require that their majors take statistics courses.

These days, social scientists work in a wide variety of areas that use statistical methods, such as governmental agencies, business organizations, and health care facilities. For example, social scientists in government agencies dealing with human welfare or environmental issues or public health policy invariably need to use statistical methods or at least read reports that contain statistics. Medical sociologists often must evaluate recommendations from studies that contain quantitative investigations of new therapies or new ways of caring for the elderly. Some social scientists help managers to evaluate employee performance using quantitative benchmarks and to determine factors that help predict sales of products. In fact, increasingly many jobs for social scientists expect a knowledge of statistical methods as a basic work tool. As the joke goes, "What did the sociologist who passed statistics say to the sociologist who failed it? 'I'll have a Big Mac, fries, and a Coke.' "

But an understanding of statistics is important even if you never use statistical methods in your career. Every day you are exposed to an explosion of information, from advertising, news reporting, political campaigning, surveys about opinions on controversial issues, and other communications containing statistical arguments. Statistics helps you make sense of this information and better understand the world. You will find concepts from this text helpful in judging the information you will encounter in your everyday life.

We realize you are not reading this book in hopes of becoming a statistician. In addition, you may suffer from math phobia and feel fear at what lies ahead. Please be assured that you can read this book and learn the primary concepts and methods of statistics with little knowledge of mathematics. Just because you may have had difficulty in math courses before does not mean you will be at a disadvantage here. To understand this book, logical thinking and perseverance are more important than mathematics. In our experience, the most important factor in how well you do in a statistics course is how much time you spend on the course—attending class, doing homework, reading and re-reading this text, studying your class notes, working together with your fellow students, getting help from your professor or teaching assistant—not your mathematical knowledge or your gender or your race or whether you feel fear of statistics at the beginning.

Don't be frustrated if learning comes slowly and you need to read a chapter a few times before it starts to make sense. Just as you would not expect to take a single course in a foreign language and be able to speak that language fluently, the same is true with the language of statistics. Once you have completed even a portion of this text, however, you will better understand how to make sense of statistical information.

## Data

Information gathering is at the heart of all sciences, providing the ***observations*** used in statistical analyses. The observations gathered on the characteristics of interest are collectively called ***data***.

For example, a study might conduct a survey of 1000 people to observe characteristics such as opinion about the legalization of marijuana, political party affiliation, political ideology, how often attend religious services, number of years of education, annual income, marital status, race, and gender. The data for a particular person would consist of observations such as (opinion = do not favor legalization, party = Republican, ideology = conservative, religiosity = once a week, education = 14 years, annual income in range 40–60 thousand dollars, marital status = married, race = white, gender = female). Looking at the data in the right way helps us learn about how such characteristics are related. We can then answer questions such as, "Do people who attend church more often tend to be more politically conservative?"

To generate data, the social sciences use a wide variety of methods, including surveys, experiments, and direct observation of behavior in natural settings. In addition, social scientists often analyze data already recorded for other purposes, such as police records, census materials, and hospital files. Existing archived collections of data are called ***databases***. Many databases are now available on the Internet. A very important database for social scientists contains results since 1972 of the General Social Survey.

### EXAMPLE 1.1    The General Social Survey (GSS)

Every other year, the National Opinion Research Center at the University of Chicago conducts the General Social Survey (GSS). This survey of about 2000 adults provides data about opinions and behaviors of the American public. Social scientists use it to investigate how adult Americans answer a wide diversity of questions, such as, "Do you believe in life after death?," "Would you be willing to pay higher prices in order to protect the environment?," and "Do you think a preschool child is likely to suffer if his or her mother works?" Similar surveys occur in other countries, such as the General Social Survey administered by Statistics Canada, the British Social Attitudes Survey, and the Eurobarometer survey and European Social Survey for nations in the European Union.

It is easy to get summaries of data from the GSS database. We'll demonstrate, using a question it asked in one survey, "About how many good friends do you have?"

- Go to the Web site sda.berkeley.edu/GSS/ at the Survey Documentation and Analysis site at the University of California, Berkeley.
- Click on *New SDA*.
- The GSS name for the question about number of good friends is NUMFREND. Type NUMFREND as the *Row* variable name. Click on *Run the table*.

Now you'll see a table that shows the possible values for 'number of good friends' and the number of people and the percentage who made each possible response. The most common responses were 2 and 3 (about 16% made each of these responses). ■

## What Is Statistics?

In this text, we use the term "statistics" in the broad sense to refer to methods for obtaining and analyzing data.

| Statistics |
| --- |
| *Statistics* consists of a body of methods for obtaining and analyzing data. |

Specifically, statistics provides methods for

1. *Design*: Planning how to gather data for research studies
2. *Description*: Summarizing the data
3. *Inference*: Making predictions based on the data

*Design* refers to planning how to obtain the data. For a survey, for example, the design aspects would specify how to select the people to interview and would construct the questionnaire to administer.

*Description* refers to summarizing data, to help understand the information they provide. For example, an analysis of the number of good friends based on the GSS data might start with a list of the number reported for each of the people who responded to that question that year. The raw data are a complete listing of observations, person by person. These are not easy to comprehend, however. We get bogged down in numbers. For presentation of results, instead of listing *all* observations, we could summarize the data with a graph or table showing the percentages reporting 1 good friend, 2 good friends, 3,..., and so on. Or we could report the average number of good friends, which was 6, or the most common response, which was 2. Graphs, tables and numerical summaries are called *descriptive statistics*.

*Inference* refers to making predictions based on data. For instance, for the GSS data on reported number of good friends, 6.2% reported having only 1 good friend. Can we use this information to predict the percentage of the more than 200 million adults in the U.S. at that time who had only 1 good friend? A method presented in this book allows us to predict that that percentage is no greater than 8%. Predictions made using data are called *statistical inferences*.

*Description* and *inference* are the two types of *statistical analysis*—ways of analyzing the data. Social scientists use descriptive and inferential statistics to answer questions about social phenomena. For instance, "Is having the death penalty available for punishment associated with a reduction in violent crime?" "Does student performance in schools depend on the amount of money spent per student, the size of the classes, or the teachers' salaries?"

## 1.2 DESCRIPTIVE STATISTICS AND INFERENTIAL STATISTICS

Section 1.1 explained that statistics consists of methods for *designing* studies and *analyzing* data collected in the studies. Methods for analyzing data include descriptive methods for summarizing the data and inferential methods for making predictions. A statistical analysis is classified as **descriptive** or **inferential**, according to whether its main purpose is to describe the data or to make predictions. To explain this distinction further, we next define the *population* and the *sample*.

### Populations and Samples

The entities that a study observes are called the **subjects** for the study. Usually the subjects are people, such as in the GSS, but they might instead be families, schools, cities, or companies, for instance.

> **Population and Sample**
>
> The **population** is the total set of subjects of interest in a study. A **sample** is the subset of the population on which the study collects data.

In the 2004 GSS, the sample was the 2813 adult Americans who participated in the survey. The population was all adult Americans at that time—more than 200 million people.

The ultimate goal of any study is to learn about populations. But it is almost always necessary, and more practical, to observe only samples from those populations. For example, the GSS and polling organizations such as the Gallup poll usually select samples of about 1000–3000 Americans to collect information about opinions and beliefs of the population of *all* Americans.

> **Descriptive Statistics**
>
> **Descriptive statistics** summarize the information in a collection of data.

Descriptive statistics consist of graphs, tables, and numbers such as averages and percentages. The main purpose of descriptive statistics is to reduce the data to simpler and more understandable forms without distorting or losing much information.

Although data are usually available only for a sample, descriptive statistics are also useful when data are available for the entire population, such as in a census. By contrast, inferential statistics apply when data are available only for a sample but we want to make a prediction about the entire population.

> **Inferential Statistics**
>
> **Inferential statistics** provide predictions about a population, based on data from a sample of that population.

### EXAMPLE 1.2 Belief in Heaven

In two of its surveys, the GSS asked, "Do you believe in heaven?" The population of interest was the collection of all adults in the United States. In the most recent survey in which this was asked, 86% of the 1158 sampled subjects answered *yes*. We would be interested, however, not only in those 1158 people but in the *entire population* of all adults in the U.S.

Inferential statistics provide a prediction about the larger population using the sample data. An inferential method presented in Chapter 5 predicts that the population percentage that believe in heaven falls between 84% and 88%. That is, the sample value of 86% has a "margin of error" of 2%. Even though the sample size was tiny compared to the population size, we can conclude that a large percentage of the population believed in heaven. ■

Inferential statistical analyses can predict characteristics of entire populations quite well by selecting samples that are small relative to the population size. That's why many polls sample only about a thousand people, even if the population has millions of people. In this book, we'll see why this works.

In the past quarter-century, social scientists have increasingly recognized the power of inferential statistical methods. Presentation of these methods occupies a large portion of this textbook, beginning in Chapter 5.

## Parameters and Statistics

---

**Parameters and Statistics**

---

A *parameter* is a numerical summary of the population. A *statistic* is a numerical summary of the sample data.

---

Example 1.2 estimated the percentage of Americans who believe in heaven. The parameter was the population percentage who believed in heaven. Its value was unknown. The inference about this parameter was based on a statistic—the percentage of the 1158 subjects interviewed in the survey who answered *yes*, namely, 86%. Since this number *describes* a characteristic of the sample, it is a descriptive statistic.

In practice, the main interest is in the values of the parameters, not the values of the statistics for the particular sample selected. For example, in viewing results of a poll before an election, we're more interested in the *population* percentages favoring the various candidates than in the *sample* percentages for the people interviewed. The sample and statistics describing it are important only insofar as they help us make inferences about unknown population parameters.

An important aspect of statistical inference involves reporting the likely *precision* of the sample statistic that estimates the population parameter. For Example 1.2 on belief in heaven, an inferential statistical method predicted how close the *sample* value of 86% was likely to be to the unknown percentage of the *population* believing in heaven. The reported margin of error was 2%.

When data exist for an entire population, such as in a census, it's possible to find the actual values of the parameters of interest. Then there is no need to use inferential statistical methods.

## Defining Populations: Actual and Conceptual

Usually the population to which inferences apply is an actual set of subjects. In Example 1.2, it was adult residents of the U.S. Sometimes, though, the generalizations refer to a *conceptual* population—one that does not actually exist but is hypothetical.

For example, suppose a consumer organization evaluates gas mileage for a new model of an automobile by observing the average number of miles per gallon for five sample autos driven on a standardized 100-mile course. Their inferences refer to the performance on this course for the conceptual population of *all* autos of this model that will be or could hypothetically be manufactured.

## 1.3 THE ROLE OF COMPUTERS IN STATISTICS

Over time, ever more powerful computers reach the market, and powerful and easy-to-use software is further developed for statistical methods. This software provides an enormous boon to the use of statistics.

### Statistical Software

SPSS (Statistical Package for the Social Sciences), SAS, MINITAB, and Stata are the most popular statistical software on college campuses. It is much easier to apply statistical methods using these software than using hand calculation. Moreover, many methods presented in this text are too complex to do by hand or with hand calculators.

Most chapters of this text, including all those that present methods requiring considerable computation, show examples of the output of statistical software. One purpose of this textbook is to teach you what to look for in output and how to interpret it. Knowledge of computer programming is not necessary for using statistical software or for reading this book.

The text appendix explains how to use SPSS and SAS, organized by chapter. You can refer to this appendix as you read each chapter to learn how to use them to perform the analyses of that chapter.

### Data Files

Figure 1.1 shows an example of data organized in a ***data file*** for analysis by statistical software. A data file has the form of a spreadsheet:

- Any one row contains the observations for a particular subject in the sample.
- Any one column contains the observations for a particular characteristic.

Figure 1.1 is a window for editing data in SPSS. It shows data for the first ten subjects in a sample, for the characteristics sex, racial group, marital status, age, and annual income (in thousands of dollars). Some of the data are numerical, and some consist of labels. Chapter 2 introduces the types of data for data files.

### Uses and Misuses of Statistical Software

A note of caution: The easy access to statistical methods using software has dangers as well as benefits. It is simple to apply inappropriate methods. A computer performs the analysis requested whether or not the assumptions required for its proper use are satisfied.

Incorrect analyses result when researchers take insufficient time to understand the statistical method, the assumptions for its use, or its appropriateness for the specific problem. It is vital to understand the method before using it. Just knowing how to use statistical software does not guarantee a proper analysis. You'll need a good background in statistics to understand which method to select, which options to choose in that method, and how to make valid conclusions from the output. The main purpose of this text is to give you this background.

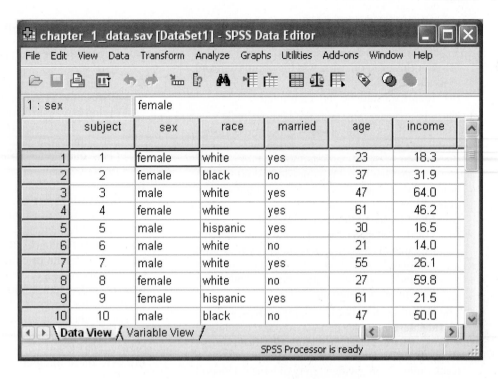

**FIGURE 1.1:** Example of Part of a SPSS Data File

## 1.4 CHAPTER SUMMARY

The field of statistics includes methods for

- designing research studies,
- describing the data, and
- making inferences (predictions) using the data.

Statistical methods normally are applied to observations in a **sample** taken from the **population** of interest. **Statistics** summarize sample data, while **parameters** summarize entire populations. There are two types of statistical analyses:

- **Descriptive statistics** summarize sample or population data with numbers, tables, and graphs.
- **Inferential statistics** make predictions about population parameters, based on sample data.

A **data file** has a separate row of data for each subject and a separate column for each characteristic. Statistical methods are easy to apply to data files using software. This relieves us of computational drudgery and helps us focus on the proper application and interpretation of the methods.

## PROBLEMS

### Practicing the Basics

**1.1.** The Environmental Protection Agency (EPA) uses a few new automobiles of each brand every year to collect data on pollution emission and gasoline mileage performance. For the Toyota Prius brand, identify the (a) subject, (b) sample, (c) population.

**1.2.** In the 2006 gubernatorial election in California, an exit poll sampled 2705 of the 7 million people who voted. The poll stated that 56.5%

reported voting for the Republican candidate, Arnold Schwarzenegger. Of all 7 million voters, 55.9% voted for Schwarzenegger.

(a) For this exit poll, what was the population and what was the sample?

(b) Identify a statistic and a parameter.

**1.3.** The student government at the University of Wisconsin conducts a study about alcohol abuse among students. One hundred of the 40,858 members of the student body are sampled and asked to complete a questionnaire. One question asked is, "On how many days in the past week did you consume at least one alcoholic drink?"

(a) Identify the population of interest.

(b) For the 40,858 students, one characteristic of interest was the percentage who would respond *zero* to this question. This value is computed for the 100 students sampled. Is it a parameter or a statistic? Why?

**1.4.** The Institute for Public Opinion Research at Florida International University has conducted the FIU/Florida Poll (www.fiu.edu/orgs/ipor/ffp) of about 1200 Floridians annually since 1988 to track opinions on a wide variety of issues. The poll reported in 2006 that 67% of Floridians believe that state government should not make laws restricting access to abortion. Is 67% the value of a statistic, or of a parameter? Why?

**1.5.** A GSS asked subjects whether astrology—the study of star signs—has some scientific truth (GSS question SCITEST3). Of 1245 sampled subjects, 651 responded *definitely or probably true*, and 594 responded *definitely or probably not true*. The proportion responding *definitely or probably true* was $651/1245 = 0.523$.

(a) Describe the population of interest.

(b) For what population parameter might we want to make an inference?

(c) What sample statistic could be used in making this inference?

(d) Does the value of the statistic in (c) necessarily equal the parameter in (b)? Explain.

**1.6.** Go to the GSS Web site, sda.berkeley.edu/GSS/. By entering TVHOURS as the *Row variable*, find a summary of responses to the question, "On a typical day, about how many hours do you personally watch television?"

(a) What was the most common response?

(b) Is your answer in (a) a descriptive statistic, or an inferential statistic?

**1.7.** Go to the GSS Web site, sda.berkeley.edu/GSS/. By entering HEAVEN as the *Row variable*, you can find the percentages of people who said *definitely yes*, *probably yes*, *probably not*, and

*definitely not* when asked whether they believed in heaven.

(a) Report the percentage who gave one of the *yes* responses.

(b) To obtain data for a particular year such as 1998, enter YEAR(1998) in the *Selection filter* option box before you click on *Run the Table*. Do this for HEAVEN in 1998, and report the percentage who gave one of the *yes* responses. (This question was asked only in 1991 and 1998.)

(c) Summarize opinions in 1998 about belief in hell (variable HELL in the GSS). Was the percentage of *yes* responses higher for HEAVEN or HELL?

**1.8.** The Current Population Survey (CPS) is a monthly survey of households conducted by the U.S. Census Bureau. A CPS of 60,000 households indicated that of those households, 8.1% of the whites, 22.3% of the blacks, 20.9% of the Hispanics, and 10.2% of the Asians had annual income below the poverty level (*Statistical Abstract of the United States, 2006*).

(a) Are these numbers statistics, or parameters? Explain.

(b) A method from this text predicts that the percentage of *all* black households in the United States having income below the poverty level is at least 21% but no greater than 24%. What type of statistical method does this illustrate—descriptive or inferential? Why?

**1.9.** A BBC story (September 9, 2004) about a poll in 35 countries concerning whether people favored George W. Bush or John Kerry in the 2004 U.S. Presidential election stated that Kerry was clearly preferred. Of the sample from Germany, 74% preferred Kerry, 10% preferred Bush, with the rest undecided or not responding. Multiple choice: The results for Germany are an example of

(a) descriptive statistics for a sample.

(b) inferential statistics about a population.

(c) a data file.

(d) a population.

**1.10.** Construct a data file describing the criminal behavior of five inmates in a local prison. The characteristics measured were race (with observations for the five subjects: white, black, white, Hispanic, white), age (19, 23, 38, 20, 41), length of sentence in years (2, 1, 10, 2, 5), whether convicted on a felony (no, no, yes, no, yes), number of prior arrests (values 2, 0, 8, 1, 5), number of prior convictions (1, 0, 3, 1, 4).

## Concepts and Applications

**1.11.** The "Student survey" data file at *www.stat.ufl.edu/~aa/social/data.html*

shows responses of a class of social science graduate students at the University of Florida to a questionnaire that asked about $GE$ = gender, $AG$ = age in years, $HI$ = high school GPA (on a four-point scale), $CO$ = college GPA, $DH$ = distance (in miles) of the campus from your home town, $DR$ = distance (in miles) of the classroom from your current residence, $NE$ = number of times a week you read a newspaper, $TV$ = average number of hours per week that you watch TV, $SP$ = average number of hours per week that you participate in sports or have other physical exercise, $VE$ = whether you are a vegetarian (yes, no), $AB$ = opinion about whether abortion should be legal in the first three months of pregnancy (yes, no), $PI$ = political ideology (1 = very liberal, 2 = liberal, 3 = slightly liberal, 4 = moderate, 5 = slightly conservative, 6 = conservative, 7 = very conservative), $PA$ = political affiliation (D = Democrat, R = Republican, I = independent), $RE$ = how often you attend religious services (never, occasionally, most weeks, every week), $LD$ = belief in life after death (yes, no), $AA$ = support affirmative action (yes, no), $AH$ = number of people you know who have died from AIDS or who are HIV+. You will use this data file for exercises in future chapters.

  **(a)** Practice accessing a data file for statistical analysis with your software by going to this Web site and copying this data file. Print a copy of the data file. How many observations (rows) are in the data file?

  **(b)** Give an example of a question that could be addressed using these data with (i) descriptive statistics, (ii) inferential statistics.

**1.12.** Using a spreadsheet program (such as Microsoft Office Excel) or statistical software, your instructor will help the class create a data file consisting of the values for class members of characteristics such as those in the previous exercise. One exercise in each chapter will use this data file.

  **(a)** Copy the data file to your computer and print a copy.

  **(b)** Give an example of a question that you could address by analyzing these data with (i) descriptive statistics, (ii) inferential statistics.

**1.13.** For the statistical software your instructor has chosen for your course, find out how to access the software, enter data, and print any data files that you create. Create a data file using the data in Figure 1.1 in Section 1.3, and print it.

**1.14.** Illustrating with an example, explain the difference between

  **(a)** a *statistic* and a *parameter*.

  **(b)** *description* and *inference* as two purposes for using statistical methods.

**1.15.** You have data for a population, from a census. Explain why descriptive statistics are helpful but inferential statistics are not needed.

**1.16.** A sociologist wants to estimate the average age at marriage for women in New England in the early eighteenth century. She finds within her state archives marriage records for a large Puritan village for the years 1700–1730. She then takes a sample of those records, noting the age of the bride for each. The average age in the sample is 24.1 years. Using a statistical method from Chapter 5, the sociologist estimates the average age of brides at marriage for the population to be between 23.5 and 24.7 years.

  **(a)** What part of this example is descriptive?

  **(b)** What part of this example is inferential?

  **(c)** To what population does the inference refer?

**1.17.** In a recent survey by Eurobarometer of Europeans about energy issues and global warming,[1] one question asked, "Would you be willing to pay more for energy produced from renewable sources than for energy produced from other sources?" The percentage of *yes* responses varied among countries between 10% (in Bulgaria) to 60% (in Luxembourg). Of the 631 subjects interviewed in the UK, 45% said *yes*. It was predicted that for all 48 million adults in the UK, that percentage who would answer *yes* falls between 41% and 49%. Identify in this discussion (a) a statistic, (b) a parameter, (c) a descriptive statistical analysis, (d) an inferential statistical analysis.

**1.18.** Go to the Web site for the Gallup poll, www.galluppoll.com. From information listed on or linked from the homepage, give an example of a (a) descriptive statistical analysis, (b) inferential statistical analysis.

**1.19.** Check whether you have access to JSTOR (Journal Storage) at your school by visiting www.jstor.org. If so, click on *Browse* and then *Sociology* or another discipline of interest to you. Select a journal and a particular issue, and browse through some of the articles. Find an article that uses statistical methods. In a paragraph of 100–200 words, explain how descriptive statistics were used.

---

[1] *Attitudes towards Energy*, published January 2006 at ec.europa.eu/public_opinion

# CHAPTER 2

# Sampling and Measurement

2.1 VARIABLES AND THEIR MEASUREMENT
2.2 RANDOMIZATION
2.3 SAMPLING VARIABILITY AND POTENTIAL BIAS
2.4 OTHER PROBABILITY SAMPLING METHODS*
2.5 CHAPTER SUMMARY

To analyze social phenomena with a statistical analysis, *descriptive* methods summarize the data and *inferential* methods use sample data to make predictions about populations. In gathering data, we must decide which subjects to sample. Selecting a sample that is representative of the population is a primary topic of this chapter.

Given a sample, we must convert our ideas about social phenomena into data through deciding what to measure and how to measure it. Developing ways to measure abstract concepts such as achievement, intelligence, and prejudice is one of the most challenging aspects of social research. A measure should have *validity*, describing what it is intended to measure and accurately reflecting the concept. It should also have *reliability*, being consistent in the sense that a subject will give the same response when asked again. Invalid or unreliable data-gathering instruments render statistical manipulations of the data meaningless.

The first section of this chapter introduces definitions pertaining to measurement, such as types of data. The other sections discuss ways, good and bad, of selecting the sample.

## 2.1 VARIABLES AND THEIR MEASUREMENT

Statistical methods help us determine the factors that explain *variability* among subjects. For instance, variation occurs from student to student in their college grade point average (GPA). What is responsible for that variability? The way those students vary in how much they study per week? in how much they watch TV per day? in their IQ? in their college board score? in their high school GPA?

### Variables

Any characteristic we can measure for each subject is called a ***variable***. The name reflects that values of the characteristic *vary* among subjects.

> **Variable**
>
> A ***variable*** is a characteristic that can vary in value among subjects in a sample or population.

Different subjects may have different values of a variable. Examples of variables are income last year, number of siblings, whether employed, and gender. The values the variable can take form the ***measurement scale***. For gender, for instance, the measurement scale consists of the two labels, female and male. For number of siblings it is 0, 1, 2, 3, . . . .

The valid statistical methods for a variable depend on its measurement scale. We treat a numerical-valued variable such as annual income differently than a variable with a measurement scale consisting of categories, such as (yes, no) for whether employed. We next present ways to classify variables. The first type refers to whether the measurement scale consists of categories or numbers. Another type refers to the number of levels in that scale.

### Quantitative and Categorical Variables

A variable is called *quantitative* when the measurement scale has numerical values. The values represent different magnitudes of the variable. Examples of quantitative variables are a subject's annual income, number of siblings, age, and number of years of education completed.

A variable is called *categorical* when the measurement scale is a set of categories. For example, marital status, with categories (single, married, divorced, widowed), is categorical. For Canadians, the province of residence is categorical, with the categories Alberta, British Columbia, and so on. Other categorical variables are whether employed (yes, no), primary clothes shopping destination (local mall, local downtown, Internet, other), favorite type of music (classical, country, folk, jazz, rock), religious affiliation (Protestant, Catholic, Jewish, Muslim, other, none), and political party preference.

For categorical variables, distinct categories differ in quality, not in numerical magnitude. Categorical variables are often called *qualitative*. We distinguish between categorical and quantitative variables because different statistical methods apply to each type. Some methods apply to categorical variables and others apply to quantitative variables. For example, the *average* is a statistical summary for a quantitative variable, because it uses numerical values. It's possible to find the average for a quantitative variable such as income, but not for a categorical variable such as religious affiliation or favorite type of music.

### Nominal, Ordinal, and Interval Scales of Measurement

For a quantitative variable, the possible numerical values are said to form an *interval* scale. Interval scales have a specific numerical distance or *interval* between each pair of levels. Annual income is usually measured on an interval scale. The interval between $40,000 and $30,000, for instance, equals $10,000. We can compare outcomes in terms of how much larger or how much smaller one is than the other.

Categorical variables have two types of scales. For the categorical variables mentioned in the previous subsection, the categories are unordered. The scale does not have a "high" or "low" end. The categories are then said to form a *nominal scale*. For another example, a variable measuring primary mode of transportation to work might use the nominal scale with categories (automobile, bus, subway, bicycle, walk).

Although the different categories are often called the *levels* of the scale, for a nominal variable no level is greater than or smaller than any other level. Names or labels such as "automobile" and "bus" for mode of transportation identify the categories but do not represent different magnitudes. By contrast, each possible value of a quantitative variable is *greater than* or *less than* any other possible value.

A third type of scale falls, in a sense, between nominal and interval. It consists of categorical scales having a natural *ordering* of values. The levels form an *ordinal scale*. Examples are social class (upper, middle, lower), political philosophy (very liberal, slightly liberal, moderate, slightly conservative, very conservative), government spending on the environment (too little, about right, too much), and frequency of religious activity (never, less than once a month, about 1–3 times a month, every week, more than once a week). These scales are not nominal, because the categories are ordered. They are not interval, because there is no defined distance between levels. For example, a person categorized as very conservative is *more* conservative than a person categorized as slightly conservative, but there is no numerical value for *how much more* conservative that person is.

In summary, for ordinal variables the categories have a natural ordering, whereas for nominal variables the categories are unordered. The scales refer to the actual measurement and not to the phenomena themselves. *Place of residence* may indicate a geographic place name such as a county (nominal), the distance of that place from a point on the globe (interval), the size of the place (interval or ordinal), or other kinds of variables.

### Quantitative Aspects of Ordinal Data

As we've discussed, levels of nominal scales are qualitative, varying in quality, not in quantity. Levels of interval scales are quantitative, varying in magnitude. The position of ordinal scales on the quantitative–qualitative classification is fuzzy. Because their scale is a set of categories, they are often analyzed using the same methods as nominal scales. But in many respects, ordinal scales more closely resemble interval scales. They possess an important quantitative feature: Each level has a *greater* or *smaller* magnitude than another level.

Some statistical methods apply specifically to ordinal variables. Often, though, it's helpful to analyze ordinal scales by assigning numerical scores to categories. By treating ordinal variables as interval rather than nominal, we can use the more powerful methods available for quantitative variables.

For example, course grades (such as A, B, C, D, E) are ordinal. But we treat them as interval when we assign numbers to the grades (such as 4, 3, 2, 1, 0) to compute a grade point average. Treating ordinal variables as interval requires good judgment in assigning scores. In doing this, you can conduct a "sensitivity analysis" by checking whether conclusions would differ in any significant way for other choices of the scores.

### Discrete and Continuous Variables

One other way to classify a variable also helps determine which statistical methods are appropriate for it. This classification refers to the number of values in the measurement scale.

---

**Discrete and Continuous Variables**

A variable is *discrete* if its possible values form a set of separate numbers, such as 0, 1, 2, 3, . . . . It is *continuous* if it can take an infinite continuum of possible real number values.

---

Examples of discrete variables are the number of siblings and the number of visits to a physician last year. Any variable phrased as "the number of . . ." is discrete, because it is possible to list its possible values $\{0, 1, 2, 3, 4, \ldots\}$.

Examples of continuous variables are height, weight, and the amount of time it takes to read a passage of a book. It is impossible to write down all the distinct potential values, since they form an interval of infinitely many values. The amount of time needed to read a book, for example, could take on the value 8.6294473. . . hours.

Discrete variables have a basic unit of measurement that cannot be subdivided. For example, 2 and 3 are possible values for the number of siblings, but 2.5716 is not. For a continuous variable, by contrast, between any two possible values there is always another possible value. For example, age is continuous in the sense that an individual does not age in discrete jumps. At some well-defined point during the year in which you age from 21 to 22, you are 21.3851 years old, and similarly for every other real number between 21 and 22. A continuous, infinite collection of age values occurs between 21 and 22 alone.

Any variable with a finite number of possible values is discrete. All categorical variables, nominal or ordinal, are discrete, having a finite set of categories. Quantitative variables can be discrete or continuous; age is continuous, and number of siblings is discrete.

For quantitative variables the distinction between discrete and continuous variables can be blurry, because of how variables are actually measured. In practice, we round continuous variables when measuring them, so the measurement is actually discrete. We say that an individual is 21 years old whenever that person's age is somewhere between 21 and 22. On the other hand, some variables, although discrete, have a very large number of possible values. In measuring annual family income in dollars, the potential values are 0, 1, 2, 3, ..., up to some very large value in many millions.

What's the implication of this? Statistical methods for discrete variables are mainly used for quantitative variables that take relatively few values, such as the number of times a person has been married. Statistical methods for continuous variables are used for quantitative variables that can take lots of values, regardless of whether they are theoretically continuous or discrete. For example, statisticians treat variables such as age, income, and IQ as continuous.

In summary,

- Variables are either *quantitative* (numerical valued) or *categorical*. Quantitative variables are measured on an *interval* scale. Categorical variables with unordered categories have a *nominal* scale, and categorical variables with ordered categories have an *ordinal* scale.
- Categorical variables (nominal or ordinal) are *discrete*. Quantitative variables can be either discrete or continuous. In practice, quantitative variables that can take lots of values are treated as *continuous*.

Figure 2.1 summarizes the types of variables, in terms of the (quantitative, categorical), (nominal, ordinal, interval), and (continuous, discrete) classifications.

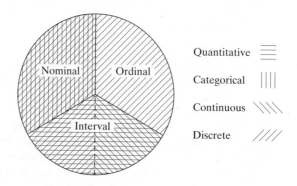

Note: Ordinal data are treated sometimes as categorical and sometimes as quantitative

**FIGURE 2.1:** Summary of Quantitative–Categorical, Nominal–Ordinal–Interval, Continuous–Discrete Classifications

## 2.2  RANDOMIZATION

Inferential statistical methods use sample statistics to make predictions about population parameters. The quality of the inferences depends on how well the sample represents the population. This section introduces an important sampling method that incorporates ***randomization***, the mechanism for achieving good sample representation.

### Simple Random Sampling

Subjects of a population to be sampled could be individuals, families, schools, cities, hospitals, records of reported crimes, and so on. *Simple random sampling* is a method of sampling for which every possible sample has equal chance of selection.

Let $n$ denote the number of subjects in the sample, called the **sample size**.

---

**Simple Random Sample**

A ***simple random sample*** of $n$ subjects from a population is one in which each possible sample of that size has the same probability (chance) of being selected.

---

For instance, suppose a researcher administers a questionnaire to one randomly selected adult in each of several households. A particular household contains four adults—mother, father, aunt, and uncle—identified as M, F, A, and U. For a simple random sample of $n = 1$ adult, each of the four adults is equally likely to be interviewed. You could select one by placing the four names on four identical ballots and selecting one blindly from a hat. For a simple random sample of $n = 2$ adults, each possible sample of size two is equally likely. The six potential samples are (M, F), (M, A), (M, U), (F, A), (F, U), and (A, U). To select the sample, you blindly select two ballots from the hat.

A simple random sample is often just called a ***random sample***. The *simple* adjective is used to distinguish this type of sampling from more complex sampling schemes presented in Section 2.4 that also have elements of randomization.

Why is it a good idea to use random sampling? Because everyone has the same chance of inclusion in the sample, so it provides fairness. This reduces the chance that the sample is seriously biased in some way, leading to inaccurate inferences about the population. Most inferential statistical methods assume randomization of the sort provided by random sampling.

### How to Select a Simple Random Sample

To select a random sample, we need a list of all subjects in the population. This list is called the ***sampling frame***. Suppose you plan to sample students at your school. The population is all students at the school. One possible sampling frame is the student directory.

The most common method for selecting a random sample is to (1) number the subjects in the sampling frame, (2) generate a set of these numbers randomly, and (3) sample the subjects whose numbers were generated. Using *random numbers* to select the sample ensures that each subject has an equal chance of selection.

---

**Random Numbers**

***Random numbers*** are numbers that are computer generated according to a scheme whereby each digit is equally likely to be any of the integers $0, 1, 2, \ldots, 9$ and does not depend on the other digits generated.

---

**TABLE 2.1: Part of a Table of Random Numbers**

| Line/Col. | (1) | (2) | (3) | (4) | (5) | (6) | (7) | (8) |
|---|---|---|---|---|---|---|---|---|
| 1 | 10480 | 15011 | 01536 | 02011 | 81647 | 91646 | 69179 | 14194 |
| 2 | 22368 | 46573 | 25595 | 85393 | 30995 | 89198 | 27982 | 53402 |
| 3 | 24130 | 48360 | 22527 | 97265 | 76393 | 64809 | 15179 | 24830 |
| 4 | 42167 | 93093 | 06243 | 61680 | 07856 | 16376 | 39440 | 53537 |
| 5 | 37570 | 39975 | 81837 | 16656 | 06121 | 91782 | 60468 | 81305 |
| 6 | 77921 | 06907 | 11008 | 42751 | 27756 | 53498 | 18602 | 70659 |

*Source*: Abridged from William H. Beyer, ed., *Handbook of Tables for Probability and Statistics*, 2nd ed., © The Chemical Rubber Co., 1968. Used by permission of the Chemical Rubber Co.

Table 2.1 shows a table containing random numbers. The numbers fluctuate according to no set pattern. Any particular number has the same chance of being a 0, 1, 2, ..., or 9. The numbers are chosen independently, so any one digit chosen has no influence on any other selection. If the first digit in a row of the table is a 9, for instance, the next digit is still just as likely to be a 9 as a 0 or 1 or any other number. Random numbers are available in published tables and can be generated with software and many statistical calculators.

Suppose you want to select a simple random sample of $n = 100$ students from a university student body of size 30,000. The sampling frame is a directory of these students. Select the students by using five-digit sequences to identify them, as follows:

1. Assign the numbers 00001 to 30000 to the students in the directory, using 00001 for the first student in the list, 00002 for the second student, and so on.
2. Starting at any point in the random number table, or by generating random numbers using software or a calculator, choose successive five-digit numbers until you obtain 100 distinct numbers between 00001 and 30000.
3. Include in the sample the students with assigned numbers equal to the random numbers selected.

For example, for the first column of five-digit numbers in Table 2.1, the first three random numbers are 10480, 22368, and 24130. The first three students selected are those numbered 10480, 22368, and 24130.

In selecting the 100 five-digit numbers, skip numbers greater than 30000, such as the next three five-digit numbers in Table 2.1, since no student in the directory has an assigned number that large. After using the first column of five-digit numbers, move to the next column of numbers and continue. If the population size were between 1000 and 9999, you would use four digits at a time. The column (or row) from which you begin selecting the numbers does not matter, since the numbers have no set pattern. Most statistical software can do this all for you.

### ⭒ Collecting Data with Sample Surveys

⚡ Many studies select a sample of people from a population and interview them to collect data. This method of data collection is called a ***sample survey***. The interview could be a personal interview, telephone interview, or self-administered questionnaire.

The General Social Survey (GSS) is an example of a sample survey. It gathers information using personal interviews of a random sample of subjects from the U.S. adult population to provide a snapshot of that population. (The survey does not use *simple* random sampling but rather a method discussed later in the chapter that incorporates multiple stages and clustering but is designed to give each family the same chance of inclusion.) National polls such as the Gallup Poll are also sample surveys. They usually use telephone interviews. Since it is often difficult to obtain a sampling frame, many telephone interviews obtain the sample with *random digit dialing*.

A variety of problems can cause responses from a sample survey to tend to favor some parts of the population over others. Then results from the sample are not representative of the population. We'll discuss some potential problems in Section 2.3.

## Collecting Data with an Experiment

In some studies, data result from a planned *experiment*. The purpose of most experiments is to compare responses of subjects on some outcome measure, under different conditions. Those conditions are levels of a variable that can influence the outcome. The scientist has the experimental control of being able to assign subjects to the conditions.

For instance, the conditions might be different drugs for treating some illness. The conditions are called **treatments**. To conduct the experiment, the researcher needs a plan for assigning subjects to the treatments. These plans are called **experimental designs**. Good experimental designs use randomization to determine which treatment a subject receives.

In the late 1980s, the Physicians' Health Study Research Group at Harvard Medical School designed an experiment to analyze whether regular intake of aspirin reduces mortality from heart disease. Of about 22,000 male physicians, half were randomly chosen to take an aspirin every other day. The remaining half took a placebo, which had no active agent. After five years, rates of heart attack were compared. By using randomization to determine who received which treatment, the researchers knew the groups would roughly balance on factors that could affect heart attack rates, such as age and quality of health. If the physicians could decide on their own which treatment to take, the groups might have been out of balance on some important factor. Suppose, for instance, younger physicians were more likely to select aspirin. Then, a lower heart attack rate among the aspirin group could occur merely because younger subjects are less likely to suffer heart attacks.

## Collecting Data with an Observational Study

In social research, it is rarely possible to conduct experiments. It's not possible to randomly assign subjects to the groups we want to compare, such as levels of gender or race or educational level or annual income. Many studies merely *observe* the outcomes for available subjects on the variables without any experimental manipulation of the subjects. Such studies are called **observational studies**. The researcher measures subjects' responses on the variables of interest but has no experimental control over the subjects.

With observational studies, comparing groups is difficult because the groups may be imbalanced on variables that affect the outcome. This is true even with random sampling. For instance, suppose we plan to compare black students, Hispanic students, and white students on some standardized test. If white students have a higher average score, a variety of variables might account for that difference, such as parents' education or parents' income or quality of school attended. This makes it difficult to compare groups with observational studies, especially when some key variables may not have been measured in the study.

Establishing cause and effect is central to science. But it's not possible to establish cause and effect definitively with a nonexperimental study, whether it be an observational study with an available sample or a sample survey using random sampling. With an observational study, there's the strong possibility that the sample does not well reflect the population. With an observational study or a sample survey, there's always the possibility that some unmeasured variable could be responsible for patterns observed in the data. With an experiment that randomly assigns subjects to treatments, those treatments should roughly balance on any unmeasured variables. For example, in the heart attack study mentioned above, the doctors taking aspirin would not tend to be younger or of better health than the doctors taking placebo. Because a randomized experiment balances the groups being compared on other factors, it's possible to study cause and effect more accurately with an experiment than with an observational study.

Whether or not a study is experimental, it's important to incorporate randomization in any study that plans to make inferences. This randomization could take the form of randomly selecting a sample for a survey, or randomly allocating subjects to different treatments for an experimental study.

## 2.3   SAMPLING VARIABILITY AND POTENTIAL BIAS

Even if a study wisely uses randomization, the results of the study still depend on which subjects are sampled. Two researchers who separately select random samples from some population may have little overlap, if any, between the two sample memberships. Therefore, the values of sample statistics will differ for the two samples, and the results of analyses based on these samples may differ.

### Sampling Error

Suppose the Gallup, Harris, Zogby, and Pew polling organizations each randomly sample 1000 adult Canadians, in order to estimate the percentage of Canadians who give the prime minister's performance in office a favorable rating. Based on the samples they select, perhaps Gallup reports an approval rating of 63%, Harris reports 68%, Zogby 65%, and Pew 64%. These differences could reflect slightly different question wording. But even if the questions are worded exactly the same, the percentages would probably differ somewhat because the samples are different.

For conclusions based on statistical inference to be worthwhile, we should know the potential *sampling error*—how much the statistic differs from the parameter it predicts because of the way results naturally exhibit variation from sample to sample.

---

**Sampling Error**

The *sampling error* of a statistic equals the error that occurs when we use a statistic based on a sample to predict the value of a population parameter.

---

Suppose that the actual percentage of the population of adult Canadians who give the prime minister a favorable rating is 66%. Then the Gallup organization, which predicted 63%, had a sampling error of $63\% - 66\% = -3\%$. The Harris organization, which predicted 68%, had a sampling error of $68\% - 66\% = 2\%$. In practice, the sampling error is unknown, because the values of population parameters are unknown.

Random sampling protects against bias, in the sense that the sampling error tends to fluctuate about 0, sometimes being positive (as in the Harris poll) and sometimes being negative (as in the Gallup poll). Random sampling also allows us to predict the likely size of the sampling error. For sample sizes of about 1000, we'll see that the sampling error for estimating percentages is usually no greater than plus or minus 3%. This bound is the *margin of error*. Variability also occurs in the values of sample statistics with nonrandom sampling, but the extent of the sampling error is not predictable as it is with random samples.

## Sampling Bias: Nonprobability Sampling

Other factors besides sampling error can cause results to vary from sample to sample. These factors can also possibly cause bias. We next discuss three types of bias. The first is called **sampling bias**.

For simple random sampling, each possible sample of *n* subjects has the same probability of selection. This is a type of **probability sampling** method, meaning that the probability any particular sample will be selected is known. Inferential statistical methods assume probability sampling. **Nonprobability sampling** methods are ones for which it is not possible to determine the probabilities of the possible samples. Inferences using such samples have unknown reliability and result in **sampling bias**.

The most common nonprobability sampling method is **volunteer sampling**. As the name implies, subjects volunteer to be in the sample. But the sample may poorly represent the population and yield misleading conclusions. For instance, a mail-in questionnaire published in *TV Guide* posed the question, "Should the President have the Line Item Veto to eliminate waste?" Of those who responded, 97% said yes. For the same question posed to a random sample, 71% said yes.[1]

Examples of volunteer sampling are visible any day on many Internet sites and television news programs. Viewers register their opinions on an issue by voting over the Internet. The viewers who respond are unlikely to be a representative cross section, but will be those who can easily access the Internet and who feel strongly enough to respond. Individuals having a particular opinion might be much more likely to respond than individuals having a different opinion. For example, one night the ABC program *Nightline* asked viewers whether the United Nations should continue to be located in the United States. Of more than 186,000 respondents, 67% wanted the United Nations out of the United States. At the same time, a poll using a random sample of about 500 respondents estimated the population percentage to be about 28%. Even though the random sample had a much smaller size, it is far more trustworthy.

A large sample does not help with volunteer sampling—the bias remains. In 1936, the newsweekly *Literary Digest* sent over 10 million questionnaires in the mail to predict the outcome of the presidential election. The questionnaires went to a relatively wealthy segment of society (those having autos or telephones), and fewer than 25% were returned. The journal used these to predict an overwhelming victory by Alfred Landon over Franklin Roosevelt. The opposite result was predicted by George Gallup with a much smaller sample in the first scientific poll taken for this purpose. In fact, Roosevelt won in a landslide.

Unfortunately, volunteer sampling is sometimes necessary. This is often true in medical studies. Suppose a study plans to investigate how well a new drug performs compared to a standard drug, for subjects who suffer from high blood pressure. The researchers are not going to be able to find a sampling frame of all who suffer from high blood pressure and take a simple random sample of them. They may, however, be able to sample such subjects at certain medical centers or using volunteers. Even then, randomization should be used wherever possible. For the study patients, they can randomly select who receives the new drug and who receives the standard one.

---

[1]D. M. Wilbur, *Public Perspective*, available at roperweb.ropercenter.uconn.edu, May–June 1993.

Even with random sampling, sampling bias can occur. One case is when the sampling frame suffers from ***undercoverage***: It lacks representation from some groups in the population. A telephone survey will not reach prison inmates or homeless people or people too poor to afford a telephone, whereas families that have many phones will tend to be over-represented. Responses by those not having a telephone might tend to be quite different from those actually sampled, leading to biased results.

### Response Bias

In a survey, the way a question is worded or asked can have a large impact on the results. For example, when a *New York Times*/CBS News poll in 2006 asked whether the interviewee would be in favor of a new gasoline tax, only 12% said yes. When the tax was presented as reducing U.S. dependence on foreign oil, 55% said yes, and when asked about a gas tax that would help reduce global warming, 59% said yes.[2]

Poorly worded or confusing questions result in ***response bias***. Even the order in which questions are asked can influence the results dramatically. During the Cold War, a study asked, "Do you think the U.S. should let Russian newspaper reporters come here and send back whatever they want?" and "Do you think Russia should let American newspaper reporters come in and send back whatever they want?" The percentage of yes responses to the first question was 36% when it was asked first and 73% when it was asked second.[3]

In an interview, characteristics of the interviewer may result in response bias. Respondents might lie if they think their belief is socially unacceptable. They may be more likely to give the answer that they think the interviewer prefers. An example is provided by a study on the effect of the interviewer's race. Following a phone interview, respondents were asked whether they thought the interviewer was black or white (all were actually black). Perceiving a white interviewer resulted in more conservative opinions. For example, 14% agreed that "American society is fair to everyone" when they thought the interviewer was black, but 31% agreed to this when they thought the interviewer was white.[4]

### Nonresponse Bias: Missing Data

Some subjects who are supposed to be in the sample may refuse to participate, or it may not be possible to reach them. This results in the problem of ***nonresponse bias***. If only half the intended sample was actually observed, we should worry about whether the half not observed differ from those observed in a way that causes biased results. Even if we select the sample randomly, the results are questionnable if there is substantial nonresponse, say over 20%.

For her book *Women in Love*, author Shere Hite surveyed women in the United States. One of her conclusions was that 70% of women who had been married at least five years have extramarital affairs. She based this conclusion on responses to questionnaires returned by 4500 women. This sounds like an impressively large sample. However, the questionnaire was mailed to about 100,000 women. We cannot know whether the 4.5% of the women who responded were representative of the 100,000 who received the questionnaire, much less the entire population of American women. This makes it dangerous to make an inference to the larger population.

---

[2]Column by T. Friedman, *New York Times*, March 2, 2006.

[3]See Crosson (1994).

[4]*Washington Post*, June 26, 1995.

*Missing data* is a problem in almost all large studies. Some subjects do not provide responses for some of the variables measured. Even in censuses, which are designed to observe everyone in a country, some people are not observed or fail to cooperate. Most software ignores cases for which observations are missing for at least one variable used in an analysis. This results in wasted information and possible bias. Statisticians have recently developed methods that replace missing observations by predicted values based on patterns in the data. See Allison (2002) for an introduction to ways of dealing with missing data.

### Summary of Types of Bias

In summary, sample surveys have potential sources of bias:

- *Sampling bias* occurs from using nonprobability samples or having undercoverage.
- *Response bias* occurs when the subject gives an incorrect response (perhaps lying), or the question wording or the way the interviewer asks the questions is confusing or misleading.
- *Nonresponse bias* occurs when some sampled subjects cannot be reached or refuse to participate or fail to answer some questions.

In any study, carefully assess the scope of conclusions. Evaluate critically the conclusions by noting the makeup of the sample. How was the sample selected? How large was it? How were the questions worded? Who sponsored and conducted the research? The less information that is available, the less you should trust it.

Finally, be wary of any study that makes inferences to a broader population than is justified by the sample chosen. Suppose a psychologist performs an experiment using a random sample of students from an introductory psychology course. With statistical inference, the sample results generalize to the population of all students in the class. For the results to be of wider interest, the psychologist might claim that the conclusions extend to *all* college students, to all young adults, or even to all adults. These generalizations may well be wrong, because the sample may differ from those populations in fundamental ways, such as in average age or socioeconomic status.

## 2.4   OTHER PROBABILITY SAMPLING METHODS*

Section 2.2 introduced *simple random sampling* and explained its importance to statistical inference. In practice, other probability sampling methods that have elements of randomness are sometimes preferable to simple random sampling or are simpler to obtain.

### Systematic Random Sampling

*Systematic random sampling* selects a subject near the beginning of the sampling frame list, skips several names and selects another subject, skips several more names and selects the next subject, and so forth. The number of names skipped at each stage depends on the desired sample size. Here's how it's done:

---

**Systematic Random Sample**

Denote the sample size by $n$ and the population size by $N$. Let $k = N/n$, the population size divided by the sample size. A *systematic random sample* (1) selects a subject at random from the first $k$ names in the sampling frame, and (2) selects every $k$th subject listed after that one. The number $k$ is called the *skip number*.

---

Suppose you want a systematic random sample of 100 students from a population of 30,000 students listed in a campus directory. Then, $n = 100$ and $N = 30,000$, so $k = 30,000/100 = 300$. The population size is 300 times the sample size, so you need to select one of every 300 students. You select one student at random, using random numbers, from the first 300 students in the directory. Then you select every 300th student after the one selected randomly. This produces a sample of size 100. The first three digits in Table 2.1 are 104, which falls between 001 and 300, so you first select the student numbered 104. The numbers of the other students selected are $104 + 300 = 404$, $404 + 300 = 704$, $704 + 300 = 1004$, $1004 + 300 = 1304$, and so on. The 100th student selected is listed in the last 300 names in the directory.

In sampling from a sampling frame, it's simpler to select a systematic random sample than a simple random sample because it uses only one random number. This method typically provides as good a representation of the population, because for alphabetic listings such as directories of names, values of most variables fluctuate randomly through the list. With this method, statistical formulas based on simple random sampling are usually valid.

A systematic random sample is not a simple random sample, because all samples of size $n$ are not equally likely. For instance, unlike in a simple random sample, two subjects listed next to each other on the list cannot both appear in the sample.

### Stratified Random Sampling

Another probability sampling method, useful in social science research for studies comparing groups, is *stratified sampling*.

---

**Stratified Random Sample**

A *stratified random sample* divides the population into separate groups, called *strata*, and then selects a simple random sample from each stratum.

---

Suppose a study in Cambridge, Massachusetts plans to compare the opinions of registered Democrats and registered Republicans about whether government should guarantee health care to all citizens. Stratifying according to political party registration, the study selects a random sample of Democrats and another random sample of Republicans.

Stratified random sampling is called *proportional* if the sampled strata proportions are the same as those in the entire population. For example, if 90% of the population of interest is Democrat and 10% is Republican, then the sampling is proportional if the sample size for Democrats is nine times the sample size for Republicans.

Stratified random sampling is called *disproportional* if the sampled strata proportions differ from the population proportions. This is useful when the population size for a stratum is relatively small. A group that comprises a small part of the population may not have enough representation in a simple random sample to allow precise inferences. It is not possible to compare accurately Democrats to Republicans, for example, if only 10 people in a sample size of 100 are Republican. By contrast, a disproportional stratified sample size of 100 might randomly sample 50 Democrats and 50 Republicans.

To implement stratification, we must know the stratum into which each subject in the sampling frame belongs. This usually restricts the variables that can be used for forming the strata. The variables must have strata that are easily identifiable. For example, it would be easy to select a stratified sample of a school population using grade level as the stratification variable, but it would be difficult to prepare an adequate sampling frame of city households stratified by household income.

## Cluster Sampling

Simple, systematic, and stratified random sampling are often difficult to implement, because they require a complete sampling frame. Such lists are easy to obtain for sampling cities or hospitals or schools, for example, but more difficult for sampling individuals or families. *Cluster sampling* is useful when a complete listing of the population is not available.

---

**Cluster Random Sample**

Divide the population into a large number of *clusters*, such as city blocks. Select a simple random sample of the clusters. Use the subjects in those clusters as the sample.

---

For example, a study might plan to sample about 1% of the families in a city, using city blocks as clusters. Using a map to identify city blocks, it could select a simple random sample of 1% of the blocks and then sample every family on each block. A study of patient care in mental hospitals in Ontario could first randomly sample mental hospitals (the clusters) and then collect data for patients within those hospitals. What's the difference between a stratified sample and a cluster sample? A stratified sample uses *every* stratum. The strata are usually groups we want to compare. By contrast, a cluster sample uses a *sample* of the clusters, rather than all of them. In cluster sampling, clusters are merely ways of easily identifying groups of subjects. The goal is not to compare the clusters but rather to use them to obtain a sample. Most clusters are not represented in the eventual sample.

Figure 2.2 illustrates the distinction among sampling subjects (simple random sample), sampling clusters of subjects (cluster random sample), and sampling subjects from within strata (stratified random sample). The figure depicts ways to survey 40 students at a school, to make comparisons among Freshmen, Sophomores, Juniors, and Seniors.

## Multistage Sampling

When conducting a survey for predicting elections, the Gallup Organization often identifies election districts as clusters and takes a simple random sample of them. But then it also takes a simple random sample of households within each selected election

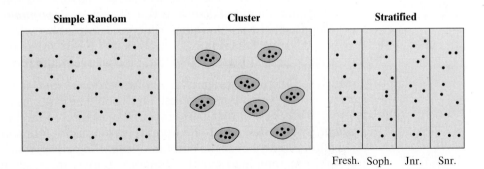

**FIGURE 2.2:** Ways of Randomly Sampling 40 Students. The figure is a schematic for a simple random sample, a cluster random sample of 8 clusters of students who live together, and a stratified random sample of 10 students from each class (Fr, So, Ju, Sr).

district. This is more feasible than sampling *every* household in the chosen districts. This is an example of *multistage sampling*, which uses combinations of sampling methods.

Here's an example of a multistage sample:

- Treat counties (or census tracts) as clusters and select a random sample of a certain number of them.
- Within each county selected, take a cluster random sample of square-block regions.
- Within each region selected, take a systematic random sample of every tenth house.
- Within each house selected, select one adult at random for the sample.

Multistage samples are common in social science research. They are simpler to implement than simple random sampling but provide a broader sampling of the population than a single method such as cluster sampling.

For statistical inference, stratified samples, cluster samples, and multistage samples use different formulas from the ones in this book. Cluster sampling requires a larger sample to achieve as much inferential precision as simple random sampling. Observations within clusters tend to be similar, because of the tendency of subjects living near one another to have similar values on opinion issues and on economic and demographic variables such as age, income, race, and occupation. So we need more data to obtain a representative cross section. By contrast, the results for stratified sampling may be more precise than those stated in this textbook for simple random sampling. Books specializing in sampling methodology provide further details (Scheaffer et al., 2005; Thompson, 2002).

## 2.5 CHAPTER SUMMARY

Statistical methods analyze data on **variables**, which are characteristics that vary among subjects. The statistical methods used depend on the type of variable:

- Numerically measured variables, such as family income and number of children in a family, are **quantitative**. They are measured on an *interval scale*.
- Variables taking value in a set of categories are **categorical**. Those measured with unordered categories, such as religious affiliation and province of residence, have a *nominal scale*. Those measured with ordered categories, such as social class and political ideology, have an *ordinal scale* of measurement.
- Variables are also classified as **discrete**, having possible values that are a set of separate numbers (such as 0, 1, 2, ...), or **continuous**, having a continuous, infinite set of possible values. Categorical variables, whether nominal or ordinal, are discrete. Quantitative variables can be of either type, but in practice are treated as continuous if they can take a large number of values.

Much social science research uses **observational studies**, which use available subjects to observe variables of interest. One should be cautious in attempting to conduct inferential analyses with data from such studies. Inferential statistical methods require **probability samples**, which incorporate randomization in some way. Random sampling allows control over the amount of **sampling error**, which describes how results can vary from sample to sample. Random samples are much more likely to be representative of the population than are nonprobability samples such as volunteer samples.

- For a **simple random sample**, every possible sample of size $n$ has the same chance of selection.

- Here are other examples of probability sampling: *Systematic* random sampling takes every *k*th subject in the sampling frame list. *Stratified* random sampling divides the population into groups (strata) and takes a random sample from each stratum. *Cluster* random sampling takes a random sample of clusters of subjects (such as city blocks) and uses subjects in those clusters as the sample. *Multistage* sampling uses combinations of these methods.

Chapter 3 introduces statistics for describing samples and corresponding parameters for describing populations. Hence, its focus is on *descriptive statistics*.

## PROBLEMS

### Practicing the Basics

**2.1.** Explain the difference between
  **(a)** Discrete and continuous variables
  **(b)** Categorical and quantitative variables
  **(c)** Nominal and ordinal variables
  Why do these distinctions matter for statistical analysis?

**2.2.** Identify each variable as categorical or quantitative:
  **(a)** Number of pets in family
  **(b)** County of residence
  **(c)** Choice of auto (domestic or import)
  **(d)** Distance (in miles) commute to work
  **(e)** Choice of diet (vegetarian, nonvegetarian)
  **(f)** Time spent in previous month browsing the World Wide Web
  **(g)** Ownership of personal computer (yes, no)
  **(h)** Number of people you have known with AIDS (0, 1, 2, 3, 4 or more)
  **(i)** Marriage form of a society (monogamy, polygyny, polyandry)

**2.3.** Which scale of measurement (nominal, ordinal, or interval) is most appropriate for
  **(a)** Attitude toward legalization of marijuana (favor, neutral, oppose)
  **(b)** Gender (male, female)
  **(c)** Number of children in family (0, 1, 2, ...)
  **(d)** Political party affiliation (Democrat, Republican, Independent)
  **(e)** Religious affiliation (Catholic, Jewish, Protestant, Muslim, other)
  **(f)** Political philosophy (very liberal, somewhat liberal, moderate, somewhat conservative, very conservative)
  **(g)** Years of school completed (0, 1, 2, 3, ...)
  **(h)** Highest degree attained (none, high school, bachelor's, master's, doctorate)
  **(i)** College major (education, anthropology, physics, sociology, ...)
  **(j)** Test score (0–100 range for scores)
  **(k)** Employment status (employed full time, employed part time, unemployed)

**2.4.** Which scale of measurement is most appropriate for
  **(a)** Occupation (plumber, teacher, secretary, ...)
  **(b)** Occupational status (blue collar, white collar)
  **(c)** Social status (lower, middle, upper class)
  **(d)** Statewide murder rate (number of murders per 1000 population)
  **(e)** County population size (number of people)
  **(f)** Population growth rate (in percentages)
  **(g)** Community size (rural, small town, large town, small city, large city)
  **(h)** Annual income (thousands of dollars per year)
  **(i)** Attitude toward affirmative action (favorable, neutral, unfavorable)
  **(j)** Lifetime number of sexual partners

**2.5.** Which scale of measurement is most appropriate for "attained education" measured as
  **(a)** Number of years (0, 1, 2, 3, ...)
  **(b)** Grade level (elementary school, middle school, high school, college, graduate school)
  **(c)** School type (public school, private school)

**2.6.** Give an example of a variable that is **(a)** categorical, **(b)** quantitative, **(c)** ordinal scale, **(d)** nominal scale, **(e)** discrete, **(f)** continuous, **(g)** quantitative and discrete.

**2.7.** A poll conducted by YouGov for the British newspaper *The Daily Telegraph* in June 2006 asked a random sample of 1962 British adults several questions about their image of the U.S. One question asked, "How would you rate George W. Bush as a world leader?" The possible choices were (great leader, reasonably satisfactory leader, pretty poor leader, terrible leader).
  **(a)** Is this four-category variable nominal, or ordinal? Why?
  **(b)** Is this variable continuous, or discrete? Why?
  **(c)** Of the 93% of the sample who responded, the percentages in the four categories were 1% (great leader), 16%, 37%, 46% (terrible leader). Are these values statistics, or parameters? Why?

**2.8.** A survey asks subjects to rate five issues according to their importance in determining voting intention for U.S. senator, using the scale (very important, somewhat important, unimportant). The issues are foreign policy, unemployment, inflation, the arms race, and civil rights. The evaluations can be treated as five variables: foreign policy evaluation, unemployment evaluation, and so on. These variables represent what scale of measurement?

**2.9.** Which of the following variables could theoretically be measured on a continuous scale? **(a)** Method of contraception used, **(b)** length of time of residence in a state, **(c)** task completion time, **(d)** intelligence, **(e)** authoritarianism, **(f)** alienation, **(g)** county of residence.

**2.10.** Which of the following variables are continuous when the measurements are as fine as possible? **(a)** Age of mother, **(b)** number of children in family, **(c)** income of spouse, **(d)** population of cities, **(e)** latitude and longitude of cities, **(f)** distance of home from place of employment, **(g)** number of foreign languages spoken.

**2.11.** A class has 50 students. Use the column of the first two digits in the random number table (Table 2.1) to select a simple random sample of three students. If the students are numbered 01 to 50, what are the numbers of the three students selected?

**2.12.** A local telephone directory has 400 pages with 130 names per page, a total of 52,000 names. Explain how you could choose a simple random sample of 5 names. Using the second column of Table 2.1 or software or a calculator, select 5 random numbers to identify subjects for the sample.

**2.13.** Explain whether an experiment or an observational study would be more appropriate to investigate the following:
**(a)** Whether or not cities with higher unemployment rates tend to have higher crime rates
**(b)** Whether a Honda Accord or a Toyota Camry gets better gas mileage
**(c)** Whether or not higher college GPAs tend to occur for students who had higher scores on college entrance exams
**(d)** Whether or not a special coupon attached to the outside of a catalog makes recipients more likely to order products from a mail-order company

**2.14.** A study is planned to study whether passive smoking (being exposed to secondhand cigarette smoke on a regular basis) leads to higher rates of lung cancer.
**(a)** One possible study is to take a sample of children, randomly select half of them for placement in an environment where they are passive smokers, and place the other half in an environment where they are not exposed

to smoke. Then 60 years later the observation is whether each has developed lung cancer. Would this study be an experimental study or an observational study? Why?
**(b)** For many reasons, including time and ethics, it is not possible to conduct the study in (a). Describe a way that *is* possible, and indicate whether it would be an experimental or observational study.

**2.15.** Table 2.2 shows the result of the 2000 Presidential election and the predictions of several organizations in the days before the election. The sample sizes were typically about 2000. The percentages for each poll do not sum to 100 because of voters reporting as undecided or favoring another candidate.
**(a)** What factors cause the results to vary somewhat among organizations?
**(b)** Identify the sampling error for the Gallup poll.

**TABLE 2.2**

| Poll | Predicted Vote | | |
|------|------|------|------|
| | Gore | Bush | Nader |
| Gallup | 46 | 48 | 4 |
| Harris | 47 | 47 | 5 |
| ABC | 45 | 48 | 3 |
| CBS | 45 | 44 | 4 |
| NBC | 44 | 47 | 3 |
| Pew Research | 47 | 49 | 4 |
| **Actual vote** | 48.4 | 47.9 | 2.7 |

*Source*: www.ncpp.org/

**2.16.** The BBC in Britain requested viewers to call the network and indicate their favorite poem. Of more than 7500 callers, more than twice as many voted for Rudyard Kipling's *If* than for any other poem. The BBC reported that this was the clear favorite.
**(a)** Explain what it means to call this a "volunteer sample."
**(b)** If the BBC truly wanted to determine Brits' favorite poem, how could it more reliably do so?

**2.17.** A Roper Poll was designed to determine the percentage of Americans who express some doubt that the Nazi Holocaust occurred. In response to the question, "Does it seem possible or does it seem impossible to you that the Nazi extermination of the Jews never happened?" 22% said it was possible the Holocaust never happened. The Roper organization later admitted that the question was worded in a confusing manner. When the poll asked, "Does it seem possible to you that the Nazi extermination of the Jews never happened, or do you feel certain that it happened?" only 1%

said it was possible it never happened.[5] Use this example to explain the concept of response bias.

**2.18.** Refer to Exercise 2.12 about selecting 5 of 52,000 names on 400 pages of a directory.
 **(a)** Select five numbers to identify subjects for a systematic random sample of five names from the directory.
 **(b)** Is cluster sampling applicable? How could it be carried out, and what would be the advantages and disadvantages?

**2.19.** You plan to sample from the 5000 students at a college, to compare the proportions of men and women who believe that the legal age for alcohol should be changed to 18. Explain how you would proceed if you want a systematic random sample of 100 students.

**2.20.** You plan to sample from the 3500 undergraduate students enrolled at the University of Rochester, to compare the proportions of female and male students who would like to see the U.S. have a female President.
 **(a)** Suppose that you use random numbers to select students, but you stop selecting females as soon as you have 40, and you stop selecting males as soon as you have 40. Is the resulting sample a simple random sample? Why or why not?
 **(b)** What type of sample is the sample in (a)? What advantage might it have over a simple random sample?

**2.21.** Clusters versus strata:
 **(a)** With a cluster random sample, do you take a sample of (i) the clusters? (ii) the subjects within every cluster?
 **(b)** With a stratified random sample, do you take a sample of (i) the strata? (ii) the subjects within every stratum?
 **(c)** Summarize the main differences between cluster sampling and stratified sampling in terms of whether you sample the groups or sample from within the groups that form the clusters or strata.

### Concepts and Applications

**2.22.** Refer to the *Student survey* data file introduced in Exercise 1.11 (page 8). For each variable in the data set, indicate whether it is:
 **(a)** Categorical or quantitative
 **(b)** Nominal, ordinal, or interval

**2.23.** Repeat the previous exercise for the data file created in Exercise 1.12 (page 9).

**2.24.** You are directing a study to determine the factors that relate to good academic performance at your school.
 **(a)** Describe how you might select a sample of 100 students for the study.
 **(b)** List some variables that you would measure. For each, provide the scale you would use to measure it, and indicate whether statistical analysis could treat it as (i) categorical or quantitative, (ii) nominal, ordinal, or interval, (iii) continuous or discrete.
 **(c)** Give an example of a research question that could be addressed using data on the variables you listed in (b).

**2.25.** With *quota sampling* a researcher stands at a street corner and conducts interviews until obtaining a quota representing the relative sizes of various groups in the population. For instance, the quota might be 50 factory workers, 100 housewives, 60 elderly people, 30 blacks, and so forth. Is this a probability or nonprobability sampling method? Explain, and discuss potential advantages or disadvantages of this method. (Professional pollsters such as Gallup used this method until 1948, when they incorrectly predicted that Dewey would defeat Truman in a landslide in the presidential election.)

**2.26.** When the Yankelovich polling organization asked,[6] "Should laws be passed to eliminate all possibilities of special interests giving huge sums of money to candidates?" 80% of the sample answered *yes*. When they posed the question, "Should laws be passed to prohibit interest groups from contributing to campaigns, or do groups have a right to contribute to the candidate they support?" only 40% said *yes*. Explain what this example illustrates, and use your answer to differentiate between sampling error and response bias in survey results.

**2.27.** In each of the following situations, evaluate whether the method of sample selection is appropriate for obtaining information about the population of interest. How would you improve the sample design?
 **(a)** A newspaper wants to determine whether its readers believe that government expenditures should be reduced by cutting benefits for the disabled. They provide an Internet address for readers to vote *yes* or *no*. Based on 1434 Internet votes, they report that 93% of the city's residents believe that benefits should be reduced.
 **(b)** A congresswoman reports that letters to her office are running 3 to 1 in opposition to

---

[5] *Newsweek*, July 25, 1994.
[6] *Source*: *A Mathematician Reads the Newspaper*, by J. A. Paulos, Basic Books, 1995, p. 15.

the passage of stricter gun control laws. She concludes that approximately 75% of her constituents oppose stricter gun control laws.

**(c)** An anthropology professor wanted to compare attitudes toward premarital sex of physical science majors and social science majors. She administered a questionnaire to her large class of Anthropology 437, Comparative Human Sexuality. She found no appreciable difference between her physical science and social science majors in their attitudes, so she concluded that the two student groups were about the same in their relative acceptance of premarital sex.

**(d)** A questionnaire was mailed to a simple random sample of 500 household addresses in a city. Ten were returned as bad addresses, 63 were returned completed, and the rest were not returned. The researcher analyzed the 63 cases and reported that they represent a "simple random sample of city households."

**(e)** A principal in a large high school is interested in student attitudes toward a proposed achievement test to determine whether a student should graduate. She lists all of the first-period classes, assigning a number to each. Then, using a random number table, she chooses a class at random and interviews every student in that class about the proposed test.

**2.28.** A content analysis of a daily newspaper studies the percentage of newspaper space devoted to news about entertainment. The sampling frame consists of the daily editions of the newspaper for the previous year. What potential problem might there be in using a systematic sample with skip number equal to 7 or a multiple of 7?

**2.29.** In a systematic random sample, every subject has the same chance of selection, but the sample is not a simple random sample. Explain why.

**2.30.** With a total sample of size 100, we want to compare Native Americans to other Americans on the percentage favoring legalized gambling. Why might it be useful to take a disproportional stratified random sample?

**2.31.** In a cluster random sample with equal-sized clusters, every subject has the same chance of selection. However, the sample is not a simple random sample. Explain why not.

**2.32.** Find an example of results of an Internet poll. Do you trust the results of the poll? If not, explain why not.

**2.33.** To sample residents of registered nursing homes in Yorkshire, UK, I construct a list of all nursing homes in the county, which I number from 1 to 110. Beginning randomly, I choose every tenth home

on the list, ending up with 11 homes. I then obtain lists of residents from those 11 homes, and I select a simple random sample from each list. What kinds of sampling have I used?

*For multiple-choice questions 2.34–2.37, select the best response.*

**2.34.** A simple random sample of size $n$ is one in which:
   **(a)** Every $n$th member is selected from the population.
   **(b)** Each possible sample of size $n$ has the same chance of being selected.
   **(c)** There must be exactly the same proportion of women in the sample as is in the population.
   **(d)** You keep sampling until you have a fixed number of people having various characteristics (e.g., males, females).
   **(e)** A particular minority group member of the population is less likely to be chosen than a particular majority group member.
   **(f)** All of the above
   **(g)** None of the above

**2.35.** If we use random numbers to take a simple random sample of 50 students from the 20,000 students at a university,
   **(a)** It is impossible to get the random number 11111, because it is not a random sequence.
   **(b)** If we get 20001 for the first random number, for the second random number that number is less likely to occur than the other possible five-digit random numbers.
   **(c)** The draw 12345 is no more or less likely than the draw 11111.
   **(d)** Since the sample is random, it is *impossible* that it will be non-representative, such as having only females in the sample.

**2.36.** Crosson (1994, p. 168) described an analysis of published medical studies involving treatments for heart attacks. In the studies having randomization and strong controls for bias, the new therapy provided improved treatment 9% of the time. In studies without randomization or other controls for bias, the new therapy provided improved treatment 58% of the time. Select the correct response(s).
   **(a)** This result suggests it is better not to use randomization in medical studies, because it is harder to show that new ideas are beneficial.
   **(b)** Many newspaper articles that suggest that a particular food, drug, or environmental agent is harmful or beneficial should be viewed skeptically, unless we learn more about the statistical design and analysis for the study.
   **(c)** This result suggests that you should be skeptical about published results of medical studies that are not randomized, controlled studies.

**(d)** Controlling for biases, both suspected and unsuspected, is necessary in medical research but not in social research, because the social sciences deal in subjective rather than objective truth.

**2.37.** A recent GSS asked subjects if they supported legalizing abortion in each of seven different circumstances. The percentage who supported legalization varied between 45% (if the woman wants it for any reason) to 92% (if the woman's health is seriously endangered by the pregnancy). This indicates that

**(a)** Responses can depend greatly on the question wording.

**(b)** Surveys sample only a small part of the population and can never be trusted.

**(c)** The sample must not have been randomly selected.

**(d)** The sample must have had problems with bias resulting from subjects not telling the truth.

**2.38.** An interviewer stands at an entrance to a popular shopping mall and conducts interviews. True or false: Because we cannot predict who will be interviewed, the sample obtained is an example of a random sample. Explain.

**2.39.** In a recent Miss America beauty pageant, television viewers could cast their vote on whether to cancel the swimwear parade by phoning a number the network provided. About 1 million viewers called and registered their opinion, of whom 79% said they wanted to see the contestants dressed as bathing beauties. True or false: Since everyone had a chance to call, this was a simple random sample of all the viewers of this program. Explain.

**\*2.40.** An interval scale for which ratios are valid is called a *ratio scale*. Such scales have a well-defined 0 point, so, for instance, one can regard the value 20 as twice the quantity of the value 10. Explain why annual income is measured on a ratio scale, but temperature (in Fahrenheit or Centigrade) is not. Is IQ, as a measure of intelligence, a ratio-scale variable?

---

\*Exercises marked with an asterisk are of greater difficulty or introduce new and optional material.

# Descriptive Statistics

We've seen that statistical methods are *descriptive* or *inferential*. The purpose of descriptive statistics is to summarize data, to make it easier to assimilate the information. This chapter presents basic methods of descriptive statistics.

We first present tables and graphs that describe the data by showing the number of times various outcomes occurred. Quantitative variables also have two key features to describe numerically:

- The ***center*** of the data—a typical observation
- The ***variability*** of the data—the spread around the center

We'll learn how to describe quantitative data with statistics that summarize the center, statistics that summarize the variability, and finally with statistics that specify certain positions in the data set that summarize both center and variability.

## 3.1   DESCRIBING DATA WITH TABLES AND GRAPHS

Tables and graphs are useful for all types of data. We'll begin with categorical variables.

### Relative Frequencies: Categorical Data

For categorical data, we list the categories and show the frequency (the number of observations) in each category. To make is easier to compare different categories, we also report proportions or percentages, also called ***relative frequencies***.

---

**Relative Frequency**

The ***relative frequency*** for a category is the ***proportion*** or ***percentage*** of the observations that fall in that category.

---

The *proportion* equals the number of observations in a category divided by the total number of observations. It is a number between 0 and 1 that expresses the share of the observations in that category. The *percentage* is the proportion multiplied by 100.

**EXAMPLE 3.1    Household Structure in the U.S.**

Table 3.1 lists the different types of households in the United States in 2005. Of 111.1 million households, for example, 24.1 million were a married couple with children. The proportion 24.1/111.1 = 0.22 were a married couple with children.

**TABLE 3.1:** U.S. Household Structure, 2005

| Type of Family | Number (millions) | Proportion | Percentage |
|---|---|---|---|
| Married couple with children | 24.1 | 0.22 | 22 |
| Married couple, no children | 31.1 | 0.28 | 28 |
| Single householder, no spouse | 19.1 | 0.17 | 17 |
| Living alone | 30.1 | 0.27 | 27 |
| Other households | 6.7 | 0.06 | 6 |
| Total | 111.1 | 1.00 | 100 |

*Source*: U.S. Census Bureau, *2005 American Community Survey,* Tables B11001, C11003.

A percentage is the proportion multiplied by 100. That is, the decimal place is moved two positions to the right. For example, since 0.22 is the proportion of families that are married couples with children, the percentage is 100(0.22) = 22%. Table 3.1 shows the proportions and percentages for all the categories.    ■

The sum of the proportions equals 1.00. The sum of the percentages equals 100. (In practice, the values may sum to a slightly different number, such as 99.9 or 100.1, because of rounding.)

It is sufficient in such a table to report the percentages (or proportions) and the total sample size, since each frequency equals the corresponding proportion multiplied by the total sample size. For instance, the frequency of married couples with children equals 0.22(111.1) = 24 million. When presenting the percentages but not the frequencies, always also include the total sample size.

### Frequency Distributions and Bar Graphs: Categorical Data

Table 3.1 lists the categories for household structure and the number of households of each type. Such a listing is called a *frequency distribution*.

---

**Frequency Distribution**

A *frequency distribution* is a listing of possible values for a variable, together with the number of observations at each value. A corresponding *relative frequency distribution* lists the possible values together with their proportions or percentages.

---

To construct a frequency distribution for a categorical variable, list the categories and count the number of observations in each.

To more easily get a feel for the data, it's helpful to look at a graph of the relative frequency distribution. A ***bar graph*** has a rectangular bar drawn over each category. The height of the bar shows the relative frequency in that category. Figure 3.1 is a bar graph for the data in Table 3.1. The bars are separated to emphasize that the variable is categorical rather than quantitative. Since household structure is a nominal variable, there is no particular natural order for the bars. The order of presentation for an ordinal variable is the natural ordering of the categories.

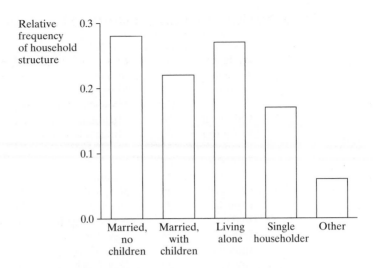

**FIGURE 3.1:** Relative Frequency of U.S. Household Structure Types, 2005

Another type of graph, the *pie chart*, is a circle having a "slice of the pie" for each category. The size of a slice represents the percentage of observations in the category. The bar graph is more precise than the pie chart for visual comparison of categories with similar relative frequencies.

### Frequency Distributions: Quantitative Data

Frequency distributions and graphs also are useful for quantitative variables. The next example illustrates.

### EXAMPLE 3.2     Statewide Violent Crime Rates

Table 3.2 lists all 50 states in the United States and their 2005 violent crime rates. This rate measures the number of violent crimes in that state in 2005 per 10,000 population. For instance, if a state had 12,000 violent crimes and a population size of 2,300,000, its violent crime rate was $(12,000/2,300,000) \times 10,000 = 52$. It is difficult to learn much by simply reading through the violent crime rates. Tables, graphs, and numerical measures help us more fully absorb the information in these data.

First, we can summarize the data with a frequency distribution. To do this, we divide the measurement scale for violent crime rate into a set of intervals and count the number of observations in each interval. Here, we use the intervals {0–11, 12–23, 24–35, 36–47, 48–59, 60–71, 72–83}. The values Table 3.2 reports were rounded, so for example the interval 12-23 represents values between 11.5 and 23.5. Counting the number of states with violent crime rates in each interval, we get the frequency distribution shown in Table 3.3. We see that considerable variability exists in the violent crime rates.

Table 3.3 also shows the relative frequencies, using proportions and percentages. For example, $3/50 = 0.06$ is the proportion for the interval 0–11, and $100(0.06) = 6$ is the percentage. As with any summary method, we lose some information as the cost of achieving some clarity. The frequency distribution does not identify which states have low or high violent crime rates, nor are the exact violent crime rates known. ∎

The intervals of values in frequency distributions are usually of equal width. The width equals 12 in Table 3.3. The intervals should include all possible values of the

**TABLE 3.2:** List of States with Violent Crime Rates Measured as Number of Violent Crimes per 10,000 Population

| | | | | | |
|---|---|---|---|---|---|
| Alabama | 43 | Louisiana | 65 | Ohio | 33 |
| Alaska | 59 | Maine | 11 | Oklahoma | 51 |
| Arizona | 51 | Maryland | 70 | Oregon | 30 |
| Arkansas | 46 | Massachusetts | 47 | Pennsylvania | 40 |
| California | 58 | Michigan | 51 | Rhode Island | 29 |
| Colorado | 34 | Minnesota | 26 | South Carolina | 79 |
| Connecticut | 31 | Mississippi | 33 | South Dakota | 17 |
| Delaware | 66 | Missouri | 47 | Tennessee | 69 |
| Florida | 73 | Montana | 36 | Texas | 55 |
| Georgia | 45 | Nebraska | 29 | Utah | 25 |
| Hawaii | 27 | Nevada | 61 | Vermont | 11 |
| Idaho | 24 | New Hampshire | 15 | Virginia | 28 |
| Illinois | 56 | New Jersey | 37 | Washington | 35 |
| Indiana | 35 | New Mexico | 66 | West Virginia | 26 |
| Iowa | 27 | New York | 46 | Wisconsin | 22 |
| Kansas | 40 | North Carolina | 46 | Wyoming | 26 |
| Kentucky | 26 | North Dakota | 8 | | |

**TABLE 3.3:** Frequency Distribution and Relative Frequency Distribution for Violent Crime Rates

| Violent Crime Rate | Frequency | Relative Frequency | Percentage |
|---|---|---|---|
| 0–11 | 3 | 0.06 | 6 |
| 12–23 | 3 | 0.06 | 6 |
| 24–35 | 18 | 0.36 | 36 |
| 36–47 | 11 | 0.22 | 22 |
| 48–59 | 7 | 0.14 | 14 |
| 60–71 | 6 | 0.12 | 12 |
| 72–83 | 2 | 0.04 | 4 |
| Total | 50 | 1.00 | 100.0 |

variable. In addition, any possible value must fit into one and only one interval; that is, they should be *mutually exclusive*.

## Histograms

A graph of a relative frequency distribution for a quantitative variable is called a *histogram*. Each interval has a bar over it, with height representing the number of observations in that interval. Figure 3.2 is a histogram for the violent crime rates.

Choosing intervals for frequency distributions and histograms is primarily a matter of common sense. If too few intervals are used, too much information is lost. For example, Figure 3.3 is a histogram of violent crime rates using the intervals 0–29, 30–59, 60–89. This is too crude to be very informative. If too many intervals are used, they are so narrow that the information presented is difficult to digest, and the histogram may be irregular and the overall pattern of the results may be obscured. Ideally, two observations in the same interval should be similar in a practical sense. To summarize annual income, for example, if a difference of $5000 in income is not considered practically important, but a difference of $15,000 is notable, we might

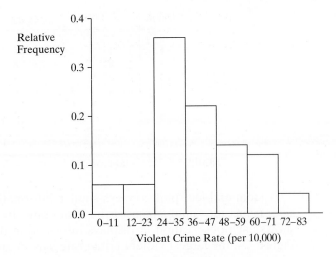

**FIGURE 3.2:** Histogram of Relative Frequencies for Statewide Violent Crime Rates

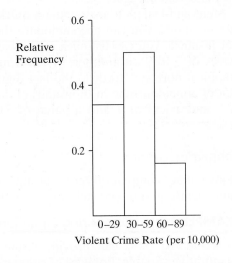

**FIGURE 3.3:** Histogram of Relative Frequencies for Violent Crime Rates, Using Too Few Intervals

choose intervals of width less than $15,000, such as $0–$9999, $10,000–$19,999, $20,000–$29,999, and so forth. Statistical software can automatically choose intervals for us and construct frequency distributions and histograms.

For a discrete variable with relatively few values, a histogram has a separate bar for each possible value. For a continuous variable or a discrete variable with many possible values, you need to divide the possible values into intervals, as we did with the violent crime rates.

### Stem-and-Leaf Plots

Figure 3.4 shows an alternative graphical representation of the violent crime rate data. This figure, called a ***stem-and-leaf plot***, represents each observation by its leading digit(s) (the *stem*) and by its final digit (the *leaf*). Each stem is a number to the left of the vertical bar and a leaf is a number to the right of it. For instance, on the second line, the stem of 1 and the leaves of 1, 1, 5, and 7 represent the violent crime rates 11, 11, 15, 17. The plot arranges the leaves in order on each line, from smallest to largest.

| Stem | Leaf |
|------|------|
| 0 | 8 |
| 1 | 1  1  5  7 |
| 2 | 2  4  5  6  6  6  6  7  7  8  9  9 |
| 3 | 0  1  3  3  4  5  5  6  7 |
| 4 | 0  0  3  5  6  6  6  7  7 |
| 5 | 1  1  1  5  6  8  9 |
| 6 | 1  5  6  6  9 |
| 7 | 0  3  9 |

**FIGURE 3.4:** Stem-and-Leaf Plot for Violent Crime Rate Data in Table 3.2

A stem-and-leaf plot conveys similar information as a histogram. Turned on its side, it has the same shape as the histogram. In fact, since the stem-and-leaf plot shows each observation, it displays information that is lost with a histogram. From Figure 3.4, the largest violent crime rate was 79 and the smallest was 8 (shown as 08 with a stem of 0 and leaf of 8). It is not possible to determine these exact values from the histogram in Figure 3.2.

Stem-and-leaf plots are useful for quick portrayals of small data sets. As the sample size increases, you can accommodate the increase in leaves by splitting the stems. For instance, you can list each stem twice, putting leaves of 0 to 4 on one line and leaves of 5 to 9 on another. When a number has several digits, it is simplest for graphical portrayal to drop the last digit or two. For instance, for a stem-and-leaf plot of annual income in thousands of dollars, a value of $27.1 thousand has a stem of 2 and a leaf of 7 and a value of $106.4 thousand has a stem of 10 and leaf of 6.

### Comparing Groups

Many studies compare different groups on some variable. Relative frequency distributions, histograms, and stem-and-leaf plots are useful for making comparisons.

### EXAMPLE 3.3    Comparing Canadian and U.S. Murder Rates

Stem-and-leaf plots can provide visual comparisons of two small samples on a quantitative variable. For ease of comparison, the results are plotted "back to back." Each plot uses the same stem, with leaves for one sample to its left and leaves for the other sample to its right. To illustrate, Figure 3.5 shows back-to-back stem and leaf plots of recent murder rates (measured as the number of murders per 100,000 population) for the 50 states in the U.S. and for the provinces of Canada. From this figure, it is clear that the murder rates tended to be much lower in Canada, varying between 0.7 (Prince Edward Island) and 2.9 (Manitoba) whereas those in the U.S. varied between 1.6 (Maine) and 20.3 (Louisiana). ∎

### Population Distribution and Sample Data Distribution

Frequency distributions and histograms apply both to a population and to samples from that population. The first type is called the ***population distribution***, and the second type is called a ***sample data distribution***. In a sense, the sample data distribution is a blurry photo of the population distribution. As the sample size increases, the sample proportion in any interval gets closer to the true population proportion. Thus, the sample data distribution looks more like the population distribution.

| Canada | | | | | Stem | United States | | | | | | | | | |
|---|---|---|---|---|---|---|---|---|---|---|---|---|---|---|---|
| | | | | 7 | 0 | | | | | | | | | | |
| | | 3 | 2 | 1 | 1 | 6 | 7 | | | | | | | | |
| 9 | 7 | 6 | 3 | 2 | 0 | 2 | 0 | 3 | 9 | | | | | | |
| | | | | | 3 | 0 | 1 | 4 | 4 | 4 | 6 | 8 | 9 | 9 | 9 |
| | | | | | 4 | 4 | 6 | | | | | | | | |
| | | | | | 5 | 0 | 2 | 3 | 8 | | | | | | |
| | | | | | 6 | 0 | 3 | 4 | 6 | 8 | 9 | | | | |
| | | | | | 7 | 5 | | | | | | | | | |
| | | | | | 8 | 0 | 3 | 4 | 6 | 9 | | | | | |
| | | | | | 9 | 0 | 8 | | | | | | | | |
| | | | | | 10 | 2 | 2 | 3 | 4 | | | | | | |
| | | | | | 11 | 3 | 3 | 4 | 4 | 6 | 9 | | | | |
| | | | | | 12 | 7 | | | | | | | | | |
| | | | | | 13 | 1 | 3 | 5 | | | | | | | |
| | | | | | 14 | | | | | | | | | | |
| | | | | | 15 | | | | | | | | | | |
| | | | | | 16 | | | | | | | | | | |
| | | | | | 17 | | | | | | | | | | |
| | | | | | 18 | | | | | | | | | | |
| | | | | | 19 | | | | | | | | | | |
| | | | | | 20 | 3 | | | | | | | | | |

**FIGURE 3.5:** Back-to-Back Stem-and-Leaf Plots of Murder Rates from U.S. and Canada. Both share the same stems, with Canada leafs to the left and U.S. leafs to the right.

For a continuous variable, imagine the sample size increasing indefinitely, with the number of intervals simultaneously increasing, so their width narrows. Then, the shape of the sample histogram gradually approaches a smooth curve. This text uses such curves to represent population distributions. Figure 3.6 shows two sample histograms, one based on a sample of size 100 and the second based on a sample of size 500, and also a smooth curve representing the population distribution. Even if a variable is discrete, a smooth curve often approximates well the population distribution, especially when the number of possible values of the variable is large.

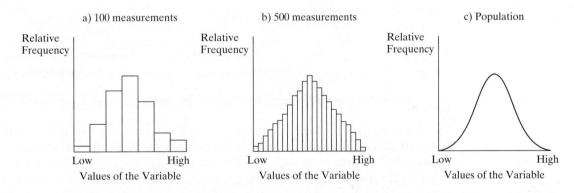

**FIGURE 3.6:** Histograms for a Continuous Variable. We use smooth curves to represent population distributions for continuous variables.

## The Shape of a Distribution

One way to summarize a sample or a population distribution is to describe its shape. A group for which the distribution is bell-shaped is fundamentally different from a group for which the distribution is U-shaped, for example. See Figure 3.7. In the U-shaped distribution, the highest points (representing the largest frequencies) are at the lowest and highest scores, whereas in the bell-shaped distribution, the highest point is near the middle value. A U-shaped distribution indicates a polarization on the variable between two sets of subjects. A bell-shaped distribution indicates that most subjects tend to fall near a central value.

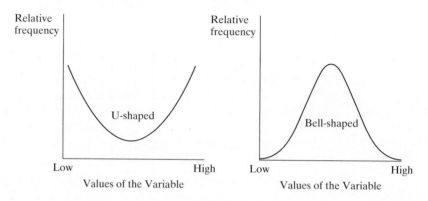

**FIGURE 3.7:** U-Shaped and Bell-Shaped Frequency Distributions

The distributions in Figure 3.7 are ***symmetric***: The side of the distribution below a central value is a mirror image of the side above that central value. Most distributions encountered in the social sciences are not symmetric. Figure 3.8 illustrates. The parts of the curve for the lowest values and the highest values are called the ***tails*** of the distribution. Often, as in Figure 3.8, one tail is much longer than the other. A distribution is said to be ***skewed to the right*** or ***skewed to the left***, according to which tail is longer.

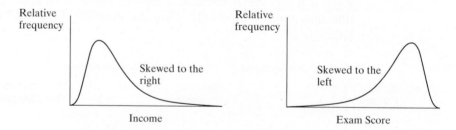

**FIGURE 3.8:** Skewed Frequency Distributions. The longer tail indicates the direction of skew.

To compare frequency distributions or histograms for two groups, you can give verbal descriptions using characteristics such as skew. It is also helpful to make numerical comparisons such as, "On the average, the murder rate for U.S. states is 5.4 higher than the murder rate for Canadian provinces." We now turn our attention to numerical descriptive statistics.

## 3.2 DESCRIBING THE CENTER OF THE DATA

This section presents statistics that describe the center of a frequency distribution for a quantitative variable. The statistics show what a *typical* observation is like.

## The Mean

The best known and most commonly used measure of the center is the ***mean***.

> **Mean**
> ___
> The ***mean*** is the sum of the observations divided by the number of observations.

The mean is often called the ***average***.

### EXAMPLE 3.4    Female Economic Activity in Europe

Table 3.4 shows an index of female economic activity for the countries of South America and of Eastern Europe in 2003. The number specifies female employment as a percentage of male employment. In Argentina, for instance, the number of females in the work force was 48% of the number of males in the work force. (The value was 83 in the United States and in Canada.)

**TABLE 3.4**: Female Economic Activity in South America and Eastern Europe; Female Employment as a Percentage of Male Employment

| South America | | Eastern Europe | |
|---|---|---|---|
| Country | Activity | Country | Activity |
| Argentina | 48 | Czech republic | 83 |
| Bolivia | 58 | Estonia | 82 |
| Brazil | 52 | Hungary | 72 |
| Chile | 50 | Latvia | 80 |
| Colombia | 62 | Lithuania | 80 |
| Ecuador | 40 | Poland | 81 |
| Guyana | 51 | Slovakia | 84 |
| Paraguay | 44 | Slovenia | 81 |
| Peru | 45 | | |
| Uruguay | 68 | | |
| Venezuela | 55 | | |

*Source: Human Development Report 2005*, United Nations Development Programme.

For the eight observations for Eastern Europe, the sum equals

$$83 + 82 + 72 + 80 + 80 + 81 + 84 + 81 = 643.$$

The mean female economic activity equals $643/8 = 80.4$. By comparison, you can check that the mean for the 11 South American countries equals $573/11 = 52.1$. Female economic activity tends to be considerably lower in South America than in Eastern Europe. ∎

We use the following notation for the mean in formulas for it and for statistics that use the mean.

---

**Notation for Observations and Sample Mean**

The sample size is symbolized by $n$. For a variable denoted by $y$, its observations are denoted by $y_1, y_2, \ldots, y_n$. The sample mean is denoted by $\bar{y}$.

---

The symbol $\bar{y}$ for the sample mean is read as "$y$-bar." Throughout the text, letters near the end of the alphabet denote variables. The $n$ sample observations on a variable $y$ are denoted by $y_1$ for the first observation, $y_2$ the second, and so forth. For example, for female economic activity in Eastern Europe, $n = 8$ and the observations are $y_1 = 83$, $y_2 = 82, \ldots, y_8 = 81$. A bar over a letter represents the sample mean for that variable. For instance, $\bar{x}$ represents the sample mean for a variable denoted by $x$.

The definition of the sample mean says that

$$\bar{y} = \frac{y_1 + y_2 + \cdots + y_n}{n}.$$

The symbol $\Sigma$ (uppercase Greek letter sigma) represents the process of summing. For instance, $\Sigma y_i$ represents the sum $y_1 + y_2 + \cdots + y_n$. This symbol stands for the sum of the $y$-values, where the index $i$ represents a typical value in the range 1 to $n$. To illustrate, for the Eastern European data,

$$\sum y_i = y_1 + y_2 + \cdots + y_8 = 83 + 82 + \cdots + 81 = 643.$$

The symbol is sometimes even further abbreviated as $\Sigma y$. Using this summation symbol, we have the shortened expression for the sample mean of $n$ observations,

$$\bar{y} = \frac{\Sigma y_i}{n}.$$

**Properties of the Mean**

Here are some properties of the mean:

- The formula for the mean uses numerical values for the observations. So the mean is appropriate only for quantitative variables. It is not sensible to compute the mean for observations on a nominal scale. For instance, for religion measured with categories such as (Protestant, Catholic, Jewish, Other), the mean religion does not make sense, even though these levels may sometimes be coded by numbers for convenience. Similarly, we cannot find the mean of observations on an ordinal rating such as excellent, good, fair, and poor, unless we assign numbers such as 4, 3, 2, 1 to the ordered levels, treating it as quantitative.
- The mean can be highly influenced by an observation that falls well above or well below the bulk of the data, called an *outlier*.

### EXAMPLE 3.5    Effect of Outlier on Mean Income

The owner of Leonardo's Pizza reports that the mean annual income of employees in the business is $40,900. In fact, the annual incomes of the seven employees are $11,200, $11,400, $11,700, $12,200, $12,300, $12,500, and $215,000. The $215,000 income is the salary of the owner's son, who happens to be an employee. The value $215,000 is an outlier. The mean computed for the other six observations alone equals $11,883, quite different from the mean of $40,900 including the outlier. ■

This example shows that the mean is not always typical of the observations in the sample. This commonly happens with small samples when at least one observation is much larger or much smaller than the others, such as in highly skewed distributions.

- ✐ The mean is pulled in the direction of the longer tail of a skewed distribution, relative to most of the data.

  In Example 3.5, the large observation $215,000 results in an extreme skewness to the right of the income distribution. This skewness pulls the mean above six of the seven observations. In general, the more highly skewed the distribution, the less typical the mean is of the data.

- The mean is the point of balance on the number line when an equal weight is at each observation point.

  For example, Figure 3.9 shows that if an equal weight is placed at each Eastern European observation on female economic activity from Example 3.4, then the line balances by placing a fulcrum at the point 80.4. The mean is the *center of gravity* (balance point) of the observations. This means that the sum of the distances to the mean from the observations *above* the mean equals the sum of the distances to the mean from the observations *below* the mean.

$\bar{y} = 80.4$

**FIGURE 3.9:** The Mean as the Center of Gravity, for Eastern Europe Data from Example 3.4. The line balances with a fulcrum at 80.4.

- Denote the sample means for two sets of data with sample sizes $n_1$ and $n_2$ by $\bar{y}_1$ and $\bar{y}_2$. The overall sample mean for the combined set of $(n_1 + n_2)$ observations is the **weighted average**

$$\bar{y} = \frac{n_1\bar{y}_1 + n_2\bar{y}_2}{n_1 + n_2}.$$

  The numerator $n_1\bar{y}_1 + n_2\bar{y}_2$ is the sum of all the observations, since $n\bar{y} = \sum y$ for each set of observations. The denominator is the total sample size.

To illustrate, for the female economic activity data in Table 3.4, the South American observations have $n_1 = 11$ and $\bar{y}_1 = 52.1$, and the Eastern European observations have $n_2 = 8$ and $\bar{y}_2 = 80.4$. The overall mean economic activity for the 19 nations equals

$$\bar{y} = \frac{n_1\bar{y}_1 + n_2\bar{y}_2}{n_1 + n_2} = \frac{11(52.1) + 8(80.4)}{11 + 8} = \frac{(573 + 643)}{19} = \frac{1216}{19} = 64.$$

The weighted average of 64 is closer to 52.1, the value for South America, than to 80.4, the value for Eastern Europe. This happens because more observations come from South America than Eastern Europe.

## The Median

The mean is a simple measure of the center. But other measures are also informative and sometimes more appropriate. Most important is the *median*. It splits the sample into two parts with equal numbers of observations, when they are ordered from lowest to highest.

---
**Median**

---

The *median* is the observation that falls in the middle of the ordered sample. When the sample size $n$ is odd, a single observation occurs in the middle. When the sample size is even, two middle observations occur, and the median is the midpoint between the two.

---

To illustrate, the ordered income observations for the seven employees in Example 3.5 are

$$\$11{,}200, \$11{,}400, \$11{,}700, \$12{,}200, \$12{,}300, \$12{,}500, \$215{,}000.$$

The median is the middle observation, $12,200. This is a more typical value for this sample than the sample mean of $40,900. When a distribution is highly skewed, the median describes a typical value better than the mean.

In Table 3.4, the ordered economic activity values for the Eastern European nations are

$$72, 80, 80, 81, 81, 82, 83, 84.$$

Since $n = 8$ is even, the median is the midpoint between the two middle values, 81 and 81, which is $(81 + 81)/2 = 81$. This is close to the sample mean of 80.4, because this data set has no outliers.

The middle observation has index $(n + 1)/2$. That is, the median is the value of observation $(n + 1)/2$ in the ordered sample. When $n = 7$, $(n + 1)/2 = (7 + 1)/2 = 4$, so the median is the fourth smallest, or equivalently fourth largest, observation. When $n$ is even, $(n + 1)/2$ falls halfway between two numbers, and the median is the midpoint of the observations with those indices. For example, when $n = 8$, $(n + 1)/2 = 4.5$, so the median is the midpoint between the 4th and 5th smallest observations.

### EXAMPLE 3.6    Median for Grouped or Ordinal Data

Table 3.5 summarizes the distribution of the highest degree completed in the U.S. population of age 25 years and over, as estimated from the 2005 American Community Survey taken by the U.S. Bureau of the Census. The possible responses form an ordinal scale. The population size was $n = 189$ (in millions). The median score is the $(n + 1)/2 = (189 + 1)/2 = 95$th lowest. Now 30 responses fall in the first category, $(30 + 56) = 86$ in the first two, $(30 + 56 + 38) = 124$ in the first three, and so forth. The 87th to 124th lowest scores fall in category 3, which therefore contains the 95th lowest, which is the median. The median response is "Some college, no degree." Equivalently, from the percentages in the last column of the table, $(15.9\% + 29.6\%) = 45.5\%$ fall in the first two categories and $(15.9\% + 29.6\% + 20.1\%) = 65.6\%$ fall in the first three, so the 50% point falls in the third category. ∎

**TABLE 3.5**: Highest Degree Completed, for a Sample of Americans

| Highest Degree | Frequency (millions) | Percentage |
|---|---|---|
| Not a high school graduate | 30 | 15.9% |
| High school only | 56 | 29.6% |
| Some college, no degree | 38 | 20.1% |
| Associate's degree | 14 | 7.4% |
| Bachelor's degree | 32 | 16.9% |
| Master's degree | 13 | 6.9% |
| Doctorate or professional | 6 | 3.2% |

## Properties of the Median

- The median, like the mean, is appropriate for quantitative variables. Since it requires only ordered observations to compute it, it is also valid for ordinal-scale data, as the previous example showed. It is not appropriate for nominal-scale data, since the observations cannot be ordered.

- For symmetric distributions, such as in Figure 3.7, the median and the mean are identical. To illustrate, the sample of observations 4, 5, 7, 9, 10 is symmetric about 7; 5 and 9 fall equally distant from it in opposite directions, as do 4 and 10. Thus, 7 is both the median and the mean.

- For skewed distributions, the mean lies toward the direction of skew (the longer tail) relative to the median. See Figure 3.10.

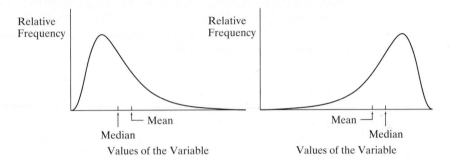

**FIGURE 3.10:** The Mean and the Median for Skewed Distributions. The mean is pulled in the direction of the longer tail.

For example, consider the violent crime rates of Table 3.2. The median is 36.5. The mean is $\bar{y} = 40.2$, somewhat larger than the median. Figure 3.2 showed that the violent crime rate values are skewed to the right. The mean is larger than the median for distributions that are skewed to the right. Income distributions tend to be skewed to the right. For example, household income in the United States in 2005 had a mean of about $61,000 and a median of about $44,000 (U.S. Bureau of the Census).

The distribution of grades on an exam tends to be skewed to the left when some students perform considerably poorer than the others. In this case, the mean is less than the median. For example, suppose that an exam scored on a scale of 0 to 100 has a median of 88 and a mean of 76. Then most students performed quite well (half being over 88), but apparently some scores were very much lower in order to bring the mean down to 76.

- The median is insensitive to the distances of the observations from the middle, since it uses only the ordinal characteristics of the data. For example, the following four sets of observations all have medians of 10:

| Set 1: | 8, | 9, | 10, | 11, | 12 |
| Set 2: | 8, | 9, | 10, | 11, | 100 |
| Set 3: | 0, | 9, | 10, | 10, | 10 |
| Set 4: | 8, | 9, | 10, | 100, | 100 |

- The median is not affected by outliers. For instance, the incomes of the seven employees in Example 3.5 have a median of $12,200 whether the largest observation is $20,000, $215,000, or $2,000,000.

## Median Compared to Mean

The median is usually more appropriate than the mean when the distribution is highly skewed, as we observed with the Leonardo's Pizza employee incomes. The mean can be greatly affected by outliers, whereas the median is not.

For the mean we need quantitative (interval-scale) data. The median also applies for ordinal scales (see Example 3.6). To use the mean for ordinal data, we must assign scores to the categories. In Table 3.5, if we assign scores 10, 12, 13, 14, 16, 18, 20 to the categories of highest degree, representing approximate number of years of education, we get a sample mean of 13.4.

The median has its own disadvantages. For discrete data that take relatively few values, quite different patterns of data can have the same median. For instance, Table 3.6, from a GSS, summarizes the 365 female responses to the question, "How many sex partners have you had in the last 12 months?" Only six distinct responses occur, and 63.8% of those are 1. The median response is 1. To find the sample mean, to sum the 365 observations we multiply each possible value by the frequency of its occurrence, and then add. That is,

$$\sum y_i = 102(0) + 233(1) + 18(2) + 9(3) + 2(4) + 1(5) = 309.$$

The sample mean response is

$$\bar{y} = \frac{\sum y_i}{n} = \frac{309}{365} = 0.85.$$

If the distribution of the 365 observations among these categories were (0, 233, 18, 9, 2, 103) (i.e., we shift 102 responses from 0 to 5), then the median would still be 1, but the mean would shift to 2.2. The mean uses the numerical values of the observations, not just their ordering.

**TABLE 3.6:** Number of Sex Partners Last Year, for Female Respondents in GSS

| Response | Frequency | Percentage |
|---|---|---|
| 0 | 102 | 27.9 |
| 1 | 233 | 63.8 |
| 2 | 18 | 4.9 |
| 3 | 9 | 2.5 |
| 4 | 2 | 0.5 |
| 5 | 1 | 0.3 |

The most extreme form of this problem occurs for **binary data**, which can take only two values, such as 0 and 1. The median equals the more common outcome, but gives no information about the relative number of observations at the two levels. For instance, consider a sample of size 5 for the variable, number of times married. The observations (1, 1, 1, 1, 1) and the observations (0, 0, 1, 1, 1) both have a median of 1. The mean is 1 for (1, 1, 1, 1, 1) and 3/5 for (0, 0, 1, 1, 1). *When observations take values of only 0 or 1, the mean equals the proportion of observations that equal 1.* Generally, for highly discrete data, the mean is more informative than the median.

In summary,

- If a distribution is highly skewed, the median is usually preferred because it better represents what is typical.

- If the distribution is close to symmetric or only mildly skewed or if it is discrete with few distinct values, the mean is usually preferred, because it uses the numerical values of all the observations.

## The Mode

Another measure, the *mode*, indicates the most common outcome.

| Mode |
|------|
| The *mode* is the value that occurs most frequently. |

The mode is most commonly used with highly discrete variables, such as with categorical data. In Table 3.5, on the highest degree completed, for instance, the mode is "High school only," since the frequency for that category is higher than the frequency for any other rating. In Table 3.6, on the number of sex partners in the last year, the mode is 1.

## Properties of the Mode

- The mode is appropriate for all types of data. For example, we might measure the mode for religion in Australia (nominal scale), for the rating given a teacher (ordinal scale), or for the number of years of education completed by Hispanic Americans (interval scale).
- A frequency distribution is called **bimodal** if two distinct mounds occur in the distribution. Bimodal distributions often occur with attitudinal variables when populations are polarized, with responses tending to be strongly in one direction or another. For instance, Figure 3.11 shows the relative frequency distribution of responses in a General Social Survey to the question, "Do you personally think it is wrong or not wrong for a woman to have an abortion if the family has a very low income and cannot afford any more children?" The relative frequencies in the two extreme categories are higher than those in the middle categories.

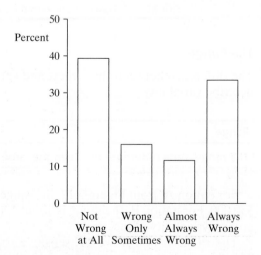

FIGURE 3.11: Bimodal Distribution for Opinion about Whether Abortion Is Wrong

- The mean, median, and mode are identical for a unimodal, symmetric distribution, such as a bell-shaped distribution.

The mean, median, and mode are complementary measures. They describe different aspects of the data. In any particular example, some or all their values may be useful. Be on the lookout for misleading statistical analyses, such as using one statistic when another would be more informative. People who present statistical conclusions often choose the statistic giving the impression they wish to convey. Recall Example 3.5 (p. 40) on Leonardo's Pizza employees, with the extreme outlying income observation. Be wary of the mean when the distribution may be highly skewed.

## 3.3 DESCRIBING VARIABILITY OF THE DATA

A measure of center alone is not adequate for numerically describing data for a quantitative variable. It describes a typical value, but not the spread of the data about that typical value. The two distributions in Figure 3.12 illustrate. The citizens of nation A and the citizens of nation B have the same mean annual income ($25,000). The distributions of those incomes differ fundamentally, however, nation B being much less variable. An income of $30,000 is extremely large for nation B, but not especially large for nation A. This section introduces statistics that describe the variability of a data set.

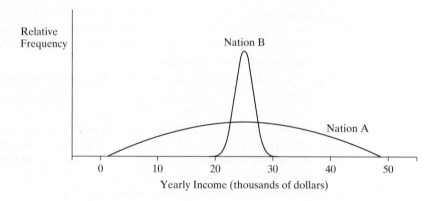

**FIGURE 3.12**: Distributions with the Same Mean but Different Variability

### The Range

The difference between the largest and smallest observations is the simplest way to describe variability.

| **Range** |
| --- |
| The *range* is the difference between the largest and smallest observations. |

For nation A, from Figure 3.12, the range of income values is about $50,000 − 0 = $50,000. For nation B, the range is about $30,000 − $20,000 = $10,000. Nation A has greater variability of incomes.

The range is not, however, sensitive to other characteristics of data variability. The three distributions in Figure 3.13 all have the same mean ($25,000) and range ($50,000), but they differ in variability about the center. In terms of distances of observations from the mean, nation A has the most variability, and nation B the least. The incomes in nation A tend to be farthest from the mean, and the incomes in nation B tend to be closest.

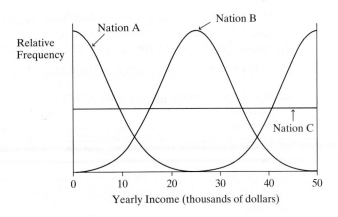

**FIGURE 3.13:** Distributions with the Same Mean and Range, but Different Variability about the Mean

## Standard Deviation

Other measures of variability are based on the deviations of the data from a measure of center such as their mean.

---

**Deviation**

The **deviation** of an observation $y_i$ from the sample mean $\bar{y}$ is $(y_i - \bar{y})$, the difference between them.

---

Each observation has a deviation. The deviation is *positive* when the observation falls *above* the mean. The deviation is *negative* when the observation falls *below* the mean. The interpretation of $\bar{y}$ as the center of gravity of the data implies that the sum of the positive deviations equals the negative of the sum of negative deviations. Thus, the sum of all the deviations about the mean, $\Sigma(y_i - \bar{y})$, equals 0. Because of this, measures of variability use either the absolute values or the squares of the deviations. The most popular measure uses the squares.

---

**Standard Deviation**

The **standard deviation** $s$ of $n$ observations is

$$s = \sqrt{\frac{\Sigma(y_i - \bar{y})^2}{n-1}} = \sqrt{\frac{\text{sum of squared deviations}}{\text{sample size} - 1}}.$$

This is the positive square root of the **variance** $s^2$, which is

$$s^2 = \frac{\Sigma(y_i - \bar{y})^2}{n-1} = \frac{(y_1 - \bar{y})^2 + (y_2 - \bar{y})^2 + \cdots + (y_n - \bar{y})^2}{n-1}.$$

---

The *variance* is approximately an average of the squared deviations. The units of measurement are the squares of those for the original data, since it uses squared deviations. This makes the variance difficult to interpret. It is why we use instead its square root, the *standard deviation*.

The expression $\Sigma(y_i - \bar{y})^2$ in these formulas is called a **sum of squares**. It represents squaring each deviation and then adding those squares. It is incorrect to first add the deviations and then square that sum; this gives a value of 0. The larger the deviations, the larger the sum of squares and the larger $s$ tends to be.

Although its formula looks complicated, the most basic interpretation of the standard deviation $s$ is quite simple: $s$ is a sort of *typical distance* of an observation from the mean. So the larger the standard deviation $s$, the greater the spread of the data.

### EXAMPLE 3.7 Comparing Variability of Quiz Scores

Each of the following sets of quiz scores for two small samples of students has a mean of 5 and a range of 10:

Sample 1: 0, 4, 4, 5, 7, 10<br>
Sample 2: 0, 0, 1, 9, 10, 10.

By inspection, sample 1 shows less variability about the mean than sample 2. Most scores in sample 1 are near the mean of 5, whereas all the scores in sample 2 are quite far from 5.

For sample 1,

$$\Sigma(y_i - \bar{y})^2 = (0 - 5)^2 + (4 - 5)^2 + (4 - 5)^2 + (5 - 5)^2$$
$$+ (7 - 5)^2 + (10 - 5)^2 = 56,$$

so the variance equals

$$s^2 = \frac{\Sigma(y_i - \bar{y})^2}{n - 1} = \frac{56}{6 - 1} = \frac{56}{5} = 11.2.$$

The standard deviation for sample 1 equals $s = \sqrt{11.2} = 3.3$. For sample 2, you can verify that $s^2 = 26.4$ and $s = \sqrt{26.4} = 5.1$. Since $3.3 < 5.1$, the standard deviations tell us that sample 1 is less variable than sample 2. ∎

Statistical software and many hand calculators can find the standard deviation. You should do the calculation yourself for a few small data sets to get a feel for what this measure represents. The answer you get may differ slightly from the value reported by software, depending on how much you round off in performing the calculation.

### Properties of the Standard Deviation

- $s \geq 0$.
- $s = 0$ only when all observations have the same value. For instance, if the ages for a sample of five students are 19, 19, 19, 19, 19, then the sample mean equals 19, each of the five deviations equals 0, and $s = 0$. This is the minimum possible variability.
- The greater the variability about the mean, the larger is the value of $s$. For example, Figure 3.5 shows that murder rates are much more variable among U.S. states than among Canadian provinces. In fact, the standard deviations are $s = 4.0$ for the United States and $s = 0.8$ for Canada.
- The reason for using $(n - 1)$, rather than $n$, in the denominator of $s$ (and $s^2$) is a technical one regarding inference about population parameters, discussed in Chapter 5. When we have data for an entire population, we replace $(n - 1)$ by the actual population size; the population variance is then precisely the mean of the squared deviations. In that case, the standard deviation can be no larger than half the range.
- If the data are rescaled, the standard deviation is also rescaled. For instance, if we change annual incomes from dollars (such as 34,000) to thousands of dollars (such as 34.0), the standard deviation also changes by a factor of 1000 (such as from 11,800 to 11.8).

### Interpreting the Magnitude of *s*

A distribution with $s = 5.1$ has greater variability than one with $s = 3.3$, but how do we interpret *how large s* = 5.1 is? We've seen that a rough answer is that *s* is a typical distance of an observation from the mean. To illustrate, suppose the first exam in your course, graded on a scale of 0 to 100, has a sample mean of 77. A value of $s = 0$ in unlikely, since every student must then score 77. A value such as $s = 50$ seems implausibly large for a typical distance from the mean. Values of *s* such as 8 or 12 seem much more realistic.

More precise ways to interpret *s* require further knowledge of the shape of the frequency distribution. The following rule provides an interpretation for many data sets.

---

**Empirical Rule**

If the histogram of the data is approximately bell shaped, then

1. About 68% of the observations fall between $\bar{y} - s$ and $\bar{y} + s$.
2. About 95% of the observations fall between $\bar{y} - 2s$ and $\bar{y} + 2s$.
3. All or nearly all observations fall between $\bar{y} - 3s$ and $\bar{y} + 3s$.

---

The rule is called the Empirical Rule because <u>many distributions seen in practice</u> (that is, *empirically*) are approximately bell shaped. Figure 3.14 is a graphical portrayal of the rule.

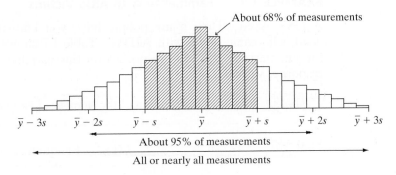

**FIGURE 3.14:** Empirical Rule: Interpretation of the Standard Deviation for a Bell-Shaped Distribution

### EXAMPLE 3.8    Describing a Distribution of SAT Scores

The Scholastic Aptitude Test (SAT, see www.collegeboard.com) has three portions: Critical Reading, Mathematics, and Writing. For each portion, the distribution of scores is approximately bell shaped. Each portion has mean about 500 and standard deviation about 100. Figure 3.15 portrays this. By the Empirical Rule, for each portion, about 68% of the scores fall between 400 and 600, because 400 and 600 are the numbers that are *one* standard deviation below and above the mean of 500. About 95% of the scores fall between 300 and 700, the numbers that are *two* standard deviations from the mean. The remaining 5% fall either below 300 or above 700. The distribution is roughly symmetric about 500, so about 2.5% of the scores fall above 700 and about 2.5% fall below 300.  ∎

The Empirical Rule applies only to distributions that are approximately bell-shaped. For other shapes, the percentage falling within two standard deviations of the mean need not be near 95%. It could be as low as 75% or as high as 100%. The

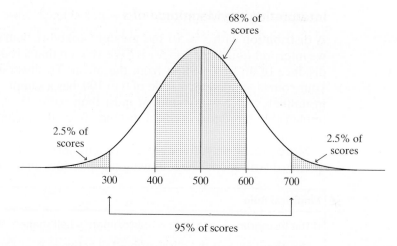

**FIGURE 3.15:** A Bell-Shaped Distribution of Scores for a Portion of the SAT, with Mean 500 and Standard Deviation 100

Empirical Rule may not work well if the distribution is highly skewed or if it is highly discrete, with the variable taking few values. The exact percentages depend on the form of the distribution, as the next example demonstrates.

## EXAMPLE 3.9    Familiarity with AIDS Victims

A GSS asked, "How many people have you known personally, either living or dead, who came down with AIDS?" Table 3.7 shows part of a computer printout for summarizing the 1598 responses on this variable. It indicates that 76% of the responses were 0.

**TABLE 3.7:** Frequency Distribution of the Number of People Known Personally with AIDS

| AIDS | Frequency | Percent |
|------|-----------|---------|
| 0 | 1214 | 76.0 |
| 1 | 204 | 12.8 |
| 2 | 85 | 5.3 |
| 3 | 49 | 3.1 |
| 4 | 19 | 1.2 |
| 5 | 13 | 0.8 |
| 6 | 5 | 0.3 |
| 7 | 8 | 0.5 |
| 8 | 1 | 0.1 |

| | | |
|------|-----------|---------|
| N | 1598 | |
| Mean | 0.47 | |
| Std Dev | 1.09 | |

The mean and standard deviation are $\bar{y} = 0.47$ and $s = 1.09$. The values 0 and 1 both fall within one standard deviation of the mean. Now 88.8% of the distribution falls at these two points, or within $\bar{y} \pm s$. This is considerably larger than the 68% that the Empirical Rule states. The Empirical Rule does not apply to this distribution, because it is not even approximately bell shaped. Instead, it is highly skewed to the right, as you can check by sketching a histogram for Table 3.7. The smallest value in the distribution (0) is less than one standard deviation below the mean; the largest value in the distribution (8) is nearly seven standard deviations above the mean.    ■

✶ Whenever the smallest or largest observation is less than a standard deviation from the mean, this is evidence of severe skew. For instance, a recent statistics exam having scale from 0 to 100 had $\bar{y} = 86$ and $s = 15$. The upper bound of 100 was less than one standard deviation above the mean. The distribution was highly skewed to the left.

✶ The standard deviation, like the mean, can be greatly affected by an outlier, especially for small data sets. For instance, the murder rates shown in Figure 3.5 for the 50 U.S. states have $\bar{y} = 7.3$ and $s = 4.0$. The distribution is somewhat irregular, but 68% of the states have murder rates within one standard deviation of the mean and 98% within two standard deviations. Now suppose we include the murder rate for the District of Columbia, which equaled 78.5, in the data set. Then $\bar{y} = 8.7$ and $s = 10.7$. The standard deviation more than doubles. Now 96.1% of the murder rates (all except D.C. and Louisiana) fall within one standard deviation of the mean.

## 3.4    MEASURES OF POSITION

Another way to describe a distribution is with a measure of **position**. This tells us the point at which a given percentage of the data fall below (or above) that point. As special cases, some measures of position describe center and some describe variability.

### Quartiles and Other Percentiles

The range uses two measures of position, the maximum value and the minimum value. The median is a measure of position, with half the data falling below it and half above it. The median is a special case of a set of measures of position called *percentiles*.

---

**Percentile**

The *pth percentile* is the point such that $p$% of the observations fall below or at that point and $(100 - p)$% fall above it.

---

Substituting $p = 50$ in this definition gives the 50th percentile. This is the median. The median is larger than 50% of the observations and smaller than the other $(100 - 50) = 50$%. Two other commonly used percentiles are the *lower quartile* and the *upper quartile*.

---

**Lower and Upper Quartiles**

The 25th percentile is called the **lower quartile**. The 75th percentile is called the **upper quartile**. One quarter of the data fall below the lower quartile. One quarter fall above the upper quartile.

---

The quartiles result from $p = 25$ and $p = 75$ in the percentile definition. The lower quartile is the median for the observations that fall below the median, that is, for the bottom half of the data. The upper quartile is the median for the observations that fall above the median, that is, for the upper half of the data. The quartiles together with the median split the distribution into four parts, each containing one-fourth of the observations. See Figure 3.16.

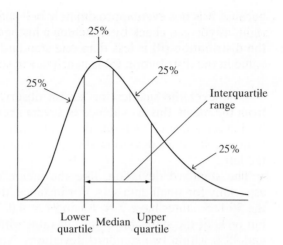

**FIGURE 3.16:** The Quartiles and the Interquartile Range

For the violent crime rates in Table 3.2, the sample size is $n = 50$ and the median equals 36.5. As with the median, the quartiles can easily be found from the stem-and-leaf plot of the data (Figure 3.4), which was

| Stem | Leaf |
|------|------|
| 0 | 8 |
| 1 | 1  1  5  7 |
| 2 | 2  4  5  6  6  6  6  7  7  8  9  9 |
| 3 | 0  1  3  3  4  5  5  6  7 |
| 4 | 0  0  3  5  6  6  6  7  7 |
| 5 | 1  1  1  5  6  8  9 |
| 6 | 1  5  6  6  9 |
| 7 | 0  3  9 |

The lower quartile is the median for the 25 observations below the median. It is the 13th smallest observation, or 27. The upper quartile is the median for the 25 observations above the median. It is the 13th largest observation, or 51.

In summary, since

lower quartile = 27, median = 36.5, upper quartile = 51,

roughly a quarter of the states had violent crime rates (i) below 27, (ii) between 27 and 36.5, (iii) between 36.5 and 51, and (iv) above 51. The distance between the upper quartile and the median, $51 - 36.5 = 14.5$, exceeds the distance $36.5 - 27 = 9.5$ between the lower quartile and the median. This commonly happens when the distribution is skewed to the right.

Software can easily find quartiles as well as other percentiles. In practice, percentiles other than the median are usually not reported for small data sets.

### Measuring Variability: Interquartile Range

The difference between the upper and lower quartiles is called the **interquartile range**, denoted by IQR. This measure describes the spread of the middle half of the observations. For the U.S. violent crime rates in Table 3.2, the interquartile range IQR = $51 - 27 = 24$. The middle half of the murder rates fall within a range of 24. Like the range and standard deviation, the IQR increases as the variability increases, and it is useful for comparing variability of different groups. For example, 12 years earlier in 1993, the quartiles of the U.S. statewide violent crime rates were 33 and 77, giving an IQR of 77 − 33 = 44 and showing quite a bit more variability.

An advantage of the IQR over the ordinary range or the standard deviation is that it is not sensitive to outliers. The U.S. violent crime rates range from 8 to 79, so the range is 71. When we include the observation for D.C., which was 161, the IQR changes only from 24 to 28. By contrast, the range changes from 71 to 153.

For bell-shaped distributions, the distance from the mean to either quartile is about 2/3rd of a standard deviation. Then IQR is roughly $(4/3)s$. The insensitivity of the IQR to outliers has recently increased its popularity, although in practice the standard deviation is still much more common.

### Box Plots: Graphing a Five-Number Summary of Positions

The median, the quartiles, and the maximum and minimum are five positions often used as a set to describe center and spread. For instance, software reports the following five-number summary for the violent crime rates (where Q1 = lower quartile, Q3 = upper quartile, regarding the median as the second quartile):

```
100% Max       79.0
 75% Q3        51.0
 50% Med       36.5
 25% Q1        27.0
  0% Min        8.0
```

The five-number summary provides a simple description of the data. It is the basis of a graphical display called the **box plot** that summarizes both the center and the variability. The *box* of a box plot contains the central 50% of the distribution, from the lower quartile to the upper quartile. The median is marked by a line drawn within the box. The lines extending from the box are called *whiskers*. These extend to the maximum and minimum, except for outliers, which are marked separately.

Figure 3.17 shows the box plot for the violent crime rates, in the format provided with SPSS software. The upper whisker and upper half of the central box are longer than the lower ones. This indicates that the right tail of the distribution, which corresponds to the relatively large values, is longer than the left tail. The plot reflects the skewness to the right of violent crime rates. (Some software also plots the mean on the box plot, representing it by a + sign.)

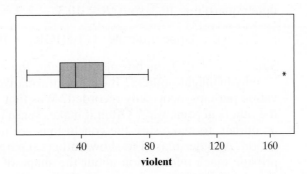

**FIGURE 3.17:** Box Plot of Violent Crime Rates of U.S. States and D.C.

Side-by-side box plots are useful for comparing two distributions. Figure 3.5 showed side-by-side stem-and-leaf plots of U.S. and Canadian murder rates. Figure 3.18 shows

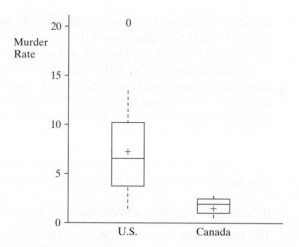

**FIGURE 3.18:** Box Plots for U.S. and Canadian Murder Rates

the side-by-side box plots. These side-by-side box plots reveal that the murder rates in the U.S. tend to be much higher and have much greater variability.

### Outliers

Box plots identify outliers separately. To explain this, we now present a formal definition of an outlier.

---

**Outlier**

An observation is an *outlier* if it falls more than 1.5(IQR) above the upper quartile or more than 1.5(IQR) below the lower quartile.

---

In box plots, the whiskers extend to the smallest and largest observations only if those values are not outliers; that is, if they are no more than 1.5(IQR) beyond the quartiles. Otherwise, the whiskers extend to the most extreme observations within 1.5(IQR), and the outliers are marked separately. For instance, the statistical software SAS marks by an O (O for outlier) a value between 1.5 and 3.0(IQR) from the box and by an asterisk (*) a value even farther away.

Figure 3.18 shows one outlier for the U.S. with a very high murder rate. This is the murder rate of 20.3 (for Louisiana). For these data, the lower quartile = 3.9 and upper quartile = 10.3, so $IQR = 10.3 - 3.9 = 6.4$. Thus,

$$\text{Upper quartile} + 1.5(IQR) = 10.3 + 1.5(6.4) = 19.9.$$

Since 20.3 > 19.9, the box plot highlights the observation of 20.3 as an outlier.

Why highlight outliers? It can be informative to investigate them. Was the observation perhaps incorrectly recorded? Was that subject fundamentally different from the others in some way? Often it makes sense to repeat a statistical analysis without an outlier, to make sure the conclusions are not overly sensitive to a single observation. Another reason to show outliers separately in a box plot is that they do not provide much information about the shape of the distribution, especially for large data sets.

In practice, the 1.5(IQR) criterion for an outlier is somewhat arbitrary. It is better to regard an observation satisfying this criterion as a *potential* outlier rather than a definite outlier. When a distribution has a long right tail, some observations may fall more than 1.5 IQR above the upper quartile even if they are not separated far from the bulk of the data.

### How Many Standard Deviations from the Mean? The *z*-Score

Another way to measure position is by the number of standard deviations that a point falls from the mean. For example, the U.S. murder rates shown in the box plot in Figure 3.18 have a mean of 7.3 and a standard deviation of 4.0. The value of 20.3 for Louisiana falls $20.3 - 7.3 = 13.0$ above the mean. Now, 13 is $13/4 = 3.25$ standard deviations. The Louisiana murder rate is 3.25 standard deviations above the mean.

The number of standard deviations that an observation falls from the mean is called its ***z-score***. For the murder rates of Figure 3.18, Louisiana has a *z*-score of

$$z = \frac{20.3 - 7.3}{4.0} = \frac{\text{Observation} - \text{Mean}}{\text{Standard Deviation}} = 3.25.$$

By the Empirical Rule, for a bell-shaped distribution it is very unusual for an observation to fall more than three standard deviations from the mean. An alternative criterion regards an observation as an outlier if it has a *z*-score larger than 3 in absolute value. By this criterion, the murder rate for Louisiana is an outlier.

We'll study *z*-scores in more detail in the next chapter. We'll see they are especially useful for bell-shaped distributions.

## 3.5    BIVARIATE DESCRIPTIVE STATISTICS

In this chapter we've learned how to summarize categorical and quantitative variables graphically and numerically. In the next three chapters we'll learn about basic ideas of statistical inference for a categorical or quantitative variable. Most studies have more than one variable, however, and Chapters 7–16 present methods that can handle two or more variables at a time.

### Association between Response and Explanatory Variables

With multivariable analyses, the main focus is on studying *associations* among the variables. There is said to be an ***association*** between two variables if certain values of one variable tend to go with certain values of the other.

For example, consider "religious affiliation," with categories (Protestant, Catholic, Other) and "ethnic group," with categories (Anglo-American, African-American, Hispanic). In the United States, Anglo-Americans are more likely to be Protestant than are Hispanics, who are overwhelmingly Catholic. African-Americans are even more likely to be Protestant. An association exists between religious affiliation and ethnic group, because the proportion of people having a particular religious affiliation changes as ethnic group changes.

An analysis of association between two variables is called a ***bivariate*** analysis, because there are two variables. Usually one is an outcome variable on which comparisons are made at levels of the other variable. The outcome variable is called the ***response variable***. The variable that defines the groups is called the ***explanatory variable***. The analysis studies how the outcome on the response variable *depends on* or is *explained by* the value of the explanatory variable. For example, when we describe how religious affiliation depends on ethnic group, religious affiliation is the response variable. In a comparison of men and women on income, income is the response variable and gender is the explanatory variable. Income may depend on gender, not gender on income.

Often, the response variable is called the ***dependent variable*** and the explanatory variable is called the ***independent variable***. The terminology *dependent variable* refers to the goal of investigating the degree to which the response on that variable *depends on* the value of the other variable. We prefer not to use these terms, since *independent* and *dependent* are used for so many other things in statistical methods.

### Comparing Two Groups Is a Bivariate Analysis

Chapter 7 will present descriptive and inferential methods for comparing two groups. For example, suppose we'd like to know whether men or women have more good friends, on the average. A GSS reports (for variable NUMFREND) that the mean number of good friends is 7.0 for men ($s = 8.4$) and 5.9 for women ($s = 6.0$). The two distributions have similar appearance, both being skewed to the right and with a median of 4.

Here, this is an analysis of two variables—number of good friends and gender. The response variable, number of good friends, is quantitative. The explanatory variable, gender, is categorical. In this case, it's common to compare means on the response variable for the categories of the categorical variable. Graphs are also useful, such as side-by-side box plots.

### Bivariate Categorical Data

Chapter 8 will present methods for analyzing association between two categorical variables. Table 3.8 is an example of such data. This table results from answers to two questions on the 2006 General Social Survey. One asked whether homosexual relations are wrong. The other asked about the fundamentalism/liberalism of the respondent's religion. A table of this kind, called a ***contingency table***, displays the number of subjects observed at combinations of possible outcomes for the two variables. It displays how outcomes of a response variable are *contingent* on the category of the explanatory variable.

**TABLE 3.8:** Cross-Classification of Religion and Opinion about Homosexual Relations

| | Opinion about Homosexual Relations | | | | |
| --- | --- | --- | --- | --- | --- |
| Religion | Always Wrong | Almost Always Wrong | Sometimes Wrong | Not Wrong at All | Total |
| Fundamentalist | 416 | 26 | 22 | 83 | 547 |
| Liberal | 213 | 29 | 52 | 292 | 586 |

Table 3.8 has eight possible combinations of responses. (Another possible outcome, "moderate" for the religion variable, is not shown here.) We could list the categories in a frequency distribution or construct a bar graph. Usually, though, it's more informative to do this for the categories of the response variable, separately for each category of the explanatory variable. For example, if we treat opinion about homosexual relations as the response variable, we could report the percentages in the four categories for homosexual relations, separately for each religious category.

Consider those who report being fundamentalist. Since $416/547 = 0.76$, 76% believe homosexual relations are always wrong. Likewise, you can check that 5% believe they are almost always wrong, 4% believe they are sometimes wrong, and 15% believe they are not wrong at all. For those who report being liberal, since $213/586 = 0.36$, 36% believe homosexual relations are always wrong. Likewise, you can check that 5% believe they are almost always wrong, 9% believe they are sometimes wrong, and 50% believe they are not wrong at all. There seems to be a definite association between opinion about homosexuality and religious beliefs, with religious fundamentalists being more negative about homosexuality. Chapter 8 will show many other ways of analyzing data of this sort.

### Bivariate Quantitative Data

When both variables are quantitative, a plot we've not yet discussed is helpful. Figure 3.19 shows an example using the software SPSS to plot data from 38 nations on fertility (the mean number of children per adult woman) and the percentage of the adult population using cell phones. (The data are shown later in the text in Table 9.13.) Here, values of cell-phone use are plotted on the horizontal axis, called the **x-axis**, and values of fertility are plotted on the vertical axis, called the **y-axis**. The values of the two variables for any particular observation form a point relative to these axes. To portray graphically the sample data, we plot the 38 observations as 38 points. For example, the point at the top left of the plot represents Pakistan, which had a fertility of 6.2 children per woman but cell-phone use of only 3.5%. This graphical plot is called a **scatterplot**.

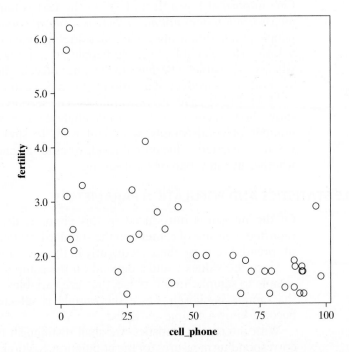

**FIGURE 3.19:** Scatterplot for Fertility and Percentage Using Cell Phones, for 38 Nations. The data are in Table 9.13 in Chapter 9.

The scatterplot shows a tendency for nations with higher cell-phone use to have lower levels of fertility. In Chapter 9 we'll learn about two ways to describe such as a trend. One way, called the ***correlation***, describes how strong the association is, in terms of how closely the data follow a *straight line trend*. For Figure 3.19, the correlation is $-0.63$. The negative value means that fertility tends to go *down* as cell-phone use goes *up*. By contrast, cell-phone use and GDP (gross domestic product, per capita) have a positive correlation of 0.83. As one goes up, the other also tends to go up.

The correlation takes values between $-1$ and $+1$. The larger it is in absolute value, that is, the farther from 0, the stronger the association. Cell-phone use is a bit more strongly associated with GDP than with fertility, because the correlation of 0.83 is larger in absolute value than the correlation of $-0.63$.

The second useful tool for describing the trend is ***regression analysis***. This provides a straight-line formula for predicting the value of the response variable from a given value of the explanatory variable. For Figure 3.19, this equation is

$$\text{Predicted fertility} = 3.4 - 0.02 \text{ (cell-phone use)}.$$

For a country with no cell-phone use, the predicted fertility is $3.4 - 0.02(0) = 3.4$ children per mother. For a country with 100% of adults using cell phones, the predicted fertility is only $3.4 - 0.02(100) = 1.4$ children per mother.

Chapter 9 shows how to find the correlation and the regression line. Later chapters show how to extend the analysis to handle categorical as well as quantitative variables.

### Analyzing More than Two Variables

This section has taken a quick look at analyzing associations between two variables. One important lesson from later in the text is that, *just because two variables have an association does not mean there is a causal connection*. For example, having more people in a nation using cell phones does not mean this is the reason the fertility rate is lower (for example, because people are talking on cell phones rather than doing what causes babies.) Perhaps high values on cell-phone use and low values on fertility are both a by-product of a nation being more economically advanced.

Most studies have *several* variables. The second half of this book (Chapters 10–16) shows how to conduct *multivariate* analyses. For example, to study what affects the number of good friends, we might want to simultaneously consider gender, age, whether married, educational level, whether attend religious services regularly, and whether live in urban or rural setting.

## 3.6  SAMPLE STATISTICS AND POPULATION PARAMETERS

Of the measures introduced in this chapter, the mean $\bar{y}$ is the most commonly reported measure of center and the standard deviation $s$ is the most common measure of spread. We'll use them frequently in the rest of the text.

Since the values $\bar{y}$ and $s$ depend on the sample selected, they vary in value from sample to sample. In this sense, they are variables. Their values are unknown before the sample is chosen. Once the sample is selected and they are computed, they become known sample statistics.

With inferential statistics, we shall distinguish between sample statistics and the corresponding measures for the population. Section 1.2 introduced the term *parameter* for a summary measure of the population. A statistic describes a sample, while a parameter describes the population from which the sample was taken. In this text, lowercase Greek letters usually denote population parameters and Roman letters denote the sample statistics.

> **Notation for Parameters**
>
> $\mu$ (Greek mu) and $\sigma$ (Greek lowercase sigma) denote the mean and standard deviation of a variable for the population.

We call $\mu$ and $\sigma$ the **population mean** and **population standard deviation**. The population mean is the average of the observations for the entire population. The population standard deviation describes the variability of those observations about the population mean.

Whereas the statistics $\bar{y}$ and $s$ are variables, with values depending on the sample chosen, the parameters $\mu$ and $\sigma$ are constants. This is because $\mu$ and $\sigma$ refer to just one particular group of observations, namely, the observations for the entire population. The parameter values are usually unknown, which is the reason for sampling and calculating sample statistics to estimate their values. Much of the rest of this text deals with ways of making inferences about unknown parameters (such as $\mu$) using sample statistics (such as $\bar{y}$). Before studying these inferential methods, though, you need to learn some basic ideas of *probability*, which serves as the foundation for the methods. Probability is the subject of the next chapter.

## 3.7    CHAPTER SUMMARY

This chapter introduced ***descriptive statistics***—ways of *describing* data to summarize key characteristics of the data.

### 3.7.1    Overview of Tables and Graphs

- A ***frequency distribution*** summarizes the counts for possible values or intervals of values. A ***relative frequency*** distribution reports this information using percentages or proportions.
- A ***bar graph*** uses bars over possible values to portray a frequency distribution for a categorical variable. For a quantitative variable, a similar graphic is called a ***histogram***. It shows whether the distribution is approximately bell shaped, U shaped, skewed to the right (longer tail pointing to the right), or whatever.
- The ***stem-and-leaf plot*** is an alternative portrayal of data for a quantitative variable. It groups together observations having the same leading digit (stem), and shows also their final digit (leaf). For small samples, it displays the individual observations.
- The ***box plot*** portrays the quartiles, the extreme values, and any outliers. The box plot and the stem-and-leaf plot also can provide back-to-back comparisons of two groups.

Stem-and-leaf plots and box plots, simple as they are, are relatively recent innovations in statistics. They were introduced by the great statistician John Tukey (see Tukey 1977), who also introduced the terminology "software." See Cleveland (1994) and Tufte (2001) for other innovative ways to present data graphically.

### 3.7.2    Overview of Measures of Center

***Measures of center*** describe the center of the data, in terms of a typical observation.

- The ***mean*** is the sum of the observations divided by the sample size. It is the center of gravity of the data.
- The ***median*** divides the ordered data set into two parts of equal numbers of observations, half below and half above that point.

- The lower quarter of the observations fall below the *lower quartile*, and the upper quarter fall above the *upper quartile*. These are the 25th and 75th *percentiles*. The median is the 50th percentile. The quartiles and median split the data into four equal parts. They are less affected than the mean by outliers or extreme skew.
- The *mode* is the most commonly occurring value. It is valid for any type of data, though usually used with categorical data or discrete variables taking relatively few values.

### 3.7.3 Overview of Measures of Variability

*Measures of variability* describe the spread of the data.

- The *range* is the difference between the largest and smallest observations. The *interquartile range* is the range of the middle half of the data between the upper and lower quartiles. It is less affected by outliers.
- The *variance* averages the squared deviations about the mean. Its square root, the *standard deviation*, is easier to interpret, describing a typical distance from the mean.
- The *Empirical Rule* states that for a bell-shaped distribution, about 68% of the observations fall within one standard deviation of the mean, about 95% fall within two standard deviations, and nearly all, if not all, fall within three standard deviations.

Table 3.9 summarizes the measures of center and variability. A *statistic* summarizes a sample. A *parameter* summarizes a population. *Statistical inference* uses statistics to make predictions about parameters.

**TABLE 3.9:** Summary of Measures of Center and Variability

| Measure | Definition | Interpretation |
|---|---|---|
| **Center** | | |
| Mean | $\bar{y} = \Sigma y_i / n$ | Center of gravity |
| Median | Middle observation of ordered sample | 50th percentile, splits sample into two equal parts |
| Mode | Most frequently occurring value | Most likely outcome, valid for all types of data |
| **Variability** | | |
| Standard deviation | $s = \sqrt{\Sigma(y_i - \bar{y})^2/(n-1)}$ | Empirical Rule: If bell shaped, 68%, 95% within $s$, $2s$ of $\bar{y}$ |
| Range | Difference between largest and smallest observation | Greater with more variability |
| Interquartile range | Difference between upper quartile (75th percentile) and lower quartile (25th percentile) | Encompasses middle half of data |

### 3.7.4 Overview of Bivariate Descriptive Statistics

*Bivariate statistics* are used to analyze data on two variables together.

- Many studies analyze how the outcome on a *response variable* depends on the value of an explanatory variable.

- For categorical variables, a ***contingency table*** shows the number of observations at the combinations of possible outcomes for the two variables.
- For quantitative variables, a ***scatterplot*** graphs the observations, showing a point for each observation. The response variable is plotted on the *y*-axis and the explanatory variable is plotted on the *x*-axis.
- For quantitative variables, the ***correlation*** describes the strength of straight-line association. It falls between $-1$ and $+1$ and indicates whether the response variable tends to increase (positive correlation) or decrease (negative correlation) as the explanatory variable increases.
- A ***regression analysis*** provides a straight-line formula for predicting the value of the response variable using the explanatory variable. We study correlation and regression in detail in Chapter 9.

## PROBLEMS

### Practicing the Basics

**3.1.** Table 3.10 shows the number (in millions) of the foreign-born population of the United States in 2004, by place of birth.
  (a) Construct a relative frequency distribution.
  (b) Sketch the data in a bar graph.
  (c) Is "Place of birth" quantitative or categorical?
  (d) Use whichever of the following measures is relevant for these data: mean, median, mode.

**TABLE 3.10**

| Place of Birth | Number |
| --- | --- |
| Europe | 4.7 |
| Asia | 8.7 |
| Caribbean | 3.3 |
| Central America | 12.9 |
| South America | 2.1 |
| Other | 2.6 |
| **Total** | 34.3 |

*Source: Statistical Abstract of the United States, 2006.*

**3.2.** According to www.adherents.com, in 2006 the number of followers of the world's five largest religions were 2.1 billion for Christianity, 1.3 billion for Islam, 0.9 billion for Hinduism, 0.4 billion for Confucianism, and 0.4 billion for Buddhism.
  (a) Construct a relative frequency distribution.
  (b) Sketch a bar graph.
  (c) Can you find a mean, median, or mode for these data? If so, do so and interpret.

**3.3.** A teacher shows her class the scores on the midterm exam in the stem-and-leaf plot:

```
6 | 5 8 8
7 | 0 1 1 3 6 7 7 9
8 | 1 2 2 3 3 3 4 6 7 7 7 8 9
9 | 0 1 1 2 3 4 4 5 8
```

  (a) Identify the number of students and the minimum and maximum scores.
  (b) Sketch a histogram with four intervals.

**3.4.** According to the *2005 American Community Survey*, in 2005 the United States had 30.1 million households with one person, 37.0 million with two persons, 17.8 million with three persons, 15.3 million with four persons, and 10.9 million with five or more persons.
  (a) Construct a relative frequency distribution.
  (b) Sketch a histogram. What is its shape?
  (c) Report and interpret the (i) median, (ii) mode of household size.

**3.5.** Copy the "2005 statewide crime" data file from the text Web site (www.stat.ufl.edu/~aa/social/data.html). Use the variable, murder rate (per 100,000 population). In this exercise, do not use the observation for D.C. Using software,
  (a) Construct a relative frequency distribution.
  (b) Construct a histogram. How would you describe the shape of the distribution?
  (c) Construct a stem-and-leaf plot. How does this plot compare to the histogram in (b)?

**3.6.** The OECD (Organization for Economic Cooperation and Development) consists of advanced, industrialized countries that accept the principles of representative democracy and a free market economy. Table 3.11 shows UN data for OECD nations on several variables: gross domestic product (GDP, per capita in U.S. dollars), percent unemployed, a measure of inequality based on comparing wealth of the richest 10% to the poorest 10%, public expenditure on health (as a percentage of the GDP), the number of physicians per 100,000 people, carbon dioxide emissions (per capita, in metric tons), the percentage of seats in parliament held by women, and female economic activity as

**TABLE 3.11:** UN Data for OECD Nations, Available as "OECD data" File at Text Web Site

| Nation | GDP | Unemp. | Inequal. | Health | Physicians | CO2 | Women Parl. | Fem. Econ. |
|---|---|---|---|---|---|---|---|---|
| Australia | 30,331 | 5.1 | 12.5 | 6.4 | 247 | 18 | 28.3 | 79 |
| Austria | 32,276 | 5.8 | 6.9 | 5.1 | 338 | 8.6 | 32.2 | 75 |
| Belgium | 31,096 | 8.4 | 8.2 | 6.3 | 449 | 8.3 | 35.7 | 72 |
| Canada | 31,263 | 6.8 | 9.4 | 6.9 | 214 | 17.9 | 24.3 | 83 |
| Denmark | 31,914 | 4.9 | 8.1 | 7.5 | 293 | 10.1 | 36.9 | 84 |
| Finland | 29,951 | 8.6 | 5.6 | 5.7 | 316 | 13 | 37.5 | 86 |
| France | 29,300 | 10.0 | 9.1 | 7.7 | 337 | 6.2 | 13.9 | 79 |
| Germany | 28,303 | 9.3 | 6.9 | 8.7 | 337 | 9.8 | 30.5 | 76 |
| Greece | 22,205 | 10.6 | 10.2 | 5.1 | 438 | 8.7 | 13 | 66 |
| Iceland | 33,051 | 2.5 | .. | 8.8 | 362 | 7.6 | 33.3 | 87 |
| Ireland | 38,827 | 4.3 | 9.4 | 5.8 | 279 | 10.3 | 14.2 | 72 |
| Italy | 28,180 | 7.7 | 11.6 | 6.3 | 420 | 7.7 | 16.1 | 61 |
| Japan | 29,251 | 4.4 | 4.5 | 6.4 | 198 | 9.7 | 10.7 | 65 |
| Luxembourg | 69,961 | 4.6 | .. | 6.2 | 266 | 22 | 23.3 | 68 |
| Netherlands | 31,789 | 6.2 | 9.2 | 6.1 | 315 | 8.7 | 34.2 | 76 |
| New Zealand | 23,413 | 3.6 | 12.5 | 6.3 | 237 | 8.8 | 32.2 | 81 |
| Norway | 38,454 | 4.6 | 6.1 | 8.6 | 313 | 9.9 | 37.9 | 87 |
| Portugal | 19,629 | 7.5 | 15 | 6.7 | 342 | 5.6 | 21.3 | 79 |
| Spain | 25,047 | 9.1 | 10.3 | 5.5 | 330 | 7.3 | 30.5 | 65 |
| Sweden | 29,541 | 5.6 | 6.2 | 8 | 328 | 5.9 | 45.3 | 87 |
| Switzerland | 33,040 | 4.1 | 9 | 6.7 | 361 | 5.6 | 24.8 | 79 |
| United Kingdom | 30,821 | 4.8 | 13.8 | 6.9 | 230 | 9.4 | 18.5 | 79 |
| United States | 39,676 | 5.1 | 15.9 | 6.8 | 256 | 19.8 | 15 | 81 |

*Source*: hdr.undp.org/statistics/data

Unemp. = % Unemployed, Inequal. = Measure of inequality, Women parl. = % of seats in parliament held by women, Fem. econ. = Female economic activity (% of male rate).

a percentage of the male rate. These data are the "OECD data" file at the text Web site.

(a) Construct a stem-and-leaf plot of the GDP values, by rounding and reporting the values in thousands of dollars (e.g., replacing $19,629 by 20).

(b) Construct a histogram corresponding to the stem-and-leaf plot in (a).

(c) Identify the outlier in each plot.

**3.7.** Recently, the statewide number of abortions per 1000 women 15 to 41 years of age, for states in the Pacific region of the United States, were: Washington, 26; Oregon, 17; California, 236; Alaska, 2; and Hawaii, 6 (*Statistical Abstract of the United States, 2006*).

(a) Find the mean.

(b) Find the median. Why is it so different from the mean?

**3.8.** Global warming seems largely a result of human activity that produces carbon dioxide emissions and other greenhouse gases. The *Human Development Report 2005*, published by the United Nations Development Programme, reported per capita emissions in 2002 for the eight largest countries in population size, in metric tons (1000 kilograms) per person: Bangladesh 0.3, Brazil 1.8, China 2.3,

India 1.2, Indonesia 1.4, Pakistan 0.7, Russia 9.9, United States 20.1.

(a) For these eight values, find the mean and the median.

(b) Does any observation appear to be an outlier? Discuss its impact on how the mean compares to the median.

**3.9.** A Roper organization survey asked, "How far have environmental protection laws and regulations gone?" For the possible responses not far enough, about right, and too far, the percentages of responses were 51%, 33%, and 16%.

(a) Which response is the mode?

(b) Can you compute a mean or a median for these data? If so, do so; if not, explain why not.

**3.10.** A researcher in an alcoholism treatment center, to study the length of stay in the center for first-time patients, randomly selects ten records of individuals institutionalized within the previous two years. The lengths of stay, in days, were 11, 6, 20, 9, 13, 4, 39, 13, 44, and 7.

(a) Construct a stem-and-leaf plot.

(b) Find the mean and the standard deviation, and interpret.

(c) For a similar study 25 years ago, lengths of stay for ten sampled individuals were 32, 18,

55, 17, 24, 31, 20, 40, 24, 15. Compare results to those in the new study using (i) a back-to-back stem-and-leaf plot, (ii) the mean, (iii) the standard deviation. Interpret any differences you find.

**(d)** Actually, the new study also selected one other record. That patient is still institutionalized after 40 days. Thus, that patient's length of stay is at least 40 days, but the actual value is unknown. Can you calculate the mean or median for the complete sample of size 11 including this partial observation? Explain. (This observation is said to be *censored*, meaning that the observed value is "cut short" of its true, unknown value.)

**3.11.** Access the GSS at sda.berkeley.edu/GSS. Entering TVHOURS for the variable and year(2006) in the selection filter, you obtain data on hours per day of TV watching in the U.S. in 2006.

**(a)** Construct the relative frequency distribution for the values 0, 1, 2, 3, 4, 5, 6, 7 or more.

**(b)** How would you describe the shape of the distribution?

**(c)** Explain why the median is 2.

**(d)** The mean is larger than 2. Why do you think this is?

**3.12.** Table 3.12 shows 2003 female economic activity (number of women in labor force per 100 men in labor force), for countries in Western Europe. Construct a back-to-back stem-and-leaf plot of these values contrasted with those from South America in Table 3.4. What is your interpretation?

**3.13.** According to Statistics Canada, in 2000 household income in Canada had median $46,752 and mean $71,600. What would you predict about the shape of the distribution? Why?

**3.14.** Table 3.13 summarizes responses of 2333 subjects in the 2006 General Social Survey to the question, "About how often did you have sex during the last 12 months?"

**(a)** Report the median and the mode. Interpret.

**(b)** Treat this scale in a quantitative manner by assigning the scores 0, 0.1, 1.0, 2.5, 4.3, 10.8, and 17 to the categories, for approximate monthly frequency. Find the sample mean, and interpret.

**TABLE 3.13**

| How Often Had Sex | Frequency |
|---|---|
| Not at all | 595 |
| Once or twice | 205 |
| About once a month | 265 |
| 2 or 3 times a month | 361 |
| About once a week | 343 |
| 2 or 3 times a week | 430 |
| More than 3 times a week | 134 |

**3.15.** The 2004 GSS asked respondents "How often do you read the newspaper?" The possible responses were (every day, a few times a week, once a week, less than once a week, never), and the counts in those categories were (358, 222, 134, 121, 71).

**(a)** Identify the mode and the median response.

**(b)** Let $y$ = number of times you read the newspaper in a week, measured as described above. For the scores $(7, 3, 1, 0.5, 0)$ for the categories, find $\bar{y}$. How does it compare to the mean of 4.4 for the 1994 GSS?

**3.16.** According to the U.S. Bureau of the Census, *2005 American Community Survey*, the median earnings in the past 12 months was $32,168 for females and $41,965 for males, whereas the mean was $39,890 for females and $56,724 for males.

**(a)** Does this suggest that the distribution of income for each gender is symmetric, or skewed to the right, or skewed to the left? Explain.

**(b)** The results refer to 73.8 million females and 83.4 million males. Find the overall mean income.

**TABLE 3.12**

| Country | Female Econ. Activity | Country | Female Econ. Activity | Country | Female Econ. Activity |
|---|---|---|---|---|---|
| Austria | 66 | Germany | 71 | Norway | 86 |
| Belgium | 67 | Greece | 60 | Portugal | 72 |
| Cyprus | 63 | Ireland | 54 | Spain | 58 |
| Denmark | 85 | Italy | 60 | Sweden | 90 |
| Finland | 87 | Luxembourg | 58 | U.K. | 76 |
| France | 78 | Netherlands | 68 | | |

*Source*: *Human Development Report, 2005*, United Nations Development Programme.

**3.17.** In 2003 in the United States, the median family income was $55,800 for white families, $34,400 for black families, and $34,300 for Hispanic families (*Statistical Abstract of the United States, 2006*).
  **(a)** Identify the response variable and the explanatory variable for this analysis.
  **(b)** Is enough information given to find the median when all the data are combined from the three groups? Why or why not?
  **(c)** If the reported values were means, what else would you need to know to find the overall mean?

**3.18.** The GSS has asked, "During the past 12 months, how many people have you known personally that were victims of homicide." Table 3.14 shows a printout from analyzing responses.
  **(a)** Is the distribution bell shaped, skewed to the right, or skewed to the left?
  **(b)** Does the Empirical Rule apply to this distribution. Why or why not?
  **(c)** Report the median. If 500 observations shift from 0 to 6, how does the median change? What property does this illustrate for the median?

**3.19.** As of October 2006, an article in wikipedia.org on "Minimum wage" reported (in U.S. dollars) the minimum wage per hour for five nations: $10.00 in Australia, $10.25 in New Zealand, $10.46 in France, $10.01 in the U.K., $5.15 in the U.S. Find the median, mean, range, and standard deviation **(a)** excluding the U.S., **(b)** for all five observations. Use the data to explain the effect of outliers on these measures.

**3.20.** *National Geographic Traveler* magazine recently presented data on the annual number of vacation days averaged by residents of eight different countries. They reported 42 days for Italy, 37 for France, 35 for Germany, 34 for Brazil, 28 for Britain, 26 for Canada, 25 for Japan, and 13 for the United States.

  **(a)** Find the mean and standard deviation. Interpret.
  **(b)** Report the five-number summary. (*Hint:* You can find the lower quartile by finding the median of the four values below the median.)

**3.21.** The Human Development Index (HDI) is an index the United Nations uses to give a summary rating for each nation based on life expectancy at birth, educational attainment, and income. In 2006, the ten nations (in order) with the highest HDI rating, followed in parentheses by the percentage of seats in their parliament held by women (which is a measure of gender empowerment) were Norway 38, Iceland 33, Australia 28, Ireland 14, Sweden 45, Canada 24, Japan 11, United States 15, Switzerland 25, Netherlands 34. Find the mean and standard deviation, and interpret.

**3.22.** The *Human Development Report 2006*, published by the United Nations (UN), showed life expectancies by country. For Western Europe, the values reported were

> Denmark 77, Portugal 77, Netherlands 78, Finland 78, Greece 78, Ireland 78, UK 78, Belgium 79, France 79, Germany 79, Norway 79, Italy 80, Spain 80, Sweden 80, Switzerland 80.

For Africa, the values reported (many of which were substantially lower than five years earlier because of the prevalence of AIDS) were

> Botswana 37, Zambia 37, Zimbabwe 37, Malawi 40, Angola 41, Nigeria 43, Rwanda 44, Uganda 47, Kenya 47, Mali 48, South Africa 49, Congo 52, Madagascar 55, Senegal 56, Sudan 56, Ghana 57.

  **(a)** Which group of life expectancies do you think has the larger standard deviation? Why?
  **(b)** Find the standard deviation for each group. Compare them to illustrate that $s$ is larger for the group that shows more spread.

**TABLE 3.14**

| VICTIMS | Frequency | Percent |
|---|---|---|
| 0 | 1244 | 90.8 |
| 1 | 81 | 5.9 |
| 2 | 27 | 2.0 |
| 3 | 11 | 0.8 |
| 4 | 4 | 0.3 |
| 5 | 2 | 0.1 |
| 6 | 1 | 0.1 |

| N | Mean | Std Dev | Max | Q3 | Med | Q1 | Min |
|---|---|---|---|---|---|---|---|
| 1370 | 0.146 | 0.546 | 6 | 0 | 0 | 0 | 0 |

**3.23.** A report indicates that teacher's annual salaries in Ontario have a mean of $50,000 and standard deviation of $10,000 (Canadian dollars). Suppose the distribution has approximately a bell shape.
  **(a)** Give an interval of values that contains about (i) 68%, (ii) 95%, (iii) all or nearly all salaries.
  **(b)** Would a salary of $100,000 be unusual? Why?

**3.24.** Excluding the U.S., the national mean number of holiday and vacation days in a year for OECD nations (see Exercise 3.6) is approximately bell shaped with a mean of 35 days and standard deviation of 3 days.[1]
  **(a)** Use the Empirical Rule to describe the variability.
  **(b)** The observation for the U.S. is 19. If this is included with the other observations, will the (i) mean increase, or decrease, (ii) standard deviation increase, or decrease?
  **(c)** Using the mean and standard deviation for the other countries, how many standard deviations is the U.S. observation from the mean?

**3.25.** For GSS data on "the number of people you know who have committed suicide," 88.8% of the responses were 0, 8.8% were 1, and the other responses took higher values. The mean equals 0.145, and the standard deviation equals 0.457.
  **(a)** What percentage of observations fall within one standard deviation of the mean?
  **(b)** Is the Empirical Rule appropriate for the distribution of this variable? Why or why not?

**3.26.** The first exam in your Statistics course is graded on a scale of 0 to 100, and the mean is 76. Which value is most plausible for the standard deviation: −20, 0, 10, or 50? Why?

**3.27.** Grade point averages of graduating seniors at the University of Rochester must fall between 2.0 and 4.0. Consider the possible standard deviation values: −10.0, 0.0, 0.4, 1.5, 6.0.
  **(a)** Which is the most realistic value? Why?
  **(b)** Which value is *impossible*? Why?

**3.28.** According to the U.S. Census Bureau, the U.S. nationwide median selling price of homes sold in 2005 was $184,100. Which of the following is the most plausible value for the standard deviation: **(a)** −15,000, **(b)** 1,000, **(c)** 10,000, **(d)** 60,000, **(e)** 1,000,000? Why?

**3.29.** For all homes in Gainesville, Florida, the residential electrical consumption[2] for the year 2006 had a mean of 10,449 and a standard deviation of 7489

kilowatt-hours (kWh). The maximum usage was 336,240 kWh.
  **(a)** What shape do you expect this distribution to have? Why?
  **(b)** Do you expect this distribution to have any outliers? Explain.

**3.30.** Residential water consumption (in thousands of gallons) in Gainesville, Florida in 2006 had a mean of 78 and a standard deviation of 119. What shape do you expect this distribution to have? Why?

**3.31.** According to *Statistical Abstract of the United States 2006*, mean salary (in dollars) of secondary school teachers in 2004 in the United States varied among states with a five-number summary of

| | | |
|---|---|---|
| 100% Max | 61,800 | (Illinois) |
| 75% Q3 | 48,850 | |
| 50% Med | 42,700 | |
| 25% Q1 | 39,250 | |
| 0% Min | 33,100 | (South Dakota) |

  **(a)** Find and interpret the range.
  **(b)** Find and interpret the interquartile range.

**3.32.** Refer to the previous exercise.
  **(a)** Sketch a box plot.
  **(b)** Based on (a), predict the direction of skew for this distribution. Explain.
  **(c)** If the distribution, although skewed, is approximately bell shaped, which value is most plausible for the standard deviation: (i) 100, (ii) 1000, (iii) 7000, (iv) 25,000? Explain.

**3.33.** Table 3.15 shows part of a computer printout for analyzing the murder rates (per 100,000) in the "2005 statewide crime" data file at the text Web site. The first column refers to the entire data set, and the second column deletes the observation for D.C. For each statistic reported, evaluate the effect of including the outlying observation for D.C.

**3.34.** During a recent semester at the University of Florida, computer usage[3] of students having accounts on a mainframe computer was summarized by a mean of 1921 and a standard deviation of 11,495 kilobytes of drive usage.
  **(a)** Does the Empirical Rule apply to this distribution? Why?
  **(b)** The five-number summary was minimum = 4, $Q1 = 256$, median = 530, $Q3 = 1105$, and maximum = 320,000. What does this suggest about the shape of the distribution? Why?
  **(c)** Use the 1.5(IQR) criterion to determine if any outliers are present.

---

[1] *Source*: Table 8.9 in www.stateofworkingamerica.org, from The Economic Policy Institute.
[2] Data supplied by Todd Kamhoot, Gainesville Regional Utilities.
[3] Data supplied by Dr. Michael Conlon, University of Florida.

**TABLE 3.15**

| Variable = MURDER | | | | |
|---|---|---|---|---|
| N | 51 | | N | 50 |
| Mean | 5.6 | | Mean | 4.8 |
| Std Dev | 6.05 | | Std Dev | 2.57 |

| Quartiles | | | Quartiles | |
|---|---|---|---|---|
| 100% Max | 44 | | 100% Max | 13 |
| 75% Q3 | 6 | | 75% Q3 | 6 |
| 50% Med | 5 | | 50% Med | 5 |
| 25% Q1 | 3 | | 25% Q1 | 3 |
| 0% Min | 1 | | 0% Min | 1 |

| Range | 43 | | Range | 12 |
|---|---|---|---|---|
| Q3-Q1 | 3 | | Q3-Q1 | 3 |
| Mode | 3 | | Mode | 3 |

**3.35.** For each of the following, sketch what you expect a histogram to look like, and explain whether the mean or the median would be greater.
  (a) The selling price of new homes in 2008
  (b) The number of children ever born per woman age 40 or over
  (c) The score on an easy exam (mean = 88, standard deviation = 10, maximum possible = 100)
  (d) The number of cars owned per family
  (e) Number of months in which subject drove a car last year

**3.36.** For each of the following variables, indicate whether you would expect its relative frequency histogram to be bell shaped, U shaped, skewed to the right, or skewed to the left.
  (a) Exam score of easy exam, with mean = 88, standard deviation = 10, minimum = 65, lower quartile = 77, median = 85, upper quartile = 91, maximum = 100)
  (b) IQ for the general population
  (c) Number of times arrested in past year
  (d) Time needed to complete difficult exam (maximum time is 1 hour)
  (e) Age at death
  (f) Weekly church contribution (median is $10 and mean is $17)
  (g) Attitude toward legalization of abortion

**3.37.** For parts (a), (b), and (f) of the previous exercise, sketch box plots that would be plausible for the variable.

**3.38.** The January 2007 unemployment rates of the 27 countries in the European Union ranged from 3.2 (Denmark) to 12.6 (Poland), with lower quartile = 5.0, median = 6.7, upper quartile = 7.9, mean = 6.7, and standard deviation = 2.2. Sketch a box plot, labeling which of these values are used in the plot.

**3.39.** For the student survey data on number of times a week reading a newspaper, referred to in Exercise 1.11, Figure 3.20 shows a computer printout of the stem-and-leaf plot and the box plot.
  (a) From the box plot, identify the minimum, lower quartile, median, upper quartile, and maximum.
  (b) Identify these five numbers using the stem-and-leaf plot.
  (c) Do the data appear to contain any outliers? If so, identify.
  (d) The standard deviation is one of the following values—0.3, 3, 13, 23. Which do you think it is, and why?

```
Stem Leaf                      Boxplot
 14 00                            0
 13
 12 0                            0
 11
 10
  9
  8
  7 000000000                    |
  6 000                          |
  5 000000000                +------+
  4 0000                      |  +   |
  3 0000000000000            *------*
  2 000000000                +------+
  1 000000                       |
  0 0000                         |
```

**FIGURE 3.20**

**3.40.** Infant mortality rates (number of infant deaths, per 1000 live births) are reported by the UN. In their 2006 report, the values for Africa had a five-number summary of

$$\text{min} = 54, Q1 = 76, \text{median} = 81,$$
$$Q3 = 101, \text{max} = 154.$$

The values for Western Europe had a five-number summary of

$$\text{min} = 3, Q1 = 4, \text{median} = 4, Q3 = 4, \text{max} = 5.$$

Sketch side-by-side box plots, and use them to describe differences between the distributions. (The plot for Europe shows that the quartiles, like the median, are less useful when the data are highly discrete.)

**3.41.** In 2004, the five-number summary for the statewide percentage of people without health insurance had a minimum of 8.9% (Minnesota), $Q1 = 11.6$, Med = 14.2, $Q3 = 17.0$, and maximum of 25.0% (Texas) (*Statistical Abstract of the United States, 2006*).
  (a) Sketch a box plot.

**(b)** Do you think that the distribution is symmetric, skewed to the right, or skewed to the left? Why?

**3.42.** High school graduation rates in the U.S. in 2004 had a minimum of 78.3 (Texas), lower quartile of 83.6, median of 87.2, upper quartile of 88.8, and maximum of 92.3 (Minnesota) (*Statistical Abstract of the United States, 2006*).
  **(a)** Report and interpret the range and the interquartile range.
  **(b)** Are there any outliers according to the 1.5(IQR) criterion?

**3.43.** Using software, analyze the murder rates from the "2005 statewide crime" data file at the text website.
  **(a)** Using the data set without D.C., find the five-number summary.
  **(b)** Construct a box plot, and interpret.
  **(c)** Repeat the analyses, including the D.C. observation, and compare results.

**3.44.** A report by the OECD[4] indicated that annual water consumption for nations in the OECD (see Exercise 3.6) was skewed to the right, with values (in cubic meters per capita) having a median of about 500 and ranging from about 200 in Denmark to 1700 in the U.S. Consider the possible values for the IQR: $-10, 0, 10, 350, 1500$. Which is the most realistic value? Why?

**3.45.** According to values from the *Human Development Report*, published by the United Nations (hdr.undp.org), carbon dioxide emissions in 2005 for the 25 nations in the European Union (EU) as of 2005 had a mean of 8.3 and standard deviation of 3.3, in metric tons per capita. All values were below 12, except Luxembourg which had a value of 21.1.
  **(a)** How many standard deviations above the mean was the value for Luxembourg?
  **(b)** Sweden's observation was 5.8. How many standard deviations below the mean was it?
  **(c)** The carbon dioxide emissions were 16.5 for Canada and 20.1 for the U.S. Relative to the distribution for the EU, find and interpret the *z*-score for (i) Canada, (ii) the U.S.

**3.46.** The United Nations publication *Energy Statistics Yearbook* (unstats.un.org/unsd/energy) lists consumption of energy. For the 25 nations that made up the EU in 2006, the energy values (in kilograms per capita) had a mean of 4998 and a standard deviation of 1786.
  **(a)** Italy had a value of 4222. How many standard deviations from the mean was it?
  **(b)** The value for the U.S. was 11,067. Relative to the distribution for the EU, find its *z*-score. Interpret.
  **(c)** If the distribution of EU energy values were bell shaped, would a value of 11,067 be unusually high? Why?

**3.47.** A study compares Democrats and Republicans on their opinions about national health insurance (favor or oppose).
  **(a)** Identify the response variable and the explanatory variable.
  **(b)** Explain how the data could be summarized in a contingency table.

**3.48.** Table 3.16 shows reported happiness for those subjects in the 2004 GSS who said that they attend religious services rarely or frequently (variables ATTEND and HAPPY).
  **(a)** Identify the response variable and the explanatory variable.
  **(b)** At each level of religious attendance, find the percentage who reported being very happy.
  **(c)** Does there seem to be an association between these variables? Why?

**3.49.** For recent United Nations data for several nations, a prediction equation relating fertility (the mean number of children per adult woman) and percentage of people using the Internet is

Predicted fertility $= 3.2 - 0.04$ (Internet use).

  **(a)** Compare the predicted fertility of a nation with 50% use of the Internet (the United States) to a nation with 0% use (Yemen).
  **(b)** The correlation is $-0.55$. Explain what the negative value represents.

**3.50.** Refer to the previous exercise. A prediction equation relating fertility and percentage of people using contraceptive methods is:

Predicted fertility $= 6.6$

$- 0.065$ (contraceptive use)

and the correlation is $-0.89$.

**TABLE 3.16**

| Religious Attendance | Happiness | | | Total |
|---|---|---|---|---|
| | Very Happy | Pretty Happy | Not Too Happy | |
| Nearly every week or more | 200 | 220 | 29 | 449 |
| Never or less than once a year | 72 | 185 | 53 | 310 |

[4] *OECD Key Environmental Indicators 2005.*

(a) What type of pattern would you expect for the points in a scatterplot for these data?

(b) Which variable seems to be more strongly associated with fertility—Internet use or contraceptive use? Why?

**3.51.** For the data for OECD nations in Table 3.11 in Exercise 3.6, use software to construct a scatterplot relating $y$ = carbon dioxide emissions and $x$ = GDP.

(a) Based on this plot, would you expect the correlation between these variables to be positive or negative? Why?

(b) Do you see an observation that falls apart from the others? Identify the nation.

**3.52.** Refer to the previous exercise. The correlation with carbon dioxide emissions is 0.03 for female economic activity and $-0.52$ with number of physicians. Which variable is more strongly associated with carbon dioxide emissions? Why?

**3.53.** What is the difference between the descriptive measures symbolized by

(a) $\bar{y}$ and $\mu$?

(b) $s$ and $\sigma$?

## Concepts and Applications

**3.54.** For the "Student survey" data file at the text Web site (see Exercise 1.11 on page 8), use software to conduct graphical and numerical summaries for

(a) distance from home town,

(b) weekly hours of TV watching. Describe the shapes of the distributions, and summarize your findings.

**3.55.** Refer to the data file your class created for Exercise 1.12 (page 9). For variables chosen by your instructor, conduct descriptive statistical analyses. In your report, give an example of a research question that could be addressed using your analyses, identifying response and explanatory variables. Summarize and interpret your findings.

**3.56.** Table 3.17 shows annual gun death rates (including homicide, suicide, and accidental deaths) per

100,000 population in advanced industrialized nations. Prepare a report in which you summarize the data using graphical and numerical methods from this chapter.

**3.57.** For the "2005 statewide crime" dataset at the text Web site, consider violent crime rate and percentage with income below the poverty level. Pose a research question for these variables relating to the direction of their association, identifying the response variable and explanatory variable. Using software, construct a scatterplot and find the correlation. Interpret, and indicate what the scatterplot and correlation suggest about the research question.

**3.58.** Refer to Exercise 3.6. Pose a research question relating to the correlation between public expenditure on health and the number of physicians per 100,000 people. Using software, analyze data in Table 3.11 to address this question, and summarize your analyses and conclusions.

**3.59.** Zagat restaurant guides publish ratings of restaurants for many large cities around the world (see www.zagat.com). The review for each restaurant gives a verbal summary as well as a 0-to-30-point rating of the quality of food, decor, service and the cost of a dinner with one drink and tip. Figure 3.21 shows side-by-side box plots of the cost for Italian restaurants in Boston, London, and New York (Little Italy and Greenwich Village neighborhoods). Summarize what you learn from these plots.

**3.60.** Refer to the previous exercise. The data are available in the "Zagat data" file at the text Web site. For the 83 restaurants listed in London, the quality of food rating has a correlation of 0.61 with decor rating, 0.81 with service rating, and 0.53 with cost rating. Summarize what you learn from these correlations.

**3.61.** Exercise 3.21 introduced the Human Development Index (HDI). Go to hdr.undp.org/statistics/data/ and get the latest HDI ratings for Sub-Saharan African nations and separately for Westernized

**TABLE 3.17**

| Nation | Gun Deaths | Nation | Gun Deaths | Nation | Gun Deaths |
|---|---|---|---|---|---|
| Australia | 1.7 | Greece | 1.8 | Norway | 2.6 |
| Austria | 3.6 | Iceland | 2.7 | Portugal | 2.1 |
| Belgium | 3.7 | Ireland | 1.5 | Spain | 0.7 |
| Canada | 3.1 | Italy | 2.0 | Sweden | 2.1 |
| Denmark | 1.8 | Japan | 0.1 | Switzerland | 6.2 |
| Finland | 4.4 | Luxembourg | 1.9 | U.K. | 0.3 |
| France | 4.9 | Netherlands | 0.8 | U.S. | 9.4 |
| Germany | 1.5 | New Zealand | 2.3 | | |

*Source*: Small Arms Survey, Geneva, 2007.

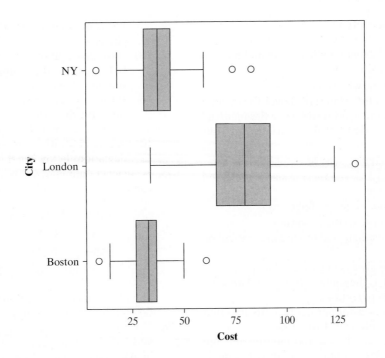

**FIGURE 3.21**

nations listed at the site as "High-income OECD." (One way to do this is to click on "Access a wide range of data tools" and then "Build table" and make the appropriate choices.) Using graphical and numerical methods of this chapter, summarize the data.

**3.62.** The incomes of players on the New York Yankees baseball team in 2006 can be summarized by the numbers[5] $2,925,000 and $7,095,078. One of these was the median and one was the mean. Which value do you think was the mean? Why?

**3.63.** In 2001, the U.S. Federal Reserve sampled about 4000 households to estimate overall net worth of a family. The Reserve reported the summaries $86,100 and $395,500. One of these was the mean, and one was the median. Which do you think was the median? Why?

**3.64.** A U.S. Federal Reserve study in 2000 indicated that for those families with annual incomes above $100,000, their median net worth was about $500,000 both in 1995 and in 1998, but their mean net worth rose from $1.4 million in 1995 to $1.7 million in 1998. A newspaper story about this said that the mean uses "a calculation that captures the huge gains made by the wealthiest Americans." Why would the median not necessarily capture those gains?

**3.65.** The fertility rate (mean number of children per adult woman) varies in Western European countries between a low of 1.3 (Italy and Spain) and a high of 1.9 (Ireland). For each woman, the number of children is a whole number, such as 0 or 1 or 2. Explain why it makes sense to measure a mean number of children per adult woman (which is not a whole number); for example, to compare these rates among European countries or with Canada (1.5), the U.S. (2.0), and Mexico (2.4).

**3.66.** According to a report from the U.S. National Center for Health Statistics, for males age 25–34 years, 2% of their heights are 64 inches or less, 8% are 66 inches or less, 27% are 68 inches or less, 39% are 69 inches or less, 54% are 70 inches or less, 68% are 71 inches or less, 80% are 72 inches or less, 93% are 74 inches or less, and 98% are 76 inches or less. These are called *cumulative percentages*.

(a) Find the median male height.

(b) Nearly all the heights fall between 60 and 80 inches, with fewer than 1% falling outside that range. If the heights are approximately bell shaped, give a rough approximation for the standard deviation. Explain your reasoning.

**3.67.** Give an example of a variable for which the mode applies, but not the mean or median.

**3.68.** Give an example of a variable having a distribution that you expect to be

(a) approximately symmetric,

(b) skewed to the right,

[5]http://usatoday.com/sports/baseball/salaries/

(c) skewed to the left,

(d) bimodal,

(e) skewed to the right, with a mode and median of 0 but a positive mean.

**3.69.** To measure center, why is the
  (a) median sometimes preferred over the mean?
  (b) Mean sometimes preferred over the median? In each case, give an example to illustrate your answer.

**3.70.** To measure variability, why is
  (a) The standard deviation $s$ usually preferred over the range?
  (b) The IQR sometimes preferred to $s$?

**3.71.** Answer true or false to the following:
  (a) The mean, median, and mode can never all be the same.
  (b) The mean is always one of the data points.
  (c) The median is the same as the second quartile and the 50th percentile.
  (d) For 67 sentences for murder recently imposed using U.S. Sentencing Commission guidelines, the median length was 160 months and the mean was 251 months. This distribution is probably skewed to the right.

*For multiple-choice problems 3.72–3.74, select the best response.*

**3.72.** In Canada, based on the 2001 census, for the categories (Catholic, Protestant, Other Christian, Muslim, Jewish, None, Other) for religious affiliation, the relative frequencies were (42%, 28%, 4%, 2%, 1%, 16%, 7%) (*Statistics Canada*).
  (a) The median religion is Protestant.
  (b) Only 2.7% of the subjects fall within one standard deviation of the mean.
  (c) The mode is Catholic.
  (d) The Jewish response is an outlier.

**3.73.** The 2004 GSS asked whether having sex before marriage is (always wrong, almost always wrong, wrong only sometimes, not wrong at all). The response counts in these four categories were (238, 79, 157, 409). This distribution is
  (a) Skewed to the right
  (b) Approximately bell shaped
  (c) Bimodal
  (d) Shape does not make sense, since the variable is nominal

**3.74.** In a study of graduate students who took the Graduate Record Exam (GRE), the Educational Testing Service reported that for the quantitative exam, U.S. citizens had a mean of 529 and standard deviation of 127, whereas the non-U.S. citizens had a mean of 649 and standard deviation of 129.
  (a) Both groups had about the same amount of variability in their scores, but non-U.S. citizens

performed better, on the average, than U.S. citizens.
  (b) If the distribution of scores was approximately bell shaped, then almost no U.S. citizens scored below 400.
  (c) If the scores range between 200 and 800, then probably the scores for non-U.S. citizens were symmetric and bell shaped.
  (d) A non-U.S. citizen who scored three standard deviations below the mean had a score of 200.

**3.75.** A teacher summarizes grades on the midterm exam by

$$\text{Min} = 26, \text{Q1} = 67, \text{Median} = 80,$$
$$\text{Q3} = 87, \text{Max} = 100,$$
$$\text{Mean} = 76, \text{Mode} = 100,$$
$$\text{Standard dev.} = 76, \text{IQR} = 20.$$

She incorrectly recorded one of these. Which one do you think it was? Why?

**3.76.** Ten people are randomly selected in Florida and another ten people are randomly selected in Alabama. Table 3.18 provides summary information on mean income. The mean is higher in Alabama both in rural areas and in urban areas. Which state has the larger overall mean income? (The reason for this apparent paradox is that mean urban incomes are larger than mean rural incomes for both states and the Florida sample has a higher proportion of urban residents.)

**TABLE 3.18**

| State | Rural | | Urban | |
|---|---|---|---|---|
| Florida | $26,000 | ($n = 3$) | $39,000 | ($n = 7$) |
| Alabama | $27,000 | ($n = 8$) | $40,000 | ($n = 2$) |

**3.77.** Refer to Table 3.2 (page 34). Explain why the mean of these 50 observations is not necessarily the same as the violent crime rate for the entire U.S. population.

**3.78.** For a sample with mean $\bar{y}$, adding a constant $c$ to each observation changes the mean to $\bar{y} + c$, and the standard deviation $s$ is unchanged. Multiplying each observation by $c$ changes the mean to $c\bar{y}$ and the standard deviation to $|c|s$.
  (a) Scores on a difficult exam have a mean of 57 and a standard deviation of 20. The teacher boosts all the scores by 20 points before awarding grades. Report the mean and standard deviation of the boosted scores.
  (b) Suppose that annual income of Canadian lawyers has a mean of $100,000 and a standard deviation of $30,000. Values are converted to

British pounds for presentation to a British audience. If one British pound equals $2.00, report the mean and standard deviation in British currency.

**(c)** Observations from a survey that asks about the number of miles travelled each day on mass transit are to be converted to kilometer units (1 mile = 1.6 kilometers). Explain how to find the mean and standard deviation of the converted observations.

*3.79. Show that $\Sigma(y_i - \bar{y})$ must equal 0 for any collection of observations $y_1, y_2, \ldots, y_n$.

*3.80. The Russian mathematician Tchebysheff proved that for any $k > 1$, the proportion of observations that fall more than $k$ standard deviations from the mean can be no greater than $1/k^2$. This holds for *any* distribution, not just bell-shaped ones.

**(a)** Find the upper bound for the proportion of observations falling (i) more than two standard deviations from the mean, (ii) more than three standard deviations from the mean, (iii) more than ten standard deviations from the mean.

**(b)** Compare the upper bound for $k = 2$ to the approximate proportion falling more than two standard deviations from the mean in a bell-shaped distribution. Why is there a difference?

*3.81. The *least squares* property of the mean states that the data fall closer to $\bar{y}$ than to any other number $c$, in the sense that the sum of squares of deviations of the data about their mean is smaller than the sum of squares of their deviations about $c$. That is,

$$\Sigma(y_i - \bar{y})^2 < \Sigma(y_i - c)^2.$$

If you have studied calculus, prove this property by treating $f(c) = \Sigma(y_i - c)^2$ as a function of $c$ and deriving the value of $c$ that provides a minimum. (*Hint*: Take the derivative of $f(c)$ with respect to $c$ and set it equal to zero.)

# CHAPTER 4

# Probability Distributions

Compared to most mathematical sciences, statistics is young. Most methods discussed in this book were developed within the past century. By contrast, probability, the subject of this chapter, has a long history. For instance, mathematicians used probability in France in the seventeenth century to evaluate various gambling strategies. Probability is a highly developed subject, but this chapter limits attention to the basics that we'll need for statistical inference.

Following a brief introduction to probability in Section 4.1, Sections 4.2 and 4.3 introduce *probability distributions*, which provide probabilities for all the possible outcomes of a variable. The *normal distribution*, described by a bell-shaped curve, is the most important probability distribution for statistical analysis. Sections 4.4 and 4.5 introduce the *sampling distribution*, a fundamentally important type of probability distribution for statistical inference. It enables us to predict how close a sample mean falls to the population mean. We'll see that the main reason for the importance of the normal distribution is the remarkable result that sampling distributions are often bell shaped.

## 4.1 INTRODUCTION TO PROBABILITY

In Chapter 2 we learned that randomness is a key component of good ways to gather data. Consider a hypothetical random sample or randomized experiment. For each observation, the possible outcomes are known, but it's uncertain which will occur.

### Probability as a Long-Run Relative Frequency

For a particular possible outcome for a random phenomenon, the *probability* of that outcome is the proportion of times that the outcome would occur in a very long sequence of observations.

---
**Probability**

With a random sample or randomized experiment, the **probability** an observation has a particular outcome is the proportion of times that outcome would occur in a very long sequence of observations.

---

Later in this chapter, we'll analyze data for the 2006 California gubernatorial election, for which the winner was the Republican candidate, Arnold Schwarzenegger.

Imagine the process of interviewing a random sample of voters in that election and asking whom they voted for. As we interview more and more people, the sample proportion who say they voted for Schwarzenegger gets closer and closer to the population proportion who voted for him. They are the same after we have interviewed everyone in the population of all voters. Suppose that population proportion is 0.56. Then, the probability that a randomly selected person voted for Schwarzenegger is 0.56.

Why does probability refer to the *long run*? Because you need a large number of observations to accurately assess a probability. If you sample only ten people and they are all right-handed, you can't conclude that the probability of being right-handed equals 1.0.

This book defines a probability as a proportion, so it is a number between 0 and 1. In practice, probabilities are often expressed also as percentages, then falling between 0 and 100. For example, if a weather forecaster says that the probability of rain today is 70%, this means that in a long series of days with atmospheric conditions like those today, rain occurs on 70% of the days.

This *long-run* approach to defining probability is not always helpful. If you decide to start a new business, you won't have a long run of trials with which to estimate the probability that the business is successful. You must then rely on *subjective* information rather than solely on *objective* data. In the subjective approach, the probability of an outcome is defined to be your degree of belief that the outcome will occur, based on the available information. A branch of statistics uses subjective probability as its foundation. It is called **Bayesian statistics**, in honor of a British clergyman (Thomas Bayes) who discovered a probability rule on which it is based. This approach is beyond our scope in this text.

### Basic Probability Rules

It's not the purpose of this text to go into detail about the many rules for finding probabilities. Here, we'll briefly mention four rules that are especially useful. We won't try to explain them with precise, mathematical reasoning, because for our purposes it suffices to have an intuitive feel for what each rule says.

Let $P(A)$ denote the probability of a possible outcome or set of outcomes denoted by the letter $A$. Then

1. **$P(\text{not } A) = 1 - P(A)$.**

   If you know the probability a particular outcome occurs, then the probability it does *not* occur is 1 minus that probability. Suppose $A$ represents the outcome that a randomly selected voter cast his or her vote for Schwarzenegger. If $P(A) = 0.56$, then $1 - 0.56 = 0.44$ is the probability of *not* voting for Schwarzenegger, that is, voting instead for the Democratic candidate or some other candidate on the ballot.

2. **If $A$ and $B$ are distinct possible outcomes (with no overlap), then $P(A \text{ or } B) = P(A) + P(B)$.**

   Suppose you take a survey to estimate the population proportion of people who believe that embryonic stem cell research should be banned by the federal government. Let $A$ represent your getting a sample proportion estimate that is much too low, being more than 0.10 *below* the population proportion. Let $B$ represent your sample proportion estimate being much too high—at least 0.10 *above* the population proportion. Using methods from this chapter, perhaps you find that $P(A) = P(B) = 0.03$. Then the overall probability your sample proportion is in error by more than 0.10 (without specifying the direction of error) is

$$P(A \text{ or } B) = P(A) + P(B) = 0.03 + 0.03 = 0.06.$$

3. **If A and B are possible outcomes, then P(A and B) = P(A) × P(B given A).**

   From U.S. Census data, the probability that a randomly selected American adult is married equals 0.56. Of those who are married, General Social Surveys indicate that the probability a person reports being *very happy* when asked to choose among (very happy, pretty happy, not too happy) is about 0.40; that is, given you are married, the probability of being very happy is 0.40. So

   $$P(\text{married and very happy}) =$$
   $$P(\text{married}) \times P(\text{very happy given married}) = 0.56 \times 0.40 = 0.22.$$

   About 22% of the adult population is both married *and* very happy.

   In some cases, A and B are "independent," in the sense that whether one occurs does not depend on whether the other does. That is, $P(B \text{ given } A) = P(B)$, so the previous rule simplifies:

4. **If A and B are independent, then P(A and B) = P(A) × P(B).**

   For example, an inference method presented in the next chapter often is used with the probability of a correct inference set at 0.95. Suppose A represents an inference about men in the population of interest (such as a prediction about the proportion of men who vote for Schwarzenegger) being correct. Let B represent a separate inference about women being correct. Then, since these are independent samples and inferences, the probability that *both* inferences are correct is

   $$P(A \text{ and } B) = P(A) \times P(B) = 0.95 \times 0.95 = 0.90.$$

## 4.2  PROBABILITY DISTRIBUTIONS FOR DISCRETE AND CONTINUOUS VARIABLES

A variable can take at least two different values. For a random sample or randomized experiment, each possible outcome has a probability that it occurs. The variable itself is sometimes then referred to as a ***random variable***. This terminology emphasizes that the outcome varies from observation to observation according to random variation that can be summarized by probabilities. We'll continue to use the simpler "variable" terminology.

Recall from Section 2.1 that a variable is *discrete* if the possible outcomes are a set of separate values, for example, a variable expressed as "the number of ..." with possible values 0, 1, 2, .... It is *continuous* if the possible outcomes are an infinite continuum. A ***probability distribution*** lists the possible outcomes and their probabilities. We'll next see how this is done for discrete and for continuous variables.

### Probability Distributions for Discrete Variables

The probability distribution of a *discrete* variable assigns a probability to each possible value of the variable. Each probability is a number between 0 and 1. The sum of the probabilities of all possible values equals 1.

Let $P(y)$ denote the probability of a possible outcome for a variable $y$. Then

$$0 \le P(y) \le 1 \text{ and } \Sigma_{\text{all } y} P(y) = 1,$$

where the sum is over all the possible values of the variable.

### EXAMPLE 4.1    Ideal Number of Children for a Family

Let $y$ denote the response to the question, "What do you think is the ideal number of children for a family to have?" This is a discrete variable, taking the possible values 0, 1, 2, 3, and so forth. According to results from a GSS for a randomly chosen person in the U.S. the probability distribution of $y$ is approximately as Table 4.1 shows. The

**TABLE 4.1**: Probability Distribution of $y$ = Ideal Number of Children for a Family

| $y$ | $P(y)$ |
| --- | --- |
| 0 | 0.01 |
| 1 | 0.03 |
| 2 | 0.60 |
| 3 | 0.23 |
| 4 | 0.12 |
| 5 | 0.01 |
| Total | 1.0 |

table displays the recorded $y$-values and their probabilities. For instance, $P(4)$, the probability that $y = 4$ children is regarded as ideal, equals 0.12. Each probability in Table 4.1 is between 0 and 1, and the sum of the probabilities equals 1. ∎

A *histogram* can portray the probability distribution. The rectangular bar over a possible value of the variable has height equal to the probability of that value. Figure 4.1 is a histogram for the probability distribution of the ideal number of children, from Table 4.1. The bar over the value 4 has height 0.12, the probability of the outcome 4.

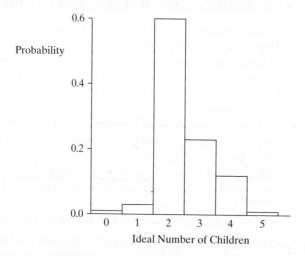

**FIGURE 4.1**: Histogram for the Probability Distribution of the Ideal Number of Children for a Family

### Probability Distributions for Continuous Variables

*Continuous* variables have an infinite continuum of possible values. Probability distributions of continuous variables assign probabilities to *intervals* of numbers. The probability that a variable falls in any particular interval is between 0 and 1, and the probability of the interval containing all the possible values equals 1.

A graph of the probability distribution of a continuous variable is a smooth, continuous curve. The *area* under the curve for an interval of values represents the probability that the variable takes a value in that interval.

**EXAMPLE 4.2     Commuting Time to Work**

A recent study about commuting time for workers in the U.S. who commute to work[1] measured $y$ = travel time (in minutes). The probability distribution of $y$ provides probabilities such as $P(y < 10)$, the probability that travel time is less than 10 minutes, or $P(30 < y < 60)$, the probability that travel time is between 30 and 60 minutes.

Figure 4.2 portrays the approximate probability distribution of $y$. The shaded area in the figure refers to the region of values higher than 45. This area equals 15% of the total area under the curve, representing the probability of 0.15 that commuting time is more than 45 minutes. Those regions in which the curve has relatively high height have the values most likely to be observed. ∎

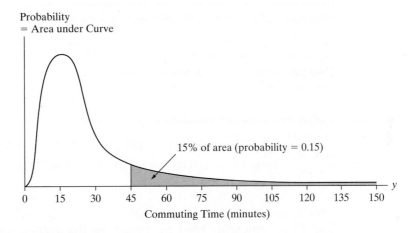

**FIGURE 4.2:** Probability Distribution of Commuting Time to Work. The area under the curve between two points represents the probability of that interval of values.

## Parameters Describe Probability Distributions

Most probability distributions have formulas for calculating probabilities. For others, tables or graphs provide the probabilities. Section 4.3 shows how to calculate probabilities for the most important probability distribution.

Section 3.1 introduced the *population distribution* of a variable. This is, equivalently, the probability distribution of the variable for a subject selected randomly from the population. For example, if 0.12 is the population proportion of adults who believe the ideal number of children is 4, then the probability that an adult selected randomly from that population believes this is also 0.12.

Like a population distribution, a probability distribution has *parameters* describing center and variability. The *mean* describes center and the *standard deviation* describes variability. The parameter values are the values these measures would assume, in the long run, if the randomized experiment or random sample repeatedly took observations on the variable $y$ having that probability distribution.

For example, suppose we take observations from the distribution in Table 4.1. Over the long run, we expect $y = 0$ to occur 1% of the time, $y = 1$ to occur 3% of the time, and so forth. In 100 observations, for instance, we expect about

one 0, 3 1's, 60 2's, 23 3's, 12 4's, and one 5.

---

[1]*Journey to Work*, issued 2004 by U.S. Census Bureau.

In that case, since the mean equals the total of the observations divided by the sample size, the mean equals

$$\frac{(1)0 + (3)1 + (60)2 + (23)3 + 12(4) + 1(5)}{100} = \frac{245}{100} = 2.45.$$

This calculation has the form

$$0(0.01) + 1(0.03) + 2(0.60) + 3(0.23) + 4(0.12) + 5(0.01),$$

the sum of the possible outcomes times their probabilities. In fact, for any discrete variable $y$, the mean of its probability distribution has this form.

---

**Mean of a Probability Distribution (Expected Value)**

The *mean of the probability distribution* for a discrete variable $y$ is

$$\mu = \sum yP(y).$$

The sum is taken over all possible values of the variable. This parameter is also called the *expected value of $y$* and is denoted by $E(y)$.

---

For Table 4.1, for example,

$$\begin{aligned}
\mu = \sum yP(y) &= 0P(0) + 1P(1) + 2P(2) + 3P(3) + 4P(4) + 5P(5) \\
&= 0(0.01) + 1(0.03) + 2(0.60) + 3(0.23) + 4(0.12) + 5(0.01) \\
&= 2.45.
\end{aligned}$$

This is also the *expected value* of $y$, $E(y) = \mu = 2.45$. The terminology reflects that $E(y)$ represents what we expect for the average value of $y$ in a long series of observations.

The **standard deviation** of a probability distribution, denoted by $\sigma$, measures its variability. The larger the value of $\sigma$, the more spread out the distribution. In a rough sense, $\sigma$ describes how far the variable $y$ tends to fall from the mean of its distribution. The Empirical Rule (Section 3.3) helps us to interpret $\sigma$. If a probability distribution is approximately bell shaped, about 68% of the probability falls between $\mu - \sigma$ and $\mu + \sigma$, about 95% falls between $\mu - 2\sigma$ and $\mu + 2\sigma$, and all or nearly all falls between $\mu - 3\sigma$ and $\mu + 3\sigma$. For example, suppose commuting time to work for a randomly selected worker in Toronto has a bell-shaped probability distribution with $\mu = 24$ minutes and $\sigma = 8$ minutes. Then there's about a 95% chance that commuting time falls between $24 - 2(8) = 8$ minutes and $24 + 2(8) = 40$ minutes.

The standard deviation is the square root of the **variance** of the probability distribution. The variance measures the average squared deviation of an observation from the mean. That is, it is the expected value of $(y - \mu)^2$. We shall not need to compute this measure, so we do not study its formula here (Exercise 4.55 shows the formula for $\sigma$ for the discrete case).

## 4.3   THE NORMAL PROBABILITY DISTRIBUTION

Some probability distributions are important because they approximate well the distributions of variables in the real world. Some are important because of their uses in statistical inference. This section introduces the **normal probability distribution**, which is important for both reasons: Its bell-shaped curve describes well many histograms of data for variables that are continuous or take a large number of possible values. It is the most important distribution for statistical inference, because we'll see it is still useful even when the sample data are *not* bell shaped.

---

**Normal Distribution**

The ***normal distribution*** is symmetric, bell shaped, and characterized by its mean $\mu$ and standard deviation $\sigma$. The probability within any particular number of standard deviations of $\mu$ is the same for all normal distributions. This probability equals 0.68 within 1 standard deviation, 0.95 within 2 standard deviations, and 0.997 within 3 standard deviations.

---

Each normal distribution is specified by two parameters—its mean $\mu$ and standard deviation $\sigma$. For any real number for $\mu$ and any nonnegative number for $\sigma$, there is a normal distribution having that mean and standard deviation. Figure 4.3 illustrates. Essentially the entire distribution falls between $\mu - 3\sigma$ and $\mu + 3\sigma$.

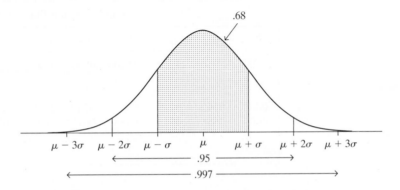

**FIGURE 4.3:** For Every Normal Distribution, the Probability Equals (Rounded) 0.68 within $\sigma$ of $\mu$, 0.95 within $2\sigma$ of $\mu$, and 0.997 within $3\sigma$ of $\mu$

For example, heights of adult females in North America have approximately a normal distribution with mean $\mu = 65.0$ inches and standard deviation $\sigma = 3.5$. The probability is nearly 1.0 that a randomly selected female has height between $\mu - 3\sigma = 65.0 - 3(3.5) = 54.5$ inches and $\mu + 3\sigma = 65.0 + 3(3.5) = 75.5$ inches. Adult male height has a normal distribution with $\mu = 70.0$ and $\sigma = 4.0$ inches. So the probability is nearly 1.0 that a randomly selected male has height between $\mu - 3\sigma = 70.0 - 3(4.0) = 58$ inches and $\mu + 3\sigma = 70.0 + 3(4.0) = 82$ inches. See Figure 4.4.

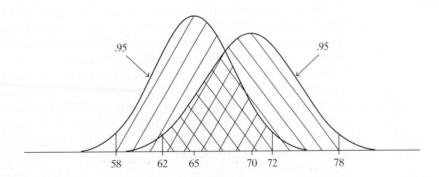

**FIGURE 4.4:** Normal Distributions for Women's Height ($\mu = 65, \sigma = 3.5$) and for Men's Height ($\mu = 70, \sigma = 4.0$)

## Tabulated Normal Tail Probabilities

For the normal distribution, for each fixed number $z$, the probability falling within $z$ standard deviations of the mean depends only on the value of $z$. This is the area under the bell-shaped normal curve between $\mu - z\sigma$ and $\mu + z\sigma$. For every normal distribution, this probability is 0.68 for $z = 1$, 0.95 for $z = 2$, and nearly 1.0 for $z = 3$.

For a normal distribution, the probability concentrated within $z\sigma$ of $\mu$ is the same for all normal curves even if $z$ is not a whole number—for instance $z = 1.43$ instead of 1, 2, or 3. Table A in Appendix A, also shown next to the inside back cover, determines probabilities for any region of values. It tabulates the probability for the values falling in the right tail, at least $z$ standard deviations above the mean. The left margin column of the table lists the values for $z$ to one decimal point, with the second decimal place listed above the columns.

**TABLE 4.2:** Part of Table A Displaying Normal Right-Tail Probabilities

| $z$ | .00 | .01 | .02 | .03 | .04 | .05 | .06 | .07 | .08 | .09 |
|-----|-----|-----|-----|-----|-----|-----|-----|-----|-----|-----|
| | | | | Second Decimal Place of $z$ | | | | | | |
| 0.0 | .5000 | .4960 | .4920 | .4880 | .4840 | .4801 | .4761 | .4721 | .4681 | .4641 |
| | | | | | .... | | | | | |
| | | | | | .... | | | | | |
| 1.4 | .0808 | .0793 | .0778 | .0764 | .0749 | .0735 | .0722 | .0708 | .0694 | .0681 |
| 1.5 | .0668 | .0655 | .0643 | .0630 | .0618 | .0606 | .0594 | .0582 | .0571 | .0559 |
| | | | | | .... | | | | | |
| | | | | | .... | | | | | |

Table 4.2 displays a small excerpt from Table A. The probability for $z = 1.43$ falls in the row labeled 1.4 and in the column labeled .03. It equals 0.0764. This means that for every normal distribution, the right-tail probability above $\mu + 1.43\sigma$ (that is, more than 1.43 standard deviations above the mean) equals 0.0764.

Since the entries in Table A are probabilities for the right half of the normal distribution above $\mu + z\sigma$, they fall between 0 and 0.50. By the symmetry of the normal curve, these right-tail probabilities also apply to the left tail below $\mu - z\sigma$. For example, the probability below $\mu - 1.43\sigma$ also equals 0.0764. The left-tail probabilities, called *cumulative probabilities*, are given by many calculators and software.

## Normal Probabilities and the Empirical Rule

The probabilities in Table A apply to the normal distribution and also apply approximately to other bell-shaped distributions. This table yields the probabilities for the Empirical Rule. That rule states that for bell-shaped histograms, about 68% of the data fall within 1 standard deviation of the mean, 95% within 2 standard deviations, and all or nearly all within 3 standard deviations.

For example, the value two standard deviations above the mean has a $z$-value of 2.00. The normal curve probability listed in Table A opposite $z = 2.00$ is 0.0228. The right-tail probability above $\mu + 2\sigma$ equals 0.0228 for every normal distribution. The left-tail probability below $\mu - 2\sigma$ also equals 0.0228, by symmetry (see Figure 4.5). The total probability more than two standard deviations from the mean is $2(0.0228) = 0.0456$. Since the probability more than two standard deviations from the mean equals 0.0456, the probability between $\mu - 2\sigma$ and $\mu + 2\sigma$ (i.e., within two standard deviations of the mean) equals $1 - 0.0456 = 0.9544$. (Here, we've used rule (1) of the probability rules at the end of Section 4.1, that $P(\text{not } A) = 1 - P(A)$.) When a

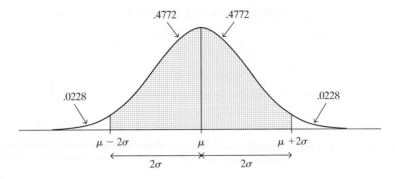

**FIGURE 4.5:** The Probability within Two Standard Deviations of the Mean for a Normal Distribution Is $1 - 2(0.0228)$, Which Is about 0.95

variable has a normal distribution, 95% of the observations fall within two standard deviations of the mean.

The probability equals 0.50 above the mean, since the normal distribution is symmetric about $\mu$. So the probability between $\mu$ and $\mu + 2\sigma$ or between $\mu - 2\sigma$ and $\mu$ equals $0.50 - 0.0228 = 0.4772$, also shown in Figure 4.5. Again, we see that the total probability within two standard deviations of the mean equals $2(0.4772) = 0.9544$, or about 95%.

The approximate percentages in the Empirical Rule are the actual percentages for the normal distribution, rounded to two decimal places. For instance, with Table A you can verify that the probability within one standard deviation of the mean of a normal distribution equals 0.68. (*Hint:* Let $z = 1.00$.) The Empirical Rule stated the percentages as being *approximate* rather than *exact*. Why? Because that rule referred to *all approximately bell-shaped distributions*, not just the normal. Not all bell-shaped distributions are normal, only those described by the mathematical formula shown in Exercise 4.56 at the end of the chapter. We won't need that formula, but we will use the probabilities tabulated for it in Table A throughout the text.

### Finding *z*-Values for Certain Tail Probabilities

Many inferential methods use $z$-values corresponding to certain normal curve probabilities. This entails the reverse use of Table A. Starting with a tail probability, which is listed in the body of Table A, we find the $z$-value that provides the number of standard deviations that that number falls from the mean.

To illustrate, let's find the $z$-value having a right-tail probability of 0.025. We look up 0.025 in the body of Table A. It corresponds to $z = 1.96$. This means that a probability of 0.025 falls above $\mu + 1.96\sigma$. Similarly, a probability of 0.025 falls below $\mu - 1.96\sigma$. So a total probability of $0.025 + 0.025 = 0.050$ falls more than $1.96\sigma$ from $\mu$. We saw in the previous subsection that 95% of a normal distribution falls within two standard deviations of the mean. More precisely, 0.9544 falls within 2.00 standard deviations, and here we've seen that 0.950 falls within 1.96 standard deviations.

To check that you understand this reasoning, verify that the $z$-value for a right-tail probability of (1) 0.05 is $z = 1.64$, (2) 0.01 is $z = 2.33$, (3) 0.005 is $z = 2.58$. Show that 90% of a normal distribution falls between $\mu - 1.64\sigma$ and $\mu + 1.64\sigma$.

### EXAMPLE 4.3    Finding the 99th Percentile of IQ Scores

Stanford-Binet IQ scores have approximately a normal distribution with mean $= 100$ and standard deviation $= 16$. What is the 99th percentile of IQ scores? In other words, what is the IQ score that falls above 99% of the scores?

To answer this, we need to find the value of $z$ such that $\mu + z\sigma$ falls above 99% of a normal distribution. We use the normal curve probability in the right tail beyond the 99th percentile. Then we can use Table A to find the $z$-value corresponding to that probability. Now, for $\mu + z\sigma$ to represent the 99th percentile, the probability below $\mu + z\sigma$ must equal 0.99, by the definition of a percentile. So 1% of the distribution is above the 99th percentile. The right-tail probability equals 0.01, as Figure 4.6 shows.

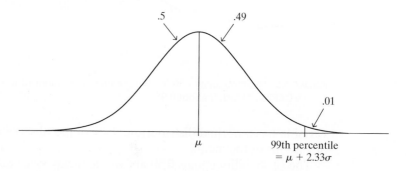

**FIGURE 4.6:** The 99th Percentile for a Normal Distribution Has 99% of the Distribution below that Point and 1% above It

The body of Table A does not contain the tail probability of exactly 0.0100. The tail probability = 0.0102 corresponds to $z = 2.32$, and tail probability = 0.0099 corresponds to $z = 2.33$. We could interpolate, but it is sufficient to use the $z$-value rounded to two decimal places. We select the one having probability closer to the desired value of 0.0100. Thus, the 99th percentile is 2.33 standard deviations above the mean. In summary, 99% of any normal distribution is located below $\mu + 2.33\sigma$, no more than 2.33 standard deviations above the mean.

For the IQ scores with mean = 100 and standard deviation = 16, the 99th percentile equals

$$\mu + 2.33\sigma = 100 + 2.33(16) = 137.$$

That is, about 99% of IQ scores fall below 137. ∎

To check that you understand the reasoning above, show that the 95th percentile of a normal distribution is $\mu + 1.64\sigma$, and show that the 95th percentile for the IQ distribution equals 126.

### z-Score Is Number of Standard Deviations from Mean

The $z$ symbol in a normal table refers to the distance between a possible value $y$ of a variable and the mean $\mu$ of its probability distribution, in terms of the *number of standard deviations* that $y$ falls from $\mu$.

### EXAMPLE 4.4    z-Scores for College Board Test Scores

Scores on each portion of the Scholastic Aptitude Test (SAT), a college entrance examination, have traditionally been approximately normal with mean $\mu = 500$ and standard deviation $\sigma = 100$. The test score of $y = 650$ has a $z$-score of $z = 1.50$, because 650 is 1.50 standard deviations above the mean. In other words, $y = 650 = \mu + z\sigma = 500 + z(100)$, where $z = 1.50$. ∎

For sample data, Section 3.4 introduced the $z$-score as a measure of position. Let's review how to find it. The distance between $y$ and the mean $\mu$ equals $y - \mu$. The $z$-score expresses this difference in units of standard deviations.

---
**z-Score**

---

The **z-score** for a value $y$ of a variable is the *number of standard deviations* that $y$ falls from $\mu$. It equals

$$z = \frac{\text{Observation} - \text{Mean}}{\text{Standard Deviation}} = \frac{y - \mu}{\sigma}.$$

---

To illustrate, when $\mu = 500$ and $\sigma = 100$, an observation of $y = 650$ has the $z$-score of

$$z = \frac{y - \mu}{\sigma} = \frac{650 - 500}{100} = 1.50.$$

*Positive z*-scores occur when the number $y$ falls *above* the mean $\mu$. *Negative z*-scores occur when the number $y$ falls *below* the mean. For example, for SAT scores with $\mu = 500$ and $\sigma = 100$, a value of $y = 350$ has a $z$-score of

$$z = \frac{y - \mu}{\sigma} = \frac{350 - 500}{100} = -1.50.$$

The test score of 350 is 1.50 standard deviations below the mean. The value $y = 350$ falls below the mean, so the $z$-score is negative.

Table A contains only positive $z$-values. Since the normal distribution is symmetric about the mean, the left-tail probability below $-z$ equals the right-tail probability above $+z$. Looking up $z = 1.50$ in Table A, we see that the probability that a SAT score falls below 350 is 0.0668, as Figure 4.7 shows. Fewer than 7% of the scores are below 350, and fewer than 7% fall above 650.

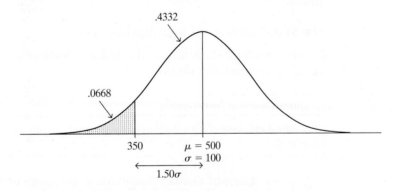

**FIGURE 4.7:** Normal Distribution for SAT Scores

The next example shows that $z$-scores provide a useful way to compare positions for different normal distributions.

### EXAMPLE 4.5    Comparing SAT and ACT Test Scores

Suppose that when you applied to college, you took a SAT exam, scoring 550. Your friend took the ACT exam, scoring 30. Which score is better?

We cannot compare the test scores of 550 and 30 directly, because they have different scales. We convert them to $z$-scores, analyzing how many standard deviations each falls from the mean. If SAT has $\mu = 500$ and $\sigma = 100$, a SAT score of $y = 550$ converts to a $z$-score of

$$z = \frac{(y - \mu)}{\sigma} = \frac{(550 - 500)}{100} = 0.50.$$

The ACT has approximately $\mu = 18$ and $\sigma = 6$, so ACT = 30 converts to a $z$-score of $(30 - 18)/6 = 2.0$.

The ACT score of 30 is relatively higher than the SAT score of 650, because 30 is 2.0 standard deviations above its mean whereas 550 is only 0.5 standard deviations above its mean. The SAT and ACT scores both have approximate normal distributions. From Table A, $z = 2.0$ has a right-tail probability of 0.0228 and $z = 0.5$ has a right-tail probability of 0.3085. Of all students taking the ACT, only about 2% scored higher than 30, whereas of all students taking the SAT, about 31% scored higher than 550. In this relative sense, the ACT score is higher. ∎

Here's a summary of how we've used $z$-scores:

---

**Using $z$-Scores to Find Probabilities or $y$-Values**

- If we have a value $y$ and need to find a probability, convert $y$ to a $z$-score using $z = (y - \mu)/\sigma$, and use a table of normal probabilities to convert it to the probability of interest.

- If we have a probability and need to find a value of $y$, convert the probability to a tail probability and find the $z$-score using a normal table, and then evaluate $y = \mu + z\sigma$.

---

For example, Example 4.6 used the equation $z = (y - \mu)/\sigma$ to determine how many standard deviations an SAT test score fell from the mean. Example 4.3 used the equation $y = \mu + z\sigma$ to find a percentile score for a normal distribution of IQ scores.

### The Standard Normal Distribution

Many inferential statistical methods use a particular normal distribution, called the **standard normal distribution**.

---

**Standard Normal Distribution**

The **standard normal distribution** is the normal distribution with mean $\mu = 0$ and standard deviation $\sigma = 1$.

---

For the standard normal distribution, the number falling $z$ standard deviations above the mean is $\mu + z\sigma = 0 + z(1) = z$. It is simply the $z$-score itself. For instance, the value of 2 is two standard deviations above the mean, and the value of $-1.3$ is 1.3 standard deviations below the mean. The original values are the same as the $z$-scores. See Figure 4.8.

When the values for an arbitrary normal distribution are converted to $z$-scores, those $z$-scores are centered around 0 and have a standard deviation of 1. The $z$-scores have the standard normal distribution.

---

**$z$-Scores and the Standard Normal Distribution**

If a variable has a normal distribution, and if its values are converted to $z$-scores by subtracting the mean and dividing by the standard deviation, then the $z$-scores have the standard normal distribution.

---

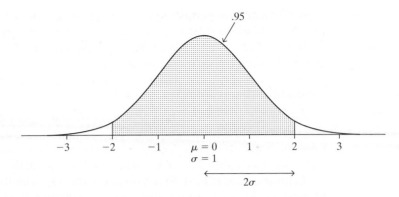

**FIGURE 4.8:** The Standard Normal Distribution Has Mean 0 and Standard Deviation 1. Its ordinary scores are the same as its **z-scores**.

Suppose we convert each SAT score $y$ to a $z$-score by using $z = (y - 500)/100$. For instance, $y = 650$ converts to $z = 1.50$, and $y = 350$ converts to $z = -1.50$. Then the entire set of $z$-scores has a normal distribution with a mean of 0 and a standard deviation of 1. This is the standard normal distribution.

Many inferential methods convert values of statistics to $z$-scores and then to normal curve probabilities. We use $z$-scores and normal probabilities often throughout the rest of the book.

## 4.4  SAMPLING DISTRIBUTIONS DESCRIBE HOW STATISTICS VARY

We've seen that probability distributions summarize probabilities of possible outcomes for a variable. So far, this chapter has treated these distributions as known. In practice, they are rarely known. We use sample data to make inferences about the parameters of those distributions. However, probability distributions with fixed parameter values are useful for many of those inferential methods. Let's look at an example that illustrates the connection between statistical inference and probability calculations with known parameter values.

### EXAMPLE 4.6    Predicting an Election from an Exit Poll

Television networks sample voters on election day to help them predict the winners early. For the fall 2006 election for Governor of California, CNN[2] reported results of an exit poll of 2705 voters. CNN stated that 56.5% reported voting for the Republican candidate, Arnold Schwarzenegger. In this example, the probability distribution for a person's vote would state the probability that a randomly selected voter voted for Schwarzenegger. This equals the proportion of the population of voters who voted for him. When the exit poll was taken, this was an unknown population parameter.

To judge whether this is sufficient information to predict the outcome of the election, the network can ask, "Suppose only half the population voted for Schwarzenegger. Would it then be surprising that 56.5% of the sampled individuals voted for him?" If this would be very unlikely, the network infers that Schwarzenegger received more than half the population votes. The inference about the election outcome is based on finding the probability of the sample result under the supposition that the population parameter, the percentage of voters preferring Schwarzenegger, equals 50%. ∎

---

[2]www.cnn.com/ELECTION/2006

Nearly 7 million people voted in this race. The exit poll sampled only 2705 voters, yet TV networks used it to predict that Schwarzenegger would win. How could there possibly have been enough information from this poll to make a prediction? We next see justification for making a prediction.

### Simulating the Estimation Process

A *simulation* can tell us how well an exit poll result approximates the population proportion voting for a candidate. We simulate the vote of a voter randomly chosen from the population by selecting a two-digit random number from a random number table (such as Table 2.2) or software. Suppose exactly 50% of the population voted for Schwarzenegger and 50% voted for the Democratic candidate, Phil Angelides. Identify all 50 two-digit numbers between 00 and 49 as Republican votes and all 50 two-digit numbers between 50 and 99 as Democrat votes. Then each candidate has a 50% chance of selection on each choice of two-digit random number.

For instance, the first two digits of the first column of Table 2.2 provide the random numbers 10, 22, 24, 42, 37, 77, and so forth. So of the first 6 voters selected, 5 voted Republican (i.e., have numbers between 00 and 49). Selecting 2705 two-digit numbers simulates the process of observing the votes of a random sample of 2705 voters of the much larger population (which is actually treated as infinite in size).

Using a computer, we selected 2705 random two-digit numbers and got 1334 Republican votes and 1371 Democrat votes. (You can try this yourself with *applets* available on the Internet. See Exercise 4.41.) The sample proportion of Republican votes was 1334/2705 = 0.493, quite close to the population proportion of 0.50. This particular estimate was good. Were we merely lucky? We repeated the process and selected 2705 more two-digit random numbers. This time the sample proportion of Republican votes was 0.511, also quite good. We next programmed the computer to perform this process of picking 2705 people a million times so we could search for a pattern in the results. Figure 4.9 shows a histogram of the million values of the sample proportion. Nearly all the simulated proportions fell between 0.47 and 0.53; that is, within 0.03 of the population proportion of 0.50. Apparently a sample of size 2705 provides quite a good estimate of a population proportion.

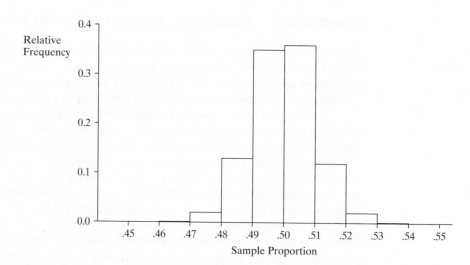

**FIGURE 4.9:** Results of Simulating the Sample Proportion Favoring the Republican Candidate, for Random Samples of 2705 Subjects from a Population in which Half Voted for Each Candidate. In nearly all cases, the sample proportion fell within 0.03 of the population proportion of 0.50.

In summary, if half the population of voters had voted for Schwarzenegger, we would have expected between about 47% and 53% of voters in an exit poll of size 2705 to have voted for him. So it would have been very unusual to observe 56.5% voting for him, as happened in the actual exit poll. If *less than half* the population voted for Schwarzenegger, it would have been even more unusual to observe this. This is the basis of the network's prediction, from its exit poll, that Schwarzenegger won the election.

It is possible to perform this simulation using any population proportion value. For instance, we could simulate sampling when the population proportion voting for the Republican is 0.45 by letting the 45 random numbers between 00 and 44 represent Republican votes and the 55 between 45 and 99 represent Democrat votes. Likewise, we could change the size of each random sample in the simulation to study the impact of the sample size. From results of the next section, for a random sample of size 2705, the sample proportion is very likely to fall within 0.03 of the population proportion, regardless of its value.

## Representing Sampling Variability by a Sampling Distribution

Voter preference is a variable, varying among voters. Likewise, so is the sample proportion voting for a given candidate a variable: Before the sample is obtained, its value is unknown, and that value varies from sample to sample. If several random samples of size $n = 2705$ each were selected, a certain predictable amount of variation would occur in the sample proportion values. A probability distribution with appearance similar to Figure 4.9 describes the variation that occurs from repeatedly selecting samples of a certain size $n$ and forming a particular statistic. This distribution is called a *sampling distribution*. It also provides probabilities of the possible values of the statistic for a *single* sample of size $n$.

---

**Sampling Distribution**

A *sampling distribution* of a statistic is the probability distribution that specifies probabilities for the possible values the statistic can take.

---

Each sample statistic has a sampling distribution. There is a sampling distribution of a sample mean, a sampling distribution of a sample proportion, a sampling distribution of a sample median, and so forth. A sampling distribution is merely a type of probability distribution. Unlike the distributions studied so far, a sampling distribution specifies probabilities not for individual observations but for possible values of a statistic computed from the observations. A sampling distribution allows us to calculate, for example, probabilities about the sample proportion of individuals who voted for the Republican in an exit poll. Before the voters are selected for the exit poll, this is a variable. It has a sampling distribution that describes the probabilities of the possible values.

The sampling distribution is important in inferential statistics because it helps us predict how close a statistic falls to the parameter it estimates. From Figure 4.9, for instance, with a sample of size 2705 the probability is apparently high that a sample proportion falls within 0.03 of the population proportion.

## EXAMPLE 4.7    Constructing a Sampling Distribution

It is sometimes possible to construct the sampling distribution without resorting to simulation or complex mathematical derivations. To illustrate, we construct the sampling distribution of the sample proportion, for an exit poll of $n = 4$ voters from a population in which half voted for each candidate. For each voter, define the $y$ variable representing the vote as follows:

$$y = 1, \text{ vote for the Republican}$$
$$y = 0, \text{ vote for the Democrat.}$$

We use a symbol with four entries to represent the $y$-values for a potential sample of size 4. For instance, $(1, 0, 0, 1)$ represents a sample in which the first and fourth subjects voted for the Republican and the second and third subjects voted for the Democrat. The 16 possible samples are

$$(1,1,1,1) \quad (1,1,1,0) \quad (1,1,0,1) \quad (1,0,1,1)$$
$$(0,1,1,1) \quad (1,1,0,0) \quad (1,0,1,0) \quad (1,0,0,1)$$
$$(0,1,1,0) \quad (0,1,0,1) \quad (0,0,1,1) \quad (1,0,0,0)$$
$$(0,1,0,0) \quad (0,0,1,0) \quad (0,0,0,1) \quad (0,0,0,0).$$

Since half the population voted for each candidate, the 16 samples are equally likely.

Now let's construct the sampling distribution of the proportion of the sample that voted for the Republican candidate. For a sample of size 4, that proportion can be 0, 0.25, 0.50, 0.75, or 1.0. The proportion 0 occurs with only one of the 16 possible samples, $(0, 0, 0, 0)$, so its probability equals $1/16 = 0.0625$. The proportion 0.25 occurs for four samples, $(1, 0, 0, 0)$, $(0, 1, 0, 0)$, $(0, 0, 1, 0)$, and $(0, 0, 0, 1)$, so its probability equals $4/16 = 0.25$. Based on this reasoning, Table 4.3 shows the probability for each possible sample proportion value.

**TABLE 4.3**: Sampling Distribution of Sample Proportion, for Random Sample of Size $n = 4$ when Population Proportion Is 0.50. For example, a sample proportion of 0.0 occurs for only 1 of 16 possible samples, namely (0, 0, 0, 0), so its probability is $1/16 = 0.0625$.

| Sample Proportion | Probability |
|---|---|
| 0.0 | 0.0625 |
| 0.25 | 0.2500 |
| 0.50 | 0.3750 |
| 0.75 | 0.2500 |
| 1.0 | 0.0625 |

Figure 4.10 portrays the sampling distribution of the sample proportion for $n = 4$. It is much more spread out than the one in Figure 4.9 for samples of size $n = 2705$, which falls nearly entirely between 0.47 and 0.53. With such a small sample ($n = 4$), the sample proportion need not be near the population proportion. This is not surprising. In practice, samples are usually much larger than $n = 4$. We used a small value in this example so it was simpler to write down all the potential samples and find probabilities for the sampling distribution. ■

With the two possible outcomes denoted by 0 and 1, Section 3.2 observed that the proportion of times that 1 occurs is the sample mean of the data. For instance, for the sample $(0, 1, 0, 0)$ in which only the second subject voted for the Republican, the sample mean equals $(0 + 1 + 0 + 0)/4 = 1/4 = 0.25$, the sample proportion voting

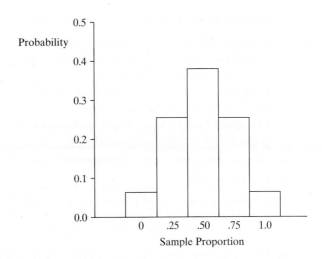

**FIGURE 4.10:** Sampling Distribution of Sample Proportion, for Random Sample of Size $n = 4$ when Population Proportion Is 0.50

for the Republican. So Figure 4.10 is also an example of a sampling distribution of a sample mean. Section 4.5 provides some general results about the sampling distribution of the sample mean.

### Repeated Sampling Interpretation of Sampling Distributions

Sampling distributions portray the sampling variability that occurs in collecting data and using sample statistics to estimate parameters. If different polling organizations each take their own exit poll and estimate the population proportion voting for the Republican candidate, they will get different estimates, because the samples have different people. Likewise, Figure 4.9 describes the variability in sample proportion values that occurs in selecting a huge number of samples of size $n = 2705$ and constructing a histogram of the sample proportions. By contrast, Figure 4.10 describes the variability for a huge number of samples of size $n = 4$.

A *sampling distribution* of a statistic based on $n$ observations is the relative frequency distribution for that statistic resulting from repeatedly taking samples of size $n$, each time calculating the statistic value. It's possible to form such a distribution empirically, as in Figure 4.9, by repeated sampling or through simulation. In practice, this is not necessary. The form of sampling distributions is often known theoretically, as shown in the previous example and in the next section. We can then find probabilities about the value of the sample statistic for one sample of the given size $n$.

## 4.5    SAMPLING DISTRIBUTIONS OF SAMPLE MEANS

Because the sample mean $\bar{y}$ is used so much, its sampling distribution merits special attention. In practice, when we analyze data and find $\bar{y}$, we don't know how close it falls to the population mean $\mu$, because we do not know the value of $\mu$. Using information about the spread of the sampling distribution, though, we can predict how close it falls. For example, the sampling distribution might tell us that with high probability, $\bar{y}$ falls within 10 units of $\mu$.

In this section we'll learn two main results about the sampling distribution of the sample mean. One provides formulas for the center and spread of the sampling distribution. The other describes its shape.

### Mean and Standard Error of Sampling Distribution of $\bar{y}$

The sample mean $\bar{y}$ is a variable, because its value varies from sample to sample. For random samples, it fluctuates around the population mean $\mu$, sometimes being smaller and sometimes being larger. In fact, the mean of the sampling distribution of $\bar{y}$ equals $\mu$. If we repeatedly took samples, then in the long run, the mean of the sample means would equal the population mean $\mu$.

The spread of the sampling distribution of $\bar{y}$ is described by its standard deviation, which is called the *standard error* of $\bar{y}$.

---

**Standard Error**
___

The standard deviation of the sampling distribution of $\bar{y}$ is called the **standard error** of $\bar{y}$. The standard error of $\bar{y}$ is denoted by $\sigma_{\bar{y}}$.

---

The standard error describes how $\bar{y}$ varies from sample to sample. Suppose we repeatedly selected samples of size $n$ from the population, finding $\bar{y}$ for each set of $n$ observations. Then, in the long run, the standard deviation of the $\bar{y}$-values would equal the standard error. The symbol $\sigma_{\bar{y}}$ (instead of $\sigma$) and the terminology *standard error* (instead of *standard deviation*) distinguish this measure from the standard deviation $\sigma$ of the population distribution.

In practice, we don't need to take samples repeatedly to find the standard error of $\bar{y}$, because a formula is available. For a random sample of size $n$, the standard error of $\bar{y}$ depends on $n$ and the population standard deviation $\sigma$ by

$$\sigma_{\bar{y}} = \frac{\sigma}{\sqrt{n}}.$$

Figure 4.11 displays a population distribution having $\sigma = 10$ and shows the sampling distribution of $\bar{y}$ for $n = 100$, for which the standard error is $\sigma_{\bar{y}} = \sigma/\sqrt{n} = 10/\sqrt{100} = 1.0$. The sampling distribution has only a tenth of the spread of the population distribution. This means that individual observations tend to vary much more than sample means vary from sample to sample.

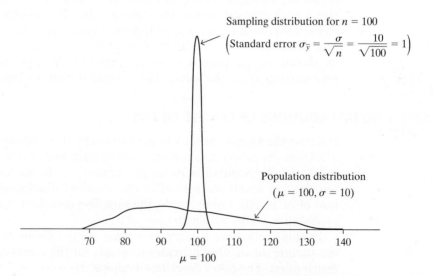

**FIGURE 4.11:** A Population Distribution and the Sampling Distribution of $\bar{y}$ for $n = 100$

In summary, the following result describes the center and spread of the sampling distribution of $\bar{y}$:

---

**Mean and Standard Error of $\bar{y}$**

---

Consider a random sample of size $n$ from a population having mean $\mu$ and standard deviation $\sigma$. The sampling distribution of $\bar{y}$ gives the probabilities for the possible values of $\bar{y}$. It has mean $\mu$ and standard error $\sigma_{\bar{y}} = \sigma/\sqrt{n}$.

---

### EXAMPLE 4.8    Standard Error of Sample Proportion in Election Exit Poll

Following Example 4.7 (page 85), we conducted a simulation to investigate how much ✶ variability to expect from sample to sample in an exit poll of 2705 voters. Instead of conducting a simulation, we can get similar information directly by finding a standard error. Knowing the standard error helps us answer the following question: If half the population voted for each candidate, how much would a sample proportion for an exit poll of 2705 voters tend to vary from sample to sample?

As in Example 4.8, let the variable $y$ equal 1 for a vote for the Republican and 0 for a vote for the Democrat. Figure 4.12 shows the distribution for which half the population voted for the Republican, so that $P(1) = 0.50$ and $P(0) = 0.50$. The mean of the distribution equals 0.50, which is the population proportion voting for the Republican. (Or, from the formula, $\mu = \Sigma yP(y) = 0(0.50) + 1(0.50) = 0.50$.) The squared deviation of $y$ from the mean, $(y - \mu)^2$, equals $(0 - 0.50)^2 = 0.25$ when $y = 0$ and it equals $(1 - 0.50)^2 = 0.25$ when $y = 1$. The variance is the expected value of this squared deviation. Thus, it equals $\sigma^2 = 0.25$. So the standard deviation of the population distribution of $y$ equals $\sigma = \sqrt{0.25} = 0.50$.

For a sample, the mean of the 0 and 1 values is the sample proportion of voters who voted for the Republican. Its sampling distribution has mean that is the mean of the population distribution of $y$, namely, $\mu = 0.50$. For repeated samples of a fixed size $n$, the sample proportions fluctuate around 0.50, being larger about half the time and smaller half the time. The standard deviation of the sampling distribution is the standard error. For a sample of size 2705, this is

$$\sigma_{\bar{y}} = \frac{\sigma}{\sqrt{n}} = \frac{0.50}{\sqrt{2705}} = 0.01.$$

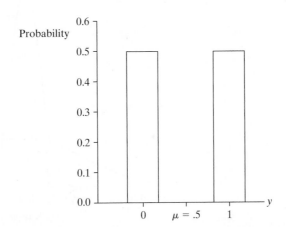

**FIGURE 4.12:** The Population Distribution when $y = 0$ or 1, with Probability 0.50 Each. This is the distribution for a vote, with 1 = vote for Republican candidate and 0 = vote for Democratic candidate.

A result from later in this section says that this sampling distribution is bell shaped. Thus, with probability close to 1.0 the sample proportion falls within three standard errors of $\mu$, that is, within $3(0.01) = 0.03$ of 0.50, or between 0.47 and 0.53. For a random sample of size 2705 from a population in which 50% voted for the Republican, it would be extremely surprising if fewer than 47% or more than 53% voted for the Republican. We've now seen how to get this result either using simulation, as shown in Figure 4.9, or using the information about the mean and standard error of the sampling distribution.   ■

### Effect of Sample Size on Sampling Distribution and Precision of Estimates

The standard error gets smaller as the sample size $n$ gets larger. The reason for this is that the denominator ($\sqrt{n}$) of the standard error formula $\sigma_{\bar{y}} = \sigma/\sqrt{n}$ increases as $n$ increases. For instance, when the population standard deviation is $\sigma = 0.50$, we've just seen that the standard error is 0.01 when $n = 2705$. When $n = 100$, a less typical size for a poll, the standard error equals

$$\sigma_{\bar{y}} = \frac{\sigma}{\sqrt{n}} = \frac{0.50}{\sqrt{n}} = \frac{0.50}{\sqrt{100}} = 0.05.$$

With $n = 100$, since three standard errors equals $3(0.05) = 0.15$, the probability is very high that the sample proportion falls within 0.15 of 0.50, or between 0.35 and 0.65.

Figure 4.13 shows the sampling distributions of the sample proportion when $n = 100$ and when $n = 2705$. As $n$ increases, the standard error decreases and the sampling distribution gets narrower. This means that the sample proportion tends to fall closer to the population proportion. It's more likely that the sample proportion closely approximates an unknown population proportion when $n = 2705$ than when $n = 100$. This agrees with our intuition that larger samples provide more precise estimates of population characteristics.

In summary, error results from estimating $\mu$ by $\bar{y}$, because we sampled only part of the population. This error, which is the **sampling error**, tends to decrease as the sample size $n$ increases. The standard error is fundamental to inferential procedures that predict the sampling error in using $\bar{y}$ to estimate $\mu$.

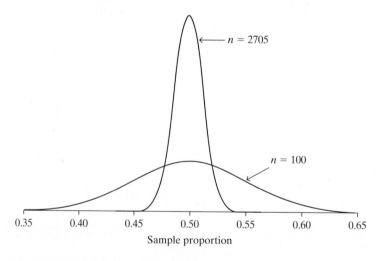

**FIGURE 4.13:** The Sampling Distributions of the Sample Proportion, when $n = 100$ and when $n = 2705$. These refer to sampling from the population distribution in Figure 4.12.

## Sampling Distribution of Sample Mean Is Approximately Normal

For the population distribution for the vote in an election, shown in Figure 4.12, the outcome has only two possible values. It is highly discrete. Nevertheless, the two sampling distributions shown in Figure 4.13 have bell shapes. This is a consequence of the second main result of this section, which describes the *shape* of the sampling distribution of $\bar{y}$. This result can be proven mathematically, and it is often called the *Central Limit Theorem*.

---

**Central Limit Theorem**

For random sampling with a large sample size $n$, the sampling distribution of the sample mean $\bar{y}$ is approximately a normal distribution.

---

Here are some implications and interpretations of this result:

- The approximate normality of the sampling distribution applies *no matter what the shape* of the population distribution. This is quite remarkable. For large random samples, the sampling distribution of $\bar{y}$ is approximately normal even if the population distribution is highly skewed, U shaped, or highly discrete such as the binary distribution in Figure 4.12. We'll see that this enables us to make inferences even when the population distribution is highly irregular. This is helpful, because many social science variables are very skewed or highly discrete.

  Figure 4.14 displays sampling distributions of $\bar{y}$ for four different shapes for the population distribution, shown at the top of the figure. Below them are

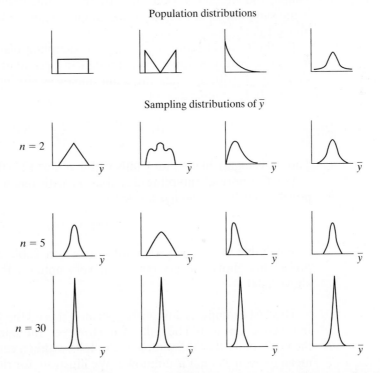

**FIGURE 4.14:** Four Different Population Distributions and the Corresponding Sampling Distributions of $\bar{y}$. As $n$ increases, the sampling distributions get narrower and have more of a bell shape.

portrayed the sampling distributions for random samples of sizes $n = 2, 5$, and 30. As $n$ increases, the sampling distribution has more of a bell shape.

- How large $n$ must be before the sampling distribution is bell shaped largely depends on the skewness of the population distribution. If the *population* distribution is bell shaped, then the sampling distribution is bell shaped for *all* sample sizes. The rightmost panel of Figure 4.14 illustrates. More skewed distributions require larger sample sizes. For most cases, a sample size of about 30 is sufficient (although it may not be large enough for precise inference). So, in practice for random sampling, the sampling distribution is nearly always approximately bell shaped.

- We could verify the Central Limit Theorem empirically by repeatedly selecting random samples, calculating $\bar{y}$ for each sample of $n$ observations. Then the histogram of the $\bar{y}$-values would be approximately a normal curve about $\mu$ with standard error equal to $\sigma/\sqrt{n}$, the population standard deviation divided by the square root of the sample size of each sample.

- Knowing that the sampling distribution of $\bar{y}$ is approximately normal helps us to find probabilities for possible values of $\bar{y}$. For instance, $\bar{y}$ almost certainly falls within $3\sigma_{\bar{y}} = 3\sigma/\sqrt{n}$ of $\mu$. We'll see that reasoning of this nature is vital to inferential statistical methods.

### EXAMPLE 4.9   Is Sample Mean Income of Migrant Workers Near Population Mean?

For the population of migrant workers in California, suppose that weekly income has a distribution that is skewed to the right with a mean of $\mu = \$380$ and a standard deviation of $\sigma = \$80$. A researcher, unaware of these values, plans to randomly sample 100 migrant workers and use the sample mean income $\bar{y}$ to estimate $\mu$. What is the sampling distribution of the sample mean? What is the probability that $\bar{y}$ falls above $\$400$?

By the Central Limit Theorem, the sampling distribution of the sample mean $\bar{y}$ is approximately normal, even though the population distribution is skewed. The sampling distribution has the same mean as the population distribution, namely, $\mu = \$380$. Its standard error is

$$\sigma_{\bar{y}} = \frac{\sigma}{\sqrt{n}} = \frac{80}{\sqrt{100}} = 8.0 \text{ dollars.}$$

Thus, it is highly likely that $\bar{y}$ falls within about $\$24$ (three standard errors) of $\mu$.

For the normal sampling distribution with mean 380 and standard error 8, the possible $\bar{y}$ value of 400 has a $z$-score of

$$z = (400 - 380)/8 = 2.5.$$

From a table of normal probabilities (such as Table A), the corresponding right-tail probability above 400 is 0.0062. It is very unlikely that the sample mean would fall above $\$400$. ∎

This last example is unrealistic, because it used the value of the population mean $\mu$. In practice, this would be unknown. However, the sampling distribution of $\bar{y}$ provides the probability that the sample mean falls within a certain distance of the population mean $\mu$, even when $\mu$ is unknown. We illustrate for the study of income of California migrant workers. Let's calculate the probability that the sample mean weekly income $\bar{y}$ falls within $\$10$ of the true mean income $\mu$ for all such workers.

Now the sampling distribution of $\bar{y}$ is approximately normal in shape and is centered about $\mu$. We saw in the previous example that when $n = 100$, the standard error is $\sigma_{\bar{y}} = \$8.0$. Hence, the probability that $\bar{y}$ falls within \$10 of $\mu$ is the probability that a normally distributed variable falls within $10/8 = 1.25$ standard deviations of its mean. That is, the number of standard errors that $\mu + 10$ (or $\mu - 10$) falls from $\mu$ is

$$z = \frac{(\mu + 10) - \mu}{8} = \frac{10}{8} = 1.25,$$

as Figure 4.15 shows. From a normal table, the probability that $\bar{y}$ falls *more than* 1.25 standard errors from $\mu$ (in either direction) is $2(0.1056) = 0.21$. Thus, the probability that $\bar{y}$ falls no more than \$10 from $\mu$ equals $1 - 0.21 = 0.79$.

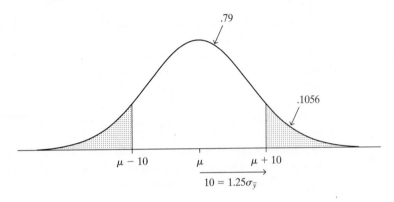

**FIGURE 4.15:** Sampling Distribution of $\bar{y}$ for Unknown $\mu$ and Standard Error $\sigma_{\bar{y}} = 8$

This example is still unrealistic, because it used the population standard deviation $\sigma$. In practice, we'd estimate this value. The next chapter shows that, to conduct inference, we can estimate $\sigma$ by the sample standard deviation $s$.

To get a feel for the Central Limit Theorem and how sampling distributions become more bell shaped as $n$ increases, it can be very helpful to use an applet on the Internet. We strongly recommend that you try Exercises 4.41 and 4.42.

## 4.6  REVIEW: POPULATION, SAMPLE DATA, AND SAMPLING DISTRIBUTIONS

Sampling distributions are fundamental to statistical inference and methodology presented in the rest of this text. Because of this, we now review and elaborate on the distinction between the sampling distribution and the two types of distributions presented in Section 3.1—the *population* distribution and the *sample data* distribution.

Here is a capsule description of the three types of distribution:

- *Population distribution*: This is the distribution from which we select the sample. It is usually unknown. We make inferences about its characteristics, such as the parameters $\mu$ and $\sigma$ that describe its center and spread. Denote the population size by $N$.

- *Sample data distribution*: This is the distribution of data that we actually observe; that is, the sample observations $y_1, y_2, \ldots, y_n$. We can describe it by statistics such as the sample mean $\bar{y}$ and sample standard deviation $s$. The larger the sample size $n$, the closer the sample data distribution resembles the population distribution, and the closer the sample statistics such as $\bar{y}$ fall to the population parameters such as $\mu$.

- *Sampling distribution* of a statistic: This is the probability distribution for the possible values of a sample statistic, such as $\bar{y}$. A sampling distribution describes the variability that occurs in the statistic's value among samples of a certain size. This distribution determines the probability that the statistic falls within a certain distance of the population parameter it estimates.

### EXAMPLE 4.10    Three Distributions for a General Social Survey Item

In 2006, the GSS asked about the number of hours a week spent on the World Wide Web, excluding e-mail (variable denoted WWWHR). The *sample data distribution* for the $n = 2778$ subjects in the sample was very highly skewed to the right. It is described by the sample mean $\bar{y} = 5.7$ and sample standard deviation $s = 10.5$.

Because the GSS cannot sample the entire population of adult Americans ($N$ of about 200 million), we don't know the *population distribution*. Because the sample data distribution had a large sample size, probably the population distribution looks like it. Most likely the population distribution would also be highly skewed to the right. Its mean and standard deviation would be similar to the sample values. Values such as $\mu = 6.0$ and $\sigma = 10.3$ would be realistic.

If the GSS repeatedly took random samples of 2778 adult Americans, the sample mean time $\bar{y}$ spent on the WWW would vary from survey to survey. The *sampling distribution* describes how $\bar{y}$ would vary. For example, if the population has mean $\mu = 6.0$ and standard deviation $\sigma = 10.3$, then the sampling distribution of $\bar{y}$ also has mean 6.0, and it has a standard error of

$$\sigma_{\bar{y}} = \frac{\sigma}{\sqrt{n}} = \frac{10.3}{\sqrt{2778}} = 0.20.$$

Unlike the population and sample data distributions, the sampling distribution would be bell shaped and narrow. Nearly all of that distribution would fall within $3(0.20) = 0.6$ of the mean of 6.0. So it's very likely that any sample of size 2778 would have a sample mean within 0.6 of 6.0. In summary, the sample data and population distributions are highly skewed and spread out, whereas the sampling distribution of $\bar{y}$ is approximately normal and has nearly all its probability in a narrow range. ∎

In reality, the GSS uses a multistage cluster sample rather than a simple random sample. Because of this, the true standard error is actually a bit larger than given by this formula. (This is discussed in Appendix A of the codebook at sda.berkeley.edu/GSS.) It's beyond the scope of this text to adjust standard errors for clustering effects. For purposes of illustration, we'll treat GSS data as if they come from a simple random sample, keeping in mind that in practice some adjustment may be necessary as explained at the GSS website.

### EXAMPLE 4.11    Three Distributions for Exit Poll Example

We consider, once again, the variable $y =$ vote in the 2006 California gubernatorial election for a randomly selected voter. Let $y = 1$ for Republican and $y = 0$ for another candidate. In fact, of the 6,921,442 adult residents of California who voted, 55.9% voted for Schwarzenegger. So the probability distribution for $y$ has probability 0.559 at $y = 1$ and probability 0.441 at $y = 0$. The mean of this distribution is $\mu = 0.559$, which is the population proportion of votes for Schwarzenegger. From a formula we'll study in the next chapter, the standard deviation of this distribution equals $\sigma = 0.497$.

The population distribution of candidate preference consists of $N = 6{,}921{,}442$ values of $y$, 44.1% of which are 0 and 55.9% of which are 1. This distribution is described by the parameters $\mu = 0.559$ and $\sigma = 0.497$. Figure 4.16 portrays this distribution, which is highly discrete (binary). It is not at all bell shaped.

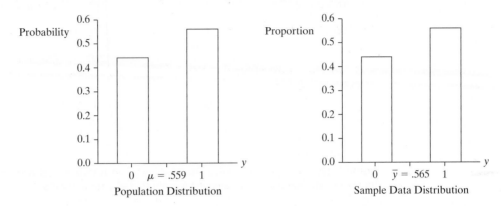

**FIGURE 4.16:** The Population ($N = 6{,}921{,}442$) and Sample Data ($n = 2705$) Distributions of Vote in 2006 California Gubernatorial Election, where 1 = Schwarzenegger and 0 = Other Candidates

Before all the votes were counted, the population distribution was unknown. When polls closed, CNN reported results of an exit poll of size $n = 2705$ to predict the outcome. A histogram of the 2705 votes in the sample describes the sample data distribution. Of the 2705 voters, 56.5% said they voted for Schwarzenegger (i.e., have $y = 1$) and 43.5% said they voted for another candidate ($y = 0$). Figure 4.16 also displays the histogram of these sample data values. Like the population distribution, the sample data distribution concentrates at $y = 0$ and $y = 1$. It is described by sample statistics such as $\bar{y} = 0.565$, which is the sample proportion voting for Schwarzenegger. The larger the sample size, the more this sample data distribution tends to resemble the population distribution, since the sample observations are a subset of the population values. If the entire population is sampled, as when all the votes are counted, then the two distributions are identical.

For a random sample of size $n = 2705$, the sampling distribution of $\bar{y}$ is approximately normal. Its mean is $\mu = 0.559$ and its standard error is

$$\sigma_{\bar{y}} = \frac{\sigma}{\sqrt{n}} = \frac{0.497}{\sqrt{2705}} = 0.01.$$

Figure 4.17 portrays this sampling distribution, relative to the population distribution of votes.

By contrast, the population distribution and sample data distribution of votes are concentrated at the values 0 and 1. The sampling distribution looks completely different from them, being much less spread out and bell shaped. The population and sample data distributions of the vote are not bell shaped. They are highly discrete, concentrated at 0 and 1. With $n = 2705$ the sample proportion can take a large number of values between 0 and 1, and its sampling distribution is essentially continuous, being approximately normal by the Central Limit Theorem. ■

## Effect of Sample Size on Sample Data and Sampling Distributions

We've seen that the sampling distribution is more nearly normal in shape for larger values of $n$. For sampling only one observation ($n = 1$), $\bar{y} = y_1$, and the sampling

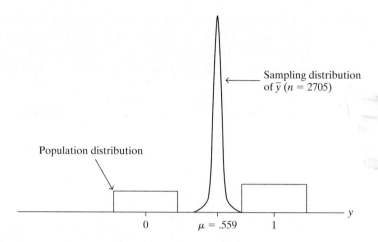

**FIGURE 4.17:** The Population Distribution (where $y = 1$ Is Vote for Schwarzenegger and $y = 0$ Is Vote for Other Candidate) and the Sampling Distribution of $\bar{y}$ for $n = 2705$

distribution of $\bar{y}$ is the same as the probability distribution for one observation on $y$. This is simply the population distribution of $y$, which need not be the least bit normal. As $n$ increases, the sampling distribution of $\bar{y}$ assumes more of a bell shape. For $n \geq 30$, the approximation is usually good. As the sample size $n$ approaches the population size $N$, the normal sampling distribution of $\bar{y}$ gets narrower and eventually converges to a spike at the single number $\mu$. When the entire population is sampled, $\bar{y} = \mu$ with probability 1 (i.e., the two measures are the same), and the sampling distribution concentrates at the point $\mu$.

Figure 4.17 showed a great difference between the population distribution and the sampling distribution of $\bar{y}$ (for $n = 2705$). Note also the great difference between the sample data distribution (Figure 4.16) and the sampling distribution (Figure 4.17). The sample data distribution looks much like the population distribution, more so as the sample size increases. The sampling distribution, on the other hand, has a bell-shaped appearance and gets narrower as $n$ increases. As Figure 4.16 shows, the sample values of $y$ can be only 0 or 1. On the other hand, sample mean values (which are sample proportions) can fall between 0 and 1. According to the sampling distribution of $\bar{y}$ for $n = 2705$, it is practically impossible that a random sample of that size has a sample mean anywhere near 0 or 1; nearly all the probability falls between 0.53 and 0.59 (within about three standard errors of the mean of the sampling distribution).

## The Key Role of Sampling Distributions in Statistical Inference

We've seen that, by the Central Limit Theorem, we can often use the normal distribution to find probabilities about $\bar{y}$. The next two chapters will show that statistical inferences rely on this theorem.

The result about sample means having approximately normal sampling distributions, for large random samples, is important also because similar results hold for many other statistics. For instance, most sample statistics used to estimate population parameters have approximately normal sampling distributions, for large random samples. The primary reason for the key role of the normal distribution is that so many statistics have approximately normal sampling distributions.

## 4.7 CHAPTER SUMMARY

For an observation in a random sample or a randomized experiment, the **probability** of a particular outcome is the proportion of times that the outcome would occur in a long sequence of observations.

- A **probability distribution** specifies probabilities for the possible values of a variable. We let $P(y)$ denote the probability of the value $y$. The probabilities are nonnegative and sum to 1.0.
- Probability distributions have summary parameters, such as the mean $\mu$ and standard deviation $\sigma$. The mean for a probability distribution of a discrete variable is

$$\mu = \sum yP(y).$$

This is also called the **expected value** of $y$.

- The **normal distribution** has a graph that is a symmetric bell-shaped curve specified by the mean $\mu$ and standard deviation $\sigma$. For any $z$, the probability falling within $z$ standard deviations of the mean is the same for every normal distribution.
- The **z-score** for an observation $y$ equals

$$z = (y - \mu)/\sigma.$$

It measures the number of standard deviations that $y$ falls from the mean $\mu$. For a normal distribution, the $z$-scores have the *standard normal distribution*, which has mean $= 0$ and standard deviation $= 1$.

- A **sampling distribution** is a probability distribution of a sample statistic, such as the sample mean or sample proportion. It specifies probabilities for the possible values of the statistic for all the possible samples.
- The sampling distribution of the sample mean $\bar{y}$ centers at the population mean $\mu$. Its standard deviation, called the **standard error**, relates to the standard deviation $\sigma$ of the population by $\sigma_{\bar{y}} = \sigma/\sqrt{n}$. As the sample size $n$ increases, the standard error decreases, so the sample mean tends to be closer to the population mean.
- The **Central Limit Theorem** states that for large random samples, the sampling distribution of the sample mean is approximately normal. This holds no matter what the shape of the population distribution. The result applies also to proportions, since the sample proportion is a special case of the sample mean for observations coded as 0 and 1 (such as for two candidates in an election).

The bell shape for the sampling distribution of many statistics is the main reason for the importance of the normal distribution. The next two chapters show how the Central Limit Theorem is the basis of methods of statistical inference.

## PROBLEMS

### Practicing the Basics

**4.1.** In a GSS, in response to the question, "Do you believe in life after death?" 907 people answered yes and 220 answered no. Based on this survey, estimate the probability that a randomly selected adult in the United States believes in life after death.

**4.2.** A GSS estimates the probability that an American adult believes in heaven is 0.85.
   (a) Estimate the probability that an American adult does not believe in heaven.
   (b) Of those who believe in heaven, about 84% believe in hell. Estimate the probability a randomly chosen American adult believes in both heaven and hell.

**4.3.** In 2000, the GSS asked subjects whether they are a member of an environmental group (variable GRNGROUP) and whether they would be very willing to pay much higher prices to protect the environment (variable GRNPRICE). Table 4.4 shows results.

(a) Explain why $96/1117 = 0.086$ estimates the probability that a randomly selected American adult is a member of an environmental group.

(b) Show that the estimated probability of being very willing to pay much higher prices to protect the environment is (i) 0.312, given that the person is a member of an environmental group, (ii) 0.086, given not a member of an environmental group.

(c) Show that the estimated probability a person is both a member of an environmental group *and* very willing to pay much higher prices to protect the environment is 0.027 (i) directly using the counts in the table, (ii) using the probability estimates from (a) and (b).

(d) Show that the estimated probability that a person answers yes to both questions or no to both questions is 0.862.

**TABLE 4.4**

| | | Pay Higher Prices | | |
|---|---|---|---|---|
| | | Yes | No | Total |
| Member of | Yes | 30 | 66 | 96 |
| Environmental | No | 88 | 933 | 1021 |
| Group | | | | |
| Total | | 118 | 999 | 1117 |

**4.4.** Let $y$ = number of languages in which a person is fluent. According to Statistics Canada, for residents of Canada this has probability distribution $P(0) = 0.02$, $P(1) = 0.81$, $P(2) = 0.17$, with negligible probability for higher values of $y$.

(a) Is $y$ a discrete or a continuous variable? Why?

(b) Construct a table showing the probability distribution of $y$.

(c) Find the probability a Canadian is *not* multilingual.

(d) Find the mean of this probability distribution.

**4.5.** Let $y$ denote the number of people known personally who were victims of homicide within the past 12 months. According to results from recent General Social Surveys, for a randomly chosen person in the U.S. the probability distribution of $y$ is approximately: $P(0) = 0.91, P(1) = 0.06, P(2) = 0.02, P(3) = 0.01$.

(a) Explain why it is not valid to find the mean of this probability distribution as $(0 + 1 + 2 + 3)/4 = 1.5$.

(b) Find the correct mean of the probability distribution.

**4.6.** A ticket for a statewide lottery costs $1. With probability 0.0000001, you win a million dollars ($1,000,000), and with probability 0.9999999 you win nothing. Let $y$ denote the winnings from buying one ticket. Construct the probability distribution for $y$. Show that the mean of the distribution equals 0.10, corresponding to an expected return of 10 cents for the dollar paid.

**4.7.** Let $y$ be the outcome of selecting a single digit from a random number table.

(a) Construct the probability distribution for $y$. (This type of distribution is called a *uniform* distribution because of the uniform spread of probabilities across the possible outcomes.)

(b) Find the mean of this probability distribution.

(c) The standard deviation $\sigma$ of this distribution is one of the following: 0.4, 2.9, 7.0, 12.0. Which do you think is correct? Why?

**4.8.** For a normal distribution, find the probability that an observation falls

(a) At least one standard deviation above the mean

(b) At least one standard deviation below the mean

(c) At least 0.67 standard deviations above the mean

**4.9.** For a normally distributed variable, verify that the probability between:

(a) $\mu - \sigma$ and $\mu + \sigma$ equals 0.68

(b) $\mu - 1.96\sigma$ and $\mu + 1.96\sigma$ equals 0.95

(c) $\mu - 3\sigma$ and $\mu + 3\sigma$ equals 0.997

(d) $\mu - 0.67\sigma$ and $\mu + 0.67\sigma$ equals 0.50

**4.10.** Find the $z$-value for which the probability that a normal variable exceeds $\mu + z\sigma$ equals

(a) 0.01
(b) 0.025
(c) 0.05
(d) 0.10
(e) 0.25
(f) 0.50

**4.11.** Find the $z$-value such that for a normal distribution the interval from $\mu - z\sigma$ to $\mu + z\sigma$ contains

(a) 50%
(b) 90%
(c) 95%
(d) 98%
(e) 99% of the probability.

**4.12.** Find the $z$-values corresponding to the

(a) 90th,
(b) 95th,
(c) 98th, and

**(d)** 99th percentiles of a normal distribution.

**4.13.** Show that if $z$ is the number such that the interval from $\mu - z\sigma$ to $\mu + z\sigma$ contains 90% of a normal distribution, then $\mu + z\sigma$ equals the 95th percentile.

**4.14.** If $z$ is the positive number such that the interval from $\mu - z\sigma$ to $\mu + z\sigma$ contains 50% of a normal distribution, then
   **(a)** Which percentile is (i) $\mu + z\sigma$? (ii) $\mu - z\sigma$?
   **(b)** Find this value of $z$.
   **(c)** Using this result, explain why the upper quartile and lower quartile of a normal distribution are $\mu + 0.67\sigma$ and $\mu - 0.67\sigma$.

**4.15.** What proportion of a normal distribution falls in the following ranges?
   **(a)** Above a $z$-score of 2.10
   **(b)** Below a $z$-score of $-2.10$
   **(c)** Above a $z$-score of $-2.10$
   **(d)** Between $z$-scores of $-2.10$ and 2.10

**4.16.** Find the $z$-score for the number that is less than only 1% of the values of a normal distribution.

**4.17.** Mensa is a society of high-IQ people whose members have a score on an IQ test at the 98th percentile or higher.
   **(a)** How many standard deviations above the mean is the 98th percentile?
   **(b)** For the normal IQ distribution with mean 100 and standard deviation 16, what is the IQ score for the 98th percentile?

**4.18.** According to a recent *Current Population Reports*, self-employed individuals in the United States work an average of 45 hours per week, with a standard deviation of 15. If this variable is approximately normally distributed, what proportion averaged more than 40 hours per week?

**4.19.** The Mental Development Index (MDI) of the Bayley Scales of Infant Development is a standardized measure used in studies with high-risk infants. It has approximately a normal distribution with a mean of 100 and a standard deviation of 16.
   **(a)** What proportion of children have a MDI of at least 120?
   **(b)** Find the MDI score that is the 90th percentile.
   **(c)** Find and interpret the lower quartile, median, and upper quartile of MDI.

**4.20.** For 5459 pregnant women using Aarhus University Hospital in Denmark in a two-year period who reported information on length of gestation until birth, the mean was 281.9 days, with standard deviation 11.4 days.[3] A baby is classified as premature if the gestation time is 258 days or less.
   **(a)** If gestation times are normally distributed, what proportion of babies would be born prematurely?

**(b)** The actual proportion born prematurely during this period was 0.036. Based on this information, how would you expect the distribution of gestation time to differ from normal?

**4.21.** Suppose that the weekly use of gasoline for motor travel by adults in North America is approximately normally distributed, with a mean of 16 gallons and a standard deviation of 5 gallons.
   **(a)** What proportion of adults use more than 20 gallons per week?
   **(b)** Assuming that the standard deviation and the normal form would remain constant, to what level must the mean reduce so that only 5% use more than 20 gallons per week?
   **(c)** If the distribution of gasoline use is not actually normal, how would you expect it to deviate from normal?

**4.22.** On the midterm exam in introductory statistics, an instructor always gives a grade of B to students who score between 80 and 90. One year, the scores have approximately a normal distribution with mean 83 and standard deviation 5. About what proportion of the students get a B?

**4.23.** For an SAT distribution ($\mu = 500, \sigma = 100$) and an ACT distribution ($\mu = 21, \sigma = 4.7$), which score is relatively higher, SAT = 600 or ACT = 29? Explain.

**4.24.** Suppose that property taxes on homes in Iowa City, Iowa have an approximately normal distribution with a mean of $2500 and a standard deviation of $1500. The property tax for one particular home is $5000.
   **(a)** Find the $z$-score corresponding to that value.
   **(b)** What proportion of the property taxes exceed $5000?
   **(c)** If the true distribution is not normal, how do you think it deviates from normal? Why?

**4.25.** An energy study in Gainesville, Florida, found that in March 2006, household use of electricity had a mean of 673 and a standard deviation of 556 kWh (kilowatt-hours).
   **(a)** If the distribution were normal, what percentage of the households had use above 1000 kWh?
   **(b)** Do you think the distribution is truly normal? Why or why not?

**4.26.** Five students, Ann, Betty, Clint, Douglas, and Edward, are rated equally qualified for admission to law school, ahead of other applicants. However, all but two positions have been filled for the entering class. Since the admissions committee can admit only two more students, it decides to randomly select two of these five candidates. For

---

this strategy, let $y$ = number of females admitted. Using the first letter of the name to denote a student, the different combinations that could be admitted are (A, B), (A, C), (A, D), (A, E), (B, C), (B, D), (B, E), (C, D), (C, E), and (D, E).

**(a)** Construct the probability distribution for $y$.

**(b)** Construct the sampling distribution of the sample *proportion* of the students selected who are female.

**4.27.** Construct the sampling distribution of the sample proportion of heads, for flipping a balanced coin:

**(a)** Once.

**(b)** Twice. (*Hint*: The possible samples are (H, H), (H, T), (T, H), (T, T).)

**(c)** Three times. (*Hint*: There are 8 possible samples.)

**(d)** Four times. (*Hint*: There are 16 possible samples.)

**(e)** Describe how the shape of the sampling distribution seems to be changing as the number of flips increases.

**4.28.** The probability distribution associated with the outcome of rolling a balanced die has probability 1/6 attached to each integer, $\{1, 2, 3, 4, 5, 6\}$. Let $(y_1, y_2)$ denote the outcomes for rolling the die twice.

**(a)** Enumerate the 36 possible $(y_1, y_2)$ pairs (e.g., (2, 1) represents a 2 followed by a 1).

**(b)** Treating the 36 pairs as equally likely, construct the sampling distribution for the sample mean $\bar{y}$ of the two numbers rolled.

**(c)** Construct a histogram of the (i) probability distribution for each roll, (ii) sampling distribution of $\bar{y}$ in (b). Describe their shapes.

**(d)** What are the means of the two distributions in (c)? Why are they the same?

**(e)** Explain why the sampling distribution of $\bar{y}$ has relatively more probability near the middle than at the minimum and maximum values. (*Hint*: Note there are many more $(y_1, y_2)$ pairs that have a sample mean near the middle than near the minimum or maximum.)

**4.29.** An exit poll of 2293 voters in the 2006 Ohio Senatorial election indicated that 44% voted for the Republican candidate, Mike DeWine, and 56% voted for the Democratic candidate, Sherrod Brown.

**(a)** If actually 50% of the population voted for DeWine, find the standard error of the sample proportion voting for him, for this exit poll. (Recall from Example 4.8 on page 91 that the population standard deviation is 0.50.)

**(b)** If actually 50% of the population voted for DeWine, would it have been surprising to obtain the results in this exit poll? Why?

**(c)** Based on your answer in (b), would you be willing to predict the outcome of this election? Explain.

**4.30.** According to *Current Population Reports*, the population distribution of number of years of education for self-employed individuals in the United States has a mean of 13.6 and a standard deviation of 3.0. Find the mean and standard error of the sampling distribution of $\bar{y}$ for a random sample of

**(a)** 9 residents,

**(b)** 36 residents,

**(c)** 100 residents. Describe the pattern as $n$ increases.

**4.31.** Refer to Exercise 4.6. The mean and standard deviation of the probability distribution for the lottery winnings $y$ are $\mu = 0.10$ and $\sigma = 316.23$. Suppose you play the lottery 1 million times. Let $\bar{y}$ denote your average winnings.

**(a)** Find the mean and standard error of the sampling distribution of $\bar{y}$.

**(b)** About how likely is it that you would "come out ahead," with your average winnings exceeding $1, the amount you paid to play each time?

**4.32.** According to recent General Social Surveys (variable PARTNERS), in the United States the distribution of $y$ = number of sex partners you have had in the past 12 months has a mean of about 1.1 and a standard deviation of about 1.1. Suppose these are the population mean and standard deviation.

**(a)** Does $y$ have a normal distribution? Explain.

**(b)** For a random sample of 2400 adults (the size of the 2006 GSS for this variable), describe the sampling distribution of $\bar{y}$ by giving its shape, mean, and standard error.

**(c)** Refer to (b). Report an interval within which the sample mean would almost surely fall.

**4.33.** The scores on the Psychomotor Development Index (PDI), a scale of infant development, are approximately normal with mean 100 and standard deviation 15.

**(a)** An infant is selected at random. Find the probability that PDI is below 90.

**(b)** A study uses a random sample of 25 infants. Specify the sampling distribution of the sample mean PDI, and find the probability that the sample mean is below 90.

**(c)** Would you be surprised to observe a PDI score of 90? Would you be surprised to observe a sample mean PDI of 90? Why?

**(d)** Sketch the population distribution for PDI. Superimpose a sketch of the sampling distribution for $n = 25$.

**4.34.** A study plans to sample randomly 100 government records of farms in Ontario to estimate the mean acreage of farms in that province. Results from an earlier study suggest that 200 acres is a reasonable guess for the population standard deviation of farm size.

(a) Find the probability that the sample mean acreage falls within 10 acres of the population mean acreage.

(b) If in reality the population standard deviation is larger than 200, would the probability be larger or smaller than you found in (a)?

**4.35.** According to the U.S. Census Bureau, in 2000 the number of people in a household had a mean of 2.6 and a standard deviation of 1.5. Suppose the Census Bureau instead had estimated this mean using a random sample of 225 homes, and that sample had a mean of 2.4 and standard deviation of 1.4.

(a) Identify the variable $y$.

(b) Describe the center and spread of the population distribution.

(c) Describe the center and spread of the sample data distribution.

(d) Describe the center and spread of the sampling distribution of the sample mean for 225 homes. What does that distribution describe?

**4.36.** The distribution of family size in a particular tribal society is skewed to the right, with $\mu = 5.2$ and $\sigma = 3.0$. These values are unknown to an anthropologist, who samples families to estimate mean family size. For a random sample of 36 families, she gets a mean of 4.6 and a standard deviation of 3.2.

(a) Identify the population distribution. State its mean and standard deviation.

(b) Identify the sample data distribution. State its mean and standard deviation.

(c) Identify the sampling distribution of $\bar{y}$. State its mean and standard error and explain what it describes.

**4.37.** Refer to the previous exercise.

(a) Find the probability that her sample mean falls within 0.5 of the population mean.

(b) Suppose she takes a random sample of size 100. Find the probability that the sample mean falls within 0.5 of the true mean, and compare the answer to that in (a).

(c) Refer to (b). If the sample were truly random, would you be surprised if the anthropologist obtained $\bar{y} = 4.0$? Why? (This could well happen if the sample were not random.)

**4.38.** At a university, 60% of the 7400 students are female. The student newspaper reports results of a survey of a random sample of 50 students about various topics involving alcohol abuse, such as participation in binge drinking. They report that their sample contained 26 females.

(a) Explain how you can set up a variable $y$ to represent gender.

(b) Identify the population distribution of gender at this university.

(c) Identify the sample data distribution of gender for this sample.

(d) The sampling distribution of the sample proportion of females in the sample is approximately a normal distribution with mean 0.60 and standard error 0.07. Explain what this means.

**4.39.** Sunshine City was designed to attract retired people. Its current population of 50,000 residents has a mean age of 60 years and a standard deviation of 16 years. The distribution of ages is skewed to the left, reflecting the predominance of older individuals. A random sample of 100 residents of Sunshine City has $\bar{y} = 58.3$ and $s = 15.0$.

(a) Describe the center and spread of the population distribution.

(b) Describe the center and spread of the sample data distribution. What shape does it probably have?

(c) Find the center and spread of the sampling distribution of $\bar{y}$ for $n = 100$. What shape does it have and what does it describe?

(d) Explain why it would not be unusual to observe a person of age 40 in Sunshine City, but it would be highly unusual to observe a sample mean of 40, for a random sample size of 100.

**4.40.** Refer to the previous exercise.

(a) Describe the sampling distribution of $\bar{y}$ for a random sample of size $n = 1$.

(b) Describe the sampling distribution of $\bar{y}$ if you sample all 50,000 residents.

## Concepts and Applications

**4.41.** You can use an *applet* on a computer or on the Internet to repeatedly generate random samples from artificial populations and analyze them to study the properties of statistical methods. To try this, go to www.prenhall.com/agresti and use the *sampling distribution* applet. Select binary for the parent population, setting the population proportion as 0.50. Select for the sample size $n = 100$.

(a) Simulate once (setting the number of simulations $N = 1$ and clicking on *Sample*) and report the counts and the proportions for the two categories. Did you get a sample proportion close to 0.50? Perform this simulation of a random sample of size 100 ten times, each time observing from the graphs the counts and the corresponding sample proportion of yes votes. Summarize.

(b) Now plot the results of simulating a random sample of size 100 and finding the sample proportion 1000 times, by setting $N = 1000$ on the menu. How does this plot reflect the Central Limit Theorem?

**4.42.** Refer to the previous exercise.

    **(a)** For this applet, select the skewed population distribution. Take 1000 samples of size 30 each. How does the empirical distribution of sample means compare to the population distribution? What does this reflect?

    **(b)** Repeat, this time choosing a sample size of only 2 for each sample. Why is the sampling distribution not symmetric and bell-shaped?

**4.43.** (*Class Exercise*) Refer to Exercises 1.11 and 1.12 (page 8). Using the population defined by your class or using the student survey, the instructor will select a variable, such as weekly time watching television.

    **(a)** Construct a histogram or stem-and-leaf plot of the population distribution of the variable for the class.

    **(b)** Using a random number table, each student should select nine students at random and compute the sample mean response for those students. (Each student should use different random numbers.) Plot a histogram of the sample means obtained by all the students. How do the spread and shape compare to the histogram in (a)? What does this illustrate?

**4.44.** (*Class Exercise*) Table 4.5 provides the ages of all 50 heads of households in a small Nova Scotian fishing village. The distribution of these ages is characterized by $\mu = 47.18$ and $\sigma = 14.74$.

    **(a)** Construct a stem-and-leaf plot of the population distribution.

    **(b)** Using a random number table, each student should select nine random numbers between 01 and 50. Using these numbers, each

student should sample nine heads of households and compute their sample mean age. Plot the empirical sampling distribution of the $\bar{y}$-values. Compare it to the distribution in (a).

    **(c)** What do you expect for the mean of the $\bar{y}$-values in a long run of repeated samples of size 9?

    **(d)** What do you expect for the standard deviation of the $\bar{y}$-values in a long run of repeated samples of size 9?

**4.45.** (*Class Exercise*) For a single toss of a coin, let $y = 1$ for a head and $y = 0$ for a tail. This simulates the vote in an election with two equally-preferred candidates.

    **(a)** Construct the probability distribution for $y$, and find its mean.

    **(b)** The coin is flipped ten times, yielding six heads and four tails. Construct the sample data distribution.

    **(c)** Each student in the class should flip a coin 10 times and calculate the proportion of heads in the sample. Summarize the empirical sampling distribution by plotting the proportions for all students. Describe the shape and spread of the sampling distribution compared to the distributions in (a) and (b).

    **(d)** If we performed the experiment of flipping the coin 10 times a very large number of times, what would we get for the (i) mean and (ii) standard deviation of the sample proportion values? You can use 0.50 as the standard deviation of the distribution in (a).

**4.46. (a)** Which distribution does the sample data distribution tend to resemble more closely—the sampling distribution or the population distribution? Explain.

    **(b)** Explain carefully the difference between a *sample data distribution* and the *sampling*

**TABLE 4.5**

| Name | Age | Name | Age | Name | Age | Name | Age |
|------|-----|------|-----|------|-----|------|-----|
| Alexander | 50 | Griffith | 66 | McTell | 49 | Staines | 33 |
| Bell | 45 | Grosvenor | 51 | MacLeod | 30 | Stewart | 36 |
| Bell | 23 | Ian | 57 | McNeil | 28 | Stewart | 25 |
| Bok | 28 | Jansch | 40 | McNeil | 31 | Thames | 29 |
| Clancy | 67 | Keelaghan | 36 | McNeil | 45 | Thomas | 57 |
| Cochran | 62 | Lavin | 38 | McNeil | 43 | Todd | 39 |
| Fairchild | 41 | Lunny | 81 | Mitchell | 43 | Trickett | 50 |
| Finney | 68 | MacColl | 27 | Muir | 54 | Trickett | 64 |
| Fisher | 37 | McCusker | 37 | Oban | 62 | Tyson | 76 |
| Francey | 60 | McCusker | 56 | Reid | 67 | Watson | 63 |
| Fricker | 41 | McDonald | 71 | Renbourn | 48 | Young | 29 |
| Gaughan | 70 | McDonald | 39 | Rogers | 32 | | |
| Graham | 47 | McDonald | 46 | Rush | 42 | | |

*distribution* of $\bar{y}$. Illustrate your answer for a variable $y$ that can take only values of 0 and 1.

**4.47.** The Palestinian Central Bureau of Statistics (www.pcbs.gov.ps) asked mothers of age 20–24 about the ideal number of children. For those living on the Gaza Strip, the probability distribution is approximately $P(1) = 0.01$, $P(2) = 0.10$, $P(3) = 0.09$, $P(4) = 0.31$, $P(5) = 0.19$, and $P(6$ or more$) = 0.29$.

(a) Because the last category is open-ended, it is not possible to calculate the mean exactly. Find a lower bound for the mean.

(b) Explain why you can find the median of the distribution, and find it.

**4.48.** For a normal distribution, show that
(a) The upper quartile equals $\mu + 0.67\sigma$.
(b) According to the 1.5(IQR) criterion, an outlier is an observation falling more than 2.7 standard deviations below or above the mean, and this happens for only 0.7% of the data.

**4.49.** In an exit poll of 1336 voters in the 2006 Senatorial election in New York State, 67% said they voted for Hillary Clinton. Based on this information, would you be willing to predict the winner of the election? Explain your reasoning.

**4.50.** For an election exit poll for a Senatorial election, find the standard error of the sample proportion voting for a candidate for whom the population proportion is 0.50, when $n = 100, 1000$, and $10,000$. In each case, predict an interval within which the sample proportion is almost certain to fall. Notice that the interval shrinks in width as the sample size increases. This is a consequence of the **law of large numbers**, which states that the sample proportion tends to get closer and closer to the population proportion as $n$ increases indefinitely.

*Select the correct response(s) in multiple-choice questions 4.51–4.52. (There may be more than one correct answer.)*

**4.51.** The standard error of a statistic describes
(a) The standard deviation of the sampling distribution of that statistic.
(b) The standard deviation of the sample data.
(c) How close that statistic is likely to fall to the parameter that it estimates.
(d) The variability in the values of the statistic for repeated random samples of size $n$.
(e) The error that occurs due to nonresponse and measurement errors.

**4.52.** The Central Limit Theorem implies that
(a) All variables have bell-shaped sample data distributions if a random sample contains at least about 30 observations.
(b) Population distributions are normal whenever the population size is large.

(c) For large random samples, the sampling distribution of $\bar{y}$ is approximately normal, regardless of the shape of the population distribution.
(d) The sampling distribution looks more like the population distribution as the sample size increases.
(e) All of the above

**4.53.** True or False: As the sample size increases, the standard error of the sampling distribution of $\bar{y}$ increases. Explain your answer.

*****4.54.** Lake Wobegon Junior College admits students only if they score above 400 on a standardized achievement test. Applicants from group A have a mean of 500 and a standard deviation of 100 on this test, and applicants from group B have a mean of 450 and a standard deviation of 100. Both distributions are approximately normal, and both groups have the same size.
(a) Find the proportion not admitted for each group.
(b) Of the students who are not admitted, what proportion are from group B?
(c) A state legislator proposes that the college lower the cutoff point for admission to 300, thinking that the proportion of the students who are not admitted who are from group B would decrease. If this policy is implemented, determine the effect on the answer to (b), and comment.

*****4.55.** The standard deviation of a discrete probability distribution is

$$\sigma = \sqrt{\sum (y - \mu)^2 P(y)}.$$

(a) Suppose $y = 1$ with probability 0.50 and $y = 0$ with probability 0.50, such as in Example 4.8 (page 91). Show that $\sigma = 0.50$.
(b) Suppose $y = 1$ with probability $\pi$ and $y = 0$ with probability $1 - \pi$, where $\pi$ represents a number between 0 and 1. Show that $\mu = \pi$ and that $\sigma = \sqrt{\pi(1 - \pi)}$.
(c) Show that the standard error of a sample proportion for a random sample of size $n$ equals $\sqrt{\pi(1 - \pi)/n}$.

*****4.56.** The curve for a normal distribution with mean $\mu$ and standard deviation $\sigma$ has mathematical formula

$$f(y) = \frac{1}{\sqrt{2\pi}\sigma} e^{-(y-\mu)^2/(2\sigma^2)}.$$

Show that this curve is symmetric, by showing that for any constant $c$, the curve has the same value at $y = \mu + c$ as at $y = \mu - c$. (The integral of $f(y)$ for $y$ between $\mu + z\sigma$ and $\infty$ equals the tail probability tabulated in Table A.)

*4.57. The standard error formula $\sigma_{\bar{y}} = \sigma/\sqrt{n}$ treats the population size $N$ as *infinitely* large relative to the sample size $n$. The formula for $\sigma_{\bar{y}}$ for a *finite* population size $N$ is

$$\sigma_{\bar{y}} = \sqrt{\frac{N-n}{N-1}}\left(\frac{\sigma}{\sqrt{n}}\right).$$

The term $\sqrt{(N-n)/(N-1)}$ is called the ***finite population correction***.

(a) When $n = 300$ students are selected from a college student body of size $N = 30{,}000$, show

that $\sigma_{\bar{y}} = 0.995\sigma/\sqrt{n}$. (In practice, $n$ is usually small relative to $N$, so the correction has little influence.)

(b) If $n = N$ (i.e., we sample the entire population), show that $\sigma_{\bar{y}} = 0$. In other words, no sampling error occurs, because $\bar{y} = \mu$.

(c) For $n = 1$, explain why the sampling distribution of $\bar{y}$ and its standard error are identical to the population distribution and its standard deviation.

# Statistical Inference: Estimation

This chapter shows how to use sample data to estimate population parameters. With quantitative variables, we estimate the population mean. A study dealing with health care issues, for example, might estimate population parameters such as the mean amount of money spent on prescription drugs during the past year and the mean number of visits to a physician. With categorical variables, we estimate population proportions for the categories. The health care study might estimate the proportions of people who (have, do not have) medical insurance and the proportions who (are satisfied, are not satisfied) with their health care.

We first learn about two types of estimates of parameters. Then, Sections 5.2 and 5.3 apply them to population means and proportions. Section 5.4 finds the sample size needed to achieve the desired precision of estimation. Section 5.5 discusses estimation of medians and other parameters.

## 5.1   POINT AND INTERVAL ESTIMATION

There are two types of estimates of parameters:

- A **_point estimate_** is a single number that is the best guess for the parameter.
- An **_interval estimate_** is an interval of numbers around the point estimate, within which the parameter value is believed to fall.

For example, a GSS asked, "Do you believe there is a life after death?" For 1958 subjects sampled, the point estimate for the proportion of all Americans who would respond _yes_ equals 0.73. An interval estimate predicts that the population proportion responding _yes_ falls between 0.71 and 0.75. That is, it predicts that the point estimate of 0.73 falls within a _margin of error_ of 0.02 of the true value. Thus, an interval estimate helps us gauge the probable precision of a point estimate.

The term _estimate_ alone is often used as short for _point estimate_. The term _estimator_ then refers to a particular type of statistic for estimating a parameter and _estimate_ refers to its value for a specific sample. For example, the sample proportion is an estimator of a population proportion. The value 0.73 is the estimate for the population proportion believing in life after death.

### Point Estimation of Parameters

Any particular parameter has many possible estimators. For a normal population distribution, for example, the center is the mean and the median, since that distribution is symmetric. So, with sample data, two possible estimators of that center are the sample mean and the sample median.

Estimates are the most common statistical inference reported by the mass media. For example, a Gallup poll in January 2007 reported that 36% of the American public approved of President George W. Bush's performance in office. This is an estimate rather than a parameter, because it was based on interviewing a sample of about 1000 people rather than the entire population.

### Unbiased and Efficient Point Estimators

A good estimator has a sampling distribution that (①) is centered around the parameter and (②) has as small a standard error as possible.

An estimator is ***unbiased*** if its sampling distribution centers around the parameter. Specifically, the parameter is the mean of the sampling distribution. From Section 4.4, for random sampling the mean of the sampling distribution of the sample mean $\bar{y}$ equals the population mean $\mu$. Thus, $\bar{y}$ is an unbiased estimator of the population mean $\mu$. Figure 5.1 illustrates. For any particular sample, the sample mean may underestimate $\mu$ or may overestimate it. If the sample mean were found repeatedly with different samples, however, the overestimates would tend to counterbalance the underestimates.

By contrast, a ***biased*** estimator tends to underestimate the parameter, on the average, or it tends to overestimate the parameter. For example, the sample range is typically smaller than the population range and it cannot be larger, because the sample minimum and maximum cannot be more extreme than the population minimum and maximum. Thus, the sample range tends to underestimate the population range. It is a biased estimator of the population range.

Suppose a population distribution is skewed to the right, as shown in Figure 5.1, and you want to estimate the population mean. If you are worried about the effects of outliers, you might decide to estimate it using the sample median rather than the sample mean. However, the population median is less than the population mean in that case, and the sample median also tends to be less than the population mean $\mu$. So the sample median is a biased estimator of $\mu$, tending on the average to underestimate $\mu$. It's better to use the sample mean, perhaps calculating it after deleting any extreme outlier if it has undue influence or may reflect an error in recording the data.

A second preferable property for an estimator is a relatively small standard error. An estimator having standard error smaller than those of other estimators is said to be ***efficient***. An efficient estimator falls closer, on the average, than other estimators to

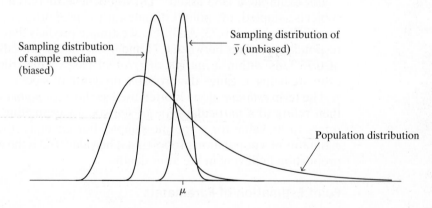

Sampling distribution of sample median (biased)

Sampling distribution of $\bar{y}$ (unbiased)

Population distribution

$\mu$

**FIGURE 5.1:** Sampling Distributions of Two Estimators of the Population Mean, for a Skewed Population Distribution

the parameter. For example, when a population distribution is normal, the standard error of the sample median is 25% larger than the standard error of the sample mean. The sample mean tends to be closer than the sample median to the population center. The sample mean is an efficient estimator. The sample median is inefficient.

In summary, a good estimator of a parameter is *unbiased*, or nearly so, and *efficient*. Statistical methods use estimators that possess these properties.

### Estimators of Mean, Standard Deviation, and Proportion

It is common, but not necessary, to use the sample analog of a population parameter as its estimator. For instance, to estimate a population proportion, the sample proportion is an estimator that is unbiased and efficient. For estimating a population mean $\mu$, the sample mean $\bar{y}$ is unbiased. It is efficient for the most common population distributions. Likewise, we use the sample standard deviation $s$ as the estimator of the population standard deviation $\sigma$.

The symbol " ˆ " over a parameter symbol is often used to represent an estimate of that parameter. The symbol " ˆ " is called a *caret* and is usually read as *hat*. For example, $\hat{\mu}$ is read as *mu-hat*. Thus, $\hat{\mu}$ denotes an estimate of the population mean $\mu$.

### Maximum Likelihood Method of Estimation*

The most important contributions to modern statistical science were made by a British statistician and geneticist, R. A. Fisher (1890–1962). While working at an agricultural research station north of London, he developed much of the theory of point estimation as well as methodology for the design of experiments and data analysis.

For point estimation, Fisher advocated the ***maximum likelihood estimate***. This estimate is the value of the parameter that is most consistent with the observed data, in the following sense: If the parameter equaled that number (i.e., the value of the estimate), the observed data would have had greater chance of occurring than if the parameter equaled any other number. For instance, a recent survey of about 1000 adult Americans reported that the maximum likelihood estimate of the population proportion who believe in astrology is 0.37. Then the observed sample would have been more likely to occur if the population proportion equals 0.37 than if it equaled any other possible value.

For many population distributions, such as the normal, the maximum likelihood estimator of a population mean is the sample mean. The primary point estimates presented in this book are, under certain population assumptions, maximum likelihood estimates. Fisher showed that, for large samples, maximum likelihood estimators have three desirable properties:

- They are efficient, for relatively large samples: Other estimators do not have smaller standard errors and do not tend to fall closer to the parameter.
- They have little, if any, bias, with the bias diminishing as the sample size increases.
- They have approximately normal sampling distributions.

### Confidence Interval Is Point Estimate ± Margin of Error

To be truly informative, an inference about a parameter should provide not only a point estimate but should also indicate how close the estimate is likely to fall to the parameter value. For example, since 1988 each year the Florida Poll conducted by Florida International University (www.fiu.edu/orgs/ipor/ffp) has asked about 1200 Floridians whether sexual relations between two adults of the same sex is wrong.

The percentage saying this is always wrong has decreased from 74% in 1988 to 54% in 2006. How accurate are these estimates? Within 2%? Within 5%? Within 10%?

The information about the precision of a point estimate determines the width of an *interval estimate* of the parameter. This consists of an interval of numbers around the point estimate. It is designed to contain the parameter with some chosen probability close to 1. Because interval estimates contain the parameter with a certain degree of confidence, they are referred to as **confidence intervals**.

---

**Confidence Interval**

A **confidence interval** for a parameter is an interval of numbers within which the parameter is believed to fall. The probability that this method produces an interval that contains the parameter is called the **confidence level**. This is a number chosen to be close to 1, such as 0.95 or 0.99.

---

The key to constructing a confidence interval is the sampling distribution of the point estimator. Often, the sampling distribution is approximately normal. The normal distribution then determines the probability that the estimator falls within a certain distance of the parameter. With probability about 0.95, the estimator falls within two standard errors. Almost certainly it falls within three standard errors. The smaller the standard error, the more precise the estimator tends to be.

In practice, often the sampling distribution is approximately normal. Then, to construct a confidence interval, we add and subtract from the point estimate some multiple (a *z*-score) of its standard error. This multiple of the standard error is the **margin of error**. That is,

A confidence interval has the form: **Point estimate ± Margin of error.**

To construct a confidence interval having "95% confidence," we take the point estimate and add and subtract a margin of error that equals about two standard errors. We'll see the details in the next two sections.

## 5.2 CONFIDENCE INTERVAL FOR A PROPORTION

For categorical data, an observation occurs in one of a set of categories. This type of measurement occurs when the variable is nominal, such as preferred candidate (Democrat, Republican, Independent), or ordinal, such as opinion about government spending (increase, keep the same, decrease). It also occurs when inherently continuous variables are measured with categorical scales, such as when annual income has categories ($0–$24,999, $25,000–$49,999, $50,000–$74,999, at least $75,000).

To summarize categorical data, we record the *proportions* (or *percentages*) of observations in the categories. For example, a study might provide a point or interval estimate of

- The proportion of Americans who have health insurance
- The proportion of Canadians who favor independent status for Quebec
- The proportion of Australians who are unemployed

### The Sample Proportion and Its Standard Error

Let $\pi$ denote a population proportion.[1] Then $\pi$ falls between 0 and 1. Its point estimator is the *sample proportion*. We denote the sample proportion by $\hat{\pi}$, since it estimates $\pi$.

---

[1] Here, $\pi$ is *not* the mathematical constant, 3.1415 . . . .

Recall that the sample proportion is a mean when we let $y = 1$ for an observation in the category of interest and $y = 0$ otherwise. (See the discussion about Table 3.6 on page 44 and following Example 4.7 on page 87.) Similarly, the population proportion $\pi$ is the mean $\mu$ of the probability distribution having probabilities

$$P(1) = \pi \quad \text{and} \quad P(0) = 1 - \pi.$$

The standard deviation of this probability distribution is $\sigma = \sqrt{\pi(1 - \pi)}$. (Exercise 4.55 in Chapter 4 derived this formula.) Since the formula for the standard error of a sample mean equals $\sigma_{\bar{y}} = \sigma/\sqrt{n}$, the standard error $\sigma_{\hat{\pi}}$ of the sample proportion $\hat{\pi}$ is

$$\sigma_{\hat{\pi}} = \sigma/\sqrt{n} = \sqrt{\frac{\pi(1 - \pi)}{n}}.$$

As the sample size increases, the standard error gets smaller. The sample proportion then tends to fall closer to the population proportion.

## Large-Sample Confidence Interval for a Proportion

Since the sample proportion $\hat{\pi}$ is a sample mean, the Central Limit Theorem applies: For large random samples, the sampling distribution of $\hat{\pi}$ is approximately normal about the parameter $\pi$ it estimates. Figure 5.2 illustrates.

Recall that 95% of a normal distribution falls within two standard deviations of the mean, or, more precisely, 1.96 standard deviations. We've just seen that the standard error of the sample proportion is $\sigma_{\hat{\pi}} = \sqrt{\pi(1 - \pi)/n}$. So, with probability 0.95, $\hat{\pi}$ falls within $1.96\sigma_{\hat{\pi}}$ units of the parameter $\pi$, that is, between $\pi - 1.96\sigma_{\hat{\pi}}$ and $\pi + 1.96\sigma_{\hat{\pi}}$, as Figure 5.2 shows.

Once the sample is selected, if $\hat{\pi}$ does fall within $1.96\sigma_{\hat{\pi}}$ units of $\pi$, then the interval from $\hat{\pi} - 1.96\sigma_{\hat{\pi}}$ to $\hat{\pi} + 1.96\sigma_{\hat{\pi}}$ contains $\pi$. See line 1 of Figure 5.2. In other words, with probability 0.95 a $\hat{\pi}$ value occurs such that the interval $\hat{\pi} \pm 1.96\sigma_{\hat{\pi}}$ contains the population proportion $\pi$.

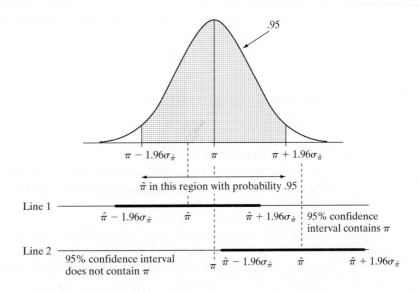

**FIGURE 5.2:** Sampling Distribution of $\hat{\pi}$ and Possible 95% Confidence Intervals for $\pi$

On the other hand, the probability is 0.05 that $\hat{\pi}$ does *not* fall within $1.96\sigma_{\hat{\pi}}$ of $\pi$. If that happens, then the interval from $\hat{\pi} - 1.96\sigma_{\hat{\pi}}$ to $\hat{\pi} + 1.96\sigma_{\hat{\pi}}$ does *not* contain $\pi$ (see Figure 5.2, line 2). Thus, the probability is 0.05 that $\hat{\pi}$ is such that $\hat{\pi} \pm 1.96\sigma_{\hat{\pi}}$ does *not* contain $\pi$.

The interval $\hat{\pi} \pm 1.96\sigma_{\hat{\pi}}$ is an interval estimate for $\pi$ with confidence level 0.95. It is called a **95% confidence interval**. In practice, the value of the standard error $\sigma_{\hat{\pi}} = \sqrt{\pi(1 - \pi)/n}$ for this formula is unknown, because it depends on the unknown parameter $\pi$. So we estimate this standard error by substituting the sample proportion, using

$$se = \sqrt{\frac{\hat{\pi}(1 - \hat{\pi})}{n}}.$$

We've used the symbol $s$ to denote a sample standard deviation, which estimates the population standard deviation $\sigma$. In the remainder of this text, we use the symbol $se$ to denote a sample estimate of a standard error.

The confidence interval formula uses this estimated standard error. In summary, the 95% confidence interval for $\pi$ is

$$\hat{\pi} \pm 1.96(se), \quad \text{where} \quad se = \sqrt{\frac{\hat{\pi}(1 - \hat{\pi})}{n}}.$$

### EXAMPLE 5.1 Estimating Proportion Who Favor Restricting Legalized Abortion

The 2006 Florida Poll (www.fiu.edu/orgs/ipor/ffp) conducted by Florida International University asked, "In general, do you think it is appropriate for state government to make laws restricting access to abortion?" Of 1200 randomly chosen adult Floridians, 396 said *yes* and 804 said *no*. We shall estimate the population proportion who would respond *yes* to this question.

Let $\pi$ represent the population proportion of adult Floridians who would respond *yes*. Of the $n = 1200$ respondents, 396 said *yes*, so $\hat{\pi} = 396/1200 = 0.33$. Then $1 - \hat{\pi} = 0.67$. That is, 33% of the sample said *yes* and 67% said *no*.

The estimated standard error of the sample proportion $\hat{\pi}$ equals

$$se = \sqrt{\frac{\hat{\pi}(1 - \hat{\pi})}{n}} = \sqrt{\frac{(0.33)(0.67)}{1200}} = \sqrt{0.000184} = 0.0136.$$

A 95% confidence interval for $\pi$ is

$$\hat{\pi} \pm 1.96(se) = 0.33 \pm 1.96(0.0136) = 0.33 \pm 0.03, \quad \text{or} \quad (0.30, 0.36).$$

The population percentage supporting restricting access to abortion appears to be at least 30% but no more than 36%. All numbers in the confidence interval (0.30, 0.36) fall below 0.50. Thus, apparently fewer than half the Florida adult population support restricting access to abortion. ∎

Results in such surveys vary greatly depending on the question wording and where the poll is conducted. For instance, when the 2006 GSS asked whether a pregnant woman should be able to obtain a legal abortion if the woman wants it for any reason (variable ABANY), 1155 said *no* and 784 said *yes*. You can check that the 95% confidence interval for the population proportion saying *no* equals (0.57, 0.62).

### EXAMPLE 5.2    Estimating Proportion Who "Oppose" from Proportion Who "Favor"

In the Florida Poll, for estimating the population proportion who supported restricting access to abortion, we obtained $se = 0.0136$ for the point estimate $\hat{\pi} = 0.33$. Similarly, the estimated standard error for $1 - \hat{\pi} = 0.67$, the proportion of voters who say *no* to restricting access to abortion, is

$$se = \sqrt{(1 - \hat{\pi})\hat{\pi}/n} = \sqrt{(0.67)(0.33)/1200} = 0.0136.$$

Both proportions have the same *se*.

A 95% confidence interval for the population proportion of *no* responses to restricting access to abortion is

$$0.67 \pm 1.96(0.0136) = 0.67 \pm 0.03, \quad \text{or} \quad (0.64, 0.70).$$

Now $0.64 = 1 - 0.36$ and $0.70 = 1 - 0.30$, where (0.30, 0.36) is the 95% confidence interval for $\pi$. Thus, inferences for the proportion $1 - \pi$ follow directly from those for the proportion $\pi$ by subtracting each endpoint of the confidence interval from 1.0. ■

If you construct a confidence interval using a hand calculator, don't round off while doing the calculation or your answer may be affected, but do round off when you report the final answer. Likewise, in reporting results from software output, you should use only the first two or three significant digits. Report the confidence interval as (0.30, 0.36) or (0.303, 0.357) rather than (0.303395, 0.356605). Software's extra precision provides accurate calculations in finding *se* and the confidence interval. However, the extra digits are distracting in reports and not useful. They do not tell us anything extra in a practical sense about the population proportion.

### Controlling the Confidence Level

With a confidence level of 0.95, that is, "95% confidence," there is a 0.05 probability that the method produces a confidence interval that does *not* contain the parameter value. In some applications, a 5% chance of an incorrect inference is unacceptable. To increase the chance of a correct inference, we use a larger confidence level, such as 0.99.

### EXAMPLE 5.3    Finding a 99% Confidence Interval

For the data in Example 5.1 (page 112), let's find a 99% confidence interval for the population proportion who favor laws restricting access to abortion. Now, 99% of a normal distribution occurs within 2.58 standard deviations of the mean. So the probability is 0.99 that the sample proportion $\hat{\pi}$ falls within 2.58 standard errors of the population proportion $\pi$. A 99% confidence interval for $\pi$ is $\hat{\pi} \pm 2.58(se)$.

In Example 5.1, the sample proportion was 0.33, with $se = 0.0136$. So the 99% confidence interval is

$$\hat{\pi} \pm 2.58(se) = 0.33 \pm 2.58(0.0136) = 0.33 \pm 0.04, \quad \text{or} \quad (0.29, 0.37).$$

Compared to the 95% confidence interval of (0.30, 0.36), this interval estimate is less precise, being a bit wider. To be more sure of enclosing the parameter, we must sacrifice precision of estimation by using a wider interval.    ∎

The general form for the confidence interval for a population proportion $\pi$ is

$$\hat{\pi} \pm z(se), \quad \text{with} \quad se = \sqrt{\hat{\pi}(1 - \hat{\pi})/n},$$

where $z$ depends on the confidence level. The higher the confidence level, the greater the chance that the confidence interval contains the parameter. High confidence levels are used in practice, so that the chance of error is small. The most common confidence level is 0.95, with 0.99 used when it is more crucial not to make an error.

The $z$-value multiplied by $se$ is the *margin of error*. With greater confidence, the confidence interval is wider because the $z$-score in the margin of error is larger—for instance, $z = 1.96$ for 95% confidence and $z = 2.58$ for 99% confidence.

Why do we settle for anything less than 100% confidence? To be absolutely 100% certain of a correct inference, the interval must contain all possible values for $\pi$. A 100% confidence interval for the population proportion in favor of limiting access to abortion goes from 0.0 to 1.0. This is not helpful. In practice, we settle for less than perfection in order to estimate much more precisely the parameter value. In forming a confidence interval, we compromise between the desired confidence that the inference is correct and the desired precision of estimation. As one gets better, the other gets worse. This is why you would not typically see a 99.9999% confidence interval. It would usually be too wide to say much about where the population parameter falls (its $z$-value is 4.9).

### Larger Sample Sizes Give Narrower Intervals

We'd expect to be able to estimate a population proportion $\pi$ more precisely with a larger sample size. The margin of error is $z(se)$, where $se = \sqrt{\hat{\pi}(1 - \hat{\pi})/n}$. The larger the value of $n$, the smaller the margin of error and the narrower the interval.

To illustrate, suppose that $\hat{\pi} = 0.33$ in Example 5.1 on estimating the proportion who favor restricting legalized abortion was based on $n = 300$, only a fourth as large as the actual sample size of $n = 1200$. Then the estimated standard error of $\hat{\pi}$ is

$$se = \sqrt{\hat{\pi}(1 - \hat{\pi})/n} = \sqrt{(0.33)(0.67)/300} = 0.027,$$

twice as large as the $se$ in Example 5.1. The resulting 95% confidence interval is

$$\hat{\pi} \pm 1.96(se) = 0.33 \pm 1.96(0.027) = 0.33 \pm 0.067.$$

This is twice as wide as the confidence interval formed from the sample of size $n = 1200$.

Since the margin of error is inversely proportional to the square root of $n$, and since $\sqrt{4n} = 2\sqrt{n}$, the sample size must *quadruple* in order to *double* the precision (i.e., halve the width). Section 5.4 shows how to find the sample size needed to achieve a certain precision.

In summary, this subsection and the previous one showed the following:

---

The **width of a confidence interval**

1. Increases as the confidence level increases
2. Decreases as the sample size increases

---

These properties apply to all confidence intervals, not just the one for a proportion.

### Error Probability = 1 − Confidence Level

The probability that an interval estimation method yields a confidence interval that does *not* contain the parameter is called the ***error probability***. This equals 1 minus the confidence level. For confidence level 0.95, the error probability equals $1 - 0.95 = 0.05$. The Greek letter $\alpha$ (alpha) denotes the error probability, and $1 - \alpha$ is the confidence level. For an error probability of $\alpha = 0.05$, the confidence level equals $1 - \alpha = 0.95$.

The $z$-value for the confidence interval is such that the probability is $\alpha$ that $\hat{\pi}$ falls *more than z* standard errors from $\pi$. The $z$-value corresponds to a total probability of $\alpha$ in the two tails of a normal distribution, or $\alpha/2$ (half the error probability) in each tail. For example, for a 95% confidence interval, $\alpha = 0.05$, and the $z$-score is the one with probability $\alpha/2 = 0.05/2 = 0.025$ in each tail. This is $z = 1.96$.

### Confidence Level Is Long-Run Proportion Correct

The confidence level for a confidence interval describes how the method performs when used over and over with many different random samples. The unknown population proportion $\pi$ is a fixed number. A confidence interval constructed from any particular sample either does or does not contain $\pi$. If we repeatedly selected random samples of that size and each time constructed a 95% confidence interval, then in the long run about 95% of the intervals would contain $\pi$. This happens because about 95% of the sample proportions would fall within $1.96(se)$ of $\pi$, as does the $\hat{\pi}$ in line 1 of Figure 5.2 (page 111). Saying that a particular interval contains $\pi$ with "95% confidence" signifies that *in the long run* 95% of such intervals would contain $\pi$. That is, 95% of the time the inference is correct.

Figure 5.3 shows the results of selecting ten separate samples and calculating the sample proportion for each and a 95% confidence interval for the population proportion. The confidence intervals jump around because $\hat{\pi}$ varies from sample to sample. However, nine of the ten intervals contain the population proportion $\pi$. On the average, only about 1 out of 20 times does a 95% confidence interval fail to contain the population parameter.

In practice, we select only *one* sample of some fixed size $n$ and construct *one* confidence interval using the observations in that sample. We do not know whether that confidence interval truly contains $\pi$. Our confidence in that interval is based on long-term properties of the procedure. We can control, by our choice of the confidence level, the chance that the interval contains $\pi$. If an error probability of 0.05 makes us nervous, we can instead form a 99% confidence interval, for which the method makes an error only 1% of the time.

### Large Sample Size Needed for Validity of Method

In practice, the probability that the confidence interval contains $\pi$ is *approximately* equal to the chosen confidence level. The approximation is better for larger samples.

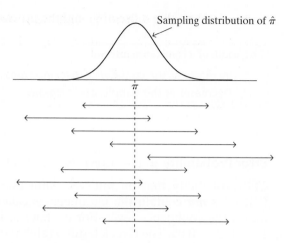

**FIGURE 5.3:** Ten 95% Confidence Intervals for a Population Proportion $\pi$. In the long run, only 5% of the intervals fail to contain $\pi$.

As $n$ increases, the sampling distribution of $\hat{\pi}$ is more closely normal in form, by the Central Limit Theorem. This is what allows us to use $z$-scores from the normal distribution in finding the margin of error. Also as $n$ increases, the *estimated* standard error $se = \sqrt{\hat{\pi}(1 - \hat{\pi})/n}$ gets closer to the *true* standard error $\sigma_{\hat{\pi}} = \sqrt{\pi(1 - \pi)/n}$.

For this reason, the confidence interval formula applies with *large* random samples. How large is "large"? A general guideline states you should have at least 15 observations both in the category of interest and not in it. This is true in most social science studies. In Example 5.1, the counts in the two categories were 396 and 804, so the sample size requirement was easily satisfied. Section 5.4 and Exercise 5.77 show methods that work well when the guideline is not satisfied.

Here is a summary of the confidence interval for a proportion:

---

**Confidence Interval for Population Proportion $\pi$**

For a random sample, a confidence interval for a population proportion $\pi$ based on a sample proportion $\hat{\pi}$ is

$$\hat{\pi} \pm z(se), \quad \text{which is} \quad \hat{\pi} \pm z\sqrt{\frac{\hat{\pi}(1 - \hat{\pi})}{n}}.$$

The $z$-value is such that the probability under a normal curve within $z$ standard errors of the mean equals the confidence level. For 95% and 99% confidence intervals, $z$ equals 1.96 and 2.58. The sample size $n$ should be sufficiently large that at least 15 observations are in the category and at least 15 are not in it.

---

## 5.3 CONFIDENCE INTERVAL FOR A MEAN

We've learned how to construct a confidence interval for a population proportion for categorical data. We now learn how to construct one for the population mean for quantitative data.

### Estimated Standard Error for the Margin of Error

Like the confidence interval for a proportion, the confidence interval for a mean has the form

**Point estimate ± Margin of error,**

where the margin of error is a multiple of the standard error. The point estimate of the population mean $\mu$ is the sample mean, $\bar{y}$. For large random samples, by the Central Limit Theorem, the sampling distribution of $\bar{y}$ is approximately normal. So, for large samples, we can again find a margin of error by multiplying a $z$-score from the normal distribution times the standard error.

From Section 4.5, the standard error of the sample mean equals

$$\sigma_{\bar{y}} = \frac{\sigma}{\sqrt{n}},$$

where $\sigma$ is the population standard deviation. Like the standard error of a sample proportion, this depends on an unknown parameter, in this case $\sigma$. In practice, we estimate $\sigma$ by the sample standard deviation $s$. So, confidence intervals use the *estimated* standard error

$$se = s/\sqrt{n}.$$

### EXAMPLE 5.4    Estimating Mean Number of Sex Partners

Some General Social Surveys ask respondents how many sex partners they have had since their eighteenth birthday. In 2006, when asked how many male sex partners they've had, the 231 females in the sample between the ages of 20 and 29 reported a mean of 4.96. A computer printout summarizes the results for this GSS variable (denoted by NUMMEN):

```
-------------------------------------------------------------------
Variable    n      Mean      StDev     SE Mean      95.0% CI
NUMMEN     231     4.96      6.81        0.45      (4.1, 5.8)
-------------------------------------------------------------------
```

How did software get the standard error reported? How do we interpret it and the confidence interval shown?

The sample standard deviation is $s = 6.81$. The sample size is $n = 231$. So the estimated standard error of the sample mean is

$$se = s/\sqrt{n} = 6.81/\sqrt{231} = 0.45.$$

In several random samples of 231 women in this age group, the sample mean number of male sex partners would vary from sample to sample with a standard deviation of about 0.45.

The 95% confidence interval reported of $(4.1, 5.8)$ is an interval estimate of $\mu$, the mean number of male sex partners since the 18th birthday for the population of adult women in the U.S. of age between 20 and 29. We can be 95% confident that this interval contains $\mu$. The point estimate of $\mu$ is 5.0, and the interval estimate predicts that $\mu$ is no smaller than 4.1 and no greater than 5.8.

This example highlights a couple of things to keep in mind in doing statistical analyses: First, the sample mean of 5.0 and standard deviation of 6.8 suggests that the distribution of the variable NUMMEN is very highly skewed to the right. The mean may be misleading as a measure of center. In fact, a look at the entire distribution of NUMMEN in 2006 (at the GSS Web site) reveals that the median response was 3, perhaps a more useful summary. It's also worth noting that the mode was 1, with 23% of the sample.

Second, the margin of error in confidence intervals refers only to sampling error. Other potential errors include those due to nonresponse or measurement error (lying or giving an inaccurate response). If such errors are not negligible, the margin of error is actually larger than reported by software using standard statistical formulas.

Finally, as mentioned in Chapters 2 and 4, the GSS uses a multistage design that incorporates cluster sampling. [2] For this design, the estimates are not quite as precise as a simple random sample would provide. For simplicity of exposition, in this text we're acting as if the GSS were a simple random sample.    ■

How did software find the margin of error for the confidence interval in the previous example? As with the proportion, for a 95% confidence interval this is roughly two times the estimated standard error. We'll next find the precise margin of error by multiplying *se* by a score that is very similar to a *z*-score unless *n* is quite small.

### The *t* Distribution

We'll now learn about a confidence interval that applies for *any* random sample size. To achieve this generality, it has the disadvantage of assuming that the population distribution is normal. In that case, the sampling distribution of $\bar{y}$ is normal even for small sample sizes. (The right panel of Figure 4.14 on page 93, which showed sampling distributions for various population distributions, illustrated this.)

Suppose we knew the exact standard error of the sample mean, $\sigma_{\bar{y}} = \sigma/\sqrt{n}$. Then, with the additional assumption that the population is normal, with any *n* we could use the formula

$$\bar{y} \pm z\sigma_{\bar{y}}, \quad \text{which is} \quad \bar{y} \pm z\sigma/\sqrt{n},$$

for instance, with $z = 1.96$ for 95% confidence. In practice, we don't know the *population* standard deviation $\sigma$, so we don't know the *exact* standard error. Substituting the *sample* standard deviation *s* for $\sigma$ to get the *estimated* standard error, $se = s/\sqrt{n}$, then introduces extra error. This error can be sizeable when *n* is small. To account for this increased error, we must replace the *z*-score by a slightly larger score, called a *t*-score. The confidence interval is then a bit wider. The *t*-score is like a *z*-score, but it comes from a bell-shaped distribution that is slightly more spread out than the standard normal distribution. This distribution is called the *t **distribution***.

### Properties of the *t* Distribution

Here are the the main properties of the *t* distribution:

- The *t* distribution is bell shaped and symmetric about a mean of 0.
- The standard deviation is a bit larger than 1. The precise value depends on what is called the ***degrees of freedom***, denoted by *df*. The *t* distribution has a slightly different spread for each distinct value of *df*, and different *t*-scores apply for each *df* value.

---

[2]See sda.berkeley.edu/D3/GSS06/Doc/gs06.htm

- For inference about a population mean, the degrees of freedom equal $df = n - 1$, one less than the sample size.
- The $t$ distribution has thicker tails and is more spread out than the standard normal distribution. The larger the $df$ value, however, the more closely it resembles the standard normal. Figure 5.4 illustrates. When $df$ is about 30 or more, the two distributions are nearly identical.

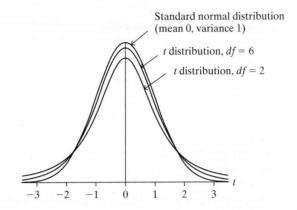

**FIGURE 5.4:** $t$ Distribution Relative to Standard Normal Distribution. The $t$ gets closer to the normal as the degrees of freedom ($df$) increase, and the two distributions are practically identical when $df > 30$.

- A $t$-score multiplied by the estimated standard error gives the margin of error for a confidence interval for the mean.

Table B at the end of the text lists $t$-scores from the $t$ distribution for various right-tail probabilities. Table 5.1 is an excerpt from that table. The column labelled $t_{.025}$ has probability 0.025 in the right tail and a two-tail probability of 0.05. This is the $t$-score used in 95% confidence intervals.

To illustrate, when the sample size is 29, the degrees of freedom are $df = n - 1 = 28$. With $df = 28$, we see that $t_{.025} = 2.048$. This means that 2.5% of the $t$ distribution falls in the right tail above 2.048. By symmetry, 2.5% also falls in the left tail below $-t_{.025} = -2.048$. See Figure 5.5. When $df = 28$, the probability equals 0.95 between

**TABLE 5.1:** Part of Table B Displaying $t$-Scores. The scores have right-tail probabilities of 0.100, 0.050, 0.025, 0.010, 0.005, and 0.001.

| | Confidence Level | | | | | |
|---|---|---|---|---|---|---|
| | 80% | 90% | 95% | 98% | 99% | 99.8% |
| $df$ | $t_{.100}$ | $t_{.050}$ | $t_{.025}$ | $t_{.010}$ | $t_{.005}$ | $t_{.001}$ |
| 1 | 3.078 | 6.314 | 12.706 | 31.821 | 63.657 | 318.3 |
| 10 | 1.372 | 1.812 | 2.228 | 2.764 | 3.169 | 4.144 |
| 28 | 1.313 | 1.701 | 2.048 | 2.467 | 2.763 | 3.408 |
| 30 | 1.310 | 1.697 | 2.042 | 2.457 | 2.750 | 3.385 |
| 100 | 1.290 | 1.660 | 1.984 | 2.364 | 2.626 | 3.174 |
| infinity | 1.282 | 1.645 | 1.960 | 2.326 | 2.576 | 3.090 |

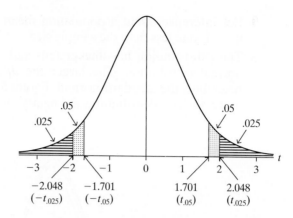

**FIGURE 5.5:** $t$ Distribution with $df = 28$

$-2.048$ and $2.048$. These are the $t$-scores for a 95% confidence interval when $n = 29$. The confidence interval is $\bar{y} \pm 2.048(se)$.

### $t$-Scores in the Confidence Interval for a Mean

Confidence intervals for a mean resemble those for proportions, except that they use the $t$ distribution instead of the standard normal.

---

**Confidence Interval for Population Mean $\mu$**

For a random sample from a normal population distribution, a 95% confidence interval for $\mu$ is

$$\bar{y} \pm t_{.025}(se), \quad \text{with} \quad se = s/\sqrt{n},$$

where $df = n - 1$ for the $t$-score.

---

Like the confidence interval for a proportion, this confidence interval has margin of error that is a score multiplied by the estimated standard error. The main difference is the substitution of the $t$-score for the $z$-score. The $t$ method also makes the assumption of a normal population distribution. This is mainly relevant for small samples. In practice, the population distribution may not be close to normal, and we discuss the importance of this assumption later in the section.

### EXAMPLE 5.5    Estimating Mean Weight Change for Anorexic Girls

This example comes from an experimental study that compared various treatments for young girls suffering from anorexia, an eating disorder. For each girl, weight was measured before and after a fixed period of treatment. The variable of interest was the change in weight, that is, weight at the end of the study minus weight at the beginning of the study. The change in weight was positive if the girl gained weight and negative if she lost weight. The treatments were designed to aid weight gain. The weight changes for the 29 girls undergoing the cognitive behavioral treatment were[3]

$$1.7, \ 0.7, \ -0.1, \ -0.7, \ -3.5, \ 14.9, \ 3.5, \ 17.1, \ -7.6, \ 1.6,$$
$$11.7, \ 6.1, \ 1.1, \ -4.0, \ 20.9, \ -9.1, \ 2.1, \ 1.4, \ -0.3, \ -3.7,$$
$$-1.4, \ -0.8, \ 2.4, \ 12.6, \ 1.9, \ 3.9, \ 0.1, \ 15.4, \ -0.7.$$

---

[3]Courtesy of Prof. Brian Everitt, Institute of Psychiatry, London.

Software used to analyze the data reports the summary results:

```
-----------------------------------------------------------
  Variable  Number of Cases    Mean    SD    SE of Mean
   CHANGE         29           3.01    7.31     1.36
-----------------------------------------------------------
```

Thus, $n = 29$ girls received this treatment. Their mean weight change was $\bar{y} = 3.01$ pounds with a standard deviation (SD) of $s = 7.31$. The sample mean had an estimated standard error of $se = s/\sqrt{n} = 7.31/\sqrt{29} = 1.36$ (reported as SE of Mean).

Let $\mu$ denote the population mean change in weight for the cognitive behavioral treatment, for the population represented by this sample. If this treatment has a beneficial effect, then $\mu$ is positive. Since $n = 29$, $df = n - 1 = 28$. For a 95% confidence interval, we use $t_{.025} = 2.048$. The 95% confidence interval is

$$\bar{y} \pm t_{.025}(se) = 3.01 \pm 2.048(1.36) = 3.0 \pm 2.8, \text{ or } (0.2, 5.8).$$

With 95% confidence, we infer that this interval contains the population mean weight change. It appears that the mean weight change is positive, but it may be rather small in practical terms. However, this experimental study used a volunteer sample, because it is not possible to identify and randomly sample a population of anorexic girls. Because of this, inferences are tentative and "95% confidence" in the results may be overly optimistic. The results are more convincing if researchers can argue that the sample was representative of the population. The study did employ randomization in assigning girls to three therapies (only one of which is considered here), which is reassuring for analyses conducted later in the text comparing therapies.

Another caveat about our conclusion is shown by Figure 5.6, a histogram that software shows for the data. This reveals that the data are skewed to the right. The assumption of a normal population distribution may be violated—more about that later. The median weight change is only 1.4 pounds, somewhat less than the mean of 3.0 because of the skew to the right. The sample median is another indication that the size of the effect could be small.                                     ■

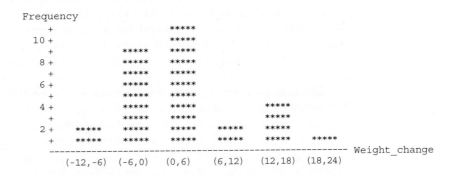

**FIGURE 5.6:** Histogram of Weight Change Values for Anorexia Study

## Effect of Confidence Level and Sample Size

We've used the $t$ distribution to find a 95% confidence interval. Other confidence levels use the same formula but with a different $t$-score.

Let $\alpha$ denote the error probability. This is the probability that the method yields a confidence interval that does not contain $\mu$. The confidence interval uses the $t$-score with tail probability $\alpha/2$ in each tail. For a 99% confidence interval, for instance, $\alpha = 1 - 0.99 = 0.01$, so $\alpha/2 = 0.005$, and the appropriate $t$-score is $t_{.005}$ for the specified $df$ value.

To be safer in estimating the population mean weight change for the anorexia study in Example 5.5, we could instead use a 99% confidence interval. Since $df = 28$ when $n = 29$, the $t$-score is $t_{.005} = 2.763$. The standard error does not change. The 99% confidence interval is

$$\bar{y} \pm 2.763(se) = 3.01 \pm 2.763(1.36), \quad \text{which is} \quad (-0.7, 6.8).$$

The confidence interval is wider than the 95% interval of (0.2, 5.8). This is the cost of having greater confidence. The 99% confidence interval contains 0. This tells us it is plausible, at the 99% confidence level, that the population mean change is 0, that is, that the therapy may not result in *any* change in the mean weight.

Like the width of the confidence interval for a proportion, the width of a confidence interval for a mean also depends on the sample size $n$. Larger sample sizes result in narrower intervals.

### Robustness for Violations of Normal Population Assumption

The assumptions for the confidence interval for a mean are (1) that randomization is used for collecting the sample, and (2) that the population distribution is normal. Under the normality assumption, the sampling distribution of $\bar{y}$ is normal even for small $n$. Likewise, the $z$-score measuring the number of standard errors that $\bar{y}$ falls from $\mu$ then has the standard normal distribution. In practice, when we use the *estimated* standard error $se = s/\sqrt{n}$ (rather than the true one, $\sigma/\sqrt{n}$), the number of $se$ that $\bar{y}$ falls from $\mu$ has the $t$ distribution.

The confidence interval in Example 5.5 estimated the mean weight change for anorexic girls. The histogram of the weight change data shown above is not precise when $n$ is as small as in that example ($n = 29$), but it showed evidence of skew. Generally, the normal population assumption seems worrisome, because many variables in the social sciences have distributions that are far from normal.

A statistical method is said to be **robust** with respect to a particular assumption if it performs adequately even when that assumption is violated. Statisticians have shown that the confidence interval for a mean using the $t$ distribution is robust against violations of the normal population assumption. Even if the population is not normal, confidence intervals based on the $t$ distribution still work quite well, especially when $n$ exceeds about 15. As the sample size gets larger, the normal population assumption becomes less important because of the Central Limit Theorem. The sampling distribution of the sample mean is then bell shaped even when the population distribution is not. The actual probability that the 95% confidence interval method provides a correct inference is close to 0.95 and gets closer as $n$ increases.

An important case when the method does not work well is when the data are extremely skewed or contain extreme outliers. Partly this is because of the effect on the method, but also because the mean itself may not then be a representative summary of the center. For this reason, the confidence interval about number of sex partners reported in Example 5.4 (page 117) has limited usefulness.

In practice, assumptions are rarely perfectly satisfied. Thus, knowing whether a statistical method is robust when a particular assumption is violated is important. The $t$ confidence interval method is *not* robust to violations of the randomization assumption. The $t$ method, like all inferential statistical methods, has questionable validity if the method for producing the data did not use randomization.

### Standard Normal Is *t* Distribution with *df* = Infinity

Look at the table of *t*-scores (Table B in the Appendix), part of which was shown in Table 5.1. As *df* increases, you move down the table. The *t*-score decreases and gets closer and closer to the *z*-score for a standard normal distribution. This reflects the *t* distribution becoming less spread out and more similar in appearance to the standard normal distribution as *df* increases. You can think of the standard normal distribution as a *t* distribution with $df = \infty$ (infinity).

For instance, when *df* increases from 1 to 100 in Table 5.1, the *t*-score $t_{.025}$ with right-tail probability equal to 0.025 decreases from 12.706 to 1.984. The *z*-score with right-tail probability of 0.025 for the standard normal distribution is $z = 1.96$. The *t*-scores are not printed for $df > 100$, but they are close to the *z*-scores. The last row of Table 5.1 and Table B lists the *z*-scores for various confidence levels, opposite $df = \infty$.

You can get *t*-scores for any *df* value using software and many calculators, so you are not restricted to Table B. For *df* values larger than shown in Table B (above 100), you can use a *z*-score to approximate the *t*-score. For a 95% confidence interval you will then use

$$\bar{y} \pm 1.96(se) \quad \text{instead of} \quad \bar{y} \pm t_{.025}(se).$$

You will not get *exactly* the same result that software would give, but it will be close enough for practical purposes. For instance, to get the confidence interval for the mean number of sex partners in Example 5.4, for which the GSS sample had $n = 231$, software uses the *t*-score for $df = 231 - 1 = 230$, which is 1.97. This is very close to the *z*-score of 1.96 from the standard normal distribution.

Why does the *t* distribution look more like the standard normal distribution as *n* (and hence *df*) increases? Because *s* is increasingly precise as a point estimate of $\sigma$ in approximating the true standard error $\sigma / \sqrt{n}$ by $se = s / \sqrt{n}$. The additional sampling error for small samples results in the *t* sampling distribution being more spread out than the standard normal.

The *t* distribution has just celebrated its 100th anniversary. It was discovered in 1908 by the statistician and chemist W. S. Gosset. At the time, Gosset was employed by Guinness Breweries in Dublin, Ireland, designing experiments pertaining to the selection, cultivation, and treatment of barley and hops for the brewing process. Due to company policy forbidding the publishing of trade secrets, Gosset used the pseudonym *Student* in articles he wrote about his discovery. The *t* distribution became known as *Student's t*, a name still sometimes used today. Confidence intervals were not introduced, however, until a series of articles by Jerzy Neyman and Egon Pearson beginning in 1928.

### A Caveat about Using Software

The examples in this section used output from statistical software to help us analyze data. We'll do this increasingly in future chapters as we cover methods that require substantial computation. You should use software yourself for some of the exercises to get a feel for how researchers analyze data in practice. Any particular software has a huge number of options and it's easy to *misuse* it. Just because results appear on an output window does not mean they are the correct ones or that the assumptions were sufficiently met to do that analysis.

When you start to use software for a given method, we suggest that you first use it for the example of that method in this book. Note whether you get the same results, as a way to check whether you are using the software correctly.

## 5.4 CHOICE OF SAMPLE SIZE

Polling organizations such as the Gallup poll take samples that typically contain about a thousand subjects. This is large enough for a sample proportion estimate to have a margin of error of about 0.03. At first glance, it seems astonishing that a sample of this size from a population of perhaps many millions is adequate for predicting outcomes of elections, summarizing opinions on controversial issues, showing relative sizes of television audiences, and so forth.

Recall that the margin of error for a confidence interval depends on the *standard error* of the point estimate. Thus, the basis for this inferential power lies in the formulas for the standard errors. As long as the sampling is properly executed, good estimates result from relatively small samples, no matter how large the population size (in fact, the methods actually treat the population size as infinite; see Exercise 57 in Chapter 4). Polling organizations use sampling methods that are more complex than simple random samples, often involving some clustering and/or stratification. However, the standard errors under their sampling plans are approximated reasonably well either by the formulas for simple random samples or by inflating those formulas by a certain factor (such as by 25%) to reflect the sample design effect.

Before data collection begins, most studies attempt to determine the sample size that will provide a certain degree of precision in estimation. A relevant measure is the value of *n* for which a confidence interval for the parameter has margin of error equal to some specified value. This section shows how they do this. The key results for finding the sample size are as follows:

- The *margin of error* depends directly on the *standard error* of the sampling distribution of the point estimator.
- The *standard error* itself depends on the *sample size*.

### Sample Size for Estimating Proportions

To determine the sample size, we must decide on the margin of error desired. In some studies, highly precise estimation is not as important as in others. An exit poll in a close election requires a precise estimate to predict the winner. If, on the other hand, the goal is to estimate the proportion of residents of Syracuse, New York, who have health insurance, a larger margin of error might be acceptable. So we must first decide whether the margin of error should be about 0.03 (three percentage points), 0.05, or whatever.

We must also specify the *probability* with which the margin of error is achieved. For example, we might decide that the error in estimating a population proportion should not exceed 0.04, with 0.95 probability. This probability must be stated, since with any sample size the error is no more than 0.04 with *some* probability, though perhaps a small one.

The next example illustrates sample size determination for estimating a population proportion.

### EXAMPLE 5.6    Sample Size for a Survey on Single-Parent Children

A social scientist wanted to estimate the proportion of school children in Boston who live with only one parent. Since her report was to be published, she wanted a reasonably precise estimate. However, since her funding was limited, she did not want to collect a larger sample than necessary. She decided to use a sample size such that, with probability 0.95, the error would not exceed 0.04. So she needed to determine *n* such that a 95% confidence interval for $\pi$ equals $\hat{\pi} \pm 0.04$.

Since the sampling distribution of the sample proportion $\hat{\pi}$ is approximately normal, $\hat{\pi}$ falls within 1.96 standard errors of $\pi$ with probability 0.95. Thus, if the sample size is such that 1.96 standard errors equals 0.04, then with probability 0.95, $\hat{\pi}$ falls within 0.04 units of $\pi$. See Figure 5.7.

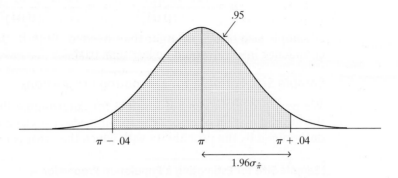

**FIGURE 5.7:** Sampling Distribution of $\hat{\pi}$ with the Error of Estimation No Greater than 0.04, with Probability 0.95

Recall that the true standard error is $\sigma_{\hat{\pi}} = \sqrt{\pi(1 - \pi)/n}$. How do we find the value of $n$ that provides a value of $\sigma_{\hat{\pi}}$ for which $0.04 = 1.96\sigma_{\hat{\pi}}$? We must solve for $n$ in the expression

$$0.04 = 1.96\sqrt{\frac{\pi(1 - \pi)}{n}}.$$

Multiplying both sides of the expression by $\sqrt{n}$ and dividing both sides by 0.04, we get

$$\sqrt{n} = \frac{1.96\sqrt{\pi(1 - \pi)}}{0.04}.$$

Squaring both sides, we obtain the result

$$n = \frac{(1.96)^2\pi(1 - \pi)}{(0.04)^2}.$$

Now we face a problem. We want to select $n$ for the purpose of estimating the population proportion $\pi$, but this formula requires the value of $\pi$. This is because the spread of the sampling distribution depends on $\pi$. The distribution is less spread out, and it is easier to estimate $\pi$, if $\pi$ is close to 0 or 1 than if it is near 0.50. Since $\pi$ is unknown, we must substitute an educated guess for it in this equation to solve for $n$.

The largest possible value for $\pi(1 - \pi)$ occurs when $\pi = 0.50$. Then $\pi(1 - \pi) = 0.25$. In fact, $\pi(1 - \pi)$ is fairly close to 0.25 unless $\pi$ is quite far from 0.50. For example, $\pi(1 - \pi) = 0.24$ when $\pi = 0.40$ or $\pi = 0.60$, and $\pi(1 - \pi) = 0.21$ when $\pi = 0.70$ or $\pi = 0.30$. Thus, another possible approach is to substitute $\pi = 0.50$ in the above equation. This yields

$$n = \frac{(1.96)^2\pi(1 - \pi)}{(0.04)^2} = \frac{(1.96)^2(0.50)(0.50)}{(0.04)^2} = 600.$$

This approach ensures that with confidence level 0.95, the margin of error will not exceed 0.04, no matter what the value of $\pi$. ∎

Obtaining $n$ by setting $\pi = 0.50$ is the "safe" approach. But this $n$ value is excessively large if $\pi$ is not near 0.50. Suppose that based on other studies the social scientist believed that $\pi$ was no higher than 0.25. Then an adequate sample size is

$$n = \frac{(1.96)^2\pi(1 - \pi)}{(0.04)^2} = \frac{(1.96)^2(0.25)(0.75)}{(0.04)^2} = 450.$$

A sample size of 600 is larger than needed. With it, the margin of error for a 95% confidence interval would be less than 0.04.

## Sample Size Formula for Estimating Proportions

We next provide a general formula for determining the sample size. Let $M$ denote the desired margin of error. The formula also uses a general $z$-score (in place of 1.96) determined by the probability with which the error is no greater than $M$.

---

**Sample Size for Estimating a Population Proportion $\pi$**

The random sample size $n$ having margin of error $M$ in estimating $\pi$ by the sample proportion $\hat{\pi}$ is

$$n = \pi(1 - \pi)\left(\frac{z}{M}\right)^2.$$

The $z$-score is the one for a confidence interval with the desired confidence level, such as $z = 1.96$ for level 0.95. You need to guess $\pi$ or take the safe approach of setting $\pi = 0.50$.

---

To illustrate, suppose the study about single-parent children wanted to estimate the population proportion to within 0.08 with a probability of at least 0.95. Then the margin of error equals $M = 0.08$, and $z = 1.96$. The required sample size using the safe approach is

$$n = \pi(1 - \pi)\left(\frac{z}{M}\right)^2 = (0.50)(0.50)\left(\frac{1.96}{0.08}\right)^2 = 150.$$

This sample size of 150 is one-fourth the sample size of 600 necessary to guarantee a margin of error no greater than $M = 0.04$. Reducing the margin of error by a factor of one-half requires quadrupling the sample size.

## Sample Size for Estimating Means

An analogous result holds for estimating a population mean $\mu$. We want to determine how large $n$ needs to be so that the sampling distribution of $\bar{y}$ has margin of error $M$. Figure 5.8 illustrates. It shows how the sampling distribution gets narrower as $n$ increases until, at the required $n$, 95% falls within the chosen margin of error. A derivation using the large-sample normal sampling distribution of $\bar{y}$ yields the following result:

---

**Sample Size for Estimating a Population Mean $\mu$**

The random sample size $n$ having margin of error $M$ in estimating $\mu$ by the sample mean $\bar{y}$ is

$$n = \sigma^2\left(\frac{z}{M}\right)^2.$$

The $z$-score is the one for a confidence interval with the desired confidence level, such as $z = 1.96$ for level 0.95. You need to guess the population standard deviation $\sigma$.

---

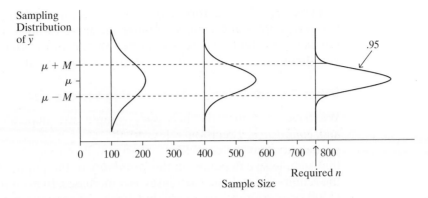

**FIGURE 5.8:** Determining $n$ So That $\bar{y}$ Has Probability 0.95 of Falling within a Margin of Error of $M$ Units of the Population Mean $\mu$

The greater the spread of the population distribution, as measured by its standard deviation $\sigma$, the larger the sample size needed to achieve a certain margin of error. If subjects have little variation (i.e., $\sigma$ is small), we need less data than if they are highly heterogenous. In practice, $\sigma$ is unknown. We need to substitute an educated guess for it, perhaps based on a previous study.

A slight complication is that since we don't know $\sigma$, for inference we actually use the $t$ distribution rather than the standard normal. But if we don't know $n$, we also don't know the degrees of freedom and the $t$-score. We saw in Table B, however, that unless $df$ is small, the $t$-score is close to the $z$-score. So we won't worry about this complication. The approximation of replacing an unknown $t$-score in the sample size formula by a $z$-score is usually much less than that involved in having to use an educated guess for $\sigma$.

### EXAMPLE 5.7   Estimating Mean Education of Native Americans

A study is planned of elderly Native Americans. Variables to be studied include educational level. How large a sample size is needed to estimate the mean number of years of attained education correct to within 1 year with probability 0.99?

Suppose the study has no prior information about the standard deviation of educational attainment for Native Americans. As a guess, perhaps nearly all values of this variable fall within a range of about 15 years, such as between 5 and 20 years. If this distribution is approximately normal, then since the range from $\mu - 3\sigma$ to $\mu + 3\sigma$ contains nearly all of a normal distribution, the range of 15 would equal about $6\sigma$. Then, $15/6 = 2.5$ is a guess for $\sigma$.

Now, for 99% confidence, the error probability is 0.01. The $z$-score is the one with probability $0.01/2 = 0.005$ in each tail, which is 2.58. Since the desired margin of error is $M = 1$ year, the required sample size is

$$n = \sigma^2 \left( \frac{z}{M} \right)^2 = (2.5)^2 \left( \frac{2.58}{1} \right)^2 = 42.$$

A more cautious approach would select a larger value for $\sigma$. For example, if the range from 5 to 20 years encloses only about 95% of the education values, we could treat this as the range from $\mu - 2\sigma$ to $\mu + 2\sigma$ and set $15 = 4\sigma$. Then $\sigma = 15/4 = 3.75$ and $n = (3.75)^2(2.58/1)^2 = 94$. If $\sigma$ is actually less than 3.75, the margin of error of a 99% confidence interval with $n = 94$ observations will be even less than 1. ∎

These sample size formulas apply to simple and systematic random sampling. Cluster samples and complex multistage samples must usually be larger to achieve the same precision, whereas stratified samples can often be smaller. In such cases, you should seek guidance from a statistical consultant.

## Other Considerations in Determining Sample Size

We have seen that the necessary sample size depends on the desired *precision* and *confidence*. Precision refers to the margin of error. Confidence refers to the probability that the confidence interval will contain the parameter. We've also seen that sample size depends on the *variability* in the population. For estimating means, the required sample size increases as $\sigma$ increases. In most social surveys, large samples (1000 or more) are necessary, but for homogeneous populations (e.g., residents of nursing homes), smaller samples are often adequate due to reduced population variability.

From a practical point of view, other considerations also affect the sample size. One consideration is the *complexity of analysis* planned. The more complex the analysis, such as the more variables analyzed simultaneously, the larger the sample needed. To analyze a single variable using a mean, a relatively small sample might be adequate. Planned comparisons of several groups using complex multivariate methods, however, require a larger sample. For instance, Example 5.7 showed we may be able to estimate mean educational attainment quite well with only 42 people. But if we also wanted to compare the mean for several ethnic and racial groups and study how the mean depends on other variables such as gender, parents' income and education, and size of the community, a larger sample would be needed.

Another consideration concerns time, money, and other *resources*. Larger samples are more expensive and more time consuming. They may require greater resources than are available. For example, sample size formulas might suggest that 1000 cases provide the desired precision. Perhaps you can afford to gather only 400. Should you go ahead with the smaller sample and sacrifice precision and/or confidence, or should you give up unless you find additional resources? You may need to answer questions such as, "Is it really crucial to study all groups, or can I reduce the sample by focusing on a couple of groups?"

In summary, no simple formula can always give an appropriate sample size. While sample size is an important matter, its choice depends on resources and the analyses planned. This requires careful judgment. A final caveat: If the study is carried out poorly, or if data are never obtained for a substantial percentage of the sample, or if some subjects lie, or if some observations are incorrectly recorded by the data collector or by the statistical analyst, then the actual probability of accuracy to within the specified margin of error may be much less than intended. When someone claims to achieve a certain precision and confidence, be skeptical unless you know that the study was substantially free of such problems.

## What If You Have Only a Small Sample?*

Sometimes, because of financial or ethical factors, it's just not possible to take as large a sample as we'd like. If $n$ must be small, how does that affect the validity of confidence interval methods? The $t$ methods for a mean can be used with any $n$. When $n$ is small, though, you need to be cautious to look for extreme outliers or great departures from the normal population assumption (such as implied by highly skewed data). These can affect the results and the validity of using the mean as a summary of center.

Recall that the confidence interval formula for a proportion requires at least 15 observations of each type. Otherwise, the sampling distribution of the sample proportion need not be close to normal, and the estimate $se = \sqrt{\hat{\pi}(1 - \hat{\pi})/n}$ of the true standard error $\sqrt{\pi(1 - \pi)/n}$ may be poor. As a result, the confidence interval formula works poorly, as the next example shows.

### EXAMPLE 5.8    What Proportion of Students Are Vegetarians?

For a class project, a student randomly sampled 20 fellow students at the University of Florida to estimate the proportion at that university who were vegetarians. Of the 20 students she sampled, none were vegetarians. Let $\pi$ denote the population proportion of vegetarians at the university. The sample proportion was $\hat{\pi} = 0/20 = 0.0$.

When $\hat{\pi} = 0.0$, then $se = \sqrt{\hat{\pi}(1 - \hat{\pi})/n} = \sqrt{(0.0)(1.0)/20} = 0.0$. The 95% confidence interval for the population proportion of vegetarians is

$$\hat{\pi} \pm 1.96(se) = 0.0 \pm 1.96(0.0), \quad \text{which is} \quad 0.0 \pm 0.0, \quad \text{or} \quad (0.0, 0.0).$$

The student concluded she could be 95% confident that $\pi$ falls between 0 and 0. But this confidence interval formula is valid only if the sample has at least 15 vegetarians and at least 15 nonvegetarians. The sample did not have at least 15 vegetarians, so the method is not appropriate. ∎

For small samples, the confidence interval formula is still valid if we use it after adding 4 artificial observations, 2 of each type. The sample of size $n = 20$ in Example 5.8 had 0 vegetarians and 20 nonvegetarians. We can apply the confidence interval formula with $0 + 2 = 2$ vegetarians and $20 + 2 = 22$ nonvegetarians. The value of the sample size for the formula is then $n = 24$. Applying the formula, we get

$$\hat{\pi} = 2/24 = 0.083, \quad se = \sqrt{\hat{\pi}(1 - \hat{\pi})/n} = \sqrt{(0.083)(0.917)/24} = 0.056.$$

The resulting 95% confidence interval is

$$\hat{\pi} \pm 1.96(se), \quad \text{which is} \quad 0.083 \pm 1.96(0.056), \quad \text{or} \quad (-0.03, 0.19).$$

A proportion cannot be negative, so we report the interval as (0.0, 0.19). We can be 95% confident that the proportion of vegetarians at the University of Florida is no greater than 0.19.

Why do we add 2 to the counts of the two types? The reason is that the confidence interval then approximates one based on a more complex method (described in Exercise 5.77) that does not require estimating the standard error.[4]

## 5.5    CONFIDENCE INTERVALS FOR MEDIAN AND OTHER PARAMETERS*

We've focused so far on estimating means and proportions. Chapter 3 showed, though, that other statistics are also useful for describing data. These other statistics also have sampling distributions. For large random samples, their sampling distributions are also approximately normal and are the basis of confidence intervals for population measures. We illustrate in this section for the median.

---

[4]See article by A. Agresti and B. Coull (who proposed this confidence interval), *American Statistician*, vol. 52, 1998, pp. 119–126.

### Inefficiency of the Sample Median for Normal Data

When the population distribution is normal and the sample is random, the standard error of the sample median has formula similar to the one for the sample mean. The standard error equals $1.25\sigma/\sqrt{n}$.

The population median for a normal distribution equals the population mean $\mu$. So the sample median and sample mean are both point estimates of the same number. The sample median is not as efficient as the sample mean because its standard error is 25% larger. When the population distribution is approximately normal, the sample mean is a better estimator of the center of that distribution. This is one reason the mean is more commonly used than the median in statistical inference.

When the population distribution is highly skewed, the population median is often a more useful summary than the population mean. We use the sample median to estimate the population median. However, the standard error formula $1.25\sigma/\sqrt{n}$ is valid only when the population distribution is approximately normal.

### Large-Sample Confidence Interval for Median

The confidence interval for the median discussed next is valid for large samples ($n$ at least about 20–30). It requires no assumption about the population distribution other than it is essentially continuous. Its logic utilizes ideas of this chapter.

By definition, the probability $\pi$ that a randomly selected observation falls below the median is 0.50. So, for a random sample of size $n$, the sample proportion $\hat{\pi}$ falling below the median has mean 0.50 and standard error $\sigma_{\hat{\pi}} = \sqrt{\pi(1 - \pi)/n} = \sqrt{0.50(0.50)/n} = 0.50/\sqrt{n}$. In particular, the probability is about 0.95 that the sample proportion of observations falling below the median is within two standard errors, or $1/\sqrt{n}$, of 0.50. The sample *number* of observations falling below the median is $n$ times the sample proportion. So the probability is about 0.95 that the number of observations falling below the median is within $n(1/\sqrt{n}) = \sqrt{n}$ of half the sample and the number of observations falling *above* the median is within $n(1/\sqrt{n}) = \sqrt{n}$ of half the sample.

Now, for an ordered sample of size $n$, the median is the middle measurement, which has index $(n + 1)/2$. The observation with index $(n + 1)/2 - \sqrt{n}$ is the lower endpoint of a 95% confidence interval for the median. The observation with index $(n + 1)/2 + \sqrt{n}$ is the upper endpoint.

### EXAMPLE 5.9    Estimating Median Shelf Time in a Library

A librarian at the University of Florida wanted to estimate various characteristics of books in one of the university's special collections. Among the questions of interest were, "How old is a typical book in the collection?" and "How long has it been since a typical book has been checked out?" We suspected that the distributions of such variables might be heavily skewed to the right. So we used the median to describe the center.

Table 5.2 shows data on $P$ = number of years since publication of book and $C$ = number of years since book checked out, for a systematic random sample of 54 books from the collection. Figure 5.9 shows a SPSS box plot for the $P$ values. The five starred values represent extreme outliers falling more than 3.0 IQR above the upper quartile. The sample median, which is 17, is more representative of the data than the sample mean of 22.6. Let's construct a 95% confidence interval for the population median of the distribution of $P$.

**TABLE 5.2:** Number of Years since Publication (*P*) and Number of Years since Checked Out (*C*) for 54 Books

| C | P | C | P | C | P | C | P | C | P |
|---|---|---|---|---|---|---|---|---|---|
| 1 | 3 | 9 | 9 | 4 | 4 | 1 | 18 | 1 | 5 |
| 30 | 30 | 0 | 17 | 2 | 7 | 0 | 12 | 1 | 13 |
| 7 | 19 | 5 | 5 | 47 | 47 | 3 | 15 | 9 | 17 |
| 11 | 140 | 2 | 19 | 5 | 8 | 2 | 10 | 11 | 18 |
| 1 | 5 | 1 | 22 | 1 | 11 | 5 | 19 | 2 | 3 |
| 2 | 97 | 0 | 10 | 1 | 21 | 7 | 7 | 4 | 19 |
| 4 | 4 | 11 | 11 | 5 | 20 | 14 | 14 | 5 | 43 |
| 2 | 19 | 10 | 10 | 10 | 10 | 0 | 18 | 10 | 17 |
| 4 | 13 | 17 | 71 | 8 | 19 | 0 | 17 | 48 | 48 |
| 2 | 19 | 11 | 11 | 6 | 6 | 7 | 20 | 4 | 4 |
| 92 | 92 | 4 | 44 | 1 | 5 | 1 | 54 | | |

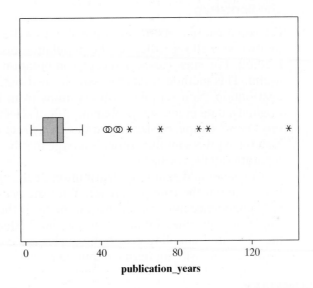

**FIGURE 5.9:** Box Plot for Number of Years since Publication for Sample of Library Books

For $n = 54$, the endpoints of a 95% confidence interval have indices

$$\frac{n+1}{2} \pm \sqrt{n} = \frac{54+1}{2} \pm \sqrt{54} = 27.5 \pm 7.3, \text{ or } (20.2, 34.8).$$

The confidence interval consists of the 20th smallest and 35th smallest (20th largest) values of the variable.

For a small sample such as this, it is simple to identify ordered values from a stem-and-leaf plot. Table 5.3 shows the part of this plot for the smallest 44 of the 54 observations, splitting stems into two. The 20th smallest observation equals 11 and the 35th smallest observation equals 19. The 95% confidence interval equals (11, 19). We can be 95% confident that the median time since publication is at least

**TABLE 5.3**: Lower Part of Stem-and-Leaf Plot for Number of Years since Publication. This does not show the long right tail of the distribution, which is not needed to find the confidence interval for the median.

| Stem | Leaf |
|------|------|
| 0 | 3  3  4  4  4 |
| 0 | 5  5  5  5  6  7  7  8  9 |
| 1 | 0  0  0  0  1  1  1  2  3  3  4 |
| 1 | 5  7  7  7  7  8  8  8  9  9  9  9  9  9  9 |
| 2 | 0  0  1  2 |

11 years and no greater than 19 years. To get a narrower interval, we need a larger sample size. ∎

### The Bootstrap

For some parameters, it is not possible to write down a confidence interval formula that works well regardless of the population distribution or sample size or sampling method. For such cases, a recent computational invention called the **bootstrap** is useful. This method treats the sample distribution as if it were the true population distribution. You sample $n$ observations from this distribution, where each of the original $n$ data points has probability $1/n$ of selection for each "new" observation. For this "new" sample of size $n$, you then construct the point estimate of the parameter. You repeat this sampling process a large number of times, for instance selecting 1000 separate samples of size $n$.

The generated sampling distribution of the point estimate values provides information about the true parameter. With the *percentile* method of bootstrapping, the 95% confidence interval for the parameter is the 95% central set of estimate values. These are the ones falling between the 2.5th percentile and 97.5th percentile of the generated sampling distribution. This is a computationally intensive process, but easily feasible with modern computing power.

## 5.6   CHAPTER SUMMARY

This chapter presented methods of estimation, focusing on the population mean $\mu$ for quantitative variables and the population proportion $\pi$ for categorical variables.

- A **point estimate** is the best single guess for the parameter value. The point estimates of the population mean $\mu$, standard deviation $\sigma$, and proportion $\pi$ are the sample values, $\bar{y}$, $s$, and $\hat{\pi}$.

- An **interval estimate**, called a **confidence interval**, is an interval of numbers within which the parameter is believed to fall. Confidence intervals for a population mean $\mu$ and for a population proportion $\pi$ have the form

$$\text{Point estimate } \pm \text{ Margin of error,}$$
$$\text{with} \quad \text{Margin of error} = \text{score} \times (se),$$

where $se$ is the estimated standard error. The score multiplied by $se$ is a $z$-score from the normal distribution for confidence intervals for proportions and a $t$-score from the $t$ distribution for confidence intervals for a mean.

- The probability that the method yields an interval that contains the parameter is called the **confidence level**. This is controlled by the choice of the $z$- or $t$-score in the margin of error. Increasing the confidence level entails the use of a larger score and, hence, the sacrifice of a wider interval.
- The **$t$ distribution** looks like the standard normal distribution, having a mean of 0 but being a bit more spread out. Its spread is determined by the **degrees of freedom**, which equal $n - 1$ for inference about a mean.
- The width of a confidence interval also depends on the standard error of the sampling distribution of the point estimate. Larger sample sizes produce smaller standard errors and narrower confidence intervals and, hence, more precise estimates.

Confidence intervals assume random sampling. For large samples, they do not need an assumption about the population distribution because the sampling distribution is roughly normal even if the population is highly nonnormal, by the Central Limit Theorem. Table 5.4 summarizes estimation methods.

**TABLE 5.4:** Summary of Estimation Methods for Means and Proportions

| Parameter | Point Estimate | Estimated Standard Error | Confidence Interval | Sample Size to Estimate to Within $M$ |
|---|---|---|---|---|
| Mean $\mu$ | $\bar{y}$ | $se = \frac{s}{\sqrt{n}}$ | $\bar{y} \pm t(se)$ | $n = \sigma^2 \left(\frac{z}{M}\right)^2$ |
| Proportion $\pi$ | $\hat{\pi}$ | $se = \sqrt{\frac{\hat{\pi}(1-\hat{\pi})}{n}}$ | $\hat{\pi} \pm z(se)$ | $n = \pi(1 - \pi)\left(\frac{z}{M}\right)^2$ |

*Note*: $z = 1.96$ for 95% confidence; for error probability $\alpha$ and confidence level $(1 - \alpha)$, $z$-score or $t$-score has right-tail probability $\alpha/2$ (e.g., $\alpha/2 = 0.025$ for 95% confidence).

Table 5.4 also shows formulas for the sample size needed to achieve a desired margin of error $M$. You must select $M$ and the confidence level, which determines the $z$-score. Also, you must substitute a guess for the population standard deviation $\sigma$ to determine the sample size for estimating a population mean $\mu$. You must substitute a guess for the population proportion $\pi$ to determine the sample size for estimating $\pi$. Substituting $\pi = 0.50$ guarantees that the sample size is large enough to give the desired precision and confidence.

## PROBLEMS

### Practicing the Basics

**5.1.** Of 577,006 people involved in motor vehicle accidents in Florida in a recent year, 412,878 were wearing seat belts (*Source*: Florida Department of Highway Safety and Motor Vehicles). Find a point estimate of the population proportion of Florida motorists wearing seat belts.

**5.2.** In response to the GSS question in 2006 about the number of hours daily spent watching TV, the responses by the seven subjects who identified themselves as Hindus were 2, 3, 2, 1, 0, 1, 4, 3.

(a) Find a point estimate of the population mean for Hindus.

(b) The margin of error for this point estimate is 1.1. Explain what this represents.

**5.3.** An Associated Press story (March 8, 2006) about a survey commissioned by the American Medical Association of a nationwide random sample of 644 college women or graduates ages 17 to 35 estimated that a proportion of 0.74 of women on Spring Break use drinking as an excuse for outrageous behavior, including public nudity and dancing on tables. Find the standard error of this estimate, and interpret.

**5.4.** A national survey conducted in July 2006 by Pew Forum on Religion & Public Life asked whether the subject favored allowing homosexual couples to enter into civil unions—legal agreements that would give them many of the same rights as married couples. Of 2003 adults interviewed, 54% said *yes*, 42% said *no*, and 4% had no opinion. Find the estimated standard error for the sample proportion answering *yes*. Interpret it.

**5.5.** When polled in 2006 and asked whether Turkey should be included in the European Union if it met all conditions set by the EU, the percentage who said *yes* was 51% in Denmark ($n = 1008$) and 42% in the UK ($n = 1312$). For the Denmark result, the report stated that the margin of error is plus or minus 3.1%. Explain how they got this result.

**5.6.** One question (coded EQUALIZE) on a recent GSS asked, "Do you think that it should be government's responsibility to reduce income differences between the rich and the poor?" Those answering *yes* included 90 of the 142 subjects who called themselves "strong Democrat" in political party identification and 26 of the 102 who called themselves "strong Republican."
  **(a)** Find the point estimate of the population proportion who would answer *yes* for each group.
  **(b)** The 95% confidence interval for the population proportion of *yes* responses is (0.55, 0.71) for strong Democrats and (0.17, 0.34) for strong Republicans. Explain how to interpret the intervals.

**5.7.** The GSS asks whether you agree or disagree with the following statement: "It is much better for everyone involved if the man is the achiever outside the home and the woman takes care of the home and family" (variable FEFAM). The sample proportion agreeing was 0.66 in 1977 and 0.36 in 2004 ($n = 883$).
  **(a)** Show that the estimated standard error in 2004 was 0.016.
  **(b)** Show that the margin of error for a 95% confidence interval using the estimate in 2004 was 0.03. Interpret.
  **(c)** Construct the 95% confidence interval for 2004, and interpret it.

**5.8.** A recent GSS asked, "If the wife in a family wants children, but the husband decides that he does not want any children, is it all right for the husband to refuse to have children?" Of 598 respondents, 366 said *yes* and 232 said *no*. Show that a 99% confidence interval for the population proportion who would say *yes* is (0.56, 0.66).

**5.9.** In 2006, the Florida Poll conducted by Florida International University asked whether current environmental regulations are too strict or not too strict. Of 1200 respondents, 229 said they were too strict. Find and interpret a (a) 95%, (b) 99% confidence interval for a relevant parameter at the time of that survey.

**5.10.** When a recent GSS asked whether the government should impose strict laws to make industry do less damage to the environment, a 95% confidence interval for the population proportion responding *yes* was (0.87, 0.90). Would a 99% confidence interval be wider or shorter? Why?

**5.11.** State the $z$-score used in finding a confidence interval for a proportion with confidence level
  **(a)** 0.98
  **(b)** 0.90
  **(c)** 0.50
  **(d)** 0.9973.

**5.12.** In the 2006 GSS, respondents were asked whether they favored or opposed the death penalty for people convicted of murder. Software shows results:

| x | n | Sample prop | 95.0% CI |
|---|---|---|---|
| 1885 | 2815 | 0.6696 | (0.652, 0.687) |

Here, $x$ refers to the number of the respondents who were in favor.
  **(a)** Show how to obtain the value reported under "Sample prop."
  **(b)** Can you conclude that more than half of all American adults are in favor? Why?
  **(c)** Find a 95% confidence interval for the proportion of American adults who *opposed* the death penalty from the confidence interval shown for the proportion in favor.

**5.13.** The GSS has asked respondents, "Do you think the use of marijuana should be made legal or not?" View results for all years at sda.berkeley.edu/GSS by entering the variables GRASS and YEAR.
  **(a)** Of the respondents in 2004, what proportion said *legal* and what proportion said *not legal*?
  **(b)** Is there enough evidence to conclude whether a majority or a minority of the population support legalization? Explain your reasoning.
  **(c)** Describe any trend you see since about 1986 in the proportion favoring legalization.

**5.14.** When the 2000 GSS asked whether human beings developed from earlier species of animals (variable SCITEST4), 53.8% of 1095 respondents answered that this was probably or definitely not true. Find a 99% confidence interval for the corresponding population proportion, and indicate whether you can conclude that a majority of Americans felt this way.

**5.15.** A study by the U.S. National Center for Health Statistics provided a point estimate of 25.5% for the percentage of adult Americans who were currently smokers. The sample size was 42,000. Assuming that this sample has the characteristics of a random sample, construct and interpret a 99% confidence interval for the population proportion of smokers. (*Note*: When $n$ is very large, even confidence intervals with large confidence levels are narrow.)

**5.16.** In the exit poll discussed in the previous chapter (page 85), of the 2705 voters sampled, 56.5% said they voted for Schwarzenegger. Is there enough evidence to predict the winner of the election? Base your decision on a 95% confidence interval, stating needed assumptions for that decision.

**5.17.** For an exit poll of people who voted in a gubernatorial election, 40% voted for Jones and 60% for Smith. Assuming this is a random sample of all voters, construct a 99% confidence interval for the proportion of votes that Jones received, if the sample size was **(a)** 400, **(b)** 40. In each case, indicate whether you would be willing to predict the winner. Explain how and why the sample size affects the inference.

**5.18.** In 2003 the Harris Poll reported results of a survey about religious beliefs. Of 2201 American adults surveyed, 27% believed in reincarnation. Treating this as a random sample, a 95% confidence interval for the population proportion of American adults believing in reincarnation is (0.25, 0.29). Without doing any calculation, explain how the interval would change if the sample size had been only a fourth as large, $n = 550$.

**5.19.** Report the $t$-score that multiplies by the standard error to form a
   **(a)** 95% confidence interval with 5 observations
   **(b)** 95% confidence interval with 15 observations
   **(c)** 95% confidence interval with 25 observations
   **(d)** 95% confidence interval with $df = 25$
   **(e)** 99% confidence interval with $df = 25$

**5.20.** Find and interpret the 95% confidence interval for $\mu$, if $\bar{y} = 70$ and $s = 10$, based on a sample size of
   **(a)** 5
   **(b)** 20.

**5.21.** The 2004 GSS asked male respondents how many female partners they have had sex with since their eighteenth birthday. The median = 6 and mode = 1 (16.0% of the sample). A computer printout summarizes other results:

```
Variable     n     Mean    StDev   SE Mean    95.0% CI
NUMWOMEN   1007   24.745   52.554   1.656    (21.5, 28.0)
```

   **(a)** Show how software got the standard error reported, and interpret.
   **(b)** Interpret the reported confidence interval.
   **(c)** State a factor that might make you skeptical about the usefulness of this confidence interval.

**5.22.** A GSS asked, "What do you think is the ideal number of children for a family to have?" The 497 females who responded had a median of 2, mean of 3.02, and standard deviation of 1.81.
   **(a)** Report the point estimate of the population mean.

**(b)** Find and interpret the standard error of the sample mean.
   **(c)** The 95% confidence interval is (2.9, 3.2). Interpret.
   **(d)** Is it plausible that the population mean = 2.0? Explain.

**5.23.** Refer to the previous exercise. For the 397 males in the sample, the mean was 2.89 and the standard deviation was 1.77.
   **(a)** Show that the standard error of the sample mean is 0.089.
   **(b)** Show that the 95% confidence interval for the population mean is (2.7, 3.1), and explain what "95% confidence" means.

**5.24.** Example 5.5 (page 120) analyzed data from a study that compared therapies for anorexia. For the 17 girls who received the family therapy, the changes in weight during the study were

$$11, 11, 6, 9, 14, -3, 0, 7, 22, -5, -4, 13, 13, 9, 4, 6, 11.$$

   **(a)** Verify that $\bar{y} = 7.29$ and $s = 7.18$ pounds.
   **(b)** Verify that the standard error of the sample mean was 1.74.
   **(c)** To use the $t$ distribution, explain why $df = 16$ and a 95% confidence interval uses the $t$-score of 2.120.
   **(d)** Let $\mu$ denote the population mean change in weight for this therapy. Verify that the 95% confidence interval for $\mu$ is (3.6, 11.0). Interpret.

**5.25.** The 2004 GSS asked, "On the average day about how many hours do you personally watch television?" Software reports:

```
Variable    N    Mean   SE Mean    95.0% CI
TVHOURS    892   2.76    0.08    (2.60, 2.93)
```

What's wrong with the interpretation, "In the long run, 95% of the time subjects watched between 2.60 and 2.93 hours of TV a day"? State the correct interpretation.

**5.26.** In response to the GSS question in 2006 about the number of hours daily spent watching TV, the responses by the 15 subjects who identified themselves as Buddhist were 0, 0, 0, 1, 1, 1, 2, 2, 2, 2, 2, 3, 4, 4, 5.
   **(a)** Estimate the mean, standard deviation, and standard error.
   **(b)** Construct a 95% confidence interval for the population mean.
   **(c)** Specify the assumptions for the method. What can you say about their validity for these data?

**5.27.** The GSS has asked subjects, "How long have you lived in the city, town or community where you live now?" The responses of 1415 subjects in one

survey had a median of 16 years, a mean of 20.3 and a standard deviation of 18.2.
   (a) Do you think that the population distribution is normal? Why or why not?
   (b) Based on your answer in (a), can you construct a 99% confidence interval for the population mean? If not, explain why not. If so, do so and interpret.

**5.28.** A recent GSS asked, "How many days in the past 7 days have you felt sad?" The 816 women who responded had a median of 1, mean of 1.81, and standard deviation of 1.98. The 633 men who responded had a median of 1, mean of 1.42, and standard deviation of 1.83.
   (a) Find a 95% confidence interval for the population mean for women. Interpret.
   (b) Explain why the $\bar{y}$- and $s$-values suggest that this variable does not have a normal distribution. Does this cause a problem with the confidence interval method in (a)? Explain.

**5.29.** The 2004 GSS asked respondents how many sex partners they had in the previous 12 months. Software reports:

```
Variable  N     Mean   StDev  SE Mean   95.0% CI
partners  2198  1.130  1.063  0.0227    (1.09, 1.18)
```

   (a) Interpret the confidence interval reported.
   (b) Based on these results, explain why the distribution was probably skewed to the right. Explain why the skew need not cause a problem with the validity of the confidence interval, unless there are extreme outliers.

**5.30.** For the "Florida student survey" data file mentioned in Exercise 1.11, software reports the results for responses on the number of times a week the subject reads a newspaper:

```
Variable  N   Mean  Std Dev  SE Mean   95.0% CI
News      60  4.1   3.0      0.387     (3.32, 4.88)
```

   (a) Interpret the confidence interval shown.
   (b) Does it seem plausible that the population distribution of this variable is normal? Why?
   (c) Explain the implications of the term "robust" regarding the normality assumption for this analysis.

**5.31.** The GSS asks respondents to rate their political views on a seven-point scale, where 1 = extremely liberal, 4 = moderate, and 7 = extremely conservative. A researcher analyzing data from the 2004 GSS gets software output:

```
Variable  N     Mean  StDev  SE Mean   99% CI
Polviews  1294  4.23  1.39   0.0387    (4.13, 4.33)
```

   (a) Show how to construct the confidence interval from the other information provided.
   (b) Would the confidence interval be wider or narrower (i) if you constructed a 95% confidence interval, (ii) if you found the 99% confidence interval only for those who called themselves *strong Democrats* on political party identification (PARTYID), for whom the mean was 3.50 with standard deviation 1.51?
   (c) What assumption are you making about the scale of measurement for political ideology when you use the sample mean and standard deviation?

**5.32.** At sda.berkeley.edu/GSS, consider responses to the question, "On how many days in the past 7 days have you felt lonely?" (coded LONELY) for the most recent survey in which this was asked.
   (a) Find a point estimate of the population mean.
   (b) Construct the 95% confidence interval, and interpret.

**5.33.** A study estimates the mean annual family income for families living in public housing in Chicago. For a random sample of 30 families, the annual incomes (in hundreds of dollars) are

```
83  90   77  100   83   64   78  92   73  122
96  60   85   86  108   70  139  56   94   84
111 93  120   70   92  100  124  59  112   79.
```

   (a) Construct a stem-and-leaf plot of the incomes. What do you predict about the shape of the population distribution?
   (b) Find and interpret point estimates of $\mu$ and $\sigma$, the population mean and standard deviation.
   (c) Construct and interpret a 95% confidence interval for $\mu$.

**5.34.** A hospital administrator wants to estimate the mean length of stay for all inpatients in that hospital. Based on a systematic random sample of 100 records of patients for the previous year, she reports that "The sample mean was 5.3. In repeated random samples of this size, the sample mean could be expected to fall within 1.0 of the true mean about 95% of the time."
   (a) Construct and interpret a 95% confidence interval for the mean.
   (b) The administrator decides that this interval is too wide, and she prefers one of only half this width. How large a sample size is needed?

**5.35.** To estimate the proportion of traffic deaths in California last year that were alcohol related, determine the necessary sample size for the estimate to be accurate to within 0.06 with probability 0.90. Based on results of a previous study, we expect the proportion to be about 0.30.

**5.36.** A television network plans to predict the outcome of an election between Jacalyn Levin and Roberto

Sanchez. They will do this with an exit poll on election day. They decide to use a random sample size for which the margin of error is 0.04 for 95% confidence intervals for population proportions.

(a) What sample size should they use?

(b) If the pollsters think that the election will be close, they might use a margin of error of 0.02. How large should the sample size be? (Note that reducing the margin of error by 50% requires quadrupling $n$.)

**5.37.** A public health unit wants to sample death records for the past year in Toronto to estimate the proportion of the deaths that were due to accidents. Health officials want the estimate to be accurate to within 0.02 with probability 0.95.

(a) Find the necessary sample size if, based on previous studies, officials believe that this proportion does not exceed 0.10.

(b) Suppose that in determining the necessary sample size, officials use the safe approach that sets $\pi = 0.50$ in the appropriate formula. Then how many records need to be sampled? Compare the result to the answer in part (a), and note the reduction in sample size that occurs by making an educated guess for $\pi$.

**5.38.** A poll in Canada indicated that 48% of Canadians favor imposing the death penalty (Canada does not have it). A report by Amnesty International on this and related polls (www.amnesty.ca) did not report the sample size but stated, "Polls of this size are considered to be accurate within 2.5 percentage points 95% of the time." About how large was the sample size?

**5.39.** The June 2003 report *Views of a Changing World* conducted by the Pew Global Attitudes Project (www.people-press.org) discussed changes in views of the U.S. by other countries. In the largest Muslim nation, Indonesia, a poll conducted in May 2003 after the Iraq war began reported that 83% had an unfavorable view of America, compared to 36% a year earlier. The 2003 result was reported to have a margin of error of 3 percentage points. Find the approximate sample size for the study.

**5.40.** An estimate is needed of the mean acreage of farms in Manitoba, Canada. The estimate should be correct to within 100 acres with probability 0.95. A preliminary study suggests that 500 acres is a reasonable guess for the standard deviation of farm size.

(a) How large a sample of farms is required?

(b) A random sample is selected of the size found in (a). The sample has a standard deviation of 300 acres, rather than 500. What is the margin of error for a 95% confidence interval for the mean acreage of farms?

**5.41.** A social scientist plans a study of adult South Africans living in townships on the outskirts of Cape Town, to investigate educational attainment (the number of years of education completed) in the black community. Many of the study's potential subjects were forced to leave Cape Town in 1966 when the government passed a law forbidding blacks to live in the inner cities. Under the apartheid system, black South African children were not required to attend school, so some residents had very little education. How large a sample size is needed so that a 95% confidence interval for the mean educational attainment has margin of error equal to 1 year? There is no information about the standard deviation of educational attainment, but researchers expect that nearly all values fall between 0 and 18 years.

**5.42.** How large a sample size is needed to estimate the mean annual income of Native Americans correct to within $1000 with probability 0.99? Suppose there is no prior information about the standard deviation of annual income of Native Americans, but we guess that about 95% of their incomes are between $6000 and $50,000 and that this distribution of incomes is approximately mound shaped.

**5.43.** An anthropologist wants to estimate the proportion of children in a tribe in the Philippines who die before reaching adulthood. For families she knew who had children born between 1980 and 1985, 3 of 30 children died before reaching adulthood. Can you use the ordinary large-sample formula to construct a 95% confidence interval for the population proportion? Why or why not? Construct an appropriate confidence interval, and interpret.

**5.44.** You randomly sample five students at your school to estimate the proportion of students who like tofu. None of the five students say they like it.

(a) Find the sample proportion who like it and its standard error. Does the usual interpretation of *se* make sense?

(b) Why is it not appropriate to use the ordinary confidence interval formula (from Section 5.1) for these data? Use a more appropriate approach, and interpret.

**5.45.** Refer to Exercise 5.33. Construct a 95% confidence interval for the median annual income of the public housing residents. Interpret.

**5.46.** Refer to Example 5.9 (page 130). Construct a 95% confidence interval for the median time since a book was last checked out. Interpret.

## Concepts and Applications

**5.47.** You can use an *applet* to repeatedly generate random samples and construct confidence intervals, to illustrate their behavior when used for many samples. To try this, go to www.prenhall.com/agresti and use the *confidence intervals for a proportion* applet. At the menu, set the population proportion value (labeled as *p*) to 0.50 and set the sample size to 200. Click on *Simulate*. The software will generate 100 samples of size 200 each. For each sample it displays the 95% and 99% confidence intervals for the population proportion and highlights the 95% intervals that fail to contain the parameter value. It also counts the number of intervals that contained the parameter value and the number that did not.

(a) In your simulation, what percentage of the 100 95% confidence intervals generated actually contained the parameter value? How many would be expected to contain the parameter?

(b) To get a feel for what happens "in the long run," click on *Simulate* 49 more times (50 times total). You will then have formed $50 \times 100 = 5000$ separate 95% confidence intervals. What percentage actually contained the true parameter value? You should see that close to 95% of the confidence intervals contained the true parameter.

5.48. Refer to the previous exercise. Using the *confidence interval for a proportion* applet, let's check that the confidence interval for a proportion may work poorly with small samples. Set $n = 10$ and $\pi = 0.90$. Click on *Simulate* to generate 100 random samples, each of size 10, forming confidence intervals for $\pi$ for each one.

(a) How many intervals failed to contain the true value, $\pi = 0.90$? How many would you expect not to contain the true value? What does this suggest? (Notice that many of the intervals contain only the value 1.0, which happens when $\hat{\pi} = 1.0$.)

(b) To see that this is not a fluke, now click on *Simulate* 49 more times so you will have a total of 5000 confidence intervals. What percentage contain $\pi = 0.90$? (*Note*: For every interval formed, the number of *failures* is smaller than 15, so the large-sample formula is not adequate.)

(c) Using the *sampling distribution* applet at the same website, select the *Binary* population distribution. Use your mouse to click on the first bar and change the proportion of 1's in the population to 0.90. (This is the value of the parameter $\pi$.) Specify $N = 1$ random sample of size $n = 10$. Click on *Sample* and it will generate the sample of size 10 and find the sample proportion and plot it on a histogram of sample proportions. Keep clicking on *Sample* 100 times, so you will have generated sample proportions for 100 samples of size 10 each. Look at the empirical sampling distribution of the sample proportion values. Is it bell shaped and symmetric? Use this to help explain why the confidence interval performs poorly in this case.

5.49. Refer to the "Student survey" data file (Exercise 1.11 on page 8). Using software, construct and interpret a 95% confidence interval for (a) the mean weekly number of hours spent watching TV, (b) the proportion believing in life after death. Interpret.

5.50. Refer to the data file created in Exercise 1.12 (page 9). For variables chosen by your instructor, pose a research question, and conduct inferential statistical analyses using basic estimation methods. Summarize and interpret your findings, and explain how you could use them to answer the research question.

5.51. In 2006, the GSS asked about the number of hours a week spent on the World Wide Web, excluding e-mail (variable denoted WWWHR). State a research question you could address about this response variable and a relevant explanatory variable. Go to sda.berkeley.edu/GSS and analyze the data. Prepare a short report summarizing your analysis and answering the question you posed.

5.52. A recent GSS asked married respondents, "Did you live with your husband/wife before you got married?" The responses were 57 *yes*, 115 *no* for those who called themselves politically liberal; and 45 *yes*, 238 *no* for those who called themselves politicaly conservative. Analyze these data, identifying the response variable and explanatory variable. Summarize your analysis in a report of no more than 300 words.

5.53. When subjects in a recent GSS were asked whether they agreed with the following statements, the (*yes*, *no*) counts under various conditions were as follows:

- Women should take care of running their homes and leave running the country up to men: (275, 1556)

- It is better for everyone involved if the man is the achiever outside the home and the woman takes care of the home and the family: (627, 1208)

- A preschool child is likely to suffer if her mother works: (776, 1054)

Analyze these data. Prepare a one-page report stating assumptions, showing results of description and inference, and summarizing conclusions.

5.54. The observations on TV watching for the seven Muslims in the GSS in a recent year were 0, 0, 2, 2, 2, 4, 6. A 95% confidence interval for the population mean is (0.3, 4.3). Suppose the observation of 6 for the seventh subject was incorrectly recorded as 60. What would have been obtained for the 95% confidence interval? Compare to the interval (0.3, 4.3). How does this warn you about potential effects of outliers on confidence intervals for means?

**5.55.** (a) Explain what it means for an estimator to be unbiased.
   (b) Explain why the sample range is a biased estimator of the population range. (*Hint*: How do the sample minimum and maximum compare to the population minimum and maximum? Explain why the sample range is typically less than the population range and cannot be larger.)

**5.56.** What is the purpose of forming a confidence interval for a parameter? What can you learn from it that you could not learn from a point estimate of the parameter?

**5.57.** An interval estimate for a mean is more informative than a point estimate, because with an interval estimate you can figure out the point estimate, but with the point estimate alone you have no idea how wide the interval estimate is.
   (a) Explain why this statement is correct, illustrating using the reported 95% confidence interval of (4.0, 5.6) for the mean number of dates in the previous month for women at a particular college.
   (b) The confidence interval in (a) used a sample size of 50. What were the sample mean and standard deviation?

**5.58.** Explain why confidence intervals are wider with
   (a) larger confidence levels,
   (b) smaller sample sizes.

**5.59.** Why would it be unusual to see a
   (a) 99.9999%,
   (b) 25% confidence interval?

**5.60.** Give an example of a study in which it would be important to have
   (a) A high degree of confidence
   (b) A high degree of precision

**5.61.** How does population heterogeneity affect the sample size required to estimate a population mean? Illustrate with an example.

**5.62.** Explain the reasoning behind the following statement: Studies about more diverse populations require larger sample sizes. Illustrate for the problem of estimating mean income for all medical doctors in the U.S. compared to estimating mean income for all entry-level employees at McDonald's restaurants in the U.S.

**5.63.** You would like to find the proportion of bills passed by Congress that were vetoed by the President in the last congressional session. After checking congressional records, you see that for the population of all 40 bills passed, 2 were vetoed. Does it make sense to construct a confidence interval using these data? Explain. (*Hint*: Identify the sample and population.)

**5.64.** The 2006 publication *Attitudes towards European Union Enlargement* from Eurobarometer states,

   > The readers are reminded that survey results are *estimations*, the accuracy of which rests upon the sample size and upon the observed percentage. With samples of about 1,000 interviews, the real percentages vary within the following confidence limits:

| Observed | Limits |
|----------|--------|
| 10% or 90% | ± 1.9 |
| 20%, 80% | ± 2.5 |
| 30%, 70% | ± 2.7 |
| 40%, 60% | ± 3.0 |
| 50% | ± 3.1 |

   (a) Explain how they got 3.0 points for 40% or 60%.
   (b) Explain why the margin of error differs for different observed percentages.
   (c) Explain why the accuracy is the same for a particular percentage and for 100 minus that value (e.g., both 40% and 60%).
   (d) Explain why it is more difficult to estimate a population proportion when it is near 0.5 than when it is near 0 or 1.

**5.65.** To use the large-sample confidence interval for $\pi$, you need at least 15 outcomes of each type. Show that the smallest value of $n$ for which the method can be used is (a) 30 when $\hat{\pi} = 0.50$, (b) 50 when $\hat{\pi} = 0.30$, (c) 150 when $\hat{\pi} = 0.10$. That is, the overall $n$ must increase as $\hat{\pi}$ moves toward 0 or 1. (When the true proportion is near 0 or 1, the sampling distribution can be highly skewed unless $n$ is quite large.)

*Select the best response in Exercises 5.66–5.69.*

**5.66.** The reason we use a $z$-score from a normal distribution in constructing a large-sample confidence interval for a proportion is that
   (a) For large random samples the sampling distribution of the sample proportion is approximately normal.
   (b) The population distribution is normal.
   (c) For large random samples the data distribution is approximately normal.
   (d) If in doubt about the population distribution, it's safest to assume that it is the normal distribution.

**5.67.** Increasing the confidence level causes the width of a confidence interval to
  (a) increase
  (b) decrease
  (c) stay the same.

**5.68.** Other things being equal, quadrupling the sample size causes the width of a confidence interval to
  (a) double
  (b) halve
  (c) be one quarter as wide
  (d) stay the same.

**5.69.** Based on responses of 1467 subjects in General Social Surveys, a 95% confidence interval for the mean number of close friends equals (6.8, 8.0). Which of the following interpretations is (are) correct?
  (a) We can be 95% confident that $\bar{y}$ is between 6.8 and 8.0.
  (b) We can be 95% confident that $\mu$ is between 6.8 and 8.0.
  (c) Ninety-five percent of the values of $y$ = number of close friends (for this sample) are between 6.8 and 8.0.
  (d) If random samples of size 1467 were repeatedly selected, then 95% of the time $\bar{y}$ would fall between 6.8 and 8.0.
  (e) If random samples of size 1467 were repeatedly selected, then in the long run 95% of the confidence intervals formed would contain the true value of $\mu$.

**5.70.** A random sample of 50 records yields a 95% confidence interval for the mean age at first marriage of women in a certain county of 21.5 to 23.0 years. Explain what is wrong with each of the following interpretations of this interval.
  (a) If random samples of 50 records were repeatedly selected, then 95% of the time the sample mean age at first marriage for women would be between 21.5 and 23.0 years.
  (b) Ninety-five percent of the ages at first marriage for women in the county are between 21.5 and 23.0 years.
  (c) We can be 95% confident that $\bar{y}$ is between 21.5 and 23.0 years.
  (d) If we repeatedly sampled the entire population, then 95% of the time the population mean would be between 21.5 and 23.5 years.

**5.71.** Refer to the previous exercise. Provide the proper interpretation.

**\*5.72.** For a random sample of $n$ subjects, explain why it is about 95% likely that the sample proportion has error no more than $1/\sqrt{n}$ in estimating the population proportion. (*Hint:* To show this "$1/\sqrt{n}$ Rule," find two standard errors when $\pi = 0.50$, and explain how this compares to two standard errors at other values of $\pi$.) Using this result, show

that $n = 1/M^2$ is a safe sample size for estimating a proportion to within $M$ with 95% confidence.

**\*5.73.** You know the sample mean of $n$ observations. Once you know $(n - 1)$ of the observations, show that you can find the remaining one. In other words, for a given value of $\bar{y}$, the values of $(n - 1)$ observations determine the remaining one. In summarizing scores on a quantitative variable, having $(n - 1)$ degrees of freedom means that only that many observations are independent.

**\*5.74.** Find the standard error of the sample proportion when $\pi = 0$ or $\pi = 1$. What does this reflect?

**\*5.75.** Let $\pi$ be the probability a randomly selected voter prefers the Republican candidate. You sample 2 people, and neither prefers, the Republican. Find the point estimate of $\pi$. Does this estimate seem sensible? Why? (The *Bayesian* estimator is an alternative one that uses a *subjective* approach, combining the sample data with your prior beliefs about $\pi$ before seeing the data. For example, if you believed $\pi$ was equally likely to fall anywhere from 0 to 1, the Bayesian estimate adds two observations, one of each type, thus yielding the estimate 1/4.)

**\*5.76.** To encourage subjects to make responses on sensitive questions, the method of ***randomized response*** is often used. The subject is asked to flip a coin, in secret. If it is a head, the subject tosses the coin once more and reports the outcome, head or tails. If, instead, the first flip is a tail, the subject reports instead the response to the sensitive question; for instance, reporting the response *head* if the true response is *yes* and reporting the response *tail* if the true response is *no*. Let $\pi$ denote the true probability of the *yes* response on the sensitive question.
  (a) Explain why the numbers in Table 5.5 are the probabilities of the four possible outcomes.
  (b) Let $p$ denote the sample proportion of subjects who report *head* for the second response. Explain why $\hat{\pi} = 2p - 0.5$ estimates $\pi$.
  (c) Using this approach, 200 subjects are asked whether they have ever knowingly cheated on their income tax. Report the estimate of $\pi$ if the number of reported heads equals (i) 50, (ii) 70, (iii) 100, (iv) 150.

**TABLE 5.5**

| First Coin | Second Response | |
|---|---|---|
| | Head | Tail |
| Head | 0.25 | 0.25 |
| Tail | $\pi/2$ | $(1 - \pi)/2$ |

**\*5.77.** To construct a large-sample confidence interval for a proportion $\pi$, it is not necessary to substitute $\hat{\pi}$ for the unknown value of $\pi$ in the formula for the standard error of $\hat{\pi}$. A less approximate method finds the endpoints for a 95% interval by determining the $\pi$ values that are 1.96 standard errors from the sample proportion, by solving for $\pi$ in the equation

$$|\hat{\pi} - \pi| = 1.96\sqrt{\frac{\pi(1 - \pi)}{n}}.$$

For Example 5.8 (page 129) with no vegetarians in a sample of size 20, substitute $\hat{\pi}$ and $n$ in this equation and show that the equation is satisfied at $\pi = 0$ and at $\pi = 0.161$. So the confidence interval is $(0, 0.161)$.

# Statistical Inference: Significance Tests

An aim of many studies is to check whether the data agree with certain predictions. The predictions typically result from the theory that drives the research. These predictions are *hypotheses* about the study population.

---

**Hypothesis**

---

In statistics, a **hypothesis** is a statement about a population. It is usually a prediction that a parameter describing some characteristic of a variable takes a particular numerical value or falls in a certain range of values.

---

Examples of hypotheses are the following: "For workers in service jobs, the mean income is the same for women and for men," and "There is no difference between Democrats and Republicans in the probabilities that they vote with their party leadership," and "Half or more of adult Canadians are satisfied with their national health service."

A **significance test** uses data to summarize the evidence about a hypothesis. It does this by comparing point estimates of parameters to the values predicted by the hypothesis. The following example illustrates concepts behind significance tests.

### EXAMPLE 6.1    Testing for Gender Bias in Selecting Managers

A large supermarket chain in Florida selected some employees to receive management training. A group of women employees claimed that males were picked at a disproportionally high rate for such training. The company denied this claim.[1] A similar claim of gender bias was made about promotions and pay for women who work for Wal-Mart.[2] How could the women employees statistically back up their assertion?

Suppose the employee pool for potential selection for management training is half male and half female. Then the company's claim of a lack of gender bias is a hypothesis. It states that, other things being equal, at each choice the probability of selecting a female equals 1/2 and the probability of selecting a male equals 1/2. If the

---

[1] *Tampa Tribune*, April 6, 1996.
[2] *New York Times*, February 7, 2007.

employees truly are selected for management training randomly in terms of gender, about half the employees picked should be females and about half should be male. The women's claim is an alternative hypothesis that the probability of selecting a male exceeds 1/2.

Suppose that nine of the ten employees chosen for management training were male. We might be inclined to believe the women's claim. However, we should analyze whether these results would be unlikely, if there were *no* gender bias. Would it be highly unusual that 9/10 of the employees chosen would have the same gender if they were truly selected at random from the employee pool? Due to sampling variation, not exactly 1/2 of the sample need be male. How far above 1/2 must the sample proportion of males chosen be before we believe the women's claim?    ■

This chapter introduces statistical methods for summarizing evidence and making decisions about hypotheses. We first present the parts that all significance tests have in common. The rest of the chapter presents significance tests about population means and population proportions. We'll also learn how to find and how to control the probability of an incorrect decision about a hypothesis.

## 6.1   THE FIVE PARTS OF A SIGNIFICANCE TEST

Now let's take a closer look at the significance test method, also called a *hypothesis test*, or *test* for short. All tests have five parts: assumptions, hypotheses, test statistic, *P*-value, and conclusion.

### Assumptions

Each test makes certain assumptions or has certain conditions for the test to be valid. These pertain to the following:

- *Type of data*: Like other statistical methods, each test applies for either quantitative data or categorical data.
- *Randomization*: Like the confidence interval method of statistical inference, a test assumes that the data were obtained using randomization, such as a random sample.
- *Population distribution*: For some tests, the variable is assumed to have a particular distribution, such as the normal distribution.
- *Sample size*: The validity of many tests improves as the sample size increases.

### Hypotheses

Each significance test has two hypotheses about the value of a parameter.

---

**Null Hypothesis, Alternative Hypothesis**

---

The **null hypothesis** is a statement that the parameter takes a particular value. The **alternative hypothesis** states that the parameter falls in some alternative range of values. Usually the value in the null hypothesis corresponds, in a certain sense, to *no effect*. The values in the alternative hypothesis then represent an effect of some type.

---

**Notation for Hypotheses**

---

The symbol $H_0$ represents the null hypothesis. The symbol $H_a$ represents the alternative hypothesis.

Consider Example 6.1 about possible gender discrimination in selecting management trainees. Let $\pi$ denote the probability that any particular selection is a male. The company claims that $\pi = 1/2$. This is an example of a null hypothesis, *no effect* referring to a lack of gender bias. The alternative hypothesis reflects the skeptical women employees' belief that this probability actually exceeds 1/2. So the hypotheses are $H_0: \pi = 1/2$ and $H_a: \pi > 1/2$. Note that $H_0$ has a *single* value whereas $H_a$ has a range of values.

A significance test analyzes the sample evidence about the null hypothesis, $H_0$. The test investigates whether the data contradict $H_0$, hence suggesting that $H_a$ is true. The approach taken is the indirect one of *proof by contradiction*. The null hypothesis is presumed to be true. Under this presumption, if the data observed would be very unusual, the evidence supports the alternative hypothesis. In the study of potential gender discrimination, we presume the null hypothesis value of $\pi = 1/2$ is true. Then we determine if the sample result of selecting 9 men for management training in 10 choices would be unusual, under this presumption. If so, then we may be inclined to believe the women's claim. But if the difference between the sample proportion of men chosen (9/10) and the $H_0$ value of 1/2 could easily be due to ordinary sampling variability, there's not enough evidence to accept the women's claim.

A researcher usually conducts a test to gauge the amount of support for the alternative hypothesis. Thus, $H_a$ is sometimes called the **research hypothesis**. The hypotheses are formulated *before* collecting or analyzing the data.

## Test Statistic

The parameter to which the hypotheses refer has a point estimate. The **test statistic** summarizes how far that estimate falls from the parameter value in $H_0$. Often this is expressed by the number of standard errors between the estimate and the $H_0$ value.

## P-Value

To interpret a test statistic value, we create a probability summary of the evidence against $H_0$. This uses the sampling distribution of the test statistic, under the presumption that $H_0$ is true. The purpose is to summarize how unusual the observed test statistic value is compared to what $H_0$ predicts.

Specifically, if the test statistic falls well out in a tail of the sampling distribution in a direction predicted by $H_a$, then it is far from what $H_0$ predicts. We can summarize how far out in the tail the test statistic falls by the tail probability of that value and of more extreme values. These are the possible test statistic values that provide *at least as much evidence against $H_0$ as the observed test statistic*, in the direction predicted by $H_a$. This probability is called the **P-value**.

---

**P-value**

The **P-value** is the probability that the test statistic equals the observed value or a value even more extreme in the direction predicted by $H_a$. It is calculated by presuming that $H_0$ is true. The P-value is denoted by P.

---

A small P-value (such as $P = 0.01$) means that the data observed would have been unusual, if $H_0$ were true. *The smaller the P-value, the stronger the evidence against $H_0$.*

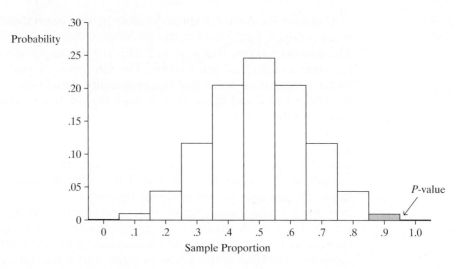

**FIGURE 6.1:** The *P*-Value Equals the Probability of the Observed Data or Even More Extreme Results. It is calculated under the presumption that $H_0$ is true, so a very small *P*-value gives strong evidence against $H_0$.

For Example 6.1 on potential gender discrimination in choosing managerial trainees, $\pi$ is the probability of selecting a male. We test $H_0$: $\pi = 1/2$ against $H_a$: $\pi > 1/2$. One possible test statistic is the sample proportion of males selected, which is $9/10 = 0.90$. The values for the sample proportion that provide this much or even more extreme evidence against $H_0$: $\pi = 1/2$ and in favor of $H_a$: $\pi > 1/2$ are the right-tail sample proportion values of 0.90 and higher. See Figure 6.1. A formula from Section 6.7 calculates this probability as 0.01, so the *P*-value equals $P = 0.01$. If the selections truly were random with respect to gender, the probability is only 0.01 of such an extreme sample result, namely, that nine or all ten selections would be males. Other things being equal, this small *P*-value provides considerable evidence against $H_0$: $\pi = 1/2$ and supporting the alternative $H_a$: $\pi > 1/2$ of discrimination against females.

By contrast, a moderate to large *P*-value means the data are consistent with $H_0$. A *P*-value such as 0.26 or 0.83 indicates that, if $H_0$ were true, the observed data would not be unusual.

## Conclusion

The *P*-value summarizes the evidence against $H_0$. Our conclusion should also *interpret* what the *P*-value tells us about the question motivating the test. Sometimes it is necessary to make a decision about the validity of $H_0$. If the *P*-value is sufficiently small, we reject $H_0$ and accept $H_a$.

Most studies require very small *P*-values, such as $P \leq 0.05$, in order to reject $H_0$. In such cases, results are said to be *significant at the 0.05 level*. This means that if $H_0$ were true, the chance of getting such extreme results as in the sample data would be no greater than 0.05.

Making a decision by rejecting or not rejecting a null hypothesis is an optional part of the significance test. We defer discussion of it until Section 6.4. Table 6.1 summarizes the parts of a significance test.

TABLE 6.1: The Five Parts of a Statistical Significance Test

1. **Assumptions**
   Type of data, randomization, population distribution, sample size condition
2. **Hypotheses**
   Null hypothesis, $H_0$ (parameter value for "no effect")
   Alternative hypothesis, $H_a$ (alternative parameter values)
3. **Test statistic**
   Compares point estimate to $H_0$ parameter value
4. ***P*-value**
   Weight of evidence against $H_0$; smaller $P$ is stronger evidence
5. **Conclusion**
   Report $P$-value
   Formal decision (optional; see Section 6.4)

## 6.2 SIGNIFICANCE TEST FOR A MEAN

For quantitative variables, significance tests usually refer to the population mean $\mu$. The five parts of the significance test follow:

### The Five Parts of a Significance Test for a Mean

#### *1.* Assumptions
The test assumes the data are obtained using randomization, such as a random sample. The quantitative variable is assumed to have a normal population distribution. We'll see that this is mainly relevant for small sample sizes and certain types of $H_a$.

#### *2.* Hypotheses
The null hypothesis about a population mean $\mu$ has the form

$$H_0 : \mu = \mu_0,$$

where $\mu_0$ is a particular value for the population mean. In other words, the hypothesized value of $\mu$ in $H_0$ is a single value. This hypothesis usually refers to *no effect* or *no change* compared to some standard. For example, Example 5.5 in the previous chapter (page 120) estimated the population mean weight change $\mu$ for teenage girls after receiving a treatment for anorexia. The hypothesis that the treatment has *no effect* is a null hypothesis, $H_0$: $\mu = 0$. Here, the $H_0$ value $\mu_0$ for the parameter $\mu$ is 0.

The alternative hypothesis contains alternative parameter values from the value in $H_0$. The most common alternative hypothesis is

$$H_a : \mu \neq \mu_0, \quad \text{such as} \quad H_a : \mu \neq 0.$$

This alternative hypothesis is called ***two sided***, because it contains values both below and above the value listed in $H_0$. For the anorexia study, $H_a$: $\mu \neq 0$ states that the treatment has *some effect*, the population mean equaling some value other than 0.

#### *3.* Test Statistic
The sample mean $\bar{y}$ estimates the population mean $\mu$. When the population distribution is normal, the sampling distribution of $\bar{y}$ is normal about $\mu$. This is also approximately true when the population distribution is *not* normal but the random sample size is relatively large, by the Central Limit Theorem.

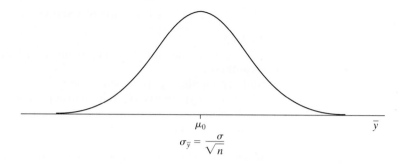

$$\sigma_{\bar{y}} = \frac{\sigma}{\sqrt{n}}$$

**FIGURE 6.2:** Sampling Distribution of $\bar{y}$ if $H_0: \mu = \mu_0$ Is True. For large random samples, it is approximately normal, centered at the null hypothesis value, $\mu_0$.

Under the presumption that $H_0: \mu = \mu_0$ is true, the center of the sampling distribution of $\bar{y}$ is the value $\mu_0$, as Figure 6.2 shows. A value of $\bar{y}$ that falls far out in the tail provides strong evidence against $H_0$, because it would be unusual if truly $\mu = \mu_0$. The evidence about $H_0$ is summarized by the number of standard errors that $\bar{y}$ falls from the null hypothesis value $\mu_0$.

Recall that the *true* standard error is $\sigma_{\bar{y}} = \sigma/\sqrt{n}$. As in Chapter 5, we substitute the sample standard deviation $s$ for the unknown population standard deviation $\sigma$ to get the *estimated* standard error, $se = s/\sqrt{n}$. The test statistic is the *t*-score

$$t = \frac{\bar{y} - \mu_0}{se}, \quad \text{where} \quad se = \frac{s}{\sqrt{n}}.$$

The farther $\bar{y}$ falls from $\mu_0$, the larger the absolute value of the $t$ test statistic. Hence, the larger the value of $|t|$, the stronger the evidence against $H_0$.

We use the symbol $t$ rather than $z$ because, as in forming a confidence interval, using $s$ to estimate $\sigma$ in the standard error introduces additional error. The null sampling distribution of the $t$ test statistic is the $t$ *distribution*, introduced in Section 5.3. It looks like the standard normal distribution, having mean equal to 0 but being more spread out, moreso for smaller $n$. It is specified by its degrees of freedom, $df = n - 1$.

### 4. P-Value

The test statistic summarizes how far the data fall from $H_0$. Different tests use different test statistics, though, and simpler interpretations result from transforming it to the probability scale of 0 to 1. The $P$-value does this.

We calculate the $P$-value under the presumption that $H_0$ is true. That is, we give the benefit of the doubt to $H_0$, analyzing how unusual the observed data would be if $H_0$ were true. The $P$-value is the probability that the test statistic equals the observed value or a value in the set of more extreme values that provide even stronger evidence against $H_0$. For $H_a: \mu \neq \mu_0$, the more extreme $t$ values are the ones even farther out in the tails of the $t$ distribution. So the $P$-value is the two-tail probability that the $t$ test statistic is at least as large in absolute value as the observed test statistic. This is also the probability that $\bar{y}$ falls at least as far from $\mu_0$ *in either direction* as the observed value of $\bar{y}$.

Figure 6.3 shows the sampling distribution of the $t$ test statistic when $H_0$ is true. A test statistic value of $t = (\bar{y} - \mu_0)/se = 0$ results when $\bar{y} = \mu_0$. This is the $t$-value most consistent with $H_0$. The $P$-value is the probability of a $t$ test statistic value at least as far from this consistent value as the one observed. To illustrate its calculation, suppose $t = 0.68$ for a sample size of 186. (This is the result in Example 6.2) This $t$-score means that the sample mean $\bar{y}$ falls 0.68 estimated standard errors above $\mu_0$.

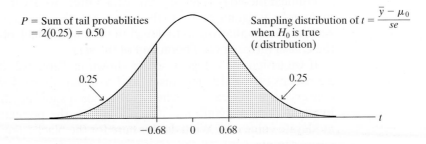

**FIGURE 6.3:** Calculation of P-Value when $t = 0.68$, for Testing $H_0: \mu = \mu_0$ against $H_a: \mu \neq \mu_0$. The P-value is the two-tail probability of a more extreme result than the observed one.

The P-value is the probability that $t \geq 0.68$ or $t \leq -0.68$ (i.e., $|t| \geq 0.68$). Since $n = 186$, $df = n - 1 = 185$ is large, and the $t$ distribution is nearly identical to the standard normal. From Table A, the probability in one tail above 0.68 is about 0.25, so the two-tail probability is about $P = 2(0.25) = 0.50$.

A more precise P-value calculation with the $t$ distribution using software gives P-value $= 0.4973545$. Round such a value, say to 0.50, before reporting it. Reporting the P-value with many decimal places, such as 0.4973545, makes it seem as if more accuracy exists than actually does. In practice, the sampling distribution is only *approximately* the $t$ distribution, because the population distribution is not exactly normal as is assumed with the $t$ test.

### 5. Conclusion

Finally, the study should interpret the P-value in context. The smaller $P$ is, the stronger the evidence against $H_0$ and in favor of $H_a$.

### EXAMPLE 6.2    Political Conservatism and Liberalism

Some political commentators have remarked that citizens of the United States are increasingly conservative, so much so that many treat *liberal* as a dirty word. We can study political ideology by analyzing response to certain items on the GSS. For instance, that survey asks (with the POLVIEWS item) where you would place yourself on a seven-point scale of political views ranging from extremely liberal, point 1, to extremely conservative, point 7. Table 6.2 shows the scale and the distribution of responses among the levels for the 2006 survey. Results are shown separately according to the three categories for the variable labelled as RACE in the GSS.

TABLE 6.2: Responses of Subjects on a Scale of Political Ideology

| Response | Black | White | Other |
|---|---|---|---|
| | | Race | |
| 1. Extremely liberal | 10 | 36 | 1 |
| 2. Liberal | 21 | 109 | 13 |
| 3. Slightly liberal | 22 | 124 | 13 |
| 4. Moderate, middle of road | 74 | 421 | 27 |
| 5. Slightly conservative | 21 | 179 | 9 |
| 6. Conservative | 27 | 176 | 7 |
| 7. Extremely conservative | 11 | 28 | 2 |
| | $n = 186$ | $n = 1073$ | $n = 72$ |

Political ideology is an ordinal scale. Often, we treat such scales in a quantitative manner by assigning scores to the categories. Then we can use quantitative summaries such as means, allowing us to detect the extent to which observations gravitate toward the conservative or the liberal end of the scale.

If we assign the category scores shown in Table 6.2, then a mean below 4 shows a propensity toward liberalism, and a mean above 4 shows a propensity toward conservatism. We can test whether these data show much evidence of either of these by conducting a significance test about how the population mean compares to the moderate value of 4. We'll do this here for the black sample and in Section 6.5 for the entire sample.

1. *Assumptions*: The sample is randomly selected. We are treating political ideology as quantitative with equally spaced scores. The $t$ test assumes a normal population distribution for political ideology. We'll discuss this assumption further at the end of this section.

2. *Hypotheses*: Let $\mu$ denote the population mean ideology for black Americans, for this seven-point scale. The null hypothesis contains one specified value for $\mu$. Since we conduct the analysis to check how, if at all, the population mean departs from the moderate response of 4, the null hypothesis is

$$H_0 : \mu = 4.0.$$

The alternative hypothesis is then

$$H_a : \mu \neq 4.0.$$

The null hypothesis states that, on the average, the population response is politically "moderate, middle of road." The alternative states that the mean falls in the liberal direction ($\mu < 4$) or in the conservative direction ($\mu > 4$).

3. *Test statistic*: The 186 observations in Table 6.2 for blacks are summarized by $\bar{y} = 4.075$ and $s = 1.512$. The estimated standard error of the sampling distribution of $\bar{y}$ is

$$se = \frac{s}{\sqrt{n}} = \frac{1.512}{\sqrt{186}} = 0.111.$$

The value of the test statistic is

$$t = \frac{\bar{y} - \mu_0}{se} = \frac{4.075 - 4.0}{0.111} = 0.68.$$

The sample mean falls 0.68 estimated standard errors above the null hypothesis value of the mean. The *df* value is $186 - 1 = 185$.

4. *P-value*: The *P*-value is the two-tail probability, presuming $H_0$ is true, that $t$ would exceed 0.68 in absolute value. From the $t$ distribution with $df = 185$ (or its standard normal approximation), this two-tail probability is $P = 0.50$. If the population mean ideology were 4.0, then the probability equals 0.50 that a sample mean for $n = 186$ subjects would fall at least as far from 4.0 as the observed $\bar{y}$ of 4.075.

5. *Conclusion*: The *P*-value of $P = 0.50$ is not small, so it does not contradict $H_0$. If $H_0$ were true, the data we observed would not be unusual. It is plausible that the population mean response for black Americans in 2006 was 4.0, not leaning toward the conservative or liberal direction. ∎

### Correspondence between Two-Sided Tests and Confidence Intervals

Conclusions using two-sided significance tests are consistent with conclusions using confidence intervals. If a test says that a particular value is believable for the parameter, then so does a confidence interval.

### EXAMPLE 6.3    Confidence Interval for Mean Political Ideology

For the data in Example 6.2, let's construct a 95% confidence interval for the population mean political ideology. With $df = 185$, the multiple of the standard error ($se = 0.111$) is $t_{.025} = 1.97$. Since $\bar{y} = 4.075$, the confidence interval is

$$\bar{y} \pm 1.97(se) = 4.075 \pm 1.97(0.111) = 4.075 \pm 0.219, \quad \text{or} \quad (3.9, 4.3).$$

At the 95% confidence level, these are the plausible values for $\mu$.

This confidence interval indicates that $\mu$ may equal 4.0, since 4.0 falls inside the confidence interval. Thus, it is not surprising that the $P$-value ($P = 0.50$) in testing $H_0: \mu = 4.0$ against $H_a: \mu \neq 4.0$ in Example 6.2 was not small. In fact;

> ⊙ Whenever the $P$-value $P > 0.05$ in a two-sided test, a 95% confidence interval for $\mu$ necessarily contains the $H_0$ value of $\mu$.

By contrast, suppose the $P$-value $= 0.02$ in testing $H_0: \mu = 4.0$. Then a 95% confidence interval would tell us that 4.0 is implausible for $\mu$, with 4.0 falling *outside* the confidence interval.

> ⊙ Whenever $P \leq 0.05$ in a two-sided test, a 95% confidence interval for $\mu$ does not contain the $H_0$ value of $\mu$.

Section 6.4 discusses further the connection between the two methods.    ∎

### One-Sided Significance Tests

A different alternative hypothesis is sometimes used when a researcher predicts a deviation from $H_0$ in a particular direction. It has the form

$$H_a : \mu > \mu_0 \quad \text{or} \quad H_a : \mu < \mu_0.$$

The alternative $H_a: \mu > \mu_0$ is used to detect whether $\mu$ is *larger* than the particular value $\mu_0$, whereas $H_a: \mu < \mu_0$ is used to detect whether $\mu$ is *smaller* than that value. These hypotheses are called **one sided**. By contrast, the *two-sided* $H_a$ is used to detect *any* type of deviation from $H_0$. This choice is made before analyzing the data.

For $H_a: \mu > \mu_0$, the $P$-value is the probability (presuming $H_0$ is true) of a $t$-score *above* the observed $t$-score; that is, to the right of it on the real number line. These $t$-scores provide more extreme evidence than the observed value in favor of $H_a$: $\mu > \mu_0$. So $P$ equals the right-tail probability under the $t$ curve, as Figure 6.4 portrays. A $t$-score of 0.68 results in $P = 0.25$ for this alternative.

For $H_a: \mu < \mu_0$, the $P$-value is the left-tail probability, (*below*) the observed $t$-score. A $t$-score of $t = -0.68$ results in $P = 0.25$ for this alternative. A $t$-score of 0.68 results in $P = 1 - 0.25 = 0.75$.

### EXAMPLE 6.4    Mean Weight Change in Anorexic Girls

Example 5.5 in Chapter 5 (page 120) analyzed data from a study comparing treatments for teenage girls suffering from anorexia. For each girl, the study observed her change in weight while receiving the therapy. Let $\mu$ denote the population mean change in

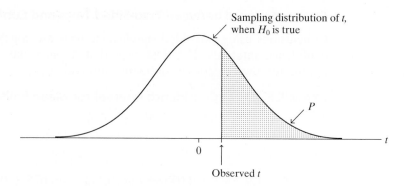

**FIGURE 6.4:** Calculation of *P*-value in Testing $H_0: \mu = \mu_0$ against $H_a: \mu > \mu_0$. The *P*-value is the probability of values to the right of the observed test statistic.

weight for the cognitive behavioral treatment. If this treatment has beneficial effect, as expected, then $\mu$ is positive. To test for no treatment effect versus a positive mean weight change, we test $H_0: \mu = 0$ against $H_a: \mu > 0$.

Software (SPSS) used to analyze the data reports:

| Variable | Number of Cases | Mean | SD | SE of Mean |
|---|---|---|---|---|
| CHANGE | 29 | 3.007 | 7.309 | 1.357 |

For the $n = 29$ girls, the sample mean weight change of 3.007 pounds had an estimated standard error of $se = 1.357$. The test statistic equals

$$t = \frac{\bar{y} - \mu_0}{se} = \frac{3.007 - 0}{1.357} = 2.22.$$

For this one-sided $H_a$, the *P*-value is the right-tail probability above 2.22. Why do we use the right tail? Because $H_a: \mu > 0$ has values *above* (that is, to the right of) the null hypothesis value of 0. It's the positive values of *t* that support this alternative hypothesis.

Now, for $n = 29$, $df = n - 1 = 28$. From Table B, $t = 2.048$ yields $P = 0.025$ for the one-sided $H_a$ and $t = 2.467$ yields $P = 0.01$. The observed $t = 2.22$ is between 2.048 and 2.467, so the *P*-value is between 0.01 and 0.025. Figure 6.5 illustrates. Table B is not detailed enough to provide the exact *P*-value. When software performs the analysis, the output reports the actual *P*-value rather than bounds for it. Most software reports the *P*-value for a two-sided alternative as the

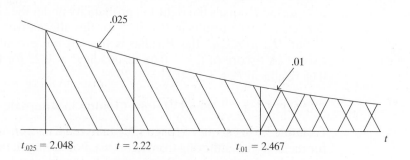

**FIGURE 6.5:** For $df = 28$, $t = 2.22$ Has a Tail Probability between 0.01 and 0.025

default, unless you request otherwise. SPSS reports results for the two-sided test and confidence interval as

| Mean | 95% CI | | t-value | df | 2-Tail Sig |
|------|--------|--------|---------|------|------------|
|      | Lower | Upper | | | |
| 3.01 | .227 | 5.787 | 2.22 | 28 | .035 |

SPSS reports $P = 0.035$ (under "2-Tail Sig"). The one-sided $P$-value is half this, or about $P = 0.02$. There is relatively strong evidence against $H_0$. It seems that the treatment has an effect.

The significance test concludes that the mean weight gain was not equal to 0. But the 95% confidence interval of (0.2, 5.8), shown also in the SPSS output, is more informative. It shows just how different from 0 the population mean change is likely to be. The effect could be very small. Also, keep in mind that this experimental study (like many medically oriented studies) had to use a volunteer sample. So these results are highly tentative, another reason that it is silly for studies like this to report $P$-values to several decimal places.    ■

### Implicit One-Sided $H_0$ for One-Sided $H_a$

From Example 6.4, the one-sided $P$-value $= 0.017$. So, if $\mu = 0$, the probability equals 0.017 of observing a sample mean weight gain of 3.01 or greater. Now, suppose $\mu < 0$; that is, the population mean weight change is negative. Then the probability of observing $\bar{y} \geq 3.01$ would be even smaller than 0.017. For example, a sample value of $\bar{y} = 3.01$ is even less likely when $\mu = -5$ than when $\mu = 0$, since 3.01 is farther out in the tail of the sampling distribution of $\bar{y}$ when $\mu = -5$ than when $\mu = 0$. Thus, rejection of $H_0: \mu = 0$ in favor of $H_a: \mu > 0$ also inherently rejects the broader null hypothesis of $H_0: \mu \leq 0$. In other words, one concludes that $\mu = 0$ is false *and* that $\mu < 0$ is false.

### The Choice of One-Sided versus Two-Sided Tests

In practice, two-sided tests are more common than one-sided tests. Even if a researcher predicts the direction of an effect, two-sided tests can also detect an effect that falls in the opposite direction. In most research articles, significance tests use two-sided $P$-values. Partly this reflects an objective approach to research that recognizes that an effect could go in either direction. In using two-sided $P$-values, researchers avoid the suspicion that they chose $H_a$ when they saw the direction in which the data occurred. That is not ethical.

Two-sided tests coincide with the usual approach in estimation. Confidence intervals are two-sided, obtained by adding and subtracting some quantity from the point estimate. One can form one-sided confidence intervals; for instance, concluding that a population mean is *at least* equal to 7 (i.e., between 7 and $\infty$). In practice, though, one-sided intervals are rarely used.

In deciding whether to use a one-sided or a two-sided $H_a$ in a particular exercise or in practice, consider the context. An exercise that says "Test whether the mean has *changed*" suggests a two-sided alternative, to allow for increase or decrease. "Test whether the mean has *increased*" suggests the one-sided $H_a: \mu > \mu_0$.

In either the one-sided or two-sided case, hypotheses always refer to population parameters, not sample statistics. So *never* express a hypothesis using sample statistic notation, such as $H_0: \bar{y} = 0$. There is no uncertainty or need to conduct statistical inference about sample statistics such as $\bar{y}$, because we can calculate their values exactly from the data.

*[handwritten margin notes: "P < 0.05 or 0.01, i.e. small 0.01" ; "significance = the strength of evidence against H₀" ; "if H₀ is true the data would be unusual and P-value must then be small — Statistical signif."]*

### The $\alpha$-Level: Using the P-Value to Make a Decision

A significance test analyzes the strength of the evidence against the null hypothesis, $H_0$. We start by presuming that $H_0$ is true. We analyze whether the data would be unusual if $H_0$ were true by finding the P-value. If the P-value is small, the data contradict $H_0$ and support $H_a$. Generally, researchers do not regard the evidence against $H_0$ as strong unless P is very small, say, $P < 0.05$ or $P < 0.01$.

Why do smaller P-values indicate stronger evidence against $H_0$? Because the data would then be more unusual if $H_0$ were true. When $H_0$ is true, the P-value is roughly equally likely to fall anywhere between 0 and 1. By contrast, when $H_0$ is false, the P-value is more likely to be near 0 than near 1.

In practice, it is sometimes necessary to decide whether the evidence against $H_0$ is strong enough to reject it. The decision is based on whether the P-value falls below a prespecified cutoff point. It's most common to reject $H_0$ if $P \leq 0.05$ and conclude that the evidence is not strong enough to reject $H_0$ if $P > 0.05$. The boundary value 0.05 is called the $\alpha$-*level* of the test.

---

**$\alpha$-Level**

The $\alpha$-*level* is a number such that we reject $H_0$ if the P-value is less than or equal to it. The $\alpha$-level is also called the **significance level**. In practice, the most common $\alpha$-levels are 0.05 and 0.01.

---

Like the choice of a confidence level for a confidence interval, the choice of $\alpha$ reflects how cautious you want to be. The smaller the $\alpha$-level, the stronger the evidence must be to reject $H_0$. To avoid bias in the decision-making process, you select $\alpha$ *before* analyzing the data.

### EXAMPLE 6.5     Adding Decisions to Previous Examples

Let's use $\alpha = 0.05$ to guide us in making a decision about $H_0$ for the examples of this section. Example 6.2 (page 149) tested $H_0$: $\mu = 4.0$ about mean political ideology. With sample mean $\bar{y} = 4.075$, the P-value was 0.50. The P-value is not small, so if truly $\mu = 4.0$, it would not be unusual to observe $\bar{y} = 4.075$. Since $P = 0.50 > 0.05$, there is insufficient evidence to reject $H_0$. It is believeable that the population mean ideology was 4.0.

Example 6.4 tested $H_0$: $\mu = 0$ about the mean weight gain for teenage girls suffering from anorexia. The P-value was 0.017. Since $P = 0.017 < 0.05$, there is sufficient evidence to reject $H_0$ in favor of $H_a$: $\mu > 0$. We conclude that the treatment results in an increase in mean weight. Such a conclusion is sometimes phrased as, "The increase in the mean weight is *statistically significant* at the 0.05 level." Since $P = 0.017$ is *not* less than 0.010, the result is *not* significant at the 0.010 level. In fact, *the P-value is the smallest level for $\alpha$ at which the results are significant.* So, with P-value $= 0.017$, we reject $H_0$ if $\alpha = 0.02$ or 0.05 or 0.10, but not if $\alpha = 0.015$ or 0.010 or 0.001. ∎

Table 6.3 summarizes significance tests for population means.

### Robustness for Violations of Normality Assumption

The $t$ test for a mean assumes that the population distribution is normal. This ensures that the sampling distribution of the sample mean $\bar{y}$ is normal (even for small $n$) and, after using $s$ to estimate $\sigma$ in finding the $se$, the $t$ test statistic has the $t$ distribution. As the sample size increases, this assumption of a normal population becomes less

**TABLE 6.3:** The Five Parts of Significance Tests for Population Means

1. **Assumptions**
   Quantitative variable
   Randomization
   Normal population (robust, especially for two-sided $H_a$, large $n$)
2. **Hypotheses**
   $H_0: \mu = \mu_0$
   $H_a: \mu \neq \mu_0$ (or $H_a: \mu > \mu_0$ or $H_a: \mu < \mu_0$)
3. **Test statistic**
   $$t = \frac{\bar{y} - \mu_0}{se} \text{ where } se = \frac{s}{\sqrt{n}}$$
4. **P-value**
   In $t$ curve, use
   $P$ = Two-tail probability for $H_a: \mu \neq \mu_0$
   $P$ = Probability to right of observed $t$-value for $H_a: \mu > \mu_0$
   $P$ = Probability to left of observed $t$-value for $H_a: \mu < \mu_0$
5. **Conclusion**
   Report $P$-value. Smaller $P$ provides stronger evidence against $H_0$ and supporting $H_a$. Can reject $H_0$ if $P \leq \alpha$-level.

important. We've seen that when $n$ is roughly about 30 or higher, an approximate normal sampling distribution occurs for $\bar{y}$ regardless of the population distribution, by the Central Limit Theorem (Section 4.5).

From Section 5.3, a statistical method is ***robust*** if it performs adequately even when an assumption is violated. Statisticians have shown that *two-sided* inferences for a mean using the $t$ distribution are robust against violations of the normal population assumption. Even if the population is not normal, two-sided $t$ tests and confidence intervals still work quite well. The test does not work so well for a one-sided test with small $n$ when the population distribution is highly skewed.

Figure 6.6 shows a histogram and a box plot of the data from the anorexia study of Example 6.4 (page 151). Figure 6.6 suggests skew to the right. The box plot highlights (as outliers) six girls who had considerable weight gains. As just mentioned, a two-sided $t$ test works quite well even if the population distribution is skewed. However, this plot makes us wary about using a one-sided test, since the sample size is not large ($n = 29$). Given this and the discussion in the previous subsection about one-sided versus two-sided tests, we're safest with that study to report a two-sided $P$-value of

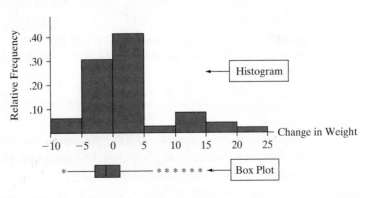

**FIGURE 6.6:** Histogram and Box Plot of Weight Change for Anorexia Sufferers

0.035. Also, as Example 5.5 (page 120) noted, the median may be a more relevant summary for these data.

## 6.3 SIGNIFICANCE TEST FOR A PROPORTION

For a categorical variable, the parameter is the population proportion for a category. For example, a significance test could analyze whether a majority of the population support embryonic stem-cell research by testing $H_0: \pi = 0.50$ against $H_a: \pi > 0.50$, where $\pi$ is the population proportion $\pi$ supporting it. The test for a proportion, like the test for a mean, finds a $P$-value for a test statistic measuring the number of standard errors a point estimate falls from a $H_0$ value.

### The Five Parts of a Significance Test for a Proportion

#### 1. Assumptions

Like other tests, this test assumes the data are obtained using randomization, such as a random sample. The sample size must be sufficiently large that the sampling distribution of $\hat{\pi}$ is approximately normal. For the most common case, in which the $H_0$ value of $\pi$ is 0.50, a sample size of at least 20 is sufficient. We'll give a precise guideline in Section 6.7, which presents a small-sample test.

#### 2. Hypotheses

The null hypothesis of a test about a population proportion has form

$$H_0 : \pi = \pi_0, \quad \text{such as} \quad H_0 : \pi = 0.50.$$

Here, $\pi_0$ denotes a particular proportion value between 0 and 1, such as 0.50. The most common alternative hypothesis is

$$H_a : \pi \neq \pi_0, \quad \text{such as} \quad H_a : \pi \neq 0.50.$$

This *two-sided* alternative states that the population proportion differs from the value in $H_0$. The *one-sided* alternatives

$$H_a : \pi > \pi_0 \quad \text{and} \quad H_a : \pi < \pi_0$$

apply when the researcher predicts a deviation in a certain direction from the $H_0$ value.

#### 3. Test Statistic

From Section 5.2, the sampling distribution of the sample proportion $\hat{\pi}$ has mean $\pi$ and standard error $\sigma_{\hat{\pi}} = \sqrt{\pi(1 - \pi)/n}$. When $H_0$ is true, $\pi = \pi_0$, so the standard error is $se_0 = \sqrt{\pi_0(1 - \pi_0)/n}$. We use the notation $se_0$ to indicate that this is the standard error under the presumption that $H_0$ is true.

The test statistic is

$$z = \frac{\hat{\pi} - \pi_0}{se_0}, \quad \text{where} \quad se_0 = \sqrt{\pi_0(1 - \pi_0)/n}.$$

This measures the number of standard errors that the sample proportion $\hat{\pi}$ falls from $\pi_0$. For large samples, if $H_0$ is true, the sampling distribution of the $z$ test statistic is the standard normal distribution.

The test statistic has a similar form as in tests for a mean:

**Form of Test Statistic**

$$z = \frac{\text{Estimate of parameter} - \text{null hypothesis value of parameter}}{\text{Standard error of estimator}}$$

Here, the estimate $\hat{\pi}$ of the proportion replaces the estimate $\bar{y}$ of the mean, and the null hypothesis proportion $\pi_0$ replaces the null hypothesis mean $\mu_0$.

### 4. P-Value

The P-Value is a one- or two-tail probability, as in tests for a mean, except using the normal rather than the $t$ distribution. For $H_a: \pi \neq \pi_0$, P is the two-tail probability. See Figure 6.7. This probability is double the single-tail probability beyond the observed $z$-value.

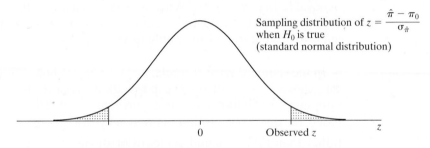

Sampling distribution of $z = \dfrac{\hat{\pi} - \pi_0}{\sigma_{\hat{\pi}}}$ when $H_0$ is true (standard normal distribution)

**FIGURE 6.7:** Calculation of P-Value in Testing $H_0: \pi = \pi_0$ against $H_a: \pi \neq \pi_0$. The two-sided alternative hypothesis uses a two-tail probability.

For one-sided alternatives, the P-value is a one-tail probability. Since $H_a: \pi > \pi_0$ predicts that the population proportion is *larger* than the $H_0$ value, its P-value is the probability *above* (i.e., to the right) of the observed $z$-value. For $H_a : \pi < \pi_0$, the P-value is the probability *below* (i.e., to the left) of the observed $z$-value.

### 5. Conclusion

As usual, the smaller the P-value, the more strongly the data contradict $H_0$ and support $H_a$. When we need to make a decision, we reject $H_0$ if $P \leq \alpha$ for a prespecified $\alpha$-level such as 0.05.

### EXAMPLE 6.6    Reduce Services or Raise Taxes?

These days, whether at the local, state, or national level, government often faces the problem of not having enough money to pay for the various services that it provides. One way to deal with this problem is to raise taxes. Another way is to reduce services. Which would you prefer? When the Florida Poll[3] asked a random sample of 1200 Floridians in 2006, 52% said raise taxes and 48% said reduce services.

Let $\pi$ denote the population proportion in Florida who would choose raising taxes. If $\pi < 0.50$, this is a minority of the population, whereas if $\pi > 0.50$, it is a majority.

---

[3]www.fiu.edu/orgs/ipor/ffp.

To analyze whether $\pi$ is in either of these ranges, we test $H_0: \pi = 0.50$ against $H_a: \pi \neq 0.50$.

The estimate of $\pi$ is $\hat{\pi} = 0.52$. Presuming $H_0: \pi = 0.50$ is true, the standard error of $\hat{\pi}$ is

$$se_0 = \sqrt{\frac{\pi_0(1 - \pi_0)}{n}} = \sqrt{\frac{(0.50)(0.50)}{1200}} = 0.0144.$$

The value of the test statistic is

$$z = \frac{\hat{\pi} - \pi_0}{se_0} = \frac{0.52 - 0.50}{0.0144} = 1.39.$$

From Table A, the two-tail $P$-value is $P = 2(0.0823) = 0.16$. If $H_0$ is true (i.e., if $\pi = 0.50$), the probability equals 0.16 that sample results would be as extreme in one direction or the other as in this sample.

This $P$-value is not small, so there is not much evidence against $H_0$. It seems believable that $\pi = 0.50$. With an $\alpha$-level such as 0.05, since $P = 0.16 > 0.05$, we would not reject $H_0$. We cannot determine whether those favoring raising taxes are a majority or minority of the population. ∎

In the standard error formula, $\sqrt{\pi(1 - \pi)/n}$, note we substituted the null hypothesis value $\pi_0 = 0.50$ for the population proportion $\pi$. The parameter values in sampling distributions for tests presume that $H_0$ is true, since the $P$-value is based on that presumption. This is why, for tests, we use $se_0 = \sqrt{\pi_0(1 - \pi_0)/n}$ rather than the estimated standard error, $se = \sqrt{\hat{\pi}(1 - \hat{\pi})/n}$. With the estimated $se$, the normal approximation for the sampling distribution of $z$ is poorer. This is especially true for proportions close to 0 or 1. The validity of the $P$-value is then poorer. By contrast, the confidence interval method does not have a hypothesized value for $\pi$, so that method uses the estimated $se$ rather than a $H_0$ value.

### Never "Accept $H_0$"

In Example 6.6, about raising taxes or reducing services, the $P$-value of 0.16 was not small. So $H_0: \pi = 0.50$ is plausible. In this case, the conclusion is sometimes reported as, "Do not reject $H_0$," since the data do not contradict $H_0$.

We say "Do not reject $H_0$" rather than "Accept $H_0$." The population proportion has many plausible values besides the number in $H_0$. For instance, a 95% confidence interval for the population proportion $\pi$ who support raising taxes rather than reducing services is

$$\hat{\pi} \pm 1.96\sqrt{\frac{\hat{\pi}(1 - \hat{\pi})}{n}} = 0.52 \pm 1.96\sqrt{\frac{(0.52)(0.48)}{1200}}, \text{ or } (0.49, 0.55).$$

This interval shows a range of plausible values for $\pi$. Even though insufficient evidence exists to conclude that $\pi \neq 0.50$, it is improper to conclude that $\pi = 0.50$.

In summary, $H_0$ contains a single value for the parameter. When the $P$-value is larger than the $\alpha$-level, saying "Do not reject $H_0$" instead of "Accept $H_0$" emphasizes that that value is merely one of many believable values. Because of sampling variability, there is a range of believable values, so we can never accept $H_0$. The reason "accept $H_a$" terminology is permissible for $H_a$ is that when the $P$-value is sufficiently small, the entire range of believable values for the parameter fall within the range of values $H_a$ specifies.

### Effect of Sample Size on *P*-Values

In Example 6.6, on raising taxes or cutting services, suppose $\hat{\pi} = 0.52$ had been based on $n = 4800$ instead of $n = 1200$. The standard error then decreases to 0.0072 (half as large), and you can verify that the test statistic $z = 2.77$. This has two-sided $P$-value $= 0.006$. That $P$-value provides strong evidence against $H_0$: $\pi = 0.50$ and suggests that a majority support raising taxes rather than cutting services. In that case, though, the 95% confidence interval for $\pi$ equals (0.506, 0.534). This indicates that $\pi$ is quite close to 0.50 in practical terms.

A given difference between an estimate and the $H_0$ value has a smaller $P$-value as the sample size increases. The larger the sample size, the more certain we can be that sample deviations from $H_0$ are indicative of true population deviations. In particular, notice that even a small difference between $\hat{\pi}$ and $\pi_0$ (or between $\bar{y}$ and $\mu_0$) can yield a small $P$-value if the sample size is very large.

## 6.4   DECISIONS AND TYPES OF ERRORS IN TESTS

When we need to decide whether the evidence against $H_0$ is strong enough to reject it, we've seen that we reject $H_0$ if $P \leq \alpha$, for a prespecified $\alpha$-level. Table 6.4 summarizes the two possible conclusions for $\alpha$-level $= 0.05$. The null hypothesis is either *rejected* or *not rejected*. If $H_0$ is rejected, then $H_a$ is accepted. If $H_0$ is not rejected, then $H_0$ is plausible, but other parameter values are also plausible. Thus, $H_0$ is never *accepted*. In this case, results are inconclusive, and the test does not identify either hypothesis as more valid.

**TABLE 6.4**: Possible Decisions in a Significance Test with $\alpha$-Level $= 0.05$

|  | Conclusion | |
| --- | --- | --- |
| $P$-Value | $H_0$ | $H_a$ |
| $P \leq 0.05$ | Reject | Accept |
| $P > 0.05$ | Do not reject | Do not accept |

It is better to report the $P$-value than to indicate merely whether the result is "statistically significant." Reporting the $P$-value has the advantage that the reader can tell whether the result is significant at any level. The $P$-values of 0.049 and 0.001 are both "significant at the 0.05 level," but the second case provides much stronger evidence than the first case. Likewise, $P$-values of 0.049 and 0.051 provide, in practical terms, the same amount of evidence about $H_0$. It is a bit artificial to call one result "significant" and the other "nonsignificant."

### Type I and Type II Errors for Decisions

Because of sampling variability, decisions in tests always have some uncertainty. The decision could be erroneous. There are two types of potential errors, conventionally called *Type I* and *Type II* errors.

---

**Type I and Type II Errors**

When $H_0$ is true, a **Type I error** occurs if $H_0$ is rejected.
When $H_0$ is false, a **Type II error** occurs if $H_0$ is not rejected.

---

There are four possible results. These refer to the two possible decisions cross-classified with the two possibilities for whether $H_0$ is true. See Table 6.5.

**TABLE 6.5:** The Four Possible Results of Making a Decision in a Test. Type I and Type II Errors Are the Two Possible Incorrect Decisions

| | | Decision | |
|---|---|---|---|
| | | *Reject $H_0$* | *Do not reject $H_0$* |
| Condition of $H_0$ | $H_0$ true | Type I error | Correct decision |
| | $H_0$ false | Correct decision | Type II error |

### Rejection Regions

The collection of test statistic values for which the test rejects $H_0$ is called the **rejection region**. For example, the rejection region for a test of level $\alpha = 0.05$ is the set of test statistic values for which $P \leq 0.05$.

For two-sided tests about a proportion, the two-tail $P$-value is $\leq 0.05$ whenever the test statistic $|z| \geq 1.96$. In other words, the rejection region consists of values of $z$ resulting from the estimate falling at least 1.96 standard errors from the $H_0$ value.

### The $\alpha$-Level Is the Probability of Type I Error

When $H_0$ is true, let's find the probability of Type I error. Suppose $\alpha = 0.05$. We've just seen that for the two-sided test about a proportion, the rejection region is $|z| \geq 1.96$. So the probability of rejecting $H_0$ is exactly 0.05, because the probability of the values in this rejection region under the standard normal curve is 0.05. But this is precisely the $\alpha$-level.

---

The probability of a Type I error is the $\alpha$-level for the test.

---

With $\alpha = 0.05$, if $H_0$ is true, the probability equals 0.05 of making a Type I error and rejecting that (true) $H_0$. We control $P$ (Type I error) by the choice of $\alpha$. The more serious the consequences of a Type I error, the smaller $\alpha$ should be. In practice, $\alpha = 0.05$ is most common, just as an error probability of 0.05 is most common with confidence intervals (that is, 95% confidence). However, this may be too high when a decision has serious implications.

For example, consider a criminal legal trial of a defendant. Let $H_0$ represent innocence and $H_a$ represent guilt. The jury rejects $H_0$ and judges the defendant to be guilty if it decides the evidence is sufficient to convict. A Type I error, rejecting a true $H_0$, occurs in convicting a defendant who is actually innocent. In a murder trial, suppose a convicted defendant gets the death penalty. Then, if a defendant is actually innocent, we would hope that the probability of conviction is much smaller than 0.05.

When we make a decision, we don't know whether we've made a Type I or Type II error, just as we don't know whether a particular confidence interval truly contains the parameter value. However, we can control the probability of an incorrect decision for either type of inference.

### As *P* (Type I Error) Goes Down, *P* (Type II Error) Goes Up

In an ideal world, Type I or Type II errors would not occur. In practice, errors do happen. We've all read about defendants who were convicted but later determined to be innocent. When we make a decision, why don't we use an extremely small $P$(Type I error), such as $\alpha = 0.000001$? For instance, why don't we make it almost impossible to convict someone who is really innocent?

When we make $\alpha$ smaller in a significance test, we need a smaller $P$-value to reject $H_0$. It then becomes harder to reject $H_0$. But this means that it will also be harder even if $H_0$ is false. The stronger the evidence required to convict someone, the more likely we will fail to convict defendants who are actually guilty. In other words, the smaller we make $P$ (Type I error), the larger $P$ (Type II error) becomes; that is, the probability of failing to reject $H_0$ even though it is false.

If we tolerate only an extremely small $P$(Type I error), such as $\alpha = 0.000001$, the test may be unlikely to reject $H_0$ even if it is false—for instance, we may be unlikely to convict someone even if he or she is guilty. This reasoning reflects the fundamental relation:

- The smaller $P$(Type I error) is, the larger $P$(Type II error) is.

Section 6.6 shows that $P$(Type II error) depends on just how far the true parameter value falls from $H_0$. If the parameter is nearly equal to the value in $H_0$, $P$(Type II error) is relatively high. If it falls far from $H_0$, $P$(Type II error) is relatively low. The farther the parameter falls from the $H_0$ value, the less likely the sample is to result in a Type II error.

For a fixed $P$(Type I error), $P$(Type II error) depends also on the sample size $n$. The larger the sample size, the more likely we are to reject a false $H_0$. To keep both $P$(Type I error) and $P$(Type II error) at low levels, it may be necessary to use a very large sample size. The $P$(Type II error) may be quite large when the sample size is small, unless the parameter falls quite far from the $H_0$ value.

Except in Section 6.6, we shall not calculate $P$(Type II error), because such calculations are complex. In practice, making a decision requires setting only $\alpha$, the $P$(Type I error).

### Equivalence between Confidence Intervals and Test Decisions

We now elaborate on the equivalence between decisions from two-sided tests and conclusions from confidence intervals, first alluded to in Example 6.3 (page 151). Consider the large-sample test of

$$H_0 : \mu = \mu_0 \qquad \text{versus} \qquad H_a : \mu \neq \mu_0.$$

When $P < 0.05$, $H_0$ is rejected at the $\alpha = 0.05$ level. This happens when the test statistic $t = (\bar{y} - \mu_0)/se$ is greater than about 1.96 in absolute value (when $n$ is large), which means that $\bar{y}$ falls more than $1.96(se)$ from $\mu_0$. But if this happens, then the 95% confidence interval for $\mu$, namely, $\bar{y} \pm 1.96(se)$, does not contain the null hypothesis value $\mu_0$. See Figure 6.8. These two inference procedures are consistent.

---

In testing $H_0$: $\mu = \mu_0$ against $H_a$: $\mu \neq \mu_0$, suppose we reject $H_0$ at the 0.05 $\alpha$-level. Then the 95% confidence interval for $\mu$ does not contain $\mu_0$. The 95% confidence interval for $\mu$ consists of those $\mu_0$ values for which we do not reject $H_0$: $\mu = \mu_0$ at the 0.05 $\alpha$-level.

---

In Example 6.2, about mean political ideology, the $P$-value for testing $H_0$: $\mu = 4.0$ against $H_a$: $\mu \neq 4.0$ was $P = 0.50$. At the $\alpha = 0.05$ level, we do not reject $H_0$: $\mu = 4.0$.

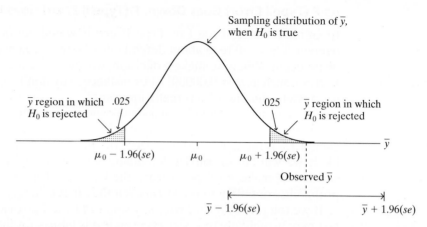

**FIGURE 6.8:** Relationship between Confidence Interval and Significance Test. The 95% confidence interval does not contain the $H_0$ value $\mu_0$ when the sample mean falls more than 1.96 standard errors from $\mu_0$, in which case the test statistic $|z| > 1.96$ and the $P$-value $< 0.05$.

It is believable that $\mu = 4.0$. Example 6.3 showed that a 95% confidence interval for $\mu$ is (3.9, 4.3), which contains $\mu_0 = 4.0$.

Rejecting $H_0$ at a particular $\alpha$-level is equivalent to the confidence interval for $\mu$ with the same error probability not containing $\mu_0$. For example, if a 99% confidence interval does not contain 0, then we would reject $H_0$: $\mu = 0$ in favor of $H_a$: $\mu \neq 0$ at the $\alpha = 0.01$ level with the test. The $\alpha$-level is both $P$(Type I error) for the test and the probability that the confidence interval method does not contain the parameter.

## Making Decisions versus Reporting the *P*-Value

The formal approach to hypothesis testing that this section has discussed was developed by the statisticians Jerzy Neyman and Egon Pearson in the late 1920s and early 1930s. In summary, this approach formulates null and alternative hypotheses, selects an $\alpha$-level for the $P$(Type I error), determines the rejection region of test statistic values that provide enough evidence to reject $H_0$, and then makes a decision about whether to reject $H_0$ according to what is actually observed for the test statistic value. With this approach, it's not even necessary to find a $P$-value. The choice of $\alpha$-level determines the rejection region, which together with the test statistic determines the decision.

The alternative approach of finding a $P$-value and using it to summarize evidence against a hypothesis is due to the great British statistician R. A. Fisher. He advocated merely reporting the $P$-value rather than using it to make a formal decision about $H_0$. Over time, this approach has gained favor, especially since software can now report precise $P$-values for a wide variety of significance tests.

This chapter has presented an amalgamation of the two approaches (the decision-based approach using an $\alpha$-level and the $P$-value approach), so you can interpret a $P$-value yet also know how to use it to make a decision if that is needed. These days, most research articles merely report the $P$-value rather than a decision about whether to reject $H_0$. From the *P*-value, readers can view the strength of evidence against $H_0$ and make their own decision, if they want to.

## 6.5 LIMITATIONS OF SIGNIFICANCE TESTS

A significance test makes an inference about whether a parameter differs from the $H_0$ value and about its direction from that value. In practice, we also want to know whether the parameter is sufficiently different from the $H_0$ value to be practically important. We'll see next that a test does not tell us as much as a confidence interval about practical importance.

### Statistical Significance versus Practical Significance

It's important to distinguish between *statistical significance* and *practical significance*. A small *P*-value, such as $P = 0.001$, is highly statistically significant. It provides strong evidence against $H_0$. It does not, however, imply an *important* finding in any practical sense. The small *P*-value merely means that if $H_0$ were true, the observed data would be very unusual. It does not mean that the true parameter value is far from $H_0$ in practical terms.

### EXAMPLE 6.7    Mean Political Ideology for All Americans

The mean political ideology of 4.08 in Example 6.2 refers to a sample of black Americans. The table also showed results for *white* and *other* categories. For a scoring of 1.0 through 7.0 for the ideology categories with 4.0 = moderate, the entire sample of 1331 observations has a mean of 4.12 and a standard deviation of 1.38. It appears that, on the average, conservatism was only slightly higher for the combined sample than for blacks alone (4.12 versus 4.08).

As in Example 6.2, we test $H_0$: $\mu = 4.0$ against $H_a$: $\mu \neq 4.0$ to analyze whether the population mean differs from the moderate ideology score of 4.0. Now, $se = s/\sqrt{n} = 1.38/\sqrt{1331} = 0.038$, and

$$t = \frac{\bar{y} - \mu_0}{se} = \frac{4.12 - 4.0}{0.038} = 3.2.$$

The two-sided *P*-value is $P = 0.001$. There is *very* strong evidence that the true mean exceeds 4.0; that is, that the true mean falls on the conservative side of moderate. But on a scale of 1.0 to 7.0, 4.12 is close to the moderate score of 4.0. Although the difference of 0.12 between the sample mean of 4.12 and the $H_0$ mean of 4.0 is highly significant statistically, the magnitude of this difference is small in practical terms. The mean response on political ideology for all Americans is essentially a moderate one. ∎

In Example 6.2, the sample mean ideology of 4.08 for $n = 186$ black Americans had $P = 0.50$, not much evidence against $H_0$. But if $\bar{y} = 4.08$ had been based on $n = 18,600$ (that is, 100 times as large as $n$ was), again with $s = 1.51$, we would have instead found $z = 6.79$ and a two-sided *P*-value of $P = 0.00000000001$. This is highly statistically significant, but not practically significant. For practical purposes, a mean of 4.08 on a scale of 1.0 to 7.0 for political ideology does not differ from 4.00.

We've seen that, with large sample sizes, $P$-values can be small even when the point estimate falls near the $H_0$-value. The size of $P$ merely summarizes the extent of evidence about $H_0$, not how far the parameter falls from $H_0$. Always inspect the difference between the estimate and the $H_0$-value to gauge the practical implications of a test result.

### Significance Tests Are Less Useful than Confidence Intervals

Null hypotheses containing single values are rarely true. That is, rarely is the parameter *exactly* equal to the value listed in $H_0$. With sufficiently large samples, so that a Type II error is unlikely, these hypotheses will normally be rejected. What is more relevant is whether the parameter is sufficiently different from the $H_0$-value to be of practical importance.

Although significance tests can be useful, most statisticians believe they have been overemphasized in social science research. It is preferable to construct confidence intervals for parameters instead of performing only significance tests. A test merely indicates whether the particular value in $H_0$ is plausible. It does not tell us which other potential values are plausible. The confidence interval, by contrast, displays the entire set of believable values. It shows the extent to which $H_0$ may be false by showing whether the values in the interval are far from the $H_0$-value. Thus, it helps us to determine whether rejection of $H_0$ has practical importance.

To illustrate, for the political ideology data in the previous example, a 95% confidence interval for $\mu$ is $\bar{y} \pm 1.96(se) = 4.12 \pm 1.96(0.038)$, or $(4.05, 4.20)$. This indicates that the difference between the population mean and the moderate score of 4.0 is small. Although the $P$-value of $P = 0.001$ provides very strong evidence against $H_0$: $\mu = 4.0$, in practical terms the confidence interval shows that $H_0$ is not wrong by much. By contrast, if $\bar{y}$ had been 6.125 (instead of 4.125), the 95% confidence interval would equal $(6.05, 6.20)$. This indicates a substantial difference from 4.0, the mean response being near the conservative score rather than the moderate score.

When a $P$-value is not small but the confidence interval is quite wide, this forces us to realize that the parameter might well fall far from $H_0$ even though we cannot reject it. This also supports why it does not make sense to "accept $H_0$," as Section 6.3 discussed.

The remainder of the text presents significance tests for a variety of situations. It is important to become familiar with these tests, if for no other reason than their frequent use in social science research. However, we'll also introduce confidence intervals that describe how far reality is from the $H_0$-value.

### Misinterpretations of Significance Tests and $P$-Values

We've seen it is improper to "accept $H_0$." We've also seen that statistical significance does not imply practical significance. Here's some other possible misinterpretations of significance tests:

- **It is misleading to report results only if they are statistically significant.** Some research journals have the policy of publishing results of a study only if the $P$-value $\leq 0.05$. Here's a danger of this policy: Suppose there truly is no effect, but 20 researchers independently conduct studies. We would expect about $20(0.05) = 1$ of them to obtain significance at the 0.05 level merely by chance. (When $H_0$ is true, about 5% of the time we get a $P$-value below 0.05 anyway.) If that researcher then submits results to a journal but the other 19 researchers do not, the article published will be a Type I error. It will report an effect when there really is not one.

- **Some tests may be statistically significant just by chance.** You should never scan software output for results that are statistically significant and report only those. If you run 100 tests, even if all the null hypotheses are correct, you would expect to get $P$-values $\leq 0.05$ about $100(0.05) = 5$ times. Be skeptical of reports of significance that might merely reflect ordinary random variability.

- **It is incorrect to interpret the $P$-value as the probability that $H_0$ is true.** The $P$-value is $P$(test statistic takes value like observed or even more extreme), presuming that $H_0$ is true. It is not $P(H_0$ true). Classical statistical methods calculate probabilities about variables and statistics (such as test statistics) that vary randomly from sample to sample, not about parameters. Statistics have sampling distributions; parameters do not. In reality, $H_0$ is not a matter of probability. It is either true or not true. We just don't know which is the case.

- **True effects may be smaller than reported estimates.** Even if a statistically significant result is a real effect, the true effect may be smaller than reported. For example, often several researchers perform similar studies, but the results that get attention are the most extreme ones. The researcher who decides to publicize the result may be the one who got the most impressive sample result, perhaps way out in the tail of the sampling distribution of all the possible results. See Figure 6.9.

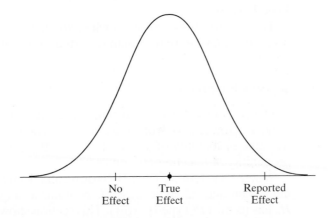

**FIGURE 6.9:** When Many Researchers Conduct Studies, the Statistically Significant Result Published Often Overestimates the True Effect

### EXAMPLE 6.8    Are Many Medical "Discoveries" Actually Type I Errors?

In medical studies, suppose that a true effect exists only 10% of the time. Suppose also that when an effect truly exists, there's a 50% chance of making a Type II error and failing to detect it. These were the hypothetical percentages used in an article in a medical journal.[4] The authors noted that many medical studies have a high Type II error rate because they are not able to use a large sample size. Assuming these rates, could a substantial percentage of medical "discoveries" actually be Type I errors?

Figure 6.10 is a ***tree diagram*** showing what we'd would expect with 1000 medical studies that test various hypotheses. If a true effect exists only 10% of the time; this would be the case for 100 of the 1000 studies. We do not get a small enough $P$-value to

---

[4]J. Sterne, G. Smith, and D. R. Cox, *British Medical Journal*, vol. 322, 2001, pp. 226–231.

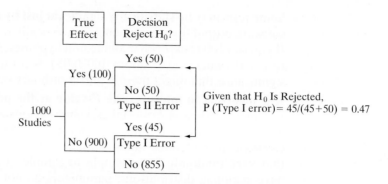

**FIGURE 6.10:** Tree Diagram of 1000 Hypothetical Medical Studies. This assumes a true effect exists 10% of the time and a 50% chance of a Type II error when an effect truly exists.

detect this true effect 50% of the time, that is, in 50 of these 100 studies. An effect will be reported for the other 50 of the 100 that do truly have an effect. For the 900 cases in which there truly is no effect, with the usual significance level of 0.05 we expect 5% of the 900 studies to incorrectly reject $H_0$. This happens for $(0.05)900 = 45$ studies. So, of the 1000 studies, we expect 50 to report an effect that is truly there, but we also expect 45 to report an effect that does not actually exist. So a proportion of $45/(45 + 50) = 0.47$ of medical studies that report effects are actually reporting Type I errors.

The moral is to be skeptical when you hear reports of new medical advances. The true effect may be weaker than reported, or there may actually be no effect at all. ∎

## 6.6 CALCULATING $P$ (TYPE II ERROR)*

We've seen that decisions in significance tests have two potential types of error. A Type I error results from rejecting $H_0$ when it is actually true. Given that $H_0$ is true, the probability of a Type I error is the $\alpha$-level of the test; when $\alpha = 0.05$, the probability of rejecting $H_0$ equals 0.05.

When $H_0$ is false, a Type II error results from *not* rejecting it. This probability has more than one value, because $H_a$ contains a range of possible values. Each value in $H_a$ has its own $P$(Type II error). This section shows how to calculate $P$(Type II error) at a particular value.

### EXAMPLE 6.9 Testing whether Astrology Really Works

One scientific test of the pseudo-science astrology used the following experiment[5]: For each of 116 adult subjects, an astrologer prepared a horoscope based on the positions of the planets and the moon at the moment of the person's birth. Each subject also filled out a California Personality Index survey. For each adult, his or her birth data and horoscope were shown to an astrologer with the results of the personality survey for that adult and for two other adults randomly selected from the experimental group. The astrologer was asked which personality chart of the three subjects was the correct one for that adult, based on his or her horoscope.

Let $\pi$ denote the probability of a correct prediction by an astrologer. If the astrologers' predictions are like random guessing, then $\pi = 1/3$. To test this against the alternative that the guesses are better than random guessing, we can test $H_0$: $\pi =$

---

[5]S. Carlson, *Nature*, vol. 318, 1985, pp. 419–425.

1/3 against $H_a$: $\pi > 1/3$. The alternative hypothesis reflects the astrologers' belief that they can predict better than random guessing. In fact, the National Council for Geocosmic Research, which supplied the astrologers for the experiment, claimed $\pi$ would be 0.50 or higher. So let's find $P$(Type II error) if actually $\pi = 0.50$, for an $\alpha = 0.05$-level test. That is, if actually $\pi = 0.50$, we'll find the probability we'd fail to reject $H_0$: $\pi = 1/3$.

To determine this, we'll first find the sample proportion values for which we would not reject $H_0$. For the test of $H_0$: $\pi = 1/3$, the sampling distribution of $\hat{\pi}$ is the curve shown on the left in Figure 6.11. With $n = 116$, this curve has standard error

$$se_0 = \sqrt{\pi_0(1 - \pi_0)/n} = \sqrt{[(1/3)(2/3)]/116} = 0.0438.$$

For $H_a$: $\pi > 1/3$, we get a $P$-value of 0.05 if the test statistic $z = 1.645$. That is, 1.645 is the $z$-score that has a right-tail probability of 0.05. So we *fail to reject $H_0$*, getting a $P$-value *above* 0.05, if $z < 1.645$. In other words, we fail to reject $H_0$: $\pi = 1/3$ if the sample proportion $\hat{\pi}$ falls less than 1.645 standard errors above 1/3, that is, if

$$\hat{\pi} < 1/3 + 1.645(se_0) = 1/3 + 1.645(0.0438) = 0.405.$$

So the right-tail probability above 0.405 is $\alpha = 0.05$ for the curve on the left in Figure 6.11.

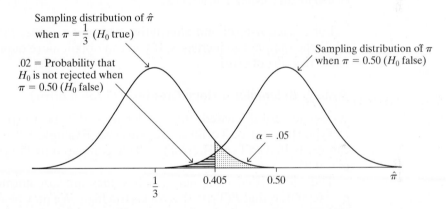

**FIGURE 6.11:** Calculation of $P$(Type II Error) for Testing $H_0$: $\pi = 1/3$ against $H_a$: $\pi > 1/3$ at $\alpha = 0.05$ Level, when True Proportion is $\pi = 0.50$. A Type II error occurs if $\hat{\pi} < 0.405$, since then $P$-value $>0.05$ even though $H_0$ is false.

To find $P$(Type II error) if $\pi$ actually equals 0.50, we must find $P(\hat{\pi} < 0.405)$ when $\pi = 0.50$. This is the left-tail probability *below* 0.405 for the curve on the right in Figure 6.11 (which is the curve that applies when $\pi = 0.50$). When $\pi = 0.50$, the standard error for a sample size of 116 is $\sqrt{[(0.50)(0.50)/116]} = 0.0464$. (This differs a bit from $se_0$ for the test statistic, which uses 1/3 instead of 0.50 for $\pi$.) For the normal distribution with a mean of 0.50 and standard error of 0.0464, the $\hat{\pi}$ value of 0.405 has a $z$-score of

$$z = \frac{0.405 - 0.50}{0.0464} = -2.04.$$

The probability that $\hat{\pi} < 0.405$ is the probability that a standard normal variable falls below $-2.04$. From Table A, the left-tail probability below $-2.04$ equals 0.02. So, for a sample of size 116, the probability of not rejecting $H_0$: $\pi = 1/3$ is 0.02, if in fact $\pi = 0.50$.

In other words, if astrologers truly had the predictive power they claimed, the chance of failing to detect this with this experiment would have only been about 0.02. To see what actually happened in the experiment, see Exercise 6.17. ■

The probability of Type II error increases when the parameter value moves closer to $H_0$. To verify this, you can check that $P$(Type II error) = 0.54 at $\pi = 0.40$. So, if the parameter falls near the $H_0$ value, there may be a substantial chance of failing to reject $H_0$. Likewise, the farther the parameter falls from $H_0$, the less likely a Type II error. Figure 6.12 plots $P$(Type II error) for the various $\pi$ values in $H_a$.

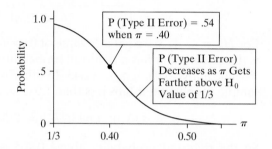

**FIGURE 6.12:** Probability of Type II Error for Testing $H_0$: $\pi = 1/3$ against $H_a$: $\pi > 1/3$ at $\alpha = 0.05$ Level, Plotted for the Potential $\pi$ Values in $H_a$

For a fixed $\alpha$-level and alternative parameter value, $P$(Type II error) decreases when the sample size increases. If you can obtain more data, you will be less likely to make this sort of error.

### Tests with Smaller $\alpha$ Have Greater $P$ (Type II error)

As Section 6.4 discussed, the smaller $\alpha = P$(Type I error) is in a test, the larger $P$(Type II error) is. To illustrate, suppose Example 6.9 used $\alpha = 0.01$. Then you can verify that $P$(Type II error) = 0.08, compared to $P$(Type II error) = 0.02 when $\alpha = 0.05$.

The reason that extremely small values are not normally used for $\alpha$, such as $\alpha = 0.0001$, is that $P$(Type II error) is too high. We may be unlikely to reject $H_0$ even if the parameter falls far from the null hypothesis. In summary, for fixed values of other factors,

- $P$(Type II error) decreases as

    — the parameter value is farther from $H_0$.

    — the sample size increases.

    — $P$(Type I error) increases.

### The Power of a Test

When $H_0$ is false, you want the probability of rejecting $H_0$ to be high. The probability of rejecting $H_0$ is called the **power** of the test. For a particular value of the parameter from within the $H_a$ range,

$$\text{Power} = 1 - P \text{ (Type II error)}.$$

In Example 6.9, for instance, the test of $H_0$: $\pi = 1/3$ has $P$(Type II error) = 0.02 at $\pi = 0.50$. Therefore, the power of the test at $\pi = 0.50$ equals $1 - 0.02 = 0.98$.

The power increases for values of the parameter falling farther from the $H_0$ value. Just as the curve for $P$(Type II error) in Figure 6.12 decreases as $\pi$ gets farther above $\pi_0 = 1/3$, the curve for the power would increase.

In practice, studies should ideally have high power. Before granting financial support for a planned study, many research agencies expect principal investigators to show that reasonable power (usually, at least 0.80) exists at values of the parameter that are considered practically significant.

When you read that results of a study are insignificant, be skeptical if no information is given about the power. The power may be low, especially if $n$ is small. For further details about calculating $P$(Type II error) or power, see Cohen (1988).

## 6.7  SMALL-SAMPLE TEST FOR A PROPORTION—THE BINOMIAL DISTRIBUTION*

For a population proportion $\pi$, Section 6.3 presented a significance test that is valid for large samples. The sampling distribution of the sample proportion $\hat{\pi}$ is then approximately normal, which justifies using a $z$ test statistic.

For small $n$, the sampling distribution of $\hat{\pi}$ occurs at only a few points. If $n = 5$, for example, the only possible values for the sample proportion $\hat{\pi}$ are 0, 1/5, 2/5, 3/5, 4/5, and 1. A continuous approximation such as the normal distribution is inappropriate. In addition, we'll see that the closer the $\pi$ is to 0 or 1 for a given sample size, the more skewed the actual sampling distribution becomes.

This section introduces a small-sample test for proportions. It uses the most important probability distribution for discrete variables, the *binomial*.

### The Binomial Distribution

For categorical data, often the following conditions hold:

1. Each observation falls into one of two categories.
2. The probabilities for the two categories are the same for each observation. We denote the probabilities by $\pi$ for category 1 and $(1 - \pi)$ for category 2.
3. The outcomes of successive observations are independent. That is, the outcome for one observation does not depend on the outcomes of other observations.

Flipping a coin repeatedly is a prototype for these conditions. For each flip, we observe whether the outcome is head (category 1) or tail (category 2). The probabilities of the outcomes are the same for each flip (0.50 for each if the coin is balanced). The outcome of a particular flip does not depend on the outcome of other flips.

Now, for $n$ observations, let $x$ denote the number that occur in category 1. For example, for $n = 5$ coin flips, $x =$ number of heads could equal 0, 1, 2, 3, 4, or 5. When the observations satisfy the above conditions, the probability distribution of $x$ is the **binomial distribution**.

The binomial variable $x$ is discrete, taking one of the integer values $0, 1, 2, \ldots, n$. The formula for the binomial probabilities follows:

---
**Probabilities for a Binomial Distribution**

---

Denote the probability of category 1, for each observation, by $\pi$. For $n$ independent observations, the probability of $x$ outcomes in category 1 is

$$P(x) = \frac{n!}{x!(n - x)!}\pi^x(1 - \pi)^{n-x}, \quad x = 0, 1, 2, \ldots, n.$$

The symbol $n!$ is called **$n$ factorial**. It represents $n! = 1 \times 2 \times 3 \cdots \times n$. For example, $1! = 1$, $2! = 1 \times 2 = 2$, $3! = 1 \times 2 \times 3 = 6$, and so forth. Also, $0!$ is defined to be 1.

---

For particular values for $\pi$ and $n$, substituting the possible values for $x$ into the formula for $P(x)$ provides the probabilities of the possible outcomes. The sum of the probabilities equals 1.0.

### EXAMPLE 6.10  Gender and Selection of Managerial Trainees

Example 6.1 (page 143) discussed a case involving potential bias against females in selection of management trainees for a large supermarket chain. The pool of employees is half female and half male. Ten trainees are supposedly selected at random from this pool. If they are truly selected at random, how many females would we expect?

The probability that any one person selected is a female is $\pi = 0.50$, the proportion of available trainees who are female. Similarly, the probability that any one person selected is male is $(1 - \pi) = 0.50$. Let $x =$ number of females selected. This has the binomial distribution with $n = 10$ and $\pi = 0.50$. For each $x$ between 0 and 10, the probability that $x$ of the ten people selected are female equals

$$P(x) = \frac{10!}{x!(10 - x)!}(0.50)^x(0.50)^{10-x}, \quad x = 0, 1, 2, \ldots, 10.$$

For example, the probability that no females are chosen ($x = 0$) equals

$$P(0) = \frac{10!}{0!10!}(0.50)^0(0.50)^{10} = (0.50)^{10} = 0.001.$$

Recall that any number raised to the power of 0 equals 1. Also, $0! = 1$, and the 10! terms in the numerator and denominator cancel, leaving $P(0) = (0.50)^{10}$. The probability that exactly one female is chosen equals

$$P(1) = \frac{10!}{1!9!}(0.50)^1(0.50)^9 = 10(0.50)(0.50)^9 = 0.010.$$

This computation simplifies considerably by using $10!/9! = 10$, since 10! is just 9! multiplied by 10. Table 6.6 lists the entire binomial distribution for $n = 10$, $\pi = 0.50$.

In Table 6.6, the probability is about 0.98 that $x$ falls between 2 and 8, inclusive. The least likely values for $x$ are 0, 1, 9, and 10, which have a combined probability of only 0.022. If the sample were randomly selected, somewhere between about two and eight females would probably be selected. It is especially unlikely that none or ten would be selected.

The probabilities for females determine those for males. For instance, the probability that nine of the ten people selected are male equals the probability that one of the ten selected is female. ∎

**TABLE 6.6:** The Binomial Distribution for $n = 10$, $\pi = 0.50$. The binomial variable $x$ can take any value between 0 and 10.

| $x$ | $P(x)$ | $x$ | $P(x)$ |
|---|---|---|---|
| 0 | 0.001 | 6 | 0.205 |
| 1 | 0.010 | 7 | 0.117 |
| 2 | 0.044 | 8 | 0.044 |
| 3 | 0.117 | 9 | 0.010 |
| 4 | 0.205 | 10 | 0.001 |
| 5 | 0.246 | | |

**Properties of the Binomial Distribution**

The binomial distribution is perfectly symmetric only when $\pi = 0.50$. In Example 6.10 with $n = 10$, for instance, since the population proportion of females equals 0.50, $x = 10$ has the same probability as $x = 0$.

The sample proportion $\hat{\pi}$ relates to $x$ by

$$\hat{\pi} = x/n.$$

For example, for $x = 1$ female chosen out of $n = 10$, $\hat{\pi} = 1/10 = 0.10$. The sampling distribution of $\hat{\pi}$ is also symmetric when $\pi = 0.50$. When $\pi \neq 0.50$, the distributions are skewed, the degree of skew increasing as $\pi$ gets closer to 0 or 1. Figure 6.13 illustrates for the sampling distribution of $\hat{\pi}$. For instance, when $\pi = 0.10$, the sample proportion $\hat{\pi}$ can't fall much below 0.10 since it must be positive, but it could fall considerably above 0.10.

The binomial distribution has mean and standard deviation

$$\mu = n\pi, \quad \sigma = \sqrt{n\pi(1 - \pi)}.$$

For example, suppose the chance of a female in any one selection for management training is 0.50, as the supermarket chain claims. Then, out of 10 trainees, we expect $\mu = n\pi = 10(0.50) = 5.0$ females.

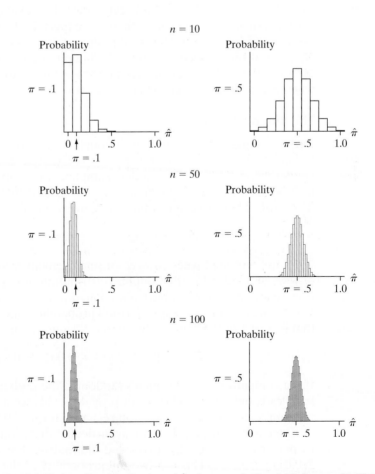

**FIGURE 6.13:** Sampling Distribution of $\hat{\pi}$ when $\pi = 0.10$ or 0.50, for $n = 10, 50, 100$

### EXAMPLE 6.11  How Much Variability Can an Exit Poll Show?

Example 4.6 (page 85) discussed an exit poll of 2705 voters for the 2006 California gubernatorial election. Let $x$ denote the number in the exit poll who voted for Arnold Schwarzenegger. In the population of nearly 7 million voters, 55.9% voted for him. If the exit poll was randomly selected, then the binomial distribution for $x$ has $n = 2705$ and $\pi = 0.559$. The distribution is described by

$$\mu = 2705(0.559) = 1512, \quad \sigma = \sqrt{2705(0.559)(0.441)} = 26.$$

Almost certainly, $x$ would fall within 3 standard deviations of the mean. This is the interval from 1434 to 1590. In fact, in that exit poll, 1528 reported voting for Schwarzenegger. ∎

We've seen (Sections 5.2, 6.3) that the sampling distribution of the sample proportion $\hat{\pi}$ has mean $\pi$ and standard error $\sigma_{\hat{\pi}} = \sqrt{\pi(1 - \pi)/n}$. To get these, we divide the binomial mean $\mu = n\pi$ and standard deviation $\sigma = \sqrt{n\pi(1 - \pi)}$ by $n$, since $\hat{\pi}$ divides $x$ by $n$.

The binomial distribution and the sampling distribution of $\hat{\pi}$ are approximately normal for large $n$. This approximation is the basis of the large-sample test of Section 6.3. How large is "large"? A guideline is that the expected number of observations should be at least 10 for both categories. For example, if $\pi = 0.50$, we need at least about $n = 20$, because then we expect $20(0.50) = 10$ observations in one category and $20(1 - 0.50) = 10$ in the other category. For testing $H_0: \pi = 0.90$ or $H_0: \pi = 0.10$, we need $n \geq 100$. The sample size requirement reflects the fact that a symmetric bell shape for the sampling distribution of $\hat{\pi}$ requires larger sample sizes when $\pi$ is near 0 or 1 than when $\pi$ is near 0.50.

### The Binomial Test

If the sample size is not large enough to use the normal test, we can use the binomial distribution directly. Refer to Example 6.10 (page 170) about potential gender discrimination. For random sampling, the probability $\pi$ that a person selected for management training is female equals 0.50. If there is bias against females, then $\pi < 0.50$. Thus, we can test the company's claim of random sampling by testing

$$H_0: \pi = 0.50 \quad \text{versus} \quad H_a: \pi < 0.50.$$

Of the ten employees chosen for management training, let $x$ denote the number of women. Under $H_0$, the sampling distribution of $x$ is the binomial distribution with $n = 10$ and $\pi = 0.50$. Table 6.6 tabulated it. As in Example 6.1 (page 143), suppose $x = 1$. The $P$-value is then the left-tail probability of an outcome at least this extreme; that is, $x = 1$ or 0. From Table 6.6, the $P$-value equals

$$P = P(0) + P(1) = 0.001 + 0.010 = 0.011.$$

If the company selected trainees randomly, the probability of choosing one or fewer females is only 0.011. This result provides evidence against the null hypothesis of a random selection process. We can reject $H_0$ for $\alpha = 0.05$, though not for $\alpha = 0.010$.

Even if we suspect bias in a particular direction, the most even-handed way to perform a test uses a two-sided alternative. For $H_a: \pi \neq 0.50$, the $P$-value is $2(0.011) = 0.022$. This is a two-tail probability of the outcome that one or fewer *of either sex* is selected. Figure 6.14 shows the formation of this $P$-value.

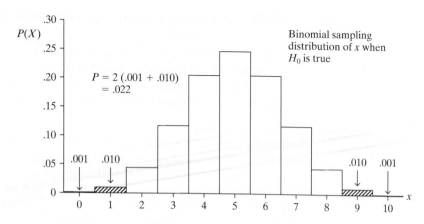

**FIGURE 6.14:** Calculation of *P*-Value in Testing $H_0$: $\pi = 0.50$ against $H_a$: $\pi \neq 0.50$, when $n = 10$ and $x = 1$

The assumptions for the binomial test are the three conditions for the binomial distribution. Here, the conditions are satisfied. Each observation has only two possible outcomes, female or male. The probability of each outcome is the same for each selection, 0.50 for selecting a female and 0.50 for selecting a male (under $H_0$). For random sampling, the outcome of any one selection does not depend on any other one.

In the rare cases that the population size is small, the binomial conditions are not all satisfied. To illustrate, suppose a population contains only four persons, of whom two are female. If we randomly sample two separate individuals, the second observation has different probabilities than the first. For example, if the first person selected was female, then the probability that the second person selected is female equals 1/3, since 1 female remains among the 3 subjects. Thus, the probabilities are not the same for each selection, which the binomial requires. For the successive observations to have essentially the same probabilities and be independent, the population size must be much larger than the sample size. The sample size should be no more than about 10% as large as the minimum of the population numbers of subjects in the two categories. This is usually easily satisfied in practice.

## 6.8   CHAPTER SUMMARY

Statistical inference uses sample data to make predictions about population parameters. Chapters 5 and 6 have introduced two inference methods—***estimation*** and ***significance tests***. The estimation method called *confidence intervals* provides a range of the most plausible values for a parameter. A significance test judges whether a particular value for the parameter is plausible. Both methods utilize the sampling distribution of the estimator of the parameter.

Significance tests have five parts:

1. ***Assumptions:***

    - Tests for *means* apply with quantitative variables, whereas tests for *proportions* apply with categorical variables.
    - Tests assume *randomization*, such as a random sample.
    - Large-sample tests about proportions require no assumption about the population distribution, because the Central Limit Theorem implies approximate normality of the sampling distribution of the sample proportion. This

justifies using the $z$ test statistic. Small-sample tests for proportions use the *binomial distribution*.

- Tests for means use the $t$ distribution for the $t$ test statistic. The test assumes the population distribution is normal. In practice, two-sided tests (like confidence intervals) are *robust* to violations of the normality assumption, especially for large samples because of the Central Limit Theorem.

2. **Null and alternative hypotheses** about the parameter: The null hypothesis has form $H_0$: $\mu = \mu_0$ for a mean and $H_0$: $\pi = \pi_0$ for a proportion. Here, $\mu_0$ and $\pi_0$ denote values hypothesized for the parameters, such as 0.50 in $H_0$: $\pi = 0.50$. The most common alternative is *two sided*, such as $H_a$: $\pi \neq 0.50$. Hypotheses such as $H_a$: $\pi > 0.50$ and $H_a$: $\pi < 0.50$ are *one sided*, designed to detect departures from $H_0$ in a particular direction.

3. A **test statistic** describes how far the point estimate falls from the $H_0$ value. The $z$ statistic for proportions and $t$ statistic for means measure the number of standard errors that the point estimate ($\hat{\pi}$ or $\bar{y}$) falls from the $H_0$-value.

4. The **P-value** describes the weight of evidence the data provide about $H_0$.

   - The $P$-value is calculated by presuming that $H_0$ is true. It equals the probability that the test statistic equals the observed value or a value even more extreme.
   - The "more extreme" results are determined by the alternative hypothesis. For two-sided $H_a$, the $P$-value is a two-tail probability.
   - Small $P$-values result when the point estimate falls far from the $H_0$ value, so that the test statistic is large. When the $P$-value is small, it would be unusual to observe such data if $H_0$ were true. The smaller the $P$-value, the stronger the evidence against $H_0$.

5. A **conclusion** based on the sample evidence about $H_0$: We report and interpret the $P$-value. Sometimes it is necessary to make a decision. If the $P$-value is less than or equal to a fixed $\alpha$-level (such as $\alpha = 0.05$), we reject $H_0$. Otherwise, we cannot reject it.

When we make a decision, two types of errors can occur.

- When $H_0$ is true, a Type I error results if we reject it.
- When $H_0$ is false, a Type II error results if we fail to reject it.

The choice of $\alpha$, the cutoff point for the $P$-value in making a decision, equals $P$(Type I error). Normally, we choose small values such as $\alpha = 0.05$ or 0.01. For fixed $\alpha$, $P$(Type II error) decreases as the distance increases between the parameter and the $H_0$ value or as the sample size increases.

Table 6.7 summarizes the five parts of the tests this chapter presented.

Sample size is a critical factor in both estimation and significance tests. With small sample sizes, confidence intervals are wide, making estimation imprecise. Small sample sizes also make it difficult to reject false null hypotheses unless the true parameter is far from the null hypothesis value. $P$(Type II error) may be high for parameter values of interest.

To introduce estimation and significance tests, Chapters 5 and 6 presented inference about a single parameter for a single variable. In practice, it is usually artificial to have a particular fixed number for the $H_0$ value of a parameter. One of the few times this happens is when the response score results from taking a difference of two

**TABLE 6.7:** Summary of Significance Tests for Means and Proportions

| Parameter | Mean | Proportion |
|---|---|---|
| 1. Assumptions | Random sample, quantitative variable normal population | Random sample, categorical variable null expected counts at least 10 |
| 2. Hypotheses | $H_0: \mu = \mu_0$ $H_a: \mu \neq \mu_0$ $H_a: \mu > \mu_0$ $H_a: \mu < \mu_0$ | $H_0: \pi = \pi_0$ $H_a: \pi \neq \pi_0$ $H_a: \pi > \pi_0$ $H_a: \pi < \pi_0$ |
| 3. Test statistic | $t = \dfrac{\bar{y} - \mu_0}{se}$ with $se = \dfrac{s}{\sqrt{n}}, df = n - 1$ | $z = \dfrac{\hat{\pi} - \pi_0}{se_0}$ with $se_0 = \sqrt{\pi_0(1 - \pi_0)/n}$ |
| 4. P-value | Two-tail probability in sampling distribution for two-sided test ($H_0: \mu \neq \mu_0$ or $H_a: \pi \neq \pi_0$); One-tail probability for one-sided test | |
| 5. Conclusion | Reject $H_0$ if P-value $\leq \alpha$-level such as 0.05 | |

values, such as the change in weight in Example 6.4 (page 151). In that case, $\mu_0 = 0$ is a natural baseline. Significance tests much more commonly refer to comparisons of means for two samples than to a fixed value of a parameter for a single sample. The next chapter shows how to compare means or proportions for two groups.

## PROBLEMS

### Practicing the Basics

**6.1.** For (a)–(c), is it a null hypothesis, or an alternative hypothesis?
  **(a)** In Canada, the proportion of adults who favor legalized gambling equals 0.50.
  **(b)** The proportion of all Canadian college students who are regular smokers now is less than 0.24 (the value it was ten years ago).
  **(c)** The mean IQ of all students at Lake Wobegon High School is larger than 100.
  **(d)** Introducing notation for a parameter, state the hypotheses in (a)–(c) in terms of the parameter values.

**6.2.** You want to know whether adults in your country think the ideal number of children is equal to 2, or higher or lower than that.
  **(a)** Define notation and state the null and alternative hypotheses for studying this.
  **(b)** For responses in a recent GSS to the question, "What do you think is the ideal number of children to have?", software shows results:

```
Test of mu = 2.0 vs mu not = 2.0

Variable   N     Mean    StDev   SE Mean    T      P-value
Children   1302  2.490   0.850   0.0236    20.80   0.0000
```

Report the test statistic value, and show how it was obtained from other values reported in the table.
  **(c)** Explain what the P-value represents and interpret its value.

**6.3.** For a test of $H_0: \mu = 0$ against $H_a: \mu \neq 0$ with $n = 1000$, the $t$ test statistic equals 1.04.
  **(a)** Find the P-value and interpret it. (*Note:* You can use the standard normal to approximate the $t$ distribution.)
  **(b)** Suppose $t = -2.50$ rather than 1.04. Find the P-value. Does this provide stronger, or weaker, evidence against the null hypothesis? Explain.
  **(c)** When $t = 1.04$, find the P-value for (i) $H_a: \mu > 0$, (ii) $H_a: \mu < 0$.

**6.4.** The P-value for a test about a mean with $n = 25$ is $P = 0.05$.
  **(a)** Find the $t$ test statistic value that has this P-value for (i) $H_a: \mu \neq 0$, (ii) $H_a: \mu > 0$, (iii) $H_a: \mu < 0$.

**(b)** Does this $P$-value provide stronger, or weaker, evidence against the null hypothesis than $P = 0.01$? Explain.

**6.5.** Find and interpret the $P$-value for testing $H_0$: $\mu = 100$ against $H_0 : \mu \neq 100$, if a sample has
**(a)** $n = 400, \bar{y} = 103, s = 40$.
**(b)** $n = 1600, \bar{y} = 103, s = 40$. Comment on the effect of $n$ on the results of a significance test.

**6.6.** Example 6.4 (page 151) described a study about therapies for teenage girls suffering from anorexia. For the 17 girls who received the family therapy, the changes in weight were

$$11, 11, 6, 9, 14, -3, 0, 7, 22, -5, -4, 13, 13, 9, 4, 6, 11.$$

Part of an SPSS printout for the data shows:

| Lower | Upper | t-value | df | 2-Tail Sig |
|-------|-------|---------|----|------------|
| 3.60  |       |         |    | .0007      |

Fill in the missing results.

**6.7.** According to a union agreement, the mean income for all senior-level assembly-line workers in a large company equals $500 per week. A representative of a women's group decides to analyze whether the mean income $\mu$ for female employees matches this norm. For a random sample of nine female employees, $\bar{y} = \$410$ and $s = \$90$.
**(a)** Test whether the mean income of female employees differs from $500 per week. Include assumptions, hypotheses, test statistic, and $P$-value. Interpret the result.
**(b)** Report the $P$-value for $H_a: \mu < 500$. Interpret.
**(c)** Report and interpret the $P$-value for $H_a$: $\mu > 500$. (*Hint*: The $P$-values for the two possible one-sided tests must sum to 1.)

**6.8.** By law, an industrial plant can discharge no more than 500 gallons of waste water per hour, on the average, into a neighboring lake. Based on other infractions they have noticed, an environmental action group believes this limit is being exceeded. Monitoring the plant is expensive, and a random sample of four hours is selected over a period of a week. Software reports:

| Variable | No. Cases | Mean | SD | SE of Mean |
|----------|-----------|------|-----|-----------|
| WASTE | 4 | 1000.0 | 400.0 | 200.0 |

**(a)** Test whether the mean discharge equals 500 gallons per hour against the alternative that the limit is being exceeded. Find the $P$-value and interpret.
**(b)** Explain why the test may be highly approximate or even invalid if the population distribution of discharge is far from normal.

**(c)** Explain how your one-sided analysis implicitly tests the broader null hypothesis that $\mu \leq 500$.

**6.9.** In response to the statement "A preschool child is likely to suffer if his or her mother works," the response categories (Strongly agree, Agree, Disagree, Strongly disagree) had counts (91, 385, 421, 99) for responses in a GSS. To treat this ordinal variable as quantitative, we assign scores to the categories. For the scores $(2, 1, -1, -2)$, which treat the distance between Agree and Disagree as twice the distance between Strongly agree and Agree or between Disagree and Strongly disagree, software reports:

| N | Mean | Std Dev | Std Err |
|------|--------|---------|---------|
| 996 | -0.052 | 1.253 | 0.0397 |

**(a)** Set up null and alternative hypotheses to test whether the population mean response differs from the neutral value, 0.
**(b)** Find the test statistic and $P$-value. Interpret, and make a decision about $H_0$, using $\alpha = 0.05$.
**(c)** Based on (b), can you "accept" $H_0$: $\mu = 0$? Why or why not?
**(d)** Construct a 95% confidence interval for $\mu$. Show the correspondence between whether 0 falls in the interval and the decision about $H_0$.

**6.10.** In Example 6.2 on political ideology (page 149), suppose we use the scores $(-3, -2, -1, 0, 1, 2, 3)$ instead of the scores $(1, 2, 3, 4, 5, 6, 7)$ used there. We then test $H_0$: $\mu = 0$. Explain the effect of the change in scores on **(a)** the sample mean and standard deviation, **(b)** the test statistic, **(c)** the $P$-value and interpretation.

**6.11.** Results of 99% confidence intervals for means are consistent with results of two-sided tests with which $\alpha$-level? Explain the connection.

**6.12.** For a test of $H_0$: $\pi = 0.50$, the $z$ test statistic equals 1.04.
**(a)** Find the $P$-value for $H_a$: $\pi > 0.50$.
**(b)** Find the $P$-value for $H_a$: $\pi \neq 0.50$.
**(c)** Find the $P$-value for $H_a$: $\pi < 0.50$.
**(d)** Do any of the $P$-values in (a), (b), or (c) give strong evidence against $H_0$? Explain.

**6.13.** For a test of $H_0$: $\pi = 0.50$, the sample proportion is 0.35 based on a sample size of 100.
**(a)** Show that the test statistic is $z = -3.0$.
**(b)** Find and interpret the $P$-value for $H_a$: $\pi < 0.50$.
**(c)** For a significance level of $\alpha = 0.05$, what decision do you make?
**(d)** If the decision in (c) was in error, what type of error was it? What could you do to reduce the chance of that type of error?

**6.14.** Same-sex marriage was legalized across Canada by the Civil Marriage Act enacted in 2005. Is this supported by a majority, or a minority, of the Canadian population? A poll conducted for the *Globe and Mail* newspaper in July 2005 of 1000 Canadians asked whether this bill should stand or be repealed. The responses were 55% should stand, 39% should repeal, 6% don't know. Let $\pi$ denote the population proportion of Canadian adults who believe it should stand. For testing $H_0 : \pi = 0.50$ against $H_a : \pi \neq 0.50$:
  (a) Find the standard error, and interpret.
  (b) Find the test statistic, and interpret.
  (c) Find the *P*-value, and interpret in context.

**6.15.** When a recent GSS asked, "Would you be willing to pay much higher taxes in order to protect the environment?" (variable GRNTAXES), 369 people answered yes and 483 answered no. Software shows the following results to analyze whether a majority or minority of Americans would answer yes:

```
-------------------------------------------------
Test of proportion = 0.5 vs not = 0.5


 N  Sample prop    95% CI     Z-Value P-Value
852   0.4331    (0.400, 0.466)  -3.91   0.000
-------------------------------------------------
```

  (a) Specify the hypotheses that are tested.
  (b) Report and interpret the test statistic value.
  (c) Report and interpret the *P*-value as a probability.
  (d) Explain an advantage of the confidence interval shown over the significance test.

**6.16.** A Pew Research Center poll (May 14, 2003) of 1201 adults asked, "All in all, do you think affirmative action programs designed to increase the number of black and minority students on college campuses are a good thing or a bad thing?" Sixty percent said good, 30% said bad, and 10% said don't know. Let $\pi$ denote the population proportion who said it is good. Find the *P*-value for testing $H_0$: $\pi = 0.50$ against $H_a$: $\pi \neq 0.50$. Interpret.

**6.17.** In the scientific test of astrology discussed in Example 6.9 (page 166), the astrologers were correct with 40 of their 116 predictions. Test $H_0$: $\pi = 1/3$ against $H_a$: $\pi > 1/3$. Find the *P*-value, make a decision using $\alpha = 0.05$, and interpret.

**6.18.** The previous exercise analyzed whether astrologers could predict the correct personality chart for a given horoscope better than by random guessing. In the words of that study, what would be a
  (a) Type I error,
  (b) Type II error?

**6.19.** A mayoral election in Madison, Wisconsin, has two candidates. Exactly half the residents currently prefer each candidate.

  (a) For a random sample of 400 voters, 230 voted for a particular candidate. Are you willing to predict the winner? Why?
  (b) For a random sample of 40 voters, 23 voted for a particular candidate. Would you be willing to predict the winner? Why? (The sample proportion is the same in (a) and (b), but the sample sizes differ.)

**6.20.** The authorship of an old document is in doubt. A historian hypothesizes that the author was a journalist named Jacalyn Levine. Upon a thorough investigation of Levine's known works, it is observed that one unusual feature of her writing was that she consistently began 6% of her sentences with the word *whereas*. To test the historian's hypothesis, it is decided to count the number of sentences in the disputed document that begin with *whereas*. Out of the 300 sentences, none do. Let $\pi$ denote the probability that any one sentence written by the unknown author of the document begins with *whereas*. Test $H_0$: $\pi = 0.06$ against $H_a$: $\pi \neq 0.06$. What assumptions are needed for your conclusion to be valid? (F. Mosteller and D. L. Wallace conducted this type of investigation to determine whether Alexander Hamilton or James Madison authored 12 of the *Federalist Papers*. See *Inference and Disputed Authorship: The Federalist*, Addison-Wesley, 1964.)

**6.21.** A multiple-choice test question has four possible responses. The question is difficult, with none of the four responses being obviously wrong, yet with only one correct answer. It first occurs on an exam taken by 400 students. Test whether more people answer the question correctly than would be expected just due to chance (i.e., if everyone randomly guessed the correct answer).
  (a) Set up the hypotheses for the test.
  (b) Of the 400 students, 125 correctly answer the question. Find the *P*-value and interpret.

**6.22.** Example 6.4 (page 151) tested a therapy for anorexia, using $H_0$: $\mu = 0$ and $H_a$: $\mu > 0$ about the population mean weight change.
  (a) In the words of that example, what would be a (i) Type I error, (ii) Type II error?
  (b) The *P*-value was 0.017. If the decision for $\alpha = 0.05$ were in error, what type of error is it?
  (c) Suppose instead $\alpha = 0.01$. What decision would you make? If it is in error, what type of error is it?

**6.23.** Jones and Smith separately conduct studies to test $H_0$: $\mu = 500$ against $H_0$: $\mu \neq 500$, each with $n = 1000$. Jones gets $\bar{y} = 519.5$, with $se = 10.0$. Smith gets $\bar{y} = 519.7$, with $se = 10.0$.
  (a) Show that $t = 1.95$ and *P*-value $= 0.051$ for Jones. Show that $t = 1.97$ and *P*-value $= 0.049$ for Smith.

**(b)** Using $\alpha = 0.050$, for each study indicate whether the result is "statistically significant."

**(c)** Using this example, explain the misleading aspects of reporting the result of a test as "$P \leq 0.05$" versus "$P > 0.05$," or as "reject $H_0$" versus "Do not reject $H_0$," without reporting the actual $P$-value.

**6.24.** Jones and Smith separately conduct studies to test $H_0: \pi = 0.50$ against $H_0: \pi \neq 0.50$, each with $n = 400$. Jones gets $\hat{\pi} = 220/400 = 0.550$. Smith gets $\hat{\pi} = 219/400 = 0.5475$.

**(a)** Show that $z = 2.00$ and $P$-value $= 0.046$ for Jones. Show that $z = 1.90$ and $P$-value $= 0.057$ for Smith.

**(b)** Using $\alpha = 0.05$, indicate in each case whether the result is "statistically significant." Interpret.

**(c)** Use this example to explain why important information is lost by reporting the result of a test as "$P$-value $\leq 0.05$" versus "$P$-value $> 0.05$," or as "reject $H_0$" versus "Do not reject $H_0$", without reporting the $P$-value.

**(d)** The 95% confidence interval for $\pi$ is (0.501, 0.599) for Jones and (0.499, 0.596) for Smith. Explain how this method shows that, in practical terms, the two studies had very similar results.

**6.25.** A study considers whether the mean score $\mu$ on a college entrance exam for students in 2007 is any different from the mean of 500 for students in 1957. Test $H_0: \mu = 500$ against $H_a: \mu \neq 500$, if for a nationwide random sample of 10,000 students who took the exam in 2007, $\bar{y} = 497$ and $s = 100$. Show that the result is highly significant statistically, but not practically significant.

**6.26.** A report released on September 25, 2006 by the Collaborative on Academic Careers in Higher Education indicated that there is a notable gap between female and male academics in their confidence that tenure rules are clear, with men feeling more confident. The 4500 faculty members in the survey were asked to evaluate policies on a scale of 1 to 5 (very unclear to very clear). The mean response about the criteria for tenure was 3.51 for females and 3.55 for males, which was indicated to meet the test for statistical significance, with the mean for females being significantly less than the mean for males. Use this study to explain the distinction between statistical significance and practical significance.

**6.27.** Refer to Example 6.8 on "medical discoveries" (page 165). Using a tree diagram, approximate $P$(Type I error) under the assumption that a true effect exists 20% of the time and that $P$(Type II error) $= 0.30$.

**6.28.** A decision is planned in a test of $H_0: \mu = 0$ against $H_a: \mu > 0$, using $\alpha = 0.05$. If $\mu = 5$, $P$(Type II error) $= 0.17$.

**(a)** Explain the meaning of this last sentence.

**(b)** If the test used $\alpha = 0.01$, would $P$(Type II error) be less than, equal to, or greater than 0.17? Explain.

**(c)** If $\mu = 10$, would $P$(Type II error) be less than, equal to, or greater than 0.17? Explain.

**6.29.** Let $\pi$ denote the proportion of schizophrenics who respond positively to treatment. A test is conducted of $H_0: \pi = 0.50$ against $H_a: \pi > 0.50$, for a sample of size 25, using $\alpha = 0.05$.

**(a)** Find the region of sample proportion values for which $H_0$ is rejected.

**(b)** Suppose that $\pi = 0.60$. Find $P$(Type II error).

**6.30.** Studies have considered whether neonatal sex differences exist in behavioral and physiological reactions to stress. One study[6] evaluated changes in heart rate for a sample of infants placed in a stressful situation. The sample mean change in heart rate was small for males compared to females: $-1.2$ compared to 10.7, each with standard deviations of about 18. Suppose we are skeptical of the result for males and plan a larger experiment to test whether the mean heart rate increases when male infants undergo the stressful experience. Let $\mu$ denote the population mean of the difference in heart rates, after versus before the stress. We'll test $H_0: \mu = 0$ against $H_a: \mu > 0$, at the $\alpha = 0.05$ level using $n = 30$ infant males. Suppose the standard deviation is 18. Find $P$(Type II error) if $\mu = 10$ by showing (a) a test statistic of $t = 1.699$ has a $P$-value of 0.05, (b) we fail to reject $H_0$ if $\bar{y} < 5.6$, (c) this happens if $\bar{y}$ falls more than 1.33 standard errors below 10, (d) this happens with probability about 0.10.

**6.31.** Refer to the previous exercise.

**(a)** Find $P$(Type II error) if $\mu = 5$. How does $P$(Type II error) depend on the value of $\mu$?

**(b)** Find $P$(Type II error) if $\mu = 10$ and $\alpha = 0.01$. How does $P$(Type II error) depend on $\alpha$?

**(c)** How does $P$(Type II error) depend on $n$?

**6.32.** A jury list contains the names of all individuals who may be called for jury duty. The proportion of women on the list is 0.53. A jury of size 12 is selected at random from the list. None selected are women.

**(a)** Find the probability of selecting 0 women.

**(b)** Test the hypothesis that the selections are random against the alternative of bias against women. Report the $P$-value, and interpret.

**6.33.** A person claiming to possess extrasensory perception (ESP) says she can guess more often than not the outcome of a flip of a balanced coin in another room, not visible to her.

---

[6]M. Davis and E. Emory, *Child Development*, vol. 66, 1995, pp. 14–27.

(a) Introduce appropriate notation, and state hypotheses for testing her claim.

(b) Of 5 coin flips, she guesses the correct result 4 times. Find the *P*-value and interpret.

**6.34.** In a CNN exit poll of 1336 voters in the 2006 Senatorial election in New York State, let $x$ = number in exit poll who voted for the Democratic candidate, Hillary Clinton.

(a) Explain why this scenario would seem to satisfy the three conditions needed to use the binomial distribution.

(b) If the population proportion voting for Clinton had been 0.50, find the mean and standard deviation of the probability distribution of $x$.

(c) For (b), using the normal distribution approximation, give an interval in which $x$ would almost certainly fall.

(d) Actually, the exit poll had $x = 895$. Explain how you could make an inference about whether $\pi$ is above or below 0.50.

**6.35.** In a given year, the probability that an American female dies in a motor vehicle accident equals 0.0001 (*Statistical Abstract of the United States*).

(a) In a city having 1 million females, find the mean and standard deviation of $x$ = number of deaths from motor vehicle accidents. State the assumptions for these to be valid. (*Hint*: Find $\mu$ and $\sigma$ for the binomial distribution.)

(b) Would it be surprising if $x = 0$? Explain. (*Hint*: How many standard deviations is 0 from the expected value?)

(c) Based on the normal approximation to the binomial, find an interval within which $x$ has probability 0.95 of occurring.

(d) The probability for American males is 0.0002. Repeat (a) for males, and compare results to those for females.

## Concepts and Applications

**6.36.** You can use an *applet* to repeatedly generate random samples and conduct significance tests, to illustrate their behavior when used for many samples. To try this, go to the *significance test for a proportion* applet at www.prenhall.com/???. Set the null hypothesis as $H_0$: $\pi = 1/3$ for a one-sided test ($\pi > 1/3$) with sample size 116, a case Example 6.9 (page 166) on the astrology experiment considered. At the menu, set the true proportion value to 0.33.

(a) Click *Simulate* and 100 samples of this size will be taken, with the *P*-value found for each sample. What percentage of the tests were significant at the 0.05 significance level?

(b) To get a feel for what happens "in the long run," do this simulation 50 times, so you will

have a total of 5000 samples of size 116. What percentage of the samples resulted in a Type I error? What percentage would you expect to do so, resulting in a Type I error?

(c) Next, change $\pi$ to 0.50, so $H_0$ is actually false. Simulate 5000 samples. What percentage of times did you make a Type II error? By Example 6.9 this should happen only about 2% of the time.

**6.37.** Refer to the "Student survey" data file (Exercise 1.11 on page 8).

(a) Test whether the population mean political ideology differs from 4.0. Report the *P*-value, and interpret.

(b) Test whether the proportion favoring legalized abortion equals, or differs from, 0.50. Report the *P*-value, and interpret.

**6.38.** Refer to the data file your class created in Exercise 1.12 (page 9). For variables chosen by your instructor, state a research question and conduct inferential statistical analyses. Also use graphical and numerical methods presented earlier in this text to describe the data and, if necessary, to check assumptions for your analyses. Prepare a report, summarizing and interpreting your findings.

**6.39.** A study considered the effects of a special class designed to improve children's verbal skills. Each child took a verbal skills test before and after attending the class for three weeks. Let $y$ = second exam score − first exam score. The scores on $y$ for a random sample of four children having learning problems were 3, 7, 3, 3. Conduct inferential statistical methods to determine whether the class has a positive effect. Summarize your analyses and interpretations in a short report. (*Note*: The scores could improve merely from the students feeling more comfortable with the testing process. A more appropriate design would also administer the exam twice to a control group that does not take the special class, comparing the changes for the experimental and control groups using methods of Chapter 7.)

**6.40.** The 49 students in a class at the University of Florida made blinded evaluations of pairs of cola drinks. For the 49 comparisons of Coke and Pepsi, Coke was preferred 29 times. In the population that this sample represents, is this strong evidence that a majority prefers one of the drinks? Refer to the following printout.

```
-----------------------------------------------
Test of parameter = 0.50 vs not = 0.50

 N  Sample prop    95.0% CI     Z-Value  P-Value
49    0.5918    (0.454, 0.729)   1.286   0.1985
-----------------------------------------------
```

Explain how each result on this printout was obtained. Summarize results in a way that would be clear to someone who is not familiar with statistical inference.

**6.41.** In the 1990s, the U.S. Justice Department and other groups studied possible abuse by Philadelphia police officers in their treatment of minorities. One study, conducted by the American Civil Liberties Union, analyzed whether African-American drivers were more likely than others in the population to be targeted by police for traffic stops. Researchers studied the results of 262 police car stops during one week in 1997. Of those, 207 of the drivers were African-American, or 79% of the total. At that time, Philadelphia's population was 42.2% African-American. Does the number of African-Americans stopped give strong evidence of possible bias, being higher than you'd expect if we take into account ordinary random variation? Explain your reasoning in a report of at most 250 words.

**6.42.** An experiment with 26 students in an Israeli classroom consisted of giving everyone a lottery ticket, and then later asking if they would be willing to exchange their ticket for another one, plus a small monetary incentive. Only 7 students agreed to the exchange. In a separate experiment, 31 students were given a new pen and then later asked to exchange it for another pen and a small monetary incentive. All 31 agreed.[7] Conduct inferential statistical methods to analyze the data. Summarize your analyses and interpretations in a short report.

**6.43.** Ideally, results of a statistical analysis should not depend greatly on a single observation. To check this, it's a good idea to conduct a *sensitivity study*: Redo the analysis after deleting an outlier from the data set or changing its value to a more typical value, and check whether results change much. For the anorexia data shown in Example 5.5 (page 120), the weight change of 20.9 pounds was a severe outlier. Suppose this observation was actually 2.9 pounds but was incorrectly recorded. Redo the one-sided test of Example 6.4 (page 151), and summarize the influence of that observation.

**6.44.** In making a decision in a test, a researcher worries about the possibility of rejecting $H_0$ when it is actually true. Explain how to control the probability of this type of error.

**6.45.** Consider the analogy between making a decision in a test and making a decision about the innocence or guilt of a defendant in a criminal trial.
   **(a)** Explain what Type I and Type II errors are in the trial.

**(b)** Explain intuitively why decreasing $P$(Type I error) increases $P$(Type II error).
**(c)** Defendants are convicted if the jury finds them to be guilty "beyond a reasonable doubt." A jury interprets this to mean that if the defendant is innocent, the probability of being found guilty should be only 1 in a billion. Describe any problems this strategy has.

**6.46.** Medical tests for diagnosing conditions such as breast cancer are fallible, just like decisions in significance tests. Identify ($H_0$ true, $H_0$ false) with disease (absent, present), and (Reject $H_0$, Do not reject $H_0$) with diagnostic test (positive, negative), where a positive diagnosis means that the test predicts that the disease is present. Explain the difference between Type I and Type II errors in this context. Explain why decreasing $P$(Type I error) increases $P$(Type II error), in this context.

**6.47.** An article in a sociology journal that deals with changes in religious beliefs over time states, "For these subjects, the difference in their mean responses on the scale of religiosity between age 16 and the current survey was significant ($P < 0.05$)."
   **(a)** Explain what it means for the result to be "significant."
   **(b)** Explain why it would have been more informative if the authors provided the actual $P$-value rather than merely indicating that it is below 0.05. What other information might they have provided?

**6.48.** An article in a political science journal states that "no significant difference was found between men and women in their voting rates ($P = 0.63$)." Can we conclude that the population voting rates are identical for men and women? Explain.

**6.49.** You conduct a significance test using software. The output reports a $P$-value of 0.4173545. In summarizing your analyses in a research article, explain why it makes more sense to report $P = 0.42$ rather than $P = 0.4173545$.

**6.50.** A research study conducts 60 significance tests. Of these, 3 are significant at the 0.05 level. The authors write a report stressing only the three "significant" results, not mentioning the other 57 tests that were "not significant." Explain what is misleading about their report.

**6.51.** Some journals have a policy of publishing research results only if they achieve statistical significance at the 0.05 $\alpha$-level.
   **(a)** Explain the dangers of this.
   **(b)** When medical stories in the mass media report supposed large dangers or benefits of certain agents (e.g., coffee drinking, fiber in cereal), later research often suggests that the effects

---

[7]M. Bar-Hillel and E. Neter, *J. Personality and Social Psych.*, vol. 70, 1996, pp. 17–27.

are smaller than first believed, or may not even exist. Explain why.

*Select the correct response(s) in Exercises 6.52–6.56. (More than one may be correct.)*

**6.52.** We analyze whether the true mean discharge of wastewater per hour from an industrial plant exceeds the company claim of 1000 gallons. For the decision in the one-sided test using $\alpha = 0.05$:
   **(a)** If the plant is not exceeding the limit, but actually $\mu = 1000$, there is only a 5% chance that we will conclude that they are exceeding the limit.
   **(b)** If the plant is exceeding the limit, there is only a 5% chance that we will conclude that they are not exceeding the limit.
   **(c)** The probability that the sample mean equals exactly the observed value would equal 0.05 if $H_0$ were true.
   **(d)** If we reject $H_0$, the probability that it is actually true is 0.05.
   **(e)** All of the above.

**6.53.** The $P$-value for testing $H_0: \mu = 100$ against $H_a: \mu \neq 100$ is $P = 0.001$. This indicates that
   **(a)** There is strong evidence that $\mu = 100$.
   **(b)** There is strong evidence that $\mu \neq 100$.
   **(c)** There is strong evidence that $\mu > 100$.
   **(d)** There is strong evidence that $\mu < 100$.
   **(e)** If $\mu$ were equal to 100, it would be unusual to obtain data such as those observed.

**6.54.** In the previous exercise, suppose the test statistic $t = 3.29$.
   **(a)** There is strong evidence that $\mu = 100$.
   **(b)** There is strong evidence that $\mu > 100$.
   **(c)** There is strong evidence that $\mu < 100$.

**6.55.** A 95% confidence interval for $\mu$ is $(96, 110)$. Which two statements about significance tests for the same data are correct?
   **(a)** In testing $H_0: \mu = 100$ against $H_a: \mu \neq 100$, $P > 0.05$.
   **(b)** In testing $H_0: \mu = 100$ against $H_a: \mu \neq 100$, $P < 0.05$.
   **(c)** In testing $H_0: \mu = \mu_0$ against $H_a: \mu \neq \mu_0$, $P > 0.05$ if $\mu_0$ is any of the numbers inside the confidence interval.
   **(d)** In testing $H_0: \mu = \mu_0$ against $H_a: \mu \neq \mu_0$, $P > 0.05$ if $\mu_0$ is any of the numbers outside the confidence interval.

**6.56.** Let $\beta$ denote $P$(Type II error). For an $\alpha = 0.05$-level test of $H_0: \mu = 0$ against $H_a: \mu > 0$ with $n = 30$ observations, $\beta = 0.36$ at $\mu = 4$. Then
   **(a)** At $\mu = 5$, $\beta > 0.36$.
   **(b)** If $\alpha = 0.01$, then at $\mu = 4$, $\beta > 0.36$.
   **(c)** If $n = 50$, then at $\mu = 4$, $\beta > 0.36$.
   **(d)** The power of the test is 0.64 at $\mu = 4$.

   **(e)** This must be false, because necessarily $\alpha + \beta = 1$.

**6.57.** Answer true or false for each of the following, and explain your answer:
   **(a)** $P$(Type II error) $= 1 - P$(Type I error).
   **(b)** If we reject $H_0$ using $\alpha = 0.01$, then we also reject it using $\alpha = 0.05$.
   **(c)** The $P$-value is the probability that $H_0$ is true. (*Hint:* Do we find probabilities about variables and their statistics, or about parameters?)
   **(d)** An article in an anthropology journal reports $P = 0.063$ for testing $H_0: \mu = 0$ against $H_a: \mu \neq 0$. If the authors had instead reported a 95% confidence interval for $\mu$, then the interval would have contained 0, and readers could have better judged just which values are plausible for $\mu$.

**6.58.** Explain the difference between one-sided and two-sided alternative hypotheses, and explain how this affects calculation of the $P$-value.

**6.59.** Explain why the terminology "do not reject $H_0$" is preferable to "accept $H_0$."

**6.60.** Your friend plans to survey students in your college to study whether a majority feel that the legal age for drinking alcohol should be reduced. He has never studied statistics. How would you explain to him the concepts of
   **(a)** null and alternative hypotheses,
   **(b)** $P$-value,
   **(c)** $\alpha$-level,
   **(d)** Type II error?

**6.61.** A random sample of size 40 has $\bar{y} = 120$. The $P$-value for testing $H_0: \mu = 100$ against $H_a: \mu \neq 100$ is $P = 0.057$. Explain what is incorrect about each of the following interpretations of this $P$-value, and provide a proper interpretation.
   **(a)** The probability that the null hypothesis is correct equals 0.057.
   **(b)** The probability that $\bar{y} = 120$ if $H_0$ is true equals 0.057.
   **(c)** If in fact $\mu \neq 100$, the probability equals 0.057 that the data would be at least as contradictory to $H_0$ as the observed data.
   **(d)** The probability of Type I error equals 0.057.
   **(e)** We can accept $H_0$ at the $\alpha = 0.05$ level.
   **(f)** We can reject $H_0$ at the $\alpha = 0.05$ level.

**\*6.62.** Refer to the previous exercise and the $P$-value of 0.057.
   **(a)** Explain why the $P$-value is the smallest $\alpha$-level at which $H_0$ can be rejected; that is, $P$ equals the smallest level at which the data are significant.
   **(b)** Refer to the correspondence between results of confidence intervals and two-sided tests. When the $P$-value is 0.057, explain why the

94.3% confidence interval is the narrowest confidence interval for $\mu$ that contains $\mu_0 = 100$.

*6.63. A researcher conducts a significance test every time she analyzes a new data set. Over time, she conducts 100 tests.
  (a) Suppose $H_0$ is true in every case. What is the distribution of the number of times she rejects $H_0$ at the 0.05 level?
  (b) Suppose she rejects $H_0$ in five of the tests. Is it plausible that $H_0$ is correct in every case? Explain.

*6.64. Each year in Liverpool, New York, a public librarian estimates the mean number of times the books in that library have been checked out in the previous year. To do this, the librarian randomly samples computer records for 100 books and forms a 95% confidence interval for the mean. This has been done for 20 years.
  (a) Find the probability that all the confidence intervals contain the true means. (*Hint*: Use the binomial distribution.)
  (b) Find the probability that at least one confidence interval does not contain the true mean.

*6.65. Suppose you wanted to test $H_0$: $\pi = 0.50$, but of the $n = 30$ observations, 0 were in the category of interest. If you found the $z$ test statistic using the $se = \sqrt{\hat{\pi}(1 - \hat{\pi})/n}$ for confidence intervals, show what happens to the test statistic. Explain why the $se_0 = \sqrt{\pi_0(1 - \pi_0)/n}$ is more appropriate for tests.

*6.66. You test $H_0$: $\pi = 0.50$ against $H_a$: $\pi > 0.50$, using $\alpha = 0.05$. In fact, $H_a$ is true. Explain why $P$(Type II error) increases toward 0.95 as $\pi$ moves down toward 0.50. (Assume $n$ and $\alpha$ stay fixed.)

*6.67. Refer to the ESP experiment in Exercise 6.33, with $n = 5$.
  (a) For what value(s) of $x$ = number of correct guesses can you reject $H_0$: $\pi = 0.50$ in favor of $H_a$: $\pi > 0.50$, using $\alpha = 0.05$?
  (b) For what value(s) of $x$ can you reject $H_0$ using $\alpha = 0.01$? (*Note*: For small samples, it may not be possible to achieve very small $P$-values.)
  (c) Suppose you test $H_0$ using $\alpha = 0.05$. If $\pi = 0.50$, what is $P$(Type I error)? (*Note*: For discrete distributions, $P$(Type I error) may be less than intended. It is better to report the $P$-value.)

# CHAPTER 7

# Comparison of Two Groups

The comparison of two groups is a very common type of analysis in the social and behavioral sciences. A study might compare mean income for men and women having similar jobs and experience. Another study might compare the proportions of Americans and Canadians who favor certain gun control laws. Means are compared for quantitative variables and proportions are compared for categorical variables.

Section 7.1 introduces some basic concepts for comparing groups. Section 7.2 illustrates these for comparing proportions and Section 7.3 for comparing means. The rest of the chapter shows some alternative methods useful for special cases.

## 7.1 PRELIMINARIES FOR COMPARING GROUPS

Do women tend to spend more time on housework than men? If so, how much more? In Great Britain in 2005, the Time Use Survey[1] studied how a random sample of Brits spend their time on a typical day. For those who reported working full time, Table 7.1 reports the mean and standard deviation of the reported average number of minutes per day spent on cooking and washing up. We use Table 7.1 to present some basic concepts for comparing groups.

TABLE 7.1: Cooking and Washing Up Minutes, per Day, for a National Survey of Men and Women Working Full Time in Great Britain

| | | Cooking and Washing Up Minutes | |
|---|---|---|---|
| Sex | Sample Size | Mean | Standard Deviation |
| Men | 1219 | 23 | 32 |
| Women | 733 | 37 | 16 |

### Bivariate Analyses with Response and Explanatory Variables

Two groups being compared constitute a ***binary*** variable —a variable having only two categories, sometimes also called ***dichotomous***. In a comparison of mean housework

---

[1] www.statistics.gov.uk

183

time for men and women, men and women are the two categories of the binary variable, sex. Methods for comparing two groups are special cases of ***bivariate*** statistical methods —an outcome variable of some type is analyzed for each category of a second variable.

From Section 3.5 (page 55), recall that an outcome variable about which comparisons are made is called a ***response variable***. The variable that defines the groups is called the ***explanatory variable***. In Table 7.1, time spent cooking and washing up is the response variable. The sex of the respondent is the explanatory variable.

### Dependent and Independent Samples

Some studies compare means or proportions at two or more points in time. For example, a ***longitudinal study*** observes subjects at several times. An example is the Framingham Heart Study, which every two years since 1948 has observed many health characteristics of more than 5000 adults from Framingham, Massachusetts. Samples that have the same subjects in each sample are called ***dependent samples***.

More generally, two samples are *dependent* when a natural matching occurs between each subject in one sample and a subject in the other sample. Usually this happens when each sample has the same subjects. But matching can also occur when the two samples have different subjects. An example is a comparison of housework time of husbands and wives, the husbands forming one sample and their wives the other.

More commonly, comparisons use ***independent samples***. This means that the observations in one sample are *independent* of those in the other sample. The subjects in the two samples are different, with no matching between one sample with the other sample. An example is Table 7.1. Subjects were randomly selected and then classified on their sex and measured on how much time they spend in various activities. The samples of men and women were independent.

Suppose you plan to analyze whether a tutoring program improves mathematical understanding. One study design administers a math achievement test to a sample of students both before and after they go though the program. The sample of test scores before the program and the sample of test scores after the program are then *dependent*, because each sample has the same subjects.

Another study design randomly splits a class of students into two groups, one of which takes the tutoring program (the *experimental* group) and one of which does not (the *control* group). After the course, both groups take the math achievement test, and mean scores are compared. The two samples are then *independent*, because they contain different subjects without a matching between samples.

These two studies are *experimental*. As mentioned at the end of Section 2.2, many social science studies are instead *observational*. For example, many comparisons of groups result from dividing a sample into subsamples according to classification on a variable such as sex or race or political party. Table 7.1 is an example of this. Such cases are examples of ***cross-sectional*** studies, which use a single survey to compare groups. If the overall sample was randomly selected, then the subsamples are independent random samples from the corresponding subpopulations.

Why do we distinguish between *independent* and *dependent* samples? Because the standard error formulas for statistics that compare means or compare proportions are different for the two types of sample. With dependent samples, matched responses are likely to be associated. In the study about a tutoring program, the students who perform relatively well on one exam probably tend to perform well on the second exam also. This affects the standard error of statistics comparing the groups.

## Difference of Estimates and Their Standard Error

To compare two populations, we can estimate the difference between their parameters. To compare population means $\mu_1$ and $\mu_2$, we treat $\mu_2 - \mu_1$ as a parameter and estimate it by the difference of sample means, $\bar{y}_2 - \bar{y}_1$. For Table 7.1, the estimated difference between the population mean daily cooking and washing up time for women and for men equals $\bar{y}_2 - \bar{y}_1 = 37 - 23 = 14$ minutes.

The sampling distribution of the estimator $\bar{y}_2 - \bar{y}_1$ has expected value $\mu_2 - \mu_1$. For large random samples, or for small random samples from normal population distributions, this sampling distribution has a normal shape, as Figure 7.1 portrays.

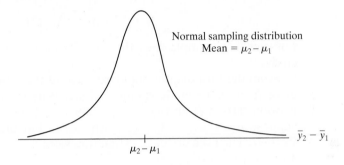

**FIGURE 7.1:** For Random Samples, the Sampling Distribution of the Difference between the Sample Means $\bar{y}_2 - \bar{y}_1$ Is Approximately Normal about $\mu_2 - \mu_1$

An estimate has a standard error that describes how precisely it estimates a parameter. Likewise, so does the difference between estimates from two samples have a standard error. For Table 7.1, the standard error of the sampling distribution of $\bar{y}_2 - \bar{y}_1$ describes how precisely $\bar{y}_2 - \bar{y}_1 = 14$ estimates $\mu_2 - \mu_1$. If many studies had been conducted in Britain comparing daily cooking and washing up time for women and men, the estimate $\bar{y}_2 - \bar{y}_1$ would not have equaled 14 minutes for each of them. The estimate would vary from study to study. The standard error describes the variability of the estimates from different potential studies of the same size.

The following general rule enables us to find the standard error when we compare estimates from independent samples:

---

**Standard Error of Difference Between Two Estimates**

For two estimates from independent samples that have estimated standard errors $se_1$ and $se_2$, the sampling distribution of their difference has

$$\text{estimated standard error} = \sqrt{(se_1)^2 + (se_2)^2}.$$

---

Each estimate has sampling error, and the variabilities add together to determine the standard error of the difference of the estimates. The standard error formula for dependent samples differs from this formula, and Section 7.4 presents it.

Recall that the estimated standard error of a sample mean equals

$$se = \frac{s}{\sqrt{n}},$$

where $s$ is the sample standard deviation. Let $n_1$ denote the sample size for the first sample and $n_2$ the sample size for the second sample. Let $s_1$ and $s_2$ denote the standard deviations. The difference $\bar{y}_2 - \bar{y}_1$ between two sample means with independent samples has estimated standard error

$$se = \sqrt{(se_1)^2 + (se_2)^2} = \sqrt{\frac{s_1^2}{n_1} + \frac{s_2^2}{n_2}}.$$

For example, from Table 7.1, the estimated standard error of the difference of 14 minutes between the sample mean cooking and washing up time for women and men equals

$$se = \sqrt{\frac{s_1^2}{n_1} + \frac{s_2^2}{n_2}} = \sqrt{\frac{(32)^2}{1219} + \frac{(16)^2}{733}} = 1.1.$$

For such large sample sizes, the estimate $\bar{y}_2 - \bar{y}_1$ would not vary much from study to study.

From the formula, the standard error of the difference is larger than the standard error for either sample estimate alone. Why is this? In practical terms, $(\bar{y}_2 - \bar{y}_1)$ is often farther from $(\mu_2 - \mu_1)$ than $\bar{y}_1$ is from $\mu_1$ or $\bar{y}_2$ is from $\mu_2$. For instance, suppose $\mu_1 = \mu_2 = 30$ (unknown to us), but the sample means are $\bar{y}_1 = 23$ and $\bar{y}_2 = 37$. Then the errors of estimation were

$$\bar{y}_1 - \mu_1 = 23 - 30 = -7 \quad \text{and} \quad \bar{y}_2 - \mu_2 = 37 - 30 = 7,$$

each estimate being off by a distance of 7. But the estimate $(\bar{y}_2 - \bar{y}_1) = 37 - 23 = 14$ falls 14 from $(\mu_2 - \mu_1) = 0$. The error of size 14 for the difference is larger than the error of size 7 for either mean individually. Suppose a sample mean that falls 7 away from a population mean is well out in the tail of a sampling distribution for a single sample mean. Then a difference between sample means that falls 14 away from the difference between population means is well out in the tail of the sampling distribution for $\bar{y}_2 - \bar{y}_1$.

### The Ratio of Parameters

Another way to compare two proportions or two means uses their *ratio*. The ratio equals 1.0 when the parameters are equal. Ratios farther from 1.0 represent larger effects.

In Table 7.1, the ratio of sample mean cooking and washing up time for women and for mean is $37/23 = 1.61$. The sample mean for women was 1.61 times the sample mean for men. This can also be expressed by saying that the mean for women was 61% higher than the mean for women.

The ratio of two proportions is often called the **relative risk**, because it is often used in public health applications to compare rates for an undesirable outcome for two groups. The ratio is often more informative than the difference when both proportions are close to zero.

For example, according to recent data from the United Nations, the annual gun homicide rate is 62.4 per one million residents in the U.S. and 1.3 per one million residents in Britain. In proportion form, the results are 0.0000624 in the U.S. and 0.0000013 in Britain. The difference between the proportions is $0.0000624 - 0.0000013 = 0.0000611$, extremely small. By contrast, the ratio is $0.000624/0.0000013 = 624/13 = 48$. The proportion of people killed by guns in the U.S. was 48 times the proportion in Britain. In this sense, the effect is large.

Software can form a confidence interval for a population ratio of means or proportions. The formulas are complex, and we will not cover them in this text.

## 7.2   CATEGORICAL DATA: COMPARING TWO PROPORTIONS

Let's now learn how to compare proportions inferentially. Let $\pi_1$ denote the proportion for the first population and $\pi_2$ the proportion for the second population. Let $\hat{\pi}_1$ and $\hat{\pi}_2$ denote the sample proportions. You may wish to review Sections 5.2 and 6.3 on inferences for proportions in the one-sample case.

### EXAMPLE 7.1   Does Prayer Help Coronary Surgery Patients?

A study used patients at six U.S. hospitals who were to receive coronary artery bypass graft surgery.[2] The patients were randomly assigned to two groups. For one group, Christian volunteers were instructed to pray for a successful surgery with a quick, healthy recovery and no complications. The praying started the night before surgery and continued for two weeks. The response was whether medical complications occurred within 30 days of the surgery. Table 7.2 summarizes results.

**TABLE 7.2:** Whether Complications Occurred for Heart Surgery Patients Who Did or Did Not Have Group Prayer

| Prayer | Complications | No Complications | Total |
|--------|---------------|------------------|-------|
| Yes    | 315           | 289              | 604   |
| No     | 304           | 293              | 597   |

Is there a difference in complication rates for the two groups? Let $\pi_1$ denote the probability for those patients who had a prayer group. Let $\pi_2$ denote the probability for the subjects not having a prayer group. From Table 7.2, the sample proportions equal

$$\hat{\pi}_1 = \frac{315}{604} = 0.522, \quad \hat{\pi}_2 = \frac{304}{597} = 0.509.$$   ■

We compare the probabilities using their difference, $\pi_2 - \pi_1$. The difference of sample proportions, $\hat{\pi}_2 - \hat{\pi}_1$, estimates $\pi_2 - \pi_1$. If $n_1$ and $n_2$ are relatively large, the estimator $\hat{\pi}_2 - \hat{\pi}_1$ has a sampling distribution that is approximately normal. See Figure 7.2. The mean of the sampling distribution is the parameter $\pi_2 - \pi_1$ to be estimated.

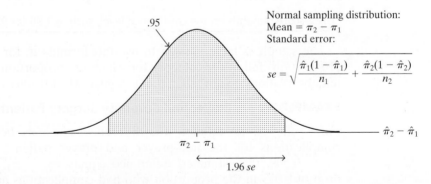

**FIGURE 7.2:** For Large Random Samples, the Sampling Distribution of the Estimator $\hat{\pi}_2 - \hat{\pi}_1$ of the Difference of Proportions Is Approximately Normal

From the rule in the box in Section 7.1 (page 185), the standard error of the difference of sample proportions equals the square root of the sum of squared

[2]H. Benson et al., *American Heart Journal*, vol. 151, 2006, pp. 934–952.

standard errors of the separate sample proportions. Recall that the estimated standard error of a single sample proportion is

$$se = \sqrt{\frac{\hat{\pi}(1 - \hat{\pi})}{n}}.$$

Therefore, the difference between two proportions has estimated standard error

$$se = \sqrt{(se_1)^2 + (se_2)^2} = \sqrt{\frac{\hat{\pi}_1(1 - \hat{\pi}_1)}{n_1} + \frac{\hat{\pi}_2(1 - \hat{\pi}_2)}{n_2}}.$$

For Table 7.2, $\hat{\pi}_2 - \hat{\pi}_1$ has estimated standard error

$$se = \sqrt{\frac{(0.522)(0.478)}{604} + \frac{(0.509)(0.491)}{597}} = 0.0288.$$

For samples of these sizes, the difference in sample proportions would not vary much from study to study.

### Confidence Interval for Difference of Proportions

As with a single proportion, the confidence interval takes the point estimate and adds and subtracts a margin of error that is a $z$-score times the estimated standard error, such as

$$(\hat{\pi}_2 - \hat{\pi}_1) \pm 1.96(se)$$

for 95% confidence.

---

**Confidence Interval for $\pi_2 - \pi_1$**

For large, independent random samples, a confidence interval for the difference $\pi_2 - \pi_1$ between two population proportions is

$$(\hat{\pi}_2 - \hat{\pi}_1) \pm z(se), \text{ where } se = \sqrt{\frac{\hat{\pi}_1(1 - \hat{\pi}_1)}{n_1} + \frac{\hat{\pi}_2(1 - \hat{\pi}_2)}{n_2}}.$$

The $z$-score depends on the confidence level, such as 1.96 for 95% confidence.

---

The sample is large enough to use this formula if, for each sample, at least ten observations fall in the category for which the proportion is estimated, and at least ten observations do not fall in that category. Most studies easily satisfy this.

### EXAMPLE 7.2 Prayer and Coronary Surgery Patients, Continued

For Table 7.2, we estimate the difference $\pi_2 - \pi_1$ between the probability of complications for the non-prayer and prayer patients. Since $\hat{\pi}_1 = 0.522$ and $\hat{\pi}_2 = 0.509$, the estimated difference equals $\hat{\pi}_2 - \hat{\pi}_1 = -0.013$. There was a drop of 0.013 in the proportion who had complications among those not receiving prayer.

To determine the precision of this estimate, we form a confidence interval. Previously we determined that $se = 0.0288$. A 95% confidence interval for $\pi_2 - \pi_1$ is

$$(\hat{\pi}_2 - \hat{\pi}_1) \pm 1.96(se), \text{ or } (0.509 - 0.522) \pm 1.96(0.0288)$$

$$= -0.013 \pm 0.057 \quad \text{or} \quad (-0.07, 0.04).$$

It seems that the difference is close to 0, so the probability of complications is similar for the two groups. ■

### Interpreting a Confidence Interval Comparing Proportions

When the confidence interval for $\pi_2 - \pi_1$ contains 0, as in the previous example, it is plausible that $\pi_2 - \pi_1 = 0$. That is, it is believable that $\pi_1 = \pi_2$. Insufficient evidence exists to conclude which of $\pi_1$ or $\pi_2$ is larger. For the confidence interval for $\pi_2 - \pi_1$ of $(-0.07, 0.04)$, we infer that $\pi_2$ may be as much as 0.07 smaller or as much as 0.04 larger than $\pi_1$.

When a confidence interval for $\pi_2 - \pi_1$ contains only *negative* values, this suggests that $\pi_2 - \pi_1$ is negative. In other words, we infer that $\pi_2$ is *smaller* than $\pi_1$. When a confidence interval for $\pi_2 - \pi_1$ contains only *positive* values, we conclude that $\pi_2 - \pi_1$ is positive; that is, $\pi_2$ is *larger* than $\pi_1$.

Which group we call Group 1 and which we call Group 2 is arbitrary. If we let Group 1 be the nonprayer group rather than the prayer group, then the estimated difference would be $+0.013$ rather than $-0.013$. The confidence interval would have been $(-0.04, 0.07)$, the negatives of the endpoints we obtained. Similarly, it does not matter whether we form a confidence interval for $\pi_2 - \pi_1$ or for $\pi_1 - \pi_2$. If the confidence interval for $\pi_2 - \pi_1$ is $(-0.07, 0.04)$, then the confidence interval for $\pi_1 - \pi_2$ is $(-0.04, 0.07)$.

The magnitude of values in the confidence interval tells you how large any true difference is. If all values in the confidence interval are near 0, such as the interval $(-0.07, 0.04)$, we infer that $\pi_2 - \pi_1$ is small in practical terms even if not exactly equal to 0.

As in the one-sample case, larger sample sizes contribute to a smaller $se$, a smaller margin of error, and narrower confidence intervals. In addition, higher confidence levels yield wider confidence intervals. For the prayer study, a 99% confidence interval equals $(-0.09, 0.06)$. This is wider than the 95% confidence interval of $(-0.07, 0.04)$.

### Significance Tests about $\pi_2 - \pi_1$

To compare population proportions $\pi_1$ and $\pi_2$, a significance test specifies $H_0: \pi_1 = \pi_2$. For the difference of proportions parameter, this hypothesis is $H_0: \pi_2 - \pi_1 = 0$, *no difference, or no effect.*

Under the presumption for $H_0$ that $\pi_1 = \pi_2$, we estimate the common value of $\pi_1$ and $\pi_2$ by the sample proportion for the entire sample. Denote this by $\hat{\pi}$. To illustrate, for the data in Table 7.2 from the prayer study, $\hat{\pi}_1 = 315/604 = 0.522$ and $\hat{\pi}_2 = 304/597 = 0.509$. For the entire sample,

$$\hat{\pi} = (315 + 304)/(604 + 597) = 619/1201 = 0.515.$$

The proportion $\hat{\pi}$ is called a *pooled estimate*, because it pools together observations from the two samples.

The test statistic measures the number of standard errors between the estimate and the $H_0$ value. Treating $\pi_2 - \pi_1$ as the parameter, we test that $\pi_2 - \pi_1 = 0$; that is, the null hypothesis value of the parameter $\pi_2 - \pi_1$ is 0. The estimated value of $\pi_2 - \pi_1$ is $\hat{\pi}_2 - \hat{\pi}_1$. The test statistic is

$$z = \frac{\text{Estimate} - \text{null hypothesis value}}{\text{Standard error}} = \frac{(\hat{\pi}_2 - \hat{\pi}_1) - 0}{se_0}.$$

Rather than use the standard error from the confidence interval, you should use an alternative formula based on the presumption stated in $H_0$ that $\pi_1 = \pi_2$. We use the notation $se_0$, because it is a $se$ that holds under $H_0$. This standard error is

$$se_0 = \sqrt{\frac{\hat{\pi}(1 - \hat{\pi})}{n_1} + \frac{\hat{\pi}(1 - \hat{\pi})}{n_2}} = \sqrt{\hat{\pi}(1 - \hat{\pi})\left(\frac{1}{n_1} + \frac{1}{n_2}\right)}.$$

For Table 7.2, the standard error estimate for the test equals

$$se_0 = \sqrt{\hat{\pi}(1 - \hat{\pi})\left(\frac{1}{n_1} + \frac{1}{n_2}\right)} = \sqrt{0.515(0.485)\left(\frac{1}{604} + \frac{1}{597}\right)}$$

$$= \sqrt{0.000832} = 0.0288.$$

The test statistic for $H_0$: $\pi_1 = \pi_2$ equals

$$z = \frac{\hat{\pi}_2 - \hat{\pi}_1}{se_0} = \frac{0.509 - 0.522}{0.0288} = -0.43.$$

The $P$-value depends in the usual way on whether the test is two sided, $H_a$: $\pi_1 \neq \pi_2$ (i.e., $\pi_2 - \pi_1 \neq 0$), or one sided, $H_a$: $\pi_1 > \pi_2$ (i.e., $\pi_2 - \pi_1 < 0$) or $H_a$: $\pi_1 < \pi_2$ ($\pi_2 - \pi_1 > 0$). Most common is the two-sided alternative. Its $P$-value is the two-tail probability from the standard normal distribution that falls beyond the observed test statistic value. A $z$-score of $-0.43$ has two-sided $P$-value equal to 0.67. There is not much evidence against $H_0$.

In summary, it is plausible that the probability of complications is the same for the prayer and nonprayer conditions. However, this study does not disprove the power of prayer. Apart from the fact that we cannot accept a null hypothesis, the experiment could not control many factors, such as whether friends and family were also praying for the patients.

The $z$ test for comparing proportions works quite well even for relatively small sample sizes. We'll give detailed guidelines in Section 8.2 when we study a more general test for comparing several groups. For simplicity, you can use the guideline for confidence intervals comparing proportions, namely that each sample should have at least 10 outcomes of each type. In practice, *two-sided* tests are robust and work well if each sample has at least five outcomes of each type.

## Contingency Tables and Conditional Probabilities

Table 7.2 is an example of a ***contingency table***. Each row is a category of the explanatory variable (whether prayed for) which defines the two groups compared. Each column is a category of the response variable (whether complications occurred). The ***cells*** of the table contain frequencies for the four possible combinations of outcomes.

The parameters $\pi_1$ and $\pi_2$ estimated using the contingency table are called ***conditional probabilities***. This term refers to probabilities for a response variable evaluated under two conditions, namely the two levels of the explanatory variable. For instance, under the condition that the subject is being prayed for, the conditional probability of developing complications is estimated to be $315/604 = 0.52$.

This section has considered binary response variables. Instead, the response could have several categories. For example, the response categories might be (No complications, Slight complications, Severe complications). Then we could compare the two groups in terms of the conditional probabilities of observations in each of the three categories. Likewise, the number of groups compared could exceed two.

Chapter 8 shows how to analyze contingency tables having more than two rows or columns.

## 7.3 QUANTITATIVE DATA: COMPARING TWO MEANS

To compare two population means $\mu_1$ and $\mu_2$, we can make inferences about their difference. You may wish to review Sections 5.3 and 6.2 on inferences for means in the one-sample case.

### Confidence Interval for $\mu_2 - \mu_1$

For large random samples, or for small random samples from normal population distributions, the sampling distribution of $(\bar{y}_2 - \bar{y}_1)$ has a normal shape. As usual, inference for means with *estimated* standard errors uses the $t$ distribution for test statistics and for the margin of error in confidence intervals. A confidence interval takes the point estimate and adds and subtracts a margin of error that is a $t$-score times the standard error.

---

**Confidence Interval for $\mu_2 - \mu_1$**

For independent random samples from two groups that have normal population distributions, a confidence interval for $\mu_2 - \mu_1$ is

$$(\bar{y}_2 - \bar{y}_1) \pm t(se), \text{ where } se = \sqrt{\frac{s_1^2}{n_1} + \frac{s_2^2}{n_2}}.$$

The $t$-score is chosen to provide the desired confidence level.

---

The formula for the degrees of freedom for the $t$-score, called the *Welch-Satterthwaite approximation*, is complex. The $df$ depends on the sample standard deviations $s_1$ and $s_2$ as well as the sample sizes $n_1$ and $n_2$. If $s_1 = s_2$ and $n_1 = n_2$, it simplifies to $df = (n_1 + n_2 - 2)$. This is the sum of the $df$ values for separate inference about each group; that is, $df = (n_1 - 1) + (n_2 - 1) = n_1 + n_2 - 2$. Generally, $df$ falls somewhere between $n_1 + n_2 - 2$ and the minimum of $(n_1 - 1)$ and $(n_2 - 1)$. Software can easily find this $df$ value, the $t$-score, and the confidence interval.

In practice, the method is robust to violations of the normal population assumption. This is expecially true when both $n_1$ and $n_2$ are at least about 30, by the Central Limit Theorem. As usual, you should be wary of extreme outliers or of extreme skew that may make the mean unsuitable as a summary measure.

### EXAMPLE 7.3    Comparing Housework Time of Men and Women

For Table 7.1 (page 183), on the daily time full-time workers spend cooking and cleaning up, denote the population mean in Britain by $\mu_1$ for men and $\mu_2$ for women. That table reported sample means of 23 minutes for 1219 men and 37 minutes for 733 women, with sample standard deviations of 32 and 16. The point estimate of $\mu_2 - \mu_1$ equals $\bar{y}_2 - \bar{y}_1 = 37 - 23 = 14$. Section 7.1 found that the estimated standard error of this difference equals

$$se = \sqrt{\frac{s_1^2}{n_1} + \frac{s_2^2}{n_2}} = \sqrt{\frac{(32)^2}{1219} + \frac{(16)^2}{733}} = 1.09.$$

The sample sizes are very large, so the $t$-score for the margin of error is essentially the $z$-score. So the 95% confidence interval for $\mu_2 - \mu_1$ is

$$(\bar{y}_2 - \bar{y}_1) \pm 1.96(se) = 14 \pm 1.96(1.09), \text{ or } 14 \pm 2, \text{ which is } (12, 16).$$

We can be 95% confident that the population mean amount of daily time spent on cooking and washing up is between 12 and 16 minutes higher for women than men. ∎

### Interpreting a Confidence Interval Comparing Means

The confidence interval (12, 16) contains only positive values. Since we took the difference between the mean for women and the mean for men, we can conclude that the population mean is higher for women. A confidence interval for $\mu_2 - \mu_1$ that contains only positive values suggests that $\mu_2 - \mu_1$ is positive, meaning that $\mu_2$ is larger than $\mu_1$. A confidence interval for $\mu_2 - \mu_1$ that contains only negative values suggests that $\mu_2$ is smaller than $\mu_1$. When the confidence interval contains 0, insufficient evidence exists to conclude which of $\mu_1$ or $\mu_2$ is larger. It is then plausible that $\mu_1 = \mu_2$.

The identification of which is group 1 and which is group 2 is arbitrary, as is whether we estimate $\mu_2 - \mu_1$ or $\mu_1 - \mu_2$. For instance, a confidence interval of (12, 16) for $\mu_2 - \mu_1$ is equivalent to one of $(-16, -12)$ for $\mu_1 - \mu_2$.

### Significance Tests about $\mu_2 - \mu_1$

To compare population means $\mu_1$ and $\mu_2$, we can also conduct a significance test of $H_0$: $\mu_1 = \mu_2$. For the difference of means parameter, this hypothesis is $H_0$: $\mu_2 - \mu_1 = 0$ (no effect).

As usual, the test statistic measures the number of standard errors between the estimate and the $H_0$ value,

$$t = \frac{\text{Estimate of parameter } - \text{ null hypothesis value of parameter}}{\text{Standard error of estimate}}.$$

Treating $\mu_2 - \mu_1$ as the parameter, we test that $\mu_2 - \mu_1 = 0$. Its estimate is $\bar{y}_2 - \bar{y}_1$. The standard error is the same as in a confidence interval. The $t$ test statistic is

$$t = \frac{(\bar{y}_2 - \bar{y}_1) - 0}{se}, \quad \text{where} \quad se = \sqrt{\frac{s_1^2}{n_1} + \frac{s_2^2}{n_2}}.$$

### EXAMPLE 7.4    Test Comparing Mean Housework for Men and Women

Using the data from Table 7.1 (page 183), we now test for a difference between the population mean cooking and washing up time, $\mu_1$ for men and $\mu_2$ for women. We test $H_0$: $\mu_1 = \mu_2$ against $H_a$: $\mu_1 \neq \mu_2$. We've seen that the estimate $\bar{y}_2 - \bar{y}_1 = 37 - 23 = 14$ has $se = 1.09$.

The test statistic equals

$$t = \frac{(\bar{y}_2 - \bar{y}_1) - 0}{se} = \frac{(37 - 23)}{1.09} = 12.8.$$

With large samples, since the $t$ distribution is essentially the same as the standard normal, $t = 12.8$ is enormous. It gives a $P$-value that is 0 to many decimal places. We conclude that the population means differ. The sample means show that the difference takes the direction of a higher mean for women. ∎

In practice, significance tests are much more common for two-sample comparisons than for one-sample analyses. It is usually artificial to test whether the population mean equals one particular value, such as in testing $H_0: \mu = \mu_0$. However, it is often relevant to test whether a *difference* exists between two population means, such as in testing $H_0: \mu_1 = \mu_2$. For instance, we may have no idea what to hypothesize for the mean amount of housework time for men, but we may want to know whether that mean (whatever its value) is the same as, larger than, or smaller than the mean for women.

### Correspondence between Confidence Intervals and Tests

For means, the equivalence between two-sided tests and confidence intervals mentioned in Sections 6.2 and 6.4 also applies in the two-sample case. For example, since the two-sided *P*-value in Example 7.4 is less than 0.05, we reject $H_0: \mu_2 - \mu_1 = 0$ at the $\alpha = 0.05$ level. Similarly, a 95% confidence interval for $\mu_2 - \mu_1$ does not contain 0, the $H_0$ value. That interval equals (12, 16).

As in one-sample inference, confidence intervals are more informative than tests. The confidence interval tells us not only that the population mean differs for men and women, but it shows us just how large that difference is likely to be, and in which direction.

## 7.4    COMPARING MEANS WITH DEPENDENT SAMPLES

*Dependent samples* occur when each observation in sample 1 matches with an observation in sample 2. The data are often called *matched pairs* data because of this matching.

### Paired Difference Scores for Matched Samples

Dependent samples commonly occur when each sample has the same subjects. Examples are *longitudinal* observational studies that observe a person's response at several points in time and experimental studies that take *repeated measures* on subjects. An example of the latter is a *cross-over* study, in which a subject receives one treatment for a period and then the other treatment. The next example illustrates.

### EXAMPLE 7.5    Cell Phone Use and Driver Reaction Time

A recent experiment[3] used a sample of college students to investigate whether cell phone use impairs drivers' reaction times. On a machine that simulated driving situations, at irregular periods a target flashed red or green. Participants were instructed to press a brake button as soon as possible when they detected a red light. Under the cell phone condition, the student carried out a conversation about a political issue on the cell phone with someone in a separate room. In the control condition, they listened to a radio broadcast or to books-on-tape while performing the simulated driving.

For each student, for a particular condition the outcome recorded in Table 7.3 is their mean response time (in milliseconds) over several trials. Figure 7.3 shows box plots of the data for the two conditions. Student 28 is an outlier under each condition. ∎

---

[3]Data courtesy of David Strayer, University of Utah. See D. Strayer and W. Johnston, *Psych. Science*, vol. 21, 2001, pp. 462–466.

**TABLE 7.3**: Reaction Times (in Milliseconds) on Driving Skills Task and Cell Phone Use (Yes or No). The difference score is the reaction time using the cell phone minus the reaction time not using it, such as 636 − 604 = 32 milliseconds.

| | Cell Phone? | | | | Cell Phone? | | |
|---|---|---|---|---|---|---|---|
| Student | No | Yes | Difference | Student | No | Yes | Difference |
| 1 | 604 | 636 | 32 | 17 | 525 | 626 | 101 |
| 2 | 556 | 623 | 67 | 18 | 508 | 501 | −7 |
| 3 | 540 | 615 | 75 | 19 | 529 | 574 | 45 |
| 4 | 522 | 672 | 150 | 20 | 470 | 468 | −2 |
| 5 | 459 | 601 | 142 | 21 | 512 | 578 | 66 |
| 6 | 544 | 600 | 56 | 22 | 487 | 560 | 73 |
| 7 | 513 | 542 | 29 | 23 | 515 | 525 | 10 |
| 8 | 470 | 554 | 84 | 24 | 499 | 647 | 148 |
| 9 | 556 | 543 | −13 | 25 | 448 | 456 | 8 |
| 10 | 531 | 520 | −11 | 26 | 558 | 688 | 130 |
| 11 | 599 | 609 | 10 | 27 | 589 | 679 | 90 |
| 12 | 537 | 559 | 22 | 28 | 814 | 960 | 146 |
| 13 | 619 | 595 | −24 | 29 | 519 | 558 | 39 |
| 14 | 536 | 565 | 29 | 30 | 462 | 482 | 20 |
| 15 | 554 | 573 | 19 | 31 | 521 | 527 | 6 |
| 16 | 467 | 554 | 87 | 32 | 543 | 536 | −7 |

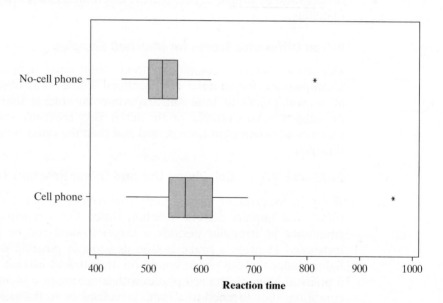

**FIGURE 7.3**: Box Plots of Observations for the Experiment on the Effects of Cell Phone Use on Reaction Times

For matched-pairs data, each observation in one sample pairs with an observation in the other sample. For each pair, we form

Difference = Observation in sample 2 − Observation in sample 1.

Table 7.3 shows the difference scores for the cell phone experiment.

Let $\bar{y}_d$ denote the sample mean of the difference scores. This estimates $\mu_d$, the population mean difference. In fact, the parameter $\mu_d$ is identical to $\mu_2 - \mu_1$, the difference between the population means for the two groups. The mean of the differences equals the difference between the means.

> For matched-pairs data, the difference between the means of the two groups equals the mean of the difference scores.

### Inferences Comparing Means Using Paired Differences

We can base analyses about $\mu_2 - \mu_1$ on inferences about $\mu_d$, using the single sample of difference scores. This simplifies the analysis, because it reduces a two-sample problem to a one-sample problem.

Let $n$ denote the number of observations in each sample. This equals the number of difference scores. The confidence interval for $\mu_d$ is

$$\bar{y}_d \pm t\left(\frac{s_d}{\sqrt{n}}\right).$$

Here, $\bar{y}_d$ and $s_d$ are the sample mean and standard deviation of the difference scores, and $t$ is the $t$-score for the chosen confidence level, having $df = n - 1$. This confidence interval has the same form as the one Section 6.3 presented for a single mean. We apply the formula to the single sample of $n$ differences rather than the original two sets of observations.

For testing $H_0: \mu_1 = \mu_2$, we express the hypothesis in terms of the difference scores as $H_0: \mu_d = 0$. The test statistic is

$$t = \frac{\bar{y}_d - 0}{se}, \quad \text{where} \quad se = s_d/\sqrt{n}.$$

This compares the sample mean of the differences to the null hypothesis value of 0, in terms of the number of standard errors between them. The standard error is the same one used for a confidence interval. Since this test uses the difference scores for the pairs of observations, it is called a ***paired-difference t test***.

### EXAMPLE 7.6    Cell Phones and Driver Reaction Time, Continued

We now analyze the matched-pairs data in Table 7.3 for the driving and cell phone experiment. The mean reaction times were 534.6 milliseconds without the cell phone and 585.2 milliseconds while using it. The 32 difference scores $(32, 67, 75, \dots)$ from Table 7.3 have a sample mean of

$$\bar{y}_d = (32 + 67 + 75 + \cdots + (-7))/32 = 50.6.$$

This equals the difference between the sample means of 585.2 and 534.6 for the two conditions. The sample standard deviation of the 32 difference scores is

$$s_d = \sqrt{\frac{(32 - 50.6)^2 + (67 - 50.6)^2 + \cdots}{32 - 1}} = 52.5.$$

The standard error of $\bar{y}_d$ is $se = s_d/\sqrt{n} = 52.5/\sqrt{32} = 9.28$.

For a 95% confidence interval for $\mu_d = \mu_2 - \mu_1$ with $df = n - 1 = 31$, we use $t_{.025} = 2.04$. The confidence interval equals

$$\bar{y}_d \pm 2.04(se) = 50.6 \pm 2.04(9.28), \quad \text{which is} \quad (31.7, 69.5).$$

We infer that the population mean reaction time when using cell phones is between about 32 and 70 milliseconds higher than when not using cell phones. The confidence interval does not contain 0. We conclude that the population mean reaction time is greater when using a cell phone.

Next consider the significance test of $H_0$: $\mu_d = 0$ (and hence equal population means for the two conditions) against $H_a$: $\mu_d \neq 0$. The test statistic is

$$t = \frac{(\bar{y}_d - 0)}{se} = \frac{50.6}{9.28} = 5.5,$$

with $df = 31$. The two-tail $P$-value equals 0.000005. There is extremely strong evidence that mean reaction time is greater when using a cell phone. Table 7.4 shows how SPSS software reports these results for its paired-samples $t$ test option.    ∎

**TABLE 7.4:** SPSS Printout for Matched-Pairs Analysis Comparing Driver Reaction Times with and without Cell Phone Use

```
-------------------------------------------------------------------
        t-tests for Paired Samples

                    Number of
    Variable          pairs        Mean      SD     SE of Mean
    NO-CELL PHONE                  534.56    66.45     11.75
                        32
    CELL PHONE                     585.19    89.65     15.85


    Paired Differences
      Mean        SD     SE of Mean     t-value   df    2-tail Sig
      50.63      52.49      9.28          5.46     31     0.000
          95% CI (31.70, 69.55)
-------------------------------------------------------------------
```

Paired-difference inferences make the usual assumptions for $t$ procedures: The observations (the difference scores) are randomly obtained from a population distribution that is normal. Confidence intervals and two-sided tests work well even if the normality assumption is violated (their *robustness* property), unless the sample size is small and the distribution is highly skewed or has severe outliers. For the study about driving and cell phones, one subject was an outlier on both reaction times. However, the difference score for that subject, which is the observation used in the analysis, is not an outlier. The article about the study did not indicate whether the subjects were randomly selected. The subjects in the experiment were probably a volunteer sample, so inferential conclusions are tentative.

### Independent versus Dependent Samples

Using dependent samples can have certain benefits. First, known sources of potential bias are controlled. Using the same subjects in each sample, for instance, keeps many other factors fixed that could affect the analysis. Suppose younger subjects tend to have faster reaction times. If group 1 has a lower sample mean than group 2, it is not because subjects in group 1 are younger, because both groups have the same subjects.

Second, the standard error of $\bar{y}_2 - \bar{y}_1$ may be smaller with dependent samples. In the cell phone study, the standard error was 9.3. If we had observed *independent* samples with the same scores as in Table 7.3, the standard error of $\bar{y}_2 - \bar{y}_1$ would have been 19.7. This is because the variability in the difference scores tends to be less than the variability in the original scores when the scores in the two samples are strongly correlated. In fact, for the data in Table 7.3, the correlation (recall Section 3.5) between the no–cell phone reaction times and the cell phone reaction times is 0.81, showing a strong positive association.

## 7.5  OTHER METHODS FOR COMPARING MEANS*

Section 7.3 presented inference comparing two means with independent samples. A slightly different inference method can be used when we expect similar variability for the two groups. For example, under a null hypothesis of "no effect," we often expect the entire distributions of the response variable to be identical for the two groups. So we expect standard deviations as well as means to be identical.

### Comparing Means while Assuming Equal Standard Deviation

In comparing the population means, this method makes the additional assumption that the population standard deviations are equal, that is, $\sigma_1 = \sigma_2$. For it, a simpler *df* expression holds for an *exact t* distribution for the test statistic. Although it seems disagreeable to make an additional assumption, confidence intervals and two-sided tests are fairly robust against violations of this and the normality assumption, particularly when the sample sizes are similar and not extremely small.

The common value $\sigma$ of $\sigma_1$ and $\sigma_2$ is estimated by

$$s = \sqrt{\frac{(n_1 - 1)s_1^2 + (n_2 - 1)s_2^2}{n_1 + n_2 - 2}} = \sqrt{\frac{\Sigma(y_1 - \bar{y}_1)^2 + \Sigma(y_2 - \bar{y}_2)^2}{n_1 + n_2 - 2}}.$$

Here, $\Sigma(y_1 - \bar{y}_1)^2$ denotes the sum of squares about the mean for the observations in the first sample, and $\Sigma(y_2 - \bar{y}_2)^2$ denotes the sum of squares about the mean for the observations in the second sample. The estimate $s$ pools information from the two samples to provide a single estimate of variability. It is called the *pooled estimate*. The term inside the square root is a weighted average of the two sample variances. When $n_1 = n_2$, it's the ordinary average. The estimate $s$ falls between $s_1$ and $s_2$. With $s$ as the estimate of $\sigma_1$ and $\sigma_2$, the estimated standard error of $\bar{y}_2 - \bar{y}_1$ simplifies to

$$se = \sqrt{\frac{s^2}{n_1} + \frac{s^2}{n_2}} = s\sqrt{\frac{1}{n_1} + \frac{1}{n_2}}.$$

The confidence interval for $\mu_2 - \mu_1$ has the usual form

$$(\bar{y}_2 - \bar{y}_1) \pm t(se).$$

The *t*-score comes from the *t* table for the desired confidence level, with $df = n_1 + n_2 - 2$. The *df* equals the total number of observations $(n_1 + n_2)$ minus the number of parameters estimated in order to calculate $s$ (namely, the two means, $\mu_1$ and $\mu_2$, estimated by $\bar{y}_1$ and $\bar{y}_2$).

To test $H_0: \mu_1 = \mu_2$, the test statistic has the usual form,

$$t = \frac{(\bar{y}_1 - \bar{y}_2)}{se}.$$

Now, *se* uses the pooled formula, as in the confidence interval. The test statistic has the *t* distribution with $df = n_1 + n_2 - 2$.

### EXAMPLE 7.7    Comparing a Therapy to a Control Group

Examples 5.5 (page 120) and 6.4 (page 151) described a study that used a cognitive behavioral therapy to treat a sample of teenage girls who suffered from anorexia. The study observed the mean weight change after a period of treatment. Studies of that type also usually have a control group that receives no treatment or a standard treatment. Then researchers can analyze how the change in weight compares for the treatment group to the control group.

In fact, the anorexia study had a control group. Teenage girls in the study were randomly assigned to the cognitive behavioral treatment (Group 1) or to the control group (Group 2). Table 7.5 summarizes the results. (The data for both groups are shown in Table 12.21 on page 396.)

**TABLE 7.5: Summary of Results Comparing Treatment Group to Control Group for Anorexia Study**

| Group | Sample Size | Mean | Standard Deviation |
|---|---|---|---|
| Treatment | 29 | 3.01 | 7.31 |
| Control | 26 | -0.45 | 7.99 |

If $H_0$ is true that the treatment has the same effect as the control, then we would expect the groups to have equal means and equal standard deviations. For these data, the pooled estimate of the assumed common standard deviation equals

$$s = \sqrt{\frac{(n_1 - 1)s_1^2 + (n_2 - 1)s_2^2}{n_1 + n_2 - 2}} = \sqrt{\frac{28(7.31)^2 + 25(7.99)^2}{29 + 26 - 2}}$$

$$= \sqrt{\frac{3092.2}{53}} = 7.64.$$

Now, $\bar{y}_1 - \bar{y}_2 = 3.01 - (-0.45) = 3.46$ has an estimated standard error of

$$se = s\sqrt{\frac{1}{n_1} + \frac{1}{n_2}} = 7.64\sqrt{\frac{1}{29} + \frac{1}{26}} = 2.06.$$

Let $\mu_1$ and $\mu_2$ denote the mean weight gains for these therapies for the hypothetical populations that the samples represent. We test $H_0: \mu_1 = \mu_2$ against $H_a: \mu_1 \neq \mu_2$. The test statistic equals

$$t = \frac{\bar{y}_1 - \bar{y}_2}{se} = \frac{3.01 - (-0.45)}{2.06} = 1.68.$$

This statistic has $df = n_1 + n_2 - 2 = 29 + 26 - 2 = 53$. From the *t*-table (Table B), the two-sided *P*-value is $P = 0.10$. There is only weak evidence of better success using the cognitive behavioral therapy.

When $df = 53$, the *t*-score for a 95% confidence interval for $(\mu_1 - \mu_2)$ is $t_{.025} = 2.006$. The interval is

$$(\bar{y}_1 - \bar{y}_2) \pm t(se) = 3.46 \pm 2.006(2.06), \text{ which is } 3.46 \pm 4.14, \text{ or } (-0.7, 7.6).$$

We conclude that the mean weight change for the cognitive behavioral therapy could be as much as 0.7 pound lower or as much as 7.6 pounds higher than the mean weight change for the control group. Since the interval contains 0, it is plausible that the population means are identical. This is consistent with the P-value exceeding 0.05 in the test. If the population mean weight change is less for the cognitive behavioral group than for the control group, it is just barely less (less than 1 pound), but if the population mean change is greater, it could be nearly 8 pounds greater. Since the sample sizes are not large, the confidence interval is relatively wide. ■

### Completely Randomized versus Randomized Block Design

The anorexia study used a *completely randomized* experimental design: Subjects were randomly assigned to the two therapies. With this design, there's the chance that the subjects selected for one therapy might differ in an important way from subjects selected for the other therapy. For moderate to large samples, factors that could influence results (such as initial weight) tend to balance by virtue of the randomization. For small samples, an imbalance could occur.

An alternative experimental design *matches* subjects in the two samples, such as by taking two girls of the same weight and randomly deciding which girl receives which therapy. This matched-pairs plan is a simple example of a **randomized block design**. Each pair of subjects forms a *block*, and within blocks subjects are randomly assigned to the treatments. With this design, we would use the methods of the previous section for dependent samples.

### Inferences Reported by Software

Table 7.6 illustrates the way SPSS reports results of two-sample $t$ tests. The table shows results of two tests for comparing means, differing in terms of whether they assume equal population standard deviations. The $t$ test just presented assumes that $\sigma_1 = \sigma_2$. The $t$ statistic that software reports for the "equal variances not assumed" case is the $t$ statistic of Section 7.3,

$$t = (\bar{y}_2 - \bar{y}_1)/se, \text{ with } se = \sqrt{\frac{s_1^2}{n_1} + \frac{s_2^2}{n_2}}.$$

When $n_1 = n_2$, the "equal variances" and "unequal variances" test statistics are identical. They are usually similar if $n_1$ and $n_2$ are close or if $s_1$ and $s_2$ are close.

**TABLE 7.6:** SPSS Output for Performing Two-Sample $t$ Tests

|  |  | t | df | Sig. (2-tailed) | Mean Difference | Std. Error Difference |
|---|---|---|---|---|---|---|
| WEIGHT CHANGE | Equal variances assumed | 1.68 | 53 | 0.099 | 3.46 | 2.06 |
|  | Equal variances not assumed | 1.67 | 50 | 0.102 | 3.46 | 2.07 |

t-test for Equality of Means

If the data show evidence of a potentially large difference in standard deviations (with, say, one sample standard deviation being at least double the other), it is better to use the approximate $t$ test (Section 7.3) that does not make the $\sigma_1 = \sigma_2$ assumption. It can yield a $t$ statistic value much different from the method that assumes $\sigma_1 = \sigma_2$ if $s_1$ and $s_2$ are quite different and the sample sizes are unequal.

Many texts and most software present a statistic denoted by $F$ for testing that the population standard deviations are equal. It's not appropriate to conduct this test in order to determine which $t$ method to use. In fact, we don't recommend this test even if your main purpose is to compare variability of two groups. The test assumes that the population distributions are normal, and it is not robust to violations of that assumption.

## Effect Size

In Example 7.7, on the anorexia study, is the estimated difference between the mean weight gains of 3.46 large or small in practical terms? Keep in mind that the size of an estimated difference depends on the units of measurement. These data were in pounds, but if converted to kilograms the estimated difference would be 1.57 and if converted to ounces it would be 55.4.

A standardized way to describe the difference divides it by the estimated standard deviation for each group. This is called the ***effect size***. With sample means of 3.01 and $-0.45$ pounds and an estimated common standard deviation of $s = 7.64$ pounds, the standardized difference is

$$\text{Effect size} = \frac{\bar{y}_1 - \bar{y}_2}{s} = \frac{3.01 - (-0.45)}{7.64} = 0.45.$$

The difference between the sample means is less than half a standard deviation, a relatively small difference. We would obtain the same value for the effect size if we measured these data in different units, such as kilograms or ounces.

## A Model for Means

In the second half of this book, we'll learn about advanced methods for analyzing associations among variables. We'll base analyses explicitly on a *model*. For two variables, a ***model*** is a simple approximation for the true relationship between those variables in the population.

Let $N(\mu, \sigma)$ denote a normal distribution with mean $\mu$ and standard deviation $\sigma$. Let $y_1$ denote a randomly selected observation from group 1 and $y_2$ a randomly selected observation from group 2. The hypothesis tested above for comparing means under the assumption $\sigma_1 = \sigma_2$ can be expressed as the model

$H_0$: Both $y_1$ and $y_2$ have a $N(\mu, \sigma)$ distribution.

$H_a$: $y_1$ has a $N(\mu_1, \sigma)$ distribution, $y_2$ has a $N(\mu_2, \sigma)$ distribution, with $\mu_1 \neq \mu_2$.

Under $H_0$, the population means are equal, with some common value $\mu$. Under $H_a$, the population means differ. This is a special case of a model Chapter 12 uses for comparing *several* means.

Sampling distributions and resulting inferences are derived under the assumed model structure. But models are merely convenient simplifications of reality. We do not expect distributions to be exactly normal, for instance. One of the key parts of becoming more comfortable using statistical methods is becoming knowledgeable about which assumptions are most important in a model and how to check such assumptions. Generally, there are benefits to using simpler models. They have fewer parameters to estimate, and inferences can be more powerful. However, when such a model is badly in error, we're better off using a more complex model.

The first significance test we discussed for comparing means used a slightly more complex model,

$H_0$: $y_1$ has a $N(\mu, \sigma_1)$ distribution, $y_2$ has a $N(\mu, \sigma_2)$ distribution.

$H_a$: $y_1$ has a $N(\mu_1, \sigma_1)$ distribution, $y_2$ has a $N(\mu_2, \sigma_2)$ distribution, with $\mu_1 \neq \mu_2$.

Again, under $H_0$ the population means are equal. But now, no assumption is made about the standard deviations being equal. If there is reason to expect the standard deviations to be very different, or if the data indicate this (with one of the sample standard deviations being at least double the other), then we're better off using analyses based on this model. If the data show that even this model is badly in error, such as when the sample data distributions are so highly skewed that the mean is an inappropriate summary, we're better off using a different model yet. The final section of this chapter presents a model that does not assume normality.

## 7.6  OTHER METHODS FOR COMPARING PROPORTIONS*

Section 7.2 presented large-sample methods for comparing proportions with independent samples. This section presents methods for comparing proportions with (1) dependent sample and (2) small samples.

### Comparing Dependent Proportions

Section 7.4 presented dependent-samples methods for comparing means. The following example illustrates dependent-samples methods for comparing proportions.

### EXAMPLE 7.8    Comparing Two Speech Recognition Systems

In recent years there have been impressive improvements in systems for automatically recognizing speech. When you call many service centers these days, before speaking with a human being you are asked to answer various questions verbally, whereas in the past you had to use the telephone dial pad.

Research in comparing the quality of different speech recognition systems often uses as a benchmark test a series of isolated words, checking how often each system makes errors recognizing the word. Table 7.7 shows an example[4] of one such test, comparing two speech recognition systems, called generalized minimal distortion segmentation (GMDS) and continuous density hidden Markov model (CDHMM).

TABLE 7.7: Results of Benchmark Test Using 2000 Words for Two Speech Recognition Systems

| GMDS | CDHMM | | Total |
| --- | --- | --- | --- |
| | Correct | Incorrect | |
| Correct | 1921 | 58 | 1979 |
| Incorrect | 16 | 5 | 21 |
| Total | 1937 | 63 | 2000 |

---

[4]From S. Chen and W. Chen, *IEEE Transactions on Speech and Audio Processing*, vol. 3, 1995, pp. 141–145.

The rows of Table 7.7 are the (correct, incorrect) categories for each word using GMDS. The columns are the same categories for CDHMM. The row marginal counts (1979, 21) are the (correct, incorrect) totals for GMDS. The column marginal counts (1937, 63) are the totals for CDHMM.

We will compare the proportion of correct responses for these two speech recognition systems. The samples are dependent, because the two systems used the same 2000 words. We'll regard these 2000 words as a random sample of the possible words on which the systems could have been tested. Let $\pi_1$ denote the population proportion correct for GMDS, and let $\pi_2$ denote the population proportion correct for CDHMM. The sample estimates are $\hat{\pi}_1 = 1979/2000 = 0.9895$ and $\hat{\pi}_2 = 1937/2000 = 0.9685$.

If the proportions correct were identical for the two systems, the number of observations in the first row of Table 7.7 would equal the number of observations in the first column. The first cell (the one containing 1921 in Table 7.7) is common to both the first row and first column, so the other cell count in the first row would equal the other cell count in the first column. That is, the number of words judged correctly by GMDS but incorrectly by CDHMM would equal the number of words judged incorrectly by GMDS but correctly by CDHMM. We can test $H_0$: $\pi_1 = \pi_2$ using the counts in those two cells. If $H_0$ is true, then of these words, we expect 1/2 to be correct for GMDS and incorrect for CDHMM and 1/2 to be incorrect for GMDS and correct for CDHMM.

As in the matched-pairs test for a mean, we reduce the inference to one about a single parameter. For the population in the two cells just mentioned, we test whether half are in each cell. In Table 7.7, of the $58 + 16 = 74$ words judged correctly by one system but incorrectly by the other, the sample proportion $58/74 = 0.784$ were correct with GMDS. Under the null hypothesis that the population proportion is 0.50, the standard error of the sample proportion for these 74 observations is $\sqrt{(0.50)(0.50)/74} = 0.058$.

From Section 6.3, the $z$ statistic for testing that the population proportion equals 0.50 is

$$z = \frac{\text{sample proportion} - H_0 \text{ proportion}}{\text{standard error}} = \frac{0.784 - 0.50}{0.058} = 4.88.$$

The two-sided $P$-value equals 0.000. This provides strong evidence against $H_0$ : $\pi_1 = \pi_2$. Based on the sample proportions, the evidence favors a greater population proportion of correct recognitions by the GMDS system. ∎

## McNemar Test for Comparing Dependent Proportions

A simple formula exists for this $z$ test statistic for comparing two dependent proportions. For a table of the form of Table 7.7, denote the cell counts in the two relevant cells by $n_{12}$ for those in row 1 and in column 2 and by $n_{21}$ for those in row 2 and in column 1. The test statistic equals

$$z = \frac{n_{12} - n_{21}}{\sqrt{n_{12} + n_{21}}}.$$

When $n_{12} + n_{21}$ exceeds about 20, this statistic has approximately a standard normal distribution when $H_0$ is true. This test is often referred to as **McNemar's test**. For smaller samples, use the binomial distribution to conduct the test.

For Table 7.7, the McNemar test uses $n_{12} = 58$, the number of words correctly recognized by GMDS and incorrectly by CDHMM, and $n_{21} = 16$, the number for the reverse. The test statistic equals

$$z = \frac{58 - 16}{\sqrt{58 + 16}} = 4.88.$$

The $P$-value is 0.000.

### Confidence Interval for Difference of Dependent Proportions

A confidence interval for the difference of proportions is more informative than a significance test. For large samples, this is

$$(\hat{\pi}_2 - \hat{\pi}_1) \pm z(se),$$

where the standard error is estimated using

$$se = \sqrt{(n_{12} + n_{21}) - (n_{12} - n_{21})^2/n}/n.$$

For Table 7.7, $\hat{\pi}_1 = 1979/2000 = 0.9895$ and $\hat{\pi}_2 = 1937/2000 = 0.9685$. The difference $\hat{\pi}_1 - \hat{\pi}_2 = 0.9895 - 0.9685 = 0.021$. For $n = 2000$ observations with $n_{12} = 58$ and $n_{21} = 16$,

$$se = \sqrt{(58 + 16) - (58 - 16)^2/2000}/2000 = 0.0043.$$

A 95% confidence interval for $\pi_1 - \pi_2$ equals $0.021 \pm 1.96(0.0043)$, or (0.013, 0.029). We conclude that the population proportion correct with the GMDS system is between about 0.01 and 0.03 higher than the population proportion correct with the CDHMM system. In summary, the difference between the population proportions seems to be quite small.

### Fisher's Exact Test for Comparing Proportions

The inferences for proportions with independent samples introduced in Section 7.2 are valid for relatively large samples. We next consider small-sample methods.

The two-sided significance test for comparing proportions with $z$ test statistic works quite well if each sample has at least about 5–10 outcomes of each type (i.e., at least 5–10 observations in each cell of the contingency table). For smaller sample sizes, the sampling distribution of $\hat{\pi}_2 - \hat{\pi}_1$ may not be close to normality. You can then compare two proportions $\pi_1$ and $\pi_2$ using a method called **Fisher's exact test**, due to the eminent statistician R. A. Fisher.

The calculations for Fisher's exact test are complex and beyond the scope of this text. The principle behind the test is straightforward, however, as Exercise 7.57 shows. Statistical software provides its $P$-value. As usual, the $P$-value is the probability of the sample result or a result even more extreme, under the presumption that $H_0$ is true. For details about Fisher's exact test, see Agresti (2007, pp. 45–48).

### EXAMPLE 7.9    Depression and Suicide among HIV Infected Persons

A recent study[5] examined rates of major depression and suicidality for HIV infected and uninfected persons in China. The study used a volunteer sample. In an attempt to

---

[5]H. Jin et al., *J. Affective Disorders*, vol. 94, 2006, pp. 269–275.

**TABLE 7.8:** Comparison of HIV-Infected and Uninfected Subjects on Whether Have Ever Attempted Suicide

```
              HIV          suicide

                   |yes      |no      |  Total
          ---------+---------+--------+
          positive |   10 |     18 |      28
          ---------+---------+--------+
          negative |    1 |     22 |      23
          ---------+---------+--------+
          Total          11         40        51



          STATISTICS FOR TABLE OF HIV BY SUICIDE
          Statistic                            Prob
          ----------------------------------------------

          Fisher's Exact Test  (Left)          0.9995
                               (Right)         0.0068
                               (2-Tail)        0.0075
```

make the sample more representative, subjects were recruited from clinics in two very different regions of China, one urban and one rural. Table 7.8 shows results based on a diagnostic interview asking whether the subject had ever attempted suicide. The table also shows output from conducting Fisher's exact test.

Denote the population proportion who had ever made a suicide attempt by $\pi_1$ for those who were HIV positive and by $\pi_2$ for those who were HIV negative. Then $\hat{\pi}_1 = 10/28 = 0.36$ and $\hat{\pi}_2 = 1/23 = 0.04$. We test $H_0: \pi_1 = \pi_2$ against $H_a: \pi_1 > \pi_2$. One of the four counts is very small, so to be safe we use Fisher's exact test.

On the printout, the right-sided alternative refers to $H_a: \pi_1 - \pi_2 > 0$; that is, $H_a: \pi_1 > \pi_2$. The P-value = 0.0068 gives very strong evidence that the population proportion attempting suicide is higher for those who are HIV positive. The P-value for the two-sided alternative equals 0.0075. This is not double the one-sided P-value because, except in certain special cases, the sampling distribution (called the **hypergeometric distribution**) is not symmetric. ∎

### Small-Sample Estimation Comparing Two Proportions

From Section 7.2, the confidence interval for comparing proportions with large samples is

$$(\hat{\pi}_2 - \hat{\pi}_1) \pm z(se), \text{ where } se = \sqrt{\frac{\hat{\pi}_1(1 - \hat{\pi}_1)}{n_1} + \frac{\hat{\pi}_2(1 - \hat{\pi}_2)}{n_2}}.$$

A simple adjustment of this formula so that it works better, even for small samples, adds one observation of each type to each sample. For the data in Table 7.8 for Example 7.9, we replace the cell counts (10, 18, 1, 22) by (11, 19, 2, 23).

Then the adjusted estimates are $\hat{\pi}_1 = (10 + 1)/(28 + 2) = 0.367$ and $\hat{\pi}_2 = (1 + 1)/(23 + 2) = 0.080$. The adjusted standard error (using $n_1 = 30$ and $n_2 = 25$) equals 0.108, and a 95% confidence interval is

$$(0.367 - 0.080) \pm 1.96(0.103), \text{ or } 0.287 \pm 0.203, \text{ which is } (0.08, 0.49).$$

Not surprisingly, with such small samples the interval is very wide.

## 7.7    NONPARAMETRIC STATISTICS FOR COMPARING GROUPS*

We have seen that many statistics have large-sample normal sampling distributions, even when population distributions are not normal. In fact, with random sampling, nearly all parameter estimators have normal distributions for large sample sizes. Small samples, though, often require additional assumptions. For instance, inferences for means using the $t$ distribution assume normal population distributions.

A body of methods exist that make *no* assumption about the shape of the population distribution. These methods are called ***nonparametric***. They contrast with the traditional (so-called *parametric*) methods that assume normal populations. Nonparametric methods are useful, for instance, when the normality assumption for methods using the $t$ distribution is badly violated. They are primarily useful for small samples, especially for one-sided tests, as parametric methods may then work poorly when the normal population assumption is badly violated. They are also useful when the two groups have highly skewed distributions, because then the mean may not be a meaningful summary measure.

### Wilcoxon-Mann-Whitney Test

To illustrate, consider the $t$ distribution method for comparing means that assumes normal population distributions with identical standard deviations (Section 7.5). These assumptions are mainly relevant for small samples, say when $n_1$ or $n_2$ is less than about 20–30. Most nonparametric comparisons of groups also assume identical shapes for the population distributions, but the shapes are not required to be normal. The model for the test is then,

$H_0$: Both $y_1$ and $y_2$ have the same distribution.

$H_a$: The distributions for $y_1$ and $y_2$ have the same shape, but the one for $y_1$ is shifted up or shifted down compared to the one for $y_2$.

The most popular test of this type is called the *Wilcoxon* test. This test is an ordinal-level method, in the sense that it uses only the rankings of the observations. The combined sample of $n_1 + n_2$ measurements are ranked from 1 to $n_1 + n_2$, and the means of the ranks are computed for observations in each sample. The test statistic compares the sample mean ranks. For large samples, a $z$ test statistic has an approximate standard normal distribution. For small samples, an exact $P$-value is based on how unusual the observed difference between the mean ranks is (under the presumption that $H_0$ is true) compared to the differences between the mean ranks for all other possible rankings.

Another nonparametric test is the *Mann-Whitney* test. It views all the pairs of observations, such that one observation is from one group and the other observation is from the other group. The test statistic is based on the number of pairs for which the observation from the first group was higher. This test is equivalent to the Wilcoxon test, giving the same $P$-value. (Frank Wilcoxon developed equivalent tests as Henry Mann and D. R. Whitney at about the same time in the late 1940s.)

For Example 7.5, comparing weight changes for a cognitive behavioral therapy group and a control group in the anorexia study (page 198), the parametric $t$ test had a two-sided $P$-value of 0.10. The large-sample version of the Wilcoxon-Mann-Whitney test reports similar results, with a two-sided $P$-value of 0.11.

Some software also can report a corresponding confidence interval for the difference between the population medians. The method assumes that the two population distributions have the same shape, but not necessarily bell shaped. The median weight change was 1.4 pounds for the cognitive behavioral therapy group and $-0.35$ pound for the control group. Software reports a 95% confidence interval for the difference between the medians of $(-0.6, 8.1)$ pounds.

### Effect Size: Proportion of Better Responses for a Group

Section 7.5 mentioned that the size of the difference between two groups is sometimes summarized by the *effect size*, which for two samples is defined as $(\bar{y}_1 - \bar{y}_2)/s$. When the distributions are very skewed or have outliers, the means are less useful and this effect size summary may be inappropriate. A nonparametric effect size measure is the proportion of pairs of observations (one from each group) for which the observation from the first group was higher. If $y_1$ denotes a randomly selected observation from group 1 and $y_2$ a randomly selected observation from group 2, then this measure estimates $P(y_1 > y_2)$.

To illustrate, suppose the anorexia study had 4 girls, 2 using a new therapy and 2 in a control group. Suppose the weight changes were

$$\text{Therapy group } (y_1): 4, 10$$

$$\text{Control group } (y_2): 2, 6.$$

There are four pairs of observations, with one from each group:

$$y_1 = 4, y_2 = 2 \text{ (Group 1 is higher)}$$
$$y_1 = 4, y_2 = 6 \text{ (Group 2 is higher)}$$
$$y_1 = 10, y_2 = 2 \text{ (Group 1 is higher)}$$
$$y_1 = 10, y_2 = 6 \text{ (Group 1 is higher)}.$$

Group 1 is higher in 3 of the 4 pairs, so the estimate of $P(y_1 > y_2)$ is 0.75. If two observations had the same value, we would count it as $y_1$ being higher for 1/2 the pair (rather than 1 or 0).

Under $H_0$ of no effect, $P(y_1 > y_2) = 0.50$. The farther $P(y_1 > y_2)$ falls from 0.50, the stronger the effect. For the full anorexia data set analyzed in Example 7.7 on page 198, the sample estimate of $P(y_1 > y_2)$ is 0.63. The estimated probability that a girl using the cognitive behavioral therapy has a larger weight gain than a girl using the control therapy is 0.63.

When the two groups have normal distributions with the same standard deviation, a connection exists between this effect size and the parametric one, $(\mu_1 - \mu_2)/\sigma$. For example, when $(\mu_1 - \mu_2)/\sigma = 0$, then $P(y_1 > y_2) = 0.50$; when $(\mu_1 - \mu_2)/\sigma = 0.5$, then $P(y_1 > y_2) = 0.64$; when $(\mu_1 - \mu_2)/\sigma = 1$, then $P(y_1 > y_2) = 0.71$; when $(\mu_1 - \mu_2)/\sigma = 2$, then $P(y_1 > y_2) = 0.92$. The effect is relatively strong if $P(y_1 > y_2)$ is larger than about 0.70 or smaller than about 0.30.

### Treating Ordinal Variables as Quantitative

Social scientists often use parametric statistical methods for quantitative data with variables that are only ordinal. They do this by assigning scores to the ordered categories. Example 6.2 (page 149), on political ideology, showed an example of this. Sometimes the choice of scores is straightforward. For categories (liberal, moderate, conservative) for political ideology, any set of equally spaced scores is sensible, such as (1, 2, 3) or (0, 5, 10). When the choice is unclear, such as with categories (not too happy, pretty happy, very happy) for happiness, it is a good idea to perform a sensitivity study. Choose two or three reasonable sets of potential scores, such as (0, 5, 10), (0, 6, 10), (0, 7, 10), and check whether the ultimate conclusions are similar for each. If not, any report should point out how conclusions depend on the scores chosen.

Alternatively, nonparametric methods are valid with ordinal data. The reason is that nonparametric methods do not use quantitative scores, but rather rankings of the observations, and rankings are ordinal information. However, this approach works best when the response variable is continuous (or nearly so), so each observation has its own rank. When used with ordered categorical responses, such methods are often less sensible than using parametric methods that treat the response as quantitative. The next example illustrates.

## EXAMPLE 7.10    Alcohol Use and Infant Malformation

Table 7.9 refers to a study of maternal drinking and congenital malformations. After the first three months of pregnancy, the women in the sample completed a questionnaire about alcohol consumption. Following childbirth, observations were recorded on presence or absence of congenital sex organ malformations. Alcohol consumption was measured as average number of drinks per day.

Is alcohol consumption associated with malformation? One approach to investigate this is to compare the mean alcohol consumption of mothers for the cases where malformation occcurred to the mean alcohol consumption of mothers for the cases where malformation did not occur. Alcohol consumption was measured by grouping values of a quantitative variable. To find means, we assign scores to alcohol consumption that are midpoints of the categories; that is, 0, 0.5, 1.5, 4.0, 7.0, the last score (for $\geq 6$) being somewhat arbitrary. The sample means are then 0.28 for the absent group and 0.40 for the present group, and the $t$ statistic of 2.56 has $P$-value of 0.01. There is strong evidence that mothers whose infants suffered malformation had a higher mean alcohol consumption.

An alternative, nonparametric, approach assigns ranks to the subjects and uses them as the category scores. For all subjects in a category, we assign the average of the ranks that would apply for a complete ranking of the sample. These are called *midranks*. For example, the 17,114 subjects at level 0 for alcohol consumption share ranks 1 through 17,114. We assign to each of them the average of these ranks, which is the midrank $(1 + 17,114)/2 = 8557.5$. The 14,502 subjects at level <1 for alcohol consumption share ranks 17,115 through $17,114 + 14,502 = 31,616$, for a midrank of

**TABLE 7.9**: Infant Malformation and Mother's Alcohol Consumption

| Malformation | Alcohol Consumption | | | | |
|---|---|---|---|---|---|
| | 0 | <1 | 1–2 | 3–5 | $\geq 6$ |
| Absent | 17,066 | 14,464 | 788 | 126 | 37 |
| Present | 48 | 38 | 5 | 1 | 1 |
| Total | 17,114 | 14,502 | 793 | 127 | 38 |

*Source*: Graubard, B. I., and Korn, E. L., *Biometrics*, vol. 43, 1987, pp. 471–476.

$(17,115 + 31,616)/2 = 24,365.5$. Similarly the midranks for the last three categories are 32,013, 32,473, and 32,555.5. Used in a large-sample Wilcoxon test, these scores yield much less evidence of an effect ($P = 0.55$).

Why does this happen? Adjacent categories having relatively few observations necessarily have similar midranks. The midranks (8557.5, 24,365.5, 32,013, 32,473, 32,555.5) are similar for the final three categories, since those categories have considerably fewer observations than the first two categories. A consequence is that this scoring scheme treats alcohol consumption level 1–2 (category 3) as much closer to consumption level $\geq 6$ (category 5) than to consumption level 0 (category 1). This seems inappropriate. It is better to use your judgment by selecting scores that reflect well the distances between categories.    ∎

Although nonparametric methods have the benefit of weaker assumptions, in practice social scientists do not use them as much as parametric methods. Partly this reflects the large sample sizes for most studies, for which assumptions about population distributions are not so vital. In addition, nonparametric methods for multivariate data sets are not as thoroughly developed as parametric methods. Most nonparametric methods are beyond the scope of this text. For details, see Hollander and Wolfe (1999).

## 7.8    CHAPTER SUMMARY

This chapter introduced methods for comparing two groups. For quantitative response variables, inferences apply to the difference $\mu_2 - \mu_1$ between population means. For categorical response variables, inferences apply to the difference $\pi_2 - \pi_1$ between population proportions.

In each case, the significance test analyzes whether 0 is a plausible difference. If the confidence interval contains 0, it is plausible that the parameters are equal. Table 7.10

**TABLE 7.10:** Summary of Comparison Methods for Two Groups, for Independent Random Samples

|  | Type of Response Variable | |
|---|:---:|:---:|
|  | Categorical | Quantitative |
| **Estimation** | | |
| 1.   Parameter | $\pi_2 - \pi_1$ | $\mu_2 - \mu_1$ |
| 2.   Point estimate | $\hat{\pi}_2 - \hat{\pi}_1$ | $\bar{y}_2 - \bar{y}_1$ |
| 3.   Standard error | $se = \sqrt{\dfrac{\hat{\pi}_1(1-\hat{\pi}_1)}{n_1} + \dfrac{\hat{\pi}_2(1-\hat{\pi}_2)}{n_2}}$ | $se = \sqrt{\dfrac{s_1^2}{n_1} + \dfrac{s_2^2}{n_2}}$ |
| 4.   Confidence interval | $(\hat{\pi}_2 - \hat{\pi}_1) \pm z(se)$ | $(\bar{y}_2 - \bar{y}_1) \pm t(se)$ |
| **Significance testing** | | |
| 1.   Assumptions | Randomization $\geq 10$ observations in each category, for each group | Randomization Normal population dist.'s (robust, especially for large $n$'s) |
| 2.   Hypotheses | $H_0: \pi_1 = \pi_2$ $(\pi_2 - \pi_1 = 0)$ $H_a: \pi_1 \neq \pi_2$ | $H_0: \mu_1 = \mu_2$ $(\mu_2 - \mu_1 = 0)$ $H_a: \mu_1 \neq \mu_2$ |
| 3.   Test statistic | $z = \dfrac{\hat{\pi}_2 - \hat{\pi}_1}{se_0}$ | $t = \dfrac{\bar{y}_2 - \bar{y}_1}{se}$ |
| 4.   $P$-value | Two-tail probability from standard normal or $t$ (Use one tail for one-sided alternative) | |

summarizes the methods for *independent* random samples, for which observations in the two samples are not matched. This is the most common case in practice.

- Both for differences of proportions and differences of means, confidence intervals have the form

$$\text{Estimated difference} \pm (\text{score})(se)$$

  using a $z$-score for proportions and $t$-score for means. In each case, the test statistic equals the estimated difference divided by the standard error.

- For *dependent* samples, each observation in one sample matches with an observation in the other sample. For quantitative variables, we compare means by analyzing the mean of difference scores computed between the paired observations. The *paired-difference* confidence interval and test procedures are the one-sample methods of Chapters 5 and 6 applied to the difference scores.

- Another approach for comparing means makes the extra assumption that the normal population distributions have equal standard deviations. This approach pools the standard deviations from the two samples to find a common estimate.

- For comparing proportions, with independent samples the small-sample test is *Fisher's exact test*. For dependent samples, *McNemar's test* compares the number of subjects who are in category 1 in the first sample and category 2 in the second sample to the number of subjects who are in category 2 in the first sample and category 1 in the second.

- *Nonparametric* statistical methods make no assumption about the shape of the population distribution. Most such methods use the ranks of the observations.

At this stage, you may feel confused about which method to use for any given situation. It may help if you use the following checklist. Ask yourself, is the analysis about

- Means or proportions (quantitative or categorical response variable)?
- Independent samples or dependent samples?
- Confidence interval or significance test?

## PROBLEMS

### Practicing the Basics

**7.1.** An Associated Press story (Feb. 23, 2007) about UCLA's annual survey of college freshmen indicated that 73% of college freshmen in 2006 considered being financially well off to be very important, compared to 42% in 1966 (the first year the survey was done). It also reported that 81% of 18- to 25-year-olds in the U.S. see getting rich as a top goal in life. Are the sample percentages of 42% in 1966 and 73% in 2006 based on independent samples or dependent samples? Explain.

**7.2.** *Transatlantic Trends* is an annual survey of American and European public opinion (see www.transatlantictrends.org), with a random sample of about 1000 adults from each of 13 European countries each year. In 2002, 38% of Europeans expressed a positive attitude about President George W. Bush's handling of international affairs. In 2006, 18% expressed a positive attitude.
  - **(a)** Explain what it would mean for these results to be based on (a) *independent* samples, (b) *dependent* samples.
  - **(b)** If we compare results in 2002 and 2006, identify the response variable and the explanatory variable, and specify whether the response variable is quantitative or categorical.

**7.3.** The National Health Interview Survey (www.cdc.gov/nchs) estimated that current cigarette smokers were 41.9% of American adults in 1965 and 21.5% in 2003.
  - **(a)** Estimate the difference between the proportions who smoked in the two years.
  - **(b)** Suppose the standard error were reported as 0.020 for each proportion. Find the standard error of the difference. Interpret.

**7.4.** When a recent Eurobarometer survey asked subjects in each European Union country whether they would be willing to pay more for energy produced from renewable sources than for energy produced from other sources, the proportion answering *yes* varied from a high of 0.52 in Denmark ($n = 1008$) to a low of 0.14 in Lithuania ($n = 1002$). For this survey:

(a) Estimate the difference between Denmark and Lithuania in the population proportion of *yes* responses.

(b) From the $se = \sqrt{\hat{\pi}(1 - \hat{\pi})/n}$ formula in Chapter 5, the proportion estimates have $se = 0.0157$ for Denmark and $se = 0.110$ for Lithuania. Use these to find the $se$ for the difference estimate in (a). Interpret this $se$.

**7.5.** The National Center for Health Statistics recently estimated that the mean weight for adult American women was 140 pounds in 1962 and 164 pounds in 2002.

(a) Suppose these estimates had standard errors of 2 pounds each year. Estimate the increase in mean weight in the population from 1962 to 2002, and find and interpret the standard error of that estimate.

(b) Show that the estimated mean in 2002 was 1.17 times the estimated mean in 1962. Express this in terms of the percentage increase.

(c) The estimated mean weights for men were 166 pounds in 1962 and 191 in 2002. Find and interpret the difference and the ratio.

**7.6.** The U.S. Census Bureau reported that in 2002 the median net worth in the U.S. was estimated to be about $89,000 for white households and $6000 for black households.

(a) Identify the response variable and the explanatory variable.

(b) Compare the groups using a (i) difference, (ii) ratio.

**7.7.** According to the U.S. Department of Justice, in 2002 the incarceration rate in the nation's prisons was 832 per 100,000 male residents, and 58 per 100,000 female residents.

(a) Find the relative risk of being incarcerated, comparing males to females. Interpret.

(b) Find the difference of proportions incarcerated. Interpret.

(c) Which measure do you think better summarizes these data? Why?

**7.8.** According to the U.S. National Center for Health Statistics, the annual probability that a male between the ages of 20 and 24 is a homicide victim is about 0.00164 for blacks and 0.00015 for whites.

(a) Compare these rates using the difference of proportions.

(b) Compare these rates using the relative risk.

(c) Which of the two measures seems to better summarize results when both proportions are very close to 0? Explain.

**7.9.** An Associated Press story (August 7, 2006) about a research study regarding the impact on teens of sexual lyrics in songs reported, "Teens who said they listened to lots of music with degrading sexual messages were almost twice as likely to start having intercourse ... within the following two years as were teens who listened to little or no sexually degrading music." The reported percentages were 51% and 29%.

(a) A 95% confidence interval for the difference between corresponding population proportions was (0.18, 0.26). Explain how to interpret it.

(b) The $P$-value is $<0.001$ for testing the null hypothesis that the corresponding population proportions are equal. Interpret.

**7.10.** For a random sample of Canadians, 60% indicate approval of the prime minister's performance. A similar poll a month later has a favorable rating of 57%. A 99% confidence interval for the change in the population proportions is $(-0.07, 0.01)$. Explain why (a) there may have been no change in support, (b) if a decrease in support occurred, it may have been fairly important, (c) if an increase in support occurred, it was probably so small as to be substantively unimportant.

**7.11.** The College Alcohol Study at the Harvard School of Public Health has interviewed random samples of students at 4-year colleges several times since 1993. Of the students who reported drinking alcohol, the percentage who reported that drinking "to get drunk" is an important reason for drinking was 39.9% of 12,708 students in 1993 and 48.2% of 8783 students in 2001.[6] For comparing results in 1993 and 2001:

(a) Show that the standard error for the estimated difference between the corresponding population proportions in 2001 and in 1993 equals 0.0069.

(b) Show that the 95% confidence interval for the difference is (0.07, 0.10). Interpret.

**7.12.** In the study mentioned in the previous exercise, the percent who said they had engaged in unplanned sexual activities because of drinking alcohol was 19.2% in 1993 and 21.3% in 2001.

(a) Specify assumptions, notation, and hypotheses for a two-sided test comparing the corresponding population proportions.

---

[6]*Journal of American College Health*, vol. 50, 2002, pp. 203–217.

**(b)** The test statistic $z = 3.8$ and the $P$-value = 0.0002. Interpret the $P$-value.

**(c)** Some might argue that the result in (b) reflects *statistical significance* but not *practical significance*. Explain the basis of this argument, and explain why you learn more from the 95% confidence interval, which is (0.009, 0.033).

**7.13.** For the Time Use Survey reported in Table 7.1 (page 183), of those working full time, 55% of 1219 men and 74% of 733 women reported spending some time on cooking and washing up during a typical day. Find and interpret a 95% confidence interval for the difference in participation rates.

**7.14.** Table 7.11 summarizes responses from General Social Surveys in 1977 and in 2006 to the question (FEFAM), "It is much better for everyone involved if the man is the achiever outside the home and the woman takes care of the home and family." Let $\pi_1$ denote the population proportion who agreed with this statement in 1977, and let $\pi_2$ denote the population proportion in 2006.

**(a)** Show that $\hat{\pi}_1 - \hat{\pi}_2 = 0.30$, with standard error 0.0163.

**(b)** Show that the 95% confidence interval for $\pi_1 - \pi_2$ is (0.27, 0.33). Interpret.

**(c)** Explain how results would differ for comparing the proportions who did *not* agree in the two years.

**TABLE 7.11**

| Year | Agree | Disagree | Total |
|------|-------|----------|-------|
| 1977 | 989 | 514 | 1503 |
| 2006 | 704 | 1264 | 1968 |

**7.15.** Refer to the previous exercise on a woman's role. In 2004, of 411 male respondents, 153 (37.2%) replied yes. Of 472 female respondents, 166 (35.2%) replied yes.

**(a)** Set up notation and specify hypotheses for the hypothesis of no difference between the population proportions of males and of females who would respond yes.

**(b)** Estimate the population proportion presuming $H_0$, find the standard error of the sample difference of proportions, and find the test statistic.

**(c)** Find the $P$-value for the two-sided alternative. Interpret.

**(d)** Of 652 respondents having less education than a college degree, 40.0% replied yes. Of 231 respondents having at least a college degree,

25.6% replied yes. Which variable, gender or educational level, seems to have had the greater influence on opinion? In other words, did opinion tend to differ more between men and women or between the most and least educated?

**7.16.** In a survey conducted by Wright State University, senior high school students were asked if they had ever used marijuana. Table 7.12 shows software output. Treating these observations as a random sample from the population of interest:

**(a)** State a research question that could be addressed with this output.

**(b)** Interpret the reported confidence interval.

**(c)** Interpret the reported $P$-value.

**TABLE 7.12**

```
Sample         yes      N      Sample prop
1. Female      445     1120      0.3973
2. Male        515     1156      0.4455

estimate for p(1) - p(2):  -0.0482
95% CI for p(1) - p(2): ( -0.0887, -0.0077)
Test for difference = 0 (vs not = 0):
z = -2.33  P-value = 0.020
```

**7.17.** A study of compulsive buying behavior (uncontrolled urges to buy) conducted a national telephone survey in 2004 of adults ages 18 and over.[7] Of 800 men, 44 were judged to be compulsive buyers according to the Compulsive Buying Scale. Of 1501 women, 90 were judged to be compulsive buyers. Conduct an inference to analyze whether one sex is more likely than the other to be a compulsive buyer. Interpret.

**7.18.** Table 7.13 shows results from a recent General Social Survey on two variables, sex and whether one believes in an afterlife (AFTERLIF). Conduct all steps of a significance test, using $\alpha = 0.05$, to compare the population proportions of females and males who would respond *yes* to belief in an afterlife. If you have made an error in your decision, what type of error is it, Type I or Type II?

**TABLE 7.13**

| Sex | Belief in Afterlife | | Total |
|-----|-----|-----|-----|
| | Yes | No or Undecided | |
| Female | 435 | 147 | 582 |
| Male | 375 | 134 | 509 |

---

[7] Koran et al., *Amer. J. Psychiatry*, vol. 163, 2006, p. 1806.

**7.19.** A GSS reported that the 486 females had a mean of 8.3 close friends ($s = 15.6$) and the 354 males had a mean of 8.9 close friends ($s = 15.5$).

(a) A 95% confidence interval for the difference between the population means for males and for females is (-1.5, 2.7). Interpret.

(b) For each sex, does it seem like the distribution of number of close friends is normal? Explain why this does not invalidate the result in (a), but may affect the usefulness of the interval.

**7.20.** Table 7.14 summarizes the number of hours spent in housework per week by gender, based on the 2002 GSS (variable RHHWORK).

(a) Estimate the difference between the population means for women and men.

(b) Show that the estimated standard error of the sample difference is 0.81. Interpret.

(c) Show that a 99% confidence interval for the difference is (2.3, 6.5). Interpret.

**TABLE 7.14**

| | | Housework Hours | |
| Gender | Sample Size | Mean | Standard Deviation |
| --- | --- | --- | --- |
| Men | 292 | 8.4 | 9.5 |
| Women | 391 | 12.8 | 11.6 |

**7.21.** A 30-month study evaluated the degree of addiction that teenagers form to nicotine once they begin experimenting with smoking.[8] The study used a random sample of 332 seventh-grade students in two Massachusetts cities who had ever used tobacco by the start of the study. The response variable was constructed from the Hooked on Nicotine Checklist (HONC). This is a list of ten questions such as "Have you ever tried to quit but couldn't?" The HONC score is the total number of questions to which a student answered *yes*. The higher the score, the greater the dependence on nicotine. There were 75 smokers and 257 ex-smokers at the end of the study. The HONC means describing nicotine addiction were 5.9 ($s = 3.3$) for the smokers and 1.0 ($s = 2.3$) for the ex-smokers.

(a) Find and interpret a point estimate to compare HONC means for smokers and ex-smokers.

(b) Software reports a 95% confidence interval of (4.1, 5.7). Interpret.

(c) Was the HONC sample data distribution for ex-smokers approximately normal? How does this affect inference?

**7.22.** Refer to Exercise 7.17, on compulsive buying behavior. The total credit card balance had a mean of $3399 and standard deviation of $5595 for 100 compulsive buyers and a mean of $2837 and standard deviation of $6335 for 1682 other respondents.

(a) Estimate the difference between the means for compulsive buyers and other respondents, and find its standard error.

(b) Compare the population means using a two-sided significance test. Interpret.

**7.23.** A recent GSS asked, "How many days in the past 7 days have you felt sad?" Software reported sample means of 1.8 for females and 1.4 for males, with a 95% confidence interval comparing them of (0.2, 0.6), a $t$ statistic of 4.8, and a $P$-value of 0.000. Interpret these results.

**7.24.** For the 2006 GSS, a comparison of females and males on the number of hours a day that the subject watched TV gave:

| Group | N | Mean | StDev | SE Mean |
| --- | --- | --- | --- | --- |
| Females | 1117 | 2.99 | 2.34 | 0.070 |
| Males | 870 | 2.86 | 2.22 | 0.075 |

(a) Conduct all parts of a significance test to analyze whether the population means differ for females and males. Interpret the $P$-value, and report the conclusion for $\alpha$-level = 0.05.

(b) If you were to construct a 95% confidence interval comparing the means, would it contain 0? Answer based on the result of (a), without finding the interval.

(c) Do you think that the distribution of TV watching is approximately normal? Why or why not? Does this affect the validity of your inferences?

**7.25.** For the 2004 GSS, Table 7.15 shows software output for evaluating the number of hours of TV watching per day by race.

**TABLE 7.15**

| Race | N | Mean | StDev | SE Mean |
| --- | --- | --- | --- | --- |
| Black | 101 | 4.09 | 3.63 | 0.3616 |
| White | 724 | 2.59 | 2.31 | 0.0859 |

```
Difference = mu (Black) - mu (White)
Estimate for difference :   1.50
95% CI for difference: (0.77, 2.23)
T-Test of difference = 0: T-value = 4.04,
P-value = 0.000
```

---

[8] J. DiFranza et al., *Archives of Pediatric and Adolescent Medicine*, vol. 156, 2002, pp. 397–403.

(a) Interpret the reported confidence interval. Can you conclude that one population mean is higher? If so, which one? Explain.

(b) Interpret the reported $P$-value.

(c) Explain the connection between the result of the significance test and the result of the confidence interval.

**7.26.** A study[9] compared personality characteristics between adult children of alcoholics and a control group matched on age and gender. For the 29 pairs of women, the authors reported a mean of 24.8 on the well-being measure for the children of alcoholics, and a mean of 29.0 for the control group. They reported $t = 2.67$ for the test comparing the means. Assuming that this is the result of a dependent-samples analysis, identify the $df$ for the $t$ test statistic, report the $P$-value, and interpret.

**7.27.** A paired-difference experiment[10] dealing with response latencies for noise detection under two conditions used a sample of twelve 9-month-old children and reported a sample mean difference of 70.1 and standard deviation of 49.4 for the differences. In their discussion, the authors reported a $t$ statistic of 4.9 having $P < 0.01$ for a two-sided alternative. Show how they constructed the $t$ statistic, and confirm the $P$-value.

**7.28.** As part of her class project, a student at the University of Florida randomly sampled 10 fellow students to investigate their most common social activities. As part of the study, she asked the students to state how many times they had done each of the following activities during the previous year: Going to a movie, going to a sporting event, or going to a party. Table 7.16 shows the data.

(a) To compare the mean movie attendance and mean sports attendance using statistical inference, should we treat the samples as independent or dependent? Why?

(b) For the analysis in (a), software shows results:

```
              N      Mean     StDev    SE Mean
movies       10    13.000    13.174     4.166
sports       10     9.000     8.380     2.650
Difference   10     4.000    16.166     5.112

95% CI for mean difference: (-7.56, 15.56)
T-Test of mean difference = 0 (vs not = 0):
       T-Value = 0.78   P-Value = 0.454
```

Interpret the 95% confidence interval shown.

(c) Show how the test statistic shown on the printout was obtained from the other information given. Report the $P$-value, and interpret in context.

**TABLE 7.16**

| Student | Activity | | |
|---------|--------|--------|---------|
| | Movies | Sports | Parties |
| 1 | 10 | 5 | 25 |
| 2 | 4 | 0 | 10 |
| 3 | 12 | 20 | 6 |
| 4 | 2 | 6 | 52 |
| 5 | 12 | 2 | 12 |
| 6 | 7 | 8 | 30 |
| 7 | 45 | 12 | 52 |
| 8 | 1 | 25 | 2 |
| 9 | 25 | 0 | 25 |
| 10 | 12 | 12 | 4 |

**7.29.** Refer to the previous exercise. For comparing parties and sports, software reports a 95% confidence interval of $(-3.33, 28.93)$ and a $P$-value of 0.106.

(a) Interpret the $P$-value.

(b) Explain the connection between the results of the test and the confidence interval.

**7.30.** A clinical psychologist wants to choose between two therapies for treating mental depression. For six patients, she randomly selects three to receive therapy A, and the other three receive therapy B. She selects small samples for ethical reasons; if her experiment indicates that one therapy is superior, that therapy will be used on her other patients having these symptoms. After one month of treatment, the improvement is measured by the change in score on a standardized scale of mental depression severity. The improvement scores are 10, 20, 30 for the patients receiving therapy A, and 30, 45, 45 for the patients receiving therapy B.

(a) Using the method that assumes a common standard deviation for the two therapies, show that the pooled $s = 9.35$ and $se = 7.64$.

(b) When the sample sizes are very small, it may be worth sacrificing some confidence to achieve more precision. Show that the 90% confidence interval for $(\mu_2 - \mu_1)$ is (3.7, 36.3). Interpret.

(c) Estimate and summarize the effect size.

**7.31.** Refer to the previous exercise. To avoid bias from the samples being unbalanced with such small $n$, the psychologist redesigned the experiment. She

[9]D. Baker and L. Stephenson, *Journal of Clinical Psychology*, vol. 51, 1995, p. 694.
[10]J. Morgan and J. Saffran, *Child Development*, vol. 66, 1995, pp. 911–936.

forms three pairs of subjects, such that the patients matched in any given pair are similar in health and socioeconomic status. For each pair, she randomly selects one subject for each therapy. Table 7.17 shows the improvement scores, and Table 7.18 shows results of using SPSS to analyze the data.

(a) Compare the means by (i) finding the difference of the sample means for the two therapies, (ii) finding the mean of the difference scores. Compare.

(b) Verify the standard deviation of the differences and standard error for the mean difference.

(c) Verify the confidence interval shown for the population mean difference. Interpret.

(d) Verify the test statistic, $df$, and $P$-value for comparing the means. Interpret.

**TABLE 7.17**

| Pair | Therapy A | Therapy B |
|------|-----------|-----------|
| 1 | 10 | 30 |
| 2 | 20 | 45 |
| 3 | 30 | 45 |

**7.32.** A study[11] of bulimia among college women considered the effect of childhood sexual abuse on various components of a Family Environment Scale. For a measure of family cohesion, the sample mean for the bulimic students was 2.0 for 13 sexually abused students and 4.8 for 17 nonabused students. Table 7.19 shows software results of a two-sample comparison of means.

(a) Assuming equal population standard deviations, construct a 95% confidence interval for the difference in mean family cohesion for sexually abused students and nonabused students. Interpret.

(b) Explain how to interpret results of significance tests from this printout.

**TABLE 7.19**

Variable: COHESION

| ABUSED | N | Mean | Std Dev | Std Error |
|--------|-----|------|---------|-----------|
| yes | 13 | 2.0 | 2.1 | 0.58 |
| no | 17 | 4.8 | 3.2 | 0.78 |

| Variances | T | DF | P-value |
|-----------|------|------|---------|
| Unequal | 2.89 | 27.5 | 0.007 |
| Equal | 2.73 | 28 | 0.011 |

**7.33.** For the survey of students described in Exercise 1.11, the responses on political ideology had a mean of 3.18 and standard deviation of 1.72 for the 51 nonvegetarian students and a mean of 2.22 and standard deviation of 0.67 for the 9 vegetarian students. When we use software to compare the means with a significance test, we obtain

| Variances | T | DF | P-value |
|-----------|-------|------|---------|
| Unequal | 2.915 | 30.9 | 0.0066 |
| Equal | 1.636 | 58.0 | 0.1073 |

Explain why the results of the two tests differ so much, and give your conclusion about whether the population means are equal.

**7.34.** In 2006, the GSS asked about the number of hours a week spent on the World Wide Web (WWW-TIME). The 1569 females had a mean of 4.9 and standard deviation of 8.6. The 1196 males had a mean of 6.2 and standard deviation of 9.9. Use these results to make an inference comparing males and females on WWWTIME in the population, assuming equal population standard deviations.

**7.35.** Two new short courses have been proposed for helping students who suffer from severe math phobia, scoring at least 8 on a measure of math phobia that falls between 0 and 10 (based on responses to

**TABLE 7.18**

t-tests for Paired Samples

| Variable | Number of pairs | Mean | SD | SE of Mean |
|----------|-----------------|--------|--------|------------|
| THERAPY A | | 20.000 | 10.000 | 5.774 |
| | 3 | | | |
| THERAPY B | | 40.000 | 8.660 | 5.000 |

Paired Differences

| Mean | SD | SE of Mean | t-value | df | 2-tail Sig |
|---------|------|------------|---------|-----|------------|
| 20.0000 | 5.00 | 2.887 | 6.93 | 2 | 0.020 |

95% CI (7.58, 32.42)

---

[11]J. Kern and T. Hastings, *J. Clinical Psychology*, vol. 51, 1995, p. 499.

10 questions). A sample of ten such students were randomly allocated to the two courses. Following the course, the drop in math phobia score was recorded. The sample values were

$$\text{Course A:} \quad 0, 2, 2, 3, 3$$
$$\text{Course B:} \quad 3, 6, 6, 7, 8.$$

**(a)** Make an inferential comparison of the means, assuming equal population standard deviations. Interpret your results.
**(b)** Using software, report and interpret the *P*-value for the two-sided Wilcoxon test.
**(c)** Find and interpret the effect size $(\bar{y}_B - \bar{y}_A)/s$.
**(d)** Estimate and interpret the effect size $P(y_B > y_A)$.

**7.36.** A GSS asked subjects whether they believed in heaven and whether they believed in hell. Of 1120 subjects, 833 believed in both, 160 believed in neither, 125 believed in heaven but not in hell, and 2 believed in hell but not in heaven.
**(a)** Display the data in a contingency table, cross classifying belief in heaven (*yes, no*) with belief in hell (*yes, no*).
**(b)** Estimate the population proportion who believe in heaven and the population proportion who believe in hell.
**(c)** Show all steps of McNemar's test to compare the population proportions, and interpret.
**(d)** Construct a 95% confidence interval to compare the population proportions, and interpret.

**7.37.** A GSS asked subjects their opinions about government spending on health and government spending on law enforcement. For each, should it increase, or should it decrease? Table 7.20 shows results.
**(a)** Find the sample proportion favoring increased spending, for each item.
**(b)** Test whether the population proportions are equal. Report the *P*-value, and interpret.
**(c)** Construct a 95% confidence interval for the difference of proportions. Interpret.

**TABLE 7.20**

| Health | Law Enforcement Spending | |
|---|---|---|
| Spending | Increase | Decrease |
| Increase | 292 | 25 |
| Decrease | 14 | 9 |

**7.38.** A study[12] used data from the Longitudinal Study of Aging to investigate how older people's health and social characteristics influence how far they

live from their children. Consider Table 7.21, which shows whether an older subject lives with a child at a given time and then again four years later. The author expected that as people aged and their health deteriorated, they would be more likely to live with children. Do these data support this belief? Justify your answer with an inferential analysis.

**TABLE 7.21**

| First | Four Years Later | |
|---|---|---|
| Survey | Yes | No |
| Yes | 423 | 138 |
| No | 217 | 2690 |

**7.39.** A study[13] investigated the sexual orientation of adults who had been raised as children in lesbian families. Twenty-five children of lesbian mothers and a control group of 20 children of heterosexual mothers were seen at age 10 and again at age about 24. At the later time, they were interviewed about their sexual identity, with possible response *Bisexual/Lesbian/Gay* or *Heterosexual*. Table 7.22 shows results, in the form of a SAS printout for conducting Fisher's exact test.
**(a)** Why is Fisher's exact test used to compare the groups?
**(b)** Report and interpret the *P*-value for the alternative that the population proportion identifying as bisexual/lesbian/gay is higher for those with lesbian mothers.

**TABLE 7.22**

```
                IDENTITY

MOTHER   | B/L/G  | HETERO |  Total
---------+--------+--------+
Lesbian  |    2 |    23 |    25
---------+--------+--------+
Heterosx |    0 |    20 |    20
---------+--------+--------+
Total         2        43      45


STATISTICS FOR TABLE OF MOTHER BY IDENTITY
Statistic                            Prob
------------------------------------------
Fisher's Exact Test (Left)          1.000
                    (Right)         0.303
                    (2-Tail)        0.495
```

**7.40.** Refer to the previous problem. The young adults were also asked whether they had ever had a same-gender sexual relationship. Table 7.23

[12]M. Silverstein, *Demography*, vol. 32, 1995, p. 35.
[13]S. Colombok and F. Tasker, *Developmental Psychology*, vol. 32, 1996, pp. 3–11.

shows results. Use software to test whether the probability of this is higher for those raised by lesbian mothers. Interpret.

**TABLE 7.23**

| Mother | Same-Gender Relationship | |
|---|---|---|
| | Yes | No |
| Lesbian | 6 | 19 |
| Heterosexual | 0 | 20 |

## Concepts and Applications

**7.41.** For the "Student survey" data file (Exercise 1.11 on page 8), compare political ideology of students identifying with the Democratic party and with the Republican
  **(a)** Using graphical and numerical summaries.
  **(b)** Using inferential statistical methods. Interpret.

**7.42.** Using software with the student survey data set (Exercise 1.11), construct a confidence interval and conduct a test:
  **(a)** To compare males and females in terms of opinions about legalized abortion. Interpret.
  **(b)** To compare the mean weekly time spent watching TV to the mean weekly time in sports and other physical exercise.

**7.43.** For the data file created in Exercise 1.12, with variables chosen by your instructor, state a research question and conduct inferential statistical analyses. Prepare a report that summarizes your findings. In this report, also use graphical and numerical methods to describe the data and, if necessary, to check assumptions you make for your analysis.

**7.44.** Exercise 3.6 in Chapter 3 on page 61 showed data on carbon dioxide emissions, a major contributor to global warming, for advanced industrialized nations. Is there a difference between European and non-European nations in their emission levels? Conduct an investigation to answer this question.

**7.45.** Pose null and alternative hypotheses about the relationship between time spent on the Internet (WWWHR for the GSS) and a binary predictor available at the GSS that you believe may be associated with Internet use. Using the most recent GSS data on these variables at sda.berkeley.edu/GSS, conduct the test. Prepare a short report summarizing your analysis. (*Note*: The GSS Web site enables you to compare means for groups, by clicking on "Comparison of means.")

**7.46.** Browse one or two daily newspapers such as *The New York Times* (hard copy or online). Copy an

article about a research study that compared two groups. Prepare a short report that answers the following questions:
  **(a)** What was the purpose of the research study?
  **(b)** Identify explanatory and response variables.
  **(c)** Can you tell whether the statistical analysis used (1) independent samples or dependent samples, or (2) a comparison of proportions or a comparison of means?

**7.47.** A recent study[14] considered whether greater levels of TV watching by teenagers were associated with a greater likelihood of committing aggressive acts over the years. The researchers randomly sampled 707 families in two counties in northern New York State and made follow-up observations over 17 years. They observed whether a sampled teenager later conducted any aggressive act against another person, according to a self report by that person or by their mother. Of 88 cases with less than 1 hour per day of TV watching, 5 had committed aggressive acts. Of 619 cases with at least 1 hour per day of TV, 154 had committed aggressive acts. Analyze these data, summarizing your analyses in a short report.

**7.48.** When asked by the GSS about the number of people with whom the subject had discussed matters of importance over the past six months (variable NUMGIVEN), the response of 0 was made by 8.9% of 1531 respondents in 1985 and by 24.6% of 1482 respondents in 2004. Analyze these data inferentially and interpret.

**7.49.** A study[15] compared substance use, delinquency, psychological well-being, and social support among various family types, for a sample of urban African-American adolescent males. The sample contained 108 subjects from single-mother households and 44 from households with both biological parents. The youths responded to a battery of questions that provides a measure of perceived parental support. This measure had sample means of 46 ($s = 9$) for the single-mother households and 42 ($s = 10$) for the households with both biological parents. Consider the conclusion, "The mean parental support was 4 units higher for the single-mother households. If the true means were equal, a difference of this size could be expected only 2% of the time. For samples of this size, 95% of the time one would expect this difference to be within 3.4 of the true value."
  **(a)** Explain how this conclusion refers to the results of (i) a confidence interval, (ii) a test.
  **(b)** Describe how you would explain the results of the study to someone who has not studied inferential statistics.

[14]J. G. Johnson et al., *Science*, vol. 295, 2002, pp. 2468–2471.

[15]M. Zimmerman et al., *Child Development*, vol. 66, 1995, pp. 1598–1613.

**7.50.** The results in Table 7.24 are from a study[16] of physical attractiveness and subjective well-being. A sample of college students were rated by a panel on their physical attractiveness. The table presents the number of dates in the past three months for students rated in the top or bottom quartile of attractiveness. Analyze these data, and interpret.

**7.51.** A report (12/04/2002) by the Pew Research Center on *What the World Thinks in 2002* reported that "the American public is strikingly at odds with publics around the world in its views about the U.S. role in the world and the global impact of American actions." Conclusions were based on polls in several countries. In Pakistan, in 2002 the percentage of interviewed subjects who had a favorable view of the U.S. was 10%, and the percentage who thought the spread of American ideas and customs was good was 2% ($n = 2032$).

(a) Do you have enough information to make an inferential comparison of the proportions? If so, do so. If not, what else would you need to know?

(b) For a separate survey in 2000, the estimated percentage who had a favorable view of the U.S. was 23%. To compare inferentially the percentages in 2000 and 2002, what more would you need to know?

**7.52.** A *Time Magazine* article titled "Wal-Mart's Gender Gap" (July 5, 2004) stated that in 2001 women managers at Wal-Mart earned \$14,500 a year less, on the average, than their male counterparts. If you were also given the standard errors of the annual mean salaries for male and female managers at Wal-Mart, would you have enough information to determine whether this is a "statistically significant" difference? Explain.

**7.53.** The International Adult Literacy Survey (www.nifl.gov/nifl/facts/IALS.html) was a 22-country study in which nationally representative samples of adults were interviewed and tested at home, using the same literacy test having scores that could range from 0-500. For those of age 16–25, some of the mean prose literacy scores were UK 273.5, New Zealand 276.8, Ireland 277.7, U.S. 277.9, Denmark 283.4, Australia 283.6, Canada 286.9, Netherlands 293.5, Norway 300.4, Sweden 312.1. The Web site does not provide sample sizes or standard deviations. Suppose each sample size was 250 and each standard deviation was 50. How far apart do two sample means have to be before you feel confident that an actual difference exists between the population means? Explain your reasoning, giving your conclusion for Canada and the U.S.

**7.54.** Table 7.25 compares two hospitals on the outcomes of patient admissions for severe pneumonia. Although patient status is an ordinal variable, two researchers who analyze the data treat it as an interval variable. The first researcher assigns the scores (0, 5, 10) to the three categories. The second researcher, believing that the middle category is much closer to the third category than to the first, uses the scores (0, 9, 10). Each researcher calculates the means for the two institutions and identifies the institution with the higher mean as the one having more success in treating its patients. Find the two means for the scoring system used by (a) the first researcher, (b) the second researcher. Interpret. (Notice that the conclusion depends on the scoring system. So if you use methods for quantitative variables with ordinal data, take care in selecting scores.)

**TABLE 7.25**

| | Patient Status | | |
| --- | --- | --- | --- |
| | Died in Hospital | Released After Lengthy Stay | Released After Brief Stay |
| Hospital A | 1 | 29 | 0 |
| Hospital B | 8 | 8 | 14 |

**7.55.** From Example 6.4 (page 151) in Chapter 6, for the cognitive behavioral therapy group the sample mean change in weight of 3.0 pounds was significantly different from 0. However, Example 7.7 (page 198) showed it is not significantly different from the mean change for the control group, even though that group had a negative sample mean change. How do you explain this paradox? (*Hint*: From Sections 7.1 and 7.3, how does the *se* value for estimating a difference between two means

**TABLE 7.24**

| | No. Dates, Men | | | No. Dates, Women | | |
| --- | --- | --- | --- | --- | --- | --- |
| Attractiveness | Mean | Std. Dev. | $n$ | Mean | Std. Dev. | $n$ |
| More | 9.7 | 10.0 | 35 | 17.8 | 14.2 | 33 |
| Less | 9.9 | 12.6 | 36 | 10.4 | 16.6 | 27 |

[16]E. Diener et al., *Journal of Personality and Social Psychology*, vol. 69, 1995, pp. 120–129.

compare to the *se* value for estimating a single mean?)

**7.56.** A survey by the Harris Poll of 2201 Americans in 2003 indicated that 51% believe in ghosts and 31% believe in astrology.
  **(a)** Is it valid to compare the proportions using inferential methods for independent samples? Explain.
  **(b)** Do you have enough information to compare them using inferential methods for dependent samples? Explain.

**7.57.** A pool of six candidates for three managerial positions includes three females and three males. Table 7.26 shows the results.
  **(a)** Denote the three females by $F_1$, $F_2$, $F_3$ and the three males by $M_1$, $M_2$, $M_3$. Identify the 20 distinct samples of size three that can be chosen from these six individuals.
  **(b)** Let $\hat{\pi}_1$ denote the sample proportion of males selected and $\hat{\pi}_2$ the sample proportion of females. For Table 7.26, $\hat{\pi}_1 - \hat{\pi}_2 = (2/3) - (1/3) = 1/3$. Of the 20 possible samples, show that 10 have $\hat{\pi}_1 - \hat{\pi}_2 \geq 1/3$. Thus, if the three managers were randomly selected, the probability would equal $10/20 = 0.50$ of obtaining $\hat{\pi}_1 - \hat{\pi}_2 \geq 1/3$. In fact, this is the reasoning that provides the one-sided *P*-value for Fisher's exact test.
  **(c)** Find the *P*-value if all three selected are male. Interpret.

**TABLE 7.26**

| Gender | Chosen for Position | |
| | Yes | No |
| --- | --- | --- |
| Male | 2 | 1 |
| Female | 1 | 2 |

**7.58.** Describe a situation in which it would be more sensible to compare means using dependent samples than independent samples.

**7.59.** An Associated Press story (Feb. 1, 2007) about a University of Chicago survey of 1600 people of ages 15 to 25 in several Midwest U.S. cities indicated that 58% of black youth, 45% of Hispanic youth, and 23% of white youth reported listening to rap music every day.
  **(a)** True or false: If a 95% confidence interval comparing the population proportions for Hispanic and white youths was (0.18, 0.26), then we can infer that at least 18% but no more than 26% of the corresponding white population listens daily to rap music.
  **(b)** The study reported that 66% of black females and 57% of black males agreed that rap music videos portray black women in bad and offensive ways. True or false: Because both these groups had the same race, inferential methods comparing them must assume dependent rather than independent samples.

**7.60.** True or false? If a 95% confidence interval for $(\mu_2 - \mu_1)$ contains only positive numbers, then we can conclude that both $\mu_1$ and $\mu_2$ are positive.

**7.61.** True or false? If you know the standard error of the sample mean for each of two independent samples, you can figure out the standard error of the difference between the sample means, even if you do not know the sample sizes.

*In Exercises 7.62–7.64, select the correct response(s). More than one may be correct.*

**7.62.** A 99% confidence interval for the difference $\pi_2 - \pi_1$ between the proportions of men and women in California who are alcoholics equals (0.02, 0.09).
  **(a)** We are 99% confident that the proportion of alcoholics is between 0.02 and 0.09.
  **(b)** We are 99% confident that the proportion of men in California who are alcoholics is between 0.02 and 0.09 larger than the proportion of women in California who are.
  **(c)** At this confidence level, there is insufficient evidence to infer that the population proportions are different.
  **(d)** We are 99% confident that a minority of California residents are alcoholics.
  **(e)** Since the confidence interval does not contain 0, it is impossible that $\pi_1 = \pi_2$.

**7.63.** To compare the population mean annual incomes for Hispanics ($\mu_1$) and for whites ($\mu_2$) having jobs in construction, we construct a 95% confidence interval for $\mu_2 - \mu_1$.
  **(a)** If the confidence interval is (3000, 6000), then at this confidence level we conclude that the population mean income is higher for whites than for Hispanics.
  **(b)** If the confidence interval is $(-1000, 3000)$, then the corresponding $\alpha = 0.05$ level test of $H_0: \mu_1 = \mu_2$ against $H_a: \mu_1 \neq \mu_2$ rejects $H_0$.
  **(c)** If the confidence interval is $(-1000, 3000)$, then it is plausible that $\mu_1 = \mu_2$.
  **(d)** If the confidence interval is $(-1000, 3000)$, then we are 95% confident that the population mean annual income for whites is between $1000 less and $3000 more than the population mean annual income for Hispanics.

**7.64.** The Wilcoxon test differs from parametric procedures (for means) in the sense that
  **(a)** It applies directly to ordinal as well as interval response variables.

**(b)** It is unnecessary to assume that the population distribution is normal.

**(c)** Random sampling is not assumed.

**\*7.65.** A test consists of 100 true–false questions. Joe did not study, so on each question, he randomly guesses the correct response.

**(a)** Find the probability that he scores at least 70, thus passing the exam. (*Hint*: Use the sampling distribution for the proportion of correct responses.)

**(b)** Jane studied a little and has a 0.60 chance of a correct response for each question. Find the probability that her score is nonetheless lower than Joe's. (*Hint*: Use the sampling distribution of the difference of sample proportions.)

**(c)** How do the answers to (a) and (b) depend on the number of questions? Explain.

**\*7.66.** Let $y_{i1}$ denote the observation for subject $i$ at time 1, $y_{i2}$ the observation for subject $i$ at time 2, and $y_i = y_{i2} - y_{i1}$.

**(a)** Letting $\bar{y}_1$, $\bar{y}_2$, and $\bar{y}_d$ denote the means of these observations, show that $\bar{y}_d = \bar{y}_2 - \bar{y}_1$.

**(b)** Is the median difference (i.e., the median of the $y_i$ values) equal to the difference between the medians of the $y_{i1}$ and $y_{i2}$ values? Show that this is true, or give a counterexample to show that it is false.

# Analyzing Association between Categorical Variables

Recall that we say there is an **association** between two variables if the distribution of the response variable changes in some way as the value of the explanatory variable changes. In comparing two groups, an association exists if the population means or population proportions differ between the groups.

This chapter presents methods for detecting and describing associations between two categorical variables. The methods of this chapter help us answer a question such as, "Is there an association between happiness and whether one is religious?" The methods of Chapter 7 for comparing two proportions are special cases of ones considered here in which both variables have only two categories.

Section 8.1 introduces terminology for categorical data analysis and defines *statistical independence*, a type of lack of association. Section 8.2 presents a significance test for determining whether two categorical variables are associated, and Section 8.3 follows up that test by a *residual analysis* that describes the nature of that association. Section 8.4 shows how to determine whether the association is strong enough to have practical importance. Sections 8.5 and 8.6 present specialized analyses for ordinal variables.

## 8.1 CONTINGENCY TABLES

Data for the analysis of categorical variables are displayed in **contingency tables**. This type of table displays the number of subjects observed at all combinations of possible outcomes for the two variables.

### EXAMPLE 8.1   Gender Gap in Political Beliefs

In recent years in the United States political commentators have discussed whether a "gender gap" exists in political beliefs. Do women and men tend to differ in their political thinking and voting behavior? To investigate this, we study Table 8.1, from the 2004 GSS. The categorical variables are gender and political party identification (SEX and PARTYID in the GSS). Subjects indicated whether they identified more strongly with the Democratic or Republican party or as Independents.

Table 8.1 contains responses for 2771 subjects, cross-classified by their gender and party ID. Table 8.1 is called a $2 \times 3$ (read "2-by-3") contingency table, meaning that

**TABLE 8.1:** Party Identification (ID) and Gender, for GSS Data

| Gender | Party Identification | | | Total |
| | Democrat | Independent | Republican | |
|---|---|---|---|---|
| Females | 573 | 516 | 422 | 1511 |
| Males | 386 | 475 | 399 | 1260 |
| Total | 959 | 991 | 821 | 2771 |

it has two rows and three columns. The row totals and the column totals are called the ***marginal distributions***. The sample marginal distribution for party identification, for instance, is the set of marginal frequencies (959, 991, 821).     ■

## Percentage Comparisons

Constructing a contingency table from a data file is the first step in investigating an association between two categorical variables. To study how party identification depends on gender, we convert the frequencies to percentages within each row, as Table 8.2 shows. For example, a proportion of $573/1511 = 0.38$, or 38% in percentage terms, identify themselves as Democrat. The percentage of males who identify themselves as Democrat equals 31% (386 out of 1260). It seems that females are more likely than males to identify as Democrats.

**TABLE 8.2:** Party Identification and Gender: Percentages Computed within Rows of Table 8.1

| Gender | Party Identification | | | Total | $n$ |
| | Democrat | Independent | Republican | | |
|---|---|---|---|---|---|
| Females | 38% | 34% | 28% | 100% | 1511 |
| Males | 31% | 38% | 32% | 101% | 1260 |

The two sets of percentages for females and males are called the ***conditional distributions*** on party identification. They refer to the sample data distribution of party ID, *conditional* on gender. The females' conditional distribution on party ID is the set of percentages (38, 34, 28) for (Democrat, Independent, Republican). The percentages sum to 100 in each row, except possibly for rounding. Figure 8.1 portrays graphically the two conditional distributions.

In a similar way, we could compute conditional distributions on gender for each party ID. The first column would indicate that 60% of the Democrats are females and 40% are males. In practice, it is standard to form the conditional distribution for the response variable, within categories of the explanatory variable. In this example, party ID is a response variable, so Table 8.2 reports percentages within rows, which tells us the percentage of (Democrats, Independents, Republicans) for each gender.

Another way to report percentages provides a single set for all cells in the table, using the total sample size as the base. To illustrate, in Table 8.1, of the 2771 subjects, 573 or 21% fall in the cell (Female, Democrat), 386 or 14% fall in the cell (Male, Democrat), and so forth. This percentage distribution is called the sample ***joint distribution***. It is useful for comparing relative frequencies of occurrences for combinations of variable levels. When we distinguish between response and explanatory variables, though, conditional distributions are more informative than the joint distribution.

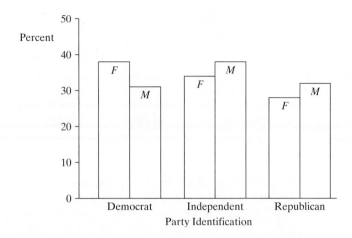

**FIGURE 8.1:** Portrayal of Conditional Distributions on Party ID in Table 8.2 for Females and Males

## Guidelines in Forming Contingency Tables

Here are some guidelines when finding proportions or percentages in contingency tables. First, as just noted, find them for the response variable within the categories of the explanatory variable. We'll construct the table so that the column variable is the response variable, as in Table 8.1. So we find proportions within each row, dividing each cell count by the row total.

Second, clearly label the variables and their categories, and give the table a title that identifies the variables and other relevant information. Third, include the total sample sizes on which the percentages or proportions are based. That way, readers can determine the cell frequencies, if they are not listed, and they can find standard errors to analyze the precision of sample proportion estimates.

## Independence and Dependence

Whether an association exists in Table 8.1 is a matter of whether females and males differ in their conditional distributions on party ID. We answer the question "Is party ID associated with gender?" with reference to the concepts of statistical *independence* and *dependence*.

---

**Statistical Independence and Statistical Dependence**

Two categorical variables are *statistically independent* if the population conditional distributions on one of them are identical at each category of the other. The variables are *statistically dependent* if the conditional distributions are not identical.

---

In other words, two variables are statistically independent if the percentage of the population in any particular category of one variable is the same for all categories of the other variable. In Table 8.2, the two conditional distributions are not identical. But that table describes a sample, and the definition of statistical independence refers to the population. If those observations were the entire population, then the variables would be statistically dependent.

For simplicity, we usually use the term *independent* rather than *statistically independent*. Table 8.3 is a hypothetical contingency table showing independence. The table contains the population data for two variables—party ID and ethnic group.

**TABLE 8.3**: Population Cross-Classification Exhibiting Statistical Independence. The conditional distribution is the same in each row, (44%, 14%, 42%).

| Ethnic Group | Party Identification | | | Total |
|---|---|---|---|---|
| | Democrat | Independent | Republican | |
| White | 440 (44%) | 140 (14%) | 420 (42%) | 1000 (100%) |
| Black | 44 (44%) | 14 (14%) | 42 (42%) | 100 (100%) |
| Hispanic | 110 (44%) | 35 (14%) | 105 (42%) | 250 (100%) |

The percentage of Democrats is the same for each ethnic group, 44%. Similarly, the percentage of Independents and the percentage of Republicans is the same for each ethnic group. The probability that a person has a particular party ID is the same for each ethnic group, and so party ID is independent of ethnic group.

Statistical independence is a symmetric property between two variables: If the conditional distributions within rows are identical, then so are the conditional distributions within columns. In Table 8.3, for example, you can check that the conditional distribution within each column equals (74%, 7%, 19%).

### EXAMPLE 8.2    What's Associated with Belief in Life after Death?

In recent General Social Surveys, the percentage of Americans who express a belief in life after death (variable AFTERLIF in the GSS) has been about 80%. This has been true both for females and for males and true for those who classify their race as black, white, or other. Thus, it appears that belief in life after death may be statistically independent of variables such as gender and race. On the other hand, whereas about 80% of Catholics and Protestants believe in an afterlife, only about 40% of Jews and 50% of those with no religion believe in an afterlife. We can't be sure, not having data for the entire population, but it seems that belief in life after death and religion are statistically dependent. ∎

## 8.2    CHI-SQUARED TEST OF INDEPENDENCE

Table 8.1 contains sample data. The definition of statistical independence refers to the population. Two variables are independent if the *population* conditional distributions on the response variable are identical. Since Table 8.1 refers to a sample, it provides evidence but does not definitively answer whether party ID and gender are independent. Even if they are independent, we would not expect the *sample* conditional distributions to be identical. Because of sampling variability, we expect sample percentages to differ from the population percentages.

We next study whether it is plausible that party ID and gender are independent. If they are truly independent, could we expect sample differences such as Table 8.2 shows between females and males in their conditional distributions merely by sampling variation? Or would differences of this size be unlikely? To address this with a significance test, we test the following:

$H_0$: The variables are statistically independent.
$H_a$: The variables are statistically dependent.

The test requires randomization—for example, random sampling or a randomized experiment. The sample size must be large, satisfying a condition stated later in the section.

## Expected Frequencies for Independence

The chi-squared test compares the observed frequencies in the contingency table with values that satisfy the null hypothesis of independence. Table 8.4 shows the observed frequencies from Table 8.1, with the values (in parentheses) that satisfy $H_0$. These $H_0$ values have the same row and column totals as the observed frequencies, but satisfy independence. They are called *expected frequencies*.

**TABLE 8.4**: Party Identification by Gender, with Expected Frequencies in Parentheses

| | Party Identification | | | |
| --- | --- | --- | --- | --- |
| Gender | Democrat | Independent | Republican | Total |
| Female | 573 (522.9) | 516 (540.4) | 422 (447.7) | 1511 |
| Male | 386 (436.1) | 475 (450.6) | 399 (373.3) | 1260 |
| Total | 959 | 991 | 821 | 2771 |

---

**Observed and Expected Frequencies**

Let $f_o$ denote an **observed** frequency in a cell of the table. Let $f_e$ denote an **expected** frequency. This is the count expected in a cell if the variables were independent. It equals the product of the row and column totals for that cell, divided by the total sample size.

---

For instance, the cell in the upper left-hand corner refers to Females who identify as Democrats. For it, $f_o = 573$. Its expected frequency is $f_e = (1511)(959)/2771 = 522.9$, the product of the row total for Females and the column total for Democrats, divided by the overall sample size.

Let's see why this rule makes sense. In the entire sample, 959 out of 2771 people (34.6%) identify as Democrats. If the variables were independent, we would expect 34.6% of males and 34.6% of females to identify as Democrats. For instance, 34.6% of the 1511 Females should be classified in the Democrat category. The expected frequency for the cell is then

$$f_e = \left( \frac{959}{2771} \right) 1511 = 0.346(1511) = 522.9.$$

## Chi-Squared Test Statistic

The test statistic for $H_0$: independence summarizes how close the expected frequencies fall to the observed frequencies. Symbolized by $\chi^2$, it is called the *chi-squared statistic*. It equals

$$\chi^2 = \sum \frac{(f_o - f_e)^2}{f_e}.$$

The summation is taken over all cells in the contingency table. For each cell, we square the difference between the observed and expected frequencies and then divide that square by the expected frequency. This is the oldest test statistic in use today; it was introduced by the British statistician Karl Pearson in 1900.

When $H_0$ is true, $f_o$ and $f_e$ tend to be close for each cell, and $\chi^2$ is relatively small. If $H_0$ is false, at least some $f_o$ and $f_e$ values tend not to be close, leading to large $(f_o - f_e)^2$ values and a large test statistic. The larger the $\chi^2$ value, the greater the evidence against $H_0$: independence.

Substituting the $f_o$ and $f_e$ values from Table 8.2 into the formula for $\chi^2$, we get

$$\chi^2 = \sum \frac{(f_o - f_e)^2}{f_e}$$

$$= \frac{(573 - 522.9)^2}{522.9} + \frac{(516 - 540.4)^2}{540.4} + \frac{(422 - 447.7)^2}{447.7}$$

$$+ \frac{(386 - 436.1)^2}{436.1} + \frac{(475 - 450.6)^2}{450.6} + \frac{(399 - 373.3)^2}{373.3}$$

$$= 4.8 + \cdots + 1.8 = 16.2.$$

The calculation is messy, but it is simple to get $\chi^2$ using software. We next study how to interpret its magnitude.

### The Chi-Squared Distribution

The sampling distribution of the $\chi^2$ test statistic indicates how large $\chi^2$ must be before strong evidence exists that $H_0$ is false. For large sample sizes, the sampling distribution is the **chi-squared probability distribution**. The name of the test and the symbol for the test statistic refer to the name of the sampling distribution. Here are the main properties of the chi-squared distribution:

- It is concentrated on the positive part of the real line. The $\chi^2$ test statistic cannot be negative, since it sums squared differences divided by positive expected frequencies. The minimum possible value, $\chi^2 = 0$, would occur if $f_o = f_e$ in each cell.

- It is skewed to the right.

- The precise shape of the distribution depends on the **degrees of freedom** (*df*). The mean $\mu = df$ and the standard deviation $\sigma = \sqrt{2df}$. Thus, the distribution tends to shift to the right and become more spread out for larger *df* values. In addition, as *df* increases, the skew lessens and the chi-squared curve becomes more bell shaped. See Figure 8.2.

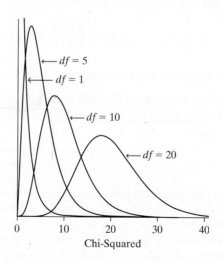

**FIGURE 8.2:** The Chi-Squared Distribution. The curve has larger mean and standard deviation as the degrees of freedom increase.

● For testing $H_0$: independence with a table having $r$ rows and $c$ columns,

$$df = (r - 1)(c - 1).$$

For a $2 \times 3$ table, $r = 2$ and $c = 3$ and $df = (2 - 1)(3 - 1) = 1 \times 2 = 2$. Larger numbers of rows and columns produce larger $df$ values. Since larger tables have more terms in the summation for the $x^2$ test statistic, the $x^2$ values also tend to be larger.

● The larger the $x^2$ value, the stronger the evidence against $H_0$: independence. The $P$-value equals the right-tail probability above the observed $x^2$ value. It measures the probability, presuming $H_0$ is true, that $x^2$ is at least as large as the observed value. Figure 8.3 depicts the $P$-value.

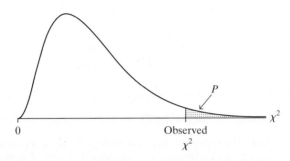

**FIGURE 8.3:** The $P$-Value for the Chi-Squared Test of Independence Is the Right-Tail Probability, above the Observed Value of the Test Statistic

Table C at the back of the text lists chi-squared values for various right-tail probabilities. These are $x^2$ test statistic values that have $P$-values equal to those probabilities. For example, Table C reports that when $df = 2$, $x^2 = 5.99$ has $P$-value $= 0.05$, and $x^2 = 9.21$ has $P$-value $= 0.01$.

## EXAMPLE 8.3    Chi-Squared Statistic for Party ID and Gender

To apply the chi-squared test to Table 8.4, we test the following:

$H_0$: Party ID and gender are statistically independent.
$H_a$: Party ID and gender are statistically dependent.

Previously, we obtained test statistic $x^2 = 16.2$. In Table C, for $df = 2$, 16.2 falls above 13.82, the chi-squared value having right-tail probability 0.001. Thus, we conclude that $P < 0.001$. Software indicates that $P = 0.0003$. This provides extremely strong evidence against $H_0$. It seems likely that party ID and gender are associated in the population. If the variables were independent, it would be highly unusual for a random sample to have this large a $x^2$ statistic.    ■

### Sample Size Requirements

The chi-squared test, like one- and two-sample $z$ tests for proportions, is a large-sample test. The chi-squared distribution is the sampling distribution of the $x^2$ test statistic only if the sample size is large. A rough guideline for this requirement is that the expected frequency $f_e$ should exceed 5 in each cell. Otherwise, the chi-squared distribution may poorly approximate the actual distribution of the $x^2$ statistic.

For 2 × 2 contingency tables, a small-sample test of independence is **Fisher's exact test**, discussed in Section 7.5. This test extends to tables of arbitrary size $r \times c$ but requires specialized software, such as SAS (the EXACT option in PROC FREQ) or SPSS (the Exact module).

If you have such software, you can use the exact test for *any* sample size. You don't need to use the chi-squared approximation. For Table 8.4, the exact test also gives *P*-value = 0.0003. Table 8.5 summarizes the five parts of the chi-squared test.

**TABLE 8.5:** The Five Parts of the Chi-Squared Test of Independence

1. Assumptions: Two categorical variables, random sampling, $f_e \geq 5$ in all cells
2. Hypotheses: $H_0$: Statistical independence of variables
   $H_a$: Statistical dependence of variables
3. Test statistic: $\chi^2 = \sum \dfrac{(f_o - f_e)^2}{f_e}$, where $f_e = \dfrac{\text{(Row total)(Column total)}}{\text{Total sample size}}$
4. P-value: $P$ = right-tail probability above observed $\chi^2$ value,
   for chi-squared distribution with $df = (r - 1)(c - 1)$
5. Conclusion:  Report *P*-value
   If decision needed, reject $H_0$ at $\alpha$-level if $P \leq \alpha$

## Using Software to Conduct Chi-Squared Tests

The chi-squared test of independence is computationally messy enough that you should use software to conduct it. Table 8.6 illustrates output for Table 8.1. SPSS lists the *P*-value under *Asymp. Sig.*, short for *asymptotic significance*, where the "asymptotic" refers to a large-sample method. Most software also reports an alternative test statistic, called the *likelihood-ratio statistic*, which usually provides similar results. Chapter 15 introduces this statistic.

**TABLE 8.6:** Printout for Chi-Squared Test of Independence

| GENDER | | democrat | indep | repub | Total |
|--------|--|---------|-------|-------|-------|
| female | Count | 573 | 516 | 422 | 1511 |
|  | Expected Count | 522.9 | 540.4 | 447.7 | |
| male | Count | 386 | 475 | 399 | 1260 |
|  | Expected Count | 436.1 | 450.6 | 373.3 | |
| Total | | 959 | 991 | 821 | 2771 |

| Statistic | Value | df | Asymp. Sig. |
|-----------|-------|-----|-------------|
| Pearson Chi-Square | 16.202 | 2 | .000 |
| Likelihood Ratio | 16.273 | 2 | .000 |

## Interpretation of Degrees of Freedom

The *df* in a chi-squared test has the following interpretation: Given the marginal totals, the cell counts in a rectangular block of size $(r - 1) \times (c - 1)$ within the contingency table determine the other cell counts.

To illustrate, in Table 8.1, suppose we know the two frequencies 573 and 516 in the upper-left-hand part of the table. This is a block of size $1 \times 2$, shown in Table 8.7. Then, given the marginal totals, we can determine all the other cell counts. For instance, since 573 of the 959 Democrats are female, the other $959 - 573 = 386$ must be male. Since 516 of the 991 Independents are female, the other $991 - 516 = 475$ must be male. Also, since the total of the female row is 1511, and since the first two cells contain 1089 (i.e., $573 + 516$) subjects, the remaining cell must have $1511 - 1089 = 422$ observations. From this and the fact that the last column has 821 observations, there must be $821 - 422 = 399$ observations in the second cell in that column.

**TABLE 8.7:** Illustration of Degrees of Freedom; a Block of $(r - 1)(c - 1)$ Cell Counts Determine the Others

| | Party Identification | | | |
|---|---|---|---|---|
| Gender | Democrat | Independent | Republican | Total |
| Female | 573 | 516 | — | 1511 |
| Male | — | — | — | 1260 |
| Total | 959 | 991 | 821 | 2771 |

Once the marginal frequencies are fixed in a contingency table, a block of only $(r - 1) \times (c - 1)$ cell counts is free to vary, since these cell counts determine the remaining ones. The degrees of freedom value equals the number of cells in this block, so $df = (r - 1)(c - 1)$. We'll see another way to interpret $df$ at the end of Section 8.3.

### Chi-Squared Tests and Treatment of Categories

In the chi-squared test, the value of the $\chi^2$ test statistic does not depend on which is the response variable and which is the explanatory variable (if either). The steps of the test and the results are identical either way. When a response variable is identified and the population conditional distributions are identical, they are said to be *homogeneous*. The chi-squared test of independence is then often referred to as a *test of homogeneity*. For example, party ID is a response variable and gender is explanatory, so we can regard the chi-squared test applied to these data as a test of homogeneity of the conditional distributions of party ID.

The chi-squared test treats the classifications as nominal. That is, $\chi^2$ takes the same value if the rows or columns are reordered in any way. If either classification is ordinal or grouped interval, the chi-squared test does not use that information. In that case, it is usually better to apply stronger statistical methods designed for the higher level of measurement. Section 8.6 presents a test of independence for ordinal variables.

## 8.3    RESIDUALS: DETECTING THE PATTERN OF ASSOCIATION

The chi-squared test of independence, like other significance tests, provides limited information. If the $P$-value has moderate size (e.g., $P > 0.10$), it is plausible that the variables are independent. If the $P$-value is very small, strong evidence exists that the variables are associated. The chi-squared test tells us nothing, however, about the nature or strength of the association. The test does not indicate whether all cells deviate greatly from independence or perhaps only one or two of the cells do so. The next two sections introduce methods to learn more about the association.

### Residual Analysis

A cell-by-cell comparison of observed and expected frequencies reveals the nature of the evidence about the association. The difference $(f_o - f_e)$ between an observed and expected cell frequency is called a *residual*.

The counts on party ID and gender are shown again below in Table 8.8. For the first cell, the residual equals $573 - 522.9 = 50.1$. The residual is positive when, as in this cell, the observed frequency $f_o$ exceeds the value $f_e$ that independence predicts. The residual is negative when the observed frequency is smaller than independence predicts.

How do we know whether a residual is large enough to indicate a departure from independence that is unlikely to be due to mere chance? A standardized form of the residual that behaves like a $z$-score provides this information.

---

**Standardized Residual**

The *standardized residual* for a cell equals

$$z = \frac{f_o - f_e}{se} = \frac{f_o - f_e}{\sqrt{f_e(1 - \text{row proportion})(1 - \text{column proportion})}}.$$

Here, $se$ denotes the standard error of $f_o - f_e$, presuming $H_0$ is true. The standardized residual is the number of standard errors that $(f_o - f_e)$ falls from the value of 0 that we expect when $H_0$ is true.

---

The $se$ uses the marginal proportions for the row and the column in which the cell falls. When $H_0$: independence is true, the standardized residuals have a large-sample standard normal distribution. They fluctuate around a mean of 0, with a standard deviation of about 1.

We use the standardized residuals in an informal manner to describe the pattern of the association among the cells. A large standardized residual provides evidence against independence in that cell. When $H_0$ is true, there is only about a 5% chance that any particular standardized residual exceeds 2 in absolute value. When we inspect many cells in a table, some standardized residuals could be large just by random variation. Values below $-3$ or above $+3$, however, are very convincing evidence of a true effect in that cell.

### EXAMPLE 8.4    Standardized Residuals for Gender and Political ID

Table 8.8 displays the standardized residuals for testing independence between gender and party affiliation. For the first cell, for instance, $f_o = 573$ and $f_e = 522.9$. The first row and first column marginal proportions equal $1511/2771 = 0.545$ and $959/2771 = 0.346$. Substituting into the formula, the standardized residual

$$z = \frac{f_o - f_e}{\sqrt{f_e(1 - \text{row prop.})(1 - \text{column prop.})}}$$

$$= \frac{573 - 522.9}{\sqrt{[522.9(1 - 0.545)(1 - 0.346)]}} = 4.0.$$

Since the standardized residual exceeds 3.0, this cell has more observations than we'd expect if the variables were truly independent.

Table 8.8 exhibits very large positive residuals for female Democrats and male Republicans. This means there were more female Democrats and male Republicans than the hypothesis of independence predicts. The table exhibits relatively large negative residuals for female Republicans and male Democrats. There were fewer

**TABLE 8.8:** Standardized Residuals (in Parentheses) for Testing Independence between Party ID and Gender

| | Party Identification | | |
|---|---|---|---|
| Gender | Democrat | Independent | Republican |
| Female | 573 (4.0) | 516 (−1.9) | 422 (−2.1) |
| Male | 386 (−4.0) | 475 (1.9) | 399 (2.1) |

female Republicans and male Democrats than we'd expect if party affiliation were independent of gender.

For each party ID, Table 8.8 contains only one nonredundant standardized residual. The one for females is the negative of the one for males. The observed counts and the expected frequencies have the same row and column totals. Thus, in a given column, if $f_o > f_e$ in one cell, the reverse must happen in the other cell. The differences $f_o − f_e$ have the same magnitude but different sign in the two cells, implying the same pattern for their standardized residuals. ■

Along with the $\chi^2$ statistic, most statistical software can provide standardized residuals. See the text appendix for details.

## Chi-Squared and Difference of Proportions for 2 × 2 Tables

As Section 7.2 showed, 2 × 2 contingency tables often compare two groups on a binary response variable. The outcomes could be, for example, (yes, no) on an opinion question. For convenience, we label the two possible outcomes for that binary variable by the generic labels *success* and *failure*.

Let $\pi_1$ represent the proportion of successes in population 1, and let $\pi_2$ represent the proportion of successes in population 2. Then $(1 − \pi_1)$ and $(1 − \pi_2)$ are the proportions of failures. Table 8.9 displays the notation. The rows are the groups to be compared and the columns are the response categories.

**TABLE 8.9:** 2 × 2 Table for Comparing Two Groups on a Binary Response Variable

| | Proportion Making Each Response | | |
|---|---|---|---|
| Group | Success | Failure | Total |
| 1 | $\pi_1$ | $1 − \pi_1$ | 1.0 |
| 2 | $\pi_2$ | $1 − \pi_2$ | 1.0 |

If the response variable is statistically independent of the populations considered, then $\pi_1 = \pi_2$. The null hypothesis of independence corresponds to the *homogeneity* hypothesis, $H_0: \pi_1 = \pi_2$. In fact, the chi-squared test of independence is equivalent to a test for equality of two population proportions. Section 7.2 presented a $z$ test statistic for this, based on dividing the difference of sample proportions by its standard error,

$$z = \frac{\hat{\pi}_2 − \hat{\pi}_1}{se}.$$

The chi-squared statistic relates to this $z$ statistic by $\chi^2 = z^2$.

The chi-squared statistic for $2 \times 2$ tables has $df = 1$. Its $P$-value from the chi-squared distribution is the same as the $P$-value for the two-sided test with the $z$ test statistic. This is because of a direct connection between the standard normal distribution and the chi-squared distribution with $df = 1$: Squaring $z$-scores with certain two-tail probabilities yields chi-squared scores with $df = 1$ having the same right-tail probabilities. For instance, $z = 1.96$ is the $z$-score with a two-tail probability of 0.05. The square of this, $(1.96)^2 = 3.84$, is the chi-squared score for $df = 1$ with a $P$-value of 0.05. (You can check this in Table C.)

### EXAMPLE 8.5 Women's and Men's Roles

Table 8.10 summarizes responses from General Social Surveys in 1977 and in 2006 to the statement (FEFAM), "It is much better for everyone involved if the man is the achiever outside the home and the woman takes care of the home and family." You can check that the sample proportions agreeing with the statement were $\hat{\pi}_1 = 0.658$ in 1977, $\hat{\pi}_2 = 0.358$ in 2006, the $se$ for the test comparing them equals 0.0171, and the $z$ test statistic for $H_0$: $\pi_1 = \pi_2$ is $z = (0.658 - 0.358)/0.0171 = 17.54$. You can also check that the chi-squared statistic for this table is $\chi^2 = 307.6$. This equals the square of the $z$ test statistic. Both statistics show extremely strong evidence against the null hypothesis of equal population proportions. ∎

**TABLE 8.10:** GSS Responses to the Statement, "It is much better for everyone involved if the man is the achiever outside the home and the woman takes care of the home and family," with Standardized Residuals in Parentheses

| Year | Agree | Disagree | Total |
|------|-------|----------|-------|
| 1977 | 989 (17.5) | 514 ($-17.5$) | 1503 |
| 2006 | 704 ($-17.5$) | 1264 (17.5) | 1968 |

### Standardized Residuals for $2 \times 2$ Tables

Let's follow up the test for Table 8.10 with a residual analysis. Table 8.10 also shows the standardized residuals. Those in the first column suggest that more subjects agreed with the statement in 1977 and fewer agreed in 2006 than we'd expect if opinion were independent of the year of the survey. Notice that *every* standardized residual equals either $+17.5$ or $-17.5$. The absolute value of the standardized residual is 17.5 in every cell.

For chi-squared tests with $2 \times 2$ tables, $df = 1$. This means that only one piece of information exists about whether an association exists. Once we find the standardized residual for one cell, other standardized residuals in the table have the same absolute value. In fact, in $2 \times 2$ tables, each standardized residual equals the $z$ test statistic (or its negative) for comparing the two proportions. The square of each standardized residual equals the $\chi^2$ test statistic.

### Chi-Squared Needed for Larger Tables Than $2 \times 2$

For a $2 \times 2$ table, why should we ever do a $z$ test if we can get the same result with chi-squared? An advantage of the $z$ test is that it also applies with one-sided alternative hypotheses, such as $H_a$: $\pi_1 > \pi_2$. The direction of the effect is lost in squaring $z$ and using $\chi^2$.

Why do we need the $\chi^2$ statistic? The reason is that a $z$ statistic can only compare a single estimate to a single $H_0$ value. Examples are a $z$ statistic for comparing a sample proportion to a $H_0$ proportion such as 0.5, or a difference of sample proportions to a $H_0$ value of 0 for $\pi_2 - \pi_1$. When a table is larger than $2 \times 2$ and thus $df > 1$, we need more than one difference parameter to describe the association. For instance, suppose Table 8.10 had three rows, for three years of data. Then $H_0$: independence corresponds to $\pi_1 = \pi_2 = \pi_3$, where $\pi_i$ is the population proportion agreeing with the statement in year $i$. The comparison parameters are $(\pi_1 - \pi_2), (\pi_1 - \pi_3)$, and $(\pi_2 - \pi_3)$. We could use a $z$ statistic for each comparison, but not a single $z$ statistic for the overall test of independence.

We can interpret the $df$ value in a chi-squared test as the number of parameters needed to determine all the comparisons for describing the contingency table. For instance, for a $3 \times 2$ table for comparing three years on a binary opinion response, $df = 2$. This means we need to know only two parameters for making comparisons to figure out the third. For instance, if we know $(\pi_1 - \pi_2)$ and $(\pi_1 - \pi_3)$, then

$$(\pi_2 - \pi_3) = (\pi_1 - \pi_3) - (\pi_1 - \pi_2).$$

## 8.4   MEASURING ASSOCIATION IN CONTINGENCY TABLES

The main questions normally addressed in analyzing a contingency table are as follows:

- *Is there an association?* The chi-squared test of independence addresses this question. The smaller the $P$-value, the stronger the evidence of association.
- *How do the data differ from what independence predicts?* The standardized residuals highlight the cells that are more likely or less likely than expected under independence.
- *How strong is the association?* To summarize this, we use a statistic such as a difference of proportions, forming a confidence interval to estimate the strength of association in the population.

Analyzing the *strength* of the association reveals whether the association is important or whether it is statistically significant but practically insignificant. This section presents two ways to measure strength of association for contingency tables.

### Measures of Association

| **Measure of Association** |
| --- |
| A *measure of association* is a statistic or a parameter that summarizes the strength of the dependence between two variables. |

Let's first consider what is meant by *strong* versus *weak* association. Table 8.11 shows two hypothetical contingency tables relating race to opinion about allowing civil unions for same-sex couples. Case A, which exhibits statistical independence, represents the weakest possible association. Both whites and blacks have 60% in favor and 40% opposed to civil unions. Opinion is not associated with race. By contrast, case B exhibits the strongest possible association. All whites favor allowing civil unions, whereas all blacks oppose it. In this table, opinion is completely dependent on race. For these subjects, if we know their race, we know their opinion.

A measure of association describes how similar a table is to the tables representing the strongest and weakest associations. It takes a range of values from one extreme

**TABLE 8.11**: Cross-Classification of Opinion about Same-Sex Civil Unions, by Race, Showing (A) No Association, (B) Maximum Association

| Case A | | Opinion | | | Case B | Opinion | | |
|--------|------|-------|--------|-------|--------|-------|--------|-------|
| | Race | Favor | Oppose | Total | | Favor | Oppose | Total |
| | White | 360 | 240 | 600 | | 600 | 0 | 600 |
| | Black | 240 | 160 | 400 | | 0 | 400 | 400 |
| | Total | 600 | 400 | 1000 | | 600 | 400 | 1000 |

to another as data range from the weakest to strongest association. It is useful for comparing associations, to determine which is stronger.

## Difference of Proportions

As Sections 7.2 and 8.3 discussed, many $2 \times 2$ tables compare two groups on a binary variable. In such cases, an easily interpretable measure of association is the difference between the proportions for a given response category. For example, we could measure the difference between the proportions of whites and blacks who favor allowing same-sex civil unions. For Table 8.11(A), this difference is

$$\frac{360}{600} - \frac{240}{400} = 0.60 - 0.60 = 0.0.$$

The population difference of proportions is 0 whenever the conditional distributions are identical, that is, when the variables are independent. The difference is 1 or $-1$ for the strongest possible association. For Table 8.11(B), for instance, the difference is

$$\frac{600}{600} - \frac{0}{400} = 1.0,$$

the maximum possible absolute value for the difference.

This measure falls between $-1$ and $+1$. In practice we don't expect data to take these extreme values, but *the stronger the association, the larger the absolute value of the difference of proportions*. The following contingency tables illustrate the increase in this measure as the degree of association increases:

| Cell Counts: | 25 25 / 25 25 | 30 20 / 20 30 | 35 15 / 15 35 | 40 10 / 10 40 | 45 5 / 5 45 | 50 0 / 0 50 |
|---|---|---|---|---|---|---|
| Difference of Proportions: | 0 | .2 | .4 | .6 | .8 | 1.0 |

For the second table, for instance, the proportion falling in the first column equals $30/(30 + 20) = 0.60$ in row 1 and $20/(20 + 30) = 0.40$ in row 2, for a difference of $0.60 - 0.40 = 0.20$.

## Chi-Squared Does Not Measure Association

A large value for $\chi^2$ in the test of independence suggests that the variables are associated. It does *not* imply, however, that the variables have a strong association. This statistic summarizes how close the observed frequencies are to the frequencies expected if the variables were independent. It merely indicates, however, how much

**TABLE 8.12**: Cross-Classifications of Opinion on Legalized Same-Sex Unions, by Race, Showing Weak but Identical Associations

| | A | | | B | | | C | | |
|---|---|---|---|---|---|---|---|---|---|
| | Yes | No | Total | Yes | No | Total | Yes | No | Total |
| White | 49 | 51 | 100 | 98 | 102 | 200 | 4,900 | 5,100 | 10,000 |
| Black | 51 | 49 | 100 | 102 | 98 | 200 | 5,100 | 4,900 | 10,000 |
| | 100 | 100 | 200 | 200 | 200 | 400 | 10,000 | 10,000 | 20,000 |

$$\chi^2 = 0.08 \qquad\qquad \chi^2 = 0.16 \qquad\qquad \chi^2 = 8.0$$
$$P\text{-value} = 0.78 \qquad P\text{-value} = 0.69 \qquad P\text{-value} = 0.005$$

evidence there is that the variables are dependent, not how strong that dependence is. For a given association, larger $\chi^2$ values occur for larger sample sizes. As with any significance test, large test statistic values can occur with weak effects, if the sample size is large.

For example, consider the hypothetical cases in Table 8.12. The association in each table is very weak—the conditional distribution for whites on opinion (49% favor, 51% oppose) is nearly identical to the conditional distribution for blacks (51% favor, 49% oppose). All three tables show exactly the same degree of association, with the difference between the proportions of blacks and whites who favor legalizing same-sex civil unions being $0.51 - 0.49 = 0.02$ in each table.

For the sample of size 200 in case A, $\chi^2 = 0.08$, which has a $P$-value $= 0.78$. For the sample of size 400 in case B, $\chi^2 = 0.16$, for which $P = 0.69$. So, when the cell counts double, $\chi^2$ doubles. Similarly, for the sample size of 20,000 (100 times as large as $n = 200$) in case C, $\chi^2 = 8.0$ (100 times as large as $\chi^2 = 0.08$), and $P = 0.005$.

In summary, for a fixed percentage assignment to the cells of a contingency table, $\chi^2$ is directly proportional to the sample size—larger values occur with larger sample sizes. Like other test statistics, the larger the $\chi^2$ statistic, the smaller the $P$-value and the stronger the evidence against the null hypothesis. However, a small $P$-value can result from a weak association when the sample size is large, as case C shows.

### The Odds Ratio*

The difference of proportions is easily interpretable. Several other measures are also reported by statistical software. This subsection presents the most important one for categorical data analysis, the *odds ratio*.

For a binary response variable, recall that we use *success* to denote the outcome of interest and *failure* the other outcome. The **odds** of success are defined to be

$$\text{Odds} = \frac{\text{Probability of success}}{\text{Probability of failure}}.$$

If the probability of success $= 0.75$, then the probability of failure equals $1 - 0.75 = 0.25$, and the odds of success $= 0.75/0.25 = 3.0$. If $P(\text{success}) = 0.50$, then odds $= 0.50/0.50 = 1.0$. If $P(\text{success}) = 0.25$, then odds $= 0.25/0.75 = 1/3$. The odds are nonnegative, with value greater than 1.0 when a success is more likely than a failure. When odds $= 3.0$, a success is three times as likely as a failure; we expect about three successes for every failure. When odds $= 1/3$, a failure is three times as likely as a success; we expect about one success for every three failures.

The probability of an outcome relates to the odds of the outcome by

$$\text{Probability} = \frac{\text{Odds}}{\text{Odds} + 1}.$$

For instance, when odds = 3, probability = $3/(3 + 1) = 0.75$.

The ratio of odds from the two rows of a $2 \times 2$ table is called the **odds ratio**. For instance, if the odds = 4.5 in row 1 and the odds = 3.0 in row 2, then the odds ratio equals $4.5/3.0 = 1.5$. The odds of success in row 1 then equal 1.5 times the odds of success in row 2. We denote the odds ratio by the Greek letter $\theta$ (theta).

### EXAMPLE 8.6    Race of Murder Victims and Offenders

For murders in the United States in 2005 having a single victim and single offender, Table 8.13 cross classifies the race of the victim by the race of the offender. We treat race of victim as the response variable. For white offenders, the proportion of victims who were white equals $3150/3380 = 0.932$ and the proportion who were black equals $230/3380 = 0.068$. The odds of a white victim equaled $0.932/0.068 = 13.7$. This equals $(3150/3380)/(230/3380) = 3150/230$. So we can calculate the odds by the ratio of the counts in the two cells in row 1, without converting them to proportions.

**TABLE 8.13**: Cross-Classification of Race of Victim and Race of Offender

| Race of Offender | Race of Victim | | Total |
|---|---|---|---|
| | White | Black | |
| White | 3150 | 230 | 3380 |
| Black | 516 | 2984 | 3500 |

*Source*: www.fbi.gov

The value 13.7 means that for white offenders, there were 13.7 white victims for every 1 black victim. For black offenders, the odds of a white victim equaled $516/2984 = 0.173$. This means there were 0.173 white victims for every 1 black victim. Equivalently, since $2984/516 = 1/0.173 = 5.8$, black offenders had 5.8 black victims for every white victim.

For Table 8.13, the odds ratio equals

$$\theta = \frac{\text{Odds for white offenders}}{\text{Odds for black offenders}} = \frac{13.7}{0.173} = 79.2.$$

For white offenders, the odds of a white victim were about 79 times the odds of a white victim for black offenders.    ∎

In summary,

---
**Odds and Odds Ratio**

The estimated **odds** for a binary response equal the number of successes divided by the number of failures.

The **odds ratio** is a measure of association for $2 \times 2$ contingency tables that equals the odds in row 1 divided by the odds in row 2.

---

### Properties of the Odds Ratio*

In Table 8.13, suppose we treat race of offender, rather than race of victim, as the response variable. When victims were white, the odds the race of offender was white equaled $3150/516 = 6.10$. When victims were black, the odds the race of offender was white equaled $230/2984 = 0.077$. The odds ratio equals $6.10/0.077 = 79.2$. For each choice of the response variable, the odds ratio is 79.2. In fact,

- The odds ratio takes the same value regardless of the choice of response variable.

Since the odds ratio treats the variables symmetrically, the odds ratio is a natural measure when there is no obvious distinction between the variables, such as when both are response variables.

- The odds ratio $\theta$ equals the ratio of the products of cell counts from diagonally opposite cells.

For Table 8.13, for instance,

$$\theta = \frac{(3150 \times 2984)}{(230 \times 516)} = 79.2.$$

Because of this property, the odds ratio is also called the **_cross-product ratio_**.

- The odds ratio can equal any nonnegative number.
- When the success probabilities are identical in the two rows of a $2 \times 2$ table (i.e., $\pi_1 = \pi_2$), then $\theta = 1$.

When $\pi_1 = \pi_2$, the odds are also equal. The odds of success do not depend on the row level of the table, and the variables are then independent, with $\theta = 1$. The value $\theta = 1$ for independence serves as a baseline for comparison. Odds ratios on each side of 1 reflect certain types of associations.

- When $\theta > 1$, the odds of success are _higher_ in row 1 than in row 2.

For instance, when $\theta = 4$, the odds of success in row 1 are four times the odds of success in row 2.

- When $\theta < 1$, the odds of success are _lower_ in row 1 than in row 2.
- Values of $\theta$ farther from 1.0 in a given direction represent stronger associations.

An odds ratio of 4 is farther from independence than an odds ratio of 2, and an odds ratio of 0.25 is farther from independence than an odds ratio of 0.50.

- Two values for $\theta$ represent the same strength of association, but in opposite directions, when one value is the reciprocal of the other.

For instance, $\theta = 4.0$ and $\theta = 1/4.0 = 0.25$ represent the same strength of association. When $\theta = 0.25$, the odds of success in row 1 are 0.25 times the odds of success in row 2. Equivalently, the odds of success in row 2 are $1/0.25 = 4.0$ times the odds of success in row 1. When the order of the rows is reversed or the order of the columns is reversed, the new value of $\theta$ is the reciprocal of the original value. This ordering of rows or columns is usually arbitrary, so whether we get 4.0 or 0.25 for the odds ratio is simply a matter of how we label the rows and columns.

In interpreting the odds ratio, be careful not to misinterpret it as a ratio of probabilities. An odds ratio of 79.2 does _not_ mean that $\pi_1$ is 79.2 times $\pi_2$. Instead, $\theta = 79.2$ means that the _odds_ in row 1 equal 79.2 times the odds in row 2. The odds ratio is a ratio of two odds, not a ratio of two probabilities. That is,

$$\theta = \frac{\text{Odds in row 1}}{\text{Odds in row 2}} = \frac{\pi_1/(1 - \pi_1)}{\pi_2/(1 - \pi_2)}, \quad \text{not} \quad \frac{\pi_1}{\pi_2}.$$

The ratio $\pi_1/\pi_2$ is itself a useful measure. Section 7.1 introduced this measure, often called the **_relative risk_**.

The sampling distribution of the sample odds ratio $\hat{\theta}$ is highly skewed unless the sample size is extremely large, in which case the distribution is approximately normal. See Exercise 8.45 for the method of constructing confidence intervals for odds ratios.

## Odds Ratios for $r \times c$ Tables*

For contingency tables with more than two rows or more than two columns, the odds ratio describes patterns in any $2 \times 2$ subtable. We illustrate using GSS data on political party ID and race, shown in Table 8.14.

**TABLE 8.14**: GSS Data from 2004 on Party Identification and Race

| Gender | Party Identification | | |
|---|---|---|---|
| | Democrat | Independent | Republican |
| Black | 250 | 106 | 17 |
| White | 640 | 783 | 775 |

Consider first the $2 \times 2$ subtable formed from the first two columns. The sample odds ratio equals $(250 \times 783)/(106 \times 640) = 2.89$. The odds that a black's response was Democrat rather than Independent equal 2.89 times the odds for whites. Of those subjects who responded Democrat or Independent, blacks were more likely than whites to respond Democrat.

The sample odds ratio for the last two columns of this table equals $(106 \times 775)/(17 \times 783) = 6.17$. The odds that a black's response was Independent rather than Republican equal 6.2 times the odds for whites. Of those subjects who responded Independent or Republican, blacks were much more likely than whites to respond Independent.

Finally, for the $2 \times 2$ subtable formed from the first and last columns, the sample odds ratio equals $(250 \times 775)/(17 \times 640) = 17.81$. The odds that a black's response was Democrat rather than Republican equal 17.8 times the odds for whites. Of those subjects who responded Democrat or Republican, blacks were much more likely than whites to respond Democrat. This is a very strong effect, far from the independence odds ratio value of 1.0.

The odds ratio value of 17.8 for the first and last columns equals (2.89)(6.17), the product of the other two odds ratios. For $2 \times 3$ tables, $df = 2$, meaning that only two bits of information exist about the association. Two of the odds ratios determine the third.

## Summary Measures of Association for $r \times c$ Tables*

Instead of studying association in $2 \times 2$ subtables, it's possible to summarize association in the entire table by a single number. One way to do this summarizes how well we can predict the value on one variable based on knowing the value on the other variable. For example, party ID and race are highly associated if race is a good predictor of party ID; that is, if knowing their race, we can make much better predictions about people's party ID than if we did not know it.

For quantitative variables, the *correlation* is such a summary measure. We'll study a similar summary measure of this type for ordinal variables (called *gamma*) in the next section. These measures describe an overall trend in the data. For nominal variables, when $r$ or $c$ exceed 2, it is usually an oversimplification to describe the table with a single measure of association. In that case, too many possible patterns of association exist to describe an $r \times c$ table well by a single number. Nominal measures based on predictive power (called *tau* and *lambda*) and gamma for ordinal data were defined in 1954 by two prominent statistician–social scientists, Leo Goodman and William Kruskal. Most software for analyzing contingency tables prints their measures and several others. Some nominal measures, such as the contingency coefficient and Cramer's $V$, are difficult to interpret (other than larger values representing stronger association) and, in our view, not especially useful.

We do not present the summary nominal measures in this text. We believe you get a better feel for the association by making percentage comparisons of conditional distributions, by viewing the pattern of standardized residuals in the cells of the table, by constructing odds ratios in $2 \times 2$ subtables, and by building models such as those presented in Chapter 15. These methods become even more highly preferred to summary measures of association when the analysis is multivariate rather than bivariate.

## 8.5 ASSOCIATION BETWEEN ORDINAL VARIABLES*

We now turn our attention to other analyses of contingency tables that apply when the variables are ordinal. The categories of ordinal variables are ordered. Statistical analyses for ordinal data take this ordering into account. This section introduces a popular ordinal measure of association, and Section 8.6 presents related methods of inference.

### EXAMPLE 8.7    How Strongly Associated Are Income and Happiness?

Table 8.15 is a contingency table with ordinal variables. These data, from the 2004 GSS, refer to the relation between family income (FINRELA) and happiness (HAPPY). This table shows results for black Americans, and Exercise 8.13 analyzes data for white Americans.

Let's first get a feel for the data by studying the conditional distributions on happiness. Table 8.15 shows these in parentheses. For instance, the conditional distribution $(24\%, 54\%, 22\%)$ displays the percentages in the happiness categories for subjects with family income below average. Only 22% are very happy, whereas 36% of the subjects at the highest income level are very happy. Conversely, a lower percentage (9%) of the high-income group are not too happy compared to those in the lowest income group (24%). The odds ratio for the four corner cells is $(16 \times 8)/(15 \times 2) = 4.3$. It seems that subjects with higher incomes tended to have greater happiness.  ■

**TABLE 8.15**: Family Income and Happiness for a GSS Sample

|  | Happiness | | | |
| --- | --- | --- | --- | --- |
| Family Income | Not Too Happy | Pretty Happy | Very Happy | Total |
| Below average | 16 (24%) | 36 (54%) | 15 (22%) | 67 (100.0%) |
| Average | 11 (16%) | 36 (53%) | 21 (31%) | 68 (100.0%) |
| Above average | 2 (9%) | 12 (55%) | 8 (36%) | 22 (100.0%) |
| Total | 29 | 84 | 44 | 157 |

Ordinal data exhibit two primary types of association between variables $x$ and $y$—*positive* and *negative*. Positive association results when subjects at the high end of the scale on $x$ tend also to be high on $y$, and those who are low on $x$ tend to be low on $y$. For example, a positive association exists between income and happiness if those with low incomes tend to have lower happiness, and those with high incomes tend to have greater happiness. Negative association occurs when subjects classified high on $x$ tend to be classified low on $y$, and those classified low on $x$ tend to be high on $y$. For example, a negative association might exist between religious fundamentalism and tolerance toward homosexuality—the more fundamentalist in religious beliefs, the less tolerance toward homosexuality.

### Concordance and Discordance

Many ordinal measures of association are based on the information about the association provided by all the pairs of observations.

---

**Concordant Pair, Discordant Pair**

A pair of observations is **concordant** if the subject who is *higher* on one variable also is *higher* on the other variable.

A pair of observations is **discordant** if the subject who is *higher* on one variable is *lower* on the other.

---

In Table 8.15, we regard *Not too happy* as the low end and *Very happy* as the high end of the scale on $y$ = happiness, and *Below average* as low and *Above average* as high on $x$ = family income. By convention, we construct contingency tables for ordinal variables so that the low end of the row variable is the first row and the low end of the column variable is the first column. (There is no standard, however, and other books or software may use a different convention.)

Consider a pair of subjects, one of whom is classified (below average, not too happy), and the other of whom is classified (average, pretty happy). The first subject is one of the 16 classified in the upper-left-hand cell of Table 8.15, and the second subject is one of the 36 classified in the middle cell. This pair of subjects is concordant, since the second subject is higher than the first subject both in happiness and in income. The subject who is higher on one variable is also higher on the other. Now, each of the 16 subjects classified (below average, not too happy) can pair with each of the 36 subjects classified (average, pretty happy). So there are $16 \times 36 = 576$ concordant pairs of subjects from these two cells.

By contrast, each of 36 subjects in the cell (below average, pretty happy) forms a discordant pair when matched with each of the 11 subjects in the cell (average, not too happy). The 36 subjects have lower income than the other 11 subjects, yet they have greater happiness. All $36 \times 11 = 396$ of these pairs of subjects are discordant.

Concordant pairs of observations provide evidence of positive association since, for such a pair, the subject who is higher on one variable also is higher on the other. On the other hand, the more prevalent the discordant pairs, the more evidence there is of a negative association.

---

**Notation for Numbers of Concordant and Discordant Pairs**

Let $C$ denote the total number of concordant pairs of observations, and let $D$ denote the total number of discordant pairs of observations.

---

A general rule for finding the number of concordant pairs $C$ is this: Start at the corner of the table for the low level for each variable (the cell in row 1 and column 1 for Table 8.15). Multiply that cell count by the count in every cell that is higher on both variables (those cells below and to the right in Table 8.15). Similarly, for every other cell, multiply the cell count by the counts in cells that are higher on both variables. (For the cells in the row or in the column at the highest level of a variable, such as row *Above average* or column *Very happy* in Table 8.15, no observations are higher on both variables.) The number of concordant pairs is the sum of these products.

In Table 8.15, the 16 subjects in the first cell are concordant when matched with the $(36 + 21 + 12 + 8)$ subjects below and to the right who are higher on each variable. Similarly, the 36 subjects in the second cell in the first row are concordant when matched with the $(21 + 8)$ subjects who are higher on each variable, and so forth. Thus,

$$C = 16(36 + 21 + 12 + 8) + 36(21 + 8) + 11(12 + 8) + 36(8) = 2784.$$

Table 8.16 portrays this calculation of the total number of concordant pairs.

**TABLE 8.16**: Illustration of Calculation of Number of Concordant Pairs, C

| | NTH | PH | VH | NTH | PH | VH | NTH | PH | VH | NTH | PH | VH |
|---|---|---|---|---|---|---|---|---|---|---|---|---|
| Below | 16 | | | | 36 | | | | | | | |
| Average | | 36 | 21 | | | 21 | 11 | | | | 36 | |
| Above | | 12 | 8 | | | 8 | | 12 | 8 | | | 8 |

$$C = 16(36+21+12+8) \quad + 36(21+8) \quad + 11(12+8) \quad + 36(8) = 2784$$

To find the total number of discordant pairs $D$, start at the corner of the table that is the high level of one variable and the low level of the other. For example, the 15 subjects in the cell (below average, very satisfied) form discordant pairs when paired with the $(11 + 36 + 2 + 12)$ subjects below and to the left in the table who are higher on income but lower on happiness. Multiply the count in each cell by the counts in all cells that are higher on income but lower in job satisfaction. The total number of discordant pairs is

$$D = 15(11 + 36 + 2 + 12) + 21(2 + 12) + 36(11 + 2) + 36(2) = 1749.$$

Table 8.17 portrays the calculation of the number of discordant pairs.

**TABLE 8.17**: Illustration of Calculation of Number of Discordant Pairs, D

| | NTH | PH | VH | NTH | PH | VH | NTH | PH | VH | NTH | PH | VH |
|---|---|---|---|---|---|---|---|---|---|---|---|---|
| Below | | | 15 | | | | | 36 | | | | |
| Average | 11 | 36 | | | | 21 | 11 | | | | 36 | |
| Above | 2 | 12 | | 2 | 12 | | 2 | | | 2 | | |

$$D = 15(11+36+2+12) \quad + 21(2+12) \quad + 36(11+2) \quad + 36(2) = 1749$$

In summary, Table 8.15 has $C = 2784$ and $D = 1749$. More pairs show evidence of a positive association (i.e., concordant pairs) than show evidence of a negative association (discordant pairs).

### Gamma

A positive difference for $C - D$ occurs when $C > D$. This indicates a positive association. A negative difference for $C - D$ reflects a negative association.

Larger sample sizes have larger numbers of pairs with, typically, larger absolute differences in $C - D$. Therefore, we standardize this difference to make it easier to interpret. To do this, we divide $C - D$ by the total number of pairs that are either concordant or discordant, $C + D$. This gives the measure of association called **gamma**. Its sample formula is

$$\hat{\gamma} = \frac{C - D}{C + D}.$$

Here are some properties of gamma:

- The value of gamma falls between $-1$ and $+1$.
- The sign of gamma indicates whether the association is positive or negative.
- The larger the absolute value of gamma, the stronger the association.

A table for which gamma equals 0.60 or $-0.60$ exhibits a stronger association than one for which gamma equals 0.30 or $-0.30$, for example. The value $+1$ represents the strongest positive association. This occurs when there are no discordant pairs ($D = 0$), so all the pairs reveal a positive association. Gamma equals $-1$ when $C = 0$, so all pairs reveal a negative association. Gamma equals 0 when $C = D$.

For Table 8.15, $C = 2784$ and $D = 1749$, so

$$\hat{\gamma} = \frac{2784 - 1749}{2784 + 1749} = 0.228.$$

This sample exhibits a positive association between family income and happiness. The higher the family income, the greater the happiness tends to be. However, the sample value is closer to 0 than to 1, so the association is relatively weak.

The calculation of gamma is rather messy. Most statistical software can find gamma for you.

### Gamma Is a Difference between Two Ordinal Proportions

Another interpretation for the magnitude of gamma follows from the expression

$$\hat{\gamma} = \frac{C - D}{C + D} = \frac{C}{C + D} - \frac{D}{C + D}.$$

Now $(C + D)$ is the total number of pairs that are concordant or discordant. The ratio $C/(C + D)$ is the proportion of those pairs that are concordant, $D/(C + D)$ is the proportion of the pairs that are discordant, and $\hat{\gamma}$ is the difference between the two proportions.

For example, suppose $\hat{\gamma} = 0.60$. Then, since 0.80 and 0.20 are the two proportions that sum to 1 and have a difference of $0.80 - 0.20 = 0.60$, 80% of the pairs are concordant and 20% are discordant. Similarly, $\hat{\gamma} = -0.333$ indicates that 1/3 of the pairs are concordant and 2/3 of the pairs are discordant, since $1/3 + 2/3 = 1$ and $1/3 - 2/3 = -0.333$.

For Table 8.15, out of the $2784 + 1749 = 4533$ pairs that are concordant or discordant, the proportion $2784/4533 = 0.614$ are concordant and the proportion $1749/4533 = 0.386$ are discordant; $\hat{\gamma} = 0.228$ is the difference between these proportions.

### Common Properties of Ordinal Measures

Gamma is one of several ordinal measures of association. Others are **Kendall's tau-b** and **tau-c**, **Spearman's rho-b**, and **rho-c**, and **Somers' d**. All these measures are similar in their basic purposes and characteristics. For lack of space, we do not define these other measures, but we will list some common properties. These properties also hold for the *correlation* for quantitative variables, which was introduced in Section 3.5 and will be used extensively in the next chapter.

- Ordinal measures of association take values between $-1$ and $+1$. The sign tells us whether the association is positive or negative.
- If the variables are statistically independent, then the population values of ordinal measures equal 0.
- The stronger the association, the larger the absolute value of the measure. Values of 1.0 and $-1.0$ represent the strongest associations.
- With the exception of Somers' $d$, the ordinal measures of association named above do not distinguish between response and explanatory variables. They take the same value when variable $y$ is the response variable as when it is the explanatory variable.

So far, we have discussed the use of ordinal measures only for description. The next section presents statistical inference, namely, confidence intervals and tests for ordinal data.

## 8.6 INFERENCE FOR ORDINAL ASSOCIATIONS*

The chi-squared test of whether two categorical variables are independent treats the variables as nominal. Other tests are usually more powerful when the variables are ordinal. This section presents such a test and shows how to construct confidence intervals for ordinal measures of association such as gamma. The inferences are best applied to a large random sample. As a rough guideline, each of $C$ and $D$ should exceed about 50.

### Confidence Intervals for Measures of Association

Confidence intervals help us gauge the strength of the association in the population. Let $\gamma$ denote the population value of gamma. For sample gamma, $\hat{\gamma}$, its sampling distribution is approximately normal about $\gamma$. Its standard error $se$ describes the variation in $\hat{\gamma}$ values around $\gamma$ among samples of the given size. The formula for $se$ is complicated but it is reported by most software. A confidence interval for $\gamma$ has the form

$$\hat{\gamma} \pm z(se).$$

### EXAMPLE 8.8    Association between Income and Happiness

For the data in Table 8.15 on family income and happiness, $\hat{\gamma} = 0.228$. We'll see in Table 8.18 that this has $se = 0.114$. A 95% confidence interval for $\gamma$ is

$$\hat{\gamma} \pm 1.96(se), \quad \text{or } 0.228 \pm 1.96(0.114), \quad \text{or } 0.228 \pm 0.223,$$

which equals $(0.005, 0.45)$. We can be 95% confident that $\gamma$ is no less than 0.005 and no greater than 0.45. It is plausible that essentially no association exists between income and happiness, but it is also plausible that a moderate positive association exists. We need a larger sample size to estimate this more precisely. ∎

### Test of Independence Using Gamma

Next we'll consider a test of independence that treats the variables as ordinal. As in the chi-squared test, the null hypothesis is that the variables are statistically independent. We express the test in terms of gamma, but a similar approach works with other ordinal measures of association. The alternative hypothesis can take the two-sided form $H_a$: $\gamma \neq 0$ or a one-sided form, $H_a$: $\gamma > 0$ or $H_a$: $\gamma < 0$, when we predict the direction of the association.

The test statistic has the $z$ statistic form. It takes the difference between $\hat{\gamma}$ and the value of 0 that gamma takes when $H_0$: independence is true and divides by the standard error,

$$z = \frac{\hat{\gamma} - 0}{se}.$$

This test statistic has approximately the standard normal distribution when $H_0$ is true. Some software also reports a $se$ and/or related $P$-value that holds only under $H_0$.

### EXAMPLE 8.9    Testing Independence between Income and Happiness

Does Table 8.15 relating family income and happiness suggest these variables are associated in the population? The chi-squared test of independence has $\chi^2 = 3.82$ with $df = 4$, for which the $P$-value equals 0.43. This test does not show any evidence of an association. The chi-squared test treats the variables as nominal, however, and ordinal-level methods are more powerful if there is a positive or negative trend.

Table 8.18 shows a printout for the analysis of Table 8.15. The $\hat{\gamma} = 0.228$ value has $se = 0.114$, labelled as *Asymp. std. error*, where *Asymp.* stands for "asympotic" or "large-sample." The test statistic equals

$$z = \frac{\hat{\gamma} - 0}{se} = \frac{0.228 - 0}{0.114} = 2.00.$$

From the standard normal table, the $P$-value for $H_a$: $\gamma \neq 0$ equals 0.046. (SPSS reports a $P$-value of 0.050, based on using a different standard error in the test statistic that only applies under $H_0$.)

TABLE 8.18: Part of a Computer Printout for Analyzing Table 8.17

|  | Value | DF | Asymp. Sig. |
|---|---|---|---|
| Pearson Chi-Square | 3.816 | 4 | 0.431 |

|  | Value | Asymp. Std. Error | Approx. sig. |
|---|---|---|---|
| Gamma | 0.2283 | 0.1139 | 0.050 |

This test shows some evidence of an association. Since the sample value of gamma was positive, it seems that a positive association exists between income and happiness. The test for $H_a$: $\gamma > 0$ has $P = 0.023$ (or 0.025 using the null $se$). ∎

### Ordinal Tests versus Pearson Chi-Squared Test

The $z$ test result for these data providing evidence of an association may seem surprising. The chi-squared statistic of $\chi^2 = 3.82$ with $df = 4$ provided no evidence ($P = 0.43$).

A test of independence based on an ordinal measure is usually preferred to the chi-squared test when both variables are ordinal. The $\chi^2$ statistic ignores the ordering of the categories, taking the same value no matter how the levels are ordered. If a positive or negative trend exists, ordinal measures are usually more powerful for detecting it. Unfortunately, the situation is not clear cut. It is possible for the chi-squared test to be more powerful even if the data are ordinal.

To explain this, we first note that the null hypothesis of independence is not equivalent to a value of 0 for population gamma. Although independence implies $\gamma = 0$, the converse is not true. Namely, $\gamma$ may equal 0 even though the variables are not statistically independent. For example, Table 8.19 shows a relationship between two variables that does not have a single trend. Over the first two columns there is a positive relationship, since $y$ increases when $x$ increases. Over the last two columns there is a negative relationship, as $y$ decreases when $x$ increases. For the entire table, $C = 25(25 + 25) = 1250 = D$, so $\gamma = 0$. The proportion of concordant pairs equals the proportion of discordant pairs. However, there is not independence, because the conditional distribution on $y$ for the low level of $x$ is completely different from the conditional distribution on $y$ for the high level of $x$.

**TABLE 8.19:** A Relationship for Which Ordinal Measures of Association Equal 0. The variables are dependent even though gamma equals 0.

|  |  | Level of y | | | |
| --- | --- | --- | --- | --- | --- |
|  |  | Very low | Low | High | Very high |
| Level of x | Low | 25 | 0 | 0 | 25 |
|  | High | 0 | 25 | 25 | 0 |

Thus, an ordinal measure of association may equal 0 when the variables are statistically dependent but the dependence does not have an overall positive or overall negative trend. The chi-squared test can perform better than the ordinal test when the relationship does not have a single trend. In practice, most relationships with ordinal variables have primarily one trend, if any. So the ordinal test is usually more powerful than the chi-squared test.

### Similar Inference Methods for Other Ordinal Measures

The inference methods for gamma apply also to other ordinal measures of association. For a confidence interval, take the sample value and add and subtract a $z$-score times the standard error, which is available using software. Test results are usually similar for any ordinal measure based on the difference between the numbers of concordant pairs and discordant pairs, such as gamma or Kendall's tau-$b$.

An alternative approach to detect trends assigns scores to the categories for each variable and uses the correlation and a $z$ test based on it. (Section 9.5 presents a closely related test.) Some software reports this as a test of *linear-by-linear association*.

Whenever possible, it is better to choose the categories for ordinal variables finely rather than crudely. For instance, it is better to use four or five categories than only two categories. Standard errors of measures tend to be smaller with more categories, for a given sample size. Thus, the finer the categorizations, the shorter the confidence interval for a population measure of association tends to be. In addition, finer measurement makes it more valid to treat the data as quantitative and use the more powerful methods presented in the following chapter for quantitative variables.

### Mixed Ordinal–Nominal Contingency Tables

For a cross-classification of an ordinal variable with a nominal variable that has only two categories, ordinal measures of association are still valid. In that case, the sign of the measure indicates which level of the nominal variable is associated with higher responses on the ordinal variable. For instance, suppose gamma = $-0.12$ for the association in a $2 \times 3$ table relating gender (female, male) to happiness (not too happy, pretty happy, very happy). Since the sign is negative, the "higher" level of gender (i.e., male) tends to occur with lower happiness. The association is weak, however.

When the nominal variable has more than two categories, it is inappropriate to use an ordinal measure such as gamma. There are specialized methods for mixed nominal–ordinal tables, but it is usually simplest to treat the ordinal variable as quantitative by assigning scores to its levels. The methods of Chapter 12, which generalize comparisons of two means to several groups, are then appropriate. Section 15.4 presents a modeling approach that does not require assigning scores to ordinal response variables.

## 8.7    CHAPTER SUMMARY

This chapter introduced analyses of association for categorical variables:

- By *describing the counts* in **contingency tables** using percentage distributions, called **conditional distributions**, across the categories of the response variable. If the population conditional distributions are identical, the two variables are **statistically independent**—the probability of any particular response is the same for each level of the explanatory variable.

- By using **chi-squared** to *test* $H_0$**:** *independence* between the variables. The $\chi^2$ test statistic compares each observed frequency $f_o$ to the expected frequency $f_e$ satisfying $H_0$, using

$$\chi^2 = \sum \frac{(f_o - f_e)^2}{f_e}.$$

  The test statistic has a large-sample chi-squared distribution. The **degrees of freedom** depend on the number of rows $r$ and the number of columns $c$, through $df = (r - 1)(c - 1)$. The *P*-value is the right-tail probability above the observed value of $\chi^2$.

- By *describing the pattern of association* using **standardized residuals** for the cells in the table. A standardized residual reports the number of standard errors that $(f_o - f_e)$ falls from 0. A value larger than about 2 or 3 in absolute value indicates that that cell provides evidence of association in a particular direction.

- By *describing the strength of association*. For $2 \times 2$ tables the **difference of proportions** is useful, as is the **odds ratio**, the ratio of odds from the two rows. Each odds measures the proportion of successes divided by the proportion of failures. When there is independence, the difference of proportions equals 0 and the odds ratio equals 1. The stronger the association, the farther the measures fall from these baseline values.

This chapter also presented methods for analyzing association between two ordinal variables.

- Many ***ordinal measures of association*** use the numbers of ***concordant pairs*** (the subject who is higher on *x* also is higher on *y*) and ***discordant pairs*** (the subject who is higher on *x* is lower on *y*).
- Of the pairs that are concordant or discordant, ***gamma*** equals the difference between the proportions of the two types. Gamma falls between $-1$ and $+1$, with larger absolute values indicating stronger association. When the variables are independent, gamma equals 0.

The chi-squared test treats the data as nominal. When the variables are ordinal, methods that use the ordinality (such as a *z* test based on sample gamma) are more powerful for detecting a positive or negative association trend.

The next chapter introduces similar methods for describing and making inferences about the association between two quantitative variables.

## PROBLEMS

### Practicing the Basics

**8.1.** GSS surveys routinely show that in the United States, about 40% of males and 40% of females believe that a women should be able to get an abortion if she wants it for any reason (variable ABANY).

   **(a)** Construct a contingency table showing the conditional distribution on whether unrestricted abortion should be legal (yes, no) by gender.

   **(b)** Based on these results, does statistical independence seem plausible between gender and opinion about unrestricted abortion? Explain.

**8.2.** Whether a woman becomes pregnant in the next year is a categorical variable with categories (yes, no), and whether she and her partner use contraceptives is another categorical variable with categories (yes, no). Would you expect these variables to be statistically independent, or associated? Explain.

**8.3.** Every year, a large-scale poll of college freshmen conducted by the Higher Education Research Institute at UCLA asks their opinions about a variety of issues. In 2002, 46% of men and 35% of women in the survey of 283,000 college freshmen indicated support for legalization of marijuana.

   **(a)** If results for the population of college freshmen were similar to these, would gender and opinion about legalizing marijuana be independent, or dependent?

   **(b)** Display hypothetical population percentages in a contingency table for which these variables would be independent.

**8.4.** Some political analysts claimed that during the presidency of George W. Bush, the popularity of the U.S. decreased dramatically around the world. In *America Against the World: How We*

*Are Different and Why We Are Disliked*,[1] the Pew Research Center summarized results of 91,000 interviews conducted in 51 nations. In Germany, for example, the study reported that those having favorable opinions of the U.S. changed between 2000 and 2006 from 78% to 37%. Show how to construct a contingency table relating opinion about the U.S. by year of survey, for Germany. For this table, identify the response variable, the explanatory variable, and the conditional distributions.

**8.5.** Based on current estimates of how well mammograms detect breast cancer, Table 8.20 shows what to expect for 100,000 adult women over the age of 40 in terms of whether a woman has breast cancer and whether a mammogram gives a positive result (i.e., indicates that the woman has breast cancer).

   **(a)** Construct the conditional distributions for the mammogram test result, given the true disease status. Does the mammogram appear to be a good diagnostic tool?

   **(b)** Construct the conditional distribution of disease status, for those who have a positive test result. Use this to explain why even a good diagnostic test can have a high false positive rate when a disease is not common.

**TABLE 8.20**

|  |  | Diagnostic Test | |
|---|---|---|---|
|  |  | Positive | Negative |
| Breast | Yes | 860 | 140 |
| Cancer | No | 11,800 | 87,120 |

**8.6.** Data posted at the FBI Web site (www.fbi.gov) indicated that of all blacks slain in 2005, 91% were slain by blacks, and of all whites slain in 2005, 83%

[1]Kohut, A. and Stokes, B. (2006). *America Against the World: How We Are Different and Why We Are Disliked*. Times Books.

were slain by whites. Let $y$ denote race of victim and $x$ denote race of murderer.

(a) Which conditional distributions do these statistics refer to, those of $y$ at given levels of $x$ or those of $x$ at given levels of $y$? Set up a contingency table showing these distributions.

(b) Are $x$ and $y$ independent or dependent? Explain.

**8.7.** How large a $\chi^2$ value provides a $P$-value of 0.05 for testing independence for the following table dimensions?

a) $2 \times 2$   b) $3 \times 3$   c) $2 \times 5$   d) $5 \times 5$
e) $3 \times 9$

**8.8.** Show that the contingency table in Table 8.21 has four degrees of freedom by showing how the four cell counts given determine the others.

**TABLE 8.21**

| 10 | 20 |  | 60 |
|----|----|----|----|
| 30 | 40 |  | 100 |
|  |  |  | 40 |
| 50 | 80 | 70 |  |

**8.9.** In 2000 the GSS asked whether a subject is willing to accept cuts in the standard of living to help the environment (GRNSOL), with categories (very willing, fairly willing, neither willing nor unwilling, not very willing, not at all willing). When this was cross-tabulated with sex, $\chi^2 = 8.0$.

(a) What are the hypotheses for the test to which refers?

(b) Report the $df$ value on which $\chi^2$ is based.

(c) What conclusion would you make, using a significance level of (i) 0.05, (ii) 0.10? State your conclusion in the context of this study.

**8.10.** Table 8.22 refers to a survey of senior high school students in Dayton, Ohio.

(a) Construct conditional distributions that treat cigarette smoking as the response variable. Interpret.

(b) Test whether cigarette use and alcohol use are statistically independent. Report the $P$-value and interpret.

**TABLE 8.22**

|  |  | Cigarette Use | |
|----|----|----|----|
|  |  | Yes | No |
| Alcohol | Yes | 1449 | 500 |
| Use | No | 46 | 281 |

*Source*: Thanks to Professor Harry Khamis for providing these data.

**8.11.** Are people happier who believe in life after death? Go to the GSS Web site sda.berkeley.edu/GSS and download the contingency table for the 2006 survey relating happiness and whether you believe in life after death (variables HAPPY and POSTLIFE, with YEAR(2006) in the 'selection filter').

(a) State a research question that could be addressed with the output.

(b) Report the conditional distributions, using happiness as the response variable, and interpret.

(c) Report the $\chi^2$ value and its $P$-value. (You can get this by checking 'Statistics'.) Interpret.

(d) Interpret the standardized residuals. (You can get them by checking 'z-statistic'.)

**8.12.** In the GSS, subjects who were married were asked the happiness of their marriage, the variable coded as HAPMAR.

(a) Go to sda.berkeley.edu/GSS/ and construct a contingency table for 2006 relating HAPMAR to family income measured as (above average, average, below average), by entering FINRELA(r: 1-2; 3; 4-5) as the row variable and YEAR(2006) in the selection filter. Use a table or graph with conditional distributions to describe the association.

(b) By checking 'Statistics,' you request the chi-squared statistic. Report it and its $df$ and $P$-value, and interpret.

**8.13.** The sample in Table 8.15 is 157 black Americans. Table 8.23 shows cell counts and standardized residuals for income and happiness for white subjects in the 2004 GSS.

(a) Explain how to interpret the Pearson chi-squared statistic and its associated $P$-value.

(b) Explain how to interpret the standardized residuals in the four corner cells.

**TABLE 8.23**

```
Rows: income   Columns: happiness

              not    pretty   very    All

below          62      187     45     294
             5.34     3.43   -7.40

average        47      270    181     498
            -2.73    -0.57   2.53

above          22      127    118     267
            -2.37    -2.88   4.73

All           131      584    131    1059

Cell Contents:       Count
                     Standardized residual

Pearson Chi-Square = 72.15, DF = 4, P-Value = 0.000
```

**8.14.** Table 8.24 shows SPSS analyses with the 2004 GSS, for variables party ID and race.
  **(a)** Report the expected frequency for the first cell, and show how SPSS obtained it.
  **(b)** Test the hypothesis of independence between party ID and race. Report the test statistic and *P*-value and interpret.
  **(c)** Use the standardized residuals (labelled ADJ RES here for "adjusted residuals" to describe the pattern of association.

**TABLE 8.24**

| | | Count<br>Exp Val<br>Adj Res | PARTY_ID | | Row |
|---|---|---|---|---|---|
| | | democr | indep | repub | Total |
| RACE | black | 250 | 106 | 17 | 373 |
| | | 129.1 | 129.0 | 114.9 | |
| | | 14.2 | -2.7 | -11.9 | |
| | white | 640 | 783 | 1775 | 2198 |
| | | 760.9 | 760.0 | 677.1 | |
| | | -14.2 | 2.7 | 11.9 | |
| | Column Total | 890 | 889 | 792 | 2571 |

| Chi-Square | Value | DF | Significance |
|---|---|---|---|
| Pearson | 234.73 | 2 | 0.0000 |

**8.15.** For a 2 × 4 cross classification of gender and religiosity (very, moderately, slightly, not at all) for recent GSS data, the standardized residual was 3.2 for females who are very religious, −3.2 for males who are very religious, −3.5 for females who are not at all religious, and 3.5 for males who are not at all religious. All other standardized residuals fell between −1.1 and 1.1. Interpret.

**8.16.** Table 8.25 is from the 2006 General Social Survey, cross-classifying happiness (HAPPY) and marital status (MARITAL).

**TABLE 8.25**

| Marital Status | Very Happy | Pretty Happy | Not Too Happy |
|---|---|---|---|
| Married | 600 (13.1) | 720 (−5.4) | 93 (−10.0) |
| Widowed | 63 (−2.2) | 142 (−0.2) | 51 (3.4) |
| Divorced | 93 (−6.1) | 304 (3.2) | 88 (3.6) |
| Separated | 19 (−2.7) | 51 (−1.2) | 31 (5.3) |
| Never Married | 144 (−7.4) | 459 (4.2) | 127 (4.0) |

  **(a)** Software reports that $\chi^2 = 236.4$. Interpret.
  **(b)** Table 8.25 also shows, in parentheses, the standardized residuals. Summarize the association by indicating which marital statuses have

strong evidence of (i) more, (ii) fewer people in the population in the *very happy* category than if the variables were independent.
  **(c)** Compare the married and divorced groups by the difference in proportions in the *very happy* category.

**8.17.** In a *USA Today*/Gallup poll in July 2006, 82% of Republicans approved of President George W. Bush's performance, whereas 9% of Democrats approved. Would you characterize the association between political party affiliation and opinion about Bush's performance as weak, or strong? Explain why.

**8.18.** In a recent GSS, the death penalty for subjects convicted of murder was favored by 74% of whites and 43% of blacks. It was favored by 75% of males and 63% of females. In this sample, which variable was more strongly associated with death penalty opinion—race or gender? Explain why.

**8.19.** Refer to Exercise 8.10, on alcohol use and cigarette use.
  **(a)** Describe the strength of association using the difference between users and nonusers of alcohol in the proportions who have used cigarettes. Interpret.
  **(b)** Describe the strength of association using the difference between users and nonusers of cigarettes in the proportions who have used alcohol. Interpret.
  **(c)** Describe the strength of association using the odds ratio. Interpret. Does the odds ratio value depend on your choice of response variable?

**8.20.** Table 8.26 cross-classifies 68,694 passengers in autos and light trucks involved in accidents in the state of Maine by whether they were wearing a seat belt and by whether they were injured or killed. Describe the association using
  **(a)** The difference between two proportions, treating whether injured or killed as the response variable.
  **(b)** The odds ratio.

**TABLE 8.26**

| | | Injury | |
|---|---|---|---|
| | | Yes | No |
| Seat Belt | Yes | 2409 | 35,383 |
| | No | 3865 | 27,037 |

*Source*: Thanks to Dr. Cristanna Cook, Medical Care Development, Augusta, Maine, for supplying these data.

**8.21.** According to the Substance Abuse and Mental Health Archive, a 2003 national household survey on drug abuse indicated that for Americans aged

26–34, 51% had used marijuana at least once in their lifetime, and 18% had used cocaine at least once.

(a) Find the odds of having used (i) marijuana, (ii) cocaine. Interpret.

(b) Find the odds ratio comparing marijuana use to cocaine use Interpret.

**8.22.** According to the U.S. Department of Justice, in 2004 the incarceration rate in the nation's prisons was 1 per 109 male residents, 1 per 1563 female residents, 1694 per 100,000 black residents, and 252 per 100,000 white residents (*Source*: www.ojp.usdoj.gov/bjs).

(a) Find the odds ratio between whether incarcerated and (i) gender, (ii) race. Interpret.

(b) According to the odds ratio, which has the stronger association with whether incarcerated, gender or race? Explain.

**8.23.** Refer to Table 8.1 (page 222) on political party ID and gender. Find and interpret the odds ratio for each 2 × 2 subtable. Explain why this analysis suggests that the last two columns show essentially no association.

**8.24.** For college freshmen in 2004, the percent who agreed that homosexual relationships should be legally prohibited was 38.0% of males and 23.4% of females (www.gseis.ucla.edu/heri/american_freshman.html).

(a) The odds ratio is 2.01. Explain what is wrong with the interpretation, "The probability of a yes response for males is 2.01 times the probability of a yes response for females." Give the correct interpretation.

(b) The odds of a yes response equaled 0.613 for males. Estimate the probability of a yes response for males.

(c) Based on the odds of 0.613 for males and the odds ratio of 2.01, show how to estimate the probability of a yes response for females.

**8.25.** Table 8.27 cross-classifies happiness with family income for the subsample of the 2004 GSS that identified themselves as Jewish.

(a) Find the number of (i) concordant pairs, (ii) discordant pairs.

(b) Find gamma and interpret.

**TABLE 8.27**

| | | HAPPY | | |
|---|---|---|---|---|
| | | Not_too | Pretty | Very |
| INCOME | Below | 1 | 2 | 1 |
| | Average | 0 | 5 | 2 |
| | Above | 2 | 4 | 0 |

(c) Show how to express gamma as a difference between two proportions.

**8.26.** For the 2006 GSS, $\hat{\gamma} = 0.22$ for the relationship between job satisfaction (SATJOB; categories very dissatisfied, little dissatisfied, moderately satisfied, very satisfied) and family income (FINRELA; below average, average, above average).

(a) Would you consider this a very strong or relatively weak association? Explain.

(b) Of the pairs that are concordant or discordant, what proportion are concordant? Discordant?

(c) Is this a stronger or a weaker association than the one between job satisfaction and happiness (variable HAPPY), which has $\hat{\gamma} = 0.40$? Explain.

**8.27.** A study on educational aspirations of high school students[2] measured aspirations using the scale (some high school, high school graduate, some college, college graduate) and family income with three ordered categories. Software provides the results shown in Table 8.28.

(a) Use gamma to summarize the association.

(b) Test independence of educational aspirations and family income using the chi-squared test. Interpret.

(c) Find the 95% confidence interval for gamma. Interpret.

(d) Conduct an alternative test of independence that takes category ordering into account. Why are results so different from the chi-squared test?

**TABLE 8.28**

| Statistic | DF | Value | Prob |
|---|---|---|---|
| Chi-Square | 6 | 8.871 | 0.181 |

| Statistic | | Value | ASE |
|---|---|---|---|
| Gamma | | 0.163 | 0.080 |

**8.28.** Refer to Exercise 8.13, on happiness and income. The analysis there does not take into account the ordinality of the variables. Using software:

(a) Summarize the strength of association by finding and interpreting gamma.

(b) Construct and interpret a 95% confidence interval for the population value of gamma.

## Concepts and Applications

**8.29.** Refer to the "Student survey" data file (Exercise 1.11 on page 8). Using software, create and

---

[2]S. Crysdale, *Intern. J. Compar. Sociol.*, vol. 16, 1975, pp. 19–36.

analyze descriptively and inferentially the contingency table relating opinion about abortion and **(a)** political affiliation, **(b)** religiosity.

**8.30.** Refer to the data file you created in Exercise 1.12. For variables chosen by your instructor, pose a research question and conduct descriptive and inferential statistical analyses. Interpret and summarize your findings in a short report.

**8.31.** In 2002 the GSS asked how housework was shared between the respondent and his or her spouse (HHWKFAIR). Possible responses were 1 = I do much more than my fair share, 2 = I do a bit more than my fair share, 3 = I do roughly my fair share, 4 = I do a bit less than my fair share, 5 = I do much less than my fair share. Table 8.29 shows results according to the respondent's sex. State a research question that could be addressed with this output, and prepare a one-page report summarizing what you learn. (The "Adj. Residual" is the standardized residual.)

**8.32.** Pose a research question about attitude regarding homosexual relations and political ideology. Using the most recent GSS data on HOMOSEX and POLVIEWS, conduct a descriptive and inferential analysis to address this question. Prepare a short report summarizing your analysis.

**8.33.** Several sociologists have reported that racial prejudice varies according to religious group. Examine this using Table 8.30, for white respondents to the 2002 GSS. The variables are Fundamentalism/Liberalism of Respondent's Religion (FUND) and response to the question (RACMAR), "Do you think there should be laws against marriages between blacks and whites?" Analyze these data. Prepare a report, describing your analyses and providing interpretations of the data.

**TABLE 8.30**

| Religious Preference | Laws against Marriage | | |
|---|---|---|---|
| | Favor | Oppose | Total |
| Fundamentalist | 39 | 142 | 181 |
| Moderate | 21 | 248 | 269 |
| Liberal | 17 | 236 | 253 |
| None | 16 | 74 | 90 |
| Total | 93 | 700 | 793 |

**8.34.** For 2006 GSS data, of those identifying as Democrats, 616 classified themselves as liberal and 262 as conservative. Of those identifying as Republicans, 94 called themselves liberal and 721 called themselves conservative. Using methods presented in this chapter, describe the strength of association.

**8.35.** A study[3] of American armed forces who had served in Iraq or Afghanistan found that the event of being attacked or ambushed was reported by 1139 of 1961 Army members who had served in Afghanistan, 789 of 883 Army members who had served in Iraq, and 764 of 805 Marines who had served in Iraq. Summarize these data using conditional distributions and measures of association.

**8.36.** Shortly before a gubernatorial election, a poll asks a random sample of 50 potential voters the following questions:

Do you consider yourself to be a Democrat (D), a Republican (R), or Independent (I)?

If you were to vote today, would you vote for the Democratic candidate (D), the

**TABLE 8.29**

| | | | HHWKFAIR | | | | | Total |
|---|---|---|---|---|---|---|---|---|
| | | | 1 | 2 | 3 | 4 | 5 | |
| sex | female | Count | 121 | 108 | 135 | 19 | 6 | 389 |
| | | % within sex | 31.1% | 27.8% | 34.7% | 4.9% | 1.5% | 100.0% |
| | | Adj. Residual | 8.0 | 5.9 | -4.2 | -7.1 | -4.9 | |
| | male | Count | 18 | 28 | 148 | 68 | 29 | 291 |
| | | % within sex | 6.2% | 9.6% | 50.9% | 23.4% | 10.0% | 100.0% |
| | | Adj. Residual | -8.0 | -5.9 | 4.2 | 7.1 | 4.9 | |

| | Value | df | Asymp. Sig. |
|---|---|---|---|
| Pearson Chi-Square | 155.8 | 4 | .000 |

| | Value | Asymp. Std. Error |
|---|---|---|
| Gamma | .690 | .038 |

Republican (R), or would you be undecided (U) about how to vote?

Do you plan on voting in the election? Yes (Y) or no (N)?

For each person interviewed, the answers to the three questions are entered in a data file. For example, the entry (D, U, N) represents a registered Democrat who is undecided and who does not expect to vote. Table 8.31 summarizes results of the 50 interviews. Using software, create a data file and conduct the following analyses:

**(a)** Construct the $3 \times 3$ contingency table relating party affiliation to intended vote. Report the conditional distributions on intended vote for each of the three party affiliations. Are they very different?

**(b)** Report the result of the test of the hypothesis that intended vote is independent of party affiliation. Provide the test statistic and the $P$-value, and interpret the result.

**(c)** Supplement the analyses in (a)–(b) to investigate the association more fully. Interpret.

#### TABLE 8.31

| | | | | |
|---|---|---|---|---|
| (D, U, N) | (R, R, Y) | (I, D, Y) | (I, U, N) | (R, U, N) |
| (I, D, N) | (R, R, Y) | (I, U, N) | (D, U, Y) | (D, R, N) |
| (I, D, N) | (D, D, Y) | (D, D, Y) | (I, D, Y) | (R, U, N) |
| (D, R, N) | (R, D, N) | (D, U, N) | (D, D, Y) | (R, R, Y) |
| (R, R, Y) | (D, D, N) | (D, D, Y) | (I, D, Y) | (R, R, N) |
| (D, D, Y) | (D, R, Y) | (I, U, N) | (D, D, N) | (D, D, Y) |
| (R, R, Y) | (R, R, Y) | (D, U, N) | (I, R, N) | (I, R, Y) |
| (R, R, Y) | (I, U, Y) | (D, D, Y) | (D, R, Y) | (D, D, N) |
| (D, D, Y) | (I, R, Y) | (R, R, Y) | (I, D, Y) | (R, R, N) |
| (R, R, Y) | (D, D, Y) | (I, D, Y) | (I, R, N) | (R, R, Y) |

**8.37. (a)** When the sample size is very large, we have not necessarily established an important result when we show a statistically significant association. Explain.

**(b)** The remarks in Sections 8.3 and 8.4 about small $P$-values not necessarily referring to an important effect apply for any significance test. Explain why, discussing the effect of $n$ on standard errors and the sizes of test statistics.

**8.38.** Answer true or false for the following. Explain your answer.

**(a)** Even when the sample conditional distributions in a contingency table are only slightly different, when the sample size is very large it is possible to have a large $\chi^2$ test statistic and a very small $P$-value for testing $H_0$: independence.

**(b)** If the odds ratio = 2.0 between gender (female, male) and opinion on some issue

(favor, oppose), then the odds ratio = $-2.0$ if we measure gender as (male, female).

**(c)** Interchanging two rows in a contingency table has no effect on the chi-squared statistic.

**(d)** Interchanging two rows in a contingency table has no effect on gamma.

**(e)** If $\gamma = 0$ for two variables, then the variables are statistically independent.

**8.39.** The correct answer in Exercise 8.38(c) implies that if the chi-squared statistic is used for a contingency table having ordered categories in both directions, then (select the correct response(s))

**(a)** The statistic actually treats the variables as nominal.

**(b)** Information about the ordering is ignored.

**(c)** The test is usually not as powerful for detecting association as a test statistic based on numbers of concordant and discordant pairs.

**(d)** The statistic cannot differentiate between positive and negative associations.

**8.40.** Each subject in a sample of 100 men and 100 women is asked to indicate which of the following factors (one or more) are responsible for increases in crime committed by teenagers: A—the increasing gap in income between the rich and poor, B—the increase in the percentage of single-parent families, C—insufficient time that parents spend with their children, D—criminal penalties given by courts are too lenient, E—increasing problems with drugs in society, F—increasing levels of violence shown on TV. To analyze whether responses differ by gender of respondent, we cross-classify the responses by gender, as Table 8.32 shows.

**(a)** Is it valid to apply the chi-squared test of independence to these data? Explain.

**(b)** Explain how this table actually provides information needed to cross-classify gender with each of six variables. Construct the contingency table relating gender to opinion about whether the increasing gap in income is responsible for increases in teenage crime.

#### TABLE 8.32

| Gender | A | B | C | D | E | F |
|---|---|---|---|---|---|---|
| Men | 60 | 81 | 75 | 63 | 86 | 62 |
| Women | 75 | 87 | 86 | 46 | 82 | 83 |

**\*8.41.** Table 8.33 exhibits the maximum possible association between two binary variables for a sample of size $n$.

**(a)** Show that $\chi^2 = n$ for this table and, hence, that the maximum value of $\chi^2$ for $2 \times 2$ tables is $n$.

**(b)** The *phi-squared* measure of association for $2 \times 2$ contingency tables has sample value

$$\hat{\phi}^2 = \frac{\chi^2}{n}.$$

Explain why this measure falls between 0 and 1, with a population value of 0 corresponding to independence. (It is a special case, for $2 \times 2$ tables, of the *Goodman and Kruskal tau* measure and of the $r^2$ measure introduced in the next chapter.)

**TABLE 8.33**

| | |
|---|---|
| $n/2$ | 0 |
| 0 | $n/2$ |

**\*8.42.** For $2 \times 2$ tables, gamma simplifies to a measure first proposed about 1900 by the statistician G. Udny Yule, who also introduced the odds ratio. In that special case, gamma is called **Yule's Q**.
  **(a)** Show that for a generic table with counts $(a, b)$ in row 1 and $(c, d)$ in row 2, the number of concordant pairs equals $ad$, the number of discordant pairs equals $bc$, and $Q = (ad - bc)/(ad + bc)$.
  **(b)** Show that the absolute value of gamma equals 1 for any $2 \times 2$ table in which one of the cell frequencies is 0.
**\*8.43.** Construct a $3 \times 3$ table for each of the following conditions:
  **(a)** Gamma equals 1. (*Hint*: There should be no discordant pairs.)

**(b)** Gamma equals $-1$.
**(c)** Gamma equals 0.

**\*8.44.** A chi-squared variable with degrees of freedom equal to $df$ has representation $z_1^2 + \ldots + z_{df}^2$, where $z_1, \ldots, z_{df}$ are independent standard normal variates.
  **(a)** If $z$ is a test statistic that has a standard normal distribution, what distribution does $z^2$ have?
  **(b)** Explain how to get the chi-squared values for $df = 1$ in Table C from $z$-scores in the standard normal table (Table A). Illustrate for the chi-squared value of 6.63 having $P$-value 0.01.
  **(c)** The chi-squared statistic for testing $H_0$: independence between belief in an afterlife (yes, no) and happiness (not too happy, pretty happy, very happy) is $\chi_1^2$ in a $2 \times 3$ table for men and $\chi_2^2$ in a $2 \times 3$ table for women. If $H_0$ is true for each gender, then what is the probability distribution of $\chi_1^2 + \chi_2^2$?

**\*8.45.** For a $2 \times 2$ table with cell counts $a, b, c, d$, the sample log odds ratio $\log \hat{\theta}$ has approximately a normal sampling distribution with estimated standard error

$$se = \sqrt{\frac{1}{a} + \frac{1}{b} + \frac{1}{c} + \frac{1}{d}}.$$

The antilogs of the endpoints of the confidence interval for $\log(\theta)$ are endpoints of the confidence interval for $\theta$. For Table 8.13 on page 236, show that $se = 0.0833$ and the 95% confidence interval for the odds ratio is (67.3, 93.2). Interpret.

# CHAPTER 9

# Linear Regression and Correlation

Chapter 8 presented methods for analyzing association between categorical response and explanatory variables. This chapter presents methods for analyzing quantitative response and explanatory variables.

Table 9.1 shows data from *Statistical Abstract of the United States* for the 50 states and the District of Columbia (D.C.) on the following:

- Murder rate: The number of murders per 100,000 people in the population
- Violent crime rate: The number of murders, forcible rapes, robberies, and aggravated assaults per 100,000 people in the population
- Percentage of the population with income below the poverty level
- Percentage of families headed by a single parent

For these quantitative variables, violent crime rate and murder rate are natural response variables. We'll treat the poverty rate and percentage of single-parent families as explanatory variables for these responses as we study methods for analyzing relationships between quantitative variables in this chapter and in some exercises. The text Web site contains two datasets on these and other variables that we will also analyze in exercises in this and later chapters.

We analyze three different, but related, aspects of such relationships:

1. We investigate *whether there is an association* between the variables by testing the hypothesis of statistical independence.
2. We study the *strength of their association* using the *correlation* measure of association.
3. We estimate a *regression equation* that predicts the value of the response variable from the value of the explanatory variable. For instance, such an equation predicts a state's murder rate using the percentage of its population living below the poverty level.

The analyses are collectively called a ***regression analysis***. Section 9.1 shows how to use a straight line for the regression equation, and Section 9.2 shows how to use data to estimate the line. Section 9.3 introduces the *linear regression model*, which takes into account variability of the data about the regression line. Section 9.4 uses the *correlation* and its square to describe the strength of association. Section 9.5 presents

TABLE 9.1: Statewide Data Used to Illustrate Regression Analyses

| State | Violent Crime | Murder Rate | Poverty Rate | Single Parent | State | Violent Crime | Murder Rate | Poverty Rate | Single Parent |
|-------|-------|-------|-------|-------|-------|-------|-------|-------|-------|
| AK | 761 | 9.0 | 9.1 | 14.3 | MT | 178 | 3.0 | 14.9 | 10.8 |
| AL | 780 | 11.6 | 17.4 | 11.5 | NC | 679 | 11.3 | 14.4 | 11.1 |
| AR | 593 | 10.2 | 20.0 | 10.7 | ND | 82 | 1.7 | 11.2 | 8.4 |
| AZ | 715 | 8.6 | 15.4 | 12.1 | NE | 339 | 3.9 | 10.3 | 9.4 |
| CA | 1078 | 13.1 | 18.2 | 12.5 | NH | 138 | 2.0 | 9.9 | 9.2 |
| CO | 567 | 5.8 | 9.9 | 12.1 | NJ | 627 | 5.3 | 10.9 | 9.6 |
| CT | 456 | 6.3 | 8.5 | 10.1 | NM | 930 | 8.0 | 17.4 | 13.8 |
| DE | 686 | 5.0 | 10.2 | 11.4 | NV | 875 | 10.4 | 9.8 | 12.4 |
| FL | 1206 | 8.9 | 17.8 | 10.6 | NY | 1074 | 13.38 | 16.4 | 12.7 |
| GA | 723 | 11.4 | 13.5 | 13.0 | OH | 504 | 6.0 | 13.0 | 11.4 |
| HI | 261 | 3.8 | 8.0 | 9.1 | OK | 635 | 8.4 | 19.9 | 11.1 |
| IA | 326 | 2.3 | 10.3 | 9.0 | OR | 503 | 4.6 | 11.8 | 11.3 |
| ID | 282 | 2.9 | 13.1 | 9.5 | PA | 418 | 6.8 | 13.2 | 9.6 |
| IL | 960 | 11.42 | 13.6 | 11.5 | RI | 402 | 3.9 | 11.2 | 10.8 |
| IN | 489 | 7.5 | 12.2 | 10.8 | SC | 1023 | 10.3 | 18.7 | 12.3 |
| KS | 496 | 6.4 | 13.1 | 9.9 | SD | 208 | 3.4 | 14.2 | 9.4 |
| KY | 463 | 6.6 | 20.4 | 10.6 | TN | 766 | 10.2 | 19.6 | 11.2 |
| LA | 1062 | 20.3 | 26.4 | 14.9 | TX | 762 | 11.9 | 17.4 | 11.8 |
| MA | 805 | 3.9 | 10.7 | 10.9 | UT | 301 | 3.1 | 10.7 | 10.0 |
| MD | 998 | 12.7 | 9.7 | 12.0 | VA | 372 | 8.3 | 9.7 | 10.3 |
| ME | 126 | 1.6 | 10.7 | 10.6 | VT | 114 | 3.6 | 10.0 | 11.0 |
| MI | 792 | 9.8 | 15.4 | 13.0 | WA | 515 | 5.2 | 12.1 | 11.7 |
| MN | 327 | 3.4 | 11.6 | 9.9 | WI | 264 | 4.4 | 12.6 | 10.4 |
| MO | 744 | 11.3 | 16.1 | 10.9 | WV | 208 | 6.9 | 22.2 | 9.4 |
| MS | 434 | 13.5 | 24.7 | 14.7 | WY | 286 | 3.4 | 13.3 | 10.8 |
|  |  |  |  |  | DC | 2922 | 78.5 | 26.4 | 22.1 |

statistical inference for a regression analysis. The final section takes a closer look at assumptions and potential pitfalls in using regression.

## 9.1    LINEAR RELATIONSHIPS

| **Notation for Response and Explanatory Variables** |
|---|
| Let $y$ denote the *response* variable and let $x$ denote the *explanatory* variable. |

We shall analyze how values of $y$ tend to change from one subset of the population to another, as defined by values of $x$. For categorical variables, we did this by comparing the conditional distributions of $y$ at the various categories of $x$, in a contingency table. For quantitative variables, a mathematical formula describes how the conditional distribution of $y$ varies according to the value of $x$. This formula describes how $y$ = statewide murder varies according to the level of $x$ = percent below the poverty level. Does the murder rate tend to be higher for states that have higher poverty levels?

### Linear Functions

Any particular formula might provide a good description or a poor one of how $y$ relates to $x$. This chapter introduces the simplest type of formula—a *straight line*. For it, $y$ is said to be a ***linear function*** of $x$.

---

**Linear Function**

---

The formula $y = \alpha + \beta x$ expresses observations on $y$ as a ***linear function*** of observations on $x$. The formula has a straight line graph with ***slope*** $\beta$ (beta) and ***y-intercept*** $\alpha$ (alpha).

---

## EXAMPLE 9.1    Example of a Linear Function

The formula $y = 3 + 2x$ is a linear function. It has the form $y = \alpha + \beta x$ with $\alpha = 3$ and $\beta = 2$. The $y$-intercept equals 3 and the slope equals 2.

Each real number $x$, when substituted into the formula $y = 3 + 2x$, yields a distinct value for $y$. For instance, $x = 0$ has $y = 3 + 2(0) = 3$, and $x = 1$ has $y = 3 + 2(1) = 5$. Figure 9.1 plots this function. The horizontal axis, the ***x-axis***, lists the possible values of $x$. The vertical axis, the ***y-axis***, lists the possible values of $y$. The axes intersect at the point where $x = 0$ and $y = 0$, called the *origin*.    ∎

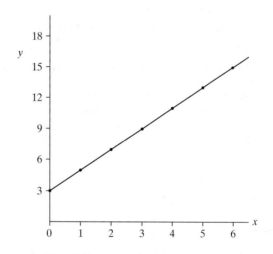

**FIGURE 9.1:** Graph of the Straight Line $y = 3 + 2x$. The $y$-intercept is 3 and the slope is 2.

### Interpreting the *y*-Intercept and Slope

At $x = 0$, the equation $y = \alpha + \beta x$ simplifies to $y = \alpha + \beta x = \alpha + \beta(0) = \alpha$. Thus, the constant $\alpha$ in this equation is the value of $y$ when $x = 0$. Now, points on the $y$-axis have $x = 0$, so the line has height $\alpha$ at the point of its intersection with the $y$-axis. Because of this, $\alpha$ is called the ***y-intercept***. The straight line $y = 3 + 2x$ intersects the $y$-axis at $\alpha = 3$, as Figure 9.1 shows.

The ***slope*** $\beta$ equals the change in $y$ for a one-unit increase in $x$. That is, for two $x$-values that differ by 1.0 (such as $x = 0$ and $x = 1$), the $y$-values differ by $\beta$. For the line $y = 3 + 2x$, $y = 3$ at $x = 0$ and $y = 5$ at $x = 1$. These $y$ values differ by $\beta = 5 - 3 = 2$. Two $x$-values that are 10 units apart differ by $10\beta$ in their $y$-values. For example, when $x = 0$, $y = 3$, and when $x = 10$, $y = 3 + 2(10) = 23$, and $23 - 3 = 20 = 10\beta$. Figure 9.2 portrays the interpretation of the $y$-intercept and slope.

To draw the straight line, we find any two separate pairs of $(x, y)$ values on the graph and then draw the line through the points. To illustrate, let's use the points just discussed: $(x = 0, y = 3)$ and $(x = 1, y = 5)$. The point on the graph with $(x = 0, y = 3)$ is three units up the $y$-axis. To find the point with $(x = 1, y = 5)$, we start at the origin $(x = 0, y = 0)$ and move one unit to the right on the $x$-axis and five units upward parallel to the $y$-axis (see Figure 9.1). After plotting the two points, drawing the straight line through the two points graphs the function $y = 3 + 2x$.

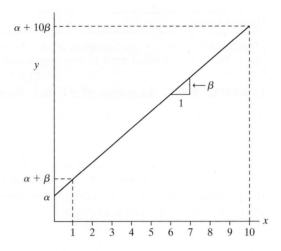

**FIGURE 9.2:** Graph of the Straight Line $y = \alpha + \beta x$. The $y$-intercept is $\alpha$ and the slope is $\beta$.

## EXAMPLE 9.2    Straight Lines for Predicting Violent Crime

For the 50 states, consider the variables $y$ = violent crime rate and $x$ = poverty rate. We'll see that the straight line $y = 210 + 25x$ approximates their relation. The $y$-intercept equals 210. This represents the violent crime rate at poverty rate $x = 0$ (unfortunately, there are no such states). The slope equals 25. When the percentage with income below the poverty level increases by 1, the violent crime rate increases by about 25 crimes a year per 100,000 population.

By contrast, if instead $x$ = percentage of the population living in urban areas, the straight line approximating the relationship is $y = 26 + 8x$. The slope of 8 is smaller than the slope of 25 when poverty rate is the predictor. An increase of 1 in the percent below the poverty level corresponds to a greater change in the violent crime rate than an increase of 1 in the percent urban. Figure 9.3 shows the lines relating the violent crime rate to poverty rate and to urban residence. Generally, the larger the absolute value of $\beta$, the steeper the line.    ■

If $\beta$ is positive, then $y$ *increases* as $x$ *increases*—the straight line goes upward, like the two lines just mentioned. Then large values of $y$ occur with large values of $x$, and small values of $y$ occur with small values of $x$. When a relationship between two variables follows a straight line with $\beta > 0$, the relationship is said to be **positive**.

If $\beta$ is negative, then $y$ *decreases* as $x$ *increases*. The straight line then goes downward, and the relationship is said to be **negative**. For instance, the equation $y = 1756 - 16x$, which has slope $-16$, approximates the relationship between $y$ = violent crime rate and $x$ = percentage of residents who are high school graduates. For each increase of 1.0 in the percent who are high school graduates, the violent crime rate decreases by about 16. Figure 9.3 also shows this line.

When $\beta = 0$, the graph is a horizontal line. The value of $y$ is constant and does not vary as $x$ varies. If two variables are independent, with the value of $y$ not depending on the value of $x$, a straight line with $\beta = 0$ represents their relationship. The line $y = 800$ shown in Figure 9.3 is an example of a line with $\beta = 0$.

## Models Are Simple Approximations for Reality

As Section 7.3 explained, a **model** is a simple approximation for the relationship between variables in the population. The linear function is the simplest mathematical

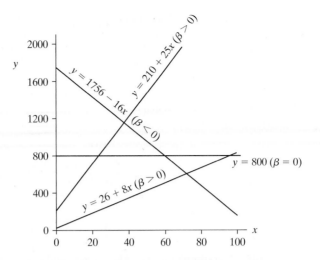

**FIGURE 9.3:** Graphs of Lines Showing Positive Relationships ($\beta > 0$), a Negative Relationship ($\beta < 0$), and Independence ($\beta = 0$)

function. It provides the simplest model for the relationship between two quantitative variables. For a given value of $x$, the model $y = \alpha + \beta x$ predicts a value for $y$. The better these predictions tend to be, the better the model.

As we mentioned in Section 3.4 and will explain further at the beginning of Chapter 10, *association does not imply causation*. For example, consider the interpretation of the slope in Example 9.2 of "When the percentage with income below the poverty level increases by 1, the violent crime rate increases by about 25 crimes a year per 100,000 population." This does not mean that if we had the ability to go to a state and increase the percentage of people living below the poverty level from 10% to 11%, we could expect the number of crimes to increase in the next year by 25 crimes per 100,000 people. It merely means that based on current data, if one state had a 10% poverty rate and one had a 11% poverty rate, we'd predict that the state with the higher poverty rate would have 25 more crimes per year per 100,000 people. But, as we'll see in Section 9.3, a sensible model is actually a bit more complex than the one we've presented so far.

## 9.2  LEAST SQUARES PREDICTION EQUATION

Using sample data, we can estimate the linear model. The process treats $\alpha$ and $\beta$ in the equation $y = \alpha + \beta x$ as unknown parameters and estimates them. The estimated linear function then provides predicted $y$-values at fixed values for $x$.

### A Scatterplot Portrays the Data

The first step of model fitting is to plot the data, to reveal whether a model with a straight line trend makes sense. The data values $(x, y)$ for any one subject form a point relative to the $x$- and $y$-axes. A plot of the $n$ observations as $n$ points is called a *scatterplot*.

### EXAMPLE 9.3    Scatterplot for Statewide Murder Rate and Poverty

For Table 9.1, let $x$ = poverty rate and $y$ = murder rate. To check whether a straight line approximates the relationship well, we first construct a scatterplot for the 51 observations. Figure 9.4 shows this plot.

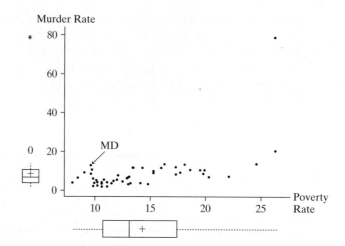

**FIGURE 9.4:** Scatterplot for $y$ = Murder Rate and $x$ = Percentage of Residents below the Poverty Level, for 50 States and D.C. Box plots are shown for murder rate to the left of the scatterplot and for poverty rate below the scatterplot.

Each point in Figure 9.4 portrays the values of poverty rate and murder rate for a given state. For Maryland, for instance, the poverty rate is $x = 9.7$, and the murder rate is $y = 12.7$. Its point $(x, y) = (9.7, 12.7)$ has coordinate 9.7 for the $x$-axis and 12.7 for the $y$-axis. This point is labeled MD in Figure 9.4.

Figure 9.4 indicates that the trend of points seems to be approximated well by a straight line. Notice, though, that one point is far removed from the rest. This is the point for the District of Columbia (D.C.). For it, the murder rate was much higher than for any state. This point lies far from the overall trend. Figure 9.4 also shows box plots for these variables. They reveal that D.C. is an extreme *outlier* on murder rate. In fact, it falls 6.5 standard deviations above the mean. We shall see that outliers can have a serious impact on a regression analysis. ∎

The scatterplot provides a visual check of whether a relationship is approximately linear. When the relationship seems highly nonlinear, it is not sensible to use a straight line model. Figure 9.5 illustrates such a case. This figure shows a negative relationship

**FIGURE 9.5:** A Nonlinear Relationship, for Which It Is Inappropriate to Use a Straight Line Model

over part of the range of $x$ values, and a positive relationship over the rest. These cancel each other out using a straight line model. For such data, a different model, presented in Section 14.5, is appropriate.

### Prediction Equation

When the scatterplot suggests that the model $y = \alpha + \beta x$ is realistic, we use the data to estimate this line. The notation

$$\hat{y} = a + bx$$

represents a *sample equation* that estimates the linear model. In the sample equation, the $y$-intercept ($a$) estimates the $y$-intercept $\alpha$ of the model and the slope ($b$) estimates the slope $\beta$. Substituting a particular $x$-value into $a + bx$ provides a value, denoted by $\hat{y}$, that predicts $y$ at that value of $x$. The sample equation $\hat{y} = a + bx$ is called the ***prediction equation***, because it provides a prediction $\hat{y}$ for the response variable at any value of $x$.

The prediction equation is the best straight line, falling closest to the points in the scatterplot, in a sense discussed later in this section. The formulas for $a$ and $b$ in the prediction equation $\hat{y} = a + bx$ are

$$b = \frac{\Sigma(x - \bar{x})(y - \bar{y})}{\Sigma(x - \bar{x})^2}, \qquad a = \bar{y} - b\bar{x}.$$

If an observation has both $x$- and $y$-values above their means, or both $x$- and $y$-values below their means, then $(x - \bar{x})(y - \bar{y})$ is positive. The slope estimate $b$ tends to be positive when most observations are like this, that is, when points with large $x$-values also tend to have large $y$-values and points with small $x$-values tend to have small $y$-values. Figure 9.4 is an example of such a case.

We shall not dwell on these formulas or even illustrate how to use them, as they are messy for hand calculation. Anyone who does any serious regression modeling uses a computer or a calculator that has these formulas programmed. To use statistical software, you supply the data file and usually select the regression method from a menu. The appendix at the end of the text provides details.

### EXAMPLE 9.4    Predicting Murder Rate from Poverty Rate

For the 51 observations on $y =$ murder rate and $x =$ poverty rate in Table 9.1, SPSS software provides the results shown in Table 9.2. Murder rate has $\bar{y} = 8.7$ and $s = 10.7$, indicating that it is probably highly skewed to the right. The box plot for murder rate in Figure 9.4 shows that the extreme outlying observation for D.C. contributes to this.

**TABLE 9.2**: Part of SPSS Printout for Fitting Linear Regression Model to Observations for 50 States and D.C. on $x =$ Percent in Poverty and $y =$ Murder Rate

| Variable | Mean | Std Deviation | | B | Std. Error |
|----------|------|---------------|---|---|------------|
| MURDER | 8.727 | 10.718 | (Constant) | -10.1364 | 4.1206 |
| POVERTY | 14.259 | 4.584 | POVERTY | 1.3230 | 0.2754 |

The estimates of $\alpha$ and $\beta$ are listed under the heading "B," the symbol that SPSS uses to denote an estimated regression coefficient. The estimated $y$-intercept is $a = -10.14$, listed opposite "(Constant)." The estimate of the slope is $b = 1.32$, listed opposite the variable name of which it is the coefficient in the prediction equation, "POVERTY." Therefore, the prediction equation is $\hat{y} = a + bx = -10.14 + 1.32x$.

The slope $b = 1.32$ is positive. So the larger the poverty rate, the larger is the predicted murder rate. The value 1.32 indicates that an increase of 1 in the percentage living below the poverty rate corresponds to an increase of 1.32 in the predicted murder rate.

Similarly, an increase of 10 in the poverty rate corresponds to a $10(1.32) = 13.2$-unit increase in predicted murder rate. If one state has a 12% poverty rate and another has a 22% poverty rate, for example, the predicted annual number of murders per 100,000 population is 13.2 higher in the second state than the first state. Since the mean murder rate is 8.7, it seems that poverty rate is an important predictor of murder rate. This differential of 13 murders per 100,000 population translates to 130 per million or 1300 per 10 million population. If the two states each had populations of 10 million, the one with the higher poverty rate would be predicted to have 1300 more murders per year. ∎

### Effect of Outliers on the Prediction Equation

Figure 9.6 plots the prediction equation from Example 9.4 over the scatterplot. The diagram shows that the observation for D.C. is a ***regression outlier***—it falls quite far from the trend that the rest of the data follow. This observation seems to have a substantial effect. The line seems to be pulled up toward it and away from the center of the general trend of points.

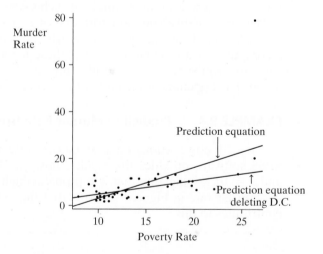

**FIGURE 9.6:** Prediction Equations Relating Murder Rate and Percentage in Poverty, with and without D.C. Observation

Let's now refit the line using the observations for the 50 states but not the one for D.C. Table 9.3 shows that the prediction equation equals $\hat{y} = -0.86 + 0.58x$. Figure 9.6 also shows this line, which passes more directly through the 50 points. The slope is 0.58, compared to 1.32 when the observation for D.C. is included. The one outlying observation has the impact of more than doubling the slope!

**TABLE 9.3:** Part of Printout for Fitting Linear Model to 50 States (but not D.C.) on $x$ = Percent in Poverty and $y$ = Murder Rate

| | Sum of Squares | df | Mean Square | Unstandardized Coefficients |  |
|---|---|---|---|---|---|
| | | | | | B |
| Regression | 307.342 | 1 | 307.34 | | |
| Residual | 470.406 | 48 | 9.80 | (Constant) | -.857 |
| Total | 777.749 | 49 | | POVERTY | .584 |

| | MURDER | PREDICT | RESIDUAL |
|---|---|---|---|
| 1 | 9.0000 | 4.4599 | 4.5401 |
| 2 | 11.6000 | 9.3091 | 2.2909 |
| 3 | 10.2000 | 10.8281 | -0.6281 |
| 4 | 8.6000 | 8.1406 | 0.4594 |

An observation is called ***influential*** if removing it results in a large change in the prediction equation. Unless the sample size is large, an observation can have a strong influence on the slope if its $x$-value is low or high compared to the rest of the data and if it is a regression outlier.

In summary, the line for the data set including D.C. seems to distort the relationship for the 50 states. It seems wiser to use the equation based on data for the 50 states alone rather than to use a single equation both for the 50 states and D.C. This line for the 50 states better represents the overall trend. In reporting these results, we would note that the murder rate for D.C. falls outside this trend, being much larger than this equation predicts.

### Prediction Errors Are Called Residuals

The prediction equation $\hat{y} = -0.86 + 0.58x$ predicts murder rates using $x$ = poverty rate. For the sample data, a comparison of the *actual* murder rates to the *predicted* values checks the goodness of the prediction equation.

For example, Massachusetts had $x = 10.7$ and $y = 3.9$. The predicted murder rate ($\hat{y}$) at $x = 10.7$ is $\hat{y} = -0.86 + 0.58x = -0.86 + 0.58(10.7) = 5.4$. The prediction error is the difference between the actual $y$-value of 3.9 and the predicted value of 5.4, or $y - \hat{y} = 3.9 - 5.4 = -1.5$. The prediction equation overestimates the murder rate by 1.5. Similarly, for Louisiana, $x = 26.4$ and $\hat{y} = -0.86 + 0.58(26.4) = 14.6$. The actual murder rate is $y = 20.3$, so the prediction is too low. The prediction error is $y - \hat{y} = 20.3 - 14.6 = 5.7$. The prediction errors are called ***residuals***.

---

**Residual**

For an observation, the difference between an observed value and the predicted value of the response variable, $y - \hat{y}$, is called the ***residual***.

---

Table 9.3 shows the murder rates, the predicted values, and the residuals for the first four states in the data file. A *positive* residual results when the observed value $y$ is *larger* than the predicted value $\hat{y}$, so $y - \hat{y} > 0$. A *negative* residual results when the observed value is smaller than the predicted value. The smaller the absolute value of the residual, the better is the prediction, since the predicted value is closer to the observed value.

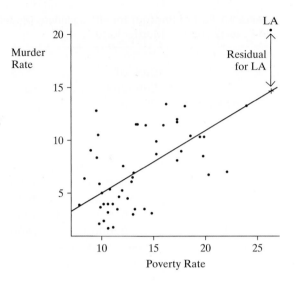

**FIGURE 9.7**: Prediction Equation and Residuals. A residual is a vertical distance between a point and the prediction line.

In a scatterplot, the residual for an observation is the vertical distance between its point and the prediction line. Figure 9.7 illustrates this. For example, the observation for Louisiana is the point with $(x, y)$ coordinates (26.4, 20.3). The prediction is represented by the point (26.4, 14.6) on the prediction line obtained by substituting $x = 26.4$ into the prediction equation $\hat{y} = -0.86 + 0.58x$. The residual is the difference between the observed and predicted points, which is the vertical distance $y - \hat{y} = 20.3 - 14.6 = 5.7$.

### Prediction Equation Has Least Squares Property

Each observation has a residual. If the prediction line falls close to the points in the scatterplot, the residuals are small. We summarize the size of the residuals by the sum of their squared values. This quantity, denoted by SSE, equals

$$\text{SSE} = \sum (y - \hat{y})^2.$$

In other words, the residual is computed for every observation in the sample, each residual is squared, and then SSE is the sum of these squares. The symbol SSE is an abbreviation for **sum of squared errors**. This terminology refers to the residual being a measure of prediction error from using $\hat{y}$ to predict $y$. Some software (such as SPSS) calls SSE the **residual sum of squares**. It describes the variation of the data around the prediction line.

The better the prediction equation, the smaller the residuals tend to be and, hence, the smaller SSE tends to be. Any particular equation has corresponding residuals and a value of SSE. The prediction equation specified by the formulas for the estimates $a$ and $b$ of $\alpha$ and $\beta$ has the *smallest* value of SSE out of all possible linear prediction equations.

---

**Least Squares Estimates**

The **least squares estimates** $a$ and $b$ are the values that provide the prediction equation $\hat{y} = a + bx$ for which the residual sum of squares, SSE $= \sum (y - \hat{y})^2$, is a minimum.

The prediction line $\hat{y} = a + bx$ is called the ***least squares line***, because it is the one with the smallest sum of squared residuals. If we square the residuals (such as those in Table 9.3) for the least squares line $\hat{y} = -0.86 + 0.58x$ and then sum them, we get

$$\text{SSE} = \sum(y - \hat{y})^2 = (4.54)^2 + (2.29)^2 + \cdots = 470.4.$$

This value is smaller than the value of SSE for *any* other straight line predictor, such as $\hat{y} = -0.88 + 0.60x$. In this sense, the data fall closer to this line than to *any* other line.

Software for regression lists the value of SSE. Table 9.3 reports it in the "Sum of Squares" column, in the row labeled "Residual." In some software, such as SAS, this is labeled as "Error" in the sum of squares column.

Besides making the errors as small as possible in this summary sense, the least squares line

- Has some positive residuals and some negative residuals, but the sum (and mean) of the residuals equals 0
- Passes through the point, $(\bar{x}, \bar{y})$

The first property tells us that the too-low predictions are balanced by the too-high predictions. Just as deviations of observations from their mean $\bar{y}$ satisfy $\sum(y - \bar{y}) = 0$, so is the prediction equation defined so that $\sum(y - \hat{y}) = 0$. The second property tells us that the line passes through the center of the data.

## 9.3   THE LINEAR REGRESSION MODEL

For the model $y = \alpha + \beta x$, each value of $x$ corresponds to a single value of $y$. Such a model is said to be ***deterministic***. It is unrealistic in social science research, because we do not expect all subjects who have the same $x$-value to have the same $y$-value. Instead, the $y$-values *vary*.

For example, let $x$ = number of years of education and $y$ = annual income. The subjects having $x = 12$ years of education do not all have the same income, because income is not completely dependent upon education. Instead, a probability distribution describes annual income for individuals with $x = 12$. This distribution refers to the variability in the $y$ values at a *fixed* value of $x$, so it is a ***conditional distribution***. A separate conditional distribution applies for those with $x = 13$ years of education, and others apply for those with other values of $x$. Each level of education has its own conditional distribution of income. For example, the mean of the conditional distribution of income would likely be higher at higher levels of education.

A ***probabilistic*** model for the relationship allows for variability in $y$ at each value of $x$. We now show how a linear function is the basis for a probabilistic model.

### Linear Regression Function

A probabilistic model uses $\alpha + \beta x$ to represent the *mean* of $y$-values, rather than $y$ itself, as a function of $x$. For a given value of $x$, $\alpha + \beta x$ represents the mean of the conditional distribution of $y$ for subjects having that value of $x$.

---

**Expected Value of $y$**

Let $E(y)$ denote the mean of a conditional distribution of $y$. The symbol $E$ represents *expected value*, which is another term for the *mean*.

We now use the equation

$$E(y) = \alpha + \beta x$$

to model the relationship between $x$ and the mean of the conditional distribution of $y$. For $y$ = annual income, in dollars, and $x$ = number of years of education, suppose $E(y) = -5000 + 3000x$. For instance, those having a high school education ($x = 12$) have a mean income of $E(y) = -5000 + 3000(12) = 31,000$ dollars. The model states that the *mean* income is 31,000, rather than stating that *every* subject with $x = 12$ has income 31,000 dollars. The model allows different subjects having $x = 12$ to have different incomes.

An equation of the form $E(y) = \alpha + \beta x$ that relates values of $x$ to the mean of the conditional distribution of $y$ is called a *regression function*.

---

**Regression Function**

A *regression function* is a mathematical function that describes how the mean of the response variable changes according to the value of an explanatory variable.

---

The function $E(y) = \alpha + \beta x$ is called a *linear* regression function, because it uses a straight line to relate the mean of $y$ to the values of $x$. The $y$-intercept $\alpha$ and the slope $\beta$ are called the **regression coefficients** for the linear regression function.

In practice, the parameters of the linear regression function are unknown. Least squares provides the sample prediction equation $\hat{y} = a + bx$. At a fixed value of $x$, $\hat{y} = a + bx$ *estimates* the mean of $y$ for all subjects in the population having that value of $x$.

### Describing Variation about the Regression Line

The linear regression model has an additional parameter $\sigma$ describing the standard deviation of each conditional distribution. That is, $\sigma$ measures the variability of the $y$ values for all subjects having the same $x$-value. We refer to $\sigma$ as the **conditional standard deviation**.

A model also assumes a particular probability distribution for the conditional distribution of $y$. This is needed to make inference about the parameters. For quantitative variables, the most common assumption is that the conditional distribution of $y$ is normal at each fixed value of $x$.

### EXAMPLE 9.5    Describing How Income Varies, for Given Education

Again, suppose $E(y) = -5000 + 3000x$ describes the relationship between mean annual income and number of years of education. Suppose also that the conditional distribution of income is normal, with $\sigma = 13,000$. According to this model, for individuals with $x$ years of education, their incomes have a normal distribution with a mean of $E(y) = -5000 + 3000x$ and a standard deviation of 13,000.

Those having a high school education ($x = 12$) have a mean income of $E(y) = -5000 + 3000(12) = 31,000$ dollars and a standard deviation of 13,000 dollars. So about 95% of the incomes fall within two standard deviations of the mean, that is, between $31,000 - 2(13,000) = 5000$ and $31,000 + 2(13,000) = 57,000$ dollars. Those with a college education ($x = 16$) have a mean annual income of $E(y) = -5000 + 3000(16) = 43,000$ dollars, with about 95% of the incomes falling between \$17,000 and \$69,000.

The slope $\beta = 3000$ implies that mean income increases \$3000 for each year increase in education. Figure 9.8 shows this regression model. That figure shows the conditional income distributions at $x = 8, 12,$ and 16 years. ∎

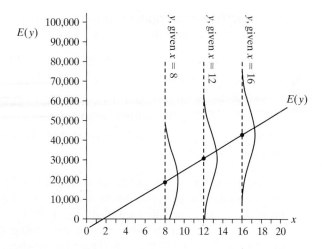

**FIGURE 9.8:** The Regression Model $E(y) = -5000 + 3000x$, with $\sigma = 13,000$, Relating $y =$ Income (in Dollars) to $x =$ Education (in Years)

In Figure 9.8, each conditional distribution is normal, and each has the same standard deviation, $\sigma = 13,000$. In practice, the distributions would not be exactly normal, and the standard deviation need not be the same for each. *Any model never holds exactly in practice.* It is merely a simple approximation for reality. For sample data, we'll learn about ways to check whether a particular model is realistic. The most important assumption is that the regression equation is linear. The scatterplot helps us check whether this assumption is badly violated, as we'll discuss later in the chapter.

### Mean Square Error: Estimating Conditional Variation

The ordinary linear regression model assumes that the standard deviation $\sigma$ of the conditional distribution of $y$ is identical at the various values of $x$. The estimate of $\sigma$ uses the numerical value for SSE $= \Sigma(y - \hat{y})^2$, which measures sample variability about the least squares line. The estimate is

$$s = \sqrt{\frac{SSE}{n - 2}} = \sqrt{\frac{\Sigma(y - \hat{y})^2}{n - 2}}.$$

If the constant variation assumption is not valid, then $s$ provides a measure of *average* variability about the line.

### EXAMPLE 9.6    TV Watching and Grade Point Averages

A survey[1] of 50 college students in an introductory psychology class observed self-reports of $y =$ high school GPA and $x =$ weekly number of hours viewing television. The study reported $\hat{y} = 3.44 - 0.03x$. For the data, software reports the following:

|  | Sum of Squares | df | Mean Square |
|---|---|---|---|
| Regression | 3.63 | 1 | 3.63 |
| Residual | 11.66 | 48 | .24 |
| Total | 15.29 | 49 |  |

---

[1]www.iusb.edu/~journal/2002/hershberger/hershberger.html

The residual sum of squares in using $x$ to predict $y$ was SSE = 11.66. The estimated conditional standard deviation is

$$s = \sqrt{\frac{\text{SSE}}{n-2}} = \sqrt{\frac{11.66}{50-2}} = 0.49.$$

At any fixed value $x$ of TV viewing, the model predicts that GPAs vary around a mean of $3.44 - 0.03x$ with a standard deviation of 0.49. At $x = 20$, for instance, the conditional distribution of GPA is estimated to have a mean of $3.44 - 0.03(20) = 2.83$ and standard deviation of 0.49. ∎

The term $(n-2)$ in the denominator of $s$ is the **degrees of freedom** (*df*) for the estimate. In general, when a regression equation has $p$ unknown parameters, then $df = n - p$. The equation $E(y) = \alpha + \beta x$ has two parameters ($\alpha$ and $\beta$), so $df = n - 2$. The table in the preceding example lists SSE = 11.66 and its $df = n - 2 = 50 - 2 = 48$. The ratio of these, $s^2 = 0.24$, is listed on the printout in the "Mean Square" column. Some software calls this the MSE, short for *mean square error*. Its square root is the estimate of the conditional standard deviation of $y$, namely $s = \sqrt{0.24} = 0.49$. (SPSS lists this under the rather misleading heading "Std. Error of the Estimate")

## Conditional Variation Tends to be Less than Marginal Variation

From Sections 3.3 and 5.1, a point estimate of the population standard deviation of a variable $y$ is

$$\sqrt{\frac{\Sigma(y - \bar{y})^2}{n - 1}}.$$

This is the standard deviation of the *marginal* distribution of $y$, because it uses only the $y$-values. It ignores values of $x$. To emphasize that this standard deviation depends on values of $y$ alone, the remainder of the text denotes it by $s_y$ in a sample and $\sigma_y$ in a population. It differs from the standard deviation of the *conditional* distribution of $y$, for a fixed value of $x$.

The sum of squares $\Sigma(y - \bar{y})^2$ in the numerator of $s_y$ is called the **total sum of squares**. In the preceding table for the 50 student GPAs, it is 15.29. Thus, the marginal standard deviation of GPA is $s_y = \sqrt{15.29/(50-1)} = 0.56$. Example 9.6 showed that the conditional standard deviation is 0.49.

Typically, less spread in $y$-values occurs at a fixed value of $x$ than totaled over all such values. We'll see that the stronger the association between $x$ and $y$, the less the conditional variability tends to be relative to the marginal variability.

For example, the *marginal* distribution of college GPAs ($y$) at your school may primarily fall between 1.0 and 4.0. Perhaps a sample has a standard deviation of $s_y = 0.60$. Suppose we could predict college GPA *perfectly* using $x =$ high school GPA, with the prediction equation $\hat{y} = 0.40 + 0.90x$. Then SSE would be 0, and the conditional standard deviation would be $s = 0$. In practice, perfect prediction would not happen. However, the stronger the association in terms of less prediction error, the smaller the conditional variability would be. See Figure 9.9, which portrays a marginal distribution that is much more spread out than each conditional distribution.

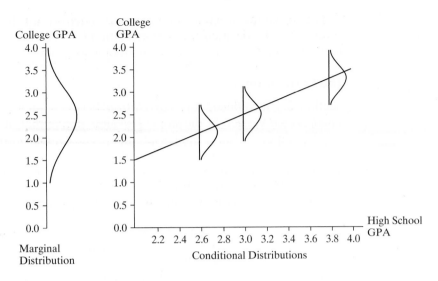

**FIGURE 9.9:** Marginal and Conditional Distributions. The marginal distribution shows the overall variability in *y* values, whereas the conditional distribution shows how *y* varies at a fixed value of *x*.

## 9.4   MEASURING LINEAR ASSOCIATION: THE CORRELATION

The linear regression model uses a straight line to describe the relationship. This section introduces two measures of the strength of association between the variables.

### The Slope and Strength of Association

The slope *b* of the prediction equation tells us the *direction* of the association. Its sign indicates whether the prediction line slopes upward or downward as *x* increases, that is, whether the association is positive or negative. The slope does not, however, directly tell us the strength of the association. The reason for this is that its numerical value is intrinsically linked to the units of measurement.

For example, consider the prediction equation $\hat{y} = -0.86 + 0.58x$ for *y* = murder rate and *x* = percent living below the poverty level. A one-unit increase in *x* corresponds to a *b* = 0.58 increase in the predicted number of murders per 100,000 people. This is equivalent to a 5.8 increase in the predicted number of murders per 1,000,000 people. So, if murder rate is the number of murders per 1,000,000 population instead of per 100,000 population, the slope is 5.8 instead of 0.58. The strength of the association is the same in each case, since the variables and data are the same. Only the units of measurement for *y* differed. In summary, the slope *b* doesn't directly indicate whether the association is strong or weak, because we can make *b* as large or as small as we like by an appropriate choice of units.

The slope *is* useful for comparing effects of two predictors having the same units. For instance, the prediction equation relating murder rate to percentage living in urban areas is 3.28 + 0.06x. A one-unit increase in the percentage living in urban areas corresponds to a 0.06 predicted increase in the murder rate, whereas a one-unit increase in the percentage below the poverty level corresponds to a 0.58 predicted increase in the murder rate. An increase of 1 in percent below the poverty level has a much greater effect on murder rate than an increase of 1 in percent urban.

The measures of association we now study do not depend on the units of measurement. Like the measures of association Chapter 8 presented for categorical data, their magnitudes indicate the strength of association.

### The Correlation

Section 3.5 introduced the **correlation** between quantitative variables. This is a _standardized_ version of the slope. Its value, unlike that of the ordinary slope $b$, does not depend on the units of measurement. The standardization adjusts the slope $b$ for the fact that the standard deviations of $x$ and $y$ depend on their units of measurement. The correlation is the value the slope would take for units such that the variables have equal standard deviations.

Let $s_x$ and $s_y$ denote the marginal sample standard deviations of $x$ and $y$,

$$s_x = \sqrt{\frac{\Sigma(x - \bar{x})^2}{n - 1}} \quad \text{and} \quad s_y = \sqrt{\frac{\Sigma(y - \bar{y})^2}{n - 1}}.$$

---

**Correlation**

The **correlation**, denoted by $r$, relates to the slope $b$ of the prediction equation $\hat{y} = a + bx$ by

$$r = \left(\frac{s_x}{s_y}\right) b.$$

---

When the sample spreads are equal ($s_x = s_y$), $r = b$. For example, when the variables are standardized by converting their values to $z$-scores, both standardized variables have standard deviations of 1.0. Because of the relationship between $r$ and $b$, the correlation is also called the **standardized regression coefficient** for the model $E(y) = \alpha + \beta x$. In practice, it's not necessary to standardize the variables, but it is often useful to interpret the correlation as the value the slope would equal if the variables were equally spread out.

The point estimate $r$ of the correlation was proposed by the British statistical scientist Karl Pearson in 1896, just four years before he developed the chi-squared test of independence for contingency tables. In fact, this estimate is sometimes called the **Pearson correlation**.

### EXAMPLE 9.7    Correlation between Murder Rate and Poverty Rate

For the data for the 50 states in Table 9.1, the prediction equation relating $y =$ murder rate to $x =$ poverty rate is $\hat{y} = -0.86 + 0.58x$. Software tells us that $s_x = 4.29$ for poverty rate and $s_y = 3.98$ for murder rate. The correlation equals

$$r = \left(\frac{s_x}{s_y}\right) b = \left(\frac{4.29}{3.98}\right)(0.58) = 0.63.$$

We will interpret this value after studying the properties of the correlation.    ∎

### Properties of the Correlation

- The correlation is valid only when a straight line is a sensible model for the relationship. Since $r$ is proportional to the slope of a linear prediction equation, it measures the _strength of the linear association_ between $x$ and $y$.

- $-1 \le r \le 1$. The correlation, unlike the slope $b$, must fall between $-1$ and $+1$. The reason will be seen later in the section.
- $r$ has the same sign as the slope $b$. Since $r$ equals $b$ multiplied by the ratio of two (positive) standard deviations, the sign is preserved. Thus, $r > 0$ when the variables are positively related, and $r < 0$ when the variables are negatively related.
- $r = 0$ for those lines having $b = 0$. When $r = 0$, there is not a linear increasing or linear decreasing trend in the relationship.
- $r = \pm 1$ when all the sample points fall exactly on the prediction line. These correspond to *perfect* positive and negative linear associations. There is then no prediction error when the prediction equation $\hat{y} = a + bx$ predicts $y$.
- The larger the absolute value of $r$, the stronger the linear association. Variables with a correlation of $-0.80$ are more strongly linearly associated than variables with a correlation of $0.40$. Figure 9.10 shows scatterplots having various values for $r$.

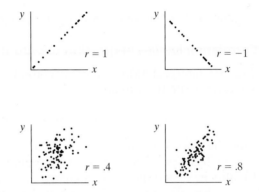

**FIGURE 9.10:** Scatterplots for Different Correlations

- The correlation, unlike the slope $b$, treats $x$ and $y$ symmetrically. The prediction equation using $y$ to predict $x$ has the same correlation as the one using $x$ to predict $y$.
- The value of $r$ does not depend on the variables' units.

For example, if $y$ is the number of murders per 1,000,000 population instead of per 100,000 population, we obtain the same value of $r = 0.63$. Also, when murder rate predicts poverty rate, the correlation is the same as when poverty rate predicts murder rate, $r = 0.63$ in both cases.

The correlation is useful for comparing associations for variables having different units. Another potential predictor for murder rate is the mean number of years of education completed by adult residents in the state. Poverty rate and education have different units, so a one-unit change in poverty rate is not comparable to a one-unit change in education. Their slopes from the separate prediction equations are not comparable. The correlations are comparable. Suppose the correlation of murder rate with education is $-0.30$. Since the correlation of murder rate with poverty rate is $0.63$, and since $0.63 > |-0.30|$, murder rate is more strongly associated with poverty rate than with education.

Many properties of the correlation are similar to those of the ordinal measure of association *gamma* (Section 8.5). It falls between $-1$ and $+1$, it is symmetric, and larger absolute values indicate stronger associations.

We emphasize that the correlation describes *linear* relationships. For curvilinear relationships, the best-fitting prediction line may be completely or nearly horizontal, and $r = 0$ when $b = 0$. See Figure 9.11. A low absolute value for $r$ does not then imply that the variables are unassociated, but that the association is not linear.

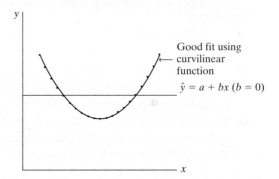

**FIGURE 9.11:** Scatterplot for Which $r = 0$, Even Though There Is a Strong Curvilinear Relationship

### Correlation Implies Regression toward the Mean

Another interpretation of the correlation relates to its standardized slope property. We can rewrite the equality

$$r = (s_x/s_y)b \quad \text{as} \quad s_x b = rs_y.$$

Now the slope $b$ is the change in $\hat{y}$ for a one-unit increase in $x$. An increase in $x$ of $s_x$ units has a predicted change of $s_x b$ units. (For instance, if $s_x = 10$, an increase of 10 units in $x$ corresponds to a change in $\hat{y}$ of $10b$.) See Figure 9.12. Since $s_x b = rs_y$, an increase of $s_x$ in $x$ corresponds to a predicted change of $r$ standard deviations in the $y$ values. The larger the absolute value of $r$, the stronger the association, in the sense that a standard deviation change in $x$ corresponds to a greater proportion of a standard deviation change in $y$.

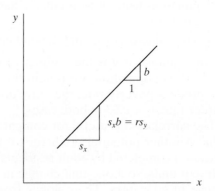

**FIGURE 9.12:** An Increase of $s_x$ Units in $x$ Corresponds to a Predicted Change of $rs_y$ Units in $y$

### EXAMPLE 9.8   Child's Height Regresses toward the Mean

The British scientist Sir Francis Galton discovered the basic ideas of regression and correlation in the 1880s. After multiplying each female height by 1.08 to account for gender differences, he noted that the correlation between $x$ = parent height (the average of father's and mother's height) and $y$ = child's height is about 0.5. From the property just discussed, a standard deviation change in parent height corresponds to half a standard deviation change in child's height.

For parents of average height, the child's height is predicted to be average. If, on the other hand, parent height is a standard deviation above average, the child is predicted to be half a standard deviation above average. If parent height is two standard deviations below average, the child is predicted to be one standard deviation below average (because the correlation is 0.5).

Since $r$ is less than 1, a $y$-value is predicted to be fewer standard deviations from its mean than $x$ is from its mean. Tall parents tend to have tall children, but on the average not quite so tall. For instance, if you consider all fathers with height 7 feet, perhaps their sons average 6 feet 5 inches—taller than average, but not so extremely tall; if you consider all fathers with height 5 feet, perhaps their sons average 5 feet 5 inches—shorter than average, but not so extremely short. In each case, Galton pointed out the *regression toward the mean*. This is the origin of the name for regression analysis. ∎

For $x$ = poverty rate and $y$ = murder rate for the 50 states, the correlation is $r = 0.63$. So a standard deviation increase in the poverty rate corresponds to a predicted 0.63 standard deviation increase in murder rate. By contrast, $r = 0.37$ between the poverty rate and the violent crime rate. This association is weaker. A standard deviation increase in poverty rate corresponds to a smaller change in the predicted violent crime rate than in the predicted murder rate (in standard deviation units).

### $r$-Squared: Proportional Reduction in Prediction Error

A related measure of association summarizes how well $x$ can predict $y$. If we can predict $y$ much better by substituting $x$-values into the prediction equation $\hat{y} = a + bx$ than without knowing the $x$-values, the variables are judged to be strongly associated. This measure of association has four elements:

- Rule 1 for predicting $y$ without using $x$.
- Rule 2 for predicting $y$ using information on $x$.
- A summary measure of prediction error for each rule, $E_1$ for errors by rule 1 and $E_2$ for errors by rule 2.
- The difference in the amount of error with the two rules is $E_1 - E_2$. Converting this reduction in error to a proportion provides the definition

$$\text{Proportional reduction in error} = \frac{E_1 - E_2}{E_1}.$$

*Rule 1* (Predicting $y$ without using $x$): The best predictor is $\bar{y}$, the sample mean.

*Rule 2* (Predicting $y$ using $x$): When the relationship between $x$ and $y$ is linear, the prediction equation $\hat{y} = a + bx$ provides the best predictor of $y$. For each subject, substituting the $x$-value into this equation provides the predicted value of $y$.

*Prediction Errors:* The prediction error for each subject is the difference between the observed and predicted values of $y$. The prediction error using rule 1 is $y - \bar{y}$, and the prediction error using rule 2 is $y - \hat{y}$, the residual. For each predictor, some prediction errors are positive, some are negative, and the sum of the errors equals 0. We summarize the prediction errors by their sum of squared values,

$$E = \sum (\text{observed } y \text{ value } - \text{ predicted } y \text{ value})^2.$$

For rule 1, the predicted values all equal $\bar{y}$. The total prediction error equals

$$E_1 = \sum (y - \bar{y})^2.$$

This is the *total sum of squares* of the $y$-values about their mean. We denote this by TSS. For rule 2, the predicted values are the $\hat{y}$-values from the prediction equation. The total prediction error equals

$$E_2 = \sum (y - \hat{y})^2.$$

We have denoted this by SSE, called the **sum of squared errors** or the **residual sum of squares**.

When $x$ and $y$ have a strong linear association, the prediction equation provides predictions ($\hat{y}$) that are much better than $\bar{y}$, in the sense that the sum of squared prediction errors is substantially less. Figure 9.13 shows graphical representations of the two predictors and their prediction errors. For rule 1, the same prediction ($\bar{y}$) applies for the value of $y$, regardless of the value of $x$. For rule 2 the prediction changes as $x$ changes, and the prediction errors tend to be smaller.

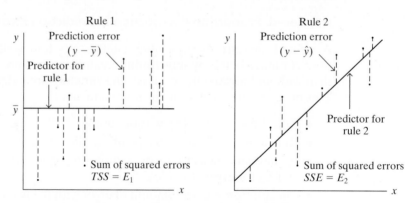

**FIGURE 9.13:** Graphical Representation of Rule 1 and Total Sum of Squares $E_1 = TSS = \sum(y - \bar{y})^2$, Rule 2 and Residual Sum of Squares $E_2 = SSE = \sum(y - \hat{y})^2$

*Definition of Measure:* The proportional reduction in error from using the linear prediction equation instead of $\bar{y}$ to predict $y$ is

$$r^2 = \frac{E_1 - E_2}{E_1} = \frac{TSS - SSE}{TSS} = \frac{\sum(y - \bar{y})^2 - \sum(y - \hat{y})^2}{\sum(y - \bar{y})^2}.$$

It is called **r-squared**, or sometimes the **coefficient of determination**.

The notation $r^2$ is used for this measure because, in fact, the proportional reduction in error equals the square of the correlation $r$. We don't need to use the sums of squares in its definition to find $r^2$, as we can square the correlation. Its defining formula is useful for interpreting $r^2$, but it is not needed for its calculation.

### EXAMPLE 9.9    $r^2$ for Murder Rate and Poverty Rate

The correlation between poverty rate and murder rate for the 50 states is $r = 0.629$. Therefore, $r^2 = (0.629)^2 = 0.395$. For predicting murder rate, the linear prediction equation $\hat{y} = -0.86 + 0.58x$ has 39.5% less error than $\bar{y}$.

Software for regression routinely provides tables that contain the sums of squares that compose $r^2$. For example, part of Table 9.3 showed

| | Sum of Squares |
|---|---|
| Regression | 307.342 |
| Residual | 470.406 |
| Total | 777.749 |

The sum of squared errors using the prediction equation is SSE $= \Sigma(y - \hat{y})^2 = 470.4$, and the total sum of squares is TSS $= \Sigma(y - \bar{y})^2 = 777.7$. Thus,

$$r^2 = \frac{\text{TSS} - \text{SSE}}{\text{TSS}} = \frac{777.7 - 470.4}{777.7} = \frac{307.3}{777.7} = 0.395.$$

In practice, it is unnecessary to perform this computation, since software reports $r$ or $r^2$ or both. ∎

### Properties of *r*-Squared

The properties of $r^2$ follow directly from those of the correlation $r$ or from its definition in terms of the sums of squares.

- Since $-1 \leq r \leq 1$, $r^2$ falls between 0 and 1.
- The minimum possible value for SSE is 0, in which case $r^2 = \text{TSS}/\text{TSS} = 1$. For SSE $= 0$, all sample points must fall exactly on the prediction line. In that case, there is no prediction error using $x$ to predict $y$. This condition corresponds to $r = \pm 1$.
- When the least squares slope $b = 0$, the $y$-intercept $a$ equals $\bar{y}$ (because $a = \bar{y} - b\bar{x}$, which equals $\bar{y}$ when $b = 0$). Then $\hat{y} = \bar{y}$ for all $x$. The two prediction rules are then identical, so that SSE $=$ TSS and $r^2 = 0$.
- Like the correlation, $r^2$ measures the strength of *linear* association. The closer $r^2$ is to 1, the stronger the linear association, in the sense that the more effective the least squares line $\hat{y} = a + bx$ is compared to $\bar{y}$ in predicting $y$.
- $r^2$ does not depend on the units of measurement, and it takes the same value when $x$ predicts $y$ as when $y$ predicts $x$.

### Sums of Squares Describe Conditional and Marginal Variability

To summarize, the correlation $r$ falls between $-1$ and $+1$. It indicates the direction of the association, positive or negative, through its sign. It is a standardized slope, equaling the slope when $x$ and $y$ are equally spread out. A one standard deviation change in $x$ corresponds to a predicted change of $r$ standard deviations in $y$. The square of the correlation has a proportional reduction in error interpretation related to predicting $y$ using $\hat{y} = a + bx$ rather than $\bar{y}$.

The total sum of squares, TSS $= \Sigma(y - \bar{y})^2$, summarizes the *variability* of the observations on $y$, since this quantity divided by $n - 1$ is the sample variance $s_y^2$ of the $y$-values. Similarly, SSE $= \Sigma(y - \hat{y})^2$ summarizes the variability around the prediction equation, which refers to variability for the conditional distributions. When $r^2 = 0.39$, the variability in $y$ using $x$ to make the predictions (via the prediction equation) is 39% less than the overall variability of the $y$ values. Thus, the $r^2$ result is often expressed as "the poverty rate explains 39% of the variability in murder rate" or "39% of the variance in murder rate is explained by its linear relationship with the poverty rate." Roughly speaking, the variance of the conditional distribution of murder rate for a given poverty rate is 39% smaller than the variance of the marginal distribution of murder rate.

This interpretation has the weakness, however, that variability is summarized by the *variance*. Many statisticians find $r^2$ to be less useful than $r$, because (being based on sums of squares) it uses the square of the original scale of measurement. It's easier to interpret the original scale than a squared scale. This is also the advantage of the standard deviation over the variance.

When two variables are strongly associated, the variation in the conditional distributions is considerably less than the variation in the marginal distribution. Figure 9.9 illustrated this.

## 9.5   INFERENCES FOR THE SLOPE AND CORRELATION

Sections 9.1–9.3 showed how a linear regression model can represent the *form* of relationships between quantitative variables. Section 9.4 used the correlation and its square to describe the *strength* of the association. These parts of a regression analysis are descriptive. We now present inferential methods for the regression model.

A test of whether the two quantitative variables are statistically independent has the same purpose as the chi-squared test for categorical variables. A confidence interval for the slope of the regression equation or the correlation tells us about the size of the effect. These inferences enable us to judge whether the variables are associated and to estimate the direction and strength of the association.

### Assumptions for Statistical Inference

Statistical inferences for regression make the following assumptions:

- The study used randomization, such as a simple random sample in a survey.
- The mean of $y$ is related to $x$ by the linear equation $E(y) = \alpha + \beta x$.
- The conditional standard deviation $\sigma$ is identical at each $x$-value.
- The conditional distribution of $y$ at each value of $x$ is normal.

The second assumption states that the linear regression function is valid. The assumption about a common $\sigma$ is one under which the least squares estimates are the best possible estimates of the regression coefficients.[2] The assumption about normality assures that the test statistic for a test of independence has a $t$ sampling distribution. In practice, none of these assumptions is ever satisfied exactly. In the final section of the chapter we'll see that the important assumptions are the first two.

---

[2] Under the assumptions of normality with common $\sigma$, least squares estimates are special cases of *maximum likelihood* estimates, introduced in Section 5.1.

## Test of Independence

Under the above assumptions, suppose the population mean of $y$ is identical at each $x$-value. In other words, the normal conditional distribution of $y$ is the same at each $x$-value. Then, the two quantitative variables are statistically independent. For the linear regression function $E(y) = \alpha + \beta x$, this means that the slope $\beta = 0$ (see Figure 9.14). The null hypothesis that the variables are statistically independent is $H_0: \beta = 0$.

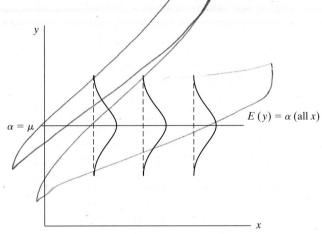

**FIGURE 9.14:** $x$ and $y$ Are Statistically Independent when the Slope $\beta = 0$ in the Regression Model $E(y) = \alpha + \beta x$

We can test independence against $H_a: \beta \neq 0$, or a one-sided alternative, $H_a: \beta > 0$ or $H_a: \beta < 0$, to predict the direction of the association. The test statistic equals

$$t = \frac{b}{se},$$

where $se$ is the standard error of the sample slope $b$. The form of the test statistic is the usual one for a $t$ or $z$ test. We take the estimate $b$ of the parameter $\beta$, subtract the null hypothesis value ($\beta = 0$), and divide by the standard error of the estimate $b$. Under the assumptions, this test statistic has the $t$ sampling distribution with $df = n - 2$. The degrees of freedom are the same as the $df$ of the conditional standard deviation estimate $s$.

The formula for the standard error of $b$ is

$$se = \frac{s}{\sqrt{\Sigma(x - \bar{x})^2}}, \quad \text{where} \quad s = \sqrt{\frac{\text{SSE}}{n - 2}}.$$

This depends on the point estimate $s$ of the standard deviation of the conditional distributions of $y$. The smaller $s$ is, the more precisely $b$ estimates $\beta$. A small $s$ occurs when the data points show little variability about the prediction equation. Also, the standard error of $b$ is inversely related to $\Sigma(x - \bar{x})^2$, the sum of squares of the observed $x$-values about their mean. This sum increases, and hence $b$ estimates $\beta$ more precisely, as the sample size $n$ increases. (The $se$ also decreases when the $x$-values are more highly spread out, but the researcher usually has no control over this except in designed experiments.)

The $P$-value for $H_a: \beta \neq 0$ is the two-tail probability from the $t$ distribution. Software provides the $P$-value. For large $df$, recall that the $t$ distribution is similar to the standard normal, so the *P*-value can be approximated using the normal probability table.

### EXAMPLE 9.10    Regression for Selling Price of Homes

What affects the selling price of a house? Table 9.4 shows observations on home sales in Gainesville, Florida, in fall 2006. This table shows data for 8 homes. The entire file for 100 home sales is the "house selling price" data file at the text Web site. Variables listed are selling price (in dollars), size of house (in square feet), annual taxes (in dollars), number of bedrooms, number of bathrooms, and whether the house is newly built. For now, we use only the data on $y$ = selling price and $x$ = size of house.

**TABLE 9.4**: Selling Prices and Related Factors for a Sample of Home Sales in Gainesville, Florida

| Home | Selling Price | Size | Taxes | Bedrooms | Bathrooms | New |
|------|--------------|------|-------|----------|-----------|-----|
| 1 | 279,900 | 2048 | 3104 | 4 | 2 | no |
| 2 | 146,500 | 912 | 1173 | 2 | 1 | no |
| 3 | 237,700 | 1654 | 3076 | 4 | 2 | no |
| 4 | 200,000 | 2068 | 1608 | 3 | 2 | no |
| 5 | 159,900 | 1477 | 1454 | 3 | 3 | no |
| 6 | 499,900 | 3153 | 2997 | 3 | 2 | yes |
| 7 | 265,500 | 1355 | 4054 | 3 | 2 | no |
| 8 | 289,900 | 2075 | 3002 | 3 | 2 | yes |

*Note*: For the complete file for 100 homes, see the text Web site.

Since these 100 observations come from one city alone, we cannot use them to make inferences about the relationship between $x$ and $y$ in general. We treat them as a random sample of a conceptual population of home sales in this market in order to analyze how these variables seem to be related.

Figure 9.15 shows a scatterplot, which displays a strong positive trend. The model $E(y) = \alpha + \beta x$ seems appropriate. Some of the points at high levels of size are

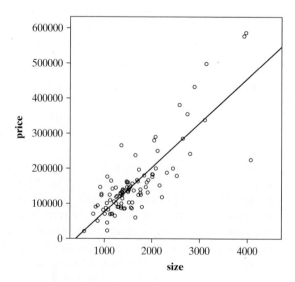

**FIGURE 9.15**: Scatterplot and Prediction Equation for $y$ = Selling Price (in Dollars) and $x$ = Size of House (in Square Feet)

regression outliers, however, and one point falls quite far below the overall trend. We discuss this abnormality in Section 14.5, which introduces an alternative model that does not assume constant variability around the regression line.

Table 9.5 shows part of a SPSS printout for a regression analysis. The prediction equation is $\hat{y} = -50,926 + 126.6x$. The predicted selling price increases by $b = 126.6$ dollars for an increase in size of a square foot. Figure 9.15 also superimposes the prediction equation over the scatterplot. In SPSS, "Beta" denotes the estimated standardized regression coefficient. For the regression model of this chapter, this is the correlation; it is not to be confused with the population slope, $\beta$, which is unknown.

**TABLE 9.5:** Information from SPSS Printout for Regression Analysis of $y$ = Selling Price and $x$ = Size of House

|  | N | Mean | Std. Deviation |
|---|---|---|---|
| price | 100 | 155331.00 | 101262.21 |
| size | 100 | 1629.28 | 666.94 |

|  | Sum of Squares | df | Mean Square |
|---|---|---|---|
| Regression | 7.057E+11 | 1 | 7.057E+11 |
| Residual | 3.094E+11 | 98 | 3157352537 |
| Total | 10.15E+11 | 99 | |

| R Square | Std. Error of the Estimate |
|---|---|
| .695 | 56190.324 |

|  | Unstandardized Coefficients | | Standardized Coefficients | | |
|---|---|---|---|---|---|
|  | B | Std. Error | Beta | t | Sig. |
| (Constant) | -50926.3 | 14896.373 | | -3.42 | .001 |
| size | 126.594 | 8.468 | .834 | 14.95 | .000 |

Table 9.5 reports that the standard error of the slope estimate is $se = 8.47$. This is listed under "Std. Error" for the size predictor. This value estimates the variability in sample slope values that would result from repeatedly selecting random samples of 100 house sales in Gainesville and calculating prediction equations.

For testing independence, $H_0$: $\beta = 0$, the test statistic is

$$t = \frac{b}{se} = \frac{126.6}{8.47} = 14.95,$$

shown in the last row of Table 9.5. Since $n = 100$, its degrees of freedom are $df = n - 2 = 98$. This is an extremely large test statistic. The $P$-value, listed in Table 9.5 under the heading "Sig", is 0.000 to three decimal places. This refers to the two-sided alternative $H_a$: $\beta \neq 0$. It is the two-tailed probability of a $t$ statistic at least as large in absolute value as the absolute value of the observed $t$, $|t| = 14.95$, presuming $H_0$ is true.

Table 9.6 shows part of a SAS printout for the same analysis. The two-sided $P$-value, listed under the heading "Pr >$|t|$," is <0.0001 to four decimal places. (It is

**TABLE 9.6:** Part of a SAS Printout for Regression Analysis of Selling Price and Size of House

| Source | DF | Sum of Squares | Mean Square |
|--------|-----|----------------|-------------|
| Model | 1 | 7.05729E11 | 7.05729E11 |
| Error | 98 | 3.094205E11 | 3157352537 |
| Corrected Total | 99 | 1.01515E12 | |

Root MSE    56,190.3

| Variable | DF | Parameter Estimate | Standard Error | t Value | Pr > \|t\| |
|----------|-----|--------------------|----------------|---------|-----------|
| Intercept | 1 | -50926 | 14896 | -3.42 | 0.0009 |
| size | 1 | 126.59411 | 8.46752 | 14.95 | <.0001 |

actually 0.0000000... to a huge number of decimal places, but SAS reports it this way rather than 0.0000 so you don't think the *P*-value is *exactly* 0.)

Both the SAS and SPSS printouts also contain a standard error and *t* test for the *y*-intercept. We won't use this information, since rarely is there any reason to test the hypothesis that a *y*-intercept equals 0. For this example, the *y*-intercept does not have any interpretation, since houses of size $x = 0$ do not exist.

In summary, there is extremely strong evidence that size of house has a positive effect on selling price. On the average, selling price increases as size increases. This is no surprise. Indeed, we would be shocked if these variables were independent. For these data, estimating the size of the effect is more relevant than testing whether it exists. ■

### Confidence Interval for the Slope

A small *P*-value for $H_0: \beta = 0$ suggests that the regression line has a nonzero slope. We should be more concerned with the size of the slope $\beta$ than in knowing merely that it is not 0. A confidence interval for $\beta$ has the formula

$$b \pm t(se).$$

The *t*-score is the value from Table B, with $df = n - 2$, for the desired confidence level. The form of the interval is similar to the confidence interval for a mean (Section 5.3), namely, take the estimate of the parameter and add and subtract a *t* multiple of the standard error. The *se* is the same as *se* in the test about $\beta$.

### EXAMPLE 9.11    Estimating the Slope for House Selling Prices

For the data on $x =$ size of house and $y =$ selling price, $b = 126.6$ and $se = 8.47$. The parameter $\beta$ refers to the change in the mean selling price (in dollars) for each 1-square-foot increase in size. For a 95% confidence interval, we use the $t_{.025}$ value for $df = n - 2 = 98$, which is $t_{.025} = 1.984$. (Table B shows $t_{.025} = 1.984$ for $df = 100$.) The interval is

$$b \pm t_{.025}(se) = 126.6 \pm 1.984(8.47)$$
$$= 126.6 \pm 16.8 \quad \text{or} \quad (110, 143).$$

We can be 95% confident that $\beta$ falls between 110 and 143. The mean selling price increases by between \$110 and \$143 for a 1-square-foot increase in house size.    ∎

In practice, we make inferences about the change in $E(y)$ for an increase in $x$ that is a relevant portion of the actual range of $x$-values. If a one-unit increase in $x$ is too small or too large in practical terms, the confidence interval for $\beta$ can be adjusted to refer to a different change in $x$. To obtain the confidence interval for a constant multiple of the slope (such as $100\beta$, the change in the mean of $y$ for an increase of 100 units in $x$), multiply the endpoints of the confidence interval for $\beta$ by the same constant.

For Table 9.4, $x$ = size of house has $\bar{x}$ = 1629 and $s_x$ = 669. A change of 1 square foot in size is small. Let's estimate the effect of a 100-square-foot increase in size. The change in the mean of $y$ is $100\beta$. The 95% confidence interval for $\beta$ is (110, 143), so the 95% confidence interval for $100\beta$ has endpoints $100(110) = 11,100$ and $100(143) = 14,300$. We infer that the mean selling price increases by at least \$11,100 and at most \$14,300, for a 100-square-foot increase in house size. For example, assuming that the linear regression model is valid, we conclude that the mean is between \$11,100 and \$14,300 higher for houses of 1700 square feet than for houses of 1600 square feet.

## Reading the Computer Printout

Let's take a closer look at the printouts in Tables 9.5 and 9.6. They contain some information we have not yet discussed. For instance, in the sum of squares table, the sum of squared errors (SSE) is 3.094 times $10^{11}$. This is a huge number because the $y$-values are very large and their deviations are squared. The estimated conditional standard deviation of $y$ is

$$s = \sqrt{\text{SSE}/(n-2)} = 56,190.$$

SAS labels this "Root MSE" for square root of the mean square error. SPSS misleadingly labels it "Std. Error of the Estimate." This is a poor label, because $s$ refers to a conditional standard deviation of selling prices (for a fixed house size), not a standard error of a statistic.

The sum of squares table also reports the total sum of squares, TSS $= \Sigma(y - \bar{y})^2 = 10.15 \times 10^{11}$. From this value and SSE,

$$r^2 = \frac{\text{TSS} - \text{SSE}}{\text{TSS}} = 0.695.$$

This is the proportional reduction in error in using house size to predict selling price. Since the slope of the prediction equation is positive, the correlation is the positive square root of this value, or 0.834. A strong positive association exists between these variables.

The total sum of squares TSS partitions into two parts, the sum of squared errors, SSE $= 3.094 \times 10^{11}$, and the difference between TSS and SSE, TSS $-$ SSE $= 7.057 \times 10^{11}$. This difference is the numerator of the $r^2$ measure. SPSS calls this the **regression sum of squares**. SAS calls it the **model sum of squares**. It represents the amount of the total variation TSS in $y$ that is explained by $x$ in using the least squares line. The ratio of this sum of squares to TSS equals $r^2$.

The table of sums of squares has an associated list of degrees of freedom values. The degrees of freedom for the total sum of squares TSS $= \Sigma(y - \bar{y})^2$ is $n - 1 = 99$, since TSS refers to variability in the *marginal* distribution of $y$, which has sample variance $s_y^2 = \text{TSS}/(n - 1)$. The degrees of freedom for SSE equals $n - 2 = 98$, since SSE refers to variability in the *conditional* distribution of $y$, which has variance estimate $s^2 = \text{SSE}/(n - 2)$ for a model having two parameters. The regression (or model) sum of squares has *df* equal to the number of explanatory variables in the regression model, in this case 1. The sum of *df* for the regression sum of squares and *df* for the residual sum of squared errors SSE equals $df = n - 1$ for the total sum of squares, in this case $1 + 98 = 99$.

### Inference for the Correlation*

The correlation $r = 0$ in the same situations in which the slope $b = 0$. Let $\rho$ (Greek letter rho) denote the correlation value in the population. Then $\rho = 0$ precisely when $\beta = 0$. In fact, a test of $H_0: \rho = 0$ using the sample value $r$ is equivalent to the $t$ test of $H_0: \beta = 0$ using the sample value $b$.

The test statistic for testing $H_0: \rho = 0$ is

$$t = \frac{r}{\sqrt{(1 - r^2)/(n - 2)}}.$$

This provides the same value as the test statistic $t = b/se$. Use either statistic to test $H_0$: independence, since each has the same $t$ sampling distribution with $df = n - 2$ and yields the same $P$-value. For example, the correlation of $r = 0.834$ for the house selling price data has

$$t = \frac{r}{\sqrt{(1 - r^2)/(n - 2)}} = \frac{0.834}{\sqrt{(1 - 0.695)/98}} = 14.95.$$

This is the same $t$ test statistic as Example 9.10 (page 278) had for testing $H_0: \beta = 0$.

For a set of variables, software can report the correlation for each pair in a **correlation matrix**. This matrix is a square table listing the variables as the rows and again as the columns. Table 9.7 shows the way software reports the correlation matrix for the variables selling price of home, size, taxes, and number of bedrooms. The

**TABLE 9.7:** Correlation Matrix for House Selling Price Data. Value under correlation is two-sided $P$-value for testing $H_0: \rho = 0$

| | | Correlations / P-value for Ho: Rho=0 | | |
|---|---|---|---|---|
| | price | size | taxes | bedrooms |
| price | 1.00000 | 0.83378 | 0.84198 | 0.39396 |
| | | <.0001 | <.0001 | <.0001 |
| size | 0.83378 | 1.00000 | 0.81880 | 0.54478 |
| | <.0001 | | <.0001 | <.0001 |
| taxes | 0.84198 | 0.81880 | 1.00000 | 0.47393 |
| | <.0001 | <.0001 | | <.0001 |
| bedrooms | 0.39396 | 0.54478 | 0.47393 | 1.00000 |
| | <.0001 | <.0001 | <.0001 | |

correlation between each pair of variables appears twice. For instance, the correlation of 0.834 between selling price and size of house occurs both in the row for "PRICE" and column for "SIZE" and in the row for "SIZE" and column for "PRICE." The *P*-value for testing $H_0$: $\rho = 0$ against $H_a$: $\rho \neq 0$ is listed beneath the correlation.

The correlations on the diagonal running from the upper left-hand corner to the lower right-hand corner of a correlation matrix all equal 1.000. This merely indicates that the correlation between a variable and itself is 1.0. For instance, if we know the value of *y*, then we can predict the value of *y* perfectly.

Constructing a confidence interval for the correlation $\rho$ is more complicated than for the slope $\beta$. The reason is that the sampling distribution of *r* is not symmetric except when $\rho = 0$. The lack of symmetry is caused by the restricted range $[-1, 1]$ for *r* values. If $\rho$ is close to 1.0, for instance, the sample *r* cannot fall much above $\rho$, but it can fall well below $\rho$. The sampling distribution of *r* is then skewed to the left. Exercise 9.64 shows how to construct confidence intervals for correlations.

### Missing Data

In a correlation analysis, some subjects may not have observations for one or more of the variables. For example, Table 9.13 in the exercises lists 10 variables for 40 nations. Observations on a few of the variables, such as literacy rate, are missing for several nations.

For statistical analyses, some software deletes all subjects for which data are missing on at least one variable. This is called ***listwise deletion***. Other software only deletes a subject for analyses for which that observation is needed. For example, this approach uses a subject in finding the correlation for two variables if that subject provides observations for both variables, regardless of whether the subject provides observations for other variables. This approach is called ***pairwise deletion***. With this approach, the sample size can be larger for each analysis.

These days, more sophisticated and better strategies exist than both of these. They are not yet available in most software, and they are beyond the scope of this text. For details, see Allison (2002).

## 9.6    MODEL ASSUMPTIONS AND VIOLATIONS

We end this chapter by reconsidering the assumptions underlying linear regression analysis. We discuss the effects of violating these assumptions and the effects of *influential* observations. Finally, we show an alternate way to express the model.

### Which Assumptions Are Important?

The linear regression model assumes that the relationship between *x* and the mean of *y* follows a straight line. The actual form is unknown. It is almost certainly not *exactly* linear. Nevertheless, a linear function often provides a decent approximation for the actual form. Figure 9.16 illustrates a straight line falling close to an actual curvilinear relationship.

The inferences discussed in the previous section are appropriate for detecting positive or negative linear associations. Suppose that instead the true relationship were U-shaped, such as in Figure 9.5. Then the variables would be statistically dependent, since the mean of *y* would change as the value of *x* changes. The *t* test of $H_0$: $\beta = 0$ might not detect it, though, because the slope *b* of the least squares line would be close to 0. In other words, a small *P*-value would probably not occur even though an association exists. In summary, $\beta = 0$ need not correspond to independence

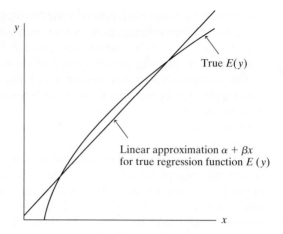

**FIGURE 9.16:** A Linear Regression Equation as an Approximation for Nonlinear Relationship

if the assumption of a linear regression model is violated. For this reason, you should always construct a scatterplot to check this fundamental assumption.

The least squares line and $r$ and $r^2$ are valid descriptive statistics no matter what the shape of the conditional distribution of $y$-values for each $x$-value. However, the statistical inferences in Section 9.5 also assume that the conditional distributions of $y$ are (1) normal, with (2) identical standard deviation $\sigma$ for each $x$-value. These assumptions are also not *exactly* satisfied in practice. For large samples, the normality assumption is relatively unimportant, because an extended Central Limit Theorem implies that sample slopes and correlations have approximately normal sampling distributions. If the assumption about common $\sigma$ is violated, other estimates may be more efficient than least squares (that is, having smaller $se$ values), but ordinary inference methods are still approximately valid.

The random sample and straight line assumptions are very important. If the true relationship deviates greatly from a straight line, for instance, it does not make sense to use a slope or a correlation to describe it. Chapter 14 discusses ways of checking the assumptions and making modifications to the analysis, if necessary.

### Extrapolation Is Dangerous

It is dangerous to apply a prediction equation to values of $x$ outside the range of observed values. The relationship might be far from linear outside that range. We might get poor or even absurd predictions by extrapolating beyond the observed range.

To illustrate, the prediction equation $\hat{y} = -0.86 + 0.58x$ in Section 9.2 relating $x$ = poverty rate to $y$ = murder rate was based on observed poverty rates between 8.0 and 26.4. It is not valid to extrapolate much below or above this range. The predicted murder rate for a poverty rate of $x = 0\%$ is $\hat{y} = -0.86$. This is an impossible value for murder rate, which cannot be negative.

### Influential Observations

The least squares method has a long history and is the standard way to fit prediction equations to data. A disadvantage of least squares, however, is that individual observations can unduly influence the results. A single observation can have a large effect if it is a *regression outlier*—having $x$-value relatively large or relatively small and falling quite far from the trend that the rest of the data follow.

Figure 9.17 illustrates this. The figure plots observations for several African and Asian nations on $y$ = crude birth rate (number of births per 1000 population size) and $x$ = number of televisions per 100 people. We added to the figure an observation on these variables for the United States, which is the outlier that is much lower than the other countries in birth rate but much higher on number of televisions. Figure 9.17 shows the prediction equations both without and with the U.S. observation. The prediction equation changes from $\hat{y} = 29.8 - 0.024x$ to $\hat{y} = 31.2 - 0.195x$. Adding only a single point to the data set causes the prediction line to tilt dramatically downward.

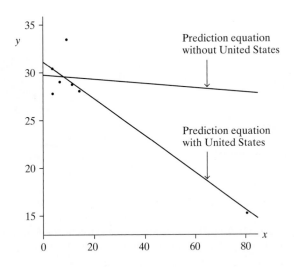

**FIGURE 9.17:** Prediction Equations for $y$ = Birth Rate and $x$ = Television Ownership, with and without Observation for United States

Section 9.2 showed a not-so-extreme version of this. The slope of the prediction equation more than doubled when we included the observation for D.C. in the data set about statewide murder rates.

When a scatterplot shows a severe regression outlier, you should investigate the reasons for it. An observation may have been incorrectly recorded. If the observation is correct, perhaps that observation is fundamentally different from the others in some way, such as the U.S. observation in Figure 9.17. It may suggest an additional predictor for the model, using methods of Chapter 11. It is often worthwhile to refit the model without one or two extreme regression outliers to see if those observations have a large effect on the fit, as we did following Example 9.4 (page 261) with the D.C. observation for the murder rates.

Observations that have a large influence on the model parameter estimates can also have a large impact on the correlation. For instance, for the data in Figure 9.17, the correlation is $-0.935$ when the U.S. is included and $-0.051$ when it is deleted from the data set. One point can make quite a difference, especially when the sample size is small.

### Factors Influencing the Correlation

Besides being influenced by outliers, the correlation depends on the range of $x$-values sampled. When a sample has a much narrower range of variation in $x$ than the population, the sample correlation tends to underestimate drastically (in absolute value) the population correlation.

Figure 9.18 shows a scatterplot of 500 points that is regular and has a correlation of $r = 0.71$. Suppose, instead, we had only sampled the middle half of the points, roughly between $x$ values of 43 and 57. Then the correlation equals only $r = 0.33$, considerably lower. For the relation between housing price and size of house, portrayed in Figure 9.15, $r = 0.834$. If we sampled only those sales in which house size is between 1300 and 2000 square feet, which include 44 of the 100 observations, $r$ decreases to 0.254.

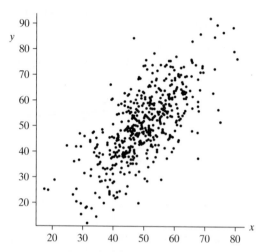

**FIGURE 9.18:** The Correlation is Affected by the Range of $x$-Values. The correlation decreases from 0.71 to 0.33 using only points with $x$ between 43 and 57.

The correlation is most appropriate as a summary measure of association when the sample $(x, y)$-values are a random sample of the population. This way, there is a representative sample of the $x$ variation as well as the $y$ variation.

### EXAMPLE 9.12 Does the SAT Predict College GPA?

Consider the association between $x$ = score on the SAT college entrance exam and $y$ = college GPA at end of second year of college. The strength of the correlation depends on the variability in SAT scores in the sample. If we study the association only for students at Harvard University, the correlation will probably be weak, because the sample SAT scores will be concentrated very narrowly at the upper end of the scale. By contrast, if we randomly sampled from the population of *all* high school students who take the SAT and placed those students in the Harvard environment, students with poor SAT scores would tend to have low GPAs at Harvard. We would then observe a much stronger correlation. ■

Other aspects of regression, such as fitting a prediction equation to the data and making inferences about the slope, remain valid when we randomly sample $y$ within a restricted range of $x$-values. We simply limit our predictions to that range. The slope of the prediction equation is not affected by a restriction in the range of $x$. For Figure 9.18, for instance, the sample slope equals 0.97 for the full data and 0.96 for the restricted middle set. The correlation makes most sense, however, when both $x$ and $y$ are random, rather than only $y$.

### Regression Model with Error Terms*

Recall that at each fixed value of $x$, the regression model permits values of $y$ to fluctuate around their mean, $E(y) = \alpha + \beta x$. Any one observation may fall above that mean (i.e., above the regression line) or below that mean (below the regression line). The standard deviation $\sigma$ summarizes the typical sizes of the deviations from the mean.

An alternative formulation for the model expresses each observation on $y$, rather than the mean $E(y)$ of the values, in terms of $x$. We've seen that the *deterministic model* $y = \alpha + \beta x$ is unrealistic, because of not allowing variability of $y$-values. To allow variability, we include a term for the deviation of the observation $y$ from the mean,

$$y = \alpha + \beta x + \varepsilon.$$

The term denoted by $\varepsilon$ (the Greek letter epsilon) represents the deviation of $y$ from the mean, $\alpha + \beta x$. Each observation has its own value for $\varepsilon$.

If $\varepsilon$ is positive, then $\alpha + \beta x + \varepsilon$ is larger than $\alpha + \beta x$, and the observation falls above the mean. See Figure 9.19. If $\varepsilon$ is negative, the observation falls below the mean. When $\varepsilon = 0$, the observation falls exactly at the mean. The mean of the $\varepsilon$-values is 0.

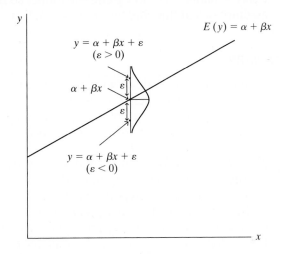

**FIGURE 9.19:** Positive and Negative $\varepsilon$-Values Correspond to Observations above and below the Mean of the Conditional Distribution

For each $x$, variability in the $y$-values corresponds to variability in $\varepsilon$. The $\varepsilon$ term is called the **error term**, since it represents the error that results from using the mean value $(\alpha + \beta x)$ of $y$ at a certain value of $x$ to predict the individual observation.

In practice, we do not know the $n$ values for $\varepsilon$, just like we do not know the parameter values and the true mean $\alpha + \beta x$. For the sample data and their prediction equation, let $e$ be such that
$$y = a + bx + e.$$

That is, $y = \hat{y} + e$, so that $e = y - \hat{y}$. Then $e$ is the *residual*, the difference between the observed and predicted values of $y$. Since $y = \alpha + \beta x + \varepsilon$, the residual $e$ estimates $\varepsilon$. We can interpret $\varepsilon$ as a **population residual**. Thus, $\varepsilon$ is the difference between the observation $y$ and the mean $\alpha + \beta x$ of all possible observations on $y$ at that value of $x$. Graphically, $\varepsilon$ is the vertical distance between the observed point and the true regression line.

In summary, we can express the regression model either as

$$E(y) = \alpha + \beta x \quad \text{or as} \quad y = \alpha + \beta x + \varepsilon.$$

We use the first equation in later chapters, because it connects better with regression models for response variables assumed to have distributions other than the normal.

Models for discrete quantitative variables and models for categorical variables are expressed in terms of their means, not in terms of $y$ itself.

### Models and Reality

We emphasize again that the regression model *approximates* the true relationship. No sensible researcher expects a relationship to be exactly linear, with exactly normal conditional distributions at each $x$ and with exactly the same standard deviation of $y$-values at each $x$-value. By definition, models merely approximate reality.

If the model seems too simple to be adequate, the scatterplot or other diagnostics may suggest improvement by using other models introduced later in this text. Such models can be fitted, rechecked, and perhaps modified further. Model building is an iterative process. Its goals are to find a realistic model that is adequate for describing the relationship and making predictions but that is still simple enough to interpret easily. Chapters 11–15 extend the model so that it applies to situations in which the assumptions of this chapter are too simplistic.

## 9.7    CHAPTER SUMMARY

Chapters 7–9 have dealt with the detection and description of *association between two variables*. Chapter 7 showed how to compare means or proportions for two groups. When the variables are statistically independent, the population means or proportions are identical for the two groups. Chapter 8 dealt with *association between two categorical variables*. Measures of association such as the difference of proportions, the odds ratio, and gamma describe the strength of association. The chi-squared statistic for nominal data or a $z$ statistic based on sample gamma for ordinal data tests the hypothesis of independence.

This chapter dealt with *association between quantitative variables*. A new element studied here was a regression model to describe the *form* of the relationship between the explanatory variable $x$ and the mean $E(y)$ of the response variable. The major aspects of the analysis are as follows:

- The **linear regression equation** $E(y) = \alpha + \beta x$ describes the *form* of the relationship. This equation is appropriate when a straight line approximates the relationship between $x$ and the mean of $y$.
- A **scatterplot** views the data and checks whether the relationship is approximately linear. If it is, the **least squares** estimates of the $y$-intercept $\alpha$ and the slope $\beta$ provide the prediction equation $\hat{y} = a + bx$ closest to the data in terms of a sum of squared residuals.
- The **correlation $r$** and its square describe the *strength* of the linear association. The correlation is a standardized slope, having the same sign as the slope but falling between $-1$ and $+1$. Its square, $r^2$, gives the proportional reduction in variability about the prediction equation compared to the variability about $\bar{y}$.
- For inference about the relationship, a $t$ test using the slope or correlation tests the **null hypothesis of independence**, namely, that the population slope and correlation equal 0. A confidence interval for the slope estimates the size of the effect.

Table 9.8 summarizes the methods studied in the past three chapters.

Chapter 11 introduces the **multiple regression** model, a generalization that permits *several* explanatory variables in the model. Chapter 12 shows how to include categorical predictors in a regression model. Chapter 13 includes both categorical

**TABLE 9.8: Summary of Tests of Independence and Measures of Association**

| | Measurement Levels of Variables | | |
| --- | --- | --- | --- |
| | Nominal | Ordinal | Interval |
| Null hypothesis | $H_0$: Independence | $H_0$: Independence | $H_0$: Independence ($\beta = 0$) |
| Test statistic | $\chi^2 = \sum \frac{(f_0 - f_e)^2}{f_e}$ | $z = \frac{\hat{\gamma}}{se}$ | $t = \frac{b}{se}, df = n - 2$ |
| Measure of association | $\hat{\pi}_2 - \hat{\pi}_1$ | $\hat{\gamma} = \frac{C - D}{C + D}$ | $r = b\left(\frac{s_x}{s_y}\right)$ |
| | Odds ratio | | $r^2 = \frac{\text{TSS} - \text{SSE}}{\text{TSS}}$ |

and quantitative predictors. Chapter 14 introduces models for more complex relationships, such as nonlinear ones. Finally, Chapter 15 presents regression models for categorical response variables. Before discussing these multivariate models, however, we introduce in the next chapter some new concepts that help us to understand and interpret multivariate relationships.

## PROBLEMS

### Practicing the Basics

**9.1.** For the following variables in a regression analysis, which variable more naturally plays the role of $x$ (explanatory variable) and which plays the role of $y$ (response variable)?
  **(a)** College grade point average (GPA) and high school GPA
  **(b)** Number of children and mother's education level
  **(c)** Annual income and number of years of education
  **(d)** Annual income and assessed value of home

**9.2.** Sketch plots of the following prediction equations, for values of $x$ between 0 and 10:
  **(a)** $\hat{y} = 7 + 0.5x$
  **(b)** $\hat{y} = 7 + x$
  **(c)** $\hat{y} = 7 - x$
  **(d)** $\hat{y} = 7 - 0.5x$
  **(e)** $\hat{y} = 7$
  **(f)** $\hat{y} = x$

**9.3.** Anthropologists often try to reconstruct information using partial human remains at burial sites. For instance, after finding a femur (thighbone), they may want to predict how tall an individual was. An equation they use to do this is $\hat{y} = 61.4 + 2.4x$, where $\hat{y}$ is the predicted height and $x$ is the length of the femur, both in centimeters.[3]
  **(a)** Identify the $y$-intercept and slope of the equation. Interpret the slope.

  **(b)** A femur found at a particular site has length of 50 cm. What is the predicted height of the person who had that femur?

**9.4.** The OECD (Organization for Economic Cooperation and Development) consists of 20 advanced, industrialized countries. For these nations,[4] the prediction equation relating $y$ = child poverty rate in 2000 to $x$ = social expenditure as a percent of gross domestic product is $\hat{y} = 22 - 1.3x$. The $y$-values ranged from 2.8% (Finland) to 21.9% (U.S.). The $x$-values ranged from 2% (U.S.) to 16% (Denmark).
  **(a)** Interpret the $y$-intercept and the slope.
  **(b)** Find the predicted poverty rates for the U.S. and for Denmark.
  **(c)** The correlation is $-0.79$. Interpret.

**9.5.** Look at Figure 2 in www.ajph.org/cgi/reprint/93/4/652?ck=nck, a scatterplot for U.S. states with correlation 0.53 between $x$ = child poverty rate and $y$ = child mortality rate. Approximate the $y$-intercept and slope of the prediction equation shown there.

**9.6.** A study[5] of mail survey response rate patterns of the elderly found a prediction equation relating $x$ = age (between about 60 and 90) and $y$ = percentage of subjects responding of $\hat{y} = 90.2 - 0.6x$.
  **(a)** Interpret the slope.
  **(b)** Find the predicted response rate for a (i) 60-year-old, (ii) 90-year-old.

**9.7.** For recent UN data from 39 countries on $y$ = per capita carbon dioxide emissions (metric tons per

---

[3]S. Junger, *Vanity Fair*, October 1999.
[4]*Source*: Figure 8H in www.stateofworkingamerica.org
[5]D. Kaldenberg et al., *Public Opinion Quarterly*, Vol. 58, 1994, p. 68.

capita) and $x$ = per capita gross domestic product (GDP, in dollars), the prediction equation was $\hat{y} = 1.26 + 0.346x$.
(a) Predict $y$ at the (i) minimum $x$-value of 0.8, (ii) maximum $x = 34.3$.
(b) For the U.S., $x = 34.3$ and $y = 19.7$. Find the predicted carbon dioxide response value. Find the residual and interpret.
(c) For Switzerland, $x = 28.1$ and $y = 5.7$. Find the predicted carbon dioxide response value and residual. Interpret.

**9.8.** A college admissions officer uses regression to approximate the relationship between $y$ = college GPA and $x$ = high school GPA (both measured on a four-point scale) for students at that college.
(a) Which equation is more realistic: $\hat{y} = 0.5 + 7.0x$, or $\hat{y} = 0.5 + 0.7x$? Why?
(b) Suppose the prediction equation is $\hat{y} = x$. Identify the $y$-intercept and slope, and interpret the slope.

**9.9.** For the data in Table 9.1 on $y$ = violent crime rate and $x$ = poverty rate, the prediction equation is $\hat{y} = 209.9 + 25.5x$.
(a) Interpret the $y$-intercept and the slope.
(b) Find the predicted violent crime rate and the residual for Massachusetts, which had $x = 10.7$ and $y = 805$. Interpret.
(c) Two states differ by 10.0 in their poverty rates. Find the difference in their predicted violent crime rates.
(d) What is the sign of the correlation between these variables? Why?

**9.10.** In the 2000 Presidential election in the U.S., the Democratic candidate was Al Gore and the Republican candidate was George W. Bush.

In Palm Beach County, Florida, initial election returns reported 3407 votes for the Reform party candidate, Pat Buchanan. Some political analysts thought that most of these votes may have actually been intended for Gore (whose name was next to Buchanan's on the ballot) but wrongly cast for Buchanan because of the design of the "butterfly ballot" used in that county, which some voters found confusing. For the 67 counties in Florida, Figure 9.20 is a scatterplot of the county-wide vote for the Reform party candidates in 2000 (Buchanan) and in 1996 (Perot).
(a) The top point is for Palm Beach county. What does it suggest?
(b) The prediction equation fitted to all but the observation for Palm Beach county is $\hat{y} = 45.7 - 0.02414x$. In Palm Beach county, $x = 30,739$. Find the predicted Buchanan vote and the residual, and interpret.
(c) Why is the top point, but not each of the two rightmost points, considered a regression outlier? (*Note*: Statistical analyses predicted that fewer than 900 of the 3407 votes were truly intended for Buchanan. Bush won the state by 537 votes and, with it, the Electoral College and the election. Other factors that played a role were 110,000 disqualified "overvote" ballots in which people mistakenly voted for more than one Presidential candidate—with Gore marked on 84,197 ballots and Bush on 37,731—often because of confusion from names being listed on more than one page of the ballot, and 61,000 "undervotes" caused by factors such as "hanging chads" from manual punch-card machines.)

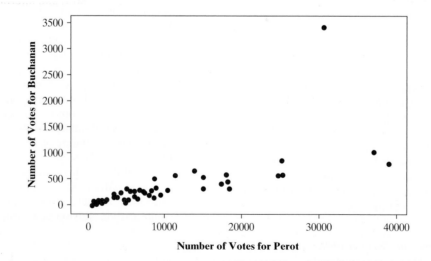

**FIGURE 9.20:** Scatterplot of Florida Countywide Vote for Reform Party Candidates Pat Buchanan in 2000 and Ross Perot in 1996

**9.11.** Figure 9.21 is a scatterplot relating $y$ = percent of people using cell phones and $x$ = per capita gross domestic product (GDP) for nations listed in the *Human Development Report*.

    **(a)** Give the approximate $x$- and $y$-coordinates for the nation that has the highest (i) cell-phone use, (ii) GDP.

    **(b)** The least squares prediction equation is $\hat{y} = -0.13 + 2.62x$. For the U.S., $x = 34.3$ and $y = 45.1$. Find the predicted cell-phone use and the residual. Interpret the residual.

    **(c)** Is the correlation positive, or negative? Explain what it means for the correlation to have this sign.

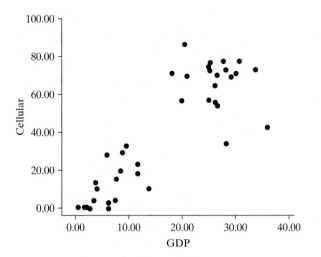

**FIGURE 9.21**

**9.12.** For nations listed in the *Human Development Report*, the correlation with percent of people using the Internet is 0.888 for per capita gross domestic product (GDP, a summary description of a nation's wealth), 0.818 for percent using cell phones, 0.669 for literacy rate, $-0.551$ for fertility rate (the mean number of children per adult woman), and 0.680 for per capita emissions of carbon dioxide.

    **(a)** Explain how to interpret the sign of the correlation between Internet use and (i) GDP, (ii) fertility rate.

    **(b)** Which variable has the (i) strongest, (ii) weakest linear association with Internet use?

**9.13.** A report summarizing the results of a study on the relationship between a verbal aptitude test $x$ and a mathematics aptitude test $y$ states that $\bar{x} = 480, \bar{y} = 500, s_x = 80, s_y = 120$, and $r = 0.60$. Using the formulas for the correlation and for the least squares estimates, find the prediction equation.

**9.14.** Table 9.16 in Exercise 9.39 shows countywide data for several variables in Florida. For those counties, Table 9.9 shows part of the printout for the regression analysis relating $y$ = median income (thousand of dollars) to $x$ = percent of residents with at least a high school education.

    **(a)** Report the prediction equation, and interpret the slope.

    **(b)** County A has 10% more of its residents than county B with at least a high school education. Find their difference in predicted median incomes.

    **(c)** Find the correlation. Interpret using (i) the sign, (ii) the magnitude, (iii) the standardized slope.

    **(d)** Find $r^2$. Explain how to interpret it.

**9.15.** A high school student analyzes whether a relationship exists between $x$ = number of books read for pleasure in the previous year and $y$ = daily average number of hours spent watching television. For her three best friends, Table 9.10 shows the observations.

    **(a)** Construct a scatterplot. From inspection of the plot, state the prediction equation, and interpret. (*Note*: You can do this without using the least squares formulas.)

    **(b)** By inspection, report the sample correlation between $x$ and $y$, and interpret.

**TABLE 9.10**

| $x$ | $y$ |
|---|---|
| 0 | 5 |
| 5 | 3 |
| 10 | 1 |

**TABLE 9.9**

| Variable | Mean | Std Dev |
|---|---|---|
| INCOME | 24.51 | 4.69 |
| EDUC | 69.49 | 8.86 |

| Variable | Parameter Estimate |
|---|---|
| (Constant) | -4.63 |
| EDUC | 0.42 |

**9.16.** For the student survey data set described in Exercise 1.11, the sample correlation between $y$ = political ideology (scored 1 to 7, with higher values representing more conservatism) and $x$ = number of times a week reading a newspaper is $r = -0.066$.
  **(a)** Would you conclude that the sample association is strong or weak?
  **(b)** Interpret the square of the correlation.
  **(c)** When $y$ is predicted using $x$ = religiosity (how often attend religious services, scored 0, 1, 2, 3), the sample correlation is $r = 0.580$. Which of these two explanatory variables seems to have a stronger linear relationship with $y$? Explain.

**9.17.** For the study in Example 9.6 (page 267) of $y$ = high school GPA and $x$ = weekly number of hours viewing television, $\hat{y} = 3.44 - 0.03x$.
  **(a)** The study reported that $r$-squared = 0.237. Interpret.
  **(b)** Report and interpret the correlation.
  **(c)** Suppose you found the correlation only for those students having TV watching of no more than 3 hours per week. Would you expect the correlation to be stronger, or weaker, than for all students? Why?

**9.18.** For students who take Statistics 101 at Lake Wobegon College in Minnesota, both $x$ = midterm exam score and $y$ = final exam score have mean = 75 and standard deviation = 10.
  **(a)** The prediction equation is $\hat{y} = 30 + 0.60x$. Find the predicted final exam score for a student who has (i) midterm score = 100, (ii) midterm score = 50. Note that the predicted final exam score regresses from the midterm score toward the mean.
  **(b)** Show that the correlation equals 0.60.
  **(c)** If instead $\hat{y} = x$, show that $r = 1.0$.
  **(d)** If instead $\hat{y} = 75$ (i.e., slope = 0), show that $r = 0.0$.

**9.19.** The prediction equation relating $x$ = years of education and $y$ = annual income (in dollars) is $\hat{y} = -20,000 + 4000x$, and the correlation equals 0.50. The standard deviations were 2.0 for $x$ and 16,000 for $y$.
  **(a)** Show how to find the correlation from the slope.
  **(b)** Results were translated to units of euros, at a time when the exchange rate was $1.25 per euro. Find the prediction equation and the correlation.

**9.20.** An article in the September 16, 2006 issue of *The Economist* showed a scatterplot for many nations relating $y$ = annual oil consumption per person (in barrels) and $x$ = GDP per person (in thousands of dollars). The $(x, y)$ values shown on the plot were approximately (3, 1) India, (8, 2) China, (9, 4) Brazil, (10, 7) Mexico, (11, 8) Russia, (20, 18)

South Korea, (29, 12) Italy, (30, 13) France, (31, 11) Britain, (31, 12) Germany, (31, 16) Japan, (34, 26) Canada, and (41, 26) the U.S. Using software,
  **(a)** Find and interpret the prediction equation.
  **(b)** Find and interpret the correlation.
  **(c)** Find and interpret the predicted value and residual for Canada.

**9.21.** For 2004 GSS data, the correlation matrix for subject's education (EDUC), mother's education (MAEDUC), and father's education (PAEDUC) is

|        | EDUC | PAEDUC | MAEDUC |
|--------|------|--------|--------|
| EDUC   | 1.00 | .40    | .38    |
| PAEDUC | .40  | 1.00   | .65    |
| MAEDUC | .38  | .65    | 1.00   |

Interpret this matrix, identifying the pair of variables with the strongest association and giving the implication of the sign of each correlation.

**9.22.** In the UN *Human Development Report*, one variable measured was $x$ = percentage of adults who use contraceptive methods. Table 9.11 shows part of a printout for a regression analysis using $y$ = fertility (mean number of children per adult woman), for 22 nations listed in that report. For those nations $x$ had a mean of 60.0 and standard deviation of 20.6.
  **(a)** State a research question that could be addressed with this output.
  **(b)** Report the prediction equation and find the predicted fertility when (i) $x = 0$, (ii) $x = 100$. Show how the difference between these can be obtained using the slope.
  **(c)** Find and interpret $r$ and $r^2$.
  **(d)** What do your analyses say about the question in (a)?

**TABLE 9.11**

| Predictor | Coef | SE Coef | t | Sig. |
|-----------|------|---------|---|------|
| Constant  | 6.6633 | 0.4771 | 13.97 | 0.000 |
| CONTRA    | -0.064843 | 0.007539 | -8.60 | 0.000 |

| Source | Sum of Squares | df |
|--------|----------------|-----|
| Regression | 37.505 | 1 |
| Residual Error | 10.138 | 20 |
| Total | 47.644 | 21 |

**9.23.** For data on several nations, we want to describe whether percentage of people using the Internet is more strongly associated with per capita GDP or with the fertility rate.
  **(a)** Can we compare the slopes when GDP and fertility each predict Internet use in separate regression equations? Why or why not?

**(b)** Let $x$ = GDP (thousands of dollars per capita). For recent data on 39 nations from the UN, for $y$ = percentage using cell phones, $\hat{y}$ = $-0.13 + 2.62x$, whereas for $y$ = percentage using Internet, $\hat{y} = -3.61 + 1.55x$. Why does it make sense to compare these slopes, thus concluding that a one-unit increase in GDP has a slightly greater impact on the percentage using cell phones than on the percentage using the Internet?

**9.24.** For the house sales data in Table 9.4, Table 9.12 shows a regression analysis relating selling price to number of bedrooms.
  **(a)** Report the prediction equation, and interpret the slope.
  **(b)** Using the sample slope and the standard deviations, find the correlation. Interpret its value.
  **(c)** Report $r^2$, and interpret its value.
  **(d)** Construct a 95% confidence interval for $\beta$, and interpret.
  **(e)** Interpret the value labeled "Root MSE."

**9.25.** Refer to the "2005 statewide crime" data set at the text Web site. For all 51 observations, use software to analyze the relationship between $y$ = murder rate and $x$ = poverty rate.
  **(a)** Construct a scatterplot. Does there seem to be a positive or a negative relationship?
  **(b)** Report the prediction equation, and find the predicted murder rate and the residual for D.C. Interpret.
  **(c)** Based on the scatterplot, would you regard D.C. as a regression outlier? Refit the model without it, and note the effect on the slope.

**9.26.** Refer to the data at the text Web site, shown in Table 9.16 in Exercise 9.39, giving county-wide data for several variables in Florida. For those data, use software to analyze $y$ = crime rate and $x$ = percentage living in an urban environment.
  **(a)** Construct a stem-and-leaf plot and a box plot for $y$. Interpret.
  **(b)** Show that $\hat{y} = 24.5 + 0.56x$. Interpret the $y$-intercept and slope.
  **(c)** Find the predicted crime rate and the residual for Alachua County. Interpret.
  **(d)** Using the slope, find the difference in predicted crime rates between counties that are 100% urban and counties that are 0% urban. Interpret.
  **(e)** Report and interpret the correlation and $r^2$.

**9.27.** Table 9.13, which is the "UN data" file at the text Web site, shows United Nations data from 2005 for several nations on a human development index (HDI, which has components referring to life expectancy at birth, educational attainment, and income per capita), the fertility rate (births per woman), percentage of women using contraception, percentage using cell phones, percentage using the Internet, per capita gross domestic product (GDP, in dollars), carbon dioxide emissions per capita (metric tons), female life expectancy, female adult literacy rate, and female economic activity rate (number of women in labor force per 100 men in labor force). This exercise uses $y$ = fertility rate and $x$ = female economic activity. Table 9.14 shows part of a SPSS printout for a regression analysis.
  **(a)** State a research question that could be addressed with this printout.
  **(b)** Report the prediction equation, and interpret.
  **(c)** Report $r$ and $r^2$, and interpret.
  **(d)** What do your analyses suggest about the question posed in (a)?

**TABLE 9.12**

| Variable | N | Mean | Std Dev |
|---|---|---|---|
| price | 100 | 155331 | 101262.2 |
| bedrooms | 100 | 3.000 | 0.651339 |

| Source | DF | Sum of Squares | Mean Square |
|---|---|---|---|
| Model | 1 | 1.575534E+11 | 1.575534E+11 |
| Error | 98 | 8.575962E+11 | 8750981211 |
| Total | 99 | 1.01515E+12 | |

Root MSE 93547    R-Square 0.1552

| Variable | Parameter Estimate | Standard Error | t | Sig. |
|---|---|---|---|---|
| Intercept | -28412 | 44303 | -0.64 | 0.5228 |
| bedrooms | 61248 | 14435 | 4.24 | <.0001 |

**TABLE 9.13:** UN Data for Several Nations, Available as "UN Data" File at Text Web site

| Nation | HDI | Fert | Cont | Cell | Inter | GDP | CO2 | Life | Liter | FemEc |
|--------|-----|------|------|------|-------|-----|-----|------|-------|-------|
| Algeria | 0.72 | 2.5 | 64 | 4.5 | .. | 2090 | 2.9 | 72.4 | 60.1 | 41 |
| Argentina | 0.86 | 2.4 | .. | .. | .. | 3524 | 3.5 | 78.2 | 97.2 | 48 |
| Australia | 0.96 | 1.7 | 76 | 71.9 | 56.7 | 26275 | 18.3 | 82.8 | .. | 79 |
| Austria | 0.94 | 1.4 | 51 | 87.9 | 46.2 | 31289 | 7.8 | 81.8 | .. | 66 |
| Belgium | 0.95 | 1.7 | 78 | 79.3 | 38.6 | 29096 | 6.8 | 82.0 | .. | 67 |
| Brazil | 0.79 | 2.3 | 77 | 26.4 | .. | 2788 | 1.8 | 74.6 | 88.6 | 52 |
| Canada | 0.95 | 1.5 | 75 | 41.9 | .. | 27079 | 16.5 | 82.4 | .. | 83 |
| Chile | 0.85 | 2 | .. | 51.1 | 27.2 | 4591 | 3.6 | 80.9 | 95.6 | 50 |
| China | 0.76 | 1.7 | 84 | 21.5 | 6.3 | 1100 | 2.7 | 73.5 | 86.5 | 86 |
| Denmark | 0.94 | 1.8 | 78 | 88.3 | 54.1 | 39332 | 8.9 | 79.4 | .. | 85 |
| Egypt | 0.66 | 3.3 | 60 | 8.4 | 4.4 | 1220 | 2.1 | 72.1 | 43.6 | 46 |
| Finland | 0.94 | 1.7 | 77 | 91.0 | 53.4 | 31058 | 12.0 | 81.7 | .. | 87 |
| France | 0.94 | 1.9 | 75 | 69.6 | 36.6 | 29410 | 6.2 | 83.0 | .. | 78 |
| Germany | 0.93 | 1.3 | 75 | 78.5 | 47.3 | 29115 | 9.8 | 81.5 | .. | 71 |
| Greece | 0.91 | 1.3 | .. | 90.2 | 15.0 | 15608 | 8.5 | 80.9 | 88.3 | 60 |
| India | 0.60 | 3.1 | 48 | 2.5 | 1.7 | 564 | 1.2 | 65.0 | 47.8 | 50 |
| Iran | 0.74 | 2.1 | 73 | 5.1 | 7.2 | 2066 | 5.3 | 71.9 | 70.4 | 39 |
| Ireland | 0.95 | 1.9 | .. | 88.0 | 31.7 | 38487 | 11.0 | 80.3 | .. | 54 |
| Israel | 0.92 | 2.9 | 68 | 96.1 | .. | 16481 | 11.0 | 81.7 | 95.6 | 69 |
| Japan | 0.94 | 1.3 | 56 | 67.9 | 48.3 | 33713 | 9.4 | 85.4 | .. | 68 |
| Malaysia | 0.80 | 2.9 | 55 | 44.2 | 34.4 | 4187 | 6.3 | 75.6 | 85.4 | 62 |
| Mexico | 0.81 | 2.4 | 68 | 29.5 | 12.0 | 6121 | 3.7 | 77.5 | 88.7 | 49 |
| Netherlands | 0.94 | 1.7 | 79 | 76.8 | 52.2 | 31532 | 9.4 | 81.1 | .. | 68 |
| NewZealand | 0.93 | 2 | 75 | 64.8 | 52.6 | 19847 | 8.7 | 81.3 | .. | 81 |
| Nigeria | 0.45 | 5.8 | 13 | 2.6 | 0.6 | 428 | 0.4 | 43.6 | 59.4 | 56 |
| Norway | 0.96 | 1.8 | 74 | 90.9 | 34.6 | 48412 | 12.2 | 81.9 | .. | 86 |
| Pakistan | 0.53 | 4.3 | 28 | 1.8 | .. | 555 | 0.7 | 63.2 | 35.2 | 44 |
| Philippines | 0.76 | 3.2 | 49 | 27.0 | .. | 989 | 0.9 | 72.5 | 92.7 | 62 |
| Russia | 0.80 | 1.3 | 73 | 24.9 | .. | 3018 | 9.9 | 72.1 | 99.2 | 83 |
| SaudiArabia | 0.77 | 4.1 | 32 | 32.1 | 6.7 | 9532 | 15.0 | 73.9 | 69.3 | 29 |
| SouthAfrica | 0.66 | 2.8 | 56 | 36.4 | .. | 3489 | 7.4 | 50.2 | 80.9 | 59 |
| Spain | 0.93 | 1.3 | 81 | 91.6 | 23.9 | 20404 | 7.3 | 83.2 | .. | 58 |
| Sweden | 0.95 | 1.6 | 78 | 98.0 | .. | 33676 | 5.8 | 82.4 | .. | 90 |
| Switzerland | 0.95 | 1.4 | 82 | 84.3 | 39.8 | 43553 | 5.7 | 83.2 | .. | 67 |
| Turkey | 0.75 | 2.5 | 64 | 39.4 | 8.5 | 3399 | 3.0 | 71.1 | 81.1 | 63 |
| UnitKingdom | 0.94 | 1.7 | 84 | 91.2 | .. | 30253 | 9.2 | 80.6 | .. | 76 |
| US | 0.94 | 2 | 76 | 54.6 | 55.6 | 37648 | 20.1 | 80.0 | .. | 83 |
| VietNam | 0.70 | 2.3 | 79 | 3.4 | 4.3 | 482 | 0.8 | 72.6 | 86.9 | 91 |
| Yemen | 0.49 | 6.2 | 21 | 3.5 | .. | 565 | 0.7 | 61.9 | 28.5 | 37 |

*Source*: *Human Development Report, 2005* available at hdr.undp.org/statistics/data

**TABLE 9.14:** Fertility Rate Regressed on Female Economic Activity

| R Square | | 0.3207 | | | |
|----------|---|--------|---|---|---|
| | B | Std. Error | t | Sig. | |
| (Constant) | 4.845 | 0.619 | 7.82 | 0.000 | |
| FEMEC | -0.039 | 0.00928 | -4.18 | 0.000 | |

**9.28.** Refer to the previous exercise. Now let the percentage using contraceptives be the explanatory variable for predicting fertility. Using software with the data at the text Web site,

(a) Construct a stem-and-leaf plot or box plot for fertility, and describe its distribution.

(b) Construct a scatterplot. Does a linear model seem appropriate?

(c) Fit the model, and interpret the parameter estimates.

(d) Can you compare the slopes of the prediction equations with the two predictors to determine which has the stronger effect? Explain.

(e) Which variable, contraceptive use or women's economic activity, seems to have the stronger association with fertility? Explain.

**9.29.** For 2428 observations from the 2004 GSS on $y$ = number of years of education (EDUC) and $x$ = number of years of mother's education (MAEDUC), $\hat{y} = 10.5 + 0.294x$, with $se = 0.0149$.

(a) Test the null hypothesis that these variables are independent, and interpret.

(b) Find a 95% confidence interval for the population slope. Interpret.

(c) The correlation equals 0.37. Explain "regression toward the mean" in terms of these variables.

**9.30.** A study was conducted using 49 Catholic female undergraduates at Texas A&M University. The variables measured refer to the parents of these students. The response variable is the number of children that the parents have. One of the explanatory variables is the mother's educational level, measured as the number of years of formal education. For these data, $\bar{x} = 9.88, s_x = 3.77, \bar{y} = 3.35, s_y = 2.19$, the prediction equation is $\hat{y} = 5.40 - 0.207x$, the standard error of the slope estimate is 0.079, and SSE = 201.95.

(a) Find the predicted numbers of children for women with (i) 8, (ii) 16 years of education.

(b) Find the correlation and interpret its value.

(c) Test the null hypothesis that mean number of children is independent of mother's educational level, and report and interpret the $P$-value.

(d) Sketch a potential scatterplot such that the analyses you conducted above would be inappropriate.

**9.31.** Is political ideology associated with income? When GSS data for 779 cases in 2004 were used to regress $y$ = political views (POLVIEWS, using scores 1–7 with 1 = extremely liberal and 7 = extremely conservative) on $x$ = respondent's income (RINCOME, using scores 1–12 for the 12

income categories), we get the results shown in Table 9.15.

(a) Show all steps of the test of the hypothesis that political views are independent of income. Interpret.

(b) What is SPSS reporting under "Beta" in this printout? How would you interpret this value?

**TABLE 9.15:** Political Views Regressed on Income

| | | | | | |
|---|---|---|---|---|---|
| R Square | | 0.00024 | | | |

| | B | Std. Error | Beta | t | Sig. |
|---|---|---|---|---|---|
| Constant | 4.12668 | 0.18271 | | 22.58 | 0.000 |
| RINCOME | 0.00739 | 0.01706 | 0.01554 | 0.43 | 0.665 |

**9.32.** Refer to the previous exercise. When political ideology is regressed on $x$ = number of hours spent in the home on religious activity in the past month (RELHRS1), we obtain

| | B | SE B | Beta | t | Sig. |
|---|---|---|---|---|---|
| Constant | 4.0115 | 0.0422 | | 95.10 | 0.0000 |
| RELHRS1 | 0.0064 | 0.0020 | 0.087 | 3.20 | 0.0015 |

(a) Report and interpret the $P$-value for testing the hypothesis that these variables are independent.

(b) Use these results to illustrate that statistical significance does not imply practical significance.

**9.33.** For the data for OECD nations in Table 3.11 on page 62, use software to construct a scatterplot relating $y$ = carbon dioxide emissions and $x$ = GDP.

(a) Based on this plot, identify a point that may have large influence in determining the correlation. Show that the correlation drops from 0.64 to 0.41 if you remove this observation from the data set.

(b) Suppose you constructed this plot using UN data for *all* data, rather than only the highly economically advanced nations that form the OECD. Would you expect the correlation to be weaker, about the same size, or stronger? Why?

## Concepts and Applications

**9.34.** For the "Student survey" data file (Exercise 1.11 on page 00), conduct regression analyses relating (i) $y$ = political ideology and $x$ = religiosity, (ii) $y$ = high school GPA and $x$ = hours of TV watching. Prepare a report

(a) Using graphical ways of portraying the individual variables and their relationship

**(b)** Interpreting descriptive statistics for summarizing the individual variables and their relationship

**(c)** Summarizing and interpreting results of inferential analyses

**9.35.** Refer to the data file you created in Exercise 1.12. For variables chosen by your instructor, pose a research question and conduct a regression and correlation analysis. Report both descriptive and inferential statistical analyses, interpreting and summarizing your findings.

**9.36.** Pose a research question about job satisfaction and educational attainment. Using the most recent GSS data on SATJOB and EDUC with the multiple regression option at sda.berkeley.edu/GSS, with scores (1, 2, 3, 4) for (very satisfied, ..., very dissatisfied), conduct a descriptive and inferential analysis to address this question. Prepare a one-page report summarizing your analysis.

**9.37.** Refer to Exercise 3.6 on page 61 of Chapter 3. Pose a research question relating to the association between the percentage of seats in parliament held by women and female economic activity. Using software, analyze data in Table 3.11 to address this question, and summarize your analyses.

**9.38.** The Zagat restaurant guides rate each restaurant on a 30-point scale for food, decor, service, and cost. The "Zagat restaurant ratings" data file at the text Web site shows 2007 ratings for Italian restaurants in Boston, London, and New York. Conduct a correlation analysis to describe the associations for restaurants in Boston between quality of the food with the ratings for decor, service, and cost.

**9.39.** Table 9.16 shows data from all 67 Florida counties on crime rate (number of crimes per 1000 residents), median income (in thousands of dollars), percentage of residents with at least a high school education (of those aged at least 25), and the percentage of the county's residents living in an urban environment. Using crime rate as the response variable and percentage urban as the predictor, analyze these data (available at the text Web site). In your report, provide interpretations of all the analyses.

**9.40.** Refer to Table 9.1 (page 256), available in the "statewide crime 2" data set at the text Web site. Pose a research question about the relationship between the murder rate and the percentage of single-parent families. Using software, conduct analyses to address this question. Write a report showing your analyses and providing interpretations.

**9.41.** Refer to the UN data for several nations shown in Table 9.13 (page 294) and given at the text Web site. Using software, obtain the correlation matrix. Which pairs of variables are highly correlated? Describe the nature of those correlations, and explain how your software handled the missing values.

**9.42.** A recent study,[6] after pointing out that diets high in fats and sugars (bad for our health) are more affordable than diets high in fruit and vegetables (good for our health), reported, "Every extra 100 g of fats and sweets eaten decreased diet costs by 0.05 to 0.4 Euros, whereas every extra 100 g of fruit and vegetables eaten increased diet costs by 0.18 to 0.29 Euros." Indicate the parameters to which these interpretations refer and the statistical inference that was performed to give this summary.

**9.43.** The headline of an article in the *Gainesville Sun* (October 17, 2003) stated, "Height can yield a taller paycheck." It described an analysis of four large studies in the U.S. and Britain by a University of Florida professor on subjects' height and salaries. The article reported that for each gender, "an inch is worth about $789 a year in salary. So, a person who is 6 feet tall will earn about $5,523 more a year than a person who is 5 foot 5."

**(a)** For the interpretation in quotes, identify the response variable and explanatory variable, and state the slope of the prediction equation, when height is measured in inches and salary in dollars.

**(b)** Explain how the value $5,523 relates to the slope.

**9.44.** In 2002, a Census Bureau survey reported that the mean total earnings that a full-time worker in the U.S. can expect to earn between ages 25 and 64 is $1.2 million for those with only a high-school education and $2.1 million for those with a college degree but no advanced degree.

**(a)** Assuming four years for a college degree and a straight line regression of $y$ = total earnings on $x$ = number years of education, what is the slope?

**(b)** If $y$ instead measures earnings per year (rather than for 40 years), then what is the slope?

**9.45.** Explain why conditional variability can be much less than marginal variability, using the relationship between $y$ = weight and $x$ = age for a sample of boys of ages 2–12, for which perhaps $\sigma_y = 30$ but the conditional $\sigma = 10$.

**9.46.** Describe a situation in which it is inappropriate to use the correlation to measure the association between two quantitative variables.

**9.47.** Annual income, in dollars, is an explanatory variable in a regression analysis. For a British version of the report on the analysis, all responses are

---

[6]E. Frazao and E. Golan, *Evidence-Based Healthcare and Public Health*, vol. 9, 2005, pp. 104–107.

**TABLE 9.16**

| County | Crime Rate | Median Income | High School | Percent Urban | County | Crime Rate | Median Income | High School | Percent Urban |
|--------|-----------|---------------|-------------|---------------|--------|-----------|---------------|-------------|---------------|
| ALACHUA | 104 | 22.1 | 82.7 | 73.2 | LAFAYETTE | 0 | 20.7 | 58.2 | 0.0 |
| BAKER | 20 | 25.8 | 64.1 | 21.5 | LAKE | 42 | 23.4 | 70.6 | 43.2 |
| BAY | 64 | 24.7 | 74.7 | 85.0 | LEE | 59 | 28.4 | 76.9 | 86.1 |
| BRADFORD | 50 | 24.6 | 65.0 | 23.2 | LEON | 107 | 27.3 | 84.9 | 82.5 |
| BREVARD | 64 | 30.5 | 82.3 | 91.9 | LEVY | 45 | 18.8 | 62.8 | 0.0 |
| BROWARD | 94 | 30.6 | 76.8 | 98.9 | LIBERTY | 8 | 22.3 | 56.7 | 0.0 |
| CALHOUN | 8 | 18.6 | 55.9 | 0.0 | MADISON | 26 | 18.2 | 56.5 | 20.3 |
| CHARLOTTE | 35 | 25.7 | 75.7 | 80.2 | MANATEE | 79 | 26.0 | 75.6 | 88.7 |
| CITRUS | 27 | 21.3 | 68.6 | 31.0 | MARION | 64 | 22.5 | 69.6 | 39.6 |
| CLAY | 41 | 34.9 | 81.2 | 65.8 | MARTIN | 53 | 31.8 | 79.7 | 83.2 |
| COLLIER | 55 | 34.0 | 79.0 | 77.6 | MONROE | 89 | 29.4 | 79.7 | 73.2 |
| COLUMBIA | 69 | 22.0 | 69.0 | 31.1 | NASSAU | 42 | 30.2 | 71.2 | 44.9 |
| DADE | 128 | 26.9 | 65.0 | 98.8 | OKALOOSA | 37 | 27.9 | 83.8 | 84.0 |
| DESOTO | 69 | 21.0 | 54.5 | 44.6 | OKEECH. | 51 | 21.4 | 59.1 | 30.1 |
| DIXIE | 49 | 15.4 | 57.7 | 0.0 | ORANGE | 93 | 30.3 | 78.8 | 93.1 |
| DUVAL | 97 | 28.5 | 76.9 | 98.8 | OSCEOLA | 78 | 27.3 | 73.7 | 66.4 |
| ESCAMBIA | 70 | 25.2 | 76.2 | 85.9 | PALM B. | 90 | 32.5 | 78.8 | 94.7 |
| FLAGLER | 34 | 28.6 | 78.7 | 63.1 | PASCO | 42 | 21.5 | 66.9 | 67.4 |
| FRANKLIN | 37 | 17.2 | 59.5 | 30.2 | PINELLAS | 70 | 26.3 | 78.1 | 99.6 |
| GADSDEN | 52 | 20.0 | 59.9 | 28.8 | POLK | 84 | 25.2 | 68.0 | 70.3 |
| GILCHRIST | 15 | 20.6 | 63.0 | 0.0 | PUTNAM | 83 | 20.2 | 64.3 | 15.7 |
| GLADES | 62 | 20.7 | 57.4 | 0.0 | SANTA R. | 43 | 27.6 | 79.9 | 57.2 |
| GULF | 19 | 21.9 | 66.4 | 35.2 | SARASOTA | 58 | 29.9 | 71.7 | 92.1 |
| HAMILTON | 6 | 18.7 | 58.4 | 0.0 | SEMINOLE | 56 | 35.6 | 78.5 | 44.4 |
| HARDEE | 57 | 22.1 | 54.8 | 16.7 | ST JOHNS | 54 | 29.9 | 81.3 | 93.2 |
| HENDRY | 47 | 24.9 | 56.6 | 44.7 | ST LUCIE | 58 | 27.7 | 84.6 | 92.8 |
| HERNANDO | 44 | 22.7 | 70.5 | 61.3 | SUMTER | 37 | 19.6 | 64.3 | 19.3 |
| HIGHLANDS | 56 | 21.1 | 68.2 | 24.8 | SUWANEE | 37 | 19.8 | 63.8 | 23.6 |
| HILLSBOR. | 110 | 28.5 | 75.6 | 89.2 | TAYLOR | 76 | 21.4 | 62.1 | 41.8 |
| HOLMES | 5 | 17.2 | 57.1 | 16.8 | UNION | 6 | 22.8 | 67.7 | 0.0 |
| INDIAN R. | 58 | 29.0 | 76.5 | 83.0 | VOLUSIA | 62 | 24.8 | 75.4 | 83.9 |
| JACKSON | 32 | 19.5 | 61.6 | 21.7 | WAKULLA | 29 | 25.0 | 71.6 | 0.0 |
| JEFFERSON | 36 | 21.8 | 64.1 | 22.3 | WALTON | 18 | 21.9 | 66.5 | 20.9 |
| | | | | | WASHINGTON | 21 | 18.3 | 60.9 | 22.9 |

*Source*: Dr. Larry Winner, University of Florida.

converted to British pounds sterling (1 pound equals about 2.0 dollars, as of 2007).
   **(a)** How, if at all, does the slope of the prediction equation change?
   **(b)** How, if at all, does the correlation change?

**9.48.** State the assumptions (a) in using the regression equation $E(y) = \alpha + \beta x$ to represent the relationship between two variables and (b) in making inferences about that equation using the least squares prediction equation. Which assumptions are most critical?

**9.49.** Refer to the previous exercise. In view of these assumptions, indicate why such a model would or would not be good in the following situations.

**(a)** $x$ = time, $y$ = percentage unemployed workers in the United States. (*Hint*: Does this continually tend to increase or decrease?)

**(b)** $x$ = income, $y$ = charitable contributions within the previous year. (*Hint*: Would poor people show as much variation as wealthy people?)

**(c)** $x$ = age, $y$ = annual medical expenses. (*Hint*: Suppose expenses tend to be relatively high for the newborn and for the elderly.)

**(d)** $x$ = per capita income, $y$ = life expectancy, for nations. (*Hint*: The increasing trend eventually levels off.)

**9.50.** For a class of 100 students, the teacher takes the 10 students who perform poorest on the midterm exam and enrolls them in a special tutoring program. The overall class mean is 70 both on the midterm and final, but the mean for the specially tutored students increases from 50 to 60. Can we conclude that the tutoring program was successful? Explain.

**9.51.** A study by the Readership Institute[7] at Northwestern University used survey data to analyze how reader behavior was influenced by the Iraq war. The response variable was a Reader Behavior Score (RBS), a combined measure summarizing newspaper use frequency, time spent with the newspaper, and how much was read. Comparing RBS scores prewar and during the war, the study noted that there was a significant increase in reading by light readers (mean RBS changing from 2.05 to 2.32, $P < 0.001$) but a significant decrease in reading by heavy readers (mean RBS changing from 5.87 to 5.66, $P < 0.001$). Would you conclude that the Iraq war caused a change in reader behavior, or could there be some other explanation?

**9.52.** Refer to Exercise 9.39. For these counties, the correlation between high school education rate and median income equals 0.79. Suppose we also have data at the individual level as well as aggregated for a county. Sketch a scatterplot to show that at the individual level, the correlation could be much weaker. (*Hint*: Show that lots of variability could exist for individuals, yet the summary values for counties could fall close to a straight line. Thus, it is misleading to extend results from the aggregate level to individuals. Making predictions about individuals based on the behavior of aggregate groups is known as the ***ecological fallacy***. See W. S. Robinson, *American Sociological Review*, vol. 15, 1950, p. 351.)

**9.53.** For which student body do you think the correlation between high-school GPA and college GPA would be higher: Yale University or the University of Bridgeport, Connecticut? Explain why.

**9.54.** Explain why the correlation between $x$ = number of years of education and $y$ = annual income is likely to be smaller if we use a random sample of adults who have a college degree than if we use a random sample of all adults.

**9.55.** Explain carefully the interpretations of the standard deviations (a) $s_y$, (b) $s_x$, (c) $s$ = square root of MSE, (d) $se$ for $b$.

**9.56.** We can regard the problem studied in Chapter 5 of estimating a single mean $\mu$ as estimating the parameter in the simple model, $E(y) = \mu$, with a single parameter. Use this fact to explain why the estimate $s_y$ of the standard deviation of the marginal distribution has $df = n - 1$.

**9.57.** The statistician George Box, who had an illustrious academic career at the University of Wisconsin, is often quoted as saying, "All models are wrong, but some models are useful." Why do you think that, in practice, (a) all models are wrong, (b) some models are *not* useful?

**9.58.** The variables $y$ = annual income (thousands of dollars), $x_1$ = number of years of education, and $x_2$ = number of years experience in job are measured for all the employees having city-funded jobs, in Knoxville, Tennessee. The following prediction equations and correlations apply.
(i.) $\hat{y} = 10 + 1.0x_1,$ $\qquad r = 0.30$
(ii.) $\hat{y} = 14 + 0.4x_2,$ $\qquad r = 0.60$
The correlation is $-0.40$ between $x_1$ and $x_2$. Which of the following statements are true? (*Hint*: Seven of the statements are true.)

**(a)** The strongest sample association is between $y$ and $x_2$.

**(b)** The weakest sample association is between $x_1$ and $x_2$.

**(c)** The prediction equation using $x_2$ to predict $x_1$ has negative slope.

**(d)** A standard deviation increase in education corresponds to a predicted increase of 0.3 standard deviations in income.

**(e)** There is a 30% reduction in error in using education, instead of $\bar{y}$, to predict income.

**(f)** Each additional year on the job corresponds to a $400 increase in predicted income.

**(g)** When $x_1$ is the predictor of $y$, the sum of squared residuals (SSE) is larger than when $x_2$ is the predictor of $y$.

**(h)** The predicted mean income for employees having 20 years of experience is $4000 higher than the predicted mean income for employees having 10 years of experience.

**(i)** If $s = 8$ for the model using $x_1$ to predict $y$, then it is not unusual to observe an income of $70,000 for an employee who has 10 years of education.

**(j)** It is possible that $s_y = 12.0$ and $s_{x_1} = 3.6$.

**(k)** It is possible that $\bar{y} = 20$ and $\bar{x}_1 = 13$.

*Select the best response(s) in Exercises 9.59–9.61. (More than one response may be correct.)*

**9.59.** One can interpret $r = 0.30$ as follows:

**(a)** A 30% reduction in error occurs in using $x$ to predict $y$.

---

**(b)** A 9% reduction in error occurs in using $x$ to predict $y$ compared to using $\bar{y}$ to predict $y$.

**(c)** 9% of the time $\hat{y} = y$.

**(d)** $y$ changes 0.30 units for every one-unit increase in $x$.

**(e)** When $x$ predicts $y$, the average residual is 0.3.

**(f)** $x$ changes exactly 0.30 standard deviations when $y$ changes one standard deviation.

**9.60.** The correlation is inappropriate as a measure of association between two quantitative variables

  **(a)** When different people measure the variables using different units

  **(b)** When the relationship is highly nonlinear.

  **(c)** When the data points fall exactly on a straight line

  **(d)** When the slope of the prediction equation is 0 using nearly all the data, but a couple of outliers are extremely high on $y$ at the high end of the $x$ scale

  **(e)** When $y$ tends to decrease as $x$ increases

  **(f)** When we have data for the entire population rather than a sample

  **(g)** When the sample has a much narrower range of $x$-values than does the population

**9.61.** The slope of the least squares prediction equation and the correlation are similar in the sense that

  **(a)** They do not depend on the units.

  **(b)** They both must fall between $-1$ and $+1$.

  **(c)** They both have the same sign.

  **(d)** They both equal 1 when there is the strongest association.

  **(e)** Their squares both have proportional reduction in error interpretations.

  **(f)** They have the same $t$ statistic value for testing $H_0$: Independence.

  **(g)** They both can be strongly affected by severe outliers.

**\*9.62.** A study in 2000 by the National Highway Traffic Safety Administration estimated that 73% of people wear seat belts, that failure to wear seat belts led to 9200 deaths in the previous year, and that that value would decrease by 270 for every 1 percentage point gain in seat belt usage. Let $\hat{y}$ = predicted number of deaths in a year and $x$ = percentage of people who wear seat belts. Find the prediction equation that yields these results.

**\*9.63.** Observations on both $x$ and $y$ are standardized, having estimated means of 0 and standard deviations of 1 (see Section 4.3). Show that the prediction equation has the form $\hat{y} = rx$, where $r$ is the sample correlation between $x$ and $y$. That is, for the standardized variables, the $y$-intercept equals 0 and the slope is the same as the correlation.

**\*9.64.** A confidence interval for a population correlation $\rho$ requires a mathematical transformation of $r$ for which the sampling distribution is approximately normal. This transformation is $T(r) = (1/2)\log_e[(1 + r)/(1 - r)]$, where $\log_e$ denotes the natural (base-$e$) logarithm. The transformation of the population value $\rho$ is denoted by $T(\rho)$. The variable $T(r)$ is approximately normally distributed about $T(\rho)$ with standard error $\sigma_T = 1/\sqrt{n - 3}$. A confidence interval for $T(\rho)$ is $T(r) \pm z\sigma_T$. Once we get the endpoints of the interval for $T(\rho)$, we substitute each endpoint for $T$ in the inverse transformation $\rho = (e^{2T} - 1)/(e^{2T} + 1)$, where $e$ denotes the exponential function (the inverse of the natural log function). These two values form the endpoints of the confidence interval for $\rho$.

  **(a)** For the correlation of 0.8338 for the data on house selling price and size of house shown partly in Table 9.4, show that $T(r) = 1.20$. Show that the standard error of $T(r)$ is 0.1015.

  **(b)** Show that a 95% confidence interval for $T(\rho)$ is (1.00, 1.40).

  **(c)** Show that the corresponding confidence interval for $\rho$ is (0.76, 0.89). (Unless $r = 0$, the confidence interval for $\rho$ is not symmetric about the point estimate $r$, because of the nonsymmetry of the sampling distribution of $r$.)

  **(d)** A confidence interval for the population value $\rho^2$ of $r^2$ follows directly by squaring the limits of the confidence interval for $\rho$. Find and interpret this confidence interval. (*Note*: When a confidence interval for $\rho$ contains 0, the lower endpoint of the confidence interval for $\rho^2$ is 0 and the upper endpoint is the larger of the squared endpoints of the confidence interval for $\rho$.)

**\*9.65.** Refer to the previous exercise. Let $\rho_1$ and $\rho_2$ denote the population correlation values between two variables for two separate populations. Let $r_1$ and $r_2$ denote sample values for independent random samples from the populations. To test $H_0$: $\rho_1 = \rho_2$, the test statistic is

$$z = \frac{T_2 - T_1}{s_{T_2 - T_1}} \quad \text{with} \quad s_{T_2 - T_1}$$

$$= \sqrt{\frac{1}{n_1 - 3} + \frac{1}{n_2 - 3}},$$

where $T_1$ and $T_2$ are the transformed values of $r_1$ and $r_2$. If $H_0$ is true, this test statistic has approximately the standard normal distribution. In Table 9.4, the correlation between housing price and size of home is $r_1 = 0.96$ for the 11 new homes and $r_2 = 0.76$ for the 89 older homes. Find the $P$-value for testing $H_0$: $\rho_1 = \rho_2$ against $H_a$: $\rho_1 \neq \rho_2$. Interpret.

*9.66. Refer to the formula $a = \bar{y} - b\bar{x}$ for the $y$-intercept.

(a) Show that substituting $x = \bar{x}$ into the prediction equation $\hat{y} = a + bx$ yields the predicted $y$-value of $\hat{y} = \bar{y}$. Show that this means that the least squares prediction equation passes through the point with coordinates $(\bar{x}, \bar{y})$, the center of gravity of the data.

(b) Show that an alternative way of expressing the regression model is as $(\hat{y} - \bar{y}) = b(x - \bar{x})$.

(c) Let $y$ = final exam score and $x$ = midterm exam score. Suppose the correlation is 0.70 and the standard deviation is the same for each set of scores. Show that $(\hat{y} - \bar{y}) = 0.70(x - \bar{x})$; that is, the predicted difference between your final exam grade and the class mean is 70% of the difference between your midterm exam score and the class mean, so your score is predicted to regress toward the mean.

*9.67. Alternative formulas for defining the correlation use terms similar to those in the equation for $b$:

$$r = \frac{\sum(x - \bar{x})(y - \bar{y})}{\sqrt{\left[\sum(x - \bar{x})^2\right]\left[\sum(y - \bar{y})^2\right]}}$$

$$= \frac{1}{n - 1}\sum\left(\frac{x - \bar{x}}{s_x}\right)\left(\frac{y - \bar{y}}{s_y}\right).$$

Roughly, the correlation is the average cross-product of the $z$-score for $x$ times the $z$-score for $y$. Using this formula, explain why (a) the correlation has the same value when $x$ predicts $y$ as when $y$ predicts $x$, (b) the correlation does not depend on the units of measurement. (*Note*: For the population, the correlation is often defined as

$$\frac{\text{Covariance of } x \text{ and } y}{(\text{Standard deviation of } x)(\text{Standard deviation of } y)}.$$

The **covariance** between $x$ and $y$ is the average of the cross-products $(x - \mu_x)(y - \mu_y)$ about the population means.)

*9.68. The values of $y$ are multiplied by a constant $c$. From their formulas, show that the standard deviation $s_y$ and the least squares slope $b$ are also then multiplied by $c$. Thus, show that $r = bs_x/s_y$ remains the same, so that $r$ does not depend on the units of measurement.

*9.69. Suppose that the linear regression model $E(y) = \alpha + \beta x$ with normality and constant standard deviation $\sigma$ is truly appropriate. Then the interval of numbers

$$\hat{y} \pm t_{.025}s\sqrt{1 + \frac{1}{n} + \frac{(x - \bar{x})^2}{\sum(x - \bar{x})^2}}$$

predicts where a new observation on $y$ will fall at that value of $x$. This interval, which for large $n$ is roughly $\hat{y} \pm 2s$, is a 95% **prediction interval** for $y$. To make an inference about the *mean* of $y$ (rather than a single value of $y$) at that value of $x$, one can use the **confidence interval**

$$\hat{y} \pm t_{.025}s\sqrt{\frac{1}{n} + \frac{(x - \bar{x})^2}{\sum(x - \bar{x})^2}}.$$

For large $n$ near $\bar{x}$ this is roughly $\hat{y} \pm 2s\sqrt{1/n}$. The $t$-value in these intervals is based on $df = n - 2$. Most software has options for calculating these formulas. Refer to the "house selling price" data file at the text Web site.

(a) Using software, find a 95% prediction interval at house size $x = 2000$.

(b) Using software, find a 95% confidence interval for the mean selling price at house size $x = 2000$.

(c) Explain intuitively why a prediction interval for a single observation is much wider than a confidence interval for the mean.

(d) Explain how prediction intervals would likely be in error if, in fact, (i) the variability in housing prices tends to increase as house size increases, (ii) the response variable is highly discrete, such as $y$ = number of children in Exercise 9.30.

# CHAPTER 10

# Introduction to Multivariate Relationships

Chapters 7–9 introduced methods for analyzing the association between two variables. In most social science research, these analyses are but the first step. Subsequent steps use multivariate methods to include in the analysis other variables that might influence that association.

For instance, Examples 8.1 and 8.3 showed that political party identification in the U.S. is associated with gender, with men more likely than women to be Republicans. To analyze why this is so, we could analyze whether differences between men and women in political ideology (measured on a conservative–liberal scale) could explain the association. For example, perhaps men tend to be more conservative than women, and being conservative tends to be associated with being Republican. If we compare men to women just for those classified as liberal in political ideology, and then again just for those classified as conservative, is it still true that men are more likely than women to be Republicans? Or could the difference between men and women on political party ID be explained by some other factor, such as income, or educational level, or religion?

Several types of research questions require adding variables to the analysis. These questions often involve notions of *causal* connections among the variables. Section 10.1 discusses causation and outlines methods for testing causal assumptions. Section 10.2 introduces *statistical control*, a fundamental tool for studying how an association changes or possibly even disappears after we remove the influence of other variables. Section 10.3 shows types of multivariate relationships that statistical control can reveal.

## 10.1 ASSOCIATION AND CAUSALITY

Causality is central to the scientific endeavor. Most people are familiar with this concept, at least in an informal sense. We know, for instance, that being exposed to a virus can cause the flu and that smoking can cause lung cancer. But how can we judge whether there is a causal relationship between two social science variables? For instance, what causes juvenile delinquency? Being poor? Coming from a single-parent home? A lack of moral and religious training? Genetic factors? A combination of these and other factors? We now look at some guidelines that help us assess a hypothesis of the form, "$X$ causes $Y$." (In this chapter, to emphasize that we are considering probabilistic properties of the variables rather than their particular values, we use uppercase notation for the variables.)

Causal relationships usually have an asymmetry, with one variable having an influence on the other, but not vice versa. An arrow drawn between two variables $X$ and $Y$, pointing to the response variable, denotes a causal association between the variables. Thus,

$$X \rightarrow Y$$

specifies that $X$ is an explanatory variable having a causal influence on $Y$. For example, suppose we suspect that being a Boy Scout has a causal effect on being a juvenile delinquent, scouts being less likely to be delinquents. We are hypothesizing that $S \rightarrow D$, where $S$ (for Scouting) and $D$ (for Delinquency) denote the binary variables "whether a Boy Scout (yes, no)" and "whether a juvenile delinquent (yes, no)."

If we suspect that one variable is causally related to another, how do we analyze whether it actually is? A relationship must satisfy three criteria to be considered a causal one. These criteria, which we'll discuss below, are

- Association between the variables
- An appropriate time order
- The elimination of alternative explanations

If all three are met, then the evidence supports the hypothesized causal relationship. If one or more criteria are not met, then we conclude there is not a causal relationship.

### Association

The first criterion for causality is *association*. We must show that $X$ and $Y$ are associated to support the hypothesis that $X$ causes $Y$. If $X \rightarrow Y$, then as $X$ changes, the distribution of $Y$ should change in some way. If scouting causes lower delinquency rates, for example, then the population proportion of delinquents should be higher for nonscouts than for scouts. For sample data a statistical test, such as a chi-squared test for categorical data or a $t$ test for the regression slope or for a comparison of means for quantitative data, analyzes whether this criterion is satisfied.

Association by itself cannot establish causality.

**Association does not imply causation.**

The remainder of this section explains why.

### Time Order

The second criterion for causality is that the two variables have the appropriate *time order*, with the cause preceding the effect. Sometimes this is just a matter of logic. For instance, race, age, and gender exist prior to current attitudes or achievements, so any causal association must treat them as causes rather than effects.

In other cases, the causal direction is not as obvious. Consider scouting and delinquency. It is logically possible that scouting reduces delinquency tendencies. On the other hand, it is also possible that delinquent boys avoid scouting but nondelinquent boys do not. Thus, the time order is not clear, and both possibilities, $S \rightarrow D$ and $D \rightarrow S$, are plausible. Just showing that an association exists does not solve this dilemma, because a lower proportion of delinquents among scout members is consistent with both explanations.

When a research study is experimental rather than observational, the time order can be fixed. For instance, does a new drug have a beneficial effect in treating a disease? We could randomly assign subjects suffering from the disease to receive either the drug or a placebo. Then, to analyze whether the drug assignment may have a causal influence on the response outcome, we would observe whether the proportion successfully treated was significantly higher for the drug treatment group. The outcome for a subject (success or not) is observed *after* the treatment, so the time order is certain.

It's difficult to study cause and effect when two variables do not have a time order but are measured together over time. The variables may be associated merely because they both have a time trend. Suppose that both the divorce rate and the crime rate have an increasing trend over a 10 year period. They will then have a positive correlation: Higher crime rates occur in years that have higher divorce rates. This does not imply that an increasing divorce rate causes the crime rate to increase. They would also be positively correlated with all other variables that have a positive time trend, such as average selling price of homes, percentage of people who use cell phones, and number of Internet searches on Google.

## Elimination of Alternative Explanation

Suppose two variables are associated and have the proper time order to satisfy a casual relation. This is still insufficient to imply causality. There may be an ***alternative explanation*** for the association.

For example, airline pilots turn on the "fasten seat belt" sign just before their planes encounter turbulence. We observe an association, greater turbulence occurring when the sign is on than when it is off. There's usually also the appropriate time order, the sign coming on, followed by turbulence shortly afterward. But this does not imply that turning on the sign causes turbulence.

An alternative explanation for an association is responsible for rejecting many hypotheses of causal relationships. Many alternative explanations involve an additional variable $Z$ or set of variables. For example, there may be a variable $Z$ that causes both $X$ and $Y$. The relationship may be ***spurious***, as defined in Section 10.3, both $X$ and $Y$ being dependent on $Z$.

With observational data, it's easy to find associations, but those associations are often explained by other variables that may not have been measured in a study. For example, some medical studies have found associations between coffee drinking and various responses, such as the likelihood of a heart attack. But after taking into account other variables associated with the extent of coffee drinking, such as country of residence, occupation, and levels of stress, such associations have disappeared or weakened considerably.

This criterion for causality of eliminating an alternative explanation is the most difficult to achieve. We may think we've found a causal relationship, but we may merely have not thought of a particular reason that can explain the association. Because of this, we can never *prove* that one variable is a cause of another. We can disprove causal hypotheses, however, by showing that empirical evidence contradicts at least one of these three criteria.

## Association, Causality, and Anecdotal Evidence

The association between smoking and lung cancer is one that is now regarded as having a causal link. The association is moderately strong, there is the proper time order (lung cancer following a period of smoking), and no alternative explanation has been found to explain the relationship. In addition, the causal link has been bolstered by biological theories that explain how smoking could cause lung cancer.

Sometimes you hear people give anecdotal evidence to attempt to disprove causal relationships. "My Uncle Reg is 85 years old, he still smokes two packs of cigarettes a day, and he's as healthy as a horse." An association does not need to be perfect, however, to be causal. Not all people who smoke two packs of cigarettes a day will get lung cancer, but a much higher percentage of them will do so than people who are nonsmokers. Perhaps Uncle Reg is still in fine health, but that should not encourage us to tempt the fates by smoking two packs a day. Anecdotal evidence is not enough to disprove causality unless it can deflate one of the three criteria for causality.

## 10.2 CONTROLLING FOR OTHER VARIABLES

A fundamental component to evaluating whether $X$ could cause $Y$ is searching for an alternative explanation. We do this by studying whether the association between $X$ and $Y$ remains when we remove the effects of other variables on this association. In a multivariate analysis, a variable is said to be *controlled* when its influence is removed.

A laboratory experiment controls variables that could affect the results by holding their values constant. For instance, an experiment in chemistry or physics might control temperature and atmospheric pressure by holding them constant in a laboratory environment during the course of the experiment. A lab experiment investigating the effect of different doses of a carcinogen on mice might control the age and diet of the mice.

### Statistical Control in Social Research

Unlike laboratory sciences, social research is usually observational rather than experimental. We cannot fix values of variables we might like to control, such as intelligence or education, before obtaining data on the variables of interest. But we can approximate an experimental type of control by grouping together observations with equal (or similar) values on the control variables. Social class or a related variable such as education or income is often a prime candidate for control in social research. To control education, for instance, we could group the sample results into those subjects with less than a high school education, those with a high school education but no college education, those with some college education, and those with at least one college degree. This is *statistical control*, rather than experimental control.

The following example illustrates statistical control in a social science setting, holding a key variable constant.

### EXAMPLE 10.1    Causal Effect of Height on Math Achievement?

Do tall students tend to be better than short students in learning math skills? We might think so looking at a random sample of students from Lake Wobegon school district who take a math achievement test. The correlation is 0.81 between height and math test score. Taller students tend to have higher scores.

Is being tall a causal influence on math achievement? Perhaps an alternative explanation for this association is that the sample has students of various ages. As age increases, both height and math test score would tend to increase. Older students tend to be taller, and older students tend to have stronger math knowledge.

We can remove the effects of age from the association by *statistical control*, studying the association between height and math test score for students of the same age. That is, we control for age by analyzing the association separately at each age level. Then variation in age cannot jointly cause both variation in height and in test score.

In fact, the achievement test was administered to students from grades 2, 5, and 8 at Lake Wobegon, so the sample contained considerable variability in the students' ages. Figure 10.1 shows a scatterplot of the observations, with labels indicating the grade for each student. The overall pattern of points shows a strong positive correlation,

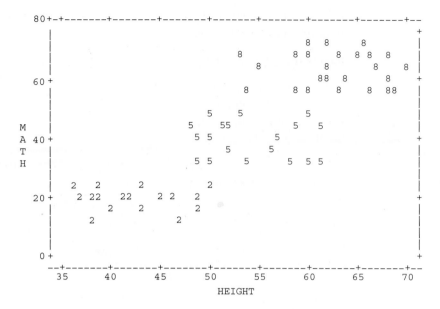

**FIGURE 10.1:** Printout Showing Relationship between Height and Math Achievement Test Score, with Observations Labeled by Grade Level. Students at a particular grade level have about the same age.

with higher math scores at higher heights. View the points within a fixed grade level (for which age is approximately constant), however, and you see random variation, with no particular pattern of increase or decrease. The correlation between height and math test score is close to zero for students of about the same age. Height does not have a causal effect on test score, because the association disappears when age is held constant. ∎

In summary, we control a variable by holding its value constant. We can then study the relationship between $X$ and $Y$ for cases with equal (or similar) values of that variable. The variable controlled is called a **control variable**. In holding the control variable constant, we remove the influence of that variable on the association between $X$ and $Y$.

### Types of Association for Statistical Control

The scatterplot in Figure 10.1 describes the association between two quantitative variables, controlling for a third variable. We can describe association between a quantitative variable and a categorical variable by comparing means. For example, at your school suppose the mean income for male faculty is higher than the mean income for female faculty. Suppose male professors tend to be older and more experienced, relatively few female professors having been hired until recent years. Then this difference would diminish and could even disappear if we control for academic rank or for number of years since received highest degree. See Exercise 18 for an example of this type. If relatively more female faculty are in low-salary colleges (Arts and Science, Education) and relatively more male faculty are in high-salary colleges (Medical School, Law, Engineering), this difference would diminish and possibly disappear if we control for college of employment.

To study the association between two categorical variables, while controlling for a third variable, we form contingency tables relating those variables separately for subjects at each level of that control variable. The separate tables that display the relationships within the fixed levels of the control variable are called ***partial tables***.

### EXAMPLE 10.2 Statistical Control for Scouting and Delinquency

Table 10.1 is a hypothetical table relating scouting to delinquency. The percentage of delinquents among scout members is lower than among nonscouts. This table is ***bivariate***, meaning that it contains data only on *two* variables. All other variables are ignored. None is controlled.

**TABLE 10.1:** Contingency Table Relating Scouting and Delinquency

|  |  | Delinquency | | |
|---|---|---|---|---|
|  |  | Yes | No | Total |
| Boy Scout | Yes | 36 (9%) | 364 (91%) | 400 |
|  | No | 60 (15%) | 340 (85%) | 400 |

In seeking a possible explanation for the association, let's control for church attendance. Perhaps boys who attend church are more likely than nonattenders to be scouts, and perhaps boys who attend church are less likely to be delinquent. Then the difference in delinquency rates between scouts and nonscouts might be due to variation in church attendance.

To control for church attendance, we examine the association between scouting and delinquency within partial tables formed by various levels of church attendance. Table 10.2 shows partial tables for three levels: Low = no more than once a year, Medium = more than once a year but less than once a week, High = at least once a week. Adding these three partial tables together produces the bivariate table (Table 10.1), which ignores church attendance. For instance, the number of Boy Scouts who are delinquents is 36 = 10 + 18 + 8.

**TABLE 10.2:** Contingency Table Relating Scouting and Delinquency, Controlling for Church Attendance

|  |  | Church Attendance | | | | | |
|---|---|---|---|---|---|---|---|
|  |  | Low | | Medium | | High | |
| Delinquency |  | Yes | No | Yes | No | Yes | No |
| Scout | Yes | 10 (20%) | 40 (80%) | 18 (12%) | 132 (88%) | 8 (4%) | 192 (96%) |
|  | No | 40 (20%) | 160 (80%) | 18 (12%) | 132 (88%) | 2 (4%) | 48 (96%) |

In each partial table, the percentage of delinquents is the same for scouts as for nonscouts. Controlling for church attendance, no association appears between scouting and delinquency. These data provide an alternative explanation for the association between scouting and delinquency, making us skeptical of any causal links. The alternative explanation is that both these variables depend on church attendance. Youngsters who attend church are less likely to be delinquents and more likely to be scouts. For a fixed level of church attendance, scouting has no association with delinquency. Since the association can be explained by a dependence on church attendance, no causal link exists between scouting and delinquency. ■

Some of the examples in this chapter use artificial data in order to clarify relationships and to make it simpler to explain the concepts. In practice, some distortion occurs because of sampling variation. Even if an association between two variables truly disappears under a control, *sample* partial tables would not look exactly like those in Table 10.2. Because of sampling variation, they would not show a *complete* lack of association. Moreover, few associations disappear *completely* under a control. There may be *some* causal connection between two variables, even within each partial table, but not as strong as the bivariate table suggests.

### Be Wary of Lurking Variables

It is not always obvious which variables require control in a study. Knowing about the theory and previous research in a field of study helps a researcher to know which variables to control. A potential pitfall of almost all social science research is the possibility that an important variable was not included in the study. If you fail to control for a variable that strongly influences the association between the variables of primary interest, you will obtain misleading results.

A variable that is *not* measured in a study (or perhaps even known about to the researchers) but that influences the association of interest is sometimes referred to as a *lurking variable*. In interpreting the positive correlation between height and math achievement in Example 10.1 (page 304), we'd be remiss if we failed to realize that the correlation could be due to a lurking variable, such as age of student.

When you read about a study that reports an association, see if you can think of a lurking variable that could be responsible for that association. For example, suppose a study reports a positive correlation between individuals' college GPA and their income later in life. Is doing well in school responsible for the higher income? An alternative explanation is that high GPA and high income could both be caused by a lurking variable such as individuals' tendency to work hard.

## 10.3    TYPES OF MULTIVARIATE RELATIONSHIPS

Section 10.2 showed that an association may change dramatically when we control for another variable. This section describes types of multivariate relationships that often occur in social science research. We denote the response variable by $Y$. In practice, there may be several explanatory variables and control variables, and we denote them by $X_1, X_2, \ldots$ .

### Spurious Associations

An association between $X_1$ and $Y$ is said to be *spurious* if both variables are dependent on a third variable $X_2$, and their association disappears when $X_2$ is controlled. Such an association results from the relationship of $X_1$ and $Y$ with the control variable $X_2$, rather than indicating a causal connection. The $X_1 Y$ association disappears when we remove the effect of $X_2$ by holding it constant. Showing that the association between two variables is spurious disproves the hypothesis of a causal connection between them.

### EXAMPLE 10.3    Examples of Spurious Associations

The association between height and mathematics achievement test score in Example 10.1 disappears at fixed levels of age. That association is spurious, with age being a common cause of both height and math achievement.

Table 10.1 (page 306) displayed an association between scouting and delinquency. Controlling for church attendance, the partial tables in Table 10.2 (page 306) showed no association. This is also consistent with spuriousness. Table 10.2 shows that as church attendance increases, the percentage of delinquents decreases (compare percentages across the partial tables) and the percentage of scout members increases. By the nature of these two associations, it is not surprising that Table 10.1 exhibits lower overall delinquency rates for scouts than nonscouts. ■

Figure 10.2 graphically depicts a spurious association, using $X_1$ = height and $Y$ = math test score. They are associated only because they both depend on a common cause, $X_2$ = age. As $X_2$ changes, it produces changes simultaneously in $X_1$ and $Y$, so that $X_1$ and $Y$ are associated. In fact, they are associated only because of their common dependence on the third variable (age).

**FIGURE 10.2:** Graphical Depiction of a Spurious Association between $X_1$ and $Y$. The association disappears when we control for $X_2$, which causally affects both $X_1$ and $Y$.

## EXAMPLE 10.4 Do Fewer Vacations Cause Increased Risk of Death?

When an association is observed between two variables, later studies often attempt to determine whether that association might be spurious by controlling for variables that could be a common cause. For example, some studies have observed an association between frequency of vacationing and quality of health. In particular, a study using a 20-year follow-up of women participants in the Framingham Heart Study found[1] that less frequent vacationing was associated with greater frequency of deaths from heart attacks.

A later study[2] questioned whether this could be a spurious association, explained by the effects of socioeconomic status (SES). For example, perhaps higher SES is responsible both for lower mortality and for more frequent vacations. But after controlling for education, family income, and other potentially important variables with a much larger data set, this study also observed higher risk of heart disease and related death for those who took less vacation time. Perhaps the association is not spurious, unless researchers find another variable to control such that the association disappears. ■

## Chain Relationships

Spurious associations are not the only ones for which the association disappears when we control for a third variable. Another way is with a *chain* of causation, in which $X_1$ affects $X_2$, which in turn affects $Y$. Figure 10.3 depicts the chain. Here, $X_1$ is an *indirect*, rather than direct, cause of $Y$. Variable $X_2$ is called an ***intervening variable*** (or sometimes a ***mediator*** variable).

$$X_1 \longrightarrow X_2 \longrightarrow Y$$

**FIGURE 10.3:** A Chain Relationship, in Which $X_1$ Indirectly Affects $Y$ through an Intervening Variable $X_2$

[1] E. D. Eaker et al., *Amer. J. Epidemiology*, vol. 135, 1992, pp. 835–864.
[2] B. B. Gump and K. A. Matthews, *Psychosomatic Medicine*, vol. 62, 2000, pp. 608–612.

## EXAMPLE 10.5    Is Education Responsible for a Long Life?

A *New York Times* article (by G. Kolata, January 3, 2007) summarized research studies dealing with human longevity. It noted that consistently across studies in many nations, life length was positively associated with educational attainment. Many researchers believe education is the most important variable in explaining how long a person lives. Is having more education responsible for having a longer life?

Establishing causal connections are difficult. In some societies, perhaps the causation could go in the other direction, with sick children not going to school or dropping out early because they were ill. Many researchers believe there could be a chain of causation, perhaps with income as an intervening variable. For example, perhaps having more education leads to greater wealth, which then (possibly for a variety of reasons, such as access to better health care) leads to living longer. Figure 10.4 depicts this causal chain model.

**FIGURE 10.4:** Example of a Chain Relationship. Income is an intervening variable, and the association between education and life length disappears when it is controlled.

Support for this model occurs if the association between education and life length disappears after controlling for income; that is, if within fixed levels of income (the intervening variable), no significant association occurs. If this happens, education does not directly affect life length, but it is an indirect cause through income.    ■

For both spurious relationships and chain relationships, an association between $Y$ and $X_1$ disappears when we control for a third variable, $X_2$. The difference between the two is in the causal order among the variables. For a spurious association, $X_2$ is causally prior to both $X_1$ and $Y$ (as in Figure 10.2), whereas in a chain association $X_2$ intervenes between the two (as in Figure 10.3).

To illustrate, a study[3] of mortality rates in the U.S. found that states that had more income inequality tended to have higher age-adjusted mortality rates. However, this association disappeared after controlling for the percentage of a state's residents that had at least a high school education. Might this reflect a chain relationship or a spurious relationship? Greater education could tend to result in less income inequality, which could in turn tend to result in lower mortality rates. Thus, the chain relationship

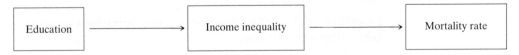

is plausible. For the relationship to be spurious, education would need to have a causal effect on both income inequality and mortality. This is also plausible. Just from viewing the association patterns, we don't know which provides a better explanation.

### Multiple Causes

Response variables in social science research almost always have more than one cause. For instance, a variety of factors likely have causal influences on responses

---

[3] A. Muller, *BMJ*, vol. 324, 2002, pp. 23–25.

such as $Y$ = juvenile delinquency or $Y$ = length of life. Figure 10.5 depicts $X_1$ and $X_2$ as separate causes of $Y$. We say that $Y$ has **multiple causes**.

**FIGURE 10.5:** Graphical Depiction of Multiple Causes of $Y$

Sometimes variables that are separate causes of $Y$ are themselves statistically independent. That is, they are *independent causes*. For instance, $X_1$ = gender and $X_2$ = race are essentially statistically independent. If they both have effects on juvenile delinquency, with delinquency rates varying both according to gender and race, they are likely to be independent causes.

In the social sciences, most explanatory variables are associated. Both being poor and being from a single-parent family may cause delinquency, but those factors are themselves probably associated. Because of complex association linkages, when we control for a variable $X_2$ or a set of variables $X_2, X_3, \ldots$, the $X_1Y$ association usually changes somewhat. Often the association decreases somewhat, although usually it does not completely disappear as in a spurious or chain relationship. Sometimes this is because $X_1$ has direct effects on $Y$ and also indirect effects through other variables. Figure 10.6 illustrates. For instance, perhaps being from a single-parent family has direct effects on delinquency but also indirect effects through being more likely to be poor. Most response variables have many causes, both direct and indirect.

**FIGURE 10.6:** Graphical Depiction of Direct and Indirect Effects of $X_1$ on $Y$

## Suppressor Variables

So far, we have discussed examples in which an association disappears or changes when we control for another variable. By contrast, occasionally two variables show no association until a third variable is controlled. That control variable is called a **suppressor variable**.

### EXAMPLE 10.6 Age Suppresses the Association between Education and Income

Is educational level positively related with income? Table 10.3 shows such a relationship, measured as binary variables, controlling for age. In each partial table, the

**TABLE 10.3:** Partial Tables Relating Education and Income, Controlling for Age

|  |  | Age = Low | | | Age = High | | |
|---|---|---|---|---|---|---|---|
|  | Income | High | Low | % High | High | Low | % High |
| Education | High | 125 | 225 | 35.7% | 125 | 25 | 83.3% |
|  | Low | 25 | 125 | 16.7% | 225 | 125 | 64.3% |

percentage of subjects at the high level of income is greater when education is high than when education is low.

Suppose now that we ignore age, adding these two partial tables together. The bivariate table for education and income is the first panel of Table 10.4. Every count equals 250. Both when education is high and when education is low, the percentage having a high income is 50%. For the bivariate table, no association exists between education and income.

**TABLE 10.4:** Bivariate Tables Relating Education, Income, and Age

| | Income | | | Income | | | Education | |
|---|---|---|---|---|---|---|---|---|
| Education | High | Low | Age | High | Low | Age | High | Low |
| High | 250 | 250 | High | 350 | 150 | High | 150 | 350 |
| Low | 250 | 250 | Low | 150 | 350 | Low | 350 | 150 |

A look at the other two bivariate tables in Table 10.4 reveals how this could happen. Age is positively associated with income but negatively associated with education. Older subjects tend to have higher income, but they tend to have lower education. Thus, when we ignore rather than control age, we give an inadvertent boost to the relative numbers of people at high incomes with low educational levels and at low incomes with high educational levels.    ■

Because of the potential for suppressor variables, it can be informative to control for other variables even when bivariate analyses do not show an association. However, see Pedhazur (1997, pp. 186–188) for a discussion of the importance of having some theoretical reason for expecting suppression effects.

## ✗ Statistical Interaction

Often the effect of an explanatory variable on a response variable changes according to the level of another explanatory variable or control variable. When the true effect of $X_1$ on $Y$ changes at different levels of $X_2$, the relationship is said to exhibit *statistical interaction*.

---
**Statistical Interaction**

---
***Statistical interaction*** exists between $X_1$ and $X_2$ in their effects on $Y$ when the true effect of one predictor on $Y$ changes as the value of the other predictor changes.

---

### EXAMPLE 10.7    Interaction between Education and Gender in Modeling Income

Consider the relationship between $Y$ = annual income (in thousands of dollars) and $X_1$ = number of years of education, by $X_2$ = gender. Many studies in the U.S. have found that the slope for a regression equation relating $Y$ to $X_1$ is larger for men than for women. Suppose that in the population, the regression equations are $E(y) = -10 + 4x_1$ for men and $E(y) = -5 + 2x_1$ for women. On the average, income for men increases by $4000 for every year of education, whereas for women it increases by $2000 for every year of education. That is, the effect of education on income varies according to gender, with the effect being greater for men than for women. So there is interaction between education and gender in their effects on income.    ■

### EXAMPLE 10.8 Interaction between SES and Age in Quality of Health

An article[4] using a sample of Canadians from the *National Population Health Survey* noted that quality of health (measured by self-rated and health indexes) tends to be positively correlated with SES (measured by years of education and annual household income). Moreover, the association strengthens with age. For example, the gap in health between low SES and high SES levels tends to be larger at older ages. Thus, there is interaction between SES and age in their effects on health. ■

To assess whether a sample shows evidence of interaction, we can compare the effect of $X_1$ on $Y$ at different levels of $X_2$. When the sample effect is similar at each level of $X_2$, it's simpler to use statistical analyses that assume an absence of interaction. The interaction is worth noting when the variability in effects is large. For instance, perhaps the association is positive at one level of $X_2$ and negative at another, or strong at one level and weak or nonexistent at another. In future chapters we'll learn how to analyze inferentially whether sample data provide strong evidence of interaction in the population.

Figure 10.7 depicts a three-variable relationship having statistical interaction. Here, $X_2$ affects the relationship between $X_1$ and $Y$. When this happens, then likewise $X_1$ affects the relationship between $X_2$ and $Y$.

**FIGURE 10.7:** Graphical Depiction of Statistical Interaction. The effect of one predictor on $Y$ depends on the level of the other predictor.

Suppose there is *no* interaction between $X_1$ and $X_2$ in their effects on $Y$. This does not mean that $X_1$ and $X_2$ have no association. There can be a lack of statistical interaction even when all the variables are associated. For instance, Tables 10.2 and 10.3 showed no interaction—in each case the association was similar in each partial table. However, in each case the predictors were associated, with each other and with the response. In Table 10.3, for instance, age was negatively associated with education and positively associated with income.

### Summary of Multivariate Relationships

In summary,

- For spurious relationships (i.e., $X_2$ affects both $X_1$ and $Y$) and chain relationships ($X_2$ intervenes between $X_1$ and $Y$), the $X_1Y$ association disappears when we control for $X_2$.
- For multiple causes, an association may change under a control but does not disappear.
- When there is a suppressor variable, an association appears only under the control.
- When there is statistical interaction, an association has different strengths and/or directions at different values of a control variable.

This list does not exhaust the possible association structures. It is even possible that, after controlling for a variable, each association in a partial table has the

---

[4]S. G. Prus, *Canadian J. on Aging*, vol. 23, Supplement, 2004, pp. S145–S153.

opposite direction as the bivariate association. This is called ***Simpson's paradox*** and is illustrated in Exercises 10.14, 10.29, and 10.30.

### Confounding Makes Assessing Effects Difficult

When two explanatory variables both have effects on a response variable but are also associated with each other, there is said to be ***confounding***. It is difficult to determine whether either of them truly causes the response, because a variable's effect could be at least partly due to its association with the other variable. We usually observe a different effect on $Y$ for a variable when we control for the other variable than when we ignore it.

Confounding is inevitable in social science research. It is the main reason it is difficult to study many issues of importance, such as what causes crime or what causes the economy to improve or what causes students to succeed in school.

## 10.4  INFERENTIAL ISSUES IN STATISTICAL CONTROL

To conduct research well, you must select the key variables, determine which variables to control, choose an appropriate model, and analyze the data and interpret the results properly. The first three sections of this chapter have bypassed inferential matters to avoid confusing them with the new concepts presented. We now discuss some inferential issues in studying associations while controlling other variables.

### Effects of Smaller Sample Size in Partial Analyses

Suppose we control for $X_2$ in studying the $X_1Y$ association. The sample size at a fixed level of $X_2$ may be much smaller than in the full data set. Even if no reduction in association occurs relative to the full data, standard errors of parameter estimators tend to be larger. Thus, confidence intervals for those parameters at fixed levels of $X_2$ tend to be wider, and test statistic values tend to be smaller.

For categorical data, for example, we could compute the $\chi^2$ statistic within a particular partial table to test whether the variables are independent at that level of $X_2$. This $\chi^2$ value may be small relative to the $\chi^2$ value for the bivariate $X_1Y$ table. This could be due partly to a weaker association, but it could also reflect the reduction in sample size. Section 8.4 showed that larger sample sizes tend to produce larger $\chi^2$ values, for a particular degree of association.

### Effects of Categorization in Controlling a Variable

For simplicity, the control variables in the examples of this chapter had only a few categories. In practice, avoid overly crude categorizations of quantitative control variables. The greater the number of control levels, the more nearly constant the control variable is within each partial table. Unless the control variable *naturally* has only two levels (e.g., gender), it is usually better to use at least three or four partial tables.

On the other hand, it's preferable not to use too many partial tables, because then each one may have a small sample size. Separate estimates may have large standard errors, resulting in imprecise inferences within the partial tables and comparisons of associations between tables. Fortunately, the advanced model-building methods presented in the rest of the text allow us to conduct statistical control and assess patterns of association and interaction without necessarily performing separate analyses at the various combinations of levels of the control variables.

### Comparing and Pooling Measures

It is often useful to compare parameter values describing the effect of a predictor on a response at different levels of a control variable. You can construct a confidence interval for a difference between two parameter values in the same way as Chapter 7 showed for a difference of proportions or a difference of means. Suppose that the two sample estimates are based on independent random samples, with standard errors $se_1$ and $se_2$. Then Section 7.1 noted that the standard error for the difference between the estimates is $\sqrt{(se_1)^2 + (se_2)^2}$. For large random samples, most estimates have approximately normal sampling distributions. Then a confidence interval for the difference between the parameters is

$$(\text{Estimate}_2 - \text{Estimate}_1) \pm z\sqrt{(se_1)^2 + (se_2)^2}.$$

If the interval does not include 0, the evidence suggests that the parameter values differ.

**EXAMPLE 10.9    Comparing Happiness Associations for Men and Women**

Is there a difference between men and women in the association between happiness and marital happiness? For data from the 2004 GSS on variables HAPPY and HAPMAR, the sample value of gamma for the $3 \times 3$ table relating these two ordinal variables is 0.674 ($se = 0.0614$, $n = 326$) for males and 0.689 ($se = 0.0599$, $n = 350$) for females.

A 95% confidence interval for the difference between the population values of gamma is

$$(0.689 - 0.674) \pm 1.96\sqrt{(0.0614)^2 + (0.0599)^2}, \quad \text{or} \quad 0.015 \pm 0.168,$$

which is $(-0.153, 0.183)$. It is plausible that the population gamma values are identical. If they are not, they are not very different. ∎

When the association between two variables is similar in the partial analyses, we can form a measure that summarizes the strength of the association, conditional on the control variable. This is referred to as a measure of *partial association*. The rest of the text shows how to do this in various situations, using models that handle all the variables at once.

## 10.5   CHAPTER SUMMARY

It is necessary to use a multivariate analysis to study effects on a response variable well. To demonstrate a causal relationship, we must show *association* between variables, ensure proper *time order*, and *eliminate alternative explanations* for the association.

To consider alternative explanations, we introduce *control variables*. We perform statistical control by analyzing associations while keeping the values of control variables essentially constant. This helps us to detect

- *Spuriousness*, in which $X_2$ jointly affects both $Y$ and $X_1$
- *Chain relationships*, in which $X_2$ is an *intervening variable*, so that $X_1$ affects $Y$ indirectly through its effects on $X_2$
- *Suppressor variables*, in which the $X_1Y$ association appears only after controlling for $X_2$
- *Statistical interaction*, in which the effect of $X_1$ on $Y$ varies according to the value of $X_2$

Table 10.5 summarizes some possible relationships. The remainder of this text presents statistical methods for multivariate relationships. As you learn about these methods, be careful not to overextend your conclusions: Realize the limitations in

**TABLE 10.5:** Some Three-Variable Relationships

| Graph | Name of Relationship | What Happens after Controlling for $X_2$ |
|---|---|---|
| $X_2 \nearrow X_1$ $\searrow Y$ | Spurious $X_1 Y$ association | Association between $X_1$ and $Y$ disappears. |
| $X_1 \longrightarrow X_2 \longrightarrow Y$ | Chain relationship; $X_2$ intervenes; $X_1$ indirectly causes $Y$ | Association between $X_1$ and $Y$ disappears. |
| $X_2$ $\downarrow$ $X_1 \longrightarrow Y$ | Interaction | Association between $X_1$ and $Y$ varies according to level of $X_2$. |
| $X_2 \searrow Y$ $X_1 \nearrow$ | Multiple causes | Association between $X_1$ and $Y$ does not change. |
| $X_1 \longrightarrow Y$ $\searrow X_2 \nearrow$ | Both direct and indirect effects of $X_1$ on $Y$ | Association between $X_1$ and $Y$ changes, but does not disappear. |

making causal inferences with inferential data, and keep in mind that any inferences you make must usually be tentative because of assumptions that may be violated or lurking variables that you did not include in your analyses. For further discussion of these points in the context of regression modeling, see Berk (2004), Freedman (2005), and Pedhazur (1997).

## PROBLEMS

### Practicing the Basics

**10.1.** State the three criteria for a causal relationship. For each, describe a relationship between two variables that is not causal because that criterion would be violated.

**10.2.** A young child wonders what causes women to have babies. For each woman who lives on her block, she observes whether her hair is gray and whether she has young children. The four women with gray hair do not have young children, whereas all five women not having gray hair have young children. Noticing this association, the child concludes that not having gray hair is what causes women to have children.
(a) Form the contingency table displaying the data.
(b) Use this example to explain why association does not imply causation.

**10.3.** For all fires in Chicago last year, data are available on $X$ = number of firefighters at the fire and $Y$ = cost of damages due to the fire. The correlation is positive.
(a) Does this mean that having more firefighters at a fire causes the damage to be worse? Explain.

(b) Identify a third variable that could be a common cause of $X$ and $Y$. Construct a hypothetical scatterplot (like Figure 10.1), identifying points according to their value on the third variable, to illustrate your argument.

**10.4.** Cities in the U.S. have a positive correlation between $Y$ = crime rate and $X$ = size of police force. Does this imply that $X$ causes $Y$? Explain.

**10.5.** An association exists between college GPA and whether a college student has ever used marijuana. Explain how
(a) The direction of a causal arrow might go in either direction.
(b) A third variable might be responsible for the association.

**10.6.** Explain what it means to *control* for a variable; use an example to illustrate.

**10.7.** Explain what is meant by a *spurious* association; draw a scatter diagram to illustrate.
(a) Illustrate using $X_1$ = shoe size, $X_2$ = age, and $Y$ = number of books one has ever read, for children from schools in Winnipeg, Canada.
(b) Illustrate using $X_1$ = height, $X_2$ = gender, and $Y$ = annual income, for a random sample of adults. Suppose that, overall, men tend

to be taller and have higher income, on the average, than females.

**10.8.** Figure 9.17 on page 285 of Chapter 9 showed a negative correlation between birth rate and television ownership. Identify a variable to help explain how this association could be spurious.

**10.9.** An Associated Press story (February 15, 2002) quoted a study at the University of California at San Diego that reported, based on a nationwide survey, that those who averaged at least 8 hours sleep a night were 12% more likely to die within six years than those who averaged 6.5 to 7.5 hours of sleep a night.

   (a) Explain how the subject's age could be positively associated both with time spent sleeping and with an increased death rate and hence could explain the association between sleeping and the death rate.

   (b) If the association disappears when we control for subject's age, do you think age is more likely to be a common cause or an intervening variable?

**10.10.** A study found that children who eat breakfast get better math grades than those who do not eat breakfast. This result was based on the association between $X$ = whether eat breakfast (yes, no) and $Y$ = grade in last math course taken. How might this result be spurious, and how could you check for that possibility?

**10.11.** Suppose race is related to frequency of juvenile arrests, with black juveniles more likely to be arrested than white juveniles. A possible chain relationship explanation is that (1) race affects family income, with blacks tending to have lower family incomes than whites, and (2) being poor increases the chance of being arrested as a juvenile. Show a figure to portray the chain relationship. To support this explanation, what would need to happen to the difference between the arrest rates for whites and blacks after controlling for family income?

**10.12.** A study at your university finds that of those who applied to its graduate school last year, the percentage admitted was *higher* for the male applicants than for the female applicants. However, for each department that received applications, the percentage admitted was *lower* for the male applicants than for the female applicants. How could this possibly happen? In your answer, explain what plays the role of the response variable, the explanatory variable, the control variable, the bivariate table, and the partial tables. (Exercise 12 in Chapter 15 shows data that have similar behavior.)

**10.13.** Table 10.6 relates occupational level (white collar, blue collar) and political party choice, controlling for income.

   (a) Construct the bivariate table between occupational level and political party, ignoring income. Is there an association? If so, describe it.

   (b) Do the partial tables display an association? Interpret them.

   (c) Using the nature of the association between income and each of the other variables, explain why the bivariate table has such different association than the partial tables.

   (d) Construct a chain diagram that might explain the relationships, identifying the intervening variable.

   (e) Show that the data are also consistent with a spurious association, and draw the corresponding diagram. Which diagram seems more appropriate? Why?

**10.14.** In murder trials[5] in 20 Florida counties in two years, the death penalty was given in 19 out of 151 cases in which a white killed a white, in 0 out of 9 cases in which a white killed a black, in 11 out of 63 cases in which a black killed a white, and in 6 out of 103 cases in which a black killed a black.

   (a) Construct partial tables relating defendant's race and the death penalty verdict, controlling for victim's race. In those tables, compare the proportions of white and black defendants who received the death penalty.

   (b) Construct the bivariate table, ignoring victim's race. Describe the association, and compare to (a).

**TABLE 10.6**

| | | High Income | | Medium High Income | | Medium Low Income | | Low Income | |
|---|---|---|---|---|---|---|---|---|---|
| | | White Collar | Blue Collar | White Collar | Blue Collar | White Collar | Blue Collar | White Collar | Blue Collar |
| Party | Democrat | 45 | 5 | 100 | 25 | 75 | 300 | 45 | 405 |
| | Republican | 405 | 45 | 300 | 75 | 25 | 100 | 5 | 45 |

[5]From M. Radelet, *American Sociological Review*, vol. 46, 1981, pp. 918–927.

(c) *Simpson's paradox* states that the associations in partial tables can all have a different direction than the association in the bivariate table. Show that these data satisfy Simpson's paradox, with white defendants having a lower or higher chance of the death penalty than black defendants according to whether we control victim's race.

(d) By describing how victim's race is associated with each of these variables, explain why the partial association differs as it does from the bivariate association.

(e) For these variables, indicate whether each of the following diagrams seems to provide a reasonable model. Give your reasoning. (Here, $P$ = death penalty, $D$ = defendant's race, $V$ = victim's race.)

(i.) $V \nearrow^{P}_{\searrow D}$     (ii.) $D \longrightarrow V \longrightarrow P$

(iii.) $\begin{array}{c} D \searrow \\ \nearrow P \\ V \end{array}$     (iv.) $D \longrightarrow P \searrow \nearrow V$

**10.15.** For the data on house sales shown partly in Table 9.4 on page 278, the number of bedrooms has a moderately strong positive correlation with selling price. Controlling for size of home, however, this association diminishes greatly.

(a) Explain how this could happen, illustrating with a diagram showing potential direct and indirect effects of number of bedrooms on selling price.

(b) Explain what it means to say that there is *confounding* in the effects of size of home and number of bedrooms in their effects on the selling price.

**10.16.** For Table 9.16 in Exercise 9.39 on page 297 in Chapter 9, giving countywide data in Florida for several variables, a moderate positive correlation ($r = 0.47$) exists between crime rate and percent who are high school graduates. The percentage living in urban areas is also strongly correlated with crime rate ($r = 0.68$) and with high school graduation rate ($r = 0.79$).

(a) Explain why the association between crime rate and high school graduation rate could

disappear, or even change direction, when we control for percentage living in urban areas.

(b) Under the control in (a), if the association disappears, which type of relationship is more plausible—a spurious relationship or a chain relationship? Explain.

**10.17.** Opposition to the legal availability of abortion is stronger among the very religious than the nonreligious, and it is also stronger among those with conservative sexual attitudes than those with more permissive attitudes. Draw a three-variable diagram of how these variables might be related, treating abortion attitude as the response variable. (*Note*: More than one diagram is plausible.)

**10.18.** Table 10.7 lists the mean salary, in thousands of dollars, of faculty on nine-month contracts in U.S. institutions of higher education in 2003–2004, by gender and academic rank.

(a) Suppose that gender is the explanatory variable. Identify the response variable and the control variable.

(b) Describe the bivariate relationship between gender and salary.

(c) Describe the relationship between gender and salary, controlling for academic rank.

(d) A hypothesis of interest for these variables is "Controlling for academic rank, annual salary and gender are independent." Draw a causal diagram that is consistent with this hypothesis. Refer to your interpretation in part (c), and comment on whether the hypothesis seems plausible.

(e) The overall difference of 12.1 thousand dollars between mean income of men and women is larger than the difference for each academic rank. Explain how this could be.

**TABLE 10.8**

| Gender | Math | | Verbal | |
|---|---|---|---|---|
| | $y = 1$ | $y = 2$ | $y = 1$ | $y = 2$ |
| Females | 100 | 50 | 50 | 100 |
| Males | 50 | 100 | 100 | 50 |

**TABLE 10.7**

| Gender | Academic Rank | | | | |
|---|---|---|---|---|---|
| | Professor | Associate | Assistant | Instructor | Overall |
| Men | 88.3 | 63.5 | 53.7 | 51.0 | 67.5 |
| Women | 76.7 | 59.1 | 49.7 | 47.4 | 55.4 |

*Source*: National Center for Education Statistics, *Digest of Education Statistics, 2004*, Table 236.

**10.19.** Table 10.8 relates $Y$ = exam score (1 = below median, 2 = above median) to gender, controlling for subject of exam (Math, Verbal). Show that subject of exam is a suppressor variable.

**10.20.** When we analyze data for the census tracts in the greater Los Angeles area, we find no significant correlation between median tax bill and median lot size. Yet a considerable positive correlation occurs when we control for the percentage of the tract used for business. Explain how the percentage of the tract used for businesses could be a suppressor variable if it is positively correlated with median tax bill and negatively correlated with median lot size.

**10.21.** According to the U.S. Census Bureau, in 2000 the population median income was estimated to be $29,661 for white females, $25,736 for black females, $40,350 for white males, $30,886 for black males. Compare the difference in median incomes between males and females for (a) white subjects (b) black subjects. If these are close estimates of the population medians, explain why there is interaction and describe its nature.

**10.22.** For lower-level managerial employees of a fast-food chain, the prediction equation relating $Y$ = annual income (thousands of dollars) to $X_1$ = number of years experience on the job equals $\hat{y} = 14.2 + 1.1x_1$ for males and $\hat{y} = 14.2 + 0.4x_1$ for females. Explain how these equations show evidence of statistical interaction.

**10.23.** A study of the association between whether a smoker (yes, no) and whether have had some form of cancer (yes, no) has odds ratio 1.1 for subjects of age less than 30, 2.4 for subjects of age 30 to 50, and 4.3 for subjects of age over 50.
   **(a)** Identify the response variable, explanatory variable, and control variable.
   **(b)** Does the study show evidence of interaction? Explain.

**10.24.** A study of students at Oregon State University found an association between frequency of church attendance and favorability toward the legalization of marijuana. Both variables were measured in ordered categories. When gender of student was controlled, the gamma measures for the two partial tables were

   Males: gamma = $-0.287$, standard error = 0.081

   Females: gamma = $-0.581$, standard error
   $= 0.091$

   **(a)** Interpret the sample gamma values.
   **(b)** These results show a slight degree of _____, since the association is somewhat stronger for females than males.
   **(c)** Construct and interpret a 95% confidence interval for the difference between the population gamma values.

## Concepts and Applications

**10.25.** Refer to the "Student survey" data file (Exercise 1.11 on page 7). Construct partial tables relating opinion about abortion to opinion about life after death, controlling for attendance at religious services, measured using the two categories, (Never or occasionally, Most weeks or every week). Prepare a report (a) posing and interpreting a possible arrow diagram, before you analyze the data, for relationships among the variables; (b) interpreting the sample associations in the bivariate table and the partial tables; (c) revising, if necessary, your arrow diagram based on the evidence in the sample data.

**10.26.** For the student survey data (Exercise 1.11), are there any pairs of variables for which you expect the association to disappear under control for a third variable? Explain.

**10.27.** Using the most recent GSS, construct a contingency table relating gender (GSS variable SEX) and party identification (PARTYID). Is there still a gender gap? Control for political ideology (POLVIEWS) by forming partial tables for the most conservative and the most liberal subjects. Does the association seem to persist for these subjects?

**10.28.** Suppose that $X_1$ = father's education is positively associated with $Y$ = son's income at age 40. However, for the regression analysis conducted separately at fixed levels of $X_2$ = son's education, the correlation does not differ significantly from zero. Do you thing this is more likely to reflect a chain relationship or a spurious relationship? Explain.

**10.29.** Table 10.9 shows the mean number of children in Canadian families, classified by whether the family was English speaking or French speaking and by whether the family lived in Quebec or in another province. Let $Y$ = number of children in family, $X_1$ = primary language of family, and $X_2$ = province (Quebec, others).
   **(a)** Describe the association between $Y$ and $X_1$, based on the overall means in this table.
   **(b)** Describe the association between $Y$ and $X_1$, controlling for $X_2$.

**TABLE 10.9**

| Province | English | French |
|---|---|---|
| Quebec | 1.64 | 1.80 |
| Other | 1.97 | 2.14 |
| **Overall** | 1.95 | 1.85 |

   **(c)** Explain how it is possible that for each level of province the mean is higher for French speaking families yet overall the mean is higher for English speaking families. (This illustrates *Simpson's paradox*. See Exercise 10.14.)

**10.30.** Eighth-grade math scores on the National Assessment of Educational Progress had means of 277 in Nebraska and 271 in New Jersey. For white students the means were 281 in Nebraska and 283 in New Jersey. For black students, the means were 236 in Nebraska and 242 in New Jersey. For other nonwhite students, the means were 259 in Nebraska and 260 in New Jersey.[6]

(a) Identify the group variable specifying the two states as the explanatory variable. What is the response variable and the control variable?

(b) Explain how it is possible for New Jersey to have the higher mean for each race yet for Nebraska to have the higher mean when the data are combined. (This illustrates *Simpson's paradox*.).

**10.31.** Example 7.1 (page 187) discussed a study that found that prayer did not reduce the incidence of complications for coronary surgery patients.

(a) Just as association does not imply causality, so does a lack of association not imply a lack of causality, because there may be an alternative explanation. Illustrate this using this study.

(b) A summary of this study in *Time Magazine* (December 4, 2006, p. 87) noted that "the prayers said by strangers were provided by the clergy and were all identical. Maybe that prevented them from being truly heartfelt. In short, the possible confounding factors in this study made it extraordinary limited." Explain what the "possible confounding" means, in the context of this study.

**10.32.** A study observes that subjects who say they exercise regularly reported only half as many serious illnesses per year, on the average, as those who say they do not exercise regularly. The results section in the article states, "We next analyzed whether age was a confounding variable affecting this association." Explain what this sentence means and how age could potentially explain the association between exercising and illnesses.

**10.33.** A research study funded by Wobegon Springs Mineral Water, Inc., discovers that the probability that a newborn child has a birth defect is lower for families that regularly buy bottled water than for families that do not. Does this association reflect a causal link between drinking bottled water and a reduction in birth defects? Why or why not?

**10.34.** The percentage of women who get breast cancer is higher now than at the beginning of this century. Suppose that cancer incidence tends to increase with age, and suppose that women tend to live longer lives now than earlier in this century. How might a comparison of breast cancer rates now with the beginning of this century show different results from these if we control for the age of the woman?

**10.35.** The crude death rate is the number of deaths in a year, per size of the population, multiplied by 1000. According to the U.S. Bureau of the Census, recently Mexico had a crude death rate of 4.6 (i.e., 4.6 deaths per 1000 population) while the United States had a crude death rate of 8.4. Could the overall death rate be higher in the United States even if the United States has a lower death rate than Mexico for people of each specific age? Explain.

**10.36.** In the United States, median age of residents is lowest in Utah. At each age level, the death rate from heart disease is higher in Utah than in Colorado; yet overall, the death rate from heart disease is lower in Utah than Colorado. Are there any contradictions here, or is this possible? Explain.

**10.37.** A study of the relationship between student's high school GPA and mother's employment (yes, no) suspects an interaction with gender of student. Controlling gender, Table 10.10 shows results.

(a) Describe the relationship between mother's employment and GPA for females and for males. Does this sample show evidence of statistical interaction? Explain.

(b) A journal article written about the study states, "Having a mother who is employed outside the home seems to have positive effects on daughter's achievement in high school, but no substantive effect on son's achievement." Explain how Table 10.10 suggests this interpretation.

**TABLE 10.10:** Mean GPA by Mother's Employment, Controlling for Gender

| Gender | Mother Employed | Mother Not Employed |
|---|---|---|
| Females | 2.94 | 2.71 |
| Males | 2.72 | 2.74 |

**10.38.** Give an example of three variables for which the effect of $X_1$ on $Y$ would be

(a) Spurious, disappearing when $X_2$ is controlled

(b) Part of a chain relationship, disappearing when an intervening variable $X_2$ is controlled

(c) Weakened, but not eliminated, when $X_2$ is controlled

(d) Unaffected by controlling $X_2$

(e) Different at different levels of $X_2$ (i.e., showing interaction)

(f) Confounded with the effect of $X_2$

**10.39.** A study of compulsive buying behavior conducted a national telephone survey in 2004 of adults ages 18 and over.[7] The study found that lower income subjects were more likely to be compulsive buyers. They reported "Compulsive buyers did not differ significantly from other respondents in mean total credit card balances, but the compulsive buyers' lower income was a confounding factor." Explain what it means to say that income was a confounding factor, and explain why a comparison of the mean total credit card balances between compulsive and noncompulsive buyers could change depending on whether income is controlled.

**10.40.** A recent study (in *Behavior Modification*, vol. 29, 2005, p. 677) reported a correlation of 0.68 between scores on an index of depression and scores on an index that measures the amount of saturated fat intake. True or false: You can conclude that if you increase your saturated fat intake by a standard deviation, your degree of depression will increase by more than half a standard deviation.

**10.41.** A study (in *Adolescence*, vol. 335, 2000, p. 445) reported a sample correlation of 0.45 between depression and loneliness and $-0.74$ between loneliness and self-esteem. True or false: By the chain law, the sample correlation between depression and self esteem was negative.

*Select the best response(s) in Exercises 10.42–10.45.*

**10.42.** For all court trials about homicides in Florida between 1976 and 1987, the difference of proportions of whites and blacks receiving the death penalty was 0.026 when the victim was black and $-0.077$ when the victim was white.[8] This shows evidence of
  **(a)** a spurious association,
  **(b)** statistical interaction,
  **(c)** a chain relationhip,
  **(d)** all of these.

**10.43.** Statistical interaction refers to which of the following?
  **(a)** Association exists between two variables.

**(b)** The effect of an explanatory variable on a response variable changes greatly over the levels of a control variable.

**(c)** The partial association is the same at each level of the control variable, but it is different from the overall bivariate association, ignoring the control variable.

**(d)** For a collection of three variables, each pair of variables is associated.

**(e)** All of the above.

**10.44.** Example 9.10 in the previous chapter used a data set on house sales to regress $Y$ = selling price of home (in dollars) to $X$ = size of house (in square feet). The prediction equation was $\hat{y} = -50,926 + 126.6x$. Now we regard size of house as $X_1$ and also consider $X_2$ = whether the house is new (yes or no). The prediction equation relating $\hat{y}$ to $x_1$ has slope 161 for new homes and 109 for older homes. This gives evidence
  **(a)** of interaction between $X_1$ and $X_2$ in their effects on $Y$
  **(b)** of a spurious association between selling price and size
  **(c)** of a chain relationship, whereby whether new affects size which affects selling price
  **(d)** that size of house does not have a causal effect on price

**10.45.** Consider the relationship between $Y$ = political party preference (Democrat, Republican) and $X_1$ = race (Black, White) and $X_2$ = gender. There is an association between $Y$ and both $X_1$ and $X_2$, with the Democrat preference being more likely for blacks than whites and for women than men.
  **(a)** $X_1$ and $X_2$ are probably independent causes of $Y$.
  **(b)** The association between $Y$ and $X_1$ is probably spurious, controlling for $X_2$.
  **(c)** Since both variables affect $Y$, there is probably interaction.
  **(d)** The variables probably satisfy a chain relationship.
  **(e)** Race is probably a suppressor variable.
  **(f)** None of the above.

---

[7]Koran et al., *American Journal of Psychiatry*, vol. 163, 2006, p. 1806.
[8]M. L. Radelet and G. L. Pierce, *Florida Law Review*, vol. 43, 1991.

# CHAPTER 11

# Multiple Regression and Correlation

Chapter 9 introduced regression modeling of the relationship between two quantitative variables. Multivariate relationships require more complex models containing several explanatory variables. Some of these may be predictors of theoretical interest, and some may be control variables.

To predict $y$ = college GPA, for example, it is sensible to use several predictors in the same model. Possibilities include $x_1$ = high school GPA, $x_2$ = math college entrance exam score, $x_3$ = verbal college entrance exam score, and $x_4$ = rating by high school guidance counselor. This chapter presents models for the relationship between a response variable $y$ and a collection of explanatory variables.

A multivariable model provides better predictions of $y$ than does a model with a single explanatory variable. Such a model also can analyze relationships between variables while controlling for other variables. This is important because Chapter 10 showed that after controlling for a variable, an association can appear quite different from when the variable is ignored. Thus, this model provides information not available with simple models that analyze only two variables at a time.

Sections 11.1 and 11.2 extend the regression model to a ***multiple regression model*** that can have multiple explanatory variables. Section 11.3 defines correlation and $r$-squared measures that describe association between $y$ and a set of explanatory variables. Section 11.4 presents inference procedures for multiple regression. Section 11.5 shows how to allow *statistical interaction* in the model, and Section 11.6 presents a test of whether a complex model provides a better fit than a simpler model. The final two sections introduce measures that summarize the association between the response variable and an explanatory variable while controlling other variables.

## 11.1 THE MULTIPLE REGRESSION MODEL

Chapter 9 modeled the relationship between the explanatory variable $x$ and the mean of the response variable $y$ by the straight line (linear) equation $E(y) = \alpha + \beta x$. We refer to this model containing a *single* predictor as a ***bivariate model***, because it contains only two variables.

### The Multiple Regression Function

Suppose there are two explanatory variables, denoted by $x_1$ and $x_2$. As in earlier chapters, we use lowercase letters to denote observations or particular values of the variables. The bivariate regression function generalizes to the *multiple regression function*

$$E(y) = \alpha + \beta_1 x_1 + \beta_2 x_2.$$

In this equation, $\alpha$, $\beta_1$, and $\beta_2$ are parameters discussed below. For particular values of $x_1$ and $x_2$, the equation specifies the population mean of $y$ for all subjects with those values of $x_1$ and $x_2$. When there are additional explanatory variables, each has a $\beta x$ term, for example, $E(y) = \alpha + \beta_1 x_1 + \beta_2 x_2 + \beta_3 x_3 + \beta_4 x_4$ with four predictors.

The multiple regression function is more difficult to portray graphically than the bivariate regression function. With two explanatory variables, the $x_1$- and $x_2$-axes are perpendicular but lie in a horizontal plane and the $y$-axis is vertical and perpendicular to both the $x_1$ and $x_2$ axes. The equation $E(y) = \alpha + \beta_1 x_1 + \beta_2 x_2$ traces a plane (a flat surface) cutting through three-dimensional space, as Figure 11.1 portrays.

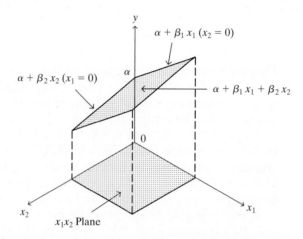

**FIGURE 11.1:** Graphical Depiction of a Multiple Regression Function with Two Explanatory Variables

The simplest interpretation treats all but one explanatory variable as control variables and fixes them at particular levels. This leaves an equation relating the mean of $y$ to the remaining explanatory variable.

### EXAMPLE 11.1    Do Higher Levels of Education Cause Higher Crime Rates?

Exercise 9.39 in Chapter 9 contains recent data on several variables for the 67 counties in the state of Florida. For each county, let $y$ = crime rate (annual number of crimes per 1000 population), $x_1$ = education (percentage of adult residents having at least a high school education), and $x_2$ = urbanization (percentage living in an urban environment).

The bivariate relationship between crime rate and education is approximated by $E(y) = -51.3 + 1.5x_1$. Surprisingly, the association is moderately *positive*, the correlation being $r = 0.47$. As the percentage of county residents having at least a high school education increases, so does the crime rate.

A closer look at the data reveals strong positive associations between crime rate and urbanization ($r = 0.68$) and between education and urbanization ($r = 0.79$). This suggests that the association between crime rate and education may be spurious.

Perhaps urbanization is a common causal factor. See Figure 11.2. As urbanization increases, both crime rate and education increase, resulting in a positive correlation between crime rate and education.

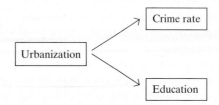

**FIGURE 11.2:** The Positive Association between Crime Rate and Education May Be Spurious, Explained by the Effects of Urbanization on Each

The relation between crime rate and both predictors considered together is approximated by the multiple regression function

$$E(y) = 58.9 - 0.6x_1 + 0.7x_2.$$

For instance, the expected crime rate for a county at the mean levels of education ($\bar{x}_1 = 70$) and urbanization ($\bar{x}_2 = 50$) is $E(y) = 58.9 - 0.6(70) + 0.7(50) = 52$ annual crimes per 1000 population.

Let's study the effect of $x_1$, controlling for $x_2$. We first set $x_2$ at its mean level of 50. Then the relationship between crime rate and education is

$$E(y) = 58.9 - 0.6x_1 + 0.7(50) = 58.9 - 0.6x_1 + 35.0 = 93.9 - 0.6x_1.$$

Figure 11.3 plots this line. Controlling for $x_2$ by fixing it at 50, the relationship between crime rate and education is negative rather than positive. The slope decreased and changed sign from 1.5 in the bivariate relationship to $-0.6$. At this fixed level of urbanization, a negative relationship exists between education and crime rate. We use the term *partial* regression equation to distinguish the equation $E(y) = 93.9 - 0.6x_1$ from the regression equation $E(y) = -51.3 + 1.5x_1$ for the *bivariate* relationship between $y$ and $x_1$. The *partial regression* equation refers to *part* of the potential observations, in this case counties having $x_2 = 50$.

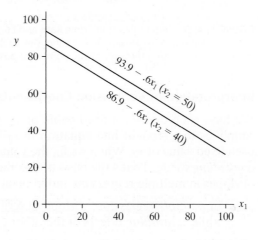

**FIGURE 11.3:** Partial Relationships between $E(y)$ and $x_1$ for the Multiple Regression Equation $E(y) = 58.9 - 0.6x_1 + 0.7x_2$. These partial regression equations fix $x_2$ to equal 50 or 40.

Next we fix $x_2$ at a different level, say $x_2 = 40$ instead of 50. Then you can check that $E(y) = 86.9 - 0.6x_1$. Thus, decreasing $x_2$ by 10 units shifts the partial line relating $y$ to $x_1$ downward by $10\beta_2 = 7.0$ units (see Figure 11.3). The slope of $-0.6$ for the partial relationship remains the same, so the line is parallel to the original one. Setting $x_2$ at a variety of values yields a collection of parallel lines, each having slope $\beta_1 = -0.6$.

Similarly, setting $x_1$ at a variety of values yields a collection of parallel lines, each having slope 0.7, relating the mean of $y$ to $x_2$. In other words, controlling for education, the slope of the partial relationship between crime rate and urbanization is $\beta_2 = 0.7$.

In summary, education has an overall positive effect on crime rate, but it has a negative effect when controlling for urbanization. The partial association has the opposite direction from the bivariate association. This is called **Simpson's paradox**. Figure 11.4 illustrates how this happens. It shows the scatterplot relating crime rate to education, portraying the overall positive association between these variables. The diagram circles the 19 counties that are highest in urbanization. That subset of points for which urbanization is nearly constant has a negative trend between crime rate and education. The high positive association between education and urbanization is reflected by the fact that most of the highlighted observations that are highest on urbanization also have high values on education. ∎

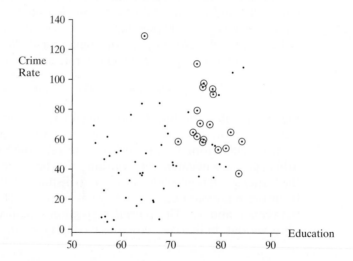

**FIGURE 11.4:** Scatterplot Relating Crime Rate and Education. The circled points are the counties highest on urbanization. A regression line fitting the circled points has negative slope, even though the regression line passing through *all* the points has positive slope (Simpson's paradox).

### Interpretation of Regression Coefficients

We have seen that for a fixed value of $x_2$, the equation $E(y) = \alpha + \beta_1 x_1 + \beta_2 x_2$ simplifies to a straight line equation in $x_1$ with slope $\beta_1$. The slope is the same for each fixed value of $x_2$. When we fix the value of $x_2$, we are holding it constant: We are *controlling* for $x_2$. That's the basis of the major difference between the interpretation of slopes in multiple regression and in bivariate regression:

- In *multiple regression*, a slope describes the effect of an explanatory variable while *controlling* effects of the other explanatory variables in the model.

- *Bivariate regression* has only a single explanatory variable. So a slope in bivariate regression describes the effect of that variable while *ignoring* all other possible explanatory variables.

The parameter $\beta_1$ measures the *partial effect* of $x_1$ on $y$, that is, the effect of a one-unit increase in $x_1$, holding $x_2$ constant. The partial effect of $x_2$ on $y$, holding $x_1$ constant, has slope $\beta_2$. Similarly, for the multiple regression model with *several* predictors, the beta coefficient of a predictor describes the change in the mean of $y$ for a one-unit increase in that predictor, controlling for the other variables in the model. The parameter $\alpha$ represents the mean of $y$ when each explanatory variable equals 0.

The parameters $\beta_1, \beta_2, \ldots$ are called **partial regression coefficients**. The adjective *partial* distinguishes these parameters from the regression coefficient $\beta$ in the *bivariate* model $E(y) = \alpha + \beta x$, which *ignores* rather than *controls* effects of other explanatory variables.

This multiple regression model assumes that the slope of the partial relationship between $y$ and each predictor is identical for *all* combinations of values of the other explanatory variables. This means that the model is appropriate when there is *no statistical interaction*, in the sense of Section 10.3. If the true partial slope between $y$ and $x_1$ is very different at $x_2 = 50$ than at $x_2 = 40$, for example, we need a more complex model. Section 11.5 will show this model.

A partial slope in a multiple regression model usually differs from the slope in the bivariate model for that predictor, but it need not. With two predictors, the partial slopes and bivariate slopes are equal if the correlation between $x_1$ and $x_2$ equals 0. When $x_1$ and $x_2$ are independent causes of $y$, the effect of $x_1$ on $y$ does not change when we control for $x_2$.

## Prediction Equation and Residuals

Corresponding to the multiple regression equation, software finds a prediction equation by estimating the model parameters using sample data. For simplicity of notation, so far we've used just two predictors. In general, let $k$ denote the number of predictors.

---

**Notation for Prediction Equation**

The prediction equation that estimates the multiple regression equation $E(y) = \alpha + \beta_1 x_1 + \beta_2 x_2 + \cdots + \beta_k x_k$ is denoted by $\hat{y} = a + b_1 x_1 + b_2 x_2 + \cdots + b_k x_k$.

---

For multiple regression, it is almost imperative to use computer software to find the prediction equation. The calculation formulas are complex and are not shown in this text.

We get the predicted value of $y$ for a subject by substituting the $x$-values for that subject into the prediction equation. Like the bivariate model, the multiple regression model has **residuals** that measure prediction errors. For a subject with predicted response $\hat{y}$ and observed response $y$, the residual is $y - \hat{y}$. The next section shows an example.

The **sum of squared errors** (SSE),

$$SSE = \sum (y - \hat{y})^2$$

summarizes the closeness of fit of the prediction equation to the response data. Most software calls SSE the ***residual sum of squares***. The formula for SSE is the same as in Chapter 9. The only difference is that the predicted value $\hat{y}$ results from using *several* explanatory variables instead of just a single predictor.

The parameter estimates in the prediction equation satisfy the ***least squares*** criterion: The prediction equation has the *smallest* SSE value of all possible equations of form $\hat{y} = a + b_1x_1 + \cdots + b_kx_k$.

## 11.2    EXAMPLE WITH MULTIPLE REGRESSION COMPUTER OUTPUT

We illustrate the methods of this chapter with the data introduced in the following example:

### EXAMPLE 11.2    Multiple Regression for Mental Health Study

A study in Alachua County, Florida, investigated the relationship between certain mental health indices and several explanatory variables. Primary interest focused on an index of mental impairment, which incorporates various dimensions of psychiatric symptoms, including aspects of anxiety and depression. This measure, which is the response variable $y$, ranged from 17 to 41 in the sample. Higher scores indicate greater psychiatric impairment.

The two explanatory variables used here are $x_1$ = life events score and $x_2$ = socioeconomic status (SES). The life events score is a composite measure of both the number and severity of major life events the subject experienced within the past three years. These events range from severe personal disruptions such as a death in the family, a jail sentence, or an extramarital affair, to less severe events such as getting a new job, the birth of a child, moving within the same city, or having a child marry. This measure[1] ranged from 3 to 97 in the sample. A high score represents a greater number and/or greater severity of these life events. The SES score is a composite index based on occupation, income, and education. Measured on a standard scale, it ranged from 0 to 100. The higher the score, the higher the status.

Table 11.1 shows data on the three variables for a random sample of 40 adults in the county. (These data are based on a larger survey. The authors thank Dr. Charles Holzer for permission to use the study as the basis of this example.) Table 11.2 summarizes the sample means and standard deviations of the three variables.    ■

### Scatterplot Matrix for Bivariate Relationships

Plots of the data provide an informal check of whether the relationships are linear. Most software can construct scatterplots on a single diagram for each pair of the variables. Figure 11.5 shows the plots for the variables from Table 11.1. This type of plot is called a ***scatterplot matrix***. Like a correlation matrix, it shows each pair of variables twice. In one plot, a variable is on the $y$-axis and in one it is on the $x$-axis. Mental impairment (the response variable) is on the $y$-axis for the plots in the first row of Figure 11.5, so these are the plots of interest to us. The plots show no evidence of nonlinearity, and models with linear effects seem appropriate. The plots suggest that life events has a mild positive effect and SES has a mild negative effect on mental impairment.

---

[1]Developed by E. Paykel et al., *Archives of General Psychiatry*, vol. 75, 1971, pp. 340–347.

**TABLE 11.1**: Scores on $y$ = Mental Impairment,
$x_1$ = Life Events, and $x_2$ = Socioeconomic Status

| $y$ | $x_1$ | $x_2$ | $y$ | $x_1$ | $x_2$ | $y$ | $x_1$ | $x_2$ |
|----|----|----|----|----|----|----|----|----|
| 17 | 46 | 84 | 26 | 50 | 40 | 30 | 44 | 53 |
| 19 | 39 | 97 | 26 | 48 | 52 | 31 | 35 | 38 |
| 20 | 27 | 24 | 26 | 45 | 61 | 31 | 95 | 29 |
| 20 | 3  | 85 | 27 | 21 | 45 | 31 | 63 | 53 |
| 20 | 10 | 15 | 27 | 55 | 88 | 31 | 42 | 7  |
| 21 | 44 | 55 | 27 | 45 | 56 | 32 | 38 | 32 |
| 21 | 37 | 78 | 27 | 60 | 70 | 33 | 45 | 55 |
| 22 | 35 | 91 | 28 | 97 | 89 | 34 | 70 | 58 |
| 22 | 78 | 60 | 28 | 37 | 50 | 34 | 57 | 16 |
| 23 | 32 | 74 | 28 | 30 | 90 | 34 | 40 | 29 |
| 24 | 33 | 67 | 28 | 13 | 56 | 41 | 49 | 3  |
| 24 | 18 | 39 | 28 | 40 | 56 | 41 | 89 | 75 |
| 25 | 81 | 87 | 29 | 5  | 40 |    |    |    |
| 26 | 22 | 95 | 30 | 59 | 72 |    |    |    |

**TABLE 11.2**: Estimated Means and Standard
Deviations of Mental Impairment, Life Events, and
Socioeconomic Status (SES)

| Variable | Mean | Standard Deviation |
|----------|------|--------------------|
| Mental Impairment | 27.30 | 5.46 |
| Life Events | 44.42 | 22.62 |
| SES | 56.60 | 25.28 |

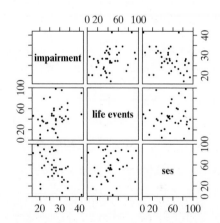

**FIGURE 11.5:** A Scatterplot Matrix: Scatterplots for Pairs of Variables from Table 11.1

## Partial Plots for Partial Relationships

The multiple regression model states that each predictor has a linear effect with common slope, controlling for the other predictors. To check this, we could use software to plot $y$ versus each predictor, for subsets of points that are nearly constant on the other predictors. With a single control variable, for example, we could sort the observations into four groups using the quartiles as boundaries, and then either construct four separate scatterplots or mark the observations on a single scatterplot according to their group. With several control variables, however, keeping them all nearly constant can reduce the sample to relatively few observations. A more informative single picture is provided by the ***partial regression plot***. It displays the relationship between the response variable and an explanatory variable after removing the effects of the other predictors in the multiple regression model. It does this by plotting the residuals from models using these two variables as responses and the other explanatory variables as predictors.

For example, here's how to find the partial regression plot for the effect of $x_1$ when the multiple regression model also has explanatory variables $x_2$ and $x_3$. Find the residuals from the model using $x_2$ and $x_3$ to predict $y$. Also find the residuals from the model using $x_2$ and $x_3$ to predict $x_1$. Then plot the residuals from the first analysis (on the $y$-axis) against the residuals from the second analysis. For these residuals, the effects of $x_2$ and $x_3$ are removed. The least squares slope for the points in this plot is necessarily the same as the estimated partial slope $b_1$ for the multiple regression model.

Figure 11.6 shows a partial regression plot (from SPSS) for $y$ = mental impairment and $x_1$ = life events, controlling for $x_2$ = SES. It plots the residuals on the $y$-axis from the model $\hat{y} = 32.2 - 0.086x_2$ using $x_2$ to predict $y$ against the residuals on the $x$-axis from the model $\hat{x}_1 = 38.2 + 0.110x_2$ using $x_2$ to predict $x_1$. Both axes have negative and positive values, because they refer to residuals. Recall that residuals (prediction errors) can be positive or negative and have a mean of 0. Figure 11.6 suggests that the partial effect of life events is approximately linear and is positive.

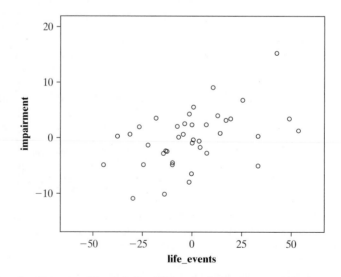

**FIGURE 11.6:** Partial Regression Plot for Mental Impairment and Life Events, Controlling for SES. This plots the residuals from regressing mental impairment on SES against the residuals from regressing life events on SES.

Figure 11.7 shows the partial regression plot for SES. It shows that its partial effect is also approximately linear but is negative. It is simple to obtain partial regression plots with standard software such as SPSS. (See the appendix.)

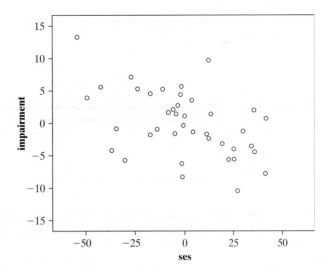

**FIGURE 11.7:** Partial Regression Plot for Mental Impairment and SES, Controlling for Life Events. This plots the residuals from regressing mental impairment on life events against the residuals from regressing SES on life events.

### Sample Computer Printouts

Tables 11.3 and 11.4 are SPSS printouts of the coefficients table for the bivariate relationships between mental impairment and the separate explanatory variables. The estimated regression coefficients fall in the column labelled "B." The prediction equations are

$$\hat{y} = 23.31 + 0.090x_1 \text{ and } \hat{y} = 32.17 - 0.086x_2.$$

In the sample, mental impairment is positively related to life events, since the coefficient of $x_1$ (0.090) is positive. The greater the number and severity of life events in the previous three years, the higher the mental impairment (i.e., the poorer the mental health) tends to be. Mental impairment is negatively related to socioeconomic status. The greater the SES level, the lower the mental impairment tends to be. The correlations between mental impairment and the explanatory variables are modest, 0.372 for life events and −0.399 for SES (listed by SPSS as "Standardized coefficients;" the "beta" label is misleading and refers to the alternate term *beta weights* for standardized regression coefficients).

**TABLE 11.3:** Bivariate Regression Analysis for $y$ = Mental Impairment (IMPAIR) and $x_1$ = Life Events (LIFE)

```
                                    Coefficients(a)
Model                    Unstandardized      Standardized
                          Coefficients        Coefficients
                        B      Std. Error        Beta        t      Sig.
1   (Constant)       23.309     1.807                      12.901   .000
    LIFE              .090       .036             .372      2.472    .018

a       Dependent Variable: IMPAIR
```

**TABLE 11.4:** Bivariate Regression Analysis for $y$ = Mental Impairment and $x_2$ = Socioeconomic Status (SES)

| | Coefficients(a) | | | | |
|---|---|---|---|---|---|
| Model | Unstandardized Coefficients | | Standardized Coefficients | | |
| | B | Std. Error | Beta | t | Sig. |
| 1 (Constant) | 32.172 | 1.988 | | 16.186 | .000 |
| SES | -.086 | .032 | -.399 | -2.679 | .011 |

a    Dependent Variable: IMPAIR

Table 11.5 shows part of a SPSS printout for the multiple regression model $E(y) = \alpha + \beta_1 x_1 + \beta_2 x_2$. The prediction equation is

$$\hat{y} = a + b_1 x_1 + b_2 x_2 = 28.230 + 0.103 x_1 - 0.097 x_2.$$

**TABLE 11.5:** Fit of Multiple Regression Model for $y$ = Mental Impairment, $x_1$ = Life Events (LIFE), and $x_2$ = Socioeconomic Status (SES)

| | Unstandardized Coefficients | | Standardized Coefficients | | |
|---|---|---|---|---|---|
| | B | Std. Error | Beta | t | Sig. |
| (Constant) | 28.230 | 2.174 | | 12.984 | .000 |
| LIFE | .103 | .032 | .428 | 3.177 | .003 |
| SES | -.097 | .029 | -.451 | -3.351 | .002 |

Dependent Variable: IMPAIR

Controlling for SES, the sample relationship between mental impairment and life events is positive, since the coefficient of life events ($b_1 = 0.103$) is positive. The estimated mean of mental impairment increases by about 0.1 for every one-unit increase in the life events score, controlling for SES. Since $b_2 = -0.097$, a negative association exists between mental impairment and SES, controlling for life events. For example, over the 100-unit range of potential SES values (from a minimum of 0 to a maximum of 100), the estimated mean mental impairment changes by $100(-0.097) = -9.7$. Since mental impairment ranges only from 17 to 41 with a standard deviation of 5.5, a decrease of 9.7 points in the mean is noteworthy.

From Table 11.1, the first subject in the sample had $y = 17$, $x_1 = 46$, and $x_2 = 84$. This subject's predicted mental impairment is

$$\hat{y} = 28.230 + 0.103(46) - 0.097(84) = 24.8.$$

The prediction error (residual) is $y - \hat{y} = 17 - 24.8 = -7.8$.

Table 11.6 summarizes some results of the regression analyses. It shows standard errors in parentheses below the parameter estimates. The partial slopes for the multiple regression model are similar to the slopes for the bivariate models. In each case, the introduction of the second predictor does little to alter the effect of the other one. This suggests that these predictors may have nearly independent sample effects on $y$. In fact, the sample correlation between $x_1$ and $x_2$ is only 0.123. The next section

**TABLE 11.6:** Summary of Regression Models for Mental Impairment

| Effect | Multiple | Life Events | SES |
|---|---|---|---|
| | | Predictors in Regression Model | |
| Intercept | 28.230 | 23.309 | 32.172 |
| Life events | 0.103 | 0.090 | — |
| | (0.032) | (0.036) | |
| SES | −0.097 | — | −0.086 |
| | (0.029) | | (0.032) |
| $R^2$ | 0.339 | 0.138 | 0.159 |
| $(n)$ | (40) | (40) | (40) |

shows how to measure the joint association of the explanatory variables with the response variable, and it shows how to interpret the $R^2$ value listed for the multiple regression model.

## 11.3  MULTIPLE CORRELATION AND $R^2$

The correlation $r$ and its square describe strength of linear association for bivariate relationships. This section presents analogous measures for the multiple regression model. They describe the strength of association between $y$ and the set of explanatory variables acting together as predictors in the model.

### The Multiple Correlation

The explanatory variables collectively are strongly associated with $y$ if the observed $y$-values correlate highly with the $\hat{y}$-values from the prediction equation. The correlation between the observed and predicted values summarizes this association.

---
**Multiple Correlation**

The **multiple correlation** for a regression model is the correlation between the observed $y$-values and the predicted $\hat{y}$-values.

---

For each subject, the prediction equation provides a predicted value $\hat{y}$. So, each subject has a $y$-value and a $\hat{y}$-value. For example, above we saw that the first subject in the sample had $y = 17$ and $\hat{y} = 24.8$. For the first three subjects in Table 11.1, the observed and predicted $y$-values are

| $y$ | $\hat{y}$ |
|---|---|
| 17 | 24.8 |
| 19 | 22.8 |
| 20 | 28.7 |

The sample correlation computed between the $y$- and $\hat{y}$-values is the multiple correlation. It is denoted by $R$.

The predicted values cannot correlate negatively with the observed values. The predictions must be at least as good as the sample mean $\bar{y}$, which is the prediction when all partial slopes $= 0$, and $\bar{y}$ has zero correlation with $y$. So $R$ always falls between 0 and 1. In this respect, the correlation between $y$ and $\hat{y}$ differs from the correlation between $y$ and a predictor $x$, which falls between $-1$ and $+1$. The larger the multiple correlation $R$, the better the predictions of $y$ by the set of explanatory variables.

## $R^2$: The Coefficient of Multiple Determination

Another measure uses the *proportional reduction in error* concept, generalizing $r^2$ for bivariate models. This measure summarizes the relative improvement in predictions using the prediction equation instead of $\bar{y}$. It has the following elements:

**Rule 1** (Predict $y$ without using $x_1, \ldots, x_k$): The best predictor is then the sample mean, $\bar{y}$.

**Rule 2** (Predict $y$ using $x_1, \ldots, x_k$): The best predictor is the prediction equation
$$\hat{y} = a + b_1 x_1 + b_2 x_2 + \cdots + b_k x_k.$$

*Prediction Errors:* The prediction error for a subject is the difference between the observed and predicted values of $y$. With rule 1, the error is $y - \bar{y}$. With rule 2, it is the residual $y - \hat{y}$. In either case, we summarize the error by the sum of the squared prediction errors. For rule 1, this is TSS $= \sum(y - \bar{y})^2$, called the *total sum of squares*. For rule 2, it is SSE $= \sum(y - \hat{y})^2$, the sum of squared errors using the prediction equation, called the *residual sum of squares*.

*Definition of Measure:* The proportional reduction in error from using the prediction equation $\hat{y} = a + b_1 x_1 + \cdots + b_k x_k$ instead of $\bar{y}$ to predict $y$ is called the **coefficient of multiple determination** or, for simplicity, **R-squared**.

---

**R-Squared: The Coefficient of Multiple Determination**

$$R^2 = \frac{\text{TSS} - \text{SSE}}{\text{TSS}} = \frac{\sum(y - \bar{y})^2 - \sum\left(y - \hat{y}\right)^2}{\sum(y - \bar{y})^2}$$

---

$R^2$ measures the proportion of the total variation in $y$ that is explained by the predictive power of all the explanatory variables, through the multiple regression model. The symbol reflects that it is the square of the multiple correlation. The uppercase notation $R^2$ distinguishes this measure from $r^2$ for the bivariate model. Their formulas are identical, and $r^2$ is the special case of $R^2$ applied to a regression model with one explanatory variable. For the multiple regression model to be useful for prediction, it should provide improved predictions relative not only to $\bar{y}$ but also to the separate bivariate models for $y$ and each explanatory variable.

## EXAMPLE 11.3  Multiple Correlation and $R^2$ for Mental Impairment

For the data on $y$ = mental impairment, $x_1$ = life events, and $x_2$ = socioeconomic status, introduced in Example 11.2, the prediction equation is $\hat{y} = 28.23 + 0.103x_1 - 0.097x_2$. Table 11.5 showed some output for this model. Software also reports ANOVA (analysis of variance) tables with sums of squares and $R$ and $R^2$ tables. Table 11.7 shows some SPSS output.

From the "Sum of Squares" column, the total sum of squares is TSS $= \sum(y - \bar{y})^2 = 1162.4$, and the residual sum of squares from using the prediction equation to predict $y$ is SSE $= \sum(y - \hat{y})^2 = 768.2$. Thus,

$$R^2 = \frac{\text{TSS} - \text{SSE}}{\text{TSS}} = \frac{1162.4 - 768.2}{1162.4} = 0.339.$$

**TABLE 11.7**: ANOVA Table and Model Summary for Regression of Mental Impairment (IMPAIR) on Life Events (LIFE) and Socioeconomic Status (SES)

```
                              ANOVA
                   Sum of
                   Squares    df   Mean Square     F       Sig.
       Regression  394.238     2    197.119      9.495     .000
       Residual    768.162    37     20.761
       Total      1162.400    39

                   Model Summary
    R      R Square   Adjusted R Square   Std. Error of the Estimate
  .582      .339           .303                   4.556

    Predictors: (Constant), SES, LIFE
    Dependent Variable: IMPAIR
```

Using life events and SES together to predict mental impairment provides a 33.9% reduction in the prediction error relative to using only $\bar{y}$. The multiple regression model provides a substantially larger reduction in error than either bivariate model (Table 11.6 reported $r^2$ values of 0.138 and 0.159 for them). It is more useful than those models for predictive purposes.

The multiple correlation between mental impairment and the two explanatory variables is $R = +\sqrt{0.339} = 0.582$. This equals the correlation between the observed $y$- and predicted $\hat{y}$-values for the model.

SPSS reports $R$ and $R^2$ in a separate "Model Summary" table, as Table 11.7 shows. Most software also reports an adjusted version of $R^2$ that is a less biased estimate of the population value. Exercise 11.61 defines this measure, and Table 11.7 reports its value of 0.303. ∎

## Properties of $R$ and $R^2$

The properties of $R^2$ are similar to those of $r^2$ for bivariate models.

- $R^2$ falls between 0 and 1.
- The larger the value of $R^2$, the better the set of explanatory variables $(x_1, \ldots, x_k)$ collectively predict $y$.
- $R^2 = 1$ only when all the residuals are 0, that is, when all $y = \hat{y}$, so that SSE = 0. In that case, the prediction equation passes through all the data points.
- $R^2 = 0$ when the predictions do not vary as any of the $x$-values vary. In that case, $b_1 = b_2 = \cdots = b_k = 0$, and $\hat{y}$ is identical to $\bar{y}$, since the explanatory variables do not add any predictive power. When this happens, the correlation between $y$ and each explanatory variable equals 0.
- $R^2$ cannot decrease when we add an explanatory variable to the model. It is impossible to explain *less* variation in $y$ by adding explanatory variables to a regression model.
- $R^2$ for the multiple regression model is at least as large as the $r^2$-values for the separate bivariate models. That is, $R^2$ for the multiple regression model is at

least as large as $r^2_{yx_1}$ for $y$ as a linear function of $x_1$, $r^2_{yx_2}$ for $y$ as a linear function of $x_2$, and so forth.

Properties of the multiple correlation $R$ follow directly from the ones for $R^2$, since $R$ is the positive square root of $R^2$. For instance, the multiple correlation for the model $E(y) = \alpha + \beta_1 x_1 + \beta_2 x_2 + \beta_3 x_3$ is at least as large as the multiple correlation for the model $E(y) = \alpha + \beta_1 x_1 + \beta_2 x_2$.

The numerator of $R^2$, TSS − SSE, summarizes the variation in $y$ explained by the multiple regression model. This difference, which equals $\sum (\hat{y} - \bar{y})^2$, is called the **regression sum of squares**. The ANOVA table in Table 11.7 lists the regression sum of squares as 394.2. (Some software, such as SAS, labels this the "Model" sum of squares.) The total sum of squares TSS of the $y$-values about $\bar{y}$ partitions into the variation explained by the regression model (regression sum of squares) plus the variation not explained by the model (the residual sum of squares, SSE).

## Multicollinearity with Many Explanatory Variables

When there are many explanatory variables but the correlations among them are strong, once you have included a few of them in the model, $R^2$ usually doesn't increase much more when you add additional ones. For example, for the "house selling price" data set at the text Web site (introduced in Example 9.10 on page 278), $r^2$ is 0.71 with the house's tax assessment as a predictor of selling price. Then $R^2$ increases to 0.77 when we add house size as a second predictor. But then it increases only to 0.79 when we add number of bathrooms, number of bedrooms, and whether the house is new as additional predictors.

When $R^2$ does not increase much, this does not mean that the additional variables are uncorrelated with $y$. It means merely that they don't add much new power for predicting $y$, given the values of the predictors already in the model. These other variables may have small associations with $y$, given the variables already in the model. This often happens in social science research when the explanatory variables are highly correlated, no one having much unique explanatory power. Section 14.3 discusses this condition, called **multicollinearity**.

Figure 11.8, which portrays the portion of the total variability in $y$ explained by each of three predictors, shows a common occurrence. The size of the set for a predictor in this figure represents the size of its $r^2$-value in predicting $y$. The amount a set for a predictor overlaps with the set for another predictor represents its association with that predictor. The part of the set for a predictor that does not overlap with other sets represents the part of the variability in $y$ explained uniquely by that predictor. In Figure 11.8, all three predictors have moderate associations with $y$, and together they explain considerable variation. Once $x_1$ and $x_2$ are in the model, however, $x_3$ explains little additional variation in $y$, because of its strong correlations with $x_1$ and $x_2$. Because of this overlap, $R^2$ increases only slightly when $x_3$ is added to a model already containing $x_1$ and $x_2$.

For predictive purposes, we gain little by adding explanatory variables to a model that are strongly correlated with ones already in the model, since $R^2$ will not increase much. Ideally, we should use explanatory variables having weak correlations with each other but strong correlations with $y$. In practice, this is not always possible, especially if we want to include certain variables in the model for theoretical reasons.

In practice, the sample size you need to do a multiple regression well gets larger when you want to use more explanatory variables. Technical difficulties caused by

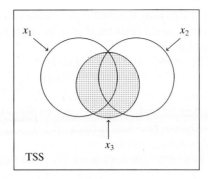

**FIGURE 11.8:** $R^2$ Does Not Increase Much when $x_3$ Is Added to the Model Already Containing $x_1$ and $x_2$

multicollinearity are less severe for larger sample sizes. Ideally, the sample size should be at least about 10 times the number of explanatory variables (for example, at least about 40 for 4 explanatory variables).

## 11.4    INFERENCE FOR MULTIPLE REGRESSION COEFFICIENTS

The multiple regression function

$$E(y) = \alpha + \beta_1 x_1 + \cdots + \beta_k x_k$$

describes the relationship between the explanatory variables and the mean of the response variable. For particular values of the explanatory variables, $\alpha + \beta_1 x_1 + \cdots + \beta_k x_k$ represents the mean of $y$ for the population having those values.

To make inferences about the parameters, we formulate the entire *multiple regression model*. This consists of this equation together with a set of assumptions:

- The population distribution of $y$ is normal, for each combination of values of $x_1, \ldots, x_k$.
- The standard deviation, $\sigma$, of the conditional distribution of responses on $y$ is the same at each combination of values of $x_1, \ldots, x_k$.
- The sample is randomly selected.

Under these assumptions, the true sampling distributions exactly equal those quoted in this section. In practice, the assumptions are never satisfied perfectly. Two-sided inferences are robust to the normality and common $\sigma$ assumptions. More important are the assumptions of randomization and that the regression function describes well how the mean of $y$ depends on the explanatory variables. We'll see ways to check the latter assumption in Section 14.2.

Two types of significance tests are used in multiple regression. The first is a global test of independence. It checks whether *any* of the explanatory variables are statistically related to $y$. The second studies the partial regression coefficients individually, to assess which explanatory variables have significant partial effects on $y$.

### Testing the Collective Influence of the Explanatory Variables

Do the explanatory variables collectively have a statistically significant effect on the response variable? We check this by testing

$$H_0 : \beta_1 = \beta_2 = \cdots = \beta_k = 0.$$

This states that the mean of $y$ does not depend on the values of $x_1, \ldots, x_k$. Under the inference assumptions, this states that $y$ is statistically independent of all $k$ explanatory variables.

The alternative hypothesis is

$$H_a : \text{At least one } \beta_i \neq 0.$$

This states that *at least one* explanatory variable is related to $y$, controlling for the others. The test judges whether using $x_1, \cdots, x_k$ together to predict $y$, with the prediction equation $\hat{y} = a + b_1 x_1 + \cdots + b_k x_k$, is better than using $\bar{y}$.

These hypotheses about $\{\beta_i\}$ are equivalent to

$$H_0 : \text{Population multiple correlation} = 0 \quad H_a : \text{Population multiple correlation} > 0.$$

The equivalence occurs because the multiple correlation equals 0 only in those situations in which all the partial regression coefficients equal 0. Also, $H_0$ is equivalent to $H_0$: population $R$-squared = 0.

For these hypotheses about the $k$ predictors, the test statistic equals

$$F = \frac{R^2/k}{(1 - R^2)/[n - (k + 1)]}.$$

The sampling distribution of this statistic is called the **F distribution**. We next study this distribution and its properties.

### The F Distribution

The symbol for the $F$ test statistic and its distribution honors the most eminent statistician in history, R. A. Fisher, who discovered the $F$ distribution in 1922. Like the chi-squared distribution, the $F$ distribution can take only nonnegative values and it is somewhat skewed to the right. Figure 11.9 illustrates.

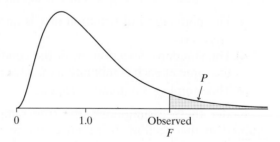

**FIGURE 11.9:** The $F$ Distribution and the $P$-Value for $F$ Tests. Larger $F$ values give stronger evidence against $H_0$.

The shape of the $F$ distribution is determined by two degrees of freedom terms, denoted by $df_1$ and $df_2$:

$$df_1 = k, \text{ the number of explanatory variables in the model.}$$
$$df_2 = n - (k + 1) = n - \text{number of parameters in regression equation.}$$

The first of these, $df_1 = k$, is the divisor of the numerator term $(R^2)$ in the $F$ test statistic. The second, $df_2 = n - (k + 1)$, is the divisor of the denominator term $(1 - R^2)$. The number of parameters in the multiple regression model is $k + 1$, representing the $k$ beta terms and the alpha term.

The mean of the $F$ distribution is approximately[2] equal to 1. The larger the $R^2$-value, the larger the ratio $R^2/(1 - R^2)$, and the larger the $F$ test statistic becomes. Thus, larger values of the $F$ test statistic provide stronger evidence against $H_0$. Under the presumption that $H_0$ is true, the $P$-value is the probability the $F$ test statistic is larger than the observed $F$-value. This is the right-tail probability under the $F$ distribution beyond the observed $F$-value, as Figure 11.9 shows.

Table D at the end of the text lists the $F$ scores having $P$-values of 0.05, 0.01, and 0.001, for various combinations of $df_1$ and $df_2$. This table allows us to determine whether $P > 0.05, 0.01 < P < 0.05, 0.001 < P < 0.01$, or $P < 0.001$. Software for regression reports the actual $P$-value.

### EXAMPLE 11.4    *F* Test for Mental Health Impairment Data

In Example 11.2 (page 326), we used multiple regression for $n = 40$ observations on $y$ = mental impairment, with $k = 2$ explanatory variables, life events and SES. The null hypothesis that mental impairment is statistically independent of life events and SES is $H_0$: $\beta_1 = \beta_2 = 0$.

In Example 11.3 (page 332), we found that this model has $R^2 = 0.339$. The $F$ test statistic value is

$$F = \frac{R^2/k}{(1 - R^2)/[n - (k + 1)]} = \frac{0.339/2}{0.661/[40 - (2 + 1)]} = 9.5.$$

The two degrees of freedom terms for the $F$ distribution are $df_1 = k = 2$ and $df_2 = n - (k + 1) = 40 - 3 = 37$, the two divisors in this statistic.

From Table D, when $df_1 = 2$ and $df_2 = 37$, the $F$-value with right-tail probability of 0.001 falls between 8.25 and 8.77. Since the observed $F$ test statistic of 9.5 falls above these two, it is farther out in the tail and has smaller tail probability than 0.001. Thus, the $P$-value is $P < 0.001$. Part of the SPSS printout in Table 11.7 showed the ANOVA table

|  | Sum of Squares | df | Mean Square | F | Sig. |
|---|---|---|---|---|---|
| Regression | 394.238 | 2 | 197.119 | 9.495 | .000 |
| Residual | 768.162 | 37 | 20.761 |  |  |

in which we see the $F$ statistic. The $P$-value, which rounded to three decimal places is $P = 0.000$, appears under the heading "Sig" in the ANOVA table.

This extremely small $P$-value provides strong evidence against $H_0$. It suggests that at least one of the explanatory variables is related to mental impairment. Equivalently, we can conclude that the population multiple correlation and $R$-squared are positive. So we obtain significantly better predictions of $y$ using the multiple regression equation than by using $\bar{y}$. ∎

Normally, unless the sample size is small and the associations are weak, this $F$ test has a small $P$-value. If we choose variables wisely for a study, at least one of them should have *some* explanatory power.

### Inferences for Individual Regression Coefficients

Suppose the $P$-value is small for the $F$ test that all the regression coefficients equal 0. This does not imply that *every* explanatory variable has an effect on $y$ (controlling for the other explanatory variables in the model), but merely that *at least one* of them has

---

[2]It equals $df_2/(df_2 - 2)$, which is usually close to 1 unless $n$ is quite small.

an effect. More narrowly focused analyses judge *which* partial effects are nonzero and estimate the sizes of those effects. These inferences make the same assumptions as the $F$ test, the most important being randomization and that the regression function describes well how the mean of $y$ depends on the explanatory variables.

Consider an arbitrary explanatory variable $x_i$, with coefficient $\beta_i$ in the multiple regression model. The test for its partial effect on $y$ has $H_0: \beta_i = 0$. If $\beta_i = 0$, the mean of $y$ is identical for all values of $x_i$, controlling for the other explanatory variables in the model. The alternative can be two sided, $H_a: \beta_i \neq 0$, or one sided, $H_a: \beta_i > 0$ or $H_a: \beta_i < 0$, to predict the direction of the partial effect.

The test statistic for $H_0: \beta_i = 0$, using sample estimate $b_i$ of $\beta_i$, is

$$t = \frac{b_i}{se},$$

where $se$ is the standard error of $b_i$. As usual, the $t$ test statistic takes the best estimate $(b_i)$ of the parameter $(\beta_i)$, subtracts the $H_0$-value of the parameter (0), and divides by the standard error. The formula for $se$ is complex, but software provides its value. If $H_0$ is true and the model assumptions hold, the $t$ statistic has the $t$ distribution with $df = n - (k + 1)$. The $df$ value is the same as $df_2$ in the $F$ test.

It is more informative to estimate the size of a partial effect than to test whether it is zero. Recall that $\beta_i$ represents the change in the mean of $y$ for a one-unit increase in $x_i$, controlling for the other variables. A confidence interval for $\beta_i$ is

$$b_i \pm t(se).$$

The $t$ score comes from the $t$ table, with $df = n - (k + 1)$. For example, a 95% confidence interval for the partial effect of $x_1$ is $b_1 \pm t_{.025}(se)$.

### EXAMPLE 11.5   Inferences for Separate Predictors of Mental Impairment

For the multiple regression model for $y$ = mental impairment, $x_1$ = life events, and $x_2$ = SES,

$$E(y) = \alpha + \beta_1 x_1 + \beta_2 x_2,$$

let's consider the effect of life events. The hypothesis that mental impairment is statistically independent of life events, controlling for SES, is $H_0: \beta_1 = 0$. If $H_0$ is true, the multiple regression equation reduces to $E(y) = \alpha + \beta_2 x_2$. If $H_0$ is false, then $\beta_1 \neq 0$ and the full model provides a better fit than the bivariate model.

Table 11.5 contained the results

|            | B       | Std. Error | t       | Sig. |
|------------|---------|------------|---------|------|
| (Constant) | 28.230  | 2.174      | 12.984  | .000 |
| LIFE       | .103    | .032       | 3.177   | .003 |
| SES        | -.097   | .029       | -3.351  | .002 |

This tells us that the point estimate of $\beta_1$ is $b_1 = 0.103$ and has standard error $se = 0.032$. The test statistic equals

$$t = \frac{b_1}{se} = \frac{0.103}{0.032} = 3.18.$$

This appears under the heading "t" in the table in the row for the variable LIFE. The statistic has $df = n - (k + 1) = 40 - 3 = 37$. The $P$-value appears under "Sig" in the row for LIFE. It is 0.003, the probability that the $t$ statistic exceeds 3.18 in absolute value. There is strong evidence that mental impairment is related to life events, controlling for SES.

A 95% confidence interval for $\beta_1$ uses $t_{0.025} = 2.026$, the $t$-value for $df = 37$ having a probability of $0.05/2 = 0.025$ in each tail. This interval equals

$$b_1 \pm t_{0.025}(se) = 0.103 \pm 2.026(0.032), \quad \text{which is} \quad (0.04, 0.17).$$

Controlling for SES, we are 95% confident that the change in mean mental impairment per one-unit increase in life events falls between 0.04 and 0.17. The interval does not contain 0. This is in agreement with rejecting $H_0$: $\beta_1 = 0$ in favor of $H_a$: $\beta_1 \neq 0$ at the $\alpha = 0.05$ level.

Since this interval contains only positive numbers, the relationship between mental impairment and life events is positive, controlling for SES. It may be simpler to interpret the interval (0.04, 0.17) by noting that an increase of 100 units in life events corresponds to anywhere from a $100(0.04) = 4$ to a $100(0.17) = 17$ unit increase in mean mental impairment. The interval is relatively wide because of the small sample size. ∎

How is the $t$ test for a partial regression coefficient different from the $t$ test of $H_0$: $\beta = 0$ for the bivariate model, $E(y) = \alpha + \beta x$, studied in Section 9.5? That $t$ test evaluates whether $y$ and $x$ are associated, *ignoring* other variables, because it applies to the bivariate model. By contrast, the test just presented evaluates whether variables are associated, *controlling* for other variables.

A note of caution: Suppose there is multicollinearity, that is, a lot of overlap among the explanatory variables in the sense that any one is well predicted by the others. Then possibly none of the individual partial effects has a small $P$-value, even if $R^2$ is large and a large $F$ statistic occurs in the global test for the $\beta$s. Any particular variable may explain uniquely little of the variation in $y$, even though together the variables explain a lot of the variation.

### Variability and Mean Squares in the ANOVA Table*

The precision of the least squares estimates relates to the size of the conditional standard deviation $\sigma$ that measures variability of $y$ at fixed values of the predictors. The smaller the variability of $y$-values about the regression equation, the smaller the standard errors become. The estimate of $\sigma$ is

$$s = \sqrt{\frac{\Sigma (y - \hat{y})^2}{n - (k + 1)}} = \sqrt{\frac{SSE}{df}}.$$

The degrees of freedom value is also $df$ for $t$ inferences for regression coefficients, and it is $df_2$ for the $F$ test about the collective effect of the predictors. (When a model has only $k = 1$ predictor, $df$ simplifies to $n - 2$, the term in the $s$ formula of Section 9.3.) Part of the SPSS printout in Table 11.7 showed the ANOVA table

|  | Sum of Squares | df | Mean Square | F | Sig. |
|---|---|---|---|---|---|
| Regression | 394.238 | 2 | 197.119 | 9.495 | .000 |
| Residual | 768.162 | 37 | 20.761 |  |  |

containing the sums of squares for the multiple regression model with the mental impairment data. We see that $SSE = 768.2$. Since $n = 40$ for $k = 2$ predictors, we have $df = n - (k + 1) = 40 - 3 = 37$ and

$$s = \sqrt{\frac{SSE}{df}} = \sqrt{\frac{768.2}{37}} = \sqrt{20.76} = 4.56.$$

If the conditional distributions are approximately bell shaped, nearly all mental impairment scores fall within about 14 units (3 standard deviations) of the mean specified by the regression function.

SPSS reports the conditional standard deviation under the heading "Std. Error of the Estimate" in the Model Summary table that also has the $R$- and $R^2$-values (see Table 11.7). This is a poor choice of label by SPSS, because $s$ refers to the variability in $y$-values, not the variability of a sampling distribution of an estimator.

The square of $s$, which estimates the conditional variance, is called the **mean square error**, often abbreviated by MSE. Software shows it in the ANOVA table in the "Mean Square" column, in the row labeled "Residual" (or "Error" in some software). For example, MSE = 20.76 in the above table. Some software (such as SAS) better labels the conditional standard deviation estimate $s$ as "Root MSE" because it is the square root of the mean square error.

### The F Statistic Is a Ratio of Mean Squares*

An alternative formula for the $F$ test statistic for testing $H_0 : \beta_1 = \cdots = \beta_k = 0$ uses the two mean squares in the ANOVA table. Specifically,

$$F = \frac{\text{Regression mean square}}{\text{Residual mean square (MSE)}} = \frac{197.1}{20.8} = 9.5.$$

This gives the same value as the $F$ test statistic formula based on $R^2$.

The regression mean square equals the regression sum of squares divided by its degrees of freedom. The $df$ equals $k$, the number of explanatory variables in the model, which is $df_1$ for the $F$ test. On the printout shown above, the regression mean square equals

$$\frac{\text{Regression SS}}{df_1} = \frac{394.2}{2} = 197.1.$$

### Relationship between F and t Statistics*

We've seen that the $F$ distribution is used to test that all partial regression coefficients equal 0. Some regression software also lists $F$ test statistics instead of $t$ test statistics for the tests about the individual regression coefficients. The two statistics are related and have the same $P$-values. The square of the $t$ statistic for testing that a partial regression coefficient equals 0 is an $F$ test statistic having the $F$ distribution with $df_1 = 1$ and $df_2 = n - (k + 1)$.

To illustrate, in Example 11.5 (page 338), for $H_0: \beta_1 = 0$ and $H_a: \beta_1 \neq 0$, the test statistic was $t = 3.18$ with $df = 37$. Alternatively, we could use $F = t^2 = 3.18^2 = 10.1$, which has the $F$ distribution with $df_1 = 1$ and $df_2 = 37$. The $P$-value for this $F$ value is 0.003, the same as Table 11.5 reports for the two-sided $t$ test.

In general, if a statistic has the $t$ distribution with $d$ degrees of freedom, then the square of that statistic has the $F$ distribution with $df_1 = 1$ and $df_2 = d$. A disadvantage of the $F$ approach is that it lacks information about the direction of the association. It cannot be used for one-sided alternative hypotheses.

## 11.5 INTERACTION BETWEEN PREDICTORS IN THEIR EFFECTS

The multiple regression equation

$$E(y) = \alpha + \beta_1 x_1 + \beta_2 x_2 + \cdots + \beta_k x_k$$

assumes that the partial relationship between $y$ and each $x_i$ is linear and that the slope $\beta_i$ of that relationship is identical for all values of the other explanatory variables. This implies a parallelism of lines relating the two variables, at various values of the other variables, as Figure 11.3 illustrated.

This model is sometimes too simple to be adequate. Often, there is **interaction**, with the relationship between two variables changing according to the value of a third variable. Section 10.3 introduced this concept.

---

**Interaction**

For quantitative variables, **interaction** exists between two explanatory variables in their effects on $y$ when the effect of one variable changes as the level of the other variable changes.

---

For example, suppose the relationship between $x_1$ and the mean of $y$ is $E(y) = 2 + 5x_1$ when $x_2 = 0$, it is $E(y) = 4 + 15x_1$ when $x_2 = 50$, and it is $E(y) = 6 + 25x_1$ when $x_2 = 100$. The slope for the partial effect of $x_1$ changes markedly as the fixed value for $x_2$ changes. There is then interaction between $x_1$ and $x_2$ in their effects on $y$.

## Cross-Product Terms

A common approach for allowing interaction introduces **cross-product terms** of the explanatory variables into the multiple regression model. With two explanatory variables, the model is

$$E(y) = \alpha + \beta_1 x_1 + \beta_2 x_2 + \beta_3 x_1 x_2.$$

This is a special case of the multiple regression model with three explanatory variables, in which $x_3$ is an artificial variable created as the cross-product $x_3 = x_1 x_2$ of the two primary explanatory variables.

Let's see why this model permits interaction. Consider how $y$ is related to $x_1$, controlling for $x_2$. We rewrite the equation in terms of $x_1$ as

$$E(y) = (\alpha + \beta_2 x_2) + (\beta_1 + \beta_3 x_2)x_1 = \alpha' + \beta' x_1,$$

where

$$\alpha' = \alpha + \beta_2 x_2 \quad \text{and} \quad \beta' = \beta_1 + \beta_3 x_2.$$

So, for fixed $x_2$, the mean of $y$ changes linearly as a function of $x_1$. The slope of the relationship is $\beta' = (\beta_1 + \beta_3 x_2)$. This depends on the value of $x_2$. As $x_2$ changes, the slope for the effect of $x_1$ changes. In summary, the mean of $y$ is a linear function of $x_1$, but the slope of the line depends on the value of $x_2$.

Note that now we can interpret $\beta_1$ as the effect of $x_1$ only when $x_2 = 0$. Unless $x_2 = 0$ is a particular value of interest for $x_2$, it is not particularly useful to form confidence intervals or perform significance tests about $\beta_2$ in this model.

Similarly, the mean of $y$ is a linear function of $x_2$, but the slope varies according to the value of $x_1$. The coefficient $\beta_2$ of $x_2$ refers to the effect of $x_2$ only at $x_1 = 0$.

## EXAMPLE 11.6    Interaction Model for Mental Impairment

For the data set on $y$ = mental impairment, $x_1$ = life events, and $x_2$ = SES, we create a third explanatory variable $x_3$ that gives the cross product of $x_1$ and $x_2$

**TABLE 11.8:** Interaction Model for $y$ = Mental Impairment, $x_1$ = Life Events, and $x_2$ = SES

|  | Sum of Squares | DF | Mean Square | F | Sig |
|---|---|---|---|---|---|
| Regression | 403.631 | 3 | 134.544 | 6.383 | 0.0014 |
| Residual | 758.769 | 36 | 21.077 |  |  |
| Total | 1162.400 | 39 |  |  |  |

| R | R Square |
|---|---|
| .589 | .347 |

|  | B | Std. Error | t | Sig |
|---|---|---|---|---|
| (Constant) | 26.036649 | 3.948826 | 6.594 | 0.0001 |
| LIFE | 0.155865 | 0.085338 | 1.826 | 0.0761 |
| SES | -0.060493 | 0.062675 | -0.965 | 0.3409 |
| LIFE*SES | -0.000866 | 0.001297 | -0.668 | 0.5087 |

for the 40 individuals. For the first subject, for example, $x_1 = 46$, $x_2 = 84$, so $x_3 = 46(84) = 3864$. Software makes it easy to create this variable without doing the calculations yourself. Table 11.8 shows part of the printout for the interaction model. The prediction equation is

$$\hat{y} = 26.0 + 0.156x_1 - 0.060x_2 - 0.00087x_1x_2.$$

Figure 11.10 portrays the relationship between predicted mental impairment and life events for a few distinct SES values. For an SES score of $x_2 = 0$, the relationship between $\hat{y}$ and $x_1$ is

$$\hat{y} = 26.0 + 0.156x_1 - 0.060(0) - 0.00087x_1(0) = 26.0 + 0.156x_1.$$

When $x_2 = 50$, the prediction equation is

$$\hat{y} = 26.0 + 0.156x_1 - 0.060(50) - 0.00087(50)x_1 = 23.0 + 0.113x_1.$$

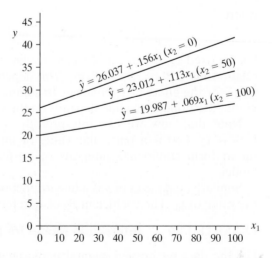

**FIGURE 11.10:** Portrayal of Interaction between $x_1$ and $x_2$ in Their Effects on $y$

When $x_2 = 100$, the prediction equation is

$$y = 20.0 + 0.069x_1.$$

The higher the value of SES, the smaller the slope between predicted mental impairment and life events, and so the weaker is the effect of life events. This suggests that subjects who possess greater resources, in the form of higher SES, are better able to withstand the mental stress of potentially traumatic life events.    ■

### Testing an Interaction Term

For two explanatory variables, the model allowing interaction is

$$E(y) = \alpha + \beta_1 x_1 + \beta_2 x_2 + \beta_3 x_1 x_2.$$

The simpler model assuming no interaction is the special case $\beta_3 = 0$. The hypothesis of no interaction is $H_0: \beta_3 = 0$. As usual, the $t$ test statistic divides the estimate of the parameter ($\beta_3$) by its standard error.

From Table 11.8, $t = -0.00087/0.0013 = -0.67$. The $P$-value for $H_a: \beta_3 \neq 0$ is $P = 0.51$. Little evidence exists of interaction. The variation in the slope of the relationship between mental impairment and life events for various SES levels could be due to sampling variability. The sample size here is small, however, and this makes it difficult to estimate effects precisely. Studies based on larger sample sizes (e.g., Holzer 1977) have shown that interaction of the type seen in this example does exist for these variables.

In Table 11.8, neither the test of $H_0: \beta_1 = 0$ or of $H_0: \beta_2 = 0$ have small $P$-values. Yet the tests of both $H_0: \beta_1 = 0$ and $H_0: \beta_2 = 0$ are highly significant for the "no interaction" model $E(y) = \alpha + \beta_1 x_1 + \beta_2 x_2$; from Table 11.5, the $P$-values are 0.003 and 0.002. This loss of significance occurs because $x_3 = x_1 x_2$ is quite strongly correlated with $x_1$ and $x_2$, with $r_{x_1 x_3} = 0.779$ and $r_{x_2 x_3} = 0.646$. These substantial correlations are not surprising, since $x_3 = x_1 x_2$ is completely determined by $x_1$ and $x_2$.

Since considerable overlap occurs in the variation in $y$ that is explained by $x_1$ and by $x_1 x_2$, and also by $x_2$ and $x_1 x_2$, the *partial* variability explained by each is relatively small. For example, much of the predictive power contained in $x_1$ is also contained in $x_2$ and $x_1 x_2$. The *unique* contribution of $x_1$ (or $x_2$) to the model is relatively small, and nonsignificant, when $x_2$ (or $x_1$) and $x_1 x_2$ are in the model.

When the evidence of interaction is weak, as it is here with a $P$-value of 0.51, it is best to drop the interaction term from the model before testing hypotheses about partial effects such as $H_0: \beta_1 = 0$ or $H_0: \beta_2 = 0$. On the other hand, *if the evidence of interaction is strong, it no longer makes sense to test these other hypotheses.* If there is interaction, then the effect of each variable exists and differs according to the level of the other variable.

### Centering the Explanatory Variables*

For the mental health data, we've seen that $x_1$ and $x_2$ are highly significant in the model with only those predictors (see Table 11.5) but lose their significance after entering the interaction term, even though the interaction is not significant (see Table 11.8). We also saw that the coefficients of $x_1$ and $x_2$ in an interaction model are not usually meaningful, because they refer to the effect of a predictor only when the other predictor equals 0.

There is an alternative way to parameterize the interaction model so that it gives estimates and significance for the effect of $x_1$ and $x_2$ similar to those for the no-interaction model. The method involves *centering* the scores for each explanatory variable around 0, by subtracting the mean. Let $x_1^C = x_1 - \mu_{x_1}$ and $x_2^C = x_2 - \mu_{x_2}$, so that each new explanatory variable has a mean of 0. Then we express the interaction model as

$$E(y) = \alpha + \beta_1 x_1^C + \beta_2 x_2^C + \beta_3 x_1^C x_2^C$$

$$= \alpha + \beta_1(x_1 - \mu_{x_1}) + \beta_2(x_2 - \mu_{x_2}) + \beta_3(x_1 - \mu_{x_1})(x_2 - \mu_{x_2}).$$

Now $\beta_1$ refers to the effect of $x_1$ at the mean of $x_2$, and $\beta_2$ refers to the effect of $x_2$ at the mean of $x_1$. Their estimates are usually similar to the estimated effects for the no-interaction model.

When we rerun the interaction model for the mental health data after centering the predictors about their sample means, that is, with

$$\text{LIFE\_CEN} = \text{LIFE} - 44.425 \text{ and SES\_CEN} = \text{SES} - 56.60,$$

we get software output

|  | B | Std. Error | t | Sig |
|---|---|---|---|---|
| (Constant) | 27.359555 | 0.731366 | 37.409 | 0.0001 |
| LIFE_CEN | 0.106850 | 0.033185 | 3.220 | 0.0027 |
| SES_CEN | -0.098965 | 0.029390 | -3.367 | 0.0018 |
| LIFE_CEN*SES_CEN | -0.000866 | 0.001297 | -0.668 | 0.5087 |

The estimate for the interaction term is the same as for the model with uncentered predictors. Now, though, the estimates (and standard errors) for the effects of $x_1$ and $x_2$ alone are similar to the values for the no-interaction model. This happens because the coefficient for a variable represents its effect at the mean of the other variable, which is typically similar to the effect for the no-interaction model. Also, the statistical significance of $x_1$ and $x_2$ is similar as in the no-interaction model.

Centering the predictor variables before using them in a model allowing interaction has two benefits. First, the estimates of the effects of $x_1$ and $x_2$ are more meaningful, being effects at the mean rather than at 0. Second, the estimates and their standard errors are similar as in the no-interaction model. The cross-product term with centered variables does not overlap with the other terms like it does in the ordinary model.

### Generalizations and Limitations*

When the number of explanatory variables exceeds two, a model allowing interaction can have cross-products for each pair of explanatory variables. For example, with three explanatory variables, an interaction model is

$$E(y) = \alpha + \beta_1 x_1 + \beta_2 x_2 + \beta_3 x_3 + \beta_4 x_1 x_2 + \beta_5 x_1 x_3 + \beta_6 x_2 x_3.$$

This is a special case of multiple regression with six explanatory variables, identifying $x_4 = x_1 x_2$, $x_5 = x_1 x_3$, and $x_6 = x_2 x_3$. Significance tests can judge which, if any, of the cross-product terms are needed in the model.

When interaction exists and the model contains cross-product terms, it is more difficult to summarize simply the relationships. One approach is to sketch a collection of lines such as those in Figure 11.10 to describe graphically how the relationship between two variables changes according to the values of other variables. Another possibility is to divide the data into groups according to the value on a control variable (e.g., high on $x_2$, medium on $x_2$, low on $x_2$) and report the slope between $y$ and $x_1$ within each subset as a means of describing the interaction.

The interaction terms in the above model are called ***second order***, to distinguish them from *higher-order* interaction terms with products of more than two variables at a time. Such terms are occasionally used in more complex models, not considered in this chapter.

## 11.6 COMPARING REGRESSION MODELS

When the number of explanatory variables increases, the multiple regression model becomes more difficult to interpret and some variables may become redundant. This is especially true when some explanatory variables are cross-products of others, to allow for interaction. Not all predictors may be needed in the model. We next present a test of whether a model fits significantly better than a simpler model containing only some of the predictors.

### Complete and Reduced Models

We refer to the full model with all the predictors as the ***complete model***. The model containing only some of these predictors is called the ***reduced model***. The reduced model is said to be *nested* within the complete model, which means that it is a special case of it.

The complete and reduced models are identical if the partial regression coefficients for the extra variables in the complete model all equal 0. In that case, none of the extra predictors increases the explained variability in $y$, in the population of interest. Testing whether the complete model is identical to the reduced model is equivalent to testing whether the extra parameters in the complete model equal 0. The alternative hypothesis is that at least one of these extra parameters is not 0, in which case the complete model is better than the reduced model.

For instance, a complete model with three explanatory variables and all the second-order interaction terms is

$$E(y) = \alpha + \beta_1 x_1 + \beta_2 x_2 + \beta_3 x_3 + \beta_4 x_1 x_2 + \beta_5 x_1 x_3 + \beta_6 x_2 x_3.$$

The reduced model without the interaction terms is

$$E(y) = \alpha + \beta_1 x_1 + \beta_2 x_2 + \beta_3 x_3.$$

The test comparing the complete model to the reduced model has $H_0$: $\beta_4 = \beta_5 = \beta_6 = 0$.

### Comparing Models by Comparing SSE or $R^2$-Values

The test statistic for comparing two regression models compares the residual sums of squares for the two models. Denote $SSE = \sum(y - \hat{y})^2$ for the reduced model by $SSE_r$ and for the complete model by $SSE_c$. Now $SSE_r \geq SSE_c$, because the reduced model has fewer predictors and tends to make poorer predictions. Even if $H_0$ were true, we would not expect the estimates of the extra parameters and the difference $(SSE_r - SSE_c)$ to equal 0. Some reduction in error occurs from fitting the extra terms because of sampling variability.

The test statistic uses the reduction in error, $SSE_r - SSE_c$, that results from adding the extra variables. An equivalent statistic uses the $R^2$-values, $R_c^2$ for the complete model and $R_r^2$ for the reduced model. The test statistic equals

$$F = \frac{(SSE_r - SSE_c)/df_1}{SSE_c/df_2} = \frac{(R_c^2 - R_r^2)/df_1}{(1 - R_c^2)/df_2}.$$

Here, $df_1$ is the number of extra terms in the complete model (e.g., 3 in the example above that adds three interaction terms to get the complete model) and $df_2$ is the usual residual $df$ for the complete model, which is $df_2 = n - (k + 1)$. A relatively large reduction in error (or relatively large increase in $R^2$) yields a large $F$ test statistic and small $P$-value. As usual for $F$ statistics, the $P$-value is the right-tail probability.

### EXAMPLE 11.7  Comparing Models for Mental Impairment

For the mental impairment data, a comparison of the complete model

$$E(y) = \alpha + \beta_1 x_1 + \beta_2 x_2 + \beta_3 x_1 x_2$$

to the reduced model

$$E(y) = \alpha + \beta_1 x_1 + \beta_2 x_2$$

analyzes whether interaction exists. The complete model has just one additional term, and the null hypothesis is $H_0: \beta_3 = 0$.

The sum of squared errors for the complete model is $SSE_c = 758.8$ (Table 11.8), while for the reduced model it is $SSE_r = 768.2$ (Table 11.7). The difference

$$SSE_r - SSE_c = 768.2 - 758.8 = 9.4$$

has $df_1 = 1$ since the complete model has one more parameter. Since the sample size is $n = 40, df_2 = n - (k + 1) = 40 - (3 + 1) = 36$, the $df$ for SSE in Table 11.8. The $F$ test statistic equals

$$F = \frac{(SSE_r - SSE_c)/df_1}{SSE_c/df_2} = \frac{9.4/1}{758.8/36} = 0.45.$$

Equivalently, the $R^2$-values for the two models are $R_r^2 = 0.339$ and $R_c^2 = 0.347$, so

$$F = \frac{\left(R_c^2 - R_r^2\right)/df_1}{(1 - R_c^2)/df_2} = \frac{(0.347 - 0.339)/1}{(1 - 0.347)/36} = 0.45.$$

From software, the $P$-value from the $F$ distribution with $df_1 = 1$ and $df_2 = 36$ is $P = 0.51$. There is little evidence that the complete model is better. The null hypothesis seems plausible, so the reduced model is adequate.

When $H_0$ contains a single parameter, the $t$ test is available. In fact, from the previous section (and Table 11.8), the $t$ statistic equals

$$t = \frac{b_3}{se} = \frac{-0.00087}{0.0013} = -0.67.$$

It also has a $P$-value of 0.51 for $H_a: \beta_3 \neq 0$. We get the same result with the $t$ test as with the $F$ test for complete and reduced models. In fact, the $F$ test statistic equals the square of the $t$ statistic. (Refer to page 340.) ∎

The $t$ test method is limited to testing one parameter at a time. The $F$ test can test *several* regression parameters together to analyze whether at least one of them is nonzero, such as in the global $F$ test of $H_0 : \beta_1 = \cdots = \beta_k = 0$ or the test comparing a complete model to a reduced model. $F$ tests are equivalent to $t$ tests only when $H_0$ contains a single parameter.

## 11.7    PARTIAL CORRELATION*

Multiple regression models describe the effect of an explanatory variable on the response variable while controlling for other variables of interest. Related measures describe the strength of the association. For example, to describe the association between mental impairment and life events, controlling for SES, we could ask, "Controlling for SES, what proportion of the variation in mental impairment does life events explain?"

These measures describe the partial association between $y$ and a particular predictor, whereas the multiple correlation and $R^2$ describe the association between $y$ and the entire set of predictors in the model. The *partial correlation* is based on the ordinary correlations between each pair of variables. For a single control variable, it is defined as follows:

---

**Partial Correlation**

The sample ***partial correlation*** between $y$ and $x_1$, controlling for $x_2$, is

$$r_{yx_1 \cdot x_2} = \frac{r_{yx_1} - r_{yx_2} r_{x_1 x_2}}{\sqrt{\left(1 - r_{yx_2}^2\right)\left(1 - r_{x_1 x_2}^2\right)}}.$$

---

In the symbol $r_{yx_1 \cdot x_2}$, the variable to the right of the dot represents the controlled variable. The analogous formula for $r_{yx_2 \cdot x_1}$ (i.e., controlling $x_1$) is

$$r_{yx_2 \cdot x_1} = \frac{r_{yx_2} - r_{yx_1} r_{x_1 x_2}}{\sqrt{\left(1 - r_{yx_1}^2\right)\left(1 - r_{x_1 x_2}^2\right)}}.$$

Since one variable is controlled, the partial correlations $r_{yx_1 \cdot x_2}$ and $r_{yx_2 \cdot x_1}$ are called ***first-order partial correlations***.

### EXAMPLE 11.8    Partial Correlation Between Education and Crime Rate

Example 11.1 (page 322) discussed a data set for counties in Florida, with $y =$ crime rate, $x_1 =$ education, and $x_2 =$ urbanization. The pairwise correlations are $r_{yx_1} = 0.468, r_{yx_2} = 0.678$, and $r_{x_1 x_2} = 0.791$. It was surprising to observe a positive correlation between crime rate and education. Can it be explained by their joint dependence on urbanization? This is plausible if the association disappears when we control for urbanization.

The partial correlation between crime rate and education, controlling for urbanization, equals

$$r_{yx_1 \cdot x_2} = \frac{r_{yx_1} - r_{yx_2} r_{x_1 x_2}}{\sqrt{\left(1 - r_{yx_2}^2\right)\left(1 - r_{x_1 x_2}^2\right)}} = \frac{0.468 - 0.678(0.791)}{\sqrt{\left(1 - 0.678^2\right)\left(1 - 0.791^2\right)}} = -0.152.$$

Not surprisingly, $r_{yx_1 \cdot x_2}$ is much smaller than $r_{yx_1}$. It even has a different direction, illustrating Simpson's paradox. The relationship between crime rate and education may well be spurious, reflecting their joint dependence on urbanization.    ■

### Interpreting Partial Correlations

The partial correlation has properties similar to those for the ordinary correlation between two variables, such as a range of $-1$ to $+1$, larger absolute values representing stronger associations, and value free of the units. We list the properties below for $r_{yx_1 \cdot x_2}$, but analogous properties apply to $r_{yx_2 \cdot x_1}$.

- $r_{yx_1 \cdot x_2}$ falls between $-1$ and $+1$.
- The larger the absolute value of $r_{yx_1 \cdot x_2}$, the stronger the association between $y$ and $x_1$, controlling for $x_2$.
- The value of a partial correlation does not depend on the units of measurement of the variables.
- $r_{yx_1 \cdot x_2}$ has the same sign as the partial slope ($b_1$) for the effect of $x_1$ in the prediction equation $\hat{y} = a + b_1 x_1 + b_2 x_2$. This happens because the same variable ($x_2$) is controlled in the model as in the correlation.
- Under the assumptions for conducting inference for multiple regression (see the beginning of Section 11.4), $r_{yx_1 \cdot x_2}$ estimates the correlation between $y$ and $x_1$ at every *fixed* value of $x_2$. If we could control $x_2$ by considering a subpopulation of subjects all having the same value on $x_2$, then $r_{yx_1 \cdot x_2}$ estimates the correlation between $y$ and $x_1$ for that subpopulation.
- The sample partial correlation is identical to the correlation computed for the points in the *partial regression plot* (Section 11.2).

### Interpreting Squared Partial Correlations

Like $r^2$ and $R^2$, the square of a partial correlation has a proportional reduction in error (PRE) interpretation. For example, the square of the value of $r_{yx_2 \cdot x_1}$ tells us that $r^2_{yx_2 \cdot x_1}$ is the proportion of variation in $y$ explained by $x_2$, controlling for $x_1$. This squared measure describes the effect of removing from consideration the portion of the total sum of squares (TSS) in $y$ that is explained by $x_1$, and then finding the proportion of the remaining unexplained variation in $y$ that is explained by $x_2$.

---

**Squared Partial Correlation**

The square of the partial correlation $r_{yx_2 \cdot x_1}$ represents the proportion of the variation in $y$ that is explained by $x_2$, out of that left unexplained by $x_1$. It equals

$$r^2_{yx_2 \cdot x_1} = \frac{R^2 - r^2_{yx_1}}{1 - r^2_{yx_1}} = \frac{\text{Partial proportion explained uniquely by } x_2}{\text{Proportion unexplained by } x_1}.$$

---

Recall from Section 9.4 that $r^2_{yx_1}$ represents the proportion of the variation in $y$ explained by $x_1$. The remaining proportion $(1 - r^2_{yx_1})$ represents the variation left unexplained. When $x_2$ is added to the model, it accounts for some additional variation. The total proportion of the variation in $y$ accounted for by $x_1$ and $x_2$ jointly is $R^2$ for the model with both $x_1$ and $x_2$ as explanatory variables. So $R^2 - r^2_{yx_1}$ is the additional proportion of the variability in $y$ explained by $x_2$, after the effects of $x_1$ have been removed or controlled. The maximum this difference could be is $1 - r^2_{yx_1}$, the proportion of variation yet to be explained after accounting for the influence of $x_1$. The additional explained variation $R^2 - r^2_{yx_1}$ divided by this maximum possible difference is a measure that has a maximum possible value of 1. In fact, as the above formula suggests, this ratio equals the squared partial correlation between $y$ and $x_2$, controlling for $x_1$.

Figure 11.11 illustrates this property of the squared partial correlation. It shows the ratio of the partial contribution of $x_2$ beyond that of $x_1$, namely, $R^2 - r^2_{yx_1}$, divided

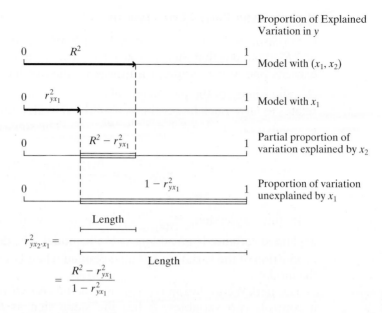

**FIGURE 11.11:** Representation of $r^2_{yx_2 \cdot x_1}$ as the Proportion of Variability That Can Be Explained by $x_2$, of that Variability Left Unexplained by $x_1$

by the proportion $(1 - r^2_{yx_1})$ left unexplained by $x_1$. Similarly, the square of $r_{yx_1 \cdot x_2}$ equals

$$r^2_{yx_1 \cdot x_2} = \frac{R^2 - r^2_{yx_2}}{1 - r^2_{yx_2}},$$

the proportion of variation in $y$ explained by $x_1$, out of that part unexplained by $x_2$.

### EXAMPLE 11.9    Partial Correlation of Life Events with Mental Impairment

We return to the mental health study, with $y$ = mental impairment, $x_1$ = life events, $x_2$ = SES. Software reports the correlation matrix

|        | IMPAIR | LIFE  | SES   |
|--------|--------|-------|-------|
| IMPAIR | 1.000  | .372  | -.399 |
| LIFE   | .372   | 1.000 | .123  |
| SES    | -.399  | .123  | 1.000 |

So $r_{yx_1} = 0.372$, $r_{yx_2} = -0.399$, and $r_{x_1x_2} = 0.123$. By its definition, the partial correlation between mental impairment and life events, controlling for SES, is

$$r_{yx_1 \cdot x_2} = \frac{r_{yx_1} - r_{yx_2}r_{x_1x_2}}{\sqrt{\left(1 - r^2_{yx_2}\right)\left(1 - r^2_{x_1x_2}\right)}} = \frac{0.372 - (-0.399)(0.123)}{\sqrt{\left[1 - (-0.399)^2\right]\left(1 - 0.123^2\right)}} = 0.463.$$

The partial correlation, like the correlation of 0.37 between mental impairment and life events, is moderately positive.

Since $r^2_{yx_1 \cdot x_2} = (0.463)^2 = 0.21$, controlling for SES, 21% of the variation in mental impairment is explained by life events. Alternatively, since $R^2 = 0.339$ (Table 11.7),

$$r^2_{yx_1 \cdot x_2} = \frac{R^2 - r^2_{yx_2}}{1 - r^2_{yx_2}} = \frac{0.339 - (-0.399)^2}{1 - (-0.399)^2} = 0.21.$$  ∎

### Higher-Order Partial Correlations

One reason we showed the connection between squared partial correlation values and $R$-squared is that this approach also works when the number of control variables exceeds one. For example, with three predictors, let $R^2_{y(x_1,x_2,x_3)}$ denote the value of $R^2$. The square of the partial correlation between $y$ and $x_3$, controlling for $x_1$ and $x_2$, relates to how much larger this is than the $R^2$-value for the model with only $x_1$ and $x_2$ as predictors, which we denote by $R^2_{y(x_1,x_2)}$. The squared partial correlation is

$$r^2_{yx_3 \cdot x_1,x_2} = \frac{R^2_{y(x_1,x_2,x_3)} - R^2_{y(x_1,x_2)}}{1 - R^2_{y(x_1,x_2)}}.$$

In this expression, $R^2_{y(x_1,x_2,x_3)} - R^2_{y(x_1,x_2)}$ is the increase in the proportion of explained variance from adding $x_3$ to the model. The denominator $1 - R^2_{y(x_1,x_2)}$ is the proportion of the variation left unexplained when $x_1$ and $x_2$ are the only predictors in the model.

The partial correlation $r_{yx_3 \cdot x_1,x_2}$ is called a **second-order partial correlation**, since it controls two variables. It has the same sign as $b_3$ in the prediction equation $\hat{y} = a + b_1 x_1 + b_2 x_2 + b_3 x_3$, which also controls $x_1$ and $x_2$ in describing the effect of $x_3$.

### Inference for Partial Correlations

Controlling for a certain set of variables, the slope of the partial effect of a predictor is 0 in the same situations in which the partial correlation between $y$ and that predictor is 0. An alternative formula for the $t$ test for a partial effect uses the partial correlation.

With $k$ predictors in the model, the equivalent $t$ test statistic is

$$t = \frac{\text{partial correlation}}{\sqrt{(1 - \text{squared partial correlation})/[n - (k + 1)]}}.$$

This statistic has the $t$ distribution with $df = n - (k + 1)$. It equals the $t$ statistic based on the partial slope estimate and, hence, has the same $P$-value.

We illustrate by testing that the population partial correlation between mental impairment and life events, controlling for SES, is 0. From Example 11.9, $r_{yx_1 \cdot x_2} = 0.463$. There are $k = 2$ explanatory variables and $n = 40$ observations. The test statistic equals

$$t = \frac{r_{yx_1 \cdot x_2}}{\sqrt{(1 - r^2_{yx_1 \cdot x_2})/[n - (k + 1)]}} = \frac{0.463}{\sqrt{[1 - (0.463)^2]/37}} = 3.18.$$

This equals the test statistic for $H_0: \beta_1 = 0$ in Table 11.5. Thus, the $P$-value is also the same, $P = 0.003$.

When no variables are controlled (i.e., the number of explanatory variables is $k = 1$), the $t$ statistic formula simplifies to

$$t = \frac{r}{\sqrt{(1 - r^2)/(n - 2)}}.$$

This is the statistic for testing that the population bivariate correlation equals 0 (Section 9.5). Confidence intervals for partial correlations are more complex. They require a log transformation such as shown for the correlation in Exercise 9.64 in Chapter 9.

## 11.8 STANDARDIZED REGRESSION COEFFICIENTS*

As in bivariate regression (recall Section 9.4), the sizes of regression coefficients in multiple regression models depend on the units of measurement for the variables. To compare the relative effects of two explanatory variables, it is appropriate to compare their coefficients only if the variables have the same units. Otherwise, *standardized* versions of the regression coefficients provide more meaningful comparisons.

---

**Standardized Regression Coefficient**

The **standardized regression coefficient** for an explanatory variable represents the change in the mean of *y*, in *y* standard deviations, for a one-standard-deviation increase in that variable, controlling for the other explanatory variables in the model. We denote them by $\beta_1^*, \beta_2^*, \ldots$

---

If $|\beta_2^*| > |\beta_1^*|$, for example, then a standard deviation increase in $x_2$ has a greater partial effect on *y* than does a standard deviation increase in $x_1$.

### The Standardization Mechanism

The standardized regression coefficients represent the values the regression coefficients take when the units are such that *y* and the explanatory variables all have equal standard deviations. We standardize the partial regression coefficients by adjusting for the differing standard deviation of *y* and each $x_i$. Let $s_y$ denote the sample standard deviation of *y*, and let $s_{x_1}, s_{x_2}, \ldots, s_{x_k}$ denote the sample standard deviations of the explanatory variables.

---

The estimates of the standardized regression coefficients are

$$b_1^* = b_1\left(\frac{s_{x_1}}{s_y}\right), \quad b_2^* = b_2\left(\frac{s_{x_2}}{s_y}\right), \ldots$$

---

### EXAMPLE 11.10    Standardized Coefficients for Mental Impairment

The prediction equation relating mental impairment to life events and SES is

$$\hat{y} = 28.23 + 0.103x_1 - 0.097x_2.$$

Table 11.2 reported the sample standard deviations $s_y = 5.5, s_{x_1} = 22.6$, and $s_{x_2} = 25.3$. Since the unstandardized coefficient of $x_1$ is $b_1 = 0.103$, the estimated standardized coefficient is

$$b_1^* = b_1\left(\frac{s_{x_1}}{s_y}\right) = 0.103\left(\frac{22.6}{5.5}\right) = 0.43.$$

Since $b_2 = -0.097$, the standardized value equals

$$b_2^* = b_2\left(\frac{s_{x_2}}{s_y}\right) = -0.097\left(\frac{25.3}{5.5}\right) = -0.45.$$

The estimated change in the mean of *y* for a standard deviation increase in $x_1$, controlling for $x_2$, has similar magnitude as the estimated change for a standard

TABLE 11.9: SPSS Printout for Fit of Multiple Regression Model to Mental Impairment Data

| | Unstandardized Coefficients | | Standardized Coefficients | | |
| --- | --- | --- | --- | --- | --- |
| | B | Std. Error | Beta | t | Sig. |
| (Constant) | 28.230 | 2.174 | | 12.984 | .000 |
| LIFE | .103 | .032 | .428 | 3.177 | .003 |
| SES | -.097 | .029 | -.451 | -3.351 | .002 |

deviation increase in $x_2$, controlling for $x_1$. However the partial effect of $x_1$ is positive, whereas the partial effect of $x_2$ is negative.

Table 11.9, which repeats Table 11.5, shows how SPSS reports the estimated standardized regression coefficients. It uses the heading BETA, reflecting the alternative name **beta weights** for these coefficients. ∎

### Properties of Standardized Regression Coefficients

For bivariate regression, standardizing the regression coefficient yields the correlation. For the multiple regression model, the standardized partial regression coefficient relates to the partial correlation (Exercise 11.65), and it usually takes a similar value.

Unlike the partial correlation, however, $b_i^*$ need not fall between $-1$ and $+1$. A value $|b_i^*| > 1$ occasionally occurs when $x_i$ is highly correlated with the set of other explanatory variables in the model. In such cases, the standard errors are usually large and the estimates are unreliable.

Since a standardized regression coefficient is a multiple of the unstandardized coefficient, one equals 0 when the other does. The test of $H_0: \beta_i^* = 0$ is equivalent to the $t$ test of $H_0: \beta_i = 0$. It is unnecessary to have separate tests for these coefficients. In the sample, the magnitudes of the $\{b_i^*\}$ have the same relative sizes as the $t$ statistics from those tests. For example, the predictor with the greatest standardized partial effect is the one that has the largest $t$ statistic, in absolute value.

### Standardized Form of Prediction Equation*

Regression equations have an expression using the standardized regression coefficients. In this equation, the variables appear in standardized form.

---

**Notation for Standardized Variables**

Let $z_y, z_{x_1}, \ldots, z_{x_k}$ denote the standardized versions of the variables $y, x_1, \ldots, x_k$. For instance, $z_y = (y - \bar{y})/s_y$ represents the number of standard deviations that an observation on $y$ falls from its mean.

---

Each subject's scores on $y, x_1, \ldots, x_k$ have corresponding $z$-scores for $z_y, z_{x_1}, \ldots, z_{x_k}$. If a subject's score on $x_1$ is such that $z_{x_1} = (x_1 - \bar{x}_1)/s_{x_1} = 2.0$, for instance, then that subject falls two standard deviations above the mean $\bar{x}_1$ on that variable.

Let $\hat{z}_y = (\hat{y} - \bar{y})/s_y$ denote the predicted $z$-score for the response variable. For the standardized variables and the estimated standardized regression coefficients, the prediction equation is

$$\hat{z}_y = b_1^* z_{x_1} + b_2^* z_{x_2} + \cdots + b_k^* z_{x_k}.$$

This equation predicts how far an observation on $y$ falls from its mean, in standard deviation units, based on how far the explanatory variables fall from their means, in standard deviation units. The standardized coefficients are the weights attached to the standardized explanatory variables in contributing to the predicted standardized response variable.

### EXAMPLE 11.11    Standardized Prediction Equation for Mental Impairment

Example 11.10 found that the estimated standardized regression coefficients for the life events and SES predictors of mental impairment are $b_1^* = 0.43$ and $b_2^* = -0.45$. The prediction equation relating the standardized variables is therefore

$$\hat{z}_y = 0.43 z_{x_1} - 0.45 z_{x_2}.$$

Consider a subject who is two standard deviations above the mean on life events but two standard deviations below the mean on SES. This subject has a predicted standardized mental impairment of

$$\hat{z}_y = 0.43(2) - 0.45(-2) = 1.8.$$

The predicted mental impairment for that subject is 1.8 standard deviations above the mean. If the distribution of mental impairment is approximately normal, this subject might well have mental health problems, since only about 4% of the scores in a normal distribution fall at least 1.8 standard deviations above their mean.    ∎

In the prediction equation with standardized variables, no intercept term appears. Why is this? When the standardized explanatory variables all equal 0, those variables all fall at their means. Then $\hat{y} = \bar{y}$, so that

$$\hat{z}_y = \frac{\hat{y} - \bar{y}}{s_y} = 0.$$

So this merely tells us that a subject who falls at the mean on each explanatory variable is predicted to fall at the mean on the response variable.

### Cautions in Comparing Standardized Regression Coefficients

To assess which predictor in a multiple regression model has the greatest impact on the response variable, it is tempting to compare their standardized regression coefficients. Make such comparisons with caution. In some cases, the observed differences in the $b_i^*$ may simply reflect sampling error. In particular, when multicollinearity exists, the standard errors are high and the estimated standardized coefficients may be unstable.

For a standardized regression coefficient to make sense, the variation in the predictor variable must be representative of the variation in the population of interest. It is inappropriate to compare the standardized effect of a predictor to others if the study purposely sampled values of that predictor in a narrow range. This comment related to a warning in Section 9.6 about the correlation: Its value depends strongly on the range of predictor values sampled.

Keep in mind also that the effects are partial ones, depending on which other variables are in the model. An explanatory variable that seems important in one system of variables may seem unimportant when other variables are controlled. For example, it is possible that $|b_2^*| > |b_1^*|$ in a model with two explanatory variables, yet when a third explanatory variable is added to the model, $|b_2^*| < |b_1^*|$.

It is unnecessary to standardize to compare the effect of the same variable for two groups, such as in comparing the results of separate regressions for females and males, since the units of measurement are the same in each group. In fact, it is usually unwise to standardize in this case, because the standardized coefficients are more susceptible than the unstandardized coefficients to differences in the standard deviations of the predictors. Two groups that have the same value for an estimated regression coefficient have different standardized coefficients if the standard deviation of the predictor differs for the two groups.

Finally, if an explanatory variable is highly correlated with the set of other explanatory variables, it is artificial to conceive of that variable changing while the others remain fixed in value. As an extreme example, suppose $y$ = height, $x_1$ = length of left leg, and $x_2$ = length of right leg. The correlation between $x_1$ and $x_2$ is extremely close to 1. It does not make much sense to imagine how $y$ changes as $x_1$ changes while $x_2$ is controlled.

## 11.9 CHAPTER SUMMARY

This chapter generalized the bivariate regression model to include additional explanatory variables. The ***multiple regression equation*** relating a response variable $y$ to a set of $k$ explanatory variables is

$$E(y) = \alpha + \beta_1 x_1 + \beta_2 x_2 + \cdots + \beta_k x_k.$$

- The $\{\beta_i\}$ are ***partial regression coefficients***. The value $\beta_i$ is the change in the mean of $y$ for a one-unit change in $x_i$, controlling for the other variables in the model.

- The ***multiple correlation*** $R$ describes the association between $y$ and the collective set of explanatory variables. It equals the correlation between the observed and predicted $y$-values. It falls between 0 and 1.

- $R^2 = (\text{TSS} - \text{SSE})/\text{TSS}$ represents the *proportional reduction in error* from predicting $y$ using the prediction equation $\hat{y} = a + b_1 x_1 + b_2 x_2 + \cdots + b_k x_k$ instead of $\bar{y}$. It equals the square of the multiple correlation.

- A ***partial correlation***, such as $r_{yx_1 \cdot x_2}$, describes the association between two variables, controlling for others. It falls between $-1$ and $+1$.

- The squared partial correlation between $y$ and $x_i$ represents the proportion of the variation in $y$ that can be explained by $x_i$, out of that part left unexplained by a set of control variables.

- An $F$ ***statistic*** tests $H_0$: $\beta_1 = \beta_2 = \cdots = \beta_k = 0$, that the response variable is independent of all the predictors. A small $P$-value suggests that at least one predictor affects the response.

- Individual $t$ tests and confidence intervals for $\{\beta_i\}$ analyze partial effects of each predictor, controlling for the other variables in the model.

- ***Interaction*** between $x_1$ and $x_2$ in their effects on $y$ means that the effect of either predictor changes as the value of the other predictor changes. We can allow this by introducing cross-products of explanatory variables to the model, such as the term $\beta_3(x_1 x_2)$.

- To ***compare regression models***, a *complete* model and a simpler *reduced* model, the $F$ test compares the SSE values or $R^2$-values.

- ***Standardized regression coefficients*** do not depend on the units of measurement. The estimated standardized coefficient $b_i^*$ describes the change in $y$, in $y$ standard deviation units, for a one-standard-deviation increase in $x_i$, controlling for the other explanatory variables.

To illustrate, with $k = 2$ explanatory variables, the prediction equation is

$$\hat{y} = a + b_1x_1 + b_2x_2.$$

Fixing $x_2$, a straight line describes the relation between $y$ and $x_1$. Its slope $b_1$ is the change in $\hat{y}$ for a one-unit increase in $x_1$, controlling for $x_2$. The multiple correlation $R$ is at least as large as the correlations between $y$ and each predictor. The squared partial correlation $r^2_{yx_2 \cdot x_1}$ is the proportion of the variation of $y$ that is explained by $x_2$, out of that part of the variation left unexplained by $x_1$. The estimated standardized regression coefficient $b_1^* = b_1(s_{x_1}/s_y)$ describes the effect of a standard deviation change in $x_1$, controlling for $x_2$.

Table 11.10 summarizes the basic properties and inference methods for these measures and those introduced in Chapter 9 for bivariate regression.

TABLE 11.10: Summary of Bivariate and Multiple Regression

| | BIVARIATE REGRESSION | MULTIPLE REGRESSION | |
|---|---|---|---|
| | | Simultaneous effect of $x_1 \ldots, x_k$ | Partial effect of one $x_i$ |
| Model Prediction equation | $E(y) = \alpha + \beta x$ $\hat{y} = a + bx$ | $E(y) = \alpha + \beta_1x_1 + \cdots + \beta_kx_k$ $\hat{y} = a + b_1x_1 + \cdots + b_kx_k$ | |
| Properties of measures | $b$ = Slope $r$ = correlation, standardized slope, $-1 \leq r \leq 1$, $r$ has the same sign as $b$ $r^2$ = PRE measure, $0 \leq r^2 \leq 1$ | $R$ = Multiple correlation, $0 \leq R \leq 1$ $R^2$ = PRE measure, $0 \leq R^2 \leq 1$ | $b_i$ = Partial slope $b_i^*$ = Standardized regression coefficient Partial correlation, $-1 \leq r_{yx_1 \cdot x_2} \leq 1$, same sign as $b_i$ and $b_i^*$, $r^2_{yx_1 \cdot x_2}$ is PRE measure |
| Tests of no association | $H_0: \beta = 0$ or $H_0: \rho = 0$, $y$ not associated with $x$ | $H_0: \beta_1 = \cdots = \beta_k = 0$ ($y$ not associated with $x_1, \ldots x_k$) | $H_0: \beta_i = 0$, or $H_0$: popul. partial corr. = 0, $y$ not associated with $x_i$, controlling for other $x$ variables |
| Test statistic | $t = \dfrac{b}{se} = \dfrac{r}{\sqrt{\dfrac{1-r^2}{n-2}}}$ $df = n - 2$ | $F = \dfrac{\text{Regression MS}}{\text{Residual MS}}$ $= \dfrac{R^2/k}{(1-R^2)/[n-(k+1)]}$, $df_1 = k$, $df_2 = n - (k + 1)$ | $t = \dfrac{b_i}{se}$ $df = n - (k + 1)$ |

The model studied in this chapter is still somewhat restrictive in the sense that all the predictors are quantitative. The next chapter shows how to include categorical predictors in the model.

## PROBLEMS

### Practicing the Basics

**11.1.** For students at Walden University, the relationship between $y$ = college GPA (with range 0–4.0) and $x_1$ = high school GPA (range 0–4.0) and $x_2$ = college board score (range 200–800) satisfies $E(y) = 0.20 + 0.50x_1 + 0.002x_2$.
  (a) Find the mean college GPA for students having (i) high school GPA = 4.0 and college board score = 800, (ii) $x_1 = 3.0$ and $x_2 = 300$.
  (b) Show that the relationship between $y$ and $x_1$ for those students with $x_2 = 500$ is $E(y) = 1.2 + 0.5x_1$.
  (c) Show that when $x_2 = 600$, $E(y) = 1.4 + 0.5x_1$. Thus, increasing $x_2$ by 100 shifts the line relating $y$ to $x_1$ upward by $100\beta_2 = 0.2$ units.
  (d) Show that setting $x_1$ at a variety of values yields a collection of parallel lines, each having slope 0.002, relating the mean of $y$ to $x_2$.

**11.2.** For recent data in Florida on $y$ = selling price of home (in dollars), $x_1$ = size of home (in square feet), $x_2$ = lot size (in square feet), the prediction equation is $\hat{y} = -10,536 + 53.8x_1 + 2.84x_2$.
  (a) A particular home of 1240 square feet on a lot of 18,000 square feet sold for $145,000. Find the predicted selling price and the residual, and interpret.
  (b) For fixed lot size, how much is the house selling price predicted to increase for each square foot increase in home size? Why?

**11.3.** Refer to the previous exercise:
  (a) For fixed home size, how much would lot size need to increase to have the same impact as a one square foot increase in home size?
  (b) Suppose house selling prices are changed from dollars to thousands of dollars. Explain why the prediction equation changes to $\hat{y} = -10.536 + 0.0538x_1 + 0.00284x_2$.

**11.4.** Use software with the "2005 statewide crime" data file at the text Web site, with murder rate (number of murders per 100,000 people) as the response variable and with percent of high school graduates and the poverty rate (percentage of the population with income below the poverty level) as explanatory variables.
  (a) Construct the partial regression plots. Interpret. Do you see any unusual observations?
  (b) Report the prediction equation. Explain how to interpret the estimated coefficients.
  (c) Redo the analyses after deleting the D.C. observation. Describe the influence of this observation on the predicted effect of poverty rate. What does this tell you about how influential outliers can be?

**11.5.** A regression analysis with recent UN data from several nations on $y$ = percentage of people who use the Internet, $x_1$ = per capita gross domestic product (in thousands of dollars), and $x_2$ = percentage of people using cell phones has results shown in Table 11.11.
  (a) Write the prediction equation.
  (b) Find the predicted Internet use for a country with per capita GDP of $10,000 and 50% using cell phones.
  (c) Find the prediction equations when cell-phone use is (i) 0 %, (ii) 100%, and use them to interpret the effect of GDP.
  (d) Use the equations in (c) to explain the "no interaction" property of the model.

**TABLE 11.11**

|             | B       | Std. Error | t     | Sig   |
|-------------|---------|------------|-------|-------|
| (Constant)  | -3.601  | 2.506      | -1.44 | 0.159 |
| GDP         | 1.2799  | 0.2703     | 4.74  | 0.000 |
| CELLULAR    | 0.1021  | 0.0900     | 1.13  | 0.264 |

R Square   .796

ANOVA

|                | Sum of Squares | DF |
|----------------|----------------|-----|
| Regression     | 10316.8        | 2  |
| Residual Error | 2642.5         | 36 |
| Total          | 12959.3        | 38 |

**11.6.** Refer to the previous exercise.
  (a) Show how to obtain $R$-squared from the sums of squares in the ANOVA table. Interpret it.
  (b) $r^2 = 0.78$ when GDP is the sole predictor. Why do you think $R^2$ does not increase much when cell-phone use is added to the model, even though it is itself highly associated with $y$ (with $r = 0.67$)? (*Hint*: Would you expect $x_1$ and $x_2$ to be highly correlated? If so, what's the effect?)

**11.7.** Table 9.16 on page 297 showed data from Florida counties on $y$ = crime rate (number per 1000 residents), $x_1$ = median income (thousands of dollars), and $x_2$ = percent in urban environment.
  (a) Figure 11.12 shows a scatterplot relating $y$ to $x_1$. Predict the sign that the estimated effect of $x_1$ has in the prediction equation $\hat{y} = a + bx_1$. Explain.
  (b) Figure 11.13 shows a partial regression plot relating $y$ to $x_1$, controlling for $x_2$. Predict the sign that the estimated effect of $x_1$ has in the prediction equation $\hat{y} = a + b_1x_1 + b_2x_2$. Explain.

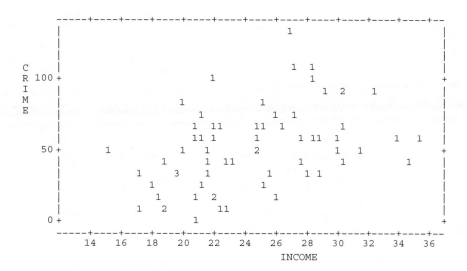

**FIGURE 11.12**

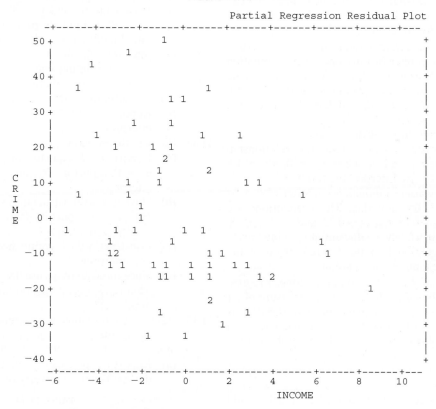

**FIGURE 11.13**

**(c)** Table 11.12 shows part of a printout for the bivariate and multiple regression models. Report the prediction equation relating $y$ to $x_1$, and interpret the slope.

**(d)** Report the prediction equation relating $y$ to both $x_1$ and $x_2$. Interpret the coefficient of $x_1$, and compare to (c).

**(e)** The correlations are $r_{yx_1} = 0.43, r_{yx_2} = 0.68, r_{x_1 x_2} = 0.73$. Use these to explain why the $x_1$ effect seems so different in (c) and (d).

**(f)** Report the prediction equations relating crime rate to income at urbanization levels of (i) 0, (ii) 50, (iii) 100. Interpret.

**TABLE 11.12**

| | B | Std. Error | t | Sig |
|---|---|---|---|---|
| (Constant) | -11.526 | 16.834 | -0.685 | 0.4960 |
| INCOME | 2.609 | 0.675 | 3.866 | 0.0003 |

| | B | Std. Error | t | Sig |
|---|---|---|---|---|
| (Constant) | 40.261 | 16.365 | 2.460 | 0.0166 |
| INCOME | -0.809 | 0.805 | -1.005 | 0.3189 |
| URBAN | 0.646 | 0.111 | 5.811 | 0.0001 |

**11.8.** Refer to the previous exercise. Using software with the "Florida crime" data file at the text website:
   (a) Construct box plots for each variable and scatterplots and partial regression plots between $y$ and each of $x_1$ and $x_2$. Interpret these plots.
   (b) Find the prediction equations for the (i) bivariate effects of $x_1$ and of $x_2$, (ii) multiple regression model. Interpret.
   (c) Find $R^2$ for the multiple regression model, and show that it is not much larger than $r^2$ for the model using urbanization alone as the predictor. Interpret.

**11.9.** Recent UN data from several nations on $y$ = crude birth rate (number of births per 1000 population size), $x_1$ = women's economic activity (female labor force as percentage of male), and $x_2$ = GNP (per capita, in thousands of dollars) has prediction equation $\hat{y} = 34.53 - 0.13x_1 - 0.64x_2$.
   (a) Interpret the coefficient of $x_1$.
   (b) Sketch on a single graph the relationship between $y$ and $x_1$ when $x_2 = 0$, $x_2 = 10$, and $x_2 = 20$. Interpret the results.
   (c) The bivariate prediction equation with $x_1$ is $\hat{y} = 37.65 - 0.31x_1$. The correlations are $r_{yx_1} = -0.58$, $r_{yx_2} = -0.72$, and $r_{x_1x_2} = 0.58$. Explain why the coefficient of $x_1$ in the bivariate equation is quite different from in the multiple predictor equation.

**11.10.** For recent UN data for several nations, a regression of carbon dioxide use ($CO_2$, a measure of air pollution) on gross domestic product (GDP) has a correlation of 0.786. With life expectancy as a second explanatory variable, the multiple correlation is 0.787.
   (a) Explain how to interpret the multiple correlation.
   (b) For predicting $CO_2$, did it help much to add life expectancy to the model? Does this mean that life expectancy is very weakly correlated with $CO_2$? Explain.

**11.11.** Table 11.13 shows a printout from fitting the multiple regression model to recent statewide data, excluding D.C., on $y$ = violent crime rate (per 100,000 people), $x_1$ = poverty rate (percentage with income below the poverty level), and $x_2$ = percent living in urban areas.

**TABLE 11.13**

| | Sum of Squares | DF | Mean Square | F | Sig |
|---|---|---|---|---|---|
| Regression | 2448368.07 | 2 | 1224184.04 | 31.249 | 0.0001 |
| Residual | 1841257.15 | 47 | 39175.68 | | |
| Total | 4289625.22 | 49 | | | |

| R | R Square | Std Error of the Estimate |
|---|---|---|
| .7555 | .5708 | 197.928 |

| | B | Std. Error | t | Sig |
|---|---|---|---|---|
| (Constant) | -498.683 | 140.988 | -3.537 | 0.0009 |
| POVERTY | 32.622 | 6.677 | 4.885 | 0.0001 |
| URBAN | 9.112 | 1.321 | 6.900 | 0.0001 |

| Correlations | VIOLENT | POVERTY | URBAN |
|---|---|---|---|
| VIOLENT | 1.0000 | .3688 | .5940 |
| POVERTY | .3688 | 1.0000 | -.1556 |
| URBAN | .5940 | -.1556 | 1.0000 |

   (a) Report the prediction equation.
   (b) Massachusetts had $y = 805$, $x_1 = 10.7$, and $x_2 = 96.2$. Find its predicted violent crime rate. Find the residual, and interpret.
   (c) Interpret the fit by showing the prediction equation relating $\hat{y}$ and $x_1$ for states with (i) $x_2 = 0$, (ii) $x_2 = 50$, (iii) $x_2 = 100$. Interpret.
   (d) Interpret the correlation matrix.
   (e) Report $R^2$ and the multiple correlation, and interpret.

**11.12.** Refer to the previous exercise.
   (a) Report the $F$ statistic for testing $H_0$: $\beta_1 = \beta_2 = 0$, report its $df$ values and $P$-value, and interpret.
   (b) Show how to construct the $t$ statistic for testing $H_0$: $\beta_1 = 0$, report its $df$ and $P$-value for $H_a$: $\beta_1 \neq 0$, and interpret.
   (c) Construct a 95% confidence interval for $\beta_1$, and interpret.
   (d) Since these analyses use data for all the states, what relevance, if any, do the inferences have in (a)–(c)?

**11.13.** Refer to the previous two exercises. When we add $x_3$ = percentage of single-parent families to the model, we get the results in Table 11.14.
   (a) Report the prediction equation and interpret the coefficient of poverty rate.

**TABLE 11.14**

| Variable | Coefficient | Std. Error |
|---|---|---|
| Intercept | -1197.538 | |
| Poverty | 18.283 | 6.136 |
| Urban | 7.712 | 1.109 |
| Single parent | 89.401 | 17.836 |
| $R^2$ | 0.722 | |
| $n$ | 50 | |

**(b)** Why do you think the effect of poverty rate is much lower after $x_3$ is added to the model?

**11.14.** Table 11.15 comes from a regression analysis of $y$ = number of children in family, $x_1$ = mother's educational level in years (MEDUC), and $x_2$ = father's socioeconomic status (FSES), for a random sample of 49 college students at Texas A&M University.

**(a)** Write the prediction equation. Interpret parameter estimates.

**(b)** Report SSE. Use it to explain the least squares property of this prediction equation.

**(c)** Explain why it is not possible that $r_{yx_1 \cdot x_2} = 0.40$.

**(d)** Can you tell from the table whether $r_{yx_1}$ is positive or negative? Explain.

**TABLE 11.15**

|  | Sum of Squares |
|---|---|
| Regression | 31.8 |
| Residual | 199.3 |
|  | b |
| (Constant) | 5.25 |
| MEDUC | −0.24 |
| FSES | 0.02 |

**11.15.** The GSS has asked subjects to rate various groups using the "feeling thermometer." The rating is between 0 and 100, more favorable as the score gets closer to 100 and less favorable as the score gets closer to 0. For a small data set from the GSS, Table 11.16 shows results of fitting the multiple regression model with feelings toward liberals as the response, using explanatory variables

**TABLE 11.16**

| Variable | Coefficient |
|---|---|
| Intercept | 135.31 |
| Ideology | −14.07 |
|  | (3.16)** |
| Religion | −2.95 |
|  | (2.26) |
| $F$ | 13.93** |
| $R^2$ | 0.799 |
| Adj. $R^2$ | 0.742 |
| ($n$) | (10) |

political ideology (scores 1 = extremely liberal, 2 = liberal, 3 = slightly liberal, 4 = moderate, 5 = slightly conservative, 6 = conservative, 7 = extremely conservative) and religious attendance,

using scores (1 = never, 2 = less than once a year, 3 = once or twice a year, 4 = several times a year, 5 = about once a month, 6 = 2–3 times a month, 7 = nearly every week, 8 = every week, 9 = several times a week). Standard errors are shown in parentheses.

**(a)** Report the prediction equation and interpret the ideology partial effect.

**(b)** Report the predicted value and residual for the first observation, for which ideology = 7, religion = 9, and feelings = 10.

**(c)** Report, and explain how to interpret, $R^2$.

**(d)** Tables of this form often put * by an effect having $P < 0.05$, ** by an effect having $P < 0.01$, and *** by an effect having $P < 0.001$. Show how this was determined for the ideology effect, and discuss the disadvantage of summarizing in this manner.

**(e)** Explain how the $F$-value can be obtained from the $R^2$-value reported. Report its $df$ values, and explain how to interpret its result.

**(f)** The estimated standardized regression coefficients are −0.79 for ideology and −0.23 for religion. Interpret.

**11.16.** Refer to Table 11.5 on page 330. Test $H_0: \beta_2 = 0$ that mental impairment is independent of SES, controlling for life events. Report the test statistic, and report and interpret the $P$-value for (a) $H_a: \beta_2 \neq 0$, (b) $H_a: \beta_2 < 0$.

**11.17.** For a random sample of 66 state precincts, data are available on

$y$ = Percentage of adult residents who are registered to vote

$x_1$ = Percentage of adult residents owning homes

$x_2$ = Percentage of adult residents who are nonwhite

$x_3$ = Median family income (thousands of dollars)

$x_4$ = Median age of residents

$x_5$ = Percentage of residents who have lived in the precinct at least 10 years.

Table 11.17 shows a portion of the printout used to analyze the data.

**(a)** Fill in all the missing values in the printout.

**(b)** Do you think it is necessary to include all five explanatory variables in the model? Explain.

**(c)** To what test does the "F" refer? Interpret the result of that test.

**(d)** To what test does the $t$-value opposite x1 refer? Interpret the result of that test.

**11.18.** Refer to the previous exercise.

**(a)** Find a 95% confidence interval for the change in the mean of $y$ for a one-unit increase in

**TABLE 11.17**

| Variable | Sum of Squares | DF | Mean Square | F | Sig | R-Square |
|---|---|---|---|---|---|---|
| | | | | | | ---- |
| Regression | ---- | --- | ---- | ---- | ---- | |
| Residual | 2940.0 | --- | ---- | | | Root MSE |
| Total | 3753.3 | --- | | | | ---- |

| Variable | Parameter Estimate | Standard Error | t | Sig |
|---|---|---|---|---|
| Intercept | 70.0000 | | | |
| x1 | 0.1000 | 0.0450 | ---- | ---- |
| x2 | -0.1500 | 0.0750 | ---- | ---- |
| x3 | 0.1000 | 0.2000 | ---- | ---- |
| x4 | -0.0400 | 0.0500 | ---- | ---- |
| x5 | 0.1200 | 0.0500 | ---- | ---- |

the percentage of adults owning homes, controlling for the other variables. Interpret.

**(b)** Find a 95% confidence interval for the change in the mean of $y$ for a 50-unit increase in the percentage of adults owning homes, controlling for the other variables. Interpret.

**11.19.** Use software with the "house selling price" data file at the text Web site to conduct a multiple regression analysis of $y$ = selling price of home (dollars), $x_1$ = size of home (square feet), $x_2$ = number of bedrooms, $x_3$ = number of bathrooms.

**(a)** Use scatterplots to display the effects of the predictors on $y$. Interpret, and explain how the highly discrete nature of $x_2$ and $x_3$ affects the plots.

**(b)** Report the prediction equation and interpret the estimated partial effect of size of home.

**(c)** Inspect the correlation matrix, and report the variable having the (i) strongest association with $y$, (ii) weakest association with $y$.

**(d)** Report $R^2$ for this model and $r^2$ for the simpler model using $x_1$ alone as the predictor. Interpret.

**11.20.** Refer to the previous exercise.

**(a)** Test the partial effect of number of bathrooms, and interpret.

**(b)** Find the partial correlation between selling price and number of bathrooms, controlling for number of bedrooms. Compare it to the correlation, and interpret.

**(c)** Find the estimated standardized regression coefficients for the model, and interpret.

**(d)** Write the prediction equation using standardized variables. Interpret.

**11.21.** Exercise 11.11 showed a regression analysis for statewide data on $y$ = violent crime rate, $x_1$ = poverty rate, and $x_2$ = percent living in urban areas. When we add an interaction term, we get the prediction equation $\hat{y} = 158.9 - 14.72x_1 - 1.29x_2 + 0.76x_1x_2$.

**(a)** As the percentage living in urban areas increases, does the effect of poverty rate tend to increase or decrease? Explain.

**(b)** Show how to interpret the prediction equation by finding how it simplifies when $x_2 = 0$, 50, and 100.

**11.22.** A study analyzes relationships among $y$ = percentage vote for Democratic candidate, $x_1$ = percentage of registered voters who are Democrats, and $x_2$ = percentage of registered voters who vote in the election, for several congressional elections in 2006. The researchers expect interaction, since they expect a higher slope between $y$ and $x_1$ at larger values of $x_2$ than at smaller values. They obtain the prediction equation $\hat{y} = 20 + 0.30x_1 + 0.05x_2 + 0.005x_1x_2$. Does this equation support the direction of their prediction? Explain.

**11.23.** Use software with the "house selling price" data file to allow interaction between number of bedrooms and number of bathrooms in their effects on selling price.

**(a)** Interpret the fit by showing the prediction equation relating $\hat{y}$ and number of bedrooms for homes with (i) two bathrooms, (ii) three bathrooms.

**(b)** Test the significance of the interaction term. Interpret.

**11.24.** A multiple regression analysis investigates the relationship between $y$ = college GPA and several explanatory variables, using a random sample of 195 students at Slippery Rock University. First, high school GPA and total SAT score are entered into the model. The sum of squared errors is SSE = 20. Next, parents' education and parents' income are added, to determine if they have an effect, controlling for high school GPA and SAT. For this expanded model SSE $= 19$. Test whether this complete model is significantly better than the one containing only high school GPA and SAT. Report and interpret the $P$-value.

**11.25.** Table 11.18 shows results of regressing $y =$ birth rate (BIRTHS, number of births per 1000 population) on $x_1 =$ women's economic activity (ECON) and $x_2 =$ literacy rate (LITERACY), using UN data for 23 nations.

(a) Report the value of each of the following:
  (i) $r_{yx_1}$    (ii) $r_{yx_2}$    (iii) $R^2$
  (iv) TSS    (v) SSE    (vi) mean square error    (vii) $s$    (viii) $s_y$
  (ix) $se$ for $b_1$    (x) $t$ for $H_0$: $\beta_1 = 0$
  (xi) $P$ for $H_0$: $\beta_1 = 0$ against $H_a$: $\beta_1 \neq 0$
  (xii) $P$ for $H_0$: $\beta_1 = 0$ against $H_a$: $\beta_1 < 0$
  (xiii) $F$ for $H_0$: $\beta_1 = \beta_2 = 0$
  (xiv) $P$ for $H_0$: $\beta_1 = \beta_2 = 0$

(b) Report the prediction equation, and interpret the signs of the estimated regression coefficients.

(c) Interpret the correlations $r_{yx_1}$ and $r_{yx_2}$.

(d) Report $R^2$, and interpret its value.

(e) Report the multiple correlation, and interpret.

(f) Though inference may not be relevant for these data, report the $F$ statistic for $H_0$: $\beta_1 = \beta_2 = 0$, report its $P$-value, and interpret.

(g) Show how to construct the $t$ statistic for $H_0$: $\beta_1 = 0$, report its $df$ and $P$-value for $H_a$: $\beta_1 \neq 0$, and interpret.

**11.26.** Refer to the previous exercise.

(a) Find the partial correlation between $y$ and $x_1$, controlling for $x_2$. Interpret the partial correlation and its square.

(b) Find the estimate of the conditional standard deviation, and interpret its value.

(c) Show how to find the estimated standardized regression coefficient for $x_1$ using the unstandardized estimate and the standard deviations, and interpret its value.

(d) Write the prediction equation using standardized variables. Interpret.

(e) Find the predicted $z$-score for a country that is one standard deviation above the mean on both predictors. Interpret.

**TABLE 11.18**

|           | Mean   | Std Deviation | N  |
|-----------|--------|---------------|----|
| BIRTHS    | 22.117 | 10.469        | 23 |
| ECON      | 47.826 | 19.872        | 23 |
| LITERACY  | 77.696 | 17.665        | 23 |

Correlations

|                 |          | BIRTHS   | ECON     | LITER    |
|-----------------|----------|----------|----------|----------|
| Correlation     | BIRTHS   | 1.00000  | -0.61181 | -0.81872 |
|                 | ECON     | -0.61181 | 1.00000  | 0.42056  |
|                 | LITERACY | -0.81872 | 0.42056  | 1.00000  |
|                 |          |          |          |          |
| Sig.(2-tailed)  | BIRTHS   | .        | 0.0019   | 0.0001   |
|                 | ECON     | 0.0019   | .        | 0.0457   |
|                 | LITERACY | 0.0001   | 0.0457   | .        |

|            | Sum of Squares | DF | Mean Square | F      | Sig    |
|------------|----------------|----|-------------|--------|--------|
| Regression | 1825.969       | 2  | 912.985     | 31.191 | 0.0001 |
| Residual   | 585.424        | 20 | 29.271      |        |        |
| Total      | 2411.393       | 22 |             |        |        |

Root MSE (Std. Error of the Estimate)  5.410    R Square  0.7572

|            | Unstandardized Coeff. B | Std. Error | Standardized Coeff. (Beta) | t      | Sig    |
|------------|-------------------------|------------|-----------------------------|--------|--------|
| (Constant) | 61.713                  | 5.2453     |                             | 11.765 | 0.0001 |
| ECON       | -0.171                  | 0.0640     | -0.325                      | -2.676 | 0.0145 |
| LITERACY   | -0.404                  | 0.0720     | -0.682                      | -5.616 | 0.0001 |

**11.27.** Refer to Examples 11.1 (page 322) and 11.8 (page 347). Explain why the partial correlation between crime rate and high school graduation rate is so different from the bivariate correlation. (This is an example of *Simpson's paradox*, which states that a bivariate association can have a different direction than a partial association.)

**11.28.** For a group of 100 children of ages varying from 3 to 15, the correlation between vocabulary score on an achievement test and height of child is 0.65. The correlation between vocabulary score and age for this sample is 0.85, and the correlation between height and age is 0.75.

(a) Show that the partial correlation between vocabulary and height, controlling for age, is 0.036. Interpret.

(b) Test whether this partial correlation is significantly nonzero. Interpret.

(c) Is it plausible that the relationship between height and vocabulary is spurious, in the sense that it is due to their joint dependence on age? Explain.

**11.29.** A multiple regression model describes the relationship among a collection of cities between $y$ = murder rate (number of murders per 100,000 residents) and

$x_1$ = Number of police officers (per 100,000 residents)

$x_2$ = Median length of prison sentence given to convicted murderers (in years)

$x_3$ = Median income of residents of city (in thousands of dollars)

$x_4$ = Unemployment rate in city

These variables are observed for a random sample of 30 cities with population size exceeding 35,000. For the model with these predictors, software reports the estimated standardized regression coefficients of $-0.075$ for $x_1$, $-0.125$ for $x_2$, $-0.30$ for $x_3$, and 0.20 for $x_4$.

(a) Write the prediction equation using standardized variables.

(b) Which explanatory variable has the greatest partial effect on $y$? Explain.

(c) Find the predicted $z$-score on murder rate for a city that is one standard deviation above the mean on $x_1$, $x_2$, and $x_3$, and one standard deviation below the mean on $x_4$. Interpret.

**11.30.** Exercise 11.11 showed a regression of violent crime rate on poverty rate and percent living in metropolitan areas. The estimated standardized regression coefficients are 0.473 for poverty rate and 0.668 for percent in metropolitan areas.

(a) Interpret the estimated standardized regression coefficients.

(b) Express the prediction equation using standardized variables, and explain how it is used.

## Concepts and Applications

**11.31.** Refer to the "Student survey" data file (Exercise 1.11 on page 8). Using software, conduct a regression analysis using $y$ = political ideology with predictors number of times per week of newspaper reading and religiosity. Prepare a report, posing a research question and summarizing your graphical analyses, bivariate models and interpretations, multiple regression models and interpretations, inferences, checks of effects of outliers, and overall summary of the relationships.

**11.32.** Repeat the previous exercise using $y$ = college GPA with predictors high school GPA and number of weekly hours of physical exercise.

**11.33.** Refer to the student data file you created in Exercise 1.12. For variables chosen by your instructor, fit a multiple regression model and conduct descriptive and inferential statistical analyses. Interpret and summarize your findings.

**11.34.** Refer to the "OECD data" file at the text Web site, shown in Table 3.11 on page 62 of Chapter 3. Pose a research question about how at least two of the variables shown in that table relate to carbon dioxide emissions. Conduct appropriate analyses to address that question, and prepare a two-page report summarizing your analyses and conclusions.

**11.35.** Using software with the "2005 statewide crime" data file at the text Web site, conduct a regression analysis of violent crime rate with predictors poverty rate, the percent living in urban areas, and percent of high school graduates. Prepare a report in which you state a research question you could answer with these data, conduct descriptive and inferential analyses, and provide interpretations and summarize your conclusions.

**11.36.** For the previous exercise, repeat the analysis, excluding the observation for D.C. Describe the effect on the various analyses of this observation.

**11.37.** Table 9.13 on page 294 in Chapter 9 is the "UN data" data file at the text Web site. Construct a multiple regression model containing two explanatory variables that provide good predictions for the fertility rate. How did you select this model? (*Hint*: One way is based on entries in the correlation matrix.)

**11.38.** In about 200 words, explain to someone who has never studied statistics what multiple regression does and how it can be useful.

**11.39.** Analyze the "house selling price" data file at the text Web site (which were introduced in Example 9.10 on page 278), using selling price of home, size of home, number of bedrooms, and taxes. Prepare a short report summarizing your analyses and conclusions.

**11.40.** For Example 11.2 on mental impairment, Table 11.19 shows the result of adding religious attendance as a predictor, measured as the approximate number of times the subject attends a religious service over the course of a year. Write a short report, interpreting the information from this table.

**TABLE 11.19**

| Variable | Coefficient |
|----------|-------------|
| Intercept | 27.422 |
| Life events | 0.0935 |
|  | $(0.0313)^{**}$ |
| SES | −0.0958 |
|  | $(0.0256)^{***}$ |
| Religious attendance | −0.0370 |
|  | (0.0219) |
| $R^2$ | 0.358 |
| (n) | (40) |

**11.41.** A study[3] of mortality rates found in the U.S. that states with higher income inequality tended to have higher mortality rates. The effect of income inequality disappeared after controlling for the percentage of a state's residents that had at least a high school education. Explain how these results relate to analyses conducted using bivariate regression and multiple regression.

**11.42.** A 2002 study[4] relating the percentage of a child's life spent in poverty to number of years of education completed by the mother and the percentage of a child's life spent in a single parent home reported the results shown in Table 11.20. Prepare a one-page report explaining how to interpret the results in this table.

**TABLE 11.20**

|  | Unstandardized Coefficients | | Standardized Coefficients | | |
|---|---|---|---|---|---|
|  | B | Std. Error | Beta | t | Sig. |
| (Constant) | 56.401 | 2.121 |  | 12.662 | .000 |
| % single parent | 0.323 | .014 | .295 | 11.362 | .000 |
| mother school | -3.330 | .152 | -.290 | -11.294 | .000 |

F 611.6 (df = 2, 4731)   Sig .000
R 0.453   R Square 0.205

[3] A. Muller, *British Medical Journal*, vol. 324, 2002, pp. 23–25.
[4] http://www.heritage.org/Research/Family/cda02-05.cfm
[5] http://www.economist.com/media/pdf/QUALITYOFLIFE.pdf

**11.43.** *The Economist* magazine[5] developed a quality-of-life index for nations as the predicted value obtained by regressing an average of life-satisfaction scores from several surveys on gross domestic product (GDP, per capita, in dollars), life expectancy (in years), an index of political freedom (from 1 = completely free to 7 = unfree), the percentage unemployed, the divorce rate (on a scale of 1 for lowest rates to 5 for highest), latitude (to distinguish between warmer and cold climes), a political stability measure, gender equality defined as the ratio of average male and female earnings, and community life (1 if country has high rate of church attendance or trade-union membership, 0 otherwise). Table 11.21 shows results of the model fit for 74 countries, for which the multiple correlation is 0.92. The study used the prediction equation to predict the quality of life in 2005 for 111 nations. The top 10 ranks were for Ireland, Switzerland, Norway, Luxembourg, Sweden, Australia, Iceland, Italy, Denmark, and Spain. Other ranks included 13 for the U.S., 14 for Canada, 15 for New Zealand, 16 for Netherlands, and 29 for the U.K.

**TABLE 11.21**

|  | Coefficient | Standard Error | t Statistic |
|---|---|---|---|
| Constant | 2.796 | 0.789 | 3.54 |
| GDP per person | 0.00003 | 0.00001 | 3.52 |
| Life expectancy | 0.045 | 0.011 | 4.23 |
| Political freedom | −0.105 | 0.056 | −1.87 |
| Unemployment | −0.022 | 0.010 | −2.21 |
| Divorce rate | −0.188 | 0.064 | −2.93 |
| Latitude | −1.353 | 0.469 | −2.89 |
| Political stability | 0.152 | 0.052 | 2.92 |
| Gender equality | 0.742 | 0.543 | 1.37 |
| Community life | 0.386 | 0.124 | 3.13 |

**(a)** Which variables would you expect to have negative effects on quality of life? Is this supported by the results?

**(b)** The study states that by itself "GDP explains more than 50% of the variation in life satisfaction." How does this relate to a summary measure of association?

**(c)** The study reported that "using so-called Beta coefficients from the regression to derive the weights of the various factors, life expectancy and GDP were the most important." Explain what was meant by this.

**(d)** Although GDP seems to be an important predictor, in a bivariate sense and a partial sense, Table 11.21 reports a very small coefficient, 0.00003. Why do you think this is?

**(e)** The study mentioned other predictors that were not included because they provided no further predictive power. For example, the study stated that education seemed to have an effect mainly through its effects on other variables in the model, such as GDP, life expectancy, and political freedom. Does this mean there is no association between education and quality of life? Explain.

**11.44.** A recent article[6] used multiple regression to predict attitudes toward homosexuality. The researchers found that the effect of number of years of education on a measure of tolerance toward homosexuality varied from essentially no effect for political conservatives to a considerably positive effect for political liberals. Explain how this is an example of statistical interaction, and explain how it would be handled by a multiple regression model.

**11.45.** In the study mentioned in the previous exercise, a separate model did not contain interaction terms. The best predictor of attitudes toward homosexuality was educational level, with an estimated standardized regression coefficient of 0.21. The authors also reported, "Controlling for other variables, an additional year of education completed was associated with a .09 rating unit increase in attitudes toward homosexuality." In comparing the effect of education with the effects of other predictors in the model, such as the age of the subject, explain the purpose of estimating standardized coefficients. Explain how to interpret the one reported for education.

**11.46.** In Exercise 11.1 on $y$ = college GPA, $x_1$ = high school GPA, and $x_2$ = college board score, $E(y) = 0.20 + 0.50x_1 + 0.002x_2$. True or false: Since $\beta_1 = 0.50$ is larger than $\beta_2 = 0.002$, this implies that $x_1$ has the greater partial effect on $y$. Explain.

**11.47.** Table 11.22 shows results of fitting various regression models to data on $y$ = college GPA, $x_1$ = high school GPA, $x_2$ = mathematics entrance exam score, and $x_3$ = verbal entrance exam score. Indicate which of the following statements are false. Give a reason for your answer.

**(a)** The correlation between $y$ and $x_1$ is positive.

**(b)** A one-unit increase in $x_1$ corresponds to a change of 0.45 in the estimated mean of $y$, controlling for $x_2$ and $x_3$.

**(c)** It follows from the sizes of the estimates for the third model that $x_1$ has the strongest partial effect on $y$.

**(d)** The value of $r^2_{yx_3}$ is 0.40.

**(e)** The partial correlation $r_{yx_1 \cdot x_2}$ is positive.

**(f)** Controlling for $x_1$, a 100-unit increase in $x_2$ corresponds to a predicted increase of 0.3 in college GPA.

**(g)** For the first model, the estimated standardized regression coefficient equals 0.50.

**11.48.** In regression analysis, which of the following statements must be false? Why?

**(a)** $r_{yx_1} = 0.01, r_{yx_2} = -0.75, R = 0.2$

**(b)** The value of the residual sum of squares, SSE, can increase as we add additional variables to the model.

**(c)** For the model $E(y) = \alpha + \beta_1 x_1$, $y$ is significantly related to $x_1$ at the 0.05 level, but when $x_2$ is added to the model, $y$ is not significantly related to $x_1$ at the 0.05 level.

**(d)** The estimated coefficient of $x_1$ is positive in the bivariate model but negative in the multiple regression model.

**(e)** When the model is refitted after $y$ is multiplied by 10, $R^2$, $r_{yx_1}$, $r_{yx_1 \cdot x_2}$, and the $F$ statistics and $t$ statistics do not change.

**(f)** The $F$ statistic for testing that all the regression coefficients equal 0 has $P < 0.05$, but none of the individual $t$ tests have $P < 0.05$.

**(g)** If you compute the standardized regression coefficient for a bivariate model, you always get the correlation.

**(h)** $r^2_{yx_1} = r^2_{yx_2} = 0.6$ and $R^2 = 1.2$.

**(i)** The correlation between $y$ and $\hat{y}$ equals $-0.10$.

**TABLE 11.22**

| Estimates | $E(y) = \alpha + \beta x_1$ | $E(y) = \alpha + \beta_1 x_1 + \beta_2 x_2$ | $E(y) = \alpha + \beta_1 x_1 + \beta_2 x_2 + \beta_3 x_3$ |
|---|---|---|---|
| Coefficient of $x_1$ | 0.450 | 0.400 | 0.340 |
| Coefficient of $x_2$ | | 0.003 | 0.002 |
| Coefficient of $x_3$ | | | 0.002 |
| $R^2$ | 0.25 | 0.34 | 0.38 |

[6]T. Shackelford and A. Besser, *Individual Differences Research*, vol. 5, 2007, pp. 106–114.

**(j)** For every $F$ test, there is an equivalent test using the $t$ distribution.

**(k)** When $|b_1| > |b_2|$ in a multiple regression prediction equation, we can conclude that $x_1$ has a stronger effect than $x_2$ on $y$.

**(l)** The estimated standardized regression coefficient for a predictor in a multiple regression model can be interpreted as the value the ordinary slope would equal for the linear prediction equation if that predictor and $y$ were scaled so they both had the same standard deviation value.

**(m)** If $\hat{y} = 31.3 + 0.15x_1 - 0.05x_2 - 0.002x_1x_2$, then the estimated effect $x_1$ on $y$ decreases as $x_2$ increases.

**(n)** Suppose $\hat{y} = 31.3 + 0.15x_1 - 0.05x_2 - 0.002x_1x_2$, with $x_1$ and $x_2$ taking values between 0 and 100. Then, since the coefficient of $x_1x_2$ is so small compared to the coefficients of $x_1$ and of $x_2$, we can conclude that the amount of interaction is negligible.

*For Exercises 11.49–11.52, select the correct answer(s) and indicate why the other responses are inappropriate. (More than one response may be correct.)*

**11.49.** If $\hat{y} = 2 + 3x_1 + 5x_2 - 8x_3$, then controlling for $x_2$ and $x_3$, the predicted mean change in $y$ when $x_1$ is increased from 10 to 20 equals
(a) 3  (b) 30  (c) 0.3  (d) Cannot be given—depends on specific values of $x_2$ and $x_3$.

**11.50.** If $\hat{y} = 2 + 3x_1 + 5x_2 - 8x_3$,
**(a)** The strongest correlation is between $y$ and $x_3$.
**(b)** The variable with the strongest partial influence on $y$ is $x_2$.
**(c)** The variable with the strongest partial influence on $y$ is $x_3$, but one cannot tell from this equation which pair has the strongest correlation.
**(d)** None of the above.

**11.51.** If $\hat{y} = 2 + 3x_1 + 5x_2 - 8x_3$,
**(a)** $r_{yx_3} < 0$
**(b)** $r_{yx_3 \cdot x_1} < 0$
**(c)** $r_{yx_3 \cdot x_1 x_2} < 0$
**(d)** Insufficient information to answer.
**(e)** Answers (a), (b), and (c) are all correct.

**11.52.** The $F$ test for comparing a complete model to a reduced model
**(a)** Can be used to test the significance of a single regression parameter in a multiple regression model
**(b)** Can be used to test $H_0: \beta_1 = \cdots = \beta_k = 0$ in a multiple regression equation

**(c)** Can be used to test $H_0$: No interaction, in the model
$$E(y) = \alpha + \beta_1x_1 + \beta_2x_2 + \beta_3x_3 + \beta_4x_1x_2 + \beta_5x_1x_3 + \beta_6x_2x_3$$

**(d)** Can be used to test whether the model $E(y) = \alpha + \beta_1x_1 + \beta_2x_2$ gives a significantly better fit than the model $E(y) = \alpha + \beta_1x_1 + \beta_2x_3$

**11.53.** Explain the difference in the purposes of the correlation, the multiple correlation, and the partial correlation.

**11.54.** Let $y$ = height, $x_1$ = length of right leg, $x_2$ = length of left leg. Describe what you expect for the relative sizes of $r_{x_1x_2}, r_{yx_2}, R$, and $r_{yx_2 \cdot x_1}$.

**11.55.** Give an example of three variables for which you expect $\beta \neq 0$ in the model $E(y) = \alpha + \beta x_1$ but $\beta_1 = 0$ in the model $E(y) = \alpha + \beta_1x_1 + \beta_2x_2$.

**11.56.** For the models $E(y) = \alpha + \beta x$ and $E(y) = \alpha + \beta_1x_1 + \beta_2x_2$, express null hypotheses in terms of correlations that are equivalent to the following:
**(a)** $H_0: \beta = 0$
**(b)** $H_0: \beta_1 = \beta_2 = 0$
**(c)** $H_0: \beta_2 = 0$

**\*11.57.** Whenever $x_1$ and $x_2$ are uncorrelated, then $R^2$ for the model $E(y) = \alpha + \beta_1x_1 + \beta_2x_2$ satisfies $R^2 = r_{yx_1}^2 + r_{yx_2}^2$. In this case, draw a figure that portrays the variability in $y$, the part of that variability explained by each of $x_1$ and $x_2$, and the total variability explained by both of them together.

**\*11.58.** Which of the following sets of correlations would you expect to yield the highest $R^2$ value? Why?
**(a)** $r_{yx_1} = 0.4$,   $r_{yx_2} = 0.4$,   $r_{x_1x_2} = 0.0$
**(b)** $r_{yx_1} = 0.4$,   $r_{yx_2} = 0.4$,   $r_{x_1x_2} = 0.5$
**(c)** $r_{yx_1} = 0.4$,   $r_{yx_2} = 0.4$,   $r_{x_1x_2} = 1.0$

**\*11.59.** Suppose the correlation between $y$ and $x_1$ equals the multiple correlation between $y$ and $x_1$ and $x_2$. What does this imply about the partial correlation $r_{yx_2 \cdot x_1}$? Interpret.

**\*11.60.** Software reports four types of sums of squares in multiple regression models. The **Type I** (sometimes called *sequential*) **sum of squares** represents the variability explained by a variable, controlling for variables previously entered into the model. The **Type III** (sometimes called *partial*) **sum of squares** represents the variability explained by that variable, controlling for all other variables in the model.
**(a)** For any multiple regression model, explain why the Type I sum of squares for $x_1$ is the regression sum of squares for the bivariate model with $x_1$ as the predictor, whereas the Type I sum of squares for $x_2$ equals the amount by which SSE decreases when $x_2$ is added to the model.

**(b)** Explain why the Type I sum of squares for the last variable entered into a model is the same as the Type III sum of squares for that variable.

*11.61. The sample value of $R^2$ tends to overestimate the population value, because the sample data fall closer to the sample prediction equation than to the true population regression equation. This bias is greater if $n$ is small or the number of predictors $k$ is large. A better estimate is **adjusted** $R^2$,

$$R^2_{adj} = 1 - \frac{s^2}{s^2_y} = R^2 - \left[\frac{k}{n - (k + 1)}\right](1 - R^2),$$

where $s^2$ is the estimated conditional variance and $s^2_y$ is the sample variance of $y$. We'll use this measure in Section 14.1.

**(a)** Suppose $R^2 = 0.339$ for a model with $k = 2$ explanatory variables, as in Table 11.5. Find $R^2_{adj}$ when $n = 10, 40$ (as in the text example), 100, and 1000. Show that $R^2_{adj}$ approaches $R^2$ in value as $n$ increases.

**(b)** Show that $R^2_{adj} < 0$ when $R^2 < k/(n - 1)$. This is undesireable, and $R^2_{adj}$ is equated to 0 in such cases. (Also, unlike $R^2$, $R^2_{adj}$ can decrease when we add an explanatory variable to a model.)

*11.62. Let $R^2_{y(x_1,...,x_k)}$ denote $R^2$ for the multiple regression model with $k$ explanatory variables. Explain why

$$r^2_{yx_k \cdot x_1,...,x_{k-1}} = \frac{R^2_{y(x_1,...,x_k)} - R^2_{y(x_1,...,x_{k-1})}}{1 - R^2_{y(x_1,...,x_{k-1})}}.$$

*11.63. The numerator $R^2 - r^2_{yx_1}$ of the squared partial correlation $r^2_{yx_2 \cdot x_1}$ gives the increase in the proportion of explained variation from adding $x_2$ to the model. This increment, denoted by $r^2_{y(x_2 \cdot x_1)}$, is called the squared **semipartial** correlation. One can use squared semipartial correlations to partition the variation in the response variable. For instance, for three explanatory variables,

$$R^2_{y(x_1,x_2,x_3)} = r^2_{yx_1} + (R^2_{y(x_1,x_2)} - r^2_{yx_1}) +$$
$$(R^2_{y(x_1,x_2,x_3)} - R^2_{y(x_1,x_2)})$$
$$= r^2_{yx_1} + r^2_{y(x_2 \cdot x_1)} + r^2_{y(x_3 \cdot x_1,x_2)}.$$

The total variation in $y$ explained by $x_1$, $x_2$, and $x_3$ together partitions into (i) the proportion explained by $x_1$ (i.e., $r^2_{yx_1}$), (ii) the proportion explained by $x_2$ beyond that explained by $x_1$ (i.e., $r^2_{y(x_2 \cdot x_1)}$), and (iii) the proportion explained by $x_3$

beyond that explained by $x_1$ and $x_2$ (i.e, $r^2_{y(x_3 \cdot x_1,x_2)}$). These correlations (each obtained by controlling for all other predictors in the model) have the same ordering as the $t$ statistics for testing partial effects, and some researchers use them as indices of importance of the predictors.

**(a)** In Example 11.2 on mental impairment, show that $r^2_{y(x_2 \cdot x_1)} = 0.20$ and $r^2_{y(x_1 \cdot x_2)} = 0.18$. Interpret.

**(b)** Explain why the squared semipartial correlation $r^2_{y(x_2 \cdot x_1)}$ cannot be larger than the squared partial correlation $r^2_{yx_2 \cdot x_1}$.

*11.64. The least squares prediction equation provides predicted values $\hat{y}$ with the strongest possible correlation with $y$, out of all possible prediction equations of that form. That is, the least squares equation yields the best prediction of $y$ in the sense that it represents the linear reduction of $x_1, \ldots, x_k$ to the single variable that is most strongly correlated with $y$. Based on this property, explain why the multiple correlation cannot decrease when one adds a variable to a multiple regression model. (*Hint*: The prediction equation for the simpler model is a special case of a prediction equation for the full model that has coefficient 0 for the added variable.)

*11.65. Let $\overline{b}^*_i$ denote the estimated standardized regression coefficient when $x_i$ is treated as the *response* variable and $y$ as an *explanatory* variable, controlling for the same set of other variables. Then $\overline{b}^*_i$ need not equal $b^*_i$. The squared partial correlation between $y$ and $x_i$, which *is* symmetric in the order of the two variables, equals

$$b^*_i \overline{b}^*_i.$$

**(a)** From this formula, explain why the partial correlation must fall between $b^*_i$ and $\overline{b}^*_i$. (*Note*: When $a = \sqrt{bc}$, $a$ is said to be the *geometric average* of $b$ and $c$.)

**(b)** Even though $b^*_i$ does not necessarily fall between $-1$ and $+1$, explain why $b^*_i \overline{b}^*_i$ cannot exceed 1.

*11.66. Chapters 12 and 13 show how to incorporate categorical predictors in regression models, and this exercise provides a preview. Table 11.23 shows part of a printout for a model for the "house selling price 2" data set at the text Web site, with $y =$ selling price of home, $x_1 =$ size of home, and $x_2 =$ whether the house is new (1 = yes, 0 = no).

**(a)** Report the prediction equation. By setting $x_2 = 0$ and then 1, construct the two separate lines for older and for new homes. Note that the model implies that the slope effect of size on selling price is the same for each.

**TABLE 11.23**

|  | B | Std. Error | t | Sig |
|---|---|---|---|---|
| (Constant) | -26.089 | 5.977 | -4.365 | 0.0001 |
| SIZE | 72.575 | 3.508 | 20.690 | 0.0001 |
| NEW | 19.587 | 3.995 | 4.903 | 0.0001 |

**(b)** Since $x_2$ takes only the values 0 and 1, explain why the coefficient of $x_2$ estimates the difference of mean selling prices between new and older homes, controlling for house size.

**\*11.67.** Refer to the previous exercise. When we add an interaction term, we get $\hat{y} = -16.6 + 66.6x_1 - 31.8x_2 + 29.4(x_1x_2)$.

**(a)** Interpret the fit by reporting the prediction equation between selling price and size of house separately for new homes ($x_2 = 1$) and for old homes ($x_2 = 0$). Interpret. (This fit is equivalent to fitting lines separately to the data for new homes and for old homes.)

**(b)** A plot of the data shows an outlier, a new home with a very high selling price. When that observation is removed from the data set and the model is refitted, $\hat{y} = -16.6 + 66.6x_1 + 9.0x_2 + 5.0(x_1x_2)$. Redo (a), and explain how an outlier can have a large impact on a regression analysis.

# Comparing Groups: Analysis of Variance (ANOVA) Methods

Chapter 7 presented methods for comparing the means of two groups. In this chapter we see how those methods extend for comparing means of *several* groups.

Chapter 8 presented methods for analyzing association between two *categorical* variables. Chapters 9 and 11 presented regression methods for analyzing association between *quantitative* variables. Methods for comparing means for several groups relate to the association between a *quantitative* response variable and *categorical* explanatory variable. The mean of the quantitative response variable is compared among groups that are categories of the explanatory variable. For example, for a comparison of mean annual income among blacks, whites, and Hispanics, the quantitative response variable is annual income and the categorical explanatory variable is racial-ethnic status.

The inferential method for comparing several means is called the ***analysis of variance***, abbreviated ***ANOVA***. Section 12.1 shows that the name refers to the way a significance test focuses on two types of variability in the data. Section 12.2 presents confidence intervals comparing group means. Section 12.3 shows that the inferences are special cases of a multiple regression analysis. Sections 12.4 and 12.5 extend the methods to incorporate additional explanatory variables—for example, to compare mean income across categories of both racial-ethnic status and gender.

Sections 12.1–12.5 present analyses for *independent samples*. As Section 7.1 explained, when each sample has the same subjects rather than unmatched samples, the samples are *dependent* and different methods apply. Sections 12.6 and 12.7 present such methods.

## 12.1 COMPARING SEVERAL MEANS: THE ANALYSIS OF VARIANCE *F* TEST

The great British statistician R. A. Fisher developed the analysis of variance method in the 1920s. The heart of this analysis is a significance test, using his *F* distribution, for detecting differences among a set of population means.

### Assumptions for the *F* Test Comparing Means

Let $g$ denote the number of groups to compare, such as $g = 3$ groups as above in comparing blacks, whites, and Hispanics. The means of the response variable for the corresponding populations are $\mu_1, \mu_2, \ldots, \mu_g$, such as $\mu_1$ for mean annual income of blacks, $\mu_2$ for mean annual income of whites, and $\mu_3$ for mean annual income of Hispanics. The sample means are $\bar{y}_1, \bar{y}_2, \ldots, \bar{y}_g$.

The analysis of variance (ANOVA) is an $F$ test for

$$H_0: \mu_1 = \mu_2 = \cdots = \mu_g$$
$$H_a: \text{at least two of the population means are unequal.}$$

If $H_0$ is false, perhaps all the population means differ, perhaps some differ, or perhaps merely one mean differs from the others. The test analyzes whether the differences observed among the sample means could have reasonably occurred by chance, if $H_0$ were true.

The assumptions for the test are as follows:

- For each group, the population distribution of the response variable $y$ is normal.
- The standard deviation of the population distribution is the same for each group. Denote the common value by $\sigma$.
- The samples from the populations are *independent* random samples.

Figure 12.1 portrays the first two assumptions. Under these assumptions, the null hypothesis states that the population distribution does not depend on the group to which a subject belongs. The ANOVA test is a *test of independence* between the quantitative response variable and the categorical explanatory variable.

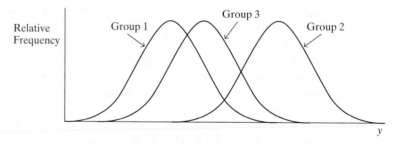

**FIGURE 12.1:** Assumptions about Population Distributions: Normal with Equal Standard Deviations, $\sigma$

The assumptions about the population distributions are stringent ones that are never satisfied exactly in practice. As usual, the random sampling assumption is the most important one. The last section of this chapter discusses the effects of violating assumptions.

### EXAMPLE 12.1 Political Ideology by Political Party

Table 12.1 summarizes observations on political ideology for three groups, based on data from subjects age 18–30 in the 2004 GSS. The three groups are the (Democrat, Independent, Republican) categories of the explanatory variable, political party identification (ID). Political ideology, the response variable, is measured on a seven-point scale, ranging from extremely liberal (1) to extremely conservative (7). For each party ID, Table 12.1 shows the number of subjects who made each response. For instance, of 91 Democrats, 9 responded extremely liberal, 20 responded liberal, ..., 0 responded extremely conservative.

Since Table 12.1 displays the data as counts in a contingency table, we could use methods for categorical data (Chapter 8). The chi-squared test treats both variables as nominal, however, whereas political ideology is ordinal. That test is not directed toward detecting whether responses have a higher or lower mean in some groups than others. Likewise, the ordinal methods of Chapter 8 (such as the gamma measure of association) are inappropriate, because they require both variables to be ordinal. Here, the groups, which are the categories of political party ID, are nominal.

**TABLE 12.1:** Political Ideology by Political Party ID, for Subjects Age 18–30

| Group (Party ID) | Political Ideology | | | | | | | Sample Size | Mean | Standard Deviation |
|---|---|---|---|---|---|---|---|---|---|---|
| | 1 | 2 | 3 | 4 | 5 | 6 | 7 | | | |
| Democrat | 9 | 20 | 17 | 36 | 4 | 5 | 0 | 91 | 3.23 | 1.28 |
| Independent | 7 | 11 | 17 | 48 | 12 | 11 | 5 | 111 | 3.90 | 1.43 |
| Republican | 0 | 2 | 7 | 23 | 23 | 17 | 2 | 74 | 4.70 | 1.10 |

*Note*: For political ideology, 1 = extremely liberal, 2 = liberal, 3 = slightly liberal, 4 = moderate, 5 = slightly conservative, 6 = conservative, 7 = extremely conservative.

When an ordinal response has several categories, in practice it is common to assign scores to its levels and treat it as a quantitative variable. This is a reasonable strategy when we would like to focus on a measure of center such as the mean rather than on the proportions in particular categories. For Table 12.1, for instance, interest might focus on how liberal or conservative the responses tend to be for each group, in some average sense, rather than on the proportions falling in each category. We analyze these data by assigning the scores (1, 2, 3, 4, 5, 6, 7) to the levels of political ideology and then comparing means. The higher the mean score, the more conservative the group's responses tended to be.

For these scores, Table 12.1 also shows the mean and standard deviation for each group. The overall sample mean is $\bar{y} = 3.89$, quite near the score of 4.0 corresponding to moderate ideology. We shall test whether the three populations have equal means. The null hypothesis is $H_0: \mu_1 = \mu_2 = \mu_3$, where $\mu_1$ is the population mean ideology for Democrats, $\mu_2$ for Independent, and $\mu_3$ for Republicans. ∎

## Variability between and within Groups

Why is a method for comparing population *means* called an analysis of *variance*? The reason is that the test statistic compares the means by using two estimates of the variance, $\sigma^2$, for each group. One estimate uses the variability *between* each sample mean $\bar{y}_i$ and the overall mean $\bar{y}$. The other estimate uses the variability *within* each group of the sample observations about their separate means—the observations from the first group about $\bar{y}_1$, the observations from the second group about $\bar{y}_2$, and so forth.

To illustrate, suppose randomly sampled observations from three groups are as shown in Figure 12.2a. It seems clear that the means of the populations these samples represent are unequal. The basis for this conclusion is that the variability *between* sample means is large and the variability of the observations *within* each sample is small.

By contrast, look at Figure 12.2b. It has the same sample means as in Figure 12.2a, so the variability *between* sample means is the same. But in Figure 12.2b the variability *within* the groups is much larger than in Figure 12.2a. The sample standard deviation for each group is much larger in Figure 12.2b. Now it is not clear whether the population means differ. Generally, the greater the variability between sample means and the smaller the variability within each group, the stronger the evidence against the null hypothesis of equal population means.

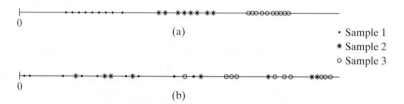

FIGURE 12.2: Two Samples. The means are the same in each case, so variability *between* groups is the same, but variability *within* groups is larger in the second set.

### The *F* Test Statistic Is a Ratio of Two Variance Estimates

For testing $H_0: \mu_1 = \mu_2 = \cdots = \mu_g$, the test statistic is the ratio of the two estimates of the population variance. The estimate that uses the variability *between* each sample mean $\bar{y}_i$ and the overall sample mean $\bar{y}$, is called the **between-groups estimate**. The estimate that uses the variability *within* each sample is called the **within-groups estimate**.

The *F* test statistic has the form

$$F = \frac{\text{Between-groups estimate of variance}}{\text{Within-groups estimate of variance}}.$$

This is called the **analysis of variance F statistic**, or **ANOVA F statistic** for short. We'll leave the computational details of the variance estimates for later in the section.

The within-groups estimate is an unbiased estimate of $\sigma^2$ regardless of whether $H_0$ is true. Because of this, we'll use it also in the formula for confidence intervals comparing means. By contrast, the between-groups estimate is unbiased only if $H_0$ is true. It then takes about the same value as the within-groups estimate. We then expect values of $F$ near 1.0, apart from sampling error. If $H_0$ is false, however, the between-groups estimate tends to overestimate $\sigma^2$. It then tends to be larger than the within-groups estimate, and the $F$ test statistic tends to be larger than 1.0, moreso with larger samples.

When $H_0$ is true, this $F$ test statistic has an $F$ sampling distribution. As in $F$ tests for multiple regression parameters (e.g., Section 11.4), the $P$-value is the right-tail probability that the $F$ test statistic exceeds the observed $F$ value. The larger the $F$ test statistic, the smaller the $P$-value.

### EXAMPLE 12.2    *F* Test Comparing Mean Political Ideology by Party ID

Software displays the results of ANOVA $F$ tests in a table similar to the one used to display sums of squares in regression analysis. This table is called an **ANOVA table**. Table 12.2 shows an ANOVA table for the $F$ test of $H_0: \mu_1 = \mu_2 = \mu_3$ comparing population mean political ideology for three political party IDs with Table 12.1.

In the ANOVA table,

- The two "mean squares" are the between-groups and within-groups estimates of the population variance $\sigma^2$.
- The $F$ test statistic is the ratio of the two mean squares.

From the Mean Square column of Table 12.2., the between-groups estimate of the variance is 44.21 and the within-groups estimate is 1.68. The $F$ test statistic is

**TABLE 12.2**: ANOVA Table for Result of $F$ Test for Table 12.1. The $F$ test statistic is the ratio of mean squares.

| Source | Sum of Squares | df | Mean Square | F | Sig |
|---|---|---|---|---|---|
| Between-Groups (Party ID) | 88.43 | 2 | 44.21 | 26.3 | .000 |
| Within-Groups (Error) | 459.52 | 273 | 1.68 | | |
| Total | 547.95 | 275 | | | |

$F = 44.21/1.68 = 26.3$. In other words, the between-groups estimate is more than 25 times the within-groups estimate. Recall that if $H_0$ is true, we expect values of $F$ near 1.0, apart from sampling error. So this test statistic gives strong evidence against $H_0$: $\mu_1 = \mu_2 = \mu_3$. Table 12.2 reports that the $P$-value is 0.000, rounded to three decimal places. We conclude that a difference exists among the population mean political ideology values for the three political party IDs.  ∎

### Within-Groups Estimate of Variance*

Now we'll see how to construct the variance estimates that form the $F$ statistic. Each estimate is a measure of variability divided by a degrees-of-freedom term.

The within-groups estimate of the population variance $\sigma^2$ pools together the sums of squares of the observations about their means. Now, for the $n_1$ observations from the first group, $\Sigma(y - \bar{y}_1)^2$ is the sum of squares of the observations about their mean. This sum of squares has $n_1 - 1$ degrees of freedom, the denominator for the sample variance $s_1^2$ for group 1. Similarly, for the $n_2$ observations from the second group, $\Sigma(y - \bar{y}_2)^2$ is the sum of squares of the observations about their sample mean, with $n_2 - 1$ degrees of freedom. The sum of these sum-of-squares terms for all the samples is called the **within-groups sum of squares**, since the sums of squares are calculated *within* each sample.

The within-groups sum of squares has degrees of freedom equal to the sum of the *df* values of the component parts:

$$df = (n_1 - 1) + (n_2 - 1) + \cdots + (n_g - 1) = (n_1 + n_2 + \cdots + n_g) - g$$

$$= N - g = \text{Total sample size} - \text{number of groups},$$

where $N$ denotes the total sample size. The ratio

$$s^2 = \frac{\text{Within-groups sum of squares}}{df} = \frac{\text{Within-groups SS}}{N - g}$$

is the within-groups estimate of the population variance $\sigma^2$ for the $g$ groups.

This estimate summarizes information about variability from the separate samples. The estimate of $\sigma^2$ using only the first group is

$$s_1^2 = \frac{\Sigma(y - \bar{y}_1)^2}{n_1 - 1}.$$

In Table 12.1, for example, this is the square of the reported standard deviation, $s_1 = 1.28$. Similarly, the sample variance for the second group is $s_2^2 = \Sigma(y - \bar{y}_2)^2/(n_2 - 1)$, and so forth for the remaining groups. Under the assumption that the population variances are identical, these terms all estimate the same parameter,

$\sigma^2$. The numerator and denominator of $s^2$ pool the information from these estimates by adding their numerators and adding their denominators. The resulting estimate relates to the separate sample variances by

$$s^2 = \frac{(n_1 - 1)s_1^2 + (n_2 - 1)s_2^2 + \cdots + (n_g - 1)s_g^2}{N - g}.$$

This estimate is a weighted average of the separate sample variances, with greater weight given to larger samples. With equal sample sizes, $s^2$ is the mean of the $g$ sample variances.

For the political ideology data in Table 12.1, we could calculate $s^2$ by calculating the within sum of squares from the raw data. Since Table 12.1 reports the standard deviations, however, it is simpler to use the formula just given, or better yet, use software. The sample sizes for the groups are $n_1 = 91, n_2 = 111, n_3 = 74$, for a total sample size of $N = 276$. From Table 12.1,

$$s^2 = \frac{(n_1 - 1)s_1^2 + (n_2 - 1)s_2^2 + (n_3 - 1)s_3^2}{N - 3}$$

$$= \frac{(91 - 1)(1.28)^2 + (111 - 1)(1.43)^2 + (74 - 1)(1.10)^2}{276 - 3} = \frac{459.5}{273} = 1.68.$$

In summary, the within-groups sum of squares equals 459.5, with $df = 273$, providing a within-groups variance estimate of 1.68. The standard deviation estimate of $s = \sqrt{1.68} = 1.30$ summarizes the three sample standard deviations from Table 12.1.

### Between-Groups Estimate of Variance*

The estimate of $\sigma^2$ based on variability between each sample mean and the overall sample mean equals

$$\frac{\sum_i n_i(\bar{y}_i - \bar{y})^2}{g - 1} = \frac{n_1(\bar{y}_1 - \bar{y})^2 + \cdots + n_g(\bar{y}_g - \bar{y})^2}{g - 1}.$$

Exercise 12.57 motivates this formula. Since this estimate describes variability among $g$ means, its

$$df = g - 1 = \text{Number of groups} - 1,$$

which is the denominator of the estimate.

The numerator of this estimate is called the **between-groups sum of squares**. The squared difference between each sample mean and the overall mean is weighted by the sample size upon which it is based. When the population means are unequal, the $\bar{y}_i$-values tend to be more variable than if the population means are equal. The farther the population means fall from the $H_0$: $\mu_1 = \cdots = \mu_g$ case, the larger the between-groups SS (sum of squares), the between-groups estimate, and the $F$ test statistic tend to be.

For Table 12.1, the overall mean $\bar{y} = 3.89$. The between-groups sum of squares equals

$$\text{Between-groups SS} = = n_1(\bar{y}_1 - \bar{y})^2 + n_2(\bar{y}_2 - \bar{y})^2 + n_3(\bar{y}_3 - \bar{y})^2$$

$$= 91(3.23 - 3.89)^2 + 111(3.90 - 3.89)^2 + 74(4.70 - 3.89)^2$$

$$= 88.43.$$

Since $g$ = number of groups = 3, this sum of squares has $df = g - 1 = 3 - 1 = 2$. The between-groups estimate of the variance is

$$\frac{\text{Between-groups SS}}{g - 1} = \frac{88.43}{2} = 44.2.$$

### Sums of Squares in ANOVA Tables*

Let's now look again at the ANOVA table (Table 12.2) for political ideology and political party ID. For the $F$ test,

$$df_1 = g - 1 = \text{No. groups} - 1 \quad \text{and} \quad df_2 = N - g$$
$$= \text{Total sample size} - \text{no. groups}.$$

These are reported in the $df$ column of the table. For these data, $df_1 = g - 1 = 3 - 1 = 2$ and $df_2 = N - g = 276 - 3 = 273$.

In the "Between-groups" row of the ANOVA table, the between-groups SS divided by $df_1$ gives a mean square, $88.43/2 = 44.21$. In the "Within-groups" row, the within-groups SS divided by $df_2$ gives the other mean square, $459.52/273 = 1.68$. The $F$ test statistic for $H_0: \mu_1 = \mu_2 = \mu_3$ is the ratio of the variance estimates, which is the ratio of the two mean squares, $F = 44.21/1.68 = 26.3$. The two $df$ terms for the test are the denominators of the two estimates of the variance.

The sum of the within-groups and between-groups sums of squares is called the **total sum of squares**. In fact, this equals

$$TSS = \sum(y - \bar{y})^2 = \text{Between-groups SS} + \text{Within-groups SS},$$

the sum of squares of the combined sample of $N$ observations about the overall mean, $\bar{y}$. Table 12.2 shows that TSS = 547.95 = 88.43 + 459.52.

The ANOVA partitions the total variability about the overall mean, TSS, into two independent parts. One part, the between-groups SS, is the portion of the total explained by the difference between each group mean and the overall mean. This is also called the *group sum of squares*, and most software replaces the "Between-groups" label in Table 12.2 by the name of the group variable (e.g., PARTY ID). The other part, the within-groups SS, is the portion of the total variability that cannot be explained by the differences among the groups. It represents the variability that remains after classifying the observations into separate groups. The within-groups sum of squares is also called the *error sum of squares*, and most software replaces the "Within-groups" label in Table 12.2 by "Error." Section 12.3 explains the analogy between these sums of squares and the sums of squares in regression analysis.

### The *F* Test versus Several *t* Tests

With two groups, Section 7.5 showed how a $t$ test can compare the means under the assumption of equal population standard deviations. In fact, if we apply the ANOVA $F$ test to data from $g = 2$ groups, the $F$ test statistic equals the square of that $t$ test statistic. The $P$-value for the $F$ test is exactly the same as the two-sided $P$-value for the $t$ test. We can use either test to conduct the analysis.

With several groups, instead of using the $F$ test, why not use a $t$ test to compare each pair of means? One reason is that using a single $F$ test rather than multiple $t$ tests enables us to control the overall probability of type I error. With an $\alpha$-level of 0.05 in the $F$ test, the probability of incorrectly rejecting a true $H_0$ is fixed at 0.05. By contrast, when we do a separate $t$ test for each pair of means, a type I error probability applies for *each* comparison. We do not then control the overall type I error rate for all the comparisons. The next section shows how these same considerations are relevant for confidence intervals.

## 12.2    MULTIPLE COMPARISONS OF MEANS

The analysis of variance $F$ test of $H_0$: $\mu_1 = \mu_2 = \cdots = \mu_g$ is a global test of independence of the response and explanatory variables, just like the $F$ test of $H_0$: $\beta_1 = \cdots = \beta_k = 0$ for multiple regression models or the chi-squared test for contingency tables. When the $P$-value is small, this does not indicate which means are different or how different they are. Confidence intervals help us to determine this. Even if the $P$-value is not small, it still is informative to estimate just how large differences in means could plausibly be.

### Confidence Intervals Comparing Means

In practice, it is more informative to estimate the population means than merely to test whether they are all equal. We can construct a confidence interval for each mean or for each difference between a pair of means.

- A confidence interval for $\mu_i$ is

$$\bar{y}_i \pm t\frac{s}{\sqrt{n_i}}.$$

In this formula, $s$ is the square root of the within-groups estimate of $\sigma^2$ that is the denominator of the ANOVA $F$ test statistic. The $t$-value for the chosen confidence level is based on $df$ for that estimate, $df = N - g$.

- A confidence interval for $\mu_i - \mu_j$ is

$$\left(\bar{y}_i - \bar{y}_j\right) \pm ts\sqrt{\frac{1}{n_i} + \frac{1}{n_j}}.$$

In this formula also, $df = N - g$ for the tabled $t$-value. Evidence exists of a difference between $\mu_i$ and $\mu_j$ when the interval does not contain 0. (For $g = 2$ groups, $df = N - g = n_1 + n_2 - 2$; this confidence interval then simplifies to the one Section 7.5 introduced for $\mu_2 - \mu_1$ assuming a common standard deviation.)

### EXAMPLE 12.3    Comparing Mean Ideology of Democrats and Republicans

For Table 12.1, let's compare population mean ideology of Democrats (group 1) and Republicans (group 3). From Table 12.1, $\bar{y}_1 = 3.23$ for $n_1 = 91$ Democrats and $\bar{y}_3 = 4.70$ for $n_3 = 74$ Republicans. From Table 12.2, the estimate of the population standard deviation is $s = \sqrt{1.68} = 1.30$, with $df = 273$. For a 95% confidence interval with $df = 273$, the $t$-score is $t_{.025} = 1.97$ (essentially the $z_{.025}$-score). The confidence interval for $\mu_3 - \mu_1$ is

$$(\bar{y}_3 - \bar{y}_1) \pm t_{.025}s\sqrt{\frac{1}{n_1} + \frac{1}{n_3}} = (4.70 - 3.23) \pm 1.97(1.30)\sqrt{\frac{1}{91} + \frac{1}{74}}$$

$$= 1.47 \pm 0.40 \quad \text{or} \quad (1.07, 1.87).$$

We infer that population mean ideology was between 1.07 and 1.87 units higher for Republicans than for Democrats. Since the interval contains only positive numbers, we conclude that $\mu_3 - \mu_1 > 0$; that is, $\mu_3$ exceeds $\mu_1$. On the average, Republicans were more conservative than Democrats, with difference about one to two categories on the seven-category scale. ■

### Error Rates with Large Numbers of Confidence Intervals

With $g$ groups, there are $g(g-1)/2$ pairs of groups to compare. When $g$ is relatively large, the number of comparisons can be very large. Confidence intervals for some pairs of means may suggest they are different *even if all of the population means are equal.*

When $g = 10$, for example, there are $g(g-1)/2 = 45$ pairs of means. Suppose we form a 95% confidence interval for the difference between each pair. The error probability of 0.05 applies for each comparison. For the 45 comparisons, we'd expect that $45(0.05) = 2.25$ of the intervals would not contain the true differences of means.

For 95% confidence intervals, the error probability of 0.05 is the probability that any particular confidence interval will not contain the true difference in population means. When we form a large number of confidence intervals, the probability that *at least* one confidence interval will be in error is much larger than the error probability for any particular interval. The larger the number of groups to compare, the greater is the chance of at least one incorrect inference.

### Bonferroni Multiple Comparisons of Means

When we plan many comparisons, methods are available that control the probability that *all* intervals will contain the true differences. Such methods are called *multiple comparison* methods. They fix the probability that *all* intervals contain the true differences of population means *simultaneously* rather than individually.

For example, with a multiple comparison method applied with $g = 10$ means and 95% confidence, the probability equals 0.95 that *all* 45 of the intervals will contain the pairwise differences $\mu_i - \mu_j$. Equivalently, the probability that *at least one* interval is in error equals 0.05. This probability is called the *multiple comparison error rate*.

We first present the *Bonferroni multiple comparison* method, since it is simple and applies to a wide variety of situations. The Bonferroni method uses the same formulas for confidence intervals introduced at the beginning of this section. However, it uses a more stringent confidence level for each interval, to ensure that the overall confidence level is sufficiently high.

To illustrate, suppose we'd like a multiple comparison error rate of 0.10, that is, a probability of 0.90 that all confidence intervals are simultaneously correct. If we plan four comparisons of means, then the Bonferroni method uses error probability $0.10/4 = 0.025$ for each one. That is, it uses a 97.5% confidence level for each interval. This approach is somewhat conservative: It ensures that the actual overall error rate is *at most* 0.10 and that the overall confidence level is *at least* 0.90. The method is based on an inequality shown by the Italian probabilist Carlo Bonferroni in 1935. It states that the probability that at least one of a set of events occurs can be no greater than the sum of the separate probabilities of the events. For instance, if the probability of an error equals 0.025 for each of four confidence intervals, then the probability that at least one of the four intervals will be in error is no greater than $(0.025 + 0.025 + 0.025 + 0.025) = 0.10$.

### EXAMPLE 12.4    Bonferroni Intervals for Political Ideology Comparisons

For the $g = 3$ party IDs in Table 12.1, let's compare the mean political ideologies: $\mu_1$ with $\mu_2$, $\mu_1$ with $\mu_3$, and $\mu_2$ with $\mu_3$. We construct confidence intervals (CIs) having overall confidence level at least 0.95. For a multiple comparison error rate of 0.05 with three comparisons, the Bonferroni method uses error probability $0.05/3 = 0.0167$

for each interval. These use the $t$-score with two-tail probability 0.0167, or single-tail probability 0.0083. For the large $df$ value here ($df = 273$), this equals 2.41, close to the $z$-score of 2.39. Recall also that $s = 1.30$.

The interval for $\mu_3 - \mu_1$, the difference between the population mean ideology of Republicans and Democrats, is

$$(\bar{y}_2 - \bar{y}_1) \pm ts\sqrt{\frac{1}{n_1} + \frac{1}{n_2}} = (4.70 - 3.23) \pm 2.41(1.30)\sqrt{\frac{1}{91} + \frac{1}{74}}$$

$$= 1.47 \pm 0.49 \quad \text{or} \quad (0.98, 1.96).$$

We construct the intervals for the other two pairs of means in a similar way. Table 12.3 displays them. None of the intervals contain 0. They show significant evidence of a difference between each pair of population means. ■

**TABLE 12.3:** Bonferroni and Tukey 95% Multiple Comparisons of Mean Political Ideology for Three Political Party ID Groups. The 95% confidence applies to the entire set of three intervals, rather than each individual interval.

| Groups | Difference of Means $\mu_i - \mu_j$ | Estimated Difference $\bar{y}_i - \bar{y}_j$ | Bonferroni 95% CI | Tukey 95% CI |
|---|---|---|---|---|
| (Independent, Democrat) | $\mu_2 - \mu_1$ | 0.67 | $(0.23, 1.11)^*$ | $(0.24, 1.10)^*$ |
| (Republican, Democrat) | $\mu_3 - \mu_1$ | 1.47 | $(0.98, 1.96)^*$ | $(0.99, 1.95)^*$ |
| (Republican, Independent) | $\mu_3 - \mu_2$ | 0.80 | $(0.33, 1.27)^*$ | $(0.34, 1.26)^*$ |

*Note*: An asterisk * indicates a significant difference.

The Bonferroni 95% multiple comparison confidence intervals are wider than separate 95% confidence intervals. For instance, the ordinary 95% confidence interval comparing Republicans and Democrats is (1.07, 1.87), whereas the Bonferroni interval is (0.98, 1.96). This is because the multiple comparison method uses a higher confidence level for each separate interval to ensure achieving the overall confidence level that applies to the entire set of comparisons.

### Tukey Multiple Comparisons of Means

Of the other methods available for multiple comparisons, we recommend **Tukey's method**. Proposed by the great statistician John Tukey, who also developed exploratory data analysis methods such as box plots and stem-and-leaf plots as well as terminology such as *software*, this method has intervals that are slightly narrower than the Bonferroni intervals. This is because they are designed to *approximate* the nominal confidence level rather than to have *at least* that level. The Tukey method uses a probability distribution (the *Studentized range*) that refers to the difference between the largest and smallest sample means. We do not present this distribution in this text, so we rely on software rather than a formula for the Tukey intervals.

Table 12.3 shows Tukey intervals for the political ideology data. For practical purposes, they provide the same conclusions as the Bonferroni intervals.

## 12.3 PERFORMING ANOVA BY REGRESSION MODELING

Chapter 11 used multiple regression to model the relationship between the mean of a quantitative response variable and a collection of *quantitative* explanatory variables. The ANOVA models the relationship between the mean of a quantitative response variable and a *categorical* explanatory variable; the categories are the groups compared. In fact, ANOVA is a special case of multiple regression. Artificial explanatory variables in a regression model can represent the groups.

### Regression with Dummy Variables

We set up an artificial variable to equal 1 if an observation comes from a particular group and 0 otherwise. With three groups, as in the political ideology and party ID example, we use two artificial variables. The first, denoted by $z_1$, equals 1 for observations from the first group and equals 0 otherwise. The second, denoted by $z_2$, equals 1 for observations from the second group and equals 0 otherwise. That is,

$$z_1 = 1 \text{ and } z_2 = 0: \text{observations from group 1}$$
$$z_1 = 0 \text{ and } z_2 = 1: \text{observations from group 2}$$
$$z_1 = 0 \text{ and } z_2 = 0: \text{observations from group 3.}$$

It is unnecessary and redundant to create a variable for the last (third) group, because values of 0 for $z_1$ and $z_2$ identify observations from it.

The artificial variables $z_1$ and $z_2$ are called **dummy variables**. They indicate the group for an observation. That is, they give a classification, not a magnitude, for the categorical predictor. Table 12.4 summarizes the dummy variables for three groups.

**TABLE 12.4:** The Two Dummy Variables for Three Groups

| Group | $z_1$ | $z_2$ |
|-------|-------|-------|
| 1 | 1 | 0 |
| 2 | 0 | 1 |
| 3 | 0 | 0 |

For the dummy variables just defined, consider the multiple regression equation

$$E(y) = \alpha + \beta_1 z_1 + \beta_2 z_2.$$

For observations from group 3, $z_1 = z_2 = 0$. The equation then simplifies to

$$E(y) = \alpha + \beta_1(0) + \beta_2(0) = \alpha.$$

So $\alpha$ represents the population mean $\mu_3$ of $y$ for the last group. For observations from group 1, $z_1 = 1$ and $z_2 = 0$, so

$$E(y) = \alpha + \beta_1(1) + \beta_2(0) = \alpha + \beta_1$$

equals the population mean $\mu_1$ for that group. Similarly, $\alpha + \beta_2$ equals the population mean $\mu_2$ for group 2 (let $z_1 = 0$ and $z_2 = 1$).

Since $\alpha + \beta_1 = \mu_1$ and $\alpha = \mu_3$, $\beta_1$ represents the difference $\mu_1 - \mu_3$. Similarly, $\beta_2 = \mu_2 - \mu_3$. Table 12.5 summarizes the parameters of the regression model and their correspondence with the population means. The $\beta$ coefficient of a dummy variable represents the difference between the mean for the group that dummy variable represents and the mean of the group not having its own dummy variable.

Dummy variable coding works because it allows the population means to take arbitrary values, with no assumed distances between groups. Using a single artificial

TABLE 12.5: Interpretation of Coefficients of Dummy Variables in Model $E(y) = \alpha + \beta_1 z_1 + \beta_2 z_2$

| Group | $z_1$ | $z_2$ | Mean of $y$ | Interpretation of $\beta$ |
|-------|-------|-------|-------------|---------------------------|
| 1 | 1 | 0 | $\mu_1 = \alpha + \beta_1$ | $\beta_1 = \mu_1 - \mu_3$ |
| 2 | 0 | 1 | $\mu_2 = \alpha + \beta_2$ | $\beta_2 = \mu_2 - \mu_3$ |
| 3 | 0 | 0 | $\mu_3 = \alpha$ | |

variable with coding such as $z = 1$ for group 1, $z = 2$ for group 2, and $z = 3$ for group 3 would not work. The model $E(y) = \alpha + \beta z$ would then assume an ordering as well as equal distances between groups. It treats the categorical variable as if it were quantitative, which is improper. Whereas it takes only one term in a regression model to represent the linear effect of a quantitative explanatory variable, it requires $g - 1$ terms to represent the $g$ categories of a categorical variable.

## EXAMPLE 12.5    Regression Model for Political Ideology and Party ID

For Table 12.1, the group variable (Party ID) has three categories. The regression model for the ANOVA procedure with $y$ = political ideology is

$$E(y) = \alpha + \beta_1 z_1 + \beta_2 z_2.$$

The dummy variables satisfy $z_1 = 1$ only for Democrats, $z_2 = 1$ only for Independents, and $z_1 = z_2 = 0$ for Republicans. Table 12.6 shows a portion of a printout for fitting this regression model. No dummy variable estimate appears in the table for Party 3 (Republicans), because it is redundant to include a dummy variable for the last group.

TABLE 12.6: Printout for Fitting Regression Model $E(y) = \alpha + \beta_1 z_1 + \beta_2 z_2$ to Data on $y$ = Political Ideology with Dummy Variables $z_1$ and $z_2$ for Party ID

```
Dependent Variable: IDEOLOGY

Parameter        Estimate    Std Error       t         Sig
(Constant)         4.534       0.0759      59.73      0.0001
PARTY      1      -0.717       0.1033      -6.94      0.0001
           2      -0.541       0.1054      -5.13      0.0001
           3       0.000       0.          0.         0.
```

The prediction equation is $\hat{y} = 4.53 - 0.72 z_1 - 0.54 z_2$. The coefficients in the prediction equation relate to the sample means in the same manner that the regression parameters relate to the population means. Just as $\alpha = \mu_3$, so does its estimate $4.53 = \bar{y}_3$, the sample mean for Republicans. Similarly, the coefficient of $z_1$ is $-0.72 = \bar{y}_1 - \bar{y}_3$ and the coefficient of $z_2$ is $-0.54 = \bar{y}_2 - \bar{y}_3$. ∎

### Regression for ANOVA Test Comparing Means

For three groups, the null hypothesis in the ANOVA $F$ test is $H_0: \mu_1 = \mu_2 = \mu_3$. If $H_0$ is true, then $\mu_1 - \mu_3 = 0$ and $\mu_2 - \mu_3 = 0$. Recall that $\mu_1 - \mu_3 = \beta_1$ and $\mu_2 - \mu_3 = \beta_2$ in the regression model $E(y) = \alpha + \beta_1 z_1 + \beta_2 z_2$ with dummy variables. So the ANOVA hypothesis is equivalent to $H_0: \beta_1 = \beta_2 = 0$ in that model. If all $\beta$-values in the model equal 0, then the mean of the response variable equals

$\alpha$ for each group. By setting up dummy variables, we can perform the ANOVA test using the $F$ test of $H_0: \beta_1 = \beta_2 = 0$ for this regression model.

The assumption from regression analysis that the conditional distributions of $y$ about the regression equation are normal with constant standard deviation implies here that the population distributions for the groups are normal, with the same standard deviation for each group. These are precisely the assumptions for the ANOVA $F$ test.

### EXAMPLE 12.6    Regression for Comparing Political Ideology Means by Party ID

Table 12.7 shows the sums of squares for fitting the regression model with dummy variables to the data on political ideology and party ID. Notice the similarity between this and the ANOVA table in Table 12.2. The "between-groups sum of squares" in ANOVA is the "regression sum of squares" (also called "model sum of squares" by some software) in the regression analysis. The "within-groups sum of squares" in ANOVA is the "residual sum of squares" (also called "sum of squared errors") and denoted by SSE. This is the variability within the groups unexplained by including parameters in the model to account for the differences between the means. The sum of squared errors divided by its degrees of freedom is the mean square error (MSE), which is the within-groups estimate $s^2 = 1.68$ of the variance of observations for each group. The regression mean square is the between-groups estimate.

**TABLE 12.7:** Printout Showing Sums of Squares for Regression Model $E(y) = \alpha + \beta_1 z_1 + \beta_2 z_2$ for Modeling Political Ideology in Terms of Party ID

|  | Sum of Squares | df | Mean Square | F Value | Sig |
|---|---|---|---|---|---|
| Regression | 88.43 | 2 | 44.21 | 26.3 | 0.000 |
| Residual | 459.52 | 273 | 1.68 | | |
| Total | 547.95 | 275 | | | |

The ratio of the regression mean square to the mean square error is the $F$ test statistic ($F = 26.3$), with $df_1 = 2$ and $df_2 = 273$, for testing $H_0: \beta_1 = \beta_2 = 0$. This hypothesis is equivalent to $H_0: \mu_1 = \mu_2 = \mu_3$ for the three party IDs. The regression analysis provides the same $F$ statistic as ANOVA did in Section 12.1.  ∎

### Why Use Regression to Do an ANOVA?

Since the ANOVA $F$ test is straightforward and since ANOVA is widely available in software, why should we care that it can be done using regression? One reason is that it's useful to have a unified approach for which most statistical methods conducted in practice are special cases. (In fact, we'll see in Chapter 14 that regression itself is a special case of a yet more general type of model that can handle response variables that do not have normal distributions, such as categorical variables.) Another reason is that being able to handle categorical predictors using a regression model gives us a mechanism for modeling *several* predictors that may be categorical or a mixture of categorical and quantitative. We'll learn about such methods in Section 12.5 and in the next chapter.

## 12.4   TWO-WAY ANALYSIS OF VARIANCE

We've seen how to compare means for groups that are categories of a categorical explanatory variable. Sometimes the groups refer to two (or more) categorical variables. For example, the groups (white men, white women, black men, black women) result from cross-classifying race and gender. The method for comparing the mean of a quantitative response variable across categories of each of two categorical variables is called a *two-way ANOVA*.

The ANOVA discussed so far, having a single explanatory variable, is called *one-way ANOVA*. It ignores other variables. Chapters 10 and 11 showed that such analyses are usually not as informative as multivariate analyses that control other variables. The rest of this chapter deals with two-way ANOVA and more complex methods for categorical explanatory and control variables.

### Main Effect Hypotheses in Two-Way ANOVA

Two-way ANOVA compares population means across categories of two explanatory variables. Each null hypothesis states that the population means are identical across categories of one categorical variable, controlling for the other one.

To illustrate two-way ANOVA, we analyze mean political ideology using explanatory variables party ID and gender. Six means result from the $2 \times 3 = 6$ combinations of their categories, as Table 12.8 shows. The subscript labels identify the groups, such as the population mean $\mu_{FD}$ for female Democrats.

**TABLE 12.8:** A Two-Way Classification of Population Mean Political Ideology by Party Identification and Gender

| Gender | Party Identification | | |
|---|---|---|---|
| | Democrat | Independent | Republican |
| Female | $\mu_{FD}$ | $\mu_{FI}$ | $\mu_{FR}$ |
| Male | $\mu_{MD}$ | $\mu_{MI}$ | $\mu_{MR}$ |

One possible analysis compares the mean political ideology for the three party IDs, controlling for gender. For females, we compare the means $\mu_{FD}$, $\mu_{FI}$, and $\mu_{FR}$ for the three party IDs; for males, we compare $\mu_{MD}$, $\mu_{MI}$, and $\mu_{MR}$. Another possible analysis compares the mean political ideology for males and females, controlling for party ID, by comparing means within each column of the table.

Table 12.9a displays a set of population means satisfying the null hypothesis that mean political ideology is identical for the three party IDs, controlling for gender.

**TABLE 12.9:** Population Mean Political Ideology Satisfying Main Effect Null Hypotheses: (a) No Effect of Party Identification, (b) No Effect of Gender

| Table | Gender | Party Identification | | |
|---|---|---|---|---|
| | | Democrat | Independent | Republican |
| **(a)** | Female | 3.0 | 3.0 | 3.0 |
| | Male | 5.0 | 5.0 | 5.0 |
| **(b)** | Female | 3.0 | 4.0 | 5.0 |
| | Male | 3.0 | 4.0 | 5.0 |

Table 12.9b displays a set of population means satisfying the null hypothesis that mean political ideology is identical for the two genders, controlling for party ID. The effects of individual predictors tested in these two null hypotheses are called ***main effects***.

### F Tests about Main Effects

The $F$ tests for two-way ANOVA have the same assumptions as the $F$ test for one-way ANOVA: randomization, a normal population distribution for each group, with the same standard deviation for each group. Now the groups are formed by the cells of the cross-classification of the two explanatory variables.

The test statistics for two-way ANOVA have complex formulas except when the sample sizes in all cells are equal. We'll rely on software. As in one-way ANOVA, the test for a predictor effect uses two estimates of the variance for each group. These estimates appear in the mean square (MS) column of the ANOVA table. For testing the main effect for a predictor, the test statistic is the ratio of mean squares,

$$F = \frac{\text{MS for the predictor}}{\text{MS error}}.$$

The MS for the predictor is a variance estimate based on between-groups variation for that predictor. That estimate tends to be inflated when $H_0$ is not true. The MS error (denoted MSE) is a within-groups variance estimate that is always unbiased and is also used in confidence intervals.

The variance estimates, listed in an ANOVA table in the Mean Square column, divide a sum of squares by its $df$ value. The degrees of freedom for the $F$ statistics are $df_1 = df$ for the numerator estimate, and $df_2 = df$ for MSE. The value of $df_1$ is always one less than the number of groups being compared; for example, $df_1 = 2$ for comparing three party IDs. As usual, larger $F$ values give stronger evidence against $H_0$, so each $P$-value is a right-tail probability.

### EXAMPLE 12.7    Two-Way ANOVA for Political Ideology by Party ID and Gender

Table 12.10 shows GSS data for political ideology by party ID and gender (with no restrictions on age). The table also shows the sample means and standard deviations of political ideology, based on scores (1, 2, 3, 4, 5, 6, 7).

**TABLE 12.10**: GSS Data on Political Ideology by Party Identification and Gender

| Party ID | Gender | Political Ideology | | | | | | | Sample Size | Mean | Std. Dev. |
|---|---|---|---|---|---|---|---|---|---|---|---|
| | | 1 | 2 | 3 | 4 | 5 | 6 | 7 | | | |
| Democrat | Female | 5 | 30 | 35 | 98 | 20 | 24 | 3 | 215 | 3.85 | 1.26 |
| | Male | 6 | 20 | 25 | 41 | 15 | 15 | 3 | 125 | 3.77 | 1.43 |
| Independent | Female | 4 | 17 | 27 | 83 | 16 | 17 | 5 | 169 | 3.95 | 1.24 |
| | Male | 4 | 16 | 20 | 59 | 21 | 23 | 1 | 144 | 4.04 | 1.30 |
| Republican | Female | 2 | 10 | 17 | 63 | 32 | 33 | 5 | 162 | 4.43 | 1.26 |
| | Male | 0 | 9 | 13 | 36 | 33 | 28 | 9 | 128 | 4.66 | 1.31 |

Software reports Table 12.11 for summarizing the analyses. The mean square error (MSE) estimates the population variance $\sigma^2$ within each cell. For testing the main

**TABLE 12.11:** ANOVA Table for Two-Way Analysis of Main Effects of Party Identification and Gender on Mean Political Ideology

Dependent Variable: IDEOLOGY

| Source | Sum of Squares | df | Mean Square | F | Sig |
|--------|------|------|------|------|------|
| Model  | 86.693   | 3   | 28.898  | 17.29 | 0.0001 |
| Error  | 1569.525 | 939 | 1.671   |       |        |
| Total  | 1656.218 | 942 |         |       |        |

| Source | Type III SS | df | Mean Square | F | Sig |
|--------|------|------|------|------|------|
| PARTY  | 84.2516 | 2 | 42.1258 | 25.20 | 0.0001 |
| GENDER | 1.3110  | 1 | 1.3110  | 0.78  | 0.3760 |

effects, it equals

$$s^2 = \text{MSE} = \frac{\text{SSE}}{df} = \frac{1569.53}{939} = 1.67.$$

For the null hypothesis of no difference in mean political ideology for the three party IDs, controlling for gender, Table 12.11 shows that the $F$ test statistic is

$$F = \frac{\text{Party ID mean square}}{\text{Mean square error}} = \frac{42.13}{1.67} = 25.2,$$

with $df_1 = 2$ and $df_2 = 939$. The $P$-value is 0.0001. Very strong evidence exists of a difference in mean political ideology among the three party IDs, controlling for gender. For the null hypothesis of no difference in mean political ideology between females and males, controlling for party ID, the $F$ test statistic is

$$F = \frac{\text{Gender mean square}}{\text{Mean square error}} = \frac{1.31}{1.67} = 0.78,$$

with $df_1 = 1$ and $df_2 = 939$. The $P$-value is $P = 0.38$. There is negligible evidence that mean political ideology varies by gender, within each party ID. ∎

### Interaction in Two-Way ANOVA

In practice, before conducting the main effects tests just described, we first test another null hypothesis. Sections 10.3 and 11.5 showed that the study of *interaction* is important whenever we analyze multivariate relationships. An absence of interaction between two explanatory variables means that the effect of either variable on the response variable (in the population) does not change for different levels of the other.

Suppose there is no interaction between gender and party ID in their effects on political ideology. Then the difference between females and males in population mean political ideology is the same for each party ID. Table 12.12 shows population means satisfying this. The difference between females and males in mean political ideology is $-1.0$ for each party. Similarly, the difference between each pair of parties in mean political ideology is the same for each gender. The difference between Republicans and Democrats, for example, equals 2.0 both for females and for males. Figure 12.3 plots the means for the party ID categories, within each gender. The ordering of

**TABLE 12.12:** Population Means for a Two-Way Classification, Displaying No Interaction

| Gender | Democrat | Independent | Republican |
|--------|----------|-------------|------------|
| Female | 3.0 | 3.5 | 5.0 |
| Male | 4.0 | 4.5 | 6.0 |

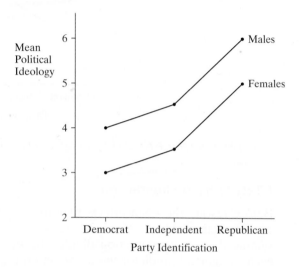

**FIGURE 12.3:** Mean Political Ideology, by Party Identification and Gender, Displaying No Interaction

categories on the horizontal axis is unimportant, since party ID is nominal. The absence of interaction is indicated by the parallel sequences of points.

By contrast, Table 12.13 and Figure 12.4 show population means displaying interaction. The difference between females and males in mean political ideology is −2 for Democrats, 0 for Independents, and +2 for Republicans. So the difference depends on the party ID. Similarly, the party ID effect on ideology differs for females and males. For females, Republicans are the most conservative, whereas for males, Democrats are the most conservative.

**TABLE 12.13:** Population Means for a Two-Way Classification, Displaying Interaction

| Gender | Democrat | Independent | Republican |
|--------|----------|-------------|------------|
| Females | 3.0 | 4.0 | 5.0 |
| Males | 5.0 | 4.0 | 3.0 |

In Table 12.13, suppose the numbers of males and females are equal for each party ID. Then the overall mean political ideology, ignoring gender, is 4.0 for each party. The overall difference in means between any two party IDs equals 0. In a one-way comparison of mean political ideology by party ID, party ID has no effect. However, in a two-way comparison, the interaction implies differing party ID effects for males and females. As in other multivariate analyses, the effect of a predictor can change dramatically when we control for another variable.

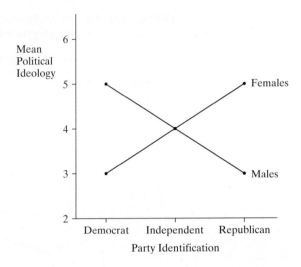

**FIGURE 12.4:** Mean Political Ideology, by Party Identification and Gender, Displaying Interaction

### $F$ Test of $H_0$: No Interaction

Before testing the main effects hypotheses in two-way ANOVA, we first test $H_0$: no interaction. The $F$ test statistic is the ratio of a mean square based on the sample degree of interaction divided by the MSE. A small $P$-value suggests that each categorical predictor has an effect on the response, but the size of effect varies according to the category of the other predictor.

When interaction exists, it is not meaningful to test the main effects hypotheses. When we reject $H_0$: no interaction, we conclude that each variable has an effect, but the nature of that effect changes according to the category of the other variable. It's then better to compare the means for one predictor separately within categories of the other. On the other hand, if the evidence of interaction is not strong (i.e., if the $P$-value is not small), we then test the two main effect hypotheses.

Table 12.10 showed the sample mean political ideology for the six combinations of party ID and gender. These means show no obvious evidence of interaction. The only sample effect that seems substantial is the difference between Republicans and Democrats, and there the effect seems similar for each gender—namely, a higher mean for Republicans. In the next section, we'll see that the test of $H_0$: no interaction has $F = 1.06$ and a $P$-value of $P = 0.34$. So a lack of interaction is plausible, and the main effect tests are valid.

Next, it's natural to use confidence intervals to find out more about the party ID effect, controlling for gender. To do this, it's helpful to study two-way ANOVA in the context of regression modeling. As in one-way ANOVA, the $F$ tests in two-way ANOVA are equivalently tests about parameters in a regression model. The next section shows how to conduct the analyses using multiple regression models with dummy variables for the categorical predictors.

## 12.5 TWO-WAY ANOVA AND REGRESSION

To conduct the $F$ tests as special cases of tests about parameters of a multiple regression model, we set up dummy variables for each predictor. We illustrate with Table 12.10, using party ID and gender (sex) as predictors of political ideology.

We use the symbol $p$ for dummy variables for party ID and $s$ as a dummy variable for sex (whether a subject is female). That is,

$$p_1 = \begin{cases} 1 & \text{if subject is Democrat} \\ 0 & \text{otherwise} \end{cases}$$

$$p_2 = \begin{cases} 1 & \text{if subject is Independent} \\ 0 & \text{otherwise.} \end{cases}$$

Both $p_1$ and $p_2$ equal 0 when the subject is Republican. Also,

$$s = \begin{cases} 1 & \text{if subject is female} \\ 0 & \text{if subject is male.} \end{cases}$$

It is redundant to include dummy variables for the final categories.

### Regression Model Assuming No Interaction

For simplicity, we'll first assume there's no interaction. In practice, we'd check this assumption first, as we discussed in the previous section. The regression model is

$$E(y) = \alpha + \beta_1 p_1 + \beta_2 p_2 + \beta_3 s.$$

To find the correspondence between the population means and the regression parameters, we substitute the possible values for the dummy variables. To illustrate, for Republicans ($p_1 = p_2 = 0$), the mean political ideology is

$$\text{Males } (s = 0) : \mu = \alpha + \beta_1(0) + \beta_2(0) + \beta_3(0) = \alpha.$$
$$\text{Females } (s = 1) : \mu = \alpha + \beta_1(0) + \beta_2(0) + \beta_3(1) = \alpha + \beta_3.$$

For the six combinations of party ID and gender, Table 12.14 shows the population means in terms of the regression parameters. For each party ID, the difference in means between females and males equals $\beta_3$. That is, the coefficient $\beta_3$ of the dummy variable $s$ for sex equals the difference between females and males in mean political ideology, controlling for party ID. The null hypothesis of no difference between females and males in the mean, controlling for party ID, is $H_0: \beta_3 = 0$.

**TABLE 12.14:** Population Means of Political Ideology for the Two-Way Classification of Party ID and Gender (Sex), Assuming No Interaction

| Gender | Party Identification | Dummy Variables $p_1$ | $p_2$ | $s$ | Population Mean of $y$ $\alpha + \beta_1 p_1 + \beta_2 p_2 + \beta_3 s$ |
|---|---|---|---|---|---|
| Female | Democrat | 1 | 0 | 1 | $\alpha + \beta_1 + \beta_3$ |
| | Independent | 0 | 1 | 1 | $\alpha + \beta_2 + \beta_3$ |
| | Republican | 0 | 0 | 1 | $\alpha + \beta_3$ |
| Male | Democrat | 1 | 0 | 0 | $\alpha + \beta_1$ |
| | Independent | 0 | 1 | 0 | $\alpha + \beta_2$ |
| | Republican | 0 | 0 | 0 | $\alpha$ |

The test of $H_0: \beta_3 = 0$ of no gender effect compares the complete model

$$E(y) = \alpha + \beta_1 p_1 + \beta_2 p_2 + \beta_3 s$$

to the reduced model,

$$E(y) = \alpha + \beta_1 p_1 + \beta_2 p_2.$$

The reduced model lacks the gender effect. The ANOVA table in Table 12.11 showed

| Source | Type III SS | df | Mean Square | F | Sig |
|--------|-------------|-----|-------------|------|--------|
| PARTY  | 84.2516     | 2   | 42.1258     | 25.20| 0.0001 |
| GENDER | 1.3110      | 1   | 1.3110      | 0.78 | 0.3760 |

The gender sum of squares of 1.31 is the amount of the variation accounted for by introducing the term $\beta_3 s$ into the model, once the other terms are already there. It represents the difference between the sums of squared errors (SSE) when these terms are omitted and when they are included. There is a difference of one parameter in the two models, so this sum of squares has $df = 1$. The table shows that the $F$ test statistic equals 0.78, with $P$-value $P = 0.38$.

In the complete model, $\beta_1$ is the difference between the means for Democrats and Republicans, and $\beta_2$ is the difference between the means for Independents and Republicans, controlling for gender. The interpretations are similar to the $\beta$-values for the regression model for one-way ANOVA, except that here we also control for gender. The null hypothesis of no differences among the parties in mean political ideology, controlling for gender, is $H_0: \beta_1 = \beta_2 = 0$. Table 12.11 or its excerpt above shows that the $F$ test statistic equals 25.2, with a $P$-value of 0.0001.

Table 12.15 shows some output for fitting the complete regression model. The prediction equation is

$$\hat{y} = 4.58 - 0.71p_1 - 0.54p_2 - 0.08s.$$

The coefficient of $s$ is $-0.08$. This is the estimated difference between females and males in mean political ideology for each party ID. The test of the gender main effect indicated that this difference is not statistically significant. The coefficient of $p_1$ is $-0.71$. This is the estimated difference between Democrats and Republicans in mean political ideology for each gender. The coefficient of $p_2$ is $-0.54$. This is the estimated difference between Independents and Republicans for each gender. The estimated difference between Democrats and Independents is $(-0.71) - (-0.54) = -0.17$ for each gender.

**TABLE 12.15**: Fit of Regression Model for Two-Way Analysis of Mean Political Ideology by Party Identification and Gender, Assuming No Interaction. The estimate is 0 at the last level of each predictor, because a dummy variable for that level is not needed and would be redundant.

---

Dependent Variable: IDEOLOGY

| Parameter | | B | Std. Error | t | Sig |
|-----------|---|--------|------------|-------|--------|
| Intercept |   | 4.5768 | 0.0897     | 51.02 | 0.0001 |
| PARTY     | 1 | -0.7112| 0.1035     | -6.87 | 0.0001 |
|           | 2 | -0.5423| 0.1054     | -5.15 | 0.0001 |
|           | 3 | 0      | .          | .     | .      |
| GENDER    | 1 | -0.0758| 0.0856     | -0.89 | 0.3760 |
|           | 2 | 0      | .          | .     | .      |

---

Substituting dummy variable values into the prediction equation yields estimated means that satisfy the no interaction model. For instance, for female Republicans, $p_1 = p_2 = 0$ and $s = 1$, so $\hat{y} = 4.58 - 0.71(0) + 0.54(0) - 0.08(1) = 4.50$.

**Regression Model with Interaction**

The model considered so far is inadequate when there is interaction. Section 11.5 showed that cross-product terms in a multiple regression model can represent interaction. Here, we take cross-products of dummy variables to obtain a regression model that allows interaction effects.

The interaction model for the two-way classification of party ID and gender is

$$E(y) = \alpha + \beta_1 p_1 + \beta_2 p_2 + \beta_3 s + \beta_4 (p_1 \times s) + \beta_5 (p_2 \times s).$$

The last two terms use cross-products for the interaction. It is not necessary to take cross-products of dummy variables from categories of the same categorical predictor, such as $p_1 \times p_2$. This is because no more than one dummy variable for a given predictor can be nonzero for any observation, since an observation cannot fall in more than one category. All such cross-products would equal 0.

Table 12.16 shows an ANOVA table for the model that allows interaction. The sum of squares for interaction, shown in the row with the product label PARTY*GENDER, is the amount of variability explained by the two interaction terms. It equals the difference between SSE without and with these terms in the model. The interaction mean square is an estimate of $\sigma^2$ based on

$$\frac{\text{Interaction SS}}{df} = \frac{3.64}{2} = 1.82.$$

We test $H_0$: no interaction, that is, $H_0$: $\beta_4 = \beta_5 = 0$, using

$$F = \frac{\text{Interaction mean square}}{\text{Mean square error}} = \frac{1.82}{1.67} = 1.09.$$

Here, $df_1 = 2$ for the interaction SS, because the model allowing interaction has two extra parameters. As usual, $df_2$ value for SSE equals the total sample size minus the number of parameters in the model. For the complete model, there are 6 parameters, so $df_2 = 943 - 6 = 937$. From the $F$ distribution with $df_1 = 2$ and $df_2 = 937$, the $P$-value is $P = 0.34$.

**TABLE 12.16:** ANOVA Table for Two-Way Analysis of Mean Political Ideology by Party Identification and Gender, Allowing Interaction

```
Dependent Variable: IDEOLOGY
              Sum of              Mean
Source        Squares     df      Square      F        Sig
Model          90.332      5      18.066     10.81    0.0001
Error        1565.886    937       1.671
Total        1656.218    942
```

| Source | Type III SS | df | Mean Square | F | Sig |
|---|---|---|---|---|---|
| PARTY | 87.795 | 2 | 43.898 | 26.27 | 0.0001 |
| GENDER | 1.488 | 1 | 1.488 | 0.89 | 0.3456 |
| PARTY*GENDER | 3.640 | 2 | 1.820 | 1.09 | 0.3370 |

There is not much evidence of interaction. It is sensible to remove the cross-product terms and use the simpler model discussed previously. Since an absence of interaction is plausible, the main effect tests presented in Table 12.11 for party ID and gender are valid. When there is not significant evidence of interaction, it is better to use the model without interaction terms in testing the main effects of the predictors and in constructing confidence intervals for the effects.

### Partial Sums of Squares

The sums of squares for party, gender, and their interaction in Tables 12.11 and 12.16 are called *partial sums of squares* (see Exercise 11.60 in Chapter 11). Some software labels them as *Type III sums of squares*. They represent the variability in $y$ explained by those terms, once the other terms are already in the model. This equals the difference between the SSE values for the model without those terms and the model with them.

Suppose each cell in the cross classification of the two predictors has the same number of observations. This happens with designed experiments that assign the same number of subjects to each cell. Then the predictors are independent, in the sense (for contingency tables in Chapter 8) that the counts in the cells of the cross classification satisfy independence. In this case, these sums of squares explain completely separate portions of the variability in $y$. They then sum to the model sum of squares (called the *regression SS* by some software). The model sum of squares equals TSS − SSE. It represents the variability explained together by all the terms in the regression model.

For survey research with observational data, predictors are rarely independent. Gender is somewhat associated with party ID, for instance. Because of this, the partial sum of squares for party ID overlaps somewhat with the partial sum of squares for gender. Consequently, the Type III sums of squares listed in Tables 12.11 and 12.16 do not add up exactly to the model sum of squares.

When the categorical predictors are associated, the partial sum of squares explained by a predictor depends on whether the interaction terms are in the model. The partial sums of squares for party and for gender differ slightly between Tables 12.11 and 12.16.

### Multiple Comparisons Following Two-Way ANOVA

In practice, we use confidence intervals to estimate the sizes of effects. Suppose $H_0$: no interaction seems plausible. Then we can treat the difference in population means between two categories for one predictor as the same at each category of the other. So we construct a single set of comparisons rather than a separate set at each category of the other variable. In Example 12.6, we estimate the differences in the mean political ideology between each pair of party IDs, controlling for gender, a total of three comparisons. We can do this using ordinary confidence intervals for regression parameters. The form is the usual one of estimate plus and minus a $t$-score times the standard error, with $df$ for $t$ being the $df$ value for the mean square error.

For instance, for the model assuming no interaction, $\hat{\beta}_1 = -0.71$ is the estimated difference between Democrats and Republicans in mean political ideology, controlling for gender. The standard error of this estimate, reported in Table 12.15, is 0.104. A 95% confidence interval is $-0.71 \pm 1.96(0.104)$, or $(-0.9, -0.5)$. Democrats are less conservative, on the average, for each gender.

The Bonferroni approach (Section 12.2) for one-way ANOVA extends to higher-way ANOVA. A comparison of all three pairs of party IDs with a multiple comparison error rate of 0.05 uses error probability $0.05/3 = 0.0167$ in determining the $t$-score for each interval. For these data, we obtain similar intervals to those shown in Table 12.3 following the one-way ANOVA.

When a practically significant degree of interaction exists, it is not appropriate to make summary comparisons of categories of one variable, controlling for the other. Instead, compare the pairs of rows separately within each column and/or compare the pairs of columns separately within each row.

### Factorial ANOVA

The methods of two-way ANOVA extend to several predictors. Categorical explanatory variables in ANOVA are often called **factors**. A multifactor ANOVA with observations from all the combinations of the factors is called **factorial ANOVA**.

For instance, with three factors, **three-way ANOVA** considers possible interactions as well as main effects for those factors. For factors denoted by A, B, and C, the full model contains a main effect for each factor, A × B, A × C, and B × C two-factor interactions, and the A × B × C three-factor interaction. The regression model has a set of dummy variables for each factor, cross-products of pairs of dummy variables for the two-factor interactions, and three-way products of dummy variables from all three factors for the three-factor interaction.

In three-way ANOVA, we first test the three-factor interaction. If the P-value is small, we compare pairs of categories for one variable at each combination of categories of the other two. Otherwise, it's better to drop the three-factor term from the model and test the two-factor interactions. Suppose, for instance, that the P-value is small for the A × B interaction but not for the others. After refitting the model with the main effects and the A × B interaction, we can test the C main effect and compare pairs of means for various pairs of categories of C. Because of the A × B interaction, we compare means from categories of A separately at each category of B, and we compare means from categories of B separately at each category of A.

When you have two or more factors, why not instead perform separate one-way ANOVAs? For instance, you could compare the mean political ideology for females and males using a one-way ANOVA, ignoring the information about party ID. Likewise, you could perform a separate one-way ANOVA to compare the means for the three party IDs, ignoring the information about gender. The main reason is that with factorial ANOVA we learn whether there is interaction. When there is, it is more informative to compare levels of one factor separately at each level of the other factor. This enables us to investigate how the effect depends on that other factor.

Another benefit of factorial ANOVA is that the residual variability, which affects the MS error and the denominators of the F test statistics, tends to decrease. When we use two or more factors to predict a response variable, we usually tend to get better predictions (that is, less residual variability) than when we use one factor. With less residual (within-groups) variability, we get larger test statistics, and hence greater power for rejecting false null hypotheses.

## 12.6   REPEATED MEASURES ANALYSIS OF VARIANCE*

The methods presented so far assume that the samples in the groups are *independent*, each group having a separate sample of subjects. In many studies, however, each group has the same subjects. Most commonly this happens when there is *repeated measurement* of the subjects over time or on several related response variables. The samples are then *dependent*, and the analysis must take this into account.

### EXAMPLE 12.8     Positive and Negative Influences on Children

A recent GSS asked subjects to respond to the following: "Children are exposed to many influences in their daily lives. What kind of influence does each of the following have on children? 1. Movies, 2. Programs on network television, 3. Rock music." The possible responses were (very negative, negative, neutral, positive, very positive). Table 12.17 shows responses for 12 of the sampled subjects, using scores $(-2, -1, 0, 1, 2)$ for the possible responses. This is part of a much larger data file for more than 1000 respondents. We analyze only this small sample here to help explain the concepts and so you can easily use your own software to try to replicate results. ■

**TABLE 12.17:** Opinions about Three Influences on Children. The scores represent $-2 =$ very negative, $-1 =$ negative, $0 =$ neutral, $1 =$ positive, $2 =$ very positive.

| Subject | Influence Movies | TV | Rock |
|---------|--------|------|------|
| 1 | $-1$ | 0 | $-1$ |
| 2 | 1 | 0 | 0 |
| 3 | 0 | 1 | $-2$ |
| 4 | 2 | 0 | 1 |
| 5 | 0 | $-1$ | $-1$ |
| 6 | $-2$ | $-2$ | $-2$ |
| 7 | $-1$ | $-1$ | 0 |
| 8 | 0 | 1 | $-1$ |
| 9 | $-1$ | $-1$ | $-1$ |
| 10 | 1 | 0 | 1 |
| 11 | 1 | 1 | $-1$ |
| 12 | $-1$ | $-1$ | $-2$ |
| Mean | $-0.08$ | $-0.25$ | $-0.75$ |

## One-Way ANOVA with Repeated Measurement

For Table 12.17, $H_0$ is the same as in ordinary one-way ANOVA: equal population means for several groups. Is there much evidence that the population means differ for the three influences? Ordinary ANOVA is inappropriate because the three samples for the categories of influence are not independent. Each sample has the same subjects.

Suppose we regard the rows of Table 12.17, like the columns, as a factor. Then the data layout resembles a two-way ANOVA. Each cell cross classifies a subject (a row) with an influence (a column). A regression model could express the expected response as a function of 2 dummy variables for the 3 influences and 11 dummy variables for the 12 subjects. The test comparing population means for the three influences is then the main effect test for the column variable in the two-way ANOVA. In fact, this is the appropriate test for data of this sort.

Table 12.18 shows the ANOVA table for a two-way ANOVA. Consider

$H_0$: Equal population means for the three influences.

The $F$ test statistic is the mean square for influence divided by the mean square error, which is $F = 1.44/0.57 = 2.55$. The $df$ values are $df_1 = 2$ and $df_2 = 22$. The $P$-value equals $P = 0.10$. The evidence against $H_0$ is not strong. But with only 12 subjects, if $H_0$ is false the power is probably low.

Table 12.19 shows that we get similar results if we use specialized software for repeated measures, such as in SPSS by using the *Repeated Measures* option after selecting *General Linear Model* in the *Analyze* menu.

**TABLE 12.18:** ANOVA Table for Repeated Measures ANOVA of Opinion Response by Influence Type. This shows results of using software for two-way ANOVA, treating the subject as a second factor.

| Source | Sum of Squares | df | Mean Square | F | Sig |
|---|---|---|---|---|---|
| Model | 27.861 | 13 | 2.143 | 3.79 | 0.003 |
| Error | 12.444 | 22 | 0.566 | | |
| Total | 40.306 | 35 | | | |

| Source | Type III SS | df | Mean Square | F | Sig |
|---|---|---|---|---|---|
| INFLUENCE | 2.889 | 2 | 1.444 | 2.55 | 0.101 |
| SUBJECT | 24.972 | 11 | 2.270 | 4.01 | 0.003 |

**TABLE 12.19:** Partial SPSS Output for Repeated Measures ANOVA of Opinion Response by Influence Type

| Source | Test of Within-Subjects Effects | | | | |
|---|---|---|---|---|---|
| | Type III Sum of Squares | df | Mean Square | F | Sig. |
| Sphericity assumed | | | | | |
| Influence | 2.889 | 2 | 1.444 | 2.55 | .101 |
| Error | 12.444 | 22 | .566 | | |

When there are only two groups, with the same subjects in each, Section 7.4 showed that inference uses the $t$ distribution with difference scores. For testing equality of means, the $F$ statistic from ANOVA then simplifies to the square of the $t$ statistic from that matched-pairs $t$ test.

## The Sphericity Assumption and Compound Symmetry

The traditional repeated measures ANOVA assumes **sphericity**. Roughly speaking, this means the following. For each pair of groups, consider the difference between two observations, one from each group. This difference is a variable, and the sphericity condition states that the standard deviation of the distribution of this difference is identical for each pair of groups. It is easier to get a feel for a special case of sphericity, called **compound symmetry**. This condition holds when the different groups have the same standard deviations and when each pair of responses has the same correlation.

If the sphericity assumption is badly violated, the $P$-value tends to be too small. Most software provides a formal significance test (Mauchly's test) of the sphericity assumption. When the data strongly contradict that assumption, an approximate test adjusts the degrees of freedom downward for the usual $F$ test statistic, using the *Greenhouse-Geisser adjustment*. The technical details for these tests and adjustments are beyond the scope of this text, but standard software reports these results.

Using a repeated measurement design can improve precision of estimation. Having the same subjects in each group helps to eliminate extraneous sources of error. For instance, other variables that affect the response have the same values for each group, so differences between group means cannot reflect differences between groups on those variables. Controlling for possibly confounding factors by keeping them fixed in each row of the data file is referred to as **blocking**. For details on the linkage of analysis of variance procedures with experimental designs, see Howell (2006), Kirk (1995), and Winer et al. (1991).

## Confidence Intervals Comparing Dependent Samples

As usual, we learn more from estimating parameters. Table 12.17 showed the sample means for the three influences. Since the sample size is small, we weaken the multiple comparison confidence level a bit so that the intervals are not overly wide. The 90% Bonferroni confidence intervals use error probability $0.10/3 = 0.0333$ for each interval. The error $df = 22$, and the $t$-score with probability $0.0333/2 = 0.0167$ in each tail is $t = 2.27$. The square root of the mean square error equals $s = \sqrt{0.566} = 0.75$. Each group has 12 observations, so the margin of error for each confidence interval is

$$ts\sqrt{\frac{1}{n_i} + \frac{1}{n_j}} = 2.27(0.75)\sqrt{\frac{1}{12} + \frac{1}{12}} = 0.70.$$

For instance, the confidence interval for the difference between the mean on movies and the mean on rock music is $(-0.08) - (-0.75) \pm 0.70$, or $(-0.03, 1.37)$. It is plausible that the means are equal, but also plausible that the mean for movies is much more in the positive direction than the mean for rock music. Table 12.20 shows all three Bonferroni comparisons. It is also plausible that the mean for TV is much more in the positive direction than the mean for rock music. Confidence intervals can convey useful information even if the overall test statistic is not significant.

**TABLE 12.20**: Bonferroni Multiple Comparison 90% Confidence Intervals for Comparing Mean Responses for Three Influences

| Influences | Difference of Means | Confidence Interval |
|---|---|---|
| Movies, TV | 0.17 | $(-0.53, 0.87)$ |
| Movies, Rock | 0.67 | $(-0.03, 1.37)$ |
| TV, Rock | 0.50 | $(-0.20, 1.20)$ |

## Fixed Effects and Random Effects

The regression model for the previous analysis is

$$E(y) = \alpha + \beta_1 m + \beta_2 t + \gamma_1 s_1 + \gamma_2 s_2 + \cdots + \gamma_{11} s_{11}.$$

Here, $y$ is the rating of an influence, $m$ is a dummy variable for movies (i.e., $m = 1$ for a response on movies, 0 otherwise), $t$ is a dummy variable for TV ($t = 1$ for a response on TV, 0 otherwise), and $m = t = 0$ for a response on rock music. Similarly, $s_1$ is a dummy variable for subject 1, equaling 1 for that subject's three responses and 0 otherwise, and likewise for 10 other subject dummy variables. We use $\gamma$ (gamma) instead of $\beta$ for the coefficients of these terms for convenience, so the index of the parameter agrees with the index of the dummy variable. As usual, each factor has one fewer dummy variable than its number of categories.

A short-hand way of writing this regression model is

$$E(y) = \alpha + \beta_j + \gamma_i.$$

Here, $\beta_j$ denotes the effect for influence $j$ and $\gamma_i$ is the effect for subject $i$, where $\beta_3 = 0$ and $\gamma_{12} = 0$ for the final category of each variable. This equation expresses the expected response in the cell in row $i$ and column $j$ in terms of a row main effect and a column main effect. Testing equality of the population mean of $y$ for the three influences corresponds to testing $H_0$: $\beta_1 = \beta_2 = 0$.

In this model, the main focus is comparing the influence parameters $\{\beta_j\}$, not the subject parameters $\{\gamma_i\}$. The $\{\gamma_i\}$ depend on which subjects are chosen for the sample. The subject effect is called a ***random effect***, because the categories of the subject factor represent a random sample of all the possible ones. By contrast, the factor that defines the groups, influence type, is called a ***fixed effect***. The analyses use *all* the categories of interest of a fixed effect rather than a random sample of them. Models studied in earlier sections of this chapter contained only fixed effects.

When the classification variables are a mixture of random and fixed effects, such as in this example, the model is called a ***mixed model***. For more complex mixed models than this one, the test statistics differ for some tests from their form when all classification variables are fixed effects. The next section discusses an important case.

## 12.7  TWO-WAY ANOVA WITH REPEATED MEASURES ON A FACTOR*

Repeated measurement data sets often have more than one fixed effect. The repeated measures usually occur across categories of one factor, but the categories of the other factor(s) have independent samples. The following example illustrates.

### EXAMPLE 12.9    Comparing Three Treatments for Anorexia

For 72 young girls suffering from anorexia, Table 12.21 shows their weights before and after an experimental period. The girls were randomly assigned to receive one of three therapies during this period. One group, a control group, received the standard therapy. The study analyzed whether one treatment is better than the others, with the girls tending to gain more weight under that treatment. Analyses of parts of this data set were presented on pages 120, 151, and 198.

Figure 12.5 shows box plots, graphically describing the response distributions before and after the experimental period for each treatment. Table 12.22 shows the summary sample means. The three treatments have similar distributions originally. This is not surprising, because subjects were randomly allocated to the three groups at that time. There is some evidence of a greater mean weight gain for the family therapy group, though there are a few low outlying weight values. ∎

### Repeated Measures on One of Two Fixed Effects

Tables 12.21 and 12.22 have two fixed effects. One of them, "Treatment," has categories (CB = cognitive behavioral, FT = family therapy, C = control). It defines three groups of girls, represented by three independent samples. The second, "Time," consists of the two times for observations, (before, after). Each time has the same subjects, so the samples at its levels are dependent. Time is called a ***within-subjects factor***, because comparisons of its categories use repeated measurements on subjects. Treatment is called a ***between-subjects factor***, because comparisons of its categories use different subjects.

**TABLE 12.21**: Weights of Anorexic Girls, in Pounds, before and after Receiving One of Three Treatments

| Cognitive Behavioral | | Family Therapy | | Control | |
|---|---|---|---|---|---|
| Weight Before | Weight After | Weight Before | Weight After | Weight Before | Weight After |
| 80.5 | 82.2 | 83.8 | 95.2 | 80.7 | 80.2 |
| 84.9 | 85.6 | 83.3 | 94.3 | 89.4 | 80.1 |
| 81.5 | 81.4 | 86.0 | 91.5 | 91.8 | 86.4 |
| 82.6 | 81.9 | 82.5 | 91.9 | 74.0 | 86.3 |
| 79.9 | 76.4 | 86.7 | 100.3 | 78.1 | 76.1 |
| 88.7 | 103.6 | 79.6 | 76.7 | 88.3 | 78.1 |
| 94.9 | 98.4 | 76.9 | 76.8 | 87.3 | 75.1 |
| 76.3 | 93.4 | 94.2 | 101.6 | 75.1 | 86.7 |
| 81.0 | 73.4 | 73.4 | 94.9 | 80.6 | 73.5 |
| 80.5 | 82.1 | 80.5 | 75.2 | 78.4 | 84.6 |
| 85.0 | 96.7 | 81.6 | 77.8 | 77.6 | 77.4 |
| 89.2 | 95.3 | 82.1 | 95.5 | 88.7 | 79.5 |
| 81.3 | 82.4 | 77.6 | 90.7 | 81.3 | 89.6 |
| 76.5 | 72.5 | 83.5 | 92.5 | 78.1 | 81.4 |
| 70.0 | 90.9 | 89.9 | 93.8 | 70.5 | 81.8 |
| 80.4 | 71.3 | 86.0 | 91.7 | 77.3 | 77.3 |
| 83.3 | 85.4 | 87.3 | 98.0 | 85.2 | 84.2 |
| 83.0 | 81.6 | | | 86.0 | 75.4 |
| 87.7 | 89.1 | | | 84.1 | 79.5 |
| 84.2 | 83.9 | | | 79.7 | 73.0 |
| 86.4 | 82.7 | | | 85.5 | 88.3 |
| 76.5 | 75.7 | | | 84.4 | 84.7 |
| 80.2 | 82.6 | | | 79.6 | 81.4 |
| 87.8 | 100.4 | | | 77.5 | 81.2 |
| 83.3 | 85.2 | | | 72.3 | 88.2 |
| 79.7 | 83.6 | | | 89.0 | 78.8 |
| 84.5 | 84.6 | | | | |
| 80.8 | 96.2 | | | | |
| 87.4 | 86.7 | | | | |

*Source*: Thanks to Professor Brian Everitt, Institute of Psychiatry, London, for these data.

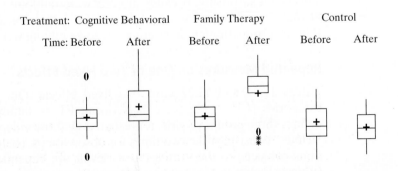

**FIGURE 12.5**: Box Plots for Weights of Anorexic Girls, by Treatment and Time of Measurement

**TABLE 12.22:** Sample Mean Weight, by Treatment and Time of Measurement, in Anorexia Study

| Treatment | Time | |
|---|---|---|
| | Before | After |
| Cognitive Behavioral (CB) | 82.7 | 85.7 |
| Family Therapy (FT) | 83.2 | 90.5 |
| Control (C) | 81.6 | 81.1 |

Although the two factors (treatment and time) are fixed effects, the analysis differs from ordinary two-way ANOVA. This is because the repeated measurements on the within-subjects factor (time) creates a third effect, a random effect for subjects. Each subject is measured at every category of time. Subjects are said to be **crossed** with the time factor. Each subject occurs at only one category of the between-subjects factor (treatment). Subjects are said to be **nested** within the treatment factor.

As in ordinary two-way ANOVA, we can test each main effect as well as their interaction. However, tests about the within-subjects factor (both its main effect and its interaction with the other fixed effect) use a different error term than the test about the between-subjects main effect. The ordinary sum of squared errors term is partitioned into two parts. One part uses the variability between mean scores of subjects. It forms an error term for testing the between-subjects factor. The other part is based on how the pattern of within-subject scores varies among subjects. It forms an error term for any test involving the within-subjects factor.

Figure 12.6 shows the partitioning of the total sum of squares for a two-way ANOVA with repeated measures on one factor. Software automatically performs this partitioning and creates $F$ statistics in the proper way for testing the main effects and interaction.

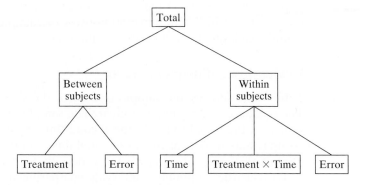

**FIGURE 12.6:** Partitioning of Variability in Two-Way ANOVA with Treatment and Time Factors and Repeated Measures on Time. Tests involving the within-subjects factor (time) use a separate error term.

### EXAMPLE 12.10    ANOVA *F* Tests Comparing Anorexia Treatments

Table 12.23 shows a SPSS printout for the analysis of the anorexia study data. Each sum of squares summarizes the variation its terms explain in a corresponding regression model. This is the reduction in SSE when we add terms to the model for that effect. Since treatment has three categories, it has two dummy variables in the regression model, and its sum of squares has $df = 2$. Since time has two levels, it has one dummy variable, and its sum of squares has $df = 1$. The interaction between these effects has two terms in the model, based on the cross-product of the two dummy variables for treatment with the dummy variable for time, so its $df = 2$.

**TABLE 12.23:** Printout for Two-Way Analysis of Variance of Table 12.21 with Treatment and Time Fixed Effects and Repeated Measures on Time

```
           Tests of Within-Subject Effects
                    Type III Sum
   Source            of Squares    df   Mean Square    F      Sig
   TIME                366.04       1     366.04     12.92   0.001
   TIME*TREATMENT      307.32       2     153.66      5.42   0.006
   Error(TIME)        1955.37      69      28.34


          Tests of Between-Subjects Effects.
                    Type III Sum
   Source            of Squares    df   Mean Square    F      Sig
   TREATMENT           644.23       2     322.12      6.20   0.003
   Error              3584.03      69      51.94
```

The error term for the between-subjects part of the table has $df = 69$, based on 28 dummy variables for the 29 subjects receiving CB therapy, 16 dummy variables for the 17 subjects receiving FT, and 25 dummy variables for the 26 subjects in group C ($28 + 16 + 25 = 69$). The remaining variability, not accounted for by this error term or by the main effects and interaction terms, is the error sum of squares for testing the within-subjects effects.

The TIME*TREATMENT row of the ANOVA table indicates that the interaction is highly significant. The $P$-value $= 0.006$. The difference between population means for the two times differs according to the treatment, and the difference between population means for a pair of treatments varies according to the time. Because of the significant interaction, we do not test the main effects. We need, instead, to use confidence intervals to describe the interaction. ∎

### Follow-Up Confidence Intervals

Table 12.22 showed the sample means for the six combinations of the two factors. The evidence of interaction is clear. The sample means for the three treatments are similar at the initial time. At the second time, by contrast, the mean for the control group is similar to its mean at the initial time, but the mean is larger for the other two treatments than their initial means, especially for the FT group.

To construct confidence intervals comparing means at the two times, for each treatment, the appropriate common standard deviation estimate is the square root of the mean square error from the within-subjects analysis. From Table 12.23, this equals $\sqrt{28.34} = 5.3$, with $df = 69$. We illustrate by constructing a 95% confidence interval comparing the two means for family therapy (FT), which 17 girls received at each time. The $t$-score for 95% confidence when $df = 69$ equals 1.99. The confidence interval has margin of error equal to this $t$-score times the root mean square error times the square root factor involving the inverse of each sample size (17 for each time). This interval equals

$$(90.5 - 83.2) \pm 1.99(5.3)\sqrt{\frac{1}{17} + \frac{1}{17}}, \text{ or } 7.3 \pm 3.6, \text{ or } (3.6, 10.9).$$

For the FT therapy, we conclude that the population mean weight is between 3.6 and 10.9 pounds higher following the treatment period. Similarly, a 95% confidence interval comparing the two means equals $(0.2, 5.8)$ for the CB therapy and $(-3.4, 2.5)$ for the control group. There is evidence of an increase, albeit a small one, for the CB therapy, but no evidence of change for the control group.

To make between-subjects comparisons of treatments, for each time, one cannot use the root mean square error from the between-subjects analysis. The reason is that these separate comparisons involve both the treatment main effect and the interaction, and these two sources of variation have different error terms in the repeated measures ANOVA. At a particular time, however, the subjects in the three treatments are independent samples. Thus, we can compare three means at a given time using a one-way ANOVA $F$ test or using confidence intervals for those data alone.

For instance, for the 72 observations at time = after, the $F$ test statistic for the one-way ANOVA comparing the three means is 8.6, with $df_1 = 2$ and $df_2 = 69$. The $P$-value is 0.0004, very strong evidence of a difference among the treatment means. For this one-way ANOVA, the square root of MSE equals $s = 7.3$. The 95% confidence interval for the difference of means between the FT and the CB treatments, based on the $17 + 29$ observations for the two groups, equals

$$(90.5 - 85.7) \pm 1.99(7.3)\sqrt{\frac{1}{17} + \frac{1}{29}}, \text{ or } 4.8 \pm 4.4, \text{ or } (0.4, 9.2).$$

We conclude that, at the follow-up time, the mean weight is between 0.4 and 9.2 pounds higher with the FT treatment than with the CB treatment. The true means may be essentially equal, but if they differ, the advantage could be quite noticeable for the family therapy. Table 12.24 shows the confidence intervals for each pair of treatments.

**TABLE 12.24:** 95% Confidence Intervals Comparing Treatment Means after the Treatment Period

| Treatments Compared | Difference of Sample Means | Confidence Interval | Bonferroni Interval |
|---|---|---|---|
| FT − CB | 4.8 | (0.4, 9.2) | (−0.7, 10.3) |
| FT − C | 9.4 | (4.9, 13.9) | (3.8, 15.0) |
| CB − C | 4.6 | (0.7, 8.5) | (−0.2, 9.4) |

In summary, there is evidence that the mean weight increases during the experimental period for both noncontrol treatments. There is marginal evidence that the mean is higher after the experiment for the FT treatment than for the CB treatment.

At this stage, further interest may relate to whether the change in means, between time = after and time = before, differed for the two noncontrol treatments. That is, do the difference scores for the FT treatment have a significantly higher mean that the difference scores for the CB treatment? The difference scores have a mean of $(90.5 - 83.2) = 7.3$ for the FT treatment and $(85.7 - 82.7) = 3.0$ for the CB treatment, and we used these as the basis of separate confidence intervals for the mean change. Since the two groups are independent samples, the variance of the difference of these means is the sum of the variances. A 95% confidence interval for the difference between the mean changes in weight is

$$(7.3 - 3.0) \pm 1.99(5.3)\sqrt{\frac{1}{17} + \frac{1}{17} + \frac{1}{29} + \frac{1}{29}}, \text{ or } 4.3 \pm 4.6, \text{ or } (-0.3, 8.8).$$

Although the mean change could be considerably larger for the FT treatment, it is also plausible that the mean changes could be identical.

### Bonferroni Multiple Comparisons of Treatments

To control the overall error rate for several comparisons, we can use the Bonferroni multiple comparison method. Suppose we use three confidence intervals to compare treatments at time = after, and three intervals to compare times within the treatments. To ensure at least 90% confidence for the entire set, since $0.10/6 = 0.0167$, we use a 98.33% confidence interval for each individual comparison.

Such intervals are wider than the ones just reported, since they use a $t$-score of 2.45 instead of 1.99. Table 12.24 shows them for the pairwise comparisons of treatments at time = after. With this more conservative approach, only the difference between the FT and C treatments is significant, with the interval not containing 0.

### More Complex Repeated Measures Analyses

Two-way ANOVA with repeated measures on a factor extends to more complex designs. Suppose, for example, that a study has three factors, A, B, and C, with repeated measures on C. That is, subjects are crossed with C but nested within combinations of levels of A and B. The between-subjects effects, namely, the A and B main effects and the A × B interaction, are tested with a mean square error based on variability between subjects. All effects involving the within-subjects factor C, namely the C main effect, the A × C interaction, the B × C interaction, and the A × B × C interaction, are tested with a separate mean square error.

In some studies with two fixed effects, repeated measures occur on both factors. For instance, we may observe the same subjects for each treatment at each of several times. Then subjects (a random effect) are crossed with both factors (fixed effects), and an observation occurs for every subject at every combination of factor levels. As in ordinary two-way ANOVA, the effects of interest refer to the fixed effects—their main effects and interaction. The complicating factor is that each test requires a separate mean square error, but software can easily conduct this analysis.

### Repeated Measures at More than Two Times

In Example 12.8 the repeated measurements occur at two times. When observations are made at several times, the repeated measures ANOVA is more complex. In particular, the results depend on assumptions about the correlation structure of the repeated measurements. The standard test for the within-subject effect assumes *sphericity*, as in one-way repeated measures ANOVA. Tests of the between-subjects effects are not affected by violation of the sphericity assumption, so no adjustment is needed for that $F$ test.

Alternative *multivariate* ANOVA (MANOVA) approaches to testing the within-subjects effects (such as the *Wilks lambda likelihood-ratio test*) make fewer assumptions but often have weaker power. Other recently developed methods allow more varied types of random effects modeling of the correlation structure for the repeated responses, providing options other than sphericity. We'll discuss such approaches in Section 16.1.

## 12.8 EFFECTS OF VIOLATIONS OF ANOVA ASSUMPTIONS

Each ANOVA method presented in this chapter assumes (in addition to randomization) that the groups have population distributions that are normal with identical standard deviations. These are stringent assumptions. As in ordinary regression assumptions, they are never exactly satisfied in practice.

### Robustness of *F* Tests

Moderate departures from normality of the population distributions can be tolerated. The $F$ distribution still provides a good approximation to the actual sampling distribution of a $F$ test statistic. This is particularly true for larger sample sizes, since the sampling distributions then have weaker dependence on the shape of the population distribution. Moderate departures from equal standard deviations can also be tolerated. When the sample sizes are identical for the groups, the $F$ test is very robust to violations of this assumption.

Constructing histograms for each sample data distribution helps to check for extreme deviations from these assumptions. Misleading results may occur in the $F$ tests if the population distributions are highly skewed and the sample size is small, or if there are relatively large differences among the population standard deviations (say, the largest sample standard deviation is several times as large as the smallest one) and the sample sizes are unequal. Section 14.5 discusses alternative regression approaches for such gross violations. When the distributions are very highly skewed, the mean may not even be an appropriate summary measure.

Confidence intervals, like tests, are not highly dependent on the normality assumption. When the standard deviations are quite different, with the ratio of the largest to smallest exceeding about 2, it is preferable to use formulas for intervals based on separate standard deviations for the groups rather than a single pooled value. For instance, the confidence interval method presented in Section 7.3 for two groups does not assume equal standard deviations.

As in other inferences, the quality of the sample is most crucial. In one-way ANOVA, for instance, conclusions may be invalid if the observations in the separate groups compared are not independent random samples. ANOVA procedures are not robust to violations of sampling assumptions.

Let's consider the validity of the assumptions for two-way ANOVA for the data in Table 12.10 on political ideology classified by party ID and gender. The sample standard deviations are similar for the six groups (between 1.24 and 1.43). Also, the sample sizes are large (125 and up), so the normality assumption is not crucial. The full GSS sample was randomly obtained, so we may regard the six samples as independent random samples. ANOVA is suitable for these data.

### The Kruskal-Wallis Test: A Nonparametric Approach

The **Kruskal-Wallis test** is an alternative to one-way ANOVA for comparing several groups. It is a nonparametric method, not requiring the normality assumption. The test statistic uses only the ordinal information in the data. It ranks the observations and compares mean ranks for the various groups. The test statistic is larger when the differences among the mean ranks are larger. It has an approximate chi-squared distribution with $df = g - 1$.

This test is especially useful for small samples in which the effects of severe departures from normality may be influential. We shall not present the test statistic here. Its result is similar to that of a chi-squared test for the effect of a categorical predictor in a model for an ordinal response presented in Section 15.4. In practice, it is more informative to use a modeling approach, because the model parameter estimates give us information about the sizes of effects. In addition, the modeling strategy adapts better to multivariate analyses.

Nonparametric tests also exist for more complex analyses. For instance, **Friedman's test** is an alternative to the $F$ test of Section 12.6 comparing groups when the same subjects occur in each. An advantage of the parametric methods is that they more easily generalize to multivariate modeling and to estimation of effects, which are more important than significance testing. Lehmann (1975) is a good source for details about nonparametric methods.

## 12.9 CHAPTER SUMMARY

This chapter presented *analysis of variance* (ANOVA) methods for comparing several groups according to their means on a quantitative response variable. The groups are categories of one or more categorical explanatory variables.

- *One-way ANOVA* methods compare means for categories of a single explanatory variable.
- *Two-way ANOVA* methods compare means across categories of each of two explanatory variables. Assuming no interaction, the main effects describe the effect of each predictor while controlling for the other one.
- *Multiple comparison* methods provide confidence intervals for the difference between each pair of means, while controlling the overall error probability. The *Bonferroni* method does this using an error probability for each comparison that equals the desired overall error probability divided by the number of comparisons.
- Analysis-of-variance methods are special cases of multiple regression analyses. *Dummy variables* in the regression model represent categories that define the groups. Each dummy variable equals 1 for a particular category and 0 otherwise.

Ordinary ANOVA methods compare groups with *independent* random samples from the groups. For some studies, different samples instead have the same subjects, such as when an experiment observes subjects repeatedly over time. Methods for *repeated measures ANOVA* result from regression models with *random effects* that represent the effects of the random sample of observed subjects. Such methods treat *within-subjects* effects (for repeated measurements on subjects) differently from *between-subjects* effects (for independent samples of subjects).

Chapters 9 and 11 presented regression models for a quantitative response variable when the explanatory variables are also *quantitative*. This chapter has modeled a quantitative response variable as a function of *categorical* explanatory variables. Table 12.25 summarizes the statistical tests discussed in Sections 12.1, 12.4, and 12.6.

**TABLE 12.25:** ANOVA Tests for Comparing Several Groups on a Response Variable

| Element of Test | One-Way ANOVA | Two-Way ANOVA | Repeated Measures ANOVA |
|---|---|---|---|
| 1. Samples | Independent | Independent | Dependent |
| 2. Hypotheses | $H_0$: Identical means $H_a$: At least two means not equal | $H_0$: Identical row means $H_0$: Identical col. means $H_0$: No Interaction | $H_0$: Identical means $H_a$: At least two means not equal |
| 3. Test statistic | $F = \dfrac{\text{Between-groups MS}}{\text{Within-groups MS}}$ $F$ distribution $df_1 = g - 1$ $df_2 = N - g$ | $F = \dfrac{\text{Effect MS}}{\text{MS error}}$ $F$ distribution $df_1 = df$ for effect $df_2 = df$ for error | $F = \dfrac{\text{Effect MS}}{\text{MS error}}$ $F$ distribution $df_1 = df$ for effect $df_2 = df$ for error |
| 4. $P$-value | Right-tail probability | Right-tail probability | Right-tail probability |

Models of the next chapter include both quantitative and categorical explanatory variables.

## PROBLEMS

### Practicing the Basics

**12.1.** A study[1] of American armed forces who had served in Iraq or Afghanistan reported that of those who had been in a firefight, the *P*-value was 0.001 for comparing the number of firefights reported by soldiers deployed in Afghanistan, soldiers deployed in Iraq, and Marines deployed in Iraq. Explain how this relates to analysis of variance, identifying the response variable, the explanatory variable, and hypotheses that could be tested to yield this *P*-value.

**12.2.** A GSS asked subjects how many good friends they have. Is this associated with the respondent's astrological sign (the 12 symbols of the Zodiac)? The ANOVA table for the GSS data reports $F = 0.61$ based on $df_1 = 11$, $df_2 = 813$.
  **(a)** Specify the null and alternative hypotheses for the ANOVA.
  **(b)** Based on what you know about the *F* distribution, would you guess that $F = 0.61$ provides strong evidence against $H_0$? Explain.
  **(c)** Software reports a *P*-value of 0.82. Explain how to interpret it.

**12.3.** For GSS data comparing the reported number of good friends for those who are (married, widowed, divorced, separated, never married), an ANOVA table reports $F = 0.80$.
  **(a)** Specify the null and alternative hypotheses for the ANOVA.
  **(b)** Based on what you know about the *F* distribution, would you guess that $F = 0.80$ provides strong evidence against $H_0$? Explain.
  **(c)** Software reports a *P*-value of 0.53. Explain how to interpret it.

**12.4.** A recent GSS asked, "What is the ideal number of kids for a family?" Do responses tend to depend on religious affiliation? Results of an ANOVA are shown in Table 12.26, for religion categories (Protestant, Catholic, Jewish, Other or none).
  **(a)** Specify the hypotheses tested in this table.

#### TABLE 12.26

| Source | SS | df | Mean Square | F | Sig |
|---|---|---|---|---|---|
| Religion | 11.72 | 3 | 3.91 | 5.48 | 0.001 |
| Error | 922.82 | 1295 | 0.71 | | |
| Total | 934.54 | 1298 | | | |

  **(b)** Report the *F* test statistic value and the *P*-value. Interpret the *P*-value.

  **(c)** Based on (b), can you conclude that *every* pair of religious affiliations has different population means for ideal family size? Explain.

**12.5.** A recent GSS asked, "How often do you go to a bar or tavern?" Table 12.27 shows descriptive statistics and an ANOVA for comparing the mean reported number of good friends at three levels of this variable.
  **(a)** State the (i) hypotheses, (ii) test statistic value, (iii) *P*-value, (iv) decision for an $\alpha = 0.05$-level test.
  **(b)** Does any aspect of the summary here suggest that an assumption for the ANOVA test may be badly violated? Explain.

#### TABLE 12.27

| | How often go to bar or tavern? | | |
|---|---|---|---|
| | Very often | Occasional | Never |
| Mean no. good friends | 12.1 | 6.4 | 6.2 |
| Standard deviation | 21.3 | 10.2 | 14.0 |
| Sample size | 41 | 166 | 215 |

| Source | Sum of Squares | df | Mean Square | F | Sig |
|---|---|---|---|---|---|
| Group | 1116.8 | 2 | 558.4 | 3.03 | 0.049 |
| Error | 77171.8 | 419 | 184.2 | | |
| Total | 78288.5 | 421 | | | |

**12.6.** Table 12.28 shows scores on the first quiz (maximum score 10 points) in a beginning French course. Students in the course are grouped as follows:
Group A:  Never studied foreign language before, but have good English skills
Group B:  Never studied foreign language before; have poor English skills
Group C:  Studied other foreign language

#### TABLE 12.28

| Group A | Group B | Group C |
|---|---|---|
| 4 | 1 | 9 |
| 6 | 5 | 10 |
| 8 | | 5 |

  **(a)** Table 12.29 provides results of an ANOVA. Report the assumptions, hypotheses, test statistic, and *P*-value. Interpret the *P*-value.
  **(b)** Suppose that the first observation in the second group was actually 9, not 1. Then the standard deviations are the same as reported

[1]C. Hoge et al., *New England J. Medic.*, vol. 351, 2004, pp. 13–21.

**TABLE 12.29**

| Source | Sum of Squares | df | Mean Square | F | Sig |
|---|---|---|---|---|---|
| Between Groups | 30.000 | 2 | 15.000 | 2.5000 | 0.1768 |
| Within Groups | 30.000 | 5 | 6.00 | | |
| Total | 60.00 | 7 | | | |

| Group | n | Mean | Standard Deviation | Standard Error |
|---|---|---|---|---|
| Grp 1 | 3 | 6.0000 | 2.0000 | 1.1547 |
| Grp 2 | 2 | 3.0000 | 2.8284 | 2.0000 |
| Grp 3 | 3 | 8.0000 | 2.6458 | 1.5275 |

in the table, but the sample means are 6, 7, and 8 rather than 6, 3, and 8. Do you think the $F$ test statistic would be larger, the same, or smaller? Explain your reasoning, without doing any calculations.

**(c)** Suppose you had the same means as shown in the table but the sample standard deviations were 1.0, 1.8, and 1.6, instead of 2.0, 2.8, and 2.6. Do you think the $F$ test statistic would be larger, the same, or smaller? Explain your reasoning.

**(d)** Suppose you had the same means and standard deviations as shown in the table but the sample sizes were 30, 20, and 30, instead of 3, 2, and 3. Do you think the $F$ test statistic would be larger, the same, or smaller? Explain your reasoning.

**(e)** In (b), (c), and (d), would the $P$-value be larger, the same, or smaller? Why?

**12.7.** Use software to reproduce the ANOVA results reported in the previous exercise.

**12.8.** A consumer protection group compares three types of front bumpers for a brand of automobile. A test is conducted by driving an automobile into a concrete wall at 15 miles per hour. The response is the amount of damage to the car, as measured by the repair costs, in hundreds of dollars. Due to the potentially large costs, the study conducts only two tests with each bumper type. Table 12.30 shows the results.

**TABLE 12.30**

| Bumper A | Bumper B | Bumper C |
|---|---|---|
| 1 | 2 | 11 |
| 3 | 4 | 15 |

**(a)** Find the within-groups sum of squares and the associated variance estimate.

**(b)** Find the between-groups sum of squares and its associated variance estimate.

**(c)** Test the hypothesis that the mean repair costs are the same for the three types of bumpers. Report the null and alternative hypotheses, test statistic, $df$ values, and $P$-value. Display results in an ANOVA table, and interpret.

**12.9.** Refer to the previous exercise. Construct 94% multiple comparison confidence intervals for the differences in mean repair costs for each pair of bumpers. Interpret the results, and indicate which types of bumpers are judged to be different in mean repair cost.

**12.10.** In a study to compare customer satisfaction at service centers for PC technical support in San Jose (California), Toronto (Canada), and Bangalore (India), each center randomly sampled 100 people who called during a two-week period. Callers rated their satisfaction on a scale of 0 to 10, with higher scores representing greater satisfaction. The sample means were 7.6 for San Jose, 7.8 for Toronto, and 7.1 for Bangalore. Table 12.31 shows the results of an ANOVA.

**TABLE 12.31**

| Source | Sum of Squares | df | Mean Square | F | Sig |
|---|---|---|---|---|---|
| Group | 26.00 | 2 | 13.00 | 27.6 | 0.000 |
| Error | 140.00 | 297 | 0.47 | | |
| Total | 60.00 | 299 | | | |

**(a)** Explain how to obtain the $F$ test statistic value reported in the table from the mean square values shown. Report the $df_1$ and $df_2$ values for the $F$ distribution, and report and interpret the $P$-value.

**(b)** Explain why the margin of error for separate 95% confidence intervals is the same (0.19) for comparing the population means for each pair of cities. Construct and interpret the three intervals.

**(c)** The margin of error for Bonferroni or for Tukey 95% multiple comparison confidence intervals is 0.23. Why is it different than in (b), and what is an advantage of this approach?

**(d)** With dummy variables to represent the service centers, the prediction equation is $\hat{y} = 7.1 + 0.5z_1 + 0.7z_2$. Show how the terms in this equation relate to the sample means of 7.6, 7.8, and 7.1.

**12.11.** The 2004 GSS asked 1829 subjects how many hours per day they watched TV, on the average. The sample means were 2.75 for whites ($n = 1435$), 4.14 for blacks ($n = 305$), and 2.61 for other ($n = 89$). The 95% confidence interval comparing the population means is (1.1, 1.7) for blacks and whites, ($-0.4$, 0.7) for whites and the other category, and (0.9, 2.1) for blacks and the other category. Based on the confidence intervals, indicate which pairs of means are significantly different, and interpret.

**12.12.** A recent GSS asked, "Would you say that you are very happy, pretty happy, or not too happy?" (variable HAPPY). The same GSS also asked, "About how many good friends do you have?" (variable NUMFREND). Table 12.32 summarizes results.
  **(a)** State a research question you could answer with these data.
  **(b)** Interpret the result of the $F$ test.
  **(c)** Software reports Tukey 95% confidence intervals of (0.3, 5.7) comparing very happy and pretty happy, ($-2.3, 6.5$) comparing very happy and not too happy, and ($-5.1, 3.3$) comparing pretty happy and not too happy. Interpret, and indicate which groups are significantly different.

**12.13.** For $g$ groups with $n = 100$ each, we plan to compare all pairs of population means. We want the probability to equal at least 0.80 that the entire set of confidence intervals contain the true differences. For the Bonferroni method, which tabled $t$-score should we use for each interval if (a) $g = 10$, (b) $g = 5$? Describe how the $t$-score depends on the number of groups, and explain the implication regarding width of the intervals.

**12.14.** A psychologist compares the mean amount of time of REM sleep for subjects under three conditions. She uses three groups of subjects, with four subjects in each group. Table 12.33 shows a SAS printout

for the analysis. Interpret all the information on this printout.

**TABLE 12.33**

| Source | DF | Sum of Squares | Mean Square | F Value | Pr > F |
|---|---|---|---|---|---|
| Model | 2 | 72.000 | 36.000 | 0.79 | 0.4813 |
| Error | 9 | 408.000 | 45.333 | | |
| Total | 11 | 480.000 | | | |

```
Bonferroni T tests for variable: TIME
   Alpha= 0.05  df= 9  MSE= 45.33333
        Critical Value of T= 2.93
   Minimum Significant Difference= 13.965
```

```
Means with the same letter are not significantly different.
Bon Grouping        Mean     N  GROUP
          A        18.000    4   3
          A
          A        15.000    4   2
          A
          A        12.000    4   1
```

**12.15.** Refer to the previous exercise.
  **(a)** Set up dummy variables for a regression model so that an $F$ test for the regression parameters is equivalent to the ANOVA $F$ test. Express $H_0$ both in terms of population means and regression parameters.
  **(b)** The prediction equation obtained in fitting the regression equation from (b) is $\hat{y} = 18 - 6z_1 - 3z_2$. Show how the parameter estimates relate to the sample means in Table 12.33.

**12.16.** Exercise 12.8 showed an ANOVA for an experiment comparing three bumpers, with sample mean damages of 2 for Bumper A, 3 for Bumper B, and 13 for Bumper C (in hundreds of dollars).
  **(a)** Set up the regression model with dummy variables for the ANOVA.
  **(b)** Show the correspondence between the null hypothesis for the means in ANOVA and the null hypothesis for the regression parameters.
  **(c)** Report the prediction equation you would obtain for the model in (a). (If you're not sure, use regression software to find it.)

**TABLE 12.32**

| | Very happy | Pretty happy | Not too happy |
|---|---|---|---|
| Mean | 10.4 | 7.4 | 8.3 |
| Standard deviation | 17.8 | 13.6 | 15.6 |
| Sample size | 276 | 468 | 87 |

| Source | Sum of Squares | df | Mean Square | F | Sig |
|---|---|---|---|---|---|
| Group | 1626.8 | 2 | 813.4 | 3.47 | 0.032 |
| Error | 193900.9 | 828 | 234.2 | | |
| Total | 195527.7 | 830 | | | |

**12.17.** When we use the 2004 GSS to evaluate how the mean number of hours a day watching TV depends on sex and race, we get the results shown in Table 12.34. The sample means were 2.71 for white females, 2.79 for white males, 4.13 for black females, and 4.16 for black males. Explain how these results are compatible with the results of the tests shown.

**TABLE 12.34**

| Source | SS | df | MS | F | Sig |
|--------|-----|-----|-----|-----|-----|
| Sex | 2.22 | 1 | 2.22 | 0.35 | 0.555 |
| Race | 489.65 | 1 | 489.65 | 76.62 | 0.000 |
| Error | 11094.16 | 1737 | 6.39 | | |
| Total | 11583.81 | 1739 | | | |

**12.18.** A recent GSS asked, "What is the ideal number of kids for a family?" Table 12.35 shows results of using the GSS to evaluate the effects of gender and race.
  (a) Explain how to interpret the results of the $F$ tests.
  (b) Let $s = 1$ for females and 0 for males, and let $r = 1$ for blacks and 0 for whites. The no interaction model has $\hat{y} = 2.42 + 0.04s + 0.37r$. Find the estimated mean for each combination of gender and race. Explain how these means satisfy "no interaction."

**TABLE 12.35**

| Source | SS | df | MS | F | P-value |
|--------|-----|-----|-----|-----|---------|
| Gender | 0.25 | 1 | 0.25 | 0.36 | 0.550 |
| Race | 16.98 | 1 | 16.98 | 24.36 | 0.000 |
| Error | 868.67 | 1246 | 0.70 | | |
| Total | 886.12 | 1248 | | | |

**12.19.** Table 12.15 on page 388 gave the prediction equation $\hat{y} = 4.58 - 0.71p_1 - 0.54p_2 - 0.08s$ relating political ideology to party ID and to sex. Find the estimated means for the six cells, and show that they satisfy a lack of interaction.

**12.20.** A regression analysis of college faculty salaries[2] included several predictors, including a dummy variable for gender (male = 1) and a dummy variable for race (nonwhite = 1). For annual income measured in thousands of dollars, the estimated coefficients were 0.76 for gender and 0.62 for race. At particular settings of the other predictors, the estimated mean salary for white females was 30.2 thousand. Find the estimated means for the other three groups.

**12.21.** When we use the 2004 GSS and regress $y = $ number of hours per day watching TV on $s = $ sex (1 = male, 0 = female) and religious affiliation ($r_1 = 1$ for Protestant, $r_2 = 1$ for Catholic, $r_3 = 1$ for Jewish, $r_1 = r_2 = r_3 = 0$ for none or other), we get $\hat{y} = 2.4 + 0.2s + 0.5r_1 + 0.8r_2 - 0.1r_3$.
  (a) Interpret the coefficient of $r_1$.
  (b) State a corresponding model for the population, and indicate which parameters must equal zero for $y$ to be independent of religious affiliation, for each sex.

**12.22.** In the U.S., the current population mean hourly wage for males is about $22 for white-collar jobs, $11 for service jobs, and $14 for blue-collar jobs. For females the means are $15 for white-collar jobs, $8 for service jobs, and $10 for blue-collar jobs.
  (a) Identify the response variable and the two factors.
  (b) Show these means in a two-way classification of the two factors.
  (c) Compare the differences between males and females for (i) white-collar jobs (ii) blue-collar jobs. Explain why there is interaction, and describe it.

**12.23.** The U.S. Census Bureau recently stated the population median income to be $29,661 for white females, $25,736 for black females, $40,350 for white males, $30,886 for black males.
  (a) Identify the response variable and the two factors, and show these medians in a two-way classification of the factors.
  (b) Explain why there is interaction in terms of the median.
  (c) Show four population median incomes that would satisfy $H_0$: no interaction.

**12.24.** Table 12.36 summarizes responses on political ideology in the 2004 GSS by religion and sex. The $P$-value is 0.03 for testing $H_0$: no interaction.

**TABLE 12.36**

| Religion | | Political Ideology Mean | Std Dev. | | Political Ideology Mean | Std. Dev. |
|----------|--------|------|----------|------|------|----------|
| Protestant | Female | 4.23 | 1.34 | Male | 4.44 | 1.41 |
| Catholic | Female | 4.10 | 1.33 | Male | 4.22 | 1.42 |
| Jewish | Female | 2.59 | 1.22 | Male | 3.82 | 1.68 |
| None | Female | 3.34 | 1.34 | Male | 3.58 | 1.42 |

[2]M. Bellas, *American Sociological Review*, vol. 59, 1994, p. 807.

Explain what this means in the context of this example, and indicate one place in the table that may be responsible for the small *P*-value.

**12.25.** Table 12.37 shows results of an ANOVA on *y* = depression index and the predictors gender and marital status (married, never married, divorced). State the sample size and fill in the blanks in the ANOVA table. Interpret results.

**TABLE 12.37**

| Source | Sum of Squares | df | Mean Square | F | Sig |
|--------|------|-----|------|-----|-----|
| Gender | 100 | — | — | — | — |
| Marital status | 200 | — | — | — | — |
| Interaction | 100 | — | — | — | — |
| Error | | — | — | | |
| Total | 4000 | 205 | | | |

**12.26.** Use software with Table 12.10 on page 383.
  **(a)** Fit the no interaction model, and verify the results given there.
  **(b)** Fit the interaction model. Show how the difference between SSE for this model and SSE for the no interaction model relates to the numerator sum of squares for testing $H_0$: no interaction.
  **(c)** Using the prediction equation for the interaction model, find the six estimated cell means, and compare them to the sample means. (*Note*: The model uses six parameters to summarize six means, so it has a perfect fit.)

**12.27.** The prediction equation $\hat{y} = 16 + 2s + 3r + 8(s \times r)$ relates *y* = annual income (thousands of dollars), *s* = sex (*s* = 1 for men, *s* = 0 for women), and *r* = race (*r* = 1 for whites, *r* = 0 for blacks). By finding the four predicted means for this equation, show that the coefficient 8 of the interaction term is the amount by which the mean for one of the four groups must increase or decrease for the interaction to disappear.

**12.28.** For the 2000 GSS, Table 12.38 shows sample means of political ideology classified by gender and by race. For $H_0$: no interaction, software reports $F = 21.7$, $df_1 = 1$ and $df_2 = 2508$, and *P*-value = 0.001.

**TABLE 12.38**

| | Race | |
|--------|--------|--------|
| Gender | Black | White |
| Female | 4.06 (n = 256) | 4.04 (n = 1144) |
| Male | 3.74 (n = 139) | 4.25 (n = 973) |

  **(a)** Suppose that instead of the two-way ANOVA, you performed a one-way ANOVA with gender as the predictor and a separate one-way ANOVA with race as the predictor. Suppose the ANOVA for gender does not show a significant effect. Explain how this could happen, even though the two-way ANOVA showed a gender effect for each race. (*Hint*: Will the overall sample means for females and males be more similar than they are for each race?)
  **(b)** Summarize what you would learn about the gender effect from a two-way ANOVA that you would fail to learn from a one-way ANOVA.

**12.29.** Refer to Table 12.17 on page 392 about three influences on children.
  **(a)** Using software, conduct the repeated measures analyses of Section 12.6.
  **(b)** Suppose you scored the influence categories $(-3, -2, 0, 2, 3)$. What would this assume about the response categories? Repeat the analyses using these scores. Are the conclusions sensitive to the choice of scores?

**12.30.** Recently the GSS asked respondents, "Compared with ten years ago, would you say that American children today are (1) much better off, (2) better off, (3) about the same, (4) worse off, or (5) much worse off?" Table 12.39 shows responses for ten of the subjects on three issues: quality of their education, safety of the neighborhoods they live in, and getting health care when they need it.
  **(a)** For each of the following, indicate whether it is a fixed effect, random effect, or response variable: (i) opinion, (ii) issue, (iii) subject.
  **(b)** Test the hypothesis that the population means are equal. Report the *P*-value, and interpret.

**TABLE 12.39**

| | Status of Children | | |
|---------|-----------|--------------|-------------|
| Subject | Education | Neighborhood | Health Care |
| 1 | 4 | 4 | 3 |
| 2 | 2 | 4 | 2 |
| 3 | 3 | 3 | 4 |
| 4 | 1 | 2 | 1 |
| 5 | 3 | 4 | 3 |
| 6 | 2 | 5 | 4 |
| 7 | 1 | 4 | 2 |
| 8 | 3 | 3 | 3 |
| 9 | 4 | 5 | 3 |
| 10 | 2 | 4 | 2 |

**12.31.** Refer to the previous exercise. The first five respondents were female, and the last five were male. Analyze these data using both gender and issue as factors.

**12.32.** The GSS asks respondents to rate various groups using the "feeling thermometer" on a scale of 0 (most unfavorable) to 100 (most favorable). We plan to study how the mean compares for rating liberals and rating conservatives, for ratings in 2006 and ratings in 1986. Explain why a two-way ANOVA using time (1986, 2006) and group rated (Liberal, Conservative) as factors would require methods for repeated measures. Identify the within-subjects and between-subjects factors.

**12.33.** Table 12.40 shows results of using SAS for analyzing the anorexia data of Table 12.21.
  **(a)** Explain how to use the information in this table to test $H_0$: no interaction between treatment and time.
  **(b)** Explain why it does not make sense to conduct the tests of the main effects.

**12.34.** Using software, conduct the repeated measures ANOVA of the anorexia data in Table 12.21 (page 396), available at the text Web site.

## Concepts and Applications

**12.35.** Refer to the "Student survey" data file (Exercise 1.11 on page 8), with response variable the number of weekly hours engaged in sports and other physical exercise. Using software, conduct an analysis of variance and follow-up estimation, and prepare a report summarizing your analyses and interpretations using
  **(a)** Gender as a predictor
  **(b)** Gender and whether a vegetarian as predictors

**12.36.** For $y$ = number of times used public transportation in previous week and $x$ = number of cars in family (which takes value 0, 1, or 2 for the given sample), explain the difference between conducting a test of independence of the variables using the ANOVA $F$ test for comparing three means and using a regression $t$ test for the coefficient of the number of cars in an ordinary regression model with a linear effect for number of cars. Give an example of three population means for which the regression test would be less appropriate than the ANOVA test. (*Hint*: What does the regression linear model assume that the ANOVA $F$ test does not?)

**12.37.** Go to the GSS Web site sda.berkeley.edu/GSS, and click on *Comparison of Means* under *Analysis*. Conduct an ANOVA for the most recent year available to compare the mean political ideology (POLVIEWS) by (a) the categories (lower, working, middle, upper) for social class (CLASS), (b) the nine regions of the country (REGION). Report results and interpret.

**12.38.** A recent GSS asked, "How often do you attend religious services?" Table 12.41 shows results of ANOVA for comparing three levels of this variable (at least 2–3 times a month for the "high" group, several times a year to about once a month for the "medium" group, and at most once a year for the "low" group) on the mean number of good friends. Use the reported results to make inferences (a significance test and estimation). Summarize your analyses and interpretations.

**12.39.** An experiment used four randomly selected groups of five individuals each. The overall sample mean was 60.
  **(a)** What did the data look like if the one-way ANOVA for comparing the means had test statistic $F = 0$?
  **(b)** What did the data look like if $F = \infty$?

### TABLE 12.40

Repeated Measures Analysis of Variance
Tests of Hypotheses for Between Subjects Effects

| Source | DF | ANOVA SS | Mean Square | F Value | Pr > F |
|--------|----|----------|-------------|---------|--------|
| TREATMNT | 2 | 644.23 | 322.12 | 6.20 | 0.0033 |
| Error | 69 | 3584.03 | 51.94 | | |

Univariate Tests of Hypotheses for Within Subject Effects
Source: TIME

| DF | ANOVA SS | Mean Square | F Value | Pr > F |
|----|----------|-------------|---------|--------|
| 1 | 275.0069444 | 275.0069444 | 9.70 | 0.0027 |

Source: TIME*TREATMNT

| DF | ANOVA SS | Mean Square | F Value | Pr > F |
|----|----------|-------------|---------|--------|
| 2 | 307.3218334 | 153.6609167 | 5.42 | 0.0065 |

Source: Error(TIME)

| DF | ANOVA SS | Mean Square |
|----|----------|-------------|
| 69 | 1955.3712221 | 28.3387134 |

**TABLE 12.41**

|  | How Often Attend Religious Services | | |
|---|---|---|---|
|  | High | Medium | Low |
| Mean number good friends | 12.1 | 6.4 | 6.2 |
| Sample size | 337 | 159 | 330 |

| Source | Sum of Squares | df | Mean Square | F | Sig |
|---|---|---|---|---|---|
| Group | 6748.2 | 2 | 3374.1 | 14.2 | 0.000 |
| Error | 196136.9 | 823 | 238.3 |  |  |
| Total | 202885.1 | 825 |  |  |  |

**12.40.** A study about smoking and personality[3] used a sample of 1638 adults in the Baltimore Longitudinal Study on Aging. The subjects formed three groups according to smoking status (never, former, current). Each subject completed a personality questionnaire that provided scores on various personality scales designed to have overall means of about 50 and standard deviations of about 10. Table 12.42 shows some results for three traits, giving the means with standard deviations in parentheses. The study measured 35 personality scales and reported an $F$ test comparing the three smoking groups for each scale. The researchers mentioned doing a Bonferroni correction for the 35 $F$ tests. If the nominal overall probability of Type I error was 0.05 for the 35 tests, how small did the $P$-value have to be for a given test to be significant? Interpret the results in the table.

**12.41.** A study[4] compared verbal memory of men and women for abstract words and for concrete words. It found a gender main effect in favor of women. It also reported, "There was no sex × word-type interaction ($F = .408$, $P = .525$), indicating that women were equally advantaged on the two kinds of words." How would you explain what this sentence means to someone who has never studied statistics?

**12.42. (a)** Explain carefully the difference between a probability of Type I error of 0.05 for a single comparison of two means and a multiple comparison error rate of 0.05 for comparing all pairs of means.

**(b)** In multiple comparisons following a one-way ANOVA with equal sample sizes, the margin of error with a 95% confidence interval for comparing each pair of means equals 10. Give three sample means illustrating that it is possible that group A is not significantly different from group B and group B is not significantly different from group C, yet group A is significantly different from group C.

**12.43.** Table 12.43 summarizes responses on political ideology in the 2004 GSS by race and gender (Recall 1 = extremely liberal, 4 = moderate, 7 = extremely conservative). Table 12.44 shows results of one-way and two-way ANOVAs comparing the four groups. Write a paragraph explaining

**TABLE 12.43**

|  |  |  | Political Ideology | |
|---|---|---|---|---|
| Race | Gender | $n$ | Mean | Standard Deviation |
| White | Female | 553 | 4.15 | 1.40 |
|  | Male | 501 | 4.42 | 1.42 |
| Black | Female | 100 | 3.95 | 1.47 |
|  | Male | 54 | 3.93 | 1.30 |

**TABLE 12.44**

1-way ANOVA

| Source | Sum of Squares | df | Mean Square | F | P |
|---|---|---|---|---|---|
| Groups | 34.46 | 3 | 11.49 | 5.78 | 0.001 |
| Error | 2393.83 | 1204 | 1.99 |  |  |
| Total | 2428.29 | 1207 |  |  |  |

2-way ANOVA

| Source | Sum of Squares | df | Mean Square | F | P |
|---|---|---|---|---|---|
| Race | 12.74 | 1 | 12.74 | 6.41 | .011 |
| Sex | 16.42 | 1 | 16.42 | 8.26 | .004 |
| Interaction | 2.66 | 1 | 2.66 | 1.34 | .248 |
| Error | 2393.83 | 1204 | 1.99 |  |  |
| Total | 2428.29 | 1207 |  |  |  |

**TABLE 12.42**

|  | Never smokers (n = 828) | Former smokers (n = 694) | Current smokers (n = 116) | $F$ |
|---|---|---|---|---|
| Neuroticism | 46.7 (9.6) | 48.5 (9.2) | 51.9 (9.9) | 17.77 |
| Extraversion | 50.4 (10.3) | 50.2 (10.0) | 50.9 (9.4) | 0.24 |
| Conscientiousness | 51.8 (10.1) | 48.9 (9.7) | 45.6 (10.3) | 29.42 |

[3] A. Terracciano and P. Costa, *Addiction*, vol. 99, 2004, pp. 472–481.

[4] D. Kimura and P. Clarke, *Psych. Reports*, vol. 91, 2002, pp. 1137–1142.

what you learn from the two-way ANOVA that you cannot learn from the one-way ANOVA.

**12.44.** Table 7.24 on page 217 summarized a study that reported the mean number of dates in the past three months. For men, the mean was 9.7 for the more attractive and 9.9 for the less attractive. For women, the mean was 17.8 for the more attractive and 10.6 for the less attractive. Identify the response variable and the factors, and indicate whether these data appear to show interaction. Explain.

**12.45.** Construct a numerical example of means for a two-way classification under the following conditions:
  **(a)** Main effects are present only for the row variable.
  **(b)** Main effects are present for each variable, with no interaction.
  **(c)** Interaction effects are present.
  **(d)** No effects of any type are present.

**12.46.** The null hypothesis of equality of means for a factor is rejected in a two-way ANOVA. Does this imply that the hypothesis will be rejected in a one-way ANOVA $F$ test if the data are collapsed over the levels of the second variable? Explain.

**12.47.** For a two-way classification of means by factors A and B, at each level of B the means are equal for the levels of A. Does this imply that the overall means are equal at the various levels of A, ignoring B? Explain the implications, in terms of how results may differ between two-way ANOVA and one-way ANOVA.

**12.48.** The 25 women faculty in the humanities division of a college have a mean salary of $66,000, whereas the five in the science division have a mean salary of $80,000. On the other hand, the 20 men in the humanities division have a mean salary of $65,000, and the 30 men in the science division have a mean salary of $79,000.
  **(a)** Construct a table of sample mean incomes for the 2 × 2 cross-classification of gender and division of college. Find the overall means for men and women. Interpret.
  **(b)** Discuss how the results of a one-way comparison of mean incomes by gender would differ

from the results of a two-way comparison of mean incomes by gender, controlling for division of college. (*Note*: This reversal of which gender has the higher mean salary, according to whether one controls division of college, illustrates *Simpson's paradox*. See Exercise 10.14 in Chapter 10.)

**12.49.** A random sample of 26 female graduate students at the University of Florida were surveyed about their attitudes toward abortion. Each received a score on abortion attitude according to how many from a list of eight possible reasons for abortion she would accept as a legitimate reason for a woman to seek abortion. Table 12.45 displays the scores, classified by religion and church attendance. Using software, analyze the data and report your findings.

**12.50.** True or false? Suppose that for subjects aged under 50, there is little difference in mean annual medical expenses for smokers and nonsmokers, but for subjects aged over 50 there is a large difference. Then there is no interaction between smoking status and age in their effects on annual medical expenses.

*Select the correct response(s) in Exercises 12.51–12.54. (More than one response may be correct.)*

**12.51.** Analysis of variance and regression are similar in the sense that
  **(a)** They both assume a quantitative response variable.
  **(b)** They both have $F$ tests for testing that the response variable is statistically independent of the explanatory variable(s).
  **(c)** For inferential purposes, they both assume that the response variable $y$ is normally distributed with the same standard deviation at all combinations of levels of the explanatory variable(s).
  **(d)** They both provide ways of partitioning the variation in $y$ into "explained" and "unexplained" components.

**12.52.** One-way ANOVA provides relatively more evidence that $H_0: \mu_1 = \cdots = \mu_g$ is false
  **(a)** The smaller the between-groups variation and the larger the within-groups variation

**TABLE 12.45**

| | | Religion | |
|---|---|---|---|
| | | Fundamentalist | Nonfundamentalist |
| Church Attendance | Frequent | 0, 3, 4, 0, 3 2, 0, 1, 1 | 2, 5, 1, 2 3, 3 |
| | Infrequent | 4, 3, 4 | 6, 8, 6, 4 6, 3, 7, 4 |

**(b)** The smaller the between-groups variation and the smaller the within-groups variation

**(c)** The larger the between-groups variation and the smaller the within-groups variation

**(d)** The larger the between-groups variation and the larger the within-groups variation

**12.53.** For four means, a multiple comparison method provides 95% confidence intervals for the differences between the six pairs. Then

**(a)** For each confidence interval, there is a 0.95 chance that it contains the population difference.

**(b)** $P$(all six confidence intervals are correct) = 0.70.

**(c)** $P$(all six confidence intervals are correct) = 0.95.

**(d)** $P$(all six confidence intervals are correct) = $(0.95)^6$.

**(e)** $P$(at least one confidence interval does not contain the true difference) = 0.05.

**(f)** The confidence intervals are wider than separate 95% confidence intervals for each difference.

**12.54.** Interaction terms are needed in a two-way ANOVA model when

**(a)** Each pair of variables is associated.

**(b)** Both explanatory variables have significant effects in the model without interaction terms.

**(c)** The difference in means between two categories of one explanatory variable varies greatly among the categories of the other explanatory variable.

**(d)** The mean square for interaction is huge compared to the mean square error.

**\*12.55.** You know the sample mean, standard deviation, and sample size for each of three groups. Can you conduct an ANOVA $F$ test comparing the population means, or would you need more information?

**\*12.56.** You form a 95% confidence interval in five different situations, with independent samples.

**(a)** Find the probability that (i) *all* five intervals contain the parameters they are designed to estimate, (ii) at least one interval is in error. (*Hint*: Use the binomial distribution.)

**(b)** If you use confidence level 0.9898 for each interval, the probability that all five intervals contain the parameters equals exactly 0.95. Explain why. (*Hint*: What is $(0.9898)^5$?) Compare 0.9898 to the confidence coefficient for each interval in the Bonferroni method.

**\*12.57.** This exercise motivates the formula for the between-groups variance estimate in one-way ANOVA. Suppose the sample sizes all equal $n$ and the population means all equal $\mu$. The sampling distribution of each $\bar{y}_i$ then has mean $\mu$ and variance $\sigma^2/n$. The sample mean of the $\bar{y}_i$ values is $\bar{y}$.

**(a)** Treating $\bar{y}_1, \bar{y}_2, \ldots, \bar{y}_g$ as $g$ observations having sample mean $\bar{y}$, explain why

$$\sum (\bar{y}_i - \bar{y})^2/(g - 1)$$

estimates the variance $\sigma^2/n$ of the sampling distribution of the $\bar{y}_i$-values.

**(b)** Using (a), explain why $\sum n(\bar{y}_i - \bar{y})^2/(g - 1)$ estimates $\sigma^2$. For the unequal sample size case, replacing $n$ by $n_i$ yields the between-groups estimate.

# CHAPTER 13

# Combining Regression and ANOVA: Quantitative and Categorical Predictors

Chapter 11 introduced multiple regression to analyze the relationship between a quantitative response variable and *quantitative* explanatory variables. Chapter 12 showed that multiple regression can also handle *categorical* explanatory variables, as in analysis of variance with dummy variables. Not surprisingly, multiple regression can also handle simultaneously quantitative and categorical explanatory variables. The model combines elements of ordinary regression analysis, for which the predictors are quantitative, and analysis of variance, for which the predictors are categorical.

### Controlling for a Covariate

One-way ANOVA compares the mean of the response variable for several groups. Two-way ANOVA compares means while controlling for another categorical variable. In many applications, it's useful to compare means while controlling for a quantitative variable. For example, in comparing mean income for men and women, we might control for possibly differing levels of job experience between men and women. The quantitative control variable is called a **covariate**. The use of regression for this type of comparison is often called **analysis of covariance**. It is one of the many statistical contributions of R. A. Fisher, the brilliant British statistician.

Because effects may change after controlling for a variable, the results of analysis of covariance may differ from the results of analysis of variance. For instance, job experience is usually positively correlated with income. If men tend to have higher levels of experience than women at a particular job, the results of a comparison of mean income for men and women will depend on whether we control for experience.

For simplicity, this chapter illustrates concepts using a single categorical predictor and a single quantitative predictor, but the basic ideas extend to multiple predictors. The first section shows graphic representations of the potential effects. Sections 13.2 and 13.3 show that regression models with dummy variables provide the basis for the analyses. Sections 13.4 and 13.5 present inferences for the models. Section 13.6 shows how to adjust the sample means of $y$ to reflect their predicted values after controlling for the covariate.

## 13.1 COMPARING MEANS AND COMPARING REGRESSION LINES

In this chapter we denote a quantitative explanatory variable by $x$ and a categorical explanatory variable by $z$. When a categorical predictor has two categories, $z$ is a dummy variable; when it has several categories, we use a set of dummy variables.

The analysis of the effect of the quantitative predictor $x$ has a regression flavor. It refers to the regression of $y$ on $x$ within each category of the categorical variable, treating $z$ as a control variable. The analysis of the effect of the categorical predictor has an ANOVA flavor. It refers to comparing the means of $y$ for the groups defined by the categorical variable, treating $x$ as the control variable.

### Comparing Regression Lines

Table 9.4 on page 278 introduced a data file on $y$ = selling price of homes. One quantitative predictor is $x$ = size of home. One categorical predictor is $z$ = whether a house is new (1 = yes, 0 = no). Studying the effect of $x$ on $y$ while controlling for $z$ is equivalent to analyzing the regression of $y$ on $x$ separately for new and older homes. We could find the best-fitting straight line for each set of points, one line for new homes and a separate line for older homes. We could then compare characteristics of the lines, for instance, whether they climb with similar or different slopes.

In this context, *no interaction* means that the true slope of the line relating expected selling price to the size of home is the same for new and older homes. Equality of slopes implies that the regression lines are parallel (see Figure 13.1a). When the $y$-intercepts are also equal, the regression lines coincide (see Figure 13.1b). If the rate of increase in selling price as a function of size of home differed for new and existing homes, then the two regression lines would not be parallel. There is then interaction (see Figure 13.1c).

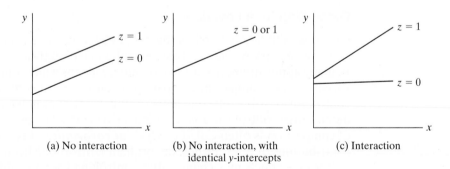

(a) No interaction  (b) No interaction, with identical $y$-intercepts  (c) Interaction

**FIGURE 13.1:** Regression Lines between Two Quantitative Variables, within Categories of a Categorical Variable with Two Categories

The effect of $x$ while controlling for $z$ may differ in substantial ways from the bivariate relationship. For instance, the effect could disappear when we control for $z$. Figure 13.2 displays a set of points having an overall positive relationship when $z$ is ignored. Within each category of $z$, however, the regression line relating $y$ to $x$ is horizontal. The overall positive trend is due to the tendency for the categories with high (low) scores on $y$ to have high (low) scores on $x$ also. Example 10.1 in Chapter 10 (page 304) presented an example of this type, with $y$ = math achievement and $x$ = height. The categorical variable was grade of school, with students coming from grades 2, 5, and 8.

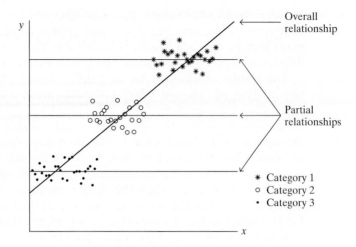

**FIGURE 13.2:** An Association between Two Quantitative Variables that Disappears after Controlling for a Categorical Variable

## Comparing Means on *y*, Controlling for *x*

Likewise, the effect of the categorical variable $z$ may change substantially when we control for $x$. For example, consider the relationship between $y$ = annual income and $z$ = gender for managerial employees of a chain of fast-food restaurants. From a two-sample comparison of men and women, mean annual income is higher for men than for women. In this company, annual income of managers tends to increase with $x$ = number of years of experience. In addition, only recently have women received many managerial appointments, so on the average they have less experience than the men. In summary, men tend to have greater experience, and greater experience tends to correlate with higher income. Perhaps this is why the overall mean annual income is higher for men. A chain relationship may exist, with gender affecting experience, which itself affects income. The difference between the mean incomes of men and women could disappear when we control for experience.

To study whether the difference in mean incomes can be explained by differing experience levels of men and women, we compare mean incomes for men and women having equal levels of experience. If there is no interaction, then the regression line between income and experience for the male employees is parallel to the one for the female employees. In that case, the difference between mean incomes for men and women is

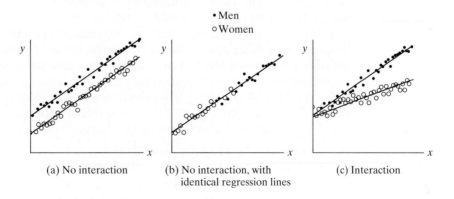

**FIGURE 13.3:** $y$ = Income by $x$ = Number of Years Experience and $z$ = Gender

identical for all fixed values of $x$ = number of years of experience. Figure 13.3a illustrates this. If the same regression line applies to each gender, as in Figure 13.3b, the mean income for each gender is identical at each level of experience. In that case, no difference occurs between male and female incomes, controlling for experience.

The results of this analysis may differ considerably from the results of the one-way analysis of variance, which compares mean incomes while ignoring rather than controlling for experience. For example, Figure 13.3b depicts a situation in which the sample mean income for men is much greater than that for women. However, the reason for the difference is that men have more experience. In fact, the same regression line fits the relationship between income and experience for both genders. It appears that the mean incomes are equal, controlling for experience.

If interaction exists, then the regression lines are not parallel. In that case, the difference between the mean incomes varies by level of experience. In Figure 13.3c, for example, the mean income for men is higher than the mean income for women at all experience levels, and the difference increases as experience increases.

## 13.2 REGRESSION WITH QUANTITATIVE AND CATEGORICAL PREDICTORS

This section presents the regression model without interaction. As in Section 12.3, we represent the categorical predictor using dummy variables, one fewer than the number of categories. We include $x$ in the model in the usual linear manner.

### Quantitative and Dummy Explanatory Variables

Suppose there are three categories for the categorical predictor, as in the following example with racial–ethnic group. The regression model is

$$E(y) = \alpha + \beta x + \beta_1 z_1 + \beta_2 z_2.$$

Here, $\beta$ (without a subscript) describes the effect of $x$ on the mean of $y$ for each group (category). Setting $(z_1 = 1, z_2 = 0)$ gives the line for category one, setting $(z_1 = 0, z_2 = 1)$ gives the line for category two, and setting $(z_1 = 0, z_2 = 0)$ gives the line for category three.

### EXAMPLE 13.1 Regression of Income on Education and Racial–Ethnic Group

For a sample of adult Americans aged over 25, Table 13.1 shows $y$ = annual income (thousands of dollars), $x$ = number of years of education (where 12 = high school graduate, 16 = college graduate), and $z$ = racial–ethnic group (black, Hispanic, white). The data exhibit patterns of a much larger sample taken by the U.S. Bureau of the Census. The sample contains $n_1 = 16$ blacks, $n_2 = 14$ Hispanics, and $n_3 = 50$ whites, for a total sample size of $N = 80$.

Table 13.2 reports the mean income and education for these subjects. Although the mean incomes differ among the three groups, these differences could result from the differing educational levels. For instance, although white subjects had higher mean incomes than blacks or Hispanics, they also had higher mean education. Perhaps the differences would disappear if we could control for education, making comparisons among the racial–ethnic groups at fixed levels of education.

For racial–ethnic status we set up the dummy variables

$z_1 = 1$ if subject is black, $z_1 = 0$ otherwise;
$z_2 = 1$ if subject is Hispanic, $z_2 = 0$ otherwise;
$z_1 = z_2 = 0$ if subject is white.

Table 13.3 shows part of a printout from using software to fit the regression model. The [race = b] and [race = h] parameters refer to the coefficients of the dummy

**TABLE 13.1:** Observations on $y$ = Annual Income (in Thousands of Dollars) and $x$ = Number of Years of Education, for Three Racial–Ethnic Groups

| Black | | Hispanic | | White | | White | | White | |
|---|---|---|---|---|---|---|---|---|---|
| $y$ | $x$ | $y$ | $x$ | $y$ | $x$ | $y$ | $x$ | $y$ | $x$ |
| 16 | 10 | 32 | 16 | 30 | 14 | 62 | 16 | 50 | 16 |
| 18 | 7 | 16 | 11 | 48 | 14 | 24 | 10 | 50 | 14 |
| 26 | 9 | 20 | 10 | 40 | 7 | 50 | 13 | 22 | 11 |
| 16 | 11 | 58 | 16 | 84 | 18 | 32 | 10 | 26 | 12 |
| 34 | 14 | 30 | 12 | 50 | 10 | 34 | 16 | 46 | 16 |
| 22 | 12 | 26 | 10 | 38 | 12 | 52 | 18 | 22 | 9 |
| 42 | 16 | 20 | 8 | 30 | 12 | 24 | 12 | 24 | 9 |
| 42 | 16 | 40 | 12 | 76 | 16 | 22 | 14 | 64 | 14 |
| 16 | 9 | 32 | 10 | 48 | 16 | 20 | 13 | 28 | 12 |
| 20 | 10 | 22 | 11 | 36 | 11 | 30 | 14 | 32 | 12 |
| 66 | 16 | 20 | 10 | 40 | 11 | 24 | 13 | 38 | 14 |
| 26 | 12 | 56 | 14 | 44 | 12 | 120 | 18 | 44 | 12 |
| 20 | 10 | 32 | 12 | 30 | 10 | 22 | 10 | 22 | 12 |
| 30 | 15 | 30 | 11 | 60 | 15 | 82 | 16 | 18 | 10 |
| 20 | 10 | | | 24 | 9 | 18 | 12 | 24 | 12 |
| 30 | 19 | | | 88 | 17 | 26 | 12 | 56 | 20 |
| | | | | 46 | 16 | 104 | 14 | | |

*Note*: The data are in the "Income, education, and racial–ethnic status" data file at the text Web site.

**TABLE 13.2:** Mean Income and Education, by Racial–Ethnic Group

| | Black | Hispanic | White | Overall |
|---|---|---|---|---|
| Mean income | $\bar{y}_1 = 27.8$ | $\bar{y}_2 = 31.0$ | $\bar{y}_3 = 42.4$ | $\bar{y} = 37.6$ |
| Mean education | $\bar{x}_1 = 12.2$ | $\bar{x}_2 = 11.6$ | $\bar{x}_3 = 13.1$ | $\bar{x} = 12.7$ |
| Sample size | $n_1 = 16$ | $n_2 = 14$ | $n_3 = 50$ | $N = 80$ |

**TABLE 13.3:** Printout for Fitting Model Assuming No Interaction to Table 13.1 on $y$ = Income and Explanatory Variables Education and Racial–Ethnic Status (with Dummy Variables for Black and Hispanic Categories)

```
                                                   95% Conf. Int.
Parameter      B       Std. Error    t      Sig    Lower   Upper
Intercept   -15.663      8.412    -1.862   .066    -32.4    1.09
education     4.432       .619     7.158   .000      3.2    5.7
[race = b]  -10.874      4.473    -2.431   .017    -19.8   -2.0
[race = h]   -4.934      4.763    -1.036   .304    -14.4    4.6
[race = w]      0          .         .       .

race=w parameter is set to zero because it is redundant

R-Squared = .462
```

variables $z_1$ for blacks and $z_2$ for Hispanics. The prediction equation is

$$\hat{y} = -15.7 + 4.4x - 10.9z_1 - 4.9z_2.$$

For blacks, $z_1 = 1$ and $z_2 = 0$, so the prediction equation is

$$\hat{y} = -15.7 + 4.4x - 10.9(1) - 4.9(0) = -26.6 + 4.4x.$$

The prediction equations for the other two racial–ethnic groups are

$$\hat{y} = -20.6 + 4.4x \quad \text{(Hispanics)}$$
$$\hat{y} = -15.7 + 4.4x \quad \text{(whites)}.$$

Figure 13.4 is a scatterplot showing the prediction equations for the three groups. The lines are parallel, since they each have the same slope, 4.4. This is the coefficient of $x$ in each prediction equation. ∎

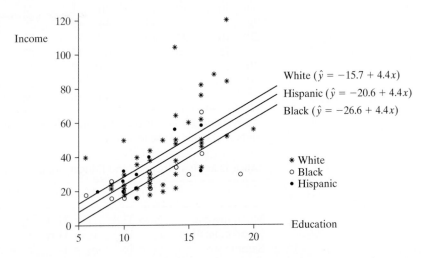

**FIGURE 13.4:** Plot of Prediction Equation for Model Assuming No Interaction. Each line has the same slope, so the lines are parallel.

## Interpretation of Parameters: No Interaction Model

Let's consider parameter interpretation. For category 1, $z_1 = 1$ and $z_2 = 0$. Then the relationship between $x$ and the mean of $y$ is

$$E(y) = \alpha + \beta x + \beta_1(1) + \beta_2(0)$$
$$= (\alpha + \beta_1) + \beta x.$$

The mean of $y$ is linearly related to $x$ with slope $\beta$ and $y$-intercept $\alpha + \beta_1$. Similarly, for category 2, $E(y) = (\alpha + \beta_2) + \beta x$. In the last category, all the dummy variables equal 0, and the regression equation reduces to $E(y) = \alpha + \beta x$.

The coefficient $\beta$ of $x$ is the slope of the regression line for each category. The equation $E(y) = \alpha + \beta x$ is the regression equation for the final category. The coefficients of the dummy variables tell us how the $y$-intercept changes for the other categories. For instance, $\beta_1$ (the coefficient of $z_1$) is the difference between the $y$-intercept for the first and the final categories. Since the regression lines are parallel, $\beta_1$ is the vertical distance between those two regression lines *at any fixed value of $x$*.

That is, controlling for $x$, $\beta_1$ is the difference between the means of $y$ for the first and last categories. Table 13.4 displays the separate equations and the parameter interpretations. Figure 13.5 graphically displays the model.

**TABLE 13.4:** Summary of Regression Equations and Parameters for Model with No Interaction, when Categorical Predictor Has Three Categories

| Category | $y$-Intercept | Slope | Mean $E(y)$ at Fixed $x$ | Difference From Mean of Category 3, Controlling for $x$ |
|---|---|---|---|---|
| 1 | $\alpha + \beta_1$ | $\beta$ | $(\alpha + \beta_1) + \beta x$ | $\beta_1$ |
| 2 | $\alpha + \beta_2$ | $\beta$ | $(\alpha + \beta_2) + \beta x$ | $\beta_2$ |
| 3 | $\alpha$ | $\beta$ | $\alpha + \beta x$ | 0 |

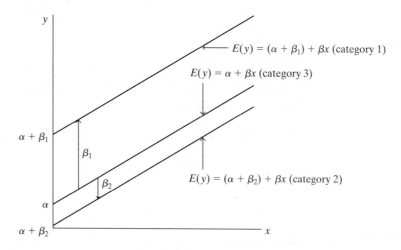

**FIGURE 13.5:** Graphic Portrayal of a Model with No Interaction, when the Categorical Predictor Has Three Categories

In summary, the coefficients of the dummy variables estimate differences in means between each category and the final category, which does not have its own dummy variable. Analogous results hold for sample prediction equations. Example 13.1 (page 416) had prediction equation

$$\hat{y} = -15.7 + 4.4x - 10.9z_1 - 4.9z_2,$$

where $z_1$ is a dummy variable for blacks and $z_2$ is one for Hispanics. The coefficient $-10.9$ of $z_1$ is the vertical distance between the lines for blacks and whites. This means that the estimated mean annual income is $10,900 lower for blacks than for whites, at each fixed level of education. Similarly, the coefficient $-4.9$ of $z_2$ represents the difference ($-$\$4900$) between the estimated mean income for Hispanics and whites, controlling for education.

## 13.3   PERMITTING INTERACTION BETWEEN QUANTITATIVE AND CATEGORICAL PREDICTORS

The analysis of covariance model that allows no interaction has the same slope for the effect of $x$ in each category of the categorical predictor. The model permitting interaction allows different slopes. To allow interaction, as usual we take cross products of the explanatory variables.

## EXAMPLE 13.2 Regression of Income on Education and Racial–Ethnic Group, Permitting Interaction

For Table 13.1, let's now allow interaction between education and racial–ethnic group in their effects on income. The model has dummy variables $z_1$ and $z_2$ for the first two racial–ethnic groups (blacks and Hispanics) and their cross-products $x \times z_1$ and $x \times z_2$ with the education predictor. Software provides the results shown in Table 13.5.

**TABLE 13.5:** Printout for Fitting Interaction Model to Table 13.1 on Income, Education, and Racial–Ethnic Status (with Dummy Variables for Black and Hispanic Categories)

| Parameter | B | Std. Error | t | Sig |
|---|---|---|---|---|
| Intercept | -25.869 | 10.498 | -2.464 | .016 |
| education | 5.210 | .783 | 6.655 | .000 |
| [race=b] | 19.333 | 18.293 | 1.057 | .294 |
| [race=h] | 9.264 | 24.282 | .382 | .704 |
| [race=w] | 0 | . | . | . |
| [race=b]*education | -2.411 | 1.418 | -1.700 | .093 |
| [race=h]*education | -1.121 | 2.006 | -.559 | .578 |
| [race=w]*education | 0 | . | . | . |

race=w parameters are set to zero because they are redundant

R-Squared    0.482

From Table 13.5, the overall prediction equation is

$$\hat{y} = -25.9 + 5.2x + 19.3z_1 + 9.3z_2 - 2.4(x \times z_1) - 1.1(x \times z_2).$$

The prediction equation with both dummy variables equal to zero ($z_1 = z_2 = 0$) refers to the final racial–ethnic category, namely, whites. For that group,

$$\hat{y} = -25.9 + 5.2x + 19.3(0) + 9.3(0) - 2.4x(0) - 1.1x(0) = -25.9 + 5.2x.$$

For the first category (blacks), $z_1 = 1$ and $z_2 = 0$, and

$$\hat{y} = -6.6 + 2.8x.$$

For the second category (Hispanics), $z_1 = 0, z_2 = 1$, and

$$\hat{y} = -16.6 + 4.1x.$$

The coefficient of $z_1$ (i.e., 19.3) again describes the difference between the $y$-intercepts for the first and the last category. However, this is the difference *only* at $x = 0$, since the equations have different slopes. Since the coefficient of $x$ (i.e., 5.2) represents the slope for the last (third) category, the coefficient of $(x \times z_1)$ (i.e., $-2.4$) represents the *difference in slopes* between the first and last categories. The two lines are parallel only when that coefficient equals 0. Similarly, for the second category, the coefficient of $z_2$ is the difference between the $y$-intercepts for the second and the last category, and the coefficient of $(x \times z_2)$ is the difference between their slopes. Table 13.6 summarizes the interpretations of the estimated parameters in the model.

**TABLE 13.6:** Summary of Prediction Equation $\hat{y} = -25.9 + 5.2x + 19.3z_1 + 9.3z_2 - 2.4(x \times z_1) - 1.1(x \times z_2)$ Allowing Interaction for $y$ = Income, $x$ = Education, and Racial–Ethnic Status ($z_1 = 1$ for Blacks and $z_2 = 1$ for Hispanics)

| Category | $y$-Intercept | Slope | Prediction Equation | Difference From Category 3 of $y$-Intercept | Slope |
|---|---|---|---|---|---|
| 1 (Black) | $-25.9 + 19.3$ | $5.2 - 2.4$ | $(-25.9 + 19.3) + (5.2 - 2.4)x$ | 19.3 | $-2.4$ |
| 2 (Hispanic) | $-25.9 + 9.3$ | $5.2 - 1.1$ | $(-25.9 + 9.3) + (5.2 - 1.1)x$ | 9.3 | $-1.1$ |
| 3 (White) | $-25.9$ | $5.2$ | $-25.9 + 5.2x$ | 0 | 0 |

Figure 13.6 plots the three prediction equations. The sample slopes are all positive. Over nearly the entire range of education values observed, whites have the highest estimated mean income, and blacks have the lowest.

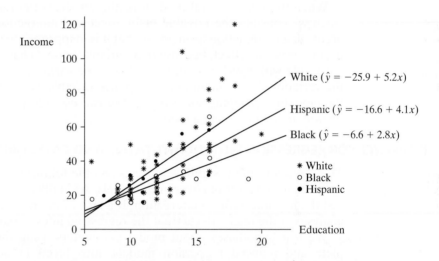

**FIGURE 13.6:** Plot of Prediction Equations for Model with Interaction Terms

When interaction exists, the difference between means of $y$ for two groups varies as a function of $x$. For example, the difference between the estimated mean of $y$ for whites and Hispanics at a particular $x$-value is

$$(-25.9 + 5.2x) - (-16.6 + 4.1x) = -9.3 + 1.1x.$$

This depends on the value of $x$. As $x$ changes, the difference in the estimated means changes. In this case, the difference between the estimated means is larger at higher levels of education. Figure 13.6 shows that the difference between the mean incomes of whites and blacks also gets larger at higher education levels.    ∎

## Comparing $R$ or $R^2$ for Different Models

To summarize how much better the model permitting interaction fits, we can check the increase in $R^2$ or in the multiple correlation $R$. Recall that $R^2$ represents the proportional reduction in error from using the prediction equation to predict the response instead of using the overall mean $\bar{y}$.

From the printout for the no-interaction model (Table 13.3), $R^2 = 0.462$. From the printout for the interaction model (Table 13.5), $R^2 = 0.482$. The corresponding multiple correlation values are $\sqrt{0.462} = 0.680$ and $\sqrt{0.482} = 0.695$. There is little gained by fitting the more complex model, as $R^2$ and $R$ do not increase much.

### Regression with Multiple Categorical and Quantitative Predictors

It is straightforward to generalize the regression models to include additional predictors of either type. To introduce additional quantitative variables, add a $\beta x$ term for each one. To introduce another categorical variable, add a set of dummy variables for its categories. To permit interaction, introduce cross-product terms: cross-products of $x$ terms for interaction between quantitative predictors, cross-products between an $x$ and a set of dummy variables for interaction between a quantitative and categorical predictor, and cross-products between dummy variables for interaction between two categorical predictors.

When there are several predictors, the number of potential models is quite large when we consider the possible main effect and interaction terms. When a variable occurs in an interaction term, recall that it is inappropriate to use the main effect term to summarize its effect, because that variable's effect changes as the value changes of a variable with which it interacts. Also, some variables may overlap considerably in the variation they explain in the response variable, so it may be possible to simplify the model by dropping some terms. We can use inference, as described in the next section, to help us select a model.

## 13.4 INFERENCE FOR REGRESSION WITH QUANTITATIVE AND CATEGORICAL PREDICTORS

This section presents significance tests and the following section presents estimation methods for analysis of covariance models. As in other multivariable models, we first test the hypothesis of no interaction. If a lack of interaction is plausible, then further analyses of the main effects treat the regression lines as parallel.

We test hypotheses about model parameters using the $F$ test comparing complete and reduced regression models, introduced in Section 11.6. For instance, the test of no interaction compares the complete model containing the interaction terms to the reduced model deleting them. The test statistic for comparing models is

$$F = \frac{(\text{SSE}_r - \text{SSE}_c)/df_1}{\text{SSE}_c/df_2} = \frac{(R_c^2 - R_r^2)/df_1}{(1 - R_c^2)/df_2},$$

where $\text{SSE}_r$ and $\text{SSE}_c$ are the residual sums of squares (i.e., the sum of squared errors) for the reduced and complete models, $df_1$ equals the difference between the number of terms in the two models, and $df_2$ is the $df$ value for the mean square for the complete model. Equivalently, we can use the second expression for the $R^2$-values of the complete and reduced models. Software presents such tests in an ANOVA table.

### Test of No Interaction

For testing $H_0$: no interaction, the model under $H_0$ is the reduced model without the cross-product terms, which has a common slope for all lines. Figure 13.7 depicts the hypotheses for this test. This test has a small $P$-value if the addition of the cross-product interaction terms provides a significant improvement in the fit.

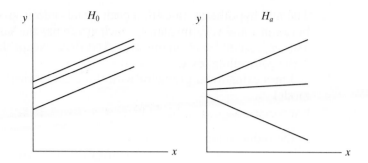

**FIGURE 13.7:** Graphical Representation of Null and Alternative Hypotheses in a Test of No Interaction, when the Categorical Predictor Has Three Categories

### EXAMPLE 13.3    Testing Interaction of Education and Racial–Ethnic Group in Their Effects on Income

For Table 13.1, we now test $H_0$: No interaction between education and racial–ethnic group, in their effects on income. The complete model

$$E(y) = \alpha + \beta x + \beta_1 z_1 + \beta_2 z_2 + \beta_3 (x \times z_1) + \beta_4 (x \times z_2),$$

contains two interaction terms. The null hypothesis is $H_0$: $\beta_3 = \beta_4 = 0$.

Table 13.7 shows how software summarizes sums of squares explained by various sets of terms in the model with interaction terms. The variability explained by the interaction terms, 691.8, equals the difference between the SSE values without and with those terms in the model. These sums of squares are **partial sums of squares**, also called **Type III sums of squares** by some software (see Section 12.5 and Exercise 11.60 in Chapter 11). They represent the variability explained after the other terms are already in the model.

**TABLE 13.7:** Computer Printout of Partial Sums of Squares Explained by Education, Racial–Ethnic Group, and Their Interaction, in the Analysis of Covariance Model Permitting Interaction

| Source | Type III Sum of Squares | df | Mean Square | F | Sig |
|---|---|---|---|---|---|
| Race | 267.319 | 2 | 133.659 | .566 | .570 |
| Education | 6373.507 | 1 | 6373.507 | 26.993 | .000 |
| Race*Education | 691.837 | 2 | 345.918 | 1.465 | .238 |
| Error | 17472.412 | 74 | 236.114 | | |
| Total | 33761.950 | 79 | | | |

For $H_0$: No interaction, the $F$ test statistic is the ratio of the interaction mean square to the MSE. Table 13.7 shows that the test statistic is $F = 345.9/236.1 = 1.46$, with a $P$-value of 0.24. There is not much evidence of interaction. We are justified in using the simpler model without cross-product terms.    ∎

### Test for Effect of Categorical Variable, Controlling for x

Possibly the model can be simplified further, if either of the main effects are not significant. Here, we test the main effect for the categorical predictor, racial–ethnic group.

The null hypothesis states that each racial–ethnic group has the same regression line between $x$ and $y$. Equivalently, each group has the same mean on $y$, controlling for $x$. This $H_0$ resembles $H_0$ in one-way ANOVA, except that this test compares the means while controlling for $x$.

For a categorical predictor with three categories, this test compares the complete model

$$E(y) = \alpha + \beta x + \beta_1 z_1 + \beta_2 z_2$$

to the reduced model

$$E(y) = \alpha + \beta x$$

lacking effects of the categorical predictor. The null hypothesis is

$$H_0 : \beta_1 = \beta_2 = 0 \quad \text{(coefficients of dummy variables} = 0).$$

The complete model represents three different but parallel regression lines between income and education, one for each racial–ethnic group. The reduced model states that the same regression line applies for all three groups. Figure 13.8 depicts this test. The $P$-value is small if the complete model with separate parallel lines provides a significantly better fit to the data than the reduced model of a common line.

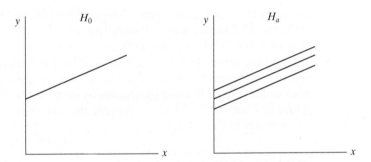

**FIGURE 13.8:** Graphical Representation of Null and Alternative Hypotheses in a Test of Equivalence of Regression Lines, when the Categorical Variable Has Three Categories (Test Assumes No Interaction)

### EXAMPLE 13.4    Testing Effect of Racial–Ethnic Group on Income, Controlling for Education

Table 13.8 shows how software reports the results of tests for the no interaction model. The $F$ statistic for the test of no effect of racial–ethnic group equals $730.29/239.00 = 3.06$. Its $P$-value equals 0.053. There is some evidence, but not strong, that the

**TABLE 13.8:** Printout of Partial Sums of Squares Explained by Education and Racial–Ethnic Group, in the Analysis of Covariance Model without Interaction

| Source | Type III Sum of Squares | df | Mean Square | F | Sig |
|---|---|---|---|---|---|
| Race | 1460.584 | 2 | 730.292 | 3.056 | .053 |
| Education | 12245.232 | 1 | 12245.232 | 51.235 | .000 |
| Error | 18164.248 | 76 | 239.003 | | |
| Total | 33761.950 | 79 | | | |

regressions of $y$ on $x$ are different for at least two of the racial–ethnic groups. The sample sizes for two of the three groups are very small, so this test does not have much power.    ∎

## Comparison with Results of ANOVA

The test just described compares the mean of $y$ among categories of a categorical variable, controlling for $x$. This is a different test than one-way ANOVA, because of the control for $x$. Table 13.9 shows the table for one-way ANOVA with these data. The $P$-value equals 0.018. Somewhat stronger evidence exists of a difference among the means when we ignore, rather than control for, education.

**TABLE 13.9:** ANOVA Printout for Fitting Model $E(y) = \alpha + \beta_1 z_1 + \beta_2 z_2$ Corresponding to One-Way ANOVA of Income by Racial–Ethnic Group

| Source | Type III Sum of Squares | df | Mean Square | F | Sig |
|--------|------------------------|-----|-------------|------|------|
| Race   | 3352.470               | 2   | 1676.235    | 4.244 | .018 |
| Error  | 30409.480              | 77  | 394.928     |      |      |
| Total  | 33761.950              | 79  |             |      |      |

Chapter 12 showed that ANOVA methods partition the total sum of squares $\sum(y - \bar{y})^2$ about the overall sample mean into component parts. The analysis of covariance, by contrast, partitions the term $\sum(x - \bar{x})(y - \bar{y})$ into component parts (Snedecor and Cochran, 1967). This term measures the *covariation* between $x$ and $y$ (Exercise 9.67 in Chapter 9). That is, it measures the way in which $x$ and $y$ vary jointly around their means $\bar{x}$ and $\bar{y}$. The cross-product $(x - \bar{x})(y - \bar{y})$ for an observation summarizes the amount by which those observations are both above or both below their means (in which case it is positive), or one above and the other below their means (in which case the cross-product is negative). The name *analysis of covariance* originates from this representation of the method.

## Test for Effect of $x$, Controlling for Categorical Variable

Assuming no interaction, we have tested for the effect of the categorical variable. Alternatively, we could test for the effect of the quantitative variable. This tests $H_0: \beta = 0$ in the model

$$E(y) = \alpha + \beta x + \beta_1 z_1 + \beta_2 z_2.$$

The hypothesis states that the straight line relating $x$ to the mean of $y$ has slope 0 for each category of the categorical variable. The null model in which $\beta = 0$ is the model for one-way ANOVA. Thus, testing the effect of $x$ corresponds to comparing the models for analysis of variance and analysis of covariance.

Since $H_0$ specifies a value for a single parameter, we can perform the test using the $t$ test. From Table 13.3, the estimated slope of 4.432 has a standard error of 0.619. The test statistic equals $t = 4.432/0.619 = 7.2$, which has a $P$-value of 0.000. The evidence is very strong that the true slope is positive. Equivalently, the square of this $t$ statistic equals the $F$ statistic of 51.2 reported for the effect of education in Table 13.8.

Table 13.10 summarizes the hypotheses, residual sums of squares, and $R^2$-values for the models of this section. In bivariate models, education is a good predictor of income ($R^2 = 0.42$), considerably better than racial–ethnic group ($R^2 = 0.10$).

**TABLE 13.10:** Summary of Comparisons of Four Models

| | Analysis of Covariance Interaction | Analysis of Covariance No Interaction | Bivariate Regression | One-Way ANOVA |
|---|---|---|---|---|
| | $E(y) = \alpha + \beta x$ $+\beta_1 z_1 + \beta_2 z_2$ $+\beta_3(xz_1) + \beta_4(xz_2)$ | $E(y) = \alpha + \beta x$ $+\beta_1 z_1 + \beta_2 z_2$ | $E(y) = \alpha + \beta x$ | $E(y) = \alpha$ $+\beta_1 z_1 + \beta_2 z_2$ |
| SSE | 17472.4 | 18164.2 | 9812.4 | 30409.5 |
| $R^2$ | 0.48 | 0.46 | 0.42 | 0.10 |
| $H_0$: No interaction $F = 1.5, P = 0.24$ | Complete model | Reduced model | — | — |
| $H_0$: $\beta_1 = \beta_2 = 0$ (Equal means, cont. for $x$) $F = 3.1, P = 0.053$ | — | Complete model | Reduced model | — |
| $H_0$: $\beta = 0$ (Zero slopes) $F = 51.2, P = 0.000$ | — | Complete model | — | Reduced model |

There is some further reduction in error from using three parallel lines, rather than one line, to predict income ($R^2 = 0.46$). This is summarized by the second test in the table, referring to the marginal evidence of the effect of the categorical predictor, controlling for the quantitative predictor. There is a highly significant effect of the quantitative predictor, controlling for the categorical one, as summarized by the third test. However, a small and insignificant reduction in error occurs by allowing different slopes for the three lines ($R^2 = 0.48$), the first test listed in the table.

## 13.5 ADJUSTED MEANS*

As usual, we learn more by estimating parameters than by testing hypotheses. This section shows how to summarize and compare means on $y$ for the categories of the categorical predictor while controlling for the quantitative covariate. These analyses can be useful when a model assuming no interaction is adequate.

### Adjusting Response Means, Controlling for the Covariate

To summarize the means of $y$ for the groups while taking into account the groups' differing means on the covariate, we can report the values expected for the means if the groups all had the same mean on $x$. These values, which adjust for the groups' differing distributions on $x$, are called *adjusted means*.

---
**Adjusted Mean**

The ***adjusted mean*** of $y$ for a particular group is the regression function for that group evaluated at the overall mean of the $x$-values for all the groups. It represents the expected value for $y$ at the mean of $x$ for the combined population.

---

Figure 13.9 illustrates the adjusted means. Since adjusted means are relevant when the no interaction model applies, this figure shows parallel lines. Let $\mu_x$ denote the

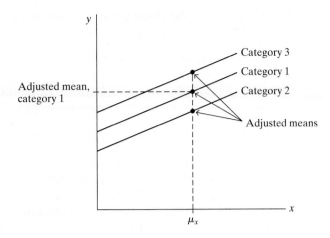

**FIGURE 13.9:** Population Adjusted Means, when a Categorical Explanatory Variable Has Three Categories

mean of $x$ for the combined population. The adjusted mean of $y$ for a particular group equals that group's regression function evaluated at $\mu_x$.

The *sample adjusted mean* of $y$ for a group is the prediction equation for that group evaluated at $\bar{x}$, the overall sample mean of $x$. This estimates the value expected for the group's mean of $y$ if the mean of $x$ for the group had equaled the overall mean.

---

**Notation for Adjusted Means**

Denote the sample adjusted mean for group $i$ by $\bar{y}'_i$. This is the value of the prediction equation for group $i$ evaluated at $\bar{x}$.

---

### EXAMPLE 13.5    Adjusted Mean Incomes, Controlling for Education

From Table 13.3, the prediction equation for the model assuming no interaction is

$$\hat{y} = -15.7 + 4.4x - 10.9z_1 - 4.9z_2.$$

Table 13.11 lists the prediction equations for the three racial–ethnic groups. The table also shows the unadjusted mean incomes and the adjusted mean incomes, controlling for education.

**TABLE 13.11:** Sample Unadjusted Mean Incomes, Adjusted Means (Controlling for Education), and Prediction Equations for Model Assuming No Interaction

| Group | Prediction Equation | Mean of $x$ | Mean of $y$ | Adjusted Mean of $y$ |
|---|---|---|---|---|
| Blacks | $\hat{y} = -26.54 + 4.43x$ | 12.2 | 27.8 | 29.7 |
| Hispanics | $\hat{y} = -20.60 + 4.43x$ | 11.6 | 31.0 | 35.6 |
| Whites | $\hat{y} = -15.66 + 4.43x$ | 13.1 | 42.5 | 40.6 |

For blacks, for instance, the prediction equation is

$$\hat{y} = -26.54 + 4.43x.$$

From Table 13.2, the mean education for the combined sample of 80 observations is $\bar{x} = 12.7$. So the sample adjusted mean income for blacks, controlling for education, is

$$\bar{y}'_1 = -26.54 + 4.43\bar{x} = -26.54 + 4.43(12.7) = 29.7.$$

Similarly, the sample adjusted means for Hispanics and whites are

$$\bar{y}'_2 = -20.60 + 4.43(12.7) = 35.6,$$
$$\bar{y}'_3 = -15.66 + 4.43(12.7) = 40.6.$$

The adjustment process adjusts an ordinary sample mean upward or downward according to whether mean education for the group is below or above average. For whites, for instance, the adjusted mean income of 40.6 is smaller than the unadjusted mean of 42.5. The reason is that the mean education for whites ($\bar{x}_3 = 13.1$) is larger than the mean education for the combined sample ($\bar{x} = 12.7$). Since a positive relationship exists between income and education, the model predicts that whites would have a lower mean income if their mean education were lower (equal to $\bar{x} = 12.7$). ∎

### Comparing Adjusted Means

The coefficients of the dummy variables in the "no interaction" model refer to differences between adjusted means. To illustrate, the estimated difference between adjusted mean incomes of blacks and whites is $\bar{y}'_1 - \bar{y}'_3 = 29.7 - 40.6 = -10.9$ (i.e., $-\$10,900$). This is precisely the coefficient of the dummy variable $z_1$ for blacks in the above prediction equation. Similarly, the estimated difference between the adjusted means of Hispanics and whites equals $\bar{y}'_2 - \bar{y}'_3 = -4.9$, which is the coefficient of $z_2$. Figure 13.10 depicts the sample adjusted means. The vertical distances between the lines represent the differences between these adjusted means.

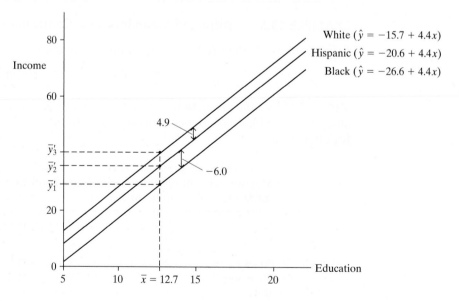

**FIGURE 13.10:** Sample Adjusted Means on Income, Controlling for Education, for Three Racial–Ethnic Groups

Since the groups had different means on the covariate (education), the adjusted means and their differences are not the same as the unadjusted means and differences.

For example, from Table 13.11, $\bar{y}_2 - \bar{y}_3 = 31.0 - 42.5 = -11.5$ is the unadjusted difference in mean income between Hispanics and whites. This is somewhat larger than the adjusted difference of $-5.0$. If whites and Hispanics had the same average educational level, the model predicts that the difference in their mean incomes would be less than half as large as it actually is in this sample.

### Graphical Interpretation

Figure 13.11 depicts the relationship between the adjusted and unadjusted means. The figure depicts the line for the first group, but the same reasoning applies to any group. The prediction equation predicts a value of $\bar{y}_i$ at the $x$-value of $x = \bar{x}_i$ for group $i$. In particular, the prediction line for the first category passes through the point with coordinates $(\bar{x}_1, \bar{y}_1)$. In other words, the *unadjusted mean* $\bar{y}_1$ is the value of the prediction equation for that group evaluated at the $x$-value of $\bar{x}_1$, the mean of the $x$-values *for that group alone* [see the point $(\bar{x}_1, \bar{y}_1)$ in Figure 13.11].

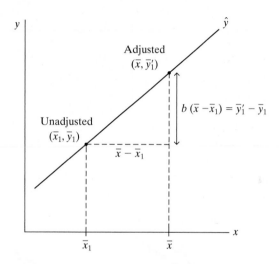

**FIGURE 13.11:** Graphical Depiction of Sample Adjusted and Unadjusted Means for the First Group. The ordinary mean is the predicted value at the mean of $x$ for that group alone, whereas the adjusted mean is the predicted value at the mean $\bar{x}$ for all the data.

The *adjusted mean* $\bar{y}_1'$ for the first group is the value of that prediction equation evaluated at the *overall mean* $\bar{x}$ for the combined sample. Hence, the prediction line for that category also passes through the point $(\bar{x}, \bar{y}_1')$, as Figure 13.11 shows. The difference between the $x$-coordinates for the points $(\bar{x}, \bar{y}_1')$ and $(\bar{x}_1, \bar{y}_1)$ is the horizontal distance $\bar{x} - \bar{x}_1$, indicated in the figure. Denoting the slope of the sample prediction equation by $b$, the vertical change in the line over the $x$ distance of $\bar{x} - \bar{x}_1$ is $b(\bar{x} - \bar{x}_1)$. That is, the predicted change in the $y$ direction for a $(\bar{x} - \bar{x}_1)$ change in the $x$-direction is $b(\bar{x} - \bar{x}_1)$. This vertical change is precisely the difference $\bar{y}_1' - \bar{y}_1$ between the $y$ coordinates of the points $(\bar{x}, \bar{y}_1')$ and $(\bar{x}_1, \bar{y}_1)$.

In summary, the difference between the adjusted and unadjusted means for the first group equals

$$\bar{y}_1' - \bar{y}_1 = b(\bar{x} - \bar{x}_1).$$

Equivalently,

$$\bar{y}_1' = \bar{y}_1 + b(\bar{x} - \bar{x}_1).$$

The process of controlling for $x$ takes the sample mean for $y$ and adjusts it by multiplying the difference $(\bar{x} - \bar{x}_1)$ in the means of $x$ by the slope $b$ of the prediction equation.

If the slope $b$ is positive, then the sample mean $\bar{y}_1$ is adjusted upward if $\bar{x} > \bar{x}_1$ (i.e., if $\bar{x} - \bar{x}_1 > 0$), as in Figure 13.11. This predicts that the mean of $y$ would have been larger had the distribution of $x$-values for that group had as large a mean as the combined samples. If group 1 is above average on $x$ (i.e., $\bar{x}_1 > \bar{x}$), then $b(\bar{x} - \bar{x}_1)$ is negative when $b > 0$, so the mean is adjusted downward.

Similar reasoning applies to other groups. Figure 13.12 depicts the adjustment process on income for the three racial–ethnic groups. The mean is adjusted down for whites and up for blacks and Hispanics.

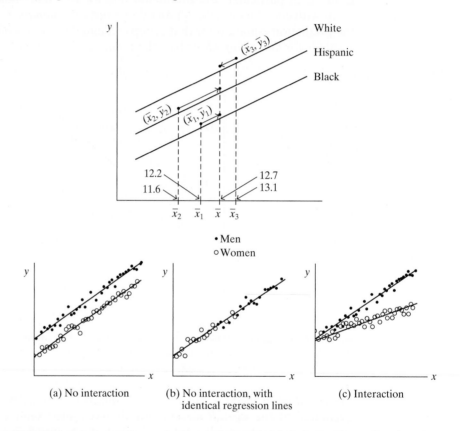

FIGURE 13.12: Adjustment Process for Income by Racial–Ethnic Group, Controlling for Education

The difference between a group's adjusted and unadjusted means depends directly on the difference between $\bar{x}$ for the combined sample and $\bar{x}_i$ for that group. The adjusted means are similar to the unadjusted means if the $\bar{x}_i$-values are close to the overall $\bar{x}$, or if the slope $b$ of the prediction equations is small.

## Multiple Comparisons of Adjusted Means

Following an analysis of variance, the Bonferroni method compares all pairs of means simultaneously with a fixed overall confidence level. This method extends directly to multiple comparison of *adjusted means*. Software for multiple regression reports standard errors for these estimates. We can form $t$ confidence intervals using these estimates and their standard errors.

**EXAMPLE 13.6    Confidence Intervals for Comparing Adjusted Mean Incomes**

Let's construct 95% confidence intervals for differences between the three pairs of adjusted mean incomes, using the Bonferroni multiple comparison approach. The error probability for each interval is $0.05/3 = 0.0167$. The $t$-score with single-tail probability $0.0167/2 = 0.0083$ and $df = 76$ (which is $df$ for SSE for the no-interaction model) is 2.45.

The estimated difference between adjusted mean incomes of Hispanics and whites is the coefficient of the dummy variable $z_2$ for Hispanics in the prediction equation. Table 13.3 showed the racial–ethnic effects

| Parameter | B | Std. Error | t | Sig |
|---|---|---|---|---|
| [race = b] | -10.874 | 4.473 | -2.431 | .017 |
| [race = h] | -4.934 | 4.763 | -1.036 | .304 |

so this coefficient is $-4.934$ and has a standard error of 4.763. The Bonferroni confidence interval equals

$$-4.934 \pm 2.45(4.763), \quad \text{or } (-16.6, 6.7).$$

Controlling for education, the difference in mean incomes for Hispanics and whites is estimated to fall between $-\$16,600$ and $\$6700$. Since the interval contains 0, it is plausible that the true adjusted mean incomes are equal. The sample contained only 14 Hispanics, so the interval is wide.

Similarly, from Table 13.3, the confidence interval comparing blacks and whites is $-10.874 \pm 2.45(4.473)$, or $(-21.8, 0.1)$. To get the standard error for the estimate $b_1 - b_2 = (-10.87 - (-4.93)) = -5.94$ comparing blacks and Hispanics, we could fit the model with one of these categories as the baseline category lacking a dummy variable. Or, we could use the general expression to get $se$ from the values $se_1$ for $b_1$ and $se_2$ for $b_2$ as

$$se = \sqrt{(se_1)^2 + (se_2)^2 - 2\text{Cov}(b_1, b_2)},$$

where $\text{Cov}(b_1, b_2)$ is taken from the *covariance matrix* of the parameter estimates, which software can provide. For these data, the standard error for $b_1 - b_2$ equals 5.67, and the confidence interval is $(-19.8, 8.0)$.

Table 13.12 summarizes the comparisons. We can be 95% confident that all three of these intervals contain the differences in population adjusted means. None of the intervals show a significant difference, which is not surprising because the $F$ test of the group effect in the previous section had a $P$-value of 0.053. Nonetheless, the intervals show that the adjusted means could be quite a bit smaller for blacks or Hispanics than for whites. More precise estimation requires a larger sample.    ∎

**TABLE 13.12:** Bonferroni Multiple Comparisons of Differences in Adjusted Mean Income by Racial–Ethnic Group, Controlling for Education

| Racial–Ethnic Groups | Estimated Difference in Adjusted Means | 95% Bonferroni Confidence Intervals |
|---|---|---|
| Blacks, Whites | $\bar{y}_1' - \bar{y}_3' = -10.9$ | $(-21.8, 0.1)$ |
| Hispanics, Whites | $\bar{y}_2' - \bar{y}_3' = -4.9$ | $(-16.6, 6.7)$ |
| Blacks, Hispanics | $\bar{y}_1' - \bar{y}_2' = -5.9$ | $(-19.8, 8.0)$ |

For the model with no interaction, testing for identical adjusted means is equivalent to testing whether the regression lines are identical. That is, two parallel lines are identical if their corresponding adjusted means are equal. Therefore, just as confidence intervals reveal which pairs of adjusted means are significantly different, so do they reveal which pairs of lines are significantly different. For example, if the interval for the difference between a pair of adjusted means does not contain 0, then the regression lines between $y$ and $x$ for those two categories are judged to have different intercepts.

### A Caution about Hypothetical Adjustment

Adjusted means can be useful for comparing several groups by adjusting for differences in the means of a covariate $x$. Use them with caution, however, when the means on $x$ are greatly different. The control process is a hypothetical one that infers what would happen *if* all groups had the same mean for $x$. If large differences exist among the groups in their means on $x$, the results of this control may be purely speculative. We must assume (1) that it makes sense to conceive of adjusting the groups on this covariate and (2) that the relationship between $y$ and $x$ would continue to have the same linear form within each category as the $x$ mean shifts for each category.

To illustrate, recall the relationship between annual income and experience and gender shown in Figure 13.3b (page 415). The same line fits the relationship between income and experience for each gender, so it is plausible that the adjusted means are equal. However, nearly all the women have less experience than the men. The conclusion that the mean incomes are equal, controlling for experience, assumes that the regression line shown also applies to women with more experience than those in the sample and to men with less experience. If it does not, then the conclusion is incorrect.

Figure 13.13 portrays a situation in which the conclusion would be misleading. The dotted lines show the relationship for each group over the $x$-region not observed. At each fixed $x$-value, a difference persists between the means of $y$. In practice, in nonexperimental research we cannot manipulate $x$-values to force groups to have the same means on covariates, so inferences about what would happen if this could be done are merely speculative.

Whenever we use adjusted means, we should check the degree to which the distributions differ on the mean of $x$. Excessively large differences may mean that

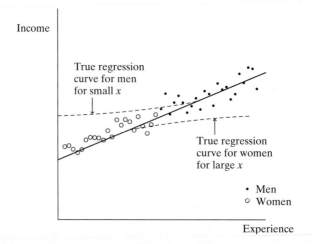

**FIGURE 13.13:** A Situation in Which Adjusted Means Are Misleading, Comparing Mean Incomes for Men and Women while Controlling for Experience

the conclusions need strong qualification. On the other hand, if relatively small differences exist among the $\bar{x}_i$, then controlling for $x$ has little effect. The results of the comparisons of adjusted means are then similar to the results of the comparisons of unadjusted means in an analysis of variance.

## 13.6   CHAPTER SUMMARY

This chapter showed that multiple regression can describe the relationship between a quantitative response variable and both quantitative and categorical explanatory variables. When the method is used to compare the mean of $y$ for different categories while controlling for a quantitative *covariate*, it is called the ***analysis of covariance***.

- The multiple regression model has linear terms (such as $\beta x$) for quantitative predictors and dummy variable terms for categorical predictors.
- There is ***no interaction*** if the slope of the line relating $x$ to the mean of $y$ is the same for each group. The model then provides a set of parallel lines. We allow interaction and different slopes by entering cross products of quantitative predictors with dummy variables in the model.
- ***Adjusted means*** summarize the means on $y$ for the groups while controlling for $x$. They represent the model's prediction for the means of $y$ at the overall mean of the $x$-values.

Adjusted means are meaningful only when there is no interaction. One can test the hypothesis of no interaction, as well as the hypothesis of equal adjusted means (or, equivalently, identical regression lines), using an $F$ test for the relevant parameters in the model. For further details about the methods of this chapter, see Blalock (1979) and Snedecor and Cochran (1967).

## PROBLEMS

### Practicing the Basics

**13.1.** The regression equation relating $y = $ education (number of years completed) to race ($z = 1$ for whites, $z = 0$ for nonwhites) in a certain country is $E(y) = 11 + 2z$. The regression equation relating education to race and to father's education ($x$) is $E(y) = 3 + 0.8x - 0.6z$.

(a) Ignoring father's education, find the mean education for whites, the mean education for nonwhites, and the difference between them.

(b) Plot the relationship between $x$ and the mean of $y$ for whites and for nonwhites.

(c) Controlling for father's education, find the difference between the mean education of whites and nonwhites.

(d) Find the mean education for whites and for nonwhites, when father's education equals 12 years.

**13.2.** Table 9.13 on page 294 showed data for several nations on various indices. Let $y = $ percentage who use the Internet, $x = $ per capita GDP (in thousands of dollars), and $z = $ whether the nation is a Western nation ($1 = $ yes, $0 = $ no).

(a) The prediction equation for the effect of $z$ is $\hat{y} = 10.5 + 30.4z$. Interpret the coefficients.

(b) The prediction equation for the effects of $x$ and $z$ is $\hat{y} = 8.3 + 0.73x + 10.9z$. Interpret the coefficients.

(c) Explain how the coefficient of $z$ could be so different in (a) and (b).

**13.3.** A regression analysis for the 100th Congress predicted the proportion of each representative's votes on abortion issues that took the "pro-choice" position (R. Tatalovich and D. Schier, *American Politics Quarterly*, vol. 21, 1993). The prediction equation was

$$\hat{y} = 0.350 + 0.011id + 0.094r + 0.005nw$$
$$+ 0.005inc + 0.063s - 0.167p,$$

where $r = $ religion (1 for non-Catholics), $s = $ sex (1 for women), $p = $ political party (1 for Democrats), $id = $ ideology is the member's ADA score (ranging from 0 at most conservative to 100 at most liberal), $nw = $ nonwhite is the percentage nonwhite of the member's district, and $inc = $ income is the median family income of the member's district.

(a) Interpret the coefficient for party.

(b) Using standardized variables, the prediction equation is

$$\hat{z}_y = 0.83z_{id} + 0.21z_r + 0.18z_{nw} + 0.05z_{inc} + 0.03z_s - 0.18z_p.$$

Comment on the relative sizes of the partial effects. Interpret the coefficient of ideology.

**13.4.** For data[1] from 27 automotive plants on $y =$ number of assembly defects per 100 cars and $x =$ time to assemble each vehicle (in hours, falling between 12 and 54), $\hat{y} = 61.3 + 0.35x$. Adding $z =$ whether facility is Japanese ($1 =$ yes, $0 =$ no) to the model, $\hat{y} = 105.0 - 0.78x - 36.2z$.

(a) Interpret the estimated partial effects.

(b) Explain why these equations satisfy Simpson's paradox, which states that a partial effect can have the reverse sign from the bivariate effect.

(c) For these data, $x$ values tended to be lower for the Japanese plants. Explain how this could be responsible for Simpson's paradox occurring.

**13.5.** Based on a national survey, Table 13.13 shows results of a prediction equation reported for $y =$ alcohol consumption, measured as the number of alcoholic drinks the subject drank during the past month (D. Umberson and M. Chen, *American Sociological Review*, vol. 59, 1994, p. 152).

(a) Setting up dummy variables $f$ for whether father died in the past three years, $s$ for sex, and $(m_1, m_2, m_3)$ for the four categories of marital status, and letting $x =$ alcohol consumption three years ago, report the prediction equation.

(b) Find the predicted alcohol consumption for a divorced male whose father died in the previous three years and whose consumption three years previously was ten drinks per month.

**TABLE 13.13**

| Explanatory Variable | Estimate | Std. Error |
|---|---|---|
| Intercept | 8.3 | |
| Death of father (0 = no) | 9.8 | 2.9 |
| Sex (0 = male) | −5.3 | 1.6 |
| Marital status (0 = married) | | |
| Divorced, separated | 7.0 | 2.0 |
| Widowed | 2.0 | 3.6 |
| Never married | 1.2 | 2.4 |
| Alcohol consumption, three years ago | 0.501 | 0.023 |

**13.6.** For the survey in the previous exercise, the sample size was 1417.

(a) Test the null hypothesis that sex has no effect on the response, controlling for the other predictors. Interpret.

(b) Construct a 95% confidence interval for the sex effect, controlling for the other predictors. Interpret.

(c) Marital status has three estimates. Dividing the coefficient of the divorced dummy variable by its standard error yields a $t$ statistic. What hypothesis does it test?

(d) What would you need to do to test the effect of marital status (all categories at once), controlling for the other variables?

**13.7.** For the "house selling price" data file at the text Web site, Table 13.14 shows results of modeling $y =$ selling price (in dollars) in terms of size of home (in square feet) and whether the home is new ($1 =$ yes; $0 =$ no).

(a) Report and interpret the prediction equation, and form separate equations relating selling price to size for new and for not new homes.

(b) Find the predicted selling price for a home of 3000 square feet that is (i) new, (ii) not new.

**TABLE 13.14**

| Parameter | B | Std. Error | t | Sig |
|---|---|---|---|---|
| Intercept | −40230.867 | 14696.140 | −2.738 | .007 |
| size | 116.132 | 8.795 | 13.204 | .000 |
| new | 57736.283 | 18653.041 | 3.095 | .003 |

**13.8.** Refer to the previous exercise. Table 13.15 shows results of fitting the model allowing interaction, where new*size refers to the cross-product term.

(a) Report the lines relating predicted selling price to size for homes that are (i) new, (ii) not new.

(b) Find the predicted selling price for a home of 3000 square feet that is (i) new, (ii) not new.

(c) Find the predicted selling price for a home of 1500 square feet that is (i) new, (ii) not new. Comparing to (b), explain how the difference in predicted selling prices changes as size of home increases.

**TABLE 13.15**

| Parameter | B | Std. Error | t | Sig |
|---|---|---|---|---|
| Intercept | −22227.808 | 15521.110 | −1.432 | .155 |
| size | 104.438 | 9.424 | 11.082 | .000 |
| new | −78527.502 | 51007.642 | −1.540 | .127 |
| new*size | 61.916 | 21.686 | 2.855 | .005 |

---

[1] *Source*: S. Chatterjee et al., *A Casebook for a First Course in Statistics and Data Analysis*, Wiley, 1995.

**13.9.** Replicate all the analyses shown in Sections 13.2–13.4 using the "Income, education, and racial–ethnic status" data file at the text Web site.

**13.10.** The printouts in Table 13.16 show results of fitting two models to data from a study of the relationship between $y$ = percentage of adults voting, percentage of adults registered to vote, and racial–ethnic representation, for a random sample of 40 precincts in the state of Texas for a gubernatorial election. Racial–ethnic representation of a precinct is the group (Anglo, black, or Mexican American) having the strongest representation in a precinct.

**(a)** State a research question that could be addressed using these data.

**(b)** Report the prediction equation for the model assuming no interaction. Interpret the parameter estimates.

**(c)** Report the prediction equation for the model allowing interaction. Interpret the parameter estimates and describe the nature of the estimated interaction.

**(d)** Test whether the regression lines for the three categories have the same slope. Report the test statistic and $P$-value, and interpret.

**(e)** For the model assuming no interaction, test whether the mean voting percentages are equal for the three categories of racial–ethnic representation, controlling for percentage registered. Report the test statistic and $P$-value, and interpret.

**(f)** Report the test statistic and $P$-value for testing the null hypothesis that percentage voting and percentage registered are independent, controlling for racial–ethnic representation. Interpret.

**(g)** Summarize what you have learned about the question posed in (a) from your analyses.

**13.11.** Refer to the previous exercise. The means of percentage registered for the three categories are $\bar{x}_1 = 76.2$, $\bar{x}_2 = 49.5$, $\bar{x}_3 = 39.7$. The overall mean $\bar{x} = 60.4$.

**(a)** Find the adjusted mean on percentage voting for Anglos. Compare it to the unadjusted mean of 52.3, and interpret.

**(b)** Sketch a plot of the no interaction model for these data, and identify on it the unadjusted and adjusted means for Anglos.

## TABLE 13.16

NO INTERACTION MODEL

| Source | Type III Sum of Squares | df | Mean Square | F | Sig |
|--------|------------------------|----|-----------|-----|-----|
| race | 40.08 | 2 | 20.04 | 1.07 | .354 |
| register | 2317.43 | 1 | 2317.43 | 123.93 | .000 |

| Source | Sum of Squares | df | Mean Square | Parameter | Estimate |
|--------|---------------|----|-----------|-----------|----------|
| Model | 7936.734 | 3 | 2645.578 | INTERCEPT | -2.7786 |
| Error | 673.166 | 36 | 18.699 | REGISTER | 0.7400 |
| Total | 8609.900 | 39 | | RACE      a | -1.3106 |
| | | | | b | -2.8522 |
| | | | | ma | 0.0000 |

INTERACTION MODEL

| Source | Type III Sum of Squares | df | Mean Square | F | Sig |
|--------|------------------------|----|-----------|-----|-----|
| race*register | 53.79 | 2 | 27.89 | 1.47 | .243 |

| Source | Sum of Squares | df | Mean Square | Parameter | Estimate |
|--------|---------------|----|-----------|-----------|----------|
| Model | 7990.523 | 5 | 1598.105 | INTERCEPT | -8.245 |
| Error | 619.377 | 34 | 18.217 | REGISTER | 0.878 |
| Total | 8609.900 | 39 | | RACE      a | 6.974 |
| | | | | b | 9.804 |
| | | | | ma | 0.000 |
| | | | | REGISTER*RACE   a | -0.175 |
| | | | | b | -0.283 |
| | | | | ma | 0.000 |

**13.12.** Table 13.1 did not report the observations for ten Asian Americans. Their $(x, y)$ values were

| Subject | 1 | 2 | 3 | 4 | 5 | 6 | 7 | 8 | 9 | 10 |
|---------|----|----|----|----|----|----|----|----|----|----|
| Education | 16 | 14 | 12 | 18 | 13 | 12 | 16 | 16 | 14 | 10 |
| Income | 70 | 42 | 24 | 56 | 32 | 38 | 58 | 82 | 36 | 20 |

Conduct the analyses for the no-interaction model shown in Sections 13.2 and 13.4, after adding these data to the "Income, education, and racial–ethnic status" data file at the text Web site. Summarize your analyses, and interpret.

**13.13.** Refer to the previous exercise. Conduct the analyses for the interaction model and for comparing that model to the no-interaction model, as shown in Sections 13.3 and 13.4, after adding these data.

**13.14.** Exercise 13.1 reported the regression equation relating $y$ = education to race ($z$ = 1 for whites) and to father's education ($x$) of $E(y) = 3 + 0.8x - 0.6z$. The mean education is 11 for nonwhites and 13 for whites. The overall mean of father's education is 12 years.
  **(a)** Find the adjusted mean educational levels for whites and nonwhites, controlling for father's education.
  **(b)** Explain why the adjusted means differ as they do from the unadjusted means.

## Concepts and Applications

**13.15.** Refer to the "Student survey" data file (Exercise 1.11). Using software, prepare a report presenting graphical, descriptive, and inferential analyses with
  **(a)** $y$ = political ideology and the predictors religiosity and whether a vegetarian
  **(b)** $y$ = college GPA with predictors high school GPA, gender, and religiosity

**13.16.** Refer to the data file your class created in Exercise 1.12. For variables chosen by your instructor, use regression analysis as the basis of descriptive and inferential statistical analyses. Summarize your findings in a report in which you state the research question posed and describe and interpret the fitted models and the related analyses.

**13.17.** Refer to the "OECD data" file at the text Web site, shown in Table 3.11 on page 62. Pose a research question about how GDP and whether a nation is in Europe relates to carbon dioxide emissions. Conduct appropriate analyses to address that question, and prepare a report summarizing your analyses and conclusions.

**13.18.** An article[2] on predicting attitudes toward homosexuality used GSS data to model a response variable with a four-point scale in which homosexual relations were scaled from 1 = always

wrong to 4 = never wrong, with $x_1$ = education (in years), $x_2$ = age, $x_3$ = political conservative (1 = yes, 0 = no), $x_4$ = religious fundamentalist (1 = yes, 0 = no), and $x_5$ = whether live in same city as when age 16 (1 = yes, 0 = no). The prediction equation allowing interaction between $x_1$ and $x_3$ is

$$\hat{y} = 0.94 + 0.13x_1 - 0.01x_2 + 1.10x_3 - 0.38x_4 - 0.15x_5 - 0.12(x_1 \times x_3).$$

  **(a)** Report the prediction equations for political conservatives and nonconservatives. Explain how these suggest that greater education corresponds to less negative views about homosexuality for nonconservatives but may have no effect for conservatives.
  **(b)** The model without interaction had fit

$$\hat{y} = 1.53 + 0.09x_1 - 0.01x_2 - 0.49x_3 - 0.39x_4 - 0.15x_5.$$

Summarize the effect of each predictor.

**13.19.** Table 13.17 shows results of fitting a regression model to data on salaries (in dollars) of about 35,000 college professors. Four predictors are categorical (binary), with dummy variable defined in parentheses. Write a short report, interpreting the effects of the predictors.

**TABLE 13.17**

| Variable | Estimate (Std. Error) |
|----------|----------------------|
| Years of experience | 162.7 (2.0) |
| Terminal degree (Ph.D. = 1) | 264.0 (40.1) |
| Degree quality | 616.8 (34.5) |
| Research productivity | 616.5 (7.7) |
| Marital status (married = 1) | 850.3 (51.2) |
| Race (nonwhite = 1) | −310.3 (107.0) |
| Gender (female = 1) | −1863.7 (62.1) |
| Intercept | 10,033.2 |

*Source*: N. Langton and J. Pfeffer, *American Sociological Review*, vol. 59, 1994, p. 236.

**13.20.** Table 13.18 is a printout based on GSS data. The response variable is an index of attitudes toward premarital, extramarital, and homosexual sex. Higher scores represent more permissive attitudes. The categorical explanatory variables are race (0 for whites, 1 for blacks), gender (0 for

---

[2]T. Shackelford and A. Besser, *Individual Differences Research*, vol. 5, 2007, pp. 106–114.

**TABLE 13.18**

Analysis of Variance

| | Sum of Squares | df | Mean Square | F |
|---|---|---|---|---|
| Regression | 2583.326 | 12 | 215.277 | 54.098 |
| Residual | 4345.534 | 1092 | 3.979 | |

| R Square | | 0.373 | | | |
|---|---|---|---|---|---|

| Variable | B | Std. Error | Beta | t | Sig |
|---|---|---|---|---|---|
| (Constant) | 9.373 | | | | |
| RACE | 0.993 | 0.2040 | 0.125 | 4.869 | .000 |
| AGE | -0.029 | 0.0042 | -0.189 | -6.957 | .000 |
| SEX | -0.289 | 0.1230 | -0.058 | -2.353 | .019 |
| EDUC | 0.073 | 0.0223 | 0.092 | 3.281 | .001 |
| REGION | 0.617 | 0.1401 | 0.115 | 4.403 | .000 |
| ATTEND | -0.286 | 0.0255 | -0.304 | -11.217 | .000 |
| R1 | -0.296 | 0.2826 | -0.049 | -1.048 | .295 |
| R2 | -0.605 | 0.2782 | -0.113 | -2.174 | .030 |
| R3 | -1.187 | 0.3438 | -0.128 | -3.454 | .001 |
| R4 | -0.127 | 0.2856 | 0.023 | 0.446 | .656 |
| R5 | 0.521 | 0.4417 | 0.034 | 1.179 | .238 |
| FREESPCH | -0.465 | 0.0581 | -0.227 | -8.011 | .000 |

males, 1 for females), region (0 for South, 1 for non-South), and religion ($r_1 = 1$ for liberal Protestant sect, $r_2 = 1$ for conservative Protestant, $r_3 = 1$ for fundamentalist Protestant sect, $r_4 = 1$ for Catholic, $r_5 = 1$ for Jewish; no religious affiliation when $r_1 = \cdots = r_5 = 0$). The quantitative explanatory variables are age, education (number of years), attendance at church (higher values represent more frequent attendance), and a variable for which higher values represent greater intolerance of freedom of speech for atheists and communists.

(a) Based on the parameter estimates, give a profile of a person you would expect to be (i) least permissive, (ii) most permissive, with respect to sexual attitudes.

(b) Summarize the main conclusions that you make from studying this printout.

**13.21.** A researcher studies factors associated with fertility (a woman's number of children) in a Latin American city. Of particular interest is whether migrants from other cities or migrants from rural areas differ from natives of the city in their family sizes. The groups to be compared are urban natives, urban migrants, and rural migrants. Since fertility is negatively related to educational level, and since education might differ among the three groups, it is decided to control that variable. Table 13.19 shows data for a random sample of married women above age 45. Analyze these data. In your report, provide graphical presentations as well as interpretations

for all your analyses, and present a summary of the main results.

**13.22.** Analyze the "house selling price 2" data file at the text Web site by modeling selling price in terms of size of house and whether it is new.

(a) Fit the model allowing interaction, and test whether the interaction term is needed in the model.

(b) Figure 13.14 shows a scatterplot, labeling the points by a 1 when the home is new and a 0 when it is not. The observation with the highest selling price is a new home that is somewhat removed from the general trend of points. Fit the interaction model after removing this single observation. Again, test whether the interaction term is needed in the model. Note what a large impact one observation can have on the conclusions.

**13.23.** For the "2005 statewide crime" data file at the text Web site let $z$ be a dummy variable for whether a state is in the South, with $z = 1$ for AL, AR, FL, GA, KY, LA, MD, MS, NC, OK, SC, TN, TX, VA, WV.

(a) Not including the observation for D.C., analyze the relationship between $y$ = violent crime rate and $z$, both ignoring and controlling for $x$ = poverty rate. Summarize your analyses and results.

(b) Repeat the analysis with D.C. in the data set, setting $z = 1$ for it. Is this observation influential?

**TABLE 13.19**

| Urban Natives | | Urban Migrants | | Rural Migrants | |
|---|---|---|---|---|---|
| Education | Fertility | Education | Fertility | Education | Fertility |
| 0 | 7 | 0 | 7 | 0 | 4 |
| 0 | 5 | 0 | 6 | 0 | 6 |
| 1 | 5 | 0 | 7 | 0 | 10 |
| 1 | 4 | 1 | 5 | 0 | 8 |
| 2 | 7 | 2 | 2 | 1 | 7 |
| 4 | 4 | 2 | 6 | 2 | 8 |
| 5 | 4 | 3 | 3 | 3 | 5 |
| 7 | 3 | 4 | 6 | 3 | 6 |
| 8 | 5 | 7 | 4 | 4 | 7 |
| 8 | 2 | 7 | 4 | 5 | 7 |
| 8 | 3 | 8 | 4 | 6 | 8 |
| 9 | 3 | 11 | 3 | 6 | 6 |
| 10 | 4 | 11 | 3 | 7 | 4 |
| 11 | 3 | 11 | 4 | 7 | 5 |
| 12 | 3 | 12 | 4 | 8 | 4 |
| | | 12 | 2 | 8 | 6 |
| | | 12 | 3 | 8 | 5 |
| | | | | 9 | 3 |
| | | | | 9 | 7 |
| | | | | 10 | 4 |

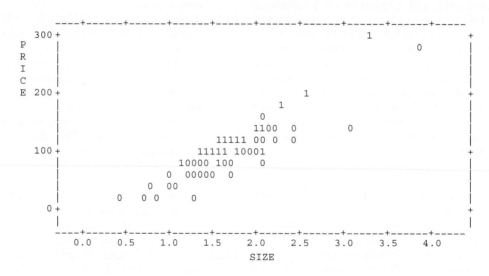

**FIGURE 13.14**

**13.24.** You have two groups, and you want to compare their regressions of $y$ on $x$, in order to test the hypothesis that the true slopes are identical for the two groups. Explain how you can do this using regression modeling.

**13.25.** In analyzing GSS data relating $y$ = frequency of having sex in the past year to frequency of going to bars, DeMaris (2004, p. 62) noted that the slope for

unmarried subjects is more than double the slope for married subjects. Introducing notation, state a model that you think would be appropriate.

**13.26.** Let $y$ = death rate and $x$ = mean age of residents, measured for each county in Louisiana and in Florida. Sketch a hypothetical scatterplot, identifying points for each state, when the mean death rate is higher in Florida than in Louisiana when mean age is ignored but lower when it is controlled. (*Hint*: When you fit a line for each state, the line should be higher for Louisiana but the *y*-values for Florida should have an overall higher mean.)

**13.27.** Draw a scatterplot with sets of points representing two groups such that $H_0$: equal means would be rejected in a one-way ANOVA but not in an analysis of covariance.

**13.28.** A regression model is fitted to annual income (thousands of dollars), using predictors age and marital status. Table 13.20 shows the sample mean incomes and the adjusted means for the model. How could the adjusted means be so different from the unadjusted means? Draw a sketch to help explain.

**TABLE 13.20**

| Group | Mean Age | Mean Income | Adjusted Mean Income |
|-------|----------|-------------|----------------------|
| Married | 44 | 40 | 30 |
| Divorced | 35 | 30 | 30 |
| Single | 26 | 20 | 30 |

*In Exercises 13.29–13.30, select the correct response(s).*

**13.29.** In the model $E(y) = \alpha + \beta_1 x + \beta_2 z$, where $z$ is a dummy variable,

**(a)** The categorical predictor has two categories.

**(b)** One line has slope $\beta_1$ and the other has slope $\beta_2$.

**(c)** $\beta_2$ is the difference between the mean of *y* for the second and first categories of the categorical variable.

**(d)** $\beta_2$ is the difference between the mean of *y* for the second and first categories of the categorical variable, controlling for *x*.

**13.30.** In the United States, the mean annual income for blacks $(\mu_1)$ is smaller than for whites $(\mu_2)$, the mean number of years of education is smaller for blacks than for whites, and annual income is positively related to number of years of education. Assuming that there is no interaction, the difference in the mean annual income between whites and blacks, controlling for education, is

**(a)** Less than $\mu_2 - \mu_1$

**(b)** Greater than $\mu_2 - \mu_1$

**(c)** Possibly equal to $\mu_2 - \mu_1$

**13.31.** Summarize the differences in purpose of a one-way analysis of variance and an analysis of covariance.

**\*13.32.** Suppose we use a centered variable for the covariate and express the interaction model when the categorical predictor has two categories as

$$E(y) = \alpha + \beta_1(x - \mu_x) + \beta_2 z + \beta_3(x - \mu_x) \times z.$$

Explain how to interpret $\beta_2$, and explain how this differs from the interpretation for the model without a centered covariate.

# C H A P T E R   14

# Model Building with Multiple Regression

14.1 MODEL SELECTION PROCEDURES
14.2 REGRESSION DIAGNOSTICS
14.3 EFFECTS OF MULTICOLLINEARITY
14.4 GENERALIZED LINEAR MODELS
14.5 NONLINEAR RELATIONSHIPS: POLYNOMIAL REGRESSION
14.6 EXPONENTIAL REGRESSION AND LOG TRANSFORMS*
14.7 CHAPTER SUMMARY

This chapter introduces tools for building regression models and evaluating the effects on their fit of unusual observations or highly correlated predictors. It also shows ways of modeling variables that badly violate the assumptions of straight line relationships with a normal response variable.

Section 14.1 discusses criteria for selecting a regression model by deciding which of a possibly large collection of variables to include in the model. Section 14.2 introduces methods for checking regression assumptions and evaluating the influence of individual observations. Section 14.3 discusses effects of multicollinearity—such strong "overlap" among the explanatory variables that no one of them seems useful when the others are also in the model. Section 14.4 introduces a generalized model that can handle response variables having distributions other than the normal. Sections 14.5 and 14.6 introduce models for nonlinear relationships.

## 14.1 MODEL SELECTION PROCEDURES

Social research studies usually have several explanatory variables. For example, for modeling mental impairment, potential predictors include income, educational attainment, an index of life events, social and environmental stress, marital status, age, self-assessment of health, number of jobs held in previous five years, number of relatives who live nearby, number of close friends, membership in social organizations, frequency of church attendance, and so forth.

Usually, the regression model for the study includes some explanatory variables for theoretical reasons. Others may be included for exploratory purposes, to check whether they explain much variation in the response variable. The model might also include terms to allow for interactions. In such situations, it can be difficult to decide which variables to use and which to exclude.

### Selecting Explanatory Variables for a Model

One possible strategy may be obvious: Include every potentially useful predictor and then delete those terms not making significant partial contributions at some preassigned $\alpha$-level. Unfortunately, this usually is inadequate. Because of correlations among the explanatory variables, any one variable may have little unique predictive power, especially when the number of predictors is large. It is conceivable that few, if any, explanatory variables would make significant *partial* contributions, given that all of the other explanatory variables are in the model.

Here are two general guidelines for selecting explanatory variables: First, include enough of them to make the model useful for theoretical purposes and to obtain good predictive power. Second, as a counterbalance to the first goal, keep the model simple. Having extra variables in the model that add little predictive power, perhaps because of overlapping a lot with the other variables, has disadvantages. The model may be more difficult to interpret because it has many more parameters to be estimated. This can result in inflated standard errors of the parameter estimates and may make it impossible to assess the partial contributions of variables that are important theoretically. To avoid multicollinearity (Section 14.3), it is helpful for the explanatory variables to be correlated with the response variable but not highly correlated among themselves.

Related to this second goal, it is best not to build complex models if the data set is small. If you have only 25 observations, you won't be able to untangle the complexity of relationships among 10 variables. Even with large data sets, it is difficult to build "believable" models containing more than about 10 explanatory variables, and with small to moderate sample sizes (say, 100 or less) it is safest to use relatively few predictors.

In attempting to obtain good predictive power, "Maximize $R^2$" is not a sensible criterion for selecting a model. Because $R^2$ cannot decrease as you add variables to a model, this approach would lead you to the most complex model in the set being considered.

Keeping these thoughts in mind, no unique or optimal approach exists for selecting predictors. For $k$ potential predictors, since each can be either included or omitted (two possibilities for each variable), there are $2^k$ potential subsets. For $k = 2$, for example, there are $2^k = 2^2 = 4$ possible models: one with both $x_1$ and $x_2$, one with $x_1$ alone, one with $x_2$ alone, and one with neither variable. The set of potential models is too large to evaluate practically if $k$ is even moderate; if $k = 7$ there are $2^7 = 128$ potential models.

Most software contains automated variable selection procedures that scan the explanatory variables to choose a subset for the model. These routines construct a model by sequentially entering or removing variables, one at a time according to some criterion. This takes much less time than fitting and comparing *all* $2^k$ possible regression models. For any particular sample and set of variables, however, different procedures may select different subsets of variables, and there is no guarantee of selecting a sensible model. Among the most popular automated variable selection methods are *backward elimination*, *forward selection*, and *stepwise regression*.

### Backward Elimination

*Backward elimination* begins by placing all of the predictors under consideration in the model. It deletes one at a time until reaching a point where the remaining variables all make significant partial contributions to predicting $y$. For most software, the variable deleted at each stage is the one that is the least significant, having the largest $P$-value in the significance test for its effect.

Specifically, here's the sequence of steps for backward elimination: The initial model contains all potential explanatory variables. If all variables make significant partial contributions at some fixed $\alpha$-level, according to the usual $t$ test or $F$ test, then that model is the final one. Otherwise, the explanatory variable having the largest $P$-value, controlling for the other variables in the model, is removed. Next, for the model with that variable removed, the partial contributions of the variables remaining in the model are reassessed, controlling for the other variables still in the model. If they are all significant, that model is the final model. Otherwise, the variable having the largest $P$-value is removed. The process continues until each remaining predictor explains a significant partial amount of the variability in $y$.

### EXAMPLE 14.1    Selecting Predictors of Home Selling Price

We refer to the 100 observations in the "house selling price" data file at the text Web site, which were introduced in Example 9.10 on page 278. We use $y$ = selling price of home, with explanatory variables the size of the home (denoted SIZE), annual taxes (TAXES), number of bedrooms (BEDS), number of bathrooms (BATHS), and a dummy variable for whether the home is new (NEW). We use backward elimination with these variables as potential predictors, requiring a variable to reach significance at the $\alpha = 0.05$ level for inclusion in the model.

Table 14.1 shows the first stage of the process, fitting the model containing all the predictors. The variable making the least partial contribution to the model is BATHS. Its $P$-value ($P = 0.85$) is the largest, and $R^2$ (not shown in Table 14.1) decreases least by dropping it from the model (from 0.7934 to 0.7933). Although number of bathrooms is moderately correlated with the selling price ($r = 0.56$), the other predictors together explain most of the same variability in selling price. Once those variables are in the model, number of bathrooms is essentially redundant.

**TABLE 14.1:** Model Fit at Initial Stage of Backward Elimination for Predicting Home Selling Price

| Variable | B | Std. Error | t | Sig |
|----------|------|-----------|-----|------|
| (Constant) | 4525.75 | 24474.05 | | |
| SIZE | 68.35 | 13.94 | 4.90 | .000 |
| NEW | 41711.43 | 16887.20 | 2.47 | .015 |
| TAXES | 38.13 | 6.81 | 5.60 | .000 |
| BATHS | -2114.37 | 11465.11 | -.18 | .854 |
| BEDS | -11259.1 | 9115.00 | -1.23 | .220 |

When we refit the model after dropping BATHS, the only nonsignificant variable is BEDS, having a $t$ statistic of $-1.31$ and $P$-value $= 0.19$. Table 14.2 shows the third stage, refitting the model after dropping BATHS and BEDS as predictors. Each variable now makes a significant contribution, controlling for the others in the model. Thus, this is the final model. Backward elimination provides the prediction equation

$$\hat{y} = -21,353.8 + 61.7(\text{SIZE}) + 46,373.7(\text{NEW}) + 37.23(\text{TAXES}).$$

Other things being equal, an extra thousand square feet of size increases the selling price by about 62 thousand dollars, and having a new home increases it by about

**TABLE 14.2:** Model Fit at Third Stage of Backward Elimination for Predicting Home Selling Price

| Variable | B | Std. Error | Std. Coeff | t | Sig |
|----------|------|-----------|-----------|-----|------|
| (Constant) | -21353.8 | 13311.49 | | | |
| SIZE | 61.70 | 12.50 | 0.406 | 4.94 | .000 |
| NEW | 46373.70 | 16459.02 | 0.144 | 2.82 | .006 |
| TAXES | 37.23 | 6.74 | 0.466 | 5.53 | .000 |

46 thousand. Using standardized variables, the equation is

$$\hat{z}_y = 0.406z_S + 0.144Z_N + 0.464z_T.$$

If we had included interactions in the original model, we would have ended up with a different final model. However, the model given here has the advantage of simplicity, and it has good predictive power ($R^2 = 0.790$, compared to 0.793 with all the predictors). In fact, the adjusted $R^2$ value (discussed later in this section) $R^2_{adj} = 0.783$ for this model is higher than $R^2_{adj} = 0.782$ for the original model.    ■

### Forward Selection and Stepwise Regression Procedures

Whereas backward elimination begins with *all* the potential explanatory variables in the model, *forward selection* begins with *none* of them. It adds one variable at a time to the model until reaching a point where no remaining variable not yet in the model makes a significant partial contribution to predicting $y$. At each step, the variable added is the one that is most significant, having the smallest $P$-value. For quantitative predictors, this is the variable having the largest $t$ test statistic, or equivalently the one providing the greatest increase in $R^2$.

To illustrate, consider again the data on selling prices of homes. Table 14.3 depicts the process. The variable most highly correlated with selling price is TAXES, so it is added first. Once TAXES is in the model, SIZE provides the greatest boost to $R^2$, and it is significant ($P = 0.000$), so it is the second variable added. Once both TAXES and SIZE are in the model, NEW provides the greatest boost to $R^2$ and it is significant ($P = 0.006$), so it is added next. At this stage, BEDS gives the greatest boost to $R^2$ (from 0.790 to 0.793), but it does not make a significant contribution ($P = 0.194$), so the final model does not include it. In this case, forward selection reaches the same final model as backward elimination.

**TABLE 14.3:** Steps of Forward Selection for Predicting Home Selling Price

| Step | Variables in Model | $P$-Value for New Term | $R^2$ |
|---|---|---|---|
| 0 | None | — | 0.000 |
| 1 | TAXES | 0.000 | 0.709 |
| 2 | TAXES, SIZE | 0.000 | 0.772 |
| 3 | TAXES, SIZE, NEW | 0.006 | 0.790 |
| 4 | TAXES, SIZE, NEW, BEDS | 0.194 | 0.793 |

Once forward selection provides a final model, not all the predictors appearing in it need necessarily be significantly related to $y$. The variability in $y$ explained by a variable entered at an early stage may overlap with the variability explained by variables added later, so it may no longer be significant. Figure 14.1 illustrates. The figure portrays the portion of the total variability in $y$ explained by each of three predictors. Variable $x_1$ explains a similar amount of variability, by itself, as $x_2$ or $x_3$. However, $x_2$ and $x_3$ between them explain much of the same variation that $x_1$ does. Once $x_2$ and $x_3$ are in the model, the unique variability explained by $x_1$ is minor.

*Stepwise regression* is a modification of forward selection that drops variables from the model if they lose their significance as other variables are added. The approach is the same as forward selection except that at each step, after entering the new variable, the procedure drops from the model any variables that no longer make

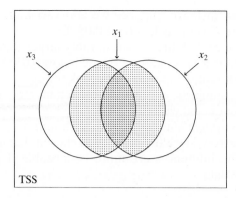

**FIGURE 14.1:** Variability in $y$ Explained by $x_1$, $x_2$, and $x_3$. Shaded portion is amount explained by $x_1$ that is also explained by $x_2$ and $x_3$.

significant partial contributions. A variable entered into the model at some stage may eventually be eliminated because of its overlap with variables entered at later stages.

For the home sales data, stepwise regression behaves the same way as forward selection. At each stage, each variable in the model makes a significant contribution, so no variables are dropped. For these variables, backward elimination, forward selection, and backward elimination all agree. This need not happen.

### Limitations and Abuses of Automatic Selection Procedures

It seems appealing to have a procedure that automatically selects variables according to established criteria. But any variable selection method should be used with caution and should not substitute for careful thought. There is no guarantee that the final model chosen will be sensible.

For instance, when it is not known whether explanatory variables interact in their effects on a response variable, one might specify all the pairwise interactions as well as the main effects as the potential explanatory variables. In this case, it is inappropriate to remove a main effect from a model that contains an interaction composed of that variable. Yet most software does not have this safeguard.

To illustrate, we used forward selection with the home sales data, including the five predictors from above as well as their 10 cross-product interaction terms. The final model had $R^2 = 0.866$, using four interaction terms (SIZE × TAXES, SIZE × NEW, TAXES × NEW, BATHS × NEW) and the TAXES main effect. It is inappropriate, however, to use these interactions as predictors without the SIZE, NEW, and BATHS main effects.

Also, a variable selection procedure may exclude an important predictor that really should be in the model according to other criteria. For instance, using backward elimination with the five predictors of home selling price and their interactions, TAXES was removed. In other words, at a certain stage, TAXES explained an insignificant part of the variation in selling price. Nevertheless, it is the best single predictor of selling price, having $r^2 = 0.709$ by itself. (Refer to step 1 of the forward selection process in Table 14.3.) Since TAXES is such an important determinant of selling price, it seems sensible that any final model should include it as a predictor.

Although $P$-values provide a guide for making decisions about adding or dropping variables in selection procedures, they are not the *true* $P$-values for the tests conducted. We add or drop a variable at each stage according to a minimum or maximum $P$-value, but the sampling distribution of the maximum or minimum of a set of $t$ or $F$ statistics differs from the sampling distribution for the statistic for an a priori chosen test.

For instance, suppose we add variables in forward selection according to whether the *P*-value is less than 0.05. Even if none of the potential predictors truly affect *y*, the probability is considerably larger than 0.05 that at least one of the separate test statistics provides a *P*-value below 0.05 (Exercise 14.48). At least one variable that is not really important may look impressive merely due to chance.

Similarly, once we choose a final model with a selection procedure, any inferences conducted with that model are highly approximate. In particular, *P*-values are likely to appear smaller than they should be and confidence intervals are likely to be too narrow, since the model was chosen that most closely reflects the data, in some sense. The inferences are more believeable if performed for that model with a new set of data.

### Exploratory versus Explanatory (Theory Driven) Research

There is a basic difference between *explanatory* and *exploratory* modes of model selection. In **explanatory research**, there is a theoretical model to test using multiple regression. We might test whether a hypothesized spurious association disappears when other variables are controlled, for example. In such research, automated selection procedures are usually not appropriate, because theory dictates which variables are in the model.

In **exploratory research**, by contrast, the goal is not to examine theoretically specified relationships but merely to find a good set of predictors. This approach searches for predictors that give a large $R^2$, without concern about theoretical explanations. Thus, educational researchers might use a variable selection procedure to search for a set of test scores and other factors that predict well how students perform in college. They should be cautious about giving causal interpretations to the effects of the different variables. For example, possibly the "best" predictor of students' success in college is whether their parents use the Internet for voice communication (with a program such as SKYPE).

In summary, automated variable selection procedures are no substitute for careful thought in formulating models. For most scientific research, they are not appropriate.

### Indices for Selecting a Model: Adjusted $R^2$, PRESS, and $C_p$

Instead of using an automated algorithm such as backward elimination to choose a method, we could ourselves try to identify a set of potentially adequate models and then use some established criterion to select among them. We have seen that maximizing $R^2$ is not a sensible criterion for selecting a model, because the most complicated model will have the largest $R^2$-value. This reflects that fact that $R^2$ has an upward bias as an estimator of the population value of $R^2$. This bias is small for large *n* but can be considerable with small *n* or with many predictors.

In comparing predictive power of different models, it is often more helpful to use *adjusted $R^2$* instead of $R^2$. This equals

$$R^2_{\text{adj}} = \frac{s_y^2 - s^2}{s_y^2} = 1 - \frac{s^2}{s_y^2},$$

where $s^2 = \Sigma(y - \hat{y})^2/[n - (k + 1)]$ is the estimated conditional variance (i.e., the mean square error, MSE) and $s_y^2 = \Sigma(y - \bar{y})^2/(n - 1)$ is the sample variance of *y*. This is a less biased estimator of the population $R^2$. Unlike ordinary $R^2$, if a term is added to a model that is not especially useful, then $R^2_{\text{adj}}$ may even *decrease*.

This happens when the new model has poorer predictive power, in the sense of a larger value of $s^2$, the MSE. For example, if the new model has the same value of SSE $= \sum(y - \hat{y})^2$, then $s^2$ will increase because the number of predictors $k$ (which is in the denominator of $s^2$) has increased.

One possible criterion for selecting a model is to choose the one having the greatest value of $R^2_{adj}$. (This is, equivalently, the model with smallest MSE value.) Table 14.4 shows the $R^2_{adj}$ values for five models for the house selling price data, in the order in which a model is built by forward selection (reverse order for backward elimination). According to this criterion, the selected model is the one with all the predictors except BATHS, which has $R^2_{adj} = 0.785$.

**TABLE 14.4:** Model Selection Criteria for Models for Home Selling Price

| Variables in Model | $R^2$ | $R^2_{adj}$ | PRESS | $C_p$ |
|---|---|---|---|---|
| TAXES | 0.709 | 0.706 | 3.17 | 36.4 |
| TAXES, SIZE | 0.772 | 0.767 | 2.73 | 9.6 |
| TAXES, SIZE, NEW | 0.790 | 0.783 | 2.67 | 3.7 |
| TAXES, SIZE, NEW, BEDS | 0.793 | 0.785 | 2.85 | 4.0 |
| TAXES, SIZE, NEW, BEDS, BATHS | 0.793 | 0.782 | 2.91 | 6.0 |

*Note:* Actual PRESS equals value reported times $10^{11}$.

Various other criteria have been proposed for selecting a model. Most of these criteria attempt to find the model for which the predicted values tend to be closest to the true expected values, in some average sense. One type of method for doing this uses **cross-validation**. For a given model, you fit the model using some of the data and then analyze how well its prediction equation predicts the rest of the data. For example, the method described next analyzes how well each observation is predicted when all the observations except that one are used to fit the model.

Suppose we fit one of the models from Table 14.4 to the house selling price data using all the data except observation 1. Using the prediction equation we get, let $\hat{y}_{(1)}$ denote the predicted selling price for observation 1. That is, we find a prediction equation using the data for observations 2, 3, ..., 100, and then we substitute the values of the explanatory variables for observation 1 into that prediction equation to get $\hat{y}_{(1)}$. Likewise, let $\hat{y}_{(2)}$ denote the prediction for observation 2 when we fit the model to observations 1, 3, 4, ..., 100, leaving out observation 2. In general, for observation $i$, we leave it out in fitting the model and then use the resulting prediction equation to get $\hat{y}_{(i)}$. Then $(y_i - \hat{y}_{(i)})$ is a type of residual, measuring how far observation $i$ falls from the value predicted for it using the prediction equation generated by the other 99 observations.

In summary, for a model for a data set with $n$ observations, we fit the model $n$ times, each time leaving out one observation and using the prediction equation to predict that observation. We then get $n$ predicted values and corresponding prediction residuals. The **predicted residual sum of squares**, denoted by PRESS, is

$$\text{PRESS} = \sum(y_i - \hat{y}_{(i)})^2.$$

The smaller the value of PRESS, the better the predictions tend to be, in a summary sense. According to this criterion, the best-fitting model is the one with the smallest value of PRESS.

Table 14.4 shows the PRESS values for five models for the house selling price data. According to this criterion, the selected model is the one with predictors TAXES, SIZE, and NEW, which has the minimum PRESS = 2.67. (The y-values were in dollars, so squared residuals tended to be huge numbers, and the actual PRESS values are the numbers reported multiplied by $10^{11}$.) This was also the model selected by backward elimination and by forward selection.

A related approach reports a statistic that describes how well each model fits compared to the full model with all the predictors. Roughly speaking, it attempts to find the simplest model that has a relatively small expected value of $[\hat{y} - E(y)]^2$, which measures the distance between a predicted value and the true mean of y at the given values of the explanatory variables. When you have a full model that you believe has sufficient terms as to eliminate important bias, you can use this statistic to search for a simpler model that also has little bias. The statistic is denoted by $C_p$, where p denotes the number of parameters in the regression model (including the y-intercept). For a given number of parameters p, smaller values of $C_p$ indicate a better fit. For the full model, necessarily $C_p = p$. A simpler model than the full one that has $C_p$ close to p provides essentially as good a fit, apart from sampling error. Models having values of $C_p$ considerably larger than p do not fit as well. In using $C_p$ to help select a model, the goal is to have the smallest number of predictors necessary to give a value of $C_p$ close to p. For that number of predictors, the selected model is the one with the minimum value of $C_p$.

Consider the models in Table 14.4. The full model shown on the last line of that table has five predictors and p = 6 parameters, so it has $C_p = 6.0$. The model removing BATHS has p = 5 parameters and has $C_p = 4.0$. The model removing BEDS has p = 4 parameters and has $C_p = 3.7$. Since $C_p$ is then close to p = 4, this model seems to fit essentially as well as the full model, apart from sampling error. The simpler models listed in the table have $C_p$ considerably larger than p ($C_p = 9.6$ with p = 3 and $C_p = 36.4$ with p = 2) and provide poorer fits.

Some software does not report PRESS or $C_p$ but does present a measure that has a similar purpose. The **AIC**, short for **Akaike information criterion**, also attempts to find a model for which the $\{\hat{y}_i\}$ tend to be closest to $\{E(y_i)\}$ in an average sense. Its formula, not considered here, penalizes a model for having more parameters than are useful for getting good predictions. The AIC is also scaled in such a way that the lower the value, the better the model. The "best" model is the one with smallest AIC. An advantage of AIC it that it is also useful for models that assume nonnormal distributions for y, in which case a sum of squared errors may not be a useful summary.

## 14.2 REGRESSION DIAGNOSTICS

Once we have selected predictors for a model, how do we know that model fits the data adequately? This section introduces diagnostics that indicate (1) when model assumptions are grossly violated and (2) when certain observations are highly influential in affecting the model fit or inference about model parameters.

Recall that inference about parameters in a regression model makes these assumptions:

- The true regression function has the form used in the model (e.g., linear).
- The conditional distribution of y is normal.
- The conditional distribution of y has constant standard deviation throughout the range of values of the explanatory variables. This condition is called *homoscedasticity*.
- The sample is randomly selected.

In practice, the assumptions are never perfectly fulfilled, but the regression model can still be useful. It is adequate to check that no assumption is grossly violated.

### Examine the Residuals

Several checks of assumptions use the residuals, $y - \hat{y}$. They represent the deviations of the observations from the prediction equation values.

One type of check concerns the normality assumption. If the observations are normally distributed about the true regression equation with constant conditional standard deviation $\sigma$, then the residuals should be approximately normally distributed. To check this, plot the residuals about their mean value 0, using a histogram or stem-and-leaf plot. They should have approximately a bell shape about 0.

A standardized version of the residual equals the residual divided by a standard deviation that describes how much residuals vary because of ordinary sampling variability. In regression, this is called[1] a ***studentized residual***. Under the normality assumption, a histogram of these residuals should have the appearance of a standard normal distribution (bell shaped with mean of 0 and standard deviation of 1). If the model holds, studentized residuals between about 2 and 3 in absolute value may be worthy of notice, but about 5% are this large simply by chance.

If a studentized residual is larger than about 3 in absolute value, the observation is a potential outlier and should be checked. If an outlier represents a measurement error, it could cause a major bias in the prediction equation. Even if it is not an error, it should be investigated. It represents an observation that is not typical of the sample data, and it may have too much impact on the model fit. Consider whether there is some reason for the peculiarity. Sometimes the outliers differ from the other observations on some variable not included in the model, and once that variable is added, they cease to be outliers.

### EXAMPLE 14.2    Residuals for Modeling Home Selling Price

For the data of Table 9.4 (page 278) with $y$ = selling price, variable selection procedures in Example 14.1 (page 443) suggested the model having predictors SIZE of home, TAXES, and whether NEW. The prediction equation is

$$\hat{y} = -21,353.8 + 61.7(\text{SIZE}) + 46,373.7(\text{NEW}) + 37.2(\text{TAXES}).$$

Figure 14.2 is a histogram of the studentized residuals for this fit, as plotted by SPSS. No severe nonnormality seems to be indicated, since they are roughly bell shaped about 0. However, the plot indicates that two observations have relatively large residuals. On further inspection, we find that observation 6 had a selling price of $499,900, which was $168,747 higher than the predicted selling price for a new home of 3153 square feet with a tax bill of $2997. The residual of $168,747 has a studentized value of 3.88. Likewise observation 64 had a selling price of $225,000, which was $165,501 lower than the predicted selling price for a non-new home of 4050 square feet with a tax bill of $4350. Its residual of −$165,501 has a studentized value of −3.93.

A severe outlier on $y$ can substantially affect the fit, especially when the values of the explanatory variables are not near their means. So we refitted the model without

---

[1] Some software, such as SPSS, reports also a *standardized residual* that is slightly different than this. It divides the ordinary residual by the square root of the mean square error, which is slightly larger than the standard error of the residual.

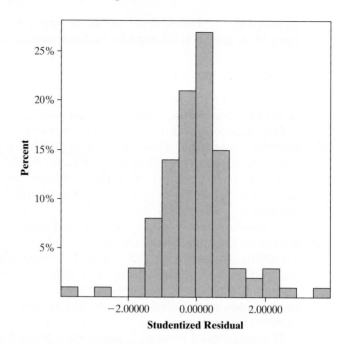

**FIGURE 14.2:** Histogram of Studentized Residuals for Multiple Regression Model Fitted to Housing Price Data, with Predictors Size, Taxes, and New

these two observations. The $R^2$-value changes from 0.79 to 0.83, and the prediction equation changes to

$$\hat{y} = -32226 + 68.9(\text{SIZE}) + 20436(\text{NEW}) + 38.3(\text{TAXES}).$$

The parameter estimates are similar for SIZE and TAXES, but the estimated effect of NEW drops from 46,374 to 20,436. Moreover, the effect of NEW is no longer significant, having a $P$-value of 0.17. Because the estimated effect of NEW is affected substantially by these two observations, we should be cautious in making conclusions about its effect. Of the 100 homes in the sample, only 11 were new. It is it difficult to make precise estimates about the NEW effect with so few new homes, and results are highly affected by a couple of unusual observations. ∎

### Plotting Residuals against Explanatory Variables

The normality assumption is not as important as the assumption that the model provides a good approximation for the true relationship between the predictors and the mean of $y$. If the model assumes a linear effect but the effect is actually strongly nonlinear, the conclusions will be faulty.

For bivariate models, the scatterplot provides a simple check on the form of the relationship. For multiple regression, it is also useful to construct a scatterplot of each explanatory variable against the response variable. This displays only the *bivariate* relationships, however, whereas the model refers to the *partial* effect of each predictor, with the others held constant. The *partial regression plot* introduced in Section 11.2 provides some information about this. It provides a summary picture of the partial relationship.

For multiple regression models, plots of the residuals (or studentized residuals) against the predicted values $\hat{y}$ or against each explanatory variable also help us check for potential problems. If the residuals appear to fluctuate randomly about 0 with no obvious trend or change in variation as the values of a particular $x_i$ increase, then no violation of assumptions is indicated. The pattern should be roughly like Figure 14.3a. In Figure 14.3c, $y$ tends to be below $\hat{y}$ for very small and very large $x_i$-values (giving negative residuals) and above $\hat{y}$ for medium-sized $x_i$-values (giving positive residuals). Such a scattering of residuals suggests that $y$ is actually nonlinearly related to $x_i$. Sections 14.5 and 14.6 show how to address nonlinearity.

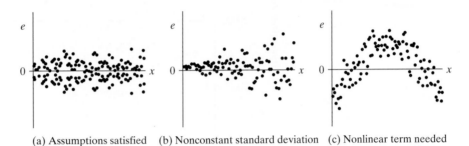

(a) Assumptions satisfied     (b) Nonconstant standard deviation     (c) Nonlinear term needed

**FIGURE 14.3:** Possible Patterns for Residuals (e), Plotted against an Explanatory Variable $x$

In practice, most response variables can take only nonnegative values. For such responses, a fairly common occurrence is that the variability increases dramatically as the mean increases. For example, consider $y$ = annual income (in dollars), using several predictors. For those subjects having $E(Y) = \$10,000$, the standard deviation of income is probably much less than for those subjects having $E(Y) = \$200,000$. Plausible standard deviations might be $4000 and $80,000. When this happens, the conditional standard deviation of $y$ is not constant, whereas ordinary regression assumes that it is. An indication that this is happening is when the residuals are more spread out as the $y_i$-values increase. If we were to plot the residuals against a predictor that has a positive partial association with $y$, such as number of years of education, the residuals would then be more spread out for larger values of the predictor, as in Figure 14.3b.

Figure 14.4 is a residual plot for the model relating selling price of home to size, taxes, and whether new. It plots the residuals against size. There is some suggestion of more variability at the higher size values. It does seem sensible that selling prices would vary more for very large homes than for very small homes. A similar picture occurs when we plot the residuals against taxes.

If the change in variability is severe, then a method other than ordinary least squares provides better estimates with more valid standard errors. Section 14.4 presents a generalized regression model that allows the variability to be greater when the mean is greater.

In practice, residual patterns are rarely as neat as the ones in Figure 14.3. Don't let a few outliers or ordinary sampling variability influence too strongly your interpretation of a plot. Also, the plots described here just scratch the surface of the graphical tools now available for diagnosing potential problems. Fox (1991) described a variety of modern graphical displays.

### Time Series Data

Some social research studies collect observations sequentially over time. For economic variables such as a stock index or the unemployment rate, for example, the observations often occur daily or monthly. The observations are then usually recorded

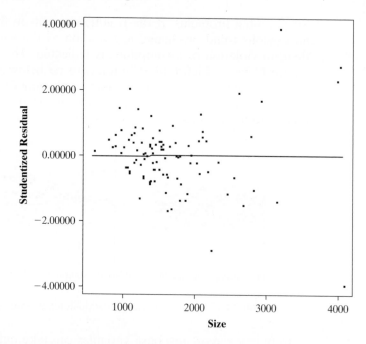

**FIGURE 14.4:** Scatterplot of Studentized Residuals of Home Selling Price Plotted against Size of Home, for Model with Predictors Size, Taxes, and Whether Home Is New

in sequence, rather than randomly sampled. Sampling subjects randomly from some population ensures that one observation is not statistically dependent on another, and this simplifies derivations of sampling distributions and their standard errors. However, neighboring observations from a time sequence are usually correlated rather than independent. For example, if the unemployment rate is relatively low in January 2008, it is probably also relatively low in February 2008.

A plot of the residuals against the time of making the observation checks for this type of dependence. Ideally, the residuals should fluctuate in a random pattern about 0 over time rather than showing a trend or periodic cycle. The methods presented in this text are based on independent observations and are inappropriate when time effects occur. For example, when observations next to each other tend to be positively correlated, the standard error of the sample mean is larger than the $\sigma/\sqrt{n}$ formula that applies for independent observations. Books specializing in time series or econometrics, such as Kennedy (2004), present methods for time series data.

### Detecting Influential Observations: Leverage

Least squares estimates of parameters in regression models can be strongly influenced by an outlier, especially when the sample size is small. A variety of statistics summarize the influence each observation has. These statistics refer to how much the predicted values $\hat{y}$ or the model parameter estimates change when the observation is removed from the data set. An observation's influence depends on two factors: (1) how far the response on $y$ falls from the overall trend in the sample, and (2) how far the values of the explanatory variables fall from their means.

The first factor on influence (how far an observation falls from the overall trend) is measured by the residual for the observation $y - \hat{y}$. The larger the residual, the farther the observation falls from the overall trend. We can search for observations with large studentized residuals (say, larger than about 3 in absolute value) to find observations that may be influential.

The second factor on influence (how far the explanatory variables fall from their means) is summarized by the **leverage** of the observation. The leverage is a nonnegative statistic such that the larger its value, the greater weight that observation receives in determining the $\hat{y}$-values (hence, it also is sometimes called a *hat value*). The formula for the leverage in multiple regression is complex. For the bivariate model, the leverage for observation $i$ simplifies to

$$h_i = \frac{1}{n} + \frac{(x_i - \bar{x})^2}{\sum(x - \bar{x})^2}.$$

So the leverage gets larger as the $x$-value gets farther from the mean, but it gets smaller as the sample size increases. When calculated for each observation in a sample, the average leverage equals $p/n$, where $p$ is the number of parameters in the model.

### Detecting Influential Observations: DFFIT and DFBETA

Most statistical software reports other diagnostics that depend on the studentized residuals and the leverages. Two popular ones are called **DFFIT** and **DFBETA**.

For a given observation, DFBETA summarizes the *effect on the model parameter estimates* of removing the observation from the data set. For the effect $\beta_j$ of $x_j$, DFBETA equals the change in the estimate $\hat{\beta}_j$ due to deleting the observation. The larger the absolute value of DFBETA, the greater the influence of the observation on that parameter estimate. Each observation has a DFBETA value for each parameter in the model.

DFFIT summarizes the *effect on the fit* of deleting the observation. It summarizes more broadly the influence of an observation, as each observation has a single DFFIT value whereas it has a separate DFBETA for each parameter. For observation $i$, DFFIT equals the change in the predicted value due to deleting that observation (i.e., $\hat{y}_i - \hat{y}_{(i)}$). The DFFIT value has the same sign as the residual. The larger its absolute value, the greater the influence that observation has on the fitted values. **Cook's distance** is an alternative measure with the same purpose, but it is based on the effect that observation $i$ has on *all* the predicted values.

### EXAMPLE 14.3    DFBETA and DFFIT for an Influential Observation

Example 14.2 (page 449) showed that observations 6 and 64 were influential on the equation for predicting home selling price using size of home, taxes, and whether the house is new. The prediction equation is

$$\hat{y} = -21,354 + 61.7(\text{SIZE}) + 46,373.7(\text{NEW}) + 37.2(\text{TAXES}).$$

For observation 6, the DFBETA values are 12.5 for size, 16,318.5 for new, and $-5.7$ for taxes. This means, for example, that if this observation is deleted from the data set, the effect of NEW changes from 46,373.7 to $46,373.7 - 16,318.5 = 30,055.2$. Observation 6 had a predicted selling price of $\hat{y} = 331,152.8$. Its DFFIT value is 29,417.0. This means that if observation 6 is deleted from the data set, then $\hat{y}$ at the predictor values for observation 6 changes to $331,152.8 - 29,417.0 = 301,735.8$. This analysis also shows that this observation is quite influential. ∎

Some software reports standardized versions of the DFBETA and DFFIT measures. The standardized DFBETA divides the change in the estimate $\hat{\beta}_j$ due to deleting the observation by the standard error of $\hat{\beta}_j$ for the adjusted data set. For observation $i$, the standardized DFFIT equals the change in the predicted value due to deleting that observation, divided by the standard error of $\hat{y}$ for the adjusted data set.

In practice, you scan or plot these diagnostic measures to see if some observations stand out from the rest, having relatively large values. Each measure has approximate cutoff points for noteworthy observations. A leverage larger than about $3p/n$ (three times the average leverage) indicates a potentially large influence. A standardized DFBETA larger than 1 suggests a substantial influence on that parameter estimate. However, the leverages, DFBETA, and DFFIT tend to decrease as $n$ increases, so normally it is a good idea to examine observations having extreme values relative to the others. Individual data points tend to have less influence for larger sample sizes.

### EXAMPLE 14.4    Influence Diagnostics for Crime Data

Table 9.1 in Chapter 9 (page 256) listed $y$ = murder rate for the 50 states and the District of Columbia (D.C.). The data are shown again in Table 14.5. That table also showed data on $x_1$ = percentage of families below the poverty level and $x_2$ = percentage of single-parent families.

The least squares fit of the multiple regression model is

$$\hat{y} = -40.7 + 0.32x_1 + 3.96x_2.$$

Table 14.5 shows the influence diagnostics for the fit of this model, including the standardized versions of DFBETA and DFFIT. The studentized residuals all fall in a reasonable range except the one for the last observation (D.C.), which equals 14.2. The observed murder rate of 78.5 for D.C. falls far above the predicted value of 55.3, causing a large positive residual. This is an extreme outlier. In addition, the leverage for D.C. equals 0.54, more than three times as large as any other leverage and nine times the average leverage of $p/n = 3/51 = 0.06$. Since D.C. has both a large studentized residual and a large leverage, it has considerable influence on the model fit.

Not surprisingly, DFFIT for D.C. is much larger than for the other observations. This suggests that the predicted values change considerably if we refit the model after removing this observation. The DFBETA value for the single-family predictor $x_2$ is much larger for D.C. than for the other observations. This suggests that the effect of $x_2$ could change substantially with the removal of D.C. By contrast, DFBETA for poverty is not so large.

These diagnostics suggest that the D.C. observation has a large influence, particularly on the coefficient of $x_2$ and on the fitted values. The prediction equation for the model fitted without the D.C. observation is

$$\hat{y} = -14.6 + 0.36x_1 + 1.52x_2.$$

Not surprisingly, the estimated effect of $x_1$ did not change much, but the coefficient of $x_2$ is now less than half as large. The standard error of the coefficient of $x_2$ also changes dramatically, decreasing from 0.44 to 0.26.    ■

An observation with a large studentized residual does not have a major influence if its values on the explanatory variables do not fall far from their means. Recall that the leverage summarizes how far the explanatory variables fall from their means. For instance, New Mexico has a relatively large negative studentized residual ($-2.25$) but a relatively small leverage (0.046), so it does not have large values of DFFIT or DFBETA. Similarly, an observation far from the mean on the explanatory variables

**TABLE 14.5:** Influence Diagnostics for Model Using Poverty Rate and Single-Parent Percentage to Predict Murder Rate for 50 U.S. States and District of Columbia

| Obs | Dep Var MURDER | Predict Value | Residual | Student Resid | Leverage h | Dffits | POVERTY Dfbeta | SINGLE Dfbeta |
|-----|------|-------|--------|-------|-------|--------|--------|--------|
| AK | 9.0 | 18.88 | -9.88 | -2.04 | 0.162 | -0.895 | 0.714 | -0.761 |
| AL | 11.6 | 10.41 | 1.18 | 0.22 | 0.031 | 0.039 | 0.024 | -0.011 |
| AR | 10.2 | 8.07 | 2.13 | 0.40 | 0.079 | 0.117 | 0.100 | -0.069 |
| AZ | 8.6 | 12.16 | -3.55 | -0.65 | 0.022 | -0.099 | -0.005 | -0.025 |
| CA | 13.1 | 14.63 | -1.53 | -0.28 | 0.034 | -0.053 | -0.027 | -0.004 |
| CO | 5.8 | 10.41 | -4.61 | -0.87 | 0.060 | -0.220 | 0.174 | -0.134 |
| CT | 6.3 | 2.04 | 4.25 | 0.79 | 0.051 | 0.185 | -0.130 | 0.015 |
| DE | 5.0 | 7.73 | -2.73 | -0.50 | 0.043 | -0.107 | 0.079 | -0.045 |
| FL | 8.9 | 6.97 | 1.92 | 0.35 | 0.048 | 0.080 | 0.059 | -0.047 |
| GA | 11.4 | 15.12 | -3.72 | -0.69 | 0.042 | -0.145 | 0.071 | -0.105 |
| HI | 3.8 | -2.07 | 5.87 | 1.11 | 0.059 | 0.279 | -0.153 | -0.058 |
| IA | 2.3 | -1.74 | 4.04 | 0.75 | 0.045 | 0.164 | -0.034 | -0.081 |
| ID | 2.9 | 1.12 | 1.77 | 0.32 | 0.035 | 0.063 | 0.012 | -0.040 |
| IL | 11.4 | 9.21 | 2.18 | 0.40 | 0.020 | 0.058 | -0.013 | 0.011 |
| IN | 7.5 | 5.99 | 1.50 | 0.27 | 0.023 | 0.043 | -0.014 | -0.000 |
| KS | 6.4 | 2.71 | 3.68 | 0.68 | 0.029 | 0.117 | 0.013 | -0.062 |
| KY | 6.6 | 7.79 | -1.19 | -0.22 | 0.088 | -0.070 | -0.061 | 0.043 |
| LA | 20.3 | 26.74 | -6.44 | -1.29 | 0.161 | -0.568 | -0.412 | -0.055 |
| MA | 3.9 | 5.91 | -2.01 | -0.37 | 0.033 | -0.068 | 0.042 | -0.014 |
| MD | 12.7 | 9.95 | 2.74 | 0.51 | 0.060 | 0.130 | -0.104 | 0.077 |
| ME | 1.6 | 4.72 | -3.12 | -0.57 | 0.031 | -0.104 | 0.058 | -0.008 |
| MI | 9.8 | 15.72 | -5.92 | -1.10 | 0.033 | -0.204 | 0.035 | -0.124 |
| MN | 3.4 | 2.23 | 1.16 | 0.21 | 0.029 | 0.037 | -0.007 | -0.013 |
| MO | 11.3 | 7.62 | 3.67 | 0.67 | 0.027 | 0.115 | 0.059 | -0.049 |
| MS | 13.5 | 25.40 | -11.90 | -2.45 | 0.126 | -0.933 | -0.623 | -0.151 |
| MT | 3.0 | 6.84 | -3.84 | -0.70 | 0.023 | -0.108 | -0.033 | 0.039 |
| NC | 11.3 | 7.87 | 3.42 | 0.62 | 0.020 | 0.090 | 0.009 | -0.013 |
| ND | 1.7 | -3.83 | 5.53 | 1.04 | 0.057 | 0.259 | 0.016 | -0.184 |
| NE | 3.9 | -0.15 | 4.05 | 0.75 | 0.039 | 0.153 | -0.047 | -0.056 |
| NH | 2.0 | -1.07 | 3.07 | 0.57 | 0.044 | 0.123 | -0.039 | -0.047 |
| NJ | 5.3 | 0.82 | 4.47 | 0.83 | 0.035 | 0.158 | -0.041 | -0.058 |
| NM | 8.0 | 19.53 | -11.53 | -2.25 | 0.046 | -0.499 | -0.017 | -0.308 |
| NV | 10.4 | 11.57 | -1.17 | -0.22 | 0.069 | -0.060 | 0.048 | -0.040 |
| NY | 13.3 | 14.85 | -1.55 | -0.28 | 0.028 | -0.048 | -0.005 | -0.019 |
| OH | 6.0 | 8.62 | -2.62 | -0.48 | 0.022 | -0.072 | 0.024 | -0.015 |
| OK | 8.4 | 9.62 | -1.22 | -0.22 | 0.067 | -0.061 | -0.051 | 0.031 |
| OR | 4.6 | 7.84 | -3.24 | -0.59 | 0.027 | -0.101 | 0.054 | -0.029 |
| PA | 6.8 | 1.55 | 5.24 | 0.97 | 0.034 | 0.183 | 0.036 | -0.115 |
| RI | 3.9 | 5.67 | -1.77 | -0.32 | 0.028 | -0.056 | 0.029 | -0.006 |
| SC | 10.3 | 13.99 | -3.69 | -0.68 | 0.038 | -0.137 | -0.084 | 0.008 |
| SD | 3.4 | 1.07 | 2.32 | 0.43 | 0.042 | 0.091 | 0.036 | -0.067 |
| TN | 10.2 | 9.92 | 0.27 | 0.05 | 0.060 | 0.013 | 0.010 | -0.006 |
| TX | 11.9 | 11.60 | 0.29 | 0.05 | 0.029 | 0.009 | 0.005 | -0.001 |
| UT | 3.1 | 2.34 | 0.75 | 0.13 | 0.032 | 0.025 | -0.010 | -0.004 |
| VA | 8.3 | 3.21 | 5.08 | 0.94 | 0.039 | 0.192 | -0.119 | 0.010 |
| VT | 3.6 | 6.08 | -2.48 | -0.46 | 0.040 | -0.094 | 0.067 | -0.028 |
| WA | 5.2 | 9.52 | -4.32 | -0.80 | 0.029 | -0.139 | 0.078 | -0.059 |
| WI | 4.4 | 4.53 | -0.13 | -0.02 | 0.023 | -0.003 | 0.000 | 0.001 |
| WV | 6.9 | 3.60 | 3.29 | 0.66 | 0.178 | 0.307 | 0.274 | -0.229 |
| WY | 3.4 | 6.34 | -2.94 | -0.54 | 0.021 | -0.079 | 0.006 | 0.012 |
| DC | 78.5 | 55.28 | 23.22 | 14.20 | 0.536 | 15.271 | -0.485 | 12.792 |

(i.e., with a large leverage) need not have a major influence, if it falls close to the prediction equation and has a small studentized residual. For instance, West Virginia has a relatively large poverty rate and its leverage of 0.18 is triple the average. However, its studentized residual is small (0.66), so it has little influence on the fit.

## 14.3   EFFECTS OF MULTICOLLINEARITY

In many social science studies using multiple regression, the explanatory variables "overlap" considerably. Each variable may be nearly redundant, in the sense that it can be predicted well using the others. If we regress an explanatory variable on the others and get a large $R^2$-value, this suggests that it may not be needed in the model once the others are there. This condition is called *multicollinearity*. This section describes the effects of multicollinearity and ways to diagnose it.

### Multicollinearity Inflates Standard Errors

Multicollinearity causes inflated standard errors for estimates of regression parameters. To show why, we first consider the regression model $E(y) = \alpha + \beta_1 x_1 + \beta_2 x_2$. The estimate of $\beta_1$ has standard error

$$se = \frac{1}{\sqrt{1 - r_{x_1 x_2}^2}} \left[ \frac{s}{\sqrt{n - 1} s_{x_1}} \right],$$

where $s$ is the estimated conditional standard deviation of $y$ and $s_{x_1}$ denotes the sample standard deviation of $x_1$ values. The effect of the correlation $r_{x_1 x_2}$ between the explanatory variables enters through the term $\sqrt{1 - r_{x_1 x_2}^2}$ in the denominator. Other things being equal, the stronger that squared correlation, the larger the standard error of $b_1$. Similarly, the standard error of the estimator of $\beta_2$ also is larger with larger values of $r_{x_1 x_2}^2$.

An analogous result applies for the model with multiple predictors. The standard error of the estimator of the coefficient $\beta_j$ of $x_j$ equals

$$se = \frac{1}{\sqrt{1 - R_j^2}} \left[ \frac{s}{\sqrt{n - 1} s_{x_j}} \right],$$

where $s_{x_j}$ is the sample standard deviation of $x_j$ and $R_j$ denotes the multiple correlation from the regression of $x_j$ on the other predictors. So when $x_j$ overlaps a lot with the other predictors, in the sense that $R_j^2$ is large for predicting $x_j$ using the other predictors, this $se$ is relatively large. Then the confidence interval for $\beta_j$ is wide, and the test of $H_0: \beta_j = 0$ has large $P$-value unless the sample size is very large.

### The VIF and Other Indicators of Multicollinearity

The quantity $1/(1 - R_j^2)$ in the above $se$ formula for the estimate of $\beta_j$ in multiple regression is called a **variance inflation factor** (VIF). It represents the multiplicative increase in the variance (squared standard error) of the estimator due to $x_j$ being correlated with the other predictors.

When any of the $R_j^2$-values from regressing each explanatory variable on the other explanatory variables in the model is close to 1, say above 0.90, multicollinearity exists. For example, if $R_j^2 > 0.90$, then VIF $> 10$ for the effect of that predictor. That is, the variance of the estimate of $\beta_j$ inflates by a factor of more than 10. The standard error inflates by a factor of more than $\sqrt{10} = 3.2$, compared to the standard error for uncorrelated predictors.

To describe the extent to which multicollinearity exists, most software can display the variance inflation factor

$$\text{VIF} = 1/(1 - R_j^2)$$

for each predictor. For example, for the model selected in Section 14.1 that predicts house selling price using taxes, size, and whether the house is new, SPSS reports as "collinearity statistics"

```
           VIF
TAXES    3.082
SIZE     3.092
NEW      1.192
```

The standard error for whether new is not affected much by correlation with the other predictors, but the other two standard errors multiply by a factor of roughly $\sqrt{3.1} = 1.76$.

Suppose a predictor is in the model primarily as a control. That is, we want to control its effects in studying effects of the variables of primary interest, but we do not need precise estimates of its effect on the response variable. Then, it is not crucial to worry about the VIF value for this predictor variable.

Even without checking VIFs, various types of behavior in a regression analysis can indicate potential problems due to multicollinearity. A warning sign occurs when the estimated coefficient for a predictor already in the model changes substantially when another variable is introduced. For example, perhaps the estimated coefficient of $x_1$ is 2.4 for the bivariate model, but when $x_2$ is added to the model, the coefficient of $x_1$ changes to 25.9.

Another indicator of multicollinearity is when a highly significant $R^2$ exists between $y$ and the explanatory variables, but individually each partial regression coefficient is not significant. In other words, $H_0: \beta_1 = \cdots = \beta_k = 0$ has a small $P$-value in the overall $F$ test, but $H_0: \beta_1 = 0$, $H_0: \beta_2 = 0$, and so forth do not have small $P$-values in the separate $t$ tests. Thus, it is difficult to assess individual partial effects when severe multicollinearity exists. Other indicators of multicollinearity are surprisingly large standard errors or standardized regression coefficients that are larger than 1 in absolute value (which is impossible for partial correlations).

Since a regression coefficient in a multiple regression model represents the effect of an explanatory variable when other variables are held constant, it has less meaning when multicollinearity exists. If $|r_{x_1 x_2}|$ is high, then as $x_1$ changes, $x_2$ also tends to change in a linear manner, and it is somewhat artificial to envision $x_1$ or $x_2$ as being held constant. Thus, the coefficients have dubious interpretations when multicollinearity exists.

## Remedial Actions when Multicollinearity Exists

Here are some remedial measures to reduce the effects of multicollinearity. First, since it may not make sense to study partial effects when the explanatory variables are highly correlated, you could use simple bivariate regression models to analyze the relationship between $y$ and each $x_i$ separately.

A better solution is to choose a subset of the explanatory variables, removing those variables that explain a small portion of the remaining unexplained variation in $y$. If $x_4$ and $x_5$ have a correlation of 0.96, it is only necessary to include one of them in the model. You could use an automated variable selection procedure to select a subset of variables, but this is primarily helpful for purely exploratory research.

Alternatively, when several predictors are highly correlated and are indicators of a common feature, you could construct a summary index by combining responses on those variables. For example, suppose that a model for predicting $y$ = opinion about president's performance in office uses 12 predictors, of which three refer to the subject's opinion about whether a woman should be able to obtain an abortion (1) when she cannot financially afford another child, (2) when she is unmarried, and (3) anytime in the first three months. Each of these items is scaled from 1 to 5, with a 5 being the most conservative response. They are likely to be highly positively correlated, contributing to multicollinearity. A possible summary measure for opinion about abortion averages (or sums) the responses to these items. Higher values on that summary index represent more conservative responses. If the items were measured on different scales, we could first standardize the scores before averaging them. Socioeconomic status is a variable of this type, summarizing the joint effects of education, income, and occupational prestige.

Often multicollinearity occurs when the predictors include interaction terms. Since cross-product terms are composed of other predictors in the model, it is not surprising that they tend to be highly correlated with the other terms. Section 11.5 noted that the effects of this are diminished if we center the predictors by subtracting their sample means before entering them in the interaction model.

Other procedures, beyond the scope of this chapter, can handle multicollinearity. For example, *factor analysis* (introduced in Chapter 16) is a method for creating artificial variables from the original ones in such a way that the new variables can be uncorrelated. In most applications, though, it is more advisable to use a subset of the variables or create some new variables directly, as just discussed.

Multicollinearity does not adversely affect all aspects of regression. Although multicollinearity makes it difficult to assess *partial* effects of explanatory variables, it does not hinder the assessment of their *joint* effects. If newly added explanatory variables overlap substantially with ones already in the model, then $R$ and $R^2$ will not increase much, but the fit will not be poorer. So the presence of multicollinearity does not diminish the predictive power of the equation. For further discussion of the effects of multicollinearity and methods for dealing with it, see DeMaris (2004), Fox (1991), and Kutner et al. (2004).

## 14.4  GENERALIZED LINEAR MODELS

The models presented in this book are special cases of **generalized linear models**. This is a broad class of models that includes ordinary regression models for response variables assumed to have a normal distribution, alternative models for continuous variables that do not assume normality, and models for discrete response variables including categorical variables. This section introduces generalized linear models. We use the acronym *GLM*.

### Nonnormal Distributions for a Response

As in other regression models, a GLM identifies a response variable $y$ and a set of explanatory variables. The regression models discussed in the past six chapters are GLMs that assume that $y$ has a normal distribution.

In many applications, the potential outcomes for $y$ are binary rather than continuous. Each observation might be labeled as a *success* or *failure*, as in the methods for proportions presented in Sections 5.2, 6.3, and 7.2. For instance, consider a study of factors that influence votes in presidential elections. For each subject, the response variable indicates the preferred candidate in the previous presidential election—the Democratic or the Republican candidate. The study uses predictors in a model for subjects' decisions about the preferred candidate. In this case, models usually assume a *binomial* distribution for $y$. The next chapter presents a GLM for binary data, called *logistic regression.*

In some applications, each observation is a count. For example, consider a study of factors associated with family size. The response for a given married couple is their number of children. The study constructs a model that uses several explanatory variables to predict the number of children. Two distributions not discussed in this text, called the *Poisson* and the *negative binomial,* are often assumed for $y$ in GLMs for count data.

Binary outcomes and counts are examples of discrete variables. Regression models that assume normal distributions are not optimal for models with discrete responses. Even when the response variable is continuous, the normal distribution is not necessarily optimal. When each observation must take a positive value, for instance, the distribution is often skewed to the right with greater variability when the mean is greater. In that case, a GLM can assume a *gamma* distribution for $y$, as discussed later in this section.

### The Link Function for a GLM

Denote the expected value of $y$, which is the mean of its probability distribution, by $\mu = E(y)$. As in ordinary regression models, in a GLM $\mu$ varies according to values of explanatory variables, which enter linearly as predictors on the right-hand side of the model equation. However, a GLM allows a function $g(\mu)$ of the mean rather than just the mean $\mu$ itself on the left-hand side. The GLM formula states that

$$g(\mu) = \alpha + \beta_1 x_1 + \beta_2 x_2 + \cdots + \beta_k x_k.$$

The function $g(\mu)$ is called the ***link function***, because it links the mean of the response variable to the explanatory variables.

The simplest possible link function is $g(\mu) = \mu$. This models the mean directly and is called the ***identity link***. It specifies a linear model for the mean response,

$$\mu = \alpha + \beta_1 x_1 + \beta_2 x_2 + \cdots + \beta_k x_k.$$

This is the form of ordinary regression models.

Other link functions permit the mean to relate nonlinearly to the predictors. For instance, the link function $g(\mu) = \log(\mu)$ models the log of the mean. The log function applies to positive numbers, so this ***log link*** is appropriate when $\mu$ cannot be negative, such as with count data. A GLM that uses the log link is often called a ***loglinear model***. It has form

$$\log(\mu) = \alpha + \beta_1 x_1 + \beta_2 x_2 + \cdots + \beta_k x_k.$$

The final section of this chapter shows an example of this model.

For binary data, the most common link function is $g(\mu) = \log[\mu/(1 - \mu)]$. This is called the ***logit link***. It is appropriate when $\mu$ falls between 0 and 1, such as a probability, in which case $\mu/(1 - \mu)$ is the *odds*. When $y$ is binary, this link is used in models for the probability of a particular outcome, for instance, to model the probability that a subject votes for the Democratic candidate. A GLM using the logit link is called a ***logistic regression model***.

### GLMs for a Response Assuming a Normal Distribution

Ordinary regression models are special cases of GLMs. They assume a normal distribution for $y$ and model the mean directly, using the identity link, $g(\mu) = \mu$. A GLM generalizes ordinary regression in two ways: First, $y$ can have a distribution other than the normal. Second, it can model a function of the mean. Both generalizations are important, especially for discrete responses.

Before GLMs were developed in the 1970s, the traditional way of analyzing "nonnormal" data involved transforming the $y$-values. The goal is to find transformed values that have an approximately normal distribution, with constant standard deviation at all levels of the predictors. Square root or log transforms are often applied to do this. If the goals of normality and constant variation are achieved, then ordinary regression methods using least squares are applicable with the transformed data. In practice, this usually does not work well. A transform that produces constant variation may not produce normality, or else simple linear models for the explanatory variables may fit poorly on that scale. Moreover, conclusions that refer to the mean response on the scale of the transformed variable are usually less relevant, and there can be technical problems such as taking logarithms of 0.

With the GLM approach, it is not necessary to transform data and use normal methods. This is because the GLM fitting process utilizes a powerful estimation method (***maximum likelihood***, see Section 5.1) for which the choice of distribution for $y$ is not restricted to normality. In addition, in GLMs the choice of link function is separate from the choice of distribution for $y$. If a certain link function makes sense for a particular type of data, it is not necessary that it also stabilize variation or produce normality.

We introduce the concept of GLMs to unify a wide variety of statistical methods. Ordinary regression models as well as models for discrete data (Chapter 15) are special cases of one highly general model. In fact, the same fitting method yields parameter estimates for all GLMs. Using GLM software, there is tremendous flexibility and power in the model-building process. You pick a probability distribution that is most appropriate for $y$. For instance, you might select the normal option for a continuous response or the binomial option for a binary response. You specify the variables that are the predictors. Finally, you pick the link function, determining which function of the mean to model. The appendix provides examples.

The next chapter introduces the most important GLM for binary response variables—the *logistic regression* model. The next subsection shows the use of GLMs for data with nonconstant variation, and the final section of the chapter shows a GLM for modeling the log link of the mean as a way of handling nonlinearity.

### GLMs for a Response Assuming a Gamma Distribution

For Example 14.2, on selling prices of homes, Figure 14.4 (page 452) showed a tendency for greater variability at higher home size values. Small homes show little variability in selling price, whereas large homes show high variability. Large homes are the ones that tend to have higher selling prices, so variability in $y$ increases as its mean increases.

This phenomenon often happens for positive-valued response variables. When the mean response is near 0, less variation occurs than when the mean response is high. For such data, least squares is not optimal. It is identical to maximum likelihood for a GLM in which $y$ is assumed to have a normal distribution with the same standard deviation $\sigma$ at all values of predictors.

An alternative approach for data of this form assumes a distribution for $y$ for which the standard deviation increases as the mean increases (i.e., that permits *heteroscedasticity*). The family of **gamma distributions** has this property. Its standard deviation increases proportionally to the mean: When the mean doubles, the standard deviation doubles. The gamma distribution is concentrated on the positive part of the line. It exhibits skewness to the right, like the chi-squared distribution, which is a special case of the gamma. (Technically, GLMs use the gamma family that has a constant *shape* parameter determining the shape of the distribution. Software estimates this parameter. SPSS reports the inverse of the estimated shape parameter. It refers to it as a *scale* parameter, terminology that conflicts with what's called the scale parameter in other sources.)

With GLMs, you can fit a regression model assuming a gamma distribution for $y$ instead of a normal distribution. Even if the data are close to normal, this alternative fit is more appropriate than the least squares fit when the standard deviation increases proportionally to the mean.

### EXAMPLE 14.5    Gamma GLM for Home Selling Price

The least squares fit of the model to the data on $y$ = selling price using predictors size of home, taxes, and whether new, discussed in Example 14.1 (page 443), is

$$\hat{y} = -21,353.8 + 61.7(\text{SIZE}) + 46,373.7(\text{NEW}) + 37.2(\text{TAXES}).$$

However, Example 14.2 (page 449) showed that two outlying observations had a substantial effect on the NEW estimate. Figure 14.4 showed that the variability in selling prices seems to increase as its mean does. This suggests that a model assuming a gamma distribution may be more appropriate. For the gamma distribution, the standard deviation increases as the mean does.

We can use software[2] to fit the GLM assuming a gamma distribution for $y$. For the GLM fit of the same model form, but assuming a gamma distribution, we get

$$\hat{y} = -940.0 + 48.7(\text{SIZE}) + 32,868.0(\text{NEW}) + 37.9(\text{TAXES}).$$

The estimated effect of TAXES is similar, but the estimated effect of SIZE is weaker and the estimated effect of NEW is much weaker. Moreover, the effect of NEW is no longer significant, as the ratio of the estimate to the standard error is 1.53. This result is similar to what Example 14.3 (page 453) obtained after deleting observation 6, an outlier corresponding to a large, new house with an unusually high selling price. The outliers are not as influential for the gamma fit, because that model expects more variability in the data when the mean is larger.

SPSS reports a scale parameter estimate of 0.0707. The larger this value, the greater the degree of skew in the gamma distributions estimated for the model. The estimated standard deviation $\hat{\sigma}$ of the conditional distribution of $Y$ relates to the estimated conditional mean $\hat{\mu}$ by

$$\hat{\sigma} = \sqrt{\text{scale}}\,\hat{\mu} = \sqrt{0.0707}\,\hat{\mu} = 0.266\hat{\mu}.$$

For example, at predictor values such that the estimated mean selling price is $\hat{\mu} = \$100,000$, the estimated standard deviation of selling prices is $\hat{\sigma} = 0.266(\$100,000) = \$26,600$. By contrast, at predictor values such that $\hat{\mu} = \$400,000$, $\hat{\sigma} = 0.266(\$400,000) = \$106,400$, four times as large. (SAS identifies the scale parameter as the

---

[2]Such as the Generalized Linear Models option in the Analyze menu of SPSS, or PROC GENMOD in SAS.

inverse of what SPSS does, so it reports an estimated scale parameter of $1/0.0707 = 14.14$. The parameter that SAS estimates is actually the ***shape parameter*** for the gamma distribution. So, with SAS, you use $\hat{\sigma} = \hat{\mu}/\sqrt{\text{scale}} = \hat{\mu}/\sqrt{14.14}$.) ∎

The traditional method of dealing with variability that increases with the mean is to transform the data, applying the log or square root to the $y$-values. Then the variability is more nearly constant, and least squares works well. There is a fundamental flaw with this approach. If the original relationship is linear, it is no longer linear after applying the transformation. If we fit a straight line and then transform back to the original scale, the fit is no longer linear. Although this approach is still used in many statistical methods textbooks, the gamma GLM approach is more elegant and preferable because of maintaining the linear relationship. Another approach that is preferable to transforming the data is the use of ***weighted least squares***, which gives more weight to observations over regions that show less variability. For further details about generalized linear models, see Gill (2000) and King (1989).

## 14.5 NONLINEAR RELATIONSHIPS: POLYNOMIAL REGRESSION

The ordinary regression model assumes that relationships are linear. The multiple regression model assumes that the partial relationship between the mean of $y$ and each quantitative explanatory variable is linear, controlling for other explanatory variables. Although social science relationships are not *exactly* linear, the degree of nonlinearity is often so minor that they can be reasonably well approximated with linear equations.

Occasionally, though, such a model is inadequate, even for approximation. A scatterplot may reveal a highly nonlinear relationship. Alternatively, the theoretical formulation of an expected relationship might predict a nonlinear relationship. For example, you might expect $y$ = annual medical expenses to have a curvilinear relationship with $x$ = age, being relatively high for the very young and the very old but lower for older children and young adults (Figure 14.5a). The relationship between $x$ = per capita income and $y$ = life expectancy for a sample of countries might be approximately a linearly increasing one, up to a certain point. However, beyond a certain level, additional income would probably result in little, if any, improvement in life expectancy (Figure 14.5b).

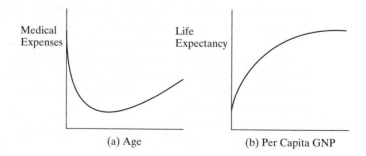

FIGURE 14.5: Two Nonlinear Relationships

Undesirable consequences may result from using straight line regression to describe relationships that are curvilinear. Measures of association designed for linearity, such as the correlation, may underestimate the true association. Estimates of the mean of $y$ at various $x$-values may be badly biased, since the prediction line may poorly approximate the true regression curve. This section and the following one present ways of modeling nonlinear relationships.

Two approaches are commonly used. The first of these uses a *polynomial* regression function. The class of polynomial functions includes a diverse set of functional patterns, including straight lines. The second approach uses a generalized linear model with a link function such as the logarithm. For example, for certain curvilinear relationships, the logarithm of the mean of the response variable is linearly related to the explanatory variables. The final section of the chapter discusses this second approach.

### Quadratic Regression Models

A ***polynomial regression function*** for a response variable $y$ and single explanatory variable $x$ has form

$$E(y) = \alpha + \beta_1 x + \beta_2 x^2 + \cdots + \beta_k x^k.$$

In this model, $x$ occurs in powers from the first ($x = x^1$) to some integer $k$. For $k = 1$, this is the straight line $E(y) = \alpha + \beta_1 x$. The index $k$, the highest power in the polynomial equation, is called the ***degree*** of the polynomial function.

The polynomial function most commonly used for nonlinear relationships is the *second-degree polynomial*

$$E(y) = \alpha + \beta_1 x + \beta_2 x^2.$$

This is called a ***quadratic regression model***. The graph of this function is parabolic, as Figure 14.6 portrays. It has a single bend, either increasing and then decreasing or else decreasing and then increasing. The shape of the parabolic curve is symmetric about a vertical axis, with its appearance when increasing a mirror image of its appearance when decreasing.

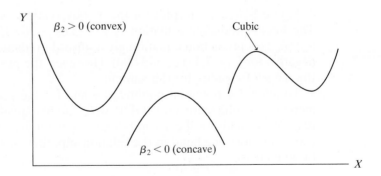

**FIGURE 14.6:** Graphs of Two Second-Degree Polynomials (Quadratic Functions) and a Third-Degree Polynomial (Cubic Function)

If a scatterplot reveals a pattern of points with one bend, then a second-degree polynomial usually improves upon the straight line fit. A third-degree polynomial $E(y) = \alpha + \beta_1 x + \beta_2 x^2 + \beta_3 x^3$, called a ***cubic function***, is a curvilinear function having *two* bends. See Figure 14.6. In general, a $k$th-degree polynomial has $(k - 1)$ bends. Of the polynomial models, the linear and quadratic equations are most useful. Rarely is it necessary to use higher than a second-degree polynomial to describe the trend.

**EXAMPLE 14.6    Fertility Predicted Using Gross Domestic Product (GDP)**

Table 14.6 shows values reported by the United Nations in 2005 for several nations on $y$ = fertility rate (the mean number of children per adult woman) and $x$ = per capita gross domestic product (GDP, in dollars). Fertility tends to decrease as GDP increases. However, a straight line model may be inadequate, since it might predict negative fertility for sufficiently high GDP. In addition, some demographers predict that after GDP passes a certain level, fertility rate may increase, since the nation's wealth makes it easier for a parent to stay home and take care of children rather than work. In the following model fitting, we will measure GDP in tens of thousands of dollars (e.g., for the U.S., 3.7648 rather than 37,648) to make the coefficients more interpretable.

**TABLE 14.6:** Data on Fertility Rate and Per Capita Gross Domestic Product GDP (in Dollars)

| Nation | GDP | Fertility Rate | Nation | GDP | Fertility Rate | Nation | GDP | Fertility Rate |
|---|---|---|---|---|---|---|---|---|
| Algeria | 2090 | 2.5 | Germany | 29115 | 1.3 | Pakistan | 555 | 4.3 |
| Argentina | 3524 | 2.4 | Greece | 15608 | 1.3 | Philippines | 989 | 3.2 |
| Australia | 26275 | 1.7 | India | 564 | 3.1 | Russia | 3018 | 1.3 |
| Austria | 31289 | 1.4 | Iran | 2066 | 2.1 | S Africa | 3489 | 2.8 |
| Belgium | 29096 | 1.7 | Ireland | 38487 | 1.9 | Saudi Ar. | 9532 | 4.1 |
| Brazil | 2788 | 2.3 | Israel | 16481 | 2.9 | Spain | 20404 | 1.3 |
| Canada | 27079 | 1.5 | Japan | 33713 | 1.3 | Sweden | 33676 | 1.6 |
| Chile | 4591 | 2.0 | Malaysia | 4187 | 2.9 | Switzerland | 43553 | 1.4 |
| China | 1100 | 1.7 | Mexico | 6121 | 2.4 | Turkey | 3399 | 2.5 |
| Denmark | 39332 | 1.8 | Netherlands | 31532 | 1.7 | UK | 30253 | 1.7 |
| Egypt | 1220 | 3.3 | New Zealand | 19847 | 2.0 | US | 37648 | 2.0 |
| Finland | 31058 | 1.7 | Nigeria | 428 | 5.8 | Viet Nam | 482 | 2.3 |
| France | 29410 | 1.9 | Norway | 48412 | 1.8 | Yemen | 565 | 6.2 |

*Source*: *Human Development Report, 2005* available at hdr.undp.org/statistics/data

Figure 14.7, a scatterplot for the 39 observations, shows a clear decreasing trend. The linear prediction equation is $\hat{y} = 3.04 - 0.415x$, and the correlation equals $-0.56$. This prediction equation gives absurd predictions for very large $x$-values; $\hat{y}$ is negative for $x > 7.3$ (i.e., $73,000$). However, the predicted values are positive over the range of $x$-values for this sample.

To allow for potential nonlinearity and for the possibility that fertility rate may increase for sufficiently large GDP, we could fit a quadratic regression model to these data. We would use the second-degree polynomial, rather than higher, because we expect at most one bend in the relationship, that is, a decrease followed potentially by an increase. ∎

**Interpreting and Fitting Quadratic Regression Models**

The quadratic regression model

$$E(y) = \alpha + \beta_1 x + \beta_2 x^2$$

plotted for the possible values of $\alpha, \beta_1$, and $\beta_2$ describes the possible parabolic shapes. Unlike straight lines, for which the slope remains constant over all $x$-values, the mean change in $y$ for a one-unit increase in $x$ *depends on the value of $x$*. For example, a straight line drawn tangent to the parabola in Figure 14.8 has positive slope for small values of $x$, zero slope where the parabola achieves its maximum value, and negative

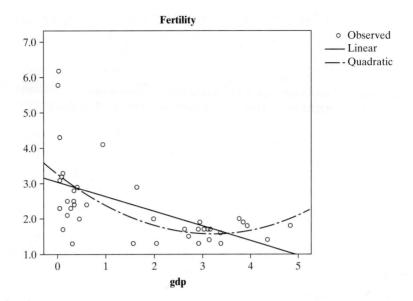

**FIGURE 14.7:** Scatterplot and Best-Fitting Straight Line and Second-Degree Polynomial for Data on Fertility Rate and Per Capita GDP

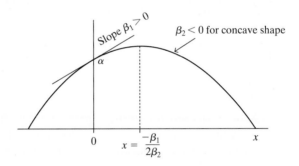

**FIGURE 14.8:** Interpretation of Parameters of Second-Degree Polynomial $E(y) = \alpha + \beta_1 x + \beta_2 x^2$

slope for large values of $x$. The rate of change of the line varies to produce a curve having a smooth bend.

The sign of the coefficient $\beta_2$ of the $x^2$-term determines whether the function is bowl shaped (opens up) relative to the $x$-axis or mound shaped (opens down). Bowl-shaped functions (also called *convex* functions) have $\beta_2 > 0$. Mound-shaped functions (also called *concave* functions) have $\beta_2 < 0$. See Figure 14.8.

As usual, the coefficient $\alpha$ is the $y$-intercept. The coefficient $\beta_1$ of $x$ is the slope of the line that is tangent to the parabola as it crosses the $y$ axis. If $\beta_1 > 0$, for example, then the parabola is sloping upward at $x = 0$ (as Figure 14.8 shows). At the point at which the slope is zero, the relationship changes direction from positive to negative or from negative to positive. This happens at $x = -\beta_1/(2\beta_2)$. This is the $x$-value at which the mean of $y$ takes its maximum if the parabola is mound-shaped and its minimum if it is bowl shaped.

To fit quadratic regression models, we treat them as a special case of the multiple regression model

$$E(y) = \alpha + \beta_1 x_1 + \beta_2 x_2 = \alpha + \beta_1 x + \beta_2 x^2$$

with two explanatory variables. We identify $x_1$ with the explanatory variable $x$ and $x_2$ with its square, $x^2$. The data for the model fit consist of the $y$-values for the subjects in the sample, the $x$-values (called $x_1$), and an artificial variable ($x_2$) consisting of the squares of the $x$-values. Software can create these squared values for us. It then uses least squares to find the best fitting function out of the class of all second-degree polynomials.

### EXAMPLE 14.7 Quadratic Regression for Fertility and GDP

Table 14.7 shows part of a printout for the quadratic regression of $y$ = fertility rate on $x$ = GDP. Here, GDP2 denotes an artificial variable constructed as the square of GDP. The prediction equation is

$$\hat{y} = 3.28 - 1.054x + 0.163x^2.$$

Figure 14.7 plots the linear and quadratic prediction equations in the scatter diagram. Since the coefficient 0.163 of $x^2$ is positive, the graph is bowl shaped (convex). Also, since the coefficient $-1.054$ of $x$ is negative, the curve is decreasing as it crosses the $y$-axis.

**TABLE 14.7:** Part of Printout for Second-Degree Polynomial Model for $y$ = Fertility Rate and $x$ = GDP

| Variable | B | Std. Error | t | Sig |
|----------|------|------------|---------|------|
| INTERCEP | 3.278 | .257 | 12.750 | .000 |
| GDP | −1.054 | 0.366 | −2.880 | .007 |
| GDP2 | .163 | 0.090 | 1.810 | .079 |
| | | | | |
| R-square | 0.375 | | | |

A bowl-shaped quadratic equation takes its minimum at $x = -\beta_1/(2\beta_2)$. For these data, we estimate this point to be $x = 1.054/[2(0.163)] = 3.23$. The predicted fertility rate increases as GDP increases above this point (i.e., \$32,300). ∎

### Description and Inference about the Nonlinear Effect

For a polynomial model, $R^2$ for multiple regression describes the strength of the association. In this context, it describes the proportional reduction in error obtained from using the polynomial model, instead of $\bar{y}$, to predict $y$. Comparing this measure to $r^2$ for the straight line model indicates how much better a fit the curvilinear model provides. Since the polynomial model has additional terms besides $x$, $R^2$ always is at least as large as $r^2$. The difference $R^2 - r^2$ measures the additional reduction in prediction error obtained by using the polynomial instead of the straight line.

For Table 14.6, the best-fitting straight line prediction equation has $r^2 = 0.318$. That line is also plotted in Figure 14.7. From Table 14.7 for the quadratic model, $R^2 = 0.375$. The best quadratic equation explains about 6% more variability in $y$ than does the best-fitting straight line equation.

If $\beta_2 = 0$, the quadratic regression equation $E(y) = \alpha + \beta_1 x + \beta_2 x^2$ reduces to the linear regression equation $E(y) = \alpha + \beta_1 x$. Therefore, to test the null hypothesis that the relationship is linear against the alternative that it is quadratic, we test $H_0: \beta_2 = 0$. The usual $t$ test for a regression coefficient does this, dividing the estimate of $\beta_2$ by its standard error. The assumptions for applying inference are the same as for ordinary regression: randomization for gathering the data, a conditional distribution of $y$-values that is normal about the mean, with constant standard deviation $\sigma$ at all $x$-values.

The set of nations in Table 14.6 is not a random sample of nations, so inference is not relevant. If it had been, the printout in Table 14.7 shows that $t = 0.163/0.090 = 1.81$, with $df = 37$. The P-value for testing $H_0: \beta_2 = 0$ against $H_a: \beta_2 \neq 0$ is $P = 0.08$. In this sense, the quadratic prediction equation apparently provides weak evidence of a better fit than the straight line equation.

### Cautions in Using Polynomial Models

Some cautions are in order before you take the conclusions in this example too seriously. The scatterplot (Figure 14.7) suggests that the variability in fertility rates is considerably higher for nations with low GDPs than it is for nations with high GDPs. The fertility rates show much greater variability when their mean is higher. A GLM that permits nonconstant standard deviation by assuming a gamma distribution for $y$, discussed in Section 14.4, provides somewhat different results, including stronger evidence of nonlinearity (Exercise 14.14).

In fact, before we conclude that fertility rate increases above a certain value, we should realize that other models for which this does not happen are also consistent with these data. For instance, Figure 14.7 suggests that a "piecewise linear" model that has a linear decrease until GDP is about \$25,000 and then a separate, nearly horizontal, line beyond that point fits quite well. A more satisfactory model for these data is one discussed in the next section of this chapter for *exponential regression*. Unless a data set is very large, several models may be consistent with the data.

In examining scatterplots, be cautious not to read too much into the data. Don't let one or two outliers suggest a curve in the trend. Good model building follows the principle of **parsimony**: Models should have no more parameters than necessary to represent the relationship adequately. One reason is that simple models are easier to understand and interpret than complex ones. Another reason is that when a model contains unnecessary variables, the standard errors of the estimates of the regression coefficients tend to inflate, hindering efforts at making precise inferences. Estimates of the conditional mean of $y$ also tend to be poorer than those obtained with well-fitting simple models.

When a polynomial regression model is valid, the regression coefficients do not have the partial slope interpretation usual for coefficients of multiple regression models. It does not make sense to refer to the change in the mean of $y$ when $x^2$ is increased one unit and $x$ is held constant. Similarly, it does not make sense to interpret the partial correlations $r_{yx^2 \cdot x}$ or $r_{yx \cdot x^2}$ as measures of association, controlling for $x$ or $x^2$. However, the coefficient $r^2_{yx^2 \cdot x}$ does measure the proportion of the variation in $y$ unaccounted for by the straight line model that is explained by the quadratic model. In Example 14.6 (page 464), applying the formula for $r^2_{yx_2 \cdot x_1}$ from Section 11.7 yields

$$r^2_{yx^2 \cdot x} = \frac{R^2 - r^2_{yx}}{1 - r^2_{yx}} = \frac{0.375 - 0.318}{1 - 0.318} = 0.08.$$

Of the variation in $y$ unexplained by the linear model, about 8% is explained by the introduction of the quadratic term.

Nonlinear relationships are also possible when there are several explanatory variables. For example, the model

$$E(y) = \alpha + \beta_1 x_1 + \beta_2 x_2 + \beta_3 x_2^2$$

allows nonlinearity in $x_2$. For fixed $x_1$, the mean of $y$ is a quadratic function of $x_2$. For fixed $x_2$, the mean of $y$ is a linear function of $x_1$ with slope $\beta_1$. This model is a special case of multiple regression with three explanatory variables, in which $x_3$ is the square of $x_2$. Models allowing both nonlinearity and interaction are also possible.

### Nonparametric Regression*

Recent advances make it possible to fit models to data without assuming particular functional forms, such as straight lines or parabolas, for the relationship. These approaches are *nonparametric*, in terms of having fewer (if any) assumptions about the functional form and the distribution of $y$. It is helpful to look at a plot of a fitted nonparametric regression model to learn about trends in the data.

One nonparametric regression method, called ***generalized additive modeling***, is a further generalization of the generalized linear model. It has the form

$$g(\mu) = f_1(x_1) + f_2(x_2) + \cdots + f_k(x_k),$$

where $f_1, \ldots, f_k$ are unspecified and potentially highly complex functions. The GLM is the special case in which each of these functions is linear. The estimated functional form of the relationship for each predictor is determined by a computer algorithm, using the sample data. As in GLMs, with this model you can select a particular link function $g$ and also a distribution for $y$. This model is useful for smoothing data to reveal overall trends.

Nonparametric regression is beyond the scope of this text. At this time, some statistical software do not yet have routines for generalized additive models. Many have related nonparametric smoothing methods that usually provide similar results. Popular smoothers are ***LOESS*** (sometimes also denoted by LOWESS and called "locally weighted scatterplot smoothing") and ***kernel*** methods that get the prediction at a particular point by smoothly averaging nearby values. The smoothed value is found by fitting a low-degree polynomial while giving more weight to observations near the point and less weight to observations further away. You can achieve greater smoothing by choosing a larger *bandwidth*, essentially by letting the weights die out more gradually as you move away from each given point.

Figure 14.9 shows two plots of nonparametric regression fits for the fertility rate data of Table 14.6. The first plot employs greater smoothing and has a curved,

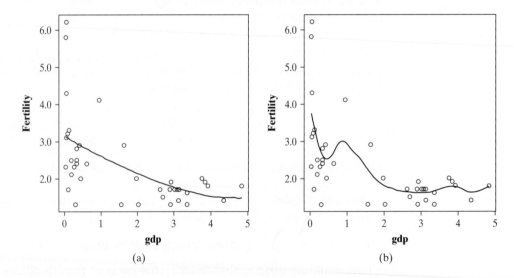

**FIGURE 14.9:** Fits of Nonparametric Regression Model to Smooth the Fertility Rate Data of Table 14.6. Fit (a) employs greater smoothing (bandwidth = 5 in SPSS) than fit (b) (bandwidth = 1 in SPSS).

decreasing trend. It is evident that the response may not eventually increase, as a quadratic model predicts. The next section discusses a model that provides a more satisfactory fit for these data.

## 14.6    EXPONENTIAL REGRESSION AND LOG TRANSFORMS*

Although polynomials provide a diverse collection of functions for modeling nonlinearity, other mathematical functions are often more appropriate. The most important case is when the mean of the response variable is an *exponential* function of the explanatory variable.

---

**Exponential Regression Function**

An **exponential regression** function has the form $E(y) = \alpha\beta^x$.

---

In this equation, the explanatory variable appears as the exponent of a parameter. Unlike a quadratic function, an exponential function can take only positive values, and it continually increases (if $\beta > 1$) or continually decreases (if $\beta < 1$). In either case, it has a convex shape, as Figure 14.10 shows. We provide interpretations for the model parameters later in this section.

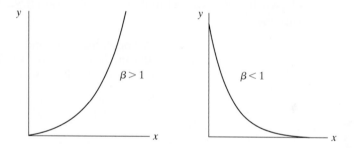

**FIGURE 14.10:** The Exponential Regression Function $E(y) = \alpha\beta^x$

For the exponential regression function, the *logarithm* of the mean is linearly related to the explanatory variable. That is, if $\mu = E(y) = \alpha\beta^x$, then

$$\log(\mu) = \log\alpha + (\log\beta)x.$$

The right-hand side of this equation has the straight line form $\alpha' + \beta'x$ with intercept $\alpha' = \log(\alpha)$ the log of the $\alpha$ parameter and slope $\beta' = \log(\beta)$ the log of the $\beta$ parameter for the exponential regression function. This model form is the special case of a generalized linear model (GLM) using the log link function. If the model holds, a plot of the log of the $y$-values should show approximately a linear relation with $x$. (Don't worry if you have forgotten your high school math about logarithms. You will not need to know this in order to understand how to fit or interpret the exponential regression model.)

It is simple to use GLM software to estimate the parameters in the model $\log[E(y)] = \alpha' + \beta'x$. The antilogs of these estimates are the estimates for the parameters in the exponential regression model $E(y) = \alpha\beta^x$, as shown Example 14.8.

### EXAMPLE 14.8    Exponential Population Growth

Exponential regression is often used to model the growth of a population over time. If the rate of growth remains constant, in percentage terms, then the size of that population grows exponentially fast. Suppose that the population size at some fixed time is $\alpha$ and the growth rate is 2% per year. After 1 year, the population is 2% larger than at the beginning of the year. This means that the population size grows by a multiplicative factor of 1.02 each year. The population size after 1 year is $\alpha(1.02)$. Similarly, the population size after 2 years is

$$(\text{Population size at end of 1 year})(1.02) = [\alpha(1.02)]1.02 = \alpha(1.02)^2.$$

After 3 years, the population size is $\alpha(1.02)^3$. After $x$ years, the population size is $\alpha(1.02)^x$. The population size after $x$ years follows an exponential function $\alpha\beta^x$ with parameters given by the initial population size $\alpha$ and the rate of growth factor, $\beta = 1.02$, corresponding to 2% growth.

Table 14.8 shows the U.S. population size (in millions) at 10-year intervals beginning in 1890. Figure 14.11 plots these values over time. Table 14.8 also shows the natural logarithm of the population sizes. (This uses the base $e$, where $e = 2.718\ldots$ is an irrational number that appears often in mathematics. The model makes sense with logs to any base, but software fits the GLM using natural logs, denoted by $\log_e$ or by $LN$.) Figure 14.12 plots these log of population size values over time. The log population sizes appear to grow approximately linearly. This suggests that population growth over this time period was approximately exponential, with a constant rate of growth. We now estimate the regression curve, treating time as the explanatory variable $x$.

**TABLE 14.8**: Population Sizes and Log Population Sizes by Decade from 1890 to 2000, with Predicted Values for Exponential Regression Model

| Year | No. Decades since 1890 $x$ | Population Size $y$ | $\log_e(y)$ | $\hat{y}$ |
|------|------|------|------|------|
| 1890 | 0 | 62.95 | 4.14 | 71.5 |
| 1900 | 1 | 75.99 | 4.33 | 81.1 |
| 1910 | 2 | 91.97 | 4.52 | 92.0 |
| 1920 | 3 | 105.71 | 4.66 | 104.4 |
| 1930 | 4 | 122.78 | 4.81 | 118.5 |
| 1940 | 5 | 131.67 | 4.88 | 134.4 |
| 1950 | 6 | 151.33 | 5.02 | 152.5 |
| 1960 | 7 | 179.32 | 5.19 | 173.0 |
| 1970 | 8 | 203.30 | 5.31 | 196.3 |
| 1980 | 9 | 226.54 | 5.42 | 222.6 |
| 1990 | 10 | 248.71 | 5.52 | 252.6 |
| 2000 | 11 | 281.42 | 5.64 | 286.6 |

*Source*: U.S. Census Bureau.

For convenience, we identify the time points $1890, 1900, \ldots, 2000$ as times $0, 1, \ldots, 11$; that is, $x$ represents the number of decades since 1890. We use software to estimate the generalized linear model $\log(\mu) = \alpha' + \beta'x$, assuming a normal distribution for $y$. The prediction equation, for natural logs, is

$$\log_e(\hat{\mu}) = 4.2698 + 0.1262x.$$

Antilogs of these estimates are the parameter estimates for the exponential regression model. For natural logs, the antilog function is the exponential function $e^x$. That is,

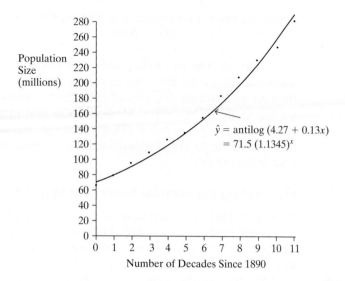

**FIGURE 14.11:** U.S. Population Size since 1890

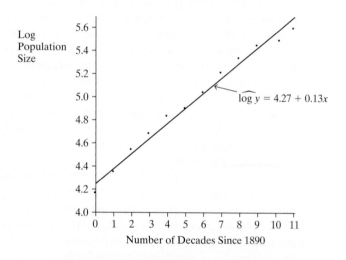

**FIGURE 14.12:** Log Population Sizes since 1890

antilog$(4.2698) = e^{4.2698} = 71.507$, and antilog$(0.1262) = e^{0.1262} = 1.1345$. (Most calculators have an $e^x$ key that provides these antilogs.) Thus, for the exponential regression model $E(y) = \alpha\beta^x$, the estimates are $\hat{\alpha} = 71.507$ and $\hat{\beta} = 1.1345$. The prediction equation is

$$\hat{y} = \hat{\alpha}\hat{\beta}^x = 71.507(1.1345)^x.$$

The predicted initial population size (in 1890) is $\hat{\alpha} = 71.5$ million. The predicted population size $x$ decades after 1890 equals $\hat{y} = 71.507(1.1345)^x$. For 2000, for instance, $x = 11$, and the predicted population size is $\hat{y} = 71.507(1.1345)^{11} = 286.6$ million. Table 14.8 shows the predicted values for each decade. Figure 14.11 plots the exponential prediction equation.

The predictions are quite good. The total sum of squares of population size values about their mean equals TSS $= 55,481$, whereas the sum of squared errors about the prediction equation is $SSE = 275$. The proportional reduction in error is $(55,481 - 275)/55,481 = 0.995$. ∎

A caution: The fit of the model $\log[E(y)] = \alpha' + \beta'x$ that you get with GLM software will *not* be the same as you get by taking logarithms of all the $y$-values and then fitting a straight line model using least squares. The latter approach[3] gives the fit for the model $E[\log(y)] = \alpha' + \beta'x$. For that model, taking antilogs does not take you back to $E(y)$, because $E[\log(y)]$ is not equivalent to $\log[E(y)]$. So in software it is preferable to use a generalized linear modeling option rather than an ordinary regression option.

### Interpreting Exponential Regression Models

Now let's take a closer look at how to interpret parameters in the exponential regression model, $E(y) = \alpha\beta^x$. The parameter $\alpha$ represents the mean of $y$ when $x = 0$. The parameter $\beta$ represents the **multiplicative** change in the mean of $y$ for a one-unit increase in $x$. The mean of $y$ at $x = 10$ equals $\beta$ *multiplied* by the mean of $y$ at $x = 9$. For instance, for the equation $\hat{y} = 71.507(1.1345)^x$, the predicted population size at a particular date equals 1.1345 times the predicted population size a decade earlier.

By contrast, the parameter $\beta$ in the *linear* model $E(y) = \alpha + \beta x$ represents the **additive** change in the mean of $y$ for a one-unit increase in $x$. In the linear model, the mean of $y$ at $x = 10$ equals $\beta$ *plus* the mean of $y$ at $x = 9$. The prediction equation for the linear model (i.e., identity link) fitted to Table 14.8 equals $\hat{y} = 49.56 + 19.50x$. This model predicts that the population size increases by 19.50 million people every decade.

In summary, for the linear model, $E(y)$ changes by the same *quantity* for each one-unit increase in $x$, whereas for the exponential model, $E(y)$ changes by the same *percentage* for each one-unit increase. For the exponential regression model with Table 14.8, the predicted population size is multiplied by 1.1345 each decade. This equation corresponds to a predicted 13.45% growth per decade.

Suppose the growth rate is 15% per decade, to choose a rounder number. This corresponds to a multiplicative factor of 1.15. After five decades, the population grows by a factor of $(1.15)^5 = 2.0$. That is, after five decades, the population size doubles. If the rate of growth remained constant at 15% per decade, the population would double every 50 years. After 100 years, the population size would be quadruple the original size; after 150 years it would be 8 times as large; after 200 years it would be 16 times its original size; and so forth.

The exponential function with $\beta > 1$ has the property that its doubling time is a constant. As can be seen from the sequence of population sizes at 50-year intervals, this is an extremely fast increase even though the annual rate of growth (1.4% annually for a decade increase of 15%) seems small. In fact, the world population has been following an exponential growth pattern, with recent rate of growth over 15% per decade.

### EXAMPLE 14.9 Exponential Regression for Fertility Rate Data

When $\beta < 1$ in the exponential regression model, $\beta' = \log(\beta) < 0$ in the log transformed GLM. In this case, the mean of $y$ *decreases* exponentially fast as $x$ increases. The curve then looks like the second curve in Figure 14.10.

In Example 14.6 with Table 14.6 (page 464), we modeled $y =$ fertility rate for several countries, with $x =$ per capita GDP. The nonparametric regression curve

---

[3]For example, as SPSS would give by selecting *Regression* in the *Analyze* menu, followed by the choice of *Curve Estimation* with the *Exponential* option.

(Figure 14.9) had appearance much like an exponentially decreasing curve. In fact, the exponential regression model provides a good fit for those data. Using the GLM with log link for $y$ = fertility rate and $x$ = per capita GDP and assuming a normal distribution for $y$, we get the prediction equation

$$\log_e(\hat{\mu}) = 1.148 - 0.206x.$$

Taking antilogs yields the exponential prediction equation

$$\hat{y} = \hat{\alpha}\hat{\beta}^x = e^{1.148}(e^{-0.206})^x = 3.15(0.81)^x.$$

The predicted fertility rate at GDP value $x + 1$ equals 81% of the predicted fertility rate at GDP value $x$; that is, it decreases by 19% for a \$10,000 increase in per capita GDP.

   With this fit, the correlation between the observed and predicted fertility rates equals 0.59, nearly as high as the value of 0.61 achieved with the quadratic model, which has an extra parameter. If we expect fertility rate to decrease continuously as GDP increases, the exponential regression model is a more realistic model than the quadratic regression model of Section 14.5, which predicted increasing fertility above a certain GDP level. Also, unlike the straight line model, the exponential regression model cannot yield negative predicted fertility rates.

   Since the scatterplot in Figure 14.7 suggests greater variability when the mean fertility rate is higher, it may be even better to assume a gamma distribution for $y$ with this exponential regression model. The prediction equation is then

$$\log_e(\hat{\mu}) = 1.112 - 0.177x, \quad \text{for which} \quad \hat{y} = e^{1.112}(e^{-0.177})^x = 3.04(0.84)^x.$$

This gives a slightly shallower rate of decrease than the fit $3.15(0.81)^x$ obtained assuming a normal response. ∎

### Transforming the Predictor to Achieve Linearity

Other transformations of the response mean or of explanatory variables are useful in some situations. For example, suppose $y$ tends to increase or decrease over a certain range of $x$-values, but once a certain $x$-value has been reached, further increases in $x$ have less effect on $y$, as in Figure 14.5b. For this concave increasing type of trend, $x$ behaves like an exponential function of $y$. Taking the logarithms of the $x$-values often linearizes the relationship. Another possible transform for this case is to invert the $x$-values (i.e., use $1/x$ as the explanatory variable).

## 14.7  CHAPTER SUMMARY

This chapter discussed issues about building regression models. We have seen how to check assumptions of the basic regression model and how to ease some restrictions of this model.

- When a large number of terms might serve as explanatory variables, the **backward elimination** and **forward selection** procedures use a sequential algorithm to select variables for the model. These are exploratory in purpose and should be used with caution.
- Plots of the **residuals** check whether the model is adequate and whether the assumptions for inferences are reasonable. Observations having a large leverage and large studentized residual have a strong influence on the model fit. The

DFBETA and DFFIT diagnostics describe which observations have a strong influence on the parameter estimates and the model fit.

- *Multicollinearity*, the condition by which the set of explanatory variables contains some redundancies, causes inflation of standard errors of estimated regression coefficients and makes it difficult to evaluate partial effects.

- *Generalized linear models* allow the response variable to have a distribution other than the normal, such as the binomial for binary data and the gamma for positive responses having greater variation at greater mean values. Such models also permit modeling a function of the mean, called the *link function*.

- *Nonlinear* relationships are modeled through the use of *polynomial* (particularly *quadratic*) functions and *exponential* functions. Quadratic functions have a parabolic appearance, whereas exponential functions have a convex increasing or convex decreasing appearance. The *exponential regression model* is a generalized linear model for the log of the mean.

## PROBLEMS

### Practicing the Basics

**14.1.** For Example 11.2 (page 326) on $y$ = mental impairment, $x_1$ = life events, and $x_2$ = SES, Table 11.5 showed the output

| | B | Std. Error | t | Sig. |
|---|---|---|---|---|
| (Constant) | 28.230 | 2.174 | 12.984 | .000 |
| LIFE | .103 | .032 | 3.177 | .003 |
| SES | -.097 | .029 | -3.351 | .002 |

and Table 11.8 showed the output for the interaction model,

| | B | Std. Error | t | Sig |
|---|---|---|---|---|
| (Constant) | 26.036649 | 3.948826 | 6.594 | 0.0001 |
| LIFE | 0.155865 | 0.085338 | 1.826 | 0.0761 |
| SES | -0.060493 | 0.062675 | -0.965 | 0.3409 |
| LIFE*SES | -0.000866 | 0.001297 | -0.668 | 0.5087 |

Table 11.4 showed that SES had $P$-value 0.011 in the bivariate model containing only that predictor,

and Table 11.3 showed that LIFE had $P$-value of 0.018 in the bivariate model containing only that predictor. Select explanatory variables from the set $x_1, x_2, x_3 = x_1x_2$, with $\alpha = 0.05$

(a) Using backward elimination

(b) Using forward selection

**14.2.** Table 11.21 on page 363 showed results of a multiple regression using nine predictors of the quality of life in a country.

(a) In backward elimination with these nine predictors, can you predict which variable would be deleted (i) first? (ii) second? Explain.

(b) In forward selection with these nine predictors, can you predict which variable would be added first? Explain.

**14.3.** For the "house selling price 2" data file at the text Web site, Table 14.9 shows a correlation matrix and a model fit using four predictors of selling price. With these four predictors.

(a) For backward elimination, which variable would be deleted first? Why?

**TABLE 14.9**

Correlation coefficients

| | price | size | beds | baths | new |
|---|---|---|---|---|---|
| price | 1.00000 | 0.89881 | 0.59027 | 0.71370 | 0.35655 |
| size | 0.89881 | 1.00000 | 0.66911 | 0.66248 | 0.17629 |
| beds | 0.59027 | 0.66911 | 1.00000 | 0.33380 | 0.26721 |
| baths | 0.71370 | 0.66248 | 0.33380 | 1.00000 | 0.18207 |
| new | 0.35655 | 0.17629 | 0.26721 | 0.18207 | 1.00000 |

| Variable | Estimate | Std. Error | t | Sig |
|---|---|---|---|---|
| INTERCEP | -41.795 | 12.104 | 3.45 | 0.0009 |
| SIZE | 64.761 | 5.630 | 11.50 | 0.0001 |
| BEDS | -2.766 | 3.960 | 0.70 | 0.4868 |
| BATHS | 19.203 | 5.650 | 3.40 | 0.0010 |
| NEW | 18.984 | 3.873 | 4.90 | 0.0001 |

**(b)** For forward selection, which variable would be added first? Why?

**(c)** Why do you think that BEDS has such a large *P*-value in the multiple regression model, even though it has a substantial correlation with PRICE?

**14.4.** Refer to the previous exercise. Using software with this data file and these four predictors, find the model that would be selected using each of the following criteria: **(a)** $R^2_{adj}$, **(b)** PRESS, **(c)** $C_p$.

**14.5.** Use software with the "statewide crime 2" data file at the text Web site, excluding the observation for D.C. Let $y$ = murder rate. For the five predictors in that data file (excluding violent crime rate), with $\alpha = 0.10$ in tests,

**(a)** Use backward elimination to select a model. Interpret.

**(b)** Use forward selection to select a model. Interpret.

**(c)** Use stepwise regression. Interpret.

**(d)** Compare results of the three selection procedures. How is it possible that a variable (percent with a high school education) can be the first variable dropped in (a) yet the second added in (b)?

**(e)** Now include the D.C. observation. Repeat (a) and (b), and compare to results excluding D.C. What does this suggest about the influence outliers can have on automatic selection procedures?

**14.6.** Figure 14.13 is a plot of the residuals versus the predicted *y*-values for the model discussed

in Example 13.1 (page 416) relating income to education and racial–ethnic group. The numbers indicate the number of cases at each point. What does this plot suggest?

**14.7.** For the 2005 data for the 21 nations in Table 9.13 not missing observations on literacy, Table 14.10 shows a printout of various diagnostics from fitting the multiple regression model relating fertility (mean number of births per woman) to literacy rate and women's economic activity.

**(a)** Study the studentized residuals. Are there any apparent outliers?

**(b)** Which, if any, observations have relatively large leverage values?

**(c)** Based on the answers in (a) and (b), does it seem as if any observations may be especially influential? Explain.

**(d)** Study the DFFIT values. Identify an observation that may have a strong influence on the fitted values.

**(e)** Study the DFBETA values. Identify an observation that is influential for the literacy estimate but not for the economic activity estimate.

**14.8.** For the "2005 statewide crime" data file, fit the linear regression model with $y$ = violent crime rate and $x$ = percent urban for all 51 observations.

**(a)** Plot the studentized residuals. Are there any clear regression outliers?

**(b)** Are there any observations with noticeable leverage?

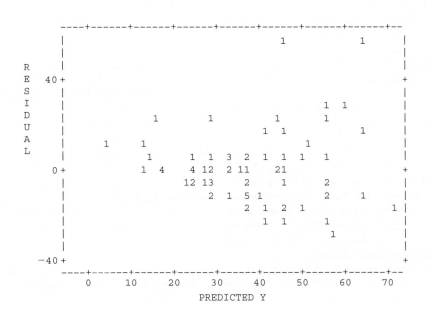

**FIGURE 14.13**

TABLE 14.10

| Obs | Residual | Studentized Residual | Leverage h | DFFIT | DFBETA fem_econ | DFBETA Literacy |
|---|---|---|---|---|---|---|
| 1 | -1.1374 | -1.3088 | 0.0935 | -0.4204 | 0.1989 | 0.0726 |
| 2 | 0.2782 | 0.3216 | 0.1792 | 0.1503 | -0.1001 | 0.1226 |
| 6 | -0.1299 | -0.1424 | 0.0915 | -0.0452 | 0.0235 | -0.0302 |
| 8 | -0.1695 | -0.1921 | 0.1490 | -0.0804 | 0.0496 | -0.0640 |
| 9 | -0.5515 | -0.6682 | 0.2378 | -0.3732 | -0.3215 | 0.1017 |
| 11 | -0.9491 | -1.1198 | 0.1589 | -0.4868 | -0.0620 | 0.3707 |
| 15 | -1.0803 | -1.2174 | 0.0665 | -0.3249 | 0.0285 | -0.1583 |
| 16 | -0.9529 | -1.1093 | 0.1372 | -0.4424 | -0.1055 | 0.3435 |
| 17 | -1.1469 | -1.3358 | 0.1118 | -0.4738 | 0.3516 | -0.1326 |
| 19 | 0.8765 | 0.9912 | 0.0982 | 0.3270 | 0.0799 | 0.1407 |
| 21 | 0.4208 | 0.4559 | 0.0596 | 0.1148 | 0.0142 | 0.0336 |
| 22 | -0.0490 | -0.0543 | 0.1102 | -0.0191 | 0.0119 | -0.0133 |
| 25 | 2.2503 | 3.0631 | 0.0867 | 0.9438 | 0.3476 | -0.6337 |
| 27 | -0.2954 | -0.3522 | 0.2273 | -0.1910 | -0.0300 | 0.1562 |
| 28 | 1.0084 | 1.1396 | 0.0808 | 0.3380 | -0.0232 | 0.1929 |
| 29 | -0.4741 | -0.5551 | 0.1901 | -0.2689 | -0.1750 | -0.0323 |
| 30 | 0.7329 | 0.8843 | 0.2165 | 0.4648 | -0.4057 | 0.1705 |
| 31 | 0.1204 | 0.1292 | 0.0512 | 0.0300 | 0.0015 | 0.0057 |
| 35 | -0.1409 | -0.1517 | 0.0571 | -0.0373 | -0.0119 | -0.0014 |
| 38 | 0.1027 | 0.1294 | 0.3124 | 0.0872 | 0.0780 | -0.0270 |
| 39 | 1.2868 | 1.7217 | 0.2847 | 1.0862 | 0.0098 | -0.8342 |

(c) Based on (a) and (b), does it seem as if any observations may be particularly influential? Explain.

(d) Study the DFFIT values. Which, if any, observations have a strong influence on the fitted values?

(e) Study the DFBETA values. For each term, which if any observations have a strong influence on the parameter estimate?

(f) Remove the observation that seems most influential, and refit the model. Is the prediction equation substantively different in any way?

14.9. In Exercise 14.3, backward elimination and forward selection choose the model with predictors SIZE, BATHS, and NEW.

(a) Fit this model with the "house selling price 2" data set. Inspect the leverages, DFFIT, and DFBETA values for SIZE. Refit the model without the three highly influential observations. Compare the prediction equation, standard errors, and $R^2$ to the fit for the complete data set. Summarize the influence of the influential observations.

(b) For this model, report the VIF values. Interpret them, and indicate whether the degree of multicollinearity is severe.

14.10. For the "house selling price 2" data file, fit the model to y = selling price (in thousands of dollars) using house size (in thousands of square feet), whether the house is new, and their interaction.

(a) Show that the interaction term is highly significant.

(b) Show that observation 5 is highly influential in affecting the fit in (a).

(c) Show that the interaction effect is not significant when observation 5 is removed from the data set.

(d) Now fit the model in (a) using a GLM assuming a gamma distribution for y. Note how the estimated interaction effect differs considerably from that in (a), and note that is not significant. (Observation 5, highly influential for ordinary least squares, is not so influential in this analysis. See also Exercise 13.22.)

14.11. Three variables have population correlations $\rho_{x_1 x_2} = 0.85$, $\rho_{yx_1} = 0.65$, and $\rho_{yx_2} = 0.65$. For these, the partial correlations are $\rho_{yx_1 \cdot x_2} = \rho_{yx_2 \cdot x_1} = 0.244$. In a sample, $r_{x_1 x_2} = 0.90$, $r_{yx_1} = 0.70$ and $r_{yx_2} = 0.60$, not far from the population values. For these, the sample partial correlations are $r_{yx_1 \cdot x_2} = 0.46$ and $r_{yx_2 \cdot x_1} = -0.10$. What does this large difference suggest about standard errors of partial correlations when multicollinearity exists? (An unwary observer might conclude that the partial effects of $x_1$ and $x_2$ have opposite signs and that the partial effect of $x_1$ is much stronger, when they are identical in the population.)

**14.12.** $y$ = height, $x_1$ = length of left leg, and $x_2$ = length of right leg are measured for 100 adults. The model $E(y) = \alpha + \beta_1 x_1 + \beta_2 x_2$ is fitted to the data, and neither $H_0: \beta_1 = 0$ nor $H_0: \beta_2 = 0$ have $P$-values below 0.05.
  **(a)** Does this imply that length of leg is not a good predictor of height? Why?
  **(b)** Does this imply that $H_0: \beta_1 = \beta_2 = 0$ would not have a $P$-value below 0.05? Why?
  **(c)** Suppose $r_{yx_1} = 0.901$, $r_{yx_2} = 0.902$, and $r_{x_1 x_2} = 0.999$. Using forward selection and the potential predictors $x_1$ and $x_2$ with $\alpha = 0.05$ for tests, which model would be selected? Why?

**14.13.** Refer to the plot of residuals in Figure 14.13 for Exercise 14.6.
  **(a)** Explain why a more valid fit may result from assuming that income has a gamma distribution, rather than a normal distribution.
  **(b)** Table 14.11 shows results for the normal GLM and the gamma GLM. Summarize how results differ for the two models.
  **(c)** Interpret the scale parameter estimate by estimating the standard deviation of income when its conditional mean is (i) 20, (ii) 50 thousand dollars.

**14.14.** Refer to the data from Example 14.6 on fertility rates and GDP (page 464). To allow for greater variation at higher values of mean fertility, fit a quadratic GLM with a gamma distribution for fertility rate and the identity link function. Find the GDP value at which predicted fertility rate takes its minimum value. Compare estimates and their significance to those using least squares.

**14.15.** Table 14.12 shows the results of fitting two models to 54 observations on $y$ = mental health score, $x_1$ = degree of social interaction, and $x_2$ = SES. The variables $x_1$ and $x_2$ are measured on scales of 0–100, and larger $y$-scores represent better mental health. The variable symbol x1**2 represents $x_1^2$, and x1 * x2 represents $x_1 x_2$.
  **(a)** When model 1 is fitted, which best describes the result over the range 0–100 of $x_1$-values?

i) $\hat{y}$ is a bowl-shaped function of $x_1$, first decreasing and then increasing.
ii) $\hat{y}$ is an increasing bowl-shaped function of $x_1$.
iii) $\hat{y}$ is a mound-shaped function of $x_1$, first increasing and then decreasing.
iv) $\hat{y}$ is an increasing mound-shaped function of $x_1$.

  **(b)** When model 2 is fitted, which best describes the result over the observed ranges?
i) $\hat{y}$ is a linear function of $x_1$ with positive slope that is the same for all $x_2$.
ii) $\hat{y}$ is a linear function of $x_1$ with positive slope for some values of $x_2$ and negative slope for others.
iii) $\hat{y}$ is a linear function of $x_1$ with positive slope, but the magnitude of that slope is smaller for larger values of $x_2$.
iv) $\hat{y}$ is a quadratic function of $x_1$ and $x_2$.

**TABLE 14.12**

| Model | Variable | Estimate | Model | Variable | Estimate |
|---|---|---|---|---|---|
| 1. | Intercept | 15 | 2. | Intercept | 16 |
| | x1 | 0.200 | | x1 | 0.07 |
| | x1**2 | −.001 | | x2 | 0.04 |
| | | | | x1*x2 | −.0006 |

**14.16.** Sketch the following mathematical functions on the same set of axes, for values of $x$ between 0 and 4. Use these curves to describe how the coefficients of $x$ and $x^2$ affect their shape.
  **(a)** $\hat{y} = 10 + 4x$  **(b)** $\hat{y} = 10 + 4x + x^2$
  **(c)** $\hat{y} = 10 + 4x - x^2$  **(d)** $\hat{y} = 10 - 4x$
  **(e)** $\hat{y} = 10 - 4x + x^2$  **(f)** $\hat{y} = 10 - 4x - x^2$

**14.17.** For the "house selling price" data file, Table 14.13 shows results of fitting the quadratic regression model.
  **(a)** Interpret the coefficients of this equation. What shape does it have?
  **(b)** Find the predicted selling price for homes with (i) $s$ = 1000 square feet, (ii) $s$ = 2000 square

**TABLE 14.11**

| | NORMAL GLM | | | GAMMA GLM | | |
|---|---|---|---|---|---|---|
| Parameter | B | se | Sig | B | se | Sig |
| Intercept | −15.663 | 8.412 | .066 | −1.927 | 5.169 | .709 |
| education | 4.432 | .619 | .000 | 3.289 | .412 | .000 |
| [race = b] | −10.874 | 4.473 | .017 | −8.905 | 2.842 | .002 |
| [race = h] | −4.934 | 4.763 | .304 | −5.953 | 3.187 | .062 |
| [race = w] | 0 | . | . | 0 | . | . |
| (Scale) | | | | .117 | | |

feet, (iii) $s = 3000$ square feet. Explain why the effect of a 1000-square-foot increase in $s$ increases as $s$ increases.

**TABLE 14.13**

| Variable | Estimate | Std. Error | t | Sig |
|---|---|---|---|---|
| Intercept | 5507.551 | 35626.650 | .155 | .877 |
| size | 65.156 | 36.289 | 1.795 | .076 |
| size*size | .014 | .008 | 1.740 | .085 |

**14.18.** Refer to the previous exercise.
  (a) Using size as a straight line predictor, $r^2 = 0.695$, whereas $R^2 = 0.704$ for the quadratic model. Is the degree of nonlinearity major or minor? Is the linear association strong, or weak?
  (b) Test whether the quadratic model gives a significantly better fit than the straight line model. Interpret.

**14.19.** The "statewide crime 2" data file at the text Web site illustrates how a single observation can be highly influential in determining whether the model should allow nonlinearity.
  (a) With all 51 observations, fit the quadratic model between $y$ = murder rate and $x$ = percentage in poverty. Test whether the quadratic term is needed. Report the $P$-value, and interpret.
  (b) Refit the model, deleting the observation for D.C. Report the $P$-value for testing the quadratic term, and interpret.
  (c) Compare (a) and (b), and use the scatterplot to explain how a single observation can have a large impact on whether the quadratic term seems needed. Show how you would be warned of this by influence diagnostics for the fit in (a).

**14.20.** For data from 1995 to 2001 on $y$ number of people (in millions) worldwide using the Internet, the prediction equation $\hat{y} = 20.34(1.77)^x$ fits well, where $x$ = number of years since 1995.
  (a) Predict the number using the Internet in (i) 1995 (take $x = 0$), (ii) 2001.
  (b) Interpret the estimate 1.77.
  (c) Illustrate the dangers of extrapolation, by predicting $y$ in 2010.
  (d) The straight line model fitted to the data gives $\hat{y} = -51 + 81x$. Explain why this model is inappropriate for these data.

**14.21.** For data between October 2002 and September 2006 given in the article "Wikipedia: Modelling Wikipedia's growth" at en.wikipedia.org, the number of English-language articles in Wikipedia was well approximated by $\hat{y} = 100,000(2.1)^x$, where $x$ is the time (in years) since January 1, 2003.

  (a) Interpret the values 100,000 and 2.1 in this prediction equation.
  (b) If this equation continues to hold, predict the number of English Wikipedia articles in (i) January 1, 2008, (ii) January 1, 2013. What is the danger of doing extrapolation such as in (ii)?

**14.22.** For United Nations data on $y$ = world population size (billions) between 1900 and 2000, the exponential regression model with $x$ = number of years since 1900 gives $\hat{y} = 1.4193(1.014)^x$.
  (a) Explain why the model fit corresponds to a rate of growth of 1.4% per year.
  (b) Show that the predicted population size (i) doubles after 50 years, (ii) quadruples after 100 years.
  (c) The correlation equals 0.948 between $y$ and $x$ and 0.985 between $\log(y)$ and $x$. Based on this, which model seems more appropriate? Why?

**14.23.** Draw rough sketches of the following mathematical functions on the same set of axes, for $x$ between 0 and 35.
  (a) $\hat{y} = 6(1.02)^x$. ($\hat{y}$ = predicted world population size in billions $x$ years from now, if there is a 2% rate of growth every year.)
  (b) $\hat{y} = 6(0.95)^x$. (What does this represent?)
  (c) Use these plots to explain the effect of whether $\beta > 1$ or $\beta < 1$ in the model $E(y) = \alpha\beta^x$.

**14.24.** Consider the formula $\hat{y} = 4(2)^x$.
  (a) Plot $\hat{y}$ for integer $x$ between 0 and 5.
  (b) Plot $\log_e \hat{y}$ against $x$. Report the intercept and slope of this line.

**14.25.** For white men in the United States, Table 14.14 presents the number of deaths per thousand individuals of a fixed age within a period of a year.
  (a) Plot $x$ = age against $y$ = death rate and against $\log y$. What do these plots suggest about a good model for the relationship?
  (b) Find the correlation between (i) $x$ and $y$, (ii) $x$ and $\log(y)$. What do these suggest about an appropriate model?
  (c) Using generalized linear models, find the prediction equation for the model $\log[E(y)] = \alpha + \beta x$.
  (d) Find the prediction equation for $\hat{y}$. Interpret the parameter estimates.

**TABLE 14.14**

| Age | Death Rate (per thousand) |
|---|---|
| 30 | 3 |
| 40 | 6 |
| 50 | 14 |
| 60 | 27 |
| 70 | 60 |
| 80 | 125 |

**14.26.** Consider the fertility and GDP data in Table 14.6 on page 464.
  **(a)** Using GLM software, fit the exponential regression model, assuming fertility rate has a (i) normal, (ii) gamma distribution. Interpret the effect of GDP on fertility rate for the gamma fit.
  **(b)** What advantages does the exponential regression model have over the quadratic model?

## Concepts and Applications

**14.27.** Refer to the "Student survey" data file (Exercise 1.11).
  **(a)** Conduct and interpret a regression analysis using $y$ = political ideology, selecting predictors from the variables in that file. Prepare a report describing the research question(s) posed, analyses and diagnostic checks that you conducted, and indicate how you selected a final model. Interpret results.
  **(b)** Repeat the analysis, using $y$ = college GPA.

**14.28.** Refer to the data file the class created in Exercise 1.12. Select a response variable, pose a research question, and build a model using other variables in the data set. Interpret and summarize your findings.

**14.29.** Analyze the "2005 statewide crime" data set at the text Web site, deleting the observation for D.C., with $y$ = violent crime rate. Use methods of this chapter. Prepare a report describing the analyses and diagnostic checks that you conducted, and indicate how you selected a model. Interpret results.

**14.30.** Refer to Table 11.1 and Example 11.2 (page 326). Conduct an analysis of residuals and influence diagnostics for the model predicting mental impairment using life events and SES, using the "mental impairment" data file at the text website.

**14.31.** Table 14.15 shows population size of Florida, by decade, from 1830 to 2000. Analyze these data.

**TABLE 14.15**

| Year | Population | Year | Population |
|------|-----------|------|-----------|
| 1830 | 34,730    | 1920 | 968,470   |
| 1840 | 54,477    | 1930 | 1,468,211 |
| 1850 | 87,445    | 1940 | 1,897,414 |
| 1860 | 140,424   | 1950 | 2,771,305 |
| 1870 | 187,748   | 1960 | 4,951,560 |
| 1880 | 269,493   | 1970 | 6,791,418 |
| 1890 | 391,422   | 1980 | 9,746,324 |
| 1900 | 528,542   | 1990 | 12,937,926 |
| 1910 | 752,619   | 2000 | 15,982,378 |

*Source*: U.S. Census Bureau.

**14.32.** Consider the "UN data" file at the text Web site. Using methods presented in this chapter,
  **(a)** Find a good model relating $x$ = per capita GDP to $y$ = life expectancy. (*Hint*: What does a plot of the data suggest?)
  **(b)** Find a good prediction equation for $y$ = fertility. Explain how you selected variables for the model.

**14.33.** Give an example of a response variable and a pair of explanatory variables for which an automated variable selection procedure would probably produce a model with only one predictor. Explain.

**14.34.** A sociologist's first reaction upon studying automated variable selection routines was that they had the danger of leading to "crass empiricism" in theory building. From a theoretical perspective, describe the dangers with such methods. What guidelines would you suggest for avoiding these problems?

**14.35.** Give an example of two variables you expect to have a nonlinear relationship. Describe the pattern you expect for the relationship, and explain how to model that pattern.

**14.36.** You plan to model coital frequency in the previous month as a function of age, for a sample of subjects with ages between 20 and 90. For the ordinary bivariate model, explain what might be inappropriate about the (a) constant standard deviation assumption, (b) straight line assumption. State a model that you think might be more valid. (See DeMaris [2004, p. 204] for a data set with these variables.)

**14.37.** Using the formula $s/s_j\sqrt{(n-1)(1-R_j^2)}$ for the standard error of the estimator of $\beta_j$ in multiple regression, explain how precision of estimation is affected by
  **(a)** Multicollinearity
  **(b)** The conditional variability of the response variable
  **(c)** The variability of the explanatory variables
  **(d)** The sample size

**14.38.** A recent newpaper article quoted a planner in a Florida city as saying, "This city has been growing at the rate of 4.2% per year. That's not slow growth by any means. It corresponds to 42% growth per decade." Explain what is incorrect about this statement. If, in fact, the current population size of the city is 100,000 and in each of the next 10 years the city increases in size by 4.2% relative to the previous year, then
  **(a)** What is the population size after a decade?
  **(b)** What percentage growth occurs for the decade?

**14.39.** Example 14.8 showed a predicted U.S. population size (in millions) $x$ decades after 1890 of $\hat{y} = 71.51(1.1345)^x$.
  (a) Show this is equivalent to 1.27% predicted growth *per year*. [*Hint*: $(1.0127)^{10} = 1.1345$.]
  (b) Explain why the predicted U.S. population size $x$ *years* after 1890 is $71.51(1.0127)^x$.

**14.40.** You invest $1000 in a savings account with interest compounded annually at 10%.
  (a) How much money do you have after $x$ years?
  (b) How long does it take your savings to double in size?

*For multiple choice problems 14.41–14.44, select the correct response(s).*

**14.41.** In the model $E(y) = \alpha + \beta_1 x + \beta_2 x^2$, the coefficient $\beta_2$
  (a) Is the mean change in $y$ as $x^2$ is increased one unit with $x$ held constant
  (b) Is a curvature coefficient that describes whether the regression equation is bowl shaped or mound shaped
  (c) Equals 0 if the relationship between $y$ and $x$ is linear
  (d) Equals 0 if the population value of $R^2$ for this model equals $\rho^2_{yx}$

**14.42.** The log transformation of the mean response in regression is useful when
  (a) $E(y)$ is approximately a logarithmic function of $x$.
  (b) $E(y)$ is approximately an exponential function of $x$.
  (c) $\log E(y)$ is approximately a linear function of $x$.
  (d) Unit changes in $x$ have a multiplicative, rather than additive, effect on the mean of $y$.

**14.43.** Forward selection and stepwise regression are similar in the sense that, if they have the same $\alpha$-level for testing a term,
  (a) They always select the same final regression model.
  (b) They always select the same initial regression model (when they enter the first explanatory variable).
  (c) Any variable not in the final model does not have a significant partial association with $y$, controlling for the variables in the final model.
  (d) It is impossible that all the variables listed for potential inclusion are in the final model.

**14.44.** Evidence of multicollinearity exists in a multiple regression fit when
  (a) Strong intercorrelations occur among explanatory variables.
  (b) The $R^2$-value is very large.

  (c) The $F$ test of $H_0: \beta_1 = \cdots = \beta_k = 0$ has a small $P$-value, but the individual $t$ tests of $H_0: \beta_1 = 0, \ldots, H_0: \beta_k = 0$ do not.
  (d) A predictor variable has VIF = 12.

**14.45.** True or false?
  (a) Adjusted $R^2$ can possibly *decrease* when an explanatory variable is added to a regression model.
  (b) Possible effects of an influential observation include changing a correlation from positive to negative, a $P$-value from 0.01 to 0.99, and $R^2$ from 0.01 to 0.99.
  (c) When multicollinearity exists, one can still obtain good estimates of regression parameters, but $R^2$ may be adversely affected.
  (d) If $y$ = annual medical expenses relates to $x$ = age by $E(y) = 1400 - 22x + 0.4x^2$, then the change in the mean of $y$ for every unit change in $x$ equals $-22$.

**14.46.** Select the best response for each of the following terms (not every response is used):

  | | |
  |---|---|
  | Heteroscedasticity | _____ |
  | Multicollinearity | _____ |
  | Forward selection | _____ |
  | Interaction | _____ |
  | Exponential model | _____ |
  | Stepwise regression | _____ |
  | Studentized residual | _____ |
  | Generalized linear model | _____ |

  (a) The mean of $y$ multiplies by $\beta$ for each unit increase in $x$.
  (b) The log of $E(y)$ is linearly related to the log of $x$.
  (c) A residual plot indicates that the residuals are much more spread out at high $x$ than at low $x$.
  (d) The bivariate effect of $x_1$ on $y$ differs from the partial effect of $x_1$ on $y$, controlling for $x_2$.
  (e) There are strong intercorrelations among explanatory variables.
  (f) At each stage, the variable considered for entry into the model has the smallest $P$-value in the test of its partial effect on $y$.
  (g) The response variable need not be normal, and we can model a function of the mean as a linear function of the predictors.
  (h) At each stage after entering a new variable, all variables in the model are retested to see if they still have a significant partial effect on $y$.
  (i) The slope between $E(y)$ and $x_1$ changes as the value of $x_2$ changes.
  (j) This measures the number of standard errors that an observation falls from its predicted value.

*14.47. Show that using a cross-product term to model interaction assumes that the slope of the relationship between $y$ and $x_1$ changes linearly as $x_2$ changes. How would you suggest modeling interaction if, instead, the slope of the linear relationship between $y$ and $x_1$ first increases as $x_2$ changes from low to moderate values and then decreases as $x_2$ changes from moderate to high values?

*14.48. Forward selection is used with ten potential predictors for $y$. In reality, none are truly correlated with $y$ or with each other. For a random sample, show that the probability equals 0.40 that at least one is entered into the regression model, when the criterion for admission is a $P$-value below 0.05 for the $t$ test. (*Hint:* Use the binomial distribution.)

# C H A P T E R 15

# Logistic Regression: Modeling Categorical Responses

---

**15.1 LOGISTIC REGRESSION**
**15.2 MULTIPLE LOGISTIC REGRESSION**
**15.3 INFERENCE FOR LOGISTIC REGRESSION MODELS**
**15.4 LOGISTIC REGRESSION MODELS FOR ORDINAL VARIABLES***
**15.5 LOGISTIC MODELS FOR NOMINAL RESPONSES***
**15.6 LOGLINEAR MODELS FOR CATEGORICAL VARIABLES***
**15.7 MODEL GOODNESS-OF-FIT TESTS FOR CONTINGENCY TABLES***
**15.8 CHAPTER SUMMARY**

---

The regression models studied in the past six chapters assume that the response variable is quantitative. This chapter presents generalized linear models for response variables that are categorical.

Sections 15.1–15.3 present the *logistic regression model* for *binary* response variables—variables having only two possible outcomes. For instance, logistic regression can model

- A voter's choice in a presidential election (Democrat or Republican), with predictor variables political ideology, annual income, education level, and religious affiliation
- Whether a person uses illegal drugs (yes or no), with predictors education level, whether employed, religiosity, marital status, and annual income

Multicategory versions of logistic regression can handle ordinal response variables (Section 15.4) and nominal response variables (Section 15.5). Section 15.6 introduces *loglinear models*, which describe association structure among a set of categorical response variables. Section 15.7 shows how to check the goodness of fit of models to contingency table data. The models of this chapter use the *odds ratio* to summarize associations.

## 15.1 LOGISTIC REGRESSION

For a binary response variable $y$, denote its two categories by 1 and 0. Commonly the generic terms *success* and *failure* are used for these two outcomes. Recall (from the discussion of Table 3.6 on page 44 and Example 4.7 on page 87) that the mean of 0 and 1 outcomes equals the proportion of outcomes that equal 1. Regression models for binary response variables describe the population proportions. The population proportion of successes also represents the probability $P(y = 1)$ for a randomly selected subject. This probability varies according to the values of the explanatory variables.

Models for binary data ordinarily assume a *binomial distribution* for the response variable (Section 6.7). This is natural for binary outcomes. The models are special cases of generalized linear models (Section 14.4).

### Linear Probability Model

For a single explanatory variable, the simple model

$$P(y = 1) = \alpha + \beta x$$

implies that the probability of success is a linear function of $x$. This is called the **linear probability model**.

This model is simple but often inappropriate. As Figure 15.1 shows, it implies that probabilities fall below 0 or above 1 for sufficiently small or large $x$ values, whereas probabilities must fall between 0 and 1. The model may be valid over a restricted range of $x$ values, but it is rarely adequate when the model has several predictors.

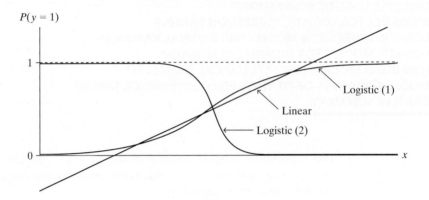

**FIGURE 15.1:** Linear and Logistic Regression Models for a (0, 1) Response, for which $E(y)$ Is $P(y = 1)$

### The Logistic Regression Model for Binary Responses

Figure 15.1 also shows more realistic response curves, which have an S-shape. With these curves, the probability of a success falls between 0 and 1 for all possible $x$-values. These curvilinear relationships are described by the formula

$$\log\left[\frac{P(y = 1)}{1 - P(y = 1)}\right] = \alpha + \beta x.$$

The ratio $P(y = 1)/[1 - P(y = 1)]$ equals the **odds**, a measure Section 8.4 introduced. For instance, when $P(y = 1) = 0.75$, the odds equals $0.75/0.25 = 3.0$, meaning that a success is three times as likely as a failure. Software uses natural logarithms (base $e$, often denoted $LN$) in fitting the model. However, we won't need to use (or understand) logarithms to interpret the model and conduct inference using it.

This formula uses the log of the odds, $\log[P(y = 1)/(1 - P(y = 1))]$, called the **logistic transformation**, or **logit** for short. The model is abbreviated as

$$\text{logit}[P(y = 1)] = \alpha + \beta x.$$

It is called the **logistic regression model**.

When the logit follows this straight line model, the probability $P(y = 1)$ itself follows a curve such as in Figure 15.1. The parameter $\beta$ indicates whether the curve goes up or goes down as $x$ increases. For $\beta > 0$, $P(y = 1)$ increases as $x$ increases, as in curve (1) in Figure 15.1. For $\beta < 0, P(y = 1)$ decreases as $x$ increases, as in curve (2) in Figure 15.1. If $\beta = 0$, $P(y = 1)$ does not change as $x$ changes, so the curve flattens to a horizontal straight line. The steepness of the curve increases as $|\beta|$ increases. For instance, $|\beta|$ for curve (2) is greater than $\beta$ for curve (1).

When $P(y = 1) = 0.50$, the odds $P(y = 1)/[1 - P(y = 1)] = 1$, and $\log[P(y = 1)/(1 - P(y = 1))] = 0$. So to find the value of $x$ at which $P(y = 1) = 0.50$, we equate this log odds value of 0 to $\alpha + \beta x$ and then solve for $x$. We then find that $P(y = 1) = 0.50$ when $x = -\alpha/\beta$.

Most software uses *maximum likelihood* (see Section 5.1) to fit the model. This method is more appropriate for binary data than least squares.

## EXAMPLE 15.1    Income and Having Travel Credit Cards

Table 15.1 shows data for a sample of 100 adults randomly selected for an Italian study on the relation between annual income and having a travel credit card, such as American Express or Diners Club. At each level of annual income (in thousands of euros), the table indicates the number of subjects in the sample and the number of those having at least one travel credit card. Let $x$ = annual income and $y$ = whether have a travel credit card (1 = yes, 0 = no). For instance, for the five observations at $x = 30$, $y = 1$ for two subjects and $y = 0$ for three subjects.

**TABLE 15.1:** Annual Income (in Thousands of Euros) and Possessing a Travel Credit Card. For example, of the five subjects with income 30 thousand euros, two possessed a travel credit card.

| Income | Number Cases | Credit Cards | Income | Number Cases | Credit Cards | Income | Number Cases | Credit Cards |
|--------|--------------|--------------|--------|--------------|--------------|--------|--------------|--------------|
| 12 | 1 | 0 | 21 | 2 | 0 | 34 | 3 | 3 |
| 13 | 1 | 0 | 22 | 1 | 1 | 35 | 5 | 3 |
| 14 | 8 | 2 | 24 | 2 | 0 | 39 | 1 | 0 |
| 15 | 14 | 2 | 25 | 10 | 2 | 40 | 1 | 0 |
| 16 | 9 | 0 | 26 | 1 | 0 | 42 | 1 | 0 |
| 17 | 8 | 2 | 29 | 1 | 0 | 47 | 1 | 0 |
| 19 | 5 | 1 | 30 | 5 | 2 | 60 | 6 | 6 |
| 20 | 7 | 0 | 32 | 6 | 6 | 65 | 1 | 1 |

*Source*: Thanks to R. Piccarreta, Bocconi University, Milan. The data were originally recorded in Italian lira but have been converted to euros.

Software provides results shown in Table 15.2 (heavily edited). The logistic prediction equation is

$$\text{logit}[\hat{P}(y = 1)] = -3.518 + 0.105x.$$

Since the estimate 0.105 of $\beta$ is positive, the estimated probability of having a credit card increases at higher levels of income. Figure 15.2 shows the prediction curve. The estimated probability equals 0.50 at $x = -\hat{\alpha}/\hat{\beta} = (3.518)/(0.105) = 33.5$. The

**TABLE 15.2:** Logistic Regression Model Output for the Italian Credit Card Data of Table 15.1. The Exp(B) term refers to exponentiating the estimate of .1054 to get an odds ratio, as explained at the end of this section.

|          | B       | S.E.   | Exp(B) |
|----------|---------|--------|--------|
| income   | .1054   | .0262  | 1.111  |
| Constant | -3.5179 | .7103  |        |

estimated probability of having a credit card is below 0.50 for incomes below 33.5 thousand euros and above 0.50 for incomes above this level. ∎

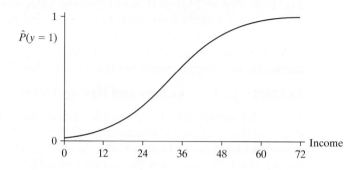

**FIGURE 15.2:** Logistic Regression Prediction Curve for Example 15.1

### Logistic Regression Equation for Probabilities

An alternative equation for logistic regression expresses the probability of success directly. It is

$$P(y = 1) = \frac{e^{\alpha + \beta x}}{1 + e^{\alpha + \beta x}}.$$

Here, $e$ raised to a power represents the antilog of that number, using natural logs. (Most calculators have an $e^x$ key that provides these antilogs, and software can report estimated probabilities based on the fit of the model.) We use this formula to estimate values of $P(y = 1)$ at particular predictor values.

From the estimates in Table 15.2, a person with annual income $x$ thousand euros has estimated probability of having a credit card equal to

$$\hat{P}(y = 1) = \frac{e^{-3.52 + 0.105x}}{1 + e^{-3.52 + 0.105x}}.$$

For subjects with income $x = 12$, the lowest income level in this sample, the estimated probability equals

$$\hat{P}(y = 1) = \frac{e^{-3.52 + 0.105(12)}}{1 + e^{-3.52 + 0.105(12)}} = \frac{e^{-2.26}}{1 + e^{-2.26}} = \frac{0.104}{1.104} = 0.094.$$

For $x = 65$, the highest income level in this sample, the estimated probability equals 0.97.

### Interpreting the Logistic Regression Model

We've seen how to estimate the probability of success, and we've seen that the sign of $\beta$ tells us whether it is increasing or decreasing as $x$ increases. How else can we interpret $\beta$? Unlike in the linear probability model, $\beta$ is not the slope for the change in $P(y = 1)$ as $x$ changes. Since the curve for $P(y = 1)$ is S-shaped, the rate at which the curve climbs or descends changes according to the value of $x$.

The simplest way to use $\beta$ to interpret the steepness of the curve uses a straight line approximation to the logistic regression curve. A straight line drawn tangent to the curve has slope $\beta P(y = 1)[1 - P(y = 1)]$, where $P(y = 1)$ is the probability at that point. Figure 15.3 illustrates. The slope is greatest when $P(y = 1) = 1/2$, where it is $\beta(1/2)(1/2) = \beta/4$. So when $P(y = 1)$ is near 1/2, one-fourth of the $\beta$ effect parameter in the logistic regression model is the approximate rate at which $P(y = 1)$ changes per one-unit increase in $x$.

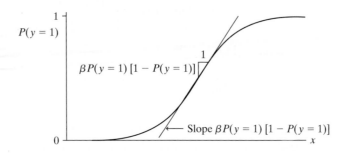

**FIGURE 15.3:** A Line Drawn Tangent to a Logistic Regression Curve Has Slope $\beta P(y = 1)[1 - P(y = 1)]$

For the Italian credit card and income data, $\hat{\beta} = 0.105$. When the estimated probability of a credit card is $\hat{P}(y = 1) = 1/2$, a line drawn tangent to the curve at that point has slope equal to $\hat{\beta}/4 = 0.105/4 = 0.026$. The rate of change in $\hat{P}(y = 1)$ for a one-thousand-euro increase in annual income is $\hat{\beta}/4 = 0.026$. At the sample mean income of $\bar{x} = 25$, the estimated probability of a credit card is $\hat{P}(y = 1) = 0.29$. Then $\hat{\beta}\hat{P}(y = 1)[1 - \hat{P}(y = 1)] = 0.105(0.29)(0.71) = 0.022$, so a one-thousand-euro increase in annual income relates approximately to a 0.022 increase in the estimated probability of having a credit card.

Software can also fit the linear probability model, $P(y = 1) = \alpha + \beta x$. The least squares fit is $\hat{P}(y = 1) = -0.159 + 0.019x$. This formula also has about a 0.02 increase in $\hat{P}(y = 1)$ per thousand-euro increase in income. However, it provides quite different predictions at the low end and high end of the income scale. For instance, it provides the absurd prediction $\hat{P}(y = 1) > 1$ when $x \geq 61$.

Another way to describe the effect of $x$ compares $\hat{P}(y = 1)$ at two different values of $x$. We've seen that when $x$ increases from its smallest to its largest value in the sample, $\hat{P}(y = 1)$ increases from 0.09 to 0.97. This is a strong effect, as there is a very large change in $\hat{P}(y = 1)$. An alternative is to instead evaluate $\hat{P}(y = 1)$ at values of $x$ that are less affected by outliers, such as the upper and lower quartiles.

### Interpretation Using the Odds and Odds Ratio

Another interpretion of the logistic regression parameter $\beta$ uses the *odds ratio* measure of association (Section 8.4). Applying antilogs to both sides of the logistic regression equation $\log[P(y = 1)/(1 - P(y = 1))] = \alpha + \beta x$ yields the model expressed in terms of the *odds*,

$$\frac{P(y = 1)}{1 - P(y = 1)} = e^{\alpha + \beta x} = e^{\alpha}(e^{\beta})^x.$$

The right-hand side of this equation has the *exponential regression* form studied in Section 14.6, a constant multiplied by another constant raised to the $x$ power. This exponential relationship implies that every unit increase in $x$ has a multiplicative effect of $e^{\beta}$ on the odds.

In Example 15.1, the antilog of $\hat{\beta}$ is $e^{\hat{\beta}} = e^{0.105} = 1.11$. When annual income increases by one thousand euros, the estimated odds of owning a credit card multiply by 1.11; that is, they increase by 11%. When $x = 25$, for example, the estimated odds of owning a travel credit card are 1.11 times what they are when $x = 24$. When $x = 25$,

$$\text{Estimated odds} = \frac{\hat{P}(y = 1)}{1 - \hat{P}(y = 1)} = e^{-3.518 + 0.105(25)} = 0.414,$$

whereas when $x = 26$,

$$\text{Estimated odds} = \frac{\hat{P}(y = 1)}{1 - \hat{P}(y = 1)} = e^{-3.518 + 0.105(26)} = 0.460,$$

which is 1.11 times the value of 0.414 at $x = 25$. In other words, $e^{0.105} = 1.11 = 0.460/0.414$ is an estimated *odds ratio*, equaling the estimated odds at $x = 26$ divided by the estimated odds at $x = 25$.

Odds ratios also apply to changes in $x$ other than 1. For example, a 10-unit change in $x$ corresponds to a change of $10\beta$ in the log odds and a multiplicative effect of $e^{10\beta} = (e^{\beta})^{10}$ on the odds. When $x = 30$, the odds equal $(1.11)^{10} = 2.9$ times the odds when $x = 20$.

Most software can report odds ratio estimates and estimated probabilities. Table 15.2 reports the estimated odds ratio for a one-unit increase in $x$ under the heading *Exp(B)*, which is notation for *exponentiating* the income estimate of 0.1054.

## 15.2 MULTIPLE LOGISTIC REGRESSION

Logistic regression can handle multiple predictors. The multiple logistic regression model has the form

$$\text{logit}[P(y = 1)] = \alpha + \beta_1 x_1 + \cdots + \beta_k x_k.$$

The formula for the probability itself is

$$P(y = 1) = \frac{e^{\alpha + \beta_1 x_1 + \cdots + \beta_k x_k}}{1 + e^{\alpha + \beta_1 x_1 + \cdots + \beta_k x_k}}.$$

Exponentiating a beta parameter provides the multiplicative effect of that predictor on the odds, controlling for the other variables. The farther a $\beta_i$ falls from 0, the stronger the effect of the predictor $x_i$, in the sense that the odds ratio falls farther from 1.

As in ordinary regression, cross-product terms allow interactions between pairs of explanatory variables. Square terms allow probabilities to increase and then decrease (or the reverse) as a predictor increases. To include categorical explanatory variables, set up dummy variables, as the next example illustrates.

### EXAMPLE 15.2    Death Penalty and Racial Predictors

Table 15.3 is a three-dimensional contingency table from a study[1] of the effects of racial characteristics on whether individuals convicted of homicide receive the death penalty. The variables in Table 15.3 are *death penalty verdict*, the response variable, having categories (yes, no), and the explanatory variables *race of defendant* and *race of victims*, each having categories (white, black). The 674 subjects were defendants in indictments involving cases with multiple murders in Florida between 1976 and 1987.

---

[1]M. L. Radelet and G. L. Pierce, *Florida Law Review*, vol. 43, 1991, pp. 1–34.

**TABLE 15.3:** Death Penalty Verdict by Defendant's Race and Victims' Race, for Cases with Multiple Murders in Florida

| Defendant's Race | Victims' Race | Death Penalty Yes | Death Penalty No | Percent Yes |
|---|---|---|---|---|
| White | White | 53 | 414 | 11.3 |
|       | Black | 0  | 16  | 0.0 |
| Black | White | 11 | 37  | 22.9 |
|       | Black | 4  | 139 | 2.8 |

For each of the four combinations of defendant's race and victims' race, Table 15.3 also lists the percentage of defendants who received the death penalty. For white defendants, the death penalty was imposed 11.3% of the time when the victims were white and 0.0% of the time when the victims were black, a difference of 11.3% − 0.0% = 11.3%. For black defendants, the death penalty was imposed 22.9% − 2.8% = 20.1% more often when the victims were white than when the victims were black. Thus, controlling for defendant's race by keeping it fixed, the percentage of *yes* death penalty verdicts was considerably higher when the victims were white than when they were black.

Now consider the association between defendant's race and the death penalty verdict, controlling for victims' race. When the victims were white, the death penalty was imposed 22.9% − 11.3% = 11.6% more often when the defendant was black than when the defendant was white. When the victims were black, the death penalty was imposed 2.8% more often when the defendant was black than when the defendant was white. In summary, controlling for victims' race, black defendants were somewhat more likely than white defendants to receive the death penalty.

For $y$ = death penalty verdict, let $y = 1$ denote the *yes* verdict. Since defendant's race and victims' race each have two categories, a single dummy variable can represent each. Let $d$ be a dummy variable for defendant's race and $v$ a dummy variable for victims' race, where

$$d = 1, \text{defendant} = \text{white}; \ d = 0, \text{defendant} = \text{black},$$
$$v = 1, \text{victims} = \text{white}; \ v = 0, \text{victims} = \text{black}.$$

The logistic model with main effects for these predictors is

$$\text{logit}[P(y = 1)] = \alpha + \beta_1 d + \beta_2 v,$$

where $\beta_1$ represents the effect of defendant's race, controlling for victims' race and $\beta_2$ represents the effect of victims' race, controlling for defendant's race. Here $e^{\beta_1}$ is the odds ratio between the response variable and defendant's race, controlling for victims' race, and $e^{\beta_2}$ is the odds ratio between the response and victims' race, controlling for defendant's race.

Table 15.4 shows output for the model fit (based on using the *generalized linear models* option from the *Analyze* menu in SPSS). The prediction equation is

$$\text{logit}[\hat{P}(y = 1)] = -3.596 - 0.868d + 2.404v.$$

Since $d = 1$ for white defendants, the *negative* coefficient of $d$ means that the estimated odds of receiving the death penalty are *lower* for white defendants than for black defendants. Since $v = 1$ for white victims, the *positive* coefficient of $v$ means

**TABLE 15.4:** Parameter Estimates for Logistic Model for Death Penalty Data. Estimates equal 0 for the "black" category of each predictor because its dummy variable value is 0.

|  | B | Std. Error | Exp(B) |
|---|---|---|---|
| (Intercept) | -3.596 | .5069 | .027 |
| [defendant=white] | -.868 | .3671 | .420 |
| [defendant=black] | 0 | . |  |
| [victim=white] | 2.404 | .6006 | 11.072 |
| [victim=black] | 0 | . |  |

that the estimated odds of receiving the death penalty are *higher* when the victims were white than when they were black.

The formula for the estimated probability of the death penalty is

$$\hat{P}(y = 1) = \frac{e^{-3.596-0.868d+2.404v}}{1 + e^{-3.596-0.868d+2.404v}}.$$

For instance, when the defendant is black and the victims were white, $d = 0$ and $v = 1$, so

$$\hat{P}(y = 1) = \frac{e^{-3.596-0.868(0)+2.404(1)}}{1 + e^{-3.596-0.868(0)+2.404(1)}} = \frac{e^{-1.192}}{1 + e^{-1.192}} = \frac{0.304}{1.304} = 0.233.$$

This is close to the sample proportion of 0.229 (Table 15.3). The estimated probabilities, unlike sample proportions, perfectly satisfy the model. The closer the sample proportions fall to the estimated probabilities, the better the model fits.

The antilog of $\hat{\beta}_1$, namely, $e^{\hat{\beta}_1} = e^{-0.868} = 0.42$, is the estimated odds ratio between defendant's race and the death penalty, controlling for victims' race. The estimated odds of the death penalty for a white defendant equal 0.42 times the estimated odds for a black defendant. We list *white* before *black* in this interpretation, because the dummy variable was set up with $d = 1$ for *white* defendants. If we instead let $d = 1$ for black defendants rather than white, then we get $\hat{\beta}_1 = 0.868$ instead of $-0.868$. Then $e^{0.868} = 2.38$, which is $1/0.42$; that is, the estimated odds of the death penalty for a black defendant equal 2.38 times the estimated odds for a white defendant, controlling for victims' race.

For victims' race, $e^{2.404} = 11.1$. Since $v = 1$ for *white* victims, the estimated odds of the death penalty when the victims were *white* equal 11.1 times the estimated odds when the victims were black, controlling for defendant's race. This is a very strong effect.

This model assumes that both explanatory variables affect the response variable, but with a lack of interaction: The effect of defendant's race on the death penalty verdict is the same for each victims' race and the effect of victims' race is the same for each defendant's race. This means that the estimated odds ratio between each predictor and the response takes the same value at each category of the other predictor. For instance, the estimated odds ratio of 11.1 between victims' race and the death penalty is the same when the defendants were white as when the defendants were black. ∎

### Effects on Odds

The parameter estimates for the logistic regression model are linear effects, but on the scale of the *log* of the odds. It is easier to understand effects on the *odds* scale than the *log odds* scale. The antilogs of the parameter estimates are multiplicative effects on the odds.

To illustrate, for the data on the death penalty, the prediction equation

$$\log[\hat{P}(y = 1)/(1 - \hat{P}(y = 1))] = -3.596 - 0.868d + 2.404v$$

refers to the log odds (i.e., logit). The corresponding prediction equation for the odds is

$$\text{odds} = e^{-3.596-0.868d+2.404v} = e^{-3.596}e^{-0.868d}e^{2.404v}.$$

For white defendants, $d = 1$, and the estimated odds equal $e^{-3.596}e^{-0.868}e^{2.404v}$. For black defendants, $d = 0$, and the estimated odds equal $e^{-3.596}e^{2.404v}$. The estimated odds for white defendants divided by the estimated odds for black defendants equal $e^{-0.868} = 0.42$. This shows why the antilog of the coefficient for $d$ in the prediction equation is the estimated odds ratio between defendant's race and death penalty verdict, for each fixed victims' race. The effect of defendant's race being white is to multiply the estimated odds of a *yes* death penalty verdict by $e^{-0.868} = 0.42$ compared to its value for black defendants. The actual values of the odds depend on victims' race, but the ratio of the odds is the same for each.

The logit model expression for the log odds is *additive*, but taking antilogs yields a *multiplicative* expression for the odds. In other words, the antilogs of the parameters are *multiplied* to obtain odds. We can use this expression to calculate odds estimates for any combination of defendant's race and victims' race. For instance, when the defendant is black ($d = 0$) and the victims were white ($v = 1$), the estimated odds of the death penalty are

$$\text{odds} = e^{-3.596-0.868d+2.404v} = e^{-3.596-0.868(0)+2.404(1)} = e^{-1.192} = 0.304.$$

Since the formula for the estimated probability of the death penalty is

$$\hat{P}(y = 1) = \frac{e^{-3.596-0.868d+2.404v}}{1 + e^{-3.596-0.868d+2.404v}},$$

we see that this probability relates to the estimated odds by

$$\hat{P}(y = 1) = \frac{\text{Odds}}{1 + \text{Odds}}.$$

This is a formula we first used in Section 8.4. For instance, when the estimated odds $= 0.304$, as in this example when $d = 0$ and $v = 1$, then $\hat{P}(y = 1) = 0.304/(1 + 0.304) = 0.233$. This is the estimated probability of the death penalty found above following the discussion of Table 15.4.

## EXAMPLE 15.3    Factors Affecting First Home Purchase

Table 15.5 summarizes logistic regression results from a study[2] of how family transitions relate to first home purchase by young married households. The response variable is whether the subject owns a home (1 = yes, 0 = no). The parameter $P(y = 1)$ is the probability of home ownership.

The model contains several explanatory variables. Two variables measure current income: husband's earnings and wife's earnings. Two variables measure marital duration: the number of years the respondent has been married and marital status two years after the year of observation. The latter is a categorical variable with levels (married, married with a working wife, single), single being the omitted category for

---

[2]From J. Henretta, *Social Forces*, vol. 66, 1987, pp. 520–536.

**TABLE 15.5:** Results of Logistic Regression for the Probability of Home Ownership

| Variable | Estimate | Std. Error |
|---|---|---|
| Intercept | −2.870 | — |
| Husband earnings ($10,000) | 0.569 | 0.088 |
| Wife earnings ($10,000) | 0.306 | 0.140 |
| No. years married | −0.039 | 0.042 |
| Married in 2 years (1 = yes) | 0.224 | 0.304 |
| Working wife in 2 years (1 = yes) | 0.373 | 0.283 |
| No. children | 0.220 | 0.101 |
| Add child in 2 years (1 = yes) | 0.271 | 0.140 |
| Head's education (no. years) | −0.027 | 0.032 |
| Parents' home ownership (1 = yes) | 0.387 | 0.176 |

the two dummy variables. Two variables measure presence of children: the number of children age 0–17 in the household and a dummy variable for whether the family has more children age 0–17 two years after the year of observation. The other variables are the household head's education and a dummy variable for whether the subject's parents owned a home in the last year that the subject lived in the parental home.

In Table 15.5, the ratio of the estimate to its standard error exceeds 2 for four of the predictors. Other things being fixed, the probability of home ownership increases with husband's earnings, wife's earnings, the number of children, and parents' home ownership. For instance, each additional child had the effect of multiplying the estimated odds of owning a home by $e^{0.220} = 1.25$; that is, the estimated odds increase by 25%. A $10,000 increase in earnings had the effect of multiplying the estimated odds of owning a home by $e^{0.569} = 1.77$ if the earnings add to husband's income and by $e^{0.306} = 1.36$ for wife's income.

From Table 15.5, number of years married, marital status in two years, and head's education show little evidence of an effect, given the other variables in the model. We could refit the model without these predictors. This more parsimonious model may yield better estimates of the effects of the significant variables. ∎

### Effects on Probabilities

We've seen that we can summarize the effects of predictors by estimating *odds ratios*. Many researchers find it easier to get a feel for the effects by viewing summaries that use the *probability* scale. Such summaries can report estimated probabilities at particular values of a predictor of interest. This evaluation is done at fixed values of the other predictors, such as at their means or at certain values of interest.

Alternatively, you can report the change in the estimated probability $\hat{P}(y = 1)$ when a predictor increases by a certain amount, such as (1) by a fixed value (e.g., 1), (2) by a standard deviation, (3) over its range from its lowest to greatest value, or (4) over its inter-quartile range from the lower quartile to the upper quartile. Approach (4) is, unlike (1), not affected by the choice of scale and, unlike (2) and (3), not affected by outliers.

To illustrate, let's investigate the effect of husband's earnings for the preceding example. Consider the estimated probability $\hat{P}(y = 1)$ of home ownership when wife's earnings = $50,000, years married = 3, the wife is working in two years, number of children = 0, add child in two years = 0, head's education = 16 years, and parents' home ownership $= 0$. When husband's earnings $= \$20,000$,

$$\hat{P}(y = 1) = \frac{e^{-2.870+0.569(2)+0.306(5)-0.039(3)+0.373(1)-0.027(16)}}{1 + e^{-2.870+0.569(2)+0.306(5)-0.039(3)+0.373(1)-0.027(16)}} = 0.41.$$

Then $\hat{P}(y = 1)$ increases to 0.55 if husband's earnings increase to $\$30,000$, to 0.79 if they increase to $\$50,000$, and to 0.98 if they increase to $\$100,000$. The effect seems quite strong.

## 15.3   INFERENCE FOR LOGISTIC REGRESSION MODELS

We next discuss statistical inference for logistic regression. As usual, inference assumes randomization for gathering the data. It also assumes a *binomial* distribution for the response variable. The model identifies $y$ as having a binomial distribution and uses the logit link function for $P(y = 1)$, which is the mean of $y$.

### Wald and Likelihood-Ratio Tests of Independence

For the bivariate logistic regression model

$$\text{logit}[P(y = 1)] = \alpha + \beta x,$$

$H_0: \beta = 0$ states that $x$ has no effect on $P(y = 1)$. This is the *independence* hypothesis. Except for very small samples, we can test $H_0$ using a $z$ test statistic, dividing the maximum likelihood estimate $\hat{\beta}$ by its standard error. Some software reports the square of this statistic, called a **Wald statistic**. This has a chi-squared distribution with $df = 1$. It has the same $P$-value as the $z$ statistic for the two-sided $H_a: \beta \neq 0$.

Most software can also report another test for this hypothesis. Called the **likelihood-ratio test**, in general it is a way to compare two models, a full model and a simpler model. It tests that the extra parameters in the full model equal zero. For example, for bivariate logistic regression it tests $H_0: \beta = 0$ by comparing the model $\text{logit}[P(y = 1)] = \alpha + \beta x$ to the simpler model $\text{logit}[P(y = 1)] = \alpha$. The test uses a key ingredient of maximum likelihood inference, the *likelihood function*. Denoted by $\ell$, this gives the probability of the observed data as a function of the parameter values. The maximum likelihood estimates maximize this function. (Specifically, the estimates are the parameter values for which the observed data are most likely; see Section 5.1.)

Let $\ell_0$ denote the maximum of the likelihood function when $H_0$ is true, and let $\ell_1$ denote the maximum without that assumption. The formula for the likelihood-ratio test statistic is

$$-2 \log\left(\frac{\ell_0}{\ell_1}\right) = (-2 \log \ell_0) - (-2 \log \ell_1).$$

It compares the maximized values of $(-2 \log \ell)$ when $H_0$ is true and when it need not be true. There is a technical reason for using $-2$ times the log of this ratio, namely, that the test statistic then has approximately a chi-squared distribution for large samples. The $df$ value equals the number of parameters in the null hypothesis.

For testing $H_0: \beta = 0$ with large samples, the Wald test and likelihood-ratio test usually provide similar results. For small to moderate sample sizes, the likelihood-ratio statistic often tends to be larger and gives a more powerful test than the Wald statistic. To be safe, use it rather than the Wald statistic.

### EXAMPLE 15.4    Inference for Income and Travel Credit Cards

Table 15.6 shows inference results for Example 15.1 (page 485) about how the probability of having a travel credit card depends on income level. $H_0$: $\beta = 0$ states that the probability of having a travel credit card is the same at all income levels.

**TABLE 15.6:** Logistic Regression Inference for Italian Credit Card Data

|          | B       | S.E.  | Wald  | df | Sig.  | 95% CI for exp(B) |       |
|----------|---------|-------|-------|----|-------|-------|-------|
| income   | .1054   | .0262 | 16.24 | 1  | .000  | 1.056 | 1.170 |
| Constant | -3.5179 | .7103 | 24.53 | 1  | .000  |       |       |

From the table, $\hat{\beta} = 0.1054$ has an estimated standard error of 0.0262. The $z$ test statistic equals $z = 0.1054/0.0262 = 4.02$. This has a $P$-value of 0.000 for $H_a$: $\beta \neq 0$. Table 15.6 reports the square of this statistic, the Wald statistic. This chi-squared statistic equals 16.2, with $df = 1$, and has the same $P$-value. There is strong evidence of a positive association between income and having a travel credit card.

The likelihood-ratio test of $H_0$: $\beta = 0$ compares the maximized value of $(-2\log \ell)$ for this model, $\text{logit}[P(y = 1)] = \alpha + \beta x$, to its maximized value for the simpler model with $\beta = 0$. In its Model Summary, SPSS reports a $-2\log \ell$ value of 97.23 for the model. Compared to the model with only an intercept term, SPSS reports (e.g., if the model is built with the "Forward:LR" method) that the change in $-2\log \ell$ would be 26.59 with $df = 1$. This is the likelihood-ratio test statistic. It also has a $P$-value of 0.000.

The result of these tests is no surprise. We would expect subjects with higher incomes to be more likely to have travel credit cards. As usual, confidence intervals are more informative. We could obtain confidence intervals for $\beta$ or for $P(y = 1)$ at various values of $x$. The formula for a confidence interval for $P(y = 1)$ is beyond the scope of this text but is simple with some software (e.g., SAS, as the appendix shows). A 95% confidence interval for the probability of having a credit card equals (0.04, 0.20) at the lowest income level of 12, (0.20, 0.40) at the mean income level of 25, and (0.78, 0.996) at the highest income level of 65. ∎

### Inference in Multiple Logistic Regression

For testing the partial effect of a predictor in a multiple logistic regression model, the parameter estimate divided by its standard error is a $z$ test statistic. The square of that, the Wald statistic, is a chi-squared statistic with $df = 1$. Most software also reports likelihood-ratio tests, which compare the $(-2\log \ell)$ values with and without the predictor in the model. This is particularly useful if a categorical predictor has several levels, in which case it has several dummy variables and the test of its effect equates several parameters to 0 in $H_0$.

### EXAMPLE 15.5    Inference for Death Penalty and Racial Predictors

For the death penalty data, Example 15.2 (page 488) used the model

$$\text{logit}[P(y = 1)] = \alpha + \beta_1 d + \beta_2 v,$$

with dummy variables $d$ and $v$ for defendant's race and victims' race. If $\beta_1 = 0$, the death penalty verdict is independent of defendant's race, controlling for victims' race. In that case, the odds ratio between the death penalty verdict and defendant's race equals $e^0 = 1$ for each victims' race.

Software (SPSS) shows the results

|  | B | Std. Error | Wald Chi-Sq. | Sig. | 95% CI for Exp(B) | |
|---|---|---|---|---|---|---|
| (Intercept) | -3.596 | .5069 | 50.33 | .000 | | |
| [defendant=white] | -.868 | .3671 | 5.59 | .018 | .20 | .86 |
| [victim=white] | 2.404 | .6006 | 16.03 | .000 | 3.41 | 35.93 |

The defendant's race effect of $-0.868$ has a standard error of 0.367. The $z$ test statistic for $H_0: \beta_1 = 0$ is $z = -0.868/0.367 = -2.36$, and the Wald statistic equals $(-2.36)^2 = 5.59$ (shown in the table). For the two-sided alternative, either statistic has a $P$-value of 0.018. Similarly, the test of $H_0: \beta_2 = 0$ has $P = 0.000$ and provides extremely strong evidence of a victims' race effect.

The parameter estimates are also the basis of confidence intervals for odds ratios. Since the estimates refer to *log* odds ratios, after constructing the interval for a $\beta_j$ we take antilogs of the endpoints to form the interval for the odds ratio. For instance, since the estimated log odds ratio of 2.404 between victims' race and the death penalty has a standard error of 0.601, a 95% confidence interval for the true log odds ratio is

$$2.404 \pm 1.96(0.601), \text{ or } (1.23, 3.58).$$

From applying the antilog (i.e., exponential function, $e^x$) to each endpoint, the confidence interval for the odds ratio equals $(e^{1.23}, e^{3.58}) = (3.4, 35.9)$, shown in the table. For a given defendant's race, when the victims were white, the estimated odds of the death penalty are between 3.4 and 35.9 times the estimated odds when the victims were black.

Most software can also provide confidence intervals for probabilities. Ninety-five percent confidence intervals for the probability of the death penalty are $(0.14, 0.37)$ for black defendants with white victims, $(0.01, 0.07)$ for black defendants with black victims, $(0.09, 0.15)$ for white defendants with white victims, and $(0.003, 0.04)$ for white defendants with black victims. ∎

### Likelihood-Ratio Test Comparing Logistic Regression Models

To compare a model with a set of predictors to a simpler model having fewer predictors, the likelihood-ratio test uses the difference in the values of $(-2 \log \ell)$ for the two models. This is an approximate chi-squared statistic with $df$ given by the number of extra parameters in the full model. This test is an analog of the $F$ test for comparing complete and reduced regression models (Section 11.6).

To illustrate, the model in Example 15.3 about home ownership (page 491) has $(-2 \log \ell) = 2931.2$. After adding five variables to the model relating to the housing market, such as the median sale price of existing homes in the area, $-2 \log \ell$ drops to 2841.1. The difference $(2931.2 - 2841.1) = 90.1$ is a chi-squared statistic with $df = 5$, since the more complex model has five additional parameters. This shows extremely strong evidence of a better fit for the more complex model ($P < 0.0001$). So at least one of these variables provides an improvement in predictive power.

A comparison of the $(-2 \log \ell)$ values for a model and for the model containing only an intercept term tests the joint effects of *all* the predictors. This test is a chi-squared analog for binary data of the $F$ test in regression of $H_0 : \beta_1 = \cdots = \beta_k = 0$ that *none* of the predictors have an effect on $y$.

## 15.4 LOGISTIC REGRESSION MODELS FOR ORDINAL VARIABLES*

Many applications have a categorical response variable with more than two categories. For instance, the GSS recently asked subjects whether government spending on the environment should increase, remain the same, or decrease. An extension of logistic regression can handle ordinal response variables.

### Cumulative Probabilities and Their Logits

Let $y$ denote an ordinal response variable. Let $P(y \leq j)$ denote the probability that the response falls in category $j$ or below (i.e., in category 1, 2, ..., or $j$). This is called a **cumulative probability**. With four categories, for example, the cumulative probabilities are

$$P(y = 1), P(y \leq 2) = P(y = 1) + P(y = 2),$$
$$P(y \leq 3) = P(y = 1) + P(y = 2) + P(y = 3),$$

and the final cumulative probability uses the entire scale, so $P(y \leq 4) = 1$.

A $c$-category response has $c$ cumulative probabilities. The order of forming the cumulative probabilities reflects the ordering of the response scale. The probabilities satisfy

$$P(y \leq 1) \leq P(y \leq 2) \leq \cdots \leq P(y \leq c) = 1.$$

The odds of response in category $j$ or below is the ratio

$$\frac{P(y \leq j)}{P(y > j)}.$$

For instance, when the odds equal 2.5, the probability of response in category $j$ or below equals 2.5 times the probability of response above category $j$. Each cumulative probability can convert to an odds.

A popular logistic model for an ordinal response uses logits of the cumulative probabilities. With $c = 4$, for example, the logits are

$$\text{logit}[P(y \leq 1)] = \log\left[\frac{P(y = 1)}{P(y > 1)}\right] = \log\left[\frac{P(y = 1)}{P(y = 2) + P(y = 3) + P(y = 4)}\right]$$

$$\text{logit}[P(y \leq 2)] = \log\left[\frac{P(y \leq 2)}{P(y > 2)}\right] = \log\left[\frac{P(y = 1) + P(y = 2)}{P(y = 3) + P(y = 4)}\right]$$

$$\text{logit}[P(y \leq 3)] = \log\left[\frac{P(y \leq 3)}{P(y > 3)}\right] = \log\left[\frac{P(y = 1) + P(y = 2) + P(y = 3)}{P(y = 4)}\right].$$

Since the final cumulative probability necessarily equals 1.0, we exclude it from the model. These logits of cumulative probabilities are called **cumulative logits**. Each cumulative logit regards the response as binary by considering whether the response is at the low end or the high end of the scale, where "low" and "high" have a different definition for each cumulative logit.

### Cumulative Logit Models for an Ordinal Response

A model can simultaneously describe the effect of an explanatory variable on all the cumulative probabilities for $y$. For each cumulative probability, the model looks like an ordinary logistic regression, where the two outcomes are low = "category $j$ or below" and high = "above category $j$." This model is

$$\text{logit}[P(y \leq j)] = \alpha_j - \beta x, \quad j = 1, 2, \ldots, c - 1.$$

For $c = 4$, for instance, this single model describes three relationships: the effect of $x$ on the odds that $y \leq 1$ instead of $y > 1$, the effect of $x$ on the odds that $y \leq 2$ instead of $y > 2$, and the effect of $x$ on the odds that $y \leq 3$ instead of $y > 3$. The model requires a separate intercept parameter $\alpha_j$ for each cumulative probability. Since the cumulative probabilities increase as $j$ increases, so do $\{\alpha_j\}$.

Why is the model written with a minus sign before $\beta$? This is not necessary, but it is how the model is parameterized by some software, such as SPSS. That way, if $\beta > 0$, then when $x$ is *higher*, cumulative probabilities are *lower*. But cumulative probabilities being lower means it is less likely to observe relatively low values and thus more likely to observe *higher* values of $y$. So this parameterization accords with the usual formulation of a positive association, in the sense that a positive $\beta$ corresponds to a positive association (higher $x$ tending to occur with higher $y$). Statistical software for fitting the model has no standard convention. Software (such as SAS) that specifies the model as $\text{logit}[P(y \leq j)] = \alpha_j + \beta x$ will report the opposite sign for $\hat{\beta}$. You should be careful to check how your software defines the model so you interpret $\hat{\beta}$ properly.

The parameter of main interest, $\beta$, describes the effect of $x$ on $y$. When $\beta = 0$, each cumulative probability does not change as $x$ changes, and the variables are independent. The effect of $x$ increases as $|\beta|$ increases. In this model, $\beta$ does not have a $j$ subscript. It has the same value for each cumulative logit. In other words, the model assumes that the effect of $x$ is the same for each cumulative probability. This cumulative logit model with this common effect is often called the ***proportional odds*** model.

Figure 15.4 depicts the model for four response categories with a quantitative predictor. The model implies a separate S-shaped curve for each of the three cumulative probabilities. For example, the curve for $P(y \leq 2)$ has the appearance of a logistic regression curve for a binary response with pair of outcomes ($y \leq 2$) and ($y > 2$). At any fixed $x$-value, the three curves have the same ordering as the cumulative probabilities, the one for $P(y \leq 1)$ being lowest.

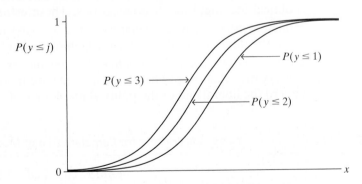

**FIGURE 15.4:** Depiction of Curves for Cumulative Probabilities in Cumulative Logit Model

The size of $|\beta|$ determines how quickly the curves climb or drop. The common value for $\beta$ means that the three response curves have the same shape. In Figure 15.4, the curve for $P(y \leq 1)$ is the curve for $P(y \leq 2)$ moved to the right and the curve for $P(y \leq 3)$ moved even further to the right. To describe the association, we can form $e^{-\beta}$ as a multiplicative effect of a one-unit increase in $x$ on the odds for the cumulative probabilities: For each $j$, the odds that $y \leq j$ multiply by $e^{-\beta}$ for each one-unit increase in $x$. (It is $e^{-\beta}$ rather than $e^{\beta}$ because of the negative sign attached to $\beta$ in the model formula.)

Model fitting treats the observations as independent from a **multinomial distribution**. This is a generalization of the *binomial distribution* from two to multiple outcome categories. Software estimates the parameters using all the cumulative probabilities at once. This provides a single estimate $\hat{\beta}$ for the effect of $x$, rather than the three separate estimates we'd get by fitting the model separately for each cumulative probability. If you reverse the order of categories of $y$ (i.e., listing from high to low instead of from low to high), the model fit is the same but the sign of $\hat{\beta}$ reverses.

### EXAMPLE 15.6 Comparing Political Ideology of Democrats and Republicans

Do Republicans tend to be more conservative than Democrats? Table 15.7, for the subjects of age 18–30 in the 2004 GSS, relates political ideology to party affiliation. We treat political ideology, which has a five-point ordinal scale, as the response variable. In Chapter 12, on ANOVA methods, we treated political ideology as quantitative by assigning scores to categories. Now we treat it as ordinal by using a cumulative logit model.

**TABLE 15.7:** Political Ideology by Party Affiliation

| Party Affiliation | Political Ideology | | | | |
|---|---|---|---|---|---|
| | Very Liberal | Slightly Liberal | Moderate | Slightly Conservative | Very Conservative |
| Democratic | 29 | 17 | 36 | 4 | 5 |
| Republican | 2 | 7 | 23 | 23 | 19 |

Let $x$ be a dummy variable for party affiliation, with $x = 1$ for Democrats and $x = 0$ for Republicans. Table 15.8 shows results of fitting the cumulative logit model. The table reports four intercept parameter estimates, because the response variable (political ideology) has five categories. These estimates are not as relevant as the estimated effect of the explanatory variable (party affiliation), which is $\hat{\beta} = -2.241$. Since the dummy variable $x$ is 1 for Democrats and since high values of $y$ represent greater conservatism, the *negative* $\hat{\beta}$ value means that Democrats tend to be *less* conservative than Republicans. Democrats are more likely than Republicans to fall toward the liberal end of the political ideology scale.

**TABLE 15.8:** Printout for Cumulative Logit Model Fitted to Table 15.7

| | Estimate | Std. Error | Wald | df | Sig. |
|---|---|---|---|---|---|
| INTERCP1 [ideology=1] | -3.051 | .336 | 82.30 | 1 | .000 |
| INTERCP2 [ideology=2] | -2.150 | .300 | 51.28 | 1 | .000 |
| INTERCP3 [ideology=3] | -.183 | .226 | .66 | 1 | .418 |
| INTERCP4 [ideology=4] | .983 | .250 | 15.41 | 1 | .000 |
| PARTY | -2.241 | .338 | 44.05 | 1 | .000 |

We can also interpret $\hat{\beta} = -2.241$ by exponentiating $-\hat{\beta}$ to form an estimated odds ratio for cumulative probabilities. For any fixed $j$, the estimated odds that a Democrat's response is in the liberal direction rather than the conservative direction (i.e., $y \leq j$ rather than $y > j$) equal $e^{-\hat{\beta}} = e^{2.241} = 9.4$ times the estimated odds for Republicans. Specifically, this odds ratio applies to each of the four cumulative probabilities for Table 15.7.

To illustrate, using the second of the four cumulative probabilities, the estimated odds that a Democrat is very liberal or slightly liberal, rather than moderate, slightly conservative, or very conservative, are 9.4 times the estimated odds that a Republican is very liberal or slightly liberal, rather than moderate, slightly conservative, or very conservative. The value 9.4 is far from the no effect value of 1.0. The sample has a strong association, Democrats tending to be more liberal than Republicans.    ■

### Inference for Effects on an Ordinal Response

When $\beta = 0$ in the cumulative logit model, the variables are independent. We test independence by testing $H_0$: $\beta = 0$. As usual, the $z$ test statistic divides $\hat{\beta}$ by its standard error. The square of that ratio is the Wald statistic, which is chi-squared with $df = 1$. Better yet, the likelihood-ratio test is based on the difference in $(-2 \log \ell)$ values with and without the predictor in the model. Most software can report both these tests.

From Table 15.8, the effect of party affiliation has estimate $\hat{\beta} = -2.241$ and standard error $= 0.338$. So $z = -2.241/0.338 = 6.63$ and the Wald statistic equals $(6.63)^2 = 44.0$. Not reported here is the likelihood-ratio test statistic for this hypothesis, which equals 51.8, based on $df = 1$. This is the difference between values of $(-2 \log \ell)$ for the model with only the intercept terms (507.8) and the full model (456.1). With either statistic, the $P$-value is 0.000 for testing $H_0$: $\beta = 0$ (independence of political ideology and party) against $H_a$: $\beta \neq 0$. These tests and $\hat{\beta}$ provide strong evidence that Democrats are politically more liberal than Republicans.

This test of independence takes into account the ordering of the response categories. It is usually more powerful than tests of independence that ignore the ordering, such as the Pearson chi-squared test of Section 8.2. When there truly is dependence, the ordinal test usually yields a smaller $P$-value.

A confidence interval for the odds ratio describes the association for the cumulative logit model. Since $\hat{\beta} = -2.241$ with $se = 0.338$, the 95% confidence interval for the population log odds ratio represented by $-\beta$ equals $2.241 \pm 1.96(0.338)$, or (1.58, 2.90). The confidence interval for the odds ratio is $(e^{1.58}, e^{2.90})$, or (4.9, 18.2). The odds that a Democrat's response falls in the liberal direction are more than about five times the odds for Republicans. To illustrate, using the second of the four cumulative probabilities, we conclude that the odds that a Democrat is very liberal or slightly liberal, rather than moderate, slightly conservative, or very conservative, fall between 4.9 and 18.2 times the odds for a Republican.

### Invariance to Choice of Response Categories

When the cumulative logit model fits well, it also fits well with similar effects for any collapsing of the response categories. For instance, if a model for categories (Very liberal, Slightly liberal, Moderate, Slightly conservative, Very conservative) fits well, approximately the same estimated effects result when we fit the model to the data after collapsing the response scale to (Liberal, Moderate, Conservative). This *invariance* to the choice of response categories is a nice feature of the model. Two researchers who use different response categories in studying an association should reach similar conclusions.

To illustrate, we collapse Table 15.7 to a three-category response, combining the two liberal categories and combining the two conservative categories. The estimated effect of party affiliation changes only from $-2.241$ (standard error $= 0.338$) to $-2.258$ (standard error $= 0.343$). Some loss of efficiency occurs in collapsing ordinal scales, resulting in larger standard errors. In practice, when observations are spread fairly evenly among the categories, the efficiency loss is minor unless the collapsing is to a binary response. It is usually inadvisable to collapse ordinal data to binary.

The cumulative logit model implies trends upward or downward among distributions of $y$ at different values of explanatory variables. When $x$ refers to two groups, as in Table 15.7, the model fits well when subjects in one group tend to make higher responses on the ordinal scale than subjects in the other group. The model does not fit well when the response distributions differ in their *variability* rather than their average. If Democrats tended to be primarily moderate in political ideology while Republicans tended to be both very conservative and very liberal (i.e., at the two extremes of the scale), then the Republicans' responses would show greater variability than the Democrats'. The two political ideology distributions would be quite different, but the model would not detect this if the average responses were similar.

### Extensions of the Model for Multiple Predictors

Cumulative logit models can handle multiple explanatory variables, which can be quantitative and/or categorical. When an explanatory variable is categorical, dummy variables represent the categories.

To check the fit of the model, we can analyze whether extra terms, such as interactions, provide a significant improvement in the model fit. One way to do this uses a likelihood-ratio test of whether the extra parameters equal 0. Some software also provides a chi-squared test for the *proportional odds* assumption that the $\beta$ effects are the same for all cumulative probabilities.

As in other statistical endeavors, there is danger in putting too much emphasis on statistical tests, whether of effects or of goodness of fit. Results are sensitive to sample size, more significant results tending to occur with larger sample sizes. Test statistics merely indicate the level of parsimony that is possible. It is important to supplement the tests with estimation methods that describe the strength of effects and with residual analyses that detect parts of the data for which the overall trend fails to hold.

### Ordinal Predictor in a Logistic Regression Model

This section has focused on modeling ordinal response variables. It is usually advisable to treat ordinal explanatory variables in a quantitative manner, for any type of regression model.

To illustrate, for Table 15.7, let's now treat party affiliation as the response variable and political ideology as the explanatory variable. Let $y = 1$ if the subject identifies as a Democrat. Rather than assign dummy variables for the categories of $x =$ political ideology, we could assign scores to the categories and assume

$$\text{logit}[P(y = 1)] = \alpha + \beta x.$$

The assignment of scores means that ideology is treated as a quantitative variable. The model is more parsimonious and simpler to interpret than if we used dummy variables.

For Table 15.7, it seems sensible to assign equally spaced scores, such as $\{1, 2, 3, 4, 5\}$. The prediction equation for the probability that party affiliation is Democrat is then

$$\text{logit}[\hat{P}(y = 1)] = 3.404 - 1.062x.$$

For this prediction equation, $e^{-1.062} = 0.35$ is the multiplicative effect of a single category increase in conservatism on the odds of being a Democrat instead of Republican. The odds of being classified Democrat multiply by 0.35 for every category increase in conservatism. Thus, the probability of being a Democrat decreases considerably as conservatism increases.

## 15.5  LOGISTIC MODELS FOR NOMINAL RESPONSES*

For nominal response variables, an extension of the binary logistic regression model provides an ordinary logistic model for each pair of response categories. The models simultaneously use all pairs of categories by specifying the odds of outcome in one category instead of another. The order of listing the categories is irrelevant, because the model treats the response scale as nominal.

### Baseline-Category Logits

Logit models for nominal response variables pair each category with a baseline category. Most software uses the last category as the baseline. With three response categories, for example, the *baseline-category logits* are

$$\log\left[\frac{P(y = 1)}{P(y = 3)}\right], \quad \log\left[\frac{P(y = 2)}{P(y = 3)}\right].$$

For $c$ outcome categories, the baseline-category logit model with a predictor $x$ is

$$\log\left[\frac{P(y = j)}{P(y = c)}\right] = \alpha_j + \beta_j x, \ j = 1, \ldots, c - 1.$$

Given that the response falls in category $j$ or the last category, this models the log odds that the response is $j$. It looks like an ordinary logistic regression model, where the two outcomes are category $j$ and category $c$.

Each logit has its own parameters. Software for multicategory logit models fits all the equations *simultaneously*, again assuming independent observations from multinomial distributions.

### EXAMPLE 15.7    Belief in Afterlife by Sex and Race

Table 15.9, from a GSS, has $y =$ belief in life after death, with categories (Yes, Undecided, No), and explanatory variables sex and race. Let $s = 1$ for females and 0 for males, and $r = 1$ for blacks and 0 for whites. With *no* as the baseline category for $y$, the model is

$$\log\left[\frac{P(y = 1)}{P(y = 3)}\right] = \alpha_1 + \beta_1^S s + \beta_1^R r,$$

$$\log\left[\frac{P(y = 2)}{P(y = 3)}\right] = \alpha_2 + \beta_2^S s + \beta_2^R r.$$

The $S$ and $R$ superscripts identify the sex and race parameters.

**TABLE 15.9:** Belief in Afterlife by Sex and Race

| | | Belief in Afterlife | | |
|---|---|---|---|---|
| Race | Sex | Yes | Undecided | No |
| Black | Female | 64 | 9 | 15 |
| | Male | 25 | 5 | 13 |
| White | Female | 371 | 49 | 74 |
| | Male | 250 | 45 | 71 |

The model assumes a lack of interaction between sex and race in their effects on belief in life after death. Table 15.10 shows the parameter estimates. The first equation refers to the odds of a *yes* rather than a *no* response on belief in the afterlife. We see that $\beta_1^S = 0.419$ and $\beta_1^R = -0.342$. Since the dummy variables are 1 for females and for blacks, given that a subject's response was *yes* or *no*, the estimated probability of a *yes* response was higher for females than for males (given race) and lower for blacks than for whites (given sex).

**TABLE 15.10:** Output for Baseline-Category Logit Model Fitted to Table 15.9. First equation uses belief categories (yes, no) and second equation uses belief categories (undecided, no). Estimates for second category of race and sex are 0 because of parameter redundancy (not having their own dummy variable).

```
------------------------------------------------
Belief                         B     Std. Error
1      Intercept           1.225      .128
       [sex=female]         .419      .171
       [sex=male]             0        .
       [race=black]        -.342      .237
       [race=white]           0        .

2      Intercept           -.487      .183
       [sex=female]         .105      .247
       [sex=male]             0        .
       [race=black]        -.271      .354
       [race=white]           0        .

The reference category is 3.
------------------------------------------------
```

The effect parameters represent log odds ratios with the baseline category. For instance, $\beta_1^S = 0.419$ is the conditional log odds ratio between sex and response categories 1 and 3 (yes and no), given race. For females, the estimated odds of response *yes* rather than *no* on life after death are $e^{0.419} = 1.52$ times those for males, controlling for race. For blacks, the estimated odds of response *yes* rather than *no* on life after death are $e^{-0.342} = 0.71$ times those for whites, controlling for sex. ∎

The choice of the baseline category is arbitrary. We can use the equations for a given choice to get equations for *any* pair of categories. For example, using properties of logarithms,

$$\log\left[\frac{P(y=1)}{P(y=2)}\right] = \log\left[\frac{P(y=1)}{P(y=3)}\right] - \log\left[\frac{P(y=2)}{P(y=3)}\right].$$

So to get the prediction equation for the log odds of belief *yes* instead of *undecided* in the previous example, we take

$$(1.225 + 0.419s - 0.342r) - (-0.487 + 0.105s - 0.271r) = 1.71 + 0.314s - 0.071r.$$

For example, the odds of response *yes* instead of *undecided* are higher for females (for whom $s = 1$) than males ($s = 0$).

Inference applies as in ordinary logistic regression, except now to test the effect of a predictor we consider all its parameters for the various equations. In Example 15.7 (page 501), the test of the sex effect has $H_0$: $\beta_1^S = \beta_2^S = 0$. The likelihood-ratio test compares the model to the simpler model dropping sex as a predictor. The test statistic equals 7.2. It has $df = 2$, since $H_0$ has 2 parameters. The $P$-value of 0.03 shows evidence of a sex effect. By contrast, the effect of race is not significant, the likelihood-ratio statistic equaling 2.0 on $df = 2$. This partly reflects the larger standard errors that the effects of race have, due to a much greater imbalance between sample sizes in the race categories than in the sex categories.

## 15.6    LOGLINEAR MODELS FOR CATEGORICAL VARIABLES*

Logistic regression models are similar in structure to ordinary regression models, both types predicting a response variable using explanatory variables. By contrast, **loglinear models** are appropriate for contingency tables in which each classification is a response variable. Loglinear analysis resembles a correlation analysis more than a regression analysis. The log-linear focus is on studying associations between pairs of variables rather than modeling the response on one of them in terms of the others.

Loglinear models are special cases of generalized linear models that assume *Poisson* distributions for cell counts in contingency tables. The Poisson distribution is defined for discrete variables, such as counts, that can take nonnegative integer values. Equivalently, given the overall sample size, they assume a *multinomial* distribution for the counts in the cells of the contingency table.

The loglinear model formulas express the logs of cell expected frequencies in terms of dummy variables for the categorical variables and interactions between those variables. The actual model formulas can be cumbersome, and this section instead uses a symbolic notation that highlights the pairs of variables that are associated. Exercise 15.39 shows why the models are called *loglinear* models.

### EXAMPLE 15.8    Students' Use of Alcohol, Cigarettes, and Marijuana

Table 15.11 is from a survey by the Wright State University School of Medicine and the United Health Services in Dayton, Ohio. The survey asked senior high school students in a nonurban area near Dayton, Ohio, whether they had ever used alcohol, cigarettes, or marijuana. Table 15.11 is a $2 \times 2 \times 2$ contingency table that cross classifies responses on these three items.

In this table, all three variables are response variables, rather than one a response and the others explanatory. The models presented in this section describe their association structure. They analyze whether each pair of variables is associated and whether the association is the same at each category of the third variable.    ■

### A Hierarchy of Loglinear Models for Three Variables

Loglinear models apply to contingency tables with any number of dimensions. We use three-way tables to introduce basic ideas, illustrating for Table 15.11. Denote the three variables by $X$, $Y$, and $Z$. (In this section, to emphasize that we are considering

**TABLE 15.11**: Alcohol (*A*), Cigarette (*C*), and Marijuana (*M*) Use for High School Seniors

| Alcohol Use | Cigarette Use | Marijuana Use | |
|---|---|---|---|
| | | Yes | No |
| Yes | Yes | 911 | 538 |
| | No | 44 | 456 |
| No | Yes | 3 | 43 |
| | No | 2 | 279 |

*Source*: I am grateful to Professor Harry Khamis, Wright State University, for these data.

probabilistic properties of the variables rather than their particular values, we use uppercase notation for the variables.)

Loglinear models describe **conditional associations** in partial tables that relate two of the variables while controlling for the third one. A pair of variables could be statistically independent at each category of the third variable. In other words, the population version of each partial table could satisfy independence. In that case, the pair is said to be **conditionally independent**, and the odds ratios equal 1 in the partial tables. Or associations might exist in some or all of the partial tables. We now introduce a hierarchy of five loglinear models, ordered in terms of the extent of association.

1. All three pairs of variables are conditionally independent. That is,
   *X* is independent of *Y*, controlling for *Z*;
   *X* is independent of *Z*, controlling for *Y*;
   *Y* is independent of *Z*, controlling for *X*.

2. Two of the pairs of variables are conditionally independent. For example,
   *X* is independent of *Z*, controlling for *Y*;
   *Y* is independent of *Z*, controlling for *X*;
   *X* and *Y* are associated, controlling for *Z*.

3. One of the pairs of variables is conditionally independent. For example,
   *X* is independent of *Z*, controlling for *Y*;
   *X* and *Y* are associated, controlling for *Z*;
   *Y* and *Z* are associated, controlling for *X*.

4. No pair of variables is conditionally independent, but the association between any two variables is the same at each category of the third. We then say there is **homogeneous association**.

5. All pairs of variables are associated, but there is *interaction*. That is, the association between each pair varies according to the category of the third variable. (Recall Section 10.3.)

Each model has a symbol that indicates the pairs of variables that are associated. Associated variables appear together in the symbol. For instance, $(XY, Z)$ denotes the model for case 2 in which *X* and *Y* are associated but the other two pairs are conditionally independent. The symbol $(XY, XZ, YZ)$ denotes the model for case 4, in which all three pairs are associated. Table 15.12 lists the symbols for the models described above. All the models provide some structure for the pattern of association except for the one symbolized by $(XYZ)$. This model fits any sample three-way table perfectly, allowing the associations to be nonhomogeneous. It is called the **saturated model**.

**TABLE 15.12:** Some Loglinear Models for Three-Dimensional Contingency Tables

| Model Symbol | Interpretation |
|---|---|
| $(X, Y, Z)$ | All pairs are conditionally independent. |
| $(XY, Z)$ | $X$ and $Y$ the only associated pair. |
| $(XY, YZ)$ | $X$ and $Z$ the only conditionally independent pair. |
| $(XY, YZ, XZ)$ | Each pair associated, controlling for the third variable. Homogeneous association. |
| $(XYZ)$ | All pairs associated, but nonhomogeneous (interaction). |

## Odds Ratio Interpretations for Loglinear Models

Interpretations of associations in loglinear models, like those in logistic regression models, can use the odds ratio. In $2 \times 2$ contingency tables, independence is equivalent to a population odds ratio of 1.0. In a three-way table, *conditional independence* between $X$ and $Y$ means that the population odds ratios in the $XY$ partial tables all equal 1.0. *Homogeneous association* means that the population odds ratios in the $XY$ partial tables are identical at each category of $Z$.

For instance, a $2 \times 2 \times 3$ table consists of three partial tables each of size $2 \times 2$, with two categories for $X$ and two categories for $Y$ measured at three levels of $Z$. Suppose the $XY$ population odds ratio is 1.0 at the first level of $Z$, 1.0 at the second level of $Z$, and 1.0 at the third level of $Z$. Then $X$ and $Y$ are conditionally independent, and loglinear model $(XZ, YZ)$ holds. If the population odds ratio $= 2.2$ at the first level of $Z$, 2.2 at the second level of $Z$, and 2.2 at the third level of $Z$, then there is conditional association but it is homogeneous. So model $(XY, XZ, YZ)$ holds. When the $XY$ odds ratios are the same at all levels of $Z$, necessarily the $XZ$ odds ratios are the same at all levels of $Y$ and the $YZ$ odds ratios are the same at all levels of $X$.

In fitting loglinear models, software provides expected frequencies having odds ratios that perfectly satisfy the model. If the model fits well, these odds ratios help us interpret the associations implied by the model.

### EXAMPLE 15.9    Estimated Odds Ratios for Substance Use Data

Denote the variables in Table 15.11 by $A$ for alcohol use, $C$ for cigarette use, and $M$ for marijuana use. Table 15.13 contains expected frequencies for the loglinear model $(AC, AM, CM)$. This model permits an association for each pair of variables. But it assumes homogeneous association, in the sense that the odds ratio between two

**TABLE 15.13:** Expected Frequencies for Loglinear Model (*AC, AM, CM*) for Alcohol (*A*), Cigarette (*C*), and Marijuana (*M*) Use for High School Seniors

| Alcohol Use | Cigarette Use | Marijuana Use | |
|---|---|---|---|
| | | Yes | No |
| Yes | Yes | 910.4 | 538.6 |
| | No | 44.6 | 455.4 |
| No | Yes | 3.6 | 42.4 |
| | No | 1.4 | 279.6 |

variables is the same at each level of the third variable. The expected frequencies are very close to the observed counts, so the model seems to fit well.

Let's study the estimated association between cigarette use and marijuana use, controlling for alcohol use, using the expected frequencies. For those who used alcohol, the estimated odds ratio between $C$ and $M$ equals

$$\frac{910.4 \times 455.4}{538.6 \times 44.6} = 17.3.$$

Similarly, for those who had not used alcohol, the estimated odds ratio between $C$ and $M$ equals

$$\frac{3.6 \times 279.6}{42.4 \times 1.4} = 17.3.$$

For each category of $A$, students who have smoked cigarettes have estimated odds of having smoked marijuana that are 17.3 times the estimated odds for students who have not smoked cigarettes. The model assumes homogeneous association, so the estimated odds ratio is the same at each category of $A$.

Software for loglinear models provides tables of model parameter estimates from which one can obtain estimated odds ratios. Table 15.14 illustrates. (Software also provides estimates for intercept and main effect parameters. They are not shown here, because interpretations use the interaction terms to describe conditional associations.) For each pair of variables, the association parameter estimate refers to the *log* odds ratio. For the $CM$ conditional association, therefore, the estimated odds ratio at each level of $A$ equals $e^{2.848} = 17.3$. Similarly, the estimated odds ratio equals $e^{2.054} = 7.8$ between $A$ and $C$ at each level of $M$, and the estimated odds ratio equals $e^{2.986} = 19.8$ between $A$ and $M$ at each level of $C$. The estimated conditional association is very strong between each pair of variables. ■

**TABLE 15.14:** Printout of Association Parameter (Log Odds Ratio) Estimates for Loglinear Model $(AC, AM, CM)$ for Substance Use Data

| Parameter | Estimate | Std. Error | z | Sig. |
|---|---|---|---|---|
| A*C | 2.0545 | 0.1741 | 11.80 | .000 |
| A*M | 2.9860 | 0.4647 | 6.43 | .000 |
| C*M | 2.8479 | 0.1638 | 17.38 | .000 |

The model $(AC, AM, CM)$ permits conditional association for each pair of variables. Other possible loglinear models for these data delete at least one of the associations. To illustrate the association patterns implied by some of these models, Table 15.15 presents estimated conditional odds ratios for the expected frequencies for the models. For example, the entry 1.0 for the $AC$ conditional association for model $(AM, CM)$ is the common value of the estimated $AC$ odds ratios at the two categories of $M$. This model implies conditional independence between alcohol use and cigarette use, controlling for marijuana use. It has estimated odds ratios of 1.0 for the $AC$ conditional association.

Table 15.15 shows that estimated conditional odds ratios equal 1.0 for each pairwise term not appearing in a model, such as the $AC$ association in model $(AM, CM)$. The odds ratios for the sample data are those reported for the saturated model $(ACM)$, which provides a perfect fit. For that model, the odds ratios between two variables

**TABLE 15.15:** Summary of Estimated Conditional Odds Ratios for Various Loglinear Models Fitted to Substance Use Data

| Model | Conditional Odds Ratio | | |
| --- | --- | --- | --- |
| | $AC$ | $AM$ | $CM$ |
| $(A, C, M)$ | 1.0 | 1.0 | 1.0 |
| $(AC, M)$ | 17.7 | 1.0 | 1.0 |
| $(AM, CM)$ | 1.0 | 61.9 | 25.1 |
| $(AC, AM, CM)$ | 7.8 | 19.8 | 17.3 |
| $(ACM)$ Level 1 | 13.8 | 24.3 | 17.5 |
| $(ACM)$ Level 2 | 7.7 | 13.5 | 9.7 |

are not the same at each level of the third variable, so they are reported separately for each level. In each case, they are strong at both levels.

Table 15.15 shows also that estimated conditional odds ratios can vary dramatically from model to model. This highlights the importance of good model selection. An estimate from this table is informative only to the extent that its model fits well. The next section shows how to check model goodness of fit.

## 15.7 MODEL GOODNESS-OF-FIT TESTS FOR CONTINGENCY TABLES*

A *goodness-of-fit test* for a model is a test of the null hypothesis that that model truly holds in the population of interest. Section 8.2 introduced the chi-squared test of independence for contingency tables. That test is a goodness-of-fit test for the loglinear model they states that the two categorical variables are statistically independent. The chi-squared statistic compares the observed frequencies to the expected frequencies that satisfy the independence model. Likewise, logistic regression and loglinear models for multidimensional contingency tables have chi-squared goodness-of-fit tests.

### Chi-Squared Goodness-of-Fit Statistics

Each model for a contingency table has a set of cell expected frequencies, which are numbers that perfectly satisfy the model and give the best fit to the observed counts. The model goodness of fit is tested by comparing the expected frequencies, denoted by $\{f_e\}$, to the observed frequencies $\{f_o\}$. Chi-squared test statistics summarize the discrepancies. Larger differences between the $\{f_o\}$ and $\{f_e\}$ yield larger values of the test statistics and stronger evidence that the model is inadequate.

Two chi-squared statistics, having similar properties, are commonly used to do this. The *Pearson statistic*

$$\chi^2 = \sum \frac{(f_o - f_e)^2}{f_e}$$

was introduced in Section 8.2 for testing independence. Another statistic, the *likelihood-ratio statistic*, is

$$G^2 = 2 \sum f_o \log\left(\frac{f_o}{f_e}\right).$$

It equals the difference between the $(-2 \log \ell)$ values for the model being tested and for the most complex model possible. Software for generalized linear models calls this statistic the *deviance*. Both $\chi^2$ and $G^2$ statistics equal 0 when there is a perfect fit (i.e., all $f_o = f_e$). Since large values indicate a poor fit, the $P$-value for testing a model is the right-tail probability above the observed value.

If the model truly holds, both test statistics have approximate chi-squared distributions. The degrees of freedom ($df$) for the statistics depend on the model fitted. The $df$ resemble the error $df$ in regression, equaling the number of responses modeled on the left-hand side of the equation minus the number of parameters on the right-hand side of the model. For logistic regression models, for instance, the number of responses modeled is the number of sample logits for the model. This equals the number of combinations of levels of explanatory variables having observations on the binary response, since there is one logit for each combination. Thus, $df$ = number of logits modeled − number of parameters. The simpler the model, in the sense of fewer parameters, the larger the $df$ for the test.

The chi-squared approximation is better for larger sample sizes. The Pearson statistic is preferred when the expected frequencies average between about 1 and 10, but neither statistic works well if most of the expected frequencies are less than about 5. It is not appropriate to use these tests if any of the predictors are not categorical. The chi-squared sampling distributions result only when they are applied to contingency tables with relatively large counts.

### EXAMPLE 15.10    Logistic Model Goodness of Fit for Death Penalty Data

Examples 15.2 (page 488) and 15.5 (page 494) used the model

$$\text{logit}[P(y = 1)] = \alpha + \beta_1 d + \beta_2 v$$

to describe how the probability of the death penalty depends on defendant's race $d$ and victims' race $v$. A goodness-of-fit test analyzes whether this model with main effects is adequate for describing the data (Table 15.3). The more complex model containing the interaction term is necessary if the main effects model fits poorly.

Software automatically finds the model expected frequencies and the goodness-of-fit statistics. For instance, this model estimated a probability of 0.233 that a black defendant receives the death penalty for having white victims. Table 15.3 showed there were 48 such black defendants, so the expected number receiving the death penalty equals $48(0.233) = 11.2$. This is the expected frequency for the cell in the table having observed frequency 11.

The $df$ equal the number of logits minus the number of parameters in the model. The death penalty data have four logits, one for each combination of defendant's race and victims' race. The model has three parameters, so both goodness-of-fit statistics have

$$df = \text{Number of logits} - \text{number of parameters} = 4 - 3 = 1.$$

Table 15.16 shows the results of chi-squared goodness-of-fit tests for the logistic model for the death penalty data. The null hypothesis for the tests is that the logistic

TABLE 15.16: Goodness-of-Fit Tests for Logistic Model with Main Effects Fitted to Death Penalty Data

| | Goodness-of-Fit Tests | | |
| --- | --- | --- | --- |
| | Value | df | Sig. |
| Likelihood Ratio | .380 | 1 | .538 |
| Pearson Chi-Square | .198 | 1 | .656 |

model with main effects truly holds; that is, no interaction occurs between defendant's race and victims' race in their effects on the death penalty verdict. The Pearson test statistic is $\chi^2 = 0.20$ and the likelihood-ratio test statistic is $G^2 = 0.38$. These test statistic values are small, so neither $P$-value is small. The model fits the data well. The null hypothesis that the model holds is plausible.    ■

### Standardized Residuals

The chi-squared statistics provide global measures of lack of fit. When the fit is poor, a closer look at the cells of the table may reveal the nature of the lack of fit. Most software for logistic and loglinear models reports **standardized residuals** (sometimes called *adjusted residuals*), which make a cell-by-cell comparison of $f_o$ and $f_e$. Each standardized residual has form

$$\text{Standardized residual} = \frac{f_o - f_e}{\text{Standard error of } (f_o - f_e)}.$$

When the model truly holds, standardized residuals behave like standard normal variables. A large standardized residual (say, exceeding 3 in absolute value) provides strong evidence of lack of fit in that cell. The standardized residuals presented in Section 8.3 are special cases for the bivariate model of independence.

For the logistic model for the death penalty data, the standardized residuals all equal $\pm 0.44$. They are small and provide no evidence of lack of fit. This is not surprising, since the goodness-of-fit statistics are small. In fact, when $df = 1$ for the goodness-of-fit test, only one standardized residual is nonredundant, and the square of any of them equals the $\chi^2$ test statistic.

### Loglinear Model Goodness of Fit

The same goodness-of-fit formulas apply to loglinear models. Likewise, standardized residuals compare individual cell counts to expected frequencies satisfying the model.

Examples 15.8 (page 503) and 15.9 (page 505) used loglinear models to describe associations among alcohol use, cigarette use, and marijuana use, for high school students. Table 15.17 displays results of Pearson $\chi^2$ and likelihood-ratio $G^2$ goodness-of-fit tests for various loglinear models, ranging from the model $(A, C, M)$ for which each pair of variables is independent to the model $(AC, AM, CM)$ for which each pair is associated but the association between two variables is the same at each level of the third. The smaller the chi-squared statistics, the better the fit. Small $P$-values contradict the null hypothesis that the model is adequate. It is usually preferable to select the simplest model that provides a decent fit to the data. If no model fits well, the standardized residuals highlight cells contributing to the lack of fit.

The chi-squared distribution falls on the positive part of the line with mean equal to the $df$ value. Hence, a value such as $G^2 = 1286.0$ based on $df = 4$ falls way out in the right-hand tail. It has a tiny $P$-value and indicates a very poor fit. From Table 15.17, the only model that passes the goodness-of-fit test is $(AC, AM, CM)$. This model allows association between all pairs of variables but assumes that the odds ratio between each pair is the same at each category of the third variable. The models that lack any associations fit poorly, having $P$-values of 0.000.

### Comparing Models by Comparing $G^2$-Values

Table 15.17 illustrates two important properties of the likelihood-ratio $G^2$ statistic. First, $G^2$ has similar properties as the SSE (sum of squared residuals) measure in

**TABLE 15.17:** Goodness-of-Fit Tests for Loglinear Models of Alcohol ($A$), Cigarette ($C$), and Marijuana ($M$) Use, with Likelihood-ratio ($G^2$) and Pearson ($\chi^2$) Chi-Squared Test Statistics

| Model | $G^2$ | $\chi^2$ | df | P-Value |
|-------|-------|----------|-----|---------|
| $(A, C, M)$ | 1286.0 | 1411.4 | 4 | .000 |
| $(A, CM)$ | 534.2 | 505.6 | 3 | .000 |
| $(C, AM)$ | 939.6 | 824.2 | 3 | .000 |
| $(M, AC)$ | 843.8 | 704.9 | 3 | .000 |
| $(AC, AM)$ | 497.4 | 443.8 | 2 | .000 |
| $(AC, CM)$ | 92.0 | 80.8 | 2 | .000 |
| $(AM, CM)$ | 187.8 | 177.6 | 2 | .000 |
| $(AC, AM, CM)$ | 0.4 | 0.4 | 1 | 0.54 |

regression. Both compare observed responses to values expected if a model holds, and both cannot increase as the model becomes more complex. For instance, $(A, CM)$ is a more complex model than $(A, C, M)$, since it allows one association. Hence, it provides a better fit and its $G^2$-value is smaller. Similarly, $G^2$ drops further for model $(AC, CM)$ and further yet for $(AC, AM, CM)$. The Pearson $\chi^2$ statistic, unlike the likelihood-ratio $G^2$, does not have this property. It could increase as a model gets more complex, although in practice this rarely happens.

The second property of $G^2$ refers to model comparison. This was first discussed at the end of Section 15.3. Section 11.6 introduced an $F$ test comparing complete and reduced regression models, based on the reduction in SSE. A similar test comparing models for categorical responses uses the reduction in $G^2$-values. To test the null hypothesis that a model truly holds versus the alternative hypothesis that a more complex model fits better, the test statistic is the difference in $G^2$-values. This difference is identical to the difference in $(-2 \log \ell)$ values for the two models. It is a chi-squared statistic with degrees of freedom equal to the difference in $df$ values for the two $G^2$-values. This is the likelihood-ratio test for comparing the models.

To illustrate, we compare models $(AC, CM)$ and $(AC, AM, CM)$. We test the null hypothesis that the reduced model $(AC, CM)$ is adequate against the alternative that the more complex model $(AC, AM, CM)$ is better. The likelihood-ratio test analyzes whether we can drop the $AM$ association from model $(AC, AM, CM)$. The test statistic is the difference between their $G^2$-values, $92.0 - 0.4 = 91.6$, based on $df = 2 - 1 = 1$. This chi-squared statistic has a P-value of $P = 0.000$. So model $(AC, AM, CM)$ fits significantly better than $(AC, CM)$.

It is not possible to use $G^2$ to compare a pair of models such as $(A, CM)$ and $(AC, AM)$. Neither is a special case of the other, since each allows association that the other excludes.

### Connection between Logistic and Loglinear Models

Any logistic regression model for a contingency table has an equivalent loglinear model. That loglinear model contains the same associations as the logistic model does between the response variable and the explanatory variables, and it contains the most general term for describing relationships among the explanatory variables.

**EXAMPLE 15.11     Loglinear Models for Death Penalty Data**

Examples 15.2 (page 488) and 15.5 (page 494) used a logistic model for the death penalty data having main effects for defendant's race and victims' race. It provides a good fit, with $G^2 = 0.38$ and $\chi^2 = 0.20$ based on $df = 1$.

Let $D$ = defendant's race, $V$ = victims' race, and $P$ = death penalty verdict. For that logistic model, $P$ is the response variable, and $D$ and $V$ have effects on $P$ but without interaction. It has precisely the same fit as the loglinear model that also allows an association between $D$ and $P$ and between $V$ and $P$ and has a term to allow an association between the explanatory variables $D$ and $V$. That is the loglinear model $(DP, VP, DV)$ that allows associations for each pair of variables. That loglinear model has the same values for $G^2$ and $\chi^2$ for testing fit, the same expected frequencies, and the same estimated odds ratios between each predictor and the death penalty outcome. You can check this, as an exercise, by using software to fit this loglinear model to the data (Table 15.3).                                               ∎

### Distinction between Logistic and Loglinear Models

Logistic models distinguish between a single response variable and a set of explanatory variables. By contrast, loglinear models treat every variable as a response variable. Although designed for a different purpose, logistic models imply association patterns among variables that are equivalent to ones expressed by loglinear models. For data in contingency tables, similar conclusions result with the two approaches.

Most applications have a single response variable. It is then more natural to use a logistic regression model than a loglinear model. The logistic analysis focuses on the effects of the predictors on the response, much as in ordinary regression modeling. For that reason, logistic regression is more important in practice. That is also why we gave it more attention than loglinear models in this chapter.

## 15.8  CHAPTER SUMMARY

Chapter 8 presented methods for analyzing association between two categorical variables. The methods of this chapter showed how to model a categorical response variable in terms of possibly *several* explanatory variables.

- For binary response variables, the ***logistic regression*** model describes how the probability of a particular category depends on explanatory variables. It uses a linear model for the ***logit*** transform of the probability, which is the log of the odds. For a quantitative explanatory variable, an S-shaped curve describes how the probability changes as the predictor changes.

- The antilog of a $\hat{\beta}$ parameter estimate in logistic regression is a multiplicative effect on the odds for the response variable, for each one-unit increase in the predictor variable of which it is a coefficient. Thus, for logistic regression the ***odds ratio*** is a natural measure of the nature and strength of an association.

- A parameter value of $\beta = 0$ corresponds to a predictor having no effect on the response. To test $H_0$: $\beta = 0$, the ***Wald test*** uses the squared ratio of $\hat{\beta}$ to its standard error. The ***likelihood-ratio test*** compares values of $(-2 \log \ell)$ for models with and without that term, where $\ell$ is the maximized *likelihood* function. The large-sample distribution of these test statistics is chi-squared with $df = 1$.

- For *ordinal* response variables, an extension of logistic regression uses *cumulative logits*, which are logits of *cumulative probabilities*. The model is called a **cumulative logit model**. The effects of predictors are the same for each cumulative probability.

- For *nominal* response variables, an extension of logistic regression forms logits by pairing each category with a baseline category. Each logit equation has separate parameters.

- **Loglinear** models are useful for investigating association patterns among a set of categorical response variables. They consider possible conditional independence patterns and use conditional odds ratios to describe association.

- For models for contingency tables, Pearson and likelihood-ratio chi-squared statistics test the goodness of fit of the model to the data.

Karl Pearson introduced the chi-squared test for bivariate contingency tables in 1900. The models presented in this chapter did not become popular until near the end of the 1900s. They are examples of **generalized linear models**, which apply to discrete as well as continuous response variables. The statistician and sociologist Leo Goodman is responsible for many of the developments in this area. Social scientists now have available a wide variety of tools for analyzing categorical data.

## PROBLEMS

### Practicing the Basics

**15.1.** A logistic regression model describes how the probability of voting for the Republican candidate in a presidential election depends on $x$, the voter's total family income (in thousands of dollars) in the previous year. The prediction equation for a particular sample is

$$\log\left[\frac{\hat{P}(y=1)}{1-\hat{P}(y=1)}\right] = -1.00 + 0.02x.$$

(a) Identify $\hat{\beta}$ and interpret its sign.

(b) Find the estimated probability of voting for the Republican candidate when (i) income = 10 thousand, (ii) income = 100 thousand.

(c) At which income level is the estimated probability of voting for the Republican candidate (i) equal to 0.50? (ii) greater than 0.50?

(d) For the region of $x$ values for which $P(y=1)$ is near 0.50, give a linear approximation for the change in the probability for an increase of one thousand dollars in income.

(e) Explain the effect of a thousand dollar increase in family income on the odds of voting Republican.

**15.2.** Refer to the previous exercise. When the explanatory variables are $x_1$ = family income, $x_2$ = number of years of education, and $s$ = sex (1 = male, 0 = female), the prediction equation is

$$\text{logit}[\hat{P}(y=1)] = -2.40 + 0.02x_1 + 0.08x_2 + 0.20s.$$

For this sample, $x_1$ ranges from 6 to 157 with a standard deviation of 25, and $x_2$ ranges from 7 to 20 with a standard deviation of 3.

(a) Find the estimated probability of voting Republican for (i) a man with 16 years of education and income 30 thousand dollars, (ii) a woman with 16 years of education and income 30 thousand dollars.

(b) Convert the probabilities in (a) to odds, and find the odds ratio, the odds for men divided by the odds for females. Interpret.

(c) Show how the odds ratio in (b) relates to the sex effect in the prediction equation.

(d) Holding the other variables constant, find the estimated effect on the odds of voting Republican of
   i) A standard deviation change in $x_2$
   ii) A standard deviation change in $x_1$
   Which predictor has the larger standardized effect? Interpret.

**15.3.** A sample of 54 elderly men are given a psychiatric examination to determine whether symptoms of senility are present. A subtest of the Wechsler Adult Intelligence Scale (WAIS) is the explanatory variable. The WAIS scores range from 4 to 20, with a mean of 11.6. Higher values indicate more effective intellectual functioning. Table 15.18 shows results.

(a) Show (i) $\hat{P}(y=1) = 0.50$ at $x = 7.2$, (ii) $\hat{P}(y=1) < 0.50$ for $x > 7.2$.

(b) Estimate the probability of senility at $x = 20$.

**TABLE 15.18**

| Variable | B | Std. Error | Wald Chi-square | Sig. |
|----------|-----|-----------|-----------------|------|
| INTERCEPT | 2.0429 | 1.0717 | 3.6338 | 0.0566 |
| WAIS | -0.2821 | 0.1007 | 7.8487 | 0.0051 |

(c) The fit of the linear probability model is $\hat{P}(y = 1) = 0.847 - 0.051x$. Estimate the probability of senility at $x = 20$. Does this make sense?

(d) Test $H_0: \beta = 0$ against $H_a : \beta \neq 0$. Report and interpret the $P$-value.

**15.4.** Refer to the previous exercise. One of the WAIS subtests, called *Picture completion*, asks questions about 20 pictures that have one vital detail missing. It is considered a test of attention to fine detail. The observations for 20 subjects on $(x, y)$, where $x =$ picture completion score and $y =$ symptoms of senility (1 = yes), are

$(7,1), (5,1), (3,1), (8,1)(1,1), (2,1)(9,1), (3,1),$
$(6,1), (4,1), (6,0), (9,0), (7,0), (7,0), (10,0),$
$(12,0), (14,0), (8,0), (8,0), (11,0).$

(a) Using software, estimate the logistic regression equation.

(b) Estimate the probability that symptoms of senility are present when (i) $x = 0$, (ii) $x = 20$.

(c) Over what range of $x$-scores is the estimated probability of senility greater than 0.50?

(d) Estimate the effect of a one-unit increase in $x$ on the odds that senility symptoms exist.

**15.5.** The final subsection of Section 15.2 used estimated probabilities to describe the effect of husband's earnings on the decision to buy a home. Perform a similar analysis to describe the effect of wife's earnings, when husband's earnings = \$50,000, years married = 3, the wife is working in two years, number of children = 0, add child in two years = 0, head's education = 16 years, and parents' home ownership = 0. Interpret.

**15.6.** Table 12.1 in Chapter 12 reported GSS data on political ideology by party affiliation of

| | 1 | 2 | 3 | 4 | 5 | 6 | 7 |
|-----------|---|----|----|----|----|----|---|
| Democrat | 9 | 20 | 17 | 36 | 4 | 5 | 0 |
| Republican | 0 | 2 | 7 | 23 | 23 | 17 | 2 |

Use logistic regression to describe the effect of ideology on the probability of being a Democrat.

(a) Report the prediction equation, and estimate the probability of Democratic affiliation at ideology level (i) 1 = extremely liberal, (ii) 7 = extremely conservative.

(b) Use the model to test whether the variables are independent. Report the test statistic and $P$-value, and interpret.

(c) Use the odds ratio to describe the effect on party affiliation of a change in ideology from (i) 1 = extremely liberal to 2 = liberal, (ii) 1 = extremely liberal to 7 = extremely conservative.

(d) Construct and interpret a 95% confidence interval for the population odds ratio in (c), case (i).

**15.7.** A study of mother's occupational status and children's schooling[3] reported the prediction equation

$$\text{logit}[\hat{P}(y = 1)] = 0.75 + 0.35b + 0.13f + 0.09m$$
$$+ 0.30fo + 0.21mo - 0.92me - 0.16s,$$

where $y = 1$ if the child obtains a high school degree, $b =$ respondent's year of birth, $f =$ father's education, $m =$ mother's education (0 to 17), $fo =$ father's occupational level, $mo =$ mother's occupational level (1 to 9), $me =$ whether mother employed (1 = yes), $s =$ number of siblings. All effects were significant at the 0.01 level.

(a) Interpret the coefficient of mother's education.

(b) Interpret the coefficient of whether mother employed.

(c) The author reported that a one-point increase in mother's occupational level is associated with a 23% increase in the odds of a high school diploma. Explain how he made this interpretation.

**15.8.** Let $P(y = 1)$ denote the probability that a randomly selected respondent supports current laws legalizing abortion, estimated using sex of respondent ($s = 0$, male; $s = 1$, female), religious affiliation ($r_1 = 1$, Protestant, 0 otherwise; $r_2 = 1$, Catholic, 0 otherwise; $r_1 = r_2 = 0$, Jewish), and political party affiliation ($p_1 = 1$, Democrat, 0 otherwise; $p_2 = 1$, Republican, 0 otherwise, $p_1 = p_2 = 0$, Independent). The logistic model with main effects has prediction equation

$$\text{logit}[\hat{P}(y = 1)] = 0.11 + 0.16s - 0.57r_1$$
$$- 0.66r_2 + 0.47p_1.$$

---

[3]M. Kalmin, *American Sociological Review*, vol. 59, 1994, p. 257.

(a) Give the effect of sex on the odds of supporting legalized abortion; that is, if the odds of support for females equal $\theta$ times the odds of support for males, report $\hat{\theta}$.

(b) Give the effect of being Democrat instead of Independent on the estimated odds of support for legalized abortion.

(c) Give the effect of being Democrat instead of Republican on the estimated odds of support for legalized abortion.

(d) Find the estimated probability of supporting legalized abortion, for (i) female Jewish Democrats, (ii) male Catholic Republicans.

15.9. Table 15.19 shows results of a study on the effects of AZT in slowing the development of AIDS symptoms. In the study, 338 veterans whose immune systems were beginning to falter after infection with the AIDS virus were randomly assigned either to receive AZT immediately or to wait until their T cells showed severe immune weakness. The response is whether they developed AIDS symptoms during the three-year study. Software reports the fit of the logistic model with main effects:

| Parameter | Estimate | Std. Error | Wald Chi-Square | Sig |
|---|---|---|---|---|
| Intercept | -1.0736 | 0.2629 | 16.6705 | .0001 |
| [azt=yes] | -0.7195 | 0.2790 | 6.6507 | .0099 |
| [race=black] | 0.0555 | 0.2886 | 0.0370 | .8476 |

**TABLE 15.19**

| Race | AZT Use | Symptoms Yes | Symptoms No |
|---|---|---|---|
| White | Yes | 14 | 93 |
| | No | 32 | 81 |
| Black | Yes | 11 | 52 |
| | No | 12 | 43 |

Source: *The New York Times*, February 15, 1991.

(a) Set up dummy variables, and report the prediction equation.

(b) Interpret the signs of the azt and race estimates.

(c) For white veterans without immediate AZT use, estimate the probability of AIDS symptoms.

(d) Find the estimated conditional odds ratio between AZT use and the development of symptoms. Interpret.

(e) Test for the effect of AZT use. Interpret.

15.10. For Table 15.11 on page 504, Table 15.20 shows a SAS printout for a logistic model treating marijuana use as the response variable.

(a) Set up dummy variables and report the prediction equation. Interpret the signs of the effects of alcohol use and cigarette use.

(b) Why are the estimates in the table equal to 0 at the second category of each predictor?

(c) Estimate the probability of having used marijuana (i) for those who have not used alcohol or cigarettes, (ii) for those who have used both alcohol and cigarettes.

(d) Show how to convert the coefficient for alcohol use to an estimated odds ratio. Interpret.

15.11. A sample of inmates being admitted to the Rhode Island Department of Corrections were asked whether they ever injected drugs and were tested for hepatitis C virus (HCV). The number who reported injecting drugs were 306 of the 887 men who tested HCV positive, 61 of the 3044 men who tested HCV negative, 110 of the 197 women who tested HCV positive, and 13 of the 288 women who tested HCV negative. The authors[4] concluded that the prevalence of HCV may be underestimated by testing only those who reported injecting drugs.

(a) Report the results as a contingency table.

(b) Define dummy variables and specify a model for which the odds ratios between HCV status and whether injected drugs are identical in the population for each sex.

(c) Fit the model in (b), and report the model-based estimate of the odds ratio in (b).

15.12. Table 15.21 refers to individuals who applied for admission into graduate school at the University of California in Berkeley. Data[5] are presented for

**TABLE 15.20**

| Parameter | | DF | Estimate | Std Err | ChiSquare | Pr > Chi |
|---|---|---|---|---|---|---|
| INTERCEPT | | 1 | -5.309 | 0.4752 | 124.820 | 0.0001 |
| ALCOHOL | yes | 1 | 2.986 | 0.4647 | 41.293 | 0.0001 |
| ALCOHOL | no | 0 | 0.000 | 0.0000 | 0. | 0. |
| CIGARETT | yes | 1 | 2.848 | 0.1638 | 302.141 | 0.0001 |
| CIGARETT | no | 0 | 0.000 | 0.0000 | 0. | 0. |

[4]G. Macolino et al., *American Journal of Public Health*, vol. 95, 2005, pp. 1739–1740.

[5]From D. Freedman, R. Pisani, and R. Purves, *Statistics*, W. W. Norton, 1978, p. 14.

five of the six largest graduate departments at the university. The variables are

A: Whether admitted (yes, no)
S: Sex of applicant (male, female)
D: Department to which application was sent $(D_1, D_2, D_3, D_4, D_5)$

(a) Construct the two-way table for sex and whether admitted, collapsing the table over department. Find the odds ratio and interpret.

(b) Treating $A$ as the response and $D$ and $S$ as categorical predictors, fit the logit model having main effects. Report the prediction equation. Interpret the coefficient of $S$ in this equation by finding the estimated conditional odds ratio between $A$ and $S$, controlling for $D$.

(c) Contrast the model estimated conditional odds ratio between $A$ and $S$ in (b) with the odds ratio reported in (a). Explain why they differ so much, satisfying Simpson's paradox.

**TABLE 15.21**

| Department | Sex | Admitted Yes | Admitted No |
|------------|-----|-----|-----|
| $D_1$ | M | 353 | 207 |
|        | F | 17 | 8 |
| $D_2$ | M | 120 | 205 |
|        | F | 202 | 391 |
| $D_3$ | M | 138 | 279 |
|        | F | 131 | 244 |
| $D_4$ | M | 53 | 138 |
|        | F | 94 | 299 |
| $D_5$ | M | 22 | 351 |
|        | F | 24 | 317 |

**15.13.** Refer to Table 8.15 on page 239 in Chapter 8. Treating happiness as the response variable, Table 15.22 shows results of fitting the cumulative logit model, using scores (1, 2, 3) for income and the chi-squared test of independence of Chapter 8.

(a) Why does the table report two intercept estimates?

(b) Report and interpret the income effect.

(c) Using the model, test the hypothesis of no income effect. Report the test statistic and $P$-value, and interpret.

(d) Suppose we instead used the Pearson chi-squared test of independence. Report the test statistic and $P$-value, and compare results to those in (c). Why are they so different?

**15.14.** Using software, replicate the results in Section 15.4 for Example 15.6 on political ideology and party affiliation.

**15.15.** Table 15.23 refers to passengers in autos and light trucks involved in accidents in the state of Maine. The table classifies subjects by sex, location of accident, seat-belt use, and a response variable having categories (1) not injured, (2) injured but not transported by emergency medical services, (3) injured and transported by emergency medical services but not hospitalized, (4) injured and hospitalized but did not die, (5) injured and died.

(a) Fit a cumulative logit model having main effects for gender ($g = 1$ for males and 0 for females), location ($r = 1$ for rural and 0 for urban), and seat-belt use ($s = 1$ for yes and 0 for no). State the prediction equation. Interpret the sign of the effect for each predictor.

(b) Report and interpret an odds ratio describing the effect of wearing a seat belt.

(c) Construct a 95% confidence interval for the true odds ratio for the effect of wearing a seat belt. Interpret.

(d) Conduct a test of the hypothesis of no effect of seat belt use on the response, controlling for gender and location. Report the $P$-value and interpret.

**15.16.** For the previous exercise, fit the model that also has the three two-way interactions. Use a likelihood-ratio test to compare this model to the main effects model. Interpret. [*Hint*: The test statistic is the difference between the $(-2 \log \ell)$ values.]

**TABLE 15.22**

|  | Estimate | Std. Error | Wald | df | Sig. |
|--|----------|------------|------|-----|------|
| INTERCP1 [happy=1] | -.792 | .415 | 3.63 | 1 | .057 |
| INTERCP2 [happy=2] | 1.681 | .435 | 14.94 | 1 | .000 |
| INCOME | .418 | .223 | 3.53 | 1 | .060 |

| Statistic | DF | Value | Sig. |
|-----------|-----|-------|------|
| Pearson Chi-square | 4 | 3.816 | 0.431 |

**TABLE 15.23**

| Gender | Location | Seat Belt | Response | | | | |
|--------|----------|-----------|------|-----|-----|-----|-----|
| | | | 1 | 2 | 3 | 4 | 5 |
| Female | Urban | No | 7287 | 175 | 720 | 91 | 10 |
| | | Yes | 11,587 | 126 | 577 | 48 | 8 |
| | Rural | No | 3246 | 73 | 710 | 159 | 31 |
| | | Yes | 6134 | 94 | 564 | 82 | 17 |
| Male | Urban | No | 10,381 | 136 | 566 | 96 | 14 |
| | | Yes | 10,969 | 83 | 259 | 37 | 1 |
| | Rural | No | 6123 | 141 | 710 | 188 | 45 |
| | | Yes | 6693 | 74 | 353 | 74 | 12 |

*Source*: Dr. Cristanna Cook, Medical Care Development, Augusta, Maine.

**15.17.** A baseline-category logit model fit predicting preference for President (Democrat, Republican, Independent) using $x$ = annual income (in \$10,000 dollars) is $\log[\hat{P}(y = 1)/\hat{P}(y = 3)] = 3.3 - 0.2x$ and $\log[\hat{P}(y = 2)/\hat{P}(y = 3)] = 1.0 + 0.3x$.
  **(a)** Use an estimated odds ratio to describe how the choice between Republican and Independent depends on income.
  **(b)** Explain how to get the prediction equation for $\log[\hat{P}(y = 2)/\hat{P}(y = 3)]$. Interpret its slope.

**15.18.** For a sample of people in Ithaca, New York, consider the most recent time each person shopped for clothes. You plan to model the choice to shop downtown (the Ithaca Common), at the Pyramid/Triphammer mall, or on the Internet, as a function of several variables, such as annual income, whether a student, and distance of residence from downtown. Explain the type of model you would use, and why.

**15.19.** Refer to the $3 \times 7$ table in Table 12.1 (page 371) on party identification and political ideology.
  **(a)** Fit a baseline-category logit model, treating party affiliation as the response. Interpret the political ideology effect for each pair of party IDs.
  **(b)** Fit a cumulative logit model, treating political ideology as the response. Interpret the party ID effects.

**15.20.** Using software, replicate the results in Section 15.5 for Example 15.7 (page 501) on belief in life after death, sex, and race.

**15.21.** Consider the fit of the model $(AC, AM, CM)$ to Table 15.11 (page 504) for the survey of high school seniors.
  **(a)** Use the expected frequencies in Table 15.13 to estimate the conditional odds ratios between $A$ and $M$ at each level of $C$.

  **(b)** Show how to obtain the estimated odds ratio in (a) from the parameter estimates for the model in Table 15.14.
  **(c)** By contrast, what is the estimated conditional odds ratio between $A$ and $M$ for the loglinear model denoted by $(AC, CM)$?

**15.22.** Refer to the loglinear model analyses reported in Section 15.6 for use of marijuana, alcohol, and cigarettes. Use software to replicate all the analyses shown there.

**15.23.** Consider a four-way cross-classification of variables $W$, $X$, $Y$, and $Z$. State the symbol for the loglinear model in which
  **(a)** All pairs of variables are independent.
  **(b)** $X$ and $Y$ are associated but other pairs of variables are independent.
  **(c)** All pairs of variables are associated, but the conditional associations are homogeneous.

**15.24.** For the logistic model reported in Exercise 15.9 on AZT use and AIDS, software reports a Pearson goodness-of-fit statistic equal to 1.39 with $df = 1$, with $P$-value 0.24. Specify $H_0$ for this test, and interpret the $P$-value.

**15.25.** Refer to the survey data for high school seniors in Table 15.11 (page 504).
  **(a)** Specify a logistic regression model for the response of whether the student has used marijuana that would have fit exactly the same as the loglinear model $(AC, AM, CM)$.
  **(b)** The Pearson and likelihood-ratio goodness-of-fit statistics for the model in (a) both equal 0.4, with $df = 1$. Interpret.

## Concepts and Applications

**15.26.** Refer to the "Student survey" data file (Exercise 1.11). Using software, conduct and interpret a logistic regression analysis using $y$ = opinion about abortion with predictors
  **(a)** political ideology
  **(b)** sex and political ideology

**15.27.** Refer to the data file you created in Exercise 1.12. For variables chosen by your instructor, fit a logistic regression model and conduct descriptive and inferential statistical analyses. Interpret and summarize your findings.

**15.28.** The data given in Exercise 10.14 in Chapter 10 came from an early study on the death penalty and racial characteristics. Analyze those data using methods of this chapter. Summarize your main findings in a way that you could present to the general public, using as little technical jargon as possible.

**15.29.** According to *The Independent* newspaper (London, March 8, 1994), the Metropolitan Police in London reported 30,475 people as missing in the year ending March 1993. For those of age 13 or less, 33 of 3271 missing males and 38 of 2486 missing females were still missing a year later. For ages 14–18, the values were 63 of 7256 males and 108 of 8877 females; for ages 19 and above, the values were 157 of 5065 males and 159 of 3520 females. Analyze and interpret these data. (Thanks to Dr. P. M. E. Altham for showing me these data.)

**15.30.** In a study of whether an educational program makes sexually active adolescents more likely to obtain condoms, adolescents were randomly assigned to two experimental groups. The educational program, involving a lecture and videotape about transmission of the HIV virus, was provided to one group but not the other. In logistic regression models, factors observed to influence a teenager to obtain condoms were sex, socioeconomic status, lifetime number of partners, and the experimental group. Table 15.24 summarizes results.

**(a)** Find the parameter estimates for the fitted model, using (1, 0) dummy variables for the first three predictors.

**TABLE 15.24**

| Variables | Odds Ratio | 95% Confidence Interval |
|---|---|---|
| Group (education versus none) | 4.04 | (1.17, 13.9) |
| Sex (males versus females) | 1.38 | (1.23, 12.88) |
| SES (high versus low) | 5.82 | (1.87, 18.28) |
| Lifetime number of Partners | 3.22 | (1.08, 11.31) |

*Source*: V. I. Rickert et al., *Clinical Pediatrics*, vol. 31, 1992, pp. 205–210.

**(b)** Explain why either the estimate of 1.38 for the odds ratio for sex or the corresponding confidence interval seems incorrect. The confidence interval is based on taking antilogs of endpoints of a confidence interval for the log odds ratio. Show that if the reported confidence interval is correct, then 1.38 is actually the *log* odds ratio, and the estimated odds ratio equals 3.98.

**15.31.** A Canadian survey of factors associated with whether a person is a hunter of wildlife showed the results in Table 15.25. Explain how to interpret the results in this table. The study abstract[6] stated, "Men are 10 times more likely to hunt wildlife than females." Comment on how this conclusion was reached, and whether it is correct.

**15.32.** A study[7] compared the relative frequency of mental health problems of various types among U.S. Army members before deployment to Iraq, U.S. Army members after serving in Iraq, U.S. Army members after serving in Afghanistan, and U.S. Marines after serving in Iraq. The study stated, "Potential differences in demographic factors among the four study groups were controlled for in our analysis with the use of logistic regression." For this study, identify the response variable, the primary explanatory variable, and likely control variables.

**15.33.** A 2006 report (http://www.oas.samhsa.gov/) by the Office of Applied Studies for the Substance Abuse and Mental Health Services Administration about factors that predict marijuana use stated, "Multiple logistic regression also confirmed that the risk of recent marijuana initiation increased with increasing age among youths aged 12 to 14, but the risk decreased with increasing age among those aged 15 to 25." What does this suggest about the way that age appears in the model used?

**15.34.** Refer to the data in Exercise 8.16 (page 249) in Chapter 8 on happiness and marital status. Using a cumulative logit model, analyze and interpret these data.

**15.35.** Refer to Table 15.4 on page 489. Show that the association between the defendant's race and the death penalty verdict satisfies Simpson's paradox. What causes this?

**15.36.** For a person, let $y = 1$ represent death during the next year and $y = 0$ represent survival. For adults in the U.K. and in the U.S., the probability of death is well approximated by the model, $\text{logit}[P(y = 1)] = -10.5 + 0.1x$, where $x = $ age in years. Show how the probability of death in the

[6]By R. Mitchell, *Crossing Boundaries*, vol. 1, 2001, 107–117.

[7]C. Hoge et al., *New England Journal of Medicine*, vol. 351, 2004, 13–21.

**TABLE 15.25**

|  | B | S.E. | Wald | Sig | Exp(B) |
|---|---|---|---|---|---|
| Constant | -5.04 | 0.16 | 943.1 | .000 | |
| Male | 2.34 | 0.15 | 259.9 | .000 | 10.39 |
| Live in rural area | 0.98 | 0.10 | 106.2 | .000 | 2.67 |
| Not married | -0.04 | 0.12 | 0.1 | .717 | .96 |
| Not employed | -0.36 | 0.12 | 8.8 | .003 | .70 |
| Age: 15 to 29 | 0.21 | 0.13 | 2.5 | .113 | 1.24 |
| Age: 50 or more | -0.27 | 0.12 | 4.7 | .030 | .77 |
| Education up to HS | 0.38 | 0.10 | 14.9 | .000 | 1.46 |
| Naturalist club member | 1.64 | 0.11 | 228.6 | .000 | .42 |

next year increases as $x$ increases from 20 to 60 to 100.

**15.37.** State the symbols for the loglinear models for categorical variables that are implied by the causal diagrams in Figure 15.5.

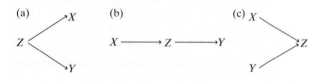

(a), (b), (c)

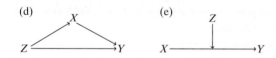

(d), (e)

**FIGURE 15.5**

**\*15.38.** For the logistic regression model, from the linear approximation $\beta/4$ for the rate of change in the probability at the $x$-value for which $P(y = 1) = 0.50$, show that $1/|\beta|$ is the approximate distance between the $x$-values at which $P(y = 1) = 1/4$ (or $P(y = 1) = 3/4$) and at which $P(y = 1) = 1/2$. Thus, the larger the value of $|\beta|$, the less the $x$-distance over which this change in probability occurs.

**\*15.39.** For a two-way contingency table, let $r_i$ denote the $i$th row total, let $c_j$ denote the $j$th column total, and let $n$ denote the total sample size. Section 8.2 showed that the cell in row $i$ and column $j$ has $f_e = r_i c_j/n$ for the independence model. Show that the log of the expected frequency has an additive formula with terms representing the influence of the $i$th row total, the $j$th column total, and the sample size. This formula is the loglinear model for independence in two-way contingency tables.

**\*15.40.** Explain what is meant by the absence of statistical interaction in modeling the relationship between a response variable $y$ and two explanatory variables $x_1$ and $x_2$ in each of the following cases. Use graphs or tables to illustrate.
**(a)** $y$, $x_1$, and $x_2$ are quantitative.
**(b)** $y$ and $x_1$ are quantitative; $x_2$ is categorical.
**(c)** $y$ is quantitative; $x_1$ and $x_2$ are categorical.
**(d)** $y$, $x_1$, and $x_2$ are binary.
**(e)** $y$ is binary, $x_1$ and $x_2$ are quantitative.

# CHAPTER 16

# An Introduction to Advanced Methodology

16.1 LONGITUDINAL DATA ANALYSIS*
16.2 MULTILEVEL (HIERARCHICAL) MODELS*
16.3 EVENT HISTORY MODELS*
16.4 PATH ANALYSIS*
16.5 FACTOR ANALYSIS*
16.6 STRUCTURAL EQUATION MODELS*
16.7 MARKOV CHAINS*

This final chapter introduces some advanced statistical methods. An introductory text such as this does not have space to present them in detail. However, a social science researcher is likely to see reference to these methods, and it is helpful to have at least a rudimentary understanding of their nature and purposes. Rather than presenting technical details, we provide an explanation of (1) what the method is used for, and (2) the types of results that can occur and their interpretations.

## 16.1 LONGITUDINAL DATA ANALYSIS*

Sections 12.6 and 12.7 introduced ANOVA methods for comparing means of *dependent* samples. Such data most commonly result from studies that observe subjects repeatedly over time, that is, in *longitudinal studies*. A few types of methods are available for such data. They vary in the assumptions they make and in how they model the correlation structure of the repeated observations.

Sections 12.6 and 12.7 presented traditional *repeated measures ANOVA*. This type of ANOVA has limitations:

- Observations on all subjects need to be made at the same time points.
- The method cannot deal with missing data. Subjects with *any* missing observations get dropped from the analysis. This can lead to significant bias when the missing data are considerable.
- The correlations among observations on the same subject are assumed to satisfy a *sphericity* structure, which is implied by common variability at all times and the same correlation between each pair of observations.

### MANOVA: Multivariate Analysis of Variance

A more general type of ANOVA does not make restrictive assumptions about the correlation pattern. It treats the set of repeated measures on a subject as a multivariate vector of responses. By doing this, standard methods are available that are designed for multivariate response data. Such methods can test hypotheses comparing the means without needing to make any assumption about the correlation structure. The tests are called MANOVA, short for ***multivariate analysis of variance***. The particular MANOVA test referred to by most software as *Wilks' lambda* is a *likelihood-ratio test*, the idea of which was introduced in Section 15.3.

The MANOVA approach has its own disadvantages, however. The main one is that it often loses power as the sacrifice for having weaker assumptions. If the assumptions for traditional repeated measures ANOVA are not badly violated, that method has higher power for testing effects. MANOVA loses power because it requires estimating a larger number of parameters. In addition, MANOVA also has the first two disadvantages mentioned above for traditional repeated measures ANOVA: Observations need to be made at the same times, and subjects with any missing observations get dropped from the analysis.

### Mixed Effects Models with Random Effects

A method developed more recently than traditional ANOVA and MANOVA does not have the disadvantages just discussed. This method allows varied types of modeling of the correlation structure for the repeated responses. It permits observations at different time points. It can accommodate subjects in the analysis when some of their observations are missing. It assumes that the missing data are *missing at random*. This means that the probability an observation is missing does not depend on the value of the unobserved response. As usual, inference assumes normality, and this assumption becomes less important with larger sample sizes.

This method uses an alternative type of model that explicitly includes ***random effects*** for the subjects. As explained in Section 12.6, a model for repeated measures data can include a dummy variable for each subject. The coefficient of a dummy variable represents the effect for a particular subject. For example, a positive effect means that each observation for that subject tends to be higher than the average for all the subjects who share the same values as that subject for the predictors. The subject factor consists of all these subject-specific effects. The effects are called *random effects*, because the subjects observed are regarded as a random sample of all the possible subjects who could have been sampled.

The distinction between random effects and other parameters in the model is that the random effects are treated as unobserved random variables rather than as parameters. That is, the terms in the model for the subjects are assumed to come from a particular probability distribution, usually the normal distribution with unknown variance. This is helpful, because otherwise the number of parameters that need to be estimated could be enormous (when $n$ is large) if each subject term were treated as a parameter rather than as a random effect.

The models also include *fixed effects* (ordinary parameters) for the predictor variables (such as treatment) for which the analyses use all the categories of interest. Because the classification variables are a mixture of random and fixed effects, the model is called a ***mixed model***.

An appealing aspect of the random effects approach to modeling is the freedom of using various correlation structures for the repeated measures on a subject. One possibility is the ***exchangeability*** structure. This assumes that all the pairwise correlations are equal for the responses of a subject at the different times. In practice, often observations closer together in time tend to be more highly correlated than observations farther apart. The ***autoregressive*** structure is a way to permit this. With it, if $\rho$ denotes the correlation for observations one unit apart in time, then the correlation is $\rho^2$ for observations two units apart in time, $\rho^3$ for observations three units apart, and so forth. It's also possible to use an ***unstructured*** approach that makes no assumption about the correlation pattern. In any of these cases, the correlations are themselves parameters to be estimated using the data.

## One-Way Repeated Measures ANOVA Using Random Effects

Let's first consider the case of one-way ANOVA with repeated measures of subjects. That is, there is one within-subjects factor but no between-subjects factor. This case was considered with traditional repeated measures ANOVA in Section 12.6. For $T$ times, the mixed model with random effects is

$$E(y) = \alpha + s_i + \beta_1 t_1 + \beta_2 t_2 + \cdots + \beta_{T-1} t_{T-1},$$

where $s_i$ is a random effect for subject $i$, $t_1$ is a dummy variable for time 1, $t_2$ is a dummy variable for time 2, and so forth. Time is a fixed effect. When $T = 2$, for example, the purpose of the study may be to compare means before and after receiving some treatment. The parameters of main interest to be estimated are the fixed effects $\{\beta_t\}$. The subject terms in the model correspond to a *random intercept* that gets added to the ordinary intercept term.

If we expect a linear trend in the means over time, we could replace the $T - 1$ fixed effects terms for the $T$ times by $\beta t$, thus using one slope parameter instead of $T - 1$ separate time parameters. Mixed models can then have a second type of random effect term to allow the slopes to vary by subject around a mean of $\beta$, that is, to allow a *random slope* as well as a random intercept.

The model just described for a within-subjects comparison of $T$ means extends to allow between-subjects effects in addition to the within-subjects effects. The next example illustrates.

## EXAMPLE 16.1    Quality of Life with Treatments for Alcohol Dependence

Gueorguieva and Krystal (2004) analyzed data from a clinical trial for the effect of using a particular drug (naltrexone) in addition to psychosocial therapy in treating 627 veterans suffering from chronic, severe alcohol dependence. The response variable was a financial satisfaction score. This was the average of four items on a quality of life scale, for which each item had potential values 1 (terrible) to 7 (delighted). For each subject, this response was observed initially and then after 4, 26, 52, and 78 weeks. The three treatments were 12 months of the drug, 3 months of the drug followed by 9 months of placebo, or 12 months of placebo. This is the between-subjects factor. Table 16.1 shows the sample mean satisfaction scores for the $3 \times 5$ combinations of treatment and time.

This data set is the sort we analyzed in Section 12.7 using ANOVA with two factors and repeated measures on one of them. Here, the repeated measures occur across

**TABLE 16.1:** Sample Mean Satisfaction for Subjects Suffering Alcohol Dependence, by Treatment and Time of Measurement. Treatment is a between-subjects factor and time is a within-subjects factor.

| Treatment | Time | | | | |
|---|---|---|---|---|---|
| | Initial | 4 Weeks | 26 Weeks | 52 Weeks | 78 Weeks |
| Long-term drug | 3.9 | 4.0 | 4.3 | 4.5 | 4.4 |
| Short-term drug | 3.7 | 4.0 | 4.1 | 4.3 | 4.3 |
| Placebo | 3.6 | 3.9 | 3.9 | 4.2 | 4.3 |

the five levels of time. Let's consider the model

$$E(y) = \alpha + s_i + \beta_1 t_1 + \beta_2 t_2 + \beta_3 t_3 + \beta_4 t_4 + \beta_5 d_1 + \beta_6 d_2 + \beta_7 t_1 \times d_1$$
$$+ \beta_8 t_1 \times d_2 + \beta_9 t_2 \times d_1 + \beta_{10} t_2 \times d_2 + \beta_{11} t_3 \times d_1 + \beta_{12} t_3 \times d_2$$
$$+ \beta_{13} t_4 \times d_1 + \beta_{14} t_4 \times d_2,$$

where $s_i$ is the effect for subject $i$, $\{t_1, t_2, t_3, t_4\}$ are dummy variables for the first four times and $\{d_1, d_2\}$ are dummy variables for the two drugs.

The traditional repeated measures ANOVA, using the Greenhouse-Geisser adjustment to account for violation of the sphericity assumption, shows no evidence of a treatment-by-time interaction ($P$-value $= 0.69$) and no evidence of a treatment effect ($P$-value $= 0.80$). There is strong evidence of a time effect ($P$-value $< 0.001$), not surprising from viewing the means in Table 16.1. We conclude that although satisfaction seems to improve over time, it may well improve just as fast for placebo as for either drug treatment. However, complete results for all five times were available for only 211 of the 627 subjects. This analysis used only the complete cases, thus ignoring the data for the 416 subjects who had some missing data.

With the mixed model approach, we treat $s_i$ as a random effect for subject $i$. Then it is not necessary to ignore the data for the subjects missing some observations. This results in greater power. When used with an unstructured pattern for the correlations, there is then slight evidence of a treatment effect ($P$-value $= 0.07$). There is still no evidence of interaction ($P$-value $= 0.63$) and very strong evidence of a time effect ($P$-value $< 0.001$).

This example shows the benefit of a mixed model approach when there are many missing observations. The traditional approach would discard much information, such that evidence about the treatment effect changes from marginal ($P = 0.07$) to very weak ($P = 0.80$). ∎

With mixed models, it's possible to use the data to predict the individual subject effects. This permits us to predict time trends at the subject level. In contrast to traditional approaches, the predicted response at each time point varies among subjects in a given treatment group.

More generally, in mixed models, the random effects can represent *clusters* rather than subjects. For example, in a study that samples families and observes the subjects in each family, a cluster consists of subjects from the same family. For given values of explanatory variables, two subjects in the same family tend to be more alike than two subjects in different families. Identifying the families in the model using a random effect for each family accounts for the correlation among subjects within a family.

More and more software can fit mixed models assuming various correlation structures for repeated measures. An example is PROC MIXED in SAS. The analysis requires some sophistication to avoid inappropriate models. You should seek a statistician's guidance before attempting to use these methods. For further details, see Fitzmaurice et al. (2004), Hedeker and Gibbons (2006), and Gueorguieva and Krystal (2004). If there are no missing data, the observations are taken at the same time, and common correlations seems like a plausible assumption, it is simpler to use traditional repeated measures ANOVA. If the sample size is small, this approach is also preferable, when its assumptions are not badly violated.

The above examples refer to continuous responses and modeling the mean. Similar approaches have been developed for categorical responses and modeling proportions using logits. For example, it is possible to include random effects in a logistic regression model to account for within-subject associations in studies with repeated measures on a binary variable. For discussion of ways of handling categorical responses in longitudinal studies, see Agresti (2007, Chapters 9 and 10).

## 16.2   MULTILEVEL (HIERARCHICAL) MODELS*

Random effects are useful for various types of models in addition to models for longitudinal data. An example is hierarchical models that describe observations having a nested nature: Units at one level are contained within units of another level. Hierarchical data are common in certain application areas, such as in educational studies.

For example, a study of student performance might measure, for each student, performance on each exam in a battery of exams. Students are nested within schools. The model could describe how the expected response for a subject depends on explanatory variables as well as how the expected response for a school depends on explanatory variables. That is, the model could analyze the effect of characteristics of a student (such as performance on past exams) and of characteristics of the school the student attends. Just as two observations for the same student (on different exams) might tend to be more alike than two observations for different students, so might two students in the same school tend to have more-alike observations than two students from different schools. This could be because students within a school tend to be similar on various socioeconomic indices.

### Modeling Observations at Two Levels

Hierarchical models contain terms for the different levels of units. For the example just mentioned, the model would contain terms for predicting an expected student response and terms for predicting the expected response within a school. Level 1 refers to measurements at the student level, and level 2 refers to measurements at the school level. Models having a hierarchical structure of this sort are called *multilevel models*.

Multilevel models often have a large number of terms. To limit the number of parameters, the model treats terms for the sampled units on which there are multiple observations as random effects rather than fixed effects. The random effects can enter the model at each level of the hierarchy.

For example, random effects for students and random effects for schools refer to different levels of the model. Level 1 random effects can account for variability among students in student-specific characteristics not measured by the explanatory variables. These might include student ability and parents' socioeconomic status. The level 2 random effects account for variability among schools due to school-specific characteristics not measured by the explanatory variables. These might include the quality of the teaching staff, the degree of drug-related problems in the school, and characteristics of the district for which the school enrolls students.

### EXAMPLE 16.2    A Two-Level Model for Student Achievement

An educational study analyzes factors that affect student performance on a statewide achievement test. Denote the test score for student $t$ in school $i$ by $y_{it}$. We'll consider a model having two levels, one for students and one for schools. When there are many schools and we can regard them as approximately a random sample of schools that the study could have analyzed, we use random effects for the schools.

The level 1 model (i.e., student level) would include a term for school $i$ and explanatory variables that have values that vary among students, such as $x_1 =$ performance on an achievement test taken in an earlier grade, $x_2 = $ GPA, $x_3 = $ race, and $x_4$ = whether the student has failed any grades. The level 1 model is

$$E(y_{it}) = \alpha + \delta_i + \beta_1 x_1 + \beta_2 x_2 + \beta_3 x_3 + \beta_4 x_4,$$

where $\delta_i$ is the effect for each student attending school $i$.

The level 2 model (i.e., school level) provides a linear predictor for the level 2 term $\delta_i$ in the level 1 model. That level 2 model has explanatory variables that vary only at the school level, such as $w_1$ = per-student expenditure of school $i$, $w_2$ = teacher's average salary, and $w_3$ = median income of families in the school district. For example, the level 2 model might be

$$\delta_i = s_i + \gamma_1 w_1 + \gamma_2 w_2 + \gamma_3 w_3.$$

The term $s_i$ is a random effect for school $i$.

Substituting the level-two model into the level 1 model, we obtain

$$E(y_{it}) = \alpha + s_i + \gamma_1 w_1 + \gamma_2 w_2 + \gamma_3 w_3 + \beta_1 x_1 + \beta_2 x_2 + \beta_3 x_3 + \beta_4 x_4.$$

Each student in school $i$ shares the random effect $s_i$. This is a mixed model, having a random effect term for schools and fixed effects consisting of explanatory variables for the schools and explanatory variables for the subjects. It can be fitted with software for mixed models or with specialized software for multilevel models (such as HLM and MLwiN). ∎

More generally, random effects can enter into each level of the model. For example, suppose there are several observations per student, such as a score for each exam in a battery of tests. Then the model can include random effects for students as well as for schools. More generally yet, a multilevel model can have more than two levels. For further details, see Gelman and Hill (2006), Raudenbush and Bryk (2002), and Snijders and Bosker (1999).

## 16.3   EVENT HISTORY MODELS*

Some studies have the objective of modeling a response variable that observes how long it takes until a certain type of event occurs. For instance, the response might be how long a person works before retiring from the work force, the age of a person when first marrying, the length of time before someone just released from prison is rearrested, or how long a person lives after being diagnosed with AIDS.

As in ordinary regression, models for the time to some event include effects of explanatory variables. A model for the length of time before rearrest, for instance, might use predictors such as number of previous arrests, whether employed, marital status, age at the time of release, and educational level.

The modeling of events occurring over time using a set of explanatory variables is called *event history analysis*. Early development of event history models took place in the 1980s in biostatistics, for modeling the length of time that a patient survives after undergoing a particular medical treatment. In this context, the analysis is called *survival analysis*. For example, survival analysis can model the amount of time until death for a patient who has had a heart transplant, using explanatory variables such as age at the time of the operation, overall quality of health, body-mass index, and whether the patient is or has been a smoker.

## Censored Data and Time-Varying Covariates

In event history analyses, the data for each subject consists of an observation of the length of time until the event of interest occurs. Two complicating factors occur that are not an issue in ordinary regression modeling.

First, for some subjects, the event has not yet occurred by the end of the observation period for the study. We cannot observe the actual time to the event for those subjects, but instead only lower bounds on those times. For instance, a study of the effects of various explanatory variables on retirement age may use a sample of adults aged at least 65. Some subjects in this sample may not have retired yet. If a 68-year-old person has not yet retired, we know only that the response variable (retirement age) takes value at least 68.

An observation of this type in which we know only a region of values in which it falls is said to be *censored*. Methods for event history analysis have special ways of handling censored data. Ignoring censored data and fitting models using only data for subjects having fully observed responses can result in a severe bias in parameter estimation.

Second, some explanatory variables for predicting the time to the event may change value over time. For instance, a study of criminal recidivism that models the length of time until rearrest may observe each month whether a person has been rearrested (the event of interest) and use explanatory variables such as whether the subject is working and whether the subject is married or living with a partner. For a particular subject, the value of explanatory variables of this type could vary over time. An explanatory variable that can vary over time is called a *time-dependent covariate*. Advanced methods for fitting event history models can handle both time-dependent and time-independent covariates.

## The Rate of Occurrence of an Event

We've considered the *length of time* until a particular event occurs as the response of interest. The most popular event history model describes, however, the *rate* of occurrence of the event.

Consider, for instance, a study about health problems of subjects admitted to a nursing home. The response is the length of time after admission before a subject requires special medical care that necessitates admission to a hospital. At a particular setting for the explanatory variables, the sample contains five subjects. The time until requiring special medical care equals 0.5 year for the first subject, 0.2 year for the second, 1.3 years for the third, and 0.1 year for the fourth. The fifth subject is a censored observation, not requiring any special medical care during the 0.4 year she had been in the home when the observation period for the study ended. Then, for these five subjects, the total number of occurrences of the event of interest is 4, and the total observation time is $(0.5 + 0.2 + 1.3 + 0.1 + 0.4) = 2.5$ years. The sample rate of occurrence is $4/2.5 = 1.6$. That is, the rate of occurrence equals 1.6 events per year of observation time. The sample number of events equals 1.6 times the total amount of time for which the entire sample of subjects were under observation.

The model formula refers to the rate of occurrence of the event rather than to the time elapsed before the event occurs. In the literature, the rate is usually called the *hazard rate* and denoted by $h$. The above calculation for a sample hazard rate implicitly assumes that this rate is constant over time. In practice, this is often not realistic. Models can allow the hazard rate to depend on time as well as on values of explanatory variables.

### The Proportional Hazards Model

Let $h(t)$ denote the hazard rate at time $t$, such as $t$ years after admission to a nursing home. The standard model for the hazard rate and a set of explanatory variables has the form

$$\log h(t) = \alpha(t) + \beta_1 x_1 + \beta_2 x_2 + \cdots + \beta_k x_k.$$

The model applies to the log of the hazard rate, because the hazard rate must be positive. Linear functions for the hazard rate itself have the disadvantage that they might provide negative predicted values, much like the linear probability model for a binary response variable. In the form of the model written here, the explanatory variables are time independent, but they can also be time dependent.

The intercept parameter $\alpha(t)$ is allowed to depend on time $t$. This permits the hazard rate itself to be time varying. Usually the primary focus is on estimating the effects of the explanatory variables on the hazard rate, not on modeling the dependence of the hazard rate on time. The geriatric study, for instance, could estimate the effects on the hazard rate of gender and age of subject. For this reason, it is common to allow $\alpha(t)$ to be an arbitrary, unspecified function. The main focus of the analysis is on estimating $\{\beta_j\}$ to make inferences about the covariate effects.

How do we interpret the covariate effects? Consider the effect of $x_1$ on the hazard rate due to increasing it by one unit while holding the other predictors constant. Denote the hazard rates at a fixed value $x_1$ and at $x_1 + 1$ by $h_1$ and $h_2$. Then

$$\log h_2(t) - \log h_1(t) = [\alpha(t) + \beta_1(x_1 + 1) + \cdots + \beta_k x_k]$$
$$- [\alpha(t) + \beta_1 x_1 + \cdots + \beta_k x_k] = \beta_1.$$

So $\beta_1$ is the change in the log hazard rate for a one-unit change in $x_1$, holding the other predictors fixed. But $\log h_2(t) - \log h_1(t) = \log[h_2(t)/h_1(t)]$, and exponentiating both sides, $h_2(t)/h_1(t) = e^{\beta_1}$, or

$$h_2(t) = e^{\beta_1} h_1(t).$$

That is, increasing $x_1$ by one unit has the effect of multiplying the hazard rate by $e^{\beta_1}$. Effects are multiplicative, as in other models that use the log to achieve linearity, such as exponential regression and logistic regression models.

The equation $h_2(t) = e^{\beta_1} h_1(t)$ illustrates that the hazard rate at one setting of explanatory variables is proportional to the hazard rate at another setting. The same proportionality constant applies at each time $t$. Because of this property, this form of model is called a ***proportional hazards model***. It is simple to interpret effects for such models, because the effect of any explanatory variable on the hazard rate is identical at all times.

In 1972 the British statistician Sir David Cox proposed and showed how to fit this form of proportional hazards model in which the dependence of the hazard on time, through $\alpha(t)$, is arbitrary. The model is called the ***Cox proportional hazards model***. It is *nonparametric*, in the sense that it makes no assumption about the probability distribution of the time to the event but instead focuses on the effects of the explanatory variables. More specialized models of proportional hazards form (or other forms) make parametric assumptions about this distribution. This is useful if the distribution of the time to the event is an important focus of the study, as it is, for example, in analyzing time to failure of electronic components.

### EXAMPLE 16.3    Modeling Time to Marital Dissolution

An article on modeling family dynamics with event history techniques analyzed data from the National Survey of Families and Households. A national probability sample of about 13,000 subjects were interviewed, and then a follow-up survey interviewed 10,000 of these subjects approximately six years later. The purpose was to analyze factors that affect the hazard rate for marital separation. The response outcome for each subject married at the beginning of the study is the number of months from then until the couple separates. People who are still in their marriage or widowed at the end of the study provide censored observations.

Table 16.2 summarizes the fit of the model. The final column of the table shows the exponentiated estimates of the regression parameters, which provide the hazard rate ratios. For instance, since $e^{0.353} = 1.42$, the estimated dissolution rate for blacks was 1.42 times the rate for whites. This is the strongest of the effects shown in the table.

**TABLE 16.2:** Estimated Effects on Hazard Rate for Marital Dissolution, Based on Cox Proportional Hazards Model

| Variable | Estimate | Std. Error | $P$-Value | $e^b$ |
|---|---|---|---|---|
| Age at marriage | −0.086 | 0.0050 | 0.000 | 0.917 |
| Year married | 0.048 | 0.0017 | 0.000 | 1.049 |
| Race (black = 1) | 0.353 | 0.0423 | 0.000 | 1.423 |
| Gender (male = 1) | −0.065 | 0.0375 | 0.083 | 0.937 |

*Source*: T. B. Heaton and V. R. A. Call, *Journal of Marriage & Family*, vol. 57, 1995, p. 1078.

As in logistic regression, significance tests of model parameters can use Wald statistics or likelihood-ratio statistics. For instance, for $H_0$: no gender effect, the Wald test statistic $z = -0.065/0.0375 = -1.73$ has two-sided $P$-value $= 0.083$. Equivalently, the square of this statistic is a chi-squared statistic with $df = 1$.    ∎

Several software programs now exist for fitting event history models, such as the SURVIVAL option with COX REGRESSION suboption on the ANALYZE menu in SPSS. See Allison (1984), DeMaris (2004, Chap. 11), and Yamaguchi (1991) for introductions to this topic.

## 16.4    PATH ANALYSIS*

Path analysis uses regression models to represent theories of causal relationships among a set of variables. Statistically, it consists merely of a series of regression analyses, but there are advantages to conducting the analyses within the path analytic framework. The primary advantage is that the researcher must specify explicitly the presumed causal relationships among the variables. This can help contribute logically to sensible theories of variable relationships.

Association is one characteristic of a cause–effect relationship. As Section 10.1 discussed, however, it is not sufficient to imply causation. Two variables that are both causally dependent on a third variable may themselves be associated. Neither is a cause of the other, however, and the association disappears when the third variable is controlled. Path analyses utilize regression models that include appropriate control variables.

An explanatory variable $x$ is a possible cause of a response variable $y$ if the proper time order occurs and if changes in $x$ give rise to changes in $y$, even when all relevant variables are controlled. If the association between two variables disappears under a control, a direct causal relationship does not exist between them. If the association does not disappear, though, the relationship is not necessarily causal. The association could disappear when other variables are controlled. So we can prove noncausality but we can never prove causality. A hypothesis of a causal relationship is bolstered, though, if the association remains after controls are introduced.

### Path Diagrams

Theoretical explanations of cause–effect relationships often hypothesize a system of relationships in which some variables, believed to be caused by others, may in turn have effects on yet other variables. A single multiple regression model is insufficient for that system, since it can handle only a single response variable. Path analysis utilizes the number of regression models necessary to include all proposed relationships in the theoretical explanation.

### EXAMPLE 16.4 Paths to Educational Attainment

Suppose a theory specifies the following:

1. A subject's educational attainment depends on several factors, including the subject's intelligence, the subject's motivation to achieve, and the parent's income level.
2. The subject's motivation to achieve itself depends on several factors, including general intelligence level and the parent's educational level.
3. The parent's income itself depends in part on the parent's educational level.

Figure 16.1 shows a graphic summary of the theory just outlined. The figure is called a *path diagram*. Such diagrams generalize the causal diagrams introduced in Chapter 10.

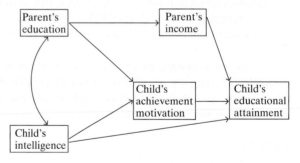

**FIGURE 16.1:** Example of Preliminary Path Diagram for Educational Attainment

In path diagrams, a cause–effect relationship is represented by a straight arrow pointing toward the effect (response) variable and leading from the causal (explanatory) variable. The response variables of the regression equations are the variables to which the arrows point. The explanatory variables for an equation with a particular response variable are those variables with arrows pointing toward that response variable. In Figure 16.1, parent's income is modeled as depending on parent's education; child's educational attainment as depending on parent's income, child's intelligence, and child's achievement motivation; and child's achievement motivation as depending on parent's education and child's intelligence. A curved line, with arrows in both directions, connects parent's education and child's intelligence. This indicates that the two variables may be associated but the model does not address their causal relationship (if any). ■

## Path Coefficients

Ordinarily in a path diagram, each arrow has a number written over it. These numbers are standardized regression coefficients for the regression equation for the response variable to which the arrows point. In the context of path analysis, they are called *path coefficients*. Figure 16.1 has three sets of coefficients to be estimated, since it refers to three separate response variables.

Denote the standardized versions of the variables in this figure by $E$, $A$, and $I$ for child's educational attainment, achievement motivation, and intelligence, and by $Pe$ and $Pi$ for parent's education and income. Also, for two variables $x$ and $y$, let $\beta^*_{yx}$ denote the standardized regression coefficient for the effect of $x$ on $y$. Then Figure 16.1 corresponds to the three regression equations

$$E(E) = \beta^*_{EI}I + \beta^*_{EA}A + \beta^*_{EPi}Pi \tag{1}$$

$$E(A) = \beta^*_{AI}I + \beta^*_{APe}Pe \tag{2}$$

$$E(Pi) = \beta^*_{PiPe}Pe. \tag{3}$$

For example, the coefficient of the path leading from parent's education to child's achievement motivation is the estimate of the standardized regression coefficient $\beta^*_{APe}$ from the multiple regression model (2) having child's achievement motivation as the response variable and parent's education and child's intelligence as the explanatory variables. Parent's income, in this model, depends only on parent's education [see (3)]. The path coefficient for that arrow is the standardized bivariate regression coefficient, which is the ordinary correlation.

The path coefficients show the direction and relative sizes of effects of explanatory variables, controlling for other variables in the sequence. Their interpretation is that of standardized regression coefficients in multiple regression (Section 11.8). For instance, a value of 0.40 means that a one standard deviation increase in the explanatory variable corresponds to a predicted increase of 0.40 standard deviations in the response variable, controlling for the other explanatory variables in that model.

Every response variable has a *residual variable path* attached to it in the path diagram. This represents the variation unexplained by its explanatory variables. Each residual variable represents the remaining portion $(1 - R^2)$ of the unexplained variation, where $R^2$ denotes the R-squared value for the regression equation for that response variable. Its path coefficient equals $\sqrt{1 - R^2}$.

## Direct and Indirect Effects

Most path models have variables that are dependent on some other variables but are, in turn, causes of other response variables. These variables are *intervening variables* (Section 10.3), since they occur in sequence between other variables. In Figure 16.1, child's achievement motivation intervenes between child's intelligence and child's educational attainment. If this causal theory is correct, child's intelligence affects his or her educational attainment in part through its effect on achievement motivation. An effect of this type, operating through an intervening variable, is said to be *indirect*. Figure 16.1 also suggests that child's intelligence has a *direct* effect on educational attainment, over and above its effect through achievement motivation. An important reason for using path analysis is that it studies the direct and indirect effects of a variable.

On the other hand, Figure 16.1 suggests that parent's education does not have a direct effect on child's educational attainment. It affects this response only through its effects on parent's income and child's achievement motivation. So if we add parent's education as a predictor to the multiple regression model (1) for response $E$, its effect should not be significant when parent's income and child's achievement motivation are also in the model.

The regression analyses conducted as part of the path analysis reveal whether significant evidence exists of the various effects. If intelligence affects educational attainment directly, as well as indirectly through its effect on motivation, then all three coefficients of parts of paths leading from intelligence to educational attainment should be significant. The direct effect would be verified by a significant partial effect for intelligence in the multiple regression model (1) containing intelligence, achievement motivation, and parent's income as predictors of educational attainment. The indirect effect would be verified by a significant partial effect for achievement motivation in that model, and a significant partial effect for intelligence on achievement motivation in the multiple regression model (2) also containing parent's education as a predictor for achievement motivation.

In conducting the regression analyses, if we find a nonsignificant path, we can erase that path from the diagram and perform the appropriate analyses again to reestimate the coefficients of the remaining paths. For small samples, though, keep in mind that a sample effect may not be significant even if it is of sufficient size to be noteworthy. To conduct a sophisticated path analysis analyzing several direct and indirect associations with any degree of precision requires a large sample size.

### EXAMPLE 16.5    Completed Path Diagram for Educational Attainment

Figure 16.2 shows the path diagram from Figure 16.1 with the path coefficients added. The residual variables for the three response variables are denoted by $R_1, R_2,$ and $R_3$. If 28% of the child's educational attainment were explained by its three predictors, for example, then the path coefficient of the residual variable $R_1$ for the child's educational attainment would be $\sqrt{1 - R^2} = \sqrt{1 - 0.28} = 0.85$.

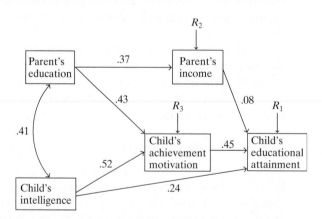

**FIGURE 16.2:** Path Diagram for Child's Educational Attainment, with Path Coefficients Added

Figure 16.2 suggests that of the three direct predictors of child's educational attainment, the child's achievement motivation had the strongest partial effect. The child's intelligence has a moderate indirect effect through increasing achievement motivation, as well as a direct effect. Parent's income is not as directly important as the child's achievement motivation or intelligence, but the parent's educational level has an important effect on the child's achievement motivation. Such conclusions are highly tentative if the path coefficients have substantial sampling error. ■

## Path Decompositions

A causal diagram is a way of hypothesizing what's responsible for an association between two variables. One of the fundamental results of path analysis decomposes the correlation between two variables in terms of component parts dealing with the various paths between those two variables.

It is easiest to illustrate this idea using a simple causal diagram. For three variables, consider the model of a chain relationship, introduced in Section 10.3. Specifically,

$$x \longrightarrow z \longrightarrow y$$

According to this model, the correlation between $x$ and $y$ is explained by the intervening variable, $z$. Controlling for $z$, that association should disappear.

The partial correlation (Section 11.7)

$$\rho_{xy \cdot z} = \frac{\rho_{xy} - \rho_{zx}\rho_{zy}}{\sqrt{\left(1 - \rho_{zx}^2\right)\left(1 - \rho_{zy}^2\right)}}$$

measures the association between $x$ and $y$, controlling for $z$. For the partial correlation $\rho_{xy \cdot z}$ to equal 0, it is necessary that

$$\rho_{xy} = \rho_{zx}\rho_{zy}.$$

That is, the correlation between $x$ and $y$ decomposes into the correlation between the intervening variable and $x$ times the correlation between the intervening variable and $y$.

A generalization of this formula holds for more complex path diagrams. Specifically, let $\beta_{z_i x}^*$ denote the path coefficient for the model in which $z_i$ is a response variable and $x$ is a predictor for it. Suppose that the $\{z_i\}$ also serve as predictors of $y$ in a separate model. Then the correlation between $x$ and $y$ decomposes into

$$\rho_{xy} = \sum_i \beta_{z_i x}^* \rho_{z_i y},$$

where the sum is over all variables $z_i$ that have a direct path to $y$. The simpler expression $\rho_{xy} = \rho_{zx}\rho_{zy}$ given previously for the chain relationship $x \longrightarrow z \longrightarrow y$ is a special case of this with only one $z_i$ variable, namely, $z$. In that case, since $x$ is the only variable in the model predicting $z$, the path coefficient of $x$ on $z$ is just the correlation between them.

How is the general decomposition useful? The equation predicts what the correlation *should* be if the causal diagram is correct. For sample data, we can compute the correlation predicted by this formula by substituting the sample estimates into the right-hand side. We then compare this predicted correlation to the actual sample correlation. If the difference between the two cannot be explained by sampling error, then the results refute the causal hypothesis that the diagram represents.

For the chain model, for instance, $r_{xy}$ should be close to $r_{zx}r_{zy}$; that is, the partial correlation $r_{xy \cdot z}$ should be close to zero. The $t$ test for $H_0$: $\rho_{xy \cdot z} = 0$ (Section 11.7) is a way of testing the model.

In summary, the basic steps in a path analysis are as follows:

1.  Set up a preliminary theory to be tested, drawing the path diagram without the path coefficients.
2.  Conduct the necessary regression modeling to estimate the path coefficients and the residual coefficients.

3. Evaluate the model, checking whether the sample results agree with it. Then reformulate the model, possibly erasing nonsignificant paths. The revised model may be the basis for future research. That research would fit models for the amended diagram and reestimate path coefficients for that diagram.

### A Caveat about Causal Modeling

We must add an important caveat here. For the path analysis decomposition formula to truly hold, we must assume that the unmeasured variables that represent the residual variation for each response variable are uncorrelated with the predictors in the regression model for that response. In Figures 16.1 and 16.2, for instance, all the other variables that affect child's educational attainment are assumed to be uncorrelated with parent's income, child's achievement motivation, and child's intelligence. In practice, it's doubtful that this would be exactly true.

The real world that social scientists study is never quite as simple as a causal diagram portrays. In any particular example, such a diagram is a crude approximation for reality. The true diagram would be highly complex. A large number of variables would likely play a role, with paths between nearly all pairs.

An analogous remark applies to regression models. Parameter estimates in prediction equations refer to the particular variables in the model. If we added other explanatory variables that affect the response variable, those estimated effects would change somewhat, because undoubtedly the added variables would be somewhat correlated with the predictors originally in the model. This is a fundamental characteristic of all social science research. No matter what you report, someone can argue that different results would occur if you had included other variables in your model.

Finally, even if data are consistent with a particular path diagram, this does not imply that the causal system represented by the diagram truly holds. Statistical methods can not directly test the hypothesized causal order. Path analysis does not infer causation from association, but merely provides structure for representing and estimating assumed causal effects. For further details about path analysis, see Duncan (1966), Freedman (2005, Chapter 5), Land (1969), and Pedhazur (1997, Chapter 18). For discussion of some of the pitfalls in attempting to use regression modeling to discover causal relationships, we recommend the books by Berk (2004), Freedman (2005), and Pedhazur (1997).

## 16.5 FACTOR ANALYSIS*

Factor analysis is a multivariate statistical method used for a wide variety of purposes. These include

1. Revealing patterns of interrelationships among variables
2. Detecting clusters of variables, each of which contains variables that are strongly intercorrelated and hence somewhat redundant
3. Reducing a large number of variables to a smaller number of statistically uncorrelated variables, the *factors* of factor analysis

The third use is helpful for handling several variables that are highly intercorrelated. For example, suppose a multiple regression model has severe multicollinearity, partly due to the large number of predictor variables used to measure each concept of interest. Factor analysis can transform a collection of highly correlated explanatory variables that are indicators of the same type to one or two factors having nearly as much predictive power. Each factor is an artificial combination of the original variables, however, and how useful this is depends on the interpretability of the factors.

## The Factor Analytic Model

The model for factor analysis expresses the expected values of a set of observable variables $x_1, \ldots, x_k$ as linear functions of a set of unobserved variables, called *factors*. The user specifies the number of factors, which we denote by $m$. This must be less than the number of variables $k$. The process uses *standardized* variables, and in fact uses only the correlation matrix for the variables.

The model consists of $k$ equations. Each one expresses a standardized variable in terms of the $m$ factors. Roughly speaking, the model says that the variables can be replaced by a smaller set of factors. The factors in the factor analysis model are artificial, unobserved variables. They are merely convenient summaries of the observed variables. In statistics, unobserved variables such as factors are sometimes referred to as **latent variables**.

The correlation of a variable with a factor is called the **loading** of the variable on that factor. After conducting a factor analysis, software shows a matrix with a row for each variable and a column for each factor that shows these factor loadings. The sum of squared loadings for a variable is called the variable's **communality**. It represents the proportion of its variability that is explained by the factors. Ideally, high communality is achieved for each variable using relatively few factors.

The fitting process also can provide equations that express the factors as linear functions of the observed variables. The coefficients in the equations depend on the sample correlations between the pairs of variables. For example, the first factor might relate to standardized versions of seven observed variables by

$$f_1 = 0.93x_1 + 0.78x_2 - 0.11x_3 + 0.02x_4 + 0.14x_5 - 0.06x_6 - 0.18x_7.$$

This equation indicates that $f_1$ primarily summarizes information provided by $x_1$ and $x_2$. The factor equations convert values on the $k$ variables for each subject to a smaller set of scores on the $m$ factors.

## Fitting the Factor Analysis Model

The researcher selects the number of factors believed adequate to explain the relationships among the observed variables. The researcher can often form a good hunch about this number by inspecting the correlation matrix for the observed variables. If different sets of variables cluster, with strong correlations between pairs of variables within each set but small correlations between variables from different sets, then one could let the number of factors equal the number of clusters.

An **exploratory** form of factor analysis searches for an appropriate number of factors. Guidance for this is provided by **eigenvalues**. The eigenvalue for a particular factor summarizes the percentage of variability of the variables explained by that factor. Factors are added to the model until additional factors provide little improvement in explained variability. A more structured, so-called **confirmatory** analysis, preselects a particular value for the number of factors. It may also assume particular structure for the factor loadings, such as taking some of them to equal 0.

The fitting process assumes that the response variables have a **multivariate normal** distribution. In particular, this implies that each individual variable has a normal distribution, and the regression relationship between each pair of variables is linear. In practice, this is unrealistic. There is a tendency for most users to go ahead and use this method regardless of the distributions, but these strong assumptions should make you wary about using the method with highly nonnormal variables (e.g., binary) or without a careful check of the effect of any obvious outliers on the ultimate conclusions.

With most exploratory factor analysis, there are so many parameters (factor loadings) that no unique solution exists. The parameters are said to be *unidentified*. For example, with given values of two variables and one factor, there are many possible solutions for the parameter estimates in

$$f_1 = \hat{\beta}_1 x_1 + \hat{\beta}_2 x_2.$$

Different solutions can give different estimated factor loadings but correspond to the same fit. After obtaining an initial solution for the factor loadings, factor analytic procedures treat each row of $m$ factor loadings as a point in $m$-dimensional space and can "rotate" the estimates to obtain more meaningful factors with simpler factor structure. The purpose of the rotation is to bring most loadings of a variable close to 0, so that each variable is highly correlated with only one or two factors. This makes it easier to interpret each factor as representing the effects of a particular subset of variables. The rotated solution reproduces the observed correlations among the observed variables just as well as the original solution.

Often, one factor is strongly related to all the variables. Ideally, after rotation, the structure of the factor loadings might appear as shown in Table 16.3. Entries of 0 in that table represent factor loadings that are not significantly different from zero. The first factor is associated with all the variables, the second factor provides information contained in $x_1, x_2, x_3$, and the third factor provides information contained in $x_4, x_5, x_6$.

**TABLE 16.3:** Simple Structure for Factor Loadings of Seven Variables on Three Factors

|  |  | Factor | | |
|---|---|:---:|:---:|:---:|
|  |  | 1 | 2 | 3 |
|  | 1 | * | * | 0 |
|  | 2 | * | * | 0 |
|  | 3 | * | * | 0 |
| Variable | 4 | * | 0 | * |
|  | 5 | * | 0 | * |
|  | 6 | * | 0 | * |
|  | 7 | * | 0 | 0 |

*Denotes a significantly nonzero loading.

In its simplest form, the fitting process derives the factors so that the correlation equals zero between each pair of them. It is also possible to use rotations for which the resulting factors are correlated (i.e., *nonorthogonal* rotations). This is often more plausible for social science applications.

### EXAMPLE 16.6   Factor Analysis of Election Variables

The correlations in Table 16.4 refer to the following eight variables, measured in an election for 147 districts in Chicago:

1. Percentage vote for Democratic candidate in mayoral election
2. Percentage vote for Democratic candidate in presidential election
3. Percentage of straight party votes
4. Median rental cost

5. Percentage homeownership
6. Percentage unemployed
7. Percentage moved in last year
8. Percentage completed more than ten years of school

**TABLE 16.4:** Correlation Matrix for Eight Variables Measured for 147 Districts in Chicago Election

|  |  | Variable Number | | | | | | | |
|---|---|---|---|---|---|---|---|---|---|
|  |  | 1 | 2 | 3 | 4 | 5 | 6 | 7 | 8 |
| Variable Number | 1 | 1.0 |  |  |  |  |  |  |  |
|  | 2 | 0.84 | 1.0 |  |  |  |  |  |  |
|  | 3 | 0.62 | 0.84 | 1.0 |  |  |  |  |  |
|  | 4 | −0.53 | −0.68 | −0.76 | 1.0 |  |  |  |  |
|  | 5 | 0.03 | −0.05 | 0.08 | −0.25 | 1.0 |  |  |  |
|  | 6 | 0.57 | 0.76 | 0.81 | −0.80 | 0.25 | 1.0 |  |  |
|  | 7 | −0.33 | −0.35 | −0.51 | 0.62 | −0.72 | −0.58 | 1.0 |  |
|  | 8 | −0.66 | −0.73 | −0.81 | 0.88 | −0.36 | −0.84 | 0.68 | 1.0 |

*Source*: Reprinted from Harman (1967, pp. 165–166) by permission of The University of Chicago Press.

The table shows that variables 1, 2, 3, and 6 are highly positively correlated, as are variables 4, 7, and 8. This suggests that two factors can represent these eight variables. Fitting the factor analysis model using the ***principal factor*** solution with two factors yields the estimated factor loadings shown in Table 16.5. The table of factor loadings has $k = 8$ rows, one for each observed variable, and $m = 2$ columns, one for each factor.

**TABLE 16.5:** Factor Loadings for a Two-Factor Solution for the Correlations in Table 16.4

|  |  | Loadings | | Communality |
|---|---|---|---|---|
|  |  | Factor 1 | Factor 2 |  |
| Variable Number | 1 | 0.69 | −0.28 | 0.55 |
|  | 2 | 0.88 | −0.48 | 1.00 |
|  | 3 | 0.87 | −0.17 | 0.79 |
|  | 4 | −0.88 | −0.09 | 0.78 |
|  | 5 | 0.28 | 0.65 | 0.50 |
|  | 6 | 0.89 | 0.01 | 0.79 |
|  | 7 | −0.66 | −0.56 | 0.75 |
|  | 8 | −0.96 | −0.15 | 0.94 |

The first factor is said to be ***bipolar*** because it contains high positive and high negative loadings. The positive correlations occur with variables 1, 2, 3, and 6, for which high scores tend to occur in districts with a heavily Democratic vote. Perhaps this factor summarizes the traditional Democratic vote. Factor 2, which is highly positively correlated with variable 5 and negatively correlated with variable 7, is interpreted as a measure of home permanency. As the score on factor 2 for a district increases, the percentage of homeownership tends to increase, and the percentage of those who have moved in the previous year tends to decrease.

Figure 16.3 plots the loadings of the variables on the two factors. Each point in Figure 16.3 represents a particular variable. For example, the point labeled 4 has as

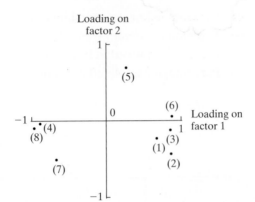

**FIGURE 16.3:** Plot of Loadings from Table 16.5 of the Eight Variables on the Two Factors

$x$-coordinate the loading of variable 4 on factor 1 ($-0.88$) and as $y$-coordinate the loading of variable 4 on factor 2 ($-0.09$). The plots shows that variables 1, 2, 3, and 6 cluster together, having similar pairs of loadings. Also, variables 4, 7, and 8 cluster together. The relatively large values for the communalities tell us that the factors explain most of the variation in the original variables.

Further analyses of these data might replace the eight variables with these two factors. They seem to have a clear interpretation. They are uncorrelated, so no redundancies occur when both are used in regression analyses. Two equations express each factor in terms of the eight variables, and these equations provide scores on the two factors for the 147 districts. ∎

A confirmatory factor analysis provides a stronger hypothesized structure before analyzing the data. For example, we could specify a structure such as in Table 16.3, such that certain factor loadings are constrained to equal 0. This makes it easier to interpret the ultimate factors. Chi-squared tests are available for checking a particular structure by testing that a set of parameters takes certain fixed values.

### Latent Class Models for Categorical Responses

Analogs of factor analysis have been developed for categorical response variables. The simplest such model is the ***latent class model***. It states that there is an unobserved latent categorical variable that explains the associations among the observed variables. Conditional on an observation falling in a particular latent category, responses on the observed variables are statistically independent.

### EXAMPLE 16.7    Latent Class Model for Abortion Attitudes

The GSS asks subjects whether they favor or oppose legalization of abortion under various conditions, such as whenever the woman wants it (variable ABANY), when the baby would have a birth defect (ABDEFECT), when the woman does not want any more children (ABNOMORE), when the mother's health is in danger (ABHLTH), when the woman is too poor to have more children (ABPOOR), when the woman is pregnant because of rape (ABRAPE), and when the woman is single and does not want to get married (ABSINGLE). Perhaps an underlying latent variable describes one's basic attitude toward legalized abortion, such that given the value of that latent variable, responses on these variables are conditionally independent.

One possible latent class model would have a single latent variable with three categories. This would result from hypothesizing that there is a class for those who nearly always oppose legalized abortion regardless of the situation, a second class for those who nearly always favor legalized abortion, and a third class for those whose response depends on the situation.  ■

This basic latent class model extends in various ways. For example, there could be two latent factors, each with its own categories. Or a *latent variable model* has a latent characteristic that varies continuously and is assumed to have a normal distribution.

### Origin and Controversy

Factor analysis was originally developed early in the twentieth century by psycho-metricians in an attempt to construct a factor or factors measuring intelligence. Charles Spearman postulated the existence of a single factor that measures general intelligence. Later, L. L. Thurstone and others hypothesized a set of group factors, each of which could be measured using a battery of tests of similar nature. For an entertaining and highly critical look at the history of this subject and the variety of potential pitfalls in using factor analysis to attempt to measure intelligence, see Gould (1981).

A danger with factor analysis is making the error of *reification*—acting as if a factor truly measures a characteristic of interest to us. In fact, we don't know this.

Also, there are statistical dangers in using this method. In any analysis dealing with unmeasured variables such as artificial factors, you could identify patterns in a factor loading matrix as suggesting certain interpretations for the factors, when actually those patterns are largely due to sampling error. One check you can do for this is to split your data set randomly into two parts and then conduct a factor analysis with each. If the results seem inconsistent in some ways, then any predictions should be very tentative and serve mainly to suggest models to check with other data sets.

For a long time, the statistical basis of factor analysis was shaky. It was not possible, for instance, to report valid standard errors for factor loadings. Recently, maximum likelihood methods have been developed that improve on many of the older methods for performing factor analysis. There has also been increasing emphasis on using factor analysis in more of a confirmatory than exploratory mode, as described in the following section. This forces a researcher to think more carefully about reasonable factor structure before performing the analysis. Then spurious conclusions are less likely. For further details, see Afifi et al. (2003), DeMaris (2002), Hagenaars and McCutcheon (2006), Harman (1967), and Thompson (2004).

## 16.6 STRUCTURAL EQUATION MODELS*

A very general model combines elements of both path analysis and factor analysis. The model is called a ***covariance structure model*** because it attempts to explain the variances and correlations among the observed variables. This explanation takes the form of a causal model relating a system of factors, some of which may be created as in factor analysis and some of which may be observed variables.

Covariance structure models have two components. The first is a ***measurement model***. It resembles a factor analysis, deriving a set of unobserved factors from the observed variables. The second component is a ***structural equation model***. It resembles a path analysis, specifying regression models for the factors derived in the measurement model.

## Measurement Model

The measurement model specifies how the observed variables relate to a set of unobserved factors, the *latent variables*. This part of the analysis resembles a factor analysis, except that the modeling has more highly specified structure. The measurement model assigns each latent variable, a priori, to a specific set of observed variables. This is accomplished by forcing certain factor loadings to equal 0, so that the latent variables are uncorrelated with other variables.

The measurement model addresses the fact that the observed variables, being subject to measurement error and problems with validity and reliability, are imperfect indicators of the concepts of true interest. For example, a study might use responses to a battery of items on a questionnaire dealing with racist attitudes as crude indicators of racism. Factor analyzing them may produce a single latent variable that is a better general measure of racism than any single item. A purpose of creating latent variables is to operationalize characteristics that are difficult to measure well, such as prejudice, anxiety, and conservatism.

## Structural Equation Model

The structural equation model uses regression models to specify causal relationships among the latent variables. One or more of the latent variables are identified as response variables, and the others are identified as explanatory variables. The latent response variables can be regressed on the latent explanatory variables as well as on other latent response variables. Unlike ordinary path analysis, this approach allows the fitting of models with two-way causation, in which latent variables may be regressed on each other.

### EXAMPLE 16.8 Covariance Structure Model for Intelligence, SES, and Achievement

Figure 16.4, based on an example in Pedhazur (1997), illustrates a covariance structure model. The model analyzes the effects of intelligence and socioeconomic status on achievement. The observed variables are the indicators of intelligence, $x_1$ = Wechsler score and $x_2$ = Stanford-Binet IQ score; the indicators of socioeconomic status, $x_3$ = father's education, $x_4$ = mother's education, and $x_5$ = parents' total income; and the indicators of achievement, $y_1$ = verbal score and $y_2$ = quantitative score on an achievement test. The achievement indicators are the response variables.

In Figure 16.4, rectangles represent observed variables and circles represent latent variables. An intelligence latent variable applies only to $x_1$ and $x_2$, the indicators of

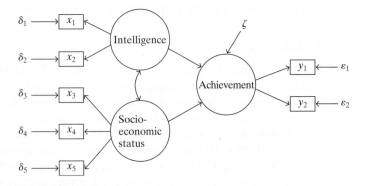

**FIGURE 16.4:** A Covariance Structure Model for Achievement, Intelligence, and Socioeconomic Status Latent Variables. It is based on five observed explanatory variables and two observed response variables.

intelligence. A socioeconomic status latent variable applies only to $x_3$, $x_4$, and $x_5$, its indicators. An achievement latent variable applies only to $y_1$ and $y_2$, the indicators of achievement. The figure depicts the dependence of the observed variables on the latent variables. The paths among the latent variables indicate that achievement is directly dependent on intelligence and socioeconomic status and that an association exists between intelligence and socioeconomic status.

As in any regression model, a variable is not completely determined by others in the system. In Figure 16.4, the $\delta$ (delta) and $\epsilon$ (epsilon) terms pointing to the observed variables are error terms, representing the variation in these variables that is unexplained by the latent variables in the measurement error model. (Recall the representation of regression models with error terms shown in Section 9.6.) The $\zeta$ (zeta) symbol represents unexplained variation in the structural equation model, the achievement latent variable not being completely determined by the intelligence and socioeconomic status latent variables.                                                ■

## Special Cases of Covariance Structure Models

Covariance structure models have the attractive features of flexibility and generality. A regression parameter can be forced to take a fixed value, such as 0. It is then called a **fixed** parameter. Or a parameter can be forced to equal another in the system. It is then called a **constrained** parameter. Or it can be completely unknown, a **free** parameter.

In Figure 16.4, in the measurement model the factor loadings of the intelligence indicators $x_1$ and $x_2$ on the socioeconomic status and achievement latent variables equal 0. So those factor loadings are fixed parameters. Similarly, the factor loadings of the socioeconomic status indicators on the intelligence and achievement latent variables equal 0, and the factor loadings of the achievement indicators on the socioeconomic status and intelligence latent variables equal 0. By contrast, in the structural equation part of the model, the regression coefficients of intelligence and socioeconomic status on achievement are free parameters.

To treat an observed variable as perfectly measured, we take the corresponding latent variable to be identical to that observed variable. This assumes a lack of error in that part of the measurement model. Ordinary regression models are special cases of covariance structure models that have a single response variable and treat all variables as perfectly measured.

Suppose we treat all the observed variables as response variables and concentrate on how to represent them by a set of latent variables. Then the model provides a structured type of factor analysis. The analysis is **confirmatory**: It has the purpose of confirming a hypothesized factor-loading pattern for prespecified latent variables. For instance, in an article dealing with racism, conservatism, affirmative action, and intellectual sophistication,[1] the authors created a factor from five measured indicators of racism. Many other variables were measured in the study, such as educational level, political conservatism, and affirmative action attitude, but those variables were forced to have loadings of 0 on the factor for racism. A chi-squared test indicated that the five indicators of racism were adequately represented by a single factor.

Confirmatory factor analysis contrasts with the **exploratory** nature of ordinary factor analysis. In an exploratory factor analysis, such as the one in Example 16.6 on page 534, we do not judge the number of important factors and their relationships with the observed variables until after viewing the matrix of factor loadings. With

---

[1] J. Sidanius et al., *Journal of Personality and Social Psychology*, vol. 70, 1996, p. 476.

exploratory factor analysis, there is greater danger of going on a fishing expedition that produces results that seem interesting but may largely reflect sampling error.

## Fitting Covariance Structure Models

The *covariance* between two variables $x$ and $y$ is the average cross product of their deviations about their means. Its population value is defined as

$$\text{Cov}(x, y) = E[(x - \mu_x)(y - \mu_y)] = \rho_{xy}\sigma_x\sigma_y.$$

That is, the covariance is completely determined by the correlation and the marginal standard deviations. A *covariance matrix* summarizes covariances for each pair in a set of variables. The entry in row $i$ and column $j$ is the covariance between variables $i$ and $j$. If we use standardized variables, then the standard deviations equal 1, and the covariance matrix is identical to the correlation matrix.

*Maximum likelihood* is the standard method for fitting covariance structure models and estimating parameters. Software for fitting the models uses the sample covariation among the observed variables to estimate parameters in the measurement model and in the structural equation model. Parameters in the structural equation model are usually the ones of ultimate interest. In the above example, these include the regression coefficients of the intelligence and socioeconomic status latent variables on the achievement latent variable.

As in ordinary regression, inference assumes normally distributed responses. A parameter estimate divided by its standard error is an approximate $z$ test statistic for a significance test. The interpretation of the magnitude of an estimate depends on whether variables are measured in the original units or in standardized form.

Unless the model fixes sufficiently many parameters, the parameters are not *identifiable*. This means there are no unique estimates, a situation that always happens with ordinary factor analysis. It is best to fix enough parameters so that this does not happen. Software provides guidance about whether identifiability is achieved. If it is not achieved, try setting additional factor loadings equal to zero or replacing a factor by observed variables in the structural equation part of the model.

Covariance structure models require specialized software. LISREL is a well-known program that fits the model using maximum likelihood. The software name is an acronym for *li*near *s*tructural *rel*ationships. Another popular program is EQS.

## Checking Model Fit

The covariance structure model and its pattern of fixed, constrained, and free parameters determines a particular pattern that the true covariance matrix of the observed variables should satisfy. How can we check the fit of the covariance structure model to the data? One way uses a large-sample chi-squared test to compare the sample covariance matrix to the estimated covariance matrix implied by the model fit. The test statistic measures how close the sample covariance matrix falls to its estimated value assuming that the model holds. The larger the statistic, the poorer the fit.

Such a goodness-of-fit test provides only a rough guide. First, the test assumes multivariate normality of the observed variables, which is at best a rough approximation for reality. Second, like other chi-squared tests, the test of fit is a *global* test. If the model fits poorly, it does not indicate what causes the lack of fit. It can be more informative to view standardized residuals that compare individual elements of the sample and model-based covariance matrix. Third, as in any test, keep in mind the dependence of results on sample size. A result may be statistically significant, for large $n$, without being practically significant.

An alternative and more informative way to check the fit is as in ordinary regression models: Compare a given model to a more complex model with additional structure that may be relevant. To test whether the more complex model gives a better fit than the reduced model, the test statistic uses the difference in goodness-of-fit chi-squared statistics for the two models.

Good aspects of covariance structure models compared to unstructured factor analysis are that (1) the models force researchers to provide theoretical underpinnings to their analyses, and (2) inferential methods provide a check of the fit of the theoretical model to the data. However, the model is complex. Any model with latent variables may require a large sample size to obtain good estimates of effects, even for a relatively modest system of variables such as Figure 16.4 portrays.

In summary, covariance structure models provide a versatile format for conducting a variety of useful analyses in social science research. The frequency of their use by social scientists has increased in recent years. Nonetheless, the complexity of the model implies that results that seem interesting are highly tentative because of the many sources of variation. We recommend that you seek guidance from a statistician or well-trained social science methodologist before using this method. For further details, see Bentler (1980), Bollen (1989), DeMaris (2002), Jöreskog and Sörbom (1997), Long (1983), and Pedhazur (1997).

## 16.7  MARKOV CHAINS*

Researchers are sometimes interested in sequences of responses over time. A study of voting patterns in presidential elections might analyze data in which subjects indicate the party for which they voted in each of the past several elections. A sequence of observations that varies randomly is called a ***stochastic process***. The possible values for the process at each step are the ***states*** of the process. For example, the possible states for the vote in an election might be (Democrat, Republican, Other, Did not vote). Stochastic models describe sequences of observations on a variable.

One of the simplest stochastic processes is the ***Markov chain***. It is appropriate if, given the behavior of the process at times $t, t-1, t-2, \ldots, 1$, the probability distribution of the outcome at time $t+1$ depends only on the outcome at time $t$. In other words, given the outcome at time $t$, the outcome at time $t+1$ is statistically independent of the outcome at all times previous to time $t$.

The Markov property is *not* that the state at time $t+1$ is *independent* of the states at time $t-1$, $t-2$, and so on; rather only that *conditional on* the value of the process at time $t$, they are independent. Letting $y_1, y_2, \ldots$ denote the successive states of the chain, $y_{t+1}$ may be associated with $y_{t-1}, y_{t-2}, \ldots$, but given $y_t$, $y_{t+1}$ is statistically independent of $y_{t-1}, y_{t-2}, \ldots$. Associations may exist, but the conditional associations (e.g., between $y_{t+1}$ and $y_{t-1}$, controlling for $y_t$) do not.

### EXAMPLE 16.9    Modeling Social Class Mobility

A study of male social class mobility considers a three-generation period, labeled by grandfather, father, and son. The study follows a family line by considering the sequence of firstborn sons at age 40 years. In each generation, the possible states of the process are upper, middle, and lower.

Suppose this process behaves like a Markov chain. Then, for example, for all fathers in a given class (such as upper), the social class of the son is statistically independent of the social class of the grandfather. Using the vertical slash | to represent *given* or *conditioned on*, the following four probabilities would be identical:

Pr(son in M | father in U, grandfather in L)
Pr(son in M | father in U, grandfather in M)
Pr(son in M | father in U, grandfather in U)
Pr(son in M | father in U) ■

### Transition Probabilities

The common probability in the above example is called the ***transition probability*** of moving from the upper class to the middle class in one generation. Denote it by $P_{UM}$. A Markov chain model studies questions such as the following:

- What is the probability of moving from one particular state to another in a particular amount of time?
- How long, on the average, does it take to move from one particular state to another?
- Are the transition probabilities between each pair of states constant over time? If they are, the process is said to have ***stationary transition probabilities***.
- Is the process a Markov chain, or is the dependence structure more complex?

The properties of a Markov chain depend on the transition probabilities. These are studied with the *transition probability matrix*, denoted by $P$. For an $s$-state chain, this matrix is an $s \times s$ table. The entry in the cell in row $i$ and column $j$ is the probability that, given that the chain is currently in state $i$, at the next time period it is in state $j$.

Table 16.6 shows the format for a transition probability matrix for the social mobility example, with a set of potential transition probabilities. The row labels refer to the father's class, and the column labels refer to the son's class. From the table, given that the father is in the upper class, then the probability is $P_{UU} = 0.45$ that the son is in the upper class, $P_{UM} = 0.48$ that the son is in the middle class, and $P_{UL} = 0.07$ that the son is in the lower class. The sum of the probabilities within each row of the matrix equals 1.0.

**TABLE 16.6:** Sample Format for Transition Probability Matrix $P$

|  |  | Time $t+1$ | | | |  | | | |
|---|---|---|---|---|---|---|---|---|---|
|  |  | $U$ | $M$ | $L$ |  |  | $U$ | $M$ | $L$ |
| Time $t$ | $U$ | $P_{UU}$ | $P_{UM}$ | $P_{UL}$ |  | $U$ | 0.45 | 0.48 | 0.07 |
|  | $M$ | $P_{MU}$ | $P_{MM}$ | $P_{ML}$ | $=$ | $M$ | 0.05 | 0.70 | 0.25 |
|  | $L$ | $P_{LU}$ | $P_{LM}$ | $P_{LL}$ |  | $L$ | 0.01 | 0.50 | 0.49 |

In practice, we estimate the transition probabilities by the sample proportion of the transitions from each state into each other state. If there are 200 father–son pairs with the father in the upper class, and if for 90 of these pairs the son is in the upper class, then $\hat{P}_{UU} = 90/200 = 0.45$.

In social science applications, it is usually unrealistic to expect transition probabilities to be stationary. This limits the usefulness of simple Markov chain models. For sample data, chi-squared tests are available of the assumptions of Markov dependence and stationary transition probabilities. Although the Markov chain model is too simplistic by itself to have much practical use, it often forms a component of a more complex and realistic model. For examples, see Bartholomew (1982), Goodman (1962), and Scheaffer and Young (2008).

## PROBLEMS

**16.1.** Summarize advantages of using a model with random effects to analyze repeated measures data compared to using traditional repeated measures ANOVA.

**16.2.** Explain what is meant by the term *mixed model*, and explain the distinction between a *fixed effect* and a *random effect*.

**16.3.** Section 16.1 noted that mixed models can use data for subjects when at least one of their observations is missing. However, the method assumes the data are *missing at random*. In Example 16.1 (page 521), suppose that subjects who drop out of the study become, over time, less financially satisfied.
  **(a)** Explain why the missing at random assumption would be violated.
  **(b)** Explain why the time effect may be overestimated using only the data observed.
  **(c)** Describe a dropout pattern such that estimates of the treatment effect would be biased.

**16.4.** Explain what a multilevel model does. Describe an application in which this type of model would be useful.

**16.5.** Refer to Table 16.2 on page 527. Interpret the estimated effect of gender on the hazard rate. Test the effect of race, and interpret.

**16.6.** A study of recidivism takes a sample of records of people who were released from prison in 2000. The response variable, measured when records are reviewed in 2008, is the number of months until the person was rearrested. In the context of this study, explain what is meant by a *censored* observation.

**16.7.** In studying the effect of race on job dismissals in the federal bureaucracy, a study[2] used event history analysis to model the hazard rate regarding termination of employment. In modeling involuntary terminations using a sample of size 2141, study authors reported $P < 0.001$ in significance tests for the partial effects of race and age. They reported an estimated effect on the hazard rate of $e^{\hat{\beta}} = 2.13$ for the coefficient of the dummy variable for being black. Explain how to interpret.

**16.8.** Let $I$ = annual income, $E$ = attained educational level, $J$ = number of years experience in job, $M$ = motivation, $A$ = age, $G$ = gender, and $P$ = parents' attained educational level. Construct a path diagram showing your opinion about the likely relationships among those variables. Specify the regression models you would need to fit to estimate the path coefficients for that diagram.

**16.9.** UN data are available for most nations on $B$ = birth rate, $G$ = per capita gross domestic product, $L$ = percent literate, $T$ = percent of homes having a television, and $C$ = percent using contraception. Draw a path diagram relating these variables. Specify the regression models you would need to fit to estimate path coefficients for your diagram.

**16.10.** The "2005 statewide crime" dataset at the text Web site has data on murder rate, percentage urban, percentage of high school graduates, and percentage in poverty. Do not use the observation for D.C. Construct a realistic path diagram for these variables. By fitting the appropriate models for these data, estimate the path coefficients, and construct the final path diagram. Interpret.

**16.11.** Refer to Example 1 of Chapter 11 (page 322), on the data for the 67 counties in Florida on $y$ = crime rate, $x_1$ = percentage of high school graduates, and $x_2$ = percentage living in an urban environment. Consider the spurious causal model for the association between crime rate and percentage of high school graduates, controlling for percentage urban. Using the "Florida crime" dataset at the text Web site, determine whether the data are consistent with this model.

**16.12.** Refer to the "2005 statewide crime" dataset at the text Web site.
  **(a)** Conduct a factor analysis. How many factors seem appropriate? Interpret the factors, using the estimated factor loadings.
  **(b)** Remove the observation for D.C., and repeat. How sensitive are the estimated factor loadings and your identification of factors to that one observation?

**16.13.** Construct a diagram representing the following covariance structure model: Three observed response variables are described by a single latent variable, and that latent variable is regressed on four observed predictors.

**16.14.** Construct a diagram representing the following covariance structure model, for variables measured for each state. The latent response variable is based on two observed indicators, violent crime rate and murder rate. The two predictor variables for that latent variable are the observed values of percentage of residents in poverty and percentage of single-parent families. These are treated as perfectly measured.

**16.15.** Refer to the previous exercise. Using software, fit this model to the "statewide crime 2" dataset at the text Web site. Interpret results.

---

[2]C. Zwerling and H. Silver, *American Sociological Review*, vol. 57, 1992, p. 651.

**16.16.** Construct a diagram representing a covariance structure model for the following: In the measurement model, a single factor represents violent crime rate and murder rate and a single factor represents percentage of high school graduates, percentage in poverty, and percentage of single-parent families. In the structural equation model, the first factor depends on the second factor as well as on the percentage of urban residents.

**16.17.** Construct a diagram representing a covariance structure model for the following: A religiosity factor is based on two indicators from the GSS about frequency of church attendance and frequency of praying. An education factor is based on two indicators from the GSS about educational attainment and parents' education. A political conservatism factor is based on two indicators from the GSS about political ideology. A government activism factor is based on three indicators from the GSS about the extent that government should be involved in reducing income inequality and helping the poorest members of society. The structural equation model predicts the political conservatism factor using the education factor and religiosity factor, predicts the government activism factor by the other three factors, and allows an association between the education and religiosity factors.

**16.18.** A variable is measured at three times, $y_1$ at time 1, $y_2$ at time 2, and $y_3$ at time 3. Suppose the chain relationship holds, with $y_1$ affecting $y_2$, which in turn affects $y_3$. Does this sequence of observations satisy Markov dependence? Explain.

**16.19.** What is wrong with this statement?: "For a Markov chain model, $y_t$ is independent of $y_{t-2}$."

# APPENDIX A

# SPSS and SAS for Statistical Analyses

Major statistical software packages have procedures for nearly all the methods presented in this text. This appendix illustrates software use for these methods.

There is insufficient space to discuss all the major packages, and we focus on SPSS and SAS. We discuss basic use of the software rather than the great variety of options provided by the procedures. For ease of reference, the material both for SAS and SPSS is organized by chapter of presentation in this text. The full data files for examples and exercises having large data sets are available at
`http://www.stat.ufl.edu/~aa/social/data.html`

## INTRODUCTION TO SPSS

**SPSS for Windows** has a graphical user interface that makes requesting statistical procedures simple. In this windows environment, SPSS provides menus and dialog boxes to save you the work of preparing code to request analyses. Our discussion below applies to version 15.0. It can help to have access to a manual such as Norusis (2006) or Green and Salkind (2007). You can also get lots of help directly from the SPSS program or at sites such as http://www.ats.ucla.edu/stat/spss/.

As of version 15.0, most of the methods described below are available in a special student version of SPSS. The GENERAL LINEAR MODEL and GENERALIZED LINEAR MODELS options in the ANALYZE menu, mentioned below for Chapters 11–15, are available in an add-on module, "SPSS Advanced Models." Particular options for modeling categorical responses (such as logistic regression and a multinomial logistic model for nominal responses) are available with another add-on, "SPSS Regression Models." These two add-ons are also part of the "SPSS Graduate Pack" that is more advanced than the ordinary student version.

## Starting and Using SPSS

When you start a session, you see a ***Data Editor window*** that contains a menu bar with a wide variety of separate menus. These include a FILE menu for creating a new file or opening an existing one, an ANALYZE menu that displays options for selecting a statistical method, a GRAPHS menu for creating a graph of some type, and menus for choosing other special features. The *Data Editor* window displays the contents of the data file. You use this to enter the data or edit existing data. The ***Output window*** shows results of the analyses after you request them from the menus. You can edit and save this for later use or printing. Other windows are available for charts and plotting data. Using the windows environment is mostly self-explanatory, but online help is readily available.

Data files have the form of a spreadsheet, each column containing a variable and each row the observations for a particular subject. You can enter the data set while in SPSS. Or you can simply call up an existing data set, which might be an ASCII file that you created with a separate editor or a file created with a spreadsheet or database program. Select FILE on the menu bar in the application window and indicate whether you want to read in a new data file (such as crime.dat) or open an existing file (such as crime.sav) or enter a new data set on the spreadsheet.

Let's go through the steps of reading a text file into the SPSS data editor. In the *Data Editor* window, go to the FILE menu and select OPEN and then DATA. Enter the FILE NAME and select the TYPE OF FILE (such as .txt file). Click on OPEN. This opens the TEXT IMPORT WIZARD. You will now be led through some steps to create the SPSS data file.

The first step asks if your text file matches a predefined format. Unless you had created a format to read the data, select NO and click NEXT. The second step asks how your variables are arranged. For files at the text Web site that are delimited by a space between each column of the data file, you select DELIMITED, tab, or space. You should also indicate here whether the variable names are at the top of the file (as at the text Web site). The third step asks whether each line represents a case (as is true for the data files at the text Web site) and whether you want to import all the cases (as you usually would). You also see here a preview of the data. The fourth step asks you to identify the delimiter between variables, which is a SPACE for the text Web site. Check the data preview and make sure it looks correct. In step 5 you have the option to change variable names and to identify the data format. SPSS should identify quantitative variables as NUMERIC and categorical variables (with labels for the categories) as STRING. At step 6, clicking on FINISH reads the data into the SPSS data editor. Check this to make sure that unintended spaces in your text file did not result in an added variable or case that needs to be deleted. A period in a cell represents a missing observation.

Figure A.1 shows an example of a Data Editor window, for the "Student survey" data file at the text Web site. For your new data file, you can redefine names and characteristics for each variable after clicking on VARIABLE VIEW. (In the Measure column, make sure SPSS has not inappropriately labeled a variable as NOMINAL that should be SCALE (interval) or ORDINAL.) You save the file by selecting the FILE menu with the *Save As* option. The name you select receives the *.sav* extension. You can access the created file later from the FILE menu.

At this point, you can select a statistical procedure from the ANALYZE menu on the *Data Editor*. When you select a procedure, a *dialog box* opens that shows you the source variables in your data set. You highlight the ones you want to use currently and click on the arrow to the right of the list to move them to the selected variables list further to the right. You then click on OK and the procedure runs, showing results in the output window. For many procedures, you can click on *Options* and an additional *subdialog box* will open that displays extra available options for the method. To save output, in the OUTPUT window, use the FILE menu and the *Save As* option. You can later access the output in the FILE menu by selecting OPEN and then OUTPUT.

## Chapter 3: Descriptive Statistics

To construct frequency distributions, histograms, and basic summary statistics, on the ANALYZE menu of the *Data Editor* window select the DESCRIPTIVE option with the FREQUENCIES suboption. A FREQUENCIES dialog box will open. Select the variables you want from the list for your file. Then clicking on *OK* provides a frequency distribution in the *Output* window. Clicking on CHARTS in the FREQUENCIES dialog box presents you with a FREQUENCIES: CHARTS dialog box containing a histogram option for quantitative variables and a bar chart option for categorical variables. You can also construct a histogram from the GRAPHS menu on the *Data Editor* window by selecting INTERACTIVE and then HISTOGRAM. Drag a variable to the *x*-axis and then select whether you want to plot counts or percentages.

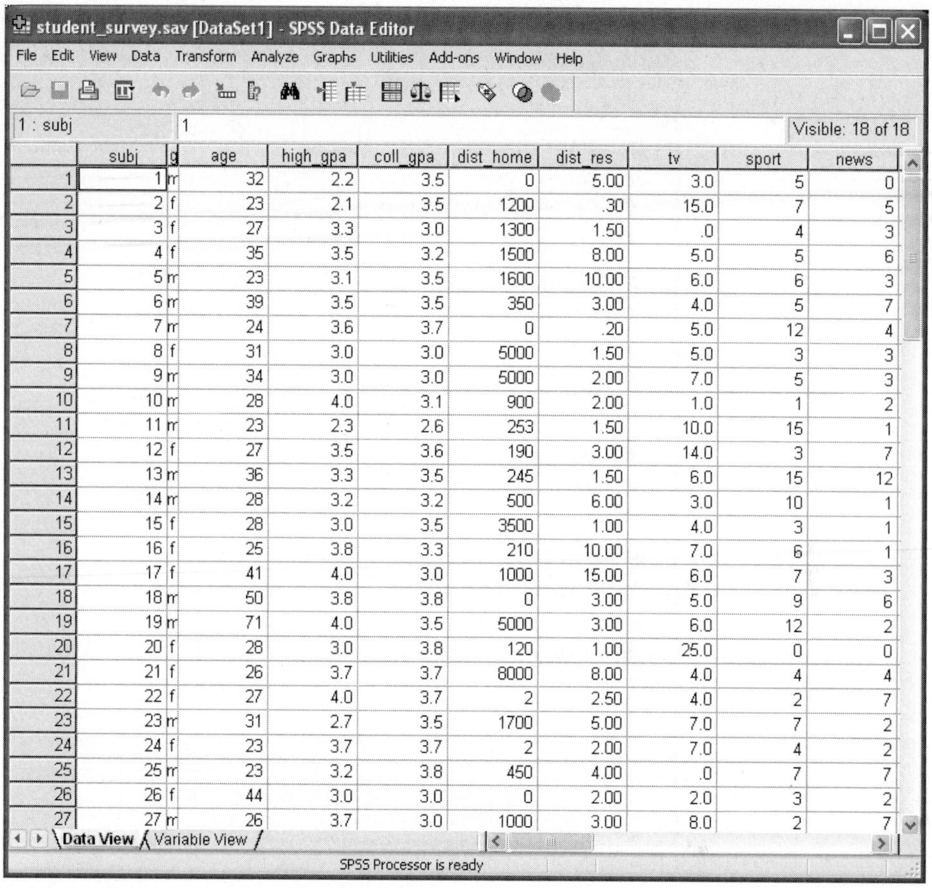


| | subj | g | age | high_gpa | coll_gpa | dist_home | dist_res | tv | sport | news |
|---|---|---|---|---|---|---|---|---|---|---|
| 1 | 1 | m | 32 | 2.2 | 3.5 | 0 | 5.00 | 3.0 | 5 | 0 |
| 2 | 2 | f | 23 | 2.1 | 3.5 | 1200 | .30 | 15.0 | 7 | 5 |
| 3 | 3 | f | 27 | 3.3 | 3.0 | 1300 | 1.50 | .0 | 4 | 3 |
| 4 | 4 | f | 35 | 3.5 | 3.2 | 1500 | 8.00 | 5.0 | 5 | 6 |
| 5 | 5 | m | 23 | 3.1 | 3.5 | 1600 | 10.00 | 6.0 | 6 | 3 |
| 6 | 6 | m | 39 | 3.5 | 3.5 | 350 | 3.00 | 4.0 | 5 | 7 |
| 7 | 7 | m | 24 | 3.6 | 3.7 | 0 | .20 | 5.0 | 12 | 4 |
| 8 | 8 | f | 31 | 3.0 | 3.0 | 5000 | 1.50 | 5.0 | 3 | 3 |
| 9 | 9 | m | 34 | 3.0 | 3.0 | 5000 | 2.00 | 7.0 | 5 | 3 |
| 10 | 10 | m | 28 | 4.0 | 3.1 | 900 | 2.00 | 1.0 | 1 | 2 |
| 11 | 11 | m | 23 | 2.3 | 2.6 | 253 | 1.50 | 10.0 | 15 | 1 |
| 12 | 12 | f | 27 | 3.5 | 3.6 | 190 | 3.00 | 14.0 | 3 | 7 |
| 13 | 13 | m | 36 | 3.3 | 3.5 | 245 | 1.50 | 6.0 | 15 | 12 |
| 14 | 14 | m | 28 | 3.2 | 3.2 | 500 | 6.00 | 3.0 | 10 | 1 |
| 15 | 15 | f | 28 | 3.0 | 3.5 | 3500 | 1.00 | 4.0 | 3 | 1 |
| 16 | 16 | f | 25 | 3.8 | 3.3 | 210 | 10.00 | 7.0 | 6 | 1 |
| 17 | 17 | f | 41 | 4.0 | 3.0 | 1000 | 15.00 | 6.0 | 7 | 3 |
| 18 | 18 | m | 50 | 3.8 | 3.8 | 0 | 3.00 | 5.0 | 9 | 6 |
| 19 | 19 | m | 71 | 4.0 | 3.5 | 5000 | 3.00 | 6.0 | 12 | 2 |
| 20 | 20 | f | 28 | 3.0 | 3.8 | 120 | 1.00 | 25.0 | 0 | 0 |
| 21 | 21 | f | 26 | 3.7 | 3.7 | 8000 | 8.00 | 4.0 | 4 | 4 |
| 22 | 22 | f | 27 | 4.0 | 3.7 | 2 | 2.50 | 4.0 | 2 | 7 |
| 23 | 23 | m | 31 | 2.7 | 3.5 | 1700 | 5.00 | 7.0 | 7 | 2 |
| 24 | 24 | f | 23 | 3.7 | 3.7 | 2 | 2.00 | 7.0 | 4 | 2 |
| 25 | 25 | m | 23 | 3.2 | 3.8 | 450 | 4.00 | .0 | 7 | 7 |
| 26 | 26 | f | 44 | 3.0 | 3.0 | 0 | 2.00 | 2.0 | 3 | 2 |
| 27 | 27 | m | 26 | 3.7 | 3.0 | 1000 | 3.00 | 8.0 | 2 | 7 |

**FIGURE A.1:** A Data Editor Window in SPSS

To construct a stem-and-leaf plot or a box plot, from the STATISTICS menu select the SUMMARIZE option with the EXPLORE suboption. The EXPLORE dialog box contains a *Plots* option; clicking on it reveals the various plot options. (The GRAPHS menu also has the option of a box plot.)

Clicking on STATISTICS in the FREQUENCIES dialog box presents you with a FREQUENCIES: STATISTICS dialog box containing options of various statistics to compute, such as measures of central tendency and variability. You can also get a basic descriptive statistic from the ANALYZE menu by selecting the DESCRIPTIVE STATISTICS option with the DESCRIPTIVES suboption.

To construct a box plot, on the GRAPHS menu in the *Data Editor* window, select CHARTBUILDER and then drag the box plot icon into the open canvas. Select the variable for the box plot and click OK. CHARTBUILDER also has options for side-by-side box plots according to the value of a categorical variable. You can also do this on the GRAPHS menu by selecting INTERACTIVE and then BOXPLOT.

To obtain correlation and regression results, on the ANALYZE menu of the *Data Editor* window select the REGRESSION option with the LINEAR suboption. You will then see a LINEAR REGRESSION dialog box in which you can identify response (dependent) and explanatory (independent) variables. See Figure A.2 for an example. The correlation is shown in the OUTPUT window in the Model Summary table under *R*, and the prediction equation is given in the *B* column of the Coefficients table.

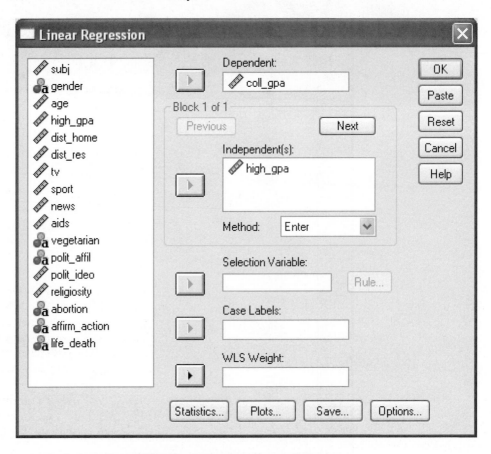

**FIGURE A.2:** Example of a SPSS Dialog Box

## Chapters 5 and 6: Estimation and Significance Tests

The ANALYZE menu on the *Data Editor* window has a COMPARE MEANS option with a ONE-SAMPLE T TEST suboption. The default with that option is a 95% confidence interval for the mean and a *t* test that the true mean equals 0. The options permit one to select a different confidence level. To test that the mean equals a constant $\mu_0$, supply that number as in the Test Value box on the ONE-SAMPLE T TEST dialog box.

Here's how to find the *t* score corresponding to a certain tail probability. We illustrate with left-tail probability = 0.025, for *df* = 226. In an empty data editor window, put 0.025 in the first column and 226 in the second column. Then on the *Transform* menu select *Compute variable*. In the Numeric Expression window, type IDF.T(var1,var2), where var1 and var2 are the names of the variables for the first two columns. Enter a name for the Target Variable. Click on OK, and the solution (−1.97052) will show up in a new column of the data file labeled with the name you gave the target variable. The code for other distributions is listed under the Functions and Special Variables menu in this dialog box, when you click on Inverse DF in the Function group menu (e.g., IDF.normal for the normal distribution).

Likewise, you can find the tail probability for a certain *t* score. To find the left-tail (i.e., cumulative) probability for a *t* score of 1.97 when *df* = 226, put 1.97 in the first column and 226 in the second column. Then on the *Transform* menu select *Compute variable*. In the Numeric Expression window, type CDF.T(var1,var2), where var1 and var2 are the names of the variables for the first two columns. Enter a name for the Target Variable. Click on OK, and the solution (0.97497) will show up in a new column of the data file labeled with the name you gave the target variable. To get the right-tail probability above the given $t$ score, subtract this cumulative probability from 1. The code for other distributions is listed under the Functions and Special Variables menu in this dialog box when you click on CDF in the Function group menu (e.g., CDF.normal for the normal distribution).

## Chapter 7: Comparison of Two Groups

The ANALYZE menu has a COMPARE MEANS option with a INDEPENDENT-SAMPLES T TEST suboption. One selects the response variable (labeled the *Test variable*) and the variable that defines the two groups to be compared (labeled the *Grouping variable*). With Define Groups under the Grouping Variable label, identify the two levels of the grouping variable that specify the groups to be compared. Click OK, and results are shown in the *Output* window. There, in the *Equal variances* row, this procedure provides the results of the $t$ test assuming the two populations have the same standard deviation value. The output provides the test statistic (labeled $t$), $df$, standard error (labeled *Std. Error Difference*), and two-sided $P$-value (labeled *Sig. (2-tailed)*). The procedure also provides the 95% confidence interval for comparing the means. Options allow you to change the confidence level. The output also shows results for the method that does not assume equal variances, in the *Unequal variances* row of the output.

The COMPARE MEANS option on the ANALYZE menu also has a PAIRED-SAMPLES T TEST suboption, which supplies the dependent-samples comparisons of means described in Section 7.4. For Fisher's exact test, see the description for the following chapter.

## Chapter 8: Analyzing Association Between Categorical Variables

The DESCRIPTIVE STATISTICS option on the ANALYZE menu has a suboption called CROSSTABS, which provides several methods for contingency tables. After identifying the row and column variables in CROSSTABS, clicking on STATISTICS provides a wide variety of options, including the chi-squared test and measures of association. The output lists the Pearson statistic, its degrees of freedom, and its $P$-value (labeled *Asymp. Sig.*).

If any expected frequencies in a $2 \times 2$ table are less than 5, Fisher's exact test results. It can also be requested by clicking on Exact in the CROSSTABS dialog box and selecting the exact test. SPSS also has an advanced module for small-sample inference (called SPSS Exact Tests) that provides exact $P$-values for various tests in CROSSTABS and NPAR TESTS procedures. For instance, the Exact Tests module provides exact tests of independence for $r \times c$ contingency tables with nominal or ordinal classifications. See the SPSS publication *SPSS Exact Tests 15.0 for Windows*.

In CROSSTABS, clicking on CELLS provides options for displaying observed and expected frequencies, as well as the standardized residuals, labeled as *Adjusted standardized*. Clicking on STATISTICS in CROSSTABS provides options of a wide variety of statistics other than chi-squared, including gamma and Kendall's tau-$b$. The output shows the measures and their standard errors (labeled *Asymp. Std. Error*), which you can use to construct confidence intervals. It also provides a test statistic for testing that the true measure equals zero, which is the ratio of the estimate to its standard error. This test uses a simpler standard error that only applies under independence and is inappropriate for confidence intervals. One option in the list of statistics, labeled *Risk*, provides as output the odds ratio and its confidence interval.

Suppose you enter the data as cell counts for the various combinations of the two variables rather than as responses on the two variables for individual subjects; for instance, perhaps you call COUNT the variable that contains these counts. Then select the WEIGHT CASES option on the DATA menu in the *Data Editor* window, and instruct SPSS to weight cases by COUNT.

### Chapter 9: Linear Regression and Correlation

To construct a scatter diagram, enter the GRAPH menu on the *Data Editor* and choose the INTERACTIVE option and then SCATTERPLOT. In the CREATE SCATTERPLOT dialog box, drag the appropriate variables to the $y$- and $x$-axes. Click on FIT in this box and then as your method select REGRESSION if you want the regression line plotted over the points or click NONE if you want only the scatterplot. Click on OK and you will see the graph in the *Output* window.

To fit the regression line, on the ANALYZE menu select REGRESSION and then LINEAR. You identify the response (Dependent) variable and the explanatory (Independent) variable. Various options are available by clicking on *Statistics* in the LINEAR REGRESSION dialog box, including estimates of the model parameters, confidence intervals for the parameters, and model fit statistics. After selecting what you want, click on CONTINUE and then back in the LINEAR REGRESSION dialog box click on OK. You'll see results in the *Output* window. Output for the estimates option includes the estimates for the prediction equation (labeled $B$), their standard errors (labeled *Std. Error*), the $t$ statistic for testing that a regression parameter equals 0 and the associated $P$-value (labeled *Sig*), and a standardized regression coefficient (labeled as *Beta*) that in this bivariate model is simply the Pearson correlation.

Output for the model fit option in a *Model Summary* table includes the $r^2$-value (labeled *R Square*) and the estimate $s$ of the conditional standard deviation (rather confusingly labeled *Std. Error of the Estimate*).

### Chapter 11: Multiple Regression and Correlation

For a multiple regression analysis, again choose REGRESSION from the ANALYZE menu with the LINEAR suboption, and add additional variables to the list of independent variables. Among the options provided by clicking on *Statistics* in the dialog box are estimates of the coefficients and confidence intervals based on them and detail about the model fit. For the *Estimates* option, the output includes standard errors of the estimates, the $t$ statistic for testing that the regression parameter equals zero and its associated two-sided $P$-value, and the estimated standardized regression coefficient (labeled *Beta*).

Requesting the *Model fit* option in the STATISTICS sub-dialog box provides additional information. For instance, the $F$ statistic provided in the *ANOVA* table is the $F$ test statistic for testing that the coefficients of the explanatory variables all equal 0. The probability labeled as *Sig* is the $P$-value for that test. Also provided in a *Model Summary* table are the multiple correlation $R$, $R^2$, and the estimate $s$ of the conditional standard deviation (poorly labeled as *Std. Error of the Estimate*).

In the ANALYZE menu in the *Data Editor* window, selecting CORRELATE and then BIVARIATE gives a BIVARIATE CORRELATIONS sub-dialog box. You select the variables you want, check PEARSON CORRELATION and then click OK, and the output window shows a correlation matrix with the $P$-values for testing the significance of each.

To construct a scatterplot matrix, from the GRAPHS menu in the *Data Editor* choose the CHART BUILDER option. Then click the GALLERY tab and select SCATTER/DOT in the Choose From list. Drag the Scatterplot Matrix icon onto the blank canvas. Drag the wanted variables to the Scattermatrix drop zone, and then click on OK. You'll see the graph in the *Output* window.

To produce all partial regression plots, click on PLOTS in the LINEAR REGRESSION dialog window and then click on *Produce all partial plots* in the LINEAR REGRESSION: PLOTS dialog box.

To obtain a partial correlation analysis, choose the PART AND PARTIAL CORRELATIONS option in the STATISTICS option box in the LINEAR REGRESSION window. Or, in the ANALYZE menu choose the CORRELATE option with the PARTIAL suboption. In the resulting PARTIAL CORRELATIONS dialog box, select the variables to correlate and select at least one variable to control. The output also provides tests of significance for these partial correlations.

To model interaction, you can construct an interaction variable within the SPSS data editor by selecting the COMPUTE VARIABLE option on the TRANSFORM menu. Provide a name for the new variable in the Target Variable box. Create the mathematical formula for the interaction term in the Numeric Expressions box, such as LIFE*SES for the explanatory variables LIFE and SES (the * symbol represents multiplication). Click OK, and in the data file in the *Data Editor* you will see a new column of observations for the new variable. This variable can then be entered into the model formula when requesting a regression equation.

Here's a second way to build an interaction term in a model, one that is especially useful for models in following chapters that also have categorical predictors. This method requires you to use the general linear model function rather than the multiple linear regression function within SPSS. This second method is well suited for forming multiple interaction terms but presents output in a slightly different form and offers fewer options for data analysis. Choose the GENERAL LINEAR MODEL in the ANALYZE menu and select the UNIVARIATE suboption. Enter the response variable into the Dependent Variable box and the explanatory variables into the Covariate(s) box. Now click on the *Model* box and select the *Custom* option. Using the Build Term(s) arrow, enter the covariates as *Main effects*. Highlight a pair of variables for which you want a cross-product and enter them by selecting *Interaction* on the Build Term(s) arrow. Or you can select the *All 2-way* option for the Build Term(s) arrow to request interaction terms for all pairs of variables. After specifying the terms for the model, click Continue and return to the UNIVARIATE dialog box. To display model parameter estimates, select the Options box and check the Parameter Estimates option. Click Continue to return to the UNIVARIATE dialog box and then click OK to perform the regression analysis.

## Chapter 12: Comparing Groups: Analysis of Variance Methods

To conduct a one-way ANOVA, on the ANALYZE menu select the COMPARE MEANS option with the ONE-WAY ANOVA suboption. Select the dependent variable and select the factor that defines the groups to be compared. (This must be coded numerically for SPSS to display it as a potential factor, even though it is treated as nominal scale! Otherwise, use the approach in the following paragraph.) Results provided include the *F* test statistic and its *P*-value, and sums of squares and mean squares for between-groups and within-groups variation. Clicking on *Post Hoc* in the ONE-WAY ANOVA dialog box provides a variety of options for multiple comparison procedures, including the Bonferroni and Tukey methods. The LSD (least significant difference) option provides ordinary confidence intervals with the confidence level applying to each interval. Clicking on *Options* in the ONE-WAY ANOVA dialog box provides the *Descriptive statistics* option of additional descriptive statistics, including the mean, standard deviation, standard error, and a 95% confidence interval for each group.

You can also conduct a one-way ANOVA on the ANALYZE menu by selecting the GENERAL LINEAR MODEL option with the UNIVARIATE suboption. With this approach, unlike the one just described, the categorical variable that is selected as the Fixed Factor can be coded with labels rather than numerically (i.e., a *string* variable in SPSS). In the UNIVARIATE dialog box, click on *Options* and you can request Descriptive statistics and Parameter estimates for displaying the regression parameter estimates from viewing the analysis as a special case of a regression analysis. Return to the UNIVARIATE dialog box and click on *Post Hoc* to select ordinary confidence intervals for comparing means (LSD) or multiple comparison intervals such as Bonferroni or Tukey.

To conduct a two-way or higher-way factorial ANOVA, on the ANALYZE menu select the GENERAL LINEAR MODEL option with the UNIVARIATE suboption. Select the dependent variable and select the Fixed Factor(s) that define the cross-classification for the means. (If you have set up dummy variables yourself, they would be entered as Covariates.) The default model is a full factorial model containing all interactions. Click on *Model* to build a customized model that contains only some or none of the interactions. Highlight variables, select Interaction or Main Effects from the Build Term(s) list, and click on the arrow to move the terms to the model list on the right. Return to the UNIVARIATE dialog box and click on *Options*. You can request Descriptive statistics, Parameter estimates, and you can select particular factors and request Display Means to see the observed and predicted means for subgroups defined by the factors. Return to the UNIVARIATE dialog box and click on *Contrasts* to display parameter estimates with standard errors, *t* statistics, and confidence intervals for comparing means for levels of each factor. Change the contrast type to *Simple* to compare each level to a baseline level, either the last (such as in setting up (1, 0) dummy variables for all levels but the last one) or the first. Return to the UNIVARIATE dialog box and click on *Post Hoc* to select confidence intervals for comparing means (LSD) or multiple comparison intervals such as Bonferroni or Tukey.

Alternatively, for one-way or factorial ANOVA, you could set up dummy variables in your data file and then use ordinary regression. On the ANALYZE menu, you would then select the REGRESSION option and LINEAR suboption, as in Chapter 11.

You can conduct repeated measures ANOVA using the GENERAL LINEAR MODEL option on the ANALYZE menu, with the REPEATED MEASURES suboption. This assumes that for each subject, each outcome for the response falls in a different column. For Example 12.8 on three influences, in a given row you would put the response for Movies in one column, for TV in a separate column, and for Rock in a third column. In the REPEATED MEASURES DEFINE FACTOR(S) dialog window, type the name and number of levels of the within-subjects factor (such as *influence* and 3) and click on *Add*. Then click on *Define* to define the model. Now, in the REPEATED MEASURES dialog box, select the between-subjects factors (if there are any), and select the response variable for each level of the within-subjects factor (such as Movies, TV, Rock). The default is a model containing all the factor interactions. Click on *Model*, and customize the model if you want to delete an interaction. Return to the REPEATED MEASURES dialog box and click on *Contrasts*, and options are provided for displaying parameter estimates and confidence intervals for contrasts comparing means in different factor levels, and for individual or Bonferroni confidence intervals. Change the contrast type to *Simple* for estimates of the between-subjects factors to refer to comparing each factor level to the first or last level. Return to the REPEATED MEASURES dialog box and click on *Options*, and you can request between-subjects observed and estimated means and various model diagnostics.

For repeated measures analyses, SPSS also reports results of standard multivariate (MANOVA) tests that do not make the assumption of sphericity for the joint distribution of the repeated responses (see Section 16.1). They are less powerful than the repeated measures ANOVA methods when the sphericity assumption is not violated.

## Chapter 13: Combining Regression and ANOVA: Quantitative and Categorical Predictors

To fit an analysis of covariance model, you can set up dummy variables for categorical predictors and use ordinary regression procedures, such as described earlier for Chapter 11. To create cross-product terms for interactions, after creating the data file, you can select COMPUTE VARIABLE on the TRANSFORM menu and create products of appropriate variables.

Alternatively, on the ANALYZE menu select the GENERAL LINEAR MODEL option with the UNIVARIATE suboption. Proceed as described for Chapter 11, now adding quantitative covariates in the Covariate(s) box. As in ANOVA, add categorical predictors to the Fixed Factor(s) box. Click on Model to build a custom model that contains only some or none of the interactions. Select *Interaction* or *Main Effects* from the Build Term(s) list, and click on the arrow to move the terms to the model list on the right.

## Chapter 14: Model Building with Multiple Regression

In the LINEAR REGRESSION dialog window for the REGRESSION choice on the ANALYZE menu, you can select a *Method* for fitting the model, among which are options such as BACKWARD, FORWARD, and STEPWISE for selecting predictors in the model (or ENTER for adding all of them).

In the LINEAR REGRESSION dialog window, you can plot studentized residuals (labelled SRESID) and request all partial regression plots by clicking on *Plots* and then making appropriate selections in the PLOTS dialog box. To obtain predicted values, residuals, studentized residuals, leverage values, and influence diagnostics, click on *Save* in the LINEAR REGRESSION dialog box. The resulting LINEAR REGRESSION: SAVE dialog box contains options for these, such as such as *Standardized DfBeta(s)* for DFBETAS and *Standardized DfFit* for DFFITS. To find variance inflation factors, click on *Statistics* in the LINEAR REGRESSION dialog box and select *Collinearity diagnostics*.

To fit generalized linear models, on the ANALYZE menu select the GENERALIZED LINEAR MODELS option and the GENERALIZED LINEAR MODELS suboption. Select the Dependent Variable and then the Distribution and Link Function. Click on the Predictors tab at the top of the dialog box and then enter quantitative variables as Covariates and categorical variables as Factors. Click on the Model tab at the top of the dialog box and enter these variables as main effects, and construct any interactions that you want in the model. Click on OK to run the model. (If you build a model assuming the gamma distribution, make sure that in the Estimation dialog box you pick Maximum Likelihood Estimate for the Scale Parameter Method.)

To fit a quadratic regression model, on the ANALYZE menu select the REGRES-SION option with the CURVE ESTIMATION suboption. Then, in the CURVE ESTIMATION dialog box, select the variables and choose the *Quadratic* model. The PLOT MODELS option provides a plot of the fitted curve. It can be useful to choose the Linear and Quadratic models so this plot shows the comparison.

To obtain a smoothing curve (a "kernel" method similar to LOESS mentioned in the text at the end of Section 14.5), on the GRAPHS menu of the data editor select INTERACTIVE and then SCATTERPLOT. After selecting the variables, click on FIT on the top of the CREATE SCATTERPLOT window and then pick SMOOTHER from the METHOD menu. Using a normal kernel provides the most smoothing and is usually a sensible choice. The Bandwidth option determines how much smoothing is done, with larger numbers providing more smoothing. After selecting the options, click on OK. You can try a few bandwidth choices, such as 1, 2, and 5, to see its effect on the smoothing.

To fit the exponential regression model, on the ANALYZE menu select the GENERALIZED LINEAR MODELS option and the GENERALIZED LINEAR MODELS suboption. Enter the response variable and select the Log link function. Click on the Predictor tab and add the quantitative predictor as a Covariate. Specify the predictor as an effect after clicking on the Model tab, and click OK to see the fit.

There is also an option for an exponential regression model by selecting the CURVE ESTIMATION suboption under the REGRESSION option in the ANA-LYZE menu. However, this provides a somewhat different fit than using GLM software, since it assumes the log of *y*, rather than *y*, is normally distributed with constant variance. As discussed following Example 14.7 (page 466), it fits the model $E[\log(Y)] = \alpha + \beta x$ rather than the model $\log[E(Y)] = \alpha + \beta x$.

## Chapter 15: Logistic Regression

To fit logistic regression models, on the ANALYZE menu select the REGRESSION option and the BINARY LOGISTIC suboption. In the LOGISTIC REGRESSION dialog box, identify the binary response (dependent) variable and the explanatory predictors (covariates). Highlight variables in the source list and click on $a * b$ to create an interaction term. Identify the explanatory variables that are categorical and for which you want dummy variables by clicking on Categorical and declaring such a covariate to be a Categorical Covariate in the LOGISTIC REGRESSION: DEFINE CATEGORICAL VARIABLES dialog box. Highlight the categorical covariate and under Change Contrast you will see several options for setting up dummy variables. The *Simple* contrast constructs them as in this text, in which the final category is the baseline.

In the LOGISTIC REGRESSION dialog box, click on *Method* for stepwise model selection procedures, such as backward elimination. Click on *Save* to save predicted probabilities, measures of influence such as leverage values and DFBETAS, and standardized residuals. Click on *Options* to open a dialog box that contains an option to construct confidence intervals for exponentiated parameters.

Another way to fit logistic regression models is with the GENERALIZED LIN-EAR MODELS option and suboption on the ANALYZE menu. You pick the binomial distribution and logit link function. It is also possible there to enter the data as the number of successes out of a certain number of trials, which is useful when the data are in contingency table form such as with the death penalty example in Table 15.3 (page 489). For example, suppose in one column you have the number of successes at each particular setting of predictors, and in a separate column you have the sample size that number of successes is based on. Then you identify the dependent variable as the variable listing the number of successes, you click the box "Variable represents binary response or number of events," and then "Number of events occurring in a set of trials," entering the variable listing the sample sizes as the "Trials variable."

You can also fit such models using the LOGLINEAR option with the LOGIT suboption in the ANALYZE menu. You identify the dependent variable, select categorical predictors as factors, and select quantitative predictors as cell covariates. The default fit is the saturated model for the factors, without including any covariates. To change this, click on *Model* and select a *Custom* model, entering the predictors and relevant interactions as terms in a customized (unsaturated) model. Clicking on *Options*, you can also display standardized residuals (called adjusted residuals) for model fits. This approach is well suited for logit models with categorical predictors, such as discussed in Section 15.2, since standard output includes observed and expected frequencies. When the data file contains the data as cell counts, such as binomial numbers of successes and failures, you weight each cell by the cell count using the WEIGHT CASES option in the DATA menu.

SPSS can also fit logistic models for categorical response variables having several response categories. On the ANALYZE menu, choose the REGRESSION option and then the ORDINAL suboption for a cumulative logit model. Select the MULTI-NOMIAL LOGISTIC suboption for a baseline-category logit model. In the latter, click on *Statistics* and check Likelihood-ratio tests under Parameters to obtain results of likelihood-ratio tests for the effects of the predictors.

For loglinear models, use the LOGLINEAR option with GENERAL suboption in the ANALYZE menu. You enter the factors for the model. The default is the saturated model, so click on *Model* and select a *Custom* model. Enter the factors as terms in a customized (unsaturated) model and then select additional interaction effects. Click on *Options* to show options for displaying observed and expected frequencies and adjusted residuals. When the data file contains the data as cell counts for the various combinations of factors rather than as responses listed for individual subjects, weight each cell by the cell count using the WEIGHT CASES option in the DATA menu.

## INTRODUCTION TO SAS

The **SAS** language consists of DATA steps that name the variables and input the data and PROC steps that request the statistical procedures. All SAS statements must end with a semicolon. The first statement, the DATA statement, assigns a name to the data set. The next statement, the INPUT statement, tells SAS the variable names and the order in which the variables are listed in the data set. The data follow the DATALINES statement, one line per subject, unless the INPUT statement ends with @@. After the data lines, a line containing only a semicolon ends the data set.

Following the data entry, PROC statements invoke the statistical procedures. A typical PROC statement lists the procedure, such as MEANS, and then also may select some options for providing greater detail than SAS provides with the default statement. The text by Schlotzhauer and Littell (1997) introduces SAS and its use for basic statistical methods. You can also get help at sites such as http://www.ats.ucla.edu/stat/sas/.

### Chapter 3: Descriptive Techniques

Table A.1 shows the format for entering the data and performing some very basic analyses, using the data set in Table 3.1 on murder rates for the 50 states. For each state, we list the state label and its value on murder rate. When you input characters rather than numbers for a variable, such as the state labels, the variable has an accompanying $ label in the INPUT statement. We enter the 50 observations as 50 lines of data, or we can enter multiple observations on a line if we enter @@ at the end of the input line, as shown in Table A.1.

**TABLE A.1**: SAS for Printing Data, Computing Basic Summary Statistics, and Preparing Plots

```
data crime ;
input  state $  murder @@;
datalines;
  AL  11.6  AK   9.0  AZ  8.6
  AR  10.2  CA  13.2  CO  5.8
  ...
;
proc print ;  var  state  murder ;
proc freq;  tables  murder ;
proc chart;  vbar  murder ;
proc means;  var  murder ;
proc univariate  plot;  var  murder ;  id  state;
run ;
```

The first procedure, PROC PRINT, prints the data set. PROC FREQ provides a frequency distribution for the variable listed following TABLES. PROC CHART provides a histogram of the variable listed in the VBAR statement. Options exist for choosing the number of bars (e.g., VBAR MURDER / LEVELS = 5) or their midpoints and for forming horizontal rather than vertical bars (HBAR instead of VBAR).

PROC MEANS provides the mean and standard deviation of the variables listed after VAR (in this case, the murder rate). The PROC UNIVARIATE statement requests a greater variety of basic statistics for a variable, including the sample size, mean, standard deviation, median, mode, range, and quartiles. The ID statement, which is optional, names STATE as the variable to identify some of the extreme observations in part of the display from this procedure. Listing the PLOT option in PROC UNIVARIATE requests stem-and-leaf and box plots for the variables listed.

### Chapters 5 and 6: Estimation and Significance Tests

The estimated standard error for a sample mean is one of the statistics provided by PROC UNIVARIATE. It is labeled as *Std Mean* in the output. We construct a confidence interval for a population mean by taking the sample mean and adding and subtracting the appropriate *t*-score times the standard error.

Table A.2 shows how to obtain the standard error and the *t*-score for the data from Example 6.4, for which $n = 29$ and $df = 28$. The two arguments for the TINV function are half the error probability and the *df* value. For instance, the statement in Table A.2 requests the *t*-score with left tail probability equal to 0.025 (for a 95% confidence interval) when $df = 28$, which equals $-2.048$. That table also shows how to input data for two dependent samples (WEIGHT1 and WEIGHT2 being the weights of anorexic girls at two times) and create a new variable (DIFF) that is the difference between WEIGHT2 and WEIGHT1.

**TABLE A.2:** SAS for Obtaining Standard Errors and *t*-Scores

```
data anorexia ;
input weight1 weight 2 ;
diff = weight2 - weight1;
datalines;
   80.5  82.2
   84.9  85.6
   . . .
;
proc univariate ; var diff ;
data findt;
       tvalue = tinv(.025, 28) ;
proc print   data = findt ;
run ;
```

## Chapter 7: Comparison of Two Groups

Table A.3 uses SAS to perform a two-sample *t* test for comparing two means (Section 7.3), using the data in Example 7.7. The input variables are THERAPY, the levels of which are the two groups to be compared, and CHANGE, the change in weight, which is the response variable. PROC SORT sorts the data into groups, according to the levels of therapy, and then PROC MEAN finds means and standard deviations for the observations in each group when you use BY followed by the group variable. The BY statement is used with SAS procedures when you want to do an analysis separately for each level of the variable specified in the BY statement.

**TABLE A.3:** SAS for Two-Sample *t* Test for Example 7.7 (see Table 12.21 for the data)

```
data depress;
input therapy $ change @@ ;
datalines;
 cogbehav 1.7
 cogbehav 0.7
. . .
 control -0.5
 control -9.3
. . .
;
proc sort; by therapy ;
proc means; by therapy ; var change ;
proc ttest; class therapy ; var change ;
run;
```

PROC TTEST is a procedure for a two-sample *t* test with independent samples. The CLASS statement names the variable that identifies the groups to be compared, and the VAR statement identifies the response variable for the analysis. The output shows the mean, standard deviation, and standard error for the response variable in each group, and provides the *t* test statistic, its *df* value, and a two-sided *P*-value, which is labeled by $Prob > |T|$. The approximate test is also provided that does not assume equal population variances for the two groups.

## Chapter 8: Analyzing Association Between Categorical Variables

Table A.4 illustrates SAS for analyzing two-way contingency tables, using data from Table 8.1. PROC FREQ conducts chi-squared tests of independence using the CHISQ option and provides the expected frequencies for the test with the EXPECTED option. The MEASURES option provides a wide assortment of measures of association (including gamma for ordinal data) and their standard errors. For 2 × 2 tables this option provides confidence intervals for the odds ratio (labeled "case-control" on output) and the relative risk. The EXACT option provides Fisher's exact test. SAS lists the category levels in alphanumeric order unless you state ORDER=DATA in the PROC directive, in which case the levels have the order in which they occur in the input data.

**TABLE A.4**: SAS for Chi-Squared Test with Table 8.1

```
data politics;
input  gender  $  party  $  count  @@;
datalines;
  Female  Democ  573  Female  Indep  516  Female  Repub  422
   Male   Democ  386   Male   Indep  475   Male   Repub  399
;
proc freq;  weight count ;
     tables  gender*party / chisq  expected  measures ;
proc genmod;  class gender party;
   model count=gender party / dist=poi link=log obstats residuals;
run;
```

You can also perform chi-squared tests using PROC GENMOD, as Table A.4 shows. This procedure, discussed in greater detail in the SAS discussion below for Chapter 14, uses a generalized linear modeling approach introduced in Section 14.4. (The code in Table A.4 views the independence hypothesis as a "loglinear model" for Poisson counts with main effects of gender and party but no interaction.) The OBSTATS and RESIDUALS options in GENMOD provide cell residuals; the output labeled *StReschi* is the standardized residual.

## Chapter 9: Linear Regression and Correlation

Table A.5 uses SAS to perform linear regression, using the "statewide crime 2" dataset, shown partly in Table 9.1. The PROC PLOT statement requests a scatterplot for murder rate and poverty rate; the first variable listed goes on the y-axis. The PROC REG statement requests a regression analysis, predicting murder rate using poverty rate. The P option following this model statement requests the predicted values and residuals for all observations. The PROC CORR statement requests the correlation between each pair of variables listed in the VAR list.

## Chapter 11: Multiple Regression and Correlation

Table A.6 uses SAS to perform multiple regression with the mental impairment data of Table 11.1. You list every explanatory variable in the model to the right of the equal sign in the model statement. The PARTIAL option provides partial regression scatterplots. The PCORR2 option provides squared partial correlations, and the STB

**TABLE A.5**: SAS for Regression Analysis with Table 9.1

```
data crime ;
input state $  violent  murder  metro  white  hs  poverty  single ;
datalines;
   AK   761     9.0  41.8   75.2   86.6    9.1   14.3
   AL   780    11.6  67.4   73.5   66.9   17.4   11.5
   AR   593    10.2  44.7   82.9   66.3   20.0   10.7
   AZ   715     8.6  84.7   88.6   78.7   15.4   12.1
   CA  1078    13.1  96.7   79.3   76.2   18.2   12.5
   ....
;
proc print  data=crime;
proc plot; plot murder*poverty ;
proc reg;  model  murder = poverty / p;
proc corr;  var violent murder metro white hs poverty single ;
run;
```

**TABLE A.6**: SAS for Multiple Regression Analysis with Table 11.1

```
data mental ;
input  impair  life   ses ;
life_cen = life - 44.425;  ses_cen = ses - 56.60;
life_ses = life_cen*ses_cen;
datalines;
   17   46    84
   19   39    97
   ....
;
proc print; var  impair   life   ses ;
proc plot ;  plot  impair*life   impair*ses ;
proc reg;  model  impair =  life   ses  /  partial   stb   pcorr2 ;
proc reg;  model  impair =  life   ses  life_ses ;
run;
```

option provides standardized regression coefficients. Following the input statement, we create centered variables by subtracting the means from the predictors and then define a variable life_ses to be the cross-product of centered life events and ses. We enter that variable in the second regression model to permit interaction in the model.

## Chapter 12: Comparing Groups: Analysis of Variance Methods

Table A.7 uses SAS to perform one-way ANOVA with Table 12.1 and two-way ANOVA with Table 12.10. The first PROC MEANS statement requests sample means on ideology for the data grouped by party. PROC GLM is a procedure for *general linear models*. It is similar in many ways to the regression procedure, PROC REG, except that PROC GLM can use CLASS statements to create dummy variables in order to include categorical predictors in the model.

**TABLE A.7**: SAS for One-Way ANOVA with Table 12.1 and Two-Way ANOVA with Table 12.10

```
data anova;
input party  $   gender  $   ideology ;
datalines;
  Dem  F  1
  Dem  F  1
  Dem  F  1
  Dem  F  1
  Dem  F  1
  Dem  F  2
  ...
  Rep  M  7
;
proc means;   by party;   var ideology;
proc glm;   class party ;
   model ideology = party   /   solution;
   means party  /   bon   tukey   alpha=.10;
proc means;   by   party   gender;   var   ideology;
proc glm;   class   party   gender;
   model ideology = party gender   /   solution;
   means party /   bon   tukey;
proc glm;   class   party   gender;
   model ideology = party gender party*gender;
run;
```

The first GLM statement requests a one-way ANOVA, comparing ideology by party. The CLASS statement requests dummy variables for the levels of party. The MEANS option provides multiple comparison confidence intervals. Here, we request the Bonferroni and Tukey methods and specify alpha = .10 for overall 90% confidence. The SOLUTION option requests the estimates for the prediction equation.

The second PROC MEANS requests sample means on ideology for each of the combinations of party and gender. Following that is a GLM statement to conduct a two-way ANOVA using party and gender as predictors of ideology, setting up dummy variables for each predictor with the CLASS statement. This is followed by a MEANS option requesting multiple comparisons across the levels of party. This analysis assumes a lack of interaction. The final GLM statement adds an interaction term to the model.

Table A.8 shows SAS for the repeated measures ANOVA with Table 12.17. Each row of the data provides the opinion responses on the three influences (movies, TV, rock) for a particular subject. You can use PROC REG or else PROC ANOVA for the modeling. The latter applies for "balanced" analyses in which the same number of responses occur at each level of a factor. This model looks like that for a standard two-way ANOVA, except that one effect is the subject effect. The analysis is followed by a multiple comparison of means across the levels of influence type.

Table A.9 shows an alternative way of inputting data for a repeated measures ANOVA. This table refers to Table 12.21, in which the groups refer to three therapies and the response is weight. Each line identifies the group into which a subject falls, and then lists successively the repeated responses by the subject, labeling them by

**TABLE A.8:** SAS for Repeated Measures ANOVA with Table 12.17

```
data repeat;
input subject  $    influ  $    opinion @@;
datalines;
   1  M  -1   1  T   0   1  R  -1
   2  M   1   2  T   0   2  R   0
  ....
  12  M  -1  12  T  -1  12  R  -2
;
proc print;
proc anova;     classes subject influ ;
    model opinion = influ subject ;
    means influ    /    tukey bon;
run;
```

**TABLE A.9:** SAS for Two-Way Repeated Measures ANOVA with Table 12.21

```
data repeat2;
input subject $ therapy $ weight1-weight2;
datalines;
   1    CB    80.5    82.2
   2    CB    84.9    85.6
   3    CB    81.5    81.4
  ....
  72     C    89.0    78.8
;
proc anova; class therapy ;
model weight1-weight2 = therapy ;
   repeated occasion  /  short printe;
means therapy / bon ;
run;
```

a name such as RESP1-RESP3 if there are three repeated responses. This table provides the analysis for a between-subjects effect (therapy) and a within-subject effect (the repeated responses on weight). The model statement indicates that the repeated responses are modeled as a function of *therapy* and that the levels at which the repeated measurements occur refer to a variable labeled as *occasion*. The analysis is followed by a Bonferroni multiple comparison of the response means by category of therapy.

This extends to more complex designs. For instance, suppose we had three factors, $A$ and $B$ being between-subjects factors and the repeated measures on a variable $y$ taken at the four levels of a factor $C$. We could use the SAS code:

```
PROC ANOVA; CLASS  A  B ;
MODEL  Y1 - Y4 = A  B  A*B ; REPEATED C ;
```

You can also conduct repeated measures ANOVA in SAS using PROC MIXED. This is a more advanced procedure that provides additional options for the covariance structure of the random effect (see Section 16.1). There are a variety of options in addition to the sphericity form of the standard analysis, and the results of tests for fixed effects depend on the choice. This procedure, unlike PROC ANOVA or GLM, can use data from subjects that have missing observations. Other advantages of PROC MIXED are that you can use continuous variables in within-subject effects, instead of only classification variables, and you can omit the between–within interaction effects from the model. See Littell et al. (2006) for details.

### Chapter 13: Combining Regression and ANOVA: Quantitative and Categorical Predictors

Table A.10 uses SAS to fit analysis of covariance models to Table 13.1. The PLOT statement requests a plot of income by education, with symbols indicating which race each observation has. The first GLM statement fits the analysis of covariance model, assuming no interaction, using a CLASS statement, to provide dummy variables for levels of race. This is followed by a request for adjusted means (also called "least squares means" and abbreviated by SAS as LSMEANS) on the response for the different levels of race, with Bonferroni multiple comparisons of them. The second GLM statement adds an interaction of race and education to the model.

**TABLE A.10:** SAS for Analysis of Covariance Models with Table 13.1

```
data ancova ;
input  income   educ   race $ ;
datalines;
 16   10   black
 18    7   black
 26    9   black
 ....
 56   20   white
;
proc plot;   plot income*educ = race;
proc glm; class race;   model income = educ race / solution;
lsmeans race    adjust=bon ;
proc glm; class race; model income=educ race educ*race / solution;
run;
```

### Chapter 14: Model Building with Multiple Regression

Table A.11 shows a variety of analyses for the house sales data. In fitting a multiple regression model, the BACKWARD, FORWARD, STEPWISE, and CP choices for the SELECTION option yield these selection procedures. The P option yields predicted values and the PRESS model diagnostic. The INFLUENCE option yields studentized residuals, leverage values, and measures of influence such as DFFITS and DFBETAS. The PLOT option following the second model statement requests plots of residuals against the predicted values and against size of home. The code sets up an artificial variable *size_2* that is the square of size. Entering it in the model, as in the third regression statement, provides a quadratic regression model.

PROC GENMOD in SAS fits generalized linear models. GENMOD specifies the distribution of the random component in the DIST option ( "nor" for normal, "gam"

**TABLE A.11:** SAS for Various Analyses Conducted with House Sales Data

```
data housing ;
input  price   size   bed   bath   new;
size_2 = size*size;
datalines;
   279900   2048   4   2   0
   146500    912   2   2   0
   ....
;
proc reg;  model price = size bed bath new  /  selection=backward;
proc reg;  model price = size bath new  /  p influence partial;
plot r.*p.  r.*size ;
proc reg;   model price = size size_2 ;
proc genmod;  model price = size  /  dist = nor  link = identity;
proc genmod;  model price = size  /  dist = gam  link = identity ;
run;
```

for gamma, "poi" for Poisson, "bin" for binomial) and specifies the link in the LINK option (including "log", "identity", and "logit"). The first GENMOD statement in Table A.11 fits the ordinary bivariate regression model to price and size. This gives the same results as using least squares with PROC REG or GLM. The second GENMOD statement fits the same type of model but instead assumes a gamma distribution for price.

Table A.12 uses GENMOD to fit an exponential regression model to the population growth data of Table 14.8. This model uses the log link.

**TABLE A.12:** SAS for Fitting Exponential Regression Model as a Generalized Linear Model to Table 14.8

```
data growth ;
input   decade   popul ;
datalines;
 0    62.95
 1    75.99
 ....
;
proc genmod;  model popul = decade  /  dist = nor  link = log ;
run;
```

### Chapter 15: Logistic Regression

You can fit logistic regression models either using software for generalized linear models or specialized software for logistic regression. Table A.13 applies PROC GENMOD and PROC LOGISTIC to Table 15.1. In the code, *credit* is a dummy variable indicating whether the subject has a credit card. There would be 100 lines of data for the 100 subjects, with a 1 in the column for credit whenever a subject had a travel credit card.

The GENMOD statement requests the binomial distribution and logit link options, which is logistic regression. PROC LOGISTIC also fits the logistic regression model.

**TABLE A.13**: SAS for Fitting Logistic Regression Model to Table 15.1

```
data binary ;
input    income    credit ;
datalines;
 12   0
 13   0
 ....
;
proc genmod descending;
    model credit/n = income  /  dist = bin  link = logit ;
proc logistic descending; model credit = income  / influence;
    output  out=predict    p=pi_hat    lower=LCL   upper=UCL;
proc print  data = predict;
run;
```

These procedures order the levels of the response variable alphanumerically, forming the logit, for instance, as

$$\log\left[\frac{P(Y = 0)}{P(Y = 1)}\right].$$

The DESCENDING option reverses the order. Following the LOGISTIC model fit, Table A.13 requests predicted probabilities and lower and upper 95% confidence limits for the true probabilities.

For PROC GENMOD and PROC LOGISTIC with binomial models, the response in the model statements can have the form of the number of successes divided by the number of cases (as data were presented in Table 15.1 and other tables). Table A.14 fits a logistic model with categorical predictors to the death penalty data in Table 15.4. Here, we set up dummy variables for the predictors when we input the data, but you can automatically do this for factors by declaring them in a CLASS statement. The OBSTATS option in GENMOD provides predicted probabilities and their confidence limits, and the RESIDUALS option provides standardized residuals (labeled *StReschi*). In models with multiple predictors, the TYPE3 option in GENMOD provides likelihood-ratio tests for testing the significance of each individual predictor in the model.

**TABLE A.14**: SAS for Fitting Logistic Model to Table 15.4

```
data death ;
input    vic   def   yes   n ;
datalines;
  1   1   53   467
  1   0   11    48
  0   1    0    16
  0   0    4   143
;
proc genmod; model yes/n = def vic / dist=bin link=logit residuals
obstats type3;
proc logistic;  model yes/n = def  vic;
```

You can fit loglinear models using either software for generalized linear models. Table A.15 uses GENMOD to fit model $(AC, AM, CM)$ to the student survey data of Table 15.11. The CLASS statement generates dummy variables for the classification factors. The $AM$ association is represented by $A * M$. The OBSTATS and RESIDUALS options provide expected frequencies (predicted values) and diagnostics, including standardized residuals.

**TABLE A.15:** SAS for Fitting Loglinear Models to Table 15.11

```
data drugs ;
input    a    $    c    $    m    $    count @@ ;
datalines;
 yes   yes   yes   911    yes   yes   no   538
 yes   no    yes    44    yes    no   no   456
 no    yes   yes     3     no   yes   no    43
 no    no    yes     2     no    no   no   279
;
proc genmod; class  a  c  m ;
 model count = a c m a*c a*m c*m / dist=poi link=log obstats residuals;
run;
```

For ordinal responses, PROC LOGISTIC provides ML fitting of the proportional odds version of cumulative logit models. PROC GENMOD fits this model using options DIST=MULTINOMIAL and LINK=CLOGIT. PROC LOGISTIC fits the baseline-category logit model for nominal responses with the option LINK=GLOGIT.

# Answers to Selected Odd-Numbered Exercises

### Chapter 1

1. **a.** An individual automobile   **b.** All automobiles of that type used in the EPA tests   **c.** All automobiles of that type that are or may be manufactured

3. **a.** All students at the University of Wisconsin   **b.** A statistic, since calculated only for the 100 sampled students

5. **a.** All adult Americans   **b.** Proportion of all adult Americans who would answer definitely or probably true   **c.** Sample proportion 0.523 estimates population proportion   **d.** No, it is an estimate of the population value but will not equal it exactly, because the sample is only a very small subset of the population.

7. **a.** 85.7%   **b.** 85.8%   **c.** 74.4%, higher for HEAVEN

9. a

15. Inferential statistics are used when you have data only for a sample and need to make predictions about the entire population.

17. **a.** The percentage in the Eurobarometer sample for a country who say "yes." **b.** The population percentage (or proportion) in a country who would say "yes." **c.** 45% of 631 sampled in the UK say "yes."   **d.** The prediction that between 41% and 49% of the UK population would say "yes."

### Chapter 2

3. **a.** Ordinal   **b.** Nominal   **c.** Interval   **d.** Nominal   **e.** Nominal   **f.** Ordinal **g.** Interval
**h.** Ordinal   **i.** Nominal   **j.** Interval   **k.** Nominal

5. **a.** Interval   **b.** Ordinal   **c.** Nominal

7. **a.** Ordinal   **b.** discrete   **c.** Statistics, because they apply to a sample of size 1962, not the entire population

9. b, c, d, e, f   **11.** Students numbered 10, 22, 24.

13. **a.** observational   **b.** experimental   **c.** observational   **d.** experimental

15. **a.** Different organizations choose different samples, and so there is sampling variability (i.e., results naturally vary from sample to sample). They may also have used slightly different sampling methods and question wording.   **b.** The difference between the predicted percentage and the actual percentage was −2.4 for Gore, 0.1 for Bush, and 1.3 for Nader.

19. Skip number is $k = 5000/100 = 50$. Pick a number at random between 01 and 50. Suppose it is 10, Then the first selection is the subject numbered 10; the next is numbered $10 + 50 = 60$; next is $60 + 50 = 110$; last is $4910 + 50 = 4960$.

21. **a.** (i) yes, (ii) no   **b.** (i) no, (ii) yes   **c.** Cluster: Samples all subjects in some of the groups; Stratified: Samples some subjects in all of the groups

25. Nonprobability

29. Because of skipping names, two subjects listed next to each other on the list cannot both be in the sample, so not all samples are equally likely.

31. Every possible sample is not equally likely. For example, the probability is 0 of a sample for which everyone is in the same cluster.

33. Cluster sampling followed by simple random sampling

35. c   **37.** a   **39.** False

## Chapter 3

1. **c.** categorical   **d.** Mode = Central America

3. **a.** 33 students, minimum = 65, maximum = 98

7. **a.** Mean = 57.4   **b.** Median = 17, very different because the outlier (California) affects the mean but not the median

9. **a.** Not far enough   **b.** Median = not far enough, mean requires scores for categories

5. **b.** 16.6   **c.** 12.0   **d.** 13.9   **e.** Mean = 27.6, Median = 24.0, Standard deviation = 12.4; the lengths of stay tended to be longer 25 years ago   **f.** Of the 11 observations, the middle in magnitude is 13.0, the median; cannot calculate mean, but substituting 40 for censored observation gives lower bound for it of 18.7.

7. **b.** Median = 2 or 3 times a month, Mode = Not at all.   **c.** Mean = 4.5

9. **a.** Mean = 73.2   **b.** Median = 16, very different because the outlier (California) affects the mean but not the median

13. Skewed right, which pulls mean out in right tail above median

15. **a.** Mode = every day, median = a few times a week

17. **a.** Response = family income in 2003, explanatory = racial–ethnic group (white, black, Hispanic)   **b.** No   **c.** The sample size for each group

19. **a.** median = \$10.13, mean = \$10.18, range = \$0.46, standard deviation = \$0.22   **b.** median = \$10.01, mean = \$9.17, range = \$5.31, standard deviation = \$2.26. The small outlier drags the mean down, but increases the range and standard deviation substantially

21. Mean = 26.7, standard deviation = 11.1

23. **a.** (i) \$40,000 to \$60,000, (ii) \$30,000 to \$70,000, (iii) \$20,000 to \$80,000   **b.** Yes, it would be five standard deviations above the mean, which would be very unusual for a bell-shaped distribution.

25. **a.** 88.8   **b.** No, the distribution is extremely skewed to the right.

27. **a.** 0.4   **b.** −10.0

29. **a.** Skewed to right   **b.** Yes, the maximum is 43.5 standard deviations above the mean.

31. **a.** \$28,700   **b.** \$9600

33. The large outlying observation increases the mean somewhat, increases the standard deviation moreso, and has a very strong effect on increasing the maximum and the range. The quartiles are unaffected.

35. Expect mean to be greater than median in cases a, b, d, since distributions are probably skewed to right; expect median to be greater in cases c, e since distributions are probably skewed to left.

**39. a.** minimum = 0, lower quartile = 2, median = 3, upper quartile = 5, maximum = 14  **c.** outliers at 12 and 14  **d.** 3

**41. b.** Skewed right

**43. a.** min = 1, LQ = 3, Median = 5, UQ = 6, max = 13  **b.** min = 1, LQ = 3, Median = 5, UQ = 6, max = 44, so the very large value affects only the maximum.

**45. a.** 3.88  **b.** 0.76  **c.** (i) 2.48, (ii) 3.58

**47. a.** Response: opinion about health insurance (favor or oppose); Explanatory: political party (Democratic, Republican)

**49. a.** 1.2 and 3.2  **b.** Nations with higher use of the Internet tend to have lower fertility rates.

**51. a.** positive  **b.** Luxembourg is extremely high on both variables.

**53. a.** Sample mean and population mean  **b.** Sample standard deviation and population standard deviation

**63.** Median = $86,100

**67.** Any nominal variable, such as religious affiliation

**69. a.** Mean can be misleading with very highly skewed distributions or extreme outliers in one direction.  **b.** Median can be uninformative with highly discrete data.

**71. a.** F  **b.** F  **c.** T  **d.** T  **73.** c

**75.** Standard deviation

**77.** Population sizes vary by state, and the overall rate gives more weight to states with larger population sizes, whereas the mean of the 50 measurements gives the same weight to each state.

## Chapter 4

**1.** 0.80

**3. b.** (i) $30/96 = 0.312$, (ii) $88/1021 = 0.086$  **c.** (i) 30/1117, (ii) (0.086)(0.312)  **d.** $(30 + 933)/1117$

**5. b.** 0.13

**7. a.** $P(0) = P(1) = \ldots = P(9) = 0.1$  **b.** 4.5  **c.** 2.9

**9. a.** $z = 1.0$ gives tail probability 0.1587, thus two-tail probability $2(0.1587) = 0.317$, or probability between $\mu - \sigma$ and $\mu + \sigma$ equal to $1 - 0.317 = 0.683$.

**11. a.** 0.67  **b.** 1.64  **c.** 1.96  **d.** 2.33  **e.** 2.58

**13.** 5% is in each tail, for which $z = 1.64$, and thus $\mu + 1.64\sigma$ is the 95th percentile.

**15. a.** 0.018  **b.** 0.018  **c.** 0.982  **d.** 0.964

**17. a.** 2.05  **b.** 133

**19. a.** 0.106  **b.** 120.5  **c.** 89, 100, 111

**21. a.** 0.21  **b.** 11.8  **c.** skewed right

**23. a.** The ACT score, which is $z = 1.7$ standard deviations above mean, compared to SAT score which is $z = 1.0$ standard deviations above mean

**25. a.** 27.8%  **b.** No, probably skewed right since mean is only 1.2 standard deviations above 0.

**27. a.** $P(0) = P(1) = 0.5$  **b.** $P(0) = 0.25, P(0.5) = 0.5, P(1) = 0.25$  **c.** $P(0) = 0.125, P(1/3) = 0.375, P(2/3) = 0.375, P(1) = 0.125$  **d.** $P(0) = 0.0625, P(0.25) = 0.250, P(0.50) = 0.375, P(0.75) = 0.250,$ $P(1) = 0.0625$  **e.** Becoming more bell shaped

**29. a.** 0.0104   **b.** Yes, the sample proportion would be 5.7 standard errors below the mean, which would happen very rarely.   **c.** Predict that Brown won

**31. a.** Mean = 0.10, standard error of $\bar{y}$ is $\sigma/\sqrt{n} = 316.23/\sqrt{1,000,000} = 0.316$.
**b.** For the sampling distribution of the sample mean, 1.0 has a $z$-score of $(1.0 - 0.10)/0.316 = 2.85$. The probability that the average exceeds 1.0 is the probability that a $z$-score exceeds 2.85, which equals 0.002.

**33. a.** $z = -0.67$, probability 0.25   **b.** By CLT, approximately normal with mean 100 and standard error $15/\sqrt{25} = 3.0$. $z = -3.33$, probability = 0.0004 below 90.   **c.** No (only 0.67 standard deviations below mean). Yes, since probability is only 0.0004 of sample mean of 90 or less.

**35. a.** Number of people in a household   **b.** mean = 2.6, standard deviation = 1.5   **c.** mean = 2.4, standard deviation = 1.4   **d.** mean = 2.6, standard error = 0.1

**37. a.** Standard error = $3.0/\sqrt{36} = 0.50$; distance of 0.5 has $z$-score of $0.5/0.5 = 1.00$, and 0.68 of a normal curve falls within 1.00 standard errors of mean.   **b.** Standard error = $3.0/\sqrt{100} = 0.30$; 0.5 has $z$-score of $0.5/0.3 = 1.67$, and 0.90 of a normal curve falls within 1.67 standard errors of mean.   **c.** Yes, because 4.0 falls $(4.0 - 5.2)/0.3 = -4.0$ standard errors from mean, which is extremely unlikely for a normal distribution.

**39. a.** Skewed left, mean 60, standard deviation 16
**b.** Mean 58.3, standard deviation 15.0, probably skewed left (It looks like the population distribution).
**c.** Mean 60, standard error 1.6, normal (by CLT)
**d.** An observation of 40 is 1.25 standard deviations below the mean, which is not unusual, but a sample mean of 40 is 12.5 standard errors below the mean of the sampling distribution of the sample mean (extremely unusual).

**47. a.** 4.41   **b.** 4

**49.** If half of population voted for Clinton, sample proportion would be 12.4 standard errors above 0.50, extremely unlikely. Predict Clinton won.

**51.** a, c, d   **53.** False

**55. a.** $\sigma^2 = (0 - 0.5)^2(0.5) + (1 - 0.5)^2(0.5) = 0.25$, and $\sigma = 0.50$
**b.** $\mu = 0(1 - \pi) + 1(\pi) = \pi$
**c.** Substitute $\sigma = \sqrt{\pi(1 - \pi)}$ (from (b)) in standard error $\sigma/\sqrt{n}$.

**57. a.** Finite population correction = $\sqrt{(30,000 - 300)/(30,000 - 1)} = \sqrt{0.99} = 0.995$.
**b.** Finite population correction = 0, so $\sigma_{\bar{Y}} = 0$.
**c.** For $n = 1$, the sample mean is a single observation from the population, so the sampling distribution is the same as the population distribution.

## Chapter 5

**1.** 0.716   **3.** 0.017   **5.** $\sqrt{(0.51)(0.49)/1008} = 0.0157$, and margin of error = $2(0.0157) = 0.031$

**7. a.** $\sqrt{(0.36)(0.64)/883} = 0.016$   **b.** $1.96(0.016) = 0.03$   **c.** $0.36 \pm 0.03$, or (0.33, 0.39)

**9.** 95% CI is $0.19 \pm 1.96(0.0113)$, which is (0.17, 0.21), and 99% CI is $0.19 \pm 2.58(0.0113)$, which is (0.16, 0.22)

**11. a.** 0.02 probability in two tails, so 0.01 in each tail, or $z = 2.33$.
**b.** 1.64   **c.** 0.67   **d.** 3.0

**13. a.** 0.364, 0.636   **b.** The 95% confidence interval of (0.33, 0.40) suggests that a minority supports legalization.   **c.** The proportion has somewhat of an increasing trend.

**15.** $0.255 \pm 2.58(0.002)$, or (0.25, 0.26)

**17. a.** $0.40 \pm 2.58\sqrt{(0.40)(0.60)/400} = 0.40 \pm 0.06$, or $(0.34, 0.46)$. Can predict Jones loses, because the interval consists entirely of numbers below 0.50, corresponding to Jones receiving a minority of the vote.
  **b.** $0.40 \pm 2.58\sqrt{(0.40)(0.60)/40} = 0.40 \pm 0.20$, or $(0.20, 0.60)$. We would not predict a winner, because the interval contains numbers both below and above 0.50. The point estimate is the same as in (a), but the interval is much wider because the sample size is so much smaller.

**19. a.** 2.776  **b.** 2.145  **c.** 2.064  **d.** 2.060  **e.** 2.787

**21. a.** $52.554/\sqrt{1007}$   **c.** The large standard deviation relative to the mean suggests the distribution is highly skewed to the right, and there may be extreme outliers.

**23. a.** $1.77/\sqrt{397}$   **b.** $2.89 \pm 1.97(0.089)$ is $(2.7, 3.1)$

**25.** The confidence interval is a prediction about the population mean, not about where values of $y$ fall for individual subjects. We can be 95% confident that the population mean TV watching falls between 2.60 and 2.93 hours per day.

**27. a.** No, the mean exceeds the median and is only $20.3/18.2 = 1.1$ standard deviations above 0, so the distribution is probably skewed to the right.   **b.** Yes, since $n$ is so large, the sampling distribution is normal by the Central Limit Theorem. The interval is $20.3 \pm 2.58(18.2)/\sqrt{1415}$, or $(19.2, 21.5)$.

**29. b.** The variable cannot take negative values, but the standard deviation has similar size as the mean. Although the population distribution and sample data distribution are probably skewed right, the sampling distribution of the sample mean is bell-shaped by the Central Limit Theorem.

**31. a.** $4.23 \pm 2.58(0.0387)$ is $4.23 \pm 0.10$, or $(4.13, 4.23)$
  **b.** (i) narrower, (ii) wider   **c.** Interval scale, with equal spacings between each pair of adjacent categories

**33. a.**

```
 5 : 69
 6 : 04
 7 : 003789
 8 : 33456
 9 : 022346
10 : 008
11 : 12
12 : 024
13 : 9
```

It is probably roughly mound shaped.   **b.** $\bar{y} = 90.0, s = 20.7$
  **c.** $se = 20.7/\sqrt{30} = 3.77$, so 95% confidence interval is $90.0 \pm 2.045(3.77) = 90.0 \pm 7.7$, or $(82.3, 97.7)$

**35.** $n = (1.64)^2(0.30)(0.70)/(0.06)^2 = 157$

**37. a.** $n = (1.96)^2(0.1)(0.9)/(0.02)^2 = 864$   **b.** $n = (1.96)^2(0.5)(0.5)/(0.02)^2 = 2401$

**39.** $n = (1.96)^2(0.83)(0.17)/(0.03)^2 = 602$

**41.** If 0 to 18 encompasses the mean plus and minus about three standard deviations, then the standard deviation is approximately 3, and we need $n = (1.96)^2(3)^2/(1)^2 = 35$.

**43.** No, do not have at least 15 in one of the categories (death before adulthood). Use formula after adding 2 outcomes of each type to get $\hat{\pi} = 5/34 = 0.147$, with $se = \sqrt{(0.147)(0.853)/34} = 0.0607$ and CI $0.147 \pm 1.96(0.0607)$, or (0.028, 0.266).

**45.** Indices of the $n = 30$ ordered observations for the interval are $(n + 1)/2 \pm \sqrt{n} = 15.5 \pm 5.5$, or 10 and 21. The 10th smallest observation is 79 and the 21st smallest (10th largest) is 96. The confidence interval is ($7900, $9600).

**49. a.** $7.27 \pm 2.00(6.72)/\sqrt{60}$, or (5.5, 9.0)   **b.** $\hat{\pi} = 31/60 = 0.517$, and CI is $0.517 \pm 1.96\sqrt{(0.517)(0.483)/60}$, or (0.39, 0.64).

**57. b.** $\bar{y} = 4.8, s = 2.89$

**59. a.** It would usually be too wide to be very useful, since we must use such a large $z$-score ($z = 3.9$) or $t$-score in forming the interval. **b.** A 25% confidence interval has too low a chance of containing the unknown parameter value.

**61.** The greater the heterogeneity, the greater the value of $\sigma$. Hence, the larger the sample size needed, since $n$ is directly proportional to $\sigma^2$. It would require a larger sample to estimate mean age to within 1 year than to estimate mean number of years of education to within 1 year, since age is much more variable.

**63.** No, statistical inference is needed when you have only a sample from the population, but here you have data for the entire population.

**65. a.** With $n = 30$ and $\hat{\pi} = 0.50$, there were $30(0.50) = 15$ in each category, which is the minimum needed to use this method.

**67.** a  **69.** b, e

**71.** We are 95% confident that the population mean age at first marriage fell between 21.5 and 23.0. If random samples of 50 records were repeatedly selected, then in the long run 95% of the confidence intervals formed would contain the population mean.

**73.** $y_n = n\bar{y} - (y_1 + y_2 + \cdots + y_{n-1})$  **75.** $\hat{\pi} = 0.0$

## Chapter 6

**1. a.** null **b.** alternative **c.** alternative **d.** $H_0: \pi = 0.50, H_a: \pi < 0.24, H_a: \mu > 100$

**3. a.** $2(0.149) = 0.30$, so it is plausible that the population mean equals 0.
**b.** $2(0.0062) = 0.012$, which is much stronger evidence against the null. Smaller $P$-values give stronger evidence.
**c.** 0.149, 0.851

**5. a.** $t = (103 - 100)/2 = 1.50, P = 2(0.067) = 0.134$ **b.** $t = 3.00, P = 0.003$. An effect of a given size has smaller $P$-value when the sample size is larger.

**7. a.** $H_0: \mu = 500, H_a: \mu \neq 500, t = (410 - 500)/30 = -3.0, df = 8, 0.01 < P < 0.02$ (actual value is 0.017, which we could report at $P = 0.02$); there is strong evidence that the mean differs from 500, and a 95% confidence interval would suggest that it is less than 500.
**b.** $P = 0.01$, very strong evidence that mean less than 500. **c.** $P = 0.99$

**9. a.** $H_0 : \mu = 0, H_a : \mu \neq 0$ **b.** Standard error $= 1.253/\sqrt{996} = 0.0397, t = (-0.052 - 0)/0.0397 = -1.31, P = 0.19$. Do not reject $H_0$. It is plausible that true mean $= 0$.

with the sample mean far from the actual population mean. Further studies in later research would reveal that the true mean is not so extreme.

**53.** b, e   **55.** a, c   **57.** F, T, F, T

**59.** The value in $H_0$ is only one of many plausible values for the parameter. A confidence interval would display a range of possible values for the parameter. The terminology "Accept $H_0$" makes it seem as if the null value is the only plausible one.

**61. a.** $H_0$ either is, or is not, correct. It is not a variable, so one cannot phrase probability statements about it.
**b.** If $H_0$ is true, the probability that $\bar{y} \geq 120$ or that $\bar{y} \leq 80$ (i.e., that $\bar{y}$ is at least 20 from $\mu_0 = 100$, so that $|z|$ is at least as large as observed) is 0.057.
**c.** This is true if "$\mu = 100$" is substituted for "$\mu \neq 100$."
**d.** The probability of Type I error equals $\alpha$ (which is not specified here), not the $P$-value. The $P$-value is compared to $\alpha$ in determining whether one can reject $H_0$.
**e.** Better to say, "We do not reject $H_0$ at the $\alpha = 0.05$ level."
**f.** No, we need $P \leq 0.05$ to be able to reject $H_0$.

**63. a.** Binomial, $n = 100$, $\pi = 0.05$
**b.** No, if $H_0$ is correct each time, the probability she would get a $P$-value $\leq 0.05$ all five times is $(0.05)^5 = 0.0000003$.

**65.** Would get $\hat{\pi} = 0.0$, $se = 0.0$, and $z = -\infty$. This cannot happen using $se_0$.

**67. a.** $x = 5$, $P$-value $= 1/32 = 0.03$.   **b.**  No value of $x$ has $P$-value $< 0.01$.   **c.** 1/32, the probability of $x$ such that the $P$-value is $\leq 0.05$.

## Chapter 7

**1.** Independent samples   **3.** $0.204$, $\sqrt{(0.02)^2 + (0.02)^2} = 0.028$

**5.** 24 pounds, $se = \sqrt{(2)^2 + (2)^2} = 2.83$   **b.** $164/140 = 1.17$, which is 17% higher
**c.** Difference $= 25$ pounds, ratio $= 1.15$

**7. a.** $832/58 = 14.3$   **b.** $0.00832 - 0.00058 = 0.00774$   **c.** relative risk

**9. a.** We can be 95% confident that the population proportion who have started sexual intercourse is between 0.18 and 0.26 higher for those who listen to lots of music with degrading sexual messages than for those who listen to little or none.
**b.** Extremely strong evidence that the population proportion who have started sexual intercourse is higher for those who listen to lots of music with degrading sexual messages.

**11. a.** $\sqrt{(0.399)(0.601)/12708 + (0.482)(0.518)/8783} = 0.0069$   **b.** $0.083 \pm 1.96$ $(0.0069) = (0.07, 0.10)$

**13.** $0.19 \pm 1.96(0.0216) = (0.15, 0.23)$

**15. b.** $\hat{\pi} = 0.36$, $se = 0.0324$, $z = 0.62$.   **c.** $P = 0.53$.   **d.** Educational level, for which the estimated difference is 0.14, compared to 0.02 for gender.

**17.** 95% confidence interval comparing proportions for women and men is $(0.060 - 0.055) \pm 1.96(0.010)$, which is $(-0.015, 0.025)$. The population proportions could be the same, and if they differ, the difference is quite small.

**19. a.** We can be 95% confident that the mean number of close friends for males is between 1.5 lower and 2.7 higher than the mean number of close friends for females.
**b.** The standard deviations exceeding the mean suggests that the distributions may be highly skewed to the right. This does not affect the method, because the

sampling distribution of the difference between the sample means is approximately bell-shaped for such large sample sizes. Extreme skew may make the means less useful than the medians, especially if there are also extreme outliers.

21. **a.** Difference between sample means = 4.9. **b.** We can be 95% confident that the population mean HONC score is between 4.1 and 5.7 higher for smokers than for ex-smokers. **c.** Probably highly skewed to the right. This does not affect inference, because the sampling distribution of the difference between sample means would be bell-shaped for such large samples.

23. There is strong evidence that the population mean is slightly higher for females, but the confidence interval shows that the difference is small.

25. **a.** Can conclude that population mean is higher for blacks.
**b.** If population means were equal, it would extremely unlikely to observe a difference as large as we did or even larger.
**c.** The 95% CI does not contain 0, and the null hypothesis of a 0 difference between the population means would be rejected at the $\alpha = 0.05$ level (since the $P$-value is smaller than 0.05).

27. Estimated standard error is $49.4/\sqrt{12} = 14.3$, and test statistic is $t = 70.1/14.3 = 4.9$.

29. **a.** The evidence is weak against $H_0$ of equal population means. **b.** The 95% confidence interval contains 0, and the hypothesis of 0 difference between population means is not rejected at the 0.05 level.

31. **a.** 20 in each case **c.** $20 \pm 4.303(2.887)$, which is $20 \pm 12.4$, or (7.6, 32.4)
**d.** $t = 20/2.887 = 6.93$, $df = 3 - 1 = 2$, $P = 2(0.01) = 0.02$, so relatively strong evidence that therapy B has higher population mean improvement scores.

33. The sample standard deviations are quite different, so we might not trust the results based on assuming equal variances. The approximate test without that assumption shows very strong evidence ($P < 0.01$) that the population means differ.

35. **a.** $t = -4.0$ ($df = 8$) and two-sided $P$-value $= 0.004$. There is very strong evidence that the mean drop was higher for course B. A 95% confidence interval for the difference in means is $(2.0 - 6.0) \pm 2.306(1)$, or $(-6.3, -1.7)$.
**c.** $4.0/1.58 = 2.5$. The difference between the sample means is 2.5 standard deviations, which is quite large.
**d.** There are $5 \times 5 = 25$ pairs of observations. B is higher on 23 pairs and gets 1/2 credit for the two pairs with $y_B = 3$ and $y_A = 3$, so the estimated probability is $24/25 = 0.96$. This is a very strong effect.

37. **a.** $\hat{\pi}_1 = (108 + 157)/294 = 265/294 = 0.90$ for environment, $\hat{\pi}_2 = 113/294 = 0.38$ for cities.
**b.** McNemar statistic $z = (n_{12} - n_{21})/\sqrt{n_{12} + n_{21}} = (5 - 157)/\sqrt{5 + 157} = -152/12.7 = -11.9$. The $P$-value is essentially 0. There is extremely strong evidence that the proportion supporting increased spending is higher for the environment.
**c.** $(0.90 - 0.38) \pm 1.96(0.031) = 0.52$, or $(0.46, 0.58)$. We conclude that the population proportion of approval is between 0.46 and 0.58 higher for spending on the environment.

39. **a.** The groups have small samples, with only 2 and 0 observations in the B/L/G category. **b.** $P$-value $= 0.30$, so not much evidence that the probabilities differ for the two groups.

**49. a.** (i) 95% CI $4 \pm 3.4$, or (0.6, 7.6) comparing population mean parental support for single-mother households and households with both biological parents. (ii) $P$-value $= 0.02$ for testing equality of population means.

**51. a.** The samples are dependent, so you need to know the sample proportions for the four possible sequences of responses on the two questions (i.e., (favorable, good), (favorable, not good), (unfavorable, good), (unfavorable, not good)). **b.** The sample size for the 2000 survey

**53.** Each standard error is 3.16. The standard error for the difference between two sample means is $\sqrt{(3.16)^2 + (3.16)^2} = 4.47$. The margin of error for a 95% confidence interval comparing two means is about $2(4.47) = 8.9$. For comparing Canada and the U.S., the interval would be $9.0 \pm 8.9$, or (0.1, 17.9), so we conclude an actual difference exists between the population means.

**55.** Since $se$ for the difference is $\sqrt{(se_1)^2 + (se_2)^2}$, the $se$ for comparing two means is larger than the $se$ for estimating one of those means. The same is true for the margins of error.

**57. a.**

| Number Males In Sample | Possible Samples Of Size 3 |
|---|---|
| 0 | $(F_1, F_2, F_3)$ |
| 1 | $(M_1, F_1, F_2)$ $(M_1, F_1, F_3)$ $(M_1, F_2, F_3)$ |
| 1 | $(M_2, F_1, F_2)$ $(M_2, F_1, F_3)$ $(M_2, F_2, F_3)$ |
| 1 | $(M_3, F_1, F_2)$ $(M_3, F_1, F_3)$ $(M_3, F_2, F_3)$ |
| 2 | $(F_1, M_1, M_2)$ $(F_1, M_1, M_3)$ $(F_1, M_2, M_3)$ |
| 2 | $(F_2, M_1, M_2)$ $(F_2, M_1, M_3)$ $(F_2, M_2, M_3)$ |
| 2 | $(F_3, M_1, M_2)$ $(F_3, M_1, M_3)$ $(F_3, M_2, M_3)$ |
| 3 | $(M_1, M_2, M_3)$ |

**b.** Each of the 20 samples is equally likely. The 10 samples with 2 or 3 males chosen have $\hat{\pi}_1 - \hat{\pi}_2 \geq 1/3$. **c.** $P = 1/20 = 0.05$.

**59. a.** False **b.** False **61.** True **63.** a, c, d

**65. a.** The sample proportion correct has approximately a normal sampling distribution with mean 0.5 and standard error $\sqrt{0.5(0.5)/100} = 0.05$. A score of 70 has $z = (0.7 - 0.5)/0.05 = 4.0$. The probability of a score of at least 70 is about 0.00003.
**b.** The sampling distribution of the difference between Jane's and Joe's proportions is approximately normal with mean $0.6 - 0.5 = 0.1$ and standard error $\sqrt{\frac{0.6(0.4)}{100} + \frac{0.5(0.5)}{100}} = 0.07$. The probability the difference is negative is the probability that a $z$-score is less than $(0 - 0.1)/0.07 = -1.43$, which is 0.08.
**c.** The standard errors decrease as the number of questions increases, and the probabilities decrease.

## Chapter 8

**1. a.** (40%, 60%) in each row **b.** Yes
**3. a.** Dependent, **b.** (40%, 60%) in each row

5. **a.** For those with breast cancer, the conditional proportion is 0.86 for a positive test and 0.14 for a negative test. For those not having breast cancer, the conditional proportion is 0.12 for a positive test and 0.88 for a negative test. Yes, it seems to perform well as a diagnostic tool.   **b.** Of those who test positive, the conditional probability of actual breast cancer is $860/12,660 = 0.068$. The 12% of false diagnoses for those who do not have breast cancer are much larger in number than the 86% of correct diagnoses for those who have it, because the number having it is relatively very small.

7. $3.84 \ (df = 1)$,   b. $9.49 \ (df = 4)$   c. $9.49$   d. $26.30$   e. $26.30$

9. **a.** $H_0$: GRNSOL is independent of sex, $H_a$: GRNSOL and sex are statistically dependent. **b.** $df = 4$ for $2 \times 5$ table **c.** (i) Cannot reject $H_0$, (ii) Reject $H_0$

13. **a.** Extremely strong evidence of association between income and happiness. **b.** The count in the first cell was 5.34 standard errors larger than we'd expect if the variables were independent. More people were (below average in income, not happy) and (above average in income, very happy) than we'd expect if variables were independent. Fewer people were (below average in income, very happy) and (above average in income, not happy) than we'd expect if variables were independent.

15. More females are very religious and more males are not at all religious than we'd expect if variables were independent. Fewer females are not at all religious and fewer males are very religious than we'd expect if variables were independent.

17. Very strong, as difference between proportions approving was 0.73.

19. **a.** $0.60$   **b.** $0.33$   **c.** $17.7$, no

21. **a.** $1.04, 0.22$   **b.** $4.7$

23. $1.37$ for Democrat and Independent, $1.40$ for Democrat and Republican, $1.03$ for Independent and Republican

23. **a.** (i) 15, (ii) 27   **b.** $-0.29$   **c.** $15/42 - 27/42$

25. **a.** Sample gamma $= 0.163$, a weak positive association. There is a slight tendency for students with higher family incomes to have higher aspirations. **b.** Test statistic $\chi^2 = 8.87, df = 6$. The $P$-value of $P = 0.18$ does not provide much evidence against the null hypothesis of independence of aspirations and family income. **c.** A 90% confidence interval for the population value of gamma is $0.163 \pm 1.96(.080) = 0.163 \pm 0.157$, or $(0.006, 0.320)$. It seems that the population value of gamma is positive, although the association may be very weak since the interval contains values very close to 0. **d.** Test based on gamma has test statistic $z = 0.163/0.080 = 2.04$, and two-sided $P$-value $2(0.0207) = 0.04$. There is evidence of a positive association. The chi-squared test ignores the ordinal nature of the variables and does not detect this evidence.

37. **a.** Size of $\chi^2$ is directly proportional to $n$, for a particular set of cell proportions; small $P$ can occur for large $n$ even when association is weak in practical terms. **b.** The standard error for $\bar{y}$ or $\hat{\pi}$ or a comparison of two values gets smaller as the sample size increases. So, for a given size of effect, the test statistic tends to be larger as the sample size is.

39. a, b, c, d

41. **a.** Each expected frequency equals $n/4$. Substituting into $\chi^2$ formula gives the result.   **b.** Since $\chi^2$ cannot exceed $n$, $\hat{\phi}^2$ cannot exceed 1. Similarly, since $\chi^2$ cannot be negative, neither can $\hat{\phi}^2$.

**43.**

| a. | L | M | H | b. | L | M | H | c. | L | M | H |
|---|---|---|---|---|---|---|---|---|---|---|---|
| Low | 10 | 0 | 0 | | 0 | 0 | 10 | | 10 | 10 | 10 |
| Medium | 0 | 10 | 0 | | 0 | 10 | 0 | | 5 | 15 | 5 |
| High | 0 | 0 | 10 | | 10 | 0 | 0 | | 10 | 5 | 10 |

**45.** CI for log odds ratio of $4.37 \pm 1.96(0.0833)$ exponentiates to CI for odds ratio of $(67.3, 93.2)$.

## Chapter 9

**1.** $y =$ college GPA in (a), number of children in (b), annual income in (c), and assessed value of home in (d).

**3. a.** $y$-intercept $= 61.4$, slope $= 2.4$, predicted height increases 2.4 cm for each 1 cm increase in femur length.   **b.** 181.4 cm

**5.** $y$-intercept about 18, slope about 0.5

**7. a.** (i) 1.5, (ii) 13.1   **b.** $\hat{y} = 13.1$, residual $= 6.6$, carbon dioxide emissions much higher than predicted for level of GDP.   **c.** $\hat{y} = 11.0$, residual $= -5.3$, carbon dioxide emissions much lower than predicted for level of GDP.

**9. a.** $209.9 =$ predicted violent crime rate for state with poverty rate $= 0$, $25.5 =$ increase in predicted violent crime rate for an increase of 1 in percentage below the poverty level.
**b.** $\hat{y} = 482.8$, $805 - 482.8 = 322.2$, so violent crime rate much higher than predicted for this level of poverty.
**c.** $10(25.5) = 255$
**d.** Positive, since it has same sign as the slope.

**11. a.** (i) $x = 20$, $y = 87$,   (ii) $x = 36$, $y = 41$   **b.** $\hat{y} = 89.7$, residual $= -44.6$, much lower use of cell phones that predicted for that GDP level.   **c.** Positive, so cell-phone use tends to increase as GDP increases.

**13.** $r = b(s_X/s_Y)$, so $b = r(s_Y/s_X) = 0.60(120/80) = 0.90$; $a = \bar{y} - b\bar{x} = 500 - 0.9(480) = 68$. Thus, $\hat{y} = a + bx = 68 + 0.9x$.

**15. a.** $\hat{y} = 5.0 - 0.4x$; predicted daily number of hours watching television decreases by 0.4 for an increase of 1 in number of books read.
**b.** $r = -1$, since the line has a negative slope and passes through all the data points.

**17. a.** There is a 23.7% reduction in error in predicting GPA using TV watching (with the linear prediction equation), compared to using the sample mean TV watching.   **b.** $-\sqrt{0.237} = -0.49$   **c.** Weaker

**19. a.** $4000(2/16,000) = 0.50$   **b.** $\hat{y} = -16,000 + 3200x$, with correlation 0.50

**21.** Strongest association between PAEDUC and MAEDUC, each variable has tendency to increase as another variable increases.

**23. a.** No, fertility and GDP have different units.   **b.** Units are same for cell-phone use and Internet use.

**25. a.** Positive   **b.** $\hat{y} = -5.18 + 1.13x$, D.C. has $\hat{y} = 15.7$ and residual 28.3.   **c.** 0.585 Yes. Now, slope $= 0.49$, less than half as large.

**27. b.** $\hat{y} = 4.845 - 0.039x$   **c.** $r = -0.57$, $r^2 = 0.32$

**29. a.** $t = 19.7$, $P$-value $= 0$ to many decimal places, extremely strong evidence of a positive association  **b.** $(0.265, 0.323)$  **c.** When mother's education is a certain number of standard deviations from the mean, the predicted education is 37% of that many standard deviations from its mean.

**31. a.** $H_0$: $\beta = 0$, $H_a$: $\beta \neq 0$, $t = 0.00739/0.1706 = 0.43$, $P$-value $= 0.66$, plausible that variables are independent, as shown also by 95% CI for $\beta$ of $(-0.03, 0.04)$  **b.** the correlation $= 0.0155$

**33. b.** Stronger, because the correlation tends to be larger when the range of $x$ values observed is larger.

**43. a.** $y = $ salary, $x = $ height, slope $= \$789$  **b.** 7($\$789$)

**47. a.** New slope $= $ old slope divided by 2.0.  **b.** Correlation does not change.

**49. a.** Over time, $y$ would fluctuate rather than follow linear trend.
**b.** Much more variability in $y$ at high levels of $x$.  **c.** Relationship may be U-shaped rather than linear.
**d.** As $x$ increases, $y$ tends to increase but eventually levels off.

**51.** Regression toward the mean

**53.** Bridgeport, because of more variability in $x = $ high school GPA values

**55. a.** Sample standard deviation of $y$ scores  **b.** Sample standard deviation of $x$ scores  **c.** Estimated standard deviation of conditional distribution of $y$ at each fixed value of $x$  **d.** Estimated standard error of sample slope $b$

**59. a.** b  **61.** c, f, g

**63.** $r = b(s_x/s_y) = b(1/1) = b$, so slope $= $ correlation. Formula for $y$-intercept is $a = \bar{y} - b\bar{x} = 0 - b(0) = 0$, so prediction equation is $\hat{y} = 0 + rx = rx$.

**67. a.** Interchange $x$ and $y$ in the formula and you get the same value.
**b.** If the units of measurement change, the $z$-score does not. For instance, if the values are doubled, then the deviation of an observation from the mean doubles, but so does the standard deviation, and the ratio of the deviation to the standard deviation does not change.

**69. c.** As the sample size increases, the width of the confidence interval for the mean goes to 0, and we can estimate the mean nearly perfectly. However large the sample size, even if we know the true mean, we cannot predict individual observations. They fluctuate around the mean with a certain variability that does not depend on the sample size.
**d.** (i) For instance, the width of the prediction interval is the same at an $x$-value that is $c$ units above $\bar{x}$ as it is at an $x$ value that is $c$ units below $\bar{x}$. But if the variability increases, the interval should be wider above the mean than below the mean.

## Chapter 10

**3. a.** No, perhaps more firefighters are called to fires that are more severe, involving larger buildings.  **b.** $Z = $ size of structure that burned

**5. b.** A third variable dealing with a factor such as the subject's natural curiosity or inquisitiveness could be positively associated with both variables. Subjects who tend to be higher in this characteristic might tend to have higher GPAs and to be more likely to experiment with marijuana.

**7. a.** Positive correlation between shoe size and number of books read is explained by age, which is strongly positively correlated with each of these.

**9. b.** Common cause

**11.** The difference would need to disappear (except for sampling error) after family income is controlled.

**13.** **a.**

|            | White C. | Blue C. |
|------------|----------|---------|
| Democrat   | 265      | 735     |
| Republican | 735      | 265     |

Yes, the percentage of white collar occupations is 26.5% for Democrats and 73.5% for Republicans.

**b.** No, conditional distributions are identical in each partial table; differences of proportions = 0 and odds ratio = 1 in each table. Controlling for income, the variables are independent.

**c.** Income tends to be higher for Republicans than Democrats, and it tends to be higher for white-collar than blue-collar occupations.

**d.** Occupation affects income, which affects party choice

**e.** Income jointly affects occupation and party choice. Chain relationship is more appropriate, since it is more plausible that occupation affects income than the reverse.

**15.** **b.** Size of home and number of bedrooms are both associated with selling price but also associated with each other. Because size of home is associated both with number of bedrooms and selling price, the effect of number of bedrooms on selling price depends on whether we control for size of home.

**19.** Ignoring the subject of the exam, there is no association, but there is a substantial association in each partial table.

**21.** **a.** $10,689,  **b.** $5150, so the effect of gender is greater for whites than for blacks.

**23.** **a.** Response = whether have cancer, explanatory = whether a smoker, control = age

**b.** Yes, the association is stronger for older subjects. Smoking seems to have a stronger effect for older subjects, who have presumably been smoking for a longer period.

**29.** **a.** Mean number of children higher for families for which English is the primary language.

**b.** For each province, the mean number of children is higher for families for which French is the primary language.

**c.** Most French-speaking families are in Quebec, where the means are lower regardless of language, and most English-speaking families are in other provinces.

**31.** **a.** Plausibly prayer has an effect only if done by a relative of the patient.

**b.** Other variables could be associated with whether one prayed and with whether the patient had complications.

**33.** Socioeconomic status may be a common cause of birth defects and of buying bottled water.

**35.** Yes, because the U.S. may have relatively more people who are old.

**37.** **a.** For females, mean GPA is higher for those with an employed mother. For males, mean GPA is about the same for those with an employed mother as for those with an nonemployed mother. Since the results differ according to gender, there is evidence of interaction.

**b.** The two means are about equal for males, yet for females the mean is higher for those with an employed mother.

**39.** Income is associated with whether one is a compulsive buyer, and both these variables are associated with credit card balance. So, the effect of whether one is a compulsive buyer on the credit card balance depends on whether income is controlled.

**41.** False   **43.** b   **45.** a

## Chapter 11

**1. a.** (i) $E(y) = 0.2 + 0.5(4.0) + 0.001(800) = 3.0$; (ii) 2.0
**b.** $E(y) = 0.2 + 0.5x_1 + 0.002(500) = 1.2 + 0.5x_1$
**c.** $E(y) = 0.2 + 0.5x_1 + 0.002(600) = 1.4 + 0.5x_1$
**d.** For instance, consider $x_1 = 3$ for which $E(y) = 1.7 + 0.002x_2$; by contrast, when $x_1 = 2$, $E(y) = 1.2 + .002x_2$, having a different $y$-intercept but the same slope of 0.002.

**3. a.** 18.9 square feet   **b.** The $y$-intercept is 10.536 thousand dollars, and a 1-unit change in $x_1$ or $x_2$ has only 1/1000 of the impact in thousands of dollars.

**5. a.** $\hat{y} = -3.601 + 1.280x_1 + 0.102x_2$   **b.** 14.3%   **c.** $\hat{y} = -3.601 + 1.280x_1$, $\hat{y} = 6.61 + 1.280x_1$, so at a fixed value of cell-phone use, Internet use is predicted to increase by 1.28% for each thousand-dollar increase in per capita GDP.   **d.** The effect of $x_1$ is the same (slope 1.28) at each fixed value of $x_2$.

**7. a.** Positive   **b.** Negative
**c.** $\hat{y} = -11.5 + 2.6x_1$; predicted crime rate increases by 2.6 (per 1000 residents) for every thousand-dollar increase in median income.
**d.** $\hat{y} = 40.3 - 0.81x_1 + 0.65x_2$; predicted crime rate decreases by 0.8 for each thousand-dollar increase in median income, controlling for level of urbanization. Compared to (c), effect is weaker and has different direction.
**e.** Urbanization is highly positively correlated both with income and with crime rate. This makes overall bivariate association between income and crime rate more positive than the partial association.
**f.** (i) $\hat{y} = 40.3 - 0.81x_1$, (ii) $\hat{y} = 40.3 - 0.81x1_1 + 0.65(50) = 73 - 0.81x_1$, (iii) $\hat{y} = 105 - 0.81x_1$. The slope stays constant, but at a fixed level of $x_1$, the crime rates are higher at higher levels of $x_2$.

**9. a.** $-0.13 = $ change in predicted birth rate for unit increase in women's economic activity, controlling for GNP.
**b.** Parallel lines, so effect of $x_1$ the same at each level of $x_2$, but at fixed $x_1$, predicted birth rates lower at higher levels of $x_2$.
**c.** $x_1$ and $x_2$ are moderately positively correlated and explain some of the same variation in $y$. Controlling for $x_2$, the effect of $x_1$ weakens.

**11. a.** $\hat{y} = -498.7 + 32.6x_1 + 9.1x_2$
**b.** $\hat{y} = -498.7 + 32.6(10.7) + 9.1(96.2) = 725.5$; residual $= 805 - 725.5 = 79.5$, so observed violent crime rate somewhat higher than model predicts.
**c.** (i) $\hat{y} = -498.7 + 32.6x_1$, (ii) $\hat{y} = -43.1 + 32.6x_1$, (iii) $\hat{y} = 412.5 + 32.6x_1$
**d.** Violent crime rate tends to increase as poverty rate increases or as percent in metropolitan areas increases; weak negative association between poverty rate and percent in metropolitan areas.
**e.** $R^2 = 0.57 = $ PRE in using $x_1$ and $x_2$ together to predict $y$, $R = \sqrt{0.57} = 0.76 = $ correlation between observed and predicted $y$-values.

**13. a.** $\hat{y} = -1197.5 + 18.3x_1 + 7.7x_2 + 89.4x_3$
**b.** $x_1$ and $x_3$ are highly positively correlated, and explain some of the same variability in $y$; controlling for $x_3$, the effect of $x_1$ weakens.

**15. a.** $\hat{y} = 135.3 - 14.07x_1 - 2.95x_2$
**b.** $\hat{y} = 135.3 - 14.07(7) - 2.95(9) = 10.3$, residual $= 10 - 10.3 = -0.3$
**c.** $R^2 = 0.799$; 80% reduction in error by predicting $y$ using $x_1$ and $x_2$ instead of $\bar{y}$.
**d.** $t = -14.07/3.16 = -4.45$, $df = 10 - 3 = 7$, $P < 0.01$ for two-sided test. Better to show actual $P$-value, since (for instance) 0.049 is not practically different from 0.051.
**e.** Using $R^2, F = [0.799/2]/[(1 - 0.799)/(10 - 3)] = 13.9, df_1 = 2, df_2 = 7, P < 0.01$; strong evidence that at least one predictor has an effect on $y$.
**f.** Ideology appears to have a stronger partial effect than religion; a standard deviation increase in ideology has a 0.79 standard deviation predicted decrease in feelings, controlling for religion.

**17. a.** $df$ values are 5, 60, 65, regression sum of squares $= 813.3$, regression mean square $= 813.3/5 = 162.7$, residual mean square $= 2940.0/60 = 49$, $F = 162.7/49 = 3.3$ with $df_1 = 5, df_2 = 60$, the $P$-value (Prob > F) is 0.01, $R^2 = 0.217$, Root MSE $= 7.0$, $t$ values are $2.22, -2.00, 0.50, -0.80, 2.40$, with $P$-values (Sig) 0.03, 0.05, 0.62, 0.43, 0.02.
**b.** No, could probably drop $x_3$ or $x_4$, or both, since the $P$-values are large for their partial tests.
**c.** The test of $H_0 : \beta_1 = \beta_2 = \ldots = \beta_5 = 0$.
There is very strong evidence that at least one predictor has an effect on $y$.
**d.** Test of $H_0 : \beta_1 = 0$; $P = 0.03$, so there is considerable evidence that $x_1$ has an effect on $y$, controlling for the other $x$s.

**21. a.** Increases   **b.** $\hat{y} = 158.9 - 14.7x_1, \hat{y} = 94.4 + 23.3x_1, \hat{y} = 29.9 + 61.3x_1$. The effect of $x_1$ moves toward the positive direction and becomes greater as $x_2$ increases.

**25. a.** (i) $-0.612$, (ii) $-0.819$, (iii) 0.757, (iv) 2411.4, (v) 585.4, (vi) 29.27, (vii) 5.41, (viii) 10.47, (ix) 0.064, (x) $-2.676$, (xi) 0.0145, (xii) 0.007, (xiii) 31.19, (xiv) 0.0001
**b.** $\hat{y} = 61.7 - 0.17x_1 - 0.40x_2$; $61.7 =$ predicted birth rate at ECON $= 0$ and LITER $= 0$ (may not be useful), $-0.17 =$ change in predicted birth rate for 1 unit increase in ECON, controlling for LITER, $-0.40 =$ change in predicted birth rate for 1-unit increase in LITER, controlling for ECON.
**c.** $-0.612$; there is a moderate negative association between birth rate and ECON; $-0.819$; there is a strong negative association between birth rate and LITER.
**d.** $R^2 = (2411.4 - 585.4)/2411.4 = 0.76$; there is a 76% reduction in error in using these two variables (instead of $\bar{y}$) to predict birth rate.
**e.** $R = \sqrt{0.76} = 0.87 =$ correlation between observed $y$-values and the predicted values $\hat{y}$.
**f.** $F = 31.2, df_1 = 2, df_2 = 20, P = 0.0001$; at least one of ECON and LITER has a significant effect.
**g.** $t = -0.171/0.064 = -2.68, df = 20, P = 0.014$; there is strong evidence of a relationship between birth rate and ECON, controlling for LITER.

**27.** Urbanization is highly positively correlated with both variables. Even though there is a weak association between crime rate and high school graduation rate at a fixed level of urbanization (since partial correlation $= -0.15$), as urbanization increases, so do both of these variables tend to increase, thus producing an overall moderate positive association (correlation = 0.47) between crime rate and high school graduation rate.

**29. a.** $\hat{z}_y = -0.075z_{x_1} - 0.125z_{x_2} - 0.30z_{x_3} + 0.20z_{x_4}$
**b.** $x_3$ has the greatest partial effect in standardized units.
**c.** $\hat{z}_y = -0.075(1) - 0.125(1) - 0.30(1) + 0.20(-1) = -0.7$, so the city is predicted to be 0.7 standard deviations below the mean in murder rate.

**43. a.** Political freedom, unemployment, divorce rate, and latitude had negative partial effects. **b.** $R^2 > 0.50$ **c.** Estimated standardized regression coefficients highest for life expectancy and GDP. A one standard deviation increase in these predictors (controlling for the others) had a greater impact than other predictors. **d.** GDP measured in per capita *dollars*, and a dollar change is extremely small. **e.** No, merely that whatever effect education has disappears after controlling for the other predictors in the model.

**45.** Different predictors have different units of measurement. Controlling the other predictors, a standard deviation increase in education corresponds to a 0.21 standard deviation increase in the predicted value of $y$.

**47. b.** The partial change is 0.34, not 0.45, which is the overall change ignoring rather than controlling the other variables.
**c.** Cannot tell, since variables have different units of measurement.
**d.** False, since this cannot exceed 0.38, the $R^2$ value for the model with $x_3$ and other variables in the model.

**49.** b  **51.** c

**53.** Correlation measures linear association between two variables, multiple correlation measures correlation between a response variable and the predicted value given by a set of explanatory variables from the estimated regression equation, partial correlation measures association between two variables while controlling for one or more other variables.

**55.** For a sample of children of various ages, $y$ = score on vocabulary achievement test, $x_1$ = height, $x_2$ = age.

**59.** $r^2_{yx_2 \cdot x_1}$, and hence its square root, equal 0.

**61. a.** 0.150, 0.303, 0.325, 0.338

**65. a.** Let $b$ denote the minimum of the two standardized estimates, and let $B$ denote the maximum. Then the squared partial correlation equals $bB$, and $bB \le BB = B^2$ and $bB \ge bb = b^2$. Thus, since the partial correlation has the same sign as the standardized coefficient, it falls between $b$ and $B$.
**b.** Because the partial correlation must fall between $-1$ and $+1$, and its square must fall between 0 and 1.

**67. a.** For new homes, $\hat{y} = -48.4 + 96.0x_1$
For older homes, $\hat{y} = -16.6 + 66.6x_1$
For new homes, the effect of size is greater than for older homes.
**b.** For new homes, $\hat{y} = -7.6 + 71.6x_1$
For older homes, $\hat{y} = -16.6 + 66.6x_1$, now only a slightly smaller effect of size than for new homes.

## Chapter 12

**1.** $y$ = number of reported firefights, explanatory variable is group (soldiers in Afghanistan, soldiers in Iraq, Marines in Iraq). Null hypothesis is that population mean number of firefights is the same for the three groups.

**3.** **a.** $H_0: \mu_1 = \mu_2 = \mu_3 = \mu_4 = \mu_5$, $H_a$: At least two population means unequal.
**b.** No, when $H_0$ is true one expects $F$ values around 1.
**c.** If $H_0$ were true, the probability of getting a $F$ test statistic of 0.80 or larger is 0.53, so there is not evidence against $H_0$.

**5.** **a.** (i) $H_0: \mu_1 = \mu_2 = \mu_3$, $H_a$: At least two population means unequal, (ii) $F = 3.03$, (iii) $P$-value $= 0.049$. At the $\alpha = 0.05$ level, there is barely enough evidence to reject $H_0$ and conclude that at least two population means differ.
**b.** For each group, the standard deviation is larger than the mean, suggesting the population distributions may have considerable skew to the right. ANOVA assumes normal population distributions.

**9.** Each CI is an ordinary 98% CI, and has plus and minus part $4.541\sqrt{4.0\left[\frac{1}{2} + \frac{1}{2}\right]} = 9.1$; only A and B are not significantly different.

**11.** **a.** Each pair except white and other. e.g., we can be 95% confident that the population mean time watching TV is between 1.1 and 1.7 hours higher for blacks than for whites.

**13.** For 10 groups, there are $10(9)/2 = 45$ comparisons. Using the Bonferroni method with error probability $0.20/45 = 0.0044$ for each guarantees at least 80% confidence for the entire set. Since $df$ is very large (990), the $t$-score is very close to the $z$-score with single-tail probability 0.0022, which is 2.84. For 5 groups, there are 10 comparisons. The Bonferroni method with error probability 0.02 for each uses the $t$-score with single-tail probability 0.01, which is 2.33. The $t$-score increases, and the confidence intervals tend to be wider, as the number of groups increases.

**15.** **a.** $E(y) = \alpha + \beta_1 z_1 + \beta_2 z_2$, where $z_1 = 1$ group 1 and 0 otherwise and $z_2 = 1$ for group 1 and 0 otherwise. $H_0 : \mu_1 = \mu_2 = \mu_3$ equivalent to $H_0 : \beta_1 = \beta_2 = 0$
**b.** 18 is mean for group 3, $-6$ is difference between mean for group 1 and group 3, and $-3$ is difference between mean for group 2 and group 3.

**17.** Large differences between sample means for whites and blacks of a given sex but small differences for females and males of a given race correspond to small $P$-value for race but not for sex.

**19.** Females ($s = 1$): 3.79, 3.96, 4.50,   Males ($s = 0$): 3.87, 4.04, 4.58. The difference between the estimated means for males and females is 0.08 for each party ID.

**21.** **a.** The estimated difference in mean TV watching between the Protestant and none or other categories of religion, controlling for sex.
**b.** $E(y) = \alpha + \beta_1 s + \beta_2 r_1 + \beta_3 r_2 + \beta_4 r_3$, need $\beta_2 = \beta_3 = \beta_4 = 0$

**23.** **a.** Response variable $=$ income, factors $=$ sex and race.
**b.** (i) \$10,689 (ii) \$5150. The difference is much greater for whites than blacks, suggesting interaction between sex and race in their effects on income.
**c.** \$30,000 for white females, \$25,000 for black females, \$40,000 for white males, \$35,000 for black males

**25.** $n = 206$, SSE $= 3600$, $df$ values are 1, 2, 2, 200, Mean Square values are 100, 100, 50, 18, $F$-values are 5.6, 5.6, 2.8, $P$-values are $P < 0.05, P < 0.01, P > 0.05$

**27.** Predicted means 16 for black women, 19 for white women, 18 for black men, 29 for white men. If the predicted value for men changes to $29 - 8 = 21$, there is no interaction.

**29.** **a.** Treats the distance between very negative and negative, and between positive and very positive, as double the distance between negative and neutral and the distance between neutral and positive.

**31.** Between-subjects: gender; within-subjects: issue. For test of interaction, $F = 1.23$, $P = 0.32$. For sex main effect, $F = 0.26$, $P = 0.62$. For issue effect, $F = 9.48$, $P = 0.002$. The margin of error for each interval comparing means for the issues is $2.12(0.719)\sqrt{\frac{1}{10} + \frac{1}{10}} = 0.7$. The sample means for the issues are 2.5, 3.8, and 2.7, so the mean for safety of neighborhoods is significantly higher than the other two means.

**39. a.** Each of the four sample means equal 60, so the between-groups SS $= 0$ and $F = 0$.
**b.** Within each group, all five observations are identical. Then the within-groups SS $= 0$, so the mean square error $= 0$ and the $F$ statistic is infinite.

**45.**

| | | a. | | | b. | | | c. | | | d. | | |
|---|---|---|---|---|---|---|---|---|---|---|---|---|---|
| | | 10 | 10 | | 10 | 20 | | 10 | 20 | | 10 | 10 | |
| | | 20 | 20 | | 30 | 40 | | 30 | 60 | | 10 | 10 | |

**47.** No, not unless at each level of B, the sample sizes are equal for each level of A.

**51.** a, b, c, d   **53.** c, e, f

**55.** You have enough information. The sample standard deviations can be combined to obtain the pooled (within-groups) estimate. The between-groups estimate can be calculated from the separate sample means, since the overall mean is a weighted average of their values.

## Chapter 13

**1. a.** 13, 11, difference $= 2$   **c.** $-.6$   **d.** 12.0, 12.6

**3. a.** The predicted proportion of pro-choice votes was 0.167 lower for Democrats, controlling for the other predictors.
**b.** Ideology seems to be, by far, the most important predictor of proportion of pro-choice votes. A standard deviation increase in ideology corresponds to a 0.83 standard deviation predicted increase in the response, controlling for the other variables in the model.

**5. a.** $\hat{y} = 8.3 + 9.8f - 5.3s + 7.0m_1 + 2.0m_2 + 1.2m_3 + 0.501x$
**b.** $\hat{y} = 8.3 + 9.8(1) + 7.0(1) + .501(10) = 30.1$

**7. a.** $\hat{y} = -40,230.9 + 116.1x + 57,736.3z$, where $z = 1$ for new and 0 for not new. For new homes, $\hat{y} = 17,505.4 + 116.1x$ and for not new homes, $\hat{y} = -40,230.9 + 116.1x$.
**b.** \$365,901 for new homes, \$308,165 for not new homes

**11. a.** Anglos: $-4.09 + 0.74(60.4) = 40.6$. From ANOVA model, unadjusted mean for Anglos equals $26.6 + 25.7 = 52.3$.

**13. a.** $F = 1.43$, $df_1 = 3$, $df_2 = 82$, $P = 0.24$
**b.** $F = 2.06$, $df_1 = 3$, $df_2 = 85$, $P = 0.11$
**c.** Test statistic $t = 7.9$, $df = 85$, $P = 0.0001$
**d.** The standard error of this estimate equals 2.20, and the $t$ score for 94% Bonferroni confidence intervals is identical to the ordinary $t$ score (when $df = 85$) for a 99% interval, which is 2.63. The interval is $-5.36 \pm 2.63(2.20)$, or $(-11.1, 0.4)$.

**25.** $E(y) = \alpha + \beta_1 x + \beta_2 z + \beta_3(xz)$, where $x = $ frequency of going to bars, $z = 1$ for married subjects and $z = 0$ for unmarried subjects.

**27.** See Figure 13.3b.    **29.** a, d

## Chapter 14

1. **a.** No interaction model with LIFE and SES predictors  **b.** No interaction model with LIFE and SES predictors

3. **a.** BEDS, because it is least significant in the model with all the predictors.
   **b.** SIZE, because it is most highly correlated with selling price and would have the smallest $P$-value.
   **c.** BEDS can be predicted well knowing SIZE, BATHS, and NEW, so it does not uniquely explain much variability in selling price.

7. **a.** Observation 25  **b.** Most noticeably, observations 38 and 39  **c.** No observations have both large studentized residuals and large leverage.  **d.** Observation 39  **e.** Observation 39

11. Partial correlations, like partial regression coefficients, have large standard errors when there is multicollinearity.

13. **a.** The variability increases as $\hat{y}$ increases, which the gamma distribution allows but the ordinary normal model (i.e., normal distribution with constant standard deviation) does not.
   **b.** For the gamma model, the estimated education effect is a bit weaker and there is stronger evidence of a difference between Hispanics and whites.
   **c.** (i) $20\sqrt{0.117} = 6.8$ thousand dollars, (ii) 17.1 thousand dollars

17. **a.** Continually increasing and "bowl shaped."  **b.** (i) \$84,764, (ii) \$192,220, (iii) \$327,877,  because with the increasing bowl shape the curve keeps climbing more quickly as $s$ increases.

21. **a.** 100,000 = predicted number of articles January 1, 2003, and predicted number is multiplied by 2.1 for each successive year.
   **b.** (i) 4,084,101 (ii) 166,798,810

23. **a.** Predicted world population size (in billions) $x$ years from now if there is a 5% decrease in population size each year.
   **c.** $\beta > 1$ ever increasing, $\beta < 1$ ever decreasing.

25. **a.** Death rate changes more quickly at higher ages, and there appears to be a linear relation between age and log of death rate, which suggest exponential model.
   **c.** $\log(\hat{\mu}) = -1.146 + 0.0747x$
   **d.** $\hat{y} = 0.318(1.0776)^x$. The death rate increases by 7.8% for each additional year of age.

33. $y$ = height, $x_1$ = length of left leg, $x_2$ = length of right leg.

35. In the U.S., for each of the past 60 years, $y$ = the cumulative federal deficit, $x$ = year. This might be well modeled by an exponential regression model.

37. Precision improves (i.e., the standard error of $b_j$ decreases) when (a) multicollinearity, as described by $R_j^2$, decreases, (b) conditional variability of the response variable decreases, (c) the variability of $x_j$ increases, (d) the sample size increases.

39. A 1.27% growth rate per year corresponds to a multiplicative effect after 10 years of $(1.0127)^{10} = 1.1345$, or 13.45%. Or, to find the yearly multiplicative factor corresponding to a 10-year multiplicative effect of 1.1345, set $1.1345 = \beta^{10}$, and solve for $\beta$; then $\log(1.1345) = 10\log(\beta)$, so $\log(\beta) = \log(1.1345)/10 = 0.01262$, and $\beta = e^{.01262} = 1.0127$.
   b. If the growth rate is 1.27% per year, then after $x$ years, the multiplicative effect is $(1.0127)^x$.

**41.** b, c, d **43.** b **45a.** True **b.** True **c.** False **d.** False

**47.** $E(y) = \alpha + \beta_1 x_1 + \beta_2 x_2 + \beta_3 x_1 x_2 + \beta_4 x_1 x_2^2$

## Chapter 15

**1. a.** Estimated probability of voting Republican increases as income increases.
**b.** (i) $e^{-1.0+0.02(10)}/[1 + e^{-1.0+0.02(10)}] = 0.31$, (ii) 0.73
**c.** (i) $1.00/0.02 = 50$ thousand, (ii) above 50 thousand
**d.** $\hat{\beta}\pi(1 - \pi) = 0.02(0.5)(0.5) = 0.005$
**e.** Odds multiply by $e^{0.02} = 1.02$ for each thousand dollar increase in family income.

**3. a.** $2.043/0.282 = 7.2$
**b.** $\hat{P}(y = 1) = e^{2.043-0.282(20)}/[1 + e^{2.043-0.282(20)}] = 0.027$
**c.** $\hat{P}(y = 1) = 0.847 - 0.051(20) = -0.17$; no, probability cannot be negative.
**d.** $z = -0.282/0.101 = -2.80$, Wald $= (-2.80)^2 = 7.8, P = 0.005$, strong evidence of a negative association between WAIS and senility.

**5.** $\hat{P}(y = 1) = 0.60$ when wife's earnings $= \$20,000$ and increases to 0.95 when wife's earnings $= \$100,000$.

**7. a.** The probability the child obtains a high school degree increases with mother's education. Estimated odds of degree multiplied by $e^{0.09} = 1.09$ for each one-unit increase in mother's education, controlling for other variables.
**b.** Probability of degree is lower when mother is employed. Estimated odds of degree when mother is employed equal $e^{-0.92} = 0.40$ times odds when mother is not employed.
**c.** $e^{0.21} = 1.23$, which corresponds to a 23% increase in the odds.

**9. a.** Let $r = 1$ for black, 0 for white, let $a = 1$ for AZT $=$ yes and 0 for AZT $=$ no. Prediction equation is logit$[\hat{P}(y = 1)] = -1.074 - 0.7195a + .0555r$.
**b.** Estimated probability of AIDS symptoms decreases with AZT use (given race) and is slightly higher for blacks, given AZT use.
**c.** $\hat{P}(y = 1) = e^{-1.074}/[1 + e^{-1.074}] = 0.25$
**d.** $e^{-0.720} = 0.49$, so estimated odds of AIDS symptoms for those using AZT are 0.49 times estimated odds for those not using AZT, controlling for race.
**e.** Wald statistic is $(-0.720/0.279)^2 = 6.65, df = 1$ $(P = .01)$, so strong evidence that AIDS symptoms are less likely for those using AZT, controlling for race.

**13. a.** There are 3 categories of happiness and 2 cumulative probabilities in the model. The logit for each cumulative probability has its own intercept term.
**b.** $\hat{\beta} = 0.418$, so happiness tends to increase with income.
**c.** Wald statistic $= (0.418/0.223)^2 = 3.53$, with $df = 1$, $P$-value $= 0.06$ for $H_a$: $\beta \neq 0$ and 0.03 for $H_a: \beta > 0$
**d.** $\chi^2 = 3.8$, $df = 4$, $P$-value $= 0.43$. The cumulative logit model treats the response as ordinal and predictor as quantitative and results in much stronger evidence of an effect than the ordinary Pearson chi-squared test of independence, which treats both variables as nominal.

**15. a.** $\hat{\beta} = -0.54$ for gender, 0.77 for location, $-0.82$ for seat belt. Controlling for the other predictors, the chance of a more serious injury is lower for males, higher in the rural location, and lower for those wearing seat belts.

**b.** $e^{-0.824} = 0.44$; for those wearing seat belts, the estimated odds of injury more serious than any fixed category are 0.44 times the estimated odds for those not wearing seat belts.

**c.** The interval $(-0.878, -0.770)$ for the $\beta$ coefficient of seat-belt use has exponentiated endpoints $(0.42, 0.46)$, which form the interval for this odds ratio.

**d.** Wald statistic $= 891.5$, $df = 1$. Extremely strong evidence of effect.

**17. a.** $e^{0.3} = 1.35$, so estimated odds of voting Republican (given that one votes either for Republican or independent) multiply by 1.35 for each $10,000 increase in annual income.

**b.** $\log[\hat{P}(y = 2)/\hat{P}(y = 1)] = (1.0 + 0.3x) - (3.3 - 0.2x) = -2.3 + 0.5x$. Given one votes for Republican or Democratic candidate, odds of voting Republican increase with income, by multiplicative factor of $e^{0.5} = 1.65$ for each $10,000 increase in annual income.

**23. a.** $(W, X, Y, Z)$,  **b.** $(XY, W, Z)$,  **c.** $(WX, WY, WZ, XY, XZ, YZ)$

**25. a.** $\text{logit}[P(y = 1)] = \alpha + \beta_1 a + \beta_2 c$, where $a$ and $c$ are dummy variables for alcohol and cigarette use (1 for yes and 0 for no)

**b.** The model fits well.

**29.** The logistic model with additive factor effects for age and gender fits well (Pearson $\chi^2 = 0.1$, $df = 2$). The estimated odds of females still being missing are $e^{0.38} = 1.46$ times those for males, given age. The estimated odds are considerably higher for those aged at least 19 than for the other two age groups, given gender.

**31.** $e^{2.34} = 10.4$, but this is a ratio of *odds*, not probabilities (which the "more likely" interpretation suggests). The odds that a male is a hunter are estimated to be 10.4 times the odds that a female is a hunter, controlling for the other variables.

**33.** The effect of age is increasing and then decreasing. If age is in the model as a quantitative variable (rather than with categories), this might be described by a quadratic term for age.

**35.** At each level of victims' race, black defendants were more likely to get the death penalty. Adding together the two partial tables (and hence ignoring rather than controlling victims' race), white defendants were more likely to get the death penalty. The association changes direction, so Simpson's paradox holds.

**37. a.** $(XZ, YZ)$  **b.** $(XZ, YZ)$,  **c.** $(XZ, YZ)$,  **d.** $(XY, XZ, YZ)$,  **e.** $(XYZ)$, there is interaction, the effect of $X$ on $Y$ varying according to the level of $Z$.

**39.** $\log(f_e) = \log(r_i) + \log(c_j) - \log(n)$, which has the form $\log(f_e) = \alpha + \beta_i + \gamma_j$ with main effects for the two classications.

# Chapter 16

**1.** Can use various correlation structures for the repeated measures on a subject, and do not need to delete subjects for which some observations are missing.

**5.** Estimated hazard rate for males is 0.94 times the rate for females. For test of race effect, $z = 0.353/0.0423 = 8.3$, $P < 0.0001$; extremely strong evidence that the rate is higher for blacks.

**7.** The estimated rate of termination for blacks was 2.13 times the estimated rate for whites, controlling for the other predictors.

**9.** G, L, T, and C all have direct effects on B, and G also has indirect effects through its effects on L, T, and C. One would need to fit the bivariate models for

L predicting G, T predicting G, and C predicting G, and the multiple regression model with G, L, T, and C all affecting B.

**11.** Yes, the effect of percentage of high school graduates weakens considerably (and is not statistically significant) after controlling for percentage urban.

**19.** $y_t$ is *conditionally* independent of $y_{t-2}$, given the outcome of $y_{t-1}$.

# Tables

**TABLE A**: Normal curve tail probabilities. Standard normal probability in right-hand tail (for negative values of $z$, probabilities are found by symmetry).

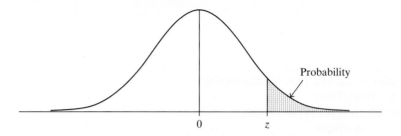

| $z$ | .00 | .01 | .02 | .03 | .04 | .05 | .06 | .07 | .08 | .09 |
|-----|-----|-----|-----|-----|-----|-----|-----|-----|-----|-----|
| | | | | | Second Decimal Place of $z$ | | | | | |
| 0.0 | .5000 | .4960 | .4920 | .4880 | .4840 | .4801 | .4761 | .4721 | .4681 | .4641 |
| 0.1 | .4602 | .4562 | .4522 | .4483 | .4443 | .4404 | .4364 | .4325 | .4286 | .4247 |
| 0.2 | .4207 | .4168 | .4129 | .4090 | .4052 | .4013 | .3974 | .3936 | .3897 | .3859 |
| 0.3 | .3821 | .3783 | .3745 | .3707 | .3669 | .3632 | .3594 | .3557 | .3520 | .3483 |
| 0.4 | .3446 | .3409 | .3372 | .3336 | .3300 | .3264 | .3228 | .3192 | .3156 | .3121 |
| 0.5 | .3085 | .3050 | .3015 | .2981 | .2946 | .2912 | .2877 | .2843 | .2810 | .2776 |
| 0.6 | .2743 | .2709 | .2676 | .2643 | .2611 | .2578 | .2546 | .2514 | .2483 | .2451 |
| 0.7 | .2420 | .2389 | .2358 | .2327 | .2296 | .2266 | .2236 | .2206 | .2177 | .2148 |
| 0.8 | .2119 | .2090 | .2061 | .2033 | .2005 | .1977 | .1949 | .1922 | .1894 | .1867 |
| 0.9 | .1841 | .1814 | .1788 | .1762 | .1736 | .1711 | .1685 | .1660 | .1635 | .1611 |
| 1.0 | .1587 | .1562 | .1539 | .1515 | .1492 | .1469 | .1446 | .1423 | .1401 | .1379 |
| 1.1 | .1357 | .1335 | .1314 | .1292 | .1271 | .1251 | .1230 | .1210 | .1190 | .1170 |
| 1.2 | .1151 | .1131 | .1112 | .1093 | .1075 | .1056 | .1038 | .1020 | .1003 | .0985 |
| 1.3 | .0968 | .0951 | .0934 | .0918 | .0901 | .0885 | .0869 | .0853 | .0838 | .0823 |
| 1.4 | .0808 | .0793 | .0778 | .0764 | .0749 | .0735 | .0722 | .0708 | .0694 | .0681 |
| 1.5 | .0668 | .0655 | .0643 | .0630 | .0618 | .0606 | .0594 | .0582 | .0571 | .0559 |
| 1.6 | .0548 | .0537 | .0526 | .0516 | .0505 | .0495 | .0485 | .0475 | .0465 | .0455 |
| 1.7 | .0446 | .0436 | .0427 | .0418 | .0409 | .0401 | .0392 | .0384 | .0375 | .0367 |
| 1.8 | .0359 | .0352 | .0344 | .0336 | .0329 | .0322 | .0314 | .0307 | .0301 | .0294 |
| 1.9 | .0287 | .0281 | .0274 | .0268 | .0262 | .0256 | .0250 | .0244 | .0239 | .0233 |
| 2.0 | .0228 | .0222 | .0217 | .0212 | .0207 | .0202 | .0197 | .0192 | .0188 | .0183 |
| 2.1 | .0179 | .0174 | .0170 | .0166 | .0162 | .0158 | .0154 | .0150 | .0146 | .0143 |
| 2.2 | .0139 | .0136 | .0132 | .0129 | .0125 | .0122 | .0119 | .0116 | .0113 | .0110 |
| 2.3 | .0107 | .0104 | .0102 | .0099 | .0096 | .0094 | .0091 | .0089 | .0087 | .0084 |
| 2.4 | .0082 | .0080 | .0078 | .0075 | .0073 | .0071 | .0069 | .0068 | .0066 | .0064 |
| 2.5 | .0062 | .0060 | .0059 | .0057 | .0055 | .0054 | .0052 | .0051 | .0049 | .0048 |
| 2.6 | .0047 | .0045 | .0044 | .0043 | .0041 | .0040 | .0039 | .0038 | .0037 | .0036 |
| 2.7 | .0035 | .0034 | .0033 | .0032 | .0031 | .0030 | .0029 | .0028 | .0027 | .0026 |
| 2.8 | .0026 | .0025 | .0024 | .0023 | .0023 | .0022 | .0021 | .0021 | .0020 | .0019 |
| 2.9 | .0019 | .0018 | .0017 | .0017 | .0016 | .0016 | .0015 | .0015 | .0014 | .0014 |
| 3.0 | .00135 | | | | | | | | | |
| 3.5 | .000233 | | | | | | | | | |
| 4.0 | .0000317 | | | | | | | | | |
| 4.5 | .00000340 | | | | | | | | | |
| 5.0 | .000000287 | | | | | | | | | |

Source: R. E. Walpole, *Introduction to Statistics* (New York: Macmillan, 1968).

**TABLE B:** *t* Distribution Critical Values

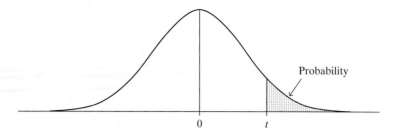

Probability

0    *t*

| df | Confidence Level | | | | | |
|---|---|---|---|---|---|---|
| | 80% | 90% | 95% | 98% | 99% | 99.8% |
| | Right-Tail Probability | | | | | |
| | $t_{.100}$ | $t_{.050}$ | $t_{.025}$ | $t_{.010}$ | $t_{.005}$ | $t_{.001}$ |
| 1 | 3.078 | 6.314 | 12.706 | 31.821 | 63.656 | 318.289 |
| 2 | 1.886 | 2.920 | 4.303 | 6.965 | 9.925 | 22.328 |
| 3 | 1.638 | 2.353 | 3.182 | 4.541 | 5.841 | 10.214 |
| 4 | 1.533 | 2.132 | 2.776 | 3.747 | 4.604 | 7.173 |
| 5 | 1.476 | 2.015 | 2.571 | 3.365 | 4.032 | 5.894 |
| 6 | 1.440 | 1.943 | 2.447 | 3.143 | 3.707 | 5.208 |
| 7 | 1.415 | 1.895 | 2.365 | 2.998 | 3.499 | 4.785 |
| 8 | 1.397 | 1.860 | 2.306 | 2.896 | 3.355 | 4.501 |
| 9 | 1.383 | 1.833 | 2.262 | 2.821 | 3.250 | 4.297 |
| 10 | 1.372 | 1.812 | 2.228 | 2.764 | 3.169 | 4.144 |
| 11 | 1.363 | 1.796 | 2.201 | 2.718 | 3.106 | 4.025 |
| 12 | 1.356 | 1.782 | 2.179 | 2.681 | 3.055 | 3.930 |
| 13 | 1.350 | 1.771 | 2.160 | 2.650 | 3.012 | 3.852 |
| 14 | 1.345 | 1.761 | 2.145 | 2.624 | 2.977 | 3.787 |
| 15 | 1.341 | 1.753 | 2.131 | 2.602 | 2.947 | 3.733 |
| 16 | 1.337 | 1.746 | 2.120 | 2.583 | 2.921 | 3.686 |
| 17 | 1.333 | 1.740 | 2.110 | 2.567 | 2.898 | 3.646 |
| 18 | 1.330 | 1.734 | 2.101 | 2.552 | 2.878 | 3.611 |
| 19 | 1.328 | 1.729 | 2.093 | 2.539 | 2.861 | 3.579 |
| 20 | 1.325 | 1.725 | 2.086 | 2.528 | 2.845 | 3.552 |
| 21 | 1.323 | 1.721 | 2.080 | 2.518 | 2.831 | 3.527 |
| 22 | 1.321 | 1.717 | 2.074 | 2.508 | 2.819 | 3.505 |
| 23 | 1.319 | 1.714 | 2.069 | 2.500 | 2.807 | 3.485 |
| 24 | 1.318 | 1.711 | 2.064 | 2.492 | 2.797 | 3.467 |
| 25 | 1.316 | 1.708 | 2.060 | 2.485 | 2.787 | 3.450 |
| 26 | 1.315 | 1.706 | 2.056 | 2.479 | 2.779 | 3.435 |
| 27 | 1.314 | 1.703 | 2.052 | 2.473 | 2.771 | 3.421 |
| 28 | 1.313 | 1.701 | 2.048 | 2.467 | 2.763 | 3.408 |
| 29 | 1.311 | 1.699 | 2.045 | 2.462 | 2.756 | 3.396 |
| 30 | 1.310 | 1.697 | 2.042 | 2.457 | 2.750 | 3.385 |
| 40 | 1.303 | 1.684 | 2.021 | 2.423 | 2.704 | 3.307 |
| 50 | 1.299 | 1.676 | 2.009 | 2.403 | 2.678 | 3.261 |
| 60 | 1.296 | 1.671 | 2.000 | 2.390 | 2.660 | 3.232 |
| 80 | 1.292 | 1.664 | 1.990 | 2.374 | 2.639 | 3.195 |
| 100 | 1.290 | 1.660 | 1.984 | 2.364 | 2.626 | 3.174 |
| ∞ | 1.282 | 1.645 | 1.960 | 2.326 | 2.576 | 3.091 |

Source: "Table of Percentage Points of the *t*-Distribution." Computed by Maxine Merrington, Biometrika, 32 (1941): 300. Reproduced by permission of the Biometrika trustees.

**TABLE C:** Chi-Squared Distribution Values for Various Right-Tail Probabilities

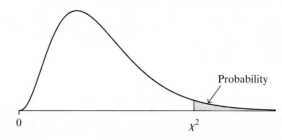

| df | \multicolumn{7}{c}{Right-Tail Probability} |
|---|---|---|---|---|---|---|---|
| | 0.250 | 0.100 | 0.050 | 0.025 | 0.010 | 0.005 | 0.001 |
| 1 | 1.32 | 2.71 | 3.84 | 5.02 | 6.63 | 7.88 | 10.83 |
| 2 | 2.77 | 4.61 | 5.99 | 7.38 | 9.21 | 10.60 | 13.82 |
| 3 | 4.11 | 6.25 | 7.81 | 9.35 | 11.34 | 12.84 | 16.27 |
| 4 | 5.39 | 7.78 | 9.49 | 11.14 | 13.28 | 14.86 | 18.47 |
| 5 | 6.63 | 9.24 | 11.07 | 12.83 | 15.09 | 16.75 | 20.52 |
| 6 | 7.84 | 10.64 | 12.59 | 14.45 | 16.81 | 18.55 | 22.46 |
| 7 | 9.04 | 12.02 | 14.07 | 16.01 | 18.48 | 20.28 | 24.32 |
| 8 | 10.22 | 13.36 | 15.51 | 17.53 | 20.09 | 21.96 | 26.12 |
| 9 | 11.39 | 14.68 | 16.92 | 19.02 | 21.67 | 23.59 | 27.88 |
| 10 | 12.55 | 15.99 | 18.31 | 20.48 | 23.21 | 25.19 | 29.59 |
| 11 | 13.70 | 17.28 | 19.68 | 21.92 | 24.72 | 26.76 | 31.26 |
| 12 | 14.85 | 18.55 | 21.03 | 23.34 | 26.22 | 28.30 | 32.91 |
| 13 | 15.98 | 19.81 | 22.36 | 24.74 | 27.69 | 29.82 | 34.53 |
| 14 | 17.12 | 21.06 | 23.68 | 26.12 | 29.14 | 31.32 | 36.12 |
| 15 | 18.25 | 22.31 | 25.00 | 27.49 | 30.58 | 32.80 | 37.70 |
| 16 | 19.37 | 23.54 | 26.30 | 28.85 | 32.00 | 34.27 | 39.25 |
| 17 | 20.49 | 24.77 | 27.59 | 30.19 | 33.41 | 35.72 | 40.79 |
| 18 | 21.60 | 25.99 | 28.87 | 31.53 | 34.81 | 37.16 | 42.31 |
| 19 | 22.72 | 27.20 | 30.14 | 32.85 | 36.19 | 38.58 | 43.82 |
| 20 | 23.83 | 28.41 | 31.41 | 34.17 | 37.57 | 40.00 | 45.32 |
| 25 | 29.34 | 34.38 | 37.65 | 40.65 | 44.31 | 46.93 | 52.62 |
| 30 | 34.80 | 40.26 | 43.77 | 46.98 | 50.89 | 53.67 | 59.70 |
| 40 | 45.62 | 51.80 | 55.76 | 59.34 | 63.69 | 66.77 | 73.40 |
| 50 | 56.33 | 63.17 | 67.50 | 71.42 | 76.15 | 79.49 | 86.66 |
| 60 | 66.98 | 74.40 | 79.08 | 83.30 | 88.38 | 91.95 | 99.61 |
| 70 | 77.58 | 85.53 | 90.53 | 95.02 | 100.4 | 104.2 | 112.3 |
| 80 | 88.13 | 96.58 | 101.8 | 106.6 | 112.3 | 116.3 | 124.8 |
| 90 | 98.65 | 107.6 | 113.1 | 118.1 | 124.1 | 128.3 | 137.2 |
| 100 | 109.1 | 118.5 | 124.3 | 129.6 | 135.8 | 140.2 | 149.5 |

Source: Calculated using *StaTable*, software from Cytel Software, Cambridge, MA.

**TABLE D:** *F* Distribution

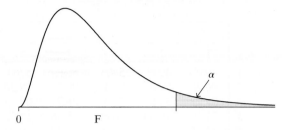

$\alpha = .05$

| $df_2$ | $df_1$ | | | | | | | | | |
|---|---|---|---|---|---|---|---|---|---|---|
| | 1 | 2 | 3 | 4 | 5 | 6 | 8 | 12 | 24 | ∞ |
| 1 | 161.4 | 199.5 | 215.7 | 224.6 | 230.2 | 234.0 | 238.9 | 243.9 | 249.0 | 254.3 |
| 2 | 18.51 | 19.00 | 19.16 | 19.25 | 19.30 | 19.33 | 19.37 | 19.41 | 19.45 | 19.50 |
| 3 | 10.13 | 9.55 | 9.28 | 9.12 | 9.01 | 8.94 | 8.84 | 8.74 | 8.64 | 8.53 |
| 4 | 7.71 | 6.94 | 6.59 | 6.39 | 6.26 | 6.16 | 6.04 | 5.91 | 5.77 | 5.63 |
| 5 | 6.61 | 5.79 | 5.41 | 5.19 | 5.05 | 4.95 | 4.82 | 4.68 | 4.53 | 4.36 |
| 6 | 5.99 | 5.14 | 4.76 | 4.53 | 4.39 | 4.28 | 4.15 | 4.00 | 3.84 | 3.67 |
| 7 | 5.59 | 4.74 | 4.35 | 4.12 | 3.97 | 3.87 | 3.73 | 3.57 | 3.41 | 3.23 |
| 8 | 5.32 | 4.46 | 4.07 | 3.84 | 3.69 | 3.58 | 3.44 | 3.28 | 3.12 | 2.93 |
| 9 | 5.12 | 4.26 | 3.86 | 3.63 | 3.48 | 3.37 | 3.23 | 3.07 | 2.90 | 2.71 |
| 10 | 4.96 | 4.10 | 3.71 | 3.48 | 3.33 | 3.22 | 3.07 | 2.91 | 2.74 | 2.54 |
| 11 | 4.84 | 3.98 | 3.59 | 3.36 | 3.20 | 3.09 | 2.95 | 2.79 | 2.61 | 2.40 |
| 12 | 4.75 | 3.88 | 3.49 | 3.26 | 3.11 | 3.00 | 2.85 | 2.69 | 2.50 | 2.30 |
| 13 | 4.67 | 3.80 | 3.41 | 3.18 | 3.02 | 2.92 | 2.77 | 2.60 | 2.42 | 2.21 |
| 14 | 4.60 | 3.74 | 3.34 | 3.11 | 2.96 | 2.85 | 2.70 | 2.53 | 2.35 | 2.13 |
| 15 | 4.54 | 3.68 | 3.29 | 3.06 | 2.90 | 2.79 | 2.64 | 2.48 | 2.29 | 2.07 |
| 16 | 4.49 | 3.63 | 3.24 | 3.01 | 2.85 | 2.74 | 2.59 | 2.42 | 2.24 | 2.01 |
| 17 | 4.45 | 3.59 | 3.20 | 2.96 | 2.81 | 2.70 | 2.55 | 2.38 | 2.19 | 1.96 |
| 18 | 4.41 | 3.55 | 3.16 | 2.93 | 2.77 | 2.66 | 2.51 | 2.34 | 2.15 | 1.92 |
| 19 | 4.38 | 3.52 | 3.13 | 2.90 | 2.74 | 2.63 | 2.48 | 2.31 | 2.11 | 1.88 |
| 20 | 4.35 | 3.49 | 3.10 | 2.87 | 2.71 | 2.60 | 2.45 | 2.28 | 2.08 | 1.84 |
| 21 | 4.32 | 3.47 | 3.07 | 2.84 | 2.68 | 2.57 | 2.42 | 2.25 | 2.05 | 1.81 |
| 22 | 4.30 | 3.44 | 3.05 | 2.82 | 2.66 | 2.55 | 2.40 | 2.23 | 2.03 | 1.78 |
| 23 | 4.28 | 3.42 | 3.03 | 2.80 | 2.64 | 2.53 | 2.38 | 2.20 | 2.00 | 1.76 |
| 24 | 4.26 | 3.40 | 3.01 | 2.78 | 2.62 | 2.51 | 2.36 | 2.18 | 1.98 | 1.73 |
| 25 | 4.24 | 3.38 | 2.99 | 2.76 | 2.60 | 2.49 | 2.34 | 2.16 | 1.96 | 1.71 |
| 26 | 4.22 | 3.37 | 2.98 | 2.74 | 2.59 | 2.47 | 2.32 | 2.15 | 1.95 | 1.69 |
| 27 | 4.21 | 3.35 | 2.96 | 2.73 | 2.57 | 2.46 | 2.30 | 2.13 | 1.93 | 1.67 |
| 28 | 4.20 | 3.34 | 2.95 | 2.71 | 2.56 | 2.44 | 2.29 | 2.12 | 1.91 | 1.65 |
| 29 | 4.18 | 3.33 | 2.93 | 2.70 | 2.54 | 2.43 | 2.28 | 2.10 | 1.90 | 1.64 |
| 30 | 4.17 | 3.32 | 2.92 | 2.69 | 2.53 | 2.42 | 2.27 | 2.09 | 1.89 | 1.62 |
| 40 | 4.08 | 3.23 | 2.84 | 2.61 | 2.45 | 2.34 | 2.18 | 2.00 | 1.79 | 1.51 |
| 60 | 4.00 | 3.15 | 2.76 | 2.52 | 2.37 | 2.25 | 2.10 | 1.92 | 1.70 | 1.39 |
| 120 | 3.92 | 3.07 | 2.68 | 2.45 | 2.29 | 2.17 | 2.02 | 1.83 | 1.61 | 1.25 |
| ∞ | 3.84 | 2.99 | 2.60 | 2.37 | 2.21 | 2.09 | 1.94 | 1.75 | 1.52 | 1.00 |

Source: From Table V of R. A. Fisher and F. Yates, *Statistical Tables for Biological, Agricultural and Medical Research*, published by Longman Group Ltd., London, 1974. (Previously published by Oliver & Boyd, Edinburgh.) Reprinted by permission of the authors and publishers.

**TABLE D:** (continued)

$\alpha = .01$

| $df_2$ | 1 | 2 | 3 | 4 | 5 | 6 | 8 | 12 | 24 | $\infty$ |
|---|---|---|---|---|---|---|---|---|---|---|
| 1 | 4052 | 4999 | 5403 | 5625 | 5764 | 5859 | 5981 | 6106 | 6234 | 6366 |
| 2 | 98.49 | 99.01 | 99.17 | 99.25 | 99.30 | 99.33 | 99.36 | 99.42 | 99.46 | 99.50 |
| 3 | 34.12 | 30.81 | 29.46 | 28.71 | 28.24 | 27.91 | 27.49 | 27.05 | 26.60 | 26.12 |
| 4 | 21.20 | 18.00 | 16.69 | 15.98 | 15.52 | 15.21 | 14.80 | 14.37 | 13.93 | 13.46 |
| 5 | 16.26 | 13.27 | 12.06 | 11.39 | 10.97 | 10.67 | 10.27 | 9.89 | 9.47 | 9.02 |
| 6 | 13.74 | 10.92 | 9.78 | 9.15 | 8.75 | 8.47 | 8.10 | 7.72 | 7.31 | 6.88 |
| 7 | 12.25 | 9.55 | 8.45 | 7.85 | 7.46 | 7.19 | 6.84 | 6.47 | 6.07 | 5.65 |
| 8 | 11.26 | 8.65 | 7.59 | 7.01 | 6.63 | 6.37 | 6.03 | 5.67 | 5.28 | 4.86 |
| 9 | 10.56 | 8.02 | 6.99 | 6.42 | 6.06 | 5.80 | 5.47 | 5.11 | 4.73 | 4.31 |
| 10 | 10.04 | 7.56 | 6.55 | 5.99 | 5.64 | 5.39 | 5.06 | 4.71 | 4.33 | 3.91 |
| 11 | 9.65 | 7.20 | 6.22 | 5.67 | 5.32 | 5.07 | 4.74 | 4.40 | 4.02 | 3.60 |
| 12 | 9.33 | 6.93 | 5.95 | 5.41 | 5.06 | 4.82 | 4.50 | 4.16 | 3.78 | 3.36 |
| 13 | 9.07 | 6.70 | 5.74 | 5.20 | 4.86 | 4.62 | 4.30 | 3.96 | 3.59 | 3.16 |
| 14 | 8.86 | 6.51 | 5.56 | 5.03 | 4.69 | 4.46 | 4.14 | 3.80 | 3.43 | 3.00 |
| 15 | 8.68 | 6.36 | 5.42 | 4.89 | 4.56 | 4.32 | 4.00 | 3.67 | 3.29 | 2.87 |
| 16 | 8.53 | 6.23 | 5.29 | 4.77 | 4.44 | 4.20 | 3.89 | 3.55 | 3.18 | 2.75 |
| 17 | 8.40 | 6.11 | 5.18 | 4.67 | 4.34 | 4.10 | 3.79 | 3.45 | 3.08 | 2.65 |
| 18 | 8.28 | 6.01 | 5.09 | 4.58 | 4.25 | 4.01 | 3.71 | 3.37 | 3.00 | 2.57 |
| 19 | 8.18 | 5.93 | 5.01 | 4.50 | 4.17 | 3.94 | 3.63 | 3.30 | 2.92 | 2.49 |
| 20 | 8.10 | 5.85 | 4.94 | 4.43 | 4.10 | 3.87 | 3.56 | 3.23 | 2.86 | 2.42 |
| 21 | 8.02 | 5.78 | 4.87 | 4.37 | 4.04 | 3.81 | 3.51 | 3.17 | 2.80 | 2.36 |
| 22 | 7.94 | 5.72 | 4.82 | 4.31 | 3.99 | 3.76 | 3.45 | 3.12 | 2.75 | 2.31 |
| 23 | 7.88 | 5.66 | 4.76 | 4.26 | 3.94 | 3.71 | 3.41 | 3.07 | 2.70 | 2.26 |
| 24 | 7.82 | 5.61 | 4.72 | 4.22 | 3.90 | 3.67 | 3.36 | 3.03 | 2.66 | 2.21 |
| 25 | 7.77 | 5.57 | 4.68 | 4.18 | 3.86 | 3.63 | 3.32 | 2.99 | 2.62 | 2.17 |
| 26 | 7.72 | 5.53 | 4.64 | 4.14 | 3.82 | 3.59 | 3.29 | 2.96 | 2.58 | 2.13 |
| 27 | 7.68 | 5.49 | 4.60 | 4.11 | 3.78 | 3.56 | 3.26 | 2.93 | 2.55 | 2.10 |
| 28 | 7.64 | 5.45 | 4.57 | 4.07 | 3.75 | 3.53 | 3.23 | 2.90 | 2.52 | 2.06 |
| 29 | 7.60 | 5.42 | 4.54 | 4.04 | 3.73 | 3.50 | 3.20 | 2.87 | 2.49 | 2.03 |
| 30 | 7.56 | 5.39 | 4.51 | 4.02 | 3.70 | 3.47 | 3.17 | 2.84 | 2.47 | 2.01 |
| 40 | 7.31 | 5.18 | 4.31 | 3.83 | 3.51 | 3.29 | 2.99 | 2.66 | 2.29 | 1.80 |
| 60 | 7.08 | 4.98 | 4.13 | 3.65 | 3.34 | 3.12 | 2.82 | 2.50 | 2.12 | 1.60 |
| 120 | 6.85 | 4.79 | 3.95 | 3.48 | 3.17 | 2.96 | 2.66 | 2.34 | 1.95 | 1.38 |
| $\infty$ | 6.64 | 4.60 | 3.78 | 3.32 | 3.02 | 2.80 | 2.51 | 2.18 | 1.79 | 1.00 |

**TABLE D:** (continued)

$\alpha = .001$

| $df_2$ | 1 | 2 | 3 | 4 | 5 | 6 | 8 | 12 | 24 | $\infty$ |
|---|---|---|---|---|---|---|---|---|---|---|
| | | | | | $df_1$ | | | | | |
| 1 | 405284 | 500000 | 540379 | 562500 | 576405 | 585937 | 598144 | 610667 | 623497 | 636619 |
| 2 | 998.5 | 999.0 | 999.2 | 999.2 | 999.3 | 999.3 | 999.4 | 999.4 | 999.5 | 999.5 |
| 3 | 167.5 | 148.5 | 141.1 | 137.1 | 134.6 | 132.8 | 130.6 | 128.3 | 125.9 | 123.5 |
| 4 | 74.14 | 61.25 | 56.18 | 53.44 | 51.71 | 50.53 | 49.00 | 47.41 | 45.77 | 44.05 |
| 5 | 47.04 | 36.61 | 33.20 | 31.09 | 29.75 | 28.84 | 27.64 | 26.42 | 25.14 | 23.78 |
| 6 | 35.51 | 27.00 | 23.70 | 21.90 | 20.81 | 20.03 | 19.03 | 17.99 | 16.89 | 15.75 |
| 7 | 29.22 | 21.69 | 18.77 | 17.19 | 16.21 | 15.52 | 14.63 | 13.71 | 12.73 | 11.69 |
| 8 | 25.42 | 18.49 | 15.83 | 14.39 | 13.49 | 12.86 | 12.04 | 11.19 | 10.30 | 9.34 |
| 9 | 22.86 | 16.39 | 13.90 | 12.56 | 11.71 | 11.13 | 10.37 | 9.57 | 8.72 | 7.81 |
| 10 | 21.04 | 14.91 | 12.55 | 11.28 | 10.48 | 9.92 | 9.20 | 8.45 | 7.64 | 6.76 |
| 11 | 19.69 | 13.81 | 11.56 | 10.35 | 9.58 | 9.05 | 8.35 | 7.63 | 6.85 | 6.00 |
| 12 | 18.64 | 12.97 | 10.80 | 9.63 | 8.89 | 8.38 | 7.71 | 7.00 | 6.25 | 5.42 |
| 13 | 17.81 | 12.31 | 10.21 | 9.07 | 8.35 | 7.86 | 7.21 | 6.52 | 5.78 | 4.97 |
| 14 | 17.14 | 11.78 | 9.73 | 8.62 | 7.92 | 7.43 | 6.80 | 6.13 | 5.41 | 4.60 |
| 15 | 16.59 | 11.34 | 9.34 | 8.25 | 7.57 | 7.09 | 6.47 | 5.81 | 5.10 | 4.31 |
| 16 | 16.12 | 10.97 | 9.00 | 7.94 | 7.27 | 6.81 | 6.19 | 5.55 | 4.85 | 4.06 |
| 17 | 15.72 | 10.66 | 8.73 | 7.68 | 7.02 | 6.56 | 5.96 | 5.32 | 4.63 | 3.85 |
| 18 | 15.38 | 10.39 | 8.49 | 7.46 | 6.81 | 6.35 | 5.76 | 5.13 | 4.45 | 3.67 |
| 19 | 15.08 | 10.16 | 8.28 | 7.26 | 6.61 | 6.18 | 5.59 | 4.97 | 4.29 | 3.52 |
| 20 | 14.82 | 9.95 | 8.10 | 7.10 | 6.46 | 6.02 | 5.44 | 4.82 | 4.15 | 3.38 |
| 21 | 14.59 | 9.77 | 7.94 | 6.95 | 6.32 | 5.88 | 5.31 | 4.70 | 4.03 | 3.26 |
| 22 | 14.38 | 9.61 | 7.80 | 6.81 | 6.19 | 5.76 | 5.19 | 4.58 | 3.92 | 3.15 |
| 23 | 14.19 | 9.47 | 7.67 | 6.69 | 6.08 | 5.65 | 5.09 | 4.48 | 3.82 | 3.05 |
| 24 | 14.03 | 9.34 | 7.55 | 6.59 | 5.98 | 5.55 | 4.99 | 4.39 | 3.74 | 2.97 |
| 25 | 13.88 | 9.22 | 7.45 | 6.49 | 5.88 | 5.46 | 4.91 | 4.31 | 3.66 | 2.89 |
| 26 | 13.74 | 9.12 | 7.36 | 6.41 | 5.80 | 5.38 | 4.83 | 4.24 | 3.59 | 2.82 |
| 27 | 13.61 | 9.02 | 7.27 | 6.33 | 5.73 | 5.31 | 4.76 | 4.17 | 3.52 | 2.75 |
| 28 | 13.50 | 8.93 | 7.19 | 6.25 | 5.66 | 5.24 | 4.69 | 4.11 | 3.46 | 2.70 |
| 29 | 13.39 | 8.85 | 7.12 | 6.19 | 5.59 | 5.18 | 4.64 | 4.05 | 3.41 | 2.64 |
| 30 | 13.29 | 8.77 | 7.05 | 6.12 | 5.53 | 5.12 | 4.58 | 4.00 | 3.36 | 2.59 |
| 40 | 12.61 | 8.25 | 6.60 | 5.70 | 5.13 | 4.73 | 4.21 | 3.64 | 3.01 | 2.23 |
| 60 | 11.97 | 7.76 | 6.17 | 5.31 | 4.76 | 4.37 | 3.87 | 3.31 | 2.69 | 1.90 |
| 120 | 11.38 | 7.31 | 5.79 | 4.95 | 4.42 | 4.04 | 3.55 | 3.02 | 2.40 | 1.56 |
| $\infty$ | 10.83 | 6.91 | 5.42 | 4.62 | 4.10 | 3.74 | 3.27 | 2.74 | 2.13 | 1.00 |

# Bibliography

Afifi, A. A., Clark, V., and May, S. (2003). *Computer-Aided Multivariate Analysis*, 4th ed. Chapman & Hall.

Agresti, A. (2007). *An Introduction to Categorical Data Analysis*, 2nd ed. Wiley.

Allison, P. D. (1984). *Event History Analysis*. Sage.

Allison, P. (2002). *Missing Data*. Sage.

Babbie, E. (2003). *The Practice of Social Research*, 10th ed. Wadsworth.

Bartholomew, D. J. (1982). *Stochastic Models for Social Processes*, 3rd ed. Wiley.

Bentler, P. M. (1980). Multivariate analysis with latent variables: Causal modelling. *Annual Review of Psychology*, 31, 419–456.

Berk, R. A. (2004). *Regression Analysis: A Constructive Critique*. Sage.

Blalock, H. M. (1979). *Social Statistics*, rev. 2nd ed. McGraw-Hill.

Bollen, K. A. (1989). *Structural Equations with Latent Variables*. Wiley.

Box, J. F. (1978). *R. A. Fisher, The Life of a Scientist*. Wiley.

Cleveland, W. S. (1994). *The Elements of Graphing Data*, 2nd ed. Chapman and Hall.

Clogg, C. C., and Shihadeh, E. S. (1994). *Statistical Models for Ordinal Variables*. Sage.

Cohen, J. (1988). *Statistical Power Analysis for the Behavioral Sciences*, 2nd ed. Lawrence Erlbaum.

Cook, R. D., and Weisberg, S. (1982). Criticism in regression. In *Sociological Methodology*. Jossey-Bass, pp. 313–361.

Crosson, C. (1994). *Tainted Truth: The Manipulation of Fact in America*. Simon & Schuster.

DeMaris, A. (1992). *Logit Modeling: Practical Applications*. Sage.

DeMaris, A. (2002). Covariance structure models. In *Handbook for Conducting Research on Human Sexuality*, eds. M. Wiederman and B. E. Bradley. Erlbaum.

DeMaris, A. (2004). *Regression with Social Data: Modeling Continuous and Limited Response Variables*. Wiley.

Draper, N. R. and Smith, H. (1998). *Applied Regression Analysis*, 3rd ed. Wiley.

Duncan, O. D. (1966). Path analysis: Sociological examples. *American Journal of Sociology*, 72, 1–16.

Eliason, S. (1993). *Maximum Likelihood Estimation: Logic and Practice*. Sage.

Fitzmaurice, G., Laird, N., and Ware, J. (2004). *Applied Longitudinal Analysis*. Wiley.

Fox, J. (1991). *Regression Diagnostics: An Introduction*. Sage.

Freedman, D. A. (2005). *Statistical Models: Theory and Practice*. Cambridge University Press.

Freund, R. J., and Littell, R. C. (2000). *SAS System for Regression*, 3rd ed. SAS Institute.

Gelman, A., and Hill, J. 2006. *Data Analysis Using Regression and Multilevel/Hierarchical Models*, Cambridge University Press.

Gill, J. (2000). *Generalized Linear Models: A Unified Approach*. Sage.

Goodman, L. A. (1962). Statistical methods for analyzing processes of change. *American Journal of Sociology*, 68, 57–78.

Gould, S. J. (1981). *The Mismeasure of Man*. W. W. Norton.

Green, S. B., and Salkind, N. J. (2007). *Using SPSS for Windows and Macintosh*, 5th ed. Prentice Hall.

Gueorguieva, R., and Krystal, J. H. (2004). Move over ANOVA. *Archives of General Psychiatry*, vol. 61, pp. 310-317.

Hagenaars, J., and McCutcheon, A. (editors). (2006). *Applied Latent Class Analysis*. Cambridge University Press.

Harman, H. (1967). *Modern Factor Analysis*, 2nd ed. University of Chicago Press.

Hedeker, D., and Gibbons, R. D. (2006). *Longitudinal Data Analysis*. Wiley.

Hollander, M., and Wolfe, D. (1999). *Nonparametric Statistical Methods*, 2nd ed. Wiley.

Holzer, C. E., III (1977). *The Impact of Life Events on Psychiatric Symptomatology*. Ph.D. dissertation, University of Florida, Gainesville.

Hosmer, D., and Lemeshow, S. (2000). *Applied Logistic Regression*, 2nd ed. Wiley.

Howell, D. C. (2006) *Statistical Methods for Psychology*, 6th ed. Wadsworth.

Jöreskog, K. G. and Sörbom, D. (1997). *LISREL 8: User's Reference Guide*. Scientific Software.

Kennedy, P. (2004) *A Guide to Econometrics*, 5th ed. Blackwell.

King, G. (1989). *Unifying Political Methodology: The Likelihood Theory of Statistical Inference*. Cambridge University Press.

Kirk, R. E. (1995) *Experimental Design: Procedures for the Behavioral Sciences*, 3rd ed. Brooks/Cole.

Kutner, M. H., Nachtsheim, C. J., and Neter, J. (2004). *Applied Linear Regression Models*, 4th ed. McGraw-Hill/Irwin.

Land, K. (1969). Principles of path analysis. In *Sociological Methodology 1969*, ed. E. Borgatta. Jossey-Bass.

Lehmann, E. L. (1975). *Nonparametrics: Statistical Methods Based on Ranks*. Holden-Day.

Littell, R., Milliken, G., Stroup, W., Wolfinger, R., and Schabenberger, O. (2006). *SAS for Mixed Models*, 2nd ed. SAS Institute.

Littell, R., Stroup, W., and Freund, R. (2002). *SAS for Linear Models*, 4th ed. SAS Institute.

Long, J. S. (1983). *Confirmatory Factor Analysis* and *Covariance Structure Models, An Introduction to LISREL*. Sage.

Norusis, M. (2006). *SPSS 14.0 Guide to Data Analysis*. Prentice Hall.

Pedhazur, E. J. (1997). *Multiple Regression in Behavioral Research*, 3rd ed. Wadsworth.

Raudenbush, S., and Bryk, A. 2002. *Hierarchical Linear Models*, 2nd ed. Sage.

Rosenberg, M. (1968). *The Logic of Survey Analysis*. Basic Books.

Scheaffer, R. L., Mendenhall, W., and Ott, L. (2005). *Elementary Survey Sampling*, 6th ed. Duxbury Press.

Scheaffer, R. L., and Young, L. (2008). *Introduction to Probability and its Applications*, 3rd ed. Wadsworth.

Schlotzhauer, S. S., and Littell, R. C. (1997). *SAS System for Elementary Statistical Analysis*, 2nd ed. SAS Institute.

Snedecor, G. W. and Cochran, W. G. (1967). *Statistical Methods*, 6th ed. Iowa State University Press.

Snijders, T. A. B., and Bosker, R. J. (1999). *Multilevel Analysis*. Sage.

Thompson, B. (2004). *Exploratory and Confirmatory Factor Analysis*. American Psychological Association.

Thompson, S. K. (2002). *Sampling*, 2nd ed. Wiley.

Tufte, E. R. (2001). *The Visual Display of Quantitative Information*, 2nd ed. Graphics Press.

Tukey, J. W. (1977). *Exploratory Data Analysis*. Addison-Wesley.

Weisberg, S. (2005). *Applied Linear Regression*, 3rd ed. Wiley.

Winer, B. J., Brown, D. R., and Michels, K. M. (1991). *Statistical Principles in Experimental Design*, 3rd ed. McGraw-Hill.

Yamaguchi, K. (1991). *Event History Analysis*. Sage.

# Index

**TABLE A:** Normal curve tail probabilities. Standard normal probability in right-hand tail (for negative values of $z$, probabilities are found by symmetry)

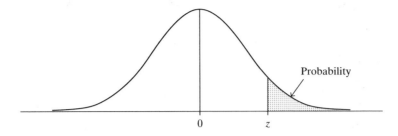

| $z$ | .00 | .01 | .02 | .03 | .04 | .05 | .06 | .07 | .08 | .09 |
|---|---|---|---|---|---|---|---|---|---|---|
| | | | | | Second Decimal Place of $z$ | | | | | |
| 0.0 | .5000 | .4960 | .4920 | .4880 | .4840 | .4801 | .4761 | .4721 | .4681 | .4641 |
| 0.1 | .4602 | .4562 | .4522 | .4483 | .4443 | .4404 | .4364 | .4325 | .4286 | .4247 |
| 0.2 | .4207 | .4168 | .4129 | .4090 | .4052 | .4013 | .3974 | .3936 | .3897 | .3859 |
| 0.3 | .3821 | .3783 | .3745 | .3707 | .3669 | .3632 | .3594 | .3557 | .3520 | .3483 |
| 0.4 | .3446 | .3409 | .3372 | .3336 | .3300 | .3264 | .3228 | .3192 | .3156 | .3121 |
| 0.5 | .3085 | .3050 | .3015 | .2981 | .2946 | .2912 | .2877 | .2843 | .2810 | .2776 |
| 0.6 | .2743 | .2709 | .2676 | .2643 | .2611 | .2578 | .2546 | .2514 | .2483 | .2451 |
| 0.7 | .2420 | .2389 | .2358 | .2327 | .2296 | .2266 | .2236 | .2206 | .2177 | .2148 |
| 0.8 | .2119 | .2090 | .2061 | .2033 | .2005 | .1977 | .1949 | .1922 | .1894 | .1867 |
| 0.9 | .1841 | .1814 | .1788 | .1762 | .1736 | .1711 | .1685 | .1660 | .1635 | .1611 |
| 1.0 | .1587 | .1562 | .1539 | .1515 | .1492 | .1469 | .1446 | .1423 | .1401 | .1379 |
| 1.1 | .1357 | .1335 | .1314 | .1292 | .1271 | .1251 | .1230 | .1210 | .1190 | .1170 |
| 1.2 | .1151 | .1131 | .1112 | .1093 | .1075 | .1056 | .1038 | .1020 | .1003 | .0985 |
| 1.3 | .0968 | .0951 | .0934 | .0918 | .0901 | .0885 | .0869 | .0853 | .0838 | .0823 |
| 1.4 | .0808 | .0793 | .0778 | .0764 | .0749 | .0735 | .0722 | .0708 | .0694 | .0681 |
| 1.5 | .0668 | .0655 | .0643 | .0630 | .0618 | .0606 | .0594 | .0582 | .0571 | .0559 |
| 1.6 | .0548 | .0537 | .0526 | .0516 | .0505 | .0495 | .0485 | .0475 | .0465 | .0455 |
| 1.7 | .0446 | .0436 | .0427 | .0418 | .0409 | .0401 | .0392 | .0384 | .0375 | .0367 |
| 1.8 | .0359 | .0352 | .0344 | .0336 | .0329 | .0322 | .0314 | .0307 | .0301 | .0294 |
| 1.9 | .0287 | .0281 | .0274 | .0268 | .0262 | .0256 | .0250 | .0244 | .0239 | .0233 |
| 2.0 | .0228 | .0222 | .0217 | .0212 | .0207 | .0202 | .0197 | .0192 | .0188 | .0183 |
| 2.1 | .0179 | .0174 | .0170 | .0166 | .0162 | .0158 | .0154 | .0150 | .0146 | .0143 |
| 2.2 | .0139 | .0136 | .0132 | .0129 | .0125 | .0122 | .0119 | .0116 | .0113 | .0110 |
| 2.3 | .0107 | .0104 | .0102 | .0099 | .0096 | .0094 | .0091 | .0089 | .0087 | .0084 |
| 2.4 | .0082 | .0080 | .0078 | .0075 | .0073 | .0071 | .0069 | .0068 | .0066 | .0064 |
| 2.5 | .0062 | .0060 | .0059 | .0057 | .0055 | .0054 | .0052 | .0051 | .0049 | .0048 |
| 2.6 | .0047 | .0045 | .0044 | .0043 | .0041 | .0040 | .0039 | .0038 | .0037 | .0036 |
| 2.7 | .0035 | .0034 | .0033 | .0032 | .0031 | .0030 | .0029 | .0028 | .0027 | .0026 |
| 2.8 | .0026 | .0025 | .0024 | .0023 | .0023 | .0022 | .0021 | .0021 | .0020 | .0019 |
| 2.9 | .0019 | .0018 | .0017 | .0017 | .0016 | .0016 | .0015 | .0015 | .0014 | .0014 |
| 3.0 | .00135 | | | | | | | | | |
| 3.5 | .000233 | | | | | | | | | |
| 4.0 | .0000317 | | | | | | | | | |
| 4.5 | .00000340 | | | | | | | | | |
| 5.0 | .000000287 | | | | | | | | | |

Source: R. E. Walpole, *Introduction to Statistics* (New York: Macmillan, 1968).

# A GUIDE TO CHOOSING A STATISTICAL METHOD

## Quantitative Response Variable (Analyzing Means)

1. If no other variables, use descriptive methods of Chapter 3 and inferential methods of Section 5.3 (confidence interval) and Section 6.2 (significance test) for a mean.

2. Categorical explanatory variable: If two levels, use methods for comparing two means from Section 7.3 (two independent samples) or Section 7.4 (two dependent samples). If several levels, use ANOVA methods for comparing several means from Sections 12.1–3 (several independent samples) or Section 12.6 (several dependent samples). These are equivalent to regression methods with dummy variables for predictors. If several categorical variables, use ANOVA methods of Sections 12.4–5 or 12.7 or use regression with dummy variables.

3. Quantitative explanatory variable: Use regression and correlation methods of Chapter 9. If several quantitative predictors, use multiple regression methods of Chapters 11 and 14.

4. Quantitative and categorical explanatory variables: Use analysis of covariance methods of Chapter 13, which are regression methods with dummy variables for categorical predictors.

## Categorical Response Variable (Analyzing Proportions)

1. If no other variable, use descriptive methods of Section 3.1 and inferential methods of Section 5.2 (confidence interval) and Section 6.3 (significance test) for proportions.

2. Categorical explanatory variable: Use contingency table methods of Chapter 8, with Section 7.2 for special case of comparing proportions for two groups and Sections 8.5–6 for ordinal classifications.

3. If binary response with quantitative explanatory variable or multiple quantitative and/or categorical predictors, use logistic regression methods of Chapter 15.

4. If ordinal response with quantitative and/or categorical predictors, use ordinal logit model of Section 15.4.